The Creative Apple

The Creative Apple

Edited by
Mark Pelczarski & Joe Tate

Creative Computing Press
Morris Plains, New Jersey

Library of Congress Number 81-70543
ISBN 0-916688-25-9

Printed in the United States of America

10 9 8 7 6 5 4 3 2

Creative Computing Press
39 East Hanover Ave.
Morris Plains, New Jersey 07950

Introduction

There are dozens of computer magazines on the stands today. But *Creative Computing* was there before Apple (the computer, not its Garden of Eden namesake). *Creative* has followed Apple's development from the original press releases, advertisements, and early versions of its Basic all the way through today's exciting developments with reviews of new products and complete, ready-to-run programs and utilities.

In this book, we've sifted through everything *Creative Computing* has published in the last four years, noting any article we could find that related in some way to the Apple. It wasn't a difficult task. Like thousands of others who read *Creative,* we had wanted to see such a book for a long time. So we set out to put together the book that we always wanted on our shelves.

We love it. We think you will, too. It was a lot of work. We didn't just reprint articles for you. We categorized, updated, verified some of the older sources, and finally settled on well over a hundred articles. These represent the most current and varied cross-section of articles and applications we could find. We used our own Apples to help with the handling of all that information, and for typing and editing the initial manuscript. What a versatile computer!

We've kept all product mentions as current as possible, although any references in the original articles to prices should be used as guidelines, not hard facts. Prices tend to change considerably with competition and demand. We also tried to present a cross-section of what's available, not an absolute, comprehensive list. Although not a "buying guide," the articles about products are a good place to start your search for what you want. Check with your dealers for comparable products and current prices.

This book will give you some idea of the wide range of applications possible with the Apple. Let the possibilities tickle your imagination! There are thousands more that haven't even been touched yet. Don't look at our chapters as absolute boundaries. In categorizing articles we'd often come up with ideas of how something in Chapter X could be used with an idea in Chapter II for an application discussed in Chapter III, and so on.

The most amazing thing about the Apple is the versatility of the machine — how much was designed into it several years back. Although some computers can claim a small degree of superiority in one area or another, none can claim such high marks across a wide range of applications. In other words, if you bought an Apple, it was a choice well made. Here's a book that will help you enjoy your Apple even more and tap its great potential.

Mark Pelczarski & Joe Tate

Contents

Contents

Chapter I
Graphics

Chapter I — Graphics

The first Apples released, back in the days when they only came with Integer BASIC, were touted for their graphic capabilities. But very few people knew how to use anything other than the low resolution (40 by 40) mode. There were special subroutines that you could load from cassette that let you use a high resolution mode, but they were difficult to use and the "hi-res" functions seemed interesting, but limited. Hah!

Those subroutines became part of Applesoft BASIC, and as more and more people started playing with hi-res graphics, more and more tricks and techniques were discovered. State-of-the-art on the Apple now rivals some of the best video arcade games. (Come to think of it, a few years ago "pong" was state-of-the-art at the arcades . . . and the Apple had all that stuff *already built in,* just waiting to be used. Now the six lowly colors provided with Apple hi-res have been mixed and matched into over a *hundred,* and the problem of mixing text and hi-res graphics has been solved many times over. Some computer artists have even claimed that with a digitizing tablet and the software that's available, the Apple is one of the most underrated graphics tools available. It's much more cost-effective than a $200,000 dedicated graphics machine, and in situations where extremely high resolution is not necessary, quite able to take over many of the high-priced systems' functions.

There's been a good cross-section of graphics articles in *Creative Computing,* especially because they run two special graphics issues a year. Included here are some reviews of graphics hardware and software, a few programs and utilities that may enhance your programming or provide some amusement, and articles on some possible interfaces you can use to extend the graphic range of your computer.

Special Notes For Chapter I

- *Apple Sketch,* by David Miller:
  Requires Applesoft, at least 32K of RAM, and a disk drive. It also happens to be attached to a nicely written article.

- *Apple Graphics Utilities,* by David Lubar:
  David Lubar recently reviewed some of the graphics software now available for the Apple. Some other areas of graphics software not covered in this article include the creation of charts and graphs from given sets of data. Dataplot from MUSE and Visiplot from Personal Software are two examples of programs in that category. (Editor's note: see the review of Visiplot at the end of this chapter.) Another would be 3-D animation routines such as 3-D Supergraphics by Paul Lutus (United Software) and Bill Budge's 3-D Game Development Tool (California Pacific). A distinction is made here between 3-D design and animation systems. Design packages can be a lot more flexible because they don't have to adhere to the extremely demanding speed requirements of animation. Of course, the design packages won't let you animate.

- *Picture Packer,* by David Lubar:
  This gives you a neat little pair of machine language programs that will work on any Apple. Even those of you who are not machine language junkies will find the steps behind the development of this utility very interesting as a description of how you can attack a programming problem.

- *Hi-Res Test for the Apple,* by Paul Hitchcock:
  Paul Hitchcock's routines in this article require Applesoft BASIC.

- *Apple II Lo-Res Shape Tables,* by David Lubar:
  This Lo-Res Shape Table routine is written for an Integer BASIC Program.

- *Apple Graphics Tablet; Apple Hi-Res Graphics Made Easy with Versa Writer; Dithering Heights:*
  These three articles describe various ways to put graphic information into your computer, other than with the keyboard, paddles, or a joystick. Of course, the possible input devices are almost endless. Sound, music, almost any kind of motion, or direct electronics from other devices can all be adapted as input. Hmmmm . . .

- Integrating CAI and Video Tape, by Marc Schwartz:
  This last article in Chapter I is about hooking your computer to a videotape machine. This can be done in two ways: the computer controls the videotape machine itself, or the computer video is sent through the videotape machine and taped. Both open a lot of possibilities — from computer aided instruction, as Marc Schwartz suggests — to creating animations on tape. Another area of interest is laser disk technology, which can allow any of thousands of frames to be instantly retrieved, presumably with possible computer interfacing controlling the retrieval. Ah, for a few dollars . . .

Apple-Sketch

When I first bought my Apple II computer a few months ago, I was very excited about using the high resolution graphics that would surely dazzle my friends. I had visions of swooping spacecraft catapulting across the screen, of finely detailed game displays; but most of all, I relished the possibility of drawing freely, in color, on the high resolution screen. What possibilities, I thought: a 45000 point display (give or take a few), with six available colors. Surely there would be an easy way to make it do my bidding! So I spent a few evenings working with my shiny new Apple, a color T.V. set, and the friendly Apple manuals, and quickly learned that things might not be very easy after all.

Apple's high resolution graphics mode consists of two areas or "pages" of memory in which to store the information that makes up a high resolution picture. The primary page picture buffer (or page 1) begins at memory location 8192 and extends up to location 16383, while the secondary page immediately follows, from locations 16384 to 24575. Six colors (black, white, green, violet, orange and blue) are available, although some limitations exist that I will talk more about later. Page one is mixture of graphics and text with four text lines residing beneath the graphics screen, although they can be removed by a simple POKE command. Page two is strictly graphics, with no text window easily available to the user. Basic statements can turn points on or off in color and can draw lines between a specified series of points. For those gamers in the crowd (like myself), binary shape tables can be created to draw, rotate, and expand a user defined shape anywhere on the screen. Sounds great, doesn't it? But let's backtrack for a moment.

To put it frankly, a single point plotted on the screen does not a picture make! A lot of careful thought and planning has to come before you can produce eye-catching drawings using this one-at-a-time method. Since many, many points must be used to produce a colorful drawing of, say, your friendly neighborhood computer, it becomes impractical (and very slow) to use a series of HPLOT statements to draw it from within a program. Who'd want to figure out where all those points should go, anyway? The method used to create shape tables is very tedious and difficult; a single mistake can put you right back where you started from.

As a result, many would-be graphics artists have become frustrated with high-

David Miller, 79 Hawley Ave., Port Chester, NY 10573.

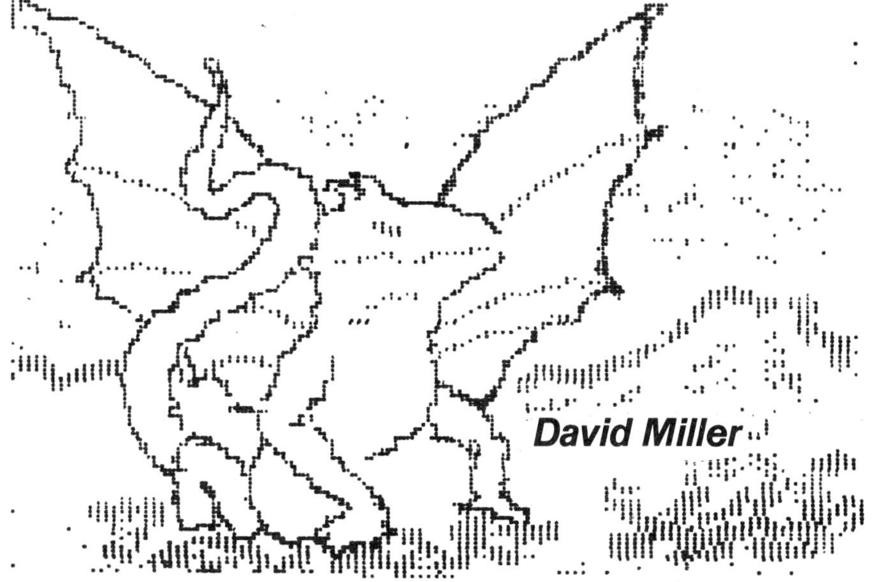

resolution graphics and shy away from using them in their programs. The more affluent, of course, buy expensive graphics tablets costing hundreds of dollars, and produce visual effects to make the rest of us turn green with envy. I soon decided to even up the score a little bit; perhaps through a little software magic, it would become possible to duplicate some of the features of the graphics tablets.

> **The method used to create shape tables is very tedious and difficult; a single mistake can put you right back where you started from.**

The result is my program, written in Applesoft to make life a little more enjoyable for the artistic Apple owner. With it you can create vivid computer art, without spending hundreds of dollars on an expensive graphics tablet, by using the Apple paddles for the drawing input. All six colors are available for either the actual drawing or for a change of background color; three pen sizes will produce thick strokes or fine detail. If you'd like to throw in some straight lines between any points on the screen, fine; and it's simple to selectively erase parts of a drawing, or the whole screen, instantly. None of this is going to do you much good if you can't preserve the results of your painstaking labor, so it is possible to save drawings on a disk and load them back into memory another time for viewing or modification. What

happens if you get stuck and can't remember how to erase the screen, or change color? Type control-H for help! and a page listing all the commands appears in place of the graphics screen; after perusing for a while, hit a key and the graphics screen is instantly restored, with any drawings intact.

When the program is run, a title page appears, followed by the command page after a key is pressed. As I said, you can pop right back here when in trouble by typing control-H. It's very helpful for beginners, but as you grow more experienced you won't be needing it anymore. Press another key and the real fun starts.

The text screen is now replaced by the black high resolution graphics screen, with a flashing white dot hiding somewhere about. If you doubt my word, turn the paddle knobs and it will magically dance across the screen. This is the point mode, as the first text line informs you, and pen position is indicated by that little blinking dot; it's color is white on a black screen and black on the others to improve visibility. To pop back into it when drawing, press P and the point will reappear. You can use it to carefully erase or chip away at parts of a drawing, or to jump quickly from place to place without drawing.

Ready to start a picture? Hit the W key and the dot stops flashing; by manipulating the paddle, you can produce a fine line of small white dots. Quickly move the pen to separate the dots, or draw slowly and carefully for a smooth white line. You can instantly change colors by pressing the first letter of the color desired (control-B for blue to differentiate it from B for black). It's just as easy to change pen size; press S and numerically choose small, medium, or large by pressing 1, 2 or 3. The point mode resumes, so press a color to begin drawing again in the new size. The pen will now be a small box instead of a single point, and a thicker line will result as you draw. Varying pen size within a drawing will produce more pleasing results, so use all three to spice up your work. The largest size, by the way, will quickly color in large areas of a picture, such as the sky.

But suppose you'd rather draw black on a white background, or blue on an orange background? No problem! Press X and then the number of the new background color you want; the screen will be instantly filled with that color, and you'll be returned to the point mode. In the process, everything on the screen is erased, so if you hit X by mistake, "return" will get you back to the point mode, safe and sound!

I'm sure that the first few attempts at a drawing will result in a meaningless clutter on the screen; it takes a lot of practice to draw easily with the paddles. By typing control-W, you can erase the whole screen instantly and start over again for (hopefully!) better results. Or you can selectively erase parts of a drawing, either by using the point or with the special erase mode. Press E and a large, blinking square will appear in place of the pen; move it carefully around to erase more quickly than with the point. The eraser is easier to locate than the point, being larger and more visible, so it could also be called a kind of extended point mode.

The line drawing mode can be used to quickly draw straight, even lines between any two points on the screen; a line is drawn in the last pen color used, and its thickness corresponds to the current pen size. After L is pressed, the flashing point reappears on the screen, and its changing X-Y coordinates are continuously displayed in the text window. To set the first endpoint, hit a key; the point will be plotted, followed by a brief pause so that the pen can be moved away. Then the flashing dot reappears, and the second endpoint can be set in the same way. The program asks if there are any corrections, and if the endpoints are exactly where you want them, depress N to draw the line and return to the point mode. Pressing Y gives the option of changing either or both of the endpoints; hit 1 to change point #1, 2 to change point #2, or B to change both. Hitting "return" when in the line drawing mode returns you to the point mode.

Okay, so now you have a great picture done that you want to show your family and friends; how can it be saved? Type control-S and enter the name you'd like it to be stored under; this name should begin with a letter, not a number or control character, although these can be used after the first letter. Hit "return", and the contents of the entire high resolution screen will be saved in a binary file on the disk. Be careful, because an unlocked file with the same name will be erased and written over! If you change

your mind about saving, hit "return" to reenter the point mode. The same process holds true for the load command (control-L), but instead of saving, a high resolution picture will be loaded into memory from the specified disk file, gradually filling the graphics screen and erasing anything previously displayed. One important note here: if you load a picture with a colored background, make sure you change the screen to the correct color first. Otherwise, the point mode will start erasing the background, as it might previously have been set for a black screen.

The final command is control-E, and it allows for a graceful, dignified exit from the program, after giving you one last chance to reconsider. More violent types will, I'm sure, use control-C or even (ugh!) reset; make your choice accordingly. And now, for the program itself:

Line 5 resets LOMEM: to 16384, above the primary page of high resolution graphics. While I was entering the program, I painfully discovered that as it

grew, it extended upward above location 8192 and into the primary high resolution page, causing the random lines to appear on the graphics screen. The last few lines of the program also acquired bad habits, playing hide and seek with me when more was added to the program. All very unpleasant, but the first line magically cures the problem. Incidentally, LOMEM: is reset to its normal value (just above 2000 with firmware Applesoft), by NEW, DEL, and by adding or changing a program line.

Lines 10-50 print the title page, wait for a key to be pressed, clear the keyboard strobe, and go to subroutine 1000, which prints out the command page.

Line 90 traps for an error that might occur during the program run; without it, the program would bomb out, and you would probably lose your picture. It sends program flow to subroutine 4000, where the error is appropriately processed.

Line 100 is initialization; it sets point and screen color, pen size, drawing modes, and D$ as Control-D for DOS commands. It clears the text screen and initializes the high resolution display; then line 105 pops the cursor down to the 21st line directly below the graphics screen and goes to subroutine 650, which

handles the point mode and pen size display.

Lines 100-200 handle the drawing, depending on the present program mode and pen size. If a key is pressed, line 110 goes to subroutine 300, which handles commands. Lines 120 and 130 read the two paddles for the X and Y pen position. If the point mode is true, line 140 plots at the present position, erases, resets the color and returns to line 110. Lines 150 and 160 draw a medium and large box in the present color, depending on pen size, if the erase mode is off. If the eraser is on, lines 170 and 180 set its color, depending on the present screen color, and 190 draws and erases it. If none of the above are true, line 200 plots the point and returns to line 110.

The following are program subroutines that are used when commands are input from the keyboard:

Lines 300-385 process commands, calling other subroutines in the process and finally returning to the main drawing section. Line 300 gets the character pressed from the keyboard and clears the keyboard strobe. The remaining lines change colors or modes, or call other subroutines if necessary, depending on the command that has been entered. If the key pressed is not a command, line 385 returns to the main drawing section.

Lines 500-530 save a picture on disk; line 520 alerts DOS with previously initialized D$ and BSAVEs the entire memory contents of high resolution page 1 under the file name input in line 510. A$2000 specifies the starting hexadecimal address (8192 decimal) and L$2000 specifies the length of the area of memory to be stored. Lines 600-630 are used in the same way to load a picture from disk into memory starting at hex location 2000, the beginning of the primary page.

Lines 650-660 set the color of the point for the point mode, depending on the present screen color. Line 660 clears the text window, sets and prints the point mode, goes to subroutine 3000 where the pen size is displayed, and returns.

Lines 700-730 are reached by control-E, and provide a dignified exit from the program. As I said before, killjoys may use "reset" or control-C if they wish.

Lines 800-840 print out the numbers for the different colors and get a character response. "Return" or CHR$ (13) pops you back into the drawing routine after resetting the point mode; an incorrect response causes line 815 to get another character. Otherwise, line 830 sets the new screen color, plots a point, and calls the special machine language routine 62454 to clear the screen in the last color HPLOTed. Finally, line 840 goes to subroutine 650, which handles the point mode restoration and pen size display.

Lines 900-940 use the same method to get a new pen size; a valid response resets

```
PRINT "80        "
]LIST

5   LOMEM: 16384
10  HOME : VTAB 10: HTAB 7: PRINT "***      APPLE-SKETCH      ***": PRINT
20  HTAB 13: PRINT "BY DAVID MILLER"
30  VTAB 19: HTAB 11: PRINT "HIT ANY KEY TO BEGIN"
40  IF  PEEK ( - 16384) < = 127 THEN 40
50  POKE  - 16368,0: GOSUB 1000
90  ONERR  GOTO 4000
100 HOME : HGR :OLDCLR = 3: HCOLOR= 3:SCRNCLR = 0:PNT = 1:ER = 0:SML = 1:
    MED = 0:LRG = 0:D$ =  CHR$ (4)
105 VTAB 21: GOSUB 650
110 IF  PEEK ( - 16384) > 127 THEN  GOSUB 300
120 X =  PDL (1) * 1.21 + 2: IF X > 277 THEN X = 277
130 Y =  PDL (0) + 2: IF Y > 157 THEN Y = 157
140 IF PNT THEN  HPLOT X,Y: HCOLOR= SCRNCLR: HPLOT X,Y: HCOLOR= OLDCLR: GOTO
    110
150 IF MED AND ER = 0 THEN  HPLOT X,Y: HPLOT X - 1,Y - 1 TO X + 1,Y - 1 TO
    X + 1,Y + 1 TO X - 1,Y + 1 TO X - 1,Y - 1: GOTO 110
160 IF LRG AND ER = 0 THEN  HPLOT X,Y: HPLOT X - 1,Y - 1 TO X + 1,Y - 1 TO
    X + 1,Y + 1 TO X - 1,Y + 1 TO X - 1,Y - 1: HPLOT X - 2,Y - 2 TO X + 2
    ,Y - 2 TO X + 2,Y + 2 TO X - 2,Y + 2 TO X - 2,Y - 2: GOTO 110
170 IF ER AND SCNRCLR = 0 THEN OLDCLR = 3
180 IF ER AND SCNRCLR < > 0 THEN OLDCLR = 0
190 IF ER THEN  HCOLOR= OLDCLR: HPLOT X,Y: HPLOT X - 1,Y - 1 TO X + 1,Y -
    1 TO X + 1,Y + 1 TO X - 1,Y + 1 TO X - 1,Y - 1: HCOLOR= SCRNCLR: HPLOT
    X,Y: HPLOT X - 1,Y - 1 TO X + 1,Y - 1 TO X + 1,Y + 1 TO X - 1,Y + 1 TO
    X - 1,Y - 1: GOTO 110
200 HPLOT X,Y: GOTO 110
299 REM  *** COMMAND SUBROUTINE
300 GET A$: POKE  - 16368,0
305 IF A$ =  CHR$ (23) THEN  HCOLOR= SCRNCLR: HPLOT 0,0: CALL 62454: HCOLOR=
    OLDCLR: RETURN
310 IF A$ = "W" THEN  HOME : VTAB 21: PRINT "COLOR=WHITE":OLDCLR = 3: HCOLOR=
    3:PNT = 0:ER = 0: GOSUB 3000: RETURN
315 IF A$ =  CHR$ (2) THEN  HOME : VTAB 21: PRINT "COLOR=BLUE":OLDCLR = 6
    : HCOLOR= 6:PNT = 0:ER = 0: GOSUB 3000: RETURN
320 IF A$ = "G" THEN  HOME : VTAB 21: PRINT "COLOR=GREEN":OLDCLR = 1: HCOLOR=
    1:PNT = 0:ER = 0: GOSUB 3000: RETURN
325 IF A$ = "E" THEN  HOME : VTAB 21: PRINT "ERASE MODE":PNT = 0:ER = 1: RETURN
330 IF A$ = "V" THEN  HOME : VTAB 21: PRINT "COLOR=VIOLET":OLDCLR = 2: HCOLOR=
    2:PNT = 0:ER = 0: GOSUB 3000: RETURN
335 IF A$ = "O" THEN  HOME : VTAB 21: PRINT "COLOR=ORANGE":OLDCLR = 5: HCOLOR=
    5:PNT = 0:ER = 0: GOSUB 3000: RETURN
340 IF A$ = "B" THEN  HOME : VTAB 21: PRINT "COLOR=BLACK":OLDCLR = 0: HCOLOR=
    0:PNT = 0:ER = 0: GOSUB 3000: RETURN
345 IF A$ =  CHR$ (12) THEN  HOME : VTAB 21: GOSUB 600: RETURN
350 IF A$ = "S" THEN  HOME : VTAB 21: GOSUB 900: RETURN
355 IF A$ = "P" THEN  HOME : VTAB 21: GOSUB 650: RETURN
360 IF A$ =  CHR$ (8) THEN  GOSUB 1000: GOSUB 650: RETURN
365 IF A$ =  CHR$ (19) THEN  HOME : VTAB 21: GOSUB 500: RETURN
370 IF A$ = "L" THEN  GOSUB 2000: RETURN
375 IF A$ = "X" THEN  GOSUB 800
380 IF A$ =  CHR$ (5) THEN  GOSUB 700
385 RETURN
500 REM   *** SAVE PICTURE
510 PRINT "READY TO SAVE PICTURE      ";: INVERSE : PRINT "RETURN";: NORMAL
    : PRINT " TO EXIT": INPUT "PICTURE NAME ? ";PICTURE$
515 IF PICTURE$ = "" THEN  GOSUB 650: RETURN
520 PRINT D$;"BSAVE ";PICTURE$;", A$2000, L$2000"
530 PRINT PICTURE$;" SAVED. ": FOR I = 1 TO 3000: NEXT I: GOSUB 650: RETURN

600 REM   *** LOAD PICTURE
610 PRINT "READY TO LOAD PICTURE      ";: INVERSE : PRINT "RETURN";: NORMAL
    : PRINT " TO EXIT": INPUT "PICTURE NAME ? ";PICTURE$
615 IF PICTURE$ = "" THEN  GOSUB 650: RETURN
620 PRINT D$;"BLOAD ";PICTURE$;", A$2000"
630 PRINT PICTURE$;" LOADED. ": FOR I = 1 TO 3000: NEXT I: GOSUB 650: RETURN

649 REM  ***  SET POINT MODE COLOR
650 IF SCNRCLR = 0 THEN OLDCLR = 3: GOTO 660
655 OLDCLR = 0
660 HCOLOR= OLDCLR:PNT = 1: HOME : VTAB 21: PRINT "POINT MODE": GOSUB 300
    0: RETURN
669 REM  ***  CTRL-E  EXIT PROGRAM?
700 HOME : VTAB 21: PRINT "REALLY EXIT THE PROGRAM (Y/N) ? ";
705 GET A$
710 IF A$ = "Y" THEN  TEXT : HOME : GOTO 4100
720 IF A$ = "N" THEN  GOSUB 650: RETURN
730 GOTO 705
799 REM  *** CHANGE BACKGROUND COLOR
800 HOME : VTAB 21: PRINT "BLACK-0    GREEN-1    VIOLET-2    WHITE-3": PRINT
    "ORANGE-5    BLUE-6    ";: INVERSE : PRINT "RETURN";: NORMAL : PRINT "
    TO EXIT"
810 PRINT "NEW BACKGROUND COLOR # ";
815 GET Z$: IF Z$ =  CHR$ (13) THEN 840
820 IF  ASC (Z$) < 48 OR  ASC (Z$) > 54 OR Z$ = "4" THEN 815
830 SCRNCLR =  VAL (Z$): HCOLOR= SCRNCLR: HPLOT 0,0: CALL 62454: HCOLOR= O
    LDCLR
```

pen size and goes to subroutine 650, which handles point mode and pen size display. An incorrect response causes line 905 to get another character.

Lines 1000-1210 display the command page. Line 1000 puts the screen back into the text mode and clears it; after the commands are printed, line 1200 waits for a key to be pressed. Then 1210 clears the keyboard strobe and uses POKE-16304,0 to restore the high resolution graphics screen without clearing it to black (which is what another HGR command would do).

Lines 2000-2470 handle the line drawing, displaying the X and Y coordinates for each point and HPLOTing the lines. Lines 2060 and 2070 read the paddles for point #1, and 2190 and 2200 read them for point #2.

Lines 3000-3030 check for the current pen size and display it beneath the lower right of the graphics screen.

Finally, lines 4000-4070 handle any DOS errors that might occur when loading or saving picutres. Line 4010 sets A to the Apple error code for the trapped

error, which is stored in decimal location 222; it also sets B equal to the line that the error occurred on. Then it clears the text screen and tabs down to the top of the text window, ready to print a message based on the error. The lines after handle:

1. Attempts to load a picture not on disk (DOS "file not found" error).

2. Attempts to save on a write protected disk, such as the DOS master or one with a write protect tab covered.

3. An I/O error, usually encountered when the disk drive door is left open.

4. Attemts to save on a filled disk, or with too little space left to hold the picture.

5. Attempts to save under a file name on disk that is locked.

6. The use of an illegal file name, usually beginning with a number or a control character.

7. Attempts to load a Basic or text file as a picture (believe me, that just won't work!)

8. Control-C: returns the text mode and ends.

As far as I can see, those are the only errors that would normally occur when running the program; all other input is handled by GET and thrown out if inappropriate. If all else fails, line 4060 tells you what error occurred and where before stopping the program. Before

```
840   GOSUB 650: RETURN
899   REM  *** CHANGE PEN SIZE
900   PRINT "READY TO CHANGE PEN SIZE": PRINT "SMALL(1) - MEDIUM(2) - LARGE
      (3) ?";
905   GET A$
910   IF A$ = "1" THEN SML = 1:MED = 0:LRG = 0: GOSUB 650: RETURN
920   IF A$ = "2" THEN SML = 0:MED = 1:LRG = 0: GOSUB 650: RETURN
930   IF A$ = "3" THEN SML = 0:MED = 0:LRG = 1: GOSUB 650: RETURN
940   GOTO 905
999   REM  *** COMMAND PAGE
1000  TEXT : HOME : HTAB 6: PRINT "***    LIST OF COMMANDS    ***": PRINT : PRINT
1010  INVERSE : PRINT "CTRL"; : NORMAL : PRINT " B - SETS DRAWING COLOR TO
      BLUE"
1020  PRINT   TAB( 6);"W - SETS DRAWING COLOR TO WHITE"
1030  PRINT   TAB( 6);"B - SETS DRAWING COLOR TO BLACK"
1040  PRINT   TAB( 6);"O - SETS DRAWING COLOR TO ORANGE"
1050  PRINT   TAB( 6);"G - SETS DRAWING COLOR TO GREEN"
1060  PRINT   TAB( 6);"V - SETS DRAWING COLOR TO VIOLET"
1070  PRINT
1080  PRINT   TAB( 6);"P - CHANGES TO POINT MODE"
1090  PRINT   TAB( 6);"E - CHANGES TO ERASE MODE"
1100  PRINT   TAB( 6);"L - CHANGES TO LINE DRAWING MODE"
1110  PRINT   TAB( 6);"X - CHANGES BACKGROUND COLOR"
1120  PRINT   TAB( 6);"S - CHANGES PEN DRAWING SIZE"
1130  PRINT
1140  INVERSE : PRINT "CTRL"; : NORMAL : PRINT " W - WIPE SCREEN CLEAR, STA
      RT OVER"
1150  INVERSE : PRINT "CTRL"; : NORMAL : PRINT " S - SAVE CURRENT PICTURE O
      N DISK"
1160  INVERSE : PRINT "CTRL"; : NORMAL : PRINT " L - LOAD PICTURE FROM DISK
      "
1170  INVERSE : PRINT "CTRL"; : NORMAL : PRINT " H - DISPLAY THIS PAGE OF C
      OMMANDS"
1180  INVERSE : PRINT "CTRL"; : NORMAL : PRINT " E - EXIT THE PROGRAM"
1190  PRINT : PRINT  TAB( 6);"HIT ANY KEY WHEN READY..."
1200  IF  PEEK ( - 16384) <  = 127 THEN 1200
1210  POKE  - 16368,0: POKE  - 16304,0: RETURN
2000  REM  *** DRAW LINE
2010 LINE$ = "                    "
2020 CH = 0:X1 = 0:X2 = 0:Y1 = 0:Y2 = 0:QX = 0:QY = 0
2030  HOME : VTAB 21: PRINT "LINE DRAWING MODE        "; : INVERSE : PRINT
      "RETURN"; : NORMAL : PRINT " TO EXIT"
2040  VTAB 22: PRINT "POINT #1: X=      Y=      <HIT KEY TO SET"
2050  IF  PEEK ( - 16384) > 127 THEN  GET A$: POKE  - 16368,0: VTAB 22: HTAB
      25: PRINT LINE$:QX = X1:QY = Y1: GOSUB 2430: GOTO 2150
2060 X1 =  PDL (1) * 1.21 + 2: IF X1 > 277 THEN X1 = 277
2070 Y1 =  PDL (0) + 2: IF Y1 > 157 THEN Y1 = 157
2075  VTAB 22: HTAB 13: PRINT  INT (X1);
2080  IF X1 < 10 THEN  PRINT "   "
2090  IF X1 >  = 10 AND X1 < 100 THEN  PRINT "  "
2100  IF X1 >  = 100 THEN  PRINT " "
2105  VTAB 22: HTAB 20: PRINT  INT (Y1);
2110  IF Y1 < 10 THEN  PRINT "   "
2120  IF Y1 >  = 10 AND Y1 < 100 THEN  PRINT "  "
2130  IF Y1 >  = 100 THEN  PRINT " "
2140  HCOLOR= OLDCLR: HPLOT X1,Y1: HCOLOR= SCRNCLR: HPLOT X1,Y1: GOTO 2050

2150  IF CH = 1 THEN 2290
2160  IF A$ =  CHR$ (13) THEN 2300
2170  VTAB 23: PRINT "POINT #2: X=      Y=      <HIT KEY TO SET"
2180  IF  PEEK ( - 16384) > 127 THEN  GET A$: POKE  - 16368,0: VTAB 23: HTAB
      25: PRINT LINE$:QX = X2:QY = Y2: GOSUB 2430: GOTO 2280
2190 X2 =  PDL (1) * 1.21 + 2: IF X2 > 277 THEN X2 = 277
2200 Y2 =  PDL (0) + 2: IF Y2 > 157 THEN Y2 = 157
2205  VTAB 23: HTAB 13: PRINT  INT (X2);
2210  IF X2 < 10 THEN  PRINT "   "
2220  IF X2 >  = 10 AND X2 < 100 THEN  PRINT "  "
2230  IF X2 >  = 100 THEN  PRINT " "
2235  VTAB 23: HTAB 20: PRINT  INT (Y2);
2240  IF Y2 < 10 THEN  PRINT "   "
```

running the program, I suggest taking a CATALOG of the disk to see what pictures are available, and which are locked (it would be a good idea to lock an important picture to prevent accidental erasure). Since you won't be able to save onto a locked file name, you'd have to save under another name to preserve your present version without losing the program.

Once a picture has been saved on disk, it can be recalled from a Basic program and displayed using the same technique as in subroutine 600. The program should initialize the string D$ as control-D or CHR$(4), then set the primary page of high resolution graphics and load the picture into memory using DOS commands.

There are a few limitations to what you can do with this program. One problem arises in that the Apple paddles are not very sturdy and tend to become worn with usage. Theoretically, they should produce a steady stream of values from 0 to 255. When new, yes. After a few weeks of Space Invaders and assorted other

If all else fails, line 4060 tells you what error occurred.

paddle games, no. Presently, my PDL(O) only goes up to about 180, and PDL(1) to 225. As a result, I use PDL(O) for the Y input, which only has to go about 160. Unfortunately, the screen is 280 units wide, so my PDL(1) values have to be multiplied to make the pen cover the entire screen, and in the process, some values are lost. With multiplication, I've discovered that about two out of every ten X values just cannot be produced, and it becomes impossible to draw a perfectly smooth line in the X direction. Is there a solution to the problem?

Yes, even if only a partial one, and I suggest it for those who type in this program. The first step is to find out just how your particular paddles will go. Change lines 2060 and 2070 to X1=PDL(1) and Y1=PDL(O). Then enter the line drawing mode and move your paddles clockwise from zero to the highest possible values. Say your paddles are functioning perfectly, and PDL(1) stops at 255. You *can* use the paddle values without multiplying if you leave a small margin on either side of the page. For a perfect paddle, subtract 255 from 280 and divide by 2, leaving a margin of 12.5 on each side. Let's call it 12, and change line 2060 to read:

```
2060 X1=PDL(1)+12:IF X1 > 277
     THEN X1=277
```

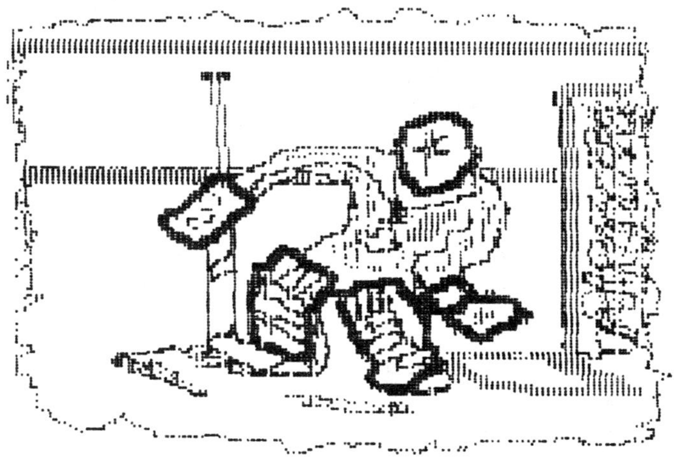

```
2250  IF Y2 >  = 10 AND Y2 < 100 THEN  PRINT " "
2260  IF Y2 >  = 100 THEN  PRINT " "
2270  HCOLOR= OLDCLR: HPLOT X2,Y2: HCOLOR= SCRNCLR: HPLOT X2,Y2: GOTO 2180
2280  IF A$ =  CHR$ (13) THEN 2300
2290  VTAB 21: HTAB 1: PRINT "ANY CORRECTIONS ? ";
2295  GET A$
2300  IF A$ =  CHR$ (13) THEN  HCOLOR= SCRNCLR: HPLOT X1,Y1: HPLOT X2,Y2: HCOLOR
      = OLDCLR: GOTO 2460
2310  IF A$ = "Y" THEN 2360
2320  IF A$ = "N" AND SML THEN  HPLOT X1,Y1 TO X2,Y2: GOTO 2450
2330  IF A$ = "N" AND MED THEN  FOR I =  - 1 TO 1: HPLOT X1 + I,Y1 + I TO
      X2 + I,Y2 + I: NEXT I: GOTO 2450
2340  IF A$ = "N" AND LRG THEN  FOR I =  - 2 TO 2: HPLOT X1 + I,Y1 + I TO
      X2 + I,Y2 + I: NEXT I: GOTO 2450
2350  GOTO 2295
2360  VTAB 21: HTAB 1: PRINT LINE$;"    ": VTAB 21: HTAB 1: PRINT "POINT 1,
      2, OR BOTH ?";
2370  GET A$
2380  IF A$ =  CHR$ (13) THEN 2300
2390  IF A$ = "1" THEN CH = 1: GOSUB 2470: HPLOT X1,Y1: HCOLOR= OLDCLR: GOTO
      2040
2400  IF A$ = "2" THEN CH = 2: GOSUB 2470: HPLOT X2,Y2: HCOLOR= OLDCLR: GOTO
      2170
2410  IF A$ = "B" THEN CH = 0: GOSUB 2470: HPLOT X1,Y1: HPLOT X2,Y2: HCOLOR=
      OLDCLR: GOTO 2040
2420  GOTO 2370
2430  IF A$ =  CHR$ (13) THEN  RETURN
2440  HCOLOR= OLDCLR: HPLOT QX,QY: FOR I = 1 TO 500: NEXT I: RETURN
2450  HOME : VTAB 21: PRINT "DONE...": FOR I = 1 TO 1000: NEXT I
2460  GOSUB 650: RETURN
2470  VTAB 21: HTAB 1: PRINT LINE$;"    ": VTAB 21: HTAB 1: PRINT "LINE D
      RAWING MODE": HCOLOR= SCRNCLR: RETURN
2999  REM  *** PEN SIZE DISPLAY
3000  VTAB 21: HTAB 25: PRINT "PEN SIZE=";
3010  IF SML THEN  PRINT "SMALL ": RETURN
3020  IF MED THEN  PRINT "MEDIUM": RETURN
3030  IF LRG THEN  PRINT "LARGE ": RETURN
4000  REM  *** ERROR TRAPPING
4010  A =  PEEK (222):B =  PEEK (218) +  PEEK (219) * 256: HOME : VTAB 21
4020  IF A = 6 THEN  PRINT "YOU DON'T HAVE THAT PICTURE ON DISK...": GOTO
      4070
4025  IF A = 4 THEN  PRINT "YOUR DISK IS WRITE PROTECTED !": PRINT "USE AN
      OTHER OR REMOVE WRITE PROTECT TAB. ": GOTO 4070
4030  IF A = 8 THEN  PRINT "I/O ERROR...IS YOUR DISK DRIVE OPEN ?": PRINT
      "IF NOT, TRY AGAIN OR USE ANOTHER DISK. ": GOTO 4070
4035  IF A = 9 THEN  PRINT "TOO MANY FILES ON DISK; DELETE SOME": PRINT "O
      R USE ANOTHER DISK. ": GOTO 4070
4040  IF A = 10 THEN  PRINT "THAT DISK FILE IS LOCKED...UNLOCK IT": PRINT
      "OR USE ANOTHER NAME FOR YOUR PICTURE. ": GOTO 4070
4045  IF A = 11 THEN  PRINT "ILLEGAL FILE NAME. ": PRINT "PLEASE BEGIN WITH
      A LETTER. ": GOTO 4070
4050  IF A = 13 THEN  PRINT "THAT FILE IS NOT A PICTURE...": GOTO 4070
4055  IF A = 255 THEN  TEXT : HOME : GOTO 4100
4060  PRINT "PROGRAM TERMINATED DUE TO ERROR ";A: PRINT "LINE # ";B: GOTO
      4100
4070  FOR I = 1 TO 3000: NEXT I: GOSUB 650: GOTO 110
4100  TEXT : END
```

Now you can get *all* of the X values between 12 and 267, and can draw a perfectly smooth line. You *won't* be able to go outside of those two margins, but they are really very small and I believe the sacrifice is worth it. Likewise, change lines 120 and 2190 to read:

```
120 X=PDL(1)+12:IF X>277 THEN X=277

2190 X2=PDL(1)+12:IF X2>277
     THEN X2=277
```

I've altered my version in the same way; as my paddle goes to 225, I add 27 to the PDL(1) values and lose a somewhat larger margin. It's all up to your personal preference; remember, these are very inexpensive input devices and it's going to take a little experimentation to get them working just right.

I'd also like to warn you that certain colors will not draw cleanly on colored backgrounds, due to the way the high resolution display works. Drawing black on an orange background, for example, produces ragged green fringes, which may also appear when erasing orange on

---

The fringe effects may be just what you want to produce a dazzling, modernistic picture.

---

another background. These color fringes appear mainly when using the colored backgrounds. They don't seem to be a problem when drawing on black or white. Consequently, I'd advise drawing on either black or white; if you'd like large areas of another color, switch to the large pen and color them in. Of course, the fringe effects may be just what you want to produce a dazzling, modernistic picture.

Don't forget, graphics tablets cost money for a good reason: they are very fast, accurate, and sophisticated. A simple Basic program, such as mine, is hard put to match their performance using very inexpensive paddles as input devices. It can, however, provide a creative challenge and hours of plain old fun if the user has just a little patience and self control (please try not to offend or abuse your poor machine in any way). I can't promise miracles, but believe me, you *can* draw good pictures if you use some imagination and creativity. I know, because I've done some myself that I like very much! Inevitably, some people just won't be able to get the knack of drawing with the paddles, no matter how hard they try. Ah well, they can always go back to playing Space Invaders.... □

THE CROWD STOPPER

David L. Ross

What do a popcorn popper, diesel engine, birthday cake, beer mug, and a corporate logo have in common? Not much, you say? No so. These items, and countless others, can be computer-animated for display on a color TV screen or monitor in a visually fascinating fashion.

But why would anyone want to animate a popper or beer mug, I hear you cry. It's an area of advertising for which the waters are virtually uncharted. Because people enjoy watching the creative process of image development on the screen, computer animation is an effective promotional tool. Whether the display is placed in a trade show exhibit, store window, building lobby, or permanent product display, the results are impressive. The creative motion on the screen attracts a crowd in a way that a static display or sign seldom does. If cleverly done, animation communicates information to viewers in an entertaining, colorful way. In effect, it's a localized "TV spot" that runs continuously and grabs the attention of passers-by—at a fraction of the cost of regular network or videotape alternatives.

We recognized the universal appeal of the TV screen in early 1979 and began to investigate the possibilities inherent in the use of computer-controlled message displays. At that time, the closest application of this nature was the continuous scrolling of text commonly seen in hotel lobbies and other public areas, announcing meeting rooms, schedules, etc. Such displays are primitive—they're visually boring and can easily be ignored by viewers. Recognizing the potential of and need for more visual impact, we began developing graphic displays to communicate key points, using

David L. Ross, President, Micro Video, P.O. Box 7357, 204E. Washington St. Ann Arbor, MI 48107.

text only where necessary. Today, our presentations are 70-80% customized color graphics.

We're building a library of animation sub-sequences that can be "dropped into" larger productions—speedboats, champagne glasses, iced cakes with burning candles, flags. We're also developing software vehicles that make program customization, such as the inclusion of corporate logos, a simpler process. A further extension of this concept is the marriage of the video game and advertising presentations, in which the viewer actually participates in the exhibit. This is becoming a powerful "draw," particularly in trade shows. Promotional messages related to the game in play and/ or the exhibitor's products and services can be entered from the keyboard, allowing "instant customization," or embedded directly in the program. The originality of this advertising concept, as well as the portability, reliability, and cost of small computers makes the Crowd Stopper an attractive alternative to videotape players or other traditional display devices.

The Popcorn Pumper—Custom Animations

Our popcorn popper animation is summarized in eight frames taken from an animated presentation developed for Wear-Ever Aluminum, Inc., a subsidiary of Alcoa, for trade show display use. Like most animations, it relies heavily on the impact of imaginative development on the screen; it has to be seen in action to fully appreciate the effects. The Popcorn Pumper is drawn on the screen in two colors—yellow and white (just like the real product)—on a black background. The base and chamber outline are built at a variable rate, with

The importance of image development is illustrated in the popcorn popper animation sequence.

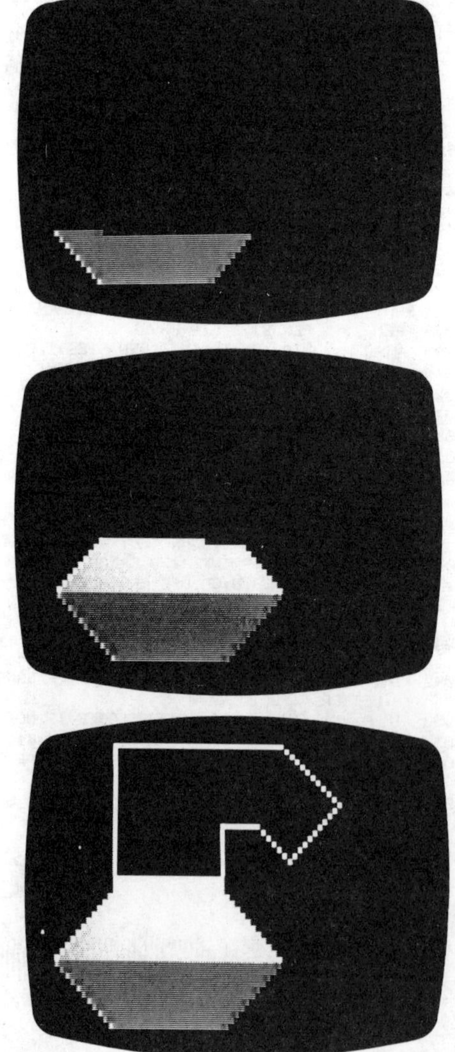

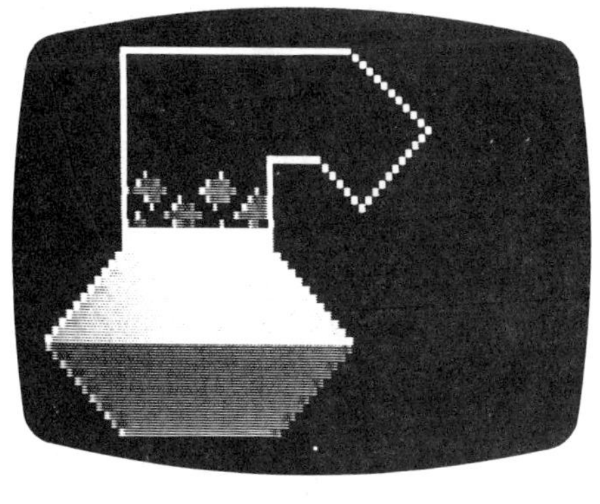

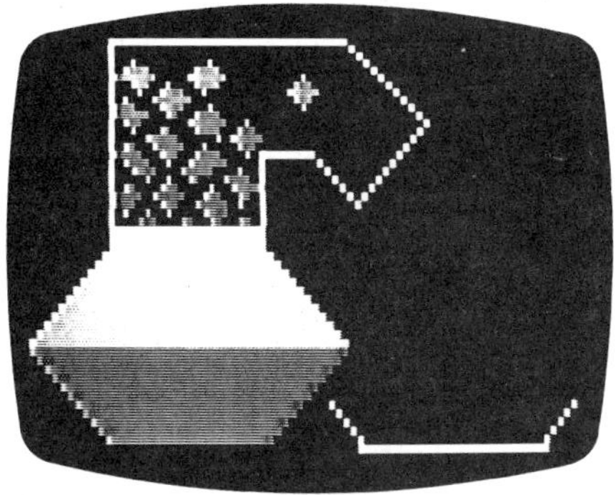

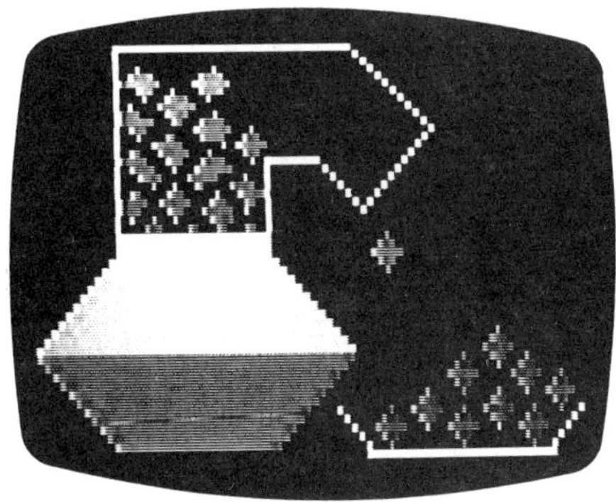

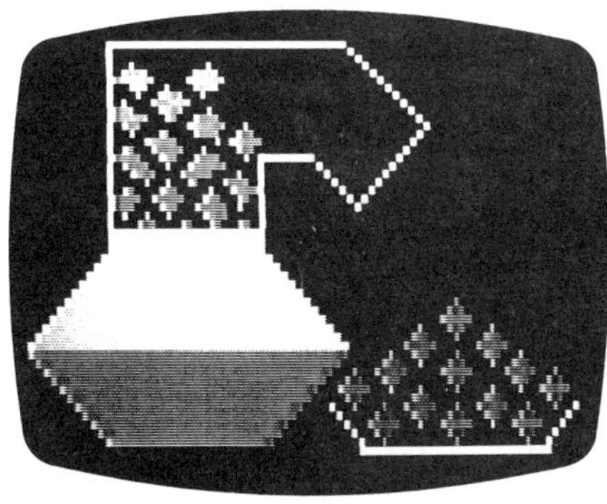

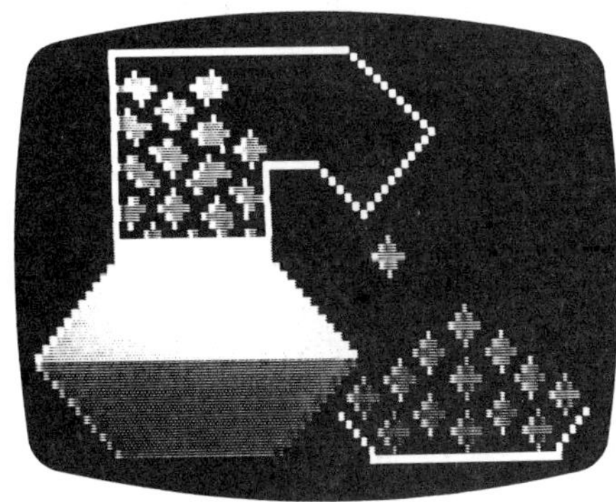

accompanying musical tones. Then we add the frenzied motion of popcorn actually "popping" in the chamber, complete with sound effects, and spill it out into the waiting bowl. Viewers invariably chuckle over this part of the presentation, and stay to watch the image development a second, third, ... time.

The popcorn popper was one of four products animated in a single program for use in Wear-Ever's Housewares Show exhibit. The presentation achieved its goal, stopping traffic in the aisle and creating interest in the Popcorn Pumper and other products Wear-ever manufactures for the home. It was so successful that the company has reused it numerous time in other trade shows.

Animations—Getting Started

To produce an effective animated display, we follow the procedures generally used in preparing speeches and written materials, with minor adaptations:

•Understand your audience. Who will primarily be viewing the presentation? Are you trying to attract the attention of adults or children? Men, women or both?

•Define your objectives. Do you want the animated presentation to sell the product or service and provide technical information as well? Or do you wish to simply stop and entertain the passing crowd? If so, for how long? What interaction with viewers do you want to effect? Will an "animated billboard" meet your goals? Or, do you want to use interactive advertising—customized video games with interweaved promotional messages—to invite participation in the exhibit and hold the viewers' interest long enough to allow company representatives to make personal contact?

•"Storyboard" the entire presentation. Try to achieve balance in the visual material, keeping it directed toward the anticipated audience and defined objectives.

•Develop the graphic images, transitions between images, and other highlighting effects, varying the animation techniques for high visual impact.

•Review the production with the client, and expect to make modifications and improvements. Seldom, if ever, is the first production the final version. Improvements can always be made.

•When approval of the presentation is final, make arrangements to watch the presentation in actual use. Is it effective? How well does it compete for people's attention in the environment in which it's being used? What portions are visually dull and need to be improved? Is the presentation meeting your defined objectives? Make note of needed modifications for future use.

An interesting phenomenon in computer-animated displays is that people's attention is generally held over multiple viewings. If you watch people in the vicinity of a presentation, you'll see their eyes continually drawn back to the screen—no matter how many times they've seen it before. You can use this as a barometer of the presentation's effectiveness.

Rules of Thumb for Successful Animation

We've evolved a set of guidelines that we believe differentiate good animated presentations from poor ones. While there are exceptions, these "rules of thumb" generally yield effective displays:

1) *Never scroll text vertically on the screen.* The human eye does not easily read material presented in this manner. More effective methods include partial screen wipes, erasing material by overwriting it in the background color, etc. The speed at which text is output to the screen and length of time it remains there are also important factors.

2) *Keep in mind that the method used to put the image on the screen is more important than the end result.* If the reverse were true, then a photograph or videotape of the actual product would be sufficient, as well as more technically accurate. Animation has the appeal of the quick sketch cartoonist at an amusement area. He holds his viewing crowds while he's drawing the picture, but tends to lose a large portion of this crowd and potential customers upon completion of the sketch.

3) *Always keep motion on the screen.* Avoid totally static screens by including at least slight movement with color changes, flashing, moving stick figures, etc. Motion ensures that viewers' eyes will stay glued to the screen—they want to see what will happen next.

4) *Avoid painfully slow image development, as it strains the viewer's interest in the display.* Faster graphics can be achieved by using broader lines or simplifying internal calculations that produce the image.

5) *Use unusual sequences to draw images.* This provides an element of surprise in the presentation and creates suspense. For example, if you need to draw a rectangular box, rather than using a single continuous line, consider drawing pairs of parallel lines going in different directions simultaneously. Or, if you want to include the American flag in your animation, don't draw it one stripe at a time—that's far too obvious. One approach you might use is to draw all red stripes simultaneously in one direction, followed by all the white stripes in the opposite direction, then add the blue field and output stars in a seemingly random fashion. The idea is to create suspense and pique the viewers' interest in whatever image you're producing.

6) *Vary the speed of the presentation.* Depending on the image and effects desired,

vary the speed accordingly. Don't draw everything as fast as possible—but allow the viewer to savor the image development. On the other hand, don't let a portion of the presentation drag enough to evoke a visual yawn.

7) *Use color for emphasis*. Color-code key concepts to improve viewer comprehension of the material. But don't carry this too far and use too many colors on a single screen simply because the computer has the capability of doing so. "Color overload" is as poor as a dull black and white presentation.

8) *Choose color combinations carefully*. Use colors that match the objects of animation if possible. Vary the color combinations throughout the presentation, but make sure all combinations are aesthetically pleasing, taking into consideration the audience, locations, and objectives.

9) *Use sound effects, if available on the computer, to highlight the animation*. In our beer mug animation, for example, sounds accompanying the graphics simulate the sounds of beer flowing into a mug, varying with the rate of flow and the fullness of the mug. Try to imitate sounds as appropriate to the image, but don't use a lot of non-related sounds, because in time they become annoying rather than entertaining. Also, don't continuously use sound for sound's sake in the presentation. Sounds add another dimension to the presentation, but too much sound will actually reduce, rather than augment, the impact.

10) *Use variety in message display*. experiment with three dimensional lettering, oversized letters, word swimming, color rolls, fades, and wipes. Words can be "shot out of cannons," color-highlighted, or "spoken" by animated characters or stick figures. Be sure that the text is readable by viewers, considering their distance from the screen, the screen size, lettering size, and duration held on the screen. You might also program the capability, as we do, of message input from the keyboard to allow last minute changes in presentation messages. This adds futher flexibility.

11) *Add humor to animations*. If your audience laughs, they'll watch longer. People love to be entertained.

12) *Pay special attention to transitions between graphic images*.Don't always clear the screen before producing another image. Allow one to evolve into another some of the time.

13) *Don't rush*. Good animations take time. Experiment with different ways of producing a single image and determine which is most visually effective, as this invariably leads to a better final result.

14) *Don't prejudge or limit your animation possibilities*. Life can be imposed even on lackluster objects such as a frying pan or toaster by the way they are drawn and the addition of a flickering flame beneath the pan or toasted bread "popping" out of the toaster.

A cardinal rule of animations is that they improve with experimentation and experience, provided enough time is allowed to do the work. Did I say "Work"? Yes, there are hours of work in every animation, but it's one of the most imaginative applications for home computers, and can give more sheer pleasure and satisfaction than other types of programming. It's enormously gratifying to watch people become enthralled with and chortle with delight over a particularly clever presentation.

So, consider the possibilities! Almost anything can be animated. We use the Interact computer, Microsoft Basic, and machine language to produce most of our animations. However, it's not so much the computer or language that you use, but the imagination that you put into programming the display that makes the difference. Give animation a try on your own computer. We think you'll find it will open up a whole new world of programming enjoyment and creativity for you. □

"AHA!!"

Apple Graphics Utilities

David Lubar

Back in the early days of the late seventies, very few people could cope with placing graphics on the Apple. We all knew it was possible, but the prospect of creating shape tables by hand was enough to dampen anyone's spirits. The picture began to brighten with the appearance of graphics utilities. *Creative Computing* published a shape table generator written by Gary D. Dawkins. Steve Wozniak of Apple furnished a shape-table program in his **Wozpak**. These programs not only allowed easy design of shapes, they also stored a series of shapes in a table, taking a major element of drudgery out of programming. Now, there are many graphics utilities on the market. Four of these programs are covered below.

Local Color

Bob Bishop, who is to Apple graphics what Wilbur and Orville were to flight, has moved the coloring book into the computer age with *Micro Painter*. The system allows you to fill in hi-res pictures with twenty-one colors. The disk includes eight drawings. When the program starts, you select a picture, either from the disk or from any disk with a drawing on it. The picture is placed on the screen, along with a flashing crosshair controlled by paddles. Colors are selected with two keystrokes. Normal blue is BB, light blue is LB, dark blue is DB, and so on. Once a color is selected, a push of the paddle button causes an area to be filled. The color spreads out in a diamond pattern, stopping whenever it encounters a black line. Once an area has been colored, it can't be easily recolored. The paint mode only functions against a white background. Colored pictures can be saved on disk.

Since most drawing programs and graphics tablets produce a white line on a

Drawing by Saul Bernstein on *Micro Painter.*

black background, Bishop has included a command which produces a negative of the screen. Thus you can draw with any graphics program, save the picture, bring it back under Micro Painter, and reverse the colors to obtain black lines on a white background.

Micro Painter also has a microscope mode which expands the picture to seven and a half times normal size. In this mode, you can examine and change individual pixels. This is handy for patching up small, enclosed areas that can't be filled in the normal mode.

It seemed to me that Micro Painter would be an ideal program to get people interested in computers. It is easy to use, fun, and produces immediate, observable results. A friend, who had very little computer experience, tried the program and had no difficulty following the instructions, which are clear and well written. She was, however, very amused by the microscope mode and the line in the instructions which said, "The Paint Brush and the area around it have been magnified seven and a half times!" After she stopped laughing, she explained that the microscope she uses at work has a resolution of 100,000X. Her amusement quickly gave way to absorbtion as she went on to color several drawings.

For beginners who want to have a new kind of fun with the Apple or advanced programmers who need to color pictures, Micro Painter is an excellent program. The instructions also include a short program in Applesoft which allows you to draw with the paddles.

Penguin Graphics

Mark Pelczarski (alias the Magic Penguin), a very talented Apple programmer, is the author of two graphics packages. *Magic Paintbrush 4.0* contains programs for drawing on the screen and for developing shape tables. There are three drawing modes. The line mode draws a line between any two points. By holding down the paddle button as you move the cursor, you can obtain curves. The fill mode also draws lines, but keeps a constant origin for the lines, allowing you to fill in an area with a series of lines. The paint mode provides a choice of nine brushes with which to paint lines or fill background. Since these brushes are stored as a shape table, the user can define his own brushes.

The shape creation routines are very nice. There are two modes, Quickdraw uses the paddles and is designed to be fast but not accurate for intricate shapes. The shapes are designed in lo-res, but can be viewed at any time on the hi-res screen. While viewing them, the paddles control scale and rotation. The other method uses keys to plot the shape. While plotting, the scale and rotation can be changed using the paddles. This is a very versatile system. For instance, you can start with a scale of four, where each point is plotted four times, then shrink the shape. The ability to alter the shape in mid-plot allows a great deal of control over the final product.

As a bonus, the disk contains five games using shapes that were created with the Magic Paintbrush: Applesoft Invader, Slot Machine, Collision, Dogfight, and Sailboat Race. The Slot Machine program is nicely done. The Invader game is rather slow, but has a hilarious ending. Collision is a good simulation of the arcade game. The games are in Basic, and don't run as fast as machine-language versions, but they make a nice extra for the package.

If you take *Magic Paintbrush*, add three dimensional graphics routines, color fills, hi-res text, and other graphics routines, you'll have Mark Pelczarski's *Graphics System*. The three-dimensional utilities verge on the phenomenal. A figure can be rotated through any dimension, distorted, moved, or scaled. You can experiment with the two figures provided on the disk or create your own. Different figures can be placed on the screen and be manipulated separately. Two-dimensional shapes can be constructed using the panel utility, then be brought into the 3-D section where vertices can be joined. The distortion subroutines were the most fascinating. Any vertex of the figure can be stretched or shrunk through left/right, forward/back, or up/down distortion. At any point, the figure can be edited, changing the length of any of the lines, or changing the connections of the vertices. It takes a few minutes to get used to the routines for creating figures, but they are well constructed. Overall, the entire 3-D set is graced with easy input routines.

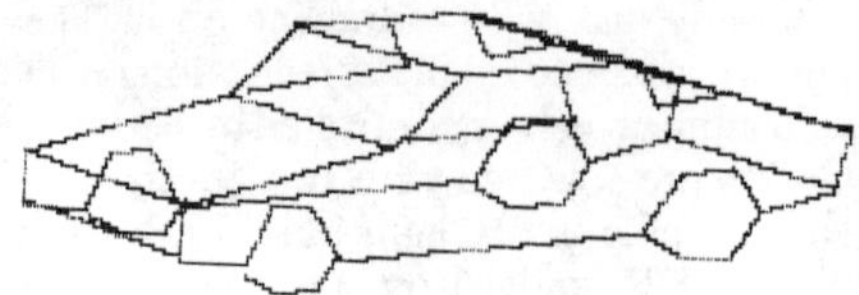

A 3-D Image by Mark Pelczarski.

The disk includes a program that shrinks a hi-res picture into one quarter of the screen. I should also mention that while the color-fill routines are not as effective as those in Micro Painter, and sometimes require several fills to cover the desired area, they do allow for over 100 colors.

Shape Up

Shape Master from **Sensational Software** is a utility specifically designed for creating and manipulating shape tables.

Shape creation is executed on hi-res grids, allowing each point to be seen in an expanded size. The user has a choice of five plotting grids, from 13-by-23 to 39-by-69, and two methods of plotting. The vector method consists of moving a cursor through the grid, and indicating which points on the path should be plotted or not plotted. This works along the lines of the traditional method where the programmer defines a series of vectors and indicates which points on the path should be plotted. At any time, you can reverse the moves, deleting the series or part of the series. The graph method allows for more flexibility. Here, individual points on the grid can be selected for plotting. Once all the desired points are chosen, the program constructs a table entry for the shape. This frees the user from worry about drawing the shape as one continous series of points. Shapes created previously can be brought into this mode for editing.

Once shapes have been created, they can be saved to a table or displayed. An entire table can be displayed, or individual shapes can be seen, scaled, and rotated. Adding to the utility of the program, any shape or group of shapes in a table can be reversed, giving a mirror image. These reversals can replace the original shapes or be appended to the table. Also, shapes within a table can be shuffled.

The authors, Doug Green and Matt Clark, have included four games and two graphics demos on the disk. The games are slow, but give good examples of what can be done with shape tables. The demos are superb. One shows a front or side view of an Atat walker from *The Empire Strikes Back* clumping along the screen. The other shows a Tie Fighter which can be rotated through three dimensions as it moves. The instructions are clear and thorough, covering all aspects of the program, and explaining how to use shapes in other programs.

End of the Rainbow

Obviously, each of the above programs has different virtues and flaws. *Micro Painter* is the best for filling areas, and the microscope mode allows for fine detailing. If you already have a good drawing program and shape-table creator, *Micro Painter* is the way to go. *Magic Paintbrush* has an excellent shape creator, and the use of definable brushes adds a lot of flexibility, but the fill routines are awkward. *Graphics System* offers a good variety of utilities, including excellent shape table routines, and is the only one of the above which includes 3-D utilities. However, it is expensive, and designed for the serious programmer who has need of these tools. *Shape Master* is designed strictly for shape tables, with no drawing routines, but it handles its functions very well. If your main concern is designing shapes for use in other programs, *Shape Master* has a lot to offer. Depending on what you already have, and what your prime needs are, each of these programs has something to offer. □

Apple Picture Packer

David Lubar

An Apple disk has a lot of space available, until you start saving hi-res pictures. Suddenly, 100K becomes very small. At best, you can store 12 pictures, along with a short program to display them. DOS 3.3 provides a bit more space, but still limits picture storage. Rather than look for more storage room, it seemed logical to try cramming the picture data into a smaller package.

While I had heard rumors that the Wizard of Cupertino knew how to fit more pictures on a disk, I'd never come across a program for doing this. I decided to give it a try. The task turned into something between an addiction and an obsession. I was never satisfied; each time I managed to reduce storage, I needed another sector—just one more, then I'd quit. And so it went for three weekends. I produced one revision after another, ending with Picture Packer 3.0. While there is still room for improvement, I believe the existing version is useful and worth sharing with the Apple community.

The program could have been written in Basic, but it would have been way too slow for any real-time application. Enter machine language—a bit tougher to write and debug, but a lot faster. My goal was to make a table that would contain 8K of hi-res data in less than 8K of space. Most pictures contain a fair amount of repetition. A look at screen memory (from $2000 to $3FFF for page one of hi-res graphics) will reveal that pictures tend to contain long strings of identical bytes.

Rather than store a series such as 00 00 00 00 44 77 00 00 00, it seemed reasonable to expect a saving of space by storing a table which said, "There are four zeroes, a 44, a 77, then three more zeroes." Using this approach, Picture Packer 1.0 was born. It made a table from screen memory. The table was composed of pairs of bytes; the first byte told how many times in a row the second byte appeared on the screen. In essence, the first byte gave the frequency of the second. For example, starting with a series of screen bytes such as 00 00 00 00 AA AA AA FF 00 00, the table would contain 04 00 03 AA 01 FF 02 00.

A test version was written to pack the lo-res screen. If it worked, the change for hi-res would be simple. The program packed a lo-res picture of 1K into a total of less than 3/4K. Feeling confident, I changed the pointers and tried packing

---

The pictures to the left were all scrunched with Picture Packer. The space scene required 14 sectors, "Adventure" took a mere 10 sectors, and "Hail to the Chief" required 19 sectors.

the hi-res screen. The first picture I tested was reduced from 32 sectors (8K requires 32 disk sectors—each disk sector contains 1/4K) down to 22 sectors. I was beginning to feel the thrill of victory when Murphy's law took effect. The next picture went from 32 sectors to 48—not exactly an economical conversion. Looking through the table and the hi-res screen, I noticed a lot of single bytes that didn't have the decency to repeat themselves and make life simple for me. The table saved space whenever there were strings of repeated bytes, but each unique byte required two bytes in the table. For example, the series 00 FF AA 38 would be packed (?) into a table as 01 00 01 FF 01 AA 01 38. Obviously, a slight change in strategy was required.

Looking at screen memory again, I noticed that there were patterns in most pictures. Some had long strings of identical bytes, others contained pairs of bytes such as AA 55 AA 55, while others had groups of four such as 38 FF AA 72 38 FF aa 72. I converted the program, making it go through the screen twice. On the first pass, it packed bytes 1,3,5 ...; on the second pass, it took care of 2,4,6 .... A series such as AA 55 AA 55 AA 55 would be represented by a table that started with 03 AA, followed by the rest of the first pass. The second pass would start with 03 55. This method succeeded in crunching pictures containing a large number of duplicate pairs.

I was faced with the unpleasant prospect of using different programs for different pictures. But there was a way around this non-utile aspect of the utility. Picture Packer 2.0 made three test packings of the screen. First, it constructed a table made by taking the bytes in order. After saving the length of this table, it did the packing in two passes, taking every second byte, then in four passes, taking every fourth byte. It compared the three table lengths and selected the method which produced the shortest table. This shortest version was repeated, and a byte was placed at the beginning of the table, telling how many passes were made. The unpacking program could use this first byte to tell what kind of table it was working with. The identification byte also served as the offset when stepping through the screen.

This version of the program produced a substantial improvement over the first version. Unfortunately, while some pictures were now being scrunched into as few as 16 sectors, others were still taking up more than 32 sectors. Looking through the table, I found the culprits were the single bytes. Each unique byte required two bytes in the table, and a series of unique bytes really killed any attempts at economy. It was time for a major change in strategy.

There had to be a way to reduce the space taken when storing a long series of unique bytes. Somehow, I had to put even more information in the table while using less space. I decided that instead of representing a series such as AA FF 35 7F as 01 AA 01 FF 01 35 01 7F, I could strip out all the 01's by using a signal byte such as FF, where FF NN would mean that the next NN bytes were unique. Had hindsight been working properly at the time, I would have seen the problem with this approach. However, logic tends to get a bit loose late at night, and I gave the method a try. The results were dismal. At times, I was using three bytes to represent a unique byte. It was rethink time again.

There were two possibilities that needed to be distinguished in the table; either a screen byte was repeated or it was unique. This information didn't require a whole byte—it could be contained in a single bit. At the moment, each frequency byte was in a range from 1 to 256 ($00 to $FF with $00 representing 256 decimal). By reducing the range to a maximum of 128, the high bit would be free. I decided to use the following convention: if the high bit was 0, the rest of the number told how many times the next byte was repeated on the screen. If the high bit was 1, then the rest of the number told how many unique bytes followed in the table. Only one more slight change was required. Since the frequency byte had to be less than $80 (the high bit of a byte has a hex value of 80 and a decimal value of 128), the allowable range had to be from $00 to $7F. To simplify testing in the program, and to allow full use of the range, the frequency was changed to represent one less than the actual count.

Where does this leave us? A series of repeated bytes would still be represented as before, though the frequency byte would be one less than its actual value. So AA AA AA AA would be represented in the table as 03 AA. A series of unique bytes such as 07 FF 35 42 would be stored as 83 07 FF 35 42. This strategy resulted in only minor changes in the original program, followed by another program which produced the final table. Since this stripped-down table would be shorter than the original version, it could be stored in the same place without overwriting any information.

Basically, any entries in the original table representing repeated bytes would be left unchanged; any series of unique bytes would be shortened considerably by the removal of all those 01's. Picture Packer 3.0 functions fairly well. Pictures with a lot of background can be packed into as few as 11 sectors, while most pictures require around 24 sectors. I managed to cram 21 pictures on one disk under DOS 3.2.1, with lengths ranging from 11 to 29 sectors. Admittedly, some pictures don't pack too well, but in most cases the program does a good job of decreasing storage requirements.

The hidden bug (there's always a hidden bug) didn't appear until after a month of trouble-free use. Suddenly, certain pictures were turning into garbage when they were unpacked. Checking through the program, I discovered that it got confused when doing more than one pass on a picture that had unique bytes at both the start and end of screen memory. The repacking of the table just counted the number of unique bytes, it didn't notice that they belonged to different passes. The problem only appeared on certain Apples. The last eight bytes of screen memory are unused. Normally, this area will contain all 00's or all FF's, depending on the brand of RAM being used. In some Apples, this area will contain FF FF 00 00 FF FF 00 00. In such cases, the final table will be messed up. The fix was simple. At the start of the program, these last eight bytes are set to zero.

Using Picture Packer 3.0

The program contains only relative branches, so it can be placed anywhere in free memory. I usually load it into $1000. With the program in memory and a picture on hi-res page 1 ($2000), you simply give the command 1000G from the monitor (assuming the program is located at $1000), or use CALL 4096 from Basic. In about five seconds, the table is ready. The end of the table is stored in the first two bytes of memory ($00,$01). To save the table on disk you need to know the length. Just subtract $40 from the value in location $01, and use that for the hi byte of the length. (Since the table always starts at $4000, the hi byte of the length will be $40 less than the ending address shown in location $01.) To get the full length, append the lo byte value from location $00. For instance, if the first two locations in memory have the values $A2, $4C, the length of the table is $0CA2. (The length is actually $0CA3, but Apple DOS always stores one more byte than requested.) To put the above example on disk, use BSAVE TITLE, A$4000, L$CA2. From Basic, the command would be PRINT D$; "BSAVE TITLE, A$4000, L"; PEEK (0) + 256 * (PEEK(1) - 64).

Once pictures have been packed, the disk displaying them need only contain the unpacking program. Again, it can reside almost anywhere in memory, as long as it doesn't conflict with program storage, screen memory, or table storage. The convenience of relocatability more than makes up for slight inefficiencies that sometimes occur in this type of code. Since the unpacker is only about $90 bytes long, it can be placed at the start of page 3 (768 decimal) without crashing any DOS hooks. To use it, just BLOAD the table and call the unpacking routine. The picture will be placed back into screen memory in several seconds. A sample program that displays a disk full of pictures is listed below.

```
10 D$="": REM  CONTROL D
20 PRINT D$;"BLOAD UNCRAM,A$1000"

30 GR : POKE -16297,0: POKE -16302
,0
40 FOR I=1 TO 21
50 PRINT D$;"BLOAD PICTURE";I
60 CALL 4096
70 NEXT I
80 END
```

A short program for displaying packed pictures.

How it Works

The program first sets bytes $3FF8-$3FFF to zero, then defines pointers for the start of screen memory and the start of the table. A flag is used to determine whether this is a test packing or the final run. Two other important variables are used. COUNT keeps track of the number of passes made during any individual packing. OFF is the offset used to get the sequence of screen bytes. This method allows the same program to be used for packing with one, two, or four passes. The main loop of the program starts by taking a byte from screen memory. Then the offset is added to the screen pointer and the next screen byte is compared with the previous byte. If they are the same, the Y register is incremented. When a different byte is found, it's time to make an entry in the table. The Y register is decremented, leaving it in a range of $00-$7F, then sent to the table, followed by the screen byte. This process is repeated until the end of the screen is reached.

Now the program has to check to see whether another pass is required for this particular packing attempt. COUNT is incremented and compared to OFF. If COUNT equals OFF, the table is done; if not, another pass is required for this packing. Once all passes have been made, the hi byte of the table length is stored. Next, OFF is doubled. This gives offsets of one,

two, and four. Finally, after all versions have been tried, the table lengths are compared. The offset from the shortest table is used, and the flag is set so the program will stop after making this table. (A second might be saved here by changing the program so the four-pass pack, if the shortest, isn't repeated since the four-pass table is already in memory.) This completes the first portion of the packing. An $FF is tacked to the table, signaling the end.

Now we have a table that contains pairs of bytes. The first byte of each pair is one less than the number of times the second byte appears on the screen. Next, the table has to be stripped down. The REPACK section first takes a frequency byte from the table. If it is not $00 or $FF, then the next screen byte is not unique. In this case, the frequency byte and screen byte are just stored in the table. If the frequency is $00, the next byte is unique. In this case, the program branches to SINGLE. Here, unique bytes are stored until a frequency other than $00 is found. Y is

used to count the number of unique bytes. When a frequency other than $00 is found, it's time to put the information in the table. Y is decremented by one, then EORed (Exclusive OR) with $80, setting the hi bit. After Y is placed in the table, the unique bytes are stored. This whole process is repeated until the table end (marked by $FF) is found. We now have a packed table representing screen memory.

Unpacker 3.0 reverses the process, turning the table into screen data. After the pointers are set up, a byte is taken from the table. If it is $80 or greater, then the next series of bytes are unique. In this case, the program branches to SING. Here, the hi bit is stripped and Y is incre-

mented by one so it will represent the actual number of unique bytes following it in the table (remember, Y was decremented by one during the packing phase). The next Y bytes are sent to the screen. Again, the offset is used to increase the screen address, allowing the program to unpack tables made with any number of passes.

In the case of repeated bytes (marked by a frequency byte that is less than $80) the next byte is sent to the screen Y times (after Y is incremented by one). When the end of screen memory is reached, a check is made to see if another pass is required. If not, the unpacking is finished.

Final Notes

As I said, the program is not perfect. I've encountered several pictures that couldn't be reduced. The packing provided no saving of space. But, in most cases, picture storage can be significantly reduced. Those of you who like to experiment might want to rewrite the program so it steps through screen memory not in ascending order, but in the same order used by the memory mapping. You could also try stepping past the unused bytes in screen memory which occur at $XX78-$XX7F and $XXF8-$XXFF.

The program puts the picture on the screen rather quickly, with visual effects that vary depending on the number of passes used. Beyond being used to store a series of pictures, the program could be handy if you have a large program or set of programs on a disk and want to add a title picture. It's no longer necessary to set aside 33 sectors for this. Also, Unpacker 3.0 is handy when you are making changes to a picture. By keeping the table in memory, a damaged picture can be quickly restored by unpacking it back to the screen.

The same approach could probably be used on the Atari. The packing would probably be even greater since Atari doesn't use the same strange odd-even hi bit technique that adds complications to Apple pictures. Any memory mapped screen could be packed this way, including the lo-res PET or TRS-80 screen (of course, a TRS-80 version would have to be rewritten in Z80 code).

I'll probably get hooked again some time and try to knock a few more sectors off the pictures. Perhaps this program can be improved. Perhaps another approach is needed. Whatever, I hope Picture Packer 3.0 and Unpacker 3.0 prove useful.

□

```
:ASM
                        1       *FICTURE PACKER 3.0
                        2               ORG     $1000
                        3       SCLO    EQU     0       ;POINTERS TO SCREEN MEMORY
                        4       SCHI    EQU     1
                        5       TABLO   EQU     2       ;POINTERS TO TABLE
                        6       TABHI   EQU     3
                        7       OFF     EQU     4       ;OFFSET FOR STEPPING
                                                                THROUGH SCREEN
                        8       COUNT   EQU     5       ;COUNTER FOR PASSES
                        9       FLAG    EQU     6       ;INDICATES TEST PASS OR
                                                                FINAL PASS
                        10      FLAG1   EQU     7
1000: A9 00             11      FIX     LDA     #$0     ;TAKES CARE OF A SMALL
1002: A2 08             12              LDX     #$08    ;BUT DEADLY BUG BY
1004: 9D F8 3F          13      FIX1    STA     $3FF8,X ;ZEROING THE LAST
1007: CA                14              DEX             ;EIGHT BYTES OF SCREEN MEMORY
1008: 10 FA             15              BPL     FIX1
100A: A9 00             16      SET     LDA     #$0
100C: 85 06             17              STA     FLAG    ;INDICATE TEST PASS
100E: A9 01             18              LDA     #$1     ;START WITH SINGLE PASS
1010: 85 04             19              STA     OFF     ;WITH OFFSET OF ONE
1012: A9 01             20      SET1    LDA     #$1     ;SET TABLE POINTERS
1014: 85 02             21              STA     TABLO
1016: A9 40             22              LDA     #$40
1018: 85 03             23              STA     TABHI
101A: A9 00             24              LDA     #0      ;SET UP COUNTER TO KEEP
101C: 85 05             25              STA     COUNT   ;TRACK OF PASSES
101E: A9 20             26      SET2    LDA     #$20    ;SET SCREEN POINTERS
1020: 85 01             27              STA     SCHI
1022: A5 05             28              LDA     COUNT   ;VALUE IN COUNTER GIVES
1024: 85 00             29              STA     SCLO    ;LO BYTE OF SCREEN START
1026: A9 00             30              LDA     #$0     ;ZERO X AND Y
1028: AA                31              TAX
1029: A8                32              TAY
102A: A1 00             33      START   LDA     (SCLO,X) ;GET A BYTE FROM THE
102C: 48                34      LOOP    PHA             ;SCREEN AND SAVE IT
102D: A5 00             35              LDA     SCLO    ;GET NEXT ADDRESS BY
102F: 18                36              CLC             ;ADDING OFFSET TO SCREEN
1030: 65 04             37              ADC     OFF     ;POINTER
1032: 85 00             38              STA     SCLO
1034: 90 08             39              BCC     CONT
1036: E6 01             40              INC     SCHI
1038: A5 01             41              LDA     SCHI    ;CHECK FOR END OF SCREEN
103A: C9 40             42              CMP     #$40
103C: F0 20             43              BEQ     DONE
103E: 68                44      CONT    PLA             ;RECOVER SCREEN BYTE
103F: C8                45              INY             ;COUNT THE FREQUENCY OR REPEATS
1040: 30 04             46              BMI     PAGE    ;MAXIMUM IS $80
1042: C1 00             47              CMP     (SCLO,X) ;LOOK FOR A DUPLICATE
                                                                SCREEN BYTE
1044: F0 E6             48              BEQ     LOOP    ;FOUND ONE
1046: 48                49      PAGE    PHA             ;SAVE SCREEN BYTE
1047: 88                50              DEY             ;ADJUST TO $00-$7F RANGE
1048: 98                51              TYA
1049: 81 02             52              STA     (TABLO,X) ;PUT FREQUENCY IN TABLE
104B: E6 02             53              INC     TABLO   ;INCREASE TABLE POINTER
104D: D0 02             54              BNE     CONT1
104F: E6 03             55              INC     TABHI
1051: 68                56      CONT1   PLA             ;RECOVER SCREEN BYTE
1052: 81 02             57              STA     (TABLO,X) ;SEND IT TO THE TABLE
1054: E6 02             58              INC     TABLO   ;INCREASE POINTER AGAIN
1056: D0 02             59              BNE     CONT2
1058: E6 03             60              INC     TABHI
105A: A0 00             61      CONT2   LDY     #$0     ;PUT FREQUENCY BACK TO 0
105C: F0 CC             62              BEQ     START   ;ALWAYS TAKEN
105E: 98                63      DONE    TYA             ;SEND FINAL FREQUENCY OF
105F: 81 02             64              STA     (TABLO,X) ;PASS TO THE TABLE
1061: E6 02             65              INC     TABLO
1063: D0 02             66              BNE     CONT5
1065: E6 03             67              INC     TABHI
1067: 68                68      CONT5   PLA             ;RECOVER FINAL SCREEN BYTE
1068: 81 02             69              STA     (TABLO,X) ;AND SEND TO TABLE
106A: E6 02             70              INC     TABLO
106C: D0 02             71              BNE     CONT6
106E: E6 03             72              INC     TABHI
1070: E6 05             73      CONT6   INC     COUNT   ;INCREASE COUNTER
1072: A5 05             74              LDA     COUNT   ;IF COUNT=OFF, THEN ALL
1074: C5 04             75              CMP     OFF     ;PASSES ARE DONE FOR THIS TRY
1076: D0 A6             76              BNE     SET2    ;IF NOT DONE, GO BACK
1078: A5 06             77              LDA     FLAG    ;TEST PASS?
107A: D0 2C             78              BNE     OUT     ;NO, GET OUT
107C: A5 03             79      NEXT    LDA     TABHI   ;YES, STORE HI BYTE OF
107E: A6 04             80              LDX     OFF     ;TABLE LENGTH FOR COMPARISON
1080: 95 06             81              STA     FLAG,X  ;AFTER ALL TRIES ARE DONE
1082: A5 04             82              LDA     OFF
```

```
1084: 0A         83                    ASL              ;DOUBLE OFFSET
1085: 85 04      84                    STA    OFF
1087: C9 08      85                    CMP    #$8       ;HAVE 1, 2, AND 4
                                                        PASSES BEEN TRIED?
1089: D0 87      86       WAY          BNE    SET1      ;NO, GO BACK
108B: A0 01      87       TEST         LDY    #$1       ;YES, CHECK STORED TABLE
108D: A5 07      88                    LDA    $7        ;LENGTHS TO FIND SHORTEST
108F: C5 08      89                    CMP    $8        ;METHOD OF PACKING
1091: 90 04      90                    BCC    TEST1
1093: A0 02      91                    LDY    #$2
1095: A5 08      92                    LDA    $8
1097: C5 0A      93       TEST1        CMP    $A
1099: 90 02      94                    BCC    TEST2
109B: A0 04      95                    LDY    #$4
109D: 84 04      96       TEST2        STY    OFF       ;SAVE OFFSET OF BEST
109F: 8C 00 40   97                    STY    $4000     ;METHOD AND PUT INTO TABLE
10A2: A9 01      98                    LDA    #1        ;SET FLAG TO INDICATE
10A4: 85 06      99                    STA    FLAG      ;THIS IS NOT A TEST PASS
10A6: D0 E1      100                   BNE    WAY       ;GO BACK FOR FINAL PACK
10A8: A9 FF      101      OUT          LDA    #$FF      ;MARK END OF TABLE
10AA: 81 02      102                   STA    (TABLO,X)
             103      *SECOND PHASE BEGINS HERE
10AC: A9 01      104      REPACK       LDA    #1        ;SET POINTERS USING
10AE: 85 02      105                   STA    TABLO     ;TABLO AND TABHI FOR ORIGINAL
10B0: 85 00      106                   STA    SCLO      ;TABLE. SCLO AND SCHI ARE
10B2: A9 40      107                   LDA    #$40      ;USED FOR NEW TABLE
10B4: 85 03      108                   STA    TABHI
10B6: 85 01      109                   STA    SCHI
10B8: A2 00      110                   LDX    #0
10BA: A1 02      111      LOOP3        LDA    (TABLO,X) ;GET FREQUENCY
10BC: F0 23      112                   BEQ    SINGLE    ;0 SIGNIFIES UNIQUE BYTE FOLLOWS
10BE: 30 20      113                   BMI    DONE2     ;END OF OLD TABLE MARKED BY $FF
10C0: 81 00      114                   STA    (SCLO,X)  ;FOR FREQUENCIES FROM 1
10C2: E6 02      115                   INC    TABLO     ;TO $FF, FREQUENCY AND
10C4: D0 02      116                   BNE    CNT1      ;SCREEN BYTE ARE SENT
10C6: E6 03      117                   INC    TABHI     ;RIGHT TO THE TABLE
10C8: E6 00      118      CNT1         INC    SCLO
10CA: D0 02      119                   BNE    CNT2
10CC: E6 01      120                   INC    SCHI
10CE: A1 02      121      CNT2         LDA    (TABLO,X)
10D0: 81 00      122                   STA    (SCLO,X)
10D2: E6 02      123                   INC    TABLO
10D4: D0 02      124                   BNE    CNT3
10D6: E6 03      125                   INC    TABHI
10D8: E6 00      126      CNT3         INC    SCLO
10DA: D0 DE      127                   BNE    LOOP3
10DC: E6 01      128                   INC    SCHI
10DE: D0 DA      129                   BNE    LOOP3     ;ALWAYS TAKEN
10E0: 60         130      DONE2        RTS              ;EXIT POINT FROM ROUTINE
10E1: A8         131      SINGLE       TAY              ;UNIQUE BYTES ARE HANDLED HERE
10E2: 85 06      132                   STA    FLAG      ;SET POINTERS FOR TEMPORARY
10E4: A9 03      133                   LDA    #3        ;STORAGE IN PAGE 3
10E6: 85 07      134                   STA    FLAG1
10E8: E6 02      135      LOOP4        INC    TABLO
10EA: D0 02      136                   BNE    CNT4
10EC: E6 03      137                   INC    TABHI
10EE: A1 02      138      CNT4         LDA    (TABLO,X) ;GET SCREEN BYTE FROM
10F0: 91 06      139                   STA    (FLAG),Y  ;TABLE AND STORE IN PAGE 3
10F2: E6 02      140                   INC    TABLO
10F4: D0 02      141                   BNE    CNT5
10F6: E6 03      142                   INC    TABHI
10F8: C8         143      CNT5         INY              ;INCREASE COUNT OF UNIQUE BYTES
10F9: 30 04      144                   BMI    PAGE2     ;VALUE CAN'T BE ABOVE $80
10FB: A1 02      145                   LDA    (TABLO,X) ;GET NEXT FREQUENCY BYTE
10FD: F0 E9      146                   BEQ    LOOP4     IF ANOTHER SINGLE, THEN GO BACK
10FF: 88         147      PAGE2        DEY              ;ADJUST FOR $00-$7F RANGE
1100: 98         148                   TYA
1101: 09 80      149                   ORA    #$80      ;SET HI BIT
1103: 81 00      150                   STA    (SCLO,X)  ;SEND IT TO NEW TABLE
1105: E6 00      151                   INC    SCLO
1107: D0 02      152                   BNE    CNT6
1109: E6 01      153                   INC    SCHI
110B: C8         154      CNT6         INY              ;RESTORE TO ORIGINAL VALUE
110C: A1 06      155      LOOP5        LDA    (FLAG,X)  ;AND USE AS COUNTER
110E: 81 00      156                   STA    (SCLO,X)  ;WHILE SENDING UNIQUE
1110: E6 06      157                   INC    FLAG      ;BYTES TO THE TABLE
1112: E6 00      158                   INC    SCLO
1114: D0 02      159                   BNE    CNT7
1116: E6 01      160                   INC    SCHI
1118: 88         161      CNT7         DEY              ;DONE WITH DATE IN PAGE 3?
1119: D0 F1      162                   BNE    LOOP5     ;NO, KEEP GOING
111B: F0 9D      163                   BEQ    LOOP3     ;YES, GET NEXT FREQUENCY
--- END ASSEMBLY ---

TOTAL ERRORS: 0

285 BYTES GENERATED THIS ASSEMBLY
```

:ASM

```
            1         *UNPACKER 3.0
            2           ORG   $900
            3  SCLO     EQU   0
            4  SCHI     EQU   1
            5  TABLO    EQU   2
            6  TABHI    EQU   3
            7  OFF      EQU   4
            8  COUNT    EQU   5
0900: AD 00 40  9  SETUP LDA   $4000   ;GET NUMBER OF PASSES
0903: 85 04    10        STA   OFF     ;FROM TABLE AND USE FOR OFFSET
0905: A9 01    11        LDA   #1      ;SET UP POINTERS TO TABLE
0907: 85 02    12        STA   TABLO
0909: A9 40    13        LDA   #$40
090B: 85 03    14        STA   TABHI
090D: A9 00    15        LDA   #0
090F: AA       16        TAX
0910: 85 05    17        STA   COUNT   ;START COUNT AT 0
0912: A9 20    18  SET2  LDA   #$20    ;SET SCREEN POINTERS
0914: 85 01    19        STA   SCHI
0916: A5 05    20        LDA   COUNT   ;USE COUNT FOR LO BYTE
0918: 85 00    21        STA   SCLO    ;OF SCREEN START
091A: A1 02    22  START1 LDA  (TABLO,X) ;GET FREQUENCY BYTE
091C: 30 3A    23        BMI   SING    ;IF HI BIT IS SET,
                                         UNIQUE BYTES FOLLOW
091E: E6 02    24        INC   TABLO   ;MOVE THROUGH TABLE TO GET
0920: D0 02    25        BNE   CON1    ;SCREEN BYTE
0922: E6 03    26        INC   TABHI
0924: A8       27  CON1  TAY           ;PUT FREQUENCY IN Y
0925: C8       28        INY           ;AND RESTORE TO ACTUAL VALUE
0926: A1 02    29        LDA   (TABLO,X) ;GET SCREEN BYTE
0928: 81 00    30  LOOP1 STA   (SCLO,X) ;SEND IT TO THE SCREEN
092A: 48       31        PHA           ;SAVE IT
092B: A5 00    32        LDA   SCLO    ;ADD OFFSET TO SCREEN POINTER
092D: 18       33        CLC
092E: 65 04    34        ADC   OFF
0930: 85 00    35        STA   SCLO
0932: 90 08    36        BCC   CON3
0934: E6 01    37        INC   SCHI
0936: A5 01    38        LDA   SCHI
0938: C9 40    39        CMP   #$40    ;END OF SCREEN?
093A: F0 0C    40        BEQ   OUT1    ;YES
093C: 68       41  CON3  PLA           ;NO, GET SCREEN BYTE BACK
093D: 88       42        DEY           ;DECREASE FREQUENCY
093E: D0 E8    43        BNE   LOOP1   ;NOT DONE, KEEP SENDING
                                         SAME BYTE TO SC
0940: E6 02    44        INC   TABLO   ;GET READY FOR NEXT ENTRY
0942: D0 D6    45        BNE   START1  ;AND GO BACK
0944: E6 03    46        INC   TABHI
0946: D0 D2    47        BNE   START1  ;ALWAYS TAKEN
0948: 68       48  OUT1  PLA           ;RESTORE STACK
0949: E6 02    49  OUT2  INC   TABLO
094B: D0 02    50        BNE   CON9
094D: E6 03    51        INC   TABHI
094F: E6 05    52  CON9  INC   COUNT   ;INCREASE COUNT AND
0951: A5 05    53        LDA   COUNT   ;CHECK WHETHER ANOTHER
0953: C5 04    54        CMP   OFF     ;PASS IS NEEDED
0955: D0 BB    55        BNE   SET2    ;YES, GO BACK
0957: 60       56        RTS           ;NO, ALL DONE
0958: 49 80    57  SING  EOR   #$80    ;REMOVE HI BIT
095A: A8       58        TAY   PUT     FREQUENCY OF UNIQUE BYTES IN Y
095B: C8       59        INY   AND     RESTORE TO ACTUAL VALUE
095C: E6 02    60        INC   TABLO   ;GET NEXT SCREEN BYTE FROM TABLE
095E: D0 02    61        BNE   LOOP5
0960: E6 03    62        INC   TABHI
0962: A1 02    63  LOOP5 LDA   (TABLO,X)
0964: 81 00    64        STA   (SCLO,X) ;SEND IT TO THE SCREEN
0966: E6 02    65        INC   TABLO
0968: D0 02    66        BNE   CON6
096A: E6 03    67        INC   TABHI
096C: A5 00    68  CON6  LDA   SCLO    ;POINT TO NEXT SCREEN LOCATION
096E: 18       69        CLC
096F: 65 04    70        ADC   OFF
0971: 85 00    71        STA   SCLO
0973: 90 08    72        BCC   CON7
0975: E6 01    73        INC   SCHI
0977: A5 01    74        LDA   SCHI
0979: C9 40    75        CMP   #$40    ;END OF SCREEN?
097B: F0 D2    76        BEQ   CON9    ;YES
097D: 88       77  CON7  DEY           ;NO, DECREASE FREQUENCY
097E: D0 E2    78        BNE   LOOP5   ;GO BACK FOR MORE UNIQUE BYTES
0980: F0 98    79        BEQ   START1  ;DONE WITH THIS SERIES

--- END ASSEMBLY ---

TOTAL ERRORS: 0

130 BYTES GENERATED THIS ASSEMBLY
```

Hi-Res Text For The Apple

Paul Hitchcock

If this hasn't happened to you yet, beware—

You're sitting in front of your Apple II Plus, the graphics master and number-cruncher *extraordinaire*. Behind you a group of friends impatiently await the unveiling of your latest *Meisterwerk*: The graphical solution of Schroedinger's wave equation. The quantum universe begins to unfurl across the screen of your monitor; you, however, secretly listen for the inevitable murmurs of astonished approval. And when the last hi-res dot winks on the screen, you turn to the audience for the expected-but-highly-deserved applause. But instead of the roar of the crowd, you are confronted with a roomful of knitted brows. Time holds its breath while your confidence ebbs away. Suddenly a question rips apart the icy silence. No, not a question, but a searing, air-ionizing laser blast aimed to demolish the foundations of your programming expertise:

"Well, *surely* it labels the axes, doesn't it?"

A red haze diffuses across your eyes; through the blur you see your friends filing silently out of the room. Your barely audible mutterings (But Applesoft doesn't include a hi-res character set...) tip-toe across the room to fall on ears that will not hear. You have just been control-C'd into the Twilight Zone.

Maybe the preceding anecdote is a *little* exaggerated, but it does emphasize an important point: a graphics display should convey all of the information a user needs to understand what the display means. That generally means graphics *and* text. Without a generous sprinkling of alphanumerics, most graphs and charts and games are, in three words, boring, dull, and boring. But even more to the point, "naked" graphics are uninformative. A quick glance at the two histograms in Figure 1 will show you precisely what I

Paul Hitchcock, 2309 Blake St., #308, Berkeley, CA 94704.

mean. Although the subject of "swimsuit sales" may not move you to the edge of your chair, at least you know what the graph is trying to say.

So how do you obtain a hi-res character set for your Apple? One inexpensive answer is found in the Apple's ability to draw user-defined, high-resolution "shapes." Listing 1 defines a table of such shapes which will give you the entire alphabet, ten digits, as well as several special characters (See Figure 2). By using the Applesoft DRAW, XDRAW, SCALE, and ROT commmands in conjunction with this table, you will be able to print text quickly and easily on the hi-res screen.

I said the shape table was inexpensive, but it's not completely free: it will cost you 641 bytes of RAM. But I think you'll agree the price is reasonable when you see how

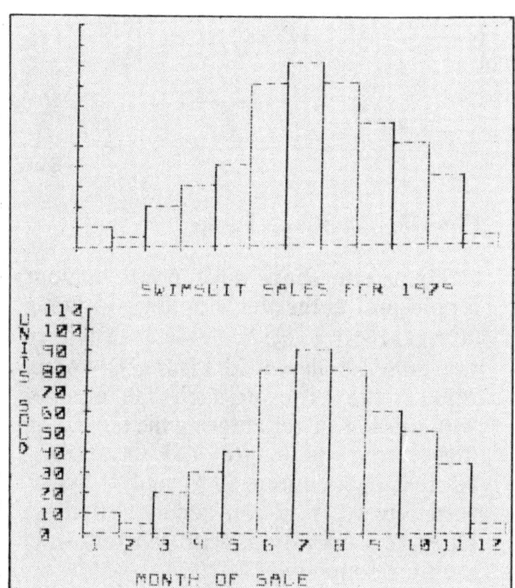

Figure 1

```
*1000.1280

1000- 38 00 78 00 7A 00 7C 00
1008- 7E 00 80 00 82 00 90 00
1010- 92 00 94 00 9C 00 A4 00
1018- A6 00 AE 00 B0 00 B5 00
1020- B9 00 C1 00 D0 00 D8 00
1028- E4 00 EF 00 F9 00 05 01
1030- 11 01 1B 01 28 01 32 01
1038- 34 01 36 01 3F 01 48 01
1040- 51 01 53 01 55 01 62 01
1048- 6F 01 79 01 84 01 90 01
1050- 99 01 A4 01 B1 01 BA 01
1058- C2 01 CF 01 D7 01 E3 01
1060- F1 01 FC 01 07 02 15 02
1068- 22 02 2D 02 37 02 43 02
1070- 4F 02 5C 02 6B 02 75 02
1078- 01 00 01 00 01 00 01 00
1080- 01 00 25 25 0E 1B 2C BE
1088- 09 3E 3E 66 49 3E 2C 00
1090- 01 00 01 00 24 2D 9F 32
1098- 36 2D 07 00 24 3F 8D 32
10A0- 36 3F 05 00 01 00 34 0E
10A8- 2D 36 24 2D 07 00 01 00
10B0- 9B 29 2D 07 00 12 37 25
10B8- 00 25 25 9E 33 37 37 04
10C0- 00 25 25 3F 3F 36 36 25
10C8- E5 93 2E 2D 25 24 04 00
10D0- 24 37 0A 36 3E 2D 07 00
10D8- 25 25 3F 3F 4E 32 3F 36
10E0- 20 20 07 00 20 24 3F 3F
10E8- 96 32 2D 2D 24 04 00 2D
10F0- 24 0E C3 36 2D 2D 36 26
10F8- 00 3F 24 2D 2D DE 2A 35
1100- 36 3F 3F 04 00 35 35 3E
1108- 3F 27 2C 0C 9F 24 2C 2D
1110- 00 25 25 3F 3F 56 31 37
1118- 37 3D 00 2D 24 3F 3F 36
1120- AD 2D 36 3F 3F 24 2D 00
1128- 2D 24 3F 3F 36 6D 31 36
1130- 04 00 01 00 01 00 2C FD
1138- 3A 3E 35 35 2D 07 00 2D

1140- 97 30 3F 2F 08 38 2F 00
1148- 3C 6F 2A 2E 37 37 3F 05
1150- 00 01 00 01 00 2D 36 E6
1158- DB 26 24 ED 23 25 20 2E
1160- 06 00 2E 2E 3E 3F 27 24
1168- 24 2D 35 35 3F 3F 00 89
1170- 32 3F 3F 24 24 2C 20 35
1178- 00 29 3E 3E 3E 27 24 24
1180- 2D 2E 06 00 AD 12 3F 3F
1188- 24 2C DD 24 20 20 07 00
1190- 45 38 3F 37 2E DD 36 26
1198- 00 2A 35 3E 3F 27 24 24
11A0- 2D 2D 06 00 20 24 0E 18
11A8- 34 2E DD 36 66 49 26 24
11B0- 00 24 2F 3D 36 36 3E 20
11B8- 07 00 09 24 36 36 3E 3F
11C0- 27 00 2C 25 0E C3 36 36
11C8- 66 51 21 27 27 3F 00 52

11D0- 31 3F 3F 24 24 34 00 3C
11D8- 3C 36 36 66 49 26 24 24
11E0- 37 07 00 2E 36 25 24 24
11E8- DE 33 3D 24 37 36 36 04
11F0- 00 09 24 3F 3F 36 36 2E
11F8- 2D 25 24 00 3B 35 20 2C
1200- 3C 3C 3F 36 36 26 00 09
1208- 24 3F 3F 36 36 2E 20 BC
1210- AD 27 25 24 00 2E 2E E6
1218- DB 26 24 24 20 35 35 3F
1220- 3F 00 BF 12 20 20 24 3C
1228- DF 24 20 20 00 24 3F 4E
1230- 09 3C 97 36 26 00 00 09
1238- 24 1E 08 33 36 36 20 20
1240- 24 04 00 09 24 1E 08 33
1248- 36 35 2E 25 2C 04 00 36
1250- 35 25 24 24 1E 08 33 36
1258- 36 25 05 00 25 25 3E 08
1260- 33 35 35 37 37 2C 2C 35
1268- 35 04 00 2D 24 1E 08 33
1270- 2E 35 36 04 00 25 25 3F
1278- 3F 95 31 37 37 2D 2D 07
1280- 00
```

Listing 1

much sparkle a bit of text will lend to your graphics displays.

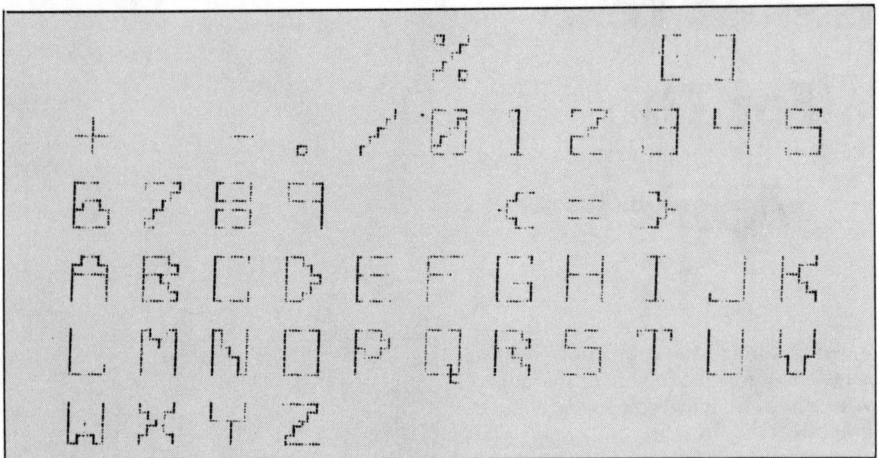

Figure 2

Entering the Shape Table

To load the shape table, power up your Apple and enter the monitor by typing "CALL-151 (return)". Enter each line of the table as shown in Listing 1, except replace the "-" after each line number with a colon. After entering the table, you must store its length and its starting address in locations $0-$1 and $E8-$E9, respectively. You can accomplish these latter two operations with the following monitor commands:

∅:8∅ ∅2 (return), and
E8:∅∅ 1∅ (return).

When you have finished the above, go back to Applesoft with CTRL C (return). Type in and RUN the short test program given in Listing 2. If your television or monitor display looks substantially like Figure 2, you're ready to save the table on tape. If it doesn't, go back and fix things up. Unless you're the type who remembers phone numbers and zip codes in hex, it's all too easy to make a mistake.

Listing 2

```
10   HGR : HCOLOR= 3
20   SCALE= 3
30   ROT= 0
40   N = 1
50   FOR J = 10 TO 135 STEP 25
60   FOR I = 7 TO 257 STEP 25
70   IF N = 60 THEN 120
80   DRAW N AT I,J
90   N = N + 1
100  NEXT I
110  NEXT J
120  END
```

Saving the Table on Tape

To save the table on tape, re-enter the monitor (CALL-151) and type

∅.1W 1∅∅∅.1280W

Put a clean tape in your recorder, start recording, and press (return). After two

beeps the cursor will reappear, indicating the table has been saved.

For your own mental well-being, it would be a good idea to make three or four copies of the shape table. I'm sure you know what I mean: you make several copies of something on tape, and each copy loads perfectly. Just make a single copy, though, and it will invariably fail to load. While Mr. Murphy might chuckle with smug satisfaction, this kind of thing turns me into a hapless psychotic.

In the future, you enter the shape table into your computer just as you would enter a cassette program, with one exception: instead of typing "LOAD", you type "SHLOAD". You can load the shape table even if you already have a program in memory, so SHLOAD can actually be activated as a program statement. However, those of you with Apples having only 16K RAM must take a special precaution before loading your tables. When you enter the table via the SHLOAD command, the Apple places the table immediately below the memory address specified by the current HIMEM setting. But when the Apple is first turned on, HIMEM is set to the highest avaialable memory address--16384, if you have a 16K machine. When you enter the hi-res graphics mode with the command HGR, all of the addresses from 8192 to 16384 (the hi-res picture bufer) are cleared, i.e., set to zero. So you must set HIMEM to 8192 (or lower) before you load your table, to avoid automatically erasing it.

Text Writing in Hi-Res

The shapes in the table are numbered, and to draw a particular shape on the screen, you refer to its number in a DRAW statement. For example, the letter "A" has the number 34, and you draw this letter at the screen coordinates X, Y with the command "DRAW 34 AT X, Y". Now the fifty-nine shapes in the table have been arranged so that the table number of a given shape is related to the ASCII number of the character the shape represents through the following formuala:

N(character)=ASC("character")-31, where N is the table number of the character enclosed in parentheses. With this function, you can forget about table numbers and can draw a character just by referring to the character itself. Again using the letter "A" as an example, the command "DRAW ASC("A")-31 AT 3∅, 5∅" will cause the letter "A" to be drawn at the screen coordinates 3∅, 5∅.

By using the above formula in conjunction with Applesoft's built-in string functions, you can easily write text strings in hi-res; Listing 3 defines a subroutine I have used in several programs for just this purpose. Before you call the subroutine though, you have to initialize four variables:

XN,YN—the coordinates of the first letter of the string

N$—the string to be printed

ZN—the horizontal/vertical printing flag. When the

flag is down (ZN= ∅), printing proceeds horizontally;

when it is up (ZN= ∅), the string will be printed in

the vertical (downward) direction.

Listing 4 provides a short example of how to use the text printing subroutine and Figure 3 shows the screen output of the program in Listing 4.

I said the shape table was inexpensive, but it's not completely free: it will cost you 641 bytes of RAM.

Advice and Limitations

You've probably noticed that I failed to include a number of special characters in the shape table (!/'/#/$/&/'/:/;/?/@). Your programs won't bomb if you include any of these characters in a text string—the illegal character will just be interpreted as a space character. The decision to omit these characters was completely arbitrary; if you want to add some (or all) of them to your table, you'll find the instructions for

```
20000   REM *HI-RES PRINTING SUBROUTINE*
20005   SCALE= 1: ROT= 0
20010   FOR CN = 1 TO  LEN (N$)
20020   Q$ =  MID$ (N$,CN)
20030   IF ZN THEN 20060
20040   DRAW  ASC (Q$) - 31 AT XN + 7 * (
CN - 1),YN
20050   GOTO 20070
20060   DRAW  ASC (Q$) - 31 AT XN,YN + 7
* (CN - 1)
20070   NEXT CN
20080   ZN = 0
20090   RETURN
```

Listing 3

doing so in the *Applesoft II Reference Manual.* Should you need only a limited number of the shape table characters for a particular application, the manual will also show you how to "cannibalize" the table to get the characters you want.

The shape table character set does suffer from one minor functional limitation: you may only print white (HCOLOR= 3) text on a black (HCOLOR= $\emptyset$) background, or vice versa. Because of the way the Apple displays colored lines in hi-res, an attempt to write text using any other color combination will result in missing line segments in all of the printed characters. In short, whatever you write will be unintelligible, although it might look pretty stylish.

As far as letter and line spacing is concerned, I've found the following rule-of-thumb to be useful: the distance between

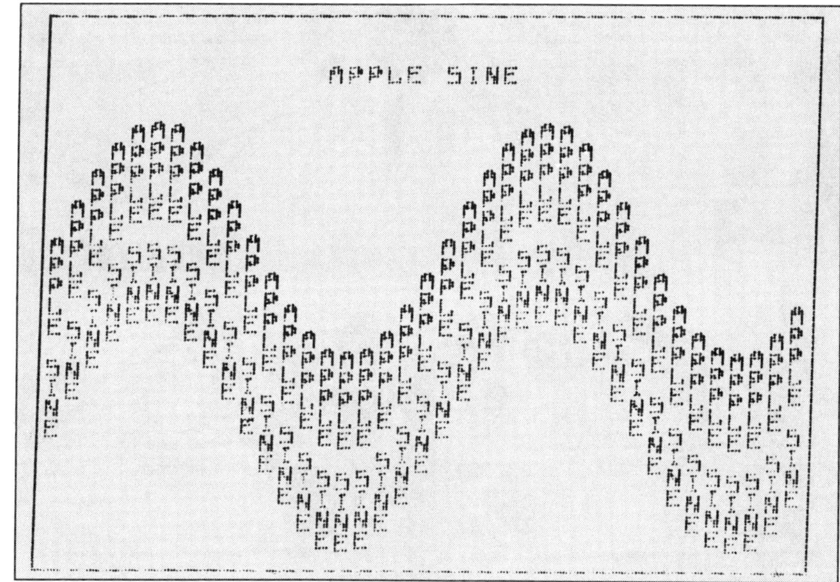

Figure 3

```
300   HGR : HCOLOR= 3
310   POKE  - 16302,0: REM  FULL SCREEN
320 ZN = 0: REM  HORIZONTAL PRINTING
330 N$ = "APPLE SINE"
340 XN = 105:YN = 20
350   GOSUB 20000
360   FOR XN = 6 TO 273 STEP 7
370 YN = 79 - 40 *  SIN (6.28 * (XN - 6)
    / 139)
380 ZN = 1: REM  VERTICAL PRINTING
390   GOSUB 20000
400   NEXT XN
410   HPLOT 2,0 TO 279,0 TO 279,191 TO 2,
191 TO 2,0
420   END
```

Listing 4

two characters or two lines of characters should be seven times the value of the SCALE; that is, if you print the first character of a text string at the coordinates X,Y, and you have previously specified that SCALE= S, the next character of the string will have the coordinates X+7*S,Y. By the way, if you follow this rule with SCALE= 1, you have room for twenty-three lines of hi-res text with forty characters per line.

The subroutine in Listing 3 represents only an elementary example of what you will be able to do with the character set. By experimenting with different letter and line spacings, you should be able to output hi-res text in nearly any conceivable format. Your graphs and your games will begin to communicate much more effectively—and isn't that what graphics is all about?

I hope you find this simple character set to be as useful as I've found it to be. So—as far as hi-res text is concerned—write soon, and write often!   □

Apple II Lo-Res Shape Tables

David Lubar

Drawing a complex shape in Lo-Res graphics requires a large number of PLOT, HLIN, and VLIN statements. Getting such a shape to move on the screen can be a slow process. While each square is drawn quickly, time is lost since the process involves interpreting the Basic command, jumping to the monitor, returning the Basic, and so on. In such cases, a Lo-Res shape table subroutine could be useful. The following article describes such a program, designed for use with Integer Basic.

I attempted to follow, to a degree, the format of Hi-Res shape tables, while eliminating some of the more difficult aspects of such tables.

What is a Shape Table?

A shape table is just a series of instuctions which are represented as numbers. In this case, the numbers contain two types of information: 1) Whether or not to plot a square at the present location; 2) Where to move next. With this information, any shape can be defined, as long as it fits within the limits of the screen. There are eight possible directions to move in the Lo-Res routine (see figure 1.) Combined with the plotting options, this gives 16 different commands. Since the Apple's monitor uses hexadecimal data, and since there are two hex digits in a byte, each byte can contain two table entries. To further simplify plotting, the table is constructed without an index. This restricts the entire table to 256 bytes, which isn't much of a limitation.

Making a Table

Each table must begin with a $00 (the "$" signifies that the number is in hex.) The end of each shape within the table is also marked with a $00. As in Hi-Res, you can't move up twice without plotting. But, since diagonal moves are allowed, you can get there by going diagonally left and up, then diagonally right and up.

Starting at the top, the values of the moves go clockwise from 0 to 7 (figure 1.) If the point is to be plotted, 8 is added to the value. Once all the values for a shape have been calculated, they are put in pairs. The routine reads each byte from right to left, so the first command of each pair should be the lower digit of the byte. For example, if the first command has a value of "8" and the second a value of "F", the table entry would be "F8". (For those who aren't familiar with hex, the values "10" through "15" are represented as "A" through "F".) Figure 2 illustrates the process of assembling a shape table.

Using the Program

Since the routine takes values from the variable table, certain variables have to be defined first. This is done with:

10 X0=Y0=SHAPE

Any variables can be used, as long as they are the same length as the ones shown above. Whenever you want to draw a shape from the table, define X0 for the X coordinate, Y0 for the Y coordinate, and SHAPE for the desired shape. The draw is done with CALL 4353. After this, X0 and Y0 will have whatever values the last move assigned to them. To draw

the shape elsewhere, X0 and Y0 must be redefined.

The table begins at location $1000, and can go up to $10FF. The routine lies directly above this point. That leaves 2K for the Basic variable table. Some refinements could be added to the program, such as error checks to make sure the squares are plotted within screen limits. If desired, a scale function could be added.

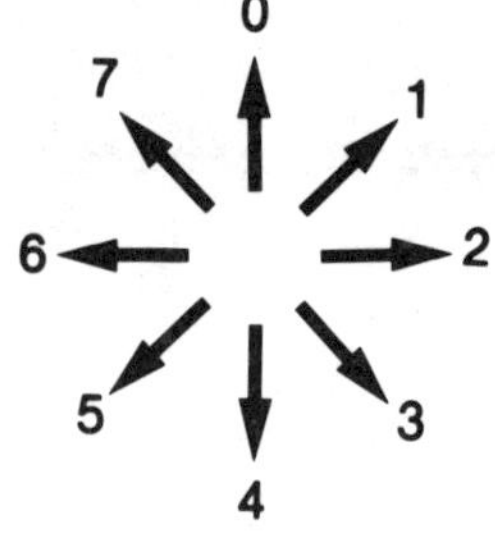

Figure 1.
Plotting Vectors

Direction	No Plot		Plot	
	Binary	Hex	Binary	Hex
↑	0000	0	1000	8
↗	0001	1	1001	9
→	0010	2	1010	A
↘	0011	3	1011	B
↓	0100	4	1100	C
↙	0101	5	1101	D
←	0110	6	1110	E
↖	0111	7	1111	F

Putting it all Together

The routine can be appended to an Integer Basic program in a number of ways. It can be loaded separately, it can be loaded with the program if the pointers are first reset, or it can be POKEd from Basic as explained in "The Apple Cart" column (*Creative Computing*, March 1980.) The table can also be POKEd from basic, or loaded in together with the routine.

If you are unfamiliar with machine language, there is an easy way to enter the routine into memory. Just go into the monitor, type "1100:" followed by the bytes shown in the hex dump (Figure 4.) Only the first memory location has to be entered. After that, whenever you hit RETURN, type another colon before beginning the next row of bytes. Once the whole routine is entered, you can check it against the disassembled listing (Figure 3) by typing "1100L". This will show the first twenty instructions. After this, type "L (RETURN)" for each additional twenty lines.

The listing shown by the Apple will contain the commands that are in the second column of Figure 3. The third column will be represented on the screen as numbers instead of the labels shown.

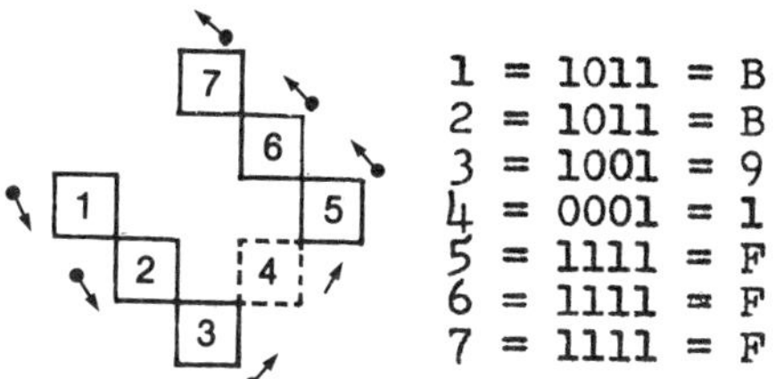

Figure 2. Sample Table Entry

Note: For last square plotted, direction of move after plot is arbitrary. Also, if there are an odd number of nybbles, the last one is completed with a 0 in the hi position.

Figure 3

These can be checked by using the symbol table at the top of Figure 3.

Practical Considerations

If a program uses very simple shapes, this routine isn't necessary. But, when you want to quickly draw and move a complicated shape, such as a person or a large spaceship, you'll find that the Lo-Res Shape Table routine allows much quicker animation than is possible in Basic. It also requires fewer program statements. Finally, as a bonus, it simplifies the creation of shapes. You don't have to worry about coordinates. All you need to know is which direction you want to move and whether you want a square at that location.

> *When you want to quickly draw and move a complicated shape, such as a person or a large spaceship, you'll find that the Lo-Res Shape Table routine allows much quicker animation than is possible in Basic.*

How it Works

This section can be skipped by anyone who prefers to avoid the company of bit hackers and other fanatics.

First, Y is loaded with the number of the shape. The routine steps through the table, decrementing Y whenever a $00 is found. When Y=0, the desired shape has been located. Each byte of the table is put in the A register, and a check is made to see if the shape is done. If not, the byte is pushed onto the stack. An AND #F gets the lo nybble. If the hi bit of the nybble is set to 1, the square will be plotted. The A register is pushed onto the stack again since the monitor PLOT routine destroys this register. The X and Y coordinates are taken from the variable table and placed in the Y and A registers. After the monitor PLOT, the nybble is pulled from the stack. An AND #$7 reduces it to the three-bit move value. The move is accomplished by incrementing or decrementing X0 and

```
* LORES SHAPE TABLE SUBROUTINE
* ENTERED FROM BASIC WITH CALL 4353
XO      EQU     $805
YO      EQU     $80C
SHAPE   EQU     $816
DATA    EQU     $1000
PLOT    EQU     $F800
        ORG     $1100
*
RTN     RTS
START   LDY     SHAPE       ;GET SHAPE NUMBER
        LDX     #$0         ;INITIALIZE COUNTER TO 0
LOOP    LDA     DATA,X      ;GET BYTE FROM SHAPE TABLE
        INX
        CMP     #$0         ;END OF A SHAPE?
        BNE     LOOP        ;NO.  KEEP LOOKING
        DEY                 ;YES.  DESIRED SHAPE IS FOUND WHEN
        BNE     LOOP        ;Y EQUALS 0
DRAW    LDA     DATA,X      ;GET BYTE TO BE PLOTTED
        CMP     #$0         ;SHAPE DONE?
        BEQ     RTN         ;YES.  GO BACK TO BASIC
        PHA                 ;NO.  SAVE BYTE
        AND     #$F         ;GET LOW NYBBLE
        CMP     #$8         ;PLOT?
        BCC     NEXT        ;NO.  SKIP PLOTTING ROUTINE
        PHA                 ;YES.  SAVE LOW NYBBLE
        LDA     YO          ;GET Y COORDINATE
        LDY     XO          ;GET X COORDINATE
        JSR     PLOT        ;MONITOR PLOT ROUTINE
        PLA                 ;RESTORE LO NYBBLE
NEXT    JSR     COORD       ;FIND NEW COORDINATES FOR X AND Y
        PLA                 ;GET ORIGINAL BYTE
        LSR                 ;SHIFT HI NYBBLE LO
        LSR
        LSR
        LSR
        CMP     #$8         ;SAME AS ABOVE
        BCC     NEXT1
        PHA
        LDA     YO
        LDY     XO
        JSR     PLOT
        PLA
NEXT1   JSR     COORD
        INX                 ;POINT TO NEXT BYTE
        JMP     DRAW        ;DO IT ALL AGAIN
*
* THE FOLLOWING SECTION HANDLES THE MOVE SET BY THE NYBBLE
*
```

—CONTINUED ON NEXT PAGE—

Y0 as necessary. Next, the stack is pulled again, getting the original byte. Four LSR's put the hi nybble into the lo position. Then the PLOT (if the hi bit of the nybble is set) and move are done. X is incremented to point to the next byte, and the routine loops back to draw.

```
COORD  AND  #$7       ;REDUCE TO 3 BIT VALUE
       CMP  #$0       ;FIND DIRECTION VALUE
       BEQ  UP
       CMP  #$1
       BEQ  DIAG1
       CMP  #$2
       BEQ  RIGHT
       CMP  #$3
       BEQ  DIAG2
       CMP  #$4
       BEQ  DOWN
       CMP  #$5
       BEQ  DIAG3
       CMP  #$6
       BEQ  LEFT
DIAG4  DEC  X0        ;IF IT REACHES HERE, A=7
       DEC  Y0
       RTS
UP     DEC  Y0
       RTS
DIAG1  INC  X0
       DEC  Y0
       RTS
RIGHT  INC  X0
       RTS
DIAG2  INC  X0
       INC  Y0
       RTS
DOWN   INC  Y0
       RTS
DIAG3  DEC  X0
       INC  Y0
       RTS
LEFT   DEC  X0
       RTS
```

Figure 3

```
1100- 60 AC 16 08 A2 00 BD 00
1108- 10 E8 C9 00 D0 F8 88 D0
1110- F5 BD 00 10 C9 00 F0 E8
1118- 48 29 0F C9 06 90 0B 48
1120- AD 0C 08 AC 05 08 20 00
1128- F8 68 20 48 11 68 4A 4A
1130- 4A 4A C9 08 90 0B 48 AD
1138- 0C 08 AC 05 08 20 00 F8
1140- 68 20 48 11 E8 4C 11 11
1148- 29 07 C9 00 F0 1F C9 01
1150- F0 1F C9 02 F0 22 C9 03
1158- F0 22 C9 04 F0 25 C9 05
1160- F0 25 C9 06 F0 28 CE 05
1168- 08 CE 0C 08 60 CE 0C 08
1170- 60 EE 05 08 CE 0C 08 60
1178- EE 05 08 60 EE 05 08 EE
1180- 0C 08 60 EE 0C 08 60 CE
1188- 05 08 FF 0C 08 60 CE 05
1190- 08 60
```

Figure 4

If LOMEM isn't set to $800, the values of X0, Y0, and SHAPE in the symbol definitions will have to be adjusted. To relocate the program, just change the value of DATA and the value of JMP DRAW.

That's all there is to it, unless, as mentioned before, you want to add error checks (including one to make sure that SHAPE isn't given a value for which there is no table entry). Happy plotting. □

Apple II Kaleidoscopes

Richard C. Vile, Jr.

Here's a colorful program that gives you a chance to explore the inner logic of folded pictures—and Integer Basic.

At one time or another, everyone has enjoyed a kaleidoscope. The symmetry of the ever-shifting patterns of color holds an endless fascination. This article will show you how to create a virtually endless variety of kaleidoscopic display programs for the Apple II low resolution graphics display. The language used for the examples will be Apple Integer Basic, although the programs could be converted to Applesoft.

The Apple II low resolution graphics display easily accomodates the generation of kaleidoscopic displays. The principle of a kaleidoscope is to replicate a basic pattern by reflection about several exes, thus producing a larger pattern with several identical subdivisions. The basic approach is illustrated in Figure 1. A square of even integral side length is sub-

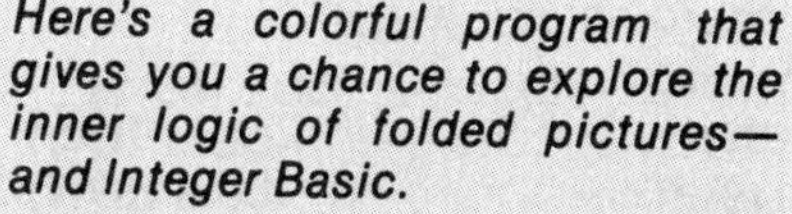

Figure 1

divided into four equal subsquares. Each of those is in turn split into two parts by drawing in the two principal diagonals of the original square. The resulting figure contains eight congruent triangles, which we number as indicated and refer to as *octants*.

Richard C. Vile, Jr., 3467 Yellowstone Dr., Ann Arbor, MI 48105.

Let us suppose that the original square is 2n units on a side. For example, the Apple II low resolution graphics display (with mixed text on the bottom four lines) is 40 units on a side: $n = 20$. Let us assume further that we divide the square into rows and columns, numbering each from 0 to $k = 2n-1$. Then for each unit in octant 1, we have the following information:

$$0 \leq ROW \leq n-1$$
$$0 \leq COL \leq n-1$$
$$ROW \leq COL$$

For any such point with co-ordinates (ROW,COL) we may systematically generate a collection of eight points which are configured kaleidoscopically as follows:

1. Form a subrectangle within the original display, with sides parallel to the original display, "equidistant" from the original sides, and with the selected point as the upper left hand corner. This yields the following points:

$$(ROW,COL)$$
$$(ROW,k-COL)$$
$$(k-ROW,COL)$$
$$(k-ROW,k-COL)$$

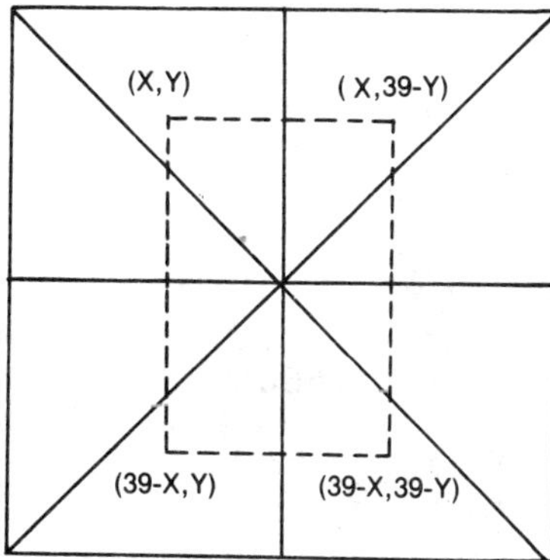

2. For each of the four corners of the square so formed, generate another point by reflection around the upper left to lower right diagonal. This point will be located in the "companion" octant. Octants x and y are companions if their numbers sum to 9 (1+8, 2+7, 3+6, 4+5). The generated point will have the co-ordinates obtained by simply interchanging the co-ordinates of the original point:

$$(COL,ROW)$$
$$(k-COL,ROW)$$
$$(COL,k-ROW)$$
$$(k-COL,k-ROW)$$

For the Apple II display, if the original point was (X,Y), we get the eight points:

(X,Y)	(Y,X)
(X,39-Y)	(39-Y,X)
(39-X,Y)	(Y,39-X)
(39-X,39-Y)	(39-Y,39-X)

The procedure is illustrated geometrically in Figure 2.

By choosing several points in the first octant, and generating the seven companion points for each, kaleidoscopic patterns may easily be created. Let's consider several ways to

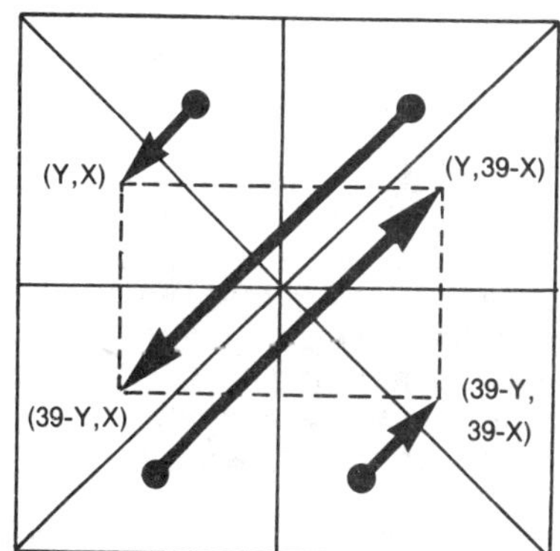

Figure 2

systematically select the "seed" points. Note: It actually does not matter where the original point is located. The eight points generated as described will all lie in the original square, and there will be one in each octant, unless ROW = COL. In that case, the reflected points coincide with the originals and only *four distinct* points appear.

How to create a virtually endless variety of kaleidoscopic display programs for the Apple II low resolution graphics display.

First Method

The first method generates one seed point for each ROW of the 40x40 display. It is accomplished by filling in detailed statements in the followint "sketch code" program:

```
For I = 0 TO 32767
FOR ROW = 0 TO 39
    Compute COL as a function
    of I and ROW.
    PLOT (ROW,COL) and its
    seven companion points.
    (Optionally) Change colors.
NEXT ROW
NEXT I
```

This technique leads to widely differing characters in the resulting kaleidoscopes, depending on the function chosen to compute COL. Here is just a sample of the possibilities:

```
COL = (ROW + I) MOD 40
COL = ABS(I-ROW) MOD 40
COL = (ROW*I) MOD 40
COL =  ABS:ROW-ABS(I-ROW))
       MOD 33
```

Note that the values computed by the functions *must* be reduced using the MOD function. If this were not done, the resulting (ROW,COL) combinations would frequently lie outside the permissible range for the screen display. The functions illustrated do not all necessarily satisfy the condition ROW $\leq$ COL, but this really does not matter as the note above indicates. Enforcing that condition by using an IF statement and recomputing the COL value when ROW > COL would not enhance the appeal of the display, but would slow its rate of production. In fact, it could in the worst case result in NO display at all if ROW > COL were always true! In practice, the inner loop in the

sketch may be replaced by one of:

```
FOR ROW = 0 TO 19
FOR ROW = 39 TO 0 STEP -1
FOR ROW = 19 TO 0 STEP -1
```

with slight but occasionally interesting differences.

Second Method

This method abandons the sequential consideration of ROWS taken by the first method and instead computes the ROW value as well as the COL value. The sketch program looks formally similar to the first, but now the inner loop index serves only to produce values for the independent variable J. The bounds of the inner loop now are chosen in such a way as to produce reasonable variety in the resulting kaleidoscope: i.e. if the inner loop runs through too many values, then the value of the outer loop index will not change rapidly enough and the same points in the display could be generated over and over.

```
FOR I = 0 TO 32767
FOR J = 0 TO 19
    Compute ROW as a function
    of I and J
    Compute COL as a function
    of I and J
    PLOT (ROW,COL) and its seven
    associates
    (Optionally) Generate color change
NEXT J
NEXT I
```

This method lends itself to considerable experimentation, since a pleasing pattern results from the appropriate *combination* of ROW and COL functions. A good way to proceed is to fix on a "good" COL function from method one and try different COL functions with it.

Third Method

This method is quite similar to the second method. It differs in that the functions used to compute ROW and COL have additional variables. For example, an extra inner loop depending on, say K, may be added and its index variable used as an extra independent variable. In addition, the variables ROW and COL may themselves be used as independent variables. An example using this technique:

```
FOR I = 0 TO 32767
  FOR J = 0 TO 39
    FOR K = 19 TO 0 STEP -1
      ROW = ABS(I-ABS(J-ABS(K-J)))MOD 21
      COL = (ROW + I + J + K) MOD 33
      PLOT "eight points"
      "Change color"
    NEXT K
  NEXT J
NEXT I
```

Subdividing the Kaleidoscope

The basic methods may be used with a *subdivided* display consisting of four subdisplays, each 20x20 in size. Since 20 is also an even number, each of the subdisplays may be used to generate its own kaleidoscope. The simplest application of this technique will generate eight points in the first subdisplay, then replicate them in the other subdisplays by applying appropriate *translations*.

In order that the first eight points lie in the upper left quadrant of the screen, the following conditions must be imposed:

$$0 \leq ROW \leq 19$$
$$0 \leq COL \leq 19$$

The eight basic points will then have coordinates:

```
(ROW,COL)        (COL,ROW)
(ROW,19-COL)     (19-COL,ROW)
(19-ROW,COL)     (COL,19-ROW)
(19-ROW,19-COL)  (19-COL,19-ROW)
```

Quadrant I
        Kaleidoscopic PLOT Points

In order to duplicate these eight points in Quadrants II, III and IV, respectively, a *translation factor* must be added to their coordinates. We illustrate how to derive these factors by discussing Quadrant II.

In Quadrant II, the row coordinate of each point corresponding to a basic point remains the same. Thus, the translation factor for the row coordinate, DR, is equal to 0. Each column coordinate of a basic point must be increased by 20 in order to obtain the corresponding point in Quadrant II. Thus the translation factor for the column coordinate, DC, is equal to 20. These facts may be summarized in the "equation":

Quadrant II←Quadrant I + (0,20)
Similarly,
    Quadrant III←Quadrant I + (20,0)
    Quadrant IV←Quadrant I + (20,20)

Applying these transformation equations to the basic eight point cluster in Quadrant I yields:

```
(ROW,COL + 20)   (COL,ROW + 20)
(ROW,39-COL)     (19-COL,ROW + 20)
(19-ROW,20 + COL) (COL,39-ROW)
(19-ROW,39-COL)  (19-COL,39-ROW)
```

Quadrant II Cluster

```
(ROW + 20,COL)     (20 + COL,ROW)
(ROW + 20,19-COL)  (39-COL,ROW)
(39-ROW,COL)       (20 + COL,19-ROW)
(39-ROW,19-COL)    (39-COL,19-ROW)
```

Quadrant III Cluster

By writing PLOT statements to generate each of the 32 points listed, the basic techniques of Methods One, Two and Three may be used to generate four-fold kaleidoscopes. It is imperative, however, that the seed point, (ROW,COL), does lie in the first quadrant; otherwise, RANGE ERRORS will result. The functions used to generate ROW and COL should therefore always reduce their results using the MOD function in order to guarantee proper location of (ROW,COL).

More Than One Function at a Time

Returning to Method One, notice how the inner loop may vary from 0 to 19 or 0 to 39. Another general technique is to use two (or more) different functions while generating ROW and COL values on a given pass through the inner loop. There are different ways to achieve the alternation; for example:

Choose randomly between the functions.

Strictly alternate between the functions.

Split the use of the functions in halves.

Use a third function to determine the alternation.

In this section we will detail the method of "splits" and the method of "leaves." The basic idea of splits is

---

The basic methods may be used with a subdivided display consisting of four subdisplays, each generating its own kaleidoscope.

---

to use one set of functions to calculate ROW and COL as long as $0 \leq J \leq SPLIT$ and then to switch to another set of functions while $SPLIT + 1 \leq J \leq 39$. SPLIT is chosen to be some value between 1 and 38 (why not 39?), and J is the index of the inner loop. When programming the splits technique, one may query the user for the value of SPLIT, choose the value of SPLIT randomly, or compute SPLIT by yet another function. An example of the latter approach is given in the listings. The idea behind leaves is to alternate (inter-*leave*) the use of the ROW and COL computing functions. The method of alternation may itself be varied, with the most popular being *strict* alternation between two sets of functions. Either the splits or the

leaves techniques may be superimposed on the three basic methods and one may use a full kaleidoscope or a four-fold kaleidoscope.

Sample Implementations

Listings 1 and 2 give examples of the splits and leaves techniques for a full screen kaleidoscope. The rest of the article contains lists of some of the functions that have been used by the author. The surface has just been scratched here; much more sophistication and control can be devised by elaborating on the methods con-

```
*** SYNTAX ERR
>LIST
   0 REM   METHOD OF SPLITS
   1 REM    SUBTITLED SNOWFLAKES
   2 REM   NOTE COMPUTATION OF SPLIT VALUE
   3 REM    AND REGENERATION OF DISPLAY
   4 KBD=-16384:CLR=-16368
  10 GR : PRINT : PRINT : PRINT
  15 COLOR= RND (15)+1
  20 FOR I=1 TO 32000
  25 SPLIT=5+(I MOD 5)*(I MOD 3) MOD 13
  30 FOR J=0 TO SPLIT
  40 ROW= ABS (I- ABS (J-I)) MOD 10+ ABS (SPLIT- ABS (J-SPLIT)) MOD
     30
  50 GOSUB 1050
  60 NEXT J
  90 FOR J=SPLIT+1 TO 19
 100 ROW= ABS ( ABS (SPLIT- ABS (I-SPLIT)) MOD 20+SPLIT- ABS (I- ABS
     (J-I)) MOD 20+SPLIT) MOD 30
 110 GOSUB 1050
 120 NEXT J
 125 IF (I MOD 8)#0 THEN 130
 126 FOR DE=1 TO 500: NEXT DE
 127 GOSUB 1070
 128 GR : COLOR=8
 130 NEXT I
1050 PLOT ROW,J: PLOT 39-ROW,J
1055 PLOT ROW,39-J: PLOT 39-ROW,39-J
1060 PLOT J,ROW: PLOT J,39-ROW
1065 PLOT 39-J,ROW: PLOT 39-J,39-ROW
1070 X= PEEK (KBD): IF X>=128 THEN GOSUB 1500
1080 IF ( RND ( PDL (0)+2)=0) THEN GOSUB 2000
1090 RETURN
1500 POKE CLR,0: IF X#141 THEN 1505: GR : COLOR=8: RETURN
1505 IF X# ASC("Q") THEN 1510: TEXT : CALL -936: END
1510 IF PEEK (KBD)<128 THEN 1510
1520 POKE CLR,0: RETURN
2000 P1= RND (4):P2= RND (4):R= RND (2)
2010 COLOR=P1*R+(1-R)*P2
2020 RETURN

>
```

Listing 1

```
>LIST
   1 REM   METHOD OF LEAVES-THREE FOLD INTERLEAVING
   2 KBD=-16384:CLR=-16368
  10 GR : PRINT : PRINT : PRINT
  15 GOSUB 1000
  20 FOR I=500 TO 32767
  25 IF I MOD 2 THEN 30
  26 FOR J=17 TO 0 STEP -1
  27 GOTO 32
  30 FOR J=0 TO 17
  32 IF I MOD 2 THEN 36
  35 ROW=((I MOD 40)* ABS (40-I) MOD 40) MOD 40: GOTO 50
  36 IF (I MOD 3) THEN 40
  38 ROW=J+(I MOD 3)+(I MOD 5): GOTO 50
  40 ROW=((I*J) MOD 20+(I+J+1) MOD 20) MOD 33
  50 PLOT ROW,J: PLOT 39-ROW,J
  55 PLOT ROW,39-J: PLOT 39-ROW,39-J
  60 PLOT J,ROW: PLOT J,39-ROW
  65 PLOT 39-J,ROW: PLOT 39-J,39-ROW
  70 X= PEEK (KBD): IF X>=128 THEN GOSUB 500
  80 IF ( RND ( PDL (0)+2)=0) THEN GOSUB 1000
  85 NEXT J
  90 NEXT I
 500 POKE CLR,0: IF X#141 THEN 510: GR : GOSUB 1000: RETURN
 510 IF X# ASC("Q") THEN 515: TEXT : CALL -936: END
 515 IF PEEK (KBD)<128 THEN 515
 520 POKE CLR,0
 530 RETURN
1000 P1= RND (4):P2= RND (4):R= RND (2)
1010 COLOR=R*P1+(1-R)*P2: RETURN
```

Listing 2

tained herein, and quite precise control over the character of the final displays arrived at. Some exercises are suggested for further exploration.

Explorations

1. Implement a 16-fold kaleidoscope.
   Hint: Use a subroutine to generate points in a 10x10 subdisplay obtained by adding appropriate DR and DC values to the basic eight points from the upper left hand 16th of the screen:

(ROW,COL)	(COL,ROW)
(ROW,9-COL)	(9-COL,ROW)
(9-ROW,COL	(COL,9-ROW)
(9-ROW,9-COL)	(9-COL,9-ROW)

   Call the subroutines from a pair of nested loops:

   ```
   FOR DR = 0 TO 30 STEP 10
     FOR DC = 0 TO 30 STEP 10
   ```

   or generate DR, DC combos randomly.
2. Implement kaleidoscopes which alternate between full screen and four-fold subdivision of the screen.
3. Implement four-fold kaleidoscopes which use different sets of functions for different subdisplays. Some symmetry may be retained by using one set of functions for quadrants I and IV and another set of functions for quadrants II and III.
4. In the splits technique, incorporate the SPLIT value into the ROW AND COL generating functions.
5. Find new variations on the basic methods.
6. If you have a disk, write a control program which allows user interaction in the selection of various combinations.
7. Use the EXEC command to switch functions dynamically while a program is running. Figure out a way to "capture" (see DOS 3.2 manual) key lines in the file to be EXEC'ed in to effect the change. Perhaps this can be combined with the CHAIN command in some clever ways.

List of Functions (Anywhere you see ROW, you can also use COL):

```
ROW = (I*J) MOD 20

ROW = (J*J + 3*J + 7) MOD 40

ROW = ABS(I - SGN(J-9)*(J+2)) MOD 35

ROW = ((I-SGN(J-9)*J) MOD 13 +((1-SGN(13-J))*(I+2))MOD 17

ROW = ABS(I - SGN(J-10)*J)MOD 25

ROW = ABS(13-I+J) MOD 20 + ABS(27-I+J) MOD 10

ROW = ABS( ABS(I - ABS(2*I-2*J))) MOD 20

ROW = ABS(2*J - ABS( 2*I - ABS(2*I-J))) MOD 33

ROW = ABS( J* (J * (J *(J MOD 40)MOD 40)MOD 40)MOD 40 - I)MOD 33

ROW = ABS( ABS(30-J)-ABS(J-ABS(17-I))+RND(2)) MOD 31

ROW = ABS( I *(J * ABS(I-J))MOD 33 - J*3) MOD 31

ROW = ABS(ABS(30-2*J)-ABS(I-ABS(J-2*J))) MOD 21

ROW = ABS(I - ABS(J-COL)) MOD (COL+1) MOD 40

ROW = ABS(COL-J)MOD 21
```

Notes:
1. The above may be varied by changing numerical coefficients.
2. Combinations of the above may be made when generating both ROW and COL by functions.
3. Complexity may be added by combining the above functions with each other and additional functions to generate new ones.
4. The values in the MOD parts of the above list may need changing for four-fold or sixteen-fold kaleidoscopes. □

Either the splits or the leaves techniques may be superimposed on the three basic methods and one may use a full kaleidoscope or a four-fold kaleidoscope.

The Apple Graphics Tablet

George Sternecker

The high resolution color capabilities of the Apple computer remain largely unexploited. Most software programs do not take advantage of the attention grabbing affects of hi-res color graphics. There is no excuse for this, since the hi-res screens can be easily utilized by various graphics tablets on the maket. Here, we will focus upon the Apple Graphics Tablet.

The Graphics Tablet is a magnetic bit pad which digitizes signals created by touching a magnetic pen to the tablet surface. The AGT consists of the bit pad itself, an overlay grid, magnetic pen, interface card, software, manual, and an anti-static cloth. The card goes into any peripheral slot in the computer (normally slot 5), and the bit pad and pen are both connected by wires to the interface card.

The tablet is 15"x15", and matches the Apple computer in color and styling. The AGT draws on HGR2, the second high resolution page, and uses the standard hi-res colors—black, white, blue, orange, green and violet. On the tablet itself is a mylar grid sheet which is aligned by using the calibration program. Every command on the AGT is displayed across the top of the grid sheet. Commands and program include reset, clear screen, pen color, recall and store picture, background color, area/distance, frames, boxes, straight lines, window, viewport, etc. The magnetic pen is used to draw on the screen, and also to execute any of these commands. The computer keyboard is used only to specify picture names and the disk drive numbers. One seldom has to leave the tablet surface while using the AGT.

The AGT is easy enough for anyone, including the computer novice, to use. The computer only "draws" when the pen

Graphics by Bob Bishop of Apple Computer.

is actually touching the surface of the AGT. When the pen is close to the surface, crosshairs appear on the video screen to indicate location. Manipulating the pen is not much harder than writing with an ordinary pen, and with a little practice, you can write cursive on the video screen with panache.

Since the AGT operates on magnetic principles, static electricity is its enemy. If the user has a static charge, or if there is a bad electrical ground, strange anomalies will appear on the screen during the drawing mode. When creating graphics, always save the picture from time to time, so that if something goes wrong, all is not lost.

Two interesting commands on the AGT are "window" and "viewport". WINDOW allows you to specify an area on the grid, and have that area equal the entire video screen. That is, a square inch could be specified as the window, and if a line were drawn across that square inch, it would extend across the entire video screen. VIEWPORT allows you to isolate a section of the grid for drawing, thus freezing the remaining portion of the hi-res screen to avoid accidentally drawing there. This feature is good for editing or for fine detail work on the screen. The AGT *will not* shrink or enlarge what is already on the hi-res screen. You can also draw a rectangle, either in outline or filled, just by specifying the two end points of one diagonal. Graphics created with the AGT can be inserted into programs by going to HGR2 and executing a BLOAD PIC (picture name).

AGT operates on Applesoft basic and requires at least one disk drive. The suggested price is $795.00, making the AGT one of the more expensive graphics tablets available. (Apple Computer Inc., 10260 Bandley Drive, Cupertino, CA 95014) □

Apple Hi-Res Graphics Made Easy with the VersaWriter

Randy Heuer

Apple II owners have a feature in their computer not found in many other personal computers. This feature is High Resolution (Hi-Res) color graphics. In the Hi-Res graphic mode the screen is subdivided into a grid of 280 x 160 pixels. Each of the pixels can be set to any of six colors (black, white, orange, blue, violet or green). However, many people writing their own programs have tended to shy away from using Hi-Res graphics. I suspect the reason for this is that the only way to access the Hi-Res features in Basic is through HPLOT statements or shape tables. With HPLOT statements you can only draw straight lines. With shape tables, you can create complex shapes but only by using cumbersome binary number tables which will frustrate most potential graphics artists.

In the past there was only one practical solution to the problem. This was the digitizer or bit-pad type device made by several companies. These devices are very nice and, if the proper software was provided, they made Hi-Res graphics much easier. How-

PHOTO 1
The Versawriter Drawing Board.

ever, for many people the cost of these devices was too prohibitive, with prices starting at over $500. In many cases this was just too much money for the privilege of using Hi-Res graphics. Most people would rather use $500+ to add a disk drive or printer. However, now there's an alternate solution to this problem.

The VersaWriter is an ingeniously simple and relatively inexpensive solution to the problem of how to handle complex Hi-Res graphics. The plotting board consists of a 14″ x 12″ plastic bed with a clear acetate overlay sheet. The original copy of the drawing or diagram is taped (masking tape preferred) to the plastic bed and then covered with a clear sheet. Instead of

---

Many people writing their own programs have tended to shy away from using Hi-Res graphics.

---

using a light or pen for tracing the figure on the plotting bed, the Versa-Writer uses a double-jointed arm attached to the top of the drawing board at one end and a free, magnifying lens with crosshairs at the other. The VersaWriter resembles a draftsman's pantograph on a smaller scale.

At each joint of the VersaWriter's arm is a potentiometer. A cable from the VersaWriter connects the potentiometer. A cable from the VersaWriter connects the potentiometers to the Apple's paddle input. Installing a VersaWriter in your Apple simply requires that you unplug your game paddles and plug the VersaWriter's single cable into the socket. No other special interface is needed.

In this day of very complex digital circuitry and other electronic overkill, the simplicity of the VersaWriter is impressive. Since the arm of the VersaWriter bends in only one direction, each point on the plotting bed corresponds to a unique set of resistances on the potentiometers. All that's needed now is the software to translate the resistances into usable screen coordinates.

The quality of this software is very important and will determine the usefulness of the device. Without user-oriented support software, devices of this type are little more than overly expensive drawing paper. Fortunately, the VersaWriter does not disappoint.

Perhaps the best way to describe some of the features of the software is to provide a list of some of the more useful commands and their actions:

Command	Effect
P	Point Cursor — Moves cursor and displays (x,y) coordinates. Permits rapid drawing of straight lines between two points.
S	Scale of Drawing — Provides independent vertical and horizontal control of drawing size on the screen.
M	Create Shape Table — Create a Hi-Res graphics binary table for use in other programs or with the Hi-Res functions.
T	Transfer Picture to Disk — Saves contents of screen on diskette.
R	Recall Picture from Disk.
Z	Color-in Enclosed Figure — "Fills in" an enclosed figure with the color of your choice.
I	Inspect Shape Table — Allows you to rotate, scale or color an existing figure.

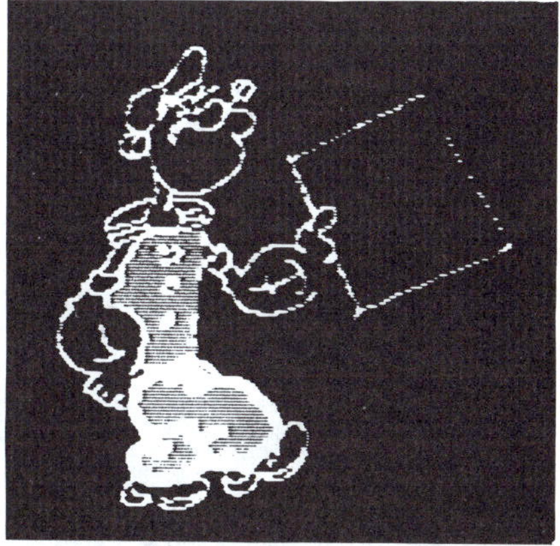

PHOTO 2
A picture of Popeye drawn using the VersaWriter. The slight distortion of the horizontal scale was probably caused by the fact that our VersaWriter was not yet calibrated when this figure was drawn."

The P (Point Cursor) command is the basic command for moving the cursor about the screen and for drawing straight lines. In addition to displaying a flashing dot at the present position of the point on the screen, a numerical readout of that position is also displayed. An option allows you to draw a straight line between any two points.

The Z command is not only useful, but genuinely fun to use. It allows you to fill in an enclosed figure with any color. Using a somewhat crude search routine to determine whether the cursor has reached the edge of the figure, this command starts filling in the figure from the present cursor position, expanding outward until reaching the edge of the figure. It's intriguing to watch the computer "color in" a drawing just as kids do with crayons.

The M command may be one of the most useful, however, it may take you a while to discover its purpose. A picture

In this day of very complex digital circuitry and other electronic overkill, the simplicity of the VersaWriter is impressive.

on the screen can be stored in the computer's memory two ways. When the entire screen is loaded or saved (R or T commands), the contents of the memory locations corresponding to the screen are copied. However, there's another way to store a figure in the Apple memory. Portions of the Hi-Res screen can be stored as shape tables. Using a somewhat complex method of binary numbers, the shape table offers some unique advantages. The primary advantage being that shapes stored in one configuration can be enlarged, rotated and moved about the screen with relative ease. The M command in the VersaWriter allows you to produce shape tables from figures you've produced on the screen.

Once a shape table has been created and stored on a disk, it can be used in other Basic programs. Using the Hi-Res functions, these shapes can

PHOTO 3

Photos 3 & 4 are examples of how even the very non-artistic author can make pretty pictures with the VersaWriter. I wonder what a person with real artistic talent could do?

be manipulated within Basic with relative ease.

To use the VersaWriter you need an Apple II computer, Disk II, Applesoft in ROM and a minimum of 32k of memory. Since the VersaWriter's software uses page one of the Hi-Res screen, ROM Applesoft must be used. This means that you must have one of the following computer configurations in order to use the VersaWriter: Apple II

PHOTO 4

with a floating point ROM card, an Apple II Plus or Apple II with a multi-language card.

Being rather simple in design, your VersaWriter should have good longevity unless you drop your 19" Color TV set on it. Of course, like any precision tool, mistreatment can damage the device. One of the programs included in the VersaWriter software package is used for calibrating the drawing board and I recommend it be run from time to time to recalibrate the device. Unless you damage the VersaWriter through mistreatment, though, I would not think

PHOTO 5

Perhaps the most useful command, the Create Shape Table (M) command is shown here scanning the letter A from the drawing in Figure 4. This process takes several minutes. However, once completed the shape table for this figure can be used in many ways (see Figure 6).

any type of maintenance would normally be necessary. The VersaWriter comes with a 90 day warranty on parts and labor.

The only real complaint I can raise about the VersaWriter is the documentation. The 8½" x 11" instruction manual is only five pages long. This is hardly adequate for the Hi-Res graphics novice. Much greater emphasis should be given to the shape table commands in particular.

Examples of how to use shape tables should be provided so the person new to Hi-Res graphics understands the differences between the screen memory and shape tables. In addition, a section on how to incorporate the VersaWriter drawing board into other programs (games, pointers, etc.) is

It's intriguing to watch the computer "color-in" a drawing just as kids do with crayons.

warranted. Altogether, I think a manual three or four times longer than the present one would not be unreasonable.

Still, the VersaWriter is a tremendous value. Its cost is $249 plus $5 shipping (and sales tax for California residents). While the VersaWriter may not be adequate for some high-precision digitizing applications (remember, the VersaWriter uses potentiometers as inputs and these analog devices are not necessarily perfectly linear throughout their range), most

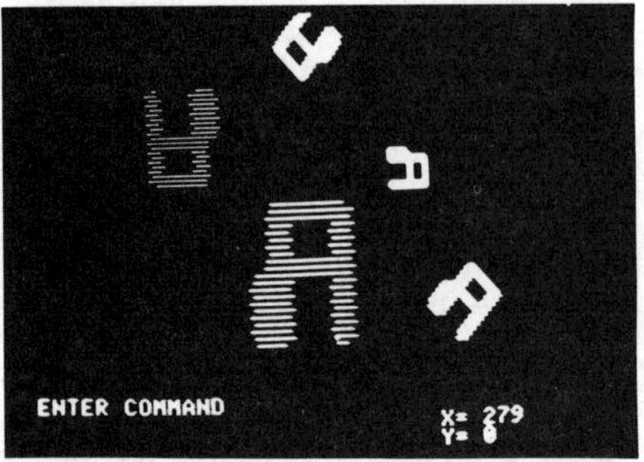

PHOTO 6

Using the shape table created by the Versawriter (in Figure 5), the A can now be enlarged, rotated, colored or moved about the screen.

people will be impressed by the capabilities of the device. We at *Creative* intend to make significant use of our VersaWriter in the future.

VersaWriter was offered briefly at an introductory price of below $200, however, this did not include applications software. The list price at this time is $250 and includes two disks of software. The applications disk includes programs to calculate distances and areas, add upper and lower case text using five character sizes, and add electronic and digital symbols for "drawing" schematic or logic diagrams.

For more information on Versa-Writer, contact either of the following: Rainbow Computing, 9719 Reseda Blvd., Northridge, CA 91324 or Peripherals Plus, 119 Maple Ave., Morristown, NJ 07960. □

Life is like playing a violin solo in public and learning the instrument as one goes on.

DITHERING HEIGHTS

Ken Recters

Is that me on TV? It sort of resembles me, but the image is just black and white with no grays. I walk a few feet further and there I am again, this time with grays, but the motion is jerky. Kind of like seeing every 10th frame of a movie.

At the Midwest Computer Show, a goodly crowd was frequently found around the Computer Station booth. People were watching those crazy images of themselves. They certainly weren't the familiar closed-circuit images produced by a camera and monitor. Something else had been added— an Apple computer. Elbowing closer to the booth, and making way for those who, with screen dumps grasped in their hands, were leaving, I got my first look at the Dithertizer II. I was impressed.

Taking input through a black and white Sanyo VC 1610X camera, the Dithertizer could put a picture on the Apple hi-res screen in less than a second. The person demonstrating the system explained that most of the existing low-cost digitizers take almost five seconds to produce a picture. The Dithertizer requires only 1/60th of a second to grab a binary picture. (The Micro Works system requires almost 5 seconds to grab an image.) The Dithertizer is fast by virtue of the fact that it uses a DMA (direct memory access) type of binary video digitizing versus a frame grabber. These binary frames are combined into dithered matrices of 2X2, 4X4, or 8X8. A 2X2 matrix requires 4 frames, a 4X4 requires 16, and an 8X8 requires 64. Increasing the size of the matrix allows for higher contrast and, therefore, more shades of gray. In other words, an 8X8 matrix provides 64 levels of gray from white to black. The actual picture takes from 1/15 of a second for the smallest matrix to 1 and 1/15 seconds for the largest matrix. Since the image could be redrawn at this rate, a slightly-less-than-real-time motion could be seen on the screen. The term "dithering" refers to the process of producing the appearance of gray scales by means of overlaying.

From what I could see, the user is given many ways to interact with the system. Intensity and contrast are controlled with the paddles. With one press of a key, the Dithertizer can switch to producing straight black and white images with no gray scales. Using the paddles, a variety of interesting contour pictures can be produced. A contour image is produced by subtracting one frame from another so that you end up with just the outline of the image, ie., you just pick up the contour edging. This requires two frames and takes 1/30th of a second to produce. Using contours, images can be produced faster than those with gray scales; you nearly have animation. Using these techniques alone or together allows the user to experiment with various artistic interpretations, or whatever else suits his fancy. Another key freezes the image. From here, it can be saved to disk. The image can also be sent to any printer capable of dumping the hi-res screen. This requires another program which is included with the package.

So, what can you do with the Dithertizer? You can make pictures of your friends, or of anything else a video camera can spy out. With a printer, the pictures could be turned into posters. And, since the scene can be saved from disk and recalled, it can be decorated later with text or shapes from a table. With the right software, many interesting things can be done to the image. With pictures on file, you can spice up your software with great graphics. According to Lynn Sullivan, president of the Computer Station, manufacturers of the Dithertizer, many "real world" applications are possible. For example, gray levels can be extracted from aerial photographs. One professor is using it for work in geology. Another is using it to study sexual response and behavior in rats. It is useful for this because it is a much more sensitive movement detector than a regular video camera.

The Dithertizer II board, with software, sells for $300. The Sanyo VC 1610X camera is $410. If you buy both, the price drops to $650. This $650 package also includes software to produce a hard-copy image on either the Paper Tiger 440 or 460 printers. An Apple Silent Writer printer can also be used by storing the hi-res page and then dumping it out. All the software commands are one letter, for example, C for contour, D for dither and P for print. The package is available from Peripherals Plus, 39 East Hanover Ave., Morris Plains, New Jersey 07950. For further information, call (201) 267-4558.

For other articles on digitizing, see "Periphicon 511 Optical Image Digitizer," *Creative Computing*, vol. 5, number 10. This review presents background information and suggests several interesting applications for computers with cameras. "Image Processing with COMPIC's Computer Portrait System," from vol. 5, number 8, presents a detailed look at the joys and woes of a computer-oriented business, as well as a complete description of the materials required for computer portraits. □

Lynn Sullivan, president of the Computer Station, as seen by the Dithertizer II.

Integrating CAI & Videotape

Marc D. Schwartz

Interactive video systems provide a lively audio-visual medium to which users can actively respond. Putting together a computer and a videotape player for instructional purposes means we can present to the student teaching materials from both videotape and computer programs. Materials can appear on the screen alternately coming from one or the other device, depending on what is needed at each step in the teaching program. A simple system consists of a computer like the Apple II, a video player and a TV monitor with a connecting interface unit that permits control of the remote TV functions from the computer keyboard or from within a computer program (see Figure 1).

With a slightly more sophisticated arrangement, it is possible to search automatically for any given frame or sequence under computer control.

There are several advantages to this combination of technologies for teaching. On the one hand, videotape can present moving, colorful, visual materials; it can permit spoken descriptions, instructions or other sounds; and it can counterbalance the more formal, text-bound character of some computer-assigned instruction. On the other hand, a computer can offer branching, programmed learning; it can generate text and graphics; it can allow for easy modification of teaching materials; it can bypass what the student already knows; it can score responses, if desired; it can be programmed to start and pause the videotape at the chosen points in the presentation.

The videotape provides a more stimulating range of visual material than is possible through the use of a computer alone, and offers spoken instruction and sound effects. Review of video materials that were not clear is possible. Furthermore, video material may be searched for and played as requested, thereby permitting audio-visual learning tailored by students to their individual needs. In addition, automatic scoring and usage tabulation can indicate points of difficulty and areas successfully mastered.

Marc D. Schwartz, 26 Trumbull St., New Haven, CT 06511.

Such an integrated system of computer and videotape thus provides a very flexible means of producing an interactive audio-visual presentation which can be suited to the needs of specific learners. Existing tapes can be adapted for use with such a system or new programs produced.

A Walkthrough

Let's walk through an example. Let's say a segment of videotape on a particular subject is presented to a student — for instance, a demonstration of how a piece of equipment works, or an analysis of a certain kind of group behavior, or a discussion of a computer program.

The more elaborate interface, permits random search and retrieval from certain low-cost videotape units.

After the segment is finished, the computer can be programmed to halt the video player and switch control of the TV screen to the computer, which offers textual instruction on the materials just presented.

The user may be asked to respond to questions about what has been presented, or given further information in textual or graphic form. An incorrect response will branch the program to either a presentation of helpful information (by computer-generated text), or will result in a "search to and play" a segment of video that contains the required information. Following a correct response or series of responses, the display is switched back to VTR for the next section of the program. Only after the student has shown that he or she understands the subject matter will the next segment of video instruction begin.

The program continues with alternating sections of video display and computer questions, the complete learning unit being summarized at the end of the videotape.

The Mechanics

The system must be synchronized so that video player and computer will work smoothly together. For example, the moment after a segment of video material has been completely presented, command of the TV display must be switched from video to computer and the video player paused. Following the CAI segment, the video player should be switched to FORWARD and the command of the TV display switched back to video.

Modes of Presentation

Using the first interface system, five modes of presentation of materials are feasible. These are 1) video display and sound (normal videotape operation), 2) computer display and sound from videotape, 3) computer display and no videotape sound (video player paused), 4) frozen-frame video display while the video player is on PAUSE. (This mode does not work well with some because their pause mode does not correctly frame the picture. With a player that frames correctly while on PAUSE, the mode is a useful one.) Keyboard control by the user of PAUSE or single-frame advance makes it possible to stop the video player when the user wants to look at certain materials in a more leisurely way. (One problem of the latter two modes is that if users repeatedly pause too long at one spot, the tape at that point will wear down and degrade the picture quality.)

The random-access video player, used with the second CAVRI computer interface, offers all the power of full branching capability. As well as those already mentioned, two additional presentational modes become possible: 6) a replay of a previous section of video, 7) branching forward or backward to hitherto unseen materials on the tape.

Interface packages to hook up an Apple II computer and video player in this fashions are available from CAVRI (Computer Assisted Video Recorded Instruction), 26 Trumbull Street, New Haven, CT 06511.

The simpler one, $295, permits alternation between computer and video player by starting and stopping the videotape. It requires an Apple II and any videotape player/recorder having a remote control socket and two audio channels.

This interface uses brief signals at selected points on audio channel 1 of the videotape to tell the computer to switch one of the relays or go on to the next step in the program. To receive the signal, the channel 1 audio-out from the video player is run into the cassette-in socket of the computer. The computer hangs in a wait loop until it receives this signal. (Audio channel 2 is used for the normal sound track of the video program.)

The more elaborate interface, at $495, permits random search and retrieval from certain low-cost videotape units. (These are the Panasonic NV8200 and NV8170, and the Sony Betamax SLO320 and 323, SLP300 and 323, and AV 2850, 2860 and 2011.)

With a relatively low expenditure of time and money, an extensive curriculum of computer assisted teaching materials can be produced

Programmed Instructions

The computer's response to the user's answers can be of three types: the pseudo-branch (especially suited to videotape materials), the branch, and the menu. In the pseudo-branch the program proceeds in the same way after the user's response, regardless of the answer given. For example, at one point in a medical program, as X-rays of the lung were being displayed on the screen, the question was posed, "In which area of the lungs can you see pneumonia?" After waiting a few moments for the user to study the X-rays,

the VP paused and control of the TV screen was switched to the computer which displayed, on the screen, the same question and four possible answers. After the user responded, regardless of the response, command of the TV display was switched back to video where the area of pneumonia was highlighted while the audio explained what characteristics of the X-ray helped identify the pneumonia as being in the mid-left lung.

A second kind of computer response to user's answers is the true branch. Here, if the user answers the question incorrectly the program branches to give him or her more information (by computer generated text) so that the question can be answered correctly. The program then returns the user to the incorrectly answered question for another try. After receiving the correct response, the program proceeds to the next step.

A third type of computer response is to offer a menu of additional information available from the computer at the user's discretion, e.g., "what tests would you like to do now, bone x-ray, cardiogram, or blood count?"

Depending on the situation, the user has the option of requesting one or more pieces of information before going on.

The Beginning of a Program

The right beginning is important for your program. One good way to begin is with a videotaped welcome to the user (spoken over a soft musical background) and a brief introduction about the program. This may be followed by an explanation of the typewriter-style keyboard, and a demonstration of how to answer questions and how to request additional information from the program as it goes along.

The user shall then be asked to carry out a few practice maneuvers. Computer-

generated instructions and questions may be displayed on the screen, with the video player automatically held in PAUSE mode while the user responds via the keyboard. If the user's response is incorrect, the program branches to re-instruct him or her on the proper use of the keyboard. If the response is correct, the program moves ahead to the formal presentation of the teaching materials.

After each videotaped presentation of teaching materials, the TV display is automatically switched to computer-generated text (while the video player pauses), and the user is asked to respond to questions about what has been presented, or asked what specific additional information he or she would like. Following one or more correct responses, the video player is switched back on to preset the next segment of the program.

An integrated system of computer and videotape provides a very flexible means of producing an interactive audio-visual presentation

Converting Previously Made Videotapes

A large number of teaching videotapes are already available. Using the method described in this article, the teaching value of those videotapes can be greatly enhanced with computer-assisted instruction by the relatively simple insertion of programmed teaching material at appropriate points on the tape.

To add computer assisted instruction to an already made videotape, I suggest the following method. Review the tape several times to select the points where CAI is to be inserted. Write the program for each CAI section. Dub the audio signals onto audio channel 1 of the videotape at the insertion points you have chosen. The tape is now ready for computer assisted/video recorded instruction.

Editing seems to go best when specific cues are selected by the author, such as a particular syllable of audio or a well-defined instant of video. (These help the author keep a chart of synchronization points for editing and review.)

Conclusion

The integration of the computer and the video player in teaching offers significant advantages. With a relatively low expenditure of time and money, an extensive curriculum of computer-assisted teaching materials can be produced or easily adapted from the large selection of video cassettes already available. The result can be a moving, complex, colorful presentation with relevant narration and sound effects, plus all the didactic power of computer-assisted instruction. □

SCHEMATIC OF COMPUTER-VIDEOPLAYER INTEGRATION

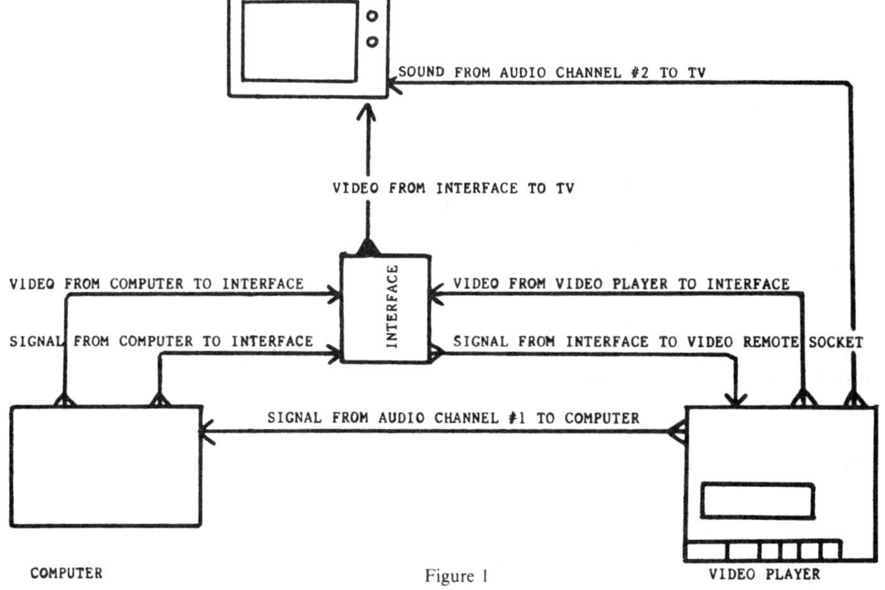

Figure 1

TEXT & GRAPHICS
Options for Apple and Epson

Alan Tobey

Two new options for owners of the Apple II computer and the Epson MX-80 printer can greatly extend the abilities and the ease of use of this popular combination. For little additional cost, these products give the user 24 different print modes with the MX-80, sophisticated graphics routines, and very simple firmware control of many of the printer's text and format features.

The full range of these features is available only to those who have both an Apple and an Epson, but users of Apples who have other graphics printers—or MX-80 owners with other computers—can take advantage of at least one part of this powerful pair.

The Grappler Interface

The Grappler Interface, from Orange Micro, is a parallel interface card for the Apple. Its on-board ROM is provided in a specific version for each compatible printer—currently all Anadex and Epson printers, IDS Paper Tigers with graphics, and the Centronics 739. The Epson MX-80 requires Graftrax-80, described below. Future graphics printers will also be accommodated.

The Grappler Interface gives the user simple control of several useful text and graphics routines. The Grappler's functions are invoked by simple commands either from the keyboard or from within a program. All commands begin with "Control-I" from Basic or "Control-Y" from Pascal or CP/M, and usually require entering just a single additional character to set each feature.

Text Features

The most important text function of the Grappler is a text screen dump routine. With only a Ctrl-I "S" command, whatever

Alan Tobey, 1228 Peralta Ave., Berkeley, CA 94706.

is on the Apple CRT text screen will be printed out automatically, with a 20-character left margin that centers the text on the printout page. (One inconvenient limitation: only the standard 40-character Apple display can be dumped; 80-column boards are not supported.) With similar commands, the Grappler can set or change left and right margins, line length and page length (with an automatic six-line skip-over-perforation feature).

> **The Grappler Interface gives the user simple control of several useful text and graphics routines.**

The screen dump routine is a very handy feature for printing out the results of programmed calculations when the printout routines have not been included in the program, or for printing partial listings of program sections you may want to think about before editing.

The text screen can be dumped any time the cursor is active (blinking), so you can, for example, print out the text screen when the program is halted for a keyboard input without disrupting further program execution. The cursor disappears while the screen is being printed, and then returns, ready for your input as if nothing had happened.

A minor annoyance is the inability of the Grappler to initiate horizontal tabs beyond the 40th column in the normal way; instead a single POKE command is required. This isn't a limitation—just a quirk the user must remember.

Graphics Features

The Grappler treats the Apple graphics in a manner similar to the way it treats the text screen. Short commands allow the Apple to send the stored contents of either hi-res graphics page one or page two to the printer, where it can be printed normally (black-on-white), inverse (white-on-black), double-size, and/or rotated 90°. In the rotated mode the printer can emulate a chart recorder by printing a series of rotated page images in sequence.

Since until now the only way to dump the Apple graphics pages to a printer has been to load (or type in) a fairly elaborate software routine, the Grappler offers tremendous advantages in convenience and savings in programming time. With the Grappler, a few keystrokes get you a graphics printout, from inside a program or as a direct command. It's so easy to do that it encourages frequent and almost whimsical use, just to have a copy of what is stored in the graphics pages. My kids love drawing pictures on the CRT with the joystick and then getting a hard-copy printout to tear off and color.

In addition to graphics dumps, the Grappler can supply the MX-80 (and "some" other printers which the manual doesn't identify) with the missing eighth bit required for TRS-80 block graphics. (The Apple II outputs only seven bits.) That is a delightful feature; one of the few advantages the TRS-80 has had to make Apple owners jealous is neatly eliminated—on paper, at least.

Orange Micro has recently revised and expanded the Grappler documentation from an early primitive version. (I originally received four pages of instructions and one page of corrections.) The current 18-page manual is written in real English—clear and unambiguous—and seems quite complete. An insert even provides a program to modify Visiplot for use with the Grappler.

The Grappler Interface should be useful to every Apple user who owns—or plans to buy—a graphics printer. With a list price of $165 ($15 less than the list for Apple's own parallel printer interface card) it's even a bargain.

Orange Micro Inc., 3150 E. La Palma, Suite G, Anaheim, CA 92806. (714) 630-3322.

Graftrax-80

Graftrax-80 is a kit that gives the Epson MX-80 printer bit-graphics capability. It does not require an Apple but will work with any computer that will drive the regular MX-80. (One exception: it will not work with the Epson 8141 serial interface.) Installing it requires pulling one IC and plugging three others into sockets provided in the MX-80, cutting one jumper wire on the circuit board of the printer, and resetting several DIP switches. Directions for doing this are very clear, and an unusually good line drawing (for once no murky photograph) makes the chance of an error virtually nil. Even a full-fledged fumblefingers should not feel intimidated.

Although Graftrax-80 is advertised as a graphics add-on, one of its most useful features is a text printout enhancement. The kit adds an italics print mode to the options already provided by the standard MX-80. This doubles (to a total of 24) the number of different print modes the MX-80 can print.

All of the regular variations and combinations of type style—using normal, emphasized, double-width, compressed and double-strike print—can also be printed in italics. This gives tremendous versatility to an already excellent printer and provides a variety of type styles for almost every conceivable purpose, from extra-bold headings to normal 80 cps print.

> ## Graftrax-80 is a kit that gives the Epson MX-80 printer bit-graphics capability.

Each print mode variation is established using simple escape codes, and with Graftrax-80 all can be turned on and off even in the middle of programmed print lines (not true with the standard MX-80). This makes sophisticated control of the printout quite simple. One example: I've set up an MX-80 to print product labels at my business. I wrote a short utility program in Applesoft that uses string concatenation to condense all the possible combinations of printer function codes into string variables. For instance, once I've set up DI$=CHR$(27)+CHR$(83)+CHR$(27)+CHR$(52)—equivalent to "ESC S ESC 4"—I can shift to double-width italic printing at any point in a printout routine with just a "PRINT DI$" statement. I load a complete routine as the beginning of a label-printing program, and then programming printout type style becomes almost as fast and as automatic as shifting to upper case.

Graftrax-80, however, is mainly a graphics enabler. Its major function is to add to the MX-80 the bit-graphics capabilities that the Epson MX-70 and MX-100 already have. In bit-graphics mode, any of the top eight printhead needles can be fired at any of 480 or 960 horizontal positions per line. This means that almost any point on the paper can be printed black or left white for truly high-resolution graphics. Graftrax-80, then, brings the MX-80 up to par with other graphics printers such as the Anadex series or the IDS Paper Tigers.

Graftrax-80 will also support TRS-80 block graphics for Apple users, independent of the Grappler. Once block graphics mode is entered via an escape code, each block graphic character is specified with a single ASCII code, so many graphics printout effects can be programmed much more quickly than in the laborious bit-plot mode.

There are several quirks of which the user should be aware. The Apple II doesn't pass the Decimal 9 or Decimal 13 character to the MX-80 with Graftrax in a way that the printer can properly interpret. The TRS-80 Model I has the same problem with Decimal 0, 10, 11 and 12. This means that certain tab and paper feed functions can't be specified conveniently; but the Graftrax manual includes reasonably short POKE routines as acceptable fixes.

Any one of its features would make Graftrax-80 well worth its additional $90 (list) cost. Together, they make an already great printer even better and put highly sophisticated printout routines within easy reach of even inexperienced programmers. I wouldn't have an MX-80 without it.

Epson America, Inc., 3415 Kashiwa St., Torrance, CA 90505. (213) 539-9140. □

```
            EPSON MX-80 PRINT MODES WITH GRAFTRAX

1. THIS IS NORMAL PRINT.

2. THIS IS NORMAL ITALIC PRINT.

3. THIS IS NORMAL EMPHASIZED PRINT.

4. THIS IS NORMAL EMPHASIZED ITALIC PRINT.

5. THIS IS NORMAL DOUBLE-STRIKE PRINT.

6. THIS IS NORMAL DOUBLE-STRIKE ITALIC PRINT.

7. THIS IS NORMAL EMPHASIZED DOUBLE-STRIKE PRINT.

8. THIS IS NORMAL EMPHASIZED DOUBLE-STRIKE ITALIC PRINT.

9. THIS IS COMPRESSED PRINT.

10. THIS IS COMPRESSED ITALIC PRINT.

11. THIS IS COMPRESSED DOUBLE-STRIKE PRINT.

12. THIS IS COMPRESSED DOUBLE-STRIKE ITALIC PRINT.

13. THIS IS DOUBLE-WIDTH PRINT.

14. THIS IS DOUBLE-WIDTH ITALIC PRINT.

15. THIS IS DOUBLE-WIDTH EMPHASIZED
    PRINT.

16. THIS IS DOUBLE-WIDTH EMPHASIZED
    ITALIC PRINT.

17. THIS IS DOUBLE-WIDTH/DOUBLE
    STRIKE PRINT.

18. THIS IS DOUBLE-WIDTH/DOUBLE
    STRIKE ITALIC PRINT.

19. THIS IS DOUBLE-WIDTH/DOUBLE
    STRIKE EMPHASIZED PRINT.

20. THIS IS DOUBLE-WIDTH/DOUBLE
    STRIKE EMPHASIZED ITALIC PRINT.

21. THIS IS DOUBLE-WIDTH COMPRESSED PRINT.

22. THIS IS DOUBLE-WIDTH COMPRESSED ITALIC PRINT.

23. THIS IS DOUBLE-WIDTH COMPRESSED DOUBLE STRIKE PRINT.

24. THIS IS DOUBLE-WIDTH COMPRESSED DOUBLE STRIKE
    ITALIC PRINT.
```

An Apple Slide Show

Mark Harris

David Lubar's article "Apple Picture Packer" in the June '81 issue of *Creative Computing* showed a way to compress Apple II high-resolution graphics for disk storage. The method is best suited for images with broad areas of single colors, a common situation in graphics. I would like to describe how to further compress a special class of pictures.

I teach Mathematics at Appalachian State University and use the Apple as a classroom tool; my most frequent use of graphics is in displaying the graph of a function or relation. A typical graph consists of two coordinate axes, a curve plotting one variable against another, and a little labeling, all against a black background. Since relatively few of the 280 x 180 pixels are being used, it is desirable to store the graph by describing only the pixels in use. With this in mind I wrote the machine language subroutines GR and LOADGR which store and load compact versions of a graph. I shall describe the strategy used in these programs a little later.

How useful are these programs? An average graph now takes only three or four sectors of disk storage, as compared to 32 for straight storage of a whole graphics page. Because of the modest space requirements, loading of the graphs is very fast, and several can be put into Apple memory at the same time. I can queue about twenty graphs in RAM and cycle through them at a fraction of a second per graph (pausing when I want to). This is the idea behind the Basic program Slide Show (Listing 1).

Mark Harris, Math Dept, Appalachian State University, Boone, NC 28608.

```
SLIDE  SHOW


10 AD = - 16300
20  HOME : VTAB 10
30 START = 24576: REM   START OF LOADGR SUBROUTINE
40 D$ = CHR$ (4): REM   CONTROL D
50 S = 1
60  DIM A(20),B(20)
70  PRINT D$;"BLOAD LOADGR.OBJ"
80  PRINT "I WILL DISPLAY GRAPHS STORED BY THE"
90  PRINT
100  PRINT "GR.OBJ0 PROGRAM AS NAME1,NAME2,..."
110  PRINT
120  INPUT "WHAT IS THE NAME? ";G$
130  PRINT : INPUT "HOW MANY GRAPHS? ";N
140 A(1) = START + 80: REM  START OF FIRST COMPACT GRAPH
150  FOR I = 1 TO N
160  PRINT D$;"BLOAD ";G$;I;",A";A(I)
170 L =  PEEK (43616) +  PEEK (43617) $ 256: REM  LENGTH OF BLOADED PROGRAM.
180 A(I + 1) = A(I) + L: REM  COMPUTE STARTING ADDRESS FOR NEXT GRAPH
190  NEXT
200  FOR I = 1 TO N
210 B(I) =  INT (A(I) / 256): REM  MSB
220 A(I) = A(I) - B(I) $ 256: REM  LSB
230  NEXT
240  HGR2 : HGR
250  POKE  - 16302,0: REM  FULL SCREEN GRAPHICS
260 PG = 1:I = 1: GOSUB 350: REM  LOAD 1ST GRAPH ON PAGE 1
270 PG = 2:I = 2: GOSUB 350: REM  LOAD 2ND GRAPH ON PAGE 2
280 X =  FRE (0): REM  A LITTLE HOUSE-CLEANING
290  GET A$: IF A$ = "S" THEN  TEXT : HOME : END
300  IF A$ =  CHR$ (27) THEN I = I + 1: GOSUB 320: REM  CHECK FOR ESC KEY
310  GOTO 280
320 AD = AD + S: POKE AD,0:S =  - S: REM  FLIPS PAGE
330 PG = (3 + S) / 2
340  IF I > N THEN I = 1
350  POKE 250,B(I): POKE 249,A(I): REM  SET UP ADDRESS OF NEXT GRAPH FOR LOADGR
360  IF PG = 1 THEN  POKE 252,32: CALL START: RETURN
370  POKE 252,64: CALL START: RETURN
```

Listing 1. A sample Applesoft program that displays compressed graphs.

About Slide Show

Use of this Applesoft program requires that several graphs first be BSAVEd under the same name followed by successive numbers, e.g. GRAPH1, GRAPH2, etc. This is done with the GR routine. Slide Show will ask for the name and number of graphs, then load them starting at address $6050 (the subroutine LOADGR is placed at $6000). Next the first two graphs are placed in hi-res pages one and two, and page one is displayed. When the ESC key is depressed, the Apple switches to page two. GRAPH3 is transferred by the LOADGR routine to page one, all done neatly behind the scenes. When ESC is hit again, GRAPH3 is displayed instantly. This loading on the hidden page continues through the entire list of graphs and then starts back with GRAPH1. The graphs appear just about as fast as the ESC key can be depressed. When you're done, just hit the "S" key.

The GR Subroutine

To compress and save a graph using the GR subroutine (Listing 2), first get the graph of your choice on hi-res page one. (I use standard HPLOTing to draw the graph and use the DOS Tool Kit "HRCG" program to label it.) Then get back to the TEXT and type BRUN GR (assuming you have saved the GR program on disk). A message giving the starting address and length of your now-compressed graph will appear on the screen. If these numbers were $0C00 and $FC, typing BSAVE GRAPH4,A$C00,L$FC would save the graph on disk under the name GRAPH4.

```
SOURCE FILE: GR
----- NEXT OBJECT FILE NAME IS GR.OBJ
0C00:                1           ORG   $0C00
00F9:                2 TBL       EQU   $F9    ;LOW BYTE OF TABLE ADDRESS
00FA:                3 TBH       EQU   $FA
00FB:                4 PGL       EQU   $FB
00FC:                5 PGH       EQU   $FC           ;CURRENT PAGE
FDED:                6 COUT      EQU   $FDED
FDDA:                7 PRBYTE    EQU   $FDDA
0C00:A2 00           8           LDX   #0
0C02:86 FB           9           STX   PGL
0C04:86 F9          10           STX   TBL
0C06:A9 20          11           LDA   #$20    ;1ST PG OF HRES GRAPHICS
0C08:85 FC          12           STA   PGH
0C0A:A9 0D          13           LDA   #$0D
0C0C:85 FA          14           STA   TBH           ;TABLE BEGINS AT $0D00
0C0E:               15 ;A ZERO BYTE MARKS END OF PAGE
0C0E:               16 ;TABLE ORGANIZATION:
0C0E:               17 ;DATA,ADRS,DTA,ADRS,...,ZBYTE,...
0C0E:A0 00          18 NWPG      LDY   #0
0C10:B1 FB          19 ZCHK      LDA   (PGL),Y
0C12:F0 0B          20           BEQ   CT
0C14:81 F9          21           STA   (TBL,X)   ;STORE NONZERO DATA
0C16:20 34 0C       22           JSR   PTR
0C19:98             23           TYA
0C1A:81 F9          24           STA   (TBL,X)   ;STORE LOW BYTE OF ADRS
0C1C:20 34 0C       25           JSR   PTR
0C1F:C8             26 CT        INY
0C20:D0 EE          27           BNE   ZCHK
0C22:A9 00          28           LDA   #0
0C24:81 F9          29           STA   (TBL,X)
0C26:20 34 0C       30           JSR   PTR
0C29:E6 FC          31           INC   PGH
0C2B:A5 FC          32           LDA   PGH
0C2D:C9 40          33           CMP   #$40
0C2F:F0 0A          34           BEQ   DONE
0C31:4C 0E 0C       35           JMP   NWPG    ;CHECK NEW PAGE
0C34:E6 F9          36 PTR       INC   TBL     ;SBR TO MOVE POINTER
0C36:D0 02          37           BNE   RET
0C38:E6 FA          38           INC   TBH
0C3A:60             39 RET       RTS
0C3B:A0 00          40 DONE      LDY   #0
0C3D:B9 59 0C       41 FTCH      LDA   MSG,Y       ;GET CHAR FOR MESSAGE
0C40:F0 07          42           BEQ   LGTH
0C42:               43 ;ZERO MARKS END OF MESSAGE:
0C42:20 ED FD       44           JSR   COUT
0C45:C8             45           INY
0C46:4C 3D 0C       46           JMP   FTCH
0C49:A5 FA          47 LGTH      LDA   TBH     ;FIND LENGTH OF TABLE
0C4B:38             48           SEC
0C4C:E9 0D          49           SBC   #$0D
0C4E:20 DA FD       50           JSR   PRBYTE
0C51:A5 F9          51           LDA   TBL
0C53:20 DA FD       52           JSR   PRBYTE
0C56:4C D0 03       53           JMP   $3D0    ;GO TO BASIC
0C59:8D 8D 8D       54 MSG       DFB   $8D,$8D,$8D
0C5C:A0 A0 A0       55           ASC   "           FINISHED."
0C5F:A0 A0 C6
0C62:C9 CE C9
0C65:D3 C8 C5
0C68:C4 AE
0C6A:8D 8D          56           DFB   $8D,$8D
0C6C:A0 A0 A0       57           ASC   "         ADDRESS = $0D00"
0C6F:A0 A0 C1
0C72:C4 C4 D2
0C75:C5 D3 D3
0C78:A0 BD A0
0C7B:A4 B0 C4
0C7E:B0 B0
0C80:8D 8D          58           DFB   $8D,$8D
0C82:A0 A0 A0       59           ASC   "         LENGTH = $"
0C85:A0 A0 CC
0C88:C5 CE C7
0C8B:D4 C8 A0
0C8E:BD A0 A4
0C91:00             60           DFB   0

### SUCCESSFUL ASSEMBLY: NO ERRORS
```

Listing 2. This machine language routine compresses hi-res data.

Packed Thoughts

An Apple Slide Show and *Picture Packer Revisited* show two excellent and diverse extensions of the packing concept. By tackling a specific area of graphics, namely plotted functions, Mr. Harris has achieved not only an extraordinary compactness of data, but also a very fast display routine. This combination need not be limited to graphs, but could also be applied, in some cases, to animation. A series of line drawings could be rapidly cycled through the screen. To carry the idea a step further, if the data were placed on the screen with an Exclusive OR, objects could be moved across a background scene. I believe readers will find many applications for the programs created by Mr. Harris.

In *Picture Packer Revisited* (see page 116), Mr. Haley has taken a quantum leap beyond the original program. His approach is elegant, and the degree of compression is impressive. One slight extension readers might wish to try would be to append a routine that turns all $00 bytes of the picture to $80. This would have no effect on the picture since $00 and $80 both produce seven unset pixels on the screen. And with no $00 bytes in the picture, $00 could be used as a signal byte. In this way, there would be no need to check for a byte which might be data or might be a flag, and BEQ could be used in place of comparing the value against $FE. Beyond this, I almost feel Mr. Haley has taken the packing con-cept as far as it can go. But such speculation usually turns out to be wrong. Which brings up a personal note.

I want to thank readers who have the curiosity and drive to push a concept beyond its limits. There is great pleasure in seeing a better way, in hearing from someone who has made an imaginative leap or found a new approach. While there is nothing wrong with using a printed program as is, there can be great rewards in asking yourself "Is this program as good as it can be?" Someone is going to surprise us. But it really shouldn't be a surprise. I've come to expect innovation and excellence from you. Thanks.—D.L.

How It Works

Each address in Apple memory consists of two bytes. The first byte is sometimes called the page number (not to be confused with the hi-res graphics pages) and the second byte gives the locations on that page. A hi-res picture occupies either memory $2000-$3FFF (hi-res page one) or $4000-5FFF (page 2). Hence a graphics page takes 32 pages of memory.

The GR program starts at the first memory page, say $2000, and finds the addresses and contents of all non-zero bytes on that page. Using a zero byte as a separator (we know it will never occur as a data byte under this scheme), the program moves on to the second page and so on up to the 32nd page. The storage format for each page is:

data byte, address byte, data byte, address byte, ... , zero byte.

Since we can keep track of the page byte and change it only when a zero byte is reached, we require only one byte for the address.

The efficiency of this method depends on the percentage of zero bytes on the graphics page. With the graphs I normally encounter, about 95% of the bytes are zero (corresponding to black background) and compact storage takes only about 10% of the original $2000 bytes. For a picture with no zero bytes, we would have a disaster; it would require more than twice the original space to store the same graph.

Other Uses

The Slide Show program illustrates one use of the LOADGR routine (Listing 3), but you may want to use it in other ways. For example, the following program puts a single graph on HGR page one and then quits:

Closing Comments

The programs listed here work well for compressing graphs which sparsely occupy an HGR page. It would be easy to change the programs to accommodate a background color other than black, but displaying staid mathematical curves against a violet page would be a little tacky.

> *The programs listed here work well for compressing graphs which sparsely occupy an HGR page.*

```
SOURCE FILE: LOADGR
                1 ###############################################################################
0000:           2 #
0000:           3 # SUBROUTINE LOADGR
0000:           4 #
0000:           5 # THIS SUBROUTINE CLEARS A HIGH-RES GRAPHICS PAGE (1 OR 2) AND LOADS A GRAPH
0000:           6 # WHICH HAS BEEN STORED BY THE GR.OBJ SUBROUTINE.
0000:           7 # TO CALL, THE PAGE # AND THE STARTING ADDRESS OF THE GRAPH MUST BE GIVEN.
0000:           8 # PAGE #: STORE $20 (FOR PAGE 1) OR $40 (FOR PAGE 2) IN PGH (DEFINED BELOW
0000:           9 # AS $FC).
0000:          10 # GRAPH ADDRESS: STORE LOW BYTE IN TBL ($F9), HIGH BYTE IN TBH ($FA).
0000:          11 #
               12 ###############################################################################
----- NEXT OBJECT FILE NAME IS LOADGR.OBJ
6000:          13          ORG  $6000
00F9:          14 TBL      EQU  $F9
00FA:          15 TBH      EQU  $FA
00FB:          16 PGL      EQU  $FB
00FC:          17 PGH      EQU  $FC
6000:18        18          CLC
6001:A5 FC     19          LDA  PGH
6003:8D 4D 60  20          STA  ADR
6006:69 20     21          ADC  #$20        ;COMPUTE END ADDRESS OF GRAPHICS PAGE
6008:8D 4E 60  22          STA  ENDADR
600B:          23 # CLEAR PAGE TO BLACK:
600B:A0 00     24          LDY  #0
600D:84 FB     25          STY  PGL
600F:A9 00     26          LDA  #0
6011:91 FB     27 LOOP     STA  (PGL),Y
6013:C8        28          INY
6014:D0 FB     29          BNE  LOOP
6016:E6 FC     30          INC  PGH
6018:A6 FC     31          LDX  PGH
601A:EC 4E 60  32          CPX  ENDADR   ;END?
601D:D0 F2     33          BNE  LOOP
601F:AA        34          TAX           ;ZERO X REG
6020:AD 4D 60  35          LDA  ADR
6023:85 FC     36          STA  PGH
6025:A1 F9     37 LOAD     LDA  (TBL,X)
6027:F0 10     38          BEQ  CHPG      ;INCREASE HIGH BYTE IF NECESSARY
6029:20 46 60  39          JSR  PTR
602C:48        40          PHA
602D:A1 F9     41          LDA  (TBL,X)
602F:A8        42          TAY
6030:68        43          PLA
6031:91 FB     44          STA  (PGL),Y
6033:20 46 60  45          JSR  PTR
6036:4C 25 60  46          JMP  LOAD
6039:E6 FC     47 CHPG     INC  PGH
603B:A5 FC     48          LDA  PGH
603D:20 46 60  49          JSR  PTR
6040:CD 4E 60  50          CMP  ENDADR   ;END?
6043:D0 E0     51          BNE  LOAD
6045:60        52          RTS
6046:E6 F9     53 PTR      INC  TBL
6048:D0 02     54          BNE  RET
604A:E6 FA     55          INC  TBH
604C:60        56 RET      RTS
604D:          57 ADR      DS   1
604E:          58 ENDADR   DS   1

### SUCCESSFUL ASSEMBLY: NO ERRORS
```

Listing 3. A routine to restore the compressed graphs.

If you want to use Slide Show as part of a presentation to an audience, you may want to substitute a paddle button for the escape key to change graphs. This allows you to face the group and control the Apple from a distance. To make this change, just replace lines 290 and 300 with:

290 IF PEEK(49249) > 127 THEN I=I+1:GOSUB 320

Both Basic programs listed in this article call the LOADGR subroutine under the name LOADGR.OBJ, so either store it that way or change the program to agree with the name you choose.

Slide Show is designed for an Apple with 48K, but the other programs can be used with less memory.

After you are finished using Slide Show, it's a good idea to type the command "FP" to restore the computer to its usual good-natured self. □

Three-Dimensional Apple Graphics

Mark Pelczarski

Welcome to the world of 3-D graphics! The words you read on this page are certainly on a two-dimensional surface, but step back a minute and survey your surroundings. The world around you has another dimension: depth. Imagine looking at a computer screen; it is definitely two-dimensional. But on the same screen you can view television shows and movies that give the illusion of that third dimension. As people on the screen move further away, they appear to get smaller, as they move closer, they appear larger. Think about it.

The program accompanying this article works on an Apple II with 48K, disk drive, and Applesoft firmware (or the language system). It allows you to create line drawings that you can rotate, scale, and move around the screen in what will appear to be three dimensions. The program is in Basic, so don't expect to be able to do rapid 3-D animations with it. It is accurate, however, and fairly easy to use.

The program was sold for a short time, and to be fair, anyone who bought a copy is welcome to contact Co-op Software about trading it in for "The Complete Graphics System," which has, among other things, a much-improved machine language version of the 3-D program. The address for Co-op Software is P.O. Box 432, West Chicago, IL 60185, and the phone number is (312) 231-0912.

Projecting 3-D Images

To start, let's look at a technique for making an object appear three-dimensional on a two-dimensional screen, trying not to worry too much about mathematics, yet. Imagine your television screen as a window, with real 3-D objects behind it. Better yet, find a window and a

Mark Pelczarski, 1206 Kings Circle, West Chicago, IL 60185.

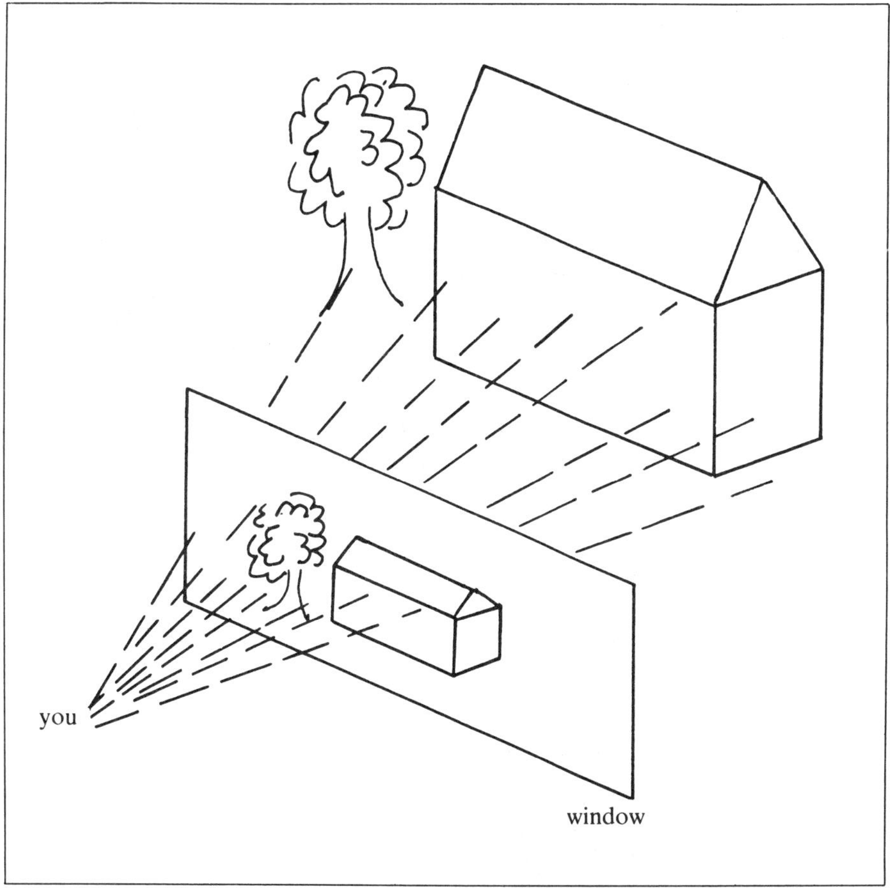

Figure 1. Projecting a 3-D subject onto a 2-D surface.

grease pencil. Sit close enough so you can reach the window, and trace what you see outside onto the surface of the window with the pencil (before you start, you'd better make sure you can erase what you draw). You should wind up with a two-dimensional (the window surface) rendition of the three-dimensional outside; and it should be pretty accurate, or, as they say in 3-D graphics-land, in "true perspective."

How does it work, and how can that idea be transferred to a computer? See the drawing in Figure 1. Light travels in a straight line from the actual object, through the window, to your eyes (technical fiends will please disallow any refraction through the window). Where the lines intersect the window, you have an outline of the objects outside, projected on a two-dimensional surface. It's the same thing that happens on film in cam-

"

eras. The mathematical key is that there are points on one side of a plane, connected with lines to a point on the other side of the plane, and where those lines intersect the plane is the two-dimensional projection. The points on one side are the object, the point on the other side is your eyes, the plane is the window, and the lines are the light.

Defining Some Program Storage

Now to set some structure to what we need for a computer rendition of all this. We'll define our objects as stick figures. We'll store a set of points with three-dimensional coordinates: X, Y, and Z. To stay somewhat consistent with what you already know about screen graphics, X will measure across the screen, left to right, Y will measure from the bottom of the screen to the top, and Z will measure the depth, from the screen surface, with positive values toward the back (see Figure 2). The point (0,0,0) will be at the center of the screen, on the screen. (Those of you familiar with 3-D coordinates will notice that the axes are tilted 90 degrees back from their usual orientation, to enable us to reference here to Z as depth.)

The points whose coordinates will be stored in memory will simply be endpoints of lines. No need to store every point of the line, since projected lines will still connect their projected endpoints. In addition to the coordinates of the endpoints, then, we'll also store a list of lines. These will be identified by the numbers of their two endpoints—sort of a three-dimensional "connect-the dots." Figure 3 shows how the cube in Figure 2 would be stored.

In a 48K Apple, there is comfortable room for 500 points and 750 lines, so define the following for storage:

X(499)—the x-coordinate of each point, 0 to 499

Y(499)—the y-coordinate of each point

Z(499)—the z-coordinate of each point

L%(749,1)—endpoints of lines 0 to 749; L%(I,0) is the number of one endpoint, and L%(I,1) is the other. The "%" makes L% an integer variable, which takes 2 bytes per element rather than 5, which it would take as a floating point variable.

The actual coordinates of an endpoint would be found using something like X(L%(I,0)), Y(L%(I,0)), and Z(L%(I,0)), where I is the number of the line, and L%(I,0) holds the point number.

If that's not confusing enough, the actual program uses an array P(499,2) for the points, rather than X, Y, and Z. If N is a point number, P(N,0) is the x-coordinate, P(N,1) is the y-coordinate, and P(N,2) is the z-coordinate. This shortens parts of the program by allowing loops, but for the purposes of this article, we'll use X, Y, and Z.

Putting an Object on the Screen

All the necessary factors are there: points are stored, the screen is the xy-plane, and your eye is somewhere out on the negative end of the z-axis (D1 is that distance in the program). When I started this part of program development, I assumed there would be some pretty heavy mathematics involved. After days of poring over old math books, going over three-dimensional equations of lines, equations for planes, techniques for finding intersections of lines and planes, all the equations for finding the projected points came down to a relatively simple relation: proportions. You need X and Y coordinates on the screen, and you have X, Y, and Z coordinates for the point you

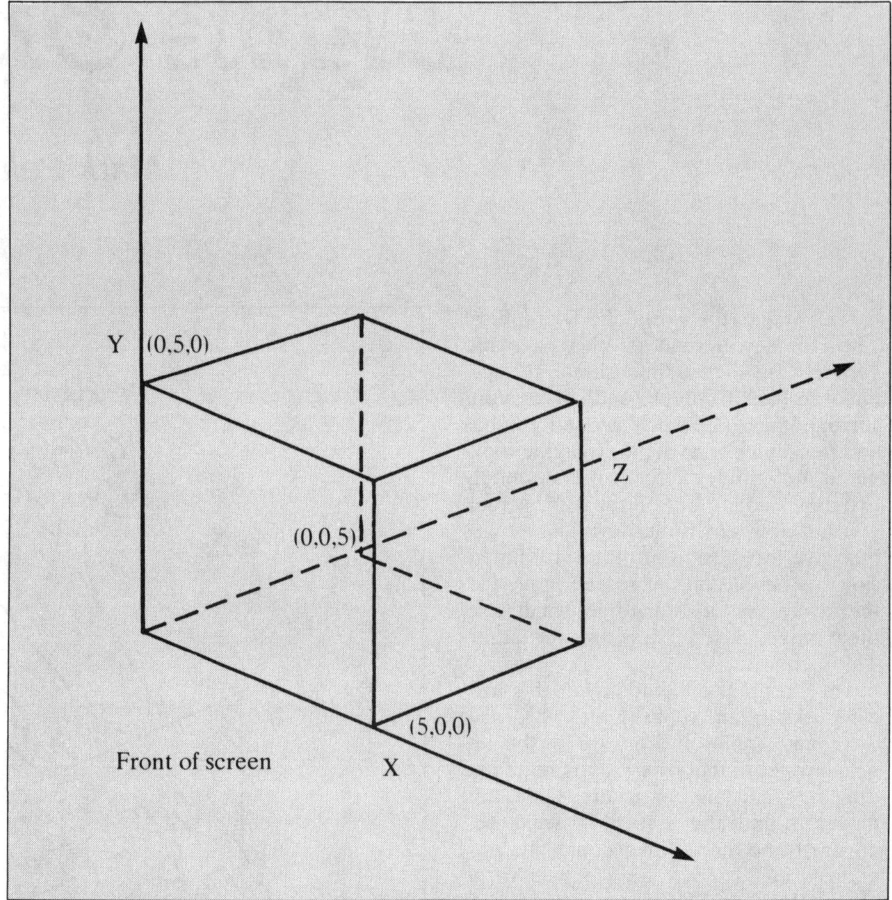

Figure 2. Axes.

	Points				Lines	
#	X	Y	Z	#	From	To
0	0	0	0	0	0	1
1	5	0	0	1	1	2
2	5	5	0	2	2	3
3	0	5	0	3	3	0
4	0	0	5	4	4	5
5	5	0	5	5	5	6
6	5	5	5	6	6	7
7	0	5	5	7	7	4
				8	0	4
				9	1	5
				10	2	6
				11	3	7

Figure 3. Points and lines for a cube.

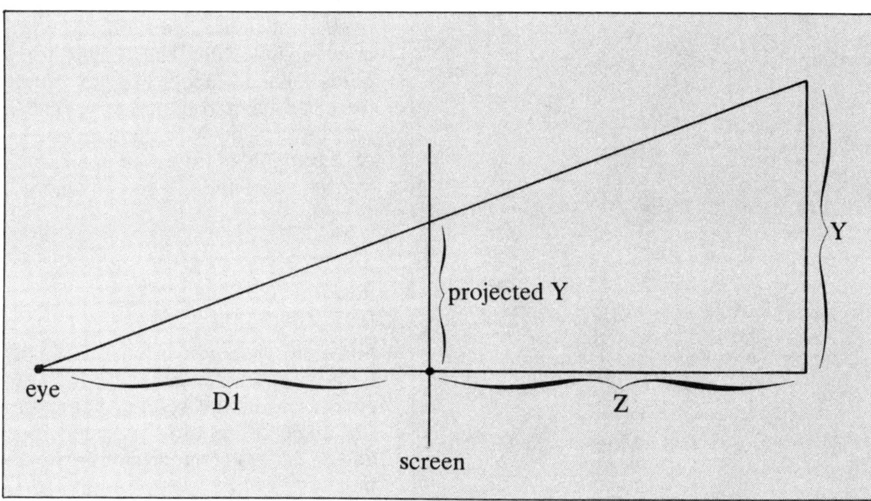

Figure 4. Projecting Y onto the screen.

want projected. Imagining the lines shown in Figure 4 gives two similar triangles. You can compute the X and Y separately; the figure and following computation shows finding Y.

$$\frac{Y}{D1+Z} = \frac{\text{project } Y}{D1}$$

or

$$\text{project } Y = \frac{Y*D1,}{D1+Z,}$$

This computation is running around somewhere in lines 4385 and 4390 of the program. Unfortunately, by then I've already changed D1 to VZ, which does some scaling for the purposes of getting a decent size on the screen. 'TR' is the point, TRanslated onto the screen. Once this is done for the X and Y coordinates of each endpoint of a line, a line is drawn connecting the translated points. The process is repeated for each set of endpoints and each line.

More Fun—Moving an Object

Just looking at a 3-D object projected on the screen isn't actually a barrel of thrills unless you can do something to it, such as move it or turn it to see another angle. It's nicer to be able to see something on the screen like the little sports car that just came around the corner outside the window. First you see its side, then the front as it turns, then it gets larger (or appears to) as it approaches and drives past. (It's a good thing the car came by; I was about to try describing the building next door doing a 90 degree turn.)

There are two approaches to viewing other angles of an object: move the object, or move your viewpoint. Moving the object requires changing all the coordinates of the object. Moving the viewpoint would seem to require movement of only one point, but it makes translation to two dimensions a little more lengthy. With this program it's more beneficial to move the object, since later we'll also talk about having more than one object on the screen and moving each independently (such as moving one box so it's on top of another).

There are three basic operations we can do with an object: shifting, rotating, and scaling. Each operation somehow affects the coordinates of each point that is stored. None of the operations affects the line information, as lines simply connect their endpoints.

Shifting

Shifting is moving an object in a direction, and is the easiest. We can shift an object left or right by adding a negative or positive number, respectively, to every x-coordinate of the object. Shifting down or up is accomplished by adding to the y-coordinates, and shifting forward (towards you) or back (away) is accomplished by modifying the z-coordinates. The effect on the screen when shifting up, down, left, or right will be to move the object in that direction, but you will also get more (or less) view of the side of the object. It is comparable to looking at a building straight-on, then looking at it from slightly down the street. Down the street you'll not only see the front, you'll see some of the side. Shifting an object forward or back will make it appear larger or smaller, as real objects appear when you're closer or further from them.

Scaling

Rotation and scaling pose a new problem: both require some type of reference point. In scaling you need a point to scale out from. In rotating, you need a point to turn the object around. In both cases, it is usually most convenient to have this point in the center of the object. Figure 5 shows examples of both operations, each done with the reference point outside the object, then inside the object. In most cases, having this point outside the object will cause rotation or scaling to throw the object right off the screen (over in the closet, on my desk, or in the kitchen).

To solve this, a center point for the figure is computed before any operations are done. This is accomplished by averaging the largest and smallest x-value, the largest and smallest y-value, then the largest and smallest z-value. In the program, it's done in lines 3032-3038, and CR(0), CR(2) are the X, Y, and Z values of the computed center.

To scale a figure, the main step is to multiply every coordinate by a scaling factor, such as 2, to double the dimensions. This operation done to the cube in Figures 2 and 3 would change all the 5's to 10's, doubling the lengths of its sides. Without regarding a center, however, you can also send objects off into neverneverland, or off the screen, whichever comes first. The apparent center of a straight multiplication is the point 0,0,0. To incorporate your own center (the one that we computed) into the scaling involves a three-step process:

Step 1—Subtract the coordinates of the center from every point. This translates the figure to an identical figure that has 0,0,0 as the center.

Step 2—Multiply every coordinate by the scaling constant. This scales it out from the point 0,0,0, which is now within the figure.

Step 3—Add the coordinates of the original center back onto every coordinate. This puts the center back where it orginally was, but the figure is now scaled outward from it.

Rotations

Rotations, like scaling, require a center. When we talk of direction, we'll use that of the part of the object closest to you (when the front rotates to the left, for example, the back goes to the right— we'll call this a left rotation). Rotations can be on any of three axes. Going around the x-axis rotates the object left or right, like a revolving door. Rotating around the z-axis moves the object clockwise or counterclockwise, like (gasp!) the hands of a clock.

Anyway, if a rotation on the z-axis is used as an example, the z-coordinates all stay the same. (Clockwise/counterclock-

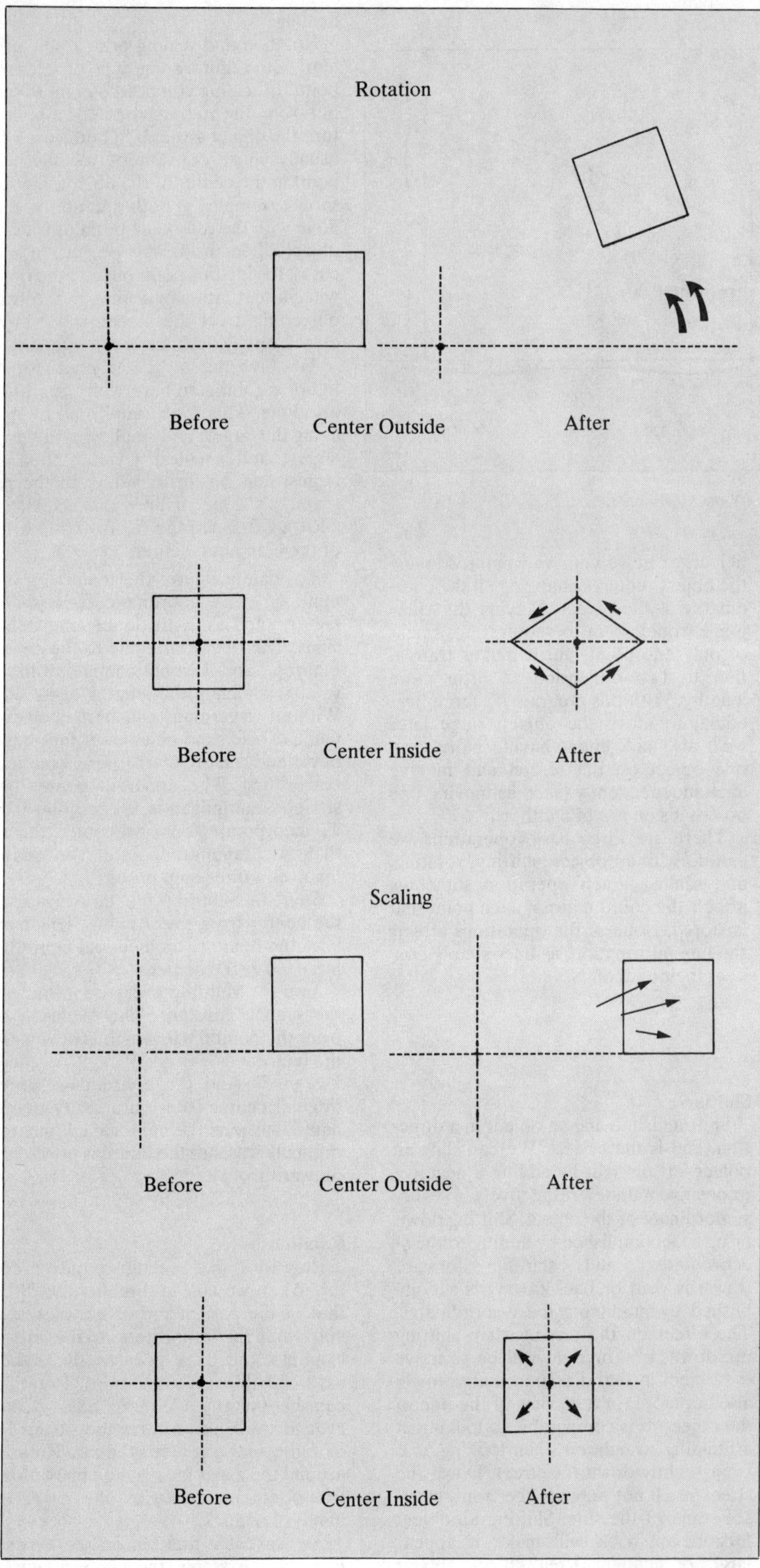

Rotation

Before Center Outside After

Before Center Inside After

Scaling

Before Center Outside After

Before Center Inside After

Figure 5. Scaling and Rotating with centers inside and outside object.

wise doesn't affect the depth of any point.) Pretend your object is a two-dimensional figure, since the z-coordinate is never involved. The X and Y coordinates change according to some old formulas from trigonometry. The formulas have to do with the sine and cosine of the angle of rotation; for short we'll say $S = \sin(a)$ and $C = \cos(a)$, where "a" is the angle:

new $X = C * X - S * Y$
new $Y = C * Y + S * X$
(new $Z = Z$)

Since this rotation is on the z-axis, the figure will move clockwise or counterclockwise on the screen, depending on the angle of rotation. A small, positive angle causes counterclockwise movement.

Similarly, rotations around the y-axis (left/right) have no effect on the y-coordinate (height of the object on the screen). Again using S and C for the sine and cosine of the angle of rotation, the formulas would be:

new $X = C * X - S * Z$
new $Z = C * Z + S * X$

The other possibility, a rotation around the x-axis, gives an up/down movement of the object. In this case the x-coordinate is unaffected. The formulas are:

new $Y = C * Y - S * Z$
new $Z = C * Z + S * Y$

If you're studying these equations, note that the plusses and minuses in the equations depend on the direction to which you assign positive angles. This is because the opposite of an angle has the same cosine ($\cos(-a) = \cos(a)$), but the opposite sine ($\sin(-a) = -\sin(a)$). In this program, down, left, and clockwise are assigned negative angles. and up, right, and counterclockwise are assigned positive angles. This is all handled internally; the program user simply specifies the direction (see lines 6075-6110).

Before a rotation is done, however, we have to do the same operation with the center. Otherwise, rotations will move around the axes, rather than turning the object in its location. The first step is to subtract the center coordinates from all the coordinates of the object. The appropriate rotation formulas are then used, rotating the translated object around one of the axes. The final step is to add the center coordinates onto the new coordinates of the object, putting it back in its original location, but now rotated.

Distortions

There is one added operation in this program, called a distortion. A distortion is scaling an object in one dimension: width, height, or depth (the X, Y, or Z coordinate, respectively). This has the effect of stretching or compacting the object in that dimension. Starting with a cube, for example, you could distort each dimension, giving a rectangular box with any width, height, and depth. Thus, with a few basic shapes, you can create a multitude of variations without having to define new figures.

Designing the Program

The basic options necessary in this program will be creating and editing figures, viewing and manipulating them, saving them for later use, and loading previous figures. Other options included in this program are the ability to clear all figures from memory, for starting over, and saving two-dimensional screen images to disk.

A feature is also included to allow more than one figure to be in memory at a time. It is arranged so that several small figures can be created or loaded from disk and each one manipulated, assembling a larger figure consisting of all small figures in memory. This large figure can be saved, with all the small figures as its parts. The information from all the small figures is kept intact, so when the large figure is re-loaded, the small figures may still be manipulated individually.

To allow this capability, two extra arrays are needed: one to hold the names of the figures in memory, and one to hold the information for first and last point number, and first and last line number. The name array is FT$ in the program, and allows up to 100 names (0-99). The information array is dimensioned FG% (99,3). The '99' allows information for up to 100 figures. If 'I' is the number of the figure, (FG%(I,0) is the starting point of the figure, FG%(I,1) is the ending point, FG%(I,2) is the starting line, and FG% (I,3) is the ending line. An example of using these would be if Figure A had 8 points (0-7) and 12 lines (0-11), and Figure B had 4 points (8-11) and 4 lines (12-15). The starting point for Figure B is 8, the ending point 11, the starting line 12, and the ending line 15.

In the program, lines 5-86 initialize storage and give the main options to the user. LOMEM is set to 16384 so that the variables will not conflict with the high-resolution graphics page. In the array dimensions, T, X, and Y are used as temporary variables, and TR, the only other array not yet mentioned, will hold the values of the three-dimensional coordinates translated to two-dimensions.

All the subroutines dealing with creating, editing, loading, and saving would be considered housekeeping subroutines, separate from the part of the program that actually lets you view and manipulate figures. Those subroutines appear in lines 170-2020. Creating a new figure is done in lines 1000-2020, with the user first entering the points, then the lines. When done entering points (in X,Y,Z coordinates), the user types 'D' for "done." The point numbers for lines are then entered, again followed by "D" when finished.

The edit subroutine is in lines 170-239. This allows the user to display the points or lines for a figure, and change any of the values assigned to them. When first creating a figure, you may find it advantageous to enter a few "dummy" points to which you won't attach lines, in case you want to use them later. Likewise, you can enter a few dummy lines (connecting point 1 to point 1, for example) for possible later use.

Other subroutines in this section are: saving a figure (lines 250-288), loading a figure (lines 300-336), re-initializing the variables (line 350), and saving a screen image (lines 400-420).

There are a couple of other subroutines following these that let you choose figures for editing and manipulating, and compute information necessary for viewing. Lines 2830 to 2875 allow you to enter a figure name for editing and manipulation. Lines 2900-2930 allow you to specify manipulating everything on the screen, or an individual figure, setting the appropriate variables based on your replies. NP, NL, and NF are the number of points, lines, and figures. SP and EP are the numbers of the starting and ending points for the current figure, and SL and EL are the numbers of the starting and ending lines.

Viewing Figures

There are a few subroutines devoted exclusively to the process of viewing figures. Lines 120-165 control this process. First, the center and the viewer's distance must be computed. This is done in the subroutine in lines 2900-3140, as earlier explained. Then, in a loop, the following occur: the points are computed and translated, lines are drawn on the screen, the user selects an option for manipulating the figure, lines are erased, and the cycle starts over with the new points being computed, lines again drawn, etc. Each process is in its own subroutine. The points are computed and translated in lines 4000-4400. The loop in that subroutine goes from the starting point of the figure to the ending point, performs the selected operation on that point (C holds the operation code), then translates that point to its two-dimensional coordinate and stores that in the TR array. After every point has been done, the subroutine returns.

Lines 5000 to 5290 draw or erase the lines on the screen. SW and FS are switches that tell it which to do. If SW is set to zero, the subroutine erases each line. If FS is set to zero, the subroutine erases the entire screen and draws the new lines. If both SW and FS are equal to 1, then the subroutine only draws the new lines. (FS is 1 when only one figure of many is being moved; that way the other figures are not erased during movement.) This subroutine loops from the starting line to the ending line, determines the endpoints by checking array TR, then checks whether the line fits on the screen. The entire section from line 5070 to 5270 checks each endpoint for being on the screen, and attempts to find a segment of the line that will fit on the screen, if possible. This prevents trouble from parts of the figure that may be above, below, or to the side of the screen.

The last subroutine, where all the decisions are made, is in lines 6000 to 6300. Choices of operation are displayed here, and other decisions are made and constants gotten within this routine. For the sake of using this program, here's a breakdown of choices:

Rotate—allows rotation of the figure. You follow by giving a direction and an angle.

Shift—moves a figure. Again, you give a direction, then the number of units the figure should be moved.

Scale—changes the size of figure. You follow by giving a constant by which the dimensions will be multiplied. The constant may be a whole number or a decimal.

Distort—scales one dimension. You choose the dimension (width, height, or depth) and the constant by which to multiply.

Move Everything/One Figure—lets you choose to have further operations affect all figures in memory or just one. Choices are given to specify all, or a single figure name.

Choose Center—allows you to select your own center for rotations and scaling. Sometimes its advantageous to keep a specific point stationary, which happens with the center in rotate/scale operations. With this option you choose the point number of the center.

Edit, Save, or Quit—returns you to main options.

Full Screen—allows you to view full screen graphics until the next keypress.

Scale View on Screen—allows you to change the size of what you see without affecting the actual coordinates. It's like using binoculars instead of increasing the size of the object. This is also helpful for increasing or decreasing the illusion of perspective; similar to viewing an object closely (more apparent perspective) or from a distance (less apparent perspective). To get more "perspective," move the object very close and scale down the view on the screen. To get less 'perspective', move the object farther away and magnify it with this option.

This program should give you a good idea of how 3-D graphics are simulated by computers, the possible operations on them, and how those operations are performed. Questions regarding the program and the techniques are welcome, and I hope you enjoy it. □

```
1   REM 3-D GRAPHICS
        COPYRIGHT 1980
        MARK PELCZARSKI
5   LOMEM: 16384: HOME :D$ =  CHR$
    (4): HGR
50  DIM CR(2),T(2),X(1),Y(1),P(49
    9,2),L%(749,1),TR(499,1),FG%
    (99,3),FT$(99)
65  GOSUB 350
70  HOME : VTAB 21: PRINT "1-CREA
    TE FIGURE, 2-EDIT FIGURE": PRINT
    "3-VIEW, 4-START OVER": PRINT
    "5-SAVE ON DISK, 6-GET FROM
    DISK": PRINT "7-SAVE 2 DIMEN
    SIONAL IMAGE, 8-QUIT";
80  INPUT C: IF C < 1 OR C > 8 THEN
    70
81  IF C = 1 THEN 1000
82  IF C = 8 THEN  TEXT : STOP
83  IF NF > 0 THEN 85
84  IF C > 1 AND C < 6 THEN  PRINT
    : PRINT "THERE ARE NO FIGURE
    S IN MEMORY.": PRINT "<PRESS
    ANY KEY>";: GET A$: GOTO 70
85  ON C GOSUB 5,170,120,350,250,
    300,400
86  GOTO 70
120 HGR :C = 1: GOSUB 2910
130 GOSUB 4000:SW = 1: GOSUB 500
    0: GOSUB 6000
155 IF FS = 1 THEN SW = 0: GOSUB
    5000
165 GOTO 130
170 GOSUB 2830:C1 = FG%(CF,0)
175 TEXT : HOME : PRINT FT$(CF)
180 PRINT "1-POINTS,2-LINES,3-CH
    ANGE,4-DONE EDITING";: INPUT
    C: IF C < 1 OR C > 4 THEN 18
    0
185 ON C GOTO 190,205,220,239
190 PRINT "#,X,Y,Z:":SW = 1:S1 =
    0: FOR I = C1 TO FG%(CF,1)
194 PRINT I - C1 + 1;: FOR I1 =
    0 TO 2: HTAB 8 + I1 * 8: PRINT
    LEFT$ ( STR$ (P(I,I1)),6);:
    NEXT : PRINT :S1 = S1 + 1: IF
    S1 = 20 THEN  PRINT "<PRESS
    A KEY>";: GET A$:S1 = 0: PRINT
196 NEXT : GOTO 180
205 C = FG%(CF,2): PRINT "#,FROM,
    TO":SW = 2:S1 = 0: FOR I = C
    TO FG%(CF,3)
212 PRINT I - C + 1,L%(I,0) - C1
    + 1,L%(I,1) - C1 + 1:S1 = S
    1 + 1: IF S1 = 20 THEN  PRINT
    "<PRESS A KEY>";: GET A$:S1 =
    0: PRINT
214 NEXT : GOTO 180
220 IF SW = 2 THEN 230
222 INPUT "POINT #";I:I = I + C1
    - 1: IF I < C1 OR I > FG%(C
    F,1) THEN 180
224 INPUT "X:";P(I,0): INPUT "Y:
    ";P(I,1): INPUT "Z:";P(I,2):
    GOTO 180
230 C = FG%(CF,2): INPUT "LINE #"
    ;I:I = I + C - 1: IF I < C OR
    I > FG%(CF,3) THEN 180
232 INPUT "FROM #";L%(I,0): INPUT
    "TO #";L%(I,1): FOR I1 = 0 TO
    1:L%(I,I1) = L%(I,I1) + C1 -
    1: NEXT : GOTO 180
239 RETURN
250 INPUT "UNDER WHAT NAME? ";A$

255 PRINT D$;"OPEN";A$
260 PRINT D$;"WRITE";A$
261 PRINT NP: PRINT NL: PRINT NF
    : IF NF < 2 THEN 270
262 FOR I = 0 TO NF - 1: PRINT F
    T$(I): FOR I1 = 0 TO 3: PRINT
    FG%(I,I1): NEXT I1,I
270 FOR I = 0 TO NP - 1: FOR I1 =
    0 TO 2: PRINT P(I,I1): NEXT
    I1,I
280 FOR I = 0 TO NL - 1: PRINT L
    %(I,0): PRINT L%(I,1): NEXT
286 PRINT D$;"CLOSE";A$
288 RETURN
300 ONERR  GOTO 302
301 INPUT "UNDER WHAT NAME?";A$:
    GOTO 304
302 PRINT A$;" WAS NOT FOUND ON
    DISK.": PRINT "<PRESS ANY KE
    Y>";: GET A$: POKE 216,0: GOTO
    70
304 PRINT "DO YOU WANT TO KEEP "
    ;A$;" AS THE NAME";: INPUT F
    T$(NF)
305 IF  LEFT$ (FT$(NF),1) = "Y" THEN
    FT$(NF) = A$: GOTO 308
306 IF  LEFT$ (FT$(NF),1) < > "
    N" THEN 304
307 INPUT "NEW NAME?";FT$(NF)
308 PRINT : PRINT D$;"OPEN";A$
309 PRINT D$;"READ";A$
310 INPUT T(0): INPUT T(1): INPUT
    T(2)
311 IF T(2) < 2 THEN 321
312 FOR I = NF + 1 TO NF + T(2)
313 INPUT FT$(I)
314 FOR I1 = 0 TO 1: INPUT FG%(I
    ,I1):FG%(I,I1) = FG%(I,I1) +
    NP: NEXT
317 FOR I1 = 2 TO 3: INPUT FG%(I
    ,I1):FG%(I,I1) = FG%(I,I1) +
    NL: NEXT I1,I
321 FOR I = NP TO NP + T(0) - 1:
    FOR I1 = 0 TO 2: INPUT P(I,
    I1): NEXT I1,I
325 FOR I = NL TO NL + T(1) - 1:
    FOR I1 = 0 TO 1: INPUT L%(I
    ,I1):L%(I,I1) = L%(I,I1) + N
    P: NEXT I1,I
331 FG%(NF,0) = NP:FG%(NF,1) = NP
    + T(0) - 1:NP = NP + T(0):F
    G%(NF,2) = NL:FG%(NF,3) = NL
    + T(1) - 1:NL = NL + T(1):C
    F = NF:NF = NF + T(2) + 1: IF
    T(2) = 1 THEN NF = NF - 1
334 PRINT D$;"CLOSE";A$
336 POKE 216,0: RETURN
350 NL = 0:NF = 0:NF = 0:VS = 0:C
    T = 3: RETURN
400 INPUT "UNDER WHAT NAME? ";A$

410 PRINT D$;"BSAVE";A$;",A8192,
    L8192"
420 RETURN
1000 HOME : TEXT :CF = NF:NF = N
    F + 1: INPUT "FIGURE NAME? "
    ;FT$(CF):FG%(CF,0) = NP:FG%(
    CF,2) = NL: PRINT "TYPE 'D'
    OR 'DONE' WHEN NO MORE POINT
    S.": ONERR  GOTO 1010
1010 PRINT "POINT #";NP - FG%(CF
    ,0) + 1: INPUT "X:";A$: IF  LEFT$
    (A$,1) = "D" THEN FG%(CF,1) =
    NP - 1: GOTO 2000
1015 IF  ASC (A$) > 57 THEN 1010
1020 P(NP,0) =  VAL (A$): INPUT "
    Y:";P(NP,1): INPUT "Z:";P(NP
    ,2):NP = NP + 1: GOTO 1010
2000 PRINT "TYPE 'D' OR 'DONE' W
    HEN NO MORE LINES.": ONERR  GOTO
    2010
2010 PRINT "LINE #";NL - FG%(CF,
    2) + 1: INPUT "FROM POINT #"
    ;A$: IF  LEFT$ (A$,1) = "D" THEN
    FG%(CF,3) = NL - 1: POKE 216
    ,0: GOTO 70
2015 IF  ASC (A$) > 57 THEN 2010
2020 L%(NL,0) =  VAL (A$): INPUT
    "TO POINT #";L%(NL,1): FOR I
    = 0 TO 1:L%(NL,I) = L%(NL,I
    ) + FG%(CF,0) - 1: NEXT :NL =
    NL + 1: GOTO 2010
2830  IF NF = 1 THEN CF = 0: RETURN
2845  INPUT "WHICH FIGURE? ";A$:I
    = 0
2855  IF FT$(I) = A$ THEN 2870
2860 I = I + 1: IF I < NF THEN 28
    55
2862  PRINT "YOU DON'T HAVE ONE H
    ERE NAMED ";A$: PRINT "<PRES
    S A KEY>";: GET A$: POP : RETURN
2870 CF = I
2875  RETURN
2900  IF NF < 2 THEN C = 1: GOTO
    2910
2905  INPUT "1-EVERYTHING, OR 2-I
    NDIVIDUAL FIGURE? ";C
2910  IF C = 1 THEN FS = 0:SP = 0
    :EP = NP - 1:SL = 0:EL = NL -
    1: GOTO 3032
2920  IF C <  > 2 THEN 2900
2930  GOSUB 2830:FS = 1:SP = FG%(
    CF,0):EP = FG%(CF,1):SL = FG
    %(CF,2):EL = FG%(CF,3)
3032  FOR I = 0 TO 2:CR(I) = 999:
    T(I) =  - 999: NEXT
3033  FOR I = SP TO EP
3034  FOR I1 = 0 TO 2
3035  IF P(I,I1) < CR(I1) THEN CR
    (I1) = P(I,I1)
3036  IF P(I,I1) > T(I1) THEN T(I
    1) = P(I,I1)
3037  NEXT I1,I
3038  FOR I = 0 TO 2:CR(I) = (CR(
    I) + T(I)) / 2: NEXT
3048  IF VS = 1 THEN 3140
3049 VS = 1:D1 = 0
3050  FOR I = SP TO EP
3060 VZ = 0: FOR I1 = 0 TO 2:VZ =
    VZ + (CR(I1) - P(I,I1)) ^ 2:
    NEXT :VZ =  SQR (VZ)
3110  IF VZ > D1 THEN D1 = VZ
3120  NEXT
3130 VZ =  - 20 * D1
3140 C = 4: RETURN
4000  FOR I = SP TO EP
4101  IF C = 4 THEN 4380
4102  FOR I1 = 0 TO 2:P(I,I1) = P
    (I,I1) - CR(I1):T(I1) = P(I,
    I1): NEXT
4110  ON C GOTO 4130,4200,4280,43
    80,4300
4130 T(1) = C1 * P(I,1) - S1 * P(
    I,2):T(2) = C1 * P(I,2) + S1
    * P(I,1): GOTO 4350
4200 T(0) = C1 * P(I,0) - S1 * P(
    I,2):T(2) = C1 * P(I,2) + S1
    * P(I,0): GOTO 4350
4280 T(0) = C1 * P(I,0) - S1 * P(
    I,1):T(1) = C1 * P(I,1) + S1
    * P(I,0): GOTO 4350
4300  IF S1 <  > 0 THEN T(S1 - 1)
    = P(I,S1 - 1) * M: GOTO 435
    0
4305  FOR I1 = 0 TO 2:T(I1) = P(I
    ,I1) * M: NEXT
4350  FOR I1 = 0 TO 2:P(I,I1) = T
    (I1) + CR(I1): NEXT
4380  IF VZ - P(I,2) >  - .001 THEN
    K = 10000 * D1: GOTO 4390
4385 K = VZ / (VZ - P(I,2))
4390 TR(I,0) = K * P(I,0):TR(I,1)
    = K * P(I,1)
4400  NEXT : RETURN
5000  IF SW = 0 THEN  HCOLOR= 0: GOTO
    5010
5005  IF FS = 0 THEN  HGR
5006  HCOLOR= 7
5010  FOR I = SL TO EL
5020 SW = 0
5030  FOR I1 = 0 TO 1
5035  IF L%(I,I1) < 0 OR L%(I,I1)
    > = NP THEN SW = 1: GOTO 5
    060
```

```
5040 X(I1) = TR(L%(I,I1),0) * CT:
     Y(I1) = TR(L%(I,i1),1) * CT
5060  NEXT
5070  FOR I1 = 0 TO 1
5090  IF SW = 1 THEN 5270
5100  IF  ABS (X(I1)) <  = 139 THEN
     5190
5110  IF  ABS (Y(I1)) <  = 95 THEN
     5150
5120  IF Y(0) = Y(1) THEN 5230
5125 YC =  SGN (Y(I1)) * 95:XC =
     (YC - Y(1)) * (X(0) - X(1)) /
     (Y(0) - Y(1)) + X(1): IF  ABS
     (XC) <  = 139 THEN 5250
5150  IF X(0) = X(1) THEN 5230
5155 XC =  SGN (X(I1)) * 139:YC =
     (XC - X(1)) * (Y(0) - Y(1)) /
     (X(0) - X(1)) + Y(1): IF  ABS
     (YC) <  = 95 THEN 5250
5180  GOTO 5230
5190  IF  ABS (Y(I1)) <  = 95 THEN
     5270
5200  IF Y(0) = Y(1) THEN 5230
5205 YC =  SGN (Y(I1)) * 95:XC =
     (YC - Y(1)) * (X(0) - X(1)) /
     (Y(0) - Y(1)) + X(1): IF  ABS
     (XC) <  = 139 THEN 5250
5230 SW = 1: GOTO 5270
5250 X(I1) = XC:Y(I1) = YC
5270  NEXT
5280  IF SW = 0 THEN  HPLOT 140 +
     X(0),96 - Y(0) TO 140 + X(1)
     ,96 - Y(1)
5290  NEXT : RETURN
6000  HOME : VTAB 21: PRINT "1-RO
     TATE, 2-SHIFT, 3-SCALE OBJEC
     T(S),": PRINT "4-DISTORT, 5-
     MOVE EVERYTHING/ONE FIGURE":
      PRINT "6-CHOOSE CENTER, 7-E
     DIT, SAVE, OR QUIT": PRINT "
     8-FULL SCREEN ";
6038  IF FS = 0 THEN  PRINT "9-SC
     ALE VIEW ON SCREEN ";
6040  INPUT C: IF FS = 0 AND C =
     9 THEN 6300
6050  ON C GOTO 6075,6142,6073,60
     71,6065,6200,6070,6250
6060  GOTO 6000
6065  GOSUB 2900: GOTO 6000
6070  POP : RETURN
6071  PRINT : INPUT "1-WIDTH, 2-H
     EIGHT, OR 3-DEPTH?";S1: IF S
     1 < 1 OR S1 > 3 THEN 6071
6073  IF C = 3 THEN S1 = 0
6074  INPUT "MULTIPLY BY? ";M:C =
     5: RETURN
6075  HOME : VTAB 21: PRINT "ROTA
     TE  1-DOWN, 2-UP, 3-LEFT, 4-
     RIGHT,": PRINT "5-CLOCKWISE,
      6-COUNTERCLOCKWISE ";: INPUT
     C: IF C < 1 OR C > 6 THEN 60
     75
6090  INPUT "ANGLE (0 - 180) ? ";
     AN: IF AN < 0 OR AN > 180 THEN
     6090
6110 AN = 3.14 * AN / 180: IF  INT
     (C / 2) * 2 <  > C THEN AN =
      - AN
6130 S1 =  SIN (AN):C1 =  COS (AN
     ):C =  INT ((C + 1) / 2): RETURN
6142  HOME : VTAB 21: PRINT "SHIF
     T  1-LEFT, 2-RIGHT, 3-DOWN,
     4-UP,": PRINT "5-CLOSER, 6-F
     ARTHER ";: INPUT C: IF C < 1
      OR C > 6 THEN 6142
6150  INPUT "HOW MANY UNITS? ";AN
     : IF  INT (C / 2) * 2 <  > C
     THEN AN =  - AN
6170 C =  INT ((C - 1) / 2):CR(C)
     = CR(C) + AN: FOR I = SP TO
     EP:P(I,C) = P(I,C) + AN: NEXT
     :C = 4: RETURN
6200  PRINT "POINT # (1-";EP - SP
      + 1;") ";: INPUT C: IF C <
     1 OR C > EP - SP + 1 THEN 62
     00
6210 C = C + SP - 1: FOR I = 0 TO
     2:CR(I) = P(C,I): NEXT : GOTO
     6000
6250  POKE  - 16302,0: GET A$: POKE
      - 16301,0: GOTO 6000
6300  INPUT "MULTIPLY BY? ";M:CT =
     CT * M:C = 4: RETURN
```

"It needs a new one of those black and green deals."

PAGE FLIPPING

David Lubar

The switches that flip between various text and graphic modes on the Apple allow for some interesting effects. At the high end, smooth animation is possible by drawing on the unseen screen, then flipping it into view. While such feats are beyond the scope of this article, a few simple techniques that show some of the potential of screen flipping will be discussed. The key numbers to keep in mind are those from 49232 to 49239. Poking any of these locations will set a specific switch. Depending on the other switches, various combinations of text and graphics will be produced. See Table 1 for a chart of the switches. Now let's put some of this information to work. Suppose you have a hi-res display, and you want a quick flash of something else. Being trite, assume the phrase 'YOU LOSE' is displayed in large block letters on the lo-res screen. The message could be flashed with the following code

```
100 POKE 49238,0 :REM TURN ON LO-
    RES
110 FOR D=1 TO 100 : NEXT D :REM
    DELAY A BIT
120 POKE 49239,0 : REM BACK TO HI-
    RES
```

Now, how does the image get on the lo-res screen? In most cases it can be drawn by the program. Even if the hi-res display is on, lo-res commands will be carried out. The computer doesn't care what is being displayed. But what if you need several different images to flash at different times, or what if there is no time for the program to create the display? The answer is a short (very short) machine language program (Listing 1) that takes a screen image from elsewhere in RAM and puts it in the lo-res memory. The nice feature of the program is that it leaves any text in the window undisturbed.

The program can be accessed from Basic. The user pokes the address of the image he has saved into locations 0 and 1. For instance, if the image is stored at $6000, the user would POKE 0,0 and POKE 1,96. The way to avoid disturbing the text window is to use some sort of signal or flag byte. In this example $AB is used since it probably won't occur in lo-res data. Whenever the routine encounters $AB, that byte isn't moved. To avoid the drudgery of putting $AB into many locations, the Basic program in Listing 2 sets up the screen image. The entire process is as follows. First, the desired lo-res image is created using graphics commands such as PLOT and VLIN. Next, the image must be moved into location $1000. This is done by entering the monitor with CALL -151 and typing 1000 < 400.7FFM. Next, get

```
:ASM
            1     *ROUTINE TO MOVE A SCREEN
            2     *IMAGE INTO LO-RES MEMORY
            3     *USER MUST PUT POINTERS
            4     *TO IMAGE INTO LOCATIONS
            5     *$00 AND $01
            6     *
            7     *PROGRAM IS RELOCATABLE
            8     *
            9             ORG   $300
            10    SRCLO   EQU   $0
            11    SRCHI   EQU   $01
            12    DESTLO  EQU   $02
            13    DESTHI  EQU   $03
            14    *
0300: A9 04   15    START   LDA   #$04     ;HI BYTE OF SCREEN START
0302: 85 03   16            STA   DESTHI   ;SET UP ZERO PAGE POINTERS
0304: AA      17            TAX            ;CONVENIENT COUNTER
0305: A9 00   18            LDA   #$0
0307: 85 02   19            STA   DESTLO
              20    *DESTLO NOW POINTS TO $400
0309: A8      21            TAY            ;ZERO OUT Y
030A: B1 00   22    LOOP    LDA   (SRCLO),Y ;GET A BYTE FROM THE SOURCE
030C: C9 AB   23            CMP   #$AB     ;SHOULD IT BE TRANSFERRED?
030E: F0 02   24            BEQ   NEXT     ;NO
0310: 91 02   25            STA   (DESTLO),Y ;YES, PUTY IT ON THE SCREEN
0312: C8      26    NEXT    INY            ;POINT TO NEXT BYTE
0313: D0 F5   27            BNE   LOOP     ;TRANSFER A FULL PAGE
0315: E6 01   28            INC   SRCHI    ;INCREASE HI BYTES OF POINTERS
0317: E6 03   29            INC   DESTHI   ;FOR NEXT PAGE
0319: CA      30            DEX            ;FOUR PAGES DONE?
031A: D0 EE   31            BNE   LOOP     ;NO
031C: 60      32            RTS            ;YES


--- END ASSEMBLY ---

TOTAL ERRORS: 0

29 BYTES GENERATED THIS ASSEMBLY
```

Listing 1.

```
1   REM   THIS PROGRAM FLAGS THE FOUR TEXT LINES IN A SCREEN IMAGE
2   REM   THE IMAGE MUST BE AT $1000
10    FOR I = 4688 TO 4688 + 47
20    FOR J = 0 TO 3
30    POKE I + J * 128,171
40    NEXT J,I
```

Listing 2.

back to Basic with 3D0G (for DOS users) or Control-C (for cassette users) and run the program in Listing 2. The image is now ready and can be saved to disk with BSAVE NAME, A$1000,L$3F8 (the last eight bytes are unneeded and will just waste an extra disk sector). For cassette, the .400.7F8W from the monitor. Later, the image can be brought into any free area of memory and put on the screen using the program in Listing 1.

Unlike the Atari, the Apple is not blessed with internal knowledge of the video signal. This means that rapid page flipping can lead to undesirable results. It works like this. The television is slaving away at what seems like high speed to us mortals. It fills the screen with lines, jumps back to the top, then does it again. To the 6502 chip in the Apple, this process takes forever. The 6502 can perform thousands of operations while the TV electron gun

```
0   REM   A SHORT AND VAGUELY INTERESTING PROGRAM BY DAVID LUBAR
1   REM   HIT ANY KEY TO STOP
2   REM   ERIC WOLCOTT HAD A HAND IN THIS
10  HGR : HCOLOR= 3: HPLOT 0,0 TO 279,191: HPLOT 279,0 TO 0,191:
  HGR2 : HPLOT 140,0 TO 140,191
50  FOR I = 768 TO 795: READ A: POKE I,A: NEXT I: CALL 768
100   DATA  173,80,192,173,87,192,173,84,192,169,11,32,168,252,17
3,85,192,169,11,32,168,252,173,0,192,16,235,96
```

Listing 3.

```
:ASM
                    1       *A FAIRLY USELESS EXAMPLE
                    2       *OF THE CONFLICT BETWEEN
                    3       *SCREEN FLIPPING AND
                    4       *RASTER SCANS
                    5       *
                    6       *RELOCATABLE CODE
                    7       *
                    8           ORG   $300
0300: AD 50 C0 9            LDA   $C050   ;TURN ON GRAPHICS MODE
0303: AD 57 C0 10           LDA   $C057   ;TURN ON HI-RES
0306: AD 54 C0 11   LOOP    LDA   $C054   ;TURN ON PAGE ONE
0309: A9 0B     12          LDA   #$0B    ;THIS VALUE SEEMS TO WORK WELL
030B: 20 A8 FC 13           JSR   $FCA8   ;MONITOR DELAY ROUTINE
030E: AD 55 C0 14           LDA   $C055   ;TURN ON PAGE TWO
0311: A9 0B     15          LDA   #$0B    ;USE SAME DELAY
0313: 20 A8 FC 16           JSR   $FCA8
0316: AD 00 C0 17           LDA   $C000   ;CHECK FOR KEYPRESS
0319: 10 EB     18          BPL   LOOP    ;NO PRESS
031B: 60        19          RTS           ;SOMEBODY WANTS OUT
--- END ASSEMBLY ---

TOTAL ERRORS: 0
28 BYTES GENERATED THIS ASSEMBLY
```

Listing 4.

is making one pass on the screen. If the computer flips pages in less time than it takes the TV to refresh the screen, alternate chunks from the two pages will be displayed. Suppose the switch takes place with a delay equal to the time the TV requires to create ten lines. The top ten lines will be from the first page. The next ten will be from the second page, and so on. Slight differences in total timing will cause the whole pattern to drift. This can be seen in the Basic program from Listing 3. The program puts lines on the two hi-res pages, then calls a machine language routine. The routine, which is poked from Basic, is shown with comments in Listing 4. To experiment with this, try changing the values used in the two delays.

This problem can produce results that range from a slight flicker to temporary disappearance of a figure on the screen. Fortunately, applications of page flipping that use Basic usually operate at a slow enough relative speed to avoid this problem.

Page flipping can be a very valuable tool on the Apple, and on other computers with similar capabilities. The potential applications are quite diverse, and there are probably many new applications that can be found for this technique. □

Notes

Chapter II
Music

Chapter II — Music

There are several music synthesizer boards available "ready-to-run" with an Apple computer. Mountain Hardware, Micro Music, and ALF all have well-known systems available. ALF has two; one has three very high quality "voices," and the other — which is less expensive and more consumer oriented — has nine voices (both use the same editor.) There are also a couple of direct-input music systems that use keyboards. Again, the versatility of the Apple is astounding.

For the less dedicated experimenter, Apple's built-in speaker allows some tone generation and sound effects (although the systems that operate through your stereo quickly spoil you). Here are some articles about the various sound options with the Apple and different approaches to computer music.

Special Notes For Chapter II

• *ALF Apple Music Synthesizer,* by Steve North:
The editor described here for the ALF three-voice system is also used in the nine-voice system. A few new features have been built into the nine-voice synthesizer, which does not have the same pure quality. However, most people won't notice a difference in sound tonal quality. The new system is also more consumer-oriented and is less expensive.

• *Computer Music — With the Accent on Music,* by Jack Citron:
This is a good article about the basics of computer music by Jack Citron (Jaxitron?). It's not specifically about the Apple, but it has some good explanations of fundamentals.

• *Sound Apple Hint:*
For those of you who don't feel it necessary to spend a couple of hundred dollars on a synthesizer board, here's a less expensive way to improve the quality of sound from your Apple.

Sound Advice

David Lubar

Computer music in the home has come a long way since the days when hobbyists placed an AM radio by the spacebar and listened to the sound of loops. There are more than a dozen systems available now, with prices ranging from around $100 to well over a $1000. Before looking at some of the new systems, it would be worthwhile to go over some definitons and guidelines. First, most systems are based on the use of a synthesizer. A few systems use digital-to-analog converters (DAC's). A synthesizer contains the hardware needed to generate a waveform. A DAC converts binary information into a variable voltage. Synthesizers have several good points; they allow high fidelity, they allow a large number of voices, and they use less memory since much of the work is done by the hardware. On the other hand, many synthesizers are limited to only one waveform. The next generation of synthesizers will have more versatility. Still, even those restricted to a single waveform can do an excellent job. DAC's also have some advantages; great versatility as far as output is concerned, simpler electronics (which means lower prices), and the potential to be adapted for other uses. Their disadvantages include less fidelity, a tendency to produce clicks (which can be filtered in either hardware or software), more use of memory space since all the work is done in memory, and a limit to the number of voices that can be played at one time. Faster processors will soon be put to use, allowing for more voices.

Whether you choose a synthesizer or a DAC, important factors will be how much you want to spend and how much can you get for your money. The professional musician will have different needs from the user who just wants something with which to experiment. Another consideration is whether the company you select gives continued support and provides a source of new material. With this in mind, on to the reviews.

Mountain Hardware

The long-awaited system from Mountain is finally available. The ads mentioned a lot of very exciting specifications, including sixteen voices and programmable waveforms. For the most part, the system fulfills these promises. But at $545, the system may be a bit high-priced for some

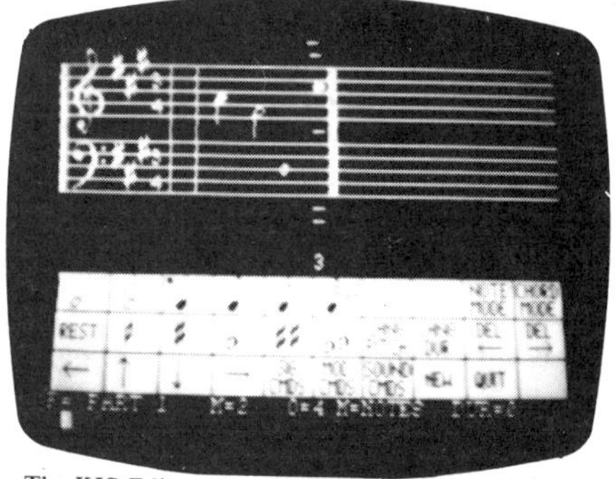

The KIS Editor displays each note as it is entered. displays each note as it is entered.

hobbyists. The hardware consists of two boards which must be plugged into consecutive slots on the Apple. Any slots other than 0 can be used. Apparently, the software checks the slots; the user doesn't have to input the slot numbers. Attached to the board are two phono jacks (plugs and cords are included) and a light pen. The light pen is used for menu selection and note entry, and works best when held slightly away from the screen instead of being pressed against the glass.

Since anyone who buys the system will want to hear it right away, Mountain included several songs on the disk with the system. This, by the way, is a double-sided disk; the song files are on the back.

To play a song, the user selects the play option with either the light pen or keyboard. The system will ask for the song name. The disk has to be flipped. Then the comp file is loaded and options are presented for changing the instrument assignments, the stereo pattern, and other parameters. Once any desired changes have been made, the disk is flipped again and the system compiles the music. This takes a minute or so, after which the music plays. The sound quality is impressive.

Music is entered with paddles or light pen by selecting options from a graphic menu. The first step is selection of a key signature. Once this is done, notes can be entered. All sharps, flats, dotted notes, and other parts of the score are all entered from the menu with light pen or paddles. Parts can be merged, up to the allowable sixteen voices. There is a provision for entering chords in any part, but the total number of notes played at any time must still be sixteen or fewer. Once a song is finished, it can be compiled and played. If it is saved in a comp file, it can be changed and then compiled. In a play file, it can be played immediately, or changes can be made.

Since the system uses digital oscillators, the waveform can be controlled through software. A table of 256 bytes defines each waveform, and the user can construct and save new waves. This method allows for a great deal of versatility in sound production.

The manual contains all the information needed to get going. The system is nice and is backed by Mountain's good reputation in the hardware field.

American Micro Products

A synthesizer board and two software packages for 48K Apples are available from this company. The board ($99.95) contains three voices and one white-noise channel. One software package, *Flash and Crash Sound Effects*, has a sound effects

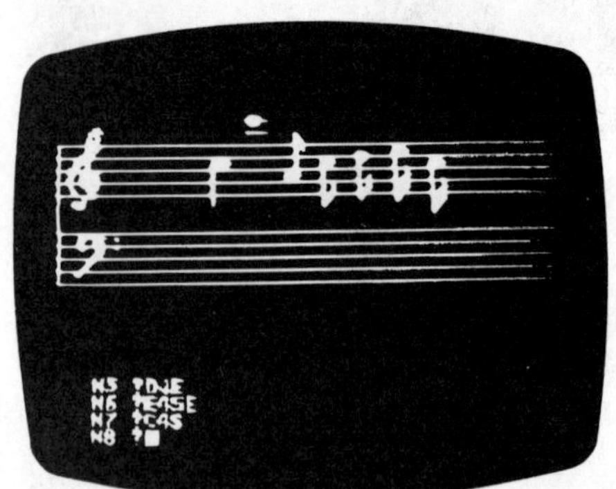

Items from the menu of the Mountain Hardware system can be selected with paddles or a light pen.

demo and documentation that shows the user how to add sound effects to his own software. Once the synthesizer is switched on, sound production is continuous. This means that it won't slow down a program. The *KIS Music Editor* ($39.95 by itself, $129.95 for *KIS* and a synthesizer) uses symbolic note entry. For example, a quarter note that was a C in the third octave would be entered as C4Q. As each note is entered, it is displayed on a high-resolution staff and played through the board. Envelope control is available through sixteen defined envelopes that can be entered along with the note code. The sound quality isn't bad, and some interesting variations are possible. A jukebox program is also on the disk, allowing for the selection and play of up to ten songs. Editing of scores is fairly simple; any note can be accessed and changed.

The boards contain drivers so they can be connected directly to eight-ohm speakers without any need for an amplifier. The boards can be combined, with each board adding three more voices. American Micro Products seems to be constantly working on new products, and they are very open to questions from users.

AlphaSyntauri Ltd.

Most music systems are not oriented toward real-time creation; in other words, you put the music in at your leisure and it comes back later. The AlphaSyntauri system allows real-time creation of music. The system consists of a keyboard and software for Apple II and Apple II plus. The user must supply his own sythesizer boards. Presently the software is configured for use with ALF boards.

One of the main features of the keyboard is velocity sensing. The speed with which any of the 61 keys is pressed controls the amplitude of the note. Since the interpretation of the keystroke is done through software, the potential exists for customizing the keyboard, using it to enter other types of input. There are also two footpedals attached to the unit. The sound of any system will only be as good as the synthesizers. In this case, with ALF boards, the sound is very good. Besides live play,

notes can be recorded on disk and replayed with different tempos. Notes can be appended to an existing score, though no editing function is available with the current software.

The software contains presets. These are defined envelopes which control six parts of the sound, including attack rate, attack volume, decay, and sustain. Eight presets come with the disk, and more can be created and saved by the user. The display consists of low-resolution graphics with bars that rise and fall according to the volume of the notes. There is a second display which gives the names of the notes being played. The system can handle six notes at a time. When more than six are struck, the bass is kept and the next-to-last high note is dropped. This works well since most music requires more sustain from the bass.

The system is nicely designed and comes with good documentation, including a thorough explanation of amplitude envelopes. The price puts it out of range of the casual user, but not beyond reach of those seriously interested in music. The AlphaSyntauri, without ALF boards, costs $1295. It should be interesting to see what happens to this price when other manufacturers enter the market.

Updates and Other Notes

Micro Music, Inc. has released *The Melodious Dictator* ($120), a program designed for ear training. At the start, the user enters his competence, from 1 to 6. A dry run shows how to use the system. A series of notes are played. The user, given the first note, must notate the rest of each sample. This is done with a paddle which moves a cursor above a section of a graphic keyboard. Unfortunately, the cursor doesn't respond very well. It blinks at a slow rate and only moves between blinks. A turn of the paddle produces no immediate results. Then, suddenly, the cursor jumps over. It might jump again before settling on a spot. This is a small problem, but might frustrate those who are more interested in music than computer graphics.

The rest of the program is well designed. A scoring system gives points for correct notes and adjusts the skill level according to performance. The key of the scale changes with each test.

So, aside from the problem with the cursor, the program is well designed. But does it work? In my case, it did. At first, I was unable to pick the right notes without many mistakes. In essence, it was a game of "Guess the Number," where the correct answer was found by narrowing down the possiblities. After a while, I began to do better, even recognzing minor thirds and

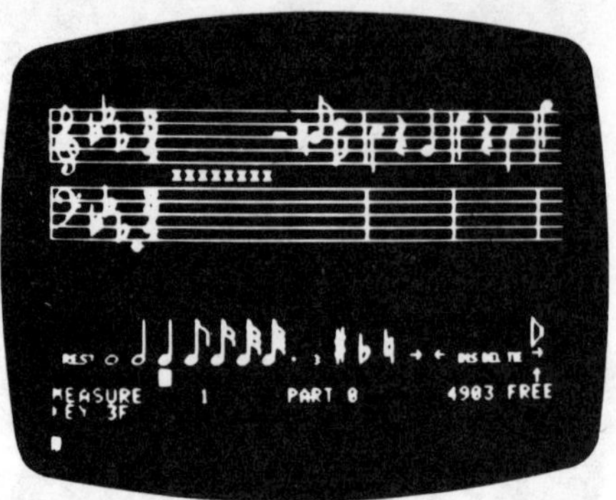

The ALF software displays the score as the song player.

other difficult (for me) intervals. The system definitely can help improve musical perception. If you want to improve your ear, and don't have a friendly pianist handy, *The Melodious Dictator* could provide a helping hand.

Now for the big news. ALF has come out with a new board that puts music within reach of a many more Apple owners. The board has nine voices and sells for $199.95 with software. The original ALF system was reviewed in June 1979 and described in greater depth in June 1980. These new boards contain more voices at a lower price. Some sacrifices had to be made to bring the user this board. Sound quality in the two upper octaves is not as precise as in the other ALF boards and there are fewer volume increments. But anyone who wants to create computer music for a reasonable price could get a lot out of this system. □

"Either get rid of the plants or stop playing the music synthesizer!"

ALF/Apple Music Synthesizer

Steve North

If you have an Apple computer, then you've probably played with programs or subroutines that make primitive music-like sounds through the Apple's built-in speaker. The ALF Apple Computer Music Synthesizer enables you to perform and experiment with high-quality computer music and is also the first significant personal computer music product to surface in at least a year.

The synthesizer card plugs into one of the Apple peripheral slots and connects to any reasonably good

ALF Music Synthesizer

audio amplifier. The board has three channels or voices, each capable of playing a single note, with direct hardware control of pitch and volume. One channel is restricted to playing square waves, while the other two may be programmed for either "normal mode" (square waves) or "pulse mode" in which the Apple controls the pulse width of the pitch generator. More complex effects can be created with the appropriate software, and more synthesizer cards can be added for more than three voices or for stereo. Our test unit had two synthesizer cards.

Given this hardware, to play music you need software to help you enter music, correct your mistakes, play the song, and then save or reload the composition for future use. ALF provides a program called ENTRY with the synthesizer card for this purpose. ENTRY is unlike any other music package we've seen for personal computers as it is graphics oriented. In the past, most computer music systems were designed for any kind of terminal or graphics device, thus, interaction was restricted to alphanumeric input/output. To enter sheet music, you had to convert the notes to a series of letters and numbers representing note value, duration, etc. This is merely a nuisance when entering the music, but a hassle when trying to debug the composition since you have to mentally convert from the alphanumeric notation back into sheet music.

By being completely graphics oriented, ENTRY avoids many of the pitfalls of other music systems. In the high-resolution graphics mode, a staff and a list of menu items are drawn on the screen. The two game

paddles are used to enter music information, while commands to the music system are typed on the keyboard.

One of the game paddles moves a "note cursor" up and down the staff. By turning the game paddle to the appropriate position, you can select a note from a range of about five octaves. Pressing the button on the paddle inputs the note and the cursor moves to the next position. The other paddle allows you to select items on the menu which appears below the staff. The items, from left to right are:

REST	Creates a rest at the current position of the note cursor of the current note duration.
	Sets the current note duration. The video-inverse block indicates the current value.
·	Dotted note.
3	Triplet.
♯ ♭ ♮	Accidental.
→	Moves note cursor right (for editing)
←	Moves note cursor left (also for editing).
INS	Selects insert mode of editing.
DEL	Deletes note under the note cursor.
TIE	Enters a tied note.
▷	Controls playing of notes during editing.

To select a menu item, the user moves the cursor (an arrow) to the appropriate item and then presses the game button. Thus entry of music is done by turning the game paddles and pressing the buttons. According to ALF, the game paddle inputs are faster than typing in alphanumeric code, once you've had practice. We also thought they were easier to understand and more fun.

The non-menu commands (entered from the keyboard) include:

NEW	Clears the workspace for a new composition.
EDIT	Changes parameters such as number of parts, speed, etc.
STEREO	Selects stereo positioning for 2 or 3 boards.
SPEED	Changes time duration of all notes.
SAVE	Saves song on cassette tape.
LOAD	Loads a song from cassette tape.
PLAY	Causes the song to be played.
DELETE	Deletes a number of items from the current cursor position forward.
LENGTH	Allows entry of notes and rests of non-standard length.
SUBROUTINE	Creates or edits a music subroutine.
PART	Moves cursor to the first item in a specified part.
MEASURE	Moves cursor to the specified measure in the current part.
QUARTER	Sets time duration of a quarter note.
KEY	Sets key signature.
TIME	Sets time signature.
TEMPO	Sets dynamic tempo during playback for systems with hardware tempo control.
POKE	Inserts non-standard item.
TRANSPOSE	Sets a transpose value for playback.

Envelope values for attack, decay, gap, release, sustain, and volume can also be input from the keyboard at the beginning of a composition and anytime later when you want to change the envelope parameters. The music system can play up to eight voices, but the voices are input one at a time, and unfortunately cannot be seen together on the same screen. However, displaying all the notes at once might actually be more difficult for the user. For instance, if two voices played the same note, it would be difficult to tell one from the other since the notes would overlap on the display.

Although it may not be apparent from this short description, ENTRY, written by John Ridges, is a very well thought out, human engineered package. For instance, the current measure number and free workspace are constantly displayed on the screen. If you enter a note duration which is too long for the current measure, the program automatically creates a tied note. When the user inputs the key signature (as in KEY: 2S for two sharps) the computer displays the key signature on the staff. As you enter notes on the

Photo of screen in entry mode

screen, or perform editing functions, they are also played through the synthesizer. Or, if you have two C-sharps in the same measure, standard music notation requires putting the # sign only before the first. If you delete the first one, the # sign automatically moves over to the second. Obviously, someone put a lot of thought and effort into this program, and it shows.

During playback, the high-resolution display of the screen is erased and a simple animated low-resolution color display of all the voices shows what's being played. The playback speed can be dynamically changed with one of the game paddles.

Besides ENTRY, ALF also supplies a shorter playback-only program (which uses less memory), a music-playing subroutine which can be incorporated into your own programs, and some sample music. The version we tried was cassette-based, but a disk version of the software is also available.

Despite the fact that Apple is probably the second best-selling personal computer, there's a noticable scarcity of plug-in options made by second sources. The ALF Music Synthesizer is the only significant one that comes to mind, other than a small assortment of serial interfaces and kluge cards. According to Philip Tubb, one of the project engineers and software designers of the synthesizer, "Don't be surprised that more people aren't making Apple peripherals. It's much, much harder than we expected. Apple's hardware and software is very poorly designed in terms of usability and expansion. Their boards are too small to fit anything on, and if you can fit it on anyway, there isn't enough power or heat dissipation. We were having quite a few problems until we switched our design over to a "mystery chip" which we're not saying anything more about at this point."

In the past year or so, computer music has more or less reached a plateau, although Philip said that "we really hope to stir things up with this Apple product, and have a few more surprises coming up (with any luck)." Probably the problem is that the companies into computer music a while ago directed their efforts at S-100 bus systems. Once sales of those systems declined, their markets dried up and so they were reluctant to develop new products. (Solid State Music has even decided to drop its old name.) Newer computers like the TRS-80, Apple, and PET are not designed for much expansion, and owners of these less expensive machines are unwilling to pay many hundreds of dollars for computer music systems. Of course, home-brewers continue to pioneer the field, but these people account for only a fractional percentage of the whole user community and thus, until their designs become actual products, have no relation to the average software-oriented computer user. It's encouraging that ALF has taken a step forward.

The ALF Apple Music Synthesizer retails for $265.00 and is available from Apple dealers or from ALF Products, Inc., 128 S. Taft, Denver, CO 80228, (303) 234-0871. The price includes the circuit card, cable, cassette, and shipping. □

Apple Music Synthesizer

Philip Tubb

Once upon a time only a few people in the world had printed books or other printed material. Eventually, printing technology advanced to the point where many people could afford to have books. Naturally, this had a great impact. Another step forward came in the form of the photocopying machine. With this technology, many people could not only possess written material, they could create their own materials to give to their friends and associates. Now, of course, printed material is quite common. We've even reached the point where the thousands

Recording technology made it possible for many people to have music, like printing technology had done earlier for text.

of local computer clubs each feel obligated to produce printed newsletters, whether or not they have anything to write.

There was a time when only a few people in the world could afford to have music. Orchestras (and even individual instruments) were expensive, and there was as yet no way to record their sounds. Recording technology made it possible for many people to have music, as printing technology had done earlier for text. Today, we still struggle to bring music to the stage that photocopiers have taken text. "One-button chords" and "rhythm masters" abound in organs which "anyone can play without lessons." Many feel that what computers have done for word-processing, they can do for music-processing, thus

Phil Tubb, 1448 Estes, Denver, CO 80215.

solving the problem of music production by the average person.

When my colleagues at ALF Products and I began work on a new computer-controlled music synthesizer (for the Apple II), we hoped to make new advancements in the area of personal music. First, the hardware had to be fairly versatile, and yet simple enough to be sufficiently low cost. Second, the software had to be easy enough for the average computer user to use. Personal-computerists are pretty good around a computer, but many are lost in the esoteric field of music. Since we made remarkable progress in the software area, I will begin with it.

FIGURE 1

The Software

In Figure 1 you will see one of the basic elements of sheet music: a note. This particular note is shown in its natural environment (a treble staff with time and key signatures) and happens to be a G and also an eighth note, plus a few other things which will come up soon. Assuming one will want to take sheet music (which is where you're likely to find notes like this one) and cause it to be performed with a computer-controlled music synthesizer, it is necessary to take lots of these notes and describe them to a music entry program. Once a song has been thus described, music production can begin.

Probably the most obvious way to get these notes into memory is to type them in with a standard ASCII keyboard, because all usable computers

seem to have such devices. Obviously, you just type EIGHTH G. It's simple. However, EIGHTH is a little long, and DOTTED THIRTYSECOND will be even worse. So, people usually abbreviate quite a bit. Let's use EG. It's harder to read, but who cares? The time savings in typing will be worth it. The various notes are Whole, Half, Eighth, Sixteenth, Thirty-second, Sixty-fourth and so on. The first letter is enough as long as we quit before we get to Sixty-fourth. Period looks great for "dotted," so the DOTTED THIRTY-SECOND G becomes T.G or maybe .TG.

Now things begin to get complicated. The note in Figure 1 isn't really a G, it's a G sharp. This is because the key signature has indicated that all C's, F's and G's will be sharp unless otherwise noted. This saves a lot of space when writing songs in which these notes are almost always sharp. There are several key signatures, in which one to six of the A through G notes are sharp or flat. In the more advanced music entry programs, one just inputs the key signature and the program figures out that it is really G sharp instead of G. But in simpler systems, and on those occasions where a note is "natural" (meaning not sharp or flat regardless of what the key signature says), or where a note must be sharp or flat even though the key signature doesn't so indicate, one must indicate this exception in some fashion. These exceptions are called accidentals. Usually this is done by adding S, F or N (Sharp, Flat or Natural). This gives us EGS. On simple music entry systems, one must always type the S, F or N; and in more advanced systems you need only type them when absolutely necessary.

Are we running out of complications? Of course not. There are many different G's in the piano scale. The scale goes A, A sharp, B, C, C sharp, D, D sharp, E, F, F sharp, G, G sharp; and then starts over at A. (Or you can use flats instead of sharps if you like: A, B flat, B, C, D flat, D, E flat, E, F, G flat, G, A flat.) Each section of the scale, from any given note up to but not including that same note again, is called an octave. Octaves are significant in that the pitch (or frequency) of any given note is always twice that of the same note in the next lower octave. Or, if you prefer, the pitch of any given note is always half that of the same note in the next higher octave. This fact comes in handy in the hardware, as you'll see later. Now, musicians like to start the octave at C. The overly-rational crowd (including myself) like to start it at A. Computer-controlled music companies often like to start their octaves at whatever their lowest note is. In any

It is difficult to remember the octave number for each note, and people often type in the wrong one, thus making the song jump up and down an octave or two on a particular note.

case, generally one winds up with "octave numbers," in which each octave is assigned a number. This is because the "traditional" notation is far too cumbersome to use. The A's in this sytem go like this (from lowest to highest pitch): A,, A, A a a' a" a"' a"" and so forth. Further, they are blessed with names like "subcontraoctave" and "four-line octave" and they switch at C, of course. The infamous Middle C (the only note most people know by name) is written c'. Rather than resort to buying an upper and lower case keyboard, and replacing the comma and apostrophe keys every other week, most people use octave numbers. So now we have EGS3, or some such. Naturally it is difficult to remember the octave number for each note, and people often type in the wrong one, thus making the song jump up and down an octave or two on a particular note.

So, you type in your EGS3's and cheerfully input the song. Of course, you'll eventually come upon a tied note, or a triplet note, or some such. There isn't any representation for these yet, but the more advanced systems come up with something. Usually the music is typed in with line

numbers, as one would in Basic or most other languages, so it can be edited later. A listing of one of these songs looks like a test print-out of a defective modem. No mere mortal can read them. This difficulty makes editing quite a task, and the problem is further compounded by the fact that most systems require a "compiling" phase in which the numeric-alphabet soup is taken from the "easy to type" format and turned into an "easy to play" format. Although this is usually necessary because the processor will need all the help it can get in order to play the song at a reasonable speed, the delay involved during the compile makes it hard to go back and forth between typing in corrections and hearing the corrections.

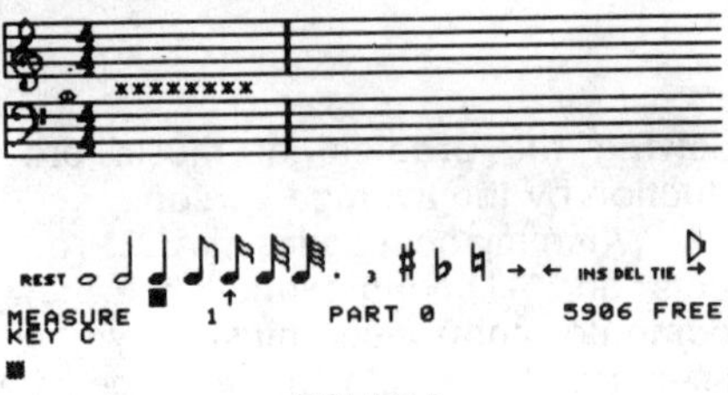

FIGURE 2

At ALF we'd been through this several times. It really is hard to use, and one's most creative impulses often die an early death in sheer frustration. A new system was needed. Fortunately, we picked the computer most likely to succeed. The high-resolution graphics meant we would be able to plot traditional (or near-traditional) music notation on the television screen. Further, the Apple has "game paddles" which are simply rotary knobs, each with a simple pushbutton just like the TV "pong" games. This indicated a possible escape from all that typing. (Really, the Apple was, and still is, the only mass-market home computer with space inside for the synthesizer.)

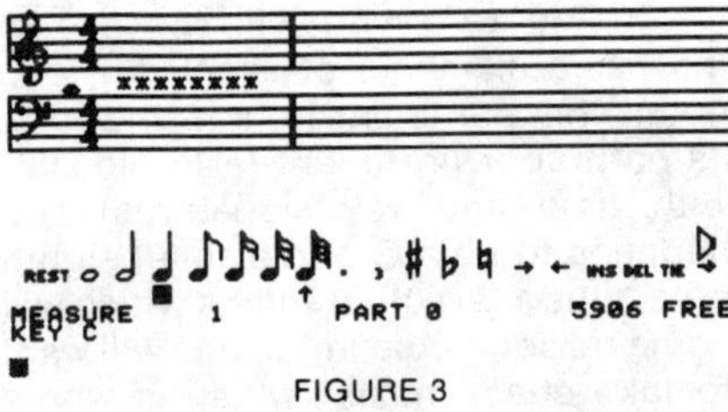

FIGURE 3

It works like this. Figure 2 is the way the screen might look when you first run our Entry program. One of the knobs (Paddle 0) changes the position of the little upward-pointing arrow. If it were turned clockwise a little, the screen would then look like Figure 3. This arrow is used to select the various "menu" items shown right above the arrow. The other knob (Paddle 1) changes the position of something we call the flying saucer cursor. Turning Paddle 1 slightly clockwise makes the

FIGURE 4

screen appear as in Figure 4. These two paddles are used for virtually all note entry. More complicated things, like key signatures, are entered using the ASCII keyboard.

The key signature shown here is the key of C, in which no notes are automatically made either sharp or flat. We want a key with three sharps. Momentarily succumbing to the omnipotent power of abbreviation, one types KEY:3S and presses return. Just

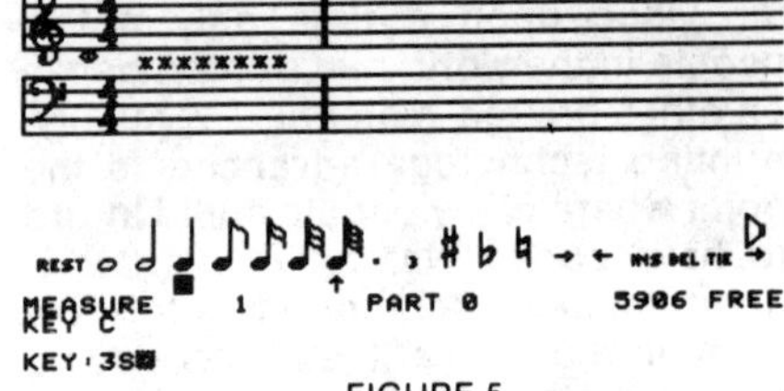

FIGURE 5

to give you the idea, Figure 5 shows the screen just before return is pressed, and Figure 6 just after. The checkerboard filled-in square is meant to

FIGURE 6

represent the text cursor on the Apple which is really filled in solid, but which flashes on and off. (For those of you dying of curiosity, these "screen photos" were printed using periods on a Hytype 1640, and reduced.) You'll notice that the cursor has moved so it is now where the 4/4 is. This cursor is always at the point where a note or special item will appear if entered. If we use Paddle 0 to aim the upward arrow under the leftward arrow, then pressing Paddle 0's button will move the cursor left one item. Figure 7 shows the screen after one such back-up.

FIGURE 7

Note that the place on the screen which originally showed KEY:C now shows KEY:3S. This spot always describes the item which the cursor is on. If we typed KEY:C and pressed return now, all would be as it was originally since the item at the cursor (KEY:3S) would be overwritten with a KEY:C. To move the cursor to the right, one positions the upward arrow under the right arrow, and presses the button. The cursor moves right once for each button press. The asterisks (*) shown where a Middle C note would go (that is, between the two staffs) each indicate some bizzare item which is not easily represented in traditional notation. In this case, they are all specifications of envelope and volume settings. After moving right past all these, the first note of the song can be entered.

FIGURE 8

By rotating Paddle 1 until the cursor is at the desired position, one selects the pitch of the note to be entered. Pressing Paddle 1's button then causes the note to be entered (see Figure 8). As the cursor moves up and down, a "click" is heard through the Apple's built-in speaker; one click at each possible note position. This allows one to position the cursor without having to look at the screen in some cases. While the Paddle 1 button is held down (and while the new note is plotted on the screen, which occurs in the blink of an eye), the synthesizer plays the appropriate pitch. This allows instant feedback so you're sure you entered the right note. If we're entering the note shown way back in Figure 1, then it will have the right pitch, but the note entered was a quarter note instead of an eighth note. This is so I can show how errors are corrected. When Paddle 1's button was pressed, the note entered was determined in pitch by the location of the flying saucer cursor, and in duration by which note has a

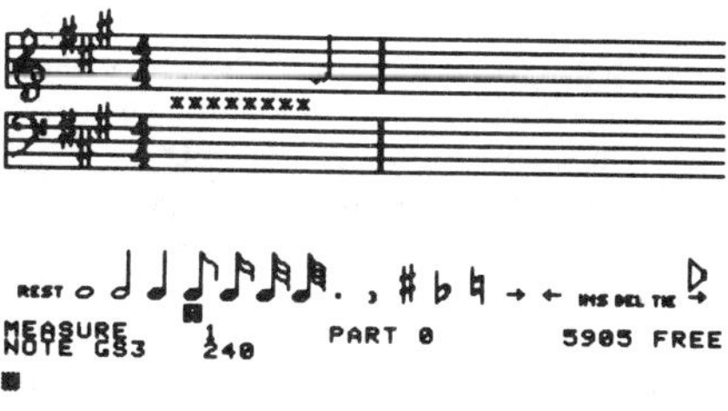

FIGURE 9

Phil Tubb hooking up his Apple/ALF synthesizer.

block under it in the menu. If we aim the arrow under left movement, press the button to back up once, and then position the arrow under the eighth note, we can then press the button to select an eighth note. The block under the quarter note disappears, and one appears under the selected note duration (see Figure 9). Now all notes entered will be eighth notes, until we change the duration again. Pressing Paddle 1's button now causes the correct note to be entered since the duration is right and Paddle 1's knob is still positioning the cursor at the same pitch. The old quarter note is wiped out (see Figure 10).

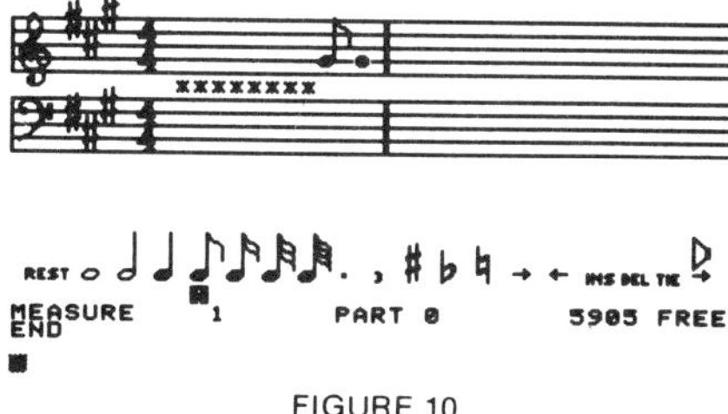

FIGURE 10

Music entry is simplified by an automatic measure bar feature. For example, if we enter a few more notes, a measure bar will appear when the measure is full (see Figure 11). The measure bar appears automatically, and serves as a quick check that you're doing all right. If we like, we can

FIGURE 11

change the time signature at any point. For example, if we type TIME:2/4 and press return, a new time signature is plotted. If we then enter a quarter note followed by a half note, the half note must be converted into two quarter notes tied together. This is done automatically by the Entry program (see Figure 12).

FIGURE 12

These measure bars are more important than you might think. Sure, they let you know you're still together with the sheet music. But in sheet music they also have to do with the accidentals. After typing TIME:2/2 for a more reasonable measure length, we can enter a few notes to explain the situation (see Figure 13). The first note is a regulation A. The next is an A

FIGURE 13

sharp. (Sharp notes are entered by using Paddle 0 to light up the block under the sharp sign in the menu before entering the note with Paddle 1's button. The block under the sharp is cleared when the note is entered, since the next note will probably not be sharp, too.) The next two notes are also A sharps, because a sharp sign continues to make other notes (of the same letter) in the measure sharp (and a flat sign makes notes flat in a similar fashion). The next note is in a new measure, so it is not sharp. Now, the next note has been entered as sharp. If we want the next note to not be sharp, we just light up the natural sign before entry. The last note is, of course, not sharp since the effect of the sharp sign is neutralized by the natural sign. This natural sign is also used to counteract the key signature.

Some of you may be wondering what happens if you move the cursor down a little more, so it would be below the staff. Figure 14 is for you.

This entry scheme is fast. You rarely do any typing. Further, you just put one hand on Paddle 0 and the other on Paddle 1, set the sheet music on the Apple, and breeze right along. But

FIGURE 14

more importantly, it looks just about like regular sheet music. Most importantly, it is really easy to edit. If you make a mistake, you must adjust a paddle knob and back up, then reenter the note. The little speaker with a right arrow under it also helps in editing.

When you use Paddle 0 to light up a block under it, the notes already entered will be played back as you move right using the right pointing arrow. When a block is not present, no playback occurs during right movement. If you want to play the song back at normal speed and with envelope and volume control, you just type PLAY. No, the sheet music notation doesn't zip across the screen while it plays. Speed problems with the Apple (or just about any processor) would degrade the quality of the playback, and a display with several notes playing

The Apple is the only mass-market home computer with space inside for the synthesizer.

simultaneously would be nearly impossible to read with Apple's graphics capabilities. We use a low-resolution display which is easy to plot and fairly easy to read. A dot for each voice moves left for lower notes and right for higher notes, and its color indicates the volume.

Obviously this entry scheme only allows one note to play at any given moment. How, then, are multiple notes played at once? Has ALF not heard of chords? The answer is really quite simple. Since each voice could well be a separate (but, it is hoped, coordinated) melody line, and since the synthesizer is capable of completely independent operation with each voice, we allow each voice to be entered separately. Not only does this make entry simple and concise, it is easy to learn and effective to use. By typing PART:1, we are magically presented with a screen that looks a lot like the screen of Figure 2, except PART 0 on the screen has changed to PART 1 and there are fewer notes of memory available. (In reality it is necessary to use the EDIT command

to create a part 1 unless a part 1 has previously been created.) The second voice (where a "voice" is a melody line or chord fragment in which at most one pitch is played at any given moment) is entered into Part 1. The third voice is entered as Part 2, and so forth. Parts 0 through 8 are available, although the ALF Apple Music Synthesizer has only three voices per card, so two or three such cards are required for six or nine voices/parts. These parts are completely independent, so you can do anything you want in them. They are virtually separate songs, although they are all played back simultaneously when you use the PLAY command.

There are a couple of ways in which the parts are not completely separate. One is an incredibly useful feature called subroutines. Those of you who program in any non-alien computer language are already familiar with subroutines and probably know what's coming up. The subroutines can be called from any part, so they are more or less part-independent. An example is in order. Let's say we want to play Row, Row, Row your Boat. If we are to do this merrily, merrily, merrily we will need subroutines, subroutines, subroutines. (Actually only one subroutine is needed but I got carried away.) Here's how it is done. First, we type SUBROUTINE:0. Really we type SUB:0 since all commands can be abbreviated as much as you like, as long as there is no confusion as to which command is desired. This is like the PART command in that it gives us a new area in which to program music. Unlike the PART command, the screen starts off "empty" (just the staffs, menu, etc.) without a key and time signature and envelope parameters. We enter the notes for row, row, row. Now we go to Part 0 using the PART:0 command, skip past the standard envelope settings, and type CALL:0. When the playback software sees this

CALL, it will trundle off to the specified subroutine (number 0, as requested, although 0 through 99 can be used) and play whatever is there. When the end of the subroutine is found, it will zip back to whatever was after the CALL. Since we need to play this section several times, we put in several more CALL:0's in Part 0. Now, in Part 1 we put a rest as long as we need for the round effect. Then several CALL:0's are needed. During playback, Part 0 will start in right away, while Part 1 rests. At the proper moment (or at the programmed moment) Part 1 will come in with the same melody. Additional parts can be added to taste. Further, we can change the envelope parameters on the various parts so they will produce different sounds. We can even change the transpose settings, which will allow one part to be played higher or lower in pitch than another, even

Music entry is simplified by an automatic measure bar feature.

though the same notes were entered (using the subroutine) for both. The contents of subroutines are not limited to notes. They can include volume and envelope changes, or other changes, as well. This allows various sound settings to be entered into subroutines which can be called whenever that sound is desired. Subroutines can even call other subroutines. We've entered the Twelve Days of Christmas using subroutines instead of entering each section several times, and you can imagine how complicated that is!

Once a song has been entered, it can, of course, be stored on cassette or on a floppy disk. It can then be read in again at any time and played back, or one could add more or perhaps change what is already there. An interesting aspect of the storage feature is that it is about the only way to record audio which does not degrade with repeated playbacks. When a tape or disk seems to be about ready to wear out (that is, becomes difficult to load) a new tape or disk, which is exactly like the original, can easily be made. Other than the now emerging digital tape recorders, all other recording methods have noise or distortion which increases with each playback (although perhaps only a little at a time), and each new copy is of less quality than the original. With a computer-controlled synthesizer, each performance can sound exactly like the original. Or, it can be different. Another interesting aspect of music data is that it can be subjected to algorithms. Programs can be written to modify the song in various ways. One popular algorithm is to flip the scale over so that all low notes are high and

68

vice-versa. If done properly, this changes minor keys to major, and major keys to minor. The results are often interesting, or at least amusing. Another possibility is changing formats. If you have an audio tape recorded with DBX or Dolby, you'd better have similar equipment for playback. However, if you have a disk of songs written for Micro Music's synthesizer, you can still play them on

Say we want to play Row, Row, Row your Boat. If we are to do this merrily, merrily, merrily we will need subroutines, subroutines, subroutines.

our synthesizer. A simple conversion program is used to change MMI's format to the ALF format, which can then be played or edited in the normal fashion. (Note that you must buy a copy of the disk, and you are then free to use it as you like. "Borrowing" a disk from a friend who has an MMI unit is in violation of copyright laws if the disk is copyrighted.) Likewise, MMI users can play ALF songs if they have an appropriate conversion program (but again, you must buy a song disk or tape). The playback will sound different on the two synthesizers, of course, because they have different capabilities. I suspect that most computer music companies will be offering conversion programs so you can use music disks available from other companies.

The various menu items on the screen are used as follows:

REST is used for entering rests. Rest duration is selected in the same fashion as when entering notes.

The seven notes shown are for selecting note duration.
- • is used for entering dotted notes.
- 3 is used for entering triplet notes.
- # is used for entering sharp notes.
- ♭ is used for entering flat notes.
- ♮ is used for entering natural notes.
- → is used to move the cursor right.
- ← is used to move the cursor left.
- INS is used to control "insert" mode. When insert mode is on, all entered items are inserted in front of the cursor, rather than over the current item.
- DEL is used to delete an item.
- TIE is used to add (tie) another note or rest duration to an existing note or rest.
- ♪ is used to turn on or off playback during right movement and DEL.

The following commands are available:
NEW is used to start fresh.
EDIT is used to change the number of parts, the suggested playback speed, or for the four text lines which are shown during playback.
STEREO is used to specify the left/right/middle playback assignments for each part (when using two or three synthesizers).
PART selects which part will be shown and available for editing.
SUBROUTINE is the same as PART, but a subroutine is selected. If not present, it is created.
GOTO is the same as PART except it puts you at the same measure you're currently at (but in the specified part).
MEASURE is used to move the cursor to any desired measure (within the current part or subroutine).
DELETE is used to delete several items from the song.

INTEGER is used to go back to Basic.
LENGTH is used to specify a note or rest length in "time periods" for unusual note durations.
LOAD is used to read a song from disk or cassette.
SAVE is used to save a song to disk or cassette.
PLAY is used to play the song.

The following commands are stored in the song data:
VOLUME selects a new volume level.
ATTACK used for envelope control.
DECAY used for envelope control.
SUSTAIN used for envelope control.
RELEASE used for envelope control.
GAP used for envelope control.
KEY specifies a new key signature.
TIME specifies a new time signature.
CALL calls a specified subroutine.

QUARTER specifies a new "time period" duration for all following quarter notes (during entry) and thus indicates the length of all menu notes.
TRANSPOSE specifies a new transpose value to be added to all following pitch values. During playback, pitches can be raised by 1 to 127 quarter steps and lowered by 1 to 128 quarter steps.
TEMPO specifies a new tempo (playback speed) when using the optional timing mode input board.
POKE is used to enter any code. This must be used with great caution, and is not recommended for general use (of course).

In addition to song data entry and editing, the software also takes on some tasks which would normally be in the hardware, but have been placed in software since it works out well. The most important of these functions is the creation of envelopes.

The term "envelope" refers to the volume contour of an individual note: the way in which it becomes loud and then dies away. For example, a plucked string becomes loud quickly, then dies away. In contrast, a piano note becomes loud quickly, stays loud (but slowly fading out) while the key is held down, then rapidly dies out when the key is released. By creatively selecting the rates and levels used, a variety of different sounds can be created.

Our software creates Attack-Decay-Sustain-Release (ADSR) envelopes, as do nearly all professional music synthesizers. This envelope has four "stages." The first is the attack stage, during which the "loudness" (or volume, but I use volume to describe the overall sound level rather than the level during individual notes) goes from its current level (which is usually zero, but can be about anything) to the currently selected "volume level" (as set by the most recent VOLUME item in the song data). The most recent ATTACK setting in the song determines the rate. In fact, the ATTACK setting is the number to be added to the volume each "time period" (yes, the same time periods used for specifying note durations). When the loudness gets to the volume level, the next stage begins. This is the decay stage, in which the loudness goes down (at a rate selected by the most recent DECAY setting) to the currently selected SUSTAIN level. The sustain level is usually some (fairly high) percentage of the current volume for piano-like sounds which hold at a high loudness level (the sustain level) after an initial "thump" (created by the attack and decay stages). In plucked-string sounds, the sustain level is selected as zero so the loudness will die out with just the "thump." Assuming that a non-zero sustain level is used, then the sustain stage occurs when the loudness simply sits around and stays at the selected sustain level. A certain amount of time before the next note begins (the time being

The term "envelope" refers to the volume contour of an individual note: the way in which it becomes loud and then dies away.

selected by the most recent GAP setting), the release stage begins. During the release stage, the loudness drops from the sustain level to a zero level at a rate specified by the most recent RELEASE setting. (It may not actually get down to zero before the next note starts, if your release rate is too slow, but it will try.)

The synthesizer software creates up to nine of these envelopes at once, all of them with independent parameter selections. Very complex sounds can be created by having more than one part play the same notes (using subroutines, of course) but with different envelope and/or transpose settings on each part. Further, parts can be delayed (using a very small rest at the beginning) for particularly devious sounds or for echo/reverb effects.

Although all this time I have been discussing the Entry program, there are five other programs supplied with the synthesizer. The programs are designed for use with Apple's Integer Basic, but versions compatible with Apple's [Microsoft] Applesoft Basic are also available for those who don't have Integer Basic. These other programs are for continuous album-style playback, simple playback (without editing capabilities), special applications (such as sound effects or song playback in your own programs), and there is an introduction program which describes, plots and plays basic synthesizer concepts.

The Hardware

The two most important parameters of a note are its pitch and duration. Using a synthesizer which has control of only pitch and duration for each note, recognizable tunes can be played. One of the easiest ways to create pitches is by division. There are simple circuits which will take an input frequency and divide it by a specified integer. (There are more complex circuits which can take an input frequency and multiply it by an integer.) Thus, the easiest way to produce a variety of frequencies (pitches) is to take a very large frequency and divide it by a variety of integers.

A sixteen-bit divider circuit can divide a frequency by any integer from 1 to 65,536. This is what we use in our synthesizer. We use an input frequency of 1,782,000 Hz (Hz is the abbreviation for Hertz, which means "cycles per second"), which is generated from a quartz crystal. This gives us output frequencies from 1,782,000/1 Hz to 1,782,000/65,536 (27.19) Hz. The piano range goes from 27.5 Hz to 4,186 Hz in 88 steps.

The notes of a piano scale are called equal tempered half steps. "Equal tempered" means the frequencies from a geometric progression, each frequency being the frequency of the previous note times a constant. "Half steps" means there are twelve notes per octave (an "octave" being the range in which the frequency of the notes doubles). (The term half step refers slightly to the fact that from one white key on a piano to the next is a "whole step" provided there is a black key in between. Since the black key's frequency is equally spaced between the white keys', and the white keys are a whole step apart, the black key must

be a half step between the white keys.) If we number the piano keys (both white and black) starting with zero and going up by ones, then to form a geometric progression with values starting at 27.5 (Hz) and doubling at each twelve note, the frequency of any note, N, must be 27.5 times 2 to the power of (N/12) Hz. The various frequencies which the synthesizer can produce with integer divisors, D, between 1 and 65,536 are: 1,782,000/D Hz; or, the divisor, D, for any desired frequency, F, will be D=INT(1,782,000/F + 0.5) MAX 1 MIN 65,536. Combining all these handy formulas, we get a formula for all piano scale divisors, D(N), where N is an integer from 0 to 87: D(N)=INT(1,782,000/(27.5 times 2 to the power of (N/12)) + 0.5) MAX 1 MIN 65,536. These divisors must be computed by the software and then programmed into the hardware. Unless we are all using Cray computers with 12.5 nanosecond clock times, some faster method than computing fractional powers will be needed. Fortunately, there is a relatively obscure but powerful algorithm for this

With a computer-controlled synthesizer, each performance can sound exactly like the original. Or, it can be different.

called a "look-up table." For those of you not familiar with this advanced programming technique, it consists of an area of memory in which is located the answer to every possible question of the nature being solved. For the piano-scale problem, there are only 88 answers, so the amount of memory required is small (176 bytes).

However, we decided to use quarter-steps, which have 24 notes per octave. (Take all those formulas above and change the 12's into 24's, then extend the range of N from 0-87 up to 0-175.) This gives us twice as many notes, but since they are twice as close together we get the same frequency range. Rather than have a range of seven octaves plus four additional notes, like a piano, we decided to add a few more high pitches to obtain eight full octaves (96 half-steps or 192 quarter-steps). Using TRANSPOSE, it is also possible to request notes even higher. Using a simple formula which takes advantage of the octave relationships, the look-up table size can be reduced. This formula is D(N+24)= INT(D(N)/2 + 0.5) when using quarter-steps (for half-steps, replace the 24 with 12). This means that if you have the divisors for the lowest octave (values of N from 0 to 23), you can compute all the others. Best accuracy is obtained using D(N+24 times A)= INT(D(N)/(2 to the power of A) + 0.5) so the rounding is done only once. Fortunately, dividing by 2 to the power of A and then rounding is quite simple in machine language. (All serious music programming is done in machine language [or, more properly, assembly language] since all high level languages present speed problems.)

By feeding the 1,782,000 Hz clock signal into three identical 16-bit programmable divider circuits, it is possible to produce three pitches at once. (The reason for choosing three sets of circuitry is, in this case, because three 16-bit dividers come in one integrated circuit package.) The next most significant aspect of a note is the duration. In our synthesizer system, this is controlled by the software. It programs the dividers for a particular pitch, then waits around for the right amount of time, and then programs the next pitch. This is done with a special "time-sharing" program which will be explained later.

Having conquered pitch and duration, the next parameter needed to improve the synthesizer is volume control. Actually, volume control is a rather insignificant feature. However, if you can control the volume quickly enough, you can make envelopes, which are vastly important and useful. It is important to create "smooth" envelopes which do not suddenly change in loudness. Sudden changes create annoying clicks, which, if you follow computer music synthesizers, you've no doubt heard in new companies' equipment. The hardware for envelope production in our synthesizer is also used for controlling volume, and consists of a special digital-to-analog converter (DAC). A DAC takes an integer, which in this case is output on the Apple bus, and creates a voltage or current as specified by the integer. For example, an input of 1 might produce 1 volt, 2 produces 2 volts, 3 3 volts, and so on. The DAC we use has an input which selects positive or negative values. This input is connected to the square wave pitch output of one of the 16-bit dividers. Thus the output of the DAC changes from positive to negative values at a rate selected by the pitch. This means the output is always centered around zero. Some systems fail to do this, and problems result. For example, a square wave changing between 0 and 5 volts has an average value (or is centered around) 2.5 volts. If a "rest" (no tone output) is implemented by stopping the programmable divider, the output will change to either

0 or 5, and thus the "center" point will change by 2.5 volts. This change produces one of those annoying clicks I mentioned earlier. Rather than stop the divider, we program the volume to zero for a rest. This eliminates the off-center click problem. Another special feature of this DAC circuit is that the outputs of the DAC are exponential. This means that if we send an arithmetic progression of integers to the DAC, it will create a geometric progression of outputs. Both frequency and volume must increase in a geometric progression in order to seem to increase at a constant rate, due to the way human hearing works.

When creating envelopes, the "time-sharing" program comes into play. The first thing this program does is start a timer in the Apple. This timer, which is controlled by one of the paddle knobs, determines the length of a "time period." The program has a "pointer" into the musical score for each part being played. The first such pointer is used to check to see what is next in the score for Part 0. If it is a subroutine call or other special function, it is done, the pointer is advanced, and the next item is done. When a note or rest is finally encountered, the proper pitch and/or volume control programming is done, and the time duration of the note or rest is copied into a special location referred to as the "time remaining." Each part has its own location for time remaining. Then, the next part is processed in the same manner, using pointers, time remaining, and other parameters associated with Part 1 rather than Part 0. If a part is holding a note, its time remaining will be non-zero. In this case, the pointer to the musical score is not needed since it is not yet time to continue with the next

item in the score. Instead, the time remaining is decremented, and the time-sharing program goes on to the next part. Eventually, the time remaining will reach zero, and it is then time for the next note. When the last part has been processed, the program waits for the Apple's timer to indicate that the full time period has been consumed. Then the whole process starts over.

In addition to checking the time remaining and the score pointer, during the processing of each part a computation is done to calculate an envelope for that part. The envelope calculation is rather simple. A "current loudness" is compared to a "desired loudness." If the current loudness is less than the desired loudness, the "attack rate" is added to the current loudness. If it is greater than the desired loudness, the "current decay rate" is subtracted. (Overshoots are detected and eliminated.) Only one addition or subtraction is done in each time period, and the new current loudness is programmed into the volume control DAC. (Each of the three pitch outputs has its own DAC.) When the current loudness reaches the desired loudness, then a new desired loudness is taken from the "current sustain level" and the current loudness tries to reach this new value. By copying the volume level into the current sustain level and the decay rate into the current decay

With a computer-controlled synthesizer, each performance can sound exactly like the original. Or, it can be different.

rate, a new note is started (and the ADS portions of the ADSR envelope will occur automatically). When it is time for the R portion to begin, a zero is copied into the desired loudness and the current sustain level, and the release rate is copied into the current decay rate. Note that the actual volume level is *never* changed directly. It is only changed by the routine which adds the attack rate (or subtracts the current decay rate) to the current loudness. This means that the volume will never change faster than the attack rate (or decay or release rate). As the desired loudness is changed, the current loudness (and thus the actual volume level) attempts to reach the desired level, but only at the programmed rates. Even a rest is created only by setting the desired loudness and current sustain levels to zero (and copying the release rate into the current decay rate).

This concludes the hardware of

our synthesizer, except to say that the three DAC outputs are connected together and zapped into levels acceptable to your stereo system. When using two synthesizers, one can be connected into the Left input and the other into the Right input on your stereo. The software is designed to let you select which synthesizer each part goes to, and thus each part's left or right positioning can be selected (or changed from time to time). When using three synthesizers, special circuitry allows one of the synthesizer's outputs to be heard on both Left and Right, thus becoming Middle (sort of).

At this point, the budget for the hardware has been reached (for a list price of $265), and further sound parameters cannot be controlled without running the price beyond most hobbyists' wildest dreams. However, the next most important feature would be control of waveforms. Like volume control, waveform control is a rather insignificant feature unless you can change the waveforms rapidly. Usually waveforms are created by filters. In an envelope generator, a DAC creates different volume levels by creating an output voltage which is specified by an input integer. In waveform control, filters are used to make certain esoteric changes in the input waveform based on an input integer. By sending the filter the same sort of numbers as one would send a volume control DAC, "wow" type sounds can be created. (However, most filters require that the current note frequency be added into the numbers usually used for envelope control.) A separate program or circuit for generating these numbers is required since you probably don't want the same pattern of numbers for the envelope and waveform control. A discussion of the basic nature of waveforms, how they affect the sound, and how they are created is beyond the scope of this article. It would be long and involved, and perhaps of little value without audible examples.

If you have questions on computer music, you can send them to: Creative Computing Magazine, Questions & Answers, Phil Tubb, P.O. Box 789-M, Morristown, NJ 07960 □

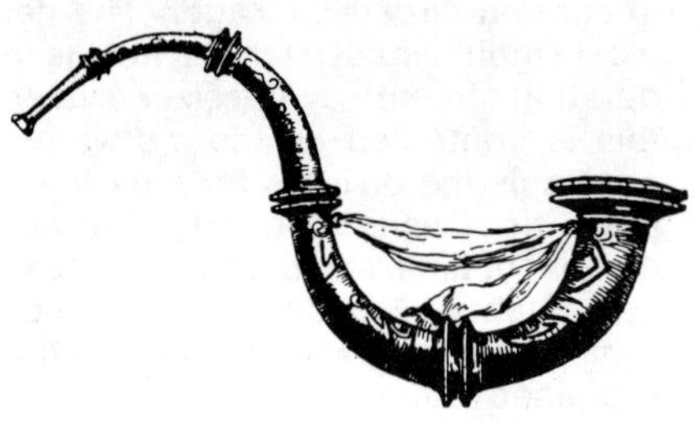

"I hate to be the one to tell you this, but for the past hour and a half you've been trying to program our candy machine."

Micro Composer
from
Micro Music, Inc.

David H. Ahl

Introduction

Micro Composer is a music system for the Apple II. The package contains a hardware music card, software on either cassette or disk, and an instruction manual. Suggested retail price is $220. Further information is available from the manufacturer, Micro Music, Inc., 309 W. Beaufort, Normal, IL 61761. Telephone (309) 452-6991.

Micro composer allows one to compose and play up to four simultaneous voices; program the pitch, rhythm and timbre of the music; specify one of seven pre-programmed tone colors for each voice or make up a new one; save and recover music from either tape or disk; and play music using the built-in amplifier circuit. The music being played or text material may be displayed on the screen during playback.

Using the System

When Micro Composer arrived, it was barely out of the postman's hands before we ripped open the box, plugged it in to our Apple and fired it up. In the front of the manual are two pages, one for installation of Micro Composer and the other describing how to run a demonstration. Hence, one can play music immediately without having to wade through pages of instructions and hours of tedious music entry. The first instruction page carries a large notice, "Before you do anything, please read this!!!!" This would be a good policy for any manufacturer to follow, but is especially welcome with a product such as this.

The manual is 28 pages long; the first 7 pages are devoted to several examples of playing, editing and composing music and are designed for the user to enter on his or her

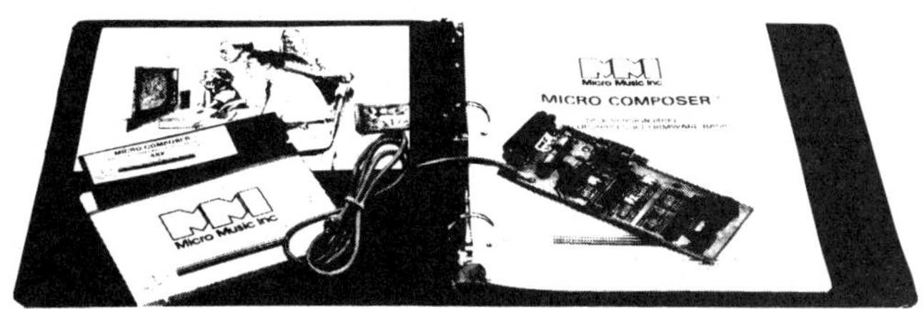
Micro Composer comes with a card for the Apple, software on cassette or disk and loose leaf instruction manual.

system. The next 12 pages describe usage of the system, its functions and commands. The remaining 8 pages contain a technical description of the system. The manual is printed on heavy card stock and is bound in a three-ring binder hence it should last through many hours of flipping pages to find out how this or that is done.

Music is entered using a simple alphanumeric coding scheme. It requires three characters to define most notes--duration, note and octave. Some examples of note coding are:

ER	Eighth Rest
QF3	Quarter note F in 3rd octave
HC4	Half note C in 4th octave
SBF3	Sixteenth note B-flat in 3rd octave
.HG1	Dotted half note G in 1st octave

Music Composer has a range of four octaves. Middle C is the first note in Octave 3. Note durations range from a thirty-second note to a whole note. Any note may be dotted except a sixteenth or thirty-second.

The first music we chose to enter was a simple piano arrangement of "The Stars and Stripes Forever." We were going along famously until the fourth measure which had a whole note tied to a half note in the next measure. Unfortunately, Micro Composer does not allow for tied notes. End of a measure—end of a note. Hence, the user is faced with either putting in a second note (untied) or a rest. In this piece, at least, rests tended to sound better.

The next piece we chose to enter was the "Triumphal March" from Aida. Here we ran into trouble in the second measure. It had a triplet, another feature not provided for in Micro Composer. We don't see any easy way around this problem; we tried an eighth and two sixteenth notes and also three sixteenth notes and a rest but neither was really satisfactory.

As mentioned earlier, Micro Composer allows for up to four polyphonic voices. In a multiple voice composition, all voices must be entered at once. In other words, one enters a chord. We had grown accustomed to entering one entire voice, or part, on the ALF system and then adding additional parts, one at a time. Perhaps it is habit, but we find the ALF approach more "natural" and easier to use. On the other hand, with Micro Composer, one hears an entire chord and can make changes immediately.

However, making changes (editing) is not one of the strong points of the system. Although the manual thoroughly describes the editing process, we found it awkward and time-consuming to use. To edit a note, one must start at the beginning of the piece, display the notes on the screen and "walk" through the piece until the error is found. Edit mode is then entered. After typing in the value of the erroneous "set" (or chord), new pitch codes must then be entered for every note in that set. In a four-voice composition, for example, to change or correct one erroneous note would require a minimum of 17 keystrokes and possibly many more. Another limitation of the editor is the inability to add a note or notes that might have been overlooked earlier in the entry process. Once, having entered a fairly long piece, we found, much to our dismay, that two measures toward the beginning were identical and we had only entered one of them. Micro Composer unfortunately would not let us insert the missing notes. Two hours of music entry down the drain. From then on we become somewhat paranoid about double and triple checking every entry before pressing return.

Another difference between Micro Composer and the ALF system is the treatment of the key signature and accidentals. With the ALF system, if a piece is in the key of E flat (3 flats), one enters 3F and the system automatically assigns a flat to the required notes. Also, an accidental assigned to one note in a measure automatically applies to other of the same note until the end of the measure. In the Micro Composer system, every note that is a sharp or flat must be specified separately. The key signature is not even specified. Also, accidentals do not carry over to other notes in the measure. This approach may be acceptable, and even desirable, when learning to read music. On the other hand, if one is not learning, this method is very time-consuming when entering music, for example, in the key of E major (4 sharps) or B flat minor (5 flats).

Playing Music

Micro Composer has a timbre command through which any one of seven timbres may be assigned to any voice. Timbres include:
1. Low string sound (bass voice only)
2. Wind-flute sound
3. Horn-brass sound
4. Bassoon-oboe sound
5. Clarinet choir sound
6. Electronic organ sound
7. Funky oboe

It's probably personal preference, but we found ourselves coming back to timbres 3, 4 and 5 most often. After setting tempo with a paddle, one may then elect to play or display-and-play. The display mode uses Apple high resolution graphics and displays all the notes being played on the bass and treble staffs. The notes progress from right to left across the screen. Although we have not used it with children learning music, this would appear to be a valuable feature. Unfortunately, music played in the display mode tends to sound somewhat staccato since with the appearance of each new note the computer must interrupt the note generation to refresh the display. In general, this is not a serious flaw although we don't advise playing music which has sixteenth or thirty-second notes in one voice against whole notes in the other voices--in the display mode the entire piece would sound like it consisted of the shorter notes.

The amplifier circuit on the board provides adequate volume for most rooms. However, if you're looking to use the system in an auditorium or noisy environment, you'll want to feed it through an external amplifier. The output signal is monophonic, a curious anachronism in a modern computer music synthesis system. We're not sure whether a second board could be added for stereo, but it doesn't seem so.

In summary

As technology rockets ahead, so do people's expectations. In the case of music synthesis systems, Hal Chamberlin's Micro Composer would have been hailed as a breakthrough just 18 months ago compared with the Solid State Music, Newtech, Software Technology and similar boards. However, Phil Tubb's ALF board for the Apple set some high standards in ease of music entry, stereo output and overall flexibility, if not in documentation (although we understand that a new ALF manual is due out shortly).

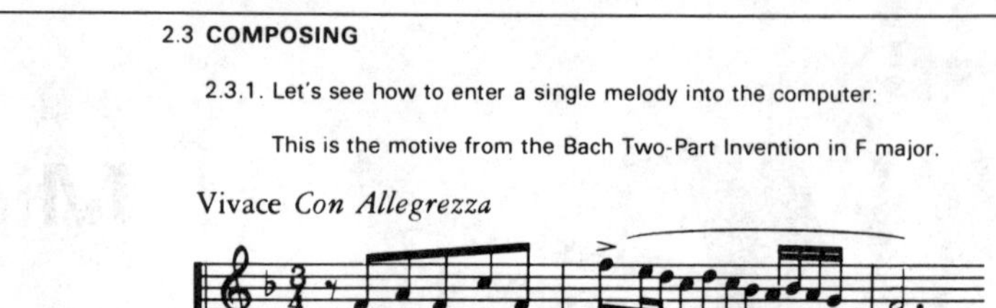

??VOICES = 1 (R)		Set up the COMPOSER for just 1 voice.
??COMPOSE ?Ø (R)		Now, we need to tell the computer we want to compose. Enter the Compose command. The "Ø" means start a new music file.

****Note: follow each pitch entered with a (R) ****

1:1?ER	Enter an Eighth Rest in set 1 of voice 1. That is what "1:1" means.
2:1?EF3	Enter an Eighth note F in the 3rd octave in set 2 of voice 1. Watch the notes appear on the screen! And hear the pitch!
3:1? EA3	And, we continue on entering in each note. We always enter the rhythm, the pitch, and the octave, in that order.
4:1? EF3	If you type a wrong code, the computer will beep, then retype the music note.
5:1? EC4	
6:1? EF3	
7:1? EF4	We have finished one measure. A Sixteenth note in set 8!
8:1? SE4	
9:1? SD4	
10:1? SC4	
11:1? SD4	
12:1? SC4	
13:1? SBF3	There is one more letter here. We need a B Flat. So we use F for flat. If we need a sharp, we would type S.
14:1? SA3	
15:1? SBF3	
16:1? SA3	
17:1? SG3	
18:1? .HF3	Put a dot before the rhythm to make a dotted value!
19:1? * (R)	An asterisk "*" tells the computer to stop composing and return to the command mode. (remember, you must press the shift key to get the asterisk.)
??METER # OF BEATS ? 3 (R) BEAT ? 4 (R)	Let's set the Meter.

Example from the instruction manual of entering three measures of music.

The key advantages of Micro Composer are good documentation, simultaneous play and display of music on two staffs, four voices on one board, no need for an external amplifier and a music entry procedure that may be helpful in learning about music (depending upon one's teaching philosophy). The disadvantages are a cumbersome editing process, awkward treatment of key signature and accidentals and an inability to handle certain musical constructions, notably tied notes and triplets.

Is Micro Composer for you? Every Apple needs music and this is certainly one way to get it.   □

Computer Music— With the Accent on Music

Jack Citron

Here's a one-of-a-kind article. First, a little music theory to fill in the technically clever but musically ignorant. And then on to Hyperwarp!

Jaxitron suggests experiments in music composition that will please a lot of you. What he ought to do is sell the package on disk...

Computer music has to sound awful! Right? Well, in the words of a song whose composer would strongly disagree and dynamically prove his point were he still with us, "It Ain't Necessarily So!" There is no law that confines the use of computers in music to experiments in sound in which all previous musical thought must be avoided. And home-computer manufacturers who advertise, "Compose your own music," are not addressing the general, music-loving public, but only one-finger pianists. Here I hope to demonstrate the computer's power to capture and convey musical concepts that can help you, as well as professional arrangers and composers, find material that would otherwise be overlooked.

From Numbers to Notes

Before going on to more interesting and creative matters, let me show the basic correspondence between musical pitch and our number system.

It seems to be common knowledge that the standard piano has 88 keys. Yet anyone who thinks numbers are pitted against the human spirit is disturbed to learn that, because the order of these keys is absolutely fixed, we can label them zero to 87 or one to 88 or in fact use any sequence of integers at all. For example, we can place zero somewhere around the center of the keyboard — say at middle C — and use negative numbers for lower pitches and positive numbers for higher ones.

In looking at a keyboard, you are immediately struck by the repetitive pattern highlighted by the black keys placed in alternating groups of two's and three's.

Jack Citron, 18136 Saticoy St., Reseda, CA 91335.

Let's extract one complete cycle of this pattern and number the keys from zero to eleven. Letting the first note be the white one just to the left of the two black keys, we force zero to correspond to the note C. The other white notes follow most unimaginatively in alphabetical order up to G but then revert to A and B as though mocking

> **And home-computer manufacturers who advertise, "Compose your own music," are not addressing the general, music-loving public, but only one-finger pianists.**

our choice of a starting point. Of course the initial note need not be C, but if it is, then the complete correspondence between numbers and notes for one "octave" becomes:

0	C	white	
1	C#		black
2	D	white	
3	D#		black
4	E	white	
5	F	white	
6	F#		black
7	G	white	
8	G#		black
9	A	white	
10	A#		black
11	B	white	

Now to cover the entire range of conventional musical pitch, the first column can be extended as required with negative and positive numbers above and below while the pitch pattern is simply repeated over and over. To change the reference pitch, you need only shift the columns with respect to each other so that zero is opposite whatever note you like.

Intervals and Scales

The word "interval" is commonly used to express the distance between two notes. Without worrying about arcane adjectives such as major, minor, augmented, diminished and perfect, we will here simply label intervals by the numeric differences involved. Thus the interval from E up to G (in the same octave) will be the difference between their assigned values — here, from 4 to 7, or +3. Similarly, the interval from G down to E will always be –3 (negative three). If you feel uncomfortable about the lack of units here, you can call them tones, half-tones or semitones (but not whole tones).

Now notice that the seven "white" notes in our setting that starts with C are numbered 0 2 4 5 7 9 11. The next white note would be 12 for the next C. It is no accident that this turns out to be the well-known major scale. But now notice that the successive intervals in this scale are 2 2 1 2 2 2, and 1 to the next C. So if you wish to express a major scale starting on D#, you can perform successive additions of the intervals beginning with the pitch 3 — that is 3, 3+2, 3+2+2, 3+2+2+1, ..., 3+2+2+1+2+2+2. The resulting numbers, 3 5 7 8 10 12 14 (and 15 to start the next octave) correspond to D#, F, G, G#, A#, C, D (and the next D#). Incidentally, throughout this article a minor technical limitation encourages my commission of a major musical sin — my typewriter as well as my computer terminal have no "flat" symbols.

Through the use of numbers, then, transposition to any key becomes a trivial matter. But more important benefits are to be gained through such calculations. Notice, for one thing, that the intervals in the scale add up to eleven (or twelve if you include the repeated "key-note" or "tonic"). By permuting these intervals in every possible way, you can use any of the 21 "modal derivatives" of a major scale. By collecting all sequences of seven positive integers that add to twelve, you make available all 462 seven-note scales in the conventional twelve-tone system of pitch. And my hand calculator tells me that amounts to 5544 scales considering transpositions to all twelve keys.

But a scale need not have exactly seven notes and the intervals need not total eleven or twelve as long as we remember that our hearing apparatus responds to the doubling of pitch as the same note.

We can form a short scale spanning any total interval. We might choose the intervals 2 1 2 or, beginning on zero, the notes 0 2 3 5. We can now treat this as a subset of a "complete" scale by repeating the *interval* sequence using one other fixed interval. That is to say, if I write 2 1 2 (2), I mean

2 1 2 (2) 2 1 2 (2) 2 1 2 (2) 2 1 2 (2) 2 1 2 . . .
C DD#F- G AA#C- D E F G- A B C D- EF#GA . . .

Notice that 2 1 2 plus the separator 2 adds to 7. If the separator interval were 1, the sequence would add to 6 so that a single repeat of the subscale would bring the whole to completion:

2 1 2 (1) 2 1 2 (1)
C DD# F — F# G# A B — C

Whenever a completed cycle brings the total spanned interval to a multiple of twelve, the total pattern will repeat (because the name of the pitch is the same for 0, 12, 24 ... and for 1, 13, 25, ... and so on).

Even if it implies some internal clash (tension!) between theory and practice, we'll stick to the statement that a melody note already present in the chord adds no tension.

Having gone this far into heresy, we might as well question whether the separator interval needs to be positive. Consider 2 1 2 (-1):

C D D# F - E F# G A - G# A# B C# - C
2 1 2 (-1) 2 1 2 (-1) 2 1 2 (-1)

Here the pattern repeats twice before adding to twelve. And this raises the obvious question about the use of negative integers in the fundamental pattern itself (not just the separator interval). Well, one could certainly object that the introduction of negative values produces a melody rather than a scale. Indeed this is true if the result is treated as a melody. But if it is used only to select notes for the actual melody, it is a scale — even though it may contain repeated pitches and retrograde motion.

Programming Fundamentals

You might now want to write some programs based on this simple arithmetic approach. Your first input as data to one program would be the subset interval sequence with the separator interval either included or given as a separate parameter. The program can then calculate the pitch numbers up to the point where the separator interval causes the next pitch to be any multiple of twelve. And, of course, if you prefer to see the output in terms of alphabetic names, you will need a conversion routine using whatever special symbols you find convenient for flats or sharps. (Because the white notes run from A to G, I call the black notes sharps so that all pitch names are two characters long with the second character being either a blank or the letter S.)

Another program can now operate on the scale making use of another input sequence to create a melody or just a suggestion for one — depending on how far your ear will allow you to go. As an example, suppose we use the previous scale developed from 2 1 2 (-1), and for the melodic input sequence we arbitrarily pick the numbers 1 3 2. The logic of the program might use these as pitch indices directly (giving the first, third and second notes — C D# D) or as *scale* intervals (that is beginning on C, an interval of one gives D, three from there in the scale gives E and two more brings us to G). Either way, there are all sorts of creative schemes you can devise to convert a short input sequence into an extended one so as to produce a long melody with a recognizable stylistic pattern based on the way your logic manipulates the numbers. Those with little musical experience will find this educational, those with more will be fascinated.

But sooner or later you will miss the all-important part of Western music that isn't there — namely harmony. (I suspect that many of you thought I would say rhythm. While ordinary rhythms are simple to the point of being trivial, more complex rhythms are indeed interesting, but they will not bring you as close to real composition as will some understanding of harmony.)

Harmony

Although no one needs to be told that melody consists of single notes ordered in time, few laymen could state clearly what harmony is. This may be because of something it shares with such deeply technical areas as high-energy physics and time-sharing computer systems — namely, it has a virtual as well as a real existence.

Harmony is made up of simultaneous groups of pitches called chords which are ordered in time, but the pitches in a chord need not be played in simultaneity. During the time a particular chord is in effect, any background containing its notes is possible. The trick behind ordinary

---

Aesthetically, the diagrams of the most symmetric states appear too simple to be pleasing, while those with less order become increasingly interesting until a point is reached where randomness becomes overpoweringly confusing and so distasteful.

---

composition in our culture is to create harmony and melody that fit together like a stage setting and story line. The harmony not only shows "where" the melody is, it also suggests where it may go next. But enough of such generalities.

Chords

Again we will use intervals, but now they are to be taken at the same point in time. For example, the interval structure 4 3 "built on" the pitch zero produces the three note chord:

0, 0+4, 0+4+3 = 0 4 7 or C E G

which is a major triad. By reversing these two intervals, we have a minor triad — i.e., 3 4 implies

0, 0+3, 0+3+4 = 0 3 7 or C D# G.

Again notice that these combinations of two numbers will let you build major or minor three-note chords on any pitch through simple addition

D# major = 3 + (4 3) = 3 7 10 or D# G A#
A# minor = 10 + (3 4) = 10 13 17 or A# C# F.

Note that the remainder modulo twelve gives the pitch name in our reference octave

10 13 17 becomes 10 1 5 or A# C# F.

Of course triads or three-note chords can be constructed from any pair of intervals — but you will find something "strange" about the musical flavor of most such structures. An interesting explanation can be given in terms of order, symmetry or what scientists might call "psychological entropy" — but we can't go into that here. For the moment just accept the fact that 3's and 4's will produce conventional results while other intervals will introduce possibilities that you may or may not be ready to appreciate.

Now you may want to write a program that will construct all possible n-note chords containing only intervals restricted to some given set. For example, if n equals four and we limit ourselves to the intervals 3 and 4, the program should find these interval sequences:

```
3 3 3    3 3 4    3 4 3    3 4 4
4 3 3    4 3 4    4 4 3    4 4 4
```

Next, each of these sequences must be tested for the presence of a subtotal within the structure that equals twelve or any multiple of twelve. If such intervals are present in a structure, there will be fewer than four unique notes. On this basis, only seven possible chords will remain here because 4 4 4 is an obvious reject. Now any of these seven chords can be built on any of the twelve different pitches through the usual summation technique.

By changing the value of n from 4 to 7 or 12, you can now find all 36 seven-note chords consisting of only threes and fours, or all four twelve-note structures containing these same intervals. And, of course, with a sense of adventure you need not be limited to just these two interval values. Further, you might introduce separator intervals to increase the already endless supply of possibilities and at the same time create new kinds of harmonic flavors. As an example,

$$m\ n\ (p\ q)\ r\ s\ t$$

would specify structures containing first three pitches using only the intervals m and/or n, separated by the interval p or q from a four-note structure limited to the intervals r, s and/or t.

The mind-boggling assortment of possibilities that you create here cries out for some sort of selection apparatus to let you pick out only the agreeable chords without actually sampling every structure found. To accomplish this, you can use the following method for measuring the "tension" in a chord structure. Structures outside any tension range of your choice can be discarded by your program.

Tension (Order in Simultaneity)

Each interval in a structure contributes to the net tension in the structure. The following table shows the value to be added for each interval, and the intervals shown are really remainders modulo twelve.

Interval	Tension Contribution
10	1
2	10
11	100
1	1000
other	0

TNSN	STRUCTURE													CLASS
232	3 3 4 4 3 3 :	C	DS	FS	AS	D	F	GS						−MI7
321	3 3 4 4 3 4 :	C	DS	FS	AS	D	F	A						−MI7
421	3 3 5 3 3 5 :	C	DS	FS	B	D	F	AS						−MA7
232	3 4 3 4 3 4 :	C	DS	G	AS	D	F	A						MI7
321	3 4 3 4 4 3 :	C	DS	G	AS	D	FS	A						MI7
232	3 4 4 3 3 4 :	C	DS	G	B	D	F	A						MI
322	3 4 4 3 3 5 :	C	DS	G	B	D	F	AS						MI
321	3 4 4 3 4 3 :	C	DS	G	B	D	FS	A						MI
411	3 4 4 3 4 4 :	C	DS	G	B	D	FS	AS						MI
331	3 5 3 3 3 5 :	C	DS	GS	B	D	F	AS						+MI
322	3 5 3 3 4 4 :	C	DS	GS	B	D	FS	AS						+MI
421	3 5 3 3 5 3 :	C	DS	GS	B	D	G	AS						+MI
1221	4 3 3 3 5 3 :	C	E	G	AS	CS	FS	A						LG7
232	4 3 3 4 4 3 :	C	E	G	AS	D	FS	A						LG7
321	4 3 3 5 3 3 :	C	E	G	AS	DS	FS	A						LG7
232	4 3 4 3 4 3 :	C	E	G	B	D	FS	A						MA7
322	4 3 4 3 4 4 :	C	E	G	B	D	FS	AS						MA7
1320	4 3 4 4 3 2 :	C	E	G	B	DS	FS	GS						MA7
321	4 3 4 4 3 3 :	C	E	G	B	DS	FS	A						MA7
411	4 3 4 4 3 4 :	C	E	G	B	DS	FS	AS						MA7
2122	4 4 2 3 5 1 :	C	E	GS	AS	CS	FS	G						+7
1133	4 4 2 4 4 1 :	C	E	GS	AS	D	FS	G						+7
1222	4 4 2 5 3 1 :	C	E	GS	AS	DS	FS	G						+7
233	4 4 3 3 4 4 :	C	E	GS	B	D	FS	AS						+MA7
322	4 4 3 3 5 3 :	C	E	GS	B	D	G	AS						+MA7
322	4 4 3 4 3 4 :	C	E	GS	B	DS	FS	AS						+MA7
411	4 4 3 4 4 3 :	C	E	GS	B	DS	G	AS						+MA7
1221	5 2 3 3 3 5 :	C	F	G	AS	CS	E	A						7+3
241	5 2 3 4 2 5 :	C	F	G	AS	D	E	A						7+3
1222	5 2 3 5 1 5 :	C	F	G	AS	DS	E	A						7+3
241	5 2 4 3 2 5 :	C	F	G	B	D	E	A						MA7+3
331	5 3 3 3 5 3 :	C	F	GS	B	D	G	AS						+MA7+3
322	5 3 3 4 4 3 :	C	F	GS	B	DS	G	AS						+MA7+3
421	5 3 3 5 3 3 :	C	F	GS	B	E	G	AS						+MA7+3

Table 1.

This is not meant to establish a linear scale, allowing us to say that this chord is twice as tense as that one. Instead it gives a logarithmic relation, and so should have psychological value! Consider as an example the seven-note structure with the interval sequence

$$4\ 3\ 4\ 3\ 4\ 3.$$

The intervals between the first note in the chord (root tone) and each of the other pitches can be tabulated

Interval from root	Remainder mod 12	Tension
4	4	0
7	7	0
11	11	100
14	2	10
18	6	0
21	9	0

Notice that if the root tone were zero, the second column (remainder mod twelve) could be interpreted as the other pitch names in the chord. From this it is clear that we do have seven unique notes.

To tabulate this information for the second chordal tone, we drop the first interval leaving 3 4 3 4 3 to form the partial sums:

Interval from 2nd note	Remainder mod 12	Tension
3	3	0
7	7	0
10	10	1
14	2	10
17	5	0

And similarly for the remaining notes:

Interval from 3rd note	Remainder mod 12	Tension
4	4	0
7	7	0
11	11	100
14	2	10

Interval from 4th note	Remainder mod 12	Tension
3	3	0
7	7	0
10	10	1

From 5th note	Remainder mod 12	Tension
4	4	0
7	7	0

From 6th note	Remainder mod 12	Tension
3	3	0

Net: 232

The tension of this chord is the sum of all the tension contributions imparted by the various intervals shown — namely, 232.

As the term tension implies, chords with lower tension values will exhibit less interval clash between pitches in the chord. Your own musical experience and taste will determine the tension range within which you will feel comfortable. You can see that the fewer notes a chord has, the better its chances of having a lower tension. But you can also see that a change in the order of the notes in a chord can alter its tension drastically.

Melody Plus Harmony

Before considering chord continuity, we can now easily link the concepts of melody and harmony using the notion of tension.

Consider as a first example a C-major triad (C E G). By measuring the intervals from each of these notes to every other note, we can assign a tension value that describes how well any note "fits" or is harmonized by this chord. Any pitch already in the chord will be given a tension of zero because it doesn't add anything (usually!). As a result, every note in the octave can be evaluated for use with this (or any other) chord. "Wrong" notes become those whose tension values exceed your personal limits. For the C-major triad:

Note	Tension
C	0
C#	1000
D	11
D#	100
E	0
F	1001
F#	110
G	0
G#	1000
A	10
A#	1
B	100

Here the tension of the pitch F, for example, was found as follows:

```
F–G = 5–7 = –2 implies 10 or a tension of      1
F–E = 5–4 =  1              1              1000
F–C = 5–0 =  5              5                 0
                                          ———
                              Total: 1001
```

For a more unusual example, consider the triad with intervals of five and six built on C (C F B) or (0 5 11).

Note	Tension
C	0
C#	1010
D	10
D#	1
E	100
F	0
F#	1000
G	10
G#	0
A	1
A#	110
B	0

The most "professional" approach would intermix both procedures letting the inherent strength of the melody or harmony alternately suggest what should come next.

Here, the chord itself has tension — a value of 100 if the C is below the B. Yet a C in the melody might seem to add considerable tension because it lies above the B in the chord. This leads to a number of additional considerations that cannot be taken up here. Even if it implies some interval clash (tension!) between theory and practice, we'll stick to the statement that a melody note already present in the chord adds no tension.

Seven-part Harmony

If you can accept the above declaration, you can see that a chord with N notes could have N melody notes that add no tension. This makes seven-note structures most attractive for connecting harmony and melody because each such structure carries its own "complete" (seven-note) scale. Using such a structure, you can take the first three or four tones as the chord to be played while the melody ranges over any part of the seven-note scale.

As a result the melody can have considerable variation in tension, and yet be controlled to the extent that its net tension cannot exceed that of the original seven-part structure. A computer listing of 34 such structures showing for each the tension, interval sequence and the corresponding pitch names if C is taken as the root tone is shown in Table 1. The list is ordered and grouped by the last column, which is labelled "class." The entries under this heading represent terminology

that is too specialized for this article, but you will notice that all structures in the same class have in common at least their first four notes.

You might also notice the structures are not completely unique. For example, the first structure built on C has exactly the same set of pitches as the sixth structure built on D# and also structure number 14 built on G#. This means that rearrangement of the same set of notes can alter the net harmonic effect. It also implies that more than one chord can harmonize the same fragment of a melody. But for that matter, if a single melodic pitch is to be harmonized, there are seven settings for each of these 34 structures, or 238 possibilities that will work. By this I mean that the melody note can be the first, second ..., sixth or seventh note in any of the 34 structures and seven times 34 is 238.

Before going further, you should validate each of these structures with your own harmonic sense. To do this, play the first three or four notes of a structure with your left hand (either simultaneously or in a fixed pattern) while picking out the entire seven-note scale (one note at a time) with your right. The scale is usually found by reordering the pitches ordinally: 1 5 2 6 3 7 4. In a few cases, this is not quite correct, but it will still give the taste of each structure. Test just one chord at a time and give your ear a good rest before changing structures. Cross off any that strike you as too unpleasant and don't be surprised if this removes quite a few — perhaps even a majority — from the list. You may be able to describe the throw-aways as having too much tension or no feeling of being in a "key." If you find you can keep only three or four out of the entire list of structures, don't worry about it. It simply shows you've led a sheltered musical life and your musical morality has persuaded you to draw the line between artistic license and unrestrained licentiousness in a conservative way.

Continuity

There are any number of programmable schemes for selecting structures and root tones for the initial composition of a harmonic continuity. Having begun this way, you must next select melody notes to fit the harmony. Conversely, a melody could be given or composed first and harmonization made to follow. The most "professional" approach would intermix both procedures letting the inherent strength of the melody or harmony alternately suggest what should come next. But in the space remaining, we will concentrate on the hardest of the basic tasks to computerize — harmonization of melody.

Given a melody, the first chore is to decide where the harmonic changes should occur. This amounts to being able to say that the first n notes will go with one chord, the next m notes with another, and so on. If your musical experience is minimal, it will be easiest to force chord changes wherever you feel a "strong" beat in keeping the rhythm — essentially the first beat of each bar of music. For the first group of melody notes, any of your allowed structures built on any possible root tone can be tested against the melody. The test must be designed to keep only those chords that satisfy certain conditions regarding the fit between harmony and melody. The creativity lies in specifying the conditions to be met. Here are just a few suggestions for tests that a chord must pass in order to harmonize a given melodic segment.

1. Entries, a, b, ... of the melody must (not) be in positions n, m, ... of the chord structure

2. More (fewer) than N melody notes must (not) have tension higher (lower) than T with respect to the first M notes of the structure

3. The root tone must be r (or s (or tones).

4. The structure number (class) must be c (or d (or ...))

You may even want to apply conditions to choose which tests to use. For example:

If there are more (fewer) than M melody notes, use test a, otherwise use test b.

In any case, conditions of this sort can be so restrictive that your program finds no structures can satisfy them. When more lenient specifications are made, chances are that more than one structure will be found to work. Your choice from this set of potential structures can be free or based on some additional tests.

Only after you have settled on the first chord are you really into the problem of continuity. All the features just discussed for finding a suitable harmony for the first fragment of the melody are now combined with considerations that take the previous chord into account, although, of course, we are now trying to fit the next group of tones in the melody. A direct approach might be to add conditions to the above set using a logical "and" to force interchordal relationships. Such conditions could include:

1. The Nth entry in the new chord should be less than (more than, exactly) P pitches above (below, in either direction) from the Mth entry in the previous one.

2. Entries x, y, ... of the previous structure should (not) be in the next one.

Another approach would be to construct a table of allowed structure changes — that is, structure type A can go to types B, C, ... A table might also contain explicit restrictions — structure type A can go to type B if the root tone moves through an interval, I. A well-thought-out table will establish a definite style in any given piece.

Order in Continuity

Another technique for controlling the style of harmonization makes use of psychological entropy (order). Suppose we are using all 34 of the seven-note structures shown above and the next section of the melody to be harmonized has only a single pitch. Without any continuity restrictions, there are 238 possible harmonizations. With relative ease, a computer can compare each of these with the previous chord and establish a distribution table of the following type.

# of changes	0	1	2	3	4	5
# of chords	4	17	43	83	79	12

A friend, having invited me over to see his new home computer, insisted on displaying its virtuosity with no less than six identically unrousing choruses of "Mary Had A Little Lamb"! Need I say more?

Here the computer found that four of the potential chords contained all seven of the pitches in the previous chord. Seventeen of the new ones had a single pitch that was not in the old one, 43 had two pitch changes, and so on. Because seven pitches out of twelve are always being used, the number of pitch changes cannot be greater than five. While 238 is not statistically large, the distribution does show typical statistical properties in that more samples fall in the inner categories than in the outer ones.

But, to get across the most fascinating property here, I must digress just a bit. There are many physical systems that display such statistical behavior. These systems can generally be described in terms of geometrical diagrams that represent some vital aspect of the property being counted — for example a cluster of arrows pointing in various directions. Generally the states more unlikely to occur — those falling in the outer columns (smaller numbers of occurrences) — exhibit high if not total symmetry (order) while the more populated distributions appear more chaotic. And *aesthetically, the diagrams of the*

most symmetric states appear too simple to be pleasing, while those with less order become increasingly interesting until a point is reached where randomness becomes overpoweringly confusing and, so, distasteful. The rightmost column usually shows a peculiar sort of order which may or may not have aesthetic value depending on its apparent simplicity. Of course there is subjectivity involved here, but the determinant of aesthetic appeal in any case is a function of the number of ways each possible state of the system can be achieved.

In the case at hand, there seems to be no convincing geometrical representation with these properties, but — and this is the source of my fascination — the ear somehow categorizes the entries just as described above with the same aesthetic result! When more than a single note is to be harmonized by one structure, the number of possibilities decreases so that you might well expect the distribution to become even less statistically valid. Yet I have found that, even with only a dozen or so possible structures, the distribution — though containing fewer than six categories — still exhibits the same aesthetic patterns.

From here, you can choose chords freely from those the computer places in the more or less ordered categories. Or you may devise some automated methodology using decision-making techniques or directed graphs taking all sorts of things into account. Arrangers will be delighted by the chord changes suggested through the statistical approach.

You might well wonder what could have caused me to try to encapsulate so much material in so short a space. The impetus came from a most unexceptional, even homespun occurrence. A friend, having invited me over to see his new home computer, insisted on displaying its virtuosity with no less than six identically unrousing choruses of "Mary Had A Little Lamb"! Need I say more? □

Sound Apple Hint

Want to hear your Apple a little more clearly? The speaker in the Apple is a 2" unit mounted facing the solid metal of the case. These two things conspire to make the sound much weaker than the speaker driver (amplifier) is capable of producing.

We found the easiest way to increase and improve the sound is to add an external speaker. A small, high effeciency, 8-ohm, 4" to 6" unit in a cabinet is your best bet. There's no point spending $30 or $40 on a high quality unit—Apple sound isn't **that** good. We bought a 5" unit from Radio Shack for $14.95 and it makes an unbelievable improvement.

To retain the portability of the Apple, we made this a plug-in unit. Since the trend these days seems to be to RCA phono plugs and jacks for extension speakers, we used them in this installation. To make the modification, unplug the speaker wire from the board on the right under the keyboard. Cut it about 3" from the plug and put in an insulated RCA phono jack. In the end leading to the Apple speaker, put in an insulated RCA phono plug. If you can't find insulated components, wrap tape around all the exposed metal. You don't want this making contact with anything else inside the Apple. When you want to use the external speaker, plug it into the jack. When you want portability, use the internal speaker.

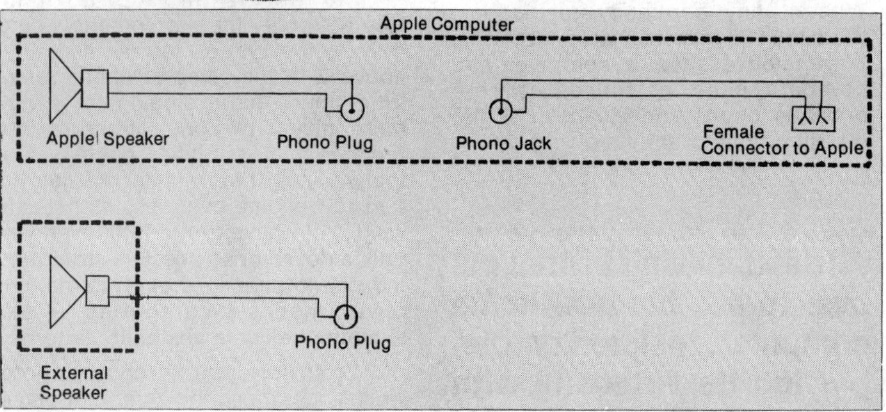

Chapter III
Education

Chapter III — Education

Welcome to the exciting field of Computers in Education. It is obvious that computers will become more a part of our everyday lives. It has even been proposed that a class society might gradually emerge that divides the population into two groups: those who use and understand computer technology and those who do not! The definition of literacy as "the ability to read and write," may soon be changed to include the words "computer programs." Proponents of computer literacy education differ only in the degree in which computers should be incorporated into the curriculum.

Donald Piele, in his series of articles, "How to Solve It With the Computer," demonstrates ways the computer can be used to improve the critical thinking of students in the 3rd through 10th grades. His emphasis is on how the computer can be used to approach new problems in a new way, not how the computer can be used to do the same old problems.

Eight lessons are presented here. Each lesson includes:
1) Classroom Procedures — an overview of how students use the computer, keep track of their own lessons, and are responsible for their assignments.
2) Programming Activities or Assignments — each suggested assignment has three levels of difficulty for: a) beginning students, b) intermediate students, and c) advanced students. At least one activity or assignment is given in each of the eight lessons. These articles include lists and runs of all programs assigned.
3) Remarks, Discussion or Related Ideas — these sections are of particular benefit to those with little or no background in computer use or in problem solving techniques. Although all graphics programs are written for the Apple, some of the programs are written in NorthStar BASIC. Apple owners must note any references for changing these programs so they will work with "Microsoft BASIC," and follow the directions given.
4) References.

In addition, in lesson five, Dr. Piele has given directions and all necessary information for holding your own computer contest. This includes everything from the contest entry form to the suggested problems, with lists and runs of sample solutions.

Other articles in this chapter include programs for keeping a grade book, determining the reading level of any reference material, and for printing a graduation card.

For classroom procedures, you should refer to both part 1 and part 2 of this series. The changes for Microsoft BASIC *must* be made for those programs to run on an Apple.

Special Notes For Chapter III

● *How to Solve It, Part 2:*

For Applesoft users, PRINT MID$(A$,X,1);"", should be used in line 110 of problem #2 instead of PRINT A$(X,X);"". If you desire to indent, use the colon (e.g., line 60 would be typed in as "60:::X=X+1" for an indentation of three spaces.) The "X MOD 35" function suggested in reference to the same problem could be done in Applesoft: X-INT(X/35)*35.

● How to Solve It, Part 3:

For Applesoft users, line 80 of the first sample solution should read: 80 IF B(I)=B THEN GOTO 130. Also, the "IF . . . THEN . . . ELSE" on line 80 of the solution to Problem #3, needs to be changed. One way is to type the following:
80 IF X/2=INT(X) THEN C=0: GOTO 90
85 C=B
90 NEXT I : RETURN
Finally, the ""A$(I,I)'' should be ""MID$(A$,I,I)'' and the back slash marks should be changed to colons.

● *How to Solve It, Part 5:*

For Applesoft users, the back slash marks in "First Head Experiment" and the "Bug-Free" programs need to be changed to colons. Also, the "X=RND(-1)" function needs to be replaced with "X=RND(-PEEK(78)-256*PEEK(79))".

● *How to Solve It, Part 6:*

This article concentrates on developing problem-solving skills by using the computer. Many of us have only thought about computer programs that: a) play games, b) do calculations, or c) keep track of records. For another type of application consider the following problem: how can a "round robin" tennis tournament be best organized so every player plays every other player?

- *How to Solve It, Part 7:*

The strengths of the computer include: "high speed computation and decision-making combined with the structures of graphs, networks, stacks, and queues and employing search, sort, merge, backtracking, recursion, and branching strategies." This article concentrates on presenting problems — and their solutions — that use the strengths of the computer. Examples include the old Water Jug Problem: "Given three jugs, one filled to capacity with 8 quarts of water (or wine?), and two empty jugs that hold 5 and 3 quarts respectively, how does one divide the liquid equally, using only those containers?" The computer programs given include lo-res graphics to represent the jugs. They then generalize the problem to N jugs with the capacities of C1, C2, etc.

- *How to Solve It, Part 8:*

Yes, the computer can indeed help students understand the proverbial story problem. A problem like: "How many chickens and how many pigs are there if there are 50 legs among 18 animals?" can not only be solved; it can also be generalized. We could ask "What is the minimum and maximum number of legs for N possible animals? List all possible combinations of these two animals, and note any patterns in the answers." There are some very good suggestions for solving these kinds of problems in the article.

To consider another kind of problem, do you think math teachers — who magically solve a quadratic equation using the quadratic formula — allow the student to know exactly what has been done? What precisely are those two numbers and how do they apply to the graph of the quadratic? The bisection method, an iterative technique for solving a quadratic, permits the student to guess and then to improve on this guess. This kind of approach encourages logical thinking and shows how the computer can be used in situations other than games, calculations, and organization of data. "More, more!" we cry.

- *A Dozen Apples for the Classroom,* by Hakansson and Roach:

Look for a traveling computer lab on the San Francisco Bay freeways. The lab is an all-in-one van that contains twelve Apple computers in three Apple Carts." The sign on the side says "L.H.S. Science Shuttle", or the Lawrence Hall of Science from the University of California at Berkeley. Each "Apple Cart", designed specifically for this program, compactly contains three computers with disk drives and three full-size color television sets — allowing for easy setup and mobility.

What can happen if one Apple computer is put into a sixth grade classroom for two hours per week for eight weeks? Such a pilot program was carried out in the spring of 1978 in Kenosha, Wisconsin for the purpose of developing logical thinking skills.

Three sample lessons are given, numbered one, five and ten, with each lesson consisting "of a simple program with a short explanation of the new statements, a sample run, and a series of simple program changes for the student to do." And you thought you had to have a computer for each student!

- *Grade Maintenance Program,* by Jim Hunter:

With this gradebook program you initially enter students' names and their roster number, and periodically add their assignment and/or test grades. The print-out includes many different options: 1) Class list with each student's average, 2) assignment or test list with student average on each, 3) ranked class list (students listed from highest average to lowest average) and 4) all of one student's grades/assignments.

Each entry of a given test or assignment may be weighted — that is, the score on the second test may be multiplied by .333 to decrease its importance to one third the other tests.

- *Reading Level Difficulty,* by Ronald Carson:

This is a surprisingly simple program to do what usually is considered to be a complex task: determining the reading level of any given text or reference.

Modifications to "increase accuracy" have been suggested by Michael Schuyler in his letter to the editor in the June, 1981 issue of *Creative Computing.* These include changing line 710 to be:
710 R=.4*(T/W*100+W/S):REM — This changes 3-letter words to a percent.
OR 710 R=.4*(T/W+W/S):REM — This leaves the percent of 3-letter words as a decimal.

- *Another Hallmark in Programming,* by Wes W. Henley, Jr.:

Because 60 columns are needed, this will not print correctly on your screen — which only has 40 columns. However, it will print correctly on any printer that uses 60 or more columns.

"I brought home a friend of mine from the arcades."

How To Solve It — With The Computer

Donald T. Piele

These are the opening words in the preface to the first edition of Professor Polya's book *How To Solve It.*[1] Upon re-reading them recently, I was struck by how well they described the mode that I prefer to use in teaching programming skills. When I have introduced computers into the classroom, I have found young students want to understand how to program a computer and enjoy the challenge of figuring out how to control it. In a small but significant way, the process of learning how to program a computer is a creative and inventive activity which exercises all aspects of the problem-solving process. Through working on programming exercises, students learn to enjoy problem-solving. Young students are especially excited about working with computers because it gives them an opportunity to test out their own ideas, something the traditional mathematics curriculum does not usually permit. Students learn that solutions to problems are not a series of rigid and meaningless operations that are blindly and uniformly followed. For this reason I believe that if small computers are used for no other function than as a vehicle for development of problem-solving skills, their use is completely justified.

The National Council of Teachers of Mathematics (NCTM) has placed the improvement of problem-solving skills as its primary objective for the 1980's. In a recent report,[2] they have recommended that:

"1. problem solving be the focus of school mathematics in the 1980's."

Donald Piele, Associate Professor of Mathematics, University of Wisconsin - Parkside, Kenosha, WI 53141.

The applications of these skills are not limited to mathematics but are in demand in all disciplines. Arthur Whimbey and Jack Lockhead write in the preface to their new book *Problem Solving and Comprehension*[3]:

"It is fascinating to imagine what might happen to our national literacy and math competency if all teachers from elementary through college level saw one of their major roles as teaching students to think carefully in acquiring and using information from the academic disciplines. This could be done by allowing more class time for students to verbally interpret and draw conclusions from reading assignments, and explain their answers to problems they solved. When a student made an error, the teacher could guide him through a correct analysis with probing, Socratic questions, while extolling the need for completeness and accuracy."

Teachers have many preconceived ideas on the role of computers in the classroom — mainly Computer Assisted Instruction. When I suggest that a black box exists that if brought into the classroom could serve as vehicle for student interaction, invite experimentation, reward careful analysis, require reading and writing, allow cooperation among students, and reward completeness and accuracy, most teachers do not think of a computer. Even advocates of computers in the classroom seldom view computers in this role. And finally, even those who understand this role have difficulty collecting enough ideas to make it work.

Objectives

The major focus of this series, then, is to give ideas and examples that support the problem-solving role for computers in the classroom. Procedures, techniques and sample problems will be given that can be used with beginning, intermediate and advanced students. For beginning students, ideas for teaching elements of the Basic language in a discovery mode will be explained. These ideas will supplement but not replace a good manual or text on the Basic language. The ideas presented here will outline an alternative to the format used in most textbooks and should be used in conjunction with reference material on Basic for a particular system.

For intermediate and advanced students, who have a working knowledge of Basic, problems for investigation will be described and complete solutions provided

The specific relationship is of little importance but the idea of looking for one is of great importance.

in Basic. Teachers using these materials in the classroom may wish to withhold the solutions for discussion with students after they have worked on the problems. Since a great deal can be learned by seeing how others solve problems, complete listings will be provided. Most of us have learned to program this way.

Lesson #1 (Beginning Students): The Process

In accord with the objectives above, the emphasis throughout this series will be on process, not answers. The personal computer is designed for interaction, and hence encourages students to experiment, revise, extend, simplify and rearrange. These are processes that are vital to problem solving. The problem that we choose to investigate will never be as important as the process that we go through to solve it. Polya's quote at the beginning of this article is the guiding principal for this series.

Keeping Records

Keeping records is very important in learning a new language and should become the primary responsibility of the student. I recommend that each student have his or her own spiral notebook which will become a personal reference manual for Basic. From the very beginning, students should record information about how to operate the system — turn it on and off, enter Basic or the system monitor, load and save programs on cassette or disk. These operations are easy to demonstrate to the entire class while the students take notes on them. I have found that it is a mistake to pass out a complete summary of this information because it bypasses a skill you want to teach — recording information. This procedure also avoids what can be a big 'turn-off' in the teaching of computer programming — information overload. By having students build their own records, this problem can be minimized and, as a bonus, they will be developing a fundamental problem-solving skill.

It is not important that they write 'textbook' descriptions of each statement. It is more important that they record what they know in their own words.

What follows is an example to illustrate the problem-solving approach to teaching the Basic language. The ideas expressed could be used with any system; however, for the purposes of illustration, the samples will be written for the Apple II system. Teachers with different systems can still use the format of the presentation but will need to change the programs.

Program 1 (Beginning Students)

Begin your first lesson in Basic by picking out a small program that contains three or four statements and ask the students to copy it in their notebooks. For example, if you are working with the Apple II system you might type in the following program:

```
10 GR

20 COLOR = 9

30 PLOT 20,20

40 END
```

Lots of information can be explored beginning with this simple program. For example, you may demonstrate what happens when you type LIST. Ask the students to record their own meaning for this command and to note that every statement and command must be ENTERed or RETURNed with a key stroke. The process of first demonstrating the command and then having the students record a description, in their own words, can be used effectively in the learning of

any interactive computer language.

Next, RUN the program. If everything was typed in correctly, the program will produce the intended results. In this example the screen will clear and a small orange square will appear in the middle of the screen. Again, it does not matter what your program does as long as it contains a small number of fundamental statements. Use graphics whenever possible because it is easy to visualize the effect of each statement. Continue discussing the program with the class and ask for their ideas on the effect of each statement.

Sample Questions

1. The first statement in the program is 10 GR. What do you think is the effect of this statement?

2. The second statement is 20 COLOR = 9. What would happen if we changed this line to 20 COLOR = 7?

3. The third statement is 30 PLOT 20,20. What does this statement do? What would happen if we changed it to 30 PLOT 10,10? What about 30 PLOT 30,30 or even 30 PLOT 20,10? What are the limits to the values in the first and second coordinates?

4. The final statement is 40 END. What would happen if we forgot it?

RUN the program a few times to test each answer. Soon the class will formulate a working definition of each statement. It is not important that they write 'textbook' descriptions of each statement. It is more important that they record what they know in their own words. Emphasize that a program is a list of statements executed in order of increasing line number and that each statement has a certain action.

System Operation and Commands

In the discussion of the program above a number of questions about the system operation and Basic commands will naturally arise. The commands RUN and LIST will be used continuously and will need to be recorded. Specific commands such as TEXT for the Apple II, which clears the GRaphics mode and allows for

the listing of the program, will become a natural part of the investigation. Questions such as how to change a line by retyping it, or how to delete or add lines to the program, are easy and natural to demonstrate in the context of this program. Finally, how to SAVE your program for later use when you will need to LOAD it again may come up in the discussion and could easily be explained at this time.

Lesson Goal

The goal of each lesson is to learn how to use the statements and commands that have been introduced and to exercise problem-solving skills. This will be done by writing a program that solves a specific problem. A typical example is:

Problem 1 (Beginning Students)
Write a program that will draw your initials in block letters on the screen.

Remarks

1. This is a clearly defined problem with a clearly defined goal and the student should have all the necessary tools to solve it. What needs to be done is to apply some problem-solving skills. Clearly, the value of the problem is not the solution but the process that each student needs to go through to solve it.

2. A fundamental skill in problem-solving is knowing how to represent information. Like most skills, it can only be developed with practice. If the problem were to represent letters on a piece of paper then the problem would be trivial because this skill has been practiced a great deal. But to carry out the same task in low resolution color graphics on the Apple II computer is quite a different problem. The student needs to first understand how positions on the screen are represented. For the Apple II the low resolution screen locations are as follows:

```
0,0  1,0  2,0 .........39,0
0,1  1,1  2,1 .........39,1
0,2  1,2  2,2 .........39,2
 .    .    .           .
 .    .    .           .
 .    .    .           .
0,39 1,39 2,39.........39,39
```

Next, the student must figure out how individual letters can be composed with an arrangement of small squares in a 40x40 grid. Finally, he or she needs to understand the Basic statements which draw the letters.

3. The opportunity to work on the computer is essential. Students work successfully in pairs if there is a limited number of machines. A sign-up schedule is advisable for the available times on the system. Deadlines for the completion of each problem should be set — one or two weeks depending on the time available for each student on the computer. All work on the problem should be recorded in the notebooks and a complete listing of the final documented program should accompany every problem solution. To insure that this is followed, establish the rule that no one can continue using the computer until their work has been recorded in their notebook in a satisfactory form. It is important to establish in the beginning that the use of the computer is a privilege that can be lost to those who do not take the work seriously. The motivation to use the computer is so strong that most behavioral problems are self correcting.

Intermediate Students

For intermediate and advanced students the emphasis will be placed on problems at the junior high level and above. It is hard to establish an absolute level of difficulty since programming skills are highly dependent upon experience which, at least for now, has very little relationship to age. In the annual computer problem-solving contest at UW-Parkside, there have been cases where students in grades 7-9 have done better than the winners in grades 10-12.

Understanding the problem-solving process is still the major objective here. The emphasis given earlier on record keeping is just as important for intermediate and advanced students as for the beginning student. Again, the problem will never be as important as the experience gained in trying to solve it. Let's begin with:

Problem 1 (Intermediate Student)

Ten people show up for the first meeting of the school computer club. Each person shakes hands with every other person exactly once. Write a program that will produce a print out of all the pairs of people who shook hands with each other and the total number.

Remarks

1. A good problem solver would first try to solve this problem with a small number of people. For example, with only three or four people it would be an easy

matter to list all the handshakes. Try it.

2. What is a good way to represent the solution? One simple idea is to use the first ten letters in the alphabet for the names of the ten students and print out pairs of letters such as AB, AC, etc. to represent handshakes between members. Deciding on a convenient representation is often a crucial part in successful problem-solving. Be flexible and actively pursue a number of alternatives.

Young students are especially excited about working with computers because it gives them an opportunity to test out their own ideas,

---

3. What is your plan of attack? Can you express it in words? The natural language is a high level language. Use it to express your plan of attack. For example:

Plan of Attack
"List the members in alphabetical order ABCDEFGHIJ. First A shakes hands with everyone to the right, AB, AC, AD, . . . AJ. Then B shakes hands with everyone to the right BC, BD, BE . . . BF. You continue shifting one position to the right and pairing that letter with all the remaining letters to the right. The last pairing is IJ. You never pair to the left because that handshake has already taken place. Continue until you reach the last handshake."

4. Finally, transform the plan of attack into an algorithm in Basic. A program that runs properly is evidence that the algorithm works and the plan has been carried out successfully.

Solutions

```
Sample Solution

10 LET A$="ABCDEFGHIJ"
20 LET L = LEN(A$)
30 FOR I = 1 TO L-1
40     FOR J = I+1 TO L
50         C=C+1
60         PRINT C," ",A$(I,I),A$(J,J)
70     NEXT J
80 NEXT I
90 END
```

Remarks

1. This program was written in North Star Basic and should be changed in line 60 for Microsoft Basic which handles strings differently.

```
60      PRINT C;" ";MID$(A$,I,1)
        ;MID$(A$,J,1)
```

2. The above program is stripped down to show only the workings of the

algorithm. Students should be required to include a statement of the problem and other personal documentation at the beginning of the program.

Suppose we had phrased the problem differently:
List out all pairs of people that can be formed from a population of 10 people.

In this form it is natural to ask:
List out all groups of size 3 that can be formed from a population of 10 people. This problem can be solved by adding another loop to the previous solution.

```
Sample Solution

10 LET A$ = "ABCDEFGHIJ"
20 LET L = LEN(A$)
30 FOR I = 1 TO L-2
40     FOR J = I+1 TO L-1
45         FOR K = J+1 TO L
50             LET C = C+1
60             PRINT C," ",A$(I,I),
                   A$(J,J),A$(K,K)
65         NEXT K
70     NEXT J
80 NEXT I
90 END
```

Remarks

1. Again this program is not complete; the output needs to be formatted.

2. As above, line 60 needs to be changed for other dialects of Basic.

The way this program is written, each time the size of the group is changed the program needs to be changed. There must be a better way to write a general program which will work for any size group. This leads to a reformulation of the problem for:

Advanced Students: Problem 1

Write a program that will list out all groups of M people that can be formed from a population of N people. For convenience you may limit N to 26. Format the output so that it prints the groupings across the page and gives the total number.

```
First Sample Solution

10 DIM A(26),A$(26)
20 A$="ABCDEFGHIJKLMNOPQRSTUVWXYZ"
30 INPUT " ENTER POPULATION
     SIZE, GROUP SIZE N,M ",N,M
40 L=1 : A(L)=1 : C=0
50 IF N-M >= A(L)-L THEN 90
60     L = L-1
70     IF L = 0 THEN 250
80     A(L) = A(L) +1 \ GOTO 50
90 IF L=M THEN 130
100     A(L+1)=A(L)+1
110     L=L+1
120     GOTO 50
130 REM ** PRINT GROUP **
140     FOR I=1 TO M
150         X=A(I) : PRINT A$(X,X),
160     NEXT I
170     PRINT
180     C=C+1
190 IF A(L)=N THEN 220
200     A(L)=A(L)+1
210     GOTO 50
220 L=L-1
230     IF L=0 THEN 250
240     GOTO 190
250     PRINT : PRINT "C(",N,",",M,
        ") = ",C
260 END
```

Remarks

1. The basic idea of this program is to build an array of length M which consists of numbers taken from 1 to N. Each number corresponds to a letter from A to Z, with 1 = A . . . 26 = Z. Thus 1234 corresponds to the group ABCD.

2. The last digit is increased until it reaches the size of N. This generates the numbers 1234, 1235, 1236 . . . 123N which correspond to the groups ABCD, ABCE, ABCF . . . ABCZ (if N = 26 and M = 4).

3. The preceding digit is now increased by one and the count continues anew: 1245, 1246, 1247 . . . 124N.

4. The numbers continue increasing in a 'speedometer like' manner until the first number is N–3. Now the last arrangement is (N–3)(N–2)(N–1)N. If N=26 this corresponds to WXYZ.

5. To carry this plan out, an array A(I) is used to hold the numbers.

6. The formatting of the output is left to the reader.

Remarks

1. This solution is written for a Basic which supports multiple line functions.

```
Second Sample Solution

10 DIM A$(26),B$(26)
20 B$="ABCDEFGHIJKLMNOPQRSTUVWXYZ"
30 A$=""
40 INPUT "ENTER POPULATION SIZE,
   GROUP SIZE  N,M ",N,M
50 X=FNF(0,0)
60 PRINT : PRINT "C(",N,",",M,")
   = ",C
70 END
80 DEF FNF(K,I)
90     L=LEN(A$)
100       IF L< M THEN 120
110 C=C+1 : PRINT A$ : RETURN 0
120 IF N-M < K-L THEN RETURN 0`
130    FOR I=K+1 TO N
140       A$=A$+B$(I,I)
150       X=FNF(I,0)
160       IF LEN(A$)=1 THEN A$=""
170       IF LEN(A$)>1 THEN A$=A$(1,
             LEN(A$)-1)
180    NEXT I
190    RETURN 0
200 FNEND
```

2. The procedure begins with the empty string A$="" and builds it up to A$="ABCD" (if M=4). Once the LEN(A$)=M, the string A$ is printed out.

3. Next, drop back to A$="ABC" and build it up again starting with one letter to the right of the last one used.

4. Statement 150 X=FNF(I,O) is embedded in the definition of the function FNF. This means that FNF is defined in terms of itself, ie., recursively.

5. Recursively defined functions can be very useful as this example shows. However it is not necessary to use recursion to solve the problem as illustrated by the first solution.

6. Again, the printout has not been formatted.

A Related Problem

A simpler problem for investigation would be:

Count the number of distinct groups of M people that can be formed from a population of size N.

Remarks

1. This problem is much easier since the groups are not required to be listed.

2. There is a natural way to view this problem which uses the notion of subgoals. For example, suppose you are asked to count the number of groups of size 3 that can be formed from 5 people. Suppose you could solve the problem if the group size was one less (4). Let C(4,2) be the number of groups of size 2 that can be chosen from 4 people, and let C(4,3) be the number of groups of size 3 that can be formed from 4 people. Now if one more person, Sam, is added to the group, Sam can join all the 2 member groups to make 3 member groups. These are all the ways in which Sam can be included in a three member group. The remaining 3 member groups (C(4,3)) are those that do not contain Sam. Thus the

---

The personal computer is designed for interaction, and hence encourages students to experiment, revise, extend, simplify and rearrange.

---

total number of 3 member groups from 5 people is given recursively by:

$$C(5,3) = C(4,2) + C(4,3)$$

3. This argument can be generalized to:

$$C(N,M) = C(N-1,M-1) + C(N-1,M).$$

4. This relationship shows how to express the problem in terms of two simpler problems. It is called a recursion relationship. It would be a mistake to have students simply program this relationship without understanding how it related to the proposed problem. Discussions, like the one above, plant ideas and procedures which will bear fruit in completely different situations. This specific relationship is of little importance but the idea of looking for one is of great importance.

5. One sample solution that uses this idea is:

```
10 INPUT "POPULATION SIZE, GROUP
   SIZE  N,M = ",N,M
20 DIM C(N,N)
30 C(0,0)=1
40 FOR I = 1 TO N
50     FOR J = 1 TO I
60        C(I,J) = C(I-1,J-1) + C(I-1,J)
70     NEXT J
80 NEXT I
90 PRINT "C(",N,",",M,") = ",C(N,M)
100 END
```

6. Another sample solution that uses a function recursively is given by:

```
10 INPUT "POPULATION SIZE,GROUP SIZE
   N,M = ",N,M
20 PRINT "C(",N,",",M,") = ",FNF(N,M)
30 END
40 DEF FNF(N,M)
50    IF M=0 THEN RETURN 1
60    IF M > N THEN RETURN 0
70    Y=FNF(N-1,M) + FNF(N-1,M-1)
80    RETURN Y
90 FNEND
```

7. Try running this second solution for N=14 and M=7. You will discover a tremendous difference in time of execution of these two solutions. Ask your advanced students to explain why. The second solution is a classic example of the poor use of recursion. In the worst case the time of execution is proportional to 2^N, while in the first solution the time of execution is proportional to N^2.

8. As a final experiment, let the students keep timed records of individual runs to 'feel' the difference between 2^N and N^2.

Conclusion

Problem-solving skills cannot be acquired just by reading problems and their solutions. Sandwiched in the middle must be discussion, trial and error, modification, generalization and more discussion. These are the activities that strengthen one's ability to solve problems because they are independent of the particular problem or its setting and can be used again in completely different problem situations.

The actual solution will never be as important as the process of arriving at it. Consequently, you should not be in a hurry to dispose of problems before they have been completely used up. Whenever you find some interesting ways to further develop these or related problems, let me hear from you. I believe we need to establish better lines of communication between all of us who want to understand and teach the problem-solving process. □

Bibliography

1) Polya, G., *How To Solve It*, Princeton University Press, 1945.
2) *An Agenda For Action: Recommendations For School Mathematics of the 1980's*, NCTM Inc., Reston, Virginia 1980.
3) Whimby, A., Lockhead, J., *Problem Solving and Comprehension*, The Franklin Institute Press, 1980.

"...It's trying to tell us it wants high tech circuitry..."

## Part II

Donald T. Piele

> *"Perhaps the most significant discovery generated by the advent of computers will turn out to be that algorithms, as objects of study, are extraordinarily rich in interesting properties; and furthermore that an algorithmic point of view is a useful way to organize knowledge in general."*
>
> *Donald Knuth, 1974*

Recently, I had the opportunity to conduct two summer programming classes for young students. One group was a class of 3rd-6th graders and the other a group of 7th-9th graders (Junior High). The classes ran for two hours each day for two weeks and included access to an Apple II computer and a Hewlett-Packard 2000 minicomputer with 10 terminals. A few of the students had previous experience with Basic programming but most were new to the subject.

Finding appropriate published classroom materials was difficult. Most textbooks on the Basic language deal primarily with the *content* of the language, but my major objective was to emphasize the *process* by which the language is used to express algorithms that solve problems. In this context the Basic language becomes a vehicle for the development of problem-solving skills rather than an object of study in its own right. To carry out this objective, I had to develop my own classroom activities.

Classroom Procedures

I began on the first day as follows.

1. Each student was given a manila folder to hold all of the classroom notes and computer printouts. It was returned each day to the classroom file. The objective was to establish the habit of keeping good records.

2. The first half hour of each day was devoted to the introduction of new Basic commands and statements that would be necessary to solve the daily problem. The students took notes from the blackboard. It is important to require that students become responsible for recording the information they will need for reference later on.

3. The next hour was spent at the terminals where the students worked in pairs. I wanted to encourage the sharing of ideas as much as possible.

4. A completed assignment consisted of a listing and run of the program including the student's name, and lesson number.

5. The last half-hour was used for a classroom demonstration of individual solutions or for class participation in a computer word or strategy game.

This format created a busy environment in which I functioned as an advisor and trouble shooter and they functioned as teams of problem solvers. In the process of working on the assignment, each team made observations, organized information, looked for patterns, made conjectures and tried them out, and used symbols to express their ideas in algorithmic form. These are precisely the skills I wanted to develop.

The student solutions tended to be very similar in the beginning. When the problems became more challenging later on, however, the programs began to represent a greater variety of strategies.

Programming Activities

The following programming activities consist of problems used in two courses described above. They include graphics problems on the Apple II for the beginning students and an investigation of algorithms for generating various sequences of numbers in a geometric design for intermediate and advanced students.

Lesson #2 (Beginning Students) Apple Graphics

In the first lesson (last month), I began with a simple program, (listed below), that used the GR, COLOR, PLOT A,B and END commands. This program illustrates how to color any position on the 40x40 low-resolution graphics screen.

When I introduced this program I made up copies of a 40x40 array with labels across the top and side, as above, and passed them out to the class. This makes it easier for students to write graphics programs at their desk. To review the coordinate system in low-resolution graphics, I used the following program and asked the class to create a small design by supplying a series of values for the COLOR and the position A,B.

```
10 GR
20 INPUT "COLOR = ",C
30 INPUT "PLOT A,B = ";A,B
40 COLOR=C
50 PLOT A,B
60 GOTO 20
70 END
```

After the students completely understood the effect of PLOT A,B, I introduced the following problem.

Donald Piele, University of Wisconsin-Parkside, Kenosha, WI 53141.

Problem #2 (Beginning Student with Apple II)

Write a program that will color the positions 3,3 and 12,14 orange and will draw the shortest green path between them. (A path is a line of color with no breaks).

Remarks

1. For beginning students, the program will simply be a series of PLOT X,Y statements that connect the two points.

2. The length of the path is equal to the number of positions plotted.

3. There is more than one "shortest" path in this problem.

4. Students who have used FOR-NEXT loops may use them to write a much shorter program.

5. For intermediate students you can upgrade the problem to: Write a program that will draw a shortest path between any two points A,B and C,D.

Print Graphics

For a computer system that has no special graphics mode, a limited form of graphics can be done with print statements. The idea hers is to use the position of the line number in the program to determine the row position and to use the position of a character in the PRINT statement to determine the column position. Beginning students are learning a lot of new procedures, so I like to use simple graphics problems that use only one statement — PRINT. For example, consider the following program that prints a block M.

```
 10 PRINT "MMMM      MMMM"
 20 PRINT "MMMMM    MMMMM"
 30 PRINT "MMMMMM  MMMMMM"
 40 PRINT "MMM MMM  MMM MMM"
 50 PRINT "MMM MMMMM  MMM"
 60 PRINT "MMM  MMMM   MMM"
 70 PRINT "MMM   MM    MMM"
 80 PRINT "MMM        MMM"
 90 PRINT "MMM        MMM"
100 END
```

There are a number of ways to pose problems that use simple line by line print graphics. For example, consider:

Problem #2 (Beginning Students)

Write a program using only print statements that will print the next term in the sequence of triangular designs:

```
  1,      3 3,      6 6 6     A A A A   ......
          3         6 6       A A A
                    6         A A
                              A
```

For numbers>9 use the alphabetic code A=10, B=11, ... Z=35.

This type of problem is one step beyond the simple printing of a design since the pattern must first be deduced. What is the next term in the sequence 1,3,6,10, ? . What is its letter equivalent? How do you make the design with print statement? These are mini-problems that must be answered in the process of solving the original problem.

Remarks

1. The next number is of course 15 which corresponds to F.

2. A typical solution is

```
10 PRINT "   F F F F F"
20 PRINT "    F F F F"
30 PRINT "     F F F"
40 PRINT "      F F"
50 PRINT "       F"
60 END
```

This problem becomes much more interesting when it is generalized for intermediate students.

Intermediate Students

Students who know how to use the TAB( ) statement and are comfortable with FOR-NEXT loops should be invited to solve

Problem #2 (Intermediate Students)

Write a program that will generate any term in the geometrical triangular sequence:

```
  1,      3 3,      6 6 6,      A A A A  ....
          3         6 6         A A A
                    6           A A
                                A
```

In going from the very concrete to the general we have made a quantum leap in the level of difficulty. But in the process, we have found a problem that requires the careful use of subgoals. The subgoals are:

1. Write an algorithm that will generate the Kth term of the triangular sequence.

2. Pass the value of this term to a procedure that will print the geometric design.

Subgoals

1. The Kth term of the triangular sequence,

```
INDEX    1    2    3    4    5.......K
      ---*----*----*----*----*....*----*
TERM     1    3    6    10   15 ......X
```

can be generated by observing that the difference between successive terms increases by 1. An algorithm that generates the value X of the Kth term of the triangular sequence is

```
30 INPUT " INDEX = ";K
40 X=0
50 FOR I = 1 TO K
60    X = X + I
70 NEXT I
```

2. The resulting value of X must now be transformed into a digit or letter from the string A$=123456789ABCDEFGHIJKLMNOPQRSTUVWXYZ". In North Star Basic and Xth number in this string is denoted by A$(X,X). In Microsoft Basic it is denoted by MID$(A$,X,1).

3. Finally, a plan of attack is needed to create the actual design.

Plan of Attack

"Begin printing K symbols in the first row with a space between each symbol. Skip down one line, tab over one position and print one less symbol than in the previous line. Continue until all K rows have been printed."

A basic program that implements this plan is the following:

```
Sample Solution:
  5 REM PROBLEM #2 (Intermediate Students) Sample Solution
 10 DIM A$(35)
 20 A$="123456789ABCDEFGHIJKLMNOPQRSTUVWXYZ"
 30 INPUT " INDEX = ";K
 35 REM *** GENERATE  K TH TERM ***
 40 X=0
 50 FOR I = 1 TO K
 60    X = X + I
 70 NEXT I
 75 REM *** GENERATE THE DESIGN ***
 80 FOR I = 1 TO K
 90    TAB(I),
100       FOR J = 1 TO K+1-I
110          PRINT A$(X,X);" ",
120       NEXT J
130    PRINT
140 NEXT I
150 END
```

Remarks

1. Line 110 will need to be replaced with MID$(A$,X,1) in Microsoft Basic.

2. As it stands now, when you try to print the 8th term (36) or higher you will get an out of bounds error.

3. One way to keep things in bounds for large values of X is to reduce X by subtracting out all multiples of 35, i.e., (X MOD 35). The idea is equivalent to starting over at 1 when you reach 36, much like a clock that starts again at 1 after passing 12.

4. When students discover that they cannot go beyond the 7th term, it is time to suggest that they look for a way to wrap the numbers around a 36 hour clock. One way to do this is to

add the lines

```
77 X = X - 35*INT(X/35)
78 IF X = 0 THEN X = 35
```

5. This additional requirement can be a bit sticky for those who are not familiar with clock arithmetic. There is a good chance that a number of students will need to do some experimenting on this problem alone. This could be viewed as an additional subgoal.

Advanced Students

For the advanced student the problem takes on added dimensions. They are given a different sequence of numbers and asked to generate the geometrical design of any term with the proper symbol, using a value which had been reduced modulo 35.

Problem #2 (Advanced Students)

Write a program that will represent any term in the sequence

```
INDEX    1     2     3     4     5
       ----*-----*-----*-----*-----
TERM     1     5    12    22    35 ....
```

graphically. Use symbols from the string

$$A\$="123456789ABC...Z"$$

to construct the figure and reduce all terms mod 35.

The added challenge to this problem is to find the geometrical design for this sequence and to write an algorithm to construct it. The difference between successive terms is different in this problem and increases by 3 instead of 1. Thus the next term is 35 + 16 or 51.

One way to view this sequence geometrically is

```
1 ,    5 5 ,    C C C ,     M M M M,
       5 5      C C C       M M M M
       5        C C C       M M M M
                  C C         M M M
                  C             M M
                                  M
```

This suggests another way to view the sequence of numbers: each design has a square top and a triangular bottom.

```
C C C
C C C      = 3 x 3, (The third Square number.)
C C C
- - -
 C C       = 3,      (The second Triangular number.)
  C
```

Thus, this Pentagonal sequence can be viewed as the sum of a Square sequence 1,4,9,16 . . . and a Triangular sequence 0,1,3,6 . . . There are two natural algorithms to generate Pentagonal numbers.

```
30 INPUT " INDEX = "; K        30 INPUT " INDEX = ";K
40 X=1                         40 X=0
50 D=1                         50 FOR I=1 TO K-1
60 FOR I =1 TO K-1             60    X=X+I
70    D = D + 3                70 NEXT I
80    X = X + D                80 X = X + K*K
90 NEXT I
```

This leads to the following sample solution:

```
10 REM PROBLEM #2 (ADVANCED STUDENTS - PENTAGONAL )
20 DIM A$(35)
30 A$="123456789ABCDEFGHIJKLMNOPQRSTUVWXYZ"
40 INPUT "INDEX = ";K
50 REM *** GENERATE THE Kth TERM ***
60 X=0
70 FOR I = 1 TO K-1
80    X=X+I
90 NEXT I
100 X = X + K*K
110 REM **** REDUCE THE TERM MOD 35 ****
120 X = X - 35*INT( X/35)
130 IF X = 0 THEN X = 35
140 REM **** GENERATE THE SQUARE TOP ****
150 FOR I=1 TO K
160    FOR J=1 TO K
170       PRINT A$(X,X);" ";
180    NEXT J
190    PRINT
200 NEXT I
210 REM **** GENERATE THE TRIANGULAR BOTTOM ***
220 FOR I=1 TO K-1
230    PRINT TAB(I);
240       FOR J=1 TO K-I
250          PRINT A$(X,X);" ";
260       NEXT J
270    PRINT
280 NEXT I
290 END
```

Remark

1. For Microsoft Basic again substitute MID$(A$,X,1) for A$(X,X).

There are many interesting sequences that can be associated with geometric shapes. Students can be asked to discover some of their own and to write the necessary program to display them. Here is one more example:

Problem #2 (Advanced Students — Hexagonal Numbers)

Write a program that will display any term in the sequence 1,6,15,28 . . . graphically using the standard technique for picking the symbol from the string A$.

```
Sample Solution:

The design is
                                      F
          6                F  F
1 ,       6  6             F  F  F  ....
          6  6 ,           F  F  F
          6                  F  F
                              F
```

The easiest way to view this sequence is by observing that it is nothing more than a Square sequence added to two Triangular sequences.

```
   F
  F F      }  Triangular part
  - - -
  F F F
  F F F    }  Square part
  F F F
  - - -
   F F     }  Triangular part
    F
```

Thus the X value of the Kth term is generated by

```
50 REM *** GENERATE THE Kth TERM
60 X=0
70 FOR I=1 TO K-1
80    X=X+I
90 NEXT I
100 X=K*K + 2*X
```

The remaining part of the program is nothing more than drawing the top triangle, the middle square, and finally the bottom triangle.

Strategy Games

Although there is a proper time and place for all types of games, the ones that I have found to be the most useful in the classroom are those that present a problem-solving challenge — better known as strategy games. They work well for me when used in moderation. You might say they have a dessert-like quality — best used at the end of a lesson.

A long time favorite of mine is a simple Nim type game played between two players, called Matches. It can be played with a pile of matches, coins, or even marks on the blackboard. The rules are very simple to understand. Each player takes turns removing 1, 2 or 3 matches from the pile until the pile is reduced to the last match. Whoever must take the last match loses the game. Every player must take something when it is his/her turn and the challenger may decide between playing first or second.

I introduce this game every chance I get to work with a group of young students — who find it fascinating until they figure out the winning strategy. By beginning with small numbers and building up one number at a time, they eventually discover the strategy themselves. Next, they realize that they can always win with any size pile if they have the option of going first or second. Before the computer was available, I would let the students play at the blackboard where the current champion would give the challenger the option of going first or second. While this usually worked well there was an occasional problem with egos.

This was the first game that I put on the Apple II when it became available three years ago. I have used it in small doses in a variety of classroom settings and I have found it to be my best dessert. It is simple enough that students immediately understand the rules, yet hard enough to keep them coming back for more. To master the game the student must make a leap from the concrete to the general by observing the pattern of losing positions. A further advantage is that the game is over quickly.

A version of this game exists in *101 Basic Computer Games* (David Ahl 1973). Here the number of options are restricted and the status of the pile is printed out after each move on paper. But with the addition of color graphics on the Apple II and the expansion of the program to include a choice for the number of matches (up to 26) and the choice of moving first or second, the game becomes much more useful as an exercise in problem-solving. It is a good example of a strategy game that the whole class can participate in at the end of the day. A typical sixth grade class will probably take a couple of weeks to master it.

A listing of 26 MATCHES is given below written in Applesoft Basic. It can be entered in Integer Basic — the original version — by deleting the letters INT in lines 430, and 470, and changing line 450 to C = RND(3) + 1. Also, all use of the command HOME should be changed to CALL –936. Finally, change the HTAB 5 in line 180 to TAB 5.   □

```
]LIST
100   REM    ***************************
110   REM    ** 2 6  M A T C H E S  ***
120   REM
130   REM        BY D.T. PIELE
140   REM
150   REM   AN APPLE REVISION OF 23 MTCH
160   REM   101 BASIC COMPUTER GAMES
170   REM    ***************************
180   TEXT : HOME : VTAB 10: HTAB 5
190   PRINT "THIS IS THE GAME OF MATCHES."
200   GOSUB 590: VTAB 12
210   PRINT "IT IS A GAME OF SKILL AND I'M GOOD."
220   GOSUB 590: VTAB 14
230   INPUT "WOULD YOU LIKE INSTRUCTIONS? (Y/N) ";A$
240   IF A$ = "Y" THEN  GOSUB 610
250   PRINT : PRINT "HOW MANY MATCHES DO YOU WANT TO BEGIN"
260   PRINT : INPUT "WITH. PICK A NUMBER UP TO 26. ";M
270   IF M < 1 OR M > 26 THEN 260
280   GR :L = 0:N = M:W = M: IF W > 13 THEN W = 13
290   REM  ***** DRAW MATCHES ******
300   FOR I = 1 TO W: COLOR= 15: VLIN 5,15 AT 3 * I: COLOR= 9: PLOT 3 * I,4
      : NEXT I
310   IF N < 14 THEN 330
320   FOR I = 1 TO N - 13: COLOR= 15: VLIN 20,30 AT 3 * I: COLOR= 9: PLOT 3
      * I,19: NEXT I
330   INPUT "DO YOU WANT TO MOVE FIRST? (Y/N) ";A$
340   IF A$ = "N" THEN 410
350   REM  **** THE HUMAN MOVES ******
360   HOME
370   PRINT "THERE ARE NOW ";M;" MATCHE(S)."
380   PRINT : INPUT "HOW MANY DO YOU WANT TO TAKE?";H
390   IF H > 3 OR H < 1 OR H > M THEN  PRINT "DON'T CHEAT NOW. TRY AGAIN.":
      GOTO 370
400   X = L + H: GOSUB 700:L = X:M = M - H: IF M = 0 THEN 530
410   REM  **** THE COMPUTER MOVES ****
420   IF M = 1 THEN 580
430   R = M - 4 *  INT (M / 4)
440   IF R < > 1 THEN 470
450   C =  INT (3 *  RND (1)) + 1
460   GOTO 480
470   C = (R + 3) - 4 *  INT ((R + 3) / 4)
480   X = L + C
490   HOME : PRINT "MY TURN, I'M THINKING.": GOSUB 590
500   GOSUB 700:L = X
510   M = M - C: IF M = 0 THEN 580
520   HOME : PRINT "I TOOK ";C;" MATCHE(S)": GOTO 370
530   REM  *** SOMEBODY WON ***
540   HOME : PRINT "I WON!!!!  BETTER LUCK NEXT TIME."
550   PRINT : INPUT "DO YOU WANT TO TRY AGAIN? (Y/N) ";A$
560   IF A$ = "N" THEN  PRINT "THANKS FOR THE GAME ": END
570   TEXT : HOME : VTAB 10: GOTO 250
580   HOME : PRINT "YOU WON!!! NICE GOING.": GOTO 550
590   FOR I = 1 TO 2000: NEXT I: RETURN
600   FOR K = 1 TO 15: NEXT K: RETURN
610   REM  **** INSTRUCTIONS ****
620   HOME : PRINT "WE BEGIN THE GAME WITH A ROW OF MATCHES."
630   GOSUB 590: PRINT
640   PRINT "WE THEN TAKE TURNS REMOVING 1,2 OR 3 ": PRINT : PRINT "MATCHES
       UNTIL THEY ARE ALL GONE."
650   GOSUB 590: PRINT
660   PRINT "WHOEVER TAKES THE LAST MATCH LOSES!!!": GOSUB 590: PRINT
670   PRINT "YOU MAY MOVE FIRST OR SECOND.": GOSUB 590: PRINT : PRINT
680   PRINT "THE BEST THINKER WILL WIN!!!": GOSUB 590: PRINT
690   RETURN
700   REM  **** REMOVING MATCHES ****
710   COLOR= 0: IF X > 13 THEN 760
720   FOR I = L TO X: FOR J = 1 TO 12
730   PLOT 3 * I,3 + J: GOSUB 600
740   NEXT J: NEXT I
750   RETURN
760   IF L > 13 THEN 790
770   FOR I = L TO 13: FOR J = 1 TO 12: PLOT 3 * I,3 + J: GOSUB 600: NEXT J
      : NEXT I
780   IF L < 13 THEN L = 13
790   FOR I = L - 12 TO X - 13: FOR J = 1 TO 12: PLOT 3 * I,18 + J: GOSUB 6
      00: NEXT J: NEXT I
800   RETURN
```


References

1) Ahl, David H., *Basic Computer Games,* p. 226, Creative Computing Press, Morristown, NJ.

2) Knuth, D.E. "Computer Science and its Relation to Mathematics", *American Mathematical Monthly,* Vol. 81, No. 4, April 1974.

## Part III

How to Solve It — With the Computer

Donald T. Piele

> *"Leibniz saw in his binary arithmetic the image of creation . . . He imagined that unity (1) represented God, and zero (0) the void; that the Supreme Being drew all beings from the void, just as 1 and 0 express all numbers in his system of numeration."*
>
> *Tobias Dantzig, 1939*

The binary number system lies at the heart of all computer operations. In this system all numbers can be expressed by a finite set of 0's and 1's which can be easily represented by a low and high voltage. Other systems, easier for humans to handle, are the decimal and hexadecimal. These systems use more symbols for each digit and consequently the same number can be expressed in a shorter length. For example, the number 111 (binary) is equivalent to 15 (decimal) and F (hexadecimal).

All three systems are used in connection with computing. Thus to be computer literate, one should understand the interrelationship of these three number systems. This months selection of problems for intermediate and advanced students will explore number systems and related problems. For the beginning student I will continue last month's exploration of Apple graphics and introduce FOR-NEXT loops.

Lesson #3 (Beginning Students)
Apple Graphics

In the previous two lessons, I introduced the graphics commands GR, COLOR, PLOT A,B and END. I showed how the program

```
10 GR              40 COLOR=C
20 INPUT "COLOR=",C    50 PLOT X,Y
30 INPUT " X,Y =",X,Y  60 END
```

will place a small colored square at the position X,Y on the 40x40 low resolution graphics screen. Thus, any one of the 1600 positions on the screen may be colored with the PLOT command; but will it take 1600 individually typed PLOT statements to cover the screen a specific color? At the rate beginning students type, it would take two weeks to write such a program. A typical solution might begin as:

```
20 COLOR=9
30 PLOT 0,0 : PLOT 1,0 : PLOT 2,0
40 PLOT 3,0 : PLOT 4,0 : PLOT 5,0
   . . . . . . . .

5360 PLOT 39,39
5370 END
```

and end after 537 lines. Clearly, the time is ripe to introduce a statement which will automate this process.

FOR-NEXT Loops

I prefer to introduce a new statement with a problem. The purpose of this problem is twofold-to introduce the new command FOR-NEXT and to exercise the problem solving process.

Donald Piele, Associate Professor of Mathematics, University of Wisconsin-Parkside, Kenosha, WI 53141.

Problem #3 (Beginning Students)
Write a small program (less than 10 statements) that will fill the screen with a single color.

Discussion:

There are two similar ways to view this problem. One strategy is to first color the positions in a given row left to right, and then to repeat the procedure for each row from top to bottom. The other strategy is to begin by coloring a column from top to bottom and then to repeat the procedure for each column from left to right. Both strategies involve the use of subgoals. Using the first strategy, the subgoal is to create a procedure for coloring a row. This can be done with a FOR-NEXT loop as follows.

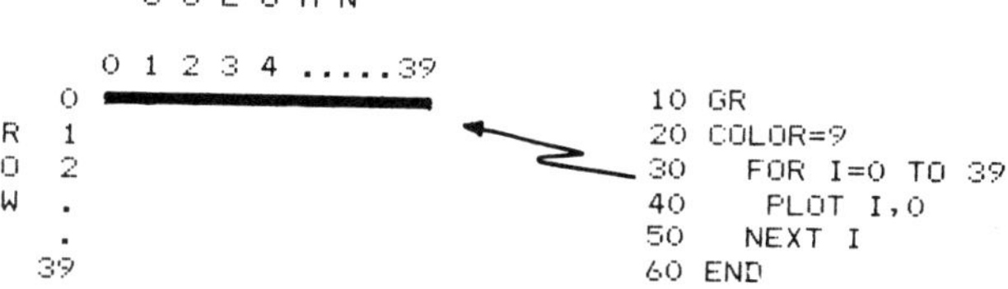

I usually key in this program, run it, and begin asking questions.
1. List all the points that are plotted. (0,0 1,0 ....38,0 39,0)
2. How can I change the program to color the second row? (40 PLOT I,1)
3. How can I change the program to color the last row? (40 PLOT I,39)
4. List the diagonal positions from the upper left corner to the bottom right corner.
(0,0 1,1 2,2 ....39,39)
5. How can I change line 40 to draw the diagonal for me? (40 PLOT I,I)
6. List the positions in the first column. (0,0 0,1 ...0,39)
7. How can I change the program to color the first column? (40 PLOT 0,I)
8. How can I change line 40 to color the last column? (40 PLOT 39,I)

When I began teaching Basic to third and fourth graders, I wondered if the use of variables, such as (I) in the above program, would be too abstract to be easily understood by young minds. My fears were quickly laid to rest as my students began to use variables with ease almost immediately. In fact, experiences with older students and adults have convinced me that the younger ones pick up the use of variables faster. I no longer keep any secrets from the younger set.

There are two commands specific to the Apple II that make drawing horizontal and vertical lines even easier. These are HLIN and VLIN. To color the first row orange simply write:

```
10 GR
20 COLOR=9
30 HLIN 0,39 AT 0
40 END
```

Similar questions and modifications can be made to this program.

1. How can I change the program to color the last row?
(30 HLIN 0,39 AT 39)

2. How can I change the program to color the first column?
(30 VLIN 0,39 AT 0)

3. How can I change the program to color the last column?
(30 VLIN 0,39 AT 39)

HLIN and VLIN can be used to construct horizontal and vertical lines of length (1-40) anywhere on the screen. For example, to draw a line in row 3 beginning in column 5 and ending in column 12 write

30 HLIN 5,12 AT 3.

The following two programs illustrate two ways of constructing this line.

```
10 GR                10 GR
20 COLOR=9           20 COLOR=9
30 FOR I=5 TO 12     30 HLIN 5,12 AT 3
40 PLOT I,3          40 END
50 NEXT I
60 END
```

```
                  C O L U M N

        0 1 2 3 4 5 6 7 8 9 10 11 12 .....39
     0
  R  1
  O  2
  W  3
     4
     .
     .
    39
```

What changes must be made to the above two programs to produce a vertical line in column 3 beginning at row 5 and ending at row 12?

```
[ 40 PLOT 3,I       30 VLIN 5,12 AT 3 ]
```

After giving the students what I consider to be enough experience with constructing lines, which are subgoals for problem #3, I prefer to say, "no more" and let the students go to work on the problem. Now they are the ones who will be asking questions — as it should be. I am available to answer their questions about all commands and statements, but it is up to them to experiment putting them together to solve the problem. Here are two ways that it could be done.

```
10 GR                10 GR
20 COLOR=9           20 COLOR=9
30 FOR I=0 TO 39     30 FOR J=0 TO 39
40   HLIN 0,39 AT I  40   FOR I=0 TO 9
50 NEXT I            50     PLOT I,J
60 END               60   NEXT I
                     70 NEXT J
                     80 END
```

These two programs use the strategy of covering the screen one row at a time. The same programs can be used to cover the screen one column at a time with the following changes:

```
[ 40 VLIN 0,39 AT I       50 PLOT J,I ]
```

Intermediate Students

The idea of representing natural numbers in different bases is fundamental in computer programming. The binary, decimal, and hexadecimal number system are introduced in all elementary assembly language programming books and in many Basic programming books. At the same time, the study of bases has diminished in mathematics textbooks along with other "new math" concepts. Lacking any immediate application and given the confusion it caused parents, the study of bases has become unpopular.

But the idea of bases is fundamental in computer programming and can be introduced to young students with a few matchboxes.

Suppose each box has the capacity to hold B matches. B is called the base for the number system and is usually expressed as a decimal number. To express the numbers in base B in sequential order, begin by adding a match one at a time to box 1. As soon as any match box is filled (contains B matches) empty it and add one match to the next higher box on its left. To represent the number of matches in each box use the following symbols:

```
Number of
  matches =   0 1 2 3 4 5 6 7 8 9 10 11 12 ....... 36

Single symbol =  0 1 2 3 4 5 6 7 8 9  A  B  C       Z
```

Each number is expressed in base B by writing the sequence of symbols associated with the number of matches in each box. For example, if the base $B = 3$, then the natural numbers would begin as 0001, 0002, and change to 0010 as the first box filled up with 3 matches, was emptied, and one match was deposited in the next higher box (#2).

It is an instructive programming exercise to implement this procedure on the computer. Arrays come in handy for storing the number of matches in each box:

B (I)= # of matches in Box I,

and string arrays are useful for holding the symbols;

```
S$="0123456789ABCDEFGHIJKLMNOPQRSTUVWXYZ".
```

(I have limited the size of the base to a maximum of 36 for practical reasons.)

Problem #3 (Intermediate Students)
Write a program that displays the natural numbers in base B in sequential order up to N digits.

Plan of Attack

Using the match box simulation, begin by depositing one match in box 1;

100 B(1)=B(1)+1.

Next check the number of matches in box 1 and continuing adding matches to box 1 if it is not filled.

IF B(1) <B THEN (print number and GOTO 100)

As soon as the first box fills up, empty it and add one match to the next higher box (#2).

B(1)=0
B(2)=B(2)+1

Continue adding matches to box 1.

IF B(2) < B THEN (print number and GOTO 100)

Otherwise, empty the matches in box 2 and add one to box 3.

B(2)=0
B(3)=B(3)+1

This same procedure is continued until a match finally reaches box N+1.

Here is a sample solution that implements this procedure.

```
      First Sample Solution

10 DIM S$(36)
20 S$="0123456789ABCDEFGHIJKLMNOPQRSTUVWXYZ"
30 INPUT "BASE =",B
40 INPUT "N PLACES = ",N
50    REM **** GENERATE THE SEQUENCE OF DIGIT****
60 B(1)=B(1)+1
70 FOR I=1 TO N
80    IF B(I)<B THEN EXIT 130
90      B(I)=0
100      B(I+1)=B(I+1) + 1
110 NEXT I
120 IF B(N+1)>0 THEN END
130    REM **** PRINT OUT ROUTINE ****
140 FOR I=N TO 1 STEP -1
150    PRINT S$( B(I)+1 , B(I)+1 ),
160 NEXT I
170    PRINT
180      GOTO 50
190 END
```

```
 |_|    |_|    |_|    |_|
Box 4  Box 3  Box 2  Box 1
```

Remarks

1. For Microsoft Basic change S$(B(I)+1,B(I)+1), in line 150 to MID$(S$,B(I)+1,1);

2. It is advisble to have the students add documentation at the beginning of their program to explain what the program is doing.

For example, I require the following:

```
1 REM ************* PROBLEM #3 **********
2 REM                BY DON PIELE
3 REM            AUGUST 28, 1980
6 PRINT "THIS PROGRAM WILL GENERATE AND PRINT THE"
7 PRINT "NATURAL NUMBERS IN BASE B UP TO N PLACES."
```

Another way to attack problem #3 is to use a coversion algorithm from the base 10 to the desired base B. To convert the number K into a base B number, first divide by B and save the quotient (INT (K/B) and the remainder (K − B*INT(K/B)). The remainder represents the value of the first "digit" (B(1)) and the quotient becomes the new number K. The process is repeated until K=0. For example, to convert 53 into base 5,

53/5= 10 remainder of 3 (=B(1))
10/5= 2 remainder of 0 (=B(2))
 2/5= 0 remainder of 2 (=B(3))
Thus 53 (base 10)= 203 (base 5).

This procedure can be implemented by changing lines 60-120 in the first sample solution and adding line 175.

```
Program Modification for Second Solution
.........................
 60 K=C
 70 FOR I=1 TO N
 80    B(I)=K-B*INT(K/B)
 90      K =INT(K/B)
100 NEXT I
110 REM
120 IF K>0 THEN END
.........................
175 C=C+1
```

Related Ideas

An unusual method for multiplying two numbers, said to be in common use in Russian villages around the turn of the century, is known today as the Russian Peasant Method. The only skills one needs to multiply with this method is to be able to add and divide by two. A description of the procedure is given below as it appeared in 1912 in *The Mathematics Teacher.*

"Having given the positive integers A and B, to multiply A by B write down A x B; under A write the exact or lower quotient obtained by dividing by 2 (INT (A/2)); under this quotient write the exact or lower quotient obtained by dividing by 2, and so on until you obtain the quotient 1. Under B write its double, under this double its double, and so on, until you have as many numbers in the second column as in the first. Next add the numbers in the second column which correspond to odd numbers in the first column. The result is the product of A x B."

Below is a specific example using 21 x 13 which illustrates the technique.

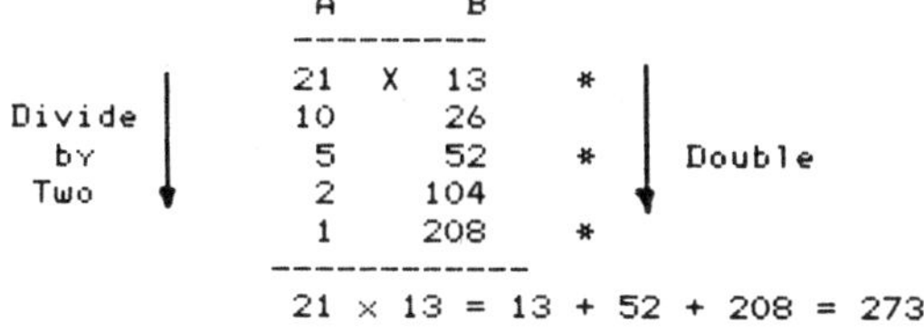

The product (21 x 13)9 is equal to the sum of all the values in column B (indicated with a *) which correspond to odd values in column A.

Russian Peasant Problem (Intermediate Students)

Write a program that uses the Russian Peasant Method to multiply two positive integers. Explain why the method works.

```
Sample Solution (Russian Peasant Problem)
  1 REM **** RUSSIAN PEASANT METHOD OF MULT ****
 10 S=0
 20 INPUT " A , B = ",A,B
 30 X=A
 40 Y=B
 50 IF X/2 <> INT(X/2) THEN S=S+Y
 60 X=INT(X/2)
 70 Y=2*Y
 80 IF X >= 1 THEN 50
 90 PRINT  A," x",B," =",S
100 END
```

Note

A justification for the Russian Peasant Method of multiplication can be given by:

(1) expressing 4 in a base 2;
 21 (base 10) = 10101 (base 2);
(2) using the appropriate powers of 2 corresponding to 10101 to write:
 $21 = 2^4 + 2^2 + 1.$

Thus, 21 x 13 = (16 + 4 + 1) x 13 = 208 + 52 + 13 = 273.

Advanced Students

The Russian Peasant Method can be used for numbers expressed in other bases besides 10. It can also be implemented for multiplying large positive integers when the digits are kept in an array. For example, if the product A x Z exceeds 8 digits (or higher depending on the Basic used), it is nesessary to store the numbers in arrays and perform array arithmetic. This suggests an extension of the previous problem to the following.

Problem #3 (Advanced Students)

Write a program that uses the Russian Peasant Method of multiplication to multiply numbers, up to 20 digits in length, in any base B.

Remarks

1. This problem reguires an extensive use of subgoals which can be implemented with subroutines or by defining functions.

2. The first task is to write a procedure which will transform any number into an array where each element of the array is written in base 10. Thus if A=123456789ABCDEF (base 16), then the corresponding array A(I) is constructed as follows,
 A(1)=16, A(2)=15, A(3)=14, ... A(16)=1.

3. A subroutine must be written that will test whether A is even or odd with respect to the base B.

4. A subroutine must be written to double the number Z (in the array with respect to the base B.

5. A subroutine must be written to divide A (in array form) by 2 and test if A is less than 1.

6. A subroutine must be written to print out the sum of all Z arrays corresponding to odd A arrays consistent with the Russian Peasant Method.

7. Finally, it is advisable to make A the smallest number since successive divisions by 2 will reduce A to 1 more quickly. Thus, a procedure should be written to check the lengths of A and Z and to make A the smallest number if necessary.

Listed below is a sample solution to this problem. I have intentionally written this program with subroutines instead of multiple-lined functions because the latter are not commonly available on the small personal computer systems. Also, for the sake of clarity, I have not attempted to combine routines that share common structures to save a few lines of programming. I have restricted the base B to < =10, but it could be expanded to 36 by changing the way the numbers are read into arrays and the way the product is printed out.

```
10 PRINT "RUSSIAN PEASANT METHOD FOR MULTIPLICATION OF A x Z"
20 PRINT "A,Z LARGE WHOLE NUMBERS IN ANY BASE B <= 10 "
30 GOTO 360
40 REM  ***** SUBROUTINE TO TEST FOR EVEN OR ODD ******
50 C=0                                    \ REM C = CARRY
60 FOR I=N TO 1 STEP -1
70   X=A(I)+C
80   IF X/2 = INT(X/2) THEN C=0 ELSE C=B
90 NEXT I \ RETURN                         \ REM IF C>0 THEN A( ) IS ODD
100 REM  ***** SUBROUTINE TO ADD Z( ) TO SUM *****
110 C=0                                    \ REM C = CARRY
120 IF M>K THEN K=M                        \ REM M=LENGTH OF Z( )
130 FOR I=1 TO K                           \ REM K=LENGTH OF SUM
140   X=S(I)+Z(I)+C                        \ REM S( )= SUM
150   R=X-B*INT(X/B)                       \ REM R = REMAINDER
160   S(I)=R   \ C = INT(X/B)
170 NEXT I
180 IF C>0 THEN S(K+1)=C
190 IF C>0 THEN K=K+1   \ RETURN
200 REM ***** SUBROUTINE TO DOUBLE Z( ) *****
210 C=0
220 FOR I=1 TO M
230   X=2*Z(I) + C
240   R=X-B*INT(X/B)
250   Z(I)=R   \ C = INT(X/B)
260 NEXT I
270 IF C>0 THEN Z(M+1)=C
280 IF C>0 THEN M=M+1   \ RETURN
290 REM ***** SUBROUTINE TO DIVIDE A( ) IN HALF (TO LOWEST INTEGER)
300 C=0 \ T=0                              \ REM T = TOTAL OF DIGITS IN A( )
310 FOR I=N TO 1 STEP -1
320   X=A(I)+C
330   IF X/2=INT(X/2) THEN C=0 ELSE C=B
340   A(I)=INT(X/2)    \ T=T+A(I)
350 NEXT I             \ RETURN
360 REM****************** M A I N   P R O G R A M ********************
370 DIM A$(20),Z$(20),T$(20),A(20),Z(40),S(40)
380 INPUT " BASE = ",B
390 INPUT "    A = ",A$
400 INPUT "    Z = ",Z$
410 N=LEN(A$) \ M=LEN(Z$)
420 IF N>M THEN K=N ELSE K=M               \ REM K = LARGEST LENGTH
430 IF M>=N THEN 460                       \ REM CHECK LENGTHS OF A AND Z
440 T$=A$ \ A$=Z$ \ Z$=T$                  \ REM EXCHANGE A AND Z
450 GOTO 410
460 FOR I= 1 TO N                          \ REM PUT A$ INTO ARRAY A( )
470   A(I)=VAL(A$(N+1-I,N+1-I))
480 NEXT I
490 FOR I=1 TO M                           \ REM PUT Z$ INTO ARRAY Z( )
500   Z(I)=VAL(Z$(M+1-I,M+1-I))
510 NEXT I
520 GOSUB 40                               \ REM TEST A( ) FOR EVEN OR ODD
530 IF C>0 THEN GOSUB 100                  \ REM IF ODD THEN ADD Z( ) TO SUM
540 GOSUB 200                              \ REM DOUBLE THE ARRAY Z( )
550 GOSUB 290                              \ REM DIVIDE A( ) IN HALF
560 IF T>0 THEN 520                        \ REM REPEAT UNTIL A( ) < 1
570 PRINT A$," x ",Z$, " = "               \ REM PRINT THE PROBLEM
580 FOR I=K TO 1 STEP -1
590   PRINT S(I),                          \ REM PRINT THE ANSWER
600 NEXT I   \ PRINT
610 END
```

```
              S A M P L E    R U N

RUSSIAN PEASANT METHOD FOR MULTIPLICATION OF A x Z
A,Z LARGE WHOLE NUMBERS IN ANY BASE B <= 10

  BASE = 10
     A = 123456789
     Z = 12345678987654321
123456789 x 12345678987654321 =
 1 5 2 4 1 5 7 8 8 5 8 4 0 5 7 3 1 1 2 6 3 5 2 6 9

  BASE = 2
     A = 1010101010101010
     Z = 1010101010101010

1010101010101010 x 1010101010101010 =
 1 1 1 0 0 0 1 1 1 0 0 0 1 1 0 0 0 1 1 1 0 0 0 1 1 1 0 0 1 0 0
```

Remarks

1. In Microsoft Basic lines 470 and 500 need to changed using the equivalence A$(I,I) =MID$(A$,I,1).

2. To upgrade this program to handle any base B, the conversion routine (lines 470-510) and the output routine (lines 580-600) both need to be changed. □

References

1) Bowden, Joseph, "The Russian Peasant Method of Multiplication" *The Mathematics Teacher*, Vol. 5, page 4-8, 1912.

2) Dantzig, Tobias, *Number, The Language of Science*, Macmillan Publishing Company, New York, 1939.

How to Solve It— With the Computer

Donald T. Piele

Part Four—Probability

> *"To sum up, we can ascertain that, approximately, the frequency of an event is to the number of all observations as the probability of the event is to the probability of the certainty, i.e., to 1. I find this correspondence between facts and logic, between possibility and realization, wonderful, indeed!"*
> *Blaise Pascal (1654)*

The development of the theory of probability is a comparatively young branch of mathematics which historians believe began with a series of letters between Pascal and Fermat in 1654. Motivated by his interest in the gambling problems suggested to him by his friend, the Chevalier de Mere, Pascal formulated many of the fundamental principles of this new science — which we now take for granted. Even the most basic idea of using a number between 0 and 1 to represent the probability of an event had not been formulated before. It was Pascal who suggested "... the most natural procedure is always to assign the number 1 to the complete certainty and to measure the degree of certainty of a random event with the fraction giving the event's share of the complete certainty."[1]

Pascal's letters were published for the first time in the small paperback, *Letters On Probability*,[1] in 1972. At the time they were written, more than 300 years earlier, it was not completely clear whether the study of the randomness was indeed a branch of mathematics. "If by mathematics one understands its traditional capital stock only, geometry, arithmetic, and algebra, there is naturally in this narrow definition no room for any new branch."I agree in this respect with Descartes, however, according to whom every study having for its aim the investigation of measure and order belongs to mathematics irrespective of the object whose measure and order it investigates.

Computers In Mathematics

Today, the network of fields linked to mathematics by this definition are huge. In fact, it is hard to exclude any area of human endeavor that does not ultimately encounter problems of measure and order. In a similar way, computers were originally designed to solve a very narrow class of computational problems in ballistics. Today, less than 35 years later, it is difficult to exclude any area of human endeavor that does not benefit by the rapid computation of measure and order provided by computers.

At the same time that computers have become indispensble tools for solving problems of measure and order, they have expanded the ways we traditionally solve problems and they have provided a completely new environment for developing the art of problem solving.

Donald Piele, University of Wisconsin-Parkside, Kenosha, WI 53141

Programming Activities

This months' activities will be taken from the world of probability. For the beginning student, I will introduce problems that use the random number generator — a function that plays an indispensable role in many computer simulations. The use of relative frequency as a measure of the probability of an event will be explored in problems for the intermediate student. Finally, the average value for the number of tries necessary to write a bug-free program will be explored by the advanced students.

Lesson #4 (Beginning Students)

In the last lesson (#3), I posed the problem of writing a program for the Apple II that would fill the screen with a single color. The intent of this problem was to introduce the FOR-NEXT statement. Now the problem will be to carry out a similar procedure in a completely random fashion.

The commonly used random number function used in Basic is denoted by RND(1). On the Apple II with Applesoft Basic, RDN(1) returns a random number between 0 and 1 every time it is encountered in the program. A simple program illustrates how this works.

```
10 PRINT RND(1)
20 GOTO 10
30 END

RUN
.53345678
.876347891
.293018028
. . . . . . . . .
```

Unfortunately, the program must be stopped (Break/ CRTL C) to read the numbers because they appear on the screen so fast. For better control of the output, I use the following program which generates 10 random numbers; the numbers multiplied by 10; and then the integer part of the numbers multiplied by 10. The following program illustrates how to use the random number generator to pick single digits at random.

```
10 REM RANDOM NUMBER
20 REM APPLESOFT BASIC
30 FOR I=1 TO 10
40    X=RND(1)
50    PRINT X, 10*X, INT(10*X)
60 NEXT I
70 END

RUN
.34753094      3.4753094      3
.89234103      8.9234103      8
.25345630      2.5345630      2
. . . . . . . .  . . . . . . . .  .
```

Integer Basic on the Apple II generates only integers, and thus the RND(X) function has a slightly different meaning. In this case RND(X) generates an integer between 0 and X-1 inclusively every time it is encountered in the program. For example, to perform the same task as above in Integer Basic, use:

```
10 REM RANDOM INTEGERS
20 REM INTEGER BASIC
30 FOR I= 1 TO 10
40    PRINT RND(10),
50 NEXT I
60 END
```

As illustrated in lesson #3, positions on the low-resolution graphics screen are located by pairs X,Y where both X and Y are integers between 0 and 39 inclusively. Thus, to pick an integer in this range at random in Applesoft Basic use INT(40*RND(1)). In Integer Basic, RND(40) accomplishes the same thing.

Problem #4 (Beginning Students)

Write a program that fills up the screen with a solid color by plotting the points at random.

Remarks

1. What does it mean to plot points on the screen at random? Discuss this question with the class and see what they think it means. As illustrated above, every point on the screen is represented by a pair of integers (X,Y) where X and Y are between 0 and 39 inclusively. If X and Y are chosen at random in this range then the point X,Y is a random point on the screen.

2. A sample solution in Applesoft Basic is:

```
10 GR
20 COLOR=9
30 X=INT(40*RND(1))
40 Y=INT(40*RND(1))
50 PLOT X,Y
60 GOTO 30
70 END
```

3. For Integer Basic lines 30 and 40 will need to be replaced by

```
30 X=RND(40)

40 Y=RND(40)
```

4. The program is caught in an endless loop which can be terminated by using the familiar CTRL C.

5 After the students have written a Basic solution to this problem I like to pose a number of follow-up questions.

a) What happens if we replace line 30 with "30 X = 20"? [A vertical line in the middle of the screen is filled at random.]

b) What happens in the original program if we replace line 40 with "40 Y = 20"? [A horizontal line in the middle of the screen is filled at random.]

c) What happens in the original program if we replace line 50 with "50 PLOT X,X"? [The diagonal line from the upper left to the lower right of the screen is filled at random.]

d) What happens in the original program if we replace line 60 with "60 GOTO 40"? [A random horizontal line is filled at random.]

e) What happens in the original program if we replace line 20 with 20 COLOR=INT(16*RND(1)) and line 60 with 60 GOTO 20. [The screen is plotted at random with random colors.]

Lesson #4 (Intermediate Students)

The simplest example of relative frequency is illustrated by the experiment of flipping a coin a fixed number of times and counting the number of heads and tails that appear. Let H be the variable that counts the number of heads and let N be the total number of tosses. The relative frequency of the occurrence of heads is defined to be H/N. Anyone who has tried this experiment with a fair coin recognizes a certain predictable behavior: The relative frequency H/N is close to 1/2 and seems to get closer the longer the experiment is performed.

This experiment can be simulated on the computer by making the random number generator act like a coin. Random numbers generated in Basic use a procedure that picks out numbers uniformly over the interval (0,1). This means that, on the average, half the numbers are less than .5. Thus, by using the statement

$$IF \; RND(1) < .5 \; THEN \; H = H + 1$$

the counter H (heads) is increased by one about 50% of the time. If the chances of a head is P, $(0 <= P <= 1)$, then the statement

$$IF \; RND(1) < P \; THEN \; H = H + 1$$

will increment the counter H by one approximately P*100% of the time.

These ideas can be put together into a simple Coin Tossing Experiment. In this experiment the probability of a head is assumed to be .5. A coin is tossed 1000 times and after every 50 tosses the total number of trials (C), the number of heads (H), and the relative frequency (H/C) are reported.

```
100 PRINT "COIN TOSSING EXPERIMENT "
110 PRINT "========================="
120 PRINT "TOSSES",TAB(7),"HEADS",TAB(14),
    "HEADS/TOSSES"
130 FOR I=1 TO 20
140 X=RND(-1)              \REM RANDOM SEED
150 X=RND(0)              \REM RANDOM NUMBER
160 C=C+1                 \REM TOTAL TOSSES
170 IF X < .5 THEN H=H+1
180 IF C/50<>INT (C/50) THEN 150
190 PRINT C,TAB(7),H,TAB(14),H/C
200 NEXT I
210 END
```

```
RUN
COIN TOSSING EXPERIMENT
=========================
TOSSES HEADS   HEADS/TOSSES
  50     30      .6
 100     51      .51
 150     76      .50666667
 200    105      .525
 250    129      .516
 300    152      .50666667
 350    182      .52
 400    203      .5075
 450    227      .50444444
 500    252      .504
 550    274      .49818182
 600    300      .5
 650    328      .50461538
 700    355      .50714286
 750    384      .512
 800    416      .52
 850    438      .51529412
 900    462      .51333333
 950    484      .50947368
1000    504      .504
```

Remarks

1. The form for the random number generator is not standard in all Basics. This program was written in NorthStar Basic. In Applesoft Basic one should use 150 X=RND(1) to generate the next random number.

2. Line 140 is used to start the program with a random seed value. This is usually handled differently in different Basics. Some Basics use the statement 140 RANDOMIZE. In Applesoft Basic this is equivalent to

$$140 \; X = RND(-PEEK(78)-256*PEEK(79)).$$

3. Line 180 is used to interrupt the experiment after every 50 tosses and print out the current value for C, H, and H/C.

Geometric Experiment

A completely different experiment can be performed by observing a series of coin tosses. Suppose instead of counting the number of heads and tails we count the number of tosses until a head occurs for the first time. This defines a new experiment called the First Head Experiment. Every time the experiment is performed we observe a number — which represents the total number of tosses needed to get a head for the first time. Thus, the outcomes of this experiment are recorded as follows.

EXPERIMENT	OUTCOME
H	1
TH	2
TTH	3
. . .	.

In this experiment, if we assume that the probability of getting a head on each toss is P, then the probability for a tail is 1-P. Under these conditions, this experiment has a Geometric distribution which I will elaborate later.

Problem #4 (Intermediate Student)
First Head Experiment

Write a program that will simulate the experiment of tossing a coin until the first head occurs. The program must allow for the entry of the probability P of a head on each toss. Perform the experiment 1000 times and keep track of the number of experiments that end after T tosses, T = 1,2,3...M. (M is the largest number of tosses needed so far.) Print out a table after every 100 experiments showing the distribution of the outcomes that end after T attempts and the relative frequency for each value of T.

Remarks:

1. The heart of this simulation is a routine that will simulate the tossing of the coin until the first head. Suppose the counter T is used to store the number of trials until the first head and that P is the probability of a head on each toss. The following few lines simulate this experiment.

```
100 PRINT "FIRST HEAD EXPERIMENT"
110 PRINT "====================="
120 PRINT "THE TOSS OF A COIN RESULTS IN EITHER A HEAD OR A TAIL."
130 PRINT "THE PROBABILITY OF HEADS IS THE NUMBER P."
140 PRINT "AN EXPERIMENT CONSISTS OF TOSSING A COIN UNTIL THE FIRST HEAD OCCURS."
150 PRINT "THE OUTCOME OF THE EXPERIMENT IS THE NUMBER OF TOSSES NEEDED."
160 PRINT
170 PRINT "THIS EXPERIMENT IS PERFORMED 1000 TIMES AND THE DISTRIBUTION "
180 PRINT "OF TOSSES IS REPORTED AFTER EVERY 100 EXPERIMENTS."
190 PRINT
200 INPUT "ENTER P THE PROBABILITY OF A HEAD ON EACH TOSS, P = ",P
210 DIM C(100)
220 X=RND(-1)                    \ REM RANDOM SEED
230 FOR J=1 TO 10
240 T=0                          \ REM T = # OF TRIALS UNTIL FIRST HEAD
250 X=RND(0)
260 T=T+1
270 IF X>P THEN 250              \ REM THE TOSS IS A TAIL
280 N=N+1                        \ REM EXPERIMENT COUNTER
290 C(T)=C(T) + 1                \ REM OUTCOME COUNTER
300 IF T>M THEN M=T              \ REM M = MAX # OF TRIALS IN ANY EXPERIMENT
310 IF N/100<>INT(N/100) THEN 240
320                              REM  PRINT OUT OF RESULTS
330 PRINT
340 PRINT "TRIAL",TAB(10),"# OF EVENTS",TAB(25),"RELATIVE FREQUENCY"
350 FOR I=1 TO M
360 PRINT I,TAB(10),C(I),TAB(25),C(I)/N
370 NEXT I
380 PRINT "==========================================="
390 PRINT "TOTALS",TAB(10),N,TAB(25),1
400 NEXT J
410 END

RUN
FIRST HEAD EXPERIMENT
=====================
THE TOSS OF A COIN RESULTS IN EITHER A HEAD OR A TAIL.
THE PROBABILITY OF HEADS IS THE NUMBER P.
EACH EXPERIMENT CONSISTS OF TOSSING A COIN UNTIL THE FIRST HEAD OCCURS.
THE OUTCOME OF THE EXPERIMENT IS THE NUMBER OF TOSSES NEEDED.

THIS EXPERIMENT IS PERFORMED 1000 TIMES AND THE DISTRIBUTION
OF TOSSES IS REPORTED AFTER EVERY 100 EXPERIMENTS.

ENTER P THE PROBABILITY OF A HEAD ON EACH TOSS, P =  .5

(ONLY THE LAST DISTRIBUTION IS PRINTED HERE)
TRIAL     # OF EVENTS     RELATIVE FREQUENCY
1         501             .501
2         245             .245
3         127             .127
4         62              .062
5         33              .033
6         17              .017
7         3               .003
8         6               .006
9         5               .005
10        1               .001
===========================================
TOTALS    1000            1
```

2. The 250-270 loop terminates whenever the random number RND(0) is less than P. This corresponds to the occurrence of a head.

3. It is convenient to use an array, such as C(T), to keep track of the number of times the experiment ends after T trials. Each time the experiment ends after T tosses, it is counted by

$$290 \; C(T) = C(T) + 1.$$

4. If N is equal to the total number of experiments performed, then C(T)/N is equal to the relative frequency of the number of experiments that end after T trials.

5. If N/100 = INT(N/100), then N is a multiple of 100. A version of this test is used to print out the distribution after every 100 experiments.

6. A sample program that solves this problem is as follows.

```
......
240 T = 0                T = TRAIL #

250 X = RND(0)           TOSS COIN

260 T = T + 1            INCREMENT TRIAL

270 IF X > P THEN 250    TOSS IS A TAIL

....                     1st HEAD OCCURS
```

Lesson #4 (Advanced Students)

The First Head Experiment serves as an introduction to a slightly different experiment which I will call the Bug-Free Program Experiment. As everyone who has ever tried to write a computer program knows, the chances that it will run correctly on the first trial is definitely below 1. We also know from experience that the chances of eliminating bugs usually improves the more times the program is modified and tried again. I will assume, for the purposes of this discussion, that the chances that a program will run perfectly   ug-free) on the Tth trail is equal to T/(T+1). Thus,

$$P(S) = T/(T+1) \text{ and}$$

$$P(F) = 1/(T+1),$$

where P(S) stands for the probability of a successful program on the Tth trial and P(F) represents the probability of a failure on the Tth trial.

This experiment is similar to the First Head Experiment described above, with one big difference. Now the probability of a success depends on the number of times the experiment has been tried. The outcome of this experiment is still the number of trials until the first success.

With this model it seems natural to wonder: How many trials, on the average, will it take to produce a bug-free program? In the language of probability, what is the expected value of the outcomes in this experiment?

The average value of the outcomes of an experiment is easy to compute. For example, assume that the outcomes of an experiment are the integers T, T = 1,2...M. Also, assume that C(T) counts the number of times T occurred. Then the average number of times that T occurs in N trials is (C(1)+2*C(2)+... M*C(M))/N.

Problem #4 (Advanced Students)

Bug-Free Program Experiment

Write a program that simulates the process of writing a program until it runs bug-free. The probability of success on the Tth trial should equal T/(T+1). Perform the experiment 1000 times and keep track of the number of programs that run after T trials where T = 1,2,3...M. (M is the largest number of attempts needed so far.) Print out a table, after every 100 experiments, showing the distribution of outcomes that end after T attempts, the relative frequency for each value of T, and the average value of T.

Remarks:

1. It would be advisable for students to write the First Head Experiment program first. With a few changes and modifications this program can be used to solve the Bug-Free Program Experiment. For example: Line 200 will no longer be needed, since the probability of success on the Tth trial is no longer fixed at P. Line 270 should be changed to read: IF X > T/(T=1) THEN 250.

2. To compute the average outcome in N experiments, the student will need to total all the outcomes. This can be done with a statement such as S = S + I*C(I) placed in the printout loop. The average value then is S/N.

3. This same average number computation could also be added into the First Head Experiment.

4. For added interest, ask students to keep track of how many attempts were made to write the Bug-Free Experiment program. Have the class make a chart of this distribution and compare it with the outcome of the Bug-Free Program experiment.

Postscript

This section is added for those interested in a more detailed mathematical treatment of the two experiments.

The First Head Experiment is an application of the Geometric distribution.[2] Before I go further, some notation may be helpful.

Notation	Meaning
H	Heads
T	Tails
P(H)= p	Probability of heads = p
P(T)= 1-p	Probability of tails = 1-p
q	q = 1-p
TTTTH	First head is on 5th trial.
P(TTTTH)	Probability of the event.
X=5	First head is on 5th trial.
P(X=5)	Probability of the event.
E(X)	Average value of X.

```
100 PRINT "BUG-FREE PROGRAM EXPERIMENT"
110 PRINT "============================="
120 PRINT "THE PROBABILITY THAT A PROGRAM IS BUG-FREE DEPENDS ON "
130 PRINT "THE NUMBER OF TIMES IT HAS BEEN REWRITTEN."
140 PRINT "EACH TIME IT IS RUN THE PROBABILITY THAT IT IS BUG "
150 PRINT "FREE IS EQUAL TO  T/(T+1) WHERE T IS THE TRIAL NUMBER."
160 PRINT
170 PRINT "AN EXPERIMENT CONSISTS OF EDITING THE PROGRAM UNTIL IT RUNS."
180 PRINT "THE OUTCOME IS THE NUMBER OF TRIALS NEEDED TO MAKE IT WORK."
190 PRINT "THIS EXPERIMENT IS PERFORMED 1000 TIMES AND THE DISTRIBUTION "
200 PRINT "OF OUTCOMES IS REPORTED AFTER EVERY 100 EXPERIMENTS."
210 PRINT "THE AVERAGE NUMBER OF TRIALS NEEDED TO PRODUCE A BUG-FREE PROGRAM"
220 PRINT "IS COMPUTED."
230 PRINT
240 DIM C(100)
250 X=RND(-1)
260 FOR J=1 TO 10
```

```
270 T=0                        \ REM T = # OF TRIALS UNTIL PROGRAM RUNS
280 X=RND(0)
290 T=T+1
300 IF X> T/(T+1) THEN 280     \ REM THE PROGRAM HAS A BUG
310 N=N+1                      \ REM EXPERIMENT COUNTER
320 C(T)=C(T) + 1              \ REM OUTCOME COUNTER
330 IF T>M THEN M=T            \ REM M = MAX # OF TRIALS IN ANY EXPERIMENT
340 IF N/100<>INT(N/100) THEN 270
350                           REM  PRINT OUT OF RESULTS
360 PRINT
370 PRINT "TRIAL",TAB(10),"# OF EVENTS",TAB(25),"RELATIVE FREQUENCY"
380 S=0
390 FOR I=1 TO M
400 PRINT I,TAB(10),C(I),TAB(25),C(I)/N
410 S=S+I*C(I)                \ REM S = SUM OF ALL OUTCOMES
420 NEXT I
430 PRINT "========================================="
440 PRINT "TOTALS",TAB(10),N,TAB(25),1
450 PRINT "AVERAGE VALUE ",S/N
460 NEXT J
470 END

RUN
BUG-FREE PROGRAM EXPERIMENT
=============================
THE PROBABILITY THAT A PROGRAM IS BUG-FREE DEPENDS ON
THE NUMBER OF TIMES IT HAS BEEN REWRITTEN.
EACH TIME IT IS RUN THE PROBABILITY THAT IT IS BUG
FREE IS EQUAL TO  T/(T+1) WHERE T IS THE TRIAL NUMBER.

AN EXPERIMENT CONSISTS OF EDITING THE PROGRAM UNTIL IT RUNS.
THE OUTCOME IS THE NUMBER OF TRIALS NEEDED TO MAKE IT WORK.
THIS EXPERIMENT IS PERFORMED 1000 TIMES AND THE DISTRIBUTION
OF OUTCOMES IS REPORTED AFTER EVERY 100 EXPERIMENTS.
THE AVERAGE NUMBER OF TRIALS NEEDED TO PRODUCE A BUG-FREE PROGRAM
IS COMPUTED.

(ONLY THE LAST DISTRIBUTION IS PRINTED HERE.)
TRIAL       # OF EVENTS       RELATIVE FREQUENCY
 1            500                .5
 2            335                .335
 3            118                .118
 4            39                 .039
 5            7                  .007
 6            1                  .001
================================================
TOTALS       1000              1
AVERAGE VALUE  1.721
```

Since all tosses of the coin are independent of one another it is true that

$$P(TTTTH) = P(T)P(T)P(T)P(T)P(H) = q^4 p.$$

If X stands for the number of tosses until the first head appears, the following probability table applies.

Outcome X	Probability
1	p
2	$q^1 p$
3	$q^2 p$
. . . .	. . .
i	$q^{i-1} p$

The average or expected outcome is determined by weighing each outcome by its probability.

$$E(X) = p + 2pq + 3pq^2 + \ldots\ldots ipq^{i-1} + \ldots$$

It can be shown, [2], that the sum of this series is $1/p$. Thus in the First Head Experiment with $p=1/2$, the average outcome $E(X) = 2$.

Bug-Free Program Experiment

The computation of the probability of each outcome is different for the Bug-Free Program Experiment. Let F represent failure and S represent success on each trial. The corresponding probabilities, P(F) and P(S), depend on the number of trails T performed

$$P(S) = T/(T+1), \quad P(F) = 1/(T+1).$$

Thus the computation of the probability for the first success occurring on the 5th trial is

$$= \frac{1}{2} \cdot \frac{1}{3} \cdot \frac{1}{4} \cdot \frac{1}{5} \cdot \frac{5}{6} = \frac{5}{6!} \quad (!=factorial)$$

If X stands for the number of trials of the program until the first success, then the following probability table applies.

Outcome X	Probability
1	1/2
2	1/3
3	1/8
.	. . .
i	$i/(i+1)!$

The average or expected number of trials for this experiment is computed by weighing each outcome with its probability.

```
E(X) = 1/2 + 2(1/3) + 3(1/8) +...+ i(i/(i+1)!) +...
```

Each term of this series may be rewritten using the identity

```
i(i/(i+1)! =   i/i! - i/(i+1)!
```

After combining terms, the series can be reduced to

```
E(X) = 1 + 1/2! + 1/3! + 1/4! + ... + 1/i! + ...
```

This familiar series is equal to e-1, where e is approximately 2.7182817. Thus, using this model, the average number of times that a computer program will need to be debugged is 1.7182817.

This is probably a well known exercise in probability, but for me it came as a delightful surprise. □

REFERENCES

1. Rényi, Alfréd, *Letters On Probability*, Wayne State University Press, Detroit, 1972.
2. Meyer, Paul, *Introductory Probability And Statistical Applications*, p. 171, Addison-Wesley Publishing Co., 1970.

## Part V

How to Solve it—
with the Computer

Donald T. Piele

For the past four years the University of Wisconsin — Parkside has conducted a computer problem solving contest for junior and senior high school students. For a period of two hours teams of up to three members each compete on interactive computer systems to solve five programming problems. The results are judged on whether they run properly using the test data supplied in the problem, are easy to read, logical, imaginative, and creative. Within two hours after the contest is over, the three best teams in each division are announced and the prizes awarded.

An Open Invitation

This year we would like to extend an invitation to schools throughout the country and the world to participate in our computer problem solving contest. We will share our 1981 contest problems with school districts, universities, or other organizations that are interested in conducting a similar local computer problem solving contest under the following guidelines.

Guidelines

1. To receive a copy of the 1981 contest problems, the director of a local organization should contact us by April 4th and agree to keep the problems confidential until Saturday, May 2, 1981. This is the date we have set for our contest this year.

2. On or after May 2, 1981, any organizations may use the problems to conduct their own contest. The results will be judged and the winners selected locally.

3. No organization that holds a local contest is required to enter their winner in the national and worldwide contest. However, to be eligible for this competition, the local contest must be held on May 2, 1981 and the set of rules (listed below) followed.

4. A national and worldwide ranking will be determined by a team of judges from the University of Wisconsin-Parkside. The first three places in each division will receive prizes from *Creative Computing* magazine. Winners will be notified by June 1, 1981 and the results will be announced in the August issue of *Creative Computing*.

Contest Rules

1. Category SR: Grades 10-12 (age < = 18)
   JR: Grades 7-9 (age < = 15)
2. Team Size: A team consists of one to three members.
3. Computer System: Any interactive computer system may be used, however, each team may use only one input device (keyboard or terminal). Hard copy must be available for listing

the programs and displaying the sample runs.

4. Time Limit: Each team will be given five problems to solve in a two hour time limit. In cases where a printer must be shared between two or more teams for the hard copy printout, time can be taken after the two hour limit to make listings and sample runs. This must be done with an official present. No program can be changed after the two hour limit.

5. Grading Procedure: The solutions will be judged as follows.

    (a) Does it run properly, using the test data provided in the problem? (12 points)

    (b) Is the program well designed and easy to read? (5 points)

    (c) Is the program imaginative, creative? (3 points)

No partial credit is given under criteria (a) for a program that does not run.

6. Multiple Sessions: It is often necessary to run more than one session during the contest to accommodate all the teams on a limited amount of hardware. In this case, those responsible for the contest must make sure that each session is run so that no one sees the problems before their turn.

7. General: No outside help is allowed during the contest, including books, programs, or people not on the team. However questions concerning the operation of computers, terminals, or printers may be answered by those conducting the contest. Also, time may be taken before the session begins to familiarize the contestants with the operation of a computer system.

Grading

We have found it helpful to have each team attach the following score sheet to each program they submit. This ensures correct identification of listings and speeds up the grading process.

Team Identification

We require that each team pick a team name for identification purposes. The Devious Debuggers, The Apple Busters, Knights of Ni, and Microbits were examples used last year. Also, each team picks a captain.

Teams enter the contest by filling out the following application form.

Contest Problems

The problems used in the third computer problem solving contest (1979) appeared in the September 1979 issue of *Creative Computing*. The fourth computer problem solving contest problems (1980) are presented here followed by a complete set of solutions and sample runs.

Donald T. Pjele, University of Wisconsin-Parkside, Kenosha, WI 53141.

SCORE SHEET

Problem Number ________________________________

Team Name   ________________________________

==

                    (For grader's use only)

                    Correctness   ______ (12 points)

                    Design and Readability ______ (5 points)

                    Imagination, Creativity______ (3 points)

                                    Total   ______

Grader________________________

==
==

                 PROGRAMMING CONTEST ENTRY FORM

TEAM NAME ____

SCHOOL NAME____

SCHOOL ADDRESS____

           ____

ADVISOR'S NAME____

ADVISOR'S PHONE #(___)___-____

DIVISION   ___ SR (Senior, grades 10-12, age < = 18)

            ___ JR (Junior, grades 7-9 , age < = 15)

TEAM MEMBERS

1.(CAPTAIN) ____

2.   ____

3.   ____

==

JUNIOR DIVISION

JR 1. Extended Fibonacci Sequences

The Fibonacci sequence 1,1,2,3,5,8,13,21,34,55 is given by the rule that the first two numbers are both 1, and each following number is the sum of the previous two numbers. For example, the first 6 terms are

```
1
1
2 = 1+1
3 = 1+2
5 = 2+3
8 = 3+5
```

To generalize this, we define the *3-Fibonacci sequence* such that the first three numbers are 1, and each following number is the sum of the previous *three* numbers. For example, the first 6 terms of the 3-Fibonacci sequence are 1,1,1,3,5,9.

You are to write a program which will print the first n terms of the 3-Fibonacci sequence, where n is given as an input value. Run your program once, with n = 20.

JR 2. Dart Throwing

Assume you are throwing darts at a 5-by-5 square checkerboard. Each throw will hit randomly at any of the 25 possible squares with equal likelihood. After throwing a certain number of darts, you count the total number of squares you hit.

Write a program to simulate this dart game by "throwing" n darts, where n is a given input value. After all n darts have been thrown, tally the results and display the dart board as in the following example:

```
    *   .   .   .   .

    .   .   *   .   *

    .   .   .   .   .

    .   *   *   .   *

    .   .   .   *   .


    NUMBER OF THROWS = 8

    NUMBER OF SQUARES HIT = 7
```

Here a "*" in a position indicates that a square has been hit (at least once), and a "." means the square has not been hit. Run program twice each for the following values of n: 10, 25, 50, 100.

JR 3. Character Replacement

Write a program which will allow 3 inputs:
  (A) An input string
  (B) A character to be replaced
  (C) A character to replace it with
The program should replace each character of the string given in (A) which matches the character given in (B) by the character given in (C). Here is an example of what your output should look like:

```
INPUT STRING    :  THE FAT FOX

REPLACE         :  F

BY              :  B

OUTPUT STRING   :  THE BAT BOX

REPLACEMENTS    :  2
```

Run your program with the above example.

JR 4. Crowded Phone Booth

Ten people named A, B, C, D, E, F, G, H, I and J are trying to get into a small phone booth which can hold only two people at a time. There are exactly 45 different ways that they can get two of the 45 into the booth. Write a program to list them. Your output should list the combinations in the form.

```
    AB    AC    AD    AE    AF    ...
```

JR 5. Twin Primes

Recall that a positive integer p > 1 is called a *prime* if its only positive factors are 1 and p. If both p and p+2 are prime, the pair p and p+2 is called a *twin prime* pair.

You are to write a program to print all twin prime pairs p and p+2 such that p+2 ≤ n, where n is a given input value, and to print the total number of prime pairs found. For example, with n = 20, your output should look like this:

```
        TWIN PRIME PAIRS NOT GREATER THAN 20

        3               5
        5               7
       11              13
       17              19


        THERE ARE 4 SUCH PAIRS
```

Run your program for n = 20, and for n = 100.

SENIOR DIVISION

SR 1. Extended Fibonacci Numbers

The Fibonacci sequence 1, 1, 2, 3, 5, 8, 13, 21, 34, 55 is given by the rule that the first two numbers are both 1, and each following number is the sum of the previous two numbers. For example, the first 6 terms are

```
1
1
2 = 1+1
3 = 1+2
5 = 2+3
8 = 3+5
```

To generalize this, we define an *m-Fibonacci sequence* (where m is an integer > 1) such that the first m numbers are 1, and each following number is the sum of the previous m numbers. For example, the first 6 terms of the 3-Fibonacci sequence are 1, 1, 1, 3, 5, 9.

You are to write a program which will print the first n terms of the m-Fibonacci sequence, where m and n are given input values with m ≤ n. *Your program should not retain more than the last m numbers displayed.* Run your program 3 times, using the following input values:

m	n
2	10
3	20
10	20

SR 2. Spirals

Write a program which will print a spiral of numbers 1 to n^2 in an n-by-n square display, where n is a given input value, n ≤ 10. For example, for n = 4 the display should look like this:

```
 7    6    5   16

 8    1    4   15

 9    2    3   14

10   11   12   13
```

and for n = 5 the display should look like this:

```
21   20   19   18   17

22    7    6    5   16

23    8    1    4   15

24    9    2    3   14

25   10   11   12   13
```

(The lines are for reference purposes only. You do not need to print them.)

Run your program twice, once with n = 4 and once with n = 5.

SR 3. Substring Replacement

Write a program which will allow three inputs:
- (A) An input string
- (B) A substring to be replaced
- (C) A substring to replace it with

The program should then replace, from left to right, each substring of the string given in (A) which matches the substring given in (B) by the substring given in (C). If a replacement is made, the string search continues beginning with the character *following* the replaced substring. Here are two examples of what your output should look like:

    Example 1:

        INPUT STRING   : HE SHUD FU
        REPLACE   : U
        BY   : OUL
        OUTPUT STRING   : HE SHOULD FOUL
        REPLACEMENTS   : 2

    Example 2:

        INPUT STRING   : FOOOOD
        REPLACE   : OO
        BY   : O
        OUTPUT STRING   : FOOD
        REPLACEMENTS   : 2

Run your program with the above examples.

SR 4. Crowded Phone Booth

There are n people (n ≤ 26) whose names are A, B, C, . . . , and a phone booth with capacity m (m ≤ n). Write a program to list all the possible ways m of these n people can get into the booth. Your output should list the combinations of names in a format similar to the following example with n = 5 and n = 3:

        ABC   ABD   ABE   ACD   ACE
        ADE   BCD   BCE   BDE   CDE

        THERE ARE 10 COMBINATIONS

Run your program with the following values of m and n:

n	m
5	3
7	4
10	2
20	19

SR 5. Twin Near Primes

A positive integer k > 1 is called a *near prime* if K is not prime but is the product of exactly two (possibly equal) primes. If both k and k+1 are near primes, the pair k and k+1 is called a *near prime pair*. You are to write a program to print all near prime pairs k and k+1 such that k+1 ≤ n, where n is a given input value, and to print the total number of near prime pairs found. For example, with n = 30, your output should look like this:

        TWIN NEAR PRIME PAIRS NOT GREATER THAN 30

            9   10
           14   15
           21   22
           25   26

        THERE ARE 4 SUCH PAIRS

Run your program for n = 30 and n = 100.

Contest Solution

The contest solutions listed below are written in North Star Basic and duplicate the logic used by the winning teams in the 1980 competition. With minor punctuation changes and string conversions, the same programs work in Applesoft Basic. These changes are noted after the listings.

```
10 PRINT "JR 1. EXTENDED FIBONACCI SEQUENCES"
20 PRINT "----------------------------------"
30 INPUT "ENTER A VALUE FOR N:",N
40 DIM A(N+3)
50 A(1)=1 \ A(2)=1 \ A(3)=1
60 FOR I=1 TO N
70    IF I < 4 THEN 90
80    A(I)=A(I-1)+A(I-2)+A(I-3)
90    PRINT A(I),
100 NEXT I
110 END
READY
RUN

JR 1. EXTENDED FIBONACCI SEQUENCES
----------------------------------
ENTER A VALUE FOR N:20
1 1 1 3 5 9 17 31 57 105 193 355 653 1201 2209 4063
7473 13745 25281 46499
READY

10 PRINT "JR 2. DART THROWING"
20 PRINT "-------------------"
30 REM         T = # OF TOSSES
40 REM         B(5,5)= THE DART BOARD
50 DIM         B(5,5)
60 REM         FNR(X) = RANDOM INTEGER BETWEEN 1 AND X
70 DEF         FNR(X) = INT(RND(0)*X) +1
75             X=RND(-1)              \ REM RANDOMIZE
80 INPUT "HOW MANY DARTS DO YOU WANT TO TOSS? ",T
90       PRINT
100      S=0
110 REM *** THROW DARTS ***
120      FOR I=1 TO T
130          B(FNR(5),FNR(5))=1
140      NEXT I
150 REM *** OUTPUT RESULTS ***
160      FOR I=1 TO 5
170         FOR J=1 TO 5
180            IF B(I,J)=0 THEN PRINT ". ",
190            IF B(I,J)=0 THEN 220
200         PRINT "* ",
210         S=S+1
220         NEXT J
230      PRINT
240      NEXT I
250      PRINT
260      PRINT "      NUMBER OF THROWS = ",T
270      PRINT "NUMBER OF SQUARES HIT = ",S
280 END
READY
RUN

JR 2. DART THROWING
-------------------
HOW MANY DARTS DO YOU WANT TO TOSS? 25

* . * * *
* . * * .
* * * . *
* * . * *
* * * * .

       NUMBER OF THROWS =  25
NUMBER OF SQUARES HIT =  19
READY
RUN

JR 2. DART THROWING
-------------------
HOW MANY DARTS DO YOU WANT TO TOSS? 25

* . . * .
. * * . *
* * * * *
. * . * *
* * * * .

       NUMBER OF THROWS =  25
NUMBER OF SQUARES HIT =  17
READY

JR 2. DART THROWING
-------------------
HOW MANY DARTS DO YOU WANT TO TOSS? 50

* * * * *
* * * * *
* * * * *
* . * * *
* * * * *
```

```
        NUMBER OF THROWS =  50
NUMBER OF SQUARES HIT =  24
READY
RUN

JR 2. DART THROWING
--------------------
HOW MANY DARTS DO YOU WANT TO TOSS? 50


* * . . *
* * * * *
. * . * *
* * * * *
* * * . *

        NUMBER OF THROWS =  50
NUMBER OF SQUARES HIT =  20
READY
RUN

JR 2. DART THROWING
--------------------
HOW MANY DARTS DO YOU WANT TO TOSS? 100


* * * * *
* * * * *
* * * * *
* * * * *
* * * * *

        NUMBER OF THROWS =  100
NUMBER OF SQUARES HIT =  25
READY


10 PRINT "JR 3. CHARACTER REPLACEMENT"
20 PRINT "---------------------------"
30      DIM A$(255), D$(255)
40      INPUT "INPUT STRING    :",A$
50      D$=A$
60      INPUT "REPLACE         :",B$
70      IF LEN(B$)=0 THEN 60
80      INPUT "BY              :",C$
90      IF LEN(C$)=0 THEN 80
100 FOR I=1 TO LEN(A$)
110     IF A$(I,I)<>B$(1,1) THEN 140
120        A$(I,I)= C$(1,1)
130        C=C+1
140     NEXT I
150     PRINT "OUTPUT  STRING :",A$
160     PRINT "REPLACEMENTS   :",C
170 END
READY
RUN

JR 3. CHARACTER REPLACEMENT
---------------------------
INPUT STRING    :THE FAT FOX
REPLACE         :F
BY              :B
OUTPUT  STRING :THE BAT BOX
REPLACEMENTS    : 2
READY


10 PRINT "JR 4. CROWDED PHONE BOOTH"
20 PRINT "-------------------------"
30 A$="ABCDEFGHIJ"
40 FOR I= 1 TO 9
50   FOR J=I+1 TO 10
60     PRINT TAB(C*4),A$(I,I),A$(J,J),
70     C=C+1
80     IF C<11 THEN 100
90     PRINT \ C=0
100    NEXT J
110 NEXT I
120 END
READY
RUN

JR 4. CROWDED PHONE BOOTH
-------------------------
AB   AC   AD   AE   AF   AG   AH   AI   AJ   BC   BD
BE   BF   BG   BH   BI   BJ   CD   CE   CF   CG   CH
CI   CJ   DE   DF   DG   DH   DI   DJ   EF   EG   EH
EI   EJ   FG   FH   FI   FJ   GH   GI   GJ   HI   HJ
IJ
READY
```

```
10  PRINT "JR 5. TWIN PRIMES"
20  PRINT "-----------------"
30  INPUT "N = ",N
40  T=0
50  PRINT "TWIN PRIME PAIRS NOT GREATER THAN ",N
60  PRINT
70     FOR I=3 TO N-2 STEP 2
80        FOR J=3 TO SQRT(I+2) STEP 2
90         IF I/J =INT(I/J) THEN EXIT 140
100        IF (I+2)/J = INT((I+2)/J) THEN EXIT 140
110       NEXT J
120    T=T+1
130 PRINT I,TAB(10),I+2
140 NEXT I
150 PRINT
160 PRINT "THERE ARE",T," SUCH PAIRS."
170 END
READY
RUN

JR 5. TWIN PRIMES
-----------------
N = 20
TWIN PRIME PAIRS NOT GREATER THAN  20
   3          5
   5          7
  11         13
  17         19

THERE ARE 4 SUCH PAIRS.
READY
RUN

JR 5. TWIN PRIMES
-----------------
N = 100
TWIN PRIME PAIRS NOT GREATER THAN  100
   3          5
   5          7
  11         13
  17         19
  29         31
  41         43
  59         61
  71         73

THERE ARE 8 SUCH PAIRS.
READY
```

```
10 PRINT "SR 1. EXTENDED FIBONACCI NUMBERS"
20 PRINT "--------------------------------"
30 INPUT "ENTER THE NUMBER OF TERMS   N = ",N
40 INPUT "ENTER A VALUE FOR THE 'M'    = ",M
50 DIM F(M)
60   FOR I=1 TO M
70     F(I)=1
80   NEXT I
90  FOR I=1 TO N
100    S=0
110      FOR J=1 TO M
120        S = S + F(J)
130        F(J-1)=F(J)
140      NEXT J
150    F(M)=S
160    PRINT F(0),
170  NEXT I
180 END
READY
RUN

SR 1. EXTENDED FIBONACCI NUMBERS
--------------------------------
ENTER THE NUMBER OF TERMS   N = 10
ENTER A VALUE FOR THE 'M'    = 2
 1 1 2 3 5 8 13 21 34 55
READY
RUN

SR 1. EXTENDED FIBONACCI NUMBERS
--------------------------------
ENTER THE NUMBER OF TERMS   N = 20
ENTER A VALUE FOR THE 'M'    = 3
1 1 1 3 5 9 17 31 57 105 193 355 653 1201 2209 4063
7473 13745 25281 46499
READY
RUN

SR 1. EXTENDED FIBONACCI NUMBERS
--------------------------------
ENTER THE NUMBER OF TERMS   N = 20
ENTER A VALUE FOR THE 'M'    = 10
1 1 1 1 1 1 1 1 1 1 10 19 37 73 145 289 577 1153 2305 4609
READY
```

```
10 PRINT "SR 2. SPIRALS"
20 PRINT "------------"
30 INPUT "WIDTH OF SQUARE :",N
40 N=INT(N)
50 DIM M(N,N)
60 Y = INT(N/2 +.5)
70 X = Y                      \ REM START AT X,Y
80 C=1 \ D=0
90  FOR S=1 TO N
100    IF INT(S/2)=S/2 THEN 120
110    RESTORE
120    FOR A = 1 TO 2
130      E=D
140      READ D
150      FOR T = 1 TO S
160        M(Y,X) = C
170        IF C=N^2 THEN 240
180        C=C+1
190        Y=Y+D
200        X=X+E
210      NEXT T
220    NEXT A
230 NEXT S
240 REM *** PRINT OUT ***
250 FOR I = 1 TO N
260    FOR J = 1 TO N
270      PRINT TAB(J*5),M(I,J),
280    NEXT J
290    PRINT \ PRINT
300 NEXT I
310 DATA 1,0,-1,0
320 END
READY
RUN

SR 2. SPIRALS
-------------
WIDTH OF SQUARE :4
        7     6     5    16

        8     1     4    15

        9     2     3    14

       10    11    12    13

READY
RUN

SR 2. SPIRALS
-------------
WIDTH OF SQUARE :5
       21    20    19    18    17

       22     7     6     5    16

       23     8     1     4    15

       24     9     2     3    14

       25    10    11    12    13

10 PRINT "SR 3. SUBSTRING REPLACEMENT"
20 PRINT "--------------------------"
30 DIM A$(200),B$(100),C$(100),D$(200)
40 INPUT "INPUT STRING    :",A$
50 INPUT "REPLACE         :",B$
60 INPUT "BY              :",C$
70 REM    R = NUMBER OF REPLACEMENTS
80 A=1
90 REM *** SEARCH FOR SUBSTRING POSITION ***
100 B=0
110 FOR I=A TO LEN(A$)-LEN(B$) + 1
120    IF A$(I,LEN(B$)+I-1)= B$ THEN B = I
130    IF A$(I,LEN(B$)+I-1) = B$ THEN EXIT 150
140 NEXT I
150 IF A>B THEN 250
160 REM *** MAKE REPLACEMENT ***
170    D$=A$
180    R=R+1
190    C=B+LEN(C$)
200 IF B + LEN(B$)<=LEN(D$) THEN 220
210    A$=D$(1,B-1)+C$ \ GOTO 250
220    A$=D$(1,B-1)+C$+D$(B+LEN(B$))
230    A=C
240    GOTO 90
250 PRINT "OUTPUT STRING   :",A$
260 PRINT "REPLACEMENTS    :",R
270 END
READY
RUN
```

```
SR 3. SUBSTRING REPLACEMENT
---------------------------
INPUT STRING    :HE SHUD FU
REPLACE         :U
BY              :OUL
OUTPUT STRING   :HE SHOULD FOUL
REPLACEMENTS    : 2
READY
RUN
```

```
SR 3. SUBSTRING REPLACEMENT
---------------------------
INPUT STRING    :FOOOOD
REPLACE         :OO
BY              :O
OUTPUT STRING   :FOOD
REPLACEMENTS    : 2
READY
```

```
10 PRINT "SR 4. CROWDED PHONE BOOTH"
20 PRINT "-------------------------"
30 DIM X(26), A$(26)
40 X(0)=64
50 INPUT "INPUT N,M ",N,M
60 IF N<M OR N>26 OR N>INT(N) OR M<1 THEN 50
65 L = INT(70/(M+2))
70    A=A+1
80    X(A)=X(A-1)
90    X(A)=X(A)+1
100 IF A < M THEN 70
110    C=C+1
120    FOR B=1 TO M
130      A$(B)=CHR$(X(B))
140    NEXT B
150 PRINT A$(1,M)," ",
155 IF C/L=INT(C/L) THEN PRINT
160 IF X(A)<A+N-M+64 THEN 90
170    A=A-1
180 IF A>0 THEN 160
190 PRINT
200 PRINT "THERE ARE",C," COMBINATIONS."
210 END
READY
RUN
```

```
SR 4. CROWDED PHONE BOOTH
-------------------------
INPUT N,M 5,3
ABC  ABD  ABE  ACD  ACE  ADE  BCD  BCE  BDE  CDE
THERE ARE 10 COMBINATIONS.
READY
RUN
```

```
SR 4. CROWDED PHONE BOOTH
-------------------------
INPUT N,M 7,4
ABCD  ABCE  ABCF  ABCG  ABDE  ABDF  ABDG  ABEF  ABEG  ABFG  ACDE
ACDF  ACDG  ACEF  ACEG  ACFG  ADEF  ADEG  ADFG  AEFG  BCDE  BCDF
BCDG  BCEF  BCEG  BCFG  BDEF  BDEG  BDFG  BEFG  CDEF  CDEG  CDFG
CEFG  DEFG
THERE ARE 35 COMBINATIONS.
READY
RUN
```

```
SR 4. CROWDED PHONE BOOTH
-------------------------
INPUT N,M 10,2
AB  AC  AD  AE  AF  AG  AH  AI  AJ  BC  BD  BE  BF  BG  BH  BI  BJ
CD  CE  CF  CG  CH  CI  CJ  DE  DF  DG  DH  DI  DJ  EF  EG  EH  EI
EJ  FG  FH  FI  FJ  GH  GI  GJ  HI  HJ  IJ
THERE ARE 45 COMBINATIONS.
READY
RUN
```

```
SR 4. CROWDED PHONE BOOTH
-------------------------
INPUT N,M 20,19
ABCDEFGHIJKLMNOPQRS    ABCDEFGHIJKLMNOPQRT    ABCDEFGHIJKLMNOPQST
ABCDEFGHIJKLMNOPRST    ABCDEFGHIJKLMNOQRST    ABCDEFGHIJKLMNPQRST
ABCDEFGHIJKLMOPQRST    ABCDEFGHIJKLNOPQRST    ABCDEFGHIJKMNOPQRST
ABCDEFGHIJLMNOPQRST    ABCDEFGHIKLMNOPQRST    ABCDEFGHJKLMNOPQRST
ABCDEFGIJKLMNOPQRST    ABCDEFHIJKLMNOPQRST    ABCDEGHIJKLMNOPQRST
ABCDFGHIJKLMNOPQRST    ABCEFGHIJKLMNOPQRST    ABDEFGHIJKLMNOPQRST
ACDEFGHIJKLMNOPQRST    BCDEFGHIJKLMNOPQRST
THERE ARE 20 COMBINATIONS.
READY
```

```
10 PRINT "SR 5. TWIN NEAR PRIMES"
20 PRINT "----------------------"
30 DIM X(100)
40 INPUT "TWIN NEAR PRIME PAIRS NOT GREATER THAN ",N
50 FOR K= 2 TO N
60    FOR B= 2 TO SQRT(K)
70        IF INT(K/B)*B < K OR K=B*B*B THEN 90
```

```
80       X(K)=X(K)+1
90    NEXT B
100      IF X(K)<>1 OR X(K-1)<>1 THEN 130
110      PRINT K-1,"  ",K
120      C=C+1
130 NEXT K
140 PRINT "THERE ARE",C," SUCH PAIRS."
150 END
READY
RUN

SR 5. TWIN NEAR PRIMES
----------------------
TWIN NEAR PRIME PAIRS NOT GREATER THAN 30
  9    10
 14    15
 21    22
 25    26
THERE ARE 4 SUCH PAIRS.
READY
RUN

SR 5. TWIN NEAR PRIMES
----------------------
TWIN NEAR PRIME PAIRS NOT GREATER THAN 100
  9    10
 14    15
 21    22
 25    26
 33    34
 34    35
 38    39
 57    58
 85    86
 86    87
 93    94
 94    95
THERE ARE 12 SUCH PAIRS.
READY
```

Applesoft Version

A minor difference between North Star and Applesoft Basic is the way each uses punctuation after PRINT and INPUT statements. North Star uses a comma (,) while Applesoft uses a semi-colon (;). For example, the following are equivalent in the two Basics.

```
     North Star                      Applesoft

10 INPUT "NAME ",A$         10 INPUT "NAME ";A$

20 PRINT "NAME = ",A$       20 PRINT "NAME = ";A$
```

(In North Star Basic either the comma (,) or the semi-colon (;) can be used since they are equivalent, but the comma appears in the listing.)

This difference between North Star and Applesoft Basic will be called 'punctuation' and line numbers where it occurs will only be listed. All other changes will be made explicit.

```
Program          Changes

JR1    Punctuation in line 30

JR2    Punctuation in lines 80,180,200,260,270

       Use RND(1) instead of RND(0) in line 70.

       Delete 75

JR3    Punctuation in lines 40,60,80,150,160.

       110 IF MID$(A$,I,1) <> LEFT$(B$,1) THEN 140

       120 A$=LEFT$(A$,I-1)+RIGHT$(C$,1)+MID$(A$,I+1)

JR4    60 PRINT TAB(C*4+1);MID$(A$,I,1);MID$(A$,J,1);

       80 IF C <10 THEN 100

JR5    Punctuation in lines 30,50,130,160

       Change SQRT in line 80 to SQR.

       90 IF I/J = INT(I/J) THEN 140
```

```
Program          Changes

SR1    Punctuation in lines 30,40

       160 PRINT F(0);"   ";

       165 IF POS(0)>35 THEN PRINT

SR2    Punctuation in line 270

       Use : instead of \ in lines 70,80

       170 IF C=INT(N*2) THEN 240

SR3    Punctuation in lines 40,50,60,250,260

       120 IF MID$(A$,I,LEN(B$))=B$ THEN B=I

       130 IF MID$(A$,I,LEN(B$))=B$ THEN 150

       210 A$=LEFT$(D$,B-1)+C$ : GOTO 250

       220 A$=LEFT$(D$,B-1)+C$+MID$(D$,B+LEN(B$))

SR4    Punctuation in lines 50,150,200

       115 A$=""

       130 A$=A$+CHR$(X(B))

SR5    Punctuation in lines 40,110,140

       Change SQRT in line 60 to SQR.
```

1980 Contest Results

In the senior division, the 1980 winners were The Knights of Ni (Dave Rosen, Eric Romesberg, and Ron Stolberg) from Prospect High School in Prospect, IL. They turned in a perfect performance — 100 points. Second place went to the Macrobytes (John Eng, Dale Smith, and Gary Steven) of Nathan Hale High School in Milwaukee, WI. Their total was 59 points. Third place was won by the Hawks (Stan Kantor, Mike Bors, and Kent Baumeister) of Main South High School, Park Ridge, IL with 37 points. Twenty teams entered the senior division contest and the average score was 27.

In the junior division, the Tutancompuns (David Nice and Robert Goll) from Lance Jr. High in Kenosha, WI took first place. They scored 96 points. Second place was awarded to the Apple Busters (Steve Scott and Dave Pagenkopf) from Wausau West Jr. High in Wausau, WI — total points 80. Third place went to the Z-80 Zappers (Arthur Claus, David Levine, and Jerry Monkman) from A.E. Stevenson High School in Prairie View, IL who scored 77 points. A total of 12 teams entered the junior division and the average score was 53 points.

Acknowledgement

I would like to pay special tribute to Tim Fossum, Associate Professor of Allied Computer Science, who has done an outstanding job as director of all of our programming contests over the past four years. He has been involved in all aspects of the contest, from thinking up problems to directing the contest and judging the results and has contributed greatly to its success.

A special thanks also goes to David Nice who wrote the Applesoft conversions listed above. □

How to Solve It— With the Computer

Donald T. Piele

> *"A problem must involve the student; they must search for the answer. Perhaps they will not reach the goal, but the search itself may prove more important than the goal."*
>
> — *F. Jacobson*

An enjoyable way to develop problem solving skills is to write computer programs. After all, sitting down with a goal in mind and trying to achieve it by fitting together elementary statements is what problem solving is all about. This application of computers is often not familiar to those who have never written programs and only think of them in terms of finished products: an interesting computer game, a business record keeping system, or a scientific program to carry out numerical calculations. But those who write programs know differently. Computer programming can be a very creative exercise which develops logical thinking and problem solving strategies. After all, the output from a computer program is only as logical as the program design. And the development of a program from start to finish exercises the full range of problem solving skills.

Assuming that this is true, what can teachers do with a computer in the classroom that will help develop an appreciation and interest in problem solving? Do the obvious! Give students problems that can be solved by a computer program. This may seem too easy to be true, but in the hands of an experienced teacher, it works.

Problem Solving — A Practical Skill

George Polya, a practitioner and teacher of problem solving skills, taught that learning to solve problems was like learning to swim. You learn by practice and imitation. In

swimming you watch what other people do with their hands and feet to keep their head above water and then you try to do the same. In the same way, to learn how to solve problems you must watch and imitate other people and then practice on your own. The teacher must instill an interest in problems in the classroom and give students lots of opportunity for imitation and practice. The teacher must have a good supply of problems and have a genuine interest in working through problem solutions. Unfortunately, both of these conditions are hard to meet. Good problems require careful and complete documentation and an understanding teacher who is interested in providing direction and encouragement. It would be very misleading to think that this approach to teaching problem solving can be implemented by simply moving a computer into the classroom. Like anything of lasting value, it requires a certain amount of dedication. Teachers who are making the effort however, are realizing for the first time the tremendous creativity and determination that students exhibit when writing programs that are uniquely their own. These teachers have found that writing computer programs can be a unique form of expression which rewards original thought yet requires careful planning and logical execution. It is my hope that the problems found in this series will be of use to teachers who are using computers in a problem solving mode.

Lesson #6 (Beginning Students)
The Setting:

Imagine a situation where a decision is made to separate things into two categories: Boys turn right, girls turn left; heads I win, tails I lose; yes I will, no I won't. The decision to divide objects, events, or actions into two categories is made by evaluating an attribute. In the examples above the attributes are: Sex (boy or girl), coin side (head, tails), response (yes, no).

How can similar decisions be made with a computer? What attributes can be distinguished by a program?

Donald T. Piele, The University of Wisconsin-Parkside, Kenosha, WI 53141.

The Problem:

Write a computer program which uses the IF...THEN... statement to decide between two courses of action.

The Discussion:

There are many ways to approach this problem. It is intentionally open ended in order to encourage the greatest possible variety of solutions. I can imagine a class where no two programs turn out alike. This would be marvelous.

Here are a few examples to show the class how it might be done. Students can use these examples to gain understanding about the use of IF...THEN...statements. Then it is up to them to create their own programs.

1. A program that accepts a number from 1 to 10 and prints out whether it is greater than 5, equal to 5, or less than 5.

```
10 INPUT "ENTER A NUMBER FROM 1 TO 10 ";N
20 IF N < 1 OR N > 10 THEN GOTO 10
30 IF N > 5 THEN PRINT "YOUR NUMBER IS GREATER THAN 5."
40 IF N = 5 THEN PRINT "YOUR NUMBER IS EQUAL TO 5."
50 IF N < 5 THEN PRINT "YOUR NUMBER IF LESS THAN 5."
60 END
```

2. A program that generates random numbers between 0 and 1 and prints H (for heads) or T (for tails) depending upon whether the number is less than or equal to .5 or greater than .5.

```
10 PRINT "COIN TOSS"
20 IF RND(1) > .5 THEN PRINT "H";
30 IF RND(1) < =.5 THEN PRINT "T";
40 GOTO 20
50 END
```

3. More imaginative solutions use the graphics capabilities of the system. In lesson #4 a program was writen for the Apple II in Applesoft Basic to color the screen a solid color by picking points X,Y at random. With one simple modification we can direct the computer to color certain portions of the screen a specific color. For example, suppose we wanted to color the right half of the screen pink and the left half blue and do it at random. This could be done by setting the color to pink (line 20 below) and changing it to blue if the X coordinate is less than 20 (line 45). Lines 30 and 40 pick a position on the low resolution graphics screen at random.

```
10 GR
20 COLOR = 11
30 X = INT(40*RND(1))
40 Y = INT(40*RND(1))
45 IF X < 20 THEN COLOR = 6
50 PLOT X,Y
60 GOTO 20
70 END
```

4. Instead of coloring the screen at random we could color it a row at a time from top to bottom and turn on a specific color depending upon the position on the screen. Can you tell what will appear when the following program is run?

```
10 GR : BLUE = 6 : PINK = 11
20 FOR Y = 0 TO 39
30    FOR X = 0 TO 39
40       COLOR = PINK
50       IF X > Y THEN COLOR = BLUE
60       PLOT X,Y
70    NEXT X
80 NEXT Y
90 END
```

Points that lie above the diagonal from the upper left corner to the bottom right corner of the screen are colored blue and those below are colored pink. What would be the outcome if the following replacements were made for line 50?

(a) 50 IF X + Y > 40 THEN COLOR = BLUE

(b) 50 IF X < 10 OR Y > 30 THEN COLOR =BLUE

(c) 50 IF X < 10 AND Y > 30 THEN COLOR = BLUE

(d) 50 IF ABS(X-Y) > 10 THEN COLOR = BLUE

(e) 50 IF Y/2 = INT(Y/2) THEN COLOR = BLUE

(f) 50 IF X*Y > 100 THEN COLOR = BLUE

The Postscript:

These examples are but a few ways to solve the original problem and learn how to write simple programs in the process. Show these to the students and then take it from there. Many of their solutions will be much more elaborate and interesting.

Lesson #6 (Intermediate Students)

The Setting:

"Years ago, when girls were called young ladies and were never permitted more violent exercises than walking, the headmistress of a boarding school wished to arrange matters so that her pupils would derive the maximum amount of companionship in their daily walks without forming boisterous groups. She therefore ordered the young ladies, of whom there were an even number (2N), to walk in pairs, but to form new pairs each day in such a way that no young lady had the same companion a second time before she had walked with every other young lady. This worked well for a day or two, but presently the young ladies began to spend more and more time each day trying to find partners. They would be nearly ready when it was discovered that the last two young ladies had already walked together. Can you help the headmistress?"

This quaint problem appears in *Mathematical Recreations*[1].

The Problem: The Daily Promenade

Write a program which will accept a value for N and prints out the daily pairings for all 2N girls. Make a complete schedule for 2N-1 days in which each girl is paired with every other girl exactly once.

The Discussion:

The hardest part of this problem is finding a suitable procedure which will generate the pairings. I expect that very few students would be able to come up with a procedure on their own. However, I wouldn't discourage anyone from trying. A more modest goal for intermediate students would be to take an established pairing technique and transform it into a computer program.

An often cited method of generating the necessary pairings is called the circle design which will be illustrated here for six

girls. Number the girls from 1 to 6 and draw a circle as shown in Figure 1. The five evenly spaced points on the circumference are labeled as shown and the center is assigned to number 6. A pairing between the six girls is represented by drawing two vertical lines between points on the upper half and the lower half of the circle. The number 6 at the center of the circle is paired to the point on the left by a horizontal line. This set of lines determines who walks with whom on one particular day. To find the next days pairings, rotate the circle counterclock-

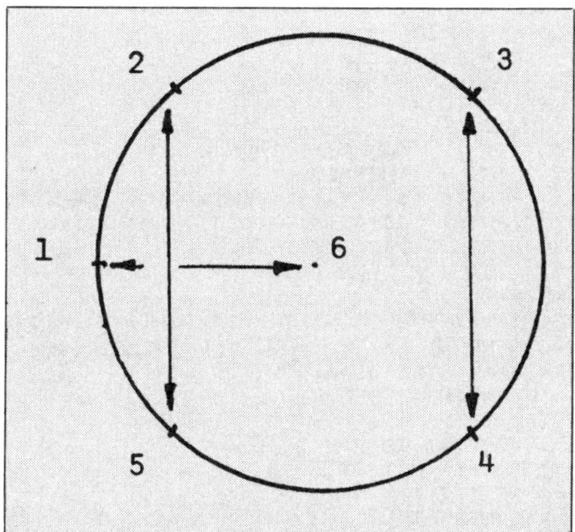

Figure 1. Pairings: 1-6, 2-5, 3-4

wise one number (1/5th of a revolution). Now the same lines can be used for matching up the girls with different partners. This is shown in Figure 2. Continue in this way through all five rotations of the circle by one number. The result will be five different pairings for the five daily promenades. The circle design works just as well for any even number of girls. Some students will have very little difficulty automating the circle design procedure. Others who are unfamiliar with how to represent information in a computer, will need further help.

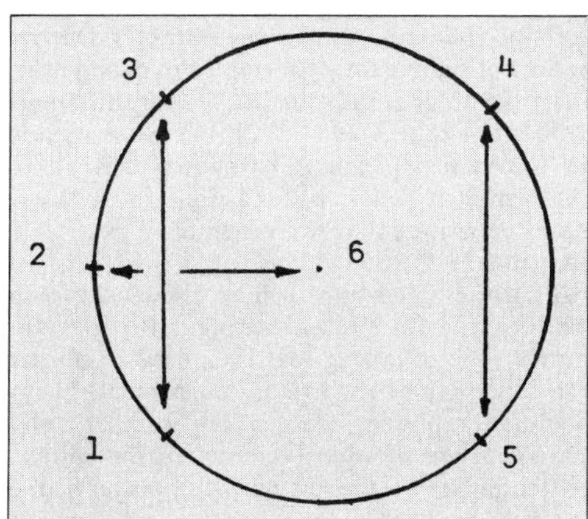

Figure 2. Rotate Figure 1 counter clockwise by one position. Pairings: 2-6, 3-1, 4-5

The Algorithm:

Step 1. The numbers from 1 to 2N that appear in the circle design are loaded into an array A(1),A(2), . . . A(2N).

Step 2. The numbers in the first half of the array are matched with numbers in the last half as follows:

A(1)-A(2N), A(2)-A(2N-1), . . . A(N)-A(2N).

We will call this pairing "the opposing ends."

Step 3. The numbers in the array elements A(1), A(2), . . . A(2N-1) are shifted to the left by one with the exception of A(1) which is cycled back and placed in A(2N-1). This is called a cyclic permutation.

Step 4. If the array has been cyclic permuted 2N-1 times then stop. If not then go back to Step 2.

The Program:

```
10 PRINT "THE DAILY PROMENADE" \ PRINT
20 INPUT "DAILY PAIRINGS FOR 2N GIRLS. N = ",N
30 DIM A(2*N)\PRINT
40 REM **** STEP 1 ****
50      FOR I=1 TO 2*N
60          A(I)=I
70      NEXT I
80 REM **** STEP 2 ****
90      K=K+1
100     PRINT "DAY ",K," : ",
110        FOR I=1 TO N
120          PRINT A(I)," -",A(2*N+1-I),"        ",
130        NEXT I
140     PRINT
150 REM **** STEP 3 ****
160        IF K=2*N-1 THEN END
170     T=A(1)
180        FOR I=1 TO 2*N-2
190          A(I)=A(I+1)
200        NEXT I
210     A(2*N-1)=T
220 GOTO 80
230 END
READY
RUN

THE DAILY PROMENADE
DAILY PAIRINGS FOR 2N GIRLS. N = 5

DAY  1 :  1 - 10    2 - 9    3 - 8    4 - 7    5 - 6
DAY  2 :  2 - 10    3 - 1    4 - 9    5 - 8    6 - 7
DAY  3 :  3 - 10    4 - 2    5 - 1    6 - 9    7 - 8
DAY  4 :  4 - 10    5 - 3    6 - 2    7 - 1    8 - 9
DAY  5 :  5 - 10    6 - 4    7 - 3    8 - 2    9 - 1
DAY  6 :  6 - 10    7 - 5    8 - 4    9 - 3    1 - 2
DAY  7 :  7 - 10    8 - 6    9 - 5    1 - 4    2 - 3
DAY  8 :  8 - 10    9 - 7    1 - 6    2 - 5    3 - 4
DAY  9 :  9 - 10    1 - 8    2 - 7    3 - 6    4 - 5
READY
```

Lesson #6 (Advanced Students)

The Setting:

The Daily Promenade Algorithm can be used to set up a round robin tournament. A tournament is called round robin if every player plays every other player exactly once. Tournaments ranging from the NCAA Fencing Championships to the summer city tennis league are set up on a round robin basis. Within divisions, the national football, basketball, and baseball leagues are basically round robin tournaments.

The Problem:

Assume that you are responsible for setting up a round robin tournament for the city tennis league. Your job is to write a computer program which will set up the schedule of matches with court assignments for each round of the tournament. The input should be the number of players (P) and the number of available courts (C), and the output should be a list of P-1 rounds so that every player plays every other player exactly once. If P is odd, then one person will of necessity draw a bye in each round. The output should fill out the following table.

```
Court #        1    2    3    4  ....... C

Round 1:       _    _    _    _          _

Round 2:       _    _    _    _          _

......

......

Round P-1      _    _    _    _          _
```

The Discussion:

Two things make this problem different from the Daily Promenade. First the number of players can be odd. This causes no great difficulty since we just have to add another "dummy" player which makes the number even. Whoever is matched with the "dummy" player draws a bye for the round. The second difference is the court assignments. Usually there are fewer than N courts so that a given round cannot be played simultaneously. This has no effect on the pairing algorithm, but it does cause a change in the way each round is printed out.

The Algorithm:

Step 1. Enter the number of players (P) and the number of courts (C). Let N = INT((P+1)/2). N is the number of matches in each round. If P is odd, then one match must be a bye. Remember whether P is odd or even.

Step 2. Print out a heading for the court numbers.

Step 3. Load the numbers from 1 to 2N in the array A.

Step 4. The numbers in the first half of the array are paired with the numbers in the last half by pairing opposing ends. Matches are assigned courts in a cyclic order 1 through C. If P is odd, then player A(2N) is the dummy and A(1) (who is paired with A(2N)) is given a bye for the round.

Step 5. The elements of A(1), A(2) . . . A(2N-1) undergo a cyclic permutation to the left. If this is the (2N-1)th permutation, then the program ends. If not, then go to Step 4.

The Program:

```
READY
RUN

ROUND ROBIN TOURNAMENT

ENTER THE NUMBER OF PLAYERS   P = 6
ENTER THE NUMBER OF COURTS    C = 3

COURT #        1         2         3

ROUND  1 :   1 - 6     2 - 5     3 - 4
ROUND  2 :   2 - 6     3 - 1     4 - 5
ROUND  3 :   3 - 6     4 - 2     5 - 1
ROUND  4 :   4 - 6     5 - 3     1 - 2
ROUND  5 :   5 - 6     1 - 4     2 - 3

ENTER THE NUMBER OF PLAYERS   P = 7
ENTER THE NUMBER OF COURTS    C = 3

COURT #        1         2         3

ROUND  1 :   2 - 7     3 - 6     4 - 5     1 - BYE
ROUND  2 :   3 - 1     4 - 7     5 - 6     2 - BYE
ROUND  3 :   4 - 2     5 - 1     6 - 7     3 - BYE
ROUND  4 :   5 - 3     6 - 2     7 - 1     4 - BYE
ROUND  5 :   6 - 4     7 - 3     1 - 2     5 - BYE
ROUND  6 :   7 - 5     1 - 4     2 - 3     6 - BYE
ROUND  7 :   1 - 6     2 - 5     3 - 4     7 - BYE

ENTER THE NUMBER OF PLAYERS   P = 8
ENTER THE NUMBER OF COURTS    C = 3

COURT #        1         2         3

ROUND  1 :   1 - 8     2 - 7     3 - 6
             4 - 5
ROUND  2 :   2 - 8     3 - 1     4 - 7
             5 - 6
ROUND  3 :   3 - 8     4 - 2     5 - 1
             6 - 7
ROUND  4 :   4 - 8     5 - 3     6 - 2
             7 - 1
ROUND  5 :   5 - 8     6 - 4     7 - 3
             1 - 2
ROUND  6 :   6 - 8     7 - 5     1 - 4
             2 - 3
ROUND  7 :   7 - 8     1 - 6     2 - 5
             3 - 4

ENTER THE NUMBER OF PLAYERS   P = 5
ENTER THE NUMBER OF COURTS    C = 2

COURT #        1         2

ROUND  1 :   2 - 5     3 - 4     1 - BYE
ROUND  2 :   3 - 1     4 - 5     2 - BYE
ROUND  3 :   4 - 2     5 - 1     3 - BYE
ROUND  4 :   5 - 3     1 - 2     4 - BYE
ROUND  5 :   1 - 4     2 - 3     5 - BYE
```

```
10  PRINT "ROUND ROBIN TOURNAMENT "\ PRINT
20  INPUT "ENTER THE NUMBER OF PLAYERS   P = ",P
30  INPUT "ENTER THE NUMBER OF COURTS    C = ",C
40  N = INT((P+1)/2) \ DIM A(2*N)
50  P1=P-2*INT(P/2)
60  REM **** STEP 2 ****
70  PRINT \ PRINT "COURT # ",
80    FOR I=1 TO C
90     PRINT TAB(14+(I-1)*9),I,
100   NEXT I
110 PRINT\PRINT
120 REM **** STEP 3 ****
130   FOR I= 1 TO 2*N
140     A(I)=I
150   NEXT I
160 REM **** STEP 4 ****
170 R = R + 1
180 PRINT "ROUND ",R," :",
190 FOR I=1 TO N
200   K=K+1
210     IF I=1 AND P1=1 THEN K = K-1
220     IF K=0 THEN 270
230     J=(K-1) - C*INT((K-1)/C)
240     PRINT TAB(12+J*9),A(I)," -",A(2*N+1-I),
250     IF K/C<>INT(K/C) THEN 270
260     IF I<N THEN PRINT
270   NEXT I
280 IF P1=1 THEN  PRINT TAB(12+(J+1)*9),A(1)," - BYE",
285 K=0 \ PRINT
290 REM **** STEP 5 ****
300   IF R=2*N-1 THEN END
310   T=A(1)
320     FOR I=1 TO 2*N-2
330       A(I)=A(I+1)
340     NEXT I
350   A(2*N-1)=T
360 GOTO 160
```

The Postscript:

The circle design certainly does produce a valid round robin tournament. We can substitute different numbers in the center and around the edges and produce a slightly different tournament. For example, if the number of player P is an even number, we can place P different numbers in the center of the design. The remaining P-1 players may be arranged through the perimeter of the circle in P-2 factorial ways (P-2 * P-3 * . . . * 2 * 1). The player in the center may choose to begin in any one of the P-1 players on the circumference of the circle. Thus there are a grand total of P*P-1*P-2! or P! (P factorial) ways of arranging for a round robin tournament for P players. Of course many of these are not significantly different. For example a tournament in which the order of the rounds is the only difference is counted as a different tournament. With this large number of round robin tournaments, can it be shown that all round robin tournaments can be derived for a circle design? Can a computer program be written that will generate all possible round robin tournaments?

All of these questions will be discussed in a future article which deals with back tracking strategies in computer programs. The following matrix is used to illustrate another way to represent a round robin tournament. The top row and left column represent the player's number and the values appearing inside the matrix represent the round number in which the player on the left plays the player at the top.   □

```
Player     1     2    3    4    5    6
         ==============================
   1     : X   : 1  : 2 : 3 : 4 : 5
   2     : 1   : X  : 3 : 4 : 5 : 2
   3     : 2   : 3  : X : 5 : 1 : 4
   4     : 3   : 4  : 5 : X : 2 : 1
   5     : 4   : 5  : 1 : 4 : X : 3
   6     : 5   : 2  : 4 : 1 : 3 : X
         ==============================
```


References

(1) Kraitchik, Maurice, *Mathematical Recreations,* W.W. Norton & Company, 1942.

(2) Freund, J.E., "Round Robin Mathematics", *The American Mathematical Monthly,* Vol. 63, page 112-114, 1957.

(3) Harary, Frank, & Moser, Leo, "The Theory of Round Robin Tournaments", *The American Mathematical Monthly,* Vol. 73, pages 231-245, 1966.

## Part VII

How to Solve It — With the Computer

Donald T. Piele

> *"The development of the electronic computer has profoundly and irrevocably changed the scientific world. In so doing it has simultaneously created numerous opportunities for the application of mathematical ideas and methods to the solution of traditional scientific problems and made possible the exploration research areas in mathematics and the sciences either previously unattainable or undreamt of. We are, in consequence, living in one of the great times of intellectual history."—Bellman, Cooke, & Lockett (1970)*

In 1970, when this paragraph first appeared in the preface to the book, *Algorithms, Graphs, And Computers* [1] , owning a computer was the privilege of government, large corporations, higher education, and other large institutions. Today, owning a computer is within the reach of local government, small businesses, primary and secondary schools, and private individuals. This has created more opportunities for the application of computer problem-solving techniques than could be imagined in 1970. As the capabilities of microcomputer systems increase in the coming years and as more people become familiar with computer programming techniques, the magnitude of the impact of computers will undoubtedly go beyond what we can imagine. Thus, for the growing number of people who are making an effort to understand how to solve problems with the computer, it is indeed a time of great intellectual growth and understanding.

Project CAMP

The idea of using computer programming to help students develop a better understanding of the problem-solving process is becoming more practical each year. But like most ideas, it is not new. Fifteen years ago, it was the major emphasis of a pre-college program named CAMP under the direction of David C. Johnson of the University of Minnesota.

Project CAMP (Computer Assisted Mathematics Program), developed at the University of Minnesota High School in the mid 1960's, was one of the first attempts to use the computer as a tool to develop problem-solving ability. The primary objectives of the project were these:

1) Test the following hypotheses:

a) The computer is an effective laboratory tool in solving mathematics problems.

b) The computer is an effective instructional aid for demonstrating and reinforcing mathematical concepts.

c) The computer is an effective tool for testing algorithms devised by students; programming the computer furthers the development of problem-solving ability.

d) The use of a computer is a means of building computational skills.

2) Identify the content in the mathematics curriculum for grades 7-12 where computer concepts can be successfully utilized in instruction.

The project produced six books, one for each grade 7-12, designed around the Basic language in a time-sharing environment. The authors gave careful attention to identifying particular problem-solving situations in which students could develop algorithms. The algorithms chosen were consistent with the mathematics curriculum of the grade level, so that no extra teaching was necessary. Thus, the topics considered in the CAP books were included in the modern mathematics books of that grade level.

The results of the experiment, as reported by the authors, indicated that the computer was an invaluable device for demonstrating mathematical concepts. The computer enabled them to do a better teaching job, because students could learn about the process for solving a problem, which is often the real goal of the lesson. It was the belief of the CAMP authors that: "A real problem can be thought of as a situation for which the student, or problem solver, does not have an established procedure or algorithm that can be automatically applied to find a solution. Students have little opportunity to develop their own algorithms in the conventional textbook problem where the algorithm is given and the exercises simply ask the student to apply it in a number of situations."

The computer also proved to be an excellent tool for teaching problem-solving. There were many instances in CAMP where students were given the opportunity to design an algorithm, program it, and then run it on the computer. If it didn't work, the student revised the procedure and tested it again, until it "worked." This type of "real world" problem-solving, which is extremely difficult for a teacher to provide, was found to be inherent in computer programming activities.

As good as the CAMP materials were for their time, the materials limited themselves to traditional mathematical algorithms usually found in mathematics textbooks. They did not introduce computer techniques and strategies that take advantage of the strengths of the computer—high speed computation and decision-making combined with the structures of graphs, networks, stacks, and queues and employing search, sort, merge, backtracking, recursion, and branching strategies. These concepts, which are currently studied in university-level data structures courses, are beginning to filter down to the pre-college level as they become needed by those interested in solving problems with the computer. As we grow in our ability to use the computer effectively, these ideas will be introduced much earlier. And it is these ideas coupled with the computer, that will give the students of the future the ability to be original problem solvers.

It is the intent of this series to give examples of these strategies in a wide variety of problem-solving settings which can be used in the classroom for students to work on and learn from.

Donald T. Piele, University of Wisconsin, Parkside, Kenosha, WI 53141.

Lesson #7 (Beginning Students)
The Setting:

The water jug problem, which will be introduced in the intermediate and advanced lessons, is the setting for a beginning graphics problem of drawing a water container on the screen and filling it to a specified level with water. To keep the problem simple, we will make the jug into a bucket that takes only three lines to draw on the screen.

Where we draw the lines depends on the amount of water we want it to hold. Thus we must first agree on how much space is to be represented by a quart of water. On the Apple II in low resolution graphics, we will arbitrarily assign 10 squares to represent one quart of water. Thus if we wanted to draw a bucket with 10 quart capacity, it would need to contain 100 squares within its boundary. One way to draw the bucket which will hold 10 quarts is to locate a 10x10 block on the screen and draw a border around it on three sides. But before we construct the bucket, we need to recall how to draw horizontal and vertical lines and use FOR/NEXT loops (see Lesson #3 Oct. 1980).

The low resolution graphics screen is a 40x40 array of points which are located at the intersection of columns and rows as follows:

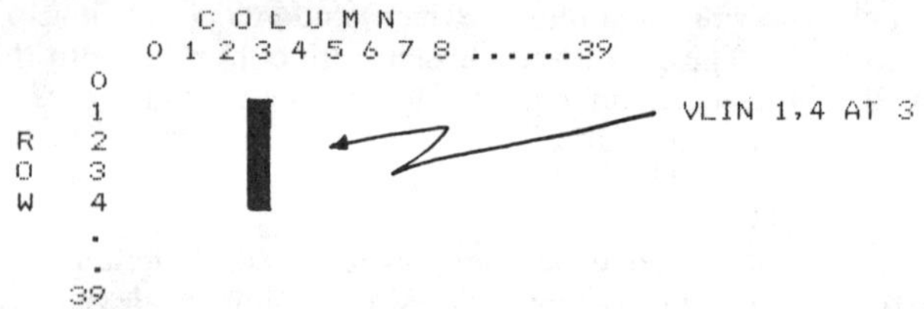

The statement VLIN A,B AT C draws a vertical line in column C beginning in row A and ending in row B. Similarly, the statement HLIN A,B AT C draws a horizontal line in row C beginning in column A and ending in column B.

The Problem:

One way to enter information into a program is to use the INPUT statement. For example, to prompt the user to enter the capacity of the bucket one could write:

INPUT "ENTER THE BUCKET CAPACITY (QUARTS):"";C

When the program is run, the words enclosed in quotes will appear on the screen while the computer waits for a numerical input which will henceforth be stored in C. The amount of water to be placed in the bucket could be entered in the same way.

INPUT "ENTER THE AMOUNT OF WATER TO POUR IN:";A

To figure out where to place the horizontal and vertical lines that form the outline of the bucket, graph paper, which shows the 40x40 array of positions on the low resolution screen, should be used. Since the rows are numbered from top to bottom, to construct two vertical lines of length C at the bottom of the graphics screen which are 10 squares apart one could write:

VLIN 39-C,39 AT 14
VLIN 39-C,39 AT 25

This forces the bottom of the bucket to be:

HLIN 15,24 AT 39.

Pouring the water into the bucket can be done by drawing one horizontal line of length 10 for each quart of water to be added from bottom to top. This is best done with a FOR/NEXT loop.

FOR I=1 TO A
HLIN 15,24 AT 39-I
NEXT I

Notice that the first quart is drawn in row 38, the second at row 37, and so on up to the last quart at row 39-A. (Refer to the low resolution screen chart if you are lost.)

The Program:

```
10 PRINT "THE WATER BUCKET "

20 INPUT "ENTER THE BUCKET CAPACITY    (QUARTS):";C

30 INPUT "ENTER THE AMOUNT OF WATER TO POUR IN:";A

40 GR

50 COLOR=15              :REM COLOR OF BUCKET

70    VLIN 39-C,39 AT 14 :REM LEFT SIDE OF BUCKET

80    VLIN 39-C,39 AT 25 :REM RIGHT SIDE OF BUCKET

90    HLIN 14,25 AT 39   :REM BOTTOM OF BUCKET

100 COLOR =4             :REM COLOR OF WATER

110   FOR I = 1 TO A     :REM POUR IN WATER

120     HLIN 15,24 AT 39-I :REM ONE QUART AT A TIME

130   NEXT I

140 END
```

Remarks:

1) There is nothing in this program to prohibit the amount of water (A) from being larger than the capacity of the bucket (C). The program will run just as well in this situation but it will look as though someone left the water outside overnight in Wisconsin in January. Of course, this can be prohibited by simply adding a statement: 35 IF A > C THEN PRINT "TOO LARGE" : GOTO 30

2) Also the program as written does not protect the user from a fatal error—entering too large a bucket for the screen. This can be protected against in the above program by adding: 25 IF C >39 THEN PRINT "TOO LARGE":GOTO 20

3) These types of safeguards are examples of good programming habits that protect the user from getting unexpected results or accidentally terminating the program.

Additional Questions:

Most computer problems easily lend themselves to further expansion and/or modification. Below are a few suggestions for The Water Bucket problem.

1) Add the ability to empty the water out of the bucket after it has been filled.

```
140 INPUT "PRESS RETURN TO EMPTY THE BUCKET ";A$

150 COLOR = 0            :REM SET COLOR TO BLACK

160   FOR I=A TO 1 STEP -1 :REM BEGIN TAKING OUT WATER

170     HLIN 15,24 AT 39-I :REM ERASE ONE QUART

180   NEXT I

190 END
```

Notice that FOR/NEXT loops can also count backwards by stepping by -1 each time. The STEP portion of the loop is optional and without it the computer assumes that the step size is +1.

2) Draw two buckets on the screen, fill one, and then empty it into the second bucket.

3) Draw two buckets of different size, fill the largest one with water, and empty as much as possible into the smaller bucket.

4) Experiment with different shapes for the containers.

Lesson #7 (Intermediate Students)
The Setting:

A popular puzzle which has amused and bemused people as far back as the 15th and 16th centuries is the Water Jug Problem. A typical version of the problem begins with a jug filled to the top with water. The amount is not important, but for the sake of discussion, let's assume the jug holds eight quarts. Two other empty jugs with capacities of perhaps five quarts and three quarts respectively are also available. The problem is to find a way to divide the water in half—four quarts to a jug. The jugs are unmarked and there are no measuring devices available. How can this job be done? This problem is represented by drawing the three jugs in their Given and Goal states.

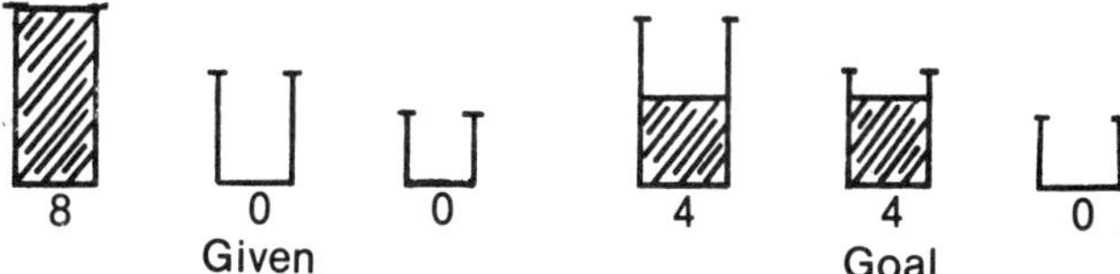

Most people attempt to solve this problem by simply adopting a method of trial and error. To keep track of the water distributions after each pouring, a chart something like the following might be constructed.

Pouring #	8-quart jug	5-quart jug	3-quart jug
0	8	0	0
1	3	5	0
2	3	2	3
3	6	2	0
4	6	0	2
5	1	5	2
6	1	4	3
7	4	4	0

The numbers in the jug capacity columns represent the amount of water in the jug at the present time. By looking back one row, it is easy to deduce which jugs were involved in the last pouring. For example, the last distribution shown is the result of pouring the contents of the three-quart jug into the eight-quart jug.

Of course, the list above is cleaned up to show only the necessary pourings that lead to a solution of the problem. In actual practice, the pourings that one must try to find the solution branch out like a tree.

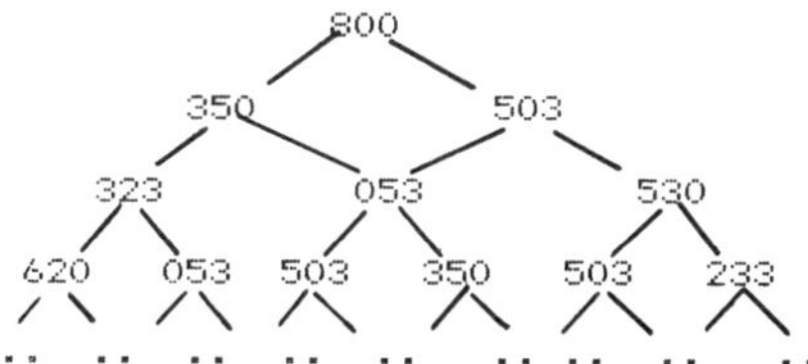

The ultimate goal, which will be carried out in the advanced problem, is to construct a procedure which will find a solution, if indeed one exists.

This problem will be broken down into two parts. The first part, which is appropriate for intermediate students, is presented first.

The Problem:

Write a computer program which will begin with any amount of water initially distributed between three jugs of eight-, five-, and three-quart capacity respectively, and will then find all possible distributions of water that can result from one pouring. Use the notation X Y Z to represent the water levels in the three jugs. For example, if X Y Z = 8 0 0, as in the initial problem, the possible distributions of water that could result from one pouring are 3 5 0 and 5 0 3.

The Discussion:

As with most problems, finding a good way to represent it is extremely important. A careful choice can make the work of finding a solution considerably easier. We begin with X Y Z

quarts of water distributed in the eight-, five-, and three-quart capacity jugs respectively. There are at most six possible new distributions that can result for three jugs. These are derived by picking any one of the three possible jugs for the source of the water (source jug) and pouring its water into either one of the remaining two jugs (sink jugs). For example, if we begin with a distribution of 4 2 2 then the six possible resulting distributions after one pouring would be:

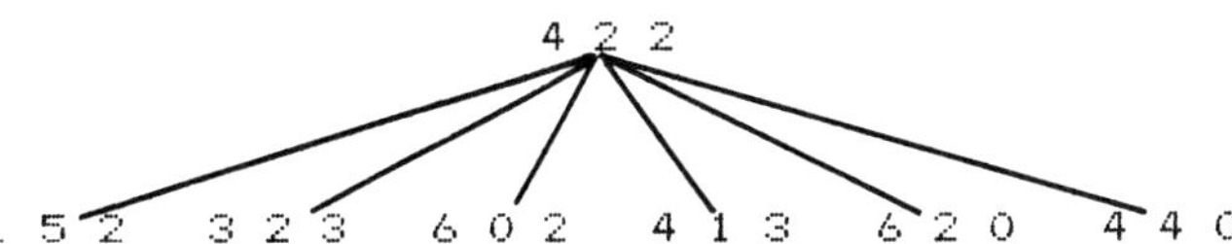

These numbers were arrived at by beginning with the jug on the left as the source and pouring into the sink jugs in order from left to right. In each transfer, one of two things happens. Either there is enough room in the sink jug for all the water to be poured into it, or some must be left behind in the source jug. Most of the work in this program is figuring out the details for each transfer and setting up the proper decisions which will produce the correct distribution of water. The six cases that must be considered for this problem are:

Pourings:	Source Jug	Sink Jugs
	1	2,3
	2	1,3
	3	1,2

The Program:

```
100 PRINT "INTERMEDIATE JUG PROBLEM"
120 PRINT "ENTER THE INITIAL WATER LEVEL IN THE THREE JUGS."
130 INPUT " 8-QUART JUG ",A(1)
140 INPUT " 5-QUART JUG ",A(2)
150 INPUT " 3-QUART JUG ",A(3)
160 PRINT
170 PRINT "HERE ARE THE POSSIBLE LEVELS AFTER ONE POURING"
180 REM *** A(1) IS THE SOURCE
190     IF A(1)=0 THEN 280        \ REM SOURCE IS EMPTY
200 REM *** POUR FROM JUG 1 TO JUG 2
210     IF A(2)=5 THEN 240        \ REM DESTINATION IS FULL
220         X=A(1)+A(2)           \ REM ADD JUG 1 AND JUG 2
230     IF X<5 THEN PRINT 0,X,A(3) ELSE PRINT X-5,5,A(3)
240 REM *** POUR FROM JUG 1 TO JUG 3
250     IF A(3)=3 THEN 280        \ REM DESTINATION IS FULL
260         X=A(1)+A(3)           \ REM ADD JUG 1 TO JUG 3
270   IF X<3 THEN PRINT 0,A(2),X ELSE PRINT X-3,A(2),3
280 REM *** A(2) IS THE SOURCE
290     IF A(2)=0 THEN 380
300 REM *** POUR FROM JUG 2 TO JUG 1
310     IF A(1)=8 THEN 340        \ REM DESTINATION IS FULL
320         X=A(1)+A(2)           \ REM ADD JUG 2 TO JUG 1
330         IF X<8 THEN PRINT X,0,A(3) ELSE PRINT 8,X-8,A(3)
340 REM *** POUR FROM JUG 2 TO JUG 3
350     IF A(3)=3 THEN 380        \ REM DESTINATION IS FULL
360         X=A(2)+A(3)           \ REM ADD JUG 2 TO JUG 3
370     IF X<3 THEN PRINT A(1),0,X ELSE PRINT A(1),X-3,3
380 REM *** A(3) IS THE SURCE
390     IF A(3)=0 THEN 480        \ REM SOURCE IS EMPTY
400 REM *** POUR FROM JUG 3 TO JUG 1
410     IF A(1)=8 THEN 440        \ REM DESTINATION IS EMPTY
420         X=A(1)+A(3)           \ REM ADD JUG 3 TO JUG 1
430     IF X<8 THEN PRINT X,A(2),0 ELSE PRINT 8,A(2),X-8
440 REM *** POUR FROM JUG 3 TO JUG 2
450     IF A(2)=5 THEN 480        \ REM DESTINATION IS FULL
460         X = A(2)+A(3)         \ REM ADD JUG 3 TO JUG 2
470     IF X<5 THEN PRINT A(1),X,0 ELSE PRINT A(1),5,X-5
480 END


READY
RUN

THE INTERMEDIATE WATER JUG PROBLEM

ENTER THE INITIAL WATER LEVEL IN THE THREE JUGS.
 8-QUART JUG 8
 5-QUART JUG 0
 3-QUART JUG 0
```

```
HERE ARE THE POSSIBLE LEVELS AFTER ONE POURING
 3 5 0
 5 0 3
READY
RUN

THE INTERMEDIATE WATER JUG PROBLEM

ENTER THE INITIAL WATER LEVEL IN THE THREE JUGS.
 8-QUART JUG 4
 5-QUART JUG 3
 3-QUART JUG 2

HERE ARE THE POSSIBLE LEVELS AFTER ONE POURING
 2 5 2
 3 3 3
 7 0 2
 4 2 3
 6 3 0
 4 5 0
READY
RUN

THE INTERMEDIATE WATER JUG PROBLEM

ENTER THE INITIAL WATER LEVEL IN THE THREE JUGS.
 8-QUART JUG 5
 5-QUART JUG 5
 3-QUART JUG 3

HERE ARE THE POSSIBLE LEVELS AFTER ONE POURING
 8 2 3
 8 5 0
READY
```

Remarks:

The program listed here was written in North Star Basic. To make it run correctly in Applesoft Basic a few simple changes are necessary.

1) In all INPUT statements the comma (,) must be changed to a semicolon (;). (See lines 130-150)

2) Applesoft does not have an ELSE statement. However, a simple modification where this occurs will produce the same effect. For example, Line 230 must be changed and 235 added:

```
230 IF X< 5 THEN PRINT 0;X;A(3) : GOTO 240
235 PRINT X-5;5;A(3)
```

Similar changes must be made in lines 270,330,370,430,470.

Lesson #7 (Advanced Students)
The Setting:

The water jug problem, introduced in the intermediate lesson, offers the advanced student a significant problem when expressed in its full generality. Rather than write a program that solves a specific water jug problem with a fixed number of jugs of specified capacity, it would be much more interesting to write a general program that will find all possible distributions of water starting from any given initial distribution of water placed in any number of different size jugs. This is the setting in which the advanced program will be introduced.

The Problem:

Write a program which will solve the general water jug problem. The user must be able to enter the number of water jugs in use, their capacity, and the initial amount of water in each. The program should then list all possible distributions of water that can be achieved by pouring water from one jug to another. Also, the program should indicate how each distribution can be reached from the initial distribution.

The Discussion:

At first glance, this appears to be a difficult problem, so we will tackle it one step at a time. There are several subgoals in this problem.

Subgoal 1 — PRINT THE DISTRIBUTION. A procedure to print out any distribution.

Subgoal 2 — POUR WATER. A procedure to perform the next scheduled pouring of water.

Subgoal 3 — CHECK FOR DUPLICATION. A procedure to check the current distribution against the master list for possible duplication.

Subgoal 4 — ADD THE DISTRIBUTION. A procedure to add a new distribution to the master list and note its predecessor.

Subgoal 5 — COPY THE DISTRIBUTION. A procedure to make a copy of the current distribution.

A successful program combines these procedures into an integrated program.

The Algorithm:

```
   1) Enter N, (the number of jugs)
Enter A (1,I), (the initial amount in each jug (I=1 to N))
Enter B(I), (the capacity of each jug (I=1 to N))
   2) COPY THE DISTRIBUTION
   3) PRINT THE DISTRIBUTION
   4) POUR WATER
   5) CHECK FOR DUPLICATION
   6) If no duplication, then ADD THE DISTRIBUTION
   7) If nothing new is added after all possible pourings have
been tried with the last distribution on the list, then END.
   8) Continue at 2.
```

The Program:

```
100 PRINT "WATER JUG PROBLEM "
110 PRINT
120 INPUT "ENTER THE NUMBER OF JUGS   ",N
130 DIM A(99,N), P(99)
140 PRINT "FOR EACH JUG ENTER HOW MUCH WATER IS INITIALLY "
150 PRINT "PRESENT IN GALLONS, AND HOW MUCH THE JUG CAN HOLD."
160 PRINT "JUG #",TAB(10),"INITIAL AMOUNT ",TAB(30),"CAPACITY
170 FOR I=1 TO N
180 PRINT I,TAB(10),\INPUT1 A(1,I)\PRINT TAB(30),\INPUT B(I)
190 NEXT I
200 PRINT
210 PRINT "INDEX",TAB(10),"JUG HOLDINGS",TAB(30),"PREVIOUS IND
220 L=1 \ P=1 \ P(1)=0
230 GOSUB 540
240 GOSUB 590
250 REM **** BEGIN TRANSFERING WATER ****
260     FOR I=1 TO N
270       IF C(I)=0 THEN 500
280         FOR J=1 TO N
290           IF I=J THEN 490
300           IF A(P,J)=B(J) THEN 490
310            GOSUB 540
320            IF A(P,I)+A(P,J)>=B(J) THEN 370
330 REM **** TRANFER FULL JUG *****
340            C(J)=A(P,J)+A(P,I)
350            C(I)=0
360            GOTO 400
370 REM **** TRANSFER PART OF A JUG ****
380            C(J)=B(J)
390            C(I)=A(P,I)+A(P,J)-B(J)
400 REM **** CHECK FOR DUPLICATION OF NODES ****
410            FOR S=1 TO L
420              FOR R =1 TO N
430                IF C(R)<>A(S,R) THEN EXIT 460
440              NEXT R
450             EXIT 490
460            NEXT S
470 REM **** NEW NODE FOUND ****
480         L=L+1 \ GOSUB 630 \ GOSUB 590
490     NEXT J
500 NEXT I
510     P=P+1
520      IF P>L THEN END
530     GOSUB 540 \ GOTO 250
540 REM **** SUBROUTINE TO MAKE COPY OF A(P, ) ****
550   FOR S=1 TO N
560      C(S)=A(P,S)
570   NEXT S
580   RETURN
590 REM **** SUBROUTINE TO PRINT OUT WATER DISTRIBUTION ****
600     PRINT L,TAB(10),
610     FOR S=1 TO N \ PRINT C(S),\NEXT S \ PRINT TAB(30),P(L)
620     RETURN
630 REM **** SUBROUTINE TO ADD NODE TO LIST ****
640     FOR S=1 TO N
650       A(L,S)=C(S)
660     NEXT S
670       P(L)=P
680       RETURN
```

```
READY
RUN

WATER JUG PROBLEM

ENTER THE NUMBER OF JUGS  3
FOR EACH JUG ENTER HOW MUCH WATER IS INITIALLY
PRESENT IN GALLONS, AND HOW MUCH THE JUG CAN HOLD.
JUG #      INITIAL AMOUNT        CAPACITY
1          ?8                    ?8
2          ?0                    ?5
3          ?0                    ?3

INDEX      JUG HOLDINGS        PREVIOUS INDEX
1            8 0 0               0
2            3 5 0               1
3            5 0 3               1
4            0 5 3               2
5            3 2 3               2
6            5 3 0               3
7            6 2 0               5
8            2 3 3               6
9            6 0 2               7
10           2 5 1               8
11           1 5 2               9
12           7 0 1               10
13           1 4 3               11
14           7 1 0               12
15           4 4 0               13
16           4 1 3               14
READY

RUN

WATER JUG PROBLEM

ENTER THE NUMBER OF JUGS  3
FOR EACH JUG ENTER HOW MUCH WATER IS INITIALLY
PRESENT IN GALLONS, AND HOW MUCH THE JUG CAN HOLD.
JUG #      INITIAL AMOUNT        CAPACITY
1          ?0                    ?19
2          ?13                   ?13
3          ?7                    ?7

INDEX      JUG HOLDINGS        PREVIOUS INDEX
1            0 13 7              0
2            13 0 7              1
3            7 13 0              1
4            19 0 1              2
5            13 7 0              2
6            19 1 0              3
7            7 6 7               3
8            6 13 1              4
9            6 7 7               5
10           12 1 7              6
11           14 6 0              7
12           12 8 0              10
13           14 0 6              11
14           5 8 7               12
15           1 13 6              13
16           5 13 2              14
17           1 12 7              15
18           18 0 2              16
19           8 12 0              17
20           18 2 0              18
21           8 5 7               19
22           11 2 7              20
23           15 5 0              21
24           11 9 0              22
25           15 0 5              23
26           4 9 7               24
27           2 13 5             25
28           4 13 3              26
29           2 11 7              27
30           17 0 3              28
31           9 11 0              29
32           17 3 0              30
33           9 4 7               31
34           10 3 7              32
35           16 4 0              33
36           10 10 0             34
37           16 0 4              35
38           3 10 7             36
39           3 13 4             37
READY
```

Remarks:

This program was also written in North Star Basic and a few changes must be made if it is to be run in Applesoft.

1) The usual punctuation mark changes from a comma (,) to a semicolon (;) in all INPUT and PRINT statements.

2) Change the EXIT 460 part of line 430 to GOTO 460. Also change line 450 GOTO 490.

3) Line 160 and 180 should be changed to read:

160 PRINT "JUG #";TAB(10);"INITIAL AMOUNT, CAPACITY"
180 PRINT I;TAB(15);INPUT A(1,I),B(I)

Postscript:

The printout for each sample run tells the whole story for each problem. The INDEX on the left lists in order all unique distributions of water in the jugs (JUG HOLDINGS). The index on the right (PREVIOUS INDEX) indicates from what previous distribution it originated. This would be important to know whenever it was necessary to reconstruct the precise sequence of pourings that leads to a given distribution. For example, to trace how the distribution 4 4 0 was derived in the first sample run, simply look to the right under the PREVIOUS INDEX to find the number 13, which corresponds to the distribution 1 4 3. This is called the ancestor of 4 4 0. Continue in the same way, reconstructing each ancestor, until you arrive back to the original distribution of 8 0 0. The result will be a subset of the original list.

```
INDEX      JUG HOLDINGS        PREVIOUS INDEX
1            8 0 0               0
2            3 5 0               1
5            3 2 3               2
7            6 2 0               5
9            6 0 2               7
11           1 5 2               9
13           1 4 3               11
15           4 4 0               13
```

Thus, the printout of this program that accompanies each problem solution tells not only which distributions are possible, but also the exact sequence of pourings that produces them. It does this for all distributions on the list—which represent the only distributions possible. Any set of numbers not on the list could never be achieved by any legal sequence of pourings.

This program also shows how to construct a tree structure which contains the important information without any duplication. For example, the printout of the first sample run represents the solution tree:

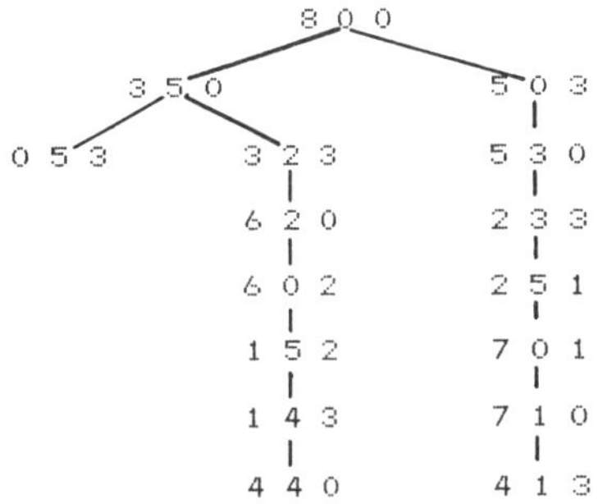

References
(1) Bellman, Cooke, Luckette, *Algorithms, Graphs, And Computers,* Academic Press, New York, 1970.

(2) La Frenz, Johnson, *Computer Assisted Mathematics Program-Algebra,* Teacher's Edition, page 4, Scott Foresman & Co. 1969.

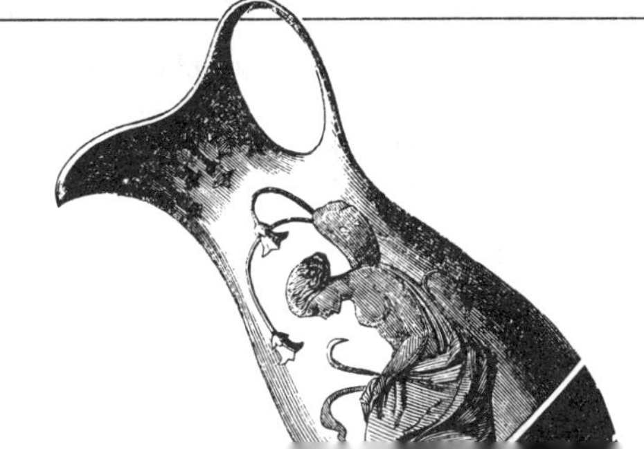

## Part VIII

How to Solve It—With the Computer

Donald T. Piele

"Learning about computers without learning how to program is like learning about cars and not learning how to drive."

—A Student

It is common today to find people in all walks of life who have a deep disdain for computers. At all grade levels in education, there are those who are openly anti-computer and are proud of it. Some teachers firmly believe that computers in the classroom will diminish the ability of students to think for themselves and will lead to their ultimate dependence on a machine.

Fortunately there is evidence of a changing attitude among many educators towards computers in the classroom. A recent study funded by the National Science Foundation has shown that there is strong support among elementary and secondary teachers, parents, and administrators for the development of computer literacy for all students. The PRISM study (Priorities in School Mathematics) [1], carried out by the National Council of Teachers of Mathematics, has made important recommendations which relate to the use of computers in the classroom. These recommendations reflect the priorities of teachers, parents, and administrators at the local school level.

The objective of the PRISM study was to provide guidelines and suggestions for curriculum changes in mathematics for the 1980's. Two of the nine major areas under investigation were problem solving and computer literacy.

Problem Solving

The one area which all respondents agreed should be emphasized in the 1980's mathematics curriculum was problem solving. Over 95% identified the goal of problem solving as the development of methods of thinking and logical reasoning. Top priority was given to the development of new materials beginning at the elementary school level.

The problem with teaching problem solving is that it is not a traditional subject which can be mastered in complete detail. This understandably makes it difficult to teach problem solving using the methods that have proven successful for more traditional subjects, such as fractions. However, many texts try to do just this. The typical "story problem," so often used in text books ostensibly to develop problem solving skills, usually turns out to be an exercise in recalling a numerical fact or in fitting the problem into a memorized pattern— hardly a genuine problem solving experience.

Donald T. Piele, The University of Wisconsin-Parkside, Kenosha, WI 53141.

Computer Programming and Problem Solving

The bond between computers and problem solving is well established. Few people would deny the value of the computer for solving problems. In fact the history of computers parallels the history of man's search for ways to automate the problem solving process. But computers do not solve problems by themselves. They need instructions from humans. Computer programming—the creative art of transforming a set of humanly constructed procedures into machine executable code—is the crucial link between man and computer.

New Problem Solving Strategies

Computers are really simple-minded. High speed computations are the thing they do best. But never underestimate the power of arithmetic if it can be done fast enough. Donald Greenspan, formerly of the University of Wisconsin and now with the University of Texas, has recently published a book which applies the computational power of the computer to the development of discrete counterparts to many classical physical phenomena [2]. Using only arithmetic he is able to establish exactly the same laws of conversation and symmetry that exist in classical continuum mechanics. The simplicity of his approach is extraordinary.

Ideas which utilize the power of high speed arithmetic will become better understood by younger students as computer programming begins to find its way into the elementary and secondary curriculum. In fact many mathematical techniques that are classically quite complicated are extremely simple when approached with the computer.

This month, I would like to focus on a set of examples that relate very closely to the kinds of problems that students are asked to solve in mathematics courses. My objective is to contrast traditional techniques for solving mathematical problems with the way in which one might solve the same problem armed with a computer. I hope to show that problem solving with the computer has the potential for providing genuine problem solving experiences which are simple, practical, and interesting.

Lesson #8 (Beginning Students)

The Setting: The proverbial "story problem" in mathematics is the bane of most students. After many tortuous experiences of trying to match up a problem with the method they have been provided with to solve it, students come away believing, at best, that problems are solved in only one way, and at worst failing even to understand the relationship between a solution and a problem. You have probably heard students argue that a wrong result must be right because, "I used the same formula you did; how could it be wrong!"

What is woefully lacking for most students is the opportunity to see solutions for problems evolve through efforts of their own and to have the opportunity to experiment with relationships and patterns. This is where the computer can be a great help. For example, consider the following problem.

The Problem: Pigs and Chickens. A boy and his sister visited a farm where they saw a pen filled with pigs and chickens. When they returned home, the boy reported that he saw 18 animals in all, and his sister remembered that she had counted a total of 50 legs. How many pigs are in the pen?

The Discussion: This problem has an interesting effect on people. Far too many who try it fail because they try to remember an algebraic formula to plug into. Others successfully set up the algebraic machinery to solve it but then fail to execute the symbol manipulations properly — usually because they have forgotten at least one crucial detail. In the algebraic setting this problem can be solved by solving the set of simultaneous linear equations:

$4P + 2C = 50$

$P + C = 18$

On the average, young kids, who have never seen algebra before, do better with this problem than adults because they look at it with an open mind.

Since this problem is presented here to illustrate more than just how to find an answer, we will convert this problem in a programming problem. This will also provide an opportunity to gain experience with the relationship between pigs, chickens, and legs which will eventually lead to insight into the problem.

The Programming Problem: Write a program which will print out the number of pigs, chickens, and the total number of legs for all combinations of pigs and chickens that add up to 18 animals.

The Algorithm: A FOR-NEXT loop can be used to compute the number of legs for each combination of pigs and chickens that add to 18. The number of chickens, of course, is 18 minus the number of pigs.

Chickens = 18-Pigs

The total number of legs is clearly,

Legs = 4*Pigs + 2*Chickens

The program:

```
10 PRINT "PIGS";TAB(15);"CHICKENS";TAB(32);
"LEGS"
20 FOR PIGS=0 TO 18
30 CHICKENS=18-PIGS
40 LEGS=4*PIGS+2*CHICKENS
50 PRINT PIGS, CHICKENS, LEGS
60 NEXT PIGS
70 END
```

RUN

PIGS	CHICKENS	LEGS
0	18	36
1	17	38
2	16	40
3	15	42
4	14	44
5	13	46
6	12	48
7	11	50
8	10	52
9	9	54
10	8	56
11	7	58
12	6	60
13	5	62
14	4	64
15	3	66
16	2	68
17	1	70
18	0	72

Remarks:

1. The program above is written in Applesoft Basic. In some forms of Basic the variables PIGS, CHICKENS, LEGS will need to be shortened to P,C,L.

2. The table printout is separated into three fields by use of the comma in Applesoft Basic. Another Basic language may require the addition of the TAB function to line up the columns.

3. The pattern that appears in this printout is very revealing. Not only is the solution (7 pigs, 11 chickens) obvious but a pattern — an increase by two in the number of legs in each row — is also clear. In fact this observation can be used to find the solution quickly using only common sense:

"If all the animals were chickens (the top row) then we would be short 14 legs (50-36). So we need to change chickens into pigs. Every time a chicken becomes a pig the number of legs increases by 2. We need 7 transformations to make up the 14 legs which means we need 7 pigs, leaving 11 chickens."

To become a good problem solver, one must be aware of the patterns and relationships that exist in almost all problems. Using the computer to display these relationships not only helps make the solution easier to find and understand, but also teaches students how to use a computer to gain insight into a problem.

Additional Problems:

1. Add more flexibility to the pigs and chickens problem by allowing the number of animals to be entered and not fixed at 18.

2. Another Problem: A carpenter agrees to work under the following conditions: He is to be paid $10 a day for his work for every day he works, but will be fined $12 for every day he misses. At the end of 30 days he has worked just enough days so as not to lose anything. Write a program which will print out the number of days worked, days absent, net pay. What is the solution?

Lesson #8 (Intermediate Students)

The Setting: The typical mathematics text does an honest job of trying to explain the origins of most algorithms before it highlights the essential part in bold type and assigns 25 problems that use it. The teacher may also do a conscientious job explaining the development of the algorithm from fundamental principles. But the student quickly learns that all you really have to know is how to plug the correct numbers into the right spots to get the assignment done. Why the algorithm works is lost in the mystery of algebraic magic.

For example, consider the quadratic formula: The roots of the quadratic equation $ax^2 + bx + c = 0$ can be expressed by the quadratic formula

$$\frac{b \pm \sqrt{b^2 - 4ac}}{2a}$$

A typical application of this formula might be to find the values of x where the curve $y = x^2 + x - 1$ crosses the x axis ($y = 0$). By simply substituting the coefficients into the quadratic formula we have:

$x = (-1 \pm \sqrt{5})/2.$

However, very little is learned about problem solving or about the meaning of the solution in the process. To most students the numbers that pop out of the quadratic formula are meaningless. It is merely a routine operation that must be performed in order to get the answers in the back of the book.

But there is a strategy which can be implemented on the computer that is completely elementary and well within the ability of intermediate students to program. It is called bisection.

The bisection strategy can be explained by playing the game of Guess. The object of this game is to guess a mystery number that lies between 0 and 100 by asking questions that can be answered either yes or no. Using the bisection strategy one can reduce the possibilities for the mystery number in half by asking: "Is the number greater than 50?" If the answer is yes, then the number has been trapped in the interval (51,100). If the answer is no, then the number is in the interval (0,50). The same strategy is repeated again on the reduced interval which contains the mystery number. In this way the size of the interval which contains the unknown number is cut in half at each stage until finally one possibility remains. This is illustrated as follows:

Trial #	Size of Interval
0	100
1	50
2	25
3	13
4	7
5	4
6	2
7	1

Including the final guess which names the mystery number, it requires at most eight questions to find the solution using the bisection technique.

This technique is also the basis of a procedure that can be used to find the real roots of any smooth function F(X). We will use the quadratic function $X^2 + X - 1$ to illustrate this idea. First, consider a table of values for this function.

X	$X^2 + X - 1$
-2	1
0	-1
1	1

This table tells us that the graph of the function is above the X axis at -2, below the X axis at 0, and above the X axis at 1. Since the quadratic function is a smooth graph and cannot make any sudden jumps in its graph, there must be a point in the interval (-2,0) where it crosses the X axis (i.e. $X^2 + X - 1 = 0$). The same must be true for the interval (0,1) (see Figure 1). The point at which this happens is called a root of the function and we can find it by using the bisection technique.

The Problem: Write a computer program that will find the roots of the quadratic function $X^2 + X - 1$ by the method of bisection. Allow the user to input values for A and B and let the program test whether the interval (A,B) contains a root.

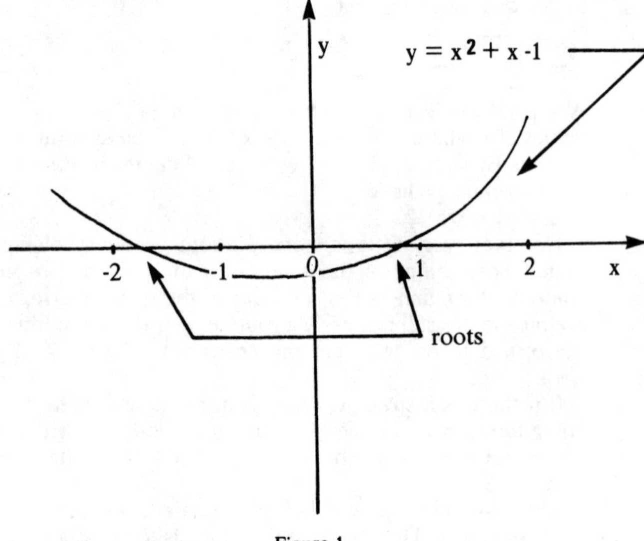

Figure 1.

The Discussion: The key to the bisection strategy is very simple. Suppose a smooth function F(X) has a different sign (+ or -) at two points X = A and X = B. For the sake of this discussion, assume that F(A)>0 and F(B)< 0. Then somewhere between A and B, F(X) must be zero. The unknown region can be cut in half by picking the midpoint C = (A + B)/2. Call C a trial root. IF F(C)=0 then the trial root is indeed a root and we are done. If not, then either F(C)>0 or F(C)< 0. IF F(C)>0, then the root must be contained in the interval (C, B) (remember F(B)< 0). IF F(C)< 0 then the root must be in the interval (A,C) (remember F(A)>0). In the first case, replace A with C and in the second case, replace B with C. Thus, in either case A or B is replaced with a new value C = (A + B)/2 so that:

(1) the region (A,B) is cut in half, and

(2) the condition that F(A) and F(B) have different signs is maintained.

We are now in a position to repeat the bisection strategy on the smaller interval (A,B). As this procedure continues, the interval (A,B) decreases in size closing in on both sides on the root. It can be stopped whenever a desired degree of accuracy is achieved.

The Algorithm: Functions are defined in Basic by use of DEF FNF (X). For the quadratic function in question we have:

DEF FNF(X) = X*X + X - 1

We must test the function initially at A and B to make sure they have different signs. This is done with the SGN ( ) function:

SGN(X) = 1 if X > 0
SGN(X) = 0 if X = 0
SGN(X) = -1 if X < 0

Thus, to begin using the bisection mehtod we must have:
SGN(FNF(A)) < > SGN(FNF(B)).

The SGN function is also used to check whether A or B is replaced with C = (A + B)/2.

IF SGN(FNF(C)) = SGN(FNF(A)) THEN A=C ELSE B=C

The absolute value function ABS(X) is used to test the size of the interval (A,B). To be accurate to 5 decimal places in an absolute sense we use the test:

IF (ABS(A-B) > .00001 THEN (continue bisecting) ELSE (print the approximate root C.)

The Program:

```
10 PRINT "BISECTION METHOD FOR FINDING ROOTS"
20 DEF FNF(X)=X*X + X - 1
30 INPUT "ENTER A,B = ",A,B
40 PRINT "TRIAL ROOT",TAB(20),"FUNCTION VALUE"
50 E=.00001
60 IF SGN(FNF(A))<>SGN(FNF(B)) THEN 90
70 PRINT "THE SIGNS ARE THE SAME, TRY AGAIN."
80 GOTO 30
90 C=(A+B)/2
100 IF FNF(C)=0 THEN 140
110 IF SGN(FNF(C))=SGN(FNF(A)) THEN A=C ELSE B=C
120 PRINT C,TAB(20),FNF(C)
130 IF ABS(A-B)>E THEN 90
140 PRINT "ROOT = ",C
150 END
```

```
BISECTION METHOD FOR FINDING ROOTS
ENTER A,B = 0,1
TRIAL ROOT              FUNCTION VALUE
 .5                      -.25
 .75                     .3125
 .625                    .015625
 .5625                   -.1210937
 .59375                  -.0537109
 .609375                 -.0192871
 .6171875                -.0018921
 .62109375               .0068512
 .61914065               .0024758
 .6181641                .000291
 .6176758                -.0008008
 .61791995               -.000255
```

```
BISECTION METHOD FOR FINDING ROOTS
ENTER A,B = -2,0
ROOT =  -1.6180345

   .61804205              .000018
   .617981               -.0001185
   .61801155             -.0000502
   .6180268              -.0000161
   .61803445              .000001
ROOT = .61803445
```

Remarks:

1. The roots computed by the quadratic formula are (-1 $\pm\sqrt{5}$)/2, which can be approximated by .618034 and - 1.618034.

2. The quadratic formula is only good for finding roots of quadratic funtions while the bisection technique can be used with any function that can be expressed in a computer language.

3. The absolute error of E = .00001 is fine for demonstration purposes, but it is not satisfactory in general. If a root is very small, for example .0002, then testing for errors of .00001 will yield an answer that is correct to only 2 significant places. To be sure of having an accuracy of at least 5 significant figures, use the relative error

E = .000001 * (ABS(A) + ABS(B))/2.

Additional Problems:

1. Replace the quadratic function X*X + X - 1 with the sine function SIN(X). The sine function is zero at X = π . Use the bisection program to obtain an approximation to π by finding a root for the sine function between 2 and 4.

2. The bisection program can also be used to find where functions intersect. For example, where does the curve Y = X intersect the curve Y = COS(X)? This happens, of course, when X = COS(X) or, expressed another way, when COS(X) - X = 0. Thus, finding the roots of the difference between the two curves is equivalent to finding where they meet. Find all points where these two functions meet.

3. Finding the fifth root of 2 is equivalent to solving the problem X^5 = 2. This is equivalent to finding a roots of the function X^5- 2 = 0. Use the bisection program to find $\sqrt[5]{2}$.

Lesson #8 (Advanced Students)

The Setting: A student working on a chemistry experiment recently has a question about a liquid dilution problem. A one-liter beaker of a concentrated solution was to be diluted with one liter of water. If the water had been added all at once, then the concentration of the liquid substance would be cut in half. But in this experiment the water was to be added very slowly, mixed completely with the concentrated liquid, and continuously discarded, so that only one liter was kept at all times. This can be seen by visualizing a full beaker (1) of a liquid solution which is being constantly diluted with water from beaker 0, instantly mixed, and the overflow discarded.

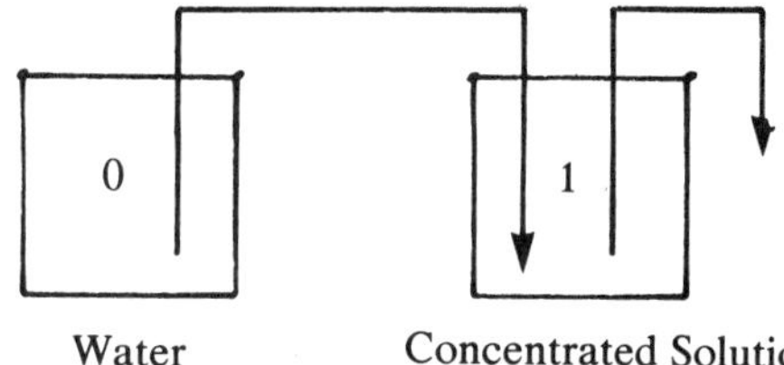

What is the concentration of the liquid after it has been diluted in this fashion with one liter of water?

Without the computer, this problem involves setting up the proper differential equation.The student who asked about the problem had no idea how to set up such a problem much less how to solve it. With a little knowledge of Basic and a computer this problem is relatively easy to understand and solve.

Problem 1: Write a computer program which simulates the dilution of the liter of a concentrated solution with one liter of water. The dilution should be carried out gradually so that a small quantity of water is added to the liquid solution, instantly mixed, and the same quantity of mixed solution discarded. What is the final concentration of the diluted solution if the initial concentration is C?

The Discussion: In the process of programming the computer to solve this problem, we actually see what is happening at each stage in the dilution. In fact, if we can compute the new concentration after the addition of a small quantity of water, then we can easily find the final concentration by simply repeating the process until all the water is added. Let M stand for the number of milliliters of water that are mixed with the dilution. (One liter = 1000 milliliters.) If M is small, then the dilution process is nearly continuous. We begin with one liter of the solution with concentration C. After adding M milliliters of water, the concentration is reduced to

C/(1 + M/1000)).

Replace the old concentration with the new by setting

C = C/(1 + M/1000).

This process of adding water, mixing the solution, and discarding an equal amount of solution must be repeated 1000/M times before the entire liter of water is used up. The resulting concentration C is a good approximation to the solution for the continuous dilution program.

The Program:

```
10 PRINT "CONTINUOUS DILUTION PROBLEM"
20 PRINT "============================="
30 INPUT "ENTER THE INITIAL CONCENTRATION       >>> ",C
40 INPUT "MILLILITERS OF WATER ADDED EACH STEP >>> ",M
50 N=1000/M            \ REM N = THE NUMBER OF STEPS
60 D=M/1000            \ REM D = WATER IN LITERS
70 T = 0               \ REM T = MILLILITERS ADDED
80 PRINT "MILLILITERS ADDED",TAB(20),"CONCENTRATION"
90 FOR I=1 TO N
100 PRINT TAB(3),T,TAB(20),C
110    C=C/(1+D)
120 T=T+M
130 NEXT I
140 PRINT TAB(3),T,TAB(10),"SOLUTION =",TAB(20),C

    CONTINUOUS DILUTION PROBLEM
    =============================
    ENTER THE INITIAL CONCENTRATION       >>> 1
    MILLILITERS OF WATER ADDED EACH STEP >>> 100
    MILLILITERS ADDED     CONCENTRATION
       0                  1
       100                .90909091
       200                .82644628
       300                .7513148
       400                .68301345
       500                .62092132
       600                .56447393
       700                .51315812
       800                .46650738
       900                .42409762
       1000   SOLUTION = .38554329
    MILLILITERS OF WATER ADDED EACH STEP >>> 50
    MILLILITERS ADDED   CONCENTRATION
       1000   SOLUTION = .37688949

    MILLILITERS OF WATER ADDED EACH STEP >>> 10
    MILLILITERS ADDED   CONCENTRATION
       1000   SOLUTION = .36971125

    MILLILITERS OF WATER ADDED EACH STEP >>> 1
    MILLILITERS ADDED   CONCENTRATION
       1000   SOLUTION = .36806335

    MILLILITERS OF WATER ADDED EACH STEP >>> .5
    MILLILITERS ADDED   CONCENTRATION
       1000   SOLUTION = .36797136
```

Remarks

1. The last four runs were made with the intermediate print out deleted.

2. Notice how little the final concentration changes in the last three runs even though the number of steps has increased 100 times.

3. The limiting value of the concentration as M approaches zero would be the exact continuous solution.

4. Those familiar with elementary differential equations will be able to understand the following argument which leads to an exact continuous solution:

Let C(I) equal the concentration at step I. Then the relationship we are using to express the new concentration from the old at each step can be written

$$C(I) = C(I-1)/(1 + D).$$

Using algebra we can rewrite this as

$$C(I)-C(I-1) = -D*C(I).$$

Let $\Delta C = C(I)-C(I-1)$, and $\Delta X = D$. We can rewrite the expression again to read

$$\frac{\Delta C}{\Delta X} = -C.$$

This difference equation leads to the differential equation

$$\frac{dC}{dX} = -C.$$

The solution of this equation is well known and given by

$$C = C_0 \, e^{-X}$$

where C_0 is the initial concentration. Substituting $C=1$ and $X=1$ into this expression, we get the exact continuous solution

$$C = .36788.$$

Problem 2: Expand Problem 1 to include a second concentrated solution which is diluted with the discarded solution from the first concentrated solution. Write a program which will simulate the dilution of each substance and find the final concentration. The initial concentration and and the step size should be entered by the user.

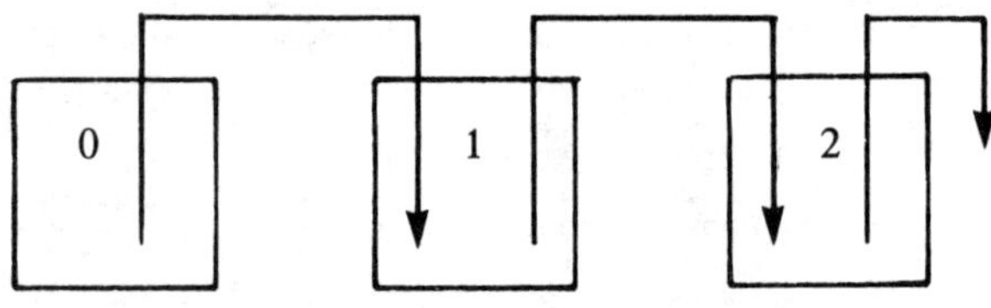

The Algorithm: Let C1 and C2 be the concentration of the first and second solution respectively. If D is the number of liters added in each step, then the concentration of the first liquid is diluted at each step to give

$$C1=C1/(1+D)$$

as before. D liters of this solution is passed on the new concentrated solution and changes its concentration to

$$C2=(C2+D*C1)/(1+D).$$

The D*C1 is the contribution from the previous beaker.
The Program:

```
10 PRINT "CONTINUOUS DILUTION PROBLEM 2 "
20 PRINT "=============================="
30 INPUT "THE INITIAL CONCENTRATION OF SOLUTION 1 >>> ",C1
40 INPUT "THE INITIAL CONCENTRATION OF SOLUTION 2 >>> ",C2
50 INPUT "MILLILITERS OF WATER ADDED EACH STEP >>> ",M
60 N=1000/M              \ REM N = THE NUMBER OF STEPS
70 D=M/1000              \ REM D = WATER IN LITERS
80 T = 0                 \ REM T = MILLILITERS ADDED
90 PRINT "MILLILITERS ADDED",TAB(20),"SOLUTION 1",
   TAB(35),"SOLUTION 2"
100 FOR I=1 TO N
110 PRINT TAB(3),T,TAB(20),C1,TAB(35),C2
120    C1=C1/(1+D)
130    C2=(C2+D*C1)/(1+D)
140 T=T+M
150 NEXT I
160 PRINT TAB(3),T,TAB(10),"ANSWER = ",TAB(20),C1,
   TAB(35),C2
170 END
```

122

```
CONTINUOUS DILUTION PROBLEM 2
=============================
THE INITIAL CONCENTRATION OF SOLUTION 1 >>> 1
THE INITIAL CONCENTRATION OF SOLUTION 2 >>> 1
MILLILITERS OF WATER ADDED EACH STEP >>> 100
MILLILITERS ADDED      SOLUTION 1      SOLUTION 2
    0                  1               1
    100                .90909091       .99173555
    200                .82644628       .97670927
    300                .7513148        .95621891
    400                .68301345       .93138209
    500                .62092132       .90315838
    600                .56447393       .87236888
    700                .51315812       .83971335
    800                .46650738       .80578554
    900                .42409762       .77108664
    1000    ANSWER =   .38554329       .73603725

MILLILITERS OF WATER ADDED EACH STEP >>> 50
MILLILITERS ADDED      SOLUTION 1      SOLUTION 2
    1000    ANSWER =   .37688949       .73583189

MILLILITERS OF WATER ADDED EACH STEP >>> 10
MILLILITERS ADDED      SOLUTION 1      SOLUTION 2
    1000    ANSWER =   .36971125       .73576197

MILLILITERS OF WATER ADDED EACH STEP >>> 1
MILLILITERS ADDED      SOLUTION 1      SOLUTION 2
    1000    ANSWER =   .36806335       .73575889

MILLILITERS OF WATER ADDED EACH STEP >>> .5
MILLILITERS ADDED      SOLUTION 1      SOLUTION 2
    1000    ANSWER =   .36797136       .73575901
```

Remarks:
1. The last four runs were made with the intermediate print out deleted.

2. The limiting values for the concentrated solutions that result when M approaches zero would be the exact continuous solutions.

3. Those familiar with differential equations will be able to understand the following argument which leads to an exact continuous solution.

As shown in the remarks following Problem 1, the concentration in the first solution satisfies the differential equation

$$\frac{dC1}{dX} = -C1.$$

The change in the concentration of the second can be derived by rewriting line 130 in the above program as

$$C2(I) = (C2(I-1) + D* C1(I))/(1 + D).$$

Let $\Delta C2 = C2(I)-C2(I-1)$ represent the change in the concentration after each step in the dilution process. Let $\Delta X = D$ and write the last expression in terms of the difference equation

$$\frac{\Delta C2}{\Delta X} = C1 - C2.$$

This leads to the second differential equation

$$\frac{dC2}{dX} = C1 - C2.$$

The two differential equations form a linear system of differential equations with the following solutions

$$C1 = C1_0 \, e^{-X}$$
$$C2 = C1_0 \, X e^{-X} + C2_0 \, e^{-X}.$$

When $X=1$, $C1_0 = 1$ and $C2_0 = 1$, we have $C1 = .36788$, $C2 = .73576$. $\square$

References
[1] *Priorities In School Mathematics*, National Council of Teachers of Mathematics, funded by the National Science Foundation, directed by Alan Osborne. Available from the ERIC Documentation Reproduction Service, P.O. Box 190, Arlington, VA 22210.
[2] Greenspan, Donald, *Arithmetic Applied Mathematics*, Pergamon Press, Elmsford, New York, 1980.

A Dozen Apples for the Classroom

Joyce Hakansson
Leslie Roach

The Science Shuttle is a unique and innovative project designed to bring computers into the school classroom. Each morning a van loaded with 12 Apple II microcomputers leaves the Lawrence Hall of Science for a school somewhere in the greater San Francisco Bay Area. Once there, two instructors unload the micros and in a half-hour set up a temporary computer laboratory within the school. During the day up to 120 students will experience the joy and excitement of learning and creating programs using interactive computers. For some students this might be a one-time introductory workshop, while for others it will be one in a series of programming and problem-solving classes.

One advantage of the Science Shuttle is that it allows us to demonstrate in local classrooms the teaching approach used at the Lawrence Hall of Science. The Lawrence Hall of Science is a science museum and a science education research center located on the University of California, Berkeley, campus. The teaching approach at the Hall is to provide people with "hands-on," participatory experiences that will promote discovery learning. For computer education, this means that the students have a chance to create, write, and debug their own computer programs while working at a computer terminal.

For the past eight years LHS has pioneered hands-on computer education through activities based on our 80 terminal time sharing system. Terminals are used as exhibits in the museum, in classes at LHS, and casually by individuals coming to the Hall. We log annually about 40,000 paid enrollments in our computer activities.

A few dozen Bay Area schools are remote users of the time sharing system, but almost none can afford to have more than one or two terminals, and cannot use our hands-on approach with a full class of students. The Science Shuttle now makes it possible for the first time to take this approach with us out to the schools. There the instructors, who are University undergraduates from various academic disciplines, encourage students to view the computer as an intellectual tool. Students are taught to develop a problem solving strategy from which they devise a logical procedure for the computer to follow. They then translate their description into a programming language, BASIC, which is understood by the machine. Debugging can be tedious, but the prospect of sharing a well-written program with others is a tempting challenge.

The Science Shuttle has allowed the Lawrence Hall's Computer Group to realize two of its long term goals: to make computers accessible to a larger number of students and to bring computers into the "average" classroom. Due to cutbacks in State funding for educational programs, many schools found that they did not have money in their budgets to transport students to us. Even when funds were available the number of classes we could teach at the Hall was severely limited by the

Joyce Hakansson, Coordinator, Computer Education; Leslie Roach, Computer Group; Lawrence Hall of Science, University of California, Berkeley, CA 94720, (415) 642-3167.

Leslie Roach and Margie Gardner show off one of the Lawrence Hall of Science "Apple Carts" and its contents as they pack up the Science Shuttle for its daily trip to a San Francisco Bay Area school. The "commuting classroom" has been booked solid since it began operation in January.

The van accommodates four carts. Each one contains three computer systems consisting of an Apple II computer, a disk drive and a color TV that serves as a monitor. Unloading the van is a one-person job. Each cart weighs about 250 lbs. when fully loaded, but the ramp and large wheels make it relatively easy to unload and wheel each one into a ground-level classroom.

size of our facility. Once portability was made possible by the microcomputer, it was only logical for us to bring our classes to schools unable to come to us. Partial support from Apple Computer Inc. has made it possible to establish the Science Shuttle.

Many educators are aware of the importance of computing, but few of them know how to bring it into the schools. The Science Shuttle is a total computing package (equipment, instructor and curriculum) at the relatively low cost of about $200 per two-hour visit. It has been a colossal success, with nearly every date booked from January 1 to the end of the school year — 6000 miles of travel and 5000 contact hours. The students enjoy the experience, the teachers become excited about it as a new teaching method, and administrators have a chance to see computers in the classroom before making a large capital investment. Often this combination has led schools to initiate their own computer education programs. □

Here goes the last of the four carts. Going out with the Science Shuttle tests an instructor's versatility. Leslie drives the van, unloads the carts and teaches the classes. If any of the equipment malfunctions, she has learned to diagnose and, in many cases, fix the problem right there. Despite all of the travelling, the equipment has held up very well.

Away they go — off to a classroom. The greatest potential hazard to the equipment is sharp bumps and jolts. To prevent damage, the TV's are firmly strapped in place. Computers and disk drives are cushioned by rubber matting and strapped onto a plywood board to form a compact unit.

A positive aspect of the program is its portability. We can teach almost anywhere. This happens to be a classroom, but we have also used libraries, multi-purpose rooms, and even outdoor patios. The carts form the base for a work station. Hollow-core doors are hinged onto the top allowing desk space for the students.

Each cart with its table-top accommodates three microcomputers. The board containing an Apple and its disk drive is placed on the table. The 13" TV monitor fits easily on top. Not much more has to be done, and it's a good thing — by this time there is a group of anxious students waiting to begin class. The set-up is completed by plugging into a power supply. Total set-up time is 20 minutes.

Groups have their choice of two programs: single-visit workshops or multi-visit programming series. In the workshops, up to 32 children at a time have an hour to an hour and a half introduction to computers. The time is spent playing interactive educational games. This is an exploratory session in which both children and local teachers have an opportunity to become acquainted with the computer. For some students, this will be their first interactive computing experience in an educational setting. The programming series, as the name suggests, is a series of classes in which the students learn problem solving and computer programming in BASIC.

Apples, con't...

BASIC syntax is learned as part of a group programming project. Students make suggestions for each statement and then test it on their computers, debugging as they go along. The programming instruction heavily emphasizes color graphics, which is one of the Apple's stong points. Students get exciting and creative results using simple syntax. Teaching programming with an emphasis on graphics is highly motivating and makes it easier for many people, especially young children, to understand the underlying concepts.

Students are encouraged to work in pairs. Working together at a computer provides a creative and dynamic learning environment from which to approach problem solving and program design. The computer's responsive interactive qualities make it an ideal playmate. Often the desire to alter a computer game leads the student naturally into the process of programming. This requires the child to develop problem solving skills, to invent logical procedures, and to learn the computer's language.

Research Questions

This pilot project suggests a number of possible topics for further investigation and research:

1. If students learn how to program a computer early, will they maintain their enthusiasm in later years?
2. If students learn how to program a computer early, will the interest and confidence level of girls, in later years, continue to match that of boys?
3. What factors influence the acceptance of microcomputers in the classroom? Graphics? Games? Programming problems?
4. What is the relationship between logical thinking skills and creative programming skill?

Conclusion

Computers have been used in education primarily as a **delivery system** for subject matter. This role will continue to be developed even

Instead of the computer programming the student, the student learns how to program the computer.

further with microcomputers. However, a new application is emerging which is fundamentally different. Instead of the computer programming the student, the student learns how to program the computer. Arthur Luehmann describes it as follows:

"Computing constitutes a new and fundamental intellectual resource. To use that resource as a mere delivery system for instruction, but not to give a student instruction in how he/she might use the resource, has been the chief failure of the CAI effort. What a loss of opportunity if the skill of computing were to be harnessed for the purpose of turning out masses of students who are unable to use computing."

The computer as an instrument for learning logical thinking and problem-solving skills is only beginning to be understood. However, with the rapid development of low cost microcomputers in the next few years, computers - and hence computer problem-solving techniques - will become a fundamental intellectual resource. □

Micros "GOTO" School

Donald T. Piele

Microcomputers can be used in the classroom for: instructional activities that we associate with CAI (Computer Assisted Instruction) or CMI (Computer Managed Instruction); enrichment activities that we associate with simulations and games; making numerical calculations for the purpose of solving mathematical problems; teaching students how to program - primarily in the BASIC language; and individual exploration of original problem-solving.

Each lesson consists of a simple program with a short explanation of the new statements, a sample run, and a series of simple program changes for the student to do.

This article is focused on the latter activity. It is a report of a pilot project in which a microcomputer was placed in a sixth grade classroom for 8 weeks for the purpose of developing logical thinking skills. The students were given instruction on how to program the APPLE II microcomputer to draw color graphics designs. They were then given similar problems to solve using the commands they had learned.

An Apple For The Teacher

In the Spring of 1978, I contacted Gordon Kunaschk, a sixth grade teacher at Bose Elementary School in Kenosha, Wisconsin. He was receptive to the idea of giving up two hours a week of class time for eight weeks to let me teach his sixth graders how to program a microcomputer. If nothing else, it would be a lesson in computer literacy. Gordie had never programmed a computer before, but he was

Don Piele, University of Wisconsin-Parkside, Kenosha, WI 53141.

willing to learn along with the kids if I was willing to provide a computer and the necessary instruction.

The Center For The Application of Computers at UW-Parkside supported the idea and supplied an APPLE II microcomputer for the project. This was a fortunate choice for us since the APPLE II system is easy to use: it is portable; it has a good keyboard; and most important of all, it has a very simple and natural set of graphics commands that allow the programmer to create pictures on a TV screen using 16 different colors. The ideas I wanted to emphasize about computer programming would be considerably enhanced by a graphics display. The basic programming construct of a loop, for example, could be visualized, and every problem to be solved by the students could be represented by a single picture.

Getting Started

My objective for bringing a microcomputer into a sixth grade classroom was to create an environment for **active problem-solving**. The BASIC programming language statements, enhanced by the graphics of the APPLE II microcomputer, form the logical building blocks. Each lesson consists of a simple program with a short explanation of the new statements, a sample run, and a series of simple program changes for the student to do. These activities allow the student to discover how the statements in the program effect its outcome. Also, problems are posed that require the student to combine statements in sequential order to solve a problem. As a result of working on these questions, the student gets a working understanding of practical problem-solving skills such as:

1. Understand the problem, its givens and goals
2. Make conjectures and probe the problem by trial and error
3. Decide on a set of possible methods of attack

4. Evaluate each possible approach for its correctness
5. Reflect on successful solutions and generalize

Each of the following exercises was designed to provide practice for these skills. They are samples taken from a larger collection and are not contiguous lessons.

Lesson #1

Key Words: GR, COLOR, PLOT

LIST	EXPLANATION
10 GR	The computer is
20 COLOR = 9	put in GRaphics mode.
20 COLOR = &	The COLOR is set to orange. There are 16 different colors to choose from.
30 PLOT 10,15	The position 10 over, 15 down from the upper left hand corner is plotted.
100 END	
RUN	

Programming the microcomputer was considered by the sixth graders to be highly motivating. They would rather spend their recess on it than go outdoors.

Your Turn (RUN the program after each change)

1. Change line 20 to . . 20 COLOR = 3
2. Change line 30 to . . . 30 PLOT 5,7
3. Add line 50 . . . . 50 PLOT 5,5
4. Add line 40 . . . . 40 COLOR = 6
5. Delete line 40 40
6. Add a point that connects 5,7 with 5,5 . . . . 60 PLOT ?,?

7. Add line 30 ......30 PLOT 39,39
8. Add line 40 ......40 PLOT 40,40
9. Delete line 40 40
10. Write a program that will display the first letter of your first name in graphics.

Lesson #5

Key Words: FOR-NEXT

LIST	EXPLANATION
10 GR 20 FOR I = o TO 15	Begin a loop with I = 0 and increase I by one each time until I = 15.
30 COLOR = I	The color changes with each pass through the loop.
40 PLOT I,15	The position to be plotted changes with each pass.
50 NEXT I	End of the loop. Go back to statement 20 if I is less than 15. Otherwise go to line 60.
100 END RUN	

Your Turn (RUN the program after each change.)
1. Change line 40 to ....40 PLOT I,10
2. Change line 40 to ....40 PLOT 20,I
3. Change line 20 to ....20 FOR I = 0 TO 39
4. Change line 40 to .....40 PLOT I,I
5. Add line 45 ....45 PLOT 39-I,I
6. Change the program to draw + in graphics.

Lesson #10

Key Words: RND, IF-THEN

LIST	EXPLANATION
10 GR 20 COLOR = 9 30 X = RND (40)	A random number is chosen from the numbers 0 to 39 and put in X.
40 Y = RND (40)	Another random number in chosen and placed in Y.
50 IF Y > 20 THEN COLOR = 3	If Y is larger than 20 then change the color to blue(3).
60 PLOT X,Y 70 GOTO 20 100 END	Go to line 20 and repeat.

RUN

Your Turn (RUN the program after each change.)
1. Change 50 to ....50 IF Y > 10 THEN COLOR = 3
2. Change 70 to ....70 GOTO 30
3. Change 70 to ....70 GOTO 20
4. Change 50 to ....50 IF X > 20 THEN COLOR = 3
5. Add 55 ....55 IF Y > 20 THEN COLOR = 13
6. Delete 55 55
7. Change 50 ......50 IF X + Y > 40 THEN COLOR = 3
8. Adjust the program to plot 4 different colors in the four different corners of the screen.

Tell & Run

In addition to the lessons, the students were given short problems to solve. They were asked to predict the output of a given program before they observed it run on the TV screen. This gave the students a chance to test their ability to reason sequentially through the statements of a program. A few examples are given below.

#1	#2
10 GR	10 GR
20 FOR I = 0 TO 10	20 FOR I = 10 to 20
30 COLOR = 9	30 COLOR = I
40 PLOT 2,I	40 HLIN 0,39 AT I
50 NEXT I	50 NEXT I
60 END	60 END

> **The original purpose for doubling up was to provide more computer time for the class each week. But it turned out to be valuable for a completely different reason - cooperation.**

Other activities reversed the process and presented a picture and asked the student to write a program that would produce the same result. Here are a few examples:

Computer As A Creative Tool

The APPLE II microcomputer was left in the classroom during the week to give the class time to experiment. Students signed up in pairs to work on the exercises together. The original purpose for doubling up was to provide more computer time for the class each week. But it turned out to be valuable for a completely different reason - cooperation. The students helped each other figure out the effect of each new command. The programming exercises facilitated discussions about the behavior of each new statement. New discoveries were shared with pride and enthusiasm.

The computer was the focus and facilitator for cooperative problem-solving.

Student Reactions

After eight weeks, the students were asked to respond to the following questionnaire, using a scale of 1 to 5 (1-strongly disagree, 5-strongly agree), with responses from the 6th grade class of 14 boys and 10 girls recorded.

Reflections

Only a small sample of the exercises done by the students are presented in this article. An entire collection of problems was prepared for the 6th grade class to be used on the APPLE II. At the present time, good materials are not readily available. This presents a formidable obstacle to the inexperienced teacher who wants to use computers in the classroom. As more classrooms begin using microcomputers and sharing their work with others, this problem will diminish.

Students in this sixth grade class were very enthusiastic about working with a microcomputer. In contrast, students at a nearby high school who had not been exposed to computers before were generally uninterested in learning how to use them. Perhaps by this time, the older students have other activities that are more relevant. Also, in the sixth grade the survey shows that boys and girls are equally confident and interested in programming the computer. However, in entries from 10th graders in an annual computer problem-solving contest held at UW-Parkside, the boys outnumber the girls 9 to 1. A recent survey in Creative Computing Magazine had a response with a distribution of 95.4% male and 4.2% female.

Programming the microcomputer was considered by the sixth graders to be highly motivating. They would rather spend their recess on it than go outdoors. Students came early to school and would hang around as long as they could after school. A sign-up sheet became a necessity. With practice, some of the students became resident 'experts' able and thrilled to help others - including the teacher. Some of the sixth graders entered our annual computer programming contest.

A Grade Maintenance Program for the Apple II with Disk Drive

Jim Hunter

One of the most laborious tasks for any teacher is maintaining accurate grade records. This program is designed to minimize the time required for that task and to maximize the accuracy with which it is done. Its features include: several output formats, weighting of individual marks, provision for missing grades and make-up work, and a turnkey approach which allows someone with little or no programming ability to operate it.

The program will be discussed with regard to its construct, its utilization, and its modification for individualized requirements. The accompanying listing of the initialization routine and the actual operations program should be referred to as the discussion proceeds. An added bonus, for those of you who do not have need of a grade keeping system, is that careful scrutiny of these listings will reveal one way in which to set up, maintain, and randomly access data files on the Apple II Disk II system. Please note that both programs are written in Applesoft, and large amounts of data may require large memory sizes in RAM. A firmware (ROM) card for Applesoft is also a big help for operating this routine quickly.

The initialization routine is the first step in running the package. You will note that, during this initialization process, you are called upon to

Jim Hunter; Byte Shop of Westminster, 14300 Beach Blvd., Westminster, CA 92683.

indicate the period number and class name. My application was at the secondary level, but by modifying the file labels, one could have grades by subject matter for an elementary class. This program is to be run one time for each disk (class/subject). After that, the main program will boot automatically with the turnkey menu.

The operator's first choice in the main menu is to "make input." This is used to enter new data or to change old information. The second main menu item ís "read output," and this is used to examine or print status reports. To exit the program, choice 3 (terminate work) is used.

The Program

Lines 10 to 120 are used to dimension all arrays and to print the main menu. Lines 1000 and 2400 are used to enter new or updated material. Lines 5000 to 7080 call the output routines. The remainder of the listing consists of several subroutines, as follows:

```
10000 GET CLASS DATA
11000 PRINT PAGE HEADINGS
12000 GET LAST ASSIGNMENT #
13000 GET LAST ROSTER #
14000 READ ROSTER NAMES
15000 SORT WEIGHTED AVERAGES
16000 LOAD GRADES INTO RAM
17000 LOAD ASSIGNMENT NAMES
18000 LOAD ASSIGNMENT WEIGHTS
19000 CRT FORMAT
```

The subroutines from 20000 to 28330 are output formatting devices. More about these formats will be discussed later. Lines 31000 to 32000 are used to turn the printer on and off.

Operation

From the main menu, the first branch loads minimal data for manipulation. The second branch, output, loads ALL files for use in the printout. It is suggested that, when running this program, the operator first make any and all inputs prior to making output runs. The input portion allows the operator to change any data, except the "classpool" information which is generated during the initialization process.

When entering new data, a code is used for a student who did not complete the work, but who will do so at a future time. For this purpose, enter "1" as the grade, and that mark will not be included in any of the averages. Later, when the work is made up, use the "input" routine to alter the mark. It will then automatically be included in the averages for the student, the class, and the assignment.

One of the problems which I encountered when developing this program was the fact that not all assignments are worth the same amount of credit. For this reason, when entering a class set of marks, you will be asked for the assignment number, assignment name, and the weighting. I used factors from .01 to 1, but the operator can choose anything which he feels comfortable with. A weighting of "1" is suggested for major assignments or exams, while ".1" might be used for quizzes or homework.

Once all new data and updates have been posted, the next logical step is to examine or print output. The output formats number four:

1. A STUDENT FILE.
2. CLASS AVERAGES BY STUDENT.
3. CLASS AVERAGES BY ASSIGNMENT.
4. RANKED AVERAGES BY STUDENT.

The first of these formats is used to evaluate the progress of an individual student. The second gives a class summary by roster number of each student's present average. My experience revealed that weekly posting of this output served two purposes. First, the students got constant feedback on their progress; and second, arguments as to what grade was being earned at progress report time were reduced to zero.

The third type of printout is the class averages by assignment. This is a useful tool to evaluate comparative difficulty of assignments. This output is primarily an instructor's tool. Finally, printout number four is a ranked output from highest to lowest. This also was posted, but I recommend that you check with your students first on that one.

Sample outputs for each format are shown with the listings. The class shown is, of course, fictitious.

Suggestions For Modifications

The most obvious area where modifications would be called for is hard copy output. The printer I was using was hooked into slot 1 with a Parallel Card from Apple. You may want to modify this portion as required. One section of the program as I use it which has been omitted is the actual assignment of grades by the computer. This is accomplished by inserting a subroutine which determines the letter grade and then changing the output statements to reflect that data.

If one were concerned with student anonymity on the ranked listing, names could be deleted and roster numbers could be used exclusively. These modifications, coupled with those mentioned in the beginning of this article, should make the program a tool which will serve the needs of teachers at all levels of instruction.

Summary

A little time spent weekly on the Apple will reap great benefits for both the teacher and the student. By ending the mystique of grades, and thus clearing away the cloud surrounding them, a teacher can spend more time doing what he is paid for...teaching.

And as for all of you non-teachers (now including myself) read over the listings here, and learn of the mysteries of file maintenance on the Apple. It took me several weeks and calls to Cupertino to arrive at this information. If it helps you, then I have served my purpose well.

Disk copies of this program are available from:

The Byte Shop of Westminster, 14300 Beach Blvd., Westminster, CA 92683.

The cost is $40, with documentation, $30 without. (This article is really all you need). □

SAMPLE PRINT OUTS
Format #1

```
PERIOD 1               ENGLISH LITERATURE
DATE OF RUN: 7 JANUARY 1979
INCLUDES ASSIGNMENTS TO #6
LAST ASSIGNMENT NAME IS:SHAKESPEARE ESSAY

ROSTER NUMBER: 3      CLAIRMONT BEVERLY

      ASSIGNMENT                STUDENT
NO.  WT.    NAME                MARK

1    .1   FIRST QUIZ              89
2    .1   SECOND QUIZ            87
3    1    CLASS ESSAY            92
4    .33  PARA DRILL            59
5    1    FIRST EXAM            92
6    .8   SHAKESPEARE ESSAY    100
AVERAGE TO DATE IS: 90.4
```

SAMPLE PRINT OUTS
Format #2

```
PERIOD 1               ENGLISH LITERATURE
DATE OF RUN: 7 JANUARY 1979
INCLUDES ASSIGNMENTS TO #6
LAST ASSIGNMENT NAME IS:SHAKESPEARE ESSAY

*********** CLASS SUMMARY ***********
ROSTER   STUDENT              CURRENT
NUMBER   NAME                 AVG

1      ABERCROMBY JOHN         89.2
2      BENNET CHRIS            71.6
3      CLAIRMONT BEVERLY       90.4
4      DEMAUPASSANT GUY *      82
5      EVERLY BOB              85
6      FRITCHMAN CLAUDE        84.6
7      GEORGE GORGEOUS         81
```

B. The * next to Guy's name means that he
    is missing an assignment.

SAMPLE PRINT OUTS
Format #3

```
PERIOD 1               ENGLISH LITERATURE
DATE OF RUN: 7 JANUARY 1979
INCLUDES ASSIGNMENTS TO #6
LAST ASSIGNMENT NAME IS:SHAKESPEARE ESSAY

********** ASSIGNMENT SUMMARY *********

      ASSIGNMENT          NUMBER    CLASS
NO.  WT.    NAME          MISSING   AVG.

1    .1   FIRST QUIZ         0       78
2    .1   SECOND QUIZ        0       86
3    1    CLASS ESSAY        0       90
4    .33  PARA DRILL         1       74
5    1    FIRST EXAM         0       95
6    .8   SHAKESPEARE ESSAY0         62

WEIGHTED CLASS AVERAGE TO DATE IS: 82
```

SAMPLE PRINT OUTS
Format #4

```
PERIOD 1               ENGLISH LITERATURE
DATE OF RUN: 7 JANUARY 1979
INCLUDES ASSIGNMENTS TO #6
LAST ASSIGNMENT NAME IS:SHAKESPEARE ESSAY

********* RANKED AVERAGES *********

CLASS        STUDENT          CURRENT
RANKING      NAME             AVG

1          CLAIRMONT BEVERLY    90.4
2          ABERCROMBY JOHN      89.2
3          EVERLY BOB           85
4          FRITCHMAN CLAUDE     84.6
5          DEMAUPASSANT GUY *   82
6          GEORGE GORGEOUS      81
7          BENNET CHRIS         71.6
```

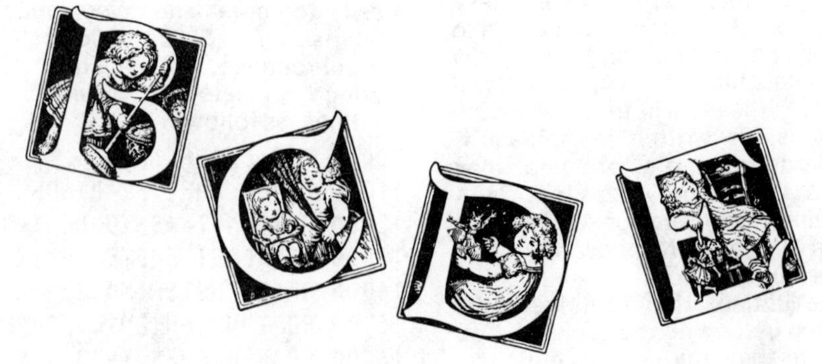

INITIALIZATION ROUTINE

```
JPR#0
JLIST

10   D$ = ""
20   PRINT "";"NOMON I,O,C"
30   HOME
40   PRINT "WHAT IS THE PERIOD NUM
     BER?"
50   INPUT P
60   PRINT "WHAT IS THE CLASS NAME
     ?"
70   INPUT CLASS$
80   PRINT D$;"OPEN CLASSPOOP$,L25
     "
90   PRINT D$;"WRITE CLASSPOOP$,R1
     "
100   PRINT P
110   PRINT D$;"WRITE CLASSPOOP$,R
      2"
120   PRINT CLASS$
130   PRINT D$;"CLOSE CLASSPOOP$"
140   PRINT D$;"OPEN ASSNAME$,L25"

150   FOR I = 1 TO 40
160   PRINT D$;"WRITE ASSNAME$,R";
      I
170   PRINT " "
180   NEXT I
190   PRINT D$;"CLOSE ASSNAME$"
200   PRINT D$;"OPEN L%,L4"
210   FOR I = 1 TO 2
220   PRINT D$;"WRITE L%,R";I
230   PRINT 0
235   NEXT I
240   PRINT D$;"CLOSE L%"
250   PRINT D$;"OPEN ASSWT%,L4"
260   FOR I = 1 TO 40
270   PRINT D$;"WRITE ASSWT%,R";I
280   PRINT 0
290   PRINT D$;"CLOSE ASSWT%"
300   PRINT D$;"OPEN NAME$,L25"
310   FOR I = 1 TO 40
320   PRINT D$;"WRITE NAME$,R";I
330   PRINT " "
340   NEXT I
350   PRINT D$;"CLOSE NAME$"
```

MAIN PROGRAM LISTING

```
JLIST

10   PRINT "";"NOMON I,O,C"
20   D$ = ""
30   DIM NAME$(40),G(40,50),W(50),ASSNAME$(50)
35   DIM AVG(40)
```

```
2170   PRINT D$;"OPEN G%";A;",L4"
2180   FOR I = 1 TO LN
2190   PRINT D$;"WRITE G%";A;",R";I
2195   PRINT G(I,A)
2200   NEXT I
2210   PRINT D$;"CLOSE G%";A
2220   PRINT D$;"APPEND ASSNAME$,L25"
2230   PRINT D$;"WRITE ASSNAME$,R";A
2240   PRINT ASSNAME$(A)
2250   PRINT D$;"CLOSE ASSNAME$"
2260   PRINT D$;"APPEND ASSWT%,L4"
2270   PRINT D$;"WRITE ASSWT%,R";A
2280   PRINT W(A)
2290   PRINT D$;"CLOSE ASSWT%"
2300   GOSUB 11000
2310   PRINT D$;"OPEN L%,L4"
2320   PRINT D$;"WRITE L%,R2"
2330   PRINT A
2340   PRINT D$;"CLOSE L%"
2350   GOSUB 11000
2360   PRINT "ANOTHER SET OF MARKS";
2370   INPUT C$
2380   IF C$ < > "Y" AND C$ < > "YES" THEN 60
2390   GOSUB 12000
2400   GOTO 2010
5000   GOSUB 11000
5010   PRINT
5020   PRINT "WHAT DO YOU WANT TO CHANGE?"
5030   PRINT : PRINT " 1.   STUDENT NAME. "
5040   PRINT " 2.   STUDENT GRADE. "
5050   PRINT " 3.   ASSIGNMENT NAME. "
5060   PRINT " 4.   ASSIGNMENT WEIGHT. "
5065   PRINT " 5.   RETURN TO MAIN MENU. "
5070   PRINT : PRINT "WHAT DO YOU WISH, MASTER"
5080   INPUT C
5090   ON C GOTO 5100,5300,5500,5700,60
5100   PRINT "WHAT ROSTER NUMBER DO YOU WISH?";
5110   INPUT N
5120   PRINT D$;"OPEN NAME$,L25"
5130   PRINT D$;"READ NAME$,R";N
5140   INPUT NAME$(N)
5150   PRINT D$;"CLOSE NAME$"
5160   PRINT "NAME NUMBER ";N;" IS NOW ";NAME$(N)
5170   PRINT "WHAT IS THE NEW NAME?";
5180   INPUT NAME$(N)
5185   IF NAME$(N) = "AVAILABLE" THEN  GOSUB 7000
5190   PRINT D$;"APPEND NAME$,L25"
5200   PRINT D$;"WRITE NAME$,R";N
5210   PRINT NAME$(N)
5230   PRINT D$;"CLOSE NAME$"
5240   PRINT : PRINT "DO YOU WANT TO CHANGE ANOTHER NAME?";
5250   INPUT C$
5260   IF C$ < > "Y" AND C$ < > "YES" THEN 5000
5270   GOTO 5100
5300   GOSUB 11000
5310   PRINT : PRINT "WHAT ROSTER NUMBERT DO YOU WANT";
5320   INPUT N
5330   PRINT : PRINT "WHAT ASSIGNMENT NUMBER DO YOU WANT";
5340   INPUT A
5350   PRINT D$;"APPEND G%";A;",L4"
5360   PRINT D$;"READ G%";A;",R";N
5370   INPUT G(N,A)
5380   PRINT D$;"CLOSE G%";A
5390   PRINT : PRINT "THE CURRENT GRADE FOR ROSTER NUMBER ";N
5400   PRINT "FOR ASSIGNMENT NUMBER ";A;" IS ";G(N,A)
5410   PRINT : PRINT "WHAT IS THE NEW GRADE";
```

```
36    DIM M(40)
37    DIM MA(50)
38    DIM X(40)
39    DIM ASSTAVG(50)
40    HOME
50    GOSUB 10000
60    GOSUB 11000
65    PRINT
70    PRINT "YOU HAVE THREE INITIAL OPTIONS:"
75 Q = 0
80    PRINT : PRINT "  1.   MAKE INPUT. "
90    PRINT "  2.   READ OUTPUT. "
100   PRINT "  3.   TERMINATE WORK. "
110   PRINT : INPUT "WHAT IS YOUR PLEASURE";C
120   ON C GOTO 1000,20000,32000
1000  HOME
1010  GOSUB 11000
1020  PRINT : PRINT "NEXT CHOICE:"
1030  PRINT "  1.   ENTER NEW DATA. "
1040  PRINT "  2.   CHANGE EXISTING DATA. "
1050  PRINT : INPUT "WHAT IS YOUR PLEASURE";C
1060  ON C GOTO 1100,5000
1100  GOSUB 11000
1110  PRINT : PRINT "WHICH OF THE FOLLOWING DO YOU WISH:"
1120  PRINT : PRINT "  1.   ENTER CLASS ROSTER. "
1130  PRINT "  2.   ENTER CLASS SET OF MARKS. "
1150  PRINT : INPUT "PICK ONE:";C
1160  ON C GOTO 1200,2000
1200  GOSUB 11000: PRINT
1210  PRINT "AS EACH NUMBER APPEARS, ENTER THE"
1220  PRINT "CORRESPONDING ROSTER NAME.   WHEN YOU"
1230  PRINT "HAVE EXHAUSTED THE NAMES, THEN TYPE"
1240  PRINT " 'LAST'. "
1250  FOR I = 1 TO 40
1260  PRINT I;
1270  INPUT NAME$(I)
1280  IF NAME$(I) = "LAST" THEN LN = I - 1
1290  IF NAME$(I) = "LAST" THEN I = 40
1300  NEXT I
1310  PRINT D$;"OPEN NAME$,L25"
1320  FOR I = 1 TO LN
1330  PRINT D$;"WRITE NAME$,R";I
1340  PRINT NAME$(I)
1350  NEXT I
1360  PRINT D$;"CLOSE NAME$"
1370  PRINT D$;"OPEN L%,L4"
1380  PRINT D$;"WRITE L%,R1"
1390  PRINT LN
1400  PRINT D$;"CLOSE L%"
1410  HOME
1420  GOTO 60
2000  GOSUB 11000: GOSUB 12000: GOSUB 13000: GOSUB 14000
2010  PRINT
2020  PRINT "THE LAST ASSIGNMENT NUMBER WAS:  ";LA
2030  PRINT "WHAT IS THIS ASSIGNMENT NUMBER"
2040  INPUT A
2050  GOSUB 11000
2060  PRINT "WHAT IS THE ASSIGNMENT NAME"
2070  INPUT ASSNAME$(A)
2080  PRINT "WHAT IS THE WEIGHTING FOR THIS WORK"
2090  INPUT W(A)
2100  GOSUB 11000
2110  PRINT : PRINT "AFTER THE ROSTER NUMBER AND NAME, YOU"
2120  PRINT "ARE TO ENTER THE SCORE FOR THAT STUDENT"
2130  FOR I = 1 TO LN
2140  PRINT I; TAB( 5)NAME$(I);
2150  INPUT G(I,A)
2160  NEXT I
5420  INPUT G(N,A)
5430  PRINT D$;"APPEND G%";A;",L4"
5440  PRINT D$;"WRITE G%";A;",R";N
5450  PRINT G(N,A)
5460  PRINT D$;"CLOSE G%";A
5470  PRINT : PRINT "DO YOU WANT TO CHANGE ANOTHER GRADE";
5480  INPUT C$
5485  IF C$ < > "Y" AND C$ < > "YES" THEN  GOTO 5000
5490  GOTO 5300
5500  GOSUB 11000
5510  PRINT : PRINT "WHAT ASSIGNMENT DO YOU WANT TO CHANGE";
5520  INPUT A
5530  PRINT D$;"APPEND ASSNAME$,L25"
5540  PRINT D$;"READ ASSNAME$,R";A
5550  INPUT ASSNAME$(A)
5560  PRINT D$;"CLOSE ASSNAME$"
5570  PRINT : PRINT "THE CURRENT NAME FOR ASSIGNMENT NO.  ";A
5580  PRINT "IS ";ASSNAME$(A)
5590  PRINT : PRINT "WHAT IS THE NEW ASSIGNMENT NAME";
5600  INPUT ASSNAME$(A)
5610  PRINT D$;"APPEND ASSNAME$,L25"
5620  PRINT D$;"WRITE ASSNAME$,R";A
5630  PRINT ASSNAME$(A)
5640  PRINT D$;"CLOSE ASSNAME$"
5650  PRINT : PRINT "DO YOU WANT TO CHANGE ANOTHER NAME";
5660  INPUT C$
5670  IF C$ < > "Y" AND C$ < > "YES" THEN 5000
5680  GOTO 5500
5700  GOSUB 11000
5710  PRINT : PRINT "WHAT ASSIGNMENT DO YOU WANT TO CHANGE"
5720  PRINT "THE WEIGHTING ON";
5730  INPUT A
5740  PRINT D$;"APPEND ASSWT%,L4"
5750  PRINT D$;"READ ASSWT%,R";A
5760  INPUT W(A)
5770  PRINT D$;"CLOSE ASSWT%"
5780  PRINT : PRINT "THE CURRENT WEIGHTING FOR ASSIGNMENT "
5785  PRINT "NUMBER ";A;" IS ";W(A)
5790  PRINT : PRINT "WHAT IS THE NEW WEIGHTING";
5800  INPUT W(A)
5810  PRINT D$;"APPEND ASSWT%,L4"
5820  PRINT D$;"WRITE ASSWT%,R";A
5830  PRINT W(A)
5840  PRINT D$;"CLOSE ASSWT%"
5850  PRINT : PRINT "DO YOU WANT TO CHANGE ANOTHER WEIGHT";
5860  INPUT C$
5870  IF C$ < > "Y" AND C$ < > "YES" THEN 5000
5880  GOTO 5700
7000  GOSUB 11000
7010  GOSUB 12000
7020  FOR A = 1 TO LA
7030  PRINT D$;"APPEND G%";A;",L4"
7040  PRINT D$;"WRITE G%";A;",R";N
7050  PRINT 0
7060  PRINT D$;"CLOSE G%";A
7070  NEXT A
7080  RETURN
9999  END
10000 REM  SUBROUTINE TO GET CLASS DATA FOR SHEET HEADINGS
10005 PRINT D$;"OPEN CLASSPOOP$,L25"
10010 FOR I = 1 TO 2
10030 PRINT D$;"READ CLASSPOOP$,R";I
10040 INPUT CLASSPOOP$(I)
10050 NEXT I
10060 PRINT D$;"CLOSE CLASSPOOP$"
10070 REM  CLASSPOOP$(1)=PERIOD
10080 REM  CLASSPOOP$(2)=CLASS$
```

```
10090 P$ = CLASSPOOP$(1)
10100 CLASS$ = CLASSPOOP$(2)
10110  RETURN
11000  REM  SUBROUTINE TO PRINT PAGE HEADINGS
11005  HOME
11010  PRINT "PERIOD ";P$;
11020  PRINT  TAB( 40 -  LEN (CLASS$))CLASS$
11030  IF Q = 0 THEN  RETURN
11040  PRINT "DATE OF RUN: ";TIME$
11050  PRINT "INCLUDES ASSIGNMENTS TO #";LA
11060  PRINT "LAST ASSIGNMENT NAME IS:";ASSNAME$(LA)
11070  RETURN
12000  REM  SUBROUTINE TO GET LAST ASSIGNMENT NUMBER
12005  PRINT D$;"OPEN L%,L4"
12010  PRINT D$;"READ L%,R2"
12020  INPUT LA
12030  PRINT D$;"CLOSE L%"
12040  RETURN
13000  REM  SUBROUTINE TO GET LAST ROSTER NUMBER
13005  PRINT D$;"OPEN L%,L4"
13010  PRINT D$;"READ L%,R1"
13020  INPUT LN
13030  PRINT D$;"CLOSE L%"
13040  RETURN
14000  REM  SUBROUTINE TO READ ROSTER NAMES
14005  PRINT D$;"OPEN NAME$,L25"
14010  FOR I = 1 TO LN
14020  PRINT D$;"READ NAME$,R";I
14030  INPUT NAME$(I)
14040  NEXT I
14050  PRINT D$;"CLOSE NAME$"
14060  RETURN
15000  REM  SUBROUTINE TO SORT WEIGHTED AVERAGES
15005 M = 0
15010 W = 0:T = 0
15020  FOR I = 1 TO LA
15025  IF G(N,I) = 1 THEN M = M + 1
15030  IF G(N,I) = 1 THEN  GOTO 15060
15040 W = W + W(I)
15050 T = T + G(N,I) * W(I)
15060  NEXT I
15070 AVG(N) =  INT ((T / (W * 100)) * 1000) / 10
15075 M(N) = M
15080  RETURN
16000  REM  SUBROUTINE TO GET ALL GRADES
16005  FOR A = 1 TO LA
16010  PRINT D$;"OPEN G%";A;",L4"
16020  FOR N = 1 TO LN
16030  PRINT D$;"READ G%";A;",R";N
16040  INPUT G(N,A)
16050  NEXT N
16060  PRINT D$;"CLOSE G%";A
16070  NEXT A
16080  RETURN
17000  REM  GET ASSIGNMENT NAMES
17010  PRINT D$;"OPEN ASSNAME$,L25"
17020  FOR I = 1 TO LA
17030  PRINT D$;"READ ASSNAME$,R";I
17040  INPUT ASSNAME$(I)
17050  NEXT I
17060  PRINT D$;"CLOSE ASSNAME$"
17070  RETURN
18000  REM  GET ASSIGNMENT WEIGHTS
18010  PRINT D$;"OPEN ASSWT%,L4"
18020  FOR I = 1 TO LA
18030  PRINT D$;"READ ASSWT%,R";I
18040  INPUT W(I)

24095  IF Q = 1 THEN  PR# 1
24100  GOSUB 11000
24110  PRINT : PRINT "********** CLASS SUMMARY **********"
24120  PRINT "ROSTER    STUDENT                 CURRENT"
24130  PRINT "NUMBER    NAME                     AVG. "
24140  PRINT
24150  FOR I = 1 TO LN
24160  PRINT I;
24170  PRINT  TAB( 7)NAME$(I);
24171  PRINT " "; : IF M(I) < 1 THEN 24180
24172  FOR J = 1 TO M(I)
24174  PRINT "*";
24176  NEXT J
24180  PRINT  TAB( 36)AVG(I)
24190  IF I / 13 =  INT (I / 13) THEN  GOSUB 19000
24200  NEXT I
24205  IF Q = 1 THEN  PR# 0
24210  PRINT : PRINT "DO YOU WANT TO SEE THEM AGAIN";
24220  INPUT C$
24230  IF C$ < > "Y" AND C$ < > "YES" THEN 20040
24240  GOTO 24100
26000  REM  SUBROUTINE TO CALCULATE CLASS AVERAGES BY ASSIGNMENT,
       AND WEIGHTED CLASS AVERAGE
26005  FOR A = 1 TO LA
26010 T = 0:NT = 0
26015 MA = 0
26020  FOR N = 1 TO LN
26025  IF G(N,A) = 1 THEN MA = MA + 1
26030  IF G(N,A) = 1 THEN  GOTO 26070
26040 T = T + G(N,A)
26050 NT = NT + 1
26060  IF NAME$(N) = "AVAILABLE" THEN NT = NT - 1
26070  NEXT N
26080 ASSTAVG(A) =  INT (T / (NT * 100) * 100)
26085 MA(A) = MA
26090  NEXT A
26095  IF Q = 1 THEN  PR# 1
26100  GOSUB 11000
26110  PRINT : PRINT "********** ASSIGNMENT SUMMARY **********"
26120  PRINT : PRINT "  ASSIGNMENT         NUMBER    CLASS"
26130  PRINT "NO.  WT.    NAME      MISSING    AVG. "
26140  PRINT
26150  FOR A = 1 TO LA
26160  PRINT A;
26170  PRINT  TAB( 6)W(A);
26180  PRINT  TAB( 10)ASSNAME$(A);
26185  PRINT  TAB( 25)MA(A);
26190  PRINT  TAB( 36)ASSTAVG(A)
26200  IF A / 13 =  INT (A / 13) THEN  GOSUB 19000
26210  NEXT A
26211 T = 0
26212 W = 0
26213  FOR I = 1 TO LA
26214 T = T + ASSTAVG(I) * W(I)
26215 W = W + W(I)
26216  NEXT I
26217 CAVG =  INT (T / (W * 100) * 100)
26218  PRINT : PRINT "WEIGHTED CLASS AVERAGE TO DATE IS: ";CAVG
26219  IF Q = 1 THEN  PR# 0
26220  PRINT : PRINT "DO YOU WANT TO SEE THEM AGAIN?";
26230  INPUT C$
26240  IF C$ < > "Y" AND C$ < > "YES" THEN  GOTO 20040
26250  GOTO 26100
28000  REM  SUBROUTINE TO OUTPUT RANKED AVERAGES
28005  FOR N = 1 TO LN
28010  GOSUB 15000
28020  NEXT N
```

134

```
18050    NEXT I
18060    PRINT D$;"CLOSE ASSWT%"
18070    RETURN
19000    REM  SUBROUTINE TO DISPLAY 13 LINES OF OUTPUT FOR CRT USE
         DELETED WITH PRINTER USAGE
19002    IF Q = 1 THEN  RETURN
19005    PRINT : PRINT "RETURN TO CONTINUE"
19010    INPUT C$
19020    HOME
19030    RETURN
20000    INPUT "DO YOU WANT HARD COPY";C$
20002    IF C$ = "Y" OR C$ = "YES" THEN Q = 1
20004    IF C$ = "Y" OR C$ = "YES" THEN  PRINT "TURN ON PRINTER NOW!
         "
20005    INPUT "WHAT IS THE DATE";TIME$
20010    GOSUB 12000: GOSUB 13000
20020    GOSUB 14000: GOSUB 16000
20030    GOSUB 17000: GOSUB 18000
20040    GOSUB 11000
20050    PRINT : PRINT "DISPLAY OF DATA IS IN FOUR FORMATS:"
20060    PRINT "  1.    STUDENT FILE. "
20070    PRINT "  2.    CLASS AVERAGES BY STUDENT. "
20080    PRINT "  3.    CLASS AVERAGES BY ASSIGNMENT. "
20090    PRINT "  4.    RANKED CLASS AVERAGES BY STUDENT. "
20095    PRINT "  5.    RETURN TO BASIC MENU. "
20097    PRINT "  6.    PRINTER ON. "
20098    PRINT "  7.    PRINTER OFF. "
20100    PRINT : PRINT "PICK ONE. ";
20110    INPUT C
20120    ON C GOTO 22000,24000,26000,28000,60,31000,31100
22000    REM  SUBROUTINE TO OUTPUT INDIVIDUAL STUDENT MARKS WITH AVE
         RAGE TO DATE
22005    GOSUB 11000
22010    PRINT : PRINT "WHAT ROSTER NUMBER DO YOU WANT TO SEE. "
22020    INPUT N
22025    IF Q = 1 THEN  PR# 1
22030    GOSUB 11000
22040    PRINT : PRINT "ROSTER NUMBER: ";N;
22050    PRINT  TAB( 40 -  LEN (NAME$(N))>NAME$(N)
22060    PRINT : PRINT "     ASSIGNMENT             STUDENT"
22070    PRINT "NO.  WT,      NAME              MARK"
22080    PRINT
22090    FOR A = 1 TO LA
22100    PRINT A; TAB( 5)W(A); TAB( 9)ASSNAME$(A);
22102    IF G(N,A) < > 1 THEN 22106
22104    PRINT  TAB( 33)"MISSING"
22105    GOTO 22115
22106    PRINT  TAB( 37)G(N,A)
22115    IF A / 13 =  INT (A / 13) THEN  GOSUB 19000
22118    NEXT A
22120    GOSUB 15000
22130    VTAB (20)
22140    PRINT "AVERAGE TO DATE IS: ";AVG(N)
22141    IF Q = 1 THEN  PR# 0
22142    PRINT "DO YOU WANT TO SEE THEM AGAIN";
22144    INPUT C$
22146    IF C$ < > "Y" AND C$ < > "YES" THEN  GOTO 20040
22148    GOTO 22030
22150    PRINT : PRINT "CHECK ANOTHER?"
22160    INPUT C$
22170    IF C$ < > "Y" AND C$ < > "YES" THEN  GOTO 20040
22180    GOTO 22000
24000    REM  SUBROUTINE TO CALCULATE AVERAGES, PRESENTED BY ROSTER
         NUMBER
24005    FOR N = 1 TO LN
24010    GOSUB 15000
24020    NEXT N

28100    FOR H = 1 TO LN
28110    P = 1
28120    FOR B = 1 TO LN
28130    IF AVG(H) > AVG(B) THEN P = P + 1
28140    IF AVG(H) = AVG(B) AND H > B THEN P = P + 1
28150    NEXT B
28160    X(P) = H
28170    NEXT H
28180    IF Q = 1 THEN  PR# 1
28200    GOSUB 11000
28210    PRINT : PRINT "********* RANKED AVERAGES *********"
28220    PRINT : PRINT "CLASS         STUDENT             CURRENT"
28230    PRINT "RANKING         NAME              AVERAGE"
28240    PRINT : FOR R = LN TO 1 STEP  - 1
28245    K =  ABS (R - LN) + 1
28250    PRINT K;
28260    PRINT  TAB( 10)NAME$(X(R));
28262    IF M(X(R)) < 1 THEN 28270
28263    PRINT " ";
28264    FOR I = 1 TO M(X(R))
28265    PRINT "*";
28266    NEXT I
28270    PRINT  TAB( 36)AVG(X(R))
28280    IF K / 13 =  INT (K / 13) THEN  GOSUB 19000
28290    NEXT R
28295    IF Q = 1 THEN  PR# 0
28300    PRINT : PRINT "DO YOU WANT TO SEE THEM AGAIN";
28310    INPUT C$
28320    IF C$ < > "Y" AND C$ < > "YES" THEN 20040
28330    GOTO 28200
29005    FOR N = 1 TO LN
31000    Q = 1
31005    GOTO 20040
31100    Q = 0
31105    GOTO 20040
32000    END
```

Reading Level Difficulty

Ronald Carlson

There are several formulas, such as Fog Index or Flesch Scale, used to estimate the reading level of text books. Most of these formulas count the number of words, syllables, sentences and polysyllabic words. Other formulas tally the occurrences of certain key words from a specific list of words.

If you have a large quantity of samples to determine the reading level or if you need to find the reading level only on occasion, this program will calculate the approximate grade level of the material.

The Fog Index, developed by Robert Gunning, is based on the following formula:

Grade Level = .4 *(W + L)

W = number of words with 3 or more syllables
L = average sentence length

There are exceptions involving words that end with -ing or -ed or capitalized words.

In my BASIC program there is a slight variation from the original formulas, inasmuch as counting syllables is a formidable task. I've used an approximation, that any word that is nine letters or longer will be three or more syllables. I also count the number of words with three or more distinct vowels and average it with the approximation by length.

So far in all of the samples I've tested, this estimation is within .5 of the grade level stated for the material. It is suggested that you take several passages, about 100 words long, throughout the book to receive an accurate measure of the grade level of that book.

Ronald Carlson, 44825 Kirk Ct., Canton, MI 48187

```
10REM
20REM READING LEVEL DIFFICULTY
30REM R. CARLSON
40REM CANTON, MICH.
50REM
60DIM A$(100)
70R1=0
80N=0
90D=0
100PRINT "DIRECTIONS"
110PRINT
120PRINT"PLEASE DELETE ALL PUNCTUATION EXCEPT AT THE END OF A SENTENCE ."
130PRINT"PLEASE TYPE A SPACE BEFORE THIS PUNCTUATION .THE ACCURACY"
140PRINT"WILL BE INCREASED IF YOU CHOOSE SEVERAL PASSAGES THROUGHOUT"
150PRINT"THE BOOK ."
160PRINT
170INPUT "HOW MANY LINES OF TEXT ",A
180PRINT"TYPE IN THE PASSAGE,ONE LINE AT A TIME."
190PRINT
200S=0
210W=0
220L=0
230T=0
240T1=0
250V=0
260FOR B=1 TO A
270INPUT A$
280X=LEN(A$)
290IF A$(X,X)="." THEN 420
300IF A$(X,X)="!" THEN 420
310IF A$(X,X)="?" THEN 420
320A$=A$+" "
330REM T IS NUMBER OF 3 SYLLABLE WORDS
340REM T1 IS THE NUMBER OF THREE SYLLABLE WORDS USING VOWELS
350REM L IS THE NUMBER OF LETTERS IN A WORD
360REM S IS THE NUMBER OF SENTENCES
370REM W IS THE NUMBER OF WORDS
380REM V IS THE NUMBER OF VOWELS /WORD
390REM D IS AN INDICATOR FOR DIFTHONGS
400REM N IS THE NUMBER OF SAMPLES
410REM R1 IS THE RUNNING TOTAL OF THE READING LEVELS
420FOR C=1TO LEN(A$)
430T$=A$(C,C)
440 IF T$="." THEN 600
450 IF T$="!" THEN 600
460 IF T$="?" THEN 600
470IF T$=" " THEN 620
480REM TRIPPING THE VARIOUS COUNTERS
490L=L+1
500IF T$="A" THEN 570
510IF T$="E" THEN 570
520IF T$="I" THEN 570
530IF T$="O" THEN 570
540IF T$="U" THEN 570
550D=0
560GOTO 680
570 D=D+1
580IF D=1 THEN V=V+1
590GOTO680
600S=S+1
610GOTO680
620W=W+1
630D=0
640IF L>=9 THEN T=T+1
650L=0
660IF V>=3 THEN T1=T1+1
670V=0
680NEXT C
690NEXT B
700T=INT((T+T1)/2)
710R=.4*(T+W/S)
720PRINT
730PRINT"THE READING LEVEL FOR THIS PASSAGE IS APPROXIMATELY ";R
740PRINT T;" THREE SYLLABLE WORDS"
750PRINT W;" WORDS IN THIS PASSAGE"
760PRINT S;" SENTENCES"
770INPUT"DO YOU HAVE MORE MATERIAL ? ",A$
```

```
780N=N+1
790R1=R1+R
800IF A$="YES" THEN 170
810PRINT
820PRINT"THE OVERALL READING LEVEL IS GRADE ";R1/N
830END
READY


RUN

DIRECTIONS

PLEASE DELETE ALL PUNCTUATION EXCEPT AT THE END OF A SENTENCE .
PLEASE TYPE A SPACE BEFORE THIS PUNCTUATION .THE ACCURACY
WILL BE INCREASED IF YOU CHOOSE SEVERAL PASSAGES THROUGHOUT
THE BOOK .

HOW MANY LINES OF TEXT 10
TYPE IN THE PASSAGE,ONE LINE AT A TIME.

?WE FEEL THIS IS MUCH TOO LITTLE COMING MUCH TOO
?LATE .IN THAT SENSE WE FEEL HIS PROGRAM IS NOT SUFFICIENTLY
?STRONG ENOUGH .WE FEEL HE SHOULD PROPOSE TO CUT DOWN
?BY AT LEAST 10 PERCENT IN TWO MONTHS RATHER THAN 50
?PERCENT IN 10 YEARS .NOW HE CAN CUT THE DEMAND BY 10
?PERCENT IN TWO MONTHS WE FEEL WITH A PROGRAM OF EDUCATING
?AMERICANS .WE CALL ON HIM TO ALLOCATE $100 MILLION
?FROM THE DEPARTMENT OF ENERGY TO EDUCATE THE AMERICAN
?PEOPLE HOW TO CONSERVE ENERGY HOW NOT TO USE
?THEIR CARS TAKE ONE MINUTE HOT SHOWERS .

THE READING LEVEL FOR THIS PASSAGE IS APPROXIMATELY  10.72
 7 THREE SYLLABLE WORDS
 99 WORDS IN THIS PASSAGE
 5 SENTENCES
DO YOU HAVE MORE MATERIAL ? NO

THE OVERALL READING LEVEL IS GRADE  10.72
READY
```

Notes

Another Hallmark in Programming

Wes W. Henley Jr.

First there was LOVE, then came LUST. Now, in a third (and final) version of greeting-card graphics, we get a bit of LUCK. □

Wes W. Henley Jr., 2144 Concord Dr., Billings, MT 59102.

```
]LIST

40    HOME
50    REM ...LUCK-PRINT (ADPD FM CREAT.COMP.APR 80.V6#4.P18.APR-FOOL-SIDE) BY W.HENLEY
60    PRINT "YOUR MESSAGE, PLEASE (IN 60 LETTERS OR"
65    INPUT "LESS): ";A$:L =  LEN (A$)
70    DIM T$(120): FOR I = 1 TO 5: PRINT : NEXT I
100   FOR J = 0 TO  INT (60 / L)
110   FOR I = 1 TO L
120  T$(J * L + I) =  MID$ (A$,I,1)
130   NEXT I: NEXT J
140  C = 0
150   PR# 1
200  A1 = 1:P = 1:C = C + 1: IF C = 37 THEN 999
205   PRINT
210   READ A:A1 = A1 + A: IF P = 1 THEN 300
240   FOR I = 1 TO A: PRINT " ";: NEXT I:P = 1: GOTO 400
300   FOR I = A1 - A TO A1 - 1: HTAB 18: PRINT T$(I);: NEXT I:P = 0
400   IF A1 > 60 THEN 200
410   GOTO 210
600   DATA  60,1,12,18,12,5,10,2,3,8,22,8,9,6,4
610   DATA  4,6,24,6,11,4,5,4,6,24,6,11,4,5
620   DATA  4,6,24,6,11,4,5,4,6,24,6,11,4,5
630   DATA  4,6,24,6,11,4,5,4,6,24,6,11,4,5
640   DATA  4,6,24,6,11,4,5,4,6,24,6,11,4,5
650   DATA  4,6,19,1,4,6,11,4,5,4,6,19,1,4,7,9,5,5
660   DATA  4,6,18,2,4,7,9,5,5,4,6,17,3,5,19,6
670   DATA  3,8,14,5,5,19,6,1,29,6,17,7,1,29,13,5,12
680   DATA  4,25,3,11,5,11,1,2,28,3,8,7,8,4
690   DATA  1,30,2,7,6,7,7,1,5,22,3,2,7,3,7,10
700   DATA  1,5,23,2,2,7,1,7,12,1,5,24,1,2,12,15
710   DATA  1,5,27,12,15,1,5,27,14,13
720   DATA  1,5,27,7,1,8,11,1,5,27,7,3,7,10
730   DATA  1,5,27,7,5,7,8,1,5,24,1,2,7,7,7,6
740   DATA  1,5,23,2,2,7,9,7,4,1,30,2,7,10,7,3
750   DATA  2,28,3,7,10,7,3,3,26,3,9,7,10,2
760   DATA  4,24,2,14,2,13,1,60
770   DATA  5000
999   FOR I = 1 TO 5: PRINT : NEXT I: PR# 0: END
```

```
CONGRATULATIONSFRIENDANDBESTWISHESONYOURNINETEEN81GRADUATION
C           NSFRIENDANDBESTWIS          ETEEN          ON
CON         IONSFRIENDANDBESTWISHE       INETEEN81       TION
CONG        TIONSFRIENDANDBESTWISHES     NINETEEN81G      ATION
CONG        TIONSFRIENDANDBESTWISHES     NINETEEN81G      ATION
CONG        TIONSFRIENDANDBESTWISHES     NINETEEN81G      ATION
CONG        TIONSFRIENDANDBESTWISHES     NINETEEN81G      ATION
CONG        TIONSFRIENDANDBESTWISHES     NINETEEN81G      ATION
CONG        TIONSFRIENDANDBESTWISHES     NINETEEN81G      ATION
CONG        TIONSFRIENDANDBESTWISHES     NINETEEN81G      ATION
CONG        TIONSFRIENDANDBESTWISHES     NINETEEN81G      ATION
CONG        TIONSFRIENDANDBESTW SHES     NINETEEN81G      ATION
CONG        TIONSFRIENDANDBESTW SHES     INETEEN81        ATION
CONG        TIONSFRIENDANDBEST  SHES     INETEEN81        ATION
CONG        TIONSFRIENDANDBES   SHESO               UATION
CON         IONSFRIENDANDB      SHESO               UATION
C                               SHESON              DUATION
C                               SHESONYOURNIN    81GRADUATION
CONG                     ISH            ETEEN              N
CO                       SHE            INETEEN          TION
C                        HE             NINETE          DUATION
C       TULATIONSFRIENDANDBEST    HE    NIN          GRADUATION
C       TULATIONSFRIENDANDBESTW   HE    N            81GRADUATION
C       TULATIONSFRIENDANDBESTWI HE            EEN81GRADUATION
C       TULATIONSFRIENDANDBESTWISHE          EEN81GRADUATION
C       TULATIONSFRIENDANDBESTWISHE           N81GRADUATION
C       TULATIONSFRIENDANDBESTWISHE     N       1GRADUATION
C       TULATIONSFRIENDANDBESTWISHE     NIN      GRADUATION
C       TULATIONSFRIENDANDBESTWISHE     NINET     ADUATION
C       TULATIONSFRIENDANDBESTWI HE     NINETEE    UATION
C       TULATIONSFRIENDANDBESTW   HE    NINETEEN8    TION
C                       HE             NINETEEN81      ION
CO                      SHE            NINETEEN81      ION
CON                     ISH            INETEEN          ON
CONG                    WI             TE                N
CONGRATULATIONSFRIENDANDBESTWISHESONYOURNINETEEN81GRADUATION
```

"Er, ahem — It's about an Apple your son gave me yesterday . . ."

Chapter IV
Word Processing

Chapter IV — Word Processing

The first article in this chapter, *(A Primer to Word Processing,* by Gordon McComb) makes a nice introduction to the joys of word processing. Having a word processor really helps if you do a lot of writing, and the Apple can be as capable as you want it to be. However, you must decide how much you are willing to invest. You can get fancy and buy an 80 column board, a lower case adapter, a letter quality printer, and word-processing software with all the bells and whistles. You may instead want to spend less than a hundred dollars and buy any of several low-priced (yet very effective) software packages that use the Apple as it is. It depends on what you need and how much you want to spend.

The next two articles *(Fundamentals of the Apple Writer* and *Lower Case Display for the Apple Writer)* deal with Apple Computer, Inc.'s own software, Apple Writer. Because it's inexpensive ($75), widely available (through Apple dealers), and very easy to use, it is probably the most popular. It also has some limitations — primarily the lack of tabbing. It does not work "as is" with the lower case video adapters on the market by Paymar, Lazer Systems, or Videx, but there is a fairly simple software conversion to fix this (see the second article.) Without the adapter, Apple Writer and most other word processors display lower case characters on the screen as upper case characters in inverse video (black letters, white background). An adapter allows both to be shown as you would expect. In either case, when copy is sent to the printer, it comes out properly.

The next two articles *(Easywriter,* and *Word Processing: Fast and Easy)* are reviews of some other word processors available for the Apple. There are several others, including Super Text II from MUSE ($150, and a lot of "bells and whistles"), and Superscribe from On-Line Systems ($89.95). The latter is interesting because it provides a lower case display without using a lower case adapter. It uses the hi-res screen for generating its own characters, and it does include a lot of nice features. Its price — allowing for what you don't have to spend for a lower case adapter — makes it the most economical choice available. Before you purchase anything, however, it's a good idea to compare the features and ease of use of each.

Through the Magic Window, by Al Evans, is a review of one of the lower case adapters mentioned earlier. When you look for such an adapter, don't just compare prices — it is also wise to look at all the options that may be available. Lazer Systems, for example, also makes a keyboard enhancer that is compatible with their lower case adapter. The enhancer allows you to use the shift keys the way you can on a normal typewriter. It also has a keyboard buffer that allows type-ahead. (The Apple normally remembers only the last character entered, so if the computer takes a moment to "think," you might lose a character. This is not a problem with slow typists.) Videx's lower case adapter is more expensive, but it also includes the shift-key modification. As always, it's best to shop around.

Finally, we present *Project 80,* by Alinsky and Gaylor. Those of you who must see exactly what your output is going to look like will need an 80 column output board or the Magic Window word processor described earlier. My complaint with Magic Window, though, is that it's difficult to proofread from the screen, because you have to simultaneously scroll up or down, and left or right. Following that is a comparative review of three such boards. My Apple has only a 40 column screen, and so I've got to trust the computer to figure the exact output. However, my applications don't require that I know exactly where words will be read to begin a new line. An 80 column board will also require you to use a monitor, instead of a regular television. A television does not have enough resolution to clearly show the smaller characters.

A Primer for Word Processing

Gordon Mc Comb

The old adage, "You can't please all the people all of the time" is definitely true about word processing programs. Whether used in education, engineering or business, the value of a word processor is beyond question. But choosing the right program for your individual needs is no easy task. A program which is perfect for one application may be worthless for another.

Enter the article you're now reading. If you don't know how merging, justification, glossaries or embedded commands can help you with your business or personal word processing needs, then by all means, read on.

Word Processing programs are among the most used programs for micro and mini computers. But many users, unsure of the meaning of certain features or the extent of their capabilities, often choose a program more or less at random. It it simply a matter of matching your needs with the capabilities of the program.

Before We Begin

In selecting the right software to satisfy your needs, two things must be taken into consideration: First, the type of documents you will be preparing; the vast majority of text written on word processors is the standard letter or manuscript variety. If your use is more specialized, you should be aware that some of the features necessary to perform complex functions are beyond the scope of many word processing programs.

For instance, if you write specifications for the construction of buildings, you will most likely want to use an extended outline form. Some programs may not be able to format text in this fashion. If you are an engineer or chemist, you will need super-

Gordon Mc Comb, 410 Escondido Avenue, Vista, CA 92083.

scripts and subscripts (letters and numbers half a line above and below regular type). Again, some programs are not capable of this.

Secondly, your computer and peripherals must support the features of the software.

A typical system might include a computer with a minimum memory of 32K, a floppy disk for data storage (either 5 1/4" or 8") and a printer.

A sufficient amount of memory is needed for the resident computer operating system, the word processing program and the text itself. With anything less than 32K, you may find yourself limited to processing only a dozen pages or so at a time.

The Printer

Your choice of a printer will be the most important factor in determining the compatibility of software and equipment. The kind of printer you choose will be dependent on the quality you need in the finished product. Daisy-wheel printers (starting at $2,000) will give you moderate speed and excellent type quality. Dot matrix printers (starting as low as $400) will give you faster speed, but less quality because the characters are composed of small dots.

Another possibility is a modified office typewriter, such as an IBM Selectric. A special base plate or hood containing dozens of "typing fingers," is attached to the typewriter and connects to the computer. The add-on plate or hood won't affect the normal operation of the typewriter, so the machine can perform double duty—as a word processing printer and a regular ofice typewriter.

Most printers may have some limitations when it comes to supporting software

features. For instance, a few daisy-wheel printers, although designed for word processing programs, aren't capable of proportional spacing (each character is spaced according to its width; "i"s take less space than "w"s) and your program may include that feature. It is unlikely that you can get a modified typewriter to print subscripts, and a dot matrix printer has trouble doing boldface. Get specifications on the printer before buying to make sure it will be able to take full advantage of the features of the program.

Inside Views

The following are features commonly found in word processing programs. Unfortunately, the terminology used for word processing features is not standard and descriptions of certain capabilities can be misleading. When buying software, ask the dealer for an explanation of the features in question. When a program is said to have "automatic indenting," will it automatically indent at the beginning of each new paragraph, or indent on *every* line? Whenever possible, try out the program before buying. Like a well-tailored suit, it should fit you well.

Password

You can control the use of your recorded documents by giving them password protection. You can select any or all of the files on a diskette to be locked in, accessible only by a coded message—and the password can be different for each document.

Upper and Lower Case

When you power up the computer and load the program, you may find a variety of ways to display the characters on the screen. Some systems may show both upper and lower case. Some may show capital letters only, and you have no way of distinguishing between upper and lower case. Still, other programs display all caps, but characters appear black within small white blocks. This is called "reverse video" and is used to denote capital letters within the text.

Upper and lower case capabilities are mainly a hardware consideration, but your program must be compatible with your hardware to operate properly. If, for example, you have modified your computer for upper and lower case, make sure the program will run with it.

However, capital letters only on the screen does not mean your computer will print out only caps. The computer itself knows the difference between upper and lower case; it's the video monitor that may be confused.

Screen Loads

The amount of text contained in an entire screen on the video monitor is called a screen load. The number of characters in a line and the number of lines per screen will vary from one computer to the next. Again, this is something inherent in the machine itself, your software won't have much control over this.

With most computers, two or three screen loads will make up one single-spaced page. The way your program handles the text is an important consideration. Some see the document as an entire page, and you "flip" through the screen pages one-by-one as you write or look over the material. This is called page scrolling. Other programs move your text one line at a time. This is called vertical line scrolling. There are no actual pages with this method; the document is one long "scroll" of text.

Wrap Around

As you type, you may notice you don't have to push the "return" or "enter" key each time you end a line. If a word exceeds the maximum screen width, it will wrap around onto the next line. The program

---

```
This  is  a  sample  of  justified
text.  Both  the  right  and  left
margins are even.   To avoid ex-
cess  space  between  words, it's
often  handy  to  have  a  hyphena-
tion  capability.  That  puts more
words on each line.


        This shows centered text.
     Good for title pages, main
              document
        headings, and more.


   This shows flush right margins.
    Instead of the typical flush
   left, it puts each line even on
              the right margin.
```

will never split a word, so as you add and delete words, the computer re-formats the text, wrapping everything around as needed.

Split Screen

Since you can view only a small portion of the document at a time, some programs have added a split screen feature that

---

You can change the way a document is printed the same way you can control its appearance on the video monitor.

---

allows you to see one part of the document while you look at or edit another part. This is a handy feature when you're moving text around, checking for continuity, transitions, etc.

Mode Control

Word processors do three basic things: write new text, edit text and jump from one part of the text to another. These functions are often referred to as "add," "change," and "cursor movement." You might also see them as "write," "edit," and "cursor control." A few programs make it possible to be in all three modes at once. Others require you to shift between modes as you work with the document. This is not as burdensome as it sounds, but check the "feel" of the program before you take it home. Some software packages have very complicated control sequences.

Cursor Control

An important aspect of your word processing system is the ease with which you can position your "pen" (cursor) at the point where you want to write or edit. You can manipulate the cursor to move left, right, up and down—all without affecting the text. You may also be able to move the cursor directly to the end or start of a line or the beginning or end of the document. Programs that are page-oriented allow the cursor to jump to any desired page.

Orientation

A program that allows you to display and change lines, either by making a change within the line, or by replacing the entire line, is a "line-oriented" word processor.

```
>*Primer on word processing._ ————————— Comment Line
>J=N LM=11 RM=74_ ┐
>C=Y LS=2         ├———————————— Embedded Commands
A PRIMER FOR WORD PROCESSING_
How to Choose the Right Word Processor_
For Your Micro or Mini Computer$

Written By_
Gordon Mc Comb$
>J=N C=N_ ————————————————————— Embedded Command
_
     The old adage, "You can't please all the people all of
the time" is definitely true about word processing
programs.  Whether used in education, engineering or
business, the value of a word processor is beyond reproach.
But choosing the right program for your individual needs is
no easy task.  What's perfect for one application may be
worthless for another._
     Enter the article you're now reading.  If you don't
know how merging, justification, glossaries or embedded
commands can help you with your business or personal word
processing needs, then by all means - read on!\
[HS>————————————┐
Mc Comb         │      [P>##] [2>]      WORD PROCESSING PRIMER_
$   Header Instruction Command └————————
]_
     WP software is some of the most utilized programs for
micro and mini computers.  But many users, unsure of the
meaning of certain features or the extend of its
ca
```

Page Number Command and Start Point

Header Text

Text and Format Lines. This is a typical printout of text, invisible (comment) lines and embedded commands. This particular document was prepared using Radio Shack's Scripsit for the TRS-80 Model 1. By following the syntax instructions for addressing the program, the user can control all margins, centering, line spacing, etc. Mastering a word processor like Scripsit takes only a couple short hours.

Often this type of program functions in the same manner as the Basic editor found in most computers. If the program allows you to move the cursor to any part of the screen display, it is character-oriented. This approach allows for faster and easier editing. Phrases such as "page-oriented" and "screen-oriented" also refer to the ability to work with a screenful of text with total cursor control.

Screen Formatting

To make it easier to visualize how a document will look when printed, many programs make it possible to change the appearance of the text on the screeen. You may be able to format the document for 10, 40, or even 100 characters wide. In the case of the line which includes more characters than the width of the screen will allow, the program will scroll the text horizontally over one character at a time as you type. This is very much like a movie panoramic effect—with words instead of mountain ranges.

Printer Formatting

You can change the way a document is printed the same way you can control its appearance on the video monitor. User-defined parameters (instructions on how to output the text) are vitally important because they control the final appearance of the document. As a minimum, you should be able to change the line spacing, line width, page length, number of lines per page, and top, left, right and bottom margins.

Other special features for formatting which may be available include:

Flush Right where the standard even margin is on the right side.

Justification, which provides even margins on both right and left sides.

Centering, which centers each line in the middle of the page—handy for titles and so forth.

Vertical Centering, which takes the entire document page and centers it in the middle of the sheet. No more top heavy letters.

Normally, the computer will set up all of the screen and printer formats when you power up the system. It will assume you want to use the program in the "normal" fashion. These are called defaults, and unless you tell the computer otherwise, it will perform all the functions as specified by the manufacturer.

Tabs and Indenting

You should be able to select tab positions the same way you do with a regular typewriter. Some programs allow only a certain number of pre-selected tabs; others make it possible to select tab stops at any character position.

Required tabs—sometimes called auto indenting—place every line at the tab position you have selected. Writers of outlines and reports will use this capability extensively.

Paragraph indenting—incorrectly called auto indenting by many manufacturers—simply indents each new paragraph. When you hit the "paragraph" key, it will automatically position only the first line at the indented position.

Local Editing

Your program should be capable of inserting and deleting characters and words. It might also be capable of dropping or adding entire lines, paragraphs and pages. These one-at-a-time changes are called local editing functions. Position the cursor where you want to make the change, key in the commands and the edited version will appear on the screen.

The simplest editing function is the strikeover feature. If you make an error, such as "the" instead of "the," position the cursor over the "e," and type in the correct spelling.

Global Editing

Let's say you must change the spelling of a person's name which occurs many times throughout a lengthy document. Instead of looking for every occurrence of the name and making each change manually with local commands, you can instruct the computer to perform a global editing function. There are three types: search or find, delete and replace. With this example, you would use the global replace function. You would tell the

3 computer screen loads = 1 single spaced page

Typical Screen and Page Configuration. The amount of text contained in one screen most likely will not equal one entire printed page. For most systems, you'll need to fill up two to four screens to equal one single-spaced typewritten page.

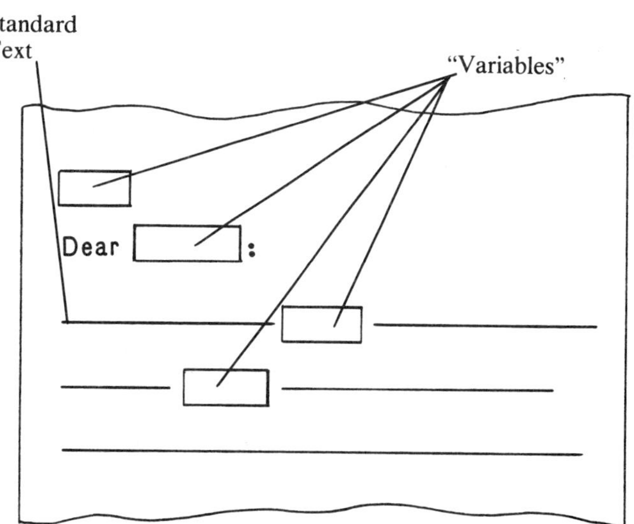

Merging Print. The operator first writes a primary document which includes the basic text plus all variable commands. Then, the user creates the secondary file document, which contains all the information that will be included in each variable slot.

computer what name to find, and how to change it. The machine does the rest.

Global search allows for easy retrieval of information. Let's say you need to make an index. Each word you want to list is keyed into the computer, which then displays every occurrence. It will continue until it reaches the end of a document. You can use global functions for correcting spelling errors, deleting redundant words, changing one vendor's name to another, etc.

Blocks

A block is any large amount of text. You define a block by putting block markers around the area with which you wish to work. The entire block can then be moved, changed or deleted at will.

For example, you need to change the position of a paragraph. You would like it better if it were at the beginning of the document, so you put markers around the paragraph, tell the computer where you want the block to be moved and give the command. Some programs refer to this feature by names such as "cut and paste," but its convenience is the same no matter what the name.

Merging

Merging has nothing to do with big business or Wall Street. It is a highly useful feature that enables the operator to create items such as personally addressed form letters in a minimum amount of time.

A typical merge feature works this way: you type out the basic letter, inserting "variable" commands in each place where names, account numbers, dates and so forth will change from letter to letter.

You then prepare a separate file of everyone's name and all the required information. Merging channels each name, account number, and date into the proper variable space.

Of course, you can also perform the same function by changing each letter manually, but merging takes only a fraction of the time.

Glossary

If you have names, sentences or paragraphs that you must write many times within the text, the glossary function will save you from entering the information each time.

You begin by making a glossary file— writing out the word(s) that you will be using often. When you prepare the document, you will now be able to refer to the glossary file, tell the computer which word(s) you want inserted, and it will do the rest. You can insert entire paragraphs with only two or three keystrokes.

Dictionary

Dictionaries, or spelling checkers, have up to 50,000-word memories (some allow you to add as many as 10,000 words of your own) that will let you know if you have made a typo or spelling mistake. If a word is misspelled, it will alert you by highlighting it, putting it in reverse video, etc.

Chaining

When you load new text material into the computer from your floppy disk, the computer automatically erases what was previously on the screen. However, by using the chain or assemble feature, you can "stack" one document on top of another. This comes in handy when you want to write material in small pieces, then combine them for a single print-out.

Directories and Menus

As you record each document on the floppy disk, you give it a name that allows you to retrieve it quickly. A directory or menu allows you to see the titles of all the documents you have saved. Some programs

Merging has nothing to do with big business or Wall Street.

will let you break from your writing, look at the directory, then continue with the writing. With others you must exit the program thereby erasing any text you have not saved.

Embedded Commands

You can instruct the computer to change the printing format while printing. This way, you can include commands for centering text, justification, indentation, etc. within the document. The printer will go through the text, changing the format as it goes without stopping for readjustment. The embedded commands will not print out unless you want them to.

Headers and Footers

At times, you may need to include the document name on each page of the manuscript. This can be done with the header and footer functions. You can instruct the computer to print out the same information on every page—either the top for a header; or the bottom for a footer. You can also specify that this function occur only on odd or even pages. This is handy when preparing a manuscript that will be printed on both sides of the paper.

Also, the program may give you the option of selecting specific pages where the header and footer are to be placed (for instance, starting on page 2, all pages thereafter except 14, 18 and 23).

Pagination

It is difficult to know where one page ends and another begins when writing with a word processor, so trying to add page numbers in the text while writing can be next to impossible. Many programs, however, will put the page numbers on for you. You can begin numbering at any point, and place the number in any position you wish.

Hyphenation

Because of the wrap-around feature of a word processor, some lines may look peculiar. A word that doesn't fit will slide to the next line, and when printed, can look awkward. Most programs will allow you to hyphenate. The computer will tell you the words that will be affected, and you tell it if you want to hyphenate and where you want to break the word.

Print Modes

If you are printing on a long roll of paper, you can instruct the computer to print continuously. If you are using single sheets, such as letterhead, you will need to instruct the computer to stop after each page so you can insert a new sheet.

Documentation and Instructions

Don't overlook this important item when choosing software. Tutorial devices, such as audio cassettes or special learning programs, help the non-computer-trained operator to understand the system better. Many word processing programs are geared for someone with little or no computer knowledge, so the instructions must be explicit and easy to understand.

A helpful sales team is also an important adjunct to your software. They may be perfectly happy to sell you the computer and the program, but will they be equally helpful when you have a question or a problem?

Miscellany

Invisible lines, sometimes called comment lines, are used by authors for reminders, notes and remarks. Invisible lines show up on the video screen and will only be printed if you specifically ask for them.

Decimal alignment neatly places each figure in a column with all decimals aligned—especially useful when preparing bills and monthly reports.

Some programs are also capable of math functions. Enter the numbers, instruct the computer to perform the arithmetic and the total will appear where you have specified.

Underlining and boldface are especially useful for emphasizing certain words or phrases. Your printer must be able to perform these functions, which usually require it to back space.

Subscript and superscript will shift the printing platen half a space up and down for printing scientific notation, equations, formulae and footnotes.

Where Do You Go From Here?

If you are considering the purchase of word processing software, you should now make a list of the features your processor must have to do the work you want done. Include the reasons for choosing certain capabilities and estimate the percentage of time you feel you will use each function. List the features you would like to have, but which are not absolutely necessary to carry out your work. Some capabilities, such as merging, math and dictionaries, are available as add-ons. If you find later that you need a feature not originally included with the program, you may be able to buy it separately.

After you have listed your feature priorities, talk with a computer and software representative to see what they have to offer you. By the way, many word processing programs are available through the mail. It is often cheaper and very convenient to buy this way, but *never* buy a program without trying it out first. Most software suppliers, understandably, don't have return policies; once you buy it, it's yours. So don't get stuck with something that won't work for you.

To some, word processing seems like a luxurious fad. People have been banging out letters and other documents on typewriters for almost 100 years, why not continue for a 100 more? But just try a good word processing program and I'll guarantee you will wonder how you ever got along without it! □

". . . and here's my computer with a joystick, and here it is with pussycat, and here . . ."

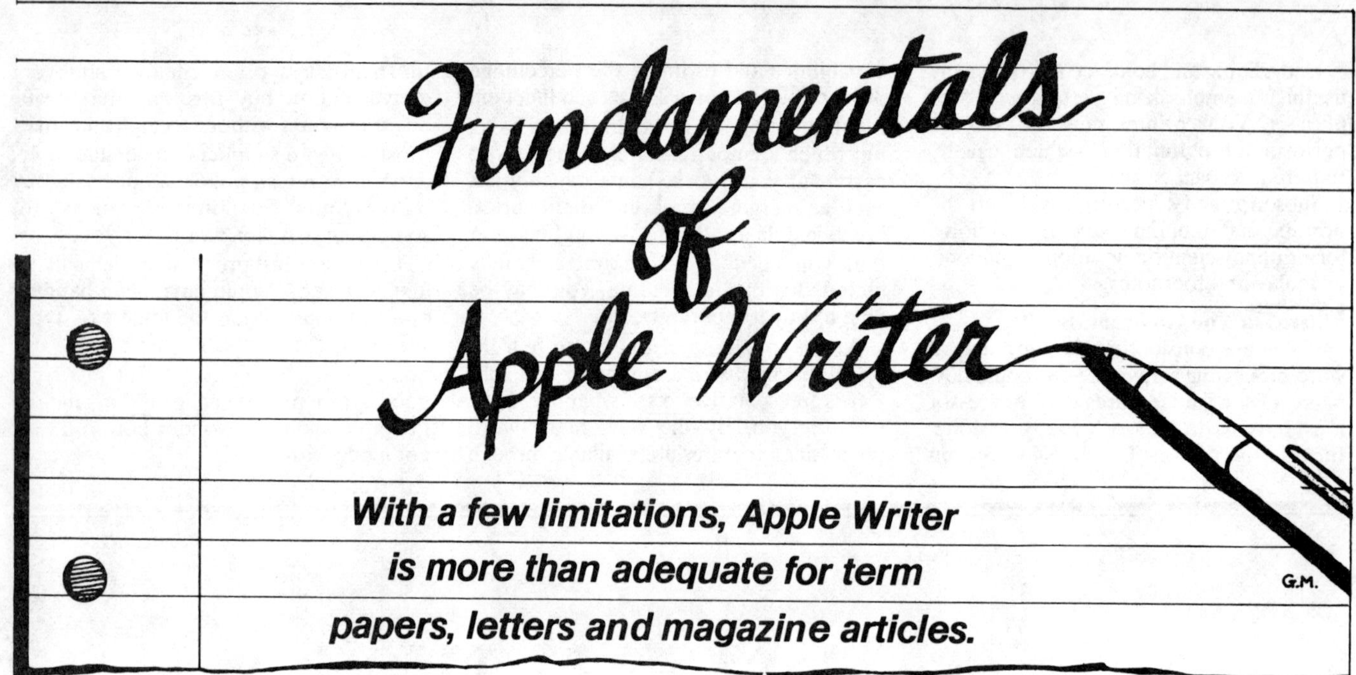

Barry D. Bayer

First there were cave drawings. And then there was hand carved type. And finally, in 1456, Johann Gutenberg launched development of the technology of moveable type, making the ability to read a perfectly printed page available to the masses.

First there was paper punched tape. And then there were the IBM magnetic tape and magnetic card 'word processors' (the MTST and MTSC). And then, in the last couple of years, the Wang, Xerox, Qyx, Redactron, and all of the other computer technology word-processing systems, which are gradually bringing us into a new era, making the ability to type a perfectly printed page available to the masses.

And indeed the modern "word processor" is one of the hottest items of office technology making the rounds today. But most of the modern word processors are nothing but computers, with software appropriate to the easy manipulation of strings. Given appropriate software the microprocessor can do anything that the big machines can, and considerably cheaper.

Barry D. Bayer, 2842 Walnut, Homewood, IL 60430.

Apple Writer comes nicely packaged, with adequate documentation And it works.

Apple Writer comes with several machine language programs duplicated on two 5¼ inch mini-floppy disks, one a write protected systems disk, and the other designed as a working copy. Instructions are given to treat the write-protected disk with great care, as it is intended to be copied when the working disk is worn. (All of the Apple Writer programs are user transferable from disk to disk, and the company even tells us how to do it. It is nice to see a software publisher who trusts us.)

Booting the system with the working disk presents a menu which permits the

operator to EDIT a file already in the computer, INITIALIZE a new file, PRINT the file in memory, SAVE the current file to disk, LOAD a file from disk to memory, or QUIT the system and return to Basic. (The actual commands used are, appropriately enough, "E," "N," "P," "S," "L," and "Q.")

Most people will probably take a quick run through the 7-page manual, and LOAD a "Tutorial" file into memory. Working through the Tutorial program gives one experience in manipulating the cursor to edit text in memory.

The initial Text mode is used to input lowercase text. Pressing the escape key once changes the cursor to an inverse video "∧", indicating that the next character typed will be printed in uppercase. (This Upper Case mode effects only the next character typed; a second character will print in lowercase.) As the Apple does not support on-screen lower case, the Apple Writer convention is that all characters appearing upper case on the 40-column screen will print lower case (on a printer that has lower case, of course) and all characters to be printed in upper case are shown on the screen in inverse video. The use of the escape key instead of the shift key, as well as the inverse video, takes some getting used to, but should be no problem to the hobbyist.

Text wraps completely around the screen, going from column 40 on one line, and continuing on column 1 of the next, without requiring a carriage return. This results in strange-looking word breaks on screen, but makes no difference when the text is finally printed.

Pressing the escape key twice in succession changes the cursor to a flashing "+", and, taking a cue from the Apple II Plus, enables the operator to move the cursor about the text using the I,J,K and M keys (they form a diamond on your typewriter keyboard) to move one line up, one space to the left, one space to the right, and one line down, respectively. This Cursor Control mode is used to get to the exact position in the text where you wish to Insert, Delete, or whatever.

The repeat key makes the cursor move faster. Control V (Vertical) to go down about 12 lines, and a control T (Top) to go up about 12 lines make big jumps possible. (The Apple Writer is big on mnemonics. Control B to the BEGINNING, Control E to the END, Control I to INSERT, Control K to KEEP (save) a portion of the file to disk, Control S to SEARCH, and the like. This sounds a bit silly, but it makes the system relatively easy to learn.) Finally, putting the cursor into Cursor Control mode, and a Control Q, will QUIT the Edit routine, and return the program to the main menu.

The Control S search-and-replace feature, although nothing new to computers or word processing, deserves a couple of sentences of its own. When properly instructed, the Apple II will search from the current cursor position to the end of the file for a given string set off by delimiters of your own choosing. Continually pressing Return will get you to each such string found, one at a time. If you have given Apple Writer a replace-ment string, you can manually order a replacement, one at a time, or can demand the computer replace each instance of the searched for string with the replacement string. Fantastic for semiautomated form letters, and for those of us who always spell a common word the same wrong way, or for changing "Lessee" to "Tenant" all the way through a form lease.

Loading or saving a file involves nothing but typing an "L" or "S", a file

---

Apple Writer will certainly make your written communication much clearer and easier.

---

name, and pressing Return. To delete a file, or to determine which files are on disk, one types a Control D, which takes you temporarily out of the program, and enables you to access DOS commands, directly. The print option causes another program named "printer" to BRUN, and presents the user with a menu having options of PRINTING a new document, CONTINUING the printing of a document already started, LOADING a file from disk for printing, RETURNing to the Editor, or QUITing the system. ("P," "C," "L," "R" or "Q," of course.)

The new-document option produces yet another menu which permits change of print parameters such as left, right, top and bottom margins, lines per page, spaces between lines, and location of printer-driver routine. The parameters are stored on disk, and will be available, in exactly the altered form, when the new document option is chosen again. The parameter menu then yields to a small menu which gives the user the choice of printing, or pressing escape, which will return to the Print menu for another try. If one chooses Print, the printing will start immediately, unless one has chosen the Single Sheet parameter, in which case the program will stop and allow the user to check paper one last time.

Apple Writer gives the user the additional formatting option of embedding format commands into the text. Each such command must be preceded by a carriage return and a "[". As these commands are part of the text (although, of course, not printed) they may be rather conveniently changed by the Search and Replace routines. These commands take precedence over the values presented in the parameter menu.

Depending on which imbedded commands have been inserted into the text while inputted, and also depending on default values entered in the parameter menu, printing can be justified left, right, centered, or full (simultaneously right and left); spacing can be single, double or more; margins can be varied, and pages numbered and titled. The operator has nothing to do but watch the printer (and feed paper if using single sheet operation.)

Apple Writer, as with all Apple-produced software that I have seen, comes nicely packaged, with adequate documentation. And it works. I suspect that a secretary in a business office might be reluctant to use it, as the inverse video can be confusing to the uninitiated, and one cannot see the typed format on the screen because of the Apple's 40 column display. Each of these are limitations of the computer, however, and not of the software. (There are a number of hardware modifications which provide lowercase characters, and even 80 column lines. The serious user may want to adapt the machine to make it look like a typewriter.)

But for someone who is willing to accept these limitations, the system is more than adequate for light typing such as term papers, complaining letters to software manufacturers, and magazine articles.

Although form letters are not provided for, as such, use of the search-and-replace routines as well as the block-insert and move commands make semi-automated form letters possible.

One disturbing feature of the entire package is the very careful DISCLAIMER OF ALL WARRANTIES AND LIABILITY emblazoned on the Copyright page of the manual. I believe that it is completely irresponsible for a software publisher to attempt to disclaim ALL warranties for a product. At the very least, a purchaser should be able to get his purchase price returned if the product doesn't work as represented in some important respect. (I wish to make clear that the Apple Writer does work, and that Apple is not the only culprit in this regard.) I imagine that Apple would probably do this voluntarily if a disastrous bug was pointed out, but any purchaser should read (and demand to see) any warranty information on any significant purchase, prior to paying, or at least have some sort of understanding with the retailer prior to purchase.

At $75 list price, the Apple Writer isn't fancy. It doesn't have a number of features such as automatic paragraph indentation, multi-file search, underscoring, and on-screen totals. But it will certainly make your written communication much clearer and easier. □

Lower-Case Display for Apple Writer

John E. Stith

Writing consumes almost all of the time I spend on my Apple II computer. Therefore, I was happy to see the arrival of several new text processor software packages for the Apple II. Unfortunately, no single package perfectly met my needs, so I decided to purchase one that came close and to modify it.

I examined three prominent text processors: Apple Writer, EasyWriter, and Super-Text. All three packages are versatile, comprehensive programs which run much faster than any Basic-language text editor and formatter I have tried, but each has its own disadvantages for my application, writing. All three packages fully support upper and lower-case print-out, but they all have their own restrictions on lower-case display on the Apple II Monitor. The following paragraphs outline the drawbacks I found in each package. These may or may not be drawbacks to other users.

Apple Writer has a convenient file format and easy-to-use upper/lower-case shifting, but has the drawback of not displaying lower-case letters on the screen during editing. (It, like EasyWriter, uses inverse letters for capitals and normal upper-case characters to represent lower-case characters.)

EasyWriter is a flexible package but has two drawbacks for me. First, it uses its own file structure, incompatible with Apple DOS 3.2, so any text I already have that I would like to use with EasyWriter

John Stith, P.O. Box 7463, Colorado Springs, CO 80933.

would have to be completely re-entered.

Therefore, I decided that, as is, no one of the three packages suited my needs. I picked the one that came closest and decided to buy and modify Apple Writer (after first calling Apple Computer and being assured that no plans existed for marketing a lower-case display version.)

> **It is more appropriate to tailor hardware/software systems to sound human-engineering concepts, rather than force the human to adapt to painful machine restrictions.**

That alone is enough to prohibit me from converting to it; but, additionally, it doesn't support lower-case screen display unless you spend more on extra hardware than the purchase price of EasyWriter.

Super-Text has a convenient file format and has upper/lower-case, on-screen display, using the Dan Paymar lower-case adapter, which costs $50 and is well worth the price. Super-Text, however,

has three significant drawbacks for my application. First, it has a cumbersome method of shifting in and out of upper case via control characters. Second, it uses embedded control characters for formatting, so it's difficult to exchange text with other ASCII computers. Third, it has no ability to print page headers automatically, a must for writing.

With the continued decrease in cost of computer capability, and the increasing cost of labor, I think it is more appropriate to tailor hardware/software systems to sound human-engineering concepts, rather than force the human to adapt to painful machine restrictions. It's obviously possible to make do with constraints such as inverse video to represent upper-case characters, or reading binary rather than decimal numbers, but I don't like to do it when it's unnecessary and time-wasting.

The Modifications

The balance of this article shows the modifications I made to Apple Writer to get around the problem of no on-screen, lower-case display. These modifications all depend on having the Dan Paymar lower-case adapter installed on the Apple II. The adapter has been described extensively in print, but, briefly, it is a small accessory that plugs into the Apple II in place of the normal character generator ROM. The Apple II operates normally, in both text and graphic modes, with the exception that lower-case characters are also included in the character set. The only limitation is that the new lower-case characters cannot

Figure 1
New Character Input and Conversion Routines for TEDITOR Program

```
18A0-   48          PHA                      ***CONVERT***
18A1-   A5 0C       LDA $0C      CONVERT CASE?
18A3-   D0 02       BNE $18A7    YES, BRANCH
18A5-   68          PLA
18A6-   60          RTS          DONE
18A7-   68          PLA
18A8-   C9 C0       CMP #$C0     UPPER CASE?
18AA-   30 12       BMI $18BE    NO, BRANCH
18AC-   C9 E0       CMP #$E0
18AE-   10 04       BPL $18B4    NO, BRANCH
18B0-   09 20       ORA #$20     CONVERT TO LOWER
18B2-   D0 0A       BNE $18BE    ALWAYS BRANCH
18B4-   C9 E0       CMP #$E0     LOWER CASE?
18B6-   30 06       BMI $18BE    NO, BRANCH
18B8-   C9 FF       CMP #$FF
18BA-   10 02       BPL $18BE    NO, BRANCH
18BC-   29 DF       AND #$DF     CONVERT TO UPPER
18BE-   60          RTS          DONE
18BF-   00          BRK          SPACE FILLER
18C0-   C9 83       CMP #$83     CTRL-C?      ***INPUT***
18C2-   D0 03       BNE $18C7    NO, BRANCH
18C4-   09 E0       ORA #$E0     YES, MAKE LOWER CASE
18C6-   60          RTS          DONE
18C7-   48          PHA
18C8-   A5 0B       LDA $0B      HAVE TO CONVERT?
18CA-   D0 08       BNE $18D4    YES, BRANCH
18CC-   68          PLA
18CD-   C9 A0       CMP #$A0     BLANK?
18CF-   D0 02       BNE $18D3    NO, BRANCH
18D1-   A9 20       LDA #$20     DON'T CARE CHARACTER
18D3-   60          RTS          DONE
18D4-   68          PLA
18D5-   C9 C0       CMP #$C0     UPPER CASE?
18D7-   30 06       BMI $18DF    NO, BRANCH
18D9-   C9 E0       CMP #$E0
18DB-   10 02       BPL $18DF    NO, BRANCH
18DD-   09 20       ORA #$20     CONVERT TO LOWER
18DF-   60          RTS          DONE
18E0-   48          PHA                      ***BELL***
18E1-   A5 70       LDA $70      POP DESIRED?
18E3-   F0 05       BEQ $18EA    NO, BRANCH
18E5-   A0 0A       LDY #$0A     LOAD DURATION
18E7-   20 E4 FB    JSR $FBE4    BELL2 IN MONITOR
18EA-   68          PLA
18EB-   60          RTS          DONE
```

Figure 1. New Character Input and Conversion Routines for TEDITOR Program.

Figure 2

Patches to Apple Writer TEDITOR Program

```
0813-   20 E0 18    JSR $18E0    CALL BELL

14FA-   4C A0 18    JMP $18A0    JUMP TO CONVERT

1501-   4C C0 18    JMP $18C0    JUMP TO INPUT

1530-   EA          NOP          ELIMINATE INVERSE CURSOR
1531-   EA          NOP
1532-   EA          NOP
1533-   EA          NOP
1534-   F0 DF       BEQ $1515    BRANCH ALWAYS

1549-   20 01 15    JSR $1501    GET CORRECT VALUE TO PRINT
154C-   20 F0 FD    JSR $FDF0    PUT IT ON SCREEN
154F-   A9 C0       LDA #$C0     RESET FOR LOWER CASE
1551-   85 0B       STA $0B
1553-   EA          NOP
```

Figure 2. Patches to Apple Writer TEDITOR Program.

Figure 3

New Character Input Routine for PRINTER Program

```
INPUT
18E0-   48          PHA
18E1-   A5 10       LDA $10      CONVERT TO LOWER CASE?
18E3-   D0 02       BNE $18E7    YES, BRANCH
18E5-   68          PLA
18E6-   60          RTS          DONE
18E7-   68          PLA
18E8-   C9 C0       CMP #$C0     UPPER CASE?
18EA-   30 06       BMI $18F2    NO, BRANCH
18EC-   C9 E0       CMP #$E0
18EE-   10 02       BPL $18F2    NO, BRANCH
18F0-   09 20       ORA #$20     CONVERT TO LOWER CASE
18F2-   60          RTS          DONE
```

Figure 3. New Character Input Routine for PRINTER Program.

be flashed or shown in inverse video.

Since Apple Computer does not provide the source code for Apple Writer, I have no absolute guarantee that the portion of memory that contains my patches will never be destroyed, but in thorough testing and in writing this article, I had no problems at all.

Figure 1, New Character Input and Conversion Routines for TEDITOR Program, shows the additional code I wrote for the text editor program. It resides at 18A0 through 18EB. (All addresses in this article are in hex.) CONVERT, located at 18A0, is the routine used during the case-change mode, changing upper case to lower case and vice versa. All other characters are left untouched. INPUT, at 18C0, is the routine that handles case shift during text entry. It traps for control-C, since that character is used as an end-of-text indicator and would accidentally truncate text if entered into the text buffer. INPUT also converts a pseudo-character, an upper-case blank, for use as a don't-care character in string searches and replacements. The third routine, BELL, at 18E0, simply sounds a pop each time a character is entered in the text-input mode, if enabled by the control-P function of Apple Writer.

BELL is optional, but if you omit it, you must also omit the patches for it in Figure 2.

Figure 2, Patches to Apple Writer TEDITOR Program, shows the changes that must be made to TEDITOR so that it calls the subroutines shown in Figure 1 at the correct times. The change at 0813 calls BELL upon character input. It is optional. The change at 14FA calls the CONVERT subroutine rather than execute the original Apple Writer version. The change at 1501 does the same for INPUT. The code at 1530 eliminates the inverse video feature. The change at 1549 causes the correct case to be displayed on the screen.

Figure 3, New Character Input Routine for PRINTER Program, shows the additional code that I wrote for the text formatter program. It resides at 18E0 through 18F2. It converts to the correct case when the page header is being entered. As in the regular editor, an ESCAPE entered causes the next input character to be upper case. In the editor, the case-change feature lets you change the case of as many characters as you want.

Figure 4, Patches to Apple Writer PRINTER Program, shows the changes that must be made to PRINTER so that it calls the subroutine in Figure 3 at the

correct time and so that it handles case conversion correctly. The value at 0F56 corrects a check for an exclamation point in the text (used for text formatting) to the correct ASCII value. The code at 1095 jumps to the new CONVERT subroutine shown in Figure 3. The code at 10C8 eliminates the inverse cursor when typing in the header. The code at 12D8 eliminates most of the printer character output conversion routine since, with these modifications, the text buffer is now in ASCII (with the most significant bit in each byte set on.) The data at 1569 corrects the values to check against for lower-case letters used in text formatting parameters. The patches at 15DF, 15E3, 15E7, and 15FC correct parameters in the routine that converts characters that follow text formatting commands into binary numbers.

How to Make the Changes

Figure 5, Modification Checklist, shows a step-by-step procedure that will allow you to take the disk supplied with Apple Writer and generate a lower-case display version on your own disk. The character representations will be different from the original Apple Writer, but if you have a lot of text to convert, you can write a short program to do it. Once you are finished, you can use the lower-case version using the same rules as published in the Apple Writer manual.

The following buffer format is provided for those individuals who would like to use Apple Writer with text already created. The program uses binary (B) files to save text on disk. The text buffer starts at 1900 and can go up to 959F. The first byte of data must be a hex 83 and the last must be a hex 60. All characters inbetween, in the lower-case version, are normal ASCII characters, with the most significant bit set on. (The unmodified Apple Writer uses the same format except that most of the characters are not in ASCII representation.) Once the text is in the buffer, do a BSAVE TEXT. YOUR FILE NAME, A$1900, L$YOUR LENGTH.

The text editor program in Apple Writer is easy to use and very powerful, but perhaps future versions of the text formatter will incorporate more advanced features.

Then you can load the file under control of Apple Writer. You may see some garbage characters at the end of the buffer because there's no hex 60 end-of-text byte, but you can quickly delete them.

If you have a lot of text files, you can use the Disk Zap program from Apple PugetSound Program Library Exchange (A.P.P.L.E.). It enables you to modify your disk directory to tell Apple DOS that your text file is a binary file and then BLOAD FILE NAME, A$1900.

As with almost any program, there are extra features that would make nice improvements. The text editor program in Apple Writer is easy to use and very powerful, but perhaps future versions of the text formatter will incorporate more advanced features such as including headers in text files, pauses while printing, skipping headers on the first page, and printing only a specified range of page numbers. The Technical Systems Consultants' Text Processing System for the Motorola 6800 is an ideal example. But Apple Writer is a great improvement over the first generation of Apple text editors and processors. I hope the addition of lower-case display capability will make it even more useful. □


```
0F56-   A1                DATA      ASCII EXCLAMATION POINT

1095-   4C E0 18          JMP $18E0  CALL INPUT

10C8-   EA                NOP        ELIMINATE INVERSE CURSOR
10C9-   EA                NOP
10CA-   EA                NOP
10CB-   EA                NOP
10CC-   F0 DF             BEQ $10AD  BRANCH ALWAYS

12D8-   4C FB 12          JMP $12FB  SKIP CONVERSION

1569-   EC                DATA       ASCII 1 (LOWER CASE L)
156A-   ED                           m
156B-   F2                           r
156C-   ED                           m
156D-   F4                           t
156E-   ED                           m
156F-   E2                           b
1570-   ED                           m
1571-   F3                           s
1572-   F0                           p
1573-   EC                           1
1574-   EA                           j
1575-   E3                           c
1576-   EA                           j
1577-   F2                           r
1578-   EA                           j
1579-   E6                           f
157A-   EA                           j
157B-   EE                           n
157C-   F0                           p

15DF-   A0                           BLANK

15E3-   B0                           0

15E7-   BA                           "9" + 1

15FC-   B0                           0
```

Figure 4. Patches to Apple Writer PRINTER Program.

Modification Checklist

1. Follow the steps outlined in the Apple Writer manual to make a copy of the Apple Writer disk. DO NOT modify the original Apple Writer disk. Also, do not LOCK the TEDITOR and PRINTER files on the working copy, yet. For all following steps that say to type in text, follow each line with a carriage return.

2. Reboot the system from the working disk copy. (Apple Writer is intended to run under DOS 3.2.)

3. In response to the editor menu, type:
Q

4. Type:
BLOAD TEDITOR

5. After the program is loaded, reset the system, placing control in the Apple monitor. (If you have an Apple II Plus, use Apple's recommended method of getting into the Apple monitor.)

6. Using the monitor, install the patches shown in figures 1 and 2 by typing the following input lines:
```
18A0: 48 A5 0C D0 02 68 60 68 C9 C0
18AA: 30 12 C9 E0 10 04 09 20 D0 0A
18B4: C9 E0 30 06 C9 FF 10 02 29 DF 60 00
18C0: C9 83 D0 03 09 E0 60 48 A5 0B
18CA: D0 08 68 C9 A0 D0 02 A9 20 60
18D4: 68 C9 C0 30 06 C9 E0 10 02 09 20 60
18E0: 48 A5 70 F0 05 A0 0A 20 E4 FB 68 60
```
At this point, you should double-check your entries by typing 18A0L and successive L's to disassemble the code and compare it to figure 1.

Figure 5. Modification Checklist.

Figure 5 - Continued

Next, type the following lines:
```
0813: 20 E0 18
14FA: 4C A0 18
1501: 4C C0 18
1530: EA EA EA EA F0
1549: 20 01 15 20 F0 FD A9 C0 85 0B EA
```
To check these inputs, type the following lines and compare the code to figure 2.
```
0813L
14FAL
1501L
1530L
1549L
```
Once you are satisfied that all of the changes were entered properly, move on to the next step. If you made errors that are too hard to correct, you can start over at step number 2.

7.   To go back to BASIC, type:
```
3D0G
```

8.   To save the new version to disk, type:
```
BSAVE TEDITOR,A$803,L$10FB
```
(This will save a few more bytes than actually necessary.)

9.   To protect your efforts, type:
```
LOCK TEDITOR
```

10.   Type:
```
BLOAD PRINTER
```

11.   After PRINTER is loaded, reset the system to get into the monitor.

12.   Using the monitor to install the patches shown in figures 3 and 4, type the following input lines:
```
18E0: 48 A5 10 D0 02 68 60 68 C9 C0
18EA: 30 06 C9 E0 10 02 09 20 60
18E0L
```
(This last entry will allow you to double-check against the code in figure 3. Reenter it if necessary.)

Now type the following lines. (Most of them are parameter changes. Enter them carefully since you won't be able to double-check by disassembling them.)
```
0F56: A1
1095: 4C E0 18
10C8: EA EA EA EA F0
12D8: 4C FB 12
1569: EC ED F2 ED F4 ED E2 ED F3 F0
1573: EC EA E3 EA F2 EA E6 EA EE F0
15DF: A0
15E3: B0
15E7: BA
15FC: B0
```
Now, use the monitor to inspect this last set of input values to make sure that you entered them correctly. If you find an incorrect value, you are running the risk that you typed in an incorrect address during the changes and therefore wiped out some random section of memory, possibly in Apple Writer itself, or DOS. Once you are satisfied that the changes were entered correctly, proceed to step number 13. If you make errors, you can reboot the system, type Q, and start over at step 10.

13.   To get back to BASIC, type:
```
3D0G
```

14.   To save the modified text processor, type:
```
BSAVE PRINTER,A$803,L$10FB
```
(This saves a few more bytes than actually necessary.)

15.   To protect your efforts, type:
```
LOCK PRINTER
```

16. Your working copy is now complete. To try it out, reboot the system using the working copy. If your Dan Paymar lower-case adapter is installed, you should see lower-case letters as you enter text in the text-insert mode.

17. Once you are satisfied that your new version is working, you can copy it to a backup disk, using the same procedure as in the Apple Writer manual. Just remember that the L field on the BSAVE commands for the TEDITOR and PRINTER programs is now $10FB rather than $1040 since both programs are now a bit longer. The control-P function in Apple Writer will now turn on a short pop that sounds each time a character is input in the text mode (unless you omitted the applicable changes.)

As I sit here in a seedy hotel room in San Francisco, I'm struck by the schism between those who take high technology, such as computers, for granted, and the rest of the world. Let me explain. Yesterday on a visit to Information Unlimited Software in Berkeley, Larry Weiss gave me a copy of EasyWriter for evaluation. Since I had an Apple with me, I decided to rev up the system tonight in my hotel room. My choice of an economical $25 room in the Hotel Victoria near Chinatown did not make this task an easy one.

First of all, my room had no TV set. The desk clerk spoke very little English and had difficulty understanding why I wanted a TV in my

With EasyWriter, characters did not get lost even at high typing speeds.

room when I could watch the color set in the lobby. Finally, after checking five rooms, a set was located which I wheeled to my room. Second problem: the room did not have a grounded outlet and I did not wish to break the grounding prong off the Apple power cord. Solution: disassemble the fluorescent light in the bathroom and jury rig the wiring to the Apple power cord. Problem 3: an antenna cable was permanently wired to the TV set (to discourage theft?) and terminated into an extremely strange connector. Problem 4: the TV did not have UHF and the Sup-R-Mod in the Apple was putting out a signal to channel 33. Solution to 3 and 4: twist the Apple cable and the TV cable together for about a 5-foot length, tune to channel 10 and a passable signal appeared. (Barely passable).

Light a cigar, pour some wine, and plunge in. Here's what I found.

EasyWriter is obviously modeled after Electric Pencil. Most of the cursor controls are the same (a,w,s,z--left, up, right and down), scrolling, insert, delete and tabs are virtually identical. Control/p exits to the print system, control/k to the disk system and control/o to Basic.

EasyWriter

David H. Ahl

There are some notable differences between EasyWriter and Electric Pencil. For example, line feed becomes shift/m on the Apple. Two line feeds are required before the entry of text and between paragraphs. Control/t is an 8-character tab; however, it seems to disappear when scrolling backwards or forward through the text. Since the Apple II has only an upper-case display, upper- and lower-case letters are defined by hitting "ESC" to make the following characters upper case. To cancel upper case, "ESC" is hit twice. Since the Apple I was using had a lower case chip in it, this did not seem to work. However, I'm sure there is a way to make it behave. I just haven't found it yet.

EasyWriter has a feature that detects the end of screen so that words are not split when they do not fit on the screen. This is called "Screen Wrap-Around." On Electric Pencil, this feature usually drops one or two characters, whereas with EasyWriter, characters did not get lost even at high typing speeds.

A little glitch: EasyWriter automatically leaves two spaces after a period which is what one usually wants. However, if a period is enclosed in quotation marks as in the above paragraph, two spaces are not wanted. To eliminate the space requires a user-defined character, a somewhat awkward thing to remember.

Moving blocks requires a sequence of eight commands, a bit unhandy. If one does much moving, it is probably something which can be memorized. However, compared to the simpler block move routine of Electric Pencil, it seems cumbersome. A further glitch is that blocks must be moved starting with the right side of a line. Thus, one cannot move a sentence from the middle of a paragraph. On the other hand, after years of using a word processing

system for many, many articles, I can't recall moving blocks more than about 10 or 12 times.

The scrolling commands are excellent. Screenfuls of text can be scrolled up, down and the last line on the top or bottom is retained to help keep one's place. This is a nice feature.

The word searching procedure allows you to search for one specific word or for groups of words using the "wild card" feature. For example T### would find any four letter word beginning with t.

Print commands can be imbedded in the text so margins can be set, skip lines, set indents, justification, line lengths, page lengths and so on throughout the text.

Text files can, of course, be saved, retrieved, revised and deleted. When you are about to do a dangerous or irreversible operation, a warning beep sounds in the speaker, a nice touch. Files may be protected or not as you wish. The disk system also permits you to format new disks, another thoughtful touch.

Blocks must be moved starting with the right side of a line. Thus, one cannot move a sentence from the middle of a paragraph.

The print subsystem permits you to specify page length, spacing between pages, line spacing and length, indent, justification and form feed (stop after each page or continuous print). Titles, headers, and page numbers can also be specified.

The print subsystem provides support for most common printers including proportional spacing units such as the Qume and Diablo.

Not-so-handy features of the print subsystem include boldface, superscripts and subscripts, and tabular formats. All of them are possible but require somewhat unusual successions of special characters.

The manual is quite complete and explains the commands and features in detail. In most cases, it gives examples as well as the description of the command.

EasyWriter was written by John Draper, who deserves a great deal of credit for this highly useful and user-oriented piece of software for the Apple II. It is available for $99.95 from many computer stores or Information Unlimited Software, 793 Vincente Ave., Berkeley, CA 94707 □

Word Processing: Fast and Easy

Dale Archibald

Let me make one thing perfectly clear: this will eventually become a review of a word processing/card file/electronic mail program for the 48K Apple II Plus or Apple II with Applesoft in ROM or a language card. The program will store about 25,000 words on a disk (30,000 on DOS 3.3).

First, however: a recent article on word processing (April, 1981, *Writer's Digest*) really made me sizzle. Writer Robin Perry proclaims "A home computer is a sophisticated toy used for games and such things as budgets, keeping track of stocks, and the like." Perry next grouped the Apple III with the Atari, PET, Heathkit, and the TRS-80 Model II calling them "some of the better-known home computers that have limited word processing capabilities."

In a sidebar, Perry says "...I feel safe in

Dale Archibald, 1817 Third Ave. N., Minneapolis, MN 55405.

recommending specific machines to you." All of them are between $6,000 and $10,000. The list includes the Apple III, the TRS-80 Model II and the Zenith/Heathkit Z89.

The Executive Secretary is reasonably simple. Considering the options it has, it's amazingly simple.

Further, Perry touts letter-quality printers for $3,000-$4,000 over $1,000 dot-matrix machines. "...the difference in price is worth it."

I emphatically disagree with Robin Perry.

Exhibit A: I am a freelance writer fulltime. Last year I sold over 175 newspaper and magazine articles to a variety of trade and consumer publications, from *Women's Wear Daily* to *Nibble*.

Exhibit B: In my office is an Apple II Plus, 48K single disk drive, MPI 88G dot-matrix printer, and a black and white video monitor. The Apple operates superbly, and has, for the most part, ever since I acquired it about it a year ago. No editor has yet complained of my dot-matrix typeface.

Exhibit C: My total system, with The Executive Secretary word processing system ($250 from Personal Business Systems, Inc., 4306 Upton Ave., So., Minneapolis, MN 55410) cost less than half what Perry recommends. And I love

it. Besides, I'd like to see Perry play Starfleet Orion on his/her Olivetti 401.

But it's possible I'm spoiled. This is the only word processing program I've ever used. I feel rather like a race car driver who's putting a test car through its paces: I work it hard in a variety of ways.

Designer John Risken gave me the uncopyable program, and installed the necessary Dan Paymar lower case adapter so that I could try it out and write about it. Bless his soul!

The $250 price tag may seem a bit steep, but consider that this program is a word processor plus form letter generator plus electronic card catalog plus report writer plus electronic mail option all in one.

Understand, please, that I am not a technical person. I am a writer. I don't have time to mess around with anything too complicated. The Executive Secretary is reasonably simple. Considering the options it has, it is amazingly simple.

Unlike some other word processing programs I've looked at for the Apple, The Executive Secretary will operate with the 40-character display and a Paymar chip; or it will use an 80-character board from Bit 3, the Smarterm from Apple, or Videoterm from Videx. The program allows either one disk or two, and can be changed to reflect new purchases.

It will support a variety of printers, parallel or serial, from the Silentype to Qume/Diablo/NEC for bidirectional printing. It will even operate the IBM ET Series typewriters.

There are 76 pages of instructions, 8 1/2 by 11", in a secretary's binder that stands next to the machine. There's also a prompt card that fits across the front of the Apple.

When you first boot The Executive Secretary, the program asks you to answer some questions. This adjusts it to your equipment.

The Commands

Beginning to type on an Executive Secretary-initialized disk is done just by typing the letter A. In place of the inverse asterisk that signals the editing mode, a short one-character underline appears. On my 40-character screen, the letters appear just as they will on the document: upper and lower case. As you type, of course, the words automatically wrap around to the next line.

Across the top of the screen reads the name of the document you've selected. Under that in inverse letters it proclaims "TYPE!' LEFT ARROW ERASES. 'ESC' ENDS." Hit Escape, and you're in the Edit mode. This allows you to move from line to line, page to page, or front to rear of the document. At the top of the screen, the inverse legend changes to "(A)DD (D)ELETE (M)ARK (P)RINT (ESC)APE."

Simply hitting A shifts you back into the Type mode. The letter D deletes one character or space to the right of the cursor. Shift D deletes a word. Control-D removes the entire line.

The character M marks three or more lines of type to move, delete, or treat as a Subfile. For example, in a lawyer's office there are often entire pages of "boiler-plate"—language that must be put into contracts. Using The Executive Secretary, these could run 3400 words long, yet be inserted just by typing, at the left margin, > sf SUBFILE or whatever name you've assigned.

Also while in the edit mode, it is possible to run a single or double spaced rough draft, line numbered or not, by touching P and answering three questions.

Other edit options include going to the numbered line selected, and a global search and replace.

Hit Escape a second time, and the latest version of your work is saved on disk.

It asks you whether you want to save the new version under the original name, under a new name, or not at all. So typing six letters on the same subject to various people is simple. Just change the addresses and names, then save each version under a new file name. Or you could type > xt NEW PERSON at the address space; as the printer arrives at that spot on the document, it would go to eXTernal file NEW PERSON and insert the correct name and address into the document. (This is for those with only one disk drive. More on this later.)

Printer Commands

The Executive Secretary uses mostly two-letter mnemonics after the right karat (>) to give commands to the printer. (For standard-sized documents, there's a ready-to-go command already set when you want to print.)

But you can customize documents as well. For instance:

•Mark Addresses to print out on envelopes after the letter is printed;

•Advance horizontally and vertically to specified places on pre-printed forms;

•Print documents to allow for bindings, with wider margins on the left side of odd-numbered pages, on the right side of even-numbered ones;

•Set left margin, top margin and bottom margin;

•Run page headers incorporating page numbers, description, etc.;

•Have abbreviations up to a line long, and insert them by typing .TE, for instance;

•Center on and center off;

•Use tabs;

•Indent;

•Have Justification on or turn justification off;

•Change a counter for things like objects or page numbers, where something else might be inserted in a sequence;

•Give special commands tailored to the particular printer, such as subscripts, superscripts, boldface or shadow printing;

•Underline if your printer is capable of doing it.

In fact, Risken seems to be adding new ones constantly.

Electronic Card Files

You can set up files with as many as 13 lines. An empty disk will hold close to 500 of these individualized cards, depending upon whether you use 13 or 16 sector disks. You assign a name to each line you want to use to get up your file. Once your master list is completed, you can sort it in alphabetical or zip code order by any line, rename lines, print mailing labels, even reports doing subtotals and totals.

The Data Factory from Micro Lab will also work with The Executive Secretary.

Form Letters

If you have two disk drives, you can draw information from the card file to print customized letters. There are special commands to the card file that mean certain subfiles will be placed into a document if something is so and something else is so, but not if something else is blank. The program will also change the all-caps structure of the address label into a regular upper and lower case name, if desired.

Visicalc Option

For those who would like to incorporate Personal Software's Visicalc formatted reports into a document, it can be accomplished with The Executive Secretary.

Conclusion

As I say, this is the only word processing system I've ever operated for any length of time. I've used it (and misused it, Risken would swear) practically every day for the last five months in as many ways as I could dream up. I have yet to lose a file of any length, although many of my word changes, line shifts, paragraph moves, etc., have caused words to drop out—as many as three lines. The latest copy of it doesn't seem to be as bad.

It doesn't have a mathematics mode, which at least one word processor does. There is one solder connection to be made for the shift key, which voids the Apple warranty. The photographs showing how this soldering job is done are terrible. And at times, when you have a variety of documents, the printer program must be fiddled with.

Overall, though, those are the only problems I find with The Executive Secretary. It is an example of the quality of the program that I can find so little even to nitpick about. It is a powerful piece of design work that can make life easier for anyone who deals with words. Risken continues to upgrade it, and promises to add further connections to other software from other firms. □

Through the Magic Window

Al Evans

From the simplest to the most sophisticated, any word processing system is basically just an electronic device for making marks on paper. One measurement of the ease of using a word processor is its "transparency"—the similarity between what appears on the screen and what is printed as final copy. From this standpoint, Magic Window, written by Gary Shannon with revision and documentation by Bill Depew, may be the best word processing system available for the standard 40-column Apple II computer.

The "virtuality" (to borrow a term from Ted Nelson) of Magic Window places you behind a window looking at a seemingly gigantic sheet of paper—say 24" by 36". You are at the keyboard of an enormously powerful typewriter, with the ability to deposit any ASCII character anywhere on this sheet in proportionately huge letters. You control the operation through the keys on the keyboard (most of them usable in two different ways), a main control menu, and subsidiary menus used for job formatting, filing, printing, and system configuration.

The Magic Window master disk boots in a single step on any Apple II system—13- or 16-sector. If a language card or compatible RAM card is installed in slot #0, the program will load there, giving the user about 10K of extra text memory. When loading is complete, Magic Window allows you to insert a text disk for automatic system configuration then displays a Subsystem Menu.

Magic Window menus are paragons of simplicity: use the arrow keys to move a white bar over the function you want, press Return to execute that function. The Subsystem Menu offers six choices: Editor Subsystem, Format Subsystem, Filer Subsystem, Printer Subsystem, Configuration Subsystem, and Exit to Basic.

The Configuration Subsystem customizes Magic Window for your computer and printer. The system will use a lower-case adapter if you have one (otherwise, capital letters are displayed in inverse characters). You can choose Upper Case Only for editing text files created from Basic programs, etc, or you can select Keypressed Sound for a "tick" each time a key is pressed (this helps establish the "typewriter" illusion).

After your system configuration is defined, it can be stored in a special file on each text disk. It can then be loaded semi-automatically during the startup process as mentioned above.

Using the Program

Now we're ready to follow a typical job through Magic Window, from formatting to printout.

The first step is to select the Format Subsysytem from the Subsystem Menu. This subsystem is used to define the "sheet of paper" you will be using: number of lines, number of characters per line, left and right margins, top and bottom margins, single or double spacing. After a format has been defined it is normally stored on the disk with the text that uses it.

The "sheet of paper" you define can be from one to 84 lines long and from 20 to 85 columns wide. This sheet can hold from one to 84 lines of text, each containing 20 to 80 characters.

After the format is set, Magic Window is ready to accept input. Select the Editor Subsystem from the Subsystem Menu and press Return. You will see one line of data showing the present cursor position on the page (line number and space number) and the number of the present page (relative to the first page of the current text). If you have entered no text, the rest of the screen is blank except for the dashes representing the edges of the "paper" and a blinking underline cursor in the center.

One unusual feature of Magic Window is that the cursor never moves; it stays right in the middle of the screen. Instead, the "paper" moves under it, just as it does on most typewriters. Any portion of the "sheet" (within the margins you have set) can be moved under the cursor. The cursor is non-destructive; it can be moved over existing text without erasing it.

Text entry is similar to other word processing systems. A carriage return is required only at the end of a paragraph. If you make a mistake, just backspace and type over it. Tabs can be set and cleared as on a typewriter, with one very handy difference—you can tab either forward or backward.

Editing can be performed any time during or after text entry. The editing

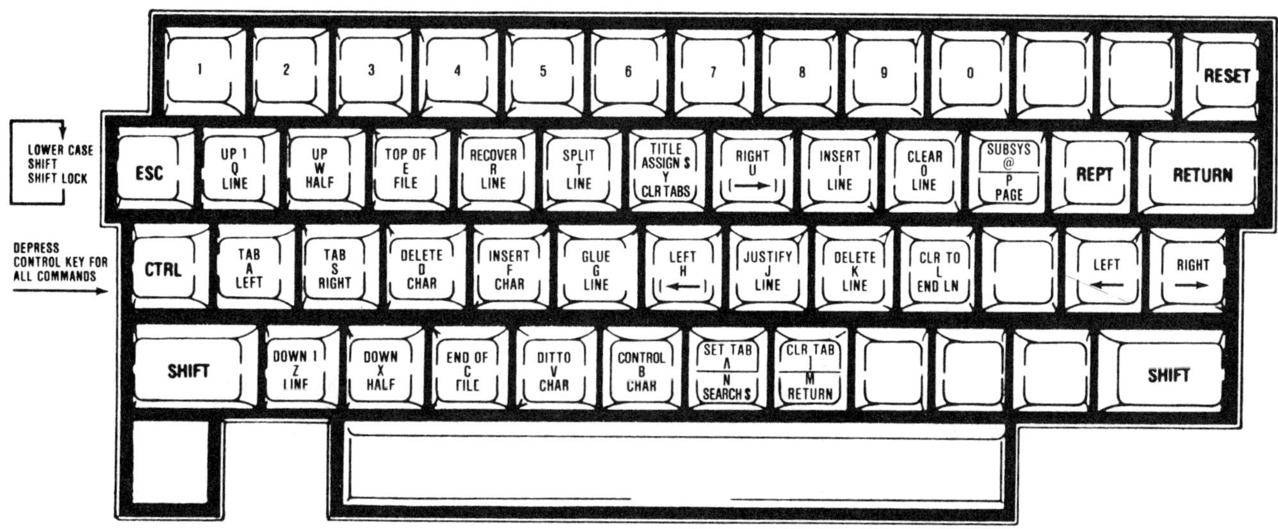

Figure 1. Magic Window editing commands. A large colored chart of these commands is supplied with the system.

commands are all control functions. For example, control-S is "tab right" and control-A is "tab left." The functions are assigned to the keys in logical patterns, rather than mnemonically. For example, control-Q is "up one line," control-W is "up half a screen," and control-E is "top of file." Similarly, control-Z is "down one line," control-X is "down half a screen," and control-C is "bottom of file." A large color chart showing all the editing commands is included with the Magic Window package (Figure 1).

Magic Window uses the so-called "split and glue" approach to editing. The "split" command (control-T) is used to isolate portions of text for alteration or deletion and to open up space for insertions of any length. The "glue" command (control-G) is then used to piece the text back together.

In addition to these functions, the Editor Subsystem has commands for inserting and deleting characters, deleting and recovering lines, copying characters from the line above, clearing the present line, and clearing from the cursor to the end of the present line. There are also commands for setting and clearing tabs, inserting blank lines, and returning to the Subsystem Menu.

Control-B allows you to insert a literal control character into the text. Control-J permits justification (flush left, flush right, flush left and right, center). Each line is adjusted individually, so that you can correct "loose lines" by hyphenating words, etc. In fact, one of the best features of Magic Window is that you can always see where the lines, paragraphs, and pages will end in your file copy.

Finally, the Editor Subsystem has a "miscellaneous" command: Control-Y, which brings up a menu which allows you to clear all tabs, assign a search string for global search, assign a title line (such as a section heading and location for a page number), and switch between two sets of characters not normally available which are assigned to shift-N, shift-M, and the "/" key. These characters include the circumflex, the tilde, the underline, the right and left curly brackets, the right and left square brackets, and the backslash.

Overall, the text editing facilities of Magic Window are comprehensive, well-designed, and very easy to use. Those familiar with other word processors will note the absence of "block move" and "global replace" functions. The system has a "global search," but the "replace" is manual. "Block moves" are accomplished by deleting groups of lines from one place in the text and recovering them in another. There is also a slightly more complicated technique which uses "unformatted" (sequential text) disk files.

When text entry is complete (or, if you're the cautious type and have entered more than you want to lose to sudden power failure), return to the Subsystem Menu and select the Filer Subsystem. This subsystem allows you to load and save two types of disk files (formatted and unformatted), to delete files, look at the directory for the current disk, change drive and slot numbers, and clear the memory for new text.

The final step in creating a document with any word processing system is printing. The Printer Subsystem, which is selected from the Subsystem Menu, permits you to print all or any part of your file on either paper or disk.

You can select upper-case-only for printout, specify a stop after each page (for sheet-fed printers), and select Mark Perforation for printing on roll paper which is later to be cut into sheets. This is also where you set the starting page number (page numbers must be in the 0-255 range).

After all the parameters are set, select Print Hardcopy. The system gives you an opportunity to set your paper to the "top-of-form" position. Since you already know what the final copy will look like, the rest is automatic.

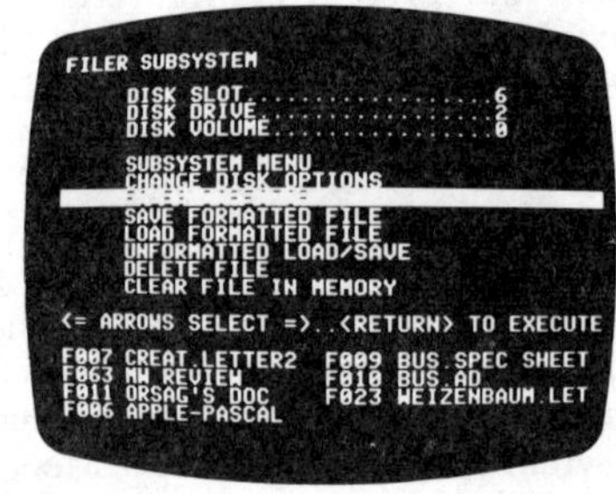

Special Features

So what does Magic Window have that other competitive systems (i.e. systems priced under $300) don't have?

In my opinion, the most important feature of this system is that it acts like a typewriter. What you see on the screen is what is finally printed on paper; there are no arcane-looking inverse chracters, lines of numbers separated by commas, flashing brackets, etc. If I were going to train somebody completely ignorant of computer systems to use an Apple word processor, this is the one I would choose. The actions taken are always visible, and operation rapidly becomes second nature.

The "typewriter" illusion is broken only by the use of the Escape key for shifting between lower case and capitals. There are systems in which the shift keys are wired to perform their normal typewriter functions. Unfortunately, this has some drawbacks. First, fewer characters can be accessed from the Apple keyboard if the shift keys are used for upper-lower case shifting. Second, many other systems I often use (for example, the Pascal 1.0 editor with the Paymar lower-case adapter and Bill Blue's ASCII Express) use the Escape key for upper-lower case control, and *any* degree of standardization is welcome. Finally, there is one definite advantage to using the Excape key: lines of mixed caps and numbers can be typed without unshifting for the numbers.

Another major advantage of Magic Window is that it reads and writes files in standard DOS 3.2 format. This means that it interfaces easily with other systems, Basic program, Visicalc, etc. For example, Magic Window comes with a listing of a short Basic program which will read a "softcopy" disk file and send it to a printer. This program can easily be modified to merge two files, for example one containing text and one containing addresses, in order to create customized form letters, etc. Magic Window "softcopy" files can also be uploaded to or downloaded from other computers using standard terminal programs.

The system has several minor, but useful, special features. As mentioned above, the program will load into the Apple language card if you have one, providing more text memory. Printer and interface commands are entered directly into the text as literal control characters, making it easy to use all of your printer's capabilities. In addition, the spaces "between the lines" are manually accessible in the double-spaced format, so that you can "fake" superscripts by placing them between two lines of text. Finally, Magic Window is a turnkey system which will boot in a single step on any Apple I, regardless of configuration.

Shortcomings

So, is this a perfect system? Well, not quite.

For one thing, the disk is "copy-protected." Protecting a disk against copying is inherently a theoretical absurdity. It doesn't hinder the knowledgeable, and causes problems for the inexperienced user, who is most likely to do the wrong thing at the wrong time and wipe out a disk.

However, I should mention that the Magic Window disk is used only once—to load the system. It is never accessed or written to during normal operation, and should therefore be safe unless exposed to stray magnetic fields, excessive heat, etc.

Line length is limited to 80 characters, which could make the system unusable in some applications. There is no way of checking how much memory is availble, but this is no problem after you learn how many pages your system will hold. Finally, there is no automatic way to change formats in the middle of a page, for example to insert a single-spaced quotation in block format within a double-spaced paper. However, this is easily accomplished by means of tab stops and manual linefeeds.

ower case plus

Leigh Goldstein

Move over Dan Paymar. There's a new kid on the block and he wants your lower case conversion business from all Apple II and Apple II Plus owners. As most of you know, the Paymar lower-case conversion has been the most widely accepted method used by Apple owners to get lower-case letters out of their machines. Being a fairly new Apple owner (four months), I was tempted by the ads I had seen in the various magazines for the Lazer System method. I sent away to Consumer Computers Mail Order, and received the kit in seven days.

Inside the box I found a software disk and the printed circuit board that was to be installed in the computer.

On my first glance through the manual I came across the word "solder," and immediately panicked. The last time I tried to solder something, I ended up spending $100 to replace the whole item. Fortunately for me though, my Apple is the latest revision, and the kit I received was specifically designed for it. If you have one of the older Apples, you must specify this fact when you order the kit.

The Apple keyboard was not constructed to allow you to enter lower case to a CRT screen. After you install the lower-case board, you must boot the software disk, which contains the programs to allow the Apple to ouput lower case. To use lower-case letters you hit the escape key twice. All typed letters will then appear in lower case. The escape key will now also function as your "shift" key. If you hold it down as you type a letter, that letter will appear in upper case. It takes a little getting used to, but it is not annoying.

In summary, I feel that the Lazer lower-case modification is well worth the money for the following reasons:

1. It is moderately easy to install; all you have to do is read carefully and stay calm.

2. The documentation is excellent.

3. It works with Pascal.

4. It is compatible with all the major word processing systems, including Apple Pie.

5. It is compatible with Mountain Computer's ROMPLUS/keyboard filter font editor (FEDIT) and their ROMWRITER EPROM programmer. This allows you to create your own fonts, view them in high resolution, and then save the font to disk.

6. It contains an expansion socket on the board which allows for future upgrades, and also offers another product called Graphics Plus—but that is another article.

My only real complaint with this system is the quality of the letter "m." It is not very sharp or clear. But that is really not a major complaint. I would not hesitate to recommend the Lazer System Lower Case Plus. It is an excellent product, and a very good value for the money.

Lazer Systems, P.O. Box 55518, Riverside, CA 92517. (714) 682-5268. $59.95.□

Leigh Goldstein, 328 E. 66 St., New York, NY 10021.

Joe Alinsky and
Winston Gayler

One of the differences between the video output of the Apple computer and that of many "professional" units is the 40-column display of the Apple. For those of us used to the "normal" 80 columns of characters, the Apple limitation can be frustrating. This is particularly true when interfacing with equipment that either offers or demands 80 columns. The reason Steve Wozniak designed the Apple with only 40 columns is good: the Apple was originally intended to be used with a standard B&W or color TV, and the bandwidth on these sets is simply not wide enough to provide the necessary resolution needed to make individual letters and characters legible at 80 columns.

With the advent of such information data banks as the Source and Micronet, a serious drawback to the 40-column display has become evident. Both the Source and Micronet require a standard 80 column terminal. (See Figure 1.) When used with the Apple, textlines are disconcertingly broken up, sometimes reducing the overall legibility of the text.

In addition, when using a text editor it is difficult to see how a page will look in the final printed version if your margins are set at 10 and 75 and your video display will not extend that far.

Three manufacturers of Apple Peripherals have addressed the problem and come up with plug-in boards that are unique in both design and operation. Yet, all three designs do display an 80-character line.

We have tested all three products from both engineering and user standpoints. Through the text and accompanying charts and photos, we have tried to provide the information that will make it easy for you to choose the board that fits your needs.

Before discussing each board separately, we have compiled a list of those features that are common to all three boards.

Common Characteristics

1) The boards plug into Apple peripheral slots (slot 3 for the Sup'r'terminal; any slot except 0 for the others).

2) All obtain power from the Apple (and all use lots of it).

3) All have composite video output, 80 columns with 24 lines of text. (The Videx board changes the number of lines depending on dot-matrix size.)

4) All display upper and lower case characters.

5) All allow keyboard selection of lower case.

6) All the boards require an actual B&W monitor, not just a TV. Even televisions with excellent resolution, displaying a good image with Apple's 40-column output will probably be disappointing with any of the 80-column boards.

7) None of the boards will handle all 128 ASCII characters from the keyboard, e.g., underscore, backslash, etc.

8) All are more difficult to read and will cause a lot more squinting than the 40-column display. One obvious reason is that the letters are smaller.

9) All the boards enable the user to view either Hi- or Lo-Res graphics on a regular television connected to the Apple video output, while viewing text on a monitor connected to the 80-column output. But, in the mixed graphics/text mode, the television set does not get the four lines of text at the bottom.

10) Once installed, it is impossible to see anything on your monitor without running the board's software or doing a PR#. All video is routed through the boards. It is possible to see the display through a separate conventional television (connected, of course, through an rf modulator). See the special note at the end of the Videx section.

11) CRT controller chip: All the units have a controller chip that provides the following hardware functions: horizontal and vertical timing; horizontal and vertical sync outputs; programmable cursor; text window manipulation; light pen register; screen memory addressing; character

Figure 1. Source Message of the Day menu on the Double Vision. Note what 80 columns does for the Source.

Joe Alinsky, P.O. Box 1411, Canoga Park, CA 91304.

Winston Gayler, 77 Ortega Ave., Mountain View, CA 94040.

generator row addressing; interface to the microprocessor bus.

Point 11 has several implications for the 80-column board user. By using a CRT LSI chip, the designer can minimize the parts count, power, and cost. Also, the user can access the programmable cursor, and future software could use the light pen input present on this chip. As a last note on this subject, one of the boards (M&R) uses the text window manipulation ability.

Videx Videoterm

Of all the boards, only the Videx provided a first class manual to accompany its product.

Included in its book were a complete schematic, theory of operation, and commented source code (how rare!). In addition, instructions are given on how to generate your own character set and instructions on directly accessing the CRT controller chip registers. As Apple recommends to all peripheral manufacturers, all firmware is contained in EPROM and a simple PR# command fires up the board.

One of the most interesting and useful features of the Videx board is the ability to control the dot matrix cell size. Table 1 indicates the choices available.

CELL SIZE (HxV)	CHAR. SIZE	SCREEN FORMAT
8x10	7x9	80x24
9x10	8x9	80x23
8x12	7x11	80x20
9x12	8x11	80x18

Table 1

Simple keyboard commands allow the user to pick any of the dot matrix cell sizes available. (See Figures 2 and 3.)

By adding an optional 2708 or 2716 EPROM, it is possible to generate your own character set. The EPROM expands this character set by 64 or 128 characters.

Any 80-column board being used with a text editor must contend with the problem of shifting between upper and lower case. Obviously, when one is entering text for later hard-copy printout, it is nice to hit

the "shift" key for upper-lower conversion as on a normal typewriter. At the very least, one should expect to strike a single key that can be reached relatively easily by the left hand little finger.

Unfortunately, Videx appears to have gone out of its way to make this a difficult task. It is necessary to hit a "ctrl A" (two keys) in order to shift. But that's not all.

Normally, after striking the "shift" key on a typewriter, it returns to lower case mode after release of the key. Not so on the Videx. The "ctrl A" arrangement is a toggle situation. Switch it "on" with a "ctrl A," and it stays in upper case until you do another "ctrl A." In order to type the word "Apple" with the "A" capitalized, it is necessary to hit four superfluous characters, (the ctrl key twice, and the "A" twice). Although a software fix to any text editor program might be possible, this is a design limitation that must be reckoned with. In talking with the manufacturer, they have indicated that a hardware fix for this might appear sometime in the future, but it is not available at this time. Those of you who decide the Videx is the board to buy should contact the manufacturer to find out when and if this mod will occur.

We discovered another problem with the "ctrl A" arrangement. It can do strange things from within a program. At one point in utilizing the Videx Videoterm with a program of ours, we found the program displaying lower case the first time it ran, upper case the second time, then lower, etc. Presumably, this was due to an embedded control A causing the toggling effect between upper and lower case.

The user should experiment with the four matrix sizes to find the one that goes best with his eyes and monitor. We found the display slightly difficult to read on a 9"

Sanyo, but it reproduced very well on a 9" Hitachi and 12" Leedex monitor. The user may also find it necessary to adjust the "height" control (usually found on the back) on his monitor.

It should also be mentioned that many functions and commands do not work with each of these boards. This is particularly true of control characters and escape functions, although on the Videoterm board such common commands as "Home," "Text" and "Vtab" do not appear on the screen. There are, however, substitute control characters that perform the same functions.

Videx provides an optional switch to allow normal viewing when the normal 40-column display is desired. We thought this was an unusual show of concern for the end user, and demonstrates good forethought on Videx's part.

Double Vision

As with the Videx, the Double Vision board plugs into any slot. However, the manner in which the board is initialized, or "fired up," differs from the Videx. Instead of a straight PR#, it is necessary to boot a disk containing the software for the board. We believe it is important to emphasize that if you are only using a monitor and are not simultaneously plugged into a standard television (through a modulator) you will not be able to see anything until you boot the Double Vision disk. If for some reason you do not wish to have 80-columns for a period of time, you will have to remove the connector from the board and re-plug it into the back of the Apple, unless of course, you have that separate TV.

Once the disk is up and running, we found the Double Vision display on the Sanyo and Hitachi to be a bit (no pun intended) better then the Videx board on these same monitors. The characters are not as close together as on the Videx. (See Figure 4.) This is probably due to the smaller 5 x 7 matrix. With the smaller matrix, any one character is less well-formed, but the whole screen of characters is easier to read.

Another plus of the Double Vision board

Figure 2. Videx with the default option of 80 characters x 24 lines. Note the narrow vertical spacing between lines.

Figure 3. Videx with the format programmed for 80 characters x 20 lines. Note that with fewer lines there is more space between lines and the true descenders are evident.

Figure 4. Double Vision: The lower case g, y, p, q, etc. are a little awkward, but the overall text is easy to read.

is that it allows escape key cursor movements. Both single key (escape D,A,C,B) and multiple key (escape I,J,K,M) cursor operations are allowed. In fact, if you don't have the autostart ROM or an Apple II Plus, the Double Vision will give you multiple key cursor moves and stop list!

As mentioned before, we feel shifting to upper case is a function that should be easy. The Double Vision board accomplishes this nicely in two ways: Escape Key: hit the escape key once and the next letter is upper case, or Shift Key: This requires a one-wire modification to your Apple. The Double Vision manual explains how this is accomplished. After the modification is complete, holding the shift key down while hitting a key prints it in upper case. Releasing it returns you to lower. This is true shift key operation. However, the shift-lock is not so easily accomplished. It is necessary to type "crtl E" to shift-lock, then "escape, ctrl z" to get back to lower case again.

We also discovered that while in the Double Vision software, neither Basic nor DOS responds to lower case.

The Double Vision uses a CRT controller chip, as do all the units, however, no instructions are given on how to access its registers.

M&R Sup'r'Terminal

The first thing you notice is its size. This is the largest board we have ever seen for the Apple. It looks like something that belongs in an S-100 bus! In addition, there is a small piggyback board that plugs into an IC socket on the Apple motherboard.

Unlike the other two boards the M&R is slot dependent; it must be plugged into slot 3. Its on-board firmware is contained in a 2716 EPROM and is activated by a PR# command (as is the Videx).

The M&R is the power-hungry champ of the three boards. We were interested in this and upon investigation, discovered that the M&R design places a power resistor on the board between the +5 and +12 volt supplies. This appears to be a method of transferring some of the +5v load to the +12v supply. Indeed, the M&R has the lowest +5v current drain of the three boards. (See Table 2.)

Checking further, we found our +5v supply near capacity (2.5 amps as specified by Apple). The 12v supply had considerable margin, as might be expected. The logic therefore, of transferring the +5v load to the 12v supply appears to be sound. However, the trade-off here is increased power dissipation (heat) inside the Apple.

Since all the boards generate a fair amount of heat (the M&R more than the others), we feel a better design for all three manufacturers would be to use power-down circuitry (again as Apple recommends) or a simple on-off switch.

The Sup'r'Terminal can be loaded with

GENERAL:			
Manufacturer	Videx	Computer Stop	M&R Enterprises
Model	Videoterm	Doublevision	Sup'r'terminal
Basic Price	$345	$295	$395

HARDWARE:			
IC Quantity	24	20	31
Sockets	Y	Y	Y
Memory Required	16K	48K	N/A
Disk Required	N	Y	N
Typical Current			
Drain +5v	400ma	400ma(570ma)	380ma(380ma)
+12v	30ma	0	190ma(210ma)
-5v	15ma	0	(1 microamp)
-12v	0	0	0
Total Power	2.4 W	2 W (2.9 W)	4.2 W (4.4 W)

Note:
Current values are average as provided by the manufacturers. Powers are derived from the currents. Values in parentheses were measured on early boards.

SOFTWARE:	2708 EPROM at C800-CBFF	1.5K of machine Code loads from disk to RAM just below DOS	2716 EPROM at C800-CFFF

Keyboard Characteristics:			
Shift Method	CTRL A	ESC or Shift Key	CTRL A or Shift Key
Shift Lock	Y	Y	Y
Cursor Escape Functions	N	Y	Y
Ctrl U copy	N	Y	Y

DISPLAY CHARACTERISTICS:			
Dot Matrix	(Varies- See Table 1)	5 x 7	5 x 8
Cursor	P	Blinking Rectangle	P
Inverse Character	Y	Y	Y (alpha only)
Control Character	Y	N	N
Graphics	Limited	N	N
True Descenders	Y	N	Y
Flashing Character	N	N	N
X-Y Cursor Addressing	Y	Y	Y

COMPATIBILITY:			
DOS 3.1	Y	N	Y
DOS 3.2	Y	Y	Y
Com Card	*	*	*
Integer Basic	Y	Y	Y
Applesoft	Y	Y	Y
Pascal	C	C	C
Peripherals	**	**	**
Unltd.Text Ed. Ver.3.0			
Apple Pi	**	**	**
Serial Card	C	N/A	C
Micromodem	C	N/A	N/A
Lower Case Basic and DOS commands	Y	N	N
"HOME." "VTAB." etc.	N	Y	N

* Only with additional software (B.I.T.S., etc.)
** Both software companies claim compatability with all the boards soon.

DOCUMENTATION:			
Schematic	Y	N	N
Source Listing	Y	N	N
Theory of Operation	Y	N	N
Manual Length (in equivalent 8 1/2 x 11 pages)	56	13	33

OPTIONS:	Graphics $25 EPROM Video Switch Plate $12	Pascal Software $25	

All table entries should be self-explanatory except the following:

ctrl U copy:
This feature which is inherent in the Apple's 40-column system allows you to copy characters from the screen using the right arrow key (ctrl U)

X-Y Cursor addressing:
A feature often found in CRT terminals that allows you to directly position the cursor via X-y coordinates.

Y   Yes
N   No
C   Claimed by the manufacturer but not tested by the authors
P   Programmable

custom character fonts (type faces) from disk or tape. Up to ten fonts can be held in a "staging area" located in RAM and then quickly transferred to the Sup'r'terminal for display. The preliminary manual includes a utility program, "Font Compressor," to aid this process. (See Figure 5.)

Figure 5. Sup'r'terminal displays good readability.

Like the Double Vision, this board adds ESC I,J,K,M cursor moves and stop list to the Apple. It also accomodates an optional one-wire hardwire modification for true shift key operation. The shift procedure is as follows: without mod: ctrl A, activates lowercase; single ctrl A, next letter is upper case; double ctrl A, caps lock. With mod:

ctrl A; activates lowercase; snift key; uppercase; double ctrl A; caps lock.

The Sup'r'Terminal does not respond to "Home," "Vtab," etc., but as on the Videx, substitute commands to provide the same functions are given in the manual. DOS and Basic will not respond to lowercase commands.

The 80-column screen does respond to the tab character (ctrl I) by moving the cursor to the next field. Tab fields are 80 characters wide.

We also noted as a handy feature the ability to program the 80-column scrolling window as can be done with the Apple's 40-column output.

We observed a couple of peculiar items with the M&R: when the Sup'r'Terminal is activated, the color of any graphics displayed on the 40-column output deteriorates, and the inverse video mode (black on white) affects only alpha characters, not numerals or symbols.

There are many good reasons for wanting 80 columns on your Apple, and if you are looking for a board to make your Apple "Professional," the chart in Table 1 should help you with your shopping. Be aware though, that product improvements are likely, so check with your dealer before deciding which board is for you. □

© Creative Computing

The Prince and the Paper

Keith E. Walker

You pays your money and you takes your chances, they say, and sooner or later you'll probably take your chances on a printer. This review will cover the Silentype printer by Apple Computer and a software package offered by Computer Station for this printer. The software package is also available for the Paper Tiger printers hooked up to an Apple II.

The Silentype printer is offered by Apple Computer for the Apple II and the new Apple III computers. The printer comes with its own special interface card and one roll of paper, which by the way, comes in 80' rolls and is 8.5" wide.

Now, I'm just a computer hacker who enjoys punching out totally incomprehensible programs that only another hacker could love. But, deep in the heart of all hackers is a yearning to write THE program that everyone simply has to have.

A printer may not help me become a better programmer, but it couldn't hurt. No more nights spent LISTing and LISTing and LISTing. Hard Copy! Just the sound of those words brings warmth to my heart.

The main reason I wanted a printer was for programming, so a letter-quality printer wasn't necessary (or affordable) and indelible copy wasn't needed. So I chose the Silentype. It is the third printer in Apple's lineup and it retails for $625 (or whatever you and your friendly merchant agree upon. Don't tell anyone, but I got mine for a *lot* less).

The printer buzzes along at the breathtaking speed of 40 characters per second (top speed) and prints those letters in a 5 x 7 dot matrix. The speed varies, though, with how dark the intensity is set. The darker the type, the slower the printing speed and vice versa.

It handles the normal ASCII character set (without true descenders on lower case), and prints in both uni-directional and bi-

Keith E. Walker, 726 5th Ave. So., Apt A, Great Falls, MT 59405.

directional formats. The maximum line length is 84 characters with 10 characters to the inch. The Silentype has the standard six lines per inch vertical spacing.

Completely devoid of any buttons or switches (inside or out), the only control on the printer is a typewriter-like platen feed. Just one little knob to worry about. All of the controls are handled with software or by directly accessing printer memory (via POKEs or control characters). This means never having to remove the cover to get at DIP switches.

As for control characters, the Silentype recognizes LF and FF (line feed and form feed) but reacts a little differently to the form feed than one would expect. All the form feed does is issue a preset number

of line feeds. With non-perforated roll type paper, a true form feed doesn't make much sense anyway. The operator can vary the number of line feeds it does by POKEing a certain address.

The other control characters handle such features as graphics screen dump, printer/CRT mirroring (this limits the printer to 40 letters per line due to the Apple screen width) and a normal 80 character width output.

What about print quality and that doggone thermal paper? Well, print quality is as good as the the average impact printer and this printer won't wake up the cat. The name Silentype is very apt. If you drag a pencil eraser across this page you'll have just about the right level of

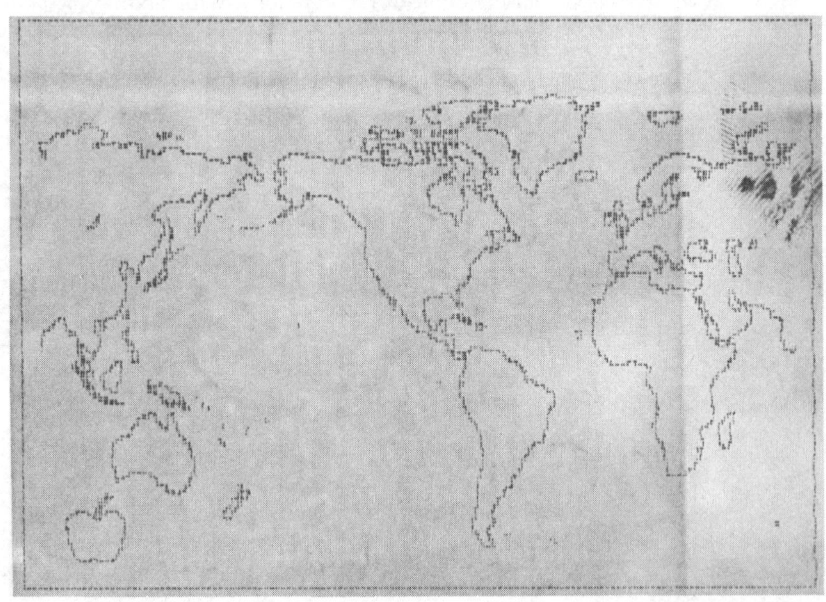

)*+,-./0123456789:;<=>?@ABCDEFGHIJKLMNOPQRSTUVWXYZ[\]^_`abcdefghijklmnopqrstuvwxy
*+,-./0123456789:;<=>?@ABCDEFGHIJKLMNOPQRSTUVWXYZ[\]^_`abcdefghijklmnopqrstuvwxyz
+,-./0123456789:;<=>?@ABCDEFGHIJKLMNOPQRSTUVWXYZ[\]^_`abcdefghijklmnopqrstuvwxyz{
,-./0123456789:;<=>?@ABCDEFGHIJKLMNOPQRSTUVWXYZ[\]^_`abcdefghijklmnopqrstuvwxyz{|
-./0123456789:;<=>?@ABCDEFGHIJKLMNOPQRSTUVWXYZ[\]^_`abcdefghijklmnopqrstuvwxyz{|}
./0123456789:;<=>?@ABCDEFGHIJKLMNOPQRSTUVWXYZ[\]^_`abcdefghijklmnopqrstuvwxyz{|}~
/0123456789:;<=>?@ABCDEFGHIJKLMNOPQRSTUVWXYZ[\]^_`abcdefghijklmnopqrstuvwxyz{|}~▓

noise. In other words, it is very, very quiet.

Contrary to what you may have heard, the Silentype doesn't use that weird feeling, scratch prone, silver paper that thermal printers used to use, but a white paper that is almost indistinguishable from the real thing.

While it is true that if you like to keep your paper in the oven or in the trunk of your car when you're not using it, the paper will turn black, but it just isn't as sensitive to heat as everyone makes it sound. The technology of paper seems to have kept pace with the rest of the microcomputer industry.

I have many list-outs that are approaching their first birthday, and there is no deterioration . . . yet. Another difficulty is trying to get something resembling a standard size sheet of paper when you have to decide where to tear the sheet (no dotted lines here!).

One more thing the Silentype doesn't offer is the extended type fonts (stretched out letters) that true impact printers offer. Those characters are great for headers and form printing.

The graphics capabilities are about average for a modern printer, but you don't have to purchase special graphics software to use it. All that you have to do is press ctrl-Q, stand back and watch. If you don't mind a little inaccuracy the Silentype will do the graphics dump bi-directionally which is pretty quick, or for a better look, you can set the printer for uni-directional printing, which isn't very fast.

Altogether, I'm very pleased with the Silentype printer, except for one very small detail. For those people lucky enough to own an Apple III computer, the Silentype can be programmed to print different fonts. Seems as though Apple could have at least offered that proper software for the Apple II.

But, where there's a need, there's a programmer, and Computer Station in St. Louis, MO, offers software to accomplish this feat. The only requirement for this software package is that you have DOS 3.3 and Apple DOS Tool Kit. Known as "Graphic Writer," it will print any of the fonts available in the DOS Took Kit (about 30 different ones), with the only limitation being that you can only print 69 letters to the lines as opposed to the normal 80. But don't be alarmed, the characters still spread fully across the page. The routine is pretty easy to incorporate into your programs and is compatible with Apple Writer (in fact, it was designed for it).

To include Graphic Writer in a program of your own, Computer Station has provided an example program. It explains with REMarks how to accomplish the task. All it involves is loading in the object code and your chosen character set and doing a few pokes to initialize the program. Computer Station didn't exactly go overboard in providing information on how the object code works, but then how many companies do?

All in all, Graphic Writer has to be one of the best things that has happened to the Silentype. With it, you can print in anything from ASCII to Katakana (Japanese characters), or even special graphics characters. And as a plus you now get true descenders on your lower case letters. Quite an impressive package.

To sum things up, I am very pleased with the Silentype printer, especially in combination with the Graphic Writer package from Computer Station. While it's true that my print-outs will get a tan if I leave them out in the sun for too long, this is a small problem to overcome. The print quality is good, the speed isn't bad and it *is* quiet. Graphic dumps are as easy as pie with control from within a program fairly easy to accomplish.

I'll give it an 85, it's got a good beat and it's easy to dance to. □

"Pemberton, I'd like to process a few words with you."

Printer Control Codes
From Within Apple Writer

J. Michael Riley

To Apple II owners whose machines are equipped with a Dan Paymar Lower Case Adapter and use Apple Writer, I highly recommend modifying the program to display lower case directly on the screen as described by John E. Stith in the February 1981 issue of *Creative Computing*. I have used the modified version for over a year and have had no problems whatever.

If your printer has the capability of varied print fonts, as mine does, you may have wondered how to send the printer the necessary control codes from within Apple Writer texts. The difficulty with direct entry of these control codes (usually ASCII control characters) is that the Apple Writer TEDITOR program uses control codes entered from the keyboard to maneuver the cursor during editing, thus effectively preventing the user from entering them into the body of the text.

I use a prehistoric IDS IP-225, which can produce enhanced (double-width) or normal characters in four different print densities under software control. The printer will also perform a carriage return without linefeed, which can be used for double-striking for emphasis, and a 1/3 linefeed, which can be used for underlining with the hyphen.

To embed these control codes in texts, you must place the necessary ASCII hexadecimal codes directly into the portion of the memory of your computer that the Apple Writer program uses for the text. The easiest way to do this is as follows:

1. Boot your system with the Apple Writer disk modified as directed in Mr. Stith's article. (The unmodified program will not work using this technique because of the way both the TEDITOR and PRINTER programs interpret and display the text memory.)

J. Michael Riley, 619 N. Cascade Ave., Suite 3, Colorado Springs, CO 80903.

2. Exit the program by pressing Q Return.

3. Enter the Apple system monitor by typing CALL -151 Return.

4. Type 1900: 83 01 02 1C 1D 1E 1F 0B 09 4B 0D 60 Return. This builds a short text in memory where Apple Writer expects to find it. Hex 83 is the beginning marker, and hex 60 is the end marker of the file. In between are the hex equivalents of the appropriate printer control codes for my printer (and many others) as follows:

```
01 = Control A = Enhanced Mode
02 = Control B = Normal Mode
1C = Control / = 8.3 Characters/inch
1D = Control ] = 10 Characters/inch
1E = Control ↑ = 12 Characters/inch
1F = Control < = 16.5 Characters/inch
0B = Control K = Vertical Tab (1/3 line
                 feed)
09 4B turns off the Apple Parallel Card
automatic linefeed
0D = Control M = Carriage Return
```

These control codes may not be applicable to your printer or printer controller card; check your manual.

5. Type 3D0G Return to re-enter Basic.

6. Type BRUN TEDITOR Return.

7. After the editor program is loaded, and the menu appears, type E Return. The text on the screen will consist of a block of inverse characters, and one flashing one (a K). Using the normal Apple Writer editing techniques, you may now add a brief explanation of each code for easier reading and use. Return to the Apple Writer menu and type S Return. Save the control codes as you would any other Apple Writer file. I saved mine right on the working master diskette under the imaginative name CONTROL CODES.

8. You may now insert any of these desired control codes within your own text by parking the cursor where you want the code, and using the Apple Writer "insert" command (Control I). When the editor asks which file to insert, respond with CONTROL CODES (or whatever name you have chosen). Then simply delete the control codes you do not want.

(Editor's Note—Readers may wish to make a series of files, with one for each control function. This way, no deletions will be required when a control file is inserted.)

I have used these codes with great success, although several of them required some experimentation before I got predictable results. For example, my printer is set up so that the controller card issues the linefeed automatically with every carriage return. This is defeated as directed in the documentation for the card, and as noted above.

Turning off the linefeed is useful for over-striking and forming composite characters. However, unless the automatic linefeed is turned back on again, the entire remainder of the text is printed with no paper advance—not too legibly, I might add. The card documentation does not specify how to restore automatic linefeed, but it happens to be with the same code as is used to turn it off.

Another subtlety of an embedded character for carriage return is that the print head returns completely to the left margin regardless of the Apple Writer margin setting. The spaces used for margin setting must be accounted for when setting up underlines or over-strikes.

This simple technique will allow you to access many of the special capabilities of your printer from within Apple Writer. It also has one unique and exciting advantage over commercially available software—it's free!

Chapter V
Business

Chapter V — Business

The most practical, useful place for a computer is in business. There is no other area in which computers are used in such numbers. Not every business needs or can afford a large mainframe machine. In many cases an Apple is quite sufficient for handling small business functions. Even in large businesses, Apples can provide easily accessible computing power, where previously it wasn't available. A small computer can be very valuable in forecasting, planning, and note-keeping. There are also the more obvious office functions — such as word processing, record maintenance, mail list processing, inventory control, and accounting — although to be fair, the utility of an Apple with some of these applications depends on the amount of data that must be handled. Still, for some larger applications, an Apple with a hard disk attached can process plenty of information quickly. The Apple can also be used as a "smart terminal" connected to other computers, for data access and exchange. The possibilities are virtually endless . . .

Since Chuck Carpenter wrote his review of *Desktop Plan* featured in this chapter, Personal Software has released *Desktop Plan II,* which includes high resolution graphing, charting of data series, and *Visicalc* compatibility. The new version sells for $199.95.

The next two articles are about Visicalc — one of the most ingenious programs I've seen on a computer. The number of possible uses for it is staggering. In a rare moment of wholehearted endorsement of a product, I have to agree with Doug Green in saying that it alone justifies the cost of a microcomputer. I just wish I had written it.

Well-Fashioned Forms, by David Lubar, concerns the data base programs that form the heart of most business applications. With a good data base system, you can store and retrieve any conceivable kind of information. When you're looking for a specific item, search routines should allow you to specify individual records, or different subsets of your information. (For example, if you kept a mailing list in your data base, you should be able to tell it to print labels for everyone in your list who lives in Illinois and who owns an Apple.) In addition you should be able to sort your data on any key, and it's nice if you have good control over the print formatting.

Because there are so many options in a data base program, they are somewhat difficult to thoroughly review. Sometimes it's even difficult to compare all the options after you've used a few different systems for months. Certain applications will work fine on one system; then a slightly different application will turn out to work much better on another system because it has some minor feature that you didn't need before. The problem in comparing, however, is that each system has its own "minor" features, and it's not always easy to anticipate which ones will be needed for future applications.

PFS is also reviewed in this article. It is only one of the dozens of data base systems available for the Apple. With the prices ranging from $100 to $250, it's best to carefully look at the options each offers . . . and doesn't offer. Check a few reviews if possible; that way it's more likely that you'll catch some of the subtle differences in the programs.

By the way, Software Publishing Corporation has released "PFS: Report," a report printing module to go along with PFS. It is also listed at $95.

A Manager and His Machine

Robert Heltman

The heartwarming story of a small computer that finds a home in big business.

Reflections after eight months: a report from a middle manager in a large corporation, who has recently incorporated an Apple into his office work life both to improve productivity and continue his education. Did it work? Let's see . . . .

This article fulfills an unwritten promise to myself and the colleagues who blessed my purchase of a portable computer at company expense. I hope it will help other executives to decide if they should take such a step and, if they do, how such a computer might be used to their advantage.

These days most executives in large organizations have access to large computers for business reports. Our paychecks arrive with the unmistakable imprint of computer preparation. More and more tasks in all areas of business are being tackled and improved by the computer.

In our Human Resources Department at General Electric in Erie, PA, we have large-scale computer systems for general employee information, equal employment opportunity tracking, payroll and exempt annual manpower review data. Many standard and special reports can be obtained periodically or overnight. The manpower data is also on-line searchable and is used to generate candidate slates and to perform various analyses.

But in my role in human resource management—and, I believe, in many other areas—there has been a sort of no man's land where certain needs and ideas just don't quite get the attention or budget priority that does, and should, go to larger projects tackled by larger computers.

Robert F. Heltman. Manager-Organization and Manpower Transportation Systems Business Division. General Electric Co.. Erie. PA 16531.

In addition, on some approved computer projects, there seem to be difficulties involved in translating the general concepts of what is needed into fully usable output. Have you ever noticed that when you meet with your systems analyst or programmer, the conversation goes something like this:
Analyst/programmer: "What do you want to be able to do?" ·
You, after some general statements: "What *can* be done?

While users need to do a better job of defining what they need it is also true that the programmer should be expected to "bring something to the party." This is most often possible when he has worked on similar applications before. However, if you are in a unique field or are developing a new application, you are often on your own.

> **I'm not an electronics expert, nor am I a computer "nut" or hobbyist. I'm a businessman pursuing productivity and better ways of doing things.**

As a new computer project gets underway, you may find that when the first output is delivered you get new ideas about what you'd *really* like to have? This goes through several cycles, while time goes by, costs rise and your programmer sincerely wishes he'd undertaken a different career—maybe milking goats in a monastery?

What these situations boil down to is this: it seems that defining and developing a new application has an interactive quality. That is, you outline what you think you want, then see the output results, which in turn triggers thoughts on what else you'd like to have. This cycles several times until you either get what you want or reach an acceptable compromise.

Last November this situation was bothering me more than usual, but so was something else. That was the growing realization that we live in the age of the "microprocessor"—that tiny computer on a thin quarter-inch-square chip that is putting "brains" into games our children get at Christmas, and products like microwaveovens, as well as into the manufacturing processess and machines that make those products. Business magazines, as well as enlishtened managers everywhere, talk about America—*our* country!—being far behind in productivity, while Japan and other nations are far ahead in robots and computers.

In the middle of all this I said to myself, "What am I doing about my own education in this new microprocessor revolution?" The answer then was, "Not enough!"

These two factors—productivity and my educational gap—concerned me so much that during last Thanksgiving vacation I dropped into my nearest computer stores. talked to the managers, and bought three books on digital electronics and small portable computers. While a lot of it was over my head, I began to get a feel for microelectronics and what could be done. For an economics/business administration major, it was at least a start.

As you can tell, I'm not an electronics expert, nor am I a computer "nut" or hobbyist. I'm a businessman pursuing productivity and better ways of doing things.

Portable computers interest me as would any superior tool or method. If factual data proved that lop-eared kangaroos improved office productivity, this article would have a report on eight months of progress in *that* field!

Next I began talking to associates at work, including old friends and new contacts at a number of company locations. My research convinced me that if I had a small portable computer, and could learn to program it, I might move toward solving both problems—component productivity readiness-to-serve, and my own educational shortfall. A portable computer was necessary because I had to get most of my learning and project application development work done at home. The normal tasks had to continue during regular business hours.

After several passes at writing a proposal, I was ready to spend the equivalent of two days talking with my division experts and management associates, who would have to approve the purchase of a computer. It was a good two days, for I continued to learn as I answered their questions.

I was fortunate in having an open-minded boss, along with reasonable and considerate associates, who were willing to listen to my story, give useful advice, and in the end, approve my purchase. In fact I became the first manager to be involved in one of several experimental pilot projects with small portable computers now under evaluation. In keeping with my plan, I purchased locally—"don't forget service!"—an Apple II with clock card, two disk drives, a 9" black and white TV monitor, Micromodem for telephone connection, and a dot/matrix printer, along with a carrying case, some mini-floppy disks, and a few more books on programming. Soon I added the Apple-soft floating point Basic language card, and an 80-column card due to growing word processing use. With company consent I carried the above home, and spent most of Christmas and New Year's vacation going to my own self-conducted school. My understanding wife began to wonder about the "electronic mistress" who kept me up late nights, but I knew I was a novice, and wanted to have some proficiency before installing the computer in my office.

Slowly, with plenty of mistakes, I learned how to operate my Apple and began writing and experimenting with simple programs. The owner and staff at the local computer store—Erie Computer Co.—were just great. As I think back about the really simple questions that had me stuck, I am amazed at how understanding and helpful they were every step of the way—even if I called at night.

Learning to make the computer work for me has been like taking a person who played beginner music on the piano years ago and giving him an organ for the task of playing Bach and Beethoven, and expecting him to compose additional music as well.

I found that it takes some time to learn the mental and manual habits of "playing" the computer. Each piece of software "music" requires learning and practice to remain proficient. In addition it can become frustrating to find that with every new piece of software comes *another* instruction manual.

I've found programming a bit like learning a foreign language; it is easier if you immerse yourself in the culture, in this case by writing short job-related programs yourself.

Frankly, I look forward to the day when we will have even higher level computer languages, and "smarter" computers that will take verbal instructions to do what one wants done.

It took me about a month of evenings and weekends before I felt confident enough to bring the Apple to my office, and have it work for me without my spending office time getting it to work. Over the following months I added one application after another.

At this point the computer is an essential part of my office life. It has proven itself invaluable, and in some ways I couldn't forecast. I'd feel lost without it. I've found it to be a practical way to "do more with less"—a situation very familiar to businessmen everywhere who are fighting off the ravages of inflation and America's rather shoddy productivity standing.

Now let's examine actual applications by looking at what I said I planned to do with the Apple in my purchase authorization last December and comparing that with actual use.

Purchase Proposal Item 1: As a "dumb" terminal, to access the manpower review data on the mainframe computer in Schenectady, via modem/telephone.

Results: This has worked out better than I originally thought due to a short "auto-dial" software program an Apple-using colleague helped me work out one Saturday at the office.

The old way was for a colleague to telephone, requesting candidates for a specific job he would describe. I would make notes on a pad, give them to an associate to search on the time-share terminal, or do so myself, then call the requesting party back, often to find him at a meeting. Usually a day or two of missed calls would pass, and if either of us had to travel, a week or so might be lost.

Now, with the special auto-dial software, when the call comes, I slip the program disk into drive #1, boot the system and it automatically dials the mainframe computer. The auto-dial program goes through six secret, and periodically changed, access codes and puts the Schenectady computer on line in about the amount of time it takes to cover the conversational pleasantries. With the phone tucked in my ear I can discuss candidate specifications and qualifications while I input the necessary

search questions via Apple and modem. It prints out the list of candidates that most closely match the requestor's needs and I then turn the list over to an associate who pulls resumes and mails them off.

The matches of candidates to specifications are a little better because the caller and I interacted with the data base at the time of the request. The matter is settled at the time of the call. There are no return calls, no lost time, no notes lying around or misplaced and no delays. This initially unforseen auto-dial program has been a real gem. It represents an increase in productivity: readiness-to-serve is greatly improved and quality of results is higher.

However, I had also wanted to do an even more automated job by tying in the clock card to make end-of-month calls to the mainframe. During plant shutdown, the same associate, Lyn Brawn, who helped me develop the auto-dial program earlier in the year, helped me put this together. We call it TAP, for Time Auto-dial Program.

There were two reasons for not getting TAP finished several months earlier. First was a bad experience, when I left my computer to finish a long printout one evening, the output appearing to be neatly piling up on the floor as I locked the door and turned out the lights. The next morning, I found a terrible mess! Because the paper holders on the printer were set with too much lateral tension, the print head impact stretched the paper causing it to form a vertical column four feet high that looped back over the printer, caught on the paper feeding in, and got bound up. The print head merrily continued to bang away, totally disintegrating paper one line high and about 80 columns wide, and spreading blackened paper dust in the process.

Was I ever peeved and upset when that greeted me the next morning! "Try not pulling the paper too tight horizontally with the feed rollers," my computer store expert told me. That has cured the problem ever since—I think. But, it has left me a bit gun-shy.

The second reason is that earlier programming attempts showed there was considerable complexity in developing the program. As one indication, we finally solved a problem of lost characters in the tenth column of each incoming message by moving a subroutine to the front of the program. The time required for the TAP program to function had been interfering with the responses from the big computer! TAP now runs successfully, and here is what it does:

1) Friendly instructions on the TV screen show the user how to enter the time the call to the mainframe computer is to be made. This can be hours or days in the future, which is nice if you are leaving town.

2) At the appointed time, the Apple will call the mainframe and get it on line.

3) Next, it will go through the six secret codes to access the manpower information files.

4) It then asks a series of end-of-period human resource questions, getting answers and storing them to disk. I've got about 24 such questions that can be changed and are loaded in advance of running the TAP program.

5) Following that, TAP electronically hangs up the telephone.

6) Finally, if I have preselected the automatic print option, the Apple will print out the results which were stored on its disk. With fear in my heart, and a more relaxed setting on the printer's paper feed rollers, I've done it this way to save me time the next day.

This program is generally set to run at the end of each month, around 8:30 p.m. with no one in attendance. Previously, the process involved someone at the terminal during work hours or on casual overtime, when telephone rates and computer charges are higher. Productivity improvement is evident.

Purchase Proposal Item 2: Tracking analysis and reporting of recruiting activities, trainees, courses, etc.

Results: Okay to "okay minus." I later learned that this activity was called "electronic filing."

Supplied with the Apple was a free piece of software called "File Cabinet." After reading the short write-up I thought, "Oh boy, this is just what I want!" I typed in all manner of data that was stockpiled just for this event. But strange wipeouts occurred when I tried to manipulate the data. "It must be me," I thought. Only later, after repeated attempts and a couple of ruined weekends, did I learn there really were bugs in this "free" program!

Since then, I've tried other electronic filing software with a "once bitten, twice shy" approach. Some of my electronic filing information is conveniently stored in letter or memo form on word processing diskettes. I find myself drifting away from letterbooks and some other filing of paper, but I wish this area was in better shape. Perhaps some reader has had more favorable and time-tested experience he or she would be willing to share.

Purchase Proposal Item 3: Specific Analyses:

Results: Use in this area has been extensive, particularly in manpower modeling. Through a friend at corporate headquarters we unearthed a model done by Hal Hayes, who retired from GE a few years ago. It was written in Basic for timesharing. Starting with it, I made some minor math modifications in the program logic and translated it into Applesoft with helpful video instructions and sounds. This has been used in internal manpower studies showing projected impacts of different levels of business on numbers of employees by level.

Another friend visited with me for a half day a few months ago then went back and designed an even more precise model which I hope to translate to Applesoft for the next organization planning study.

As a virgin effort, I wrote a model that shows the number of people by layer in the organization. It differentiates managers, foremen/supervisors and individual contributors, and prints a "half a Christmas tree" pictogram at the bottom of the one-page printout, below the calculation/information lines. This was used in a special organization planning study.

A commercially available software package based on the Troll language—for Timeshare Reactive On Line Laboratory—has been used both to plot comparative curves of various manpower data and to do multiple regression analyses for internal studies. Apple-Plot software just arrived and I'm looking forward to using it soon for bar charts and graphs.

Purchase Proposal Item 4: Mini-studies

Results: Through Erie Computer Company, a human resources software package was developed that allows a comprehensive and flexible manipulation of employee data. This is a powerful package that will enjoy continued use.

It has been used for analysis of our advanced manufacturing engineering talent and in defining and tracking our key technologists, primarily in the engineering function.

Purchase Proposal Item 5: Report updates/word processing/office management.

Results: Word processing use has grown considerably beyond what I had first anticipated. To put it in perspective it helps to look at an executive's communication options. In addition to handwritten memos, notes on the incoming letter photocopied and sent as reply, phone calls, and personal visits, he can dictate, give handwritten copy to the secretary or steno pool, use centralized word processing or, as in my case, use the computer for some tasks.

There are variables associated with this issue, such as how much travel the executive does, what internal mail delays exist between one's office and the central word processing unit if it is not in the same work area and, of course, personal habits and status concerns. These include whether the executive can or will learn new office work habits, can type, use portable or other dictation devices, writes drafts longhand, uses the secretary to administer more important projects, and ego ("I'd never be caught typing my own report"—to name a few highlights.

Without debating or justifying my position endlessly, here are a few observations: Author Alvin Toffler, in his latest book, *The Third Wave*, advises readers that as he learned more about the microelectronics revolution, which is one of the four key technologies of the future, he went out and bought a simple computer, used it as a word processor, learned to operate it in a few hours and finished the last half of his book that way. He says, "After more than a year at the keyboard I am still amazed by its speed and power . . . . This eliminates erasing, 'whiting out,' cutting, pasting, stripping, Xeroxing, or typing successive drafts". I concur, based on my portable computer experiences these past eight months.

Toffler also describes a futuristic advertisement for a group vice-president. After the normal requirements for such a position he adds the phrase "Typing Required." Get the point? Frankly, the executive who can type and use a small portable computer has a competitive advantage *today*!

What has rather naturally evolved for me is the increasing use of the word processing software. I simply find that of all the options available, I can do those letters requiring my thoughtful composition, reports, interview write-ups and speeches quicker and better myself. By way of example, I used portions of one talk already stored on a disk to draft a thirty-minute speech for my boss. It was ready for his review in a few hours. This included three printouts and rewrites. The "old way" would have meant at least a day later, to allow typing time for the secretary after getting a photocopy of old material, cutting, pasting and writing in the margins first. Talk about savings and readiness-to-serve!

While one can become familiar with the 40-column width on small computer video screens, it means mentally remembering that what is on the video tube is half as wide and twice as long as what will be printed. The difference is annoying at first, takes getting used to, and is a hindrance when you want to lay out a complex page with columns. To solve this problem, I bought the 80-column card and am now awaiting the arrival of its associated word processing software—and another instruction manual.

You may initially respond to do-it-yourself word processing with: 'What, me type?!' All I can do is report the foregoing facts, and advise you that I try to approach my job as though I were selling my services as an independent businessman. That is the acid test for deciding what is really efficient in a specific situation.

This article was done on my computer a bit at a time, often over the weekends when I frequently take the Apple home in its travel case.

As a further step toward better office management I obtained inexpensive commercial software which replaces the old hand-written "To Do" list. Many such software packages exist for under $50. While only a month into using it, and still adjusting my habits, it seems to be practical and helpful. It also allows one to enter advance dates such as quarterly reviews, employee service dates, birthdates, salary increase dates, etc., and provides early notice of same.

Another inexpensive commercial program stores several hundred names and telephone numbers, places and times calls, and prints a log of calls and a short telephone book. I group most of my outbound calls and find this program very helpful. A study of the log also shows a quarter of the calls were to parties not then present, which whets my appetite for electronic mail in the near future.

Summary

At the beginning of this commentary two objectives were mentioned—improving my component's productivity and readiness-to-serve and expanding my knowledge of computer applications.

While such evaluation is in part subjective, progress has been made on both fronts. I have no regrets and am pleased with the overall results. Objectives stated in the purchase authorization have generally been met, with some areas better and some a little short of the initial plan. And, there is still room for new and better applications.

As far as my education goes, you can conclude something about that from the above. I'll also tell you a little story. A couple of months ago I took a short Basic course taught by and for engineers here at the plant. I was able to not only keep up with the class, but could do the homework on the Apple. Some of the engineers came over and looked at my Apple set-up. That was a nice experience. I think I talk their language a little better and am a better human resource manager for technical associates as well.

I would appreciate letters from readers expressing questions, contrary findings or opinions, advice or ideas. I'm still learning.

☐

"Waddaya wanna do now — Trolls and Wizards, Fun with Math, Space Invader, Almalgamated Industries' profit and loss statement for 4th quarter FY '80. . .?"

A First Class Mailbag

Brownlee Elliott

It seems as though most of my mail these days comes with stick-on address labels printed by a computer. Now I'm not one of those multi-million dollar department stores that load suburban post offices with millions of flyers addressed to "occupant," but I have occasionally wished that my little Apple II could print address labels for me so that some of my outgoing, as well as my incoming mail, would have those neat little printed labels.

Perhaps Amy Vanderbilt would consider it gauche to address Christmas cards with computer-printed labels. Still, the music department at my church does mail out notices of concerts; and the church choir has contributed many hours of labor sorting

Brownlee Elliott, 2694 Brady Drive, Bloomfield Hills, MI 48013.

those mailing pieces by zip code so we could get a better postal rate.

And in my small business, from time to time I would like to send promotional mailings of a few hundred pieces; but I can't really afford the secretarial help to type the address labels each time, and then sort them out by zip.

So I was eager to try out a new mailing list program, "Mailbag," sold by Systems Design Lab of Redondo Beach, CA. The price was only $35, and the salesman at my friendly, local computer store thought it would exactly fill my need to deal with mailing lists of a few hundred names each.

The salesman was right—or at least mostly right. Mailbag can handle between 215 and 265 names on a 48K system in a single run; and, of course, it can handle more names than that in multiple runs. It has provisions for entering, editing, sorting, and deleting names as well as printing address labels, and can be interfaced with some word processors to produce addressed form letters.

Documentation

Like so many commercial microcomputer programs today, its documentation is weak, so let me discuss that before I describe some of the better functions in more detail. The user's manual has 23 pages, most of them devoted to a description of each of the twelve program functions in turn. In general, these descriptions are clear and complete, but occasionally an explanation will be a bit cryptic, or a piece of information will not be available.

The "Add More Names" description does not explain the use of the ESC key as a shift key, for example, and the "Build New Database" description makes only passing reference to this use of the ESC

key. Yet these are the two sections in which users will most likely be looking for that information.

The "List/Search/Print Routines" description does not clearly describe the mechanics of entering a "Search" request; users must read through the examples provided to realize how it is done. There are other instances, but like these examples, they are relatively minor, and I understand, from a phone conversation with him, that the author is aware of these weaknesses and is revising the manual.

When the manual is revised, I would like to see it include a "beginner's tutorial" to take new users through a "practice run" of the program step-by-step. I would also like to see an index. In any manual users cannot be expected to know precisely where some obscure bit of information may be located.

In any case, the documentation for this program is at least clear enough that intelligent users can make the program work reasonably well.

Program Functions

Now let me describe the various program functions in more detail. There are two routines for entering data, one (Option A) to "Add More Names," and one (Option B) to "Build a New Database." Their operation is quite straightforward: the user is presented with a menu on the left-hand side of the screen and enters the information on the right-hand side.

If an entry is too long for the space on the screen, it "wraps around" and proceeds to over-write the menu, but the computer accepts the full entry correctly. The only disadvantages are that the user must remember what the next entry is supposed to be (e.g., city or state), and that when the menu is presented for the next item, blank areas in the original menu will be filled with whatever had overwritten them (e.g., I had an "ADDRESS INC.:" for a while as a part of my menu in one run where there had been just "ADDRESS   :"). The nuisance is temporary, and disappears when the next routine is called.

Option D ("Delete Existing Names") and Option M ("Modify Existing Names") are also reasonably straightforward. Each one displays the record and gives the user the option of changing his mind and making no deletions or changes in the record. Option M presents the user with a menu on which to enter changes. It also has an undocumented but very useful feature: a carriage return leaves the rest of an item unchanged, and takes the user to the next item on the menu.

Option R ("Read Names/ Letters from Disk") and Option W ("Write Name Data to Disk") take care of file handling, saving data in text files on the disk. The users should get in the habit of routinely replacing the Mailbag disk with an ordinary DOS disk after loading the program—both to save wear and tear on the Mailbag disk and to facilitate file handling. Perhaps the hardest part of the file handling routines is remembering file names; but Mailbag has a routine, "Catalog (DOS)" which provides a list of the files on the active drive. It is also relatively simple to switch from one drive to another, though apparently not from one slot to another.

Option S is a sort program which sorts the entries into any of several possible orders: last name, title (or company—what the program calls "second name"), city, zip code, or "optional code" (an arbitrary code set up by the user).

The sort program does not specifically eliminate entries. It does not, for example, pick out only entries with zip codes less than 48000. But careful use of the list program (described below) along with the sort program will do this, since the list program can print a selected range of entries based on whatever their order happens to be at the time of the list request.

There are three other minor routines: Option G ("Global Print Functions") which sets up such parameters as mailing label size and salutation to be used on form letters; Option P ("Printer Mode On/Off"), which toggles between the screen display and the printer; and Option X ("Exit Mailbag") which takes the user out of Mailbag and into Basic.

Option X illustrates another very helpful feature of Mailbag which appears in several other places in the program: before the routine runs, the user is asked if he wants to save the data in a disk file. He does have to say "no" to this query by simply repeating the original request.

Option L ("List/Search/Print Routines"), is as the manual says, the "heart" of this

---

Perhaps Amy Vanderbilt would consider it gauche to address Christmas cards with computer-printed labels.

---

program. It can produce, either on the CRT screen or on the printer, a list of complete entries, a list of names and phone numbers, or a list of mailing labels. Any list can include all entries, or a range of entries based on the order in which they happen to be arranged at the time of the List request.

Option L can also produce a "customized" form letter, with the date, salutation, and such items as inclusion of first name, last name, and title specified. I did not test this option, so I cannot describe how well it works; but it will only work with specific word processors—those which produce text files rather than binary files (and I would assume that it does not necessarily work with all text file based processors).

I had one initial problem with the program which a more astute user might have avoided: when I printed mailing labels, every "p" was deleted, along with whatever character followed the "p." I wrote a letter to the author, and got a phone call from him the next day; the problem, as it turned out, was that I needed to make a change in one line of the program because I was using a parallel interface card. The change is explained in the manual, but I had overlooked it.

Of course, I suppose we users cannot reasonably expect complete product testing and documentation from micro-entrepreneurs the way we can expect, and even demand it, from the IBMs of the industry. But we can expect pleasant, prompt help with our problems, and it's nice to report on one company, and one author, who give such help.

So, for $35, Mailbag is a first class investment. It works well, with no bugs that I could detect. Its documentation is adequate, and presumably will be improved. It gets my—ahem—postal stamp of approval. □

"Mr. Atherton can't speak to you now. He's in combat."

Programs for the Investor

Linda Barkaszi

Cyber-Tech Stock Valuation Model
Cyber-Tech
P.O. Box 924, Chatsworth, CA 91311
TRS-80 and Apple II with ROM Applesoft
32K disk, $29.95

Any investment decision implies a forecast of future events. However, in the case of common stocks, forecasting future stock prices, earnings, and dividends is exceedingly difficult. Unlike bond interest and preferred dividends, common stock dividends and earnings of most companies have been increasing year after year. Analysts expect this growth to continue in the foreseeable future at approximately the same rate as the Gross National Product (GNP).

The price of a share of common stock depends upon the cash flow investors expect to receive if they purchase the stock, and the probability of receiving it. The expected cash flow consists of two elements: dividends and sale price. It includes the return of the original investment plus a capital gain (or, in some instances, minus a capital loss).

The *Cyber-Tech Stock Valuation Model* uses the concept of Modern Portfolio Management by first discounting the expected earnings stream to determine the time value of money. In essence, it is the present value of expected net cashflows, discounted at the cost of capital, less the initial cash outlay. Then the internal rate of return, which is the interest rate which equates the present value of expected future cash flow with the initial cost of the stock, is found. The Cyber-Tech model identifies attractive stocks as those which have the highest rate of return in each classification.

Once the cashflows are discounted and the Internal Rate of Return is found, a Security Market Line is set up, using the 15-week Treasury Bill as the risk-free rate. The Security Market Line shows the relationship between risk and return in a market. It shifts over time depending on the changes in the riskless rate of interest.

Each stock has, as an input, a risk classification (beta) based upon its expected sensitivity. Beta, which is explained thoroughly in the instruction manual, is a measure of systematic risk and is used in assigning risk classifications. Using Beta as a risk classification, the Internal Rate of Return is compared to the appropriate point on the Security Market Line. If the Internal Rate of Return is greater then the Security Market Line, an undervalued stock is identified.

The Cyber-Tech model utilizes another exciting feature; the concept of Marginal Utility Theory, or the realization that different individuals have different degrees of risk aversion and therefore have different indifference curves. The tangency point between an individual indifference curve and the Security Market Line will occur at different points because of individual preferences. The individual must determine how much risk to take in order to increase his expected return.

The program allows the user to save input and output data with automatic file naming. Printing of either input or output data can be done using either a 40- or 80-column printer. An allowance for other types of printers can be made by restructuring the program so that the printer can be used on-line full time to obtain the necessary print-outs. Complete instructions are included in the manual.

One last feature: the Cyber-Tech stock evaluation model, when used as an investment tool, is tax deductible.

Stock Market Utility Program
H&H Scientific
13507 Pendleton St., Oxon Hill, MD 20022
Apple II 48K ROM Applesoft, Disk $59.95

Stock Market Utiltiy Program, by H&H Scientific, is a set of four menu-driven programs: STK. 1, Data Corrector, EVAL, and MICROQ.

STK. 1 allows the user to enter the stock data. Data is entered chronologically, since the results are plotted on a first-in-first-out basis. Data can be either added or deleted in this section. Deleting a stock only removes its name from the list of stocks that is automatically updated. It does not delete the data file on that stock.

The Historical Stock data option in STK. 1 provides an independent means for building single data files. STK. 1 also gives the user the option to reduce files to 260 entries. Since EVAL can accept 300 entries, the maximum number that can be plotted is 280. It rewrites all stock files to the 260 most recent entries.

Data Corrector is used to correct and rewrite stock data files. You can also add or delete data elements as well as correcting another disk.

EVAL provides a comparative evaluation of stock performance. This includes simultaneous graphical display of momentum, final price, and the normalized ratio of stock price to the NYSE index average. In this program high-resolution graphics routines provide automatic vertical and horizontal scaling of the display.

MICROQ is used to build historical data files by converting stock price data obtained from CompuServe's Microquote Financial data base. The price option gives the date, volume, high/ask, low/bid and close on a daily, weekly, or monthly basis.

MICROQ requires the user to provide a means for downloading Microquote data into RAM and carrying out line-editing prior to writing to a disk file. *Data Capture 3.0*, available from Southeastern Software, fills this requirement.

In order to evaluate this package, the user must consider the cost of the two supplementary packages, *Data Capture 3.0* and access to CompuServe's Microquote, in addition to $59.95 for the software.

ANA 1
Galaxy
Dept. LP2, P.O. Box 22012,
San Diego, CA 92122
Apple II with ROM APPLESOFT
48K Disk, $49.95

ANA 1 Stock Market Analysis Program by Galaxy is one of the better stock analysis programs on the market for the Apple II. ANA 1 performs rigorous analysis on the Dow Jones Industrial Average for from six months to five years. The user can choose from up to five colors to show the relationships between a least-squares linear fit, moving averages, and filters for time, magnitude or percent changes. As many color graphs as desired can be plotted on the screen or cleared at any time.

Section 1.0 of the manual is reserved for the user. Step-by-step instructions show the command prompts with their corresponding responses underlined. Each command and its function is clearly defined. ANA 1 provides 30 two-letter commands. For example, the DL (draw line) command draws a trend line on the data. If the data is above the line, you hold. If it is below the line, you sell. The MA (moving average) command allows the user to select a moving average in order to smooth out the values of the data. This command is also used for buy/sell signals.

The user can switch between text and graphic data at any time, and change the color of the next graph whenever desired.

Section 2.0 of the manual defines the use of each command. The Data Update Program is outlined in Section 3.0. This program allows the user to add, replace, or read entries on the Dow Jones Weekly file.

Section 4.0 describes memory allocation, disk data, internal representations of the data, transformation values, graphics routines, debugging aids, and implementation of user rotuines.

Desktop/Plan is a flexible, business planning and development system. Its purpose is to assist managers and planners with the development and operation of financial "models" of business systems. The planning system is designed for execution in "desktop computers": specifically, the Apple II with DOS and a printer. Desktop/Plan provides computer assistance in performing the four major functions of financial modeling:

- Developing the model
- Executing the model
- Modifying the model
- Presenting the results

This planning system will be useful to managers and planners in businesses of all sizes. The small business manager would plan the data base model then use it to predict and measure performance. The large-company executive could use it as an adjunct to the main computer system. Any manager would have complete visibility and the flexibility to manipulate and monitor the activity of the business on a real time basis.

Desktop/Plan has many good features. It is a very comprehensive and detailed planning system. The amount of work put into the design and the practicality of the results, is a tribute to the skill of its developer, Don Williams.

Documentation

Documentation included in the manual is extensive, comprehensive and detailed. The documentation is a refreshing change from the present

Chuck Carpenter, 2228 Montclair Pl., Carrollton, TX 75006.

norm in products for personal, desktop computers. There are many good illustrations and the examples are clear. Descriptions are kept short and to the point. Additionally, there is plenty of space for user notes and comments. Nothing is crammed in or squeezed together. There are several typos and errors of omission — typical of many newly published documents. But they do not create confusion or reduce readability of the manual.

Getting Started

Introduction to the system is characteristic of the depth of coverage in the manual. The user is provided with descriptions and explanations of financial modeling, some good points on single-job applications and the significance of using desktop computers for the protection of your private data.

Other topics introduced include how to use the manual, some facts on the application of planning systems in small computers (Apple) and mainframe systems and a system overview. The system overview provides the user with a summary of each of the system options and describes various menu options and operating features. Figure 1 is a listing of the Desktop/Plan main menu. Sub-menus under each main topic further divide the selection and function capability.

Reports

Although not the first selection on the menu, reports are described first. And this is a good choice. Because the Reports function is used as a development tool, this section provides the user with needed support documentation. Instructions provided help you

```
DESKTOP/PLAN
JULY 24, 1979
1. DESIGN A MODEL
2. MODIFY A MODEL
3. EXECXUTE MODEL CALCULATIONS
4. DISPLAY MODEL VALUES
5. PRINT MODEL REPORTS
6. CONSOLIDATE MODEL VALUES
7. COPY MODEL FILE TO BACKUP DISKETTE
0. RETURN TO OPERATING SYSTEM
   ...SELECT FUNCTION DESIRED:
                            .
                            1
DEVELOP A MODEL

1. CREATE A REPORT SPECIFICATION FILE
2. CREATE A PLANNING VALUES FILE
3. CREATE A CALCULATION RULES FILE
4. RETURN TO MAIN MENU
   ...SELECT FUNCTION DESIRED:
                            .
                            3
```

Main menu and a sub-menu selection.

generate a customized blank report format. This blank format will be used to develop your unique simulation model. In this way you can build and/or modify the model according to the actual work sheet you will use (see Figure 2).

The contents and options of Reports are described along with definitions for designing a report, entering report specifications and printing the report. The sections on generating the Report are concluded with a discussion on developing and entering values. Throughout, there are illustrations, diagrams and detailed dialogue to show and tell you how to do it.

Helpful Assistance

In the introduction to Desktop/Plan it is mentioned that a user could develop financial plans without training in accounting techniques. And, you probably could do it. However, here's a book recommended to you to make the job much easier:

Finance for the Non-financial Manager

By: Herbert T. Spiro

John Wiley and Sons, Inc., 1977 Knowledge of the contents of this book will make the design of your financial plans more meaningful. The book is 230 pages of the easiest reading on financial accounting that I have ever encountered. It will provide you with knowledge of financial terminology and a basic understanding of financial management.

Making it Work

Calculation rules are given the most extensive treatment in the manual and it should be. After all, your data isn't worth much unless you can manipulate and analyze it. And, with Desktop/Plan, you can add, subtract, multiply and divide in combinations of rows and columns. You can also **fill** a line using a starting value derived elsewhere. The value can be changed in the middle of a line, too. This feature lets you input and fill across the columns with planned changes. Then, you can **interpolate** a line. By inputting a starting and ending value, you can produce a range of interpolated values for each period in between. Very handy for developing cash growth curves or product build-up curves. Finally, you can **grow** a line. If you have a growth rate planned for any period of time, this factor can be extended across the page. And, you can change the growth rate at any point. Very useful for planning percentage volume changes (increase or decrease). The grow and fill features are provided for column calculations, too.

For your specific requirements, the **custom rule** lets you provide programs to fit the personality of your operations. For instance, you can include manpower forecasting or progress curve modelling. Any number of special features (up to 20) can be implemented here. Custom rules can be used anywhere in the user's sequence of calculation rules. Adequate instructions are provided for implementing custom rules along with a warning to the 'beginner' not to take this task lightly.

Calculation rules development is described by illustrations throughout and a sample work-sheet is provided. More illustrations and examples are provided for entering and executing calculation rules. Figure 3 is a summary listing of Desktop/Plan calculation rules.

```
        COMPUTER IMAGINEERING                AUGUST 7, 1979
              DALLAS                         PAGE 1
       1ST QUARTER-FISCAL 1979

VALUES ONLY                      JANUARY  FEBRUARY    MARCH QTR TOTAL
------------------------------- --------- --------- --------- ---------
GROSS SALES                    235000.00 230000.00 237000.00         -
LESS RETURNS & ALLOWANCES           7525      6500      7000         -
                                --------- --------- --------- ---------
NET SALES                              -         -         -         -

COST OF GOODS SOLD                130000    122000    125000         -
                                --------- --------- --------- ---------
GROSS PROFIT                           -         -         -         -

     OPERATING EXPENSES
SELLING                            52000     51000     54000         -
GENERAL                            23500     22000     23000         -
ADMINISTRATIVE                     11000     11500     11200         -
DEPRECIATION                         850       800       825         -
                                --------- --------- --------- ---------
OPERATING INCOME                       -         -         -         -
OTHER INCOME                        7500      2000     20000         -
                                --------- --------- --------- ---------
NET INCOME BEFORE TAXES                -         -         -         -
ESTIMATED INCOME TAXES              9165      9464     18707         -
                                --------- --------- --------- ---------
NET INCOME                             -         -         -         -
```

Example of Desktop/Plan reports.

```
CALCULATED VALUES                JANUARY  FEBRUARY    MARCH QTR TOTAL
------------------------------- --------- --------- --------- ---------
GROSS SALES                    235000.00 230000.00 237000.00 702000.00
LESS RETURNS & ALLOWANCES           7525      6500      7000     21025
                                --------- --------- --------- ---------
NET SALES                         227475    223500    230000    680975

COST OF GOODS SOLD                130000    122000    125000    377000
                                --------- --------- --------- ---------
GROSS PROFIT                       97475    101500    105000    303975

     OPERATING EXPENSES
SELLING                            52000     51000     54000    157000
GENERAL                            23500     22000     23000     68500
ADMINISTRATIVE                     11000     11500     11200     33700
DEPRECIATION                         850       800       825      2475
                                --------- --------- --------- ---------
OPERATING INCOME                   10125     16200     15975     42300
OTHER INCOME                        7500      2000     20000     29500
                                --------- --------- --------- ---------
NET INCOME BEFORE TAXES            17625     18200     35975     71800
ESTIMATED INCOME TAXES              9165      9464     18707     37336
                                --------- --------- --------- ---------
NET INCOME                          8460      8736     17268     34464
     PREPARED WITH DESKTOP/PLAN--COMPANY CONFIDENTIAL
```

Example of a report generated with Desktop/Plan at The Computer Imagineering Store. Paul Dishman, owner of Computer Imagineering, has used Plan on the Polymorphics system. Paul indicates that Plan for the Apple II is a much expanded system. Note that top part is data before calculations and bottom section shows values after calculations.

```
          ENTER CALCULATION RULES

1-ADD 2 LINES            10-ADD 2 COLUMNS
2-ADD GROUP LINES        11-ADD GROUP COLS
3-SUBTRACT LINE          12-SUBTRACT COLS
4-MULTIPLY LINE          13-MULTIPLY COLS
5-DIVIDE LINE            14-DIVIDE COLS
6-ACCUMULATE LINES       15-COMPUTE G/R
7-EXTEND/FILL LINES      16-FILL A COLUMN
8-INTERPOLATE LINES      17-USE CUSTOM RULE
9-GROW A LINE            18-'NULL' RULE

TYPE 'END' TO QUIT ENTERING RULES
NUMBER FOR FUNCTION DESIRED:...
```

Listing of calculation options.

More Features

Other options include the ability to build sub-models, make changes to models and sub-models and print reports. Sub-models are useful for building the overall model in smaller chunks. These easy to handle sections are then linked together to make the total plan. The change function provides the capability to modify any part of your model as needed. Duplication of your model files is made using instructions included in the BACKUP section.

Two printer driver options are provided in Desktop/Plan. Both are serial and include the use of the Communications card or the High Speed Serial card. The manual describes the procedure to use for customizing your configuration. Once you make the changes, you can delete several files from the catalog. More disk space is made available on your operating diskette this way.

Addition of the capability to automatically lock and unlock files and to delete unwanted 'trials' and development 'mistakes' would be helpful. Otherwise, your diskette catalog may become cluttered with unneeded entries. You can, of course, lock, unlock and delete catalog entries using the DOS commands.

What Wasn't So Good

First, let me state that, overall, this is an excellent software package. Most of my gri es are **not** of major consequence. But, there are some things that, from my point of view, are undesirable or lacking. Here's my brief list:

- There is no summary of operation steps in the manual. If you go through from beginning to end you will eventually press all the right keys. Once you have done this, though, there is no summary to lead you through quickly the next time. Any procedure having as much detail as Plan does should have a guideline summary of steps (for use when you're part way up the learning curve).

- A disclaimer that leaves you in doubt about the ultimate usefulness of the package. To flatly state that once you purchase the package you're on your own is somewhat counter-productive. You should expect support of software that is this extensive and involved. Correction of bugs and answers to what, why and how questions are minimum requirements.

Although $95.00 is a more-than-fair price for this much planning capability, support to the customer is necessary. If the one-time charge is too low to cover follow-on service, then charge a nominal fee for the support. Most users would pay for the comfort of knowing they are not dangling loose out there.

- Master Diskette Quality. The one with my package was noisy and it had to be re-read three times in order to make a useable copy. If you want to save money in the long run use good quality diskettes. There are several manufacturers whose product quality exceeds the ANSI standards. The low-cost diskettes may be OK for the personal hobbyist. But, for revenue producing businesses that depend on reliability, don't skimp on diskette quality.

Conclusion

A final note — Desktop/Plan is not limited to financial planning. Any time-related calculation series can be implemented. For instance, production build schedules, material flow quantities and any numeric progression can be simulated. Also remember that the system can be customized. (This in addition to the special calculation features you can add.) Desktop/Plan has the potential to be a complete and creative simulation aide. In this regard, a progressive manager can take advantage of real-time data to aid in common sense decision making. □

Available from Personal Software, 592 Weddell Dr., Sunnyvale, CA 94086.

Notes

VisiCalc:
Reason Enough For Owning A Computer

Doug Green

Ideally your computer should be able to act like a cross between an electronic piece of paper and a pocket calculator. That seems to be just what the people at Personal Software, Inc. had in mind when they developed VisiCalc. VisiCalc is not merely a piece of interactive software, but in some respects is more like a separate programming language. It is extremely powerful, and handles many varied jobs with aplomb. When used properly it can save a great deal of time that would ordinarily be spent programming or using several pieces of software. VisiCalc cannot do some of the things that high level languages can do, but what it can do, it does very well indeed.

It takes much less time to learn virtually everything there is to know about the VisiCalc system than it takes for any other programming language you can think of. In my case it took about seven days averaging about one and one-half hours a day to become conversant with all that VisiCalc has to offer. This is in sharp contrast to the various high level programming languages that demand much more of the learner in exchange for their greater flexibility.

Not only does it take only a short period of time to understand the entire VisiCalc system, but it takes almost no time to begin getting results from this remarkable piece of software. This is

Doug Green, Cortland Jr.-Sr. High School, Valley View Dr., Cortland, NY 13045.

an opinion that I share with everyone that I have demonstrated this system to, as well as several people in the computer business who already use VisiCalc or supply it to other users.

A Window Into The Computer's Memory

After you load in the VisiCalc disk you will have the basic electronic sheet of paper on your screen. As you can see from Photo 1, it has 20 rows and four columns. Each location in this grid is identified by the number of the row and the letter-code at the top of the column, for example, A1. The cursor in VisiCalc is much wider than the usual single-character cursor; it takes up the entire entry that it occupies on the grid.

The amount you can store is limited more by the size of your computer's memory than it is by the VisiCalc sheet.

Any entry on the sheet can either be a number, a word, or a function of the contents of other locations. This is one of the reasons that VisiCalc is so powerful. Whenever a location is changed by the user, *all of the locations that depend on it are automatically recalculated.* It is this aspect of VisiCalc that is so striking and so useful.

Let us say you have told the VisiCalc sheet to derive column C in some way from columns A and B. Then if, for some reason, you change any of the values in columns A or B, new

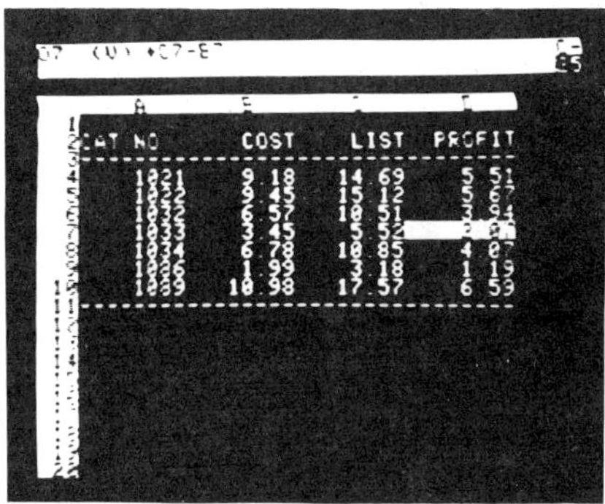

Photo 1

results in column C will be displayed automatically. This is like using FOR . . . NEXT commands in immediate mode without ever having the contents of your memory leave the screen.

Although what you see is limited by the number of spaces that can be displayed on your screen at once, the electronic sheet is actually much larger. There are 254 rows and 63 columns where information can be stored, and the amount you can store is limited more by the size of your computer's memory than it is by the VisiCalc sheet.

Keeping track of the remaining memory is very simple since it is constantly displayed in the upper right hand corner of the screen.

You may only see 20 rows of data at one time, but the number of columns can be varied by changing the width of the columns. You can also store more information in one of the grid locations than it appears able to hold. The system will remember exactly what was entered regardless of how narrow you choose to make the visible columns. The screen will display as many characters as you allow for, beginning from the left of your input.

In addition to the grid, there is space at the top of the screen where other important information is displayed.

The white bar displays the contents of the location where the cursor is currently residing. This can either be a value (v) or a label (l). These terms are analogous to numeric and alphanumeric variables that one deals with when using Basic; except just a value can be an expression referring other locations in the table.

The Clear command requires three keystrokes, a fact that saved me from clearing the VisiCalc sheet at a time when I was really trying to do something else.

Two Independently Scrollable Windows

If you are not satisfied with the information that you can see on the screen at one time, you can split the screen in either the horizontal or vertical direction and look at whatever portion of the sheet you like in either window. A common use of this feature is to display the upper left corner of your sheet in the left window while the lower right portion of your work is displayed in the right window. That way you can change your initial entries and watch your totals change at the same time. Photo 2 shows an example of how this might be put to use while analyzing the family budget for the upcoming year. Instead of wondering idly what would happen to your savings for the year if the electric bill goes up five dollars a month, you can find out just by typing over the information that you would like to see changed. As you might guess, this will change the entire row that lies beyond the changed data, along with all of the column totals that depend on these figures.

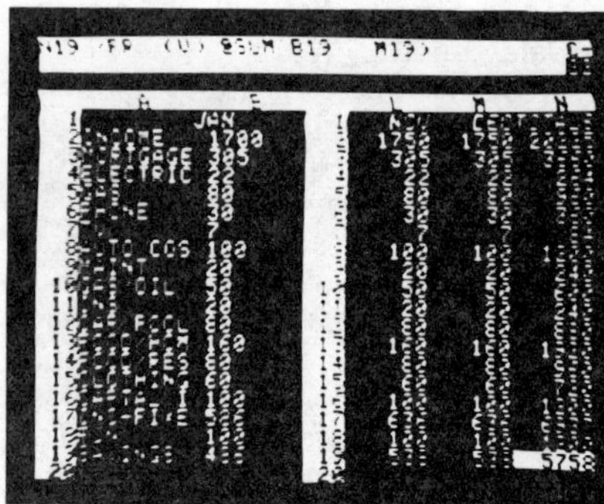

Photo 2

The Replication Feature

Another impressive feature of this system is the ability to replicate similar functions down a row, across a column, or in both directions at once. For example, if you wish to have VisiCalc derive values for column C by subtracting those in column B from the corresponding values in column A, all you need do is type in the directions for the first location in column C along with directions for replication. This will cause column C to be completed in an instant.

If you are trying to complete a table of entries that depends on the values stored in the top row and the left hand column, all you need do is supply the directions for the entry located at row two, column two along with the replication commands and the screen will fill before your eyes, much faster than most users could type in the specific formulas to perform such a task.

Cursor Control

The ← and → keys are used to move the cursor from side to side and up and down, while the space bar is used to change the direction of cursor movement from horizontal to vertical and back. For rapid movement you can hold down the repeat key. There is also a GOTO command that allows you to move the cursor to any location on the sheet with just a few keystrokes.

The little dash in the upper right hand corner of the sheet tells you which way the cursor is currently prepared to move. The letter next to this dash, either a C or an R, lets you know the current direction that the recalculation will occur in. You can instruct VisiCalc to recalculate down the columns (C) or across the rows (R). This will depend on how you have set up the entries in your table.

The ESC key is used to recover from simple typing mistakes. If you press it often enough it will erase all

VisiCalc Functions	
SUM	Calculates the sum of the values in a list
MIN	Calculates the minimum value in a list
MAX	Calculates the maximum value in a list
COUNT	Results in the number of non-blank entries in a list
AVE	Calculates the average of the non-blank values in a list. The maximum number of values in the list is 255.
NPV	Calculates the net present value of the cash flows in a list, discounted at the rate specified. The first entry in the list is the cash flow at the end of the first period, the second entry is the cash flow at the end of the second period, etc.
LOOKUP	Used with a list of items that are ranked in ascending order. This function returns the value from the list that is less than or equal to the value referenced in the command given.
PI	Returns the value of 3.1415926536
ABS	Returns the absolute value of the value given
INT	Returns the integer portion of the value given
EXP SQRT LN LOG10 SIN ASIN COS ACOS TAN ATAN	Calculates the appropriate function. The trigonometric calculations are done in radians
NA	Results of a calculation are not available. This makes all expressions using the value display as NA.
ERROR	Results in an "Error" value that makes all expressions using the value display as ERROR.
>>>>	This means that there is not enough room to display the calculated value in the room available. Making the columns wider will often allow the value to be displayed.
Scientific Notation	VisiCalc will automatically shift to scientific notation if necessary in order to display a value in the space alotted.

Table 1.

that you have typed in since you last hit the return key. As you enter data for a given location it appears on the so-called prompt line, the line between the white box at the top of the sheet and the grid. When you close an entry by hitting return, or moving the cursor to another location on the page, the contents of the prompt line are calculated (if necessary) and placed in the location on the grid that you have just dealt with.

More Functions And Commands

There are a number of other functions that are available to VisiCalc users. These are all listed in Table 1, but a few deserve special mention. The sum function is especially useful to anyone dealing with columns of numbers that must be added. (Think of all the time operators of small businesses can save by not having to bang number after number into a calculator. With VisiCalc they only need to be written once.) You can also ask for the average of a range of values along with other common functions used in business, science, and mathematics.

The list of commands is also impressive. With a few key strokes you can blank out any location, add or delete a row or column, move a row or column to a new location on the page, or repeat a number or letter across any location in the grid. This last command is especially useful for drawing lines across the page like those in Photo 1. There are a number of commands that can change the format of a given location or the entire window that the cursor is located in. The choices for these format commands include: general, integer, dollars and cents, left- or right-justified columns, and graphing. This final command can be used to construct simple bar-graphs for information displayed in a range of entries selected by the user. This is shown in Photo 3.

Other commands couple or uncouple the movements of pairs of windows, fix the titles on the screen

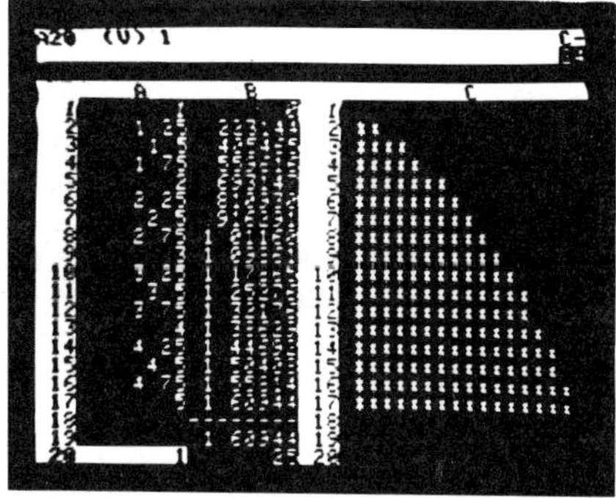

Photo 3

as the cursor moves down or to the right, and replicate formatting across a whole column or row, or the entire contents of the current window. These commands require between two and five keystrokes each depending on what is being accomplished. (The Clear command requires three keystrokes, a fact that saved me from clearing the VisiCalc sheet at a time when I was really trying to do something else.)

VisiCalc manages its own storage in its own format. It provides storage commands allowing you to save files on disks or cassette tapes, load files from a disk or a cassette, delete a file from a disk, or initialize a blank disk so that it will be ready to receive VisiCalc files for storage. It is easy to ask for a list of the file names on a given disk. You can also print the contents of your sheet on a disk as a "text file." This file can be read by other programs in Basic, for example, and the information can be further processed in this manner. (This feature permits you to perform whatever other functions you may feel are missing.)

Similar commands will result in the printing of your electronic sheet by your printer. The output will be what is actually on the sheet, as opposed to what appears in the window, so be sure to pay attention to the line width of your printer. In any case you can specify the portion of the page that will be printed with the issuance of the proper print command.

Stay Tuned

Your purchase of the VisiCalc package includes an instruction book that contains an introduction and four lessons. As I read through the book and carried out the examples I found the text to be easy to understand. The explanations were certainly cleaner and better than those I have seen in most systems programing manuals. Along with the book, which is in a handsome 10 x 7½ inch three-ring binder, you receive the VisiCalc reference card. This contains a summary of all of the VisiCalc commands and functions and is extremely useful for users who are new to the system. It would also be invaluable to infrequent users. When you send in your warranty card you will receive the first copy of the VisiCalc Newsletter free. Original owners are also protected from any defect in the disk for 90 days, and replacement thereafter for $15.00.

The people at Personal Software, Inc. are planning to improve the system and offer the updated versions to original owners at a reduced price. They also encourage users to suggest changes and additions to improve the system. As a VisiCalc user I would suggest that they add some of the more commonly used statistical functions to those listed on Table 1. The ones that I would suggest would be: standard deviation, one or more correlation co-efficients, and perhaps the ability to do a t-test and a least-squares linear regression; but new functions, must use up too much memory.

> **Whenever a location is changed by the user, *all of the locations that depend on it are automatically recalculated.***

Machines And Memory Requirements

Although the version I used was designed for an Apple system, it will soon be available for other makes of small computers including Pet and Atari. It is only available on disk and requires a minimum of 32K of RAM. Additional memory will allow for the storage of a much larger electronic sheet but all of the systems' features are available for users of 32K systems.

The version that I used (version 35) requires 23K for the resident program. This means that for a 32K system there remains only 9K for storage of the electronic sheet. This still allows for a reasonable amount of storage, but for most business applications it would be a good idea to have 48K available.

Worth The Money?

If you are in business, the chances are that the cost of a VisiCalc disk will be one business expense you will gladly bear. The current suggested retail price is $150.00. This may be a bit steep for someone who only needs to do his check book and the family budget, but for almost anyone in business, education, or any science-related field it is not only worth the initial expense, but reason enough to purchase a small computer system in the first place. □

Break Even Analysis with VisiCalc

George Blank

VisiCalc, from Software Arts, is much more than a business application for microcomputers. I like to think of it as a financial language for microcomputers, and it has a major advantage over other languages. Since the authors, Dan Bricklin and Bob Frankston, were careful to make each version compatible with the other versions, a data set that will work in one version will work in all the other versions without change. VisiCalc is currently available for the TRS-80 Model I and Model III, PET, CBM, Apple II, Atari 800, and HP-85.

The authors have also come up with a standardized data format that can be dumped directly from the computer to a printer. All you have to do to print out the data set is to save the file to the printer, using this set of commands:

```
/S
S
:P (ENTER)
```

The output will be a file such as the one included in this article. Since all data is in ASCII, I then read my VisiCalc file into the Electric Pencil word processor on my Radio Shack computer, and edit it for publication. Unfortunately, it does not work with Scripsit, as Scripsit interprets the greater than symbol as a format command, and prints an error message when it comes to a VisiCalc line.

The file is produced in reverse order, so that it is easiest to enter it into your computer by starting at the bottom and working to the top.

Commands are preceded by a slash, (/), and program lines by a greater than symbol and the letter and number of the cell where the information belongs. For example,

"   A1:" Break Even

tells the computer to put "Break Even" in cell A1. Once you can do that, all you have to do is figure out how to use the Replicate command efficiently to enter the material into your own VisiCalc file.

Although I have versions of VisiCalc for the Apple, Atari, and TRS-80, I use the TRS-80 version exclusively. I much prefer the wider screen width   (64 characters) and sharper letters from the black and white monitor. The TRS-80 version has several other advantages. It is cheaper at $99 than the $150 for the Apple version and $199 for the Atari version. Unlike the other versions, it is not copy protected, so I can put a copy of the program on each data disk. I have well over 100 diskettes, and I don't like hunting for individual ones when I can help it. I like the ability to modify my files with a good word processor such as Scripsit. In addition, the Model III, with its double density disk drives, offers more storage on each diskette.

Now for the Break Even Analysis program, which I hope is the first of many VisiCalc applications to appear in *Creative Computing*. As you enter the retail price and cost information, the program is set up to calculate the return on various quantities of goods sold. You can see the effects of changing your wholesale discount, spending more on advertising, reducing material and labor costs, or making other changes to your product strategy. You may also want to change the labels on the various fixed and variable cost categories to suit your own product.

Special Notes

The Replicate command can make it much easier to enter this program. Column C is replicated from C3 to C31 by keeping +C3 Relative and +B18 with No change. Column D is replicated by answering Relative to +C2 both times (beginning and end of the line), and answering No change to B3, B19, B9, and B16. In both cases, it is assumed that you will begin at the bottom of the listing and enter squares C2, C3 and D2 before the others in the columns.

It would even be possible to type in this program using a word processor like Scripsit, save it to disk, and read it into the VisiCalc. All you would have to do is end each line with a carriage return, and save it using the extension /VC so that VisiCalc can read it. ☐

```
">D31:+C31*B3*(.01*(100-B19))-(B9+(B16*C31))
">C31:+C30+B18
">D30:+C30*B3*(.01*(100-B19))-(B9+(B16*C30))
">C30:+C29+B18
">D29:+C29*B3*(.01*(100-B19))-(B9+(B16*C29))
">C29:+C28+B18
">D28:+C28*B3*(.01*(100-B19))-(B9+(B16*C28))
">C28:+C27+B18
">D27:+C27*B3*(.01*(100-B19))-(B9+(B16*C27))
">C27:+C26+B18
">D26:+C26*B3*(.01*(100-B19))-(B9+(B16*C26))
">C26:+C25+B18
">D25:+C25*B3*(.01*(100-B19))-(B9+(B16*C25))
">C25:+C24+B18
">D24:+C24*B3*(.01*(100-B19))-(B9+(B16*C24))
">C24:+C23+B18
">D23:+C23*B3*(.01*(100-B19))-(B9+(B16*C23))
">C23:+C22+B18
">D22:+C22*B3*(.01*(100-B19))-(B9+(B16*C22))
">C22:+C21+B18
">D21:+C21*B3*(.01*(100-B19))-(B9+(B16*C21))
```

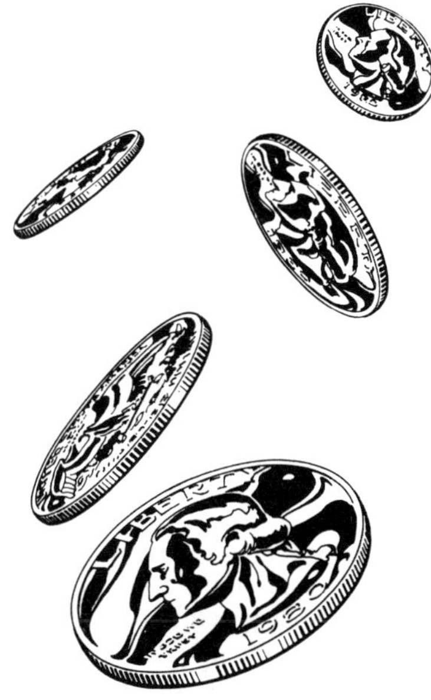

```
">C21:+C20+B18
">D20:+C20*B3*(.01*(100-B19))-(B9+(B16*C20))
">C20:+C19+B18
">D19:+C19*B3*(.01*(100-B19))-(B9+(B16*C19))
">C19:+C18+B18
">B19:50
">A19:"Discount Given (%)
">D18:+C18*B3*(.01*(100-B19))-(B9+(B16*C18))
">C18:+C17+B18
">B18:100
">A18:"Quantity Increment
">D17:+C17*B3*(.01*(100-B19))-(B9+(B16*C17))
">C17:+C16+B18
">D16:+C16*B3*(.01*(100-B19))-(B9+(B16*C16))
">C16:+C15+B18
">B16:@SUM(B12...B15)
">A16:"TOTAL VARIABLE COST
">D15:+C15*B3*(.01*(100-B19))-(B9+(B16*C15))
">C15:+C14+B18
">B15:0
">A15:"Other
">D14:+C14*B3*(.01*(100-B19))-(B9+(B16*C14))
">C14:+C13+B18
">B14:0
">A14:"Packaging
">D13:+C13*B3*(.01*(100-B19))-(B9+(B16*C13))
">C13:+C12+B18
">B13:0
">A13:"Materials
">D12:+C12*B3*(.01*(100-B19))-(B9+(B16*C12))
">C12:+C11+B18
">B12:0
">A12:"Labor
">D11:+C11*B3*(.01*(100-B19))-(B9+(B16*C11))
">C11:+C10+B18
">B11:"  (Per Unit)
">A11:"VARIABLE COSTS
">D10:+C10*B3*(.01*(100-B19))-(B9+(B16*C10))
">C10:+C9+B18
">D9:+C9*B3*(.01*(100-B19))-(B9+(B16*C9))
">C9:+C8+B18
">B9:@SUM(B6...B8)
">A9:"TOTAL FIXED COST
">D8:+C8*B3*(.01*(100-B19))-(B9+(B16*C8))
">C8:+C7+B18
">B8:0
">A8:"Other
">D7:+C7*B3*(.01*(100-B19))-(B9+(B16*C7))
">C7:+C6+B18
">B7:0
">A7:"Marketing
">D6:+C6*B3*(.01*(100-B19))-(B9+(B16*C6))
">C6:+C5+B18
">B6:0
">A6:"Development
">D5:+C5*B3*(.01*(100-B19))-(B9+(B16*C5))
">C5:+C4+B18
">B5:"  (Totals)
">A5:"FIXED COSTS
">D4:+C4*B3*(.01*(100-B19))-(B9+(B16*C4))
">C4:+C3+B18
">D3:+C3*B3*(.01*(100-B19))-(B9+(B16*C3))
">C3:+C2+B18
">B3:0
">A3:"Retail Price
">D2:+C2*B3*(.01*(100-B19))-(B9+(B16*C2))
">C2:+B18
">A2:"Product Name:
">D1:"Profit or Loss
">C1:"Units Sold
">B1:"Analysis
">A1:"   Break Even
/W1
/GOC
/GRA
/GC14
/X">A1:">A1:
```

Well-Fashioned Forms

David Lubar

A great many software companies seem to be offering some form of data-base program. These programs vary from highly-specialized software for specific types of data to general-purpose programs capable of handling a wide variety of information. Some are simple to use while others practically require a degree in computer science or the equivalent. *PFS*, a generalized data base, is user friendly and quite elegant.

This program was definitely designed with the user in mind. Its strongest feature is the way it treats information. Your data are stored in forms which you design. There are no requests for field specifications, record numbers, variable types or other parameters. To get started, all you have to do is design a form, any form at all. Each form resembles a sheet of paper, and is created right on the screen. If one page isn't enough, you can add more. The form is designed simply by typing in the headings anywhere on the screen. The only restriction is that you should leave enough space between headings to accommodate the data that will be entered. Since forms can be more than one page, this is no great restriction.

Once a form is designed, it is saved on a disk. Then, whenever you want to enter data, you just fill in the form. There are no restrictions against characters in the data; commas and quotation marks can be entered without causing any trouble. This is another sign that *PFS* was designed with the user in mind. Once any individual item has been entered, the right arrow key tabs to the next heading. This is simple and elegant. Of course, there is more to a data base than just entering information. You also have to be able to search, change, and delete items.

The search mode of *PFS* is very well designed. You can search for a complete match on any item or a combination of items from different headings, or search for partial matches. Suppose you have a mailing list stored on *PFS*, and want to find all addresses on PINE ST. (Entries are in upper case.) All you have to do is bring the form onto the screen, move the cursor to the address heading, and enter ..PINE.. as your search parameter. This would turn up any entry containing PINE as part of the address. Let's say you have a list of names where the first name comes last. To find all the SMITHs, you could search the name field for SMITH... To find all the JOHNs, the command ...JOHN would be used. Items can be entered in more than one heading, allowing, for example, a search for all SMITHs who live on PINE ST and are 65 years old. Numerical sequences can be found even if the search parameters leave out intervening characters such as commas. You can also search for numbers that are greater or less than a specific number.

Once a form has been found with a search, you can make changes, or delete an entry from the disk. The form concept allows great flexibility when making printouts. You can have the forms printed with or without headings, you can request printouts of only part of the form, you can specify a line feed or just a space between items, and you can print items found in a search or print all items. As an example, suppose you have a form containing complete ordering information for business customers. By requesting a printout of just name and address, you've turned *PFS* into a mailing-list generator.

A backup utility is provided which allows users with two drives to copy data disks. *PFS* also initializes new data disks from within the program, avoiding the need to prepare disks beforehand.

One aspect of the program might prove slightly inconvenient for experienced Apple owners. Instead of using RETURN, the program uses CONTROL-C to signal that you are done with a form. It takes a bit of getting used to. Luckily, hitting RETURN by accident does no damage. It's very hard to lose data in this program. In general, the whole system is very forgiving of mistakes. The only potential for losing data occurs if you exit the system without saving the most recent entry. In this case, you would lose only the form that was just filled.

The documentation includes an example showing how to generate a mailing label. More needs to be said about the booklet. Except for the lack of green ink, it greatly resembles Apple documentation, both in layout and quality. The pages of this spiral-bound manual are filled with screen photos and other helpful information. The user is gently stepped through all aspects of *PFS*.

While all this sounds almost too good to be true, there are some functions that are lacking in *PFS*. It has no sorting capability, and it does not allow any manipulation of numerical entries. For instance, you can't obtain the sum of all entries for a specific heading. But these limitations are minor or inconsequential in most cases, and are more than compensated for by the speed and utility of the program. For general use, whether at home or in the office, *PFS* is an outstanding program.

Creative Computing will be covering more data bases in future issues. If the above software doesn't meet your needs, keep watching. □

Evaluation of VisiTrend and VisiPlot from Personal Software

David H. Ahl

July 3, 1981. My financial officer handed me the results for the month of June. Not a remarkable event in itself, except that June 30 marks the end of our fiscal year.

Sitting at my desk, I got out my pocket calculator and started to manipulate the

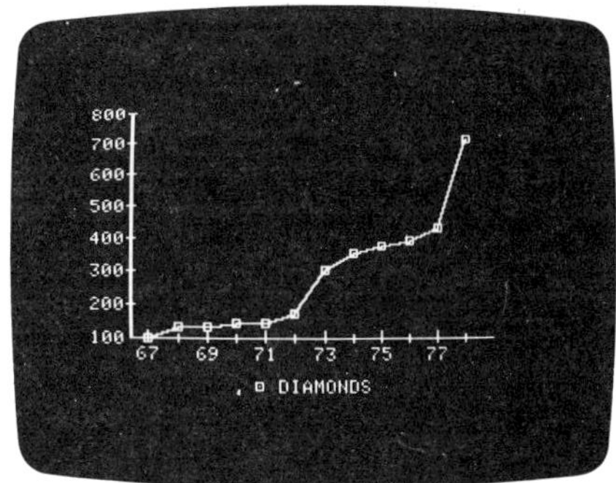

Sample line chart.

figures to develop fourth quarter, second half, and fiscal year results. I immediately realized that the job was about twice as big as it had been a year before and even considerably larger than six months earlier. The reasons: we acquired a new magazine (*Microsystems*) at the beginning of the year, started a new magazine (*SYNC*) in January, and established a new division (Education Center) in February. All this meant that I was faced with the financial figures from seven separate operating entities rather than the four that we had at the end of the previous fiscal year.

Hence I decided that it was time to learn VisiCalc, VisiPlot, and VisiTrend. Although I had a minimal working knowledge of VisiCalc, the combination Visi-

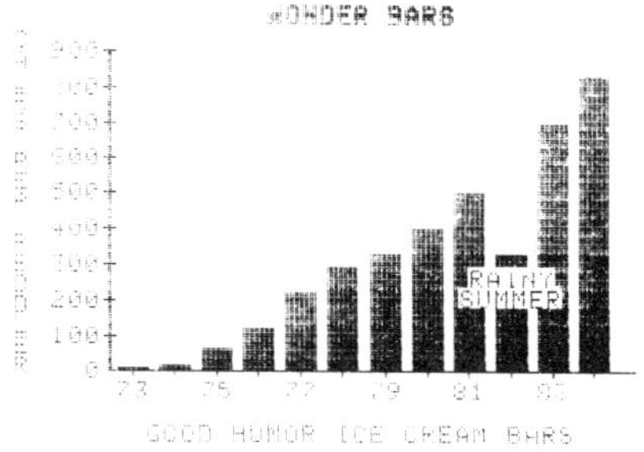

Bar chart printed by Apple Silentype printer.

Trend and VisiPlot package had just recently arrived and I hadn't even taken off its plastic wrapper.

My first chore was to get the monthly data for the entire fiscal year into VisiCalc. This I did with little difficulty. However, as I approached the end of the first quarter the speed with which the program was accepting the data slowed noticeably. Each column of the table consisted of 28 individual entries such as total sales, subscription revenue, retail sales, Periph-

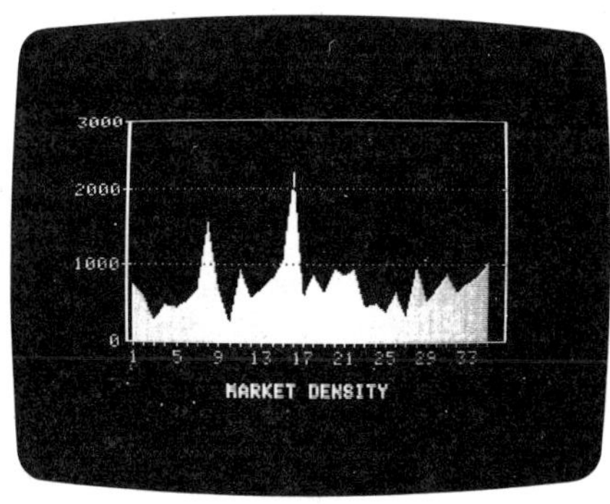

Sample area chart.

erals Plus individual sales, and the like. In addition, each column had eight calculated subtotals and eight calculated percentages. Thus, at the end of a quarter the program was dealing with approximately 40 x 3 = 120 separate pieces of data.

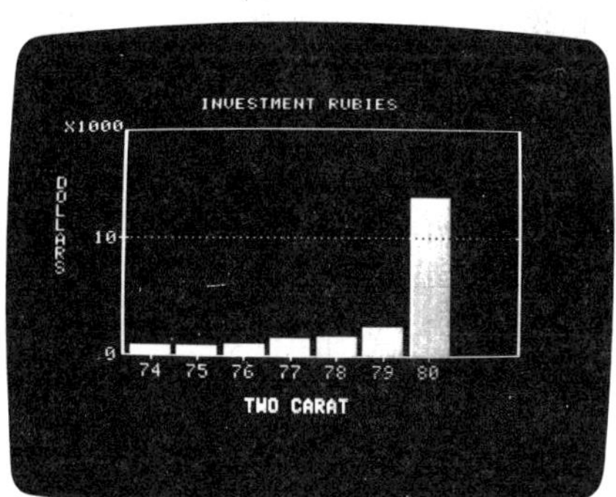

Sample bar chart.

By the end of six or seven months of data, entry had become annoyingly slow, and by the end of twelve months, it had really bogged down. Nevertheless, I was consoling myself with the thought that, once in, it was there forever for whatever analyses I may wish to do. All told, it took about two hours to enter the approximately 275 data points for a full fiscal year. I had also, in that time, entered all of the column and row titles and the various formulas for calculations of subtotals and percentages, and had printed out the resultant table.

A brief aside. Printing is probably one of the least capable attributes of VisiCalc. There is no "intelligence" whatsoever built into the print routines. For example, the printer will space across by individual spaces to "print out" a blank line. Furthermore, the routines do not take advantage of printers that do have some "intelligence" built in. I use a Diablo 1640 printer with bi-directional printing and a fairly large print buffer built in. While not as fast as a line printer, for normal correspondence the printer is more than adequate. On the other hand, VisiCalc does not take advantage of the buffer or bi-directional printing capabilities and, appears to wait for a signal from the printer that it has printed a character before sending the next one. Thus, a 60-line page that is normally printed out in about two minutes, takes over ten minutes with VisiCalc.

I don't mean to sound negative. The program is still faster, more capable, and more accurate than any alternative, particularly pocket calculator and pencil. Nevertheless, there are certain frustrations in using it.

VisiPlot

Currently available for only the Apple computer, VisiPlot is one-half of a new package from Personal Software that also includes VisiTrend. The VisiPlot portion of the package, as its name suggests, allows one to display data in graphical form on the screen and print it out on a wide variety of supported line printers. The program can make six types of charts: line, bar, area, pie, hi-lo, and scatter. In addition, it allows combining the same or different types of charts. For example, a line chart may contain one, two or three lines. A comparative bar chart may display two different bars on the same X axis or two bar charts may be displayed one above the other. A line chart may be combined with a hi-lo chart. While the possibilities are not endless, they should be sufficient to meet most normal business needs.

Like VisiCalc, the VisiTrend and VisiPlot package is entirely menu-driven. Actually, VisiTrend and VisiPlot make much more extensive use of menu commands than does VisiCalc. Menu items are selected with the right and left arrow keys and space bar. Although the commands do

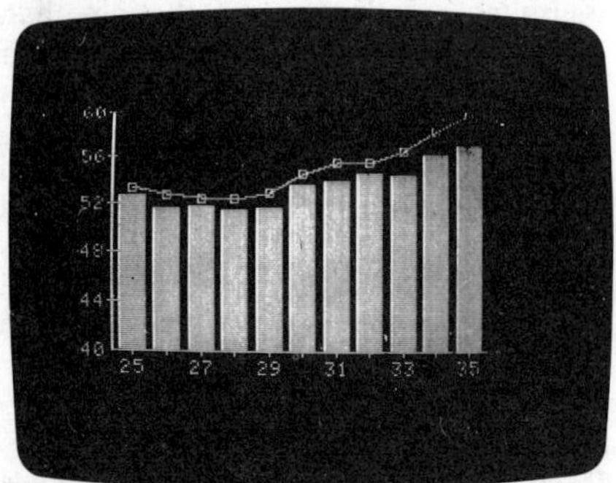

Combination line and bar chart.

what one would "naturally" expect, to provide even more help, when a one-word menu item is selected, it is highlighted in reverse video, and a more complete explanation of the item appears immediately above it. Even if one presses the wrong key, or selects an inappropriate item, there are built-in escapes and exits on every level at nearly every point. Usually, when using a program for the first time, I get into some kind of trouble that necessitates reloading the entire disk. In my first eight hours with VisiTrend and VisiPlot, this did not happen once. I am not saying that all went perfectly; however, when faced with a difficult situation, I was always able to bail out without losing any data and without having to reload the program.

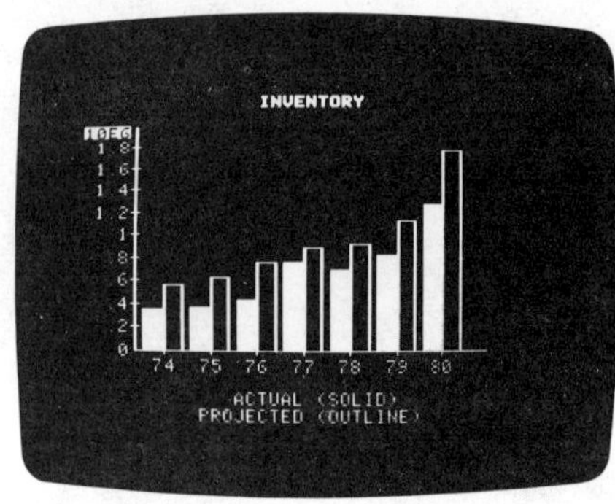

Bars may be displayed side by side for comparative purposes.

As the manual says, "Any time you seem to be at a dead end with no way to continue, press any key except reset, shift, or control." From my personal experience, I can verify that this advice really works.

A Tutorial Manual

The manual is divided into three sections. The first section (24 pages) is an introduction to VisiTrend and VisiPlot including definitions, program and disk loading instruction, and some general background about using the menu. The majority of the manual, 105 pages in all, is devoted to a tutorial in how to use VisiPlot, VisiTrend, and the data entry and edit program. This tutorial section is divided into five lessons, each of which takes about one hour to go through fairly thoroughly.

After completing two lessons in their entirety, I skipped around a bit to get to the sections describing what I really wanted to do with the data that I had. As a result, I probably missed learning about some of the features and nuances of the system. On the other hand, in a six-hour period, I was able to produce sixteen charts and run several trend projections, which was far more productive than the same six hours would have been with calculator, pencil, and graph paper.

The third section of the manual, 38 pages, is a reference guide to the use of VisiTrend and VisiPlot. I saw nothing in it that was not previously covered in the

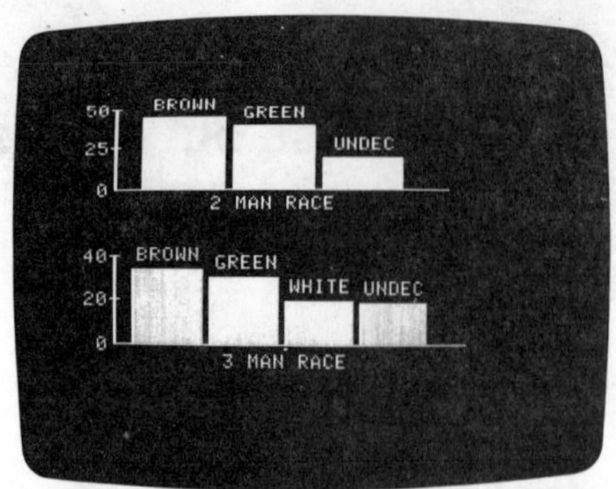

Two groups of bars may be displayed simultaneously.

tutorial section. However, it may be more efficient once one is proficient with the system, to look up desired capabilities in the reference section, rather than leafing around in the tutorial section.

Personal Software also thoughtfully includes a pocket reference card which has no less than fourteen 3 x 6" panels of information. One wonders whether pocket reference cards aren't getting a bit out of hand; but I found this one quite useful.

As the saying goes, "A picture is worth a thousand words," hence I have included a substantial number of charts with this article. Some of them are taken directly from the screen while others are printed on an Apple Silentype printer. There is little difference between the two as the print out program merely replicates the high resolution screen on the Silentype printer. Other printers that are supported by the VisiTrend/VisiPlot program include the IDS Paper Tiger 440 and 445 (with graphics option installed), the NEC Spinwriter 5510, 5515, 5520, and 5525 (with graphic option installed) and the Trendcom 200.

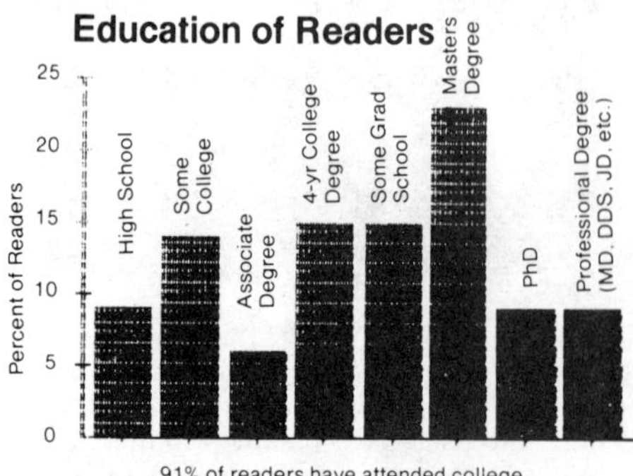

Charts may be "improved" by adding normal type.

Data Entry Surprises

The VisiTrend/VisiPlot package contains an extensive data entry and editing facility. This facility allows the user to create a new data series, and modify existing data series. The editor allows one to jump to specific places within a list, insert new data points between existing data points, delete points, format the manner in which data are displayed, print the contents of a series and the like. Like

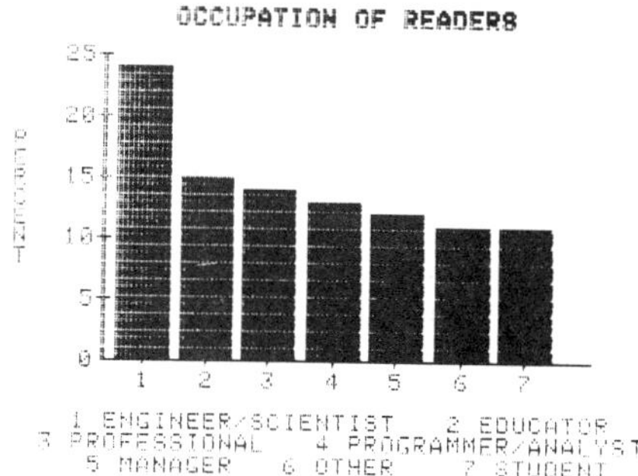

Bar chart printed by Apple Silentype printer.

the menu-driven plotting portion of the program, the data entry and editing portion of the program were simple to use.

However, I did not expect to have to use them with live data as I had all of the data that I wanted entered on a VisiCalc disk. VisiTrend/VisiPlot has the ability to accept data from VisiCalc which has been stored in the "standard" data interchange format (DIF). However, as a sentence buried in the middle of page 2-49 points out, "This means that interchange between the two products is only possible if you have a copy of the VisiCalc program at a version number higher than the 1.37." While I do, it just so happens it was not the one that I used in entering all the fiscal year data.

Even so, it appears that it would have taken at least as much time to edit the VisiCalc data for plotting as it did to enter new data. For example, my columns consist of three individual months followed by a quarterly summary. For plotting

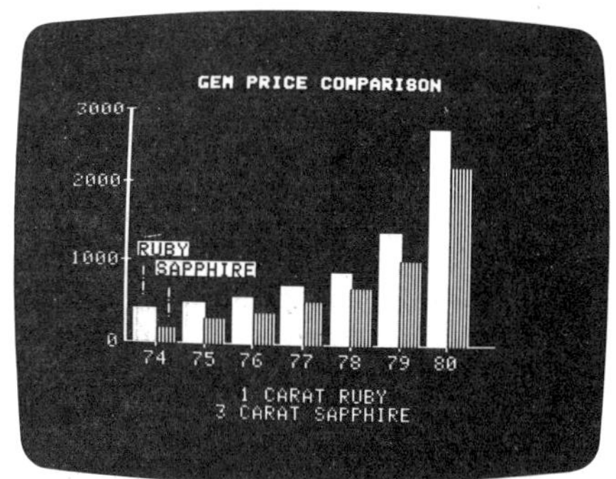

Labels may be inserted anyplace on the chart.

purposes, each of the quarterly data points would have to be edited out. Likewise, my rows include individual sales results followed by subtotals and percents for each of our seven divisions. Again the subtotals and percents would have to be deleted. I judge that re-entering the data points that I wished to plot took no more time than editing the original VisiCalc file. This, of course, would not always be true and the data interchange feature is not one to be downgraded.

As mentioned earlier, nearly every combination of charts is possible. Unfortunately, I tried to produce several that, try as I might, I could not. For example, using the VisiTrend program (more about that later) I ran a projection of sales for the next twelve months. I attempted to plot current sales for periods one to twelve and future sales for periods thirteen to twenty-four. Unfortunately, without extensive editing, this is not possible. It was easy enough to plot both sets of data on a line chart however it was not easy to plot data set one from period one to twelve and data set two from thirteen to twenty-four. Also, since most of my other charts were bar charts, I wished to present these data (twenty-four months worth) in a bar chart format. Unfortunately, I could not do it. Some experimentation indicated that the upper boundary on the number of bars that could be displayed is sixteen, however, I could not find this any place in the manual.

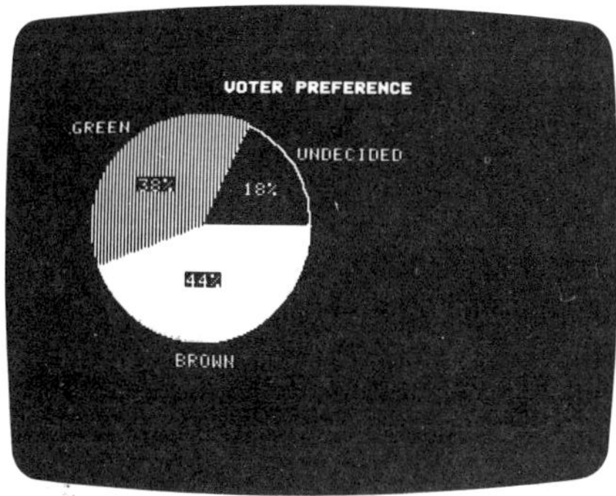

Sample pie chart.

Another minor difficulty I ran into was in the printing out of pie charts. Again, not in the manual, is the fact that a pie chart can only have eight slices and, unfortunately, I was trying to produce a ten-slice pie. Much consternation and gnashing of teeth until I figured out what was amiss and combined several of the pieces. Another small problem with pie charts: the eight different colors looked delightful on the screen, however, on the printer several of them are represented by the same method of shading. Hence, I found it was most satisfactory to use just three colors: white, black and green which, on the printer, are all distinctly different.

VisiTrend

The VisiTrend program develops ancillary data series used in analyses and forecasting techniques. The methods include derivation of moving averages, smoothing data, percent of change, leading, lagging and cumulative total functions. Additionally, new series can be created by taking ratios logs, or other mathematical or logical transformations of the data.

The program performs linear multiple regressions (using the ordinary least squares method). It also calculates and displays the major statistical measures of a multiple regression including the standard errors of the coefficients and the regression, t-statistic, R-bar squared, the F-statistic and the Durbin-Watson statistic. It also performs trend line forecasting.

Needless to say, this is an extremely comprehensive statistical package and most users will not need a fraction of what the program can deliver. Nevertheless, there are probably one or more statistical measures useful to each different user, so the program offers a complete smorgasbord.

For my purposes, I was interested in trend forecasting using linear regression and a moving average function with exponential smoothing. I had no trouble using either of these capabilities and, in about one-half hour, was able to develop several trend forecasts and moving averages. I then stored the results of these forecasts, moved back to the VisiPlot portion of the package, and plotted the results.

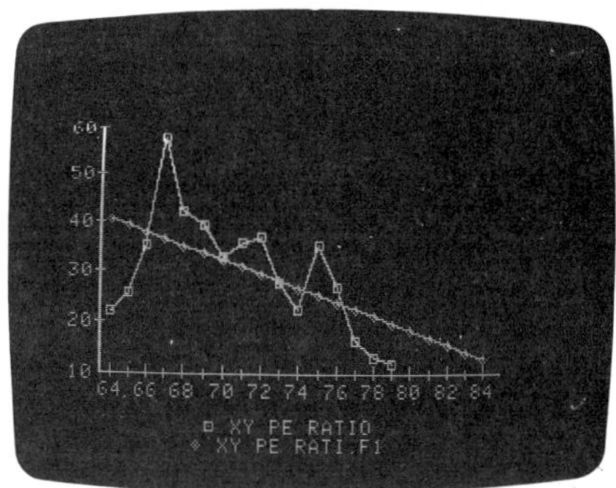

Line chart with a projection made by VisiTrend.

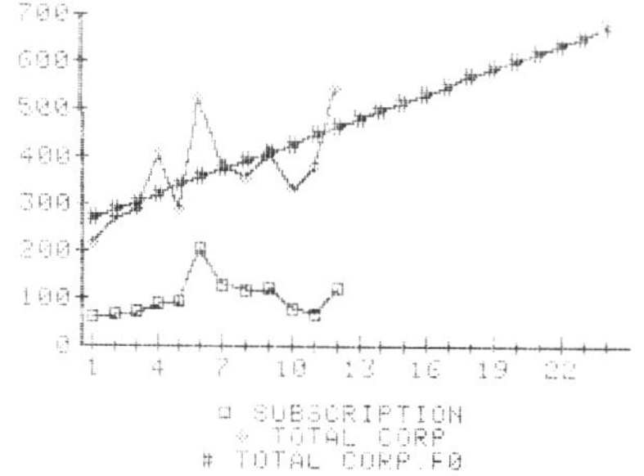

Two lines on chart with VisiTrend least squares projection.

While it is helpful to have detailed statistics, one can get overwhelmed. At one point, when I was running trend lines on virtually everything in sight, I took a break and got to thinking, "What am I going to do with all of these data?" The computer, of course, will generate anything you want. However, it is only a tool and human judgment must be used, probably more than ever before, to determine what the computer ought to be doing.

In Summary

I found the VisiTrend/VisiPlot package exceptionally user-friendly and easy to learn. The manual, particularly the tutorial section, is outstanding. While user mistakes are inevitable, the software is quite forgiving and rarely, if ever, loses any data. The package helps analyze data accurately, produces attractive charts and graphs, saves time, and is an outstanding business tool. I recommend it highly.

VisiTrend/VisiCalc is produced by VisiCorp, 1330 Bordeaux Dr., Sunnyvale CA, 94086 and is available for $259.95 at computer stores throughout the country. □

Other New Visi-Packages

VisiDex, named for the popular Rolodex information retrieval system, allows storage and retrieval of screens full of information in a free-form, unstructured manner. It can also maintain a calendar of appointments and reminders. One can think of the screen as a 5 x 7" filing card with up to twenty lines. Up to thirty-six keywords can be specified for each screen and the entire screen can be recalled by any keyword. Additional facilities include the ability to set up "templates" for applications such as mailing lists, on-screen editing, sorting keywords in alphabetical or numeric order or for print out purposes, and selective printing of partial screens. The price of VisiDex is $199.95.

VisiTerm is a communications software package designed for use with several popular modems such as the DC Hayes Micro Modem and others. The package provides full upper and lower case ASCII communications, with proportional spacing and smooth scrolling at speeds up to 1200 bps. The package is principally designed for the transmission of VisiCalc data, text, VisiPlot graphics, and related programs. The program comes with pre-defined regular, boldface, and APL characters, although it also allows the user to design his own character set. Like the other packages in the series, VisiTerm is menu driven with single stroke characters. Retail price is $149.95.

As mentioned in the VisiPlot review, VisiCalc has been updated to support a Data Interchange Format (DIF), a program independent data storage technique. The updated VisiCalc also supports Boolean functions and arithmetic comparisons as well as having 17 new simplified commands. It, like the other new Visi-series packages, is supplied on the Apple 16-sector diskette format. Price of the revised VisiCalc is $199.95. □

Notes

Chapter VI
Apple Cart

As a monthly column, Apple Cart has proven to be a valuable source of Apple information available only in *Creative Computing*. In this chapter, we've given you many months worth of material all grouped together for easy reference. Enjoy!

Using Data Files

Richard Milewski

February, 1979

In this month's Apple Cart we will provide a brief introduction to data files. It doesn't take long for even a beginning user to get the idea that a floppy disk drive added to a system can do a lot more than simply load programs more quickly than a cassette. The ability to store data on the disk opens the door to programs which can solve real world business and personal record keeping problems. Unfortunately, the books from which most beginners learn BASIC either skip data files entirely or describe file access protocols which bear little resemblance to those of the Apple II. Here, then, is our attempt.

Introduction to Data Files

Let us begin with a few informal definitions.

DATA FILE—A data storage area located on a diskette. A data file, like a program, is identified by a name. The DOS CATALOG command will produce a list of all programs and data files on a given diskette. Data files are identified by a "T" in the first column of the list. (The "T" stands for TEXT FILE.) Data files are used to increase the information storage capability of a program to store data which will be needed at a later date or to convey data from one program or set of programs to another. Smaller divisions sometimes encountered within data files are RECORDS and DATA ELEMENTS.

SERIAL ACCESS FILE—Often referred to simply as a serial file. When using a serial file, the DOS selects the next available location within the file to read or write data.

RANDOM ACCESS FILE—A data file which is divided into a number of smaller divisions called records. The use of records is much like the use of manila folders in a file drawer. Each record usually contains a number of pieces of information and while the information itself changes from record to record, the format of any record in a given data file is usually the same. For example, in an address file, name, address, city, state and zip code usually occur in identical order within each record. the chief advantage of a random access file over a serial file is that the records may be written or read in any order.

DATA ELEMENT—An item in a record. Elements may be:

Numbers—A number is any value which may be held in a simple variable (e.g., A, X, N1, P4, etc.).

Strings—A string is a sequence of characters either numbers, letters, or special characters. Note that a data element written on a file as a number can usually be read from the file as a string, but that many strings cannot be read as numbers. In general, the rules governing the input statement (and in Applesoft, the GET statement) apply.

Simple File Accessing Statements

On the Apple II the file accessing statements are the PRINT and INPUT statements. In addition some file control statements exist to perform overhead operations. These overhead operations appear in PRINT statements in which the first character printed is a control-D (shown as CHR$(4) stored in D$ in the following examples). In these examples and explanations only the basic form of each command is shown. Additional parameters are available for many of these commands, but their use is normally optional. The fundamental file accessing statements are:

OPEN (filename), L (recordsize)

The OPEN statement will create a file with the specified file name if none exists, and it prepares the system to read and/or write from the *beginning* of the file. Specifying the record size is optional and is required only for random access files.

WRITE (filename), R (record-number)

The WRITE command tells the machine that subsequent print statements contain data which is to be written to the data file. Data which is written to the file, as well as the DOS commands themselves appear on the screen in the course of program execution unless a NOMON command is given (consult your DOS manual for details on this one). Record size is required only for random access files. Note that to insure reliable operation, the WRITE command must be cancelled by printing another DOS command (simply printing a control-D will do) before attempting any input from the keyboard.

READ (filename), R (record-number)

The READ command tells the machine that subsequent input statements are to fetch data from the specified file. In the case of random access files, the data is fetched from the specified record.

CLOSE, (filename)

The CLOSE Ccommand is used to inform the system the specified data file is at least for the moment, no longer is use. It is important to close a data file after using it because the DOS stores some data in memory which is ultimately destined for the disk. This is done to maximize speed of operation. The CLOSE command insures that this information is "flushed" from memory onto the disk.

Sample Serial Access Programs

The general procedure for writing serial files is:

1. OPEN the data file.
2. WRITE the data to the file.
3. When *all* of the data has been written to the file, CLOSE the file. The following Applesoft II program will allow the user to input 10 numbers from the keyboard and write them to a the named SFILE.

```
10 D$=CHR$(4)
20 PRINT D$ "OPEN SFILE"
30 FOR I=1 TO 10
40 INPUT A
50 PRINT D$; "WRITE SFILE"
60 PRINT A
70 PRINT D$
80 NEXT I
90 PRINT D$; "CLOSE SFILE"
100 END
```

To read the data the operation is similar:

1. OPEN the file.
2. READ the data file.
3. CLOSE the data file.

The following Applesoft II program will allow the user to read the data written by the previous program. Note that by *not* using the NOMON command the data read from the file is visible on the screen.

```
10 D$=CHR$(4)
20 PRINT D$; "OPEN SFILE"
30 PRINT D$; "READ SFILE"
40 FOR I=1 TO 10
50 INPUT A
60 NEXT I
70 PRINT D$; "CLOSE SFILE"
80 END
```

Note that the above technique imposes some restrictions.

1. To read data near the end of the file, the entire file must be read.
2. To add new data to the file, the entire file must be read, then *without closing* the file, the new information must be written.

To solve the second problem, the Apple II DOS as an APPEND command which is identical to the open command except that subsequent WRITE commands place the data at the end of the file.

A more flexible way around the problem, which also permits the use of more sophisticated sorting and searching techniques uses the concept of *record*.

A record is a subdivision of a file. For purposes of this discussion each record in a given file is assumed to be of the same fixed length. Files organized into a series of records are often referred to as *randfom access* files because any record chosen at random may be read of written.

For example, given a random access file, we may

OPEN the file,
READ data from any record i the file,
WRITE data to any record in the file,
CLOSE the file when finished.

The important difference between the two file types for the purposes of sorting and searching are shown in the following example.

A	B$	Total Length
8	DOG	8, DOG☐ = 6 characters
3	HORSE	3, HORSE☐ = 8 characters
4	CAT	4, CAT☐ = 6 characters
		20 characters

where ☐ stands for a carriage return. A serial file containing the information would look like this:

1st character	11th character	21st character
8, DOG☐	3, HORSE☐	4, CAT☐

Note that we may now change "DOG" to "DUCK" without moving any of the other data in the file. This is possible because there are still 4 character positions in the first record. It is important in designing such a file to pick a record length long enough to hold the longest required data elements, but no so long as to waste disk space. Also note that one byte of space is required in each record for the endmark. We may now interchange any of the records in the file at will in order to sort the file.

We can for example, sort the file so the numeric keys are in ascending order:

1st character	11th character	21st character
3, 'HORSE☐	4, CAT☐	8, DOG☐

or sort the file to place the words in alphabetical order:

1st character	11th character	21st character
4, CAT☐	8, DOG☐	3, HORSE☐

An alternative approach which is usually much faster, especially for larger files, is to retain the original order,

1st character	11th character	21st character
8, DOG☐	3, HORSE☐	4, CAT☐

and compile an index to the file. The index consists of the record addresses in the order we wish to read them. For example:

Numeric Index = 2, 3, 1
Alphabetic Index = 3, 1, 2

Note that the use of indices permits the file to be "sorted" more than one way at a time. Alternatively the index could be used to copy the file to create another one sorted in any order for which an index exists.

Readers interested in an advance level text about sorting, searching, and information structures in general should locate a copy of *The Art of Computer Programming*, by Donald E. Knuth, Addison Wesley, 1973. Volume 3 covers Sorting and Searching.

The Exec Command

Richard Milewski

April, 1979

This month we will examine a little noticed capability of the Apple Disk II system. Buried in the middle of page 27 of the 7/78 edition of the DOS manual is a very brief description of something called the EXEC command. The DOS manual states, in part, that the command is . . . "Similar to RUN except that f [the filename] is a file containing commands (including BASIC statements) as they would be issued from the keyboard. This allows you to set up files that control the APPLE much as you would yourself."

With these few words and a brief paragraph devoted to the format of the command, the manual glosses over a facility with more potential to ease programming problems than any other command in the entire Disk Operating System. The easiest way to illustrate the use of the EXEC command is through the use of a few examples.

Program number one, the first of our examples, will create an exec file which contains the necessary commands to clear the screen, load the program from disk and list it, clear the screen again, list the disk directory (catalog), delete the program from the disk, clear the screen a third time, and, finally, list the directory again.

While this process is interesting to watch, it is of limited utility. A more useful function is performed by program number two. This program will create an exec file which will convert a collection of programs from the ROM version of Applesoft II to the cassette version (i.e. disk version). Note that the program assumes that the files are locked when the operation commences, and relocks them on completion of the conversion. The list of programs to be converted is entered as data statements beginning in line 1000. Program number three is identical to program number two except that the conversion is done in the opposite direction, i.e., from cassette Applesoft to ROM Applesoft.

Similar programs may be written to transfer programs from one disk to another, and to perform similar functions usually orchestrated from the keyboard. These techniques are particularly useful when an operation must be performed on many programs and the risk of typing errors increases.

The exec file can also be used to enter, modify, or delete lines of BASIC programs. Indeed, the possibility of creating programs which write exec files which create other programs does exist. Stopping just short of this, program number four will write an exec file which adds two subroutines to a list of programs. In this case the subroutines added are designed to disable, and re-enable the DOS so that INPUT statements will not respond to DOS commands. This exec file will add the subroutines but the subroutine calls (GOSUB statements) are not added as these would occur in different places in each program. The subroutine starting at line 30000 would be called once just before each input statement which expects input from the keyboard. The subroutine beginning at line 31000 would be called immediately after the input statement.

For those who consider self-reproduction to be the prime definition of life, we present a program/exec file combination which is 'alive,' at least within that narrow sense. Program number five will create an exec file which will destroy the program and then proceed to create a duplicate of the program which will create an exec file which will . . . ad infinitum, ad nauseam. I leave to the reader the question of determining which came first, the program or the egg-xec file, as well as the task of creating a program/exec file combination which not only 'lives,' but is capable of evolution.

Finally, program number six is a general purpose exec file creation utility. It may be used to build exec files of a non-repetitive nature.

Software

Apple owners looking for a source of programs and other information about their machines often band together to form clubs and user's groups. One of the larger of these is the Apple Corps based in San Francisco, California. They welcome membership inquiries from Apple owners around the world, and currently have a library of more than two hundred programs. Membership inquiries should be directed to:

The Apple Corps
Box 4816
San Francisco, California
94101

(A 6 by 8 inch self-addressed stamped envelope bearing 28 cents would help ensure the continued fiscal health of the club treasury.)

Other Apple owner's organizations are invited to make their existence known in this column. If there are a sufficient number, we will present a directory of Apple clubs in a future issue. Please indicate whether memberships are invited from outside your local area. (While it is nice to be able to have access to software from around the country, being able to discuss a programming problem with someone who has been there before is often a necessity for the newcomer.)■

```
10    REM   PROGRAM NUMBER ONE
20    REM
30    LET D$ =  CHR$ (4)
40    PRINT D$;"OPEN COMMANDS"
50    PRINT D$;"WRITE COMMANDS"
60    PRINT "HOME"
70    PRINT "LOAD PROGRAM NUMBER ONE"
80    PRINT "LIST"
90    PRINT "HOME"
100    PRINT "CATALOG"
110    PRINT "DELETE PROGRAM NUMBER ONE"
120    PRINT "HOME"
130    PRINT "CATALOG"
140    PRINT D$;"CLOSE COMMANDS"
150    END


10    REM   PROGRAM NUMBER TWO
20    REM
30    LET D$ =  CHR$ (4)
40    PRINT D$;"OPEN COMMANDS"
50    PRINT D$;"WRITE COMMANDS"
60    READ N$
70    IF N$ = "QUIT" THEN 9000
80    PRINT "UNLOCK ";N$
90    PRINT "LOAD ";N$
100    PRINT "CALL 3314"
110    PRINT "SAVE ";N$
120    PRINT "LOCK ";N$
130    GOTO 60
1000    REM   DATA LIST
1010    DATA   "PROGRAM ALPHA"
1020    DATA   "PROGRAM BETA"
1030    DATA   "PROGRAM GAMMA"
1040    DATA   "PROGRAM DELTA"
1050    DATA   "QUIT"
9000    PRINT D$;"CLOSE COMMANDS"
9010    PRINT D$;"EXEC COMMANDS"
9999    END


10    REM   PROGRAM NUMBER THREE
100    PRINT "CALL 54514"

        (Rest same as Program 2)


10    REM     PROGRAM NUMBER FIVE
20    REM
30    LET D$ =  CHR$ (4)
35    PRINT D$;"DELETE COMMANDS"
40    PRINT D$;"OPEN COMMANDS"
50    PRINT D$;"WRITE COMMANDS"
60    PRINT "NEW"
70    LIST
80    PRINT "RUN"
9000    PRINT D$;"CLOSE COMMANDS"
9010    PRINT D$;"EXEC COMMANDS"
9999    END


10    REM   PROGRAM NUMBER FOUR
20    REM
30    LET D$ =  CHR$ (4)
40    PRINT D$;"OPEN COMMANDS"
50    PRINT D$;"WRITE COMMANDS"
60    READ N$
70    IF N$ = "QUIT" THEN 9000
80    PRINT "UNLOCK ";N$
90    PRINT "LOAD ";N$
100    PRINT "30000 REM DISABLE"
110    PRINT "30010 DA=PEEK(54)"
120    PRINT "30020 DB=PEEK(55)"
130    PRINT "30030 DC=PEEK(56)"
140    PRINT "30040 DD=PEEK(57)"
150    PRINT "30050 PR#0:IN#0"
160    PRINT "30060 RETURN"
200    PRINT "31000 REM ENABLE"
210    PRINT "31010 POKE 54,DA"
220    PRINT "31020 POKE 55,DB"
230    PRINT "31030 POKE 56,DC"
240    PRINT "31040 POKE 57,DD"
250    PRINT "31060 RETURN"
300    PRINT "SAVE ";N$
310    PRINT "LOCK ";N$
320    GOTO 60
1000    REM   DATA LIST
1010    DATA   "PROGRAM ALPHA"
1020    DATA   "PROGRAM BETA"
1030    DATA   "PROGRAM GAMMA"
1040    DATA   "PROGRAM DELTA"
1050    DATA   "QUIT"
9000    PRINT D$;"CLOSE COMMANDS"
9010    PRINT D$;"EXEC COMMANDS"
9999    END
```

3-D Graphics

Richard Milewski

July, 1979

It is only natural with the high resolution graphics capabilities of the Apple II that considerable interest has evolved in making line drawings on the screen. Drawings of two dimensions are, of course, quite easy to produce. Three dimensional objects may be drawn by a process called projection. The study of this process, and indeed the very concept of the two dimensional perspective drawing, was one of the prime preoccupations of the worlds great artists and mathematicians during the Renaissance. Figure 1 is a woodcut done in 1525 by Albrecht Durer. Done for his treatise on geometry it shows one of the first devices for "mechanically" producing a two dimensional image of a three dimensional object. The two men are plotting the image of the lute as it would be seen from the point on the wall where the small hook is located. The string defines the path of the light from a point on the lute to the hook. As the man on the left places his end of the string on various points on the lute the man on the right notes the point at which the string passes through the plane of the image as defined by the picture frame. The hinged drawing board is then swung into place and the location of the string's intersection with the plane is marked with a dot. This device was one of the earliest pre-cursors of modern computer driven plotters.

It was not until the nineteenth century that the problem of constructing a three dimensional image from two dimensional data began to attract much attention. In 1838 Professor Wheatstone invented the reflecting stereoscope, with some minor modifications by Sir David Brewster it became an ubiquitous form of parlor entertainment through-

Figure 1. Albrecht Durer Woodcut.

out the middle nineteenth century. The operation of the stereoscope is dependant upon delivering to each eye an image which differs in angular perspective from the image delivered to the other. In the Brewster stereoscope this is done by using a lens to focus a separate image on each eye. There was a revival of popularity in stereo images in the 1950's when the technique of using crossed polarizing filters was used to produce motion pictures in three dimensions. The fad died rather quickly but a few 3D productions were done in the 1960's and in the case of one or two "adult" films as late as the early 1970's. A horror film starring Vincent Price titled "The House of Wax" stands as the most remembered of the 3D films. At about the same time as the early 3D films a fad swept the world of the pre-teenagers — Three Dimensional Comic Books! The technique was to print the comics as line drawing in red and green ink and to supply with each book a pair of cardboard framed glasses with lenses made of red and green plastic film. A whole generation of youth spent entire summers seeing the world in shades of red and green, much to the distress of their parents who were sure that the practice would result in blindness if not insanity.

3-D Images With The Apple

It is the technology of the 3D comic book which is almost directly transferrable to the high resolution screen of the APPLE II. To view the output of this month's programs it will be necessary to construct a pair of red/green glasses. Figure two shows a pair made from some red and green plastic film available at most dime stores, and a pair of 35mm slide mounts which are usually available singly for a few cents each at photo supply stores. Those of you who just happen to have a few old 3D comic books around can of course use the glasses which came with them.

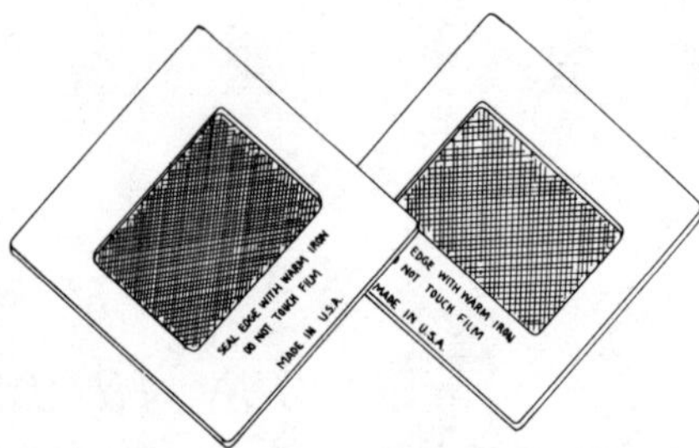

Figure 2. 3D Glasses.

The next step is to adjust the tint and color controls on your monitor so that the lines drawn in high resolution graphics will be red, green and white instead of the green, blue and white displayed by a properly adjusted set.

(Newer APPLES may produce the desired results by using the values 5 and 6 in the HCOLOR statements instead of 1 and 2.) Some fiddling with the contrast and brightness controls may also be necessary. The object is to produce red lines which are nearly invisible when viewed through the green filter and vice versa. Once this has been achieved simply run the program (HIRES Graphics in 3-D) and then view the results through the filters. It seems to work better if you don't look at the image on the screen until the filters are in place on the bridge of your nose.

The technique described above is not the only approach to the three dimensional image problem. It would seem a rather simple matter to produce 3D images using the classical two picture Brewster approach. The advantage to this approach would be the ability to produce color images in either high or low resolution graphics and the disadvantage is that the Brewster stereoscope does not lend itself to group viewing. Another

method might be to cover each half of the screen with polarizing material (cross polarized of course) and view the result with the traditional 3D movie specticles. This might, however, require more eye muscle control than most people are capable of in order to get the two images to fuse into one.

The possibilities for applications of the three dimensional images are a bit limited, but a clever programmer should be able to create a space war game with enough realism to make the player duck when attacked by an enemy missile. OK, all of you latent entrepreneurs, here's your chance! Write the ultimate space war game, send it to us, we'll review the best of the lot here and pass the best two or three onto Creative Computing Software for possible publication. Not only will you become famous, but a few royalty checks may help pay for your system.

Apple Cart 3-D Graphics

Thanks to Al Booth of San Jose, CA for bringing July Apple-Cart's missing program to our attention. And here it is:

```
10    REM   HIRES GRAPHICS IN 3D
20    REM
100   HGR : POKE  - 16302,0
500   HCOLOR= 3
505   FOR X = 10 TO 270 STEP 50
510   HPLOT X,10 TO X,180
520   HPLOT X + 1,10 TO X + 1,180
530   HPLOT X - 1,10 TO X - 1,180
590   NEXT X
1000   FOR K = 1 TO 6
1010   XL = K * 20:YL = XL * .7
1020   IP = 6 - (XL / 30)
1025   IF K / 3 =  INT (K / 3) THEN
IP = 0
1030   GOSUB 8000
1040   NEXT K
1999   END
8000   REM  COLOR SEPARATIONS
8010   HCOLOR= 2
8020   IF IP = 0 THEN   HCOLOR= 3
8025   X = 140:Y = 96
8030   GOSUB 9000
8040   XL = XL + 1
8050   GOSUB 9000
8100   IF IP = 0 THEN   RETURN
8110   HCOLOR= 1
8120   X = 140 + IP + 2
8130   GOSUB 9000
8140   XL = XL - 1
8150   GOSUB 9000
8999   RETURN
9000   REM  PLOT THE DIAMONDS
9030   HPLOT X - XL,Y TO X,Y - YL
9040   HPLOT X + XL,Y TO X,Y + YL
9050   HPLOT X - XL,Y TO X,Y + YL
9060   HPLOT X + XL,Y TO X,Y - YL
9999   RETURN
```

Apple Pascal Assembly Language

Chuck Carpenter

December, 1979

Pascal spoken here! Well, almost. After getting the new language system running with the Installation and Operating Manual, I started reading the other system manuals. There are a total of seven of them.

- Apple Language System Installation and Operating Manual.
- Three Apple BASIC manuals - Integer, Applesoft reference, and a new one, Applesoft Tutorial. This last one includes many of the Integer BASIC programs rewritten. It uses the same refreshing style found in the Integer manual with new stuff added for Applesoft.
- Three Pascal Manuals - A text by Bowles and a Users Manual by Jensen and Wirth (recognized authorities). Also included is a **preliminary** Apple Pascal Reference Manual. A permanent manual will be available and supplied free to present purchasers who send in their cards.

In addition to the generous selection of manuals, there are a number of other items in the language system package. These are:

- An autostart ROM and 16K of RAM. These are mounted on a circuit board that plugs into slot #0. If you have an Applesoft ROM card, it is replaced by the language system card. Autostart is discussed in the installation manual.
- Two new ROM's for your disk controller card so it will recognize the Pascal DOS. (Pascal has its own DOS.)
- Five Diskettes. Four containing the language system and a blank. One Pascal disk is for single drive systems. Two others are for multiple drive systems. Another is used for either and contains several system, utility and example programs. A wealth of Pascal programs are contained on these diskettes.
- One other diskette contains the two Apple BASIC languages.

```
PROGRAM GRAPH1;

   USES TURTLEGRAPHICS;

   BEGIN

   INITTURTLE;
   PENCOLOR(WHITE);

   BEGIN

     MOVE(100);
     TURN(120);
     MOVE(100);
     TURN(120);
     MOVE(100);
     READLN;
     TEXTMODE;
   END;

   END.
```

Figure 1. Simple Pascal graphics program. This program will draw an equilateral triangle. The figure will be in the upper right on the screen. Turtlegraphics starts the trace in the center of the screen and draws toward the right. The turns are counterclockwise.

```
ASM

                    1000 *******************
                    1010 * CLOCK   ROUTINE *
                    1020 * YEAR-DATE-TIME *
                    1030 *******************
                    1040
                    1050 TIME    .EQ $C400    CLOCK PROGRAM
                    1060 CHROUT  .EQ $FDED    PRNT CHAR IN A
                    1070 CLOCK   .EQ $0281    CLOCK TABLE
                    1080
                    1090         .OR $0384
                    1100
0384- A9 C4         1110 PROGRM LDA #$C4      CLOCK TO KEYBD
0386- 85 39         1120        STA $39       KSWH
0388- 20 00 C4      1130        JSR TIME      RUN CLOCK
038B- A2 04         1140        LDX #$04      INDEX COUNT
038D- BD AC 03      1150 YEAR   LDA TABLE,X   YEAR TABLE
0390- 09 80         1160        ORA #$80      NORMAL OUT
0392- 20 ED FD      1170        JSR CHROUT    PRINT IT
0395- CA            1180        DEX           TABLE DONE ?
0396- 10 F5         1190        BPL YEAR      NO-GO BACK
0398- A9 BA         1200        LDA #$BA      COLON
039A- 8D 88 02      1210        STA $0288     SWAP IT
039D- 8D 8B 02      1220        STA $028B     SWAP IT
03A0- A2 13         1230        LDX #$13      INDEX COUNT
03A2- BD 81 02      1240 TIME1  LDA CLOCK,X   DATE & TIME
03A5- 20 ED FD      1250        JSR CHROUT    PRINT IT
03A8- CA            1260        DEX           TABLE DONE ?
03A9- 10 F7         1270        BPL TIME1     NO-GO BACK
03AB- 60            1280        RTS           END IT
03AC- 39 37 39
03AF- 31            1290 TABLE  .AS '9791'    YEAR
03B0- 8D            1300        .HS 8D        CARRGE RET
                    1310        .EN


SYMBOL TABLE

TIME    C400    CHROUT FDED    CLOCK   0281
PROGRM 0384     YEAR    038D   TIME1   03A2
TABLE   03AC

:MGO PROGRM

1979 09/16 13:39:10.871
```

Figure 2. Assembled listing of the assembly language program used to print the output from a Mountain Hardware clockboard.
sample run

Apple Pascal is an extensive system. It should not be taken lightly by the novice programmer. In fact, the Apple Pascal Reference Manual states that it is for the "experienced Pascal programmer." However, not easily intimidated by such warnings, my first two Pascal programs were working within a couple of days.

Actually, the first task was to learn enough to make copies of the master diskettes. And it was a good thing to do. A couple of programs were wiped out during my learning process. After the copies were made, the rest of the system was the next major task. And what a task it is! After much trial and error, my two programs would draw a triangle and print a few lines of text. I did, however, get familiar with the text editor and many of the other Pascal system features. (Pascal includes an extensive machine language assembler too.) It will take many months to become familiar with most of this extensive and powerful programming system. We should see many new and interesting programs as Apple Pascal becomes more popular.

Figure 1 is my first attempt at a Pascal graphics program. There is plenty of information in the Apple Pascal manual on Apple Pascal commands and syntax but there are very few examples of easy-to-understand applications. So I listed one of the graphics demonstration programs and used it to figure out what to do. The program in Figure 1 is a modification of

```
:$384L

0384-    A9 C4          LDA    #$C4
0386-    85 39          STA    $39
0388-    20 00 C4       JSR    $C400
038B-    A2 04          LDX    #$04
038D-    BD AC 03       LDA    $03AC,X
0390-    09 80          ORA    #$80
0392-    20 ED FD       JSR    $FDED
0395-    CA             DEX
0396-    10 F5          BPL    $038D
0398-    A9 BA          LDA    #$BA
039A-    8D 88 02       STA    $0288
039D-    8D 8B 02       STA    $028B
03A0-    A2 13          LDX    #$13
03A2-    BD 81 02       LDA    $0281,X
03A5-    20 ED FD       JSR    $FDED
03A8-    CA             DEX
03A9-    10 F7          BPL    $03A2
03AB-    60             RTS
03AC-    39 37 39       AND    $3937,Y
03AF-    31 8D          AND    ($8D),Y
```

Figure 3. Disassembly of the clock program from the apple monitor. Only absolute addresses can be used with Apple's assembler.

a program in the textbook by Bowles. Most of the textbook programs will need to be modified to add Apple Pascal commands.

In this example, the USES TURTLEGRAPHICS command and the TEXTMODE command were the required modifications. TURTLEGRAPHICS tells Pascal it will be drawing pictures. TEXTMODE returns the screen back to the text mode. The PENCOLOR (WHITE), DRAW and TURN lines make the triangle. READLN is an input statement. This command stops the program until a key is pressed (for instance).

You can see the program doesn't look anything like BASIC. In fact, there is very little comparison between BASIC and Pascal. So if you intend to give Pascal a try, and I recommend it, expect to learn a whole new way of doing things.

Even though Pascal has a lot of appeal, and is likely to become very popular, it will not replace BASIC. And there is no reason why it should. BASIC doesn't have all the bells, whistles and structured design of many other languages but it does have universal acceptance and programming information is available to anyone. BASIC will remain a major language in the computing world for a long time. And, in that regard, this column will support both Apple BASIC's as well as Pascal. There are a number of applications where Integer BASIC is better than Applesoft. It runs faster and many things are easier to do. Furthermore, Pascal runs faster than either BASIC. Future columns will include programs doing things in each of the languages and examples of how to do the same thing in each language.

How about the native language of the Apple's 6502 microprocessor? Assembly language programming (and entry of machine language) is possible directly from the keyboard of the Apple II. Short assembly language programs are easily entered from the keyboard. Assembly into machine language is automatic with the Apple mini-assembler. Or you can enter the machine language into memory using monitor commands. For more extensive assembly language programming,

there are several 6502 assemblers available (including the one in the Apple Language System).

Machine language programs provide a convenient way to run short routines from your main programs. As an example, Figure 2 is a routine to read the clock output from the Mountain Hardware clock board. The program (using the syntax of the S-C Assembler II assembler) indexes two tables to print out the year, date and time. First, the clock is called by initializing KSWH and the jump (JSR) to TIME. This causes the clock circuits to store the clock output in the keyboard buffer area. Then, an indexing command reads the year and the contents of TABLE are printed. Because of programming conflicts, the output of the clock uses semi-colons between the hours and minutes. The next few lines of the clock routine puts colons in these memory locations. Now, the program indexes the clock output and prints the values. Note that both of the indexing routines start at the end and go in reverse. This was necessary because that's the way the clock output is stored. Also, it takes fewer instructions to index a table this way. Use 384G or CALL 900 to run this program.

Compare the listing from the S-C Assembler in Figure 2 to the listing of the same program from the Apple monitor (Figure 3). The output lacks the extended features of the S-C Assembler but does a more than creditable job. Also, the Apple assembler is available just as soon as you turn on the power to your Apple. For a shorter print out of the clock data, the program modification in Figure 4 can be used. Most of the time you only need the current date and time to the nearest minute. These programs make it possible to have some control of your programs when you are making lots of listings. The clock output from the Mountain Hardware board can be used from BASIC programs, too.

```
0398- A9 BA      1200        LDA #$BA     COLON
039A- 8D 8B 02   1210        STA $028B    SWAP IT
039D- A2 0B      1220        LDX #$0B     INDEX COUNT
039F- BD 89 02   1230 TIME1  LDA CLOCK,X  DATE & TIME
03A2- 20 ED FD   1240        JSR CHROUT   PRINT IT
03A5- CA         1250        DEX          TABLE DONE ?
03A6- 10 F7      1260        BPL TIME1    NO-GO BACK
03A8- A9 8D      1262        LDA #$8D
03AA- 20 ED FD   1264        JSR CHROUT   PRINT IT
03AD- 60         1270        RTS          END IT


:MGO PROGRM

1979 09/16 13:36

:
```

Figure 4. Example of a program modification to print out a shorter version of the Year, Date and Time program. sample run

Applesoft Keyword Search•Integer Mod Function
Pascal Revisited •Autostart Rom
Applesoft Dollar Formatter

Chuck Carpenter *January, 1980*

Applesoft — Keyword Search

Searching files for keywords is a relatively easy task, especially if you are using the Apple DOS. The program segment in Listing #1 is part of a simple text file program. As you can see from the sample run in Listing #2, this is one of the file options. The parameters and variables needed for this segment to run were established at the beginning of the main program. To help with an understanding of how this routine functions, here is a list of the variables used:

```
D$ = CHR$(4) = control D
F$ = Name of active file
K$ = Keyword to search for
K  = Keyword found flag
C  = Record counter
I & J = Local loop variables
Q$ = local response to input
     prompts
CHR$(13) = return key
```

To make it easier to follow, the program was written with a simple format and very few multiple line statements. Assume that a file exists with the name Apple Demo and that all variables have been initialized. When keyword search is selected from the options list, the title is displayed by line 6035. In line 6040, an input request is made for the keyword. Having entered the keyword, lines 6050 through 6080 open the file and READ record zero to get the record count. The READ operation is stopped in line 6090 with a control D. In lines 6100 thru 6120 the first record (or Jth record) is read in from the file and the READ is then stopped by the control D in line 6130.

String parsing, for the keyword, is accomplished in lines 6140 through 6180. The string length, minus the length of the keyword, is set in line 6140. For unformatted text, setting the record length to 80 will be wasteful. However, this allows you to edit the record easier. And, use of structured formatted records will be the more likely application for this kind of file. Line 6150 checks a sub-string of characters equal in length to the keyword. If a match is found, the record number and the record are

printed by line 6160. If no match is found, I is incremented and the next sub-string of characters is checked. This cycle is continued until all characters are checked or each occurrence of the keyword is found. If you don't want or need to find all occurrences of the keyword in a record, then add a GOTO 6190 command in line 6170.

Once the record search has been completed, J is incremented and the next record is read by line 6110. Now, the parsing process continues until all records in the file, equal to the value of C, have been read and parsed for the keyword. Lines 6200 through 6300 are a variety of options for working with the text file. If no keyword was found another one can be selected. Records containing the keyword can be edited, or simply choose to return to the file options. Note that in line 6290, GET A$ was used to accept keyboard input. Also, CHR$(13) was used to allow only the use of the return key to return to the options list. Pressing any other key will clear the screen and display the press return prompt. Try this parsing routine on your own programs. Also, rewrite it for primary and secondary keywords.

Integer BASIC — The MOD Function

One command only briefly described in the Red Book, and only casually mentioned in the Integer BASIC manual, is the MOD function. MOD is an abbreviated form of the word Modulo. It is described in the Red Book as: the remainder after the division of one expression by another expression. For example, in this statement, R=X MOD Y, R will equal the remainder when the value X is divided by the value Y. Because only integers are allowed otherwise, this is a useful way to find the remainder after a division is executed. The immediate execution mode will let you find the value by typing in PRINT (#1) MOD (#2) on your Apple and pressing return. There are several programs containing examples of the MOD function in the Red Book.

Another application for the MOD function is to POKE address data into

memory. Rather than calculating the data values of memory addresses yourself, the MOD function will help you do it. For instance, to move LOMEM you can POKE the decimal value into memory like this:

```
POKE 74, ADDR MOD 256
POLE 75, ADDR / 256
     LOMEM pointer

POKE 204, ADDR MOD 256
POKE 205, ADDR / 256
     Variables pointer
```

If you want to move LOMEM from $0800 to $0900 (the $ means a hexadecimal number), convert the address to its decimal value and include the result in place of ADDR. The HEX number $0900 is equal to 2304 decimal and will be POKEd into memory as 2304 MOD 256 = 00 and 2304 / 256 = 09. As you can see, these values equal the original HEX address: LO byte first, HI byte second. Try this with some addresses that are not as obvious; $1ABC for instance. Here's a short program to illustrate another use of the MOD function:

```
>LIST
1000 REM   *** MOD DEMO ***
1010 REM
1020 PRINT
1030 INPUT "NUMERATOR = ",N
1040 INPUT "DENOMINATOR = ",D
1050 PRINT N;" / ";D;"
     IS APPROXIMATELY"
1060 PRINT N/D;".";
1070 FOR I=1 TO 20
1080 F=N MOD D
1090 IF F>3276 THEN 1130
1100 N=F*10
1110 PRINT N/D;
1120 NEXT I
1130 PRINT
1140 GOTO 1020

>RUN

NUMERATOR = ?30000

DENOMINATOR = ?111

30000 / 111 IS APPROXIMATELY
270.27027027027027027027

NUMERATOR = ?
```

If you have an interesting idea or a question you haven't found an answer for, I'd enjoy hearing from you.

```
6000 :
6010 'REM  ** KEYWORD SEARCH **
6015  REM  *********************
6020 :
6030  HOME
6035  PRINT : PRINT "KEYWORD SEARCH - ";F$;""
6040  PRINT : INPUT "KEYWORD - ";K$
6050  LET K = 0
6060  PRINT D$"OPEN";F$;",L80"
6070  PRINT D$"READ";F$;",R";0
6080  INPUT C
6090  PRINT D$
6100  FOR J = 1 TO C
6110  PRINT D$"READ";F$;",R";J
6120  INPUT R$(J)
6130  PRINT D$
6140  FOR I = 1 TO 80 - LEN (K$)
6150  IF  MID$ (R$(J),I, LEN (K$)) < > K$ GOTO 6180
6160  PRINT : PRINT J;: PRINT " ";: PRINT R$(J)
6170  LET K = K + 1
6180  NEXT I
6190  NEXT J: PRINT
6200  IF K > 0 GOTO 6240
6210  PRINT : PRINT "NOTHING FOUND - ": PRINT "TRY ANOTHER KEY WO
     RD ? Y/N ";
6220  INPUT Q$: IF Q$ = "Y" GOTO 6000
6230  IF Q$ = "N" GOTO 6290
6240  PRINT D$"CLOSE";F$;""
6250  PRINT : PRINT "DO YOU WANT TO EDIT ? Y/N ";
6260  INPUT Q$: IF Q$ = "Y" GOTO 5000
6270  PRINT : PRINT "TRY ANOTHER KEYWORD ? Y/N ";
6280  INPUT Q$: IF Q$ = "Y" GOTO 6000
6290  PRINT : PRINT "PRESS RETURN TO CONTINUE - ";: GET A$: IF A$
     = CHR$ (13) THEN  HOME : VTAB (5): GOTO 1090
6300  HOME : GOTO 6290
```

Listing 1

```
]RUN
BUILD AND APPEND A FILE
-----------------------
ENTER THE FILE NAME - APPLE DEMO

FILE OPTIONS:

1979 10/05 08:25:43.328

  1. BUILD NEW RECORDS
  2. ADD MORE RECORDS
  3. LIST RECORDS
  4. EDIT A RECORD
  5. KEYWORD SEARCH
  0. END THE PROGRAM

FILE'APPLE DEMO'CONTAINS 6 RECORDS !

WHICH NUMBER - 3

LIST TEXT FILE - APPLE DEMO

FAST OR SLOW ? F/S F
1    WELL WELL! WHAT SHALL WE PUT IN THIS FILE?
2    BECAUSE IT'S A DEMO OF THE KEYWORD SEARCHING
3    PROGRAM SEGMENT -- I'LL JUST PUT IN A FEW
4    LINES AND SHOW HOW TO SEARCH FOR A KEYWORD.
5    ACTUALLY -- I CAN PUT IN AS MANY RECORDS AS
6    THE DISK WILL HOLD. BUT -- I'LL END IT HERE.
PRESS RETURN TO CONTINUE -
:
WHICH NUMBER - 5

KEYWORD SEARCH - APPLE DEMO

KEYWORD - KEYWORD

2 BECAUSE IT'S A DEMO OF THE KEYWORD SEARCHING

4 LINES AND SHOW HOW TO SEARCH FOR A KEYWORD.
DO YOU WANT TO EDIT ? Y/N ?N

TRY ANOTHER KEYWORD ? Y/N ?Y

KEYWORD SEARCH - APPLE DEMO

KEYWORD - APPLE

NOTHING FOUND -
TRY ANOTHER KEY WORD ? Y/N ?N

PRESS RETURN TO CONTINUE -
```

Listing 2

This circuit won't measure temperature exactly but it can be used for checking within a range. A program to read the thermal voltage could include lines like this:

```
IF X>62 AND X<68
    THEN PRINT "COOL END"
IF X>56 AND X<62
    THEN PRINT "WARM END"
```

Values used in the equalities came from an experiment where the glass bead thermistor was used as a temperature probe. Use your own values for specific applications. This circuit will have limited range because the output voltage will not go to zero. A better circuit would include a thermistor bridge with an amplifier. More linear operation and wider range temperature reading would then be possible. Notice that the supply voltage is 12 volts. The voltage was obtained by using one of the expansion connectors. A couple of 6 volt batteries would work just as well.

Any of the circuits discussed so far can be connected to a 16 pin component header. You may want to build an adapter out of a 16 pin header and a wire-wrap 16 pin socket. Solder the socket to the header, pin for pin. This way the game paddle can still be plugged in along with any special circuit you add on. Another way would be to make an extender cable. Run the cable out the back of the Apple and connect the circuits to the end of the cable. This way the cover won't have to be opened each time a new gadget is to be connected. Be sure to turn the power off before plugging in or removing any circuit from your computer.

Arley Pascal Sez

If you're experiencing problems with Pascal in your new language system, then you will appreciate these comments from N. Dealy:

1. To keep C(ompile from 'going away' or having a spectacular blow-up use the swapping or double swapping option. The directives to use are (*$S+*) and (*$S++*), respectively. These directives keep you from overflowing the 6502 and Pascal stacks.

2. Finding files is easier if you use the correct syntax from within or outside the F(ILER. Remember: Sometimes you use the suffix and sometimes you don't. You may find it handy to keep notes at hand when you first start using the system.

3. From the E(DITOR, you can write over an existing file if you Q(UIT and write to a named file. From within the editor, the system won't tell you if you already have a file by the same name. Keep a log of diskette and

file names close by if this will be a problem. From the F(ILER, unlike the E(DITOR, you are prompted if you are about to destroy something.

4. The Pascal language system does not support the clock boards. You must use the D(ATE command from the F(ILER to change the date.

5. Trying to change the name of the default volume may cause some problems. The system actually has two special volumes — the default volume and the root volume. The default volume may be changed using the 'P' filer command. Any time you specify a file without specifying the volume explicitly this is the volume that is used. On the other hand, the root volume is the volume that the system was booted from and may not be changed. The work files are always written to the root volume.

6. Direct connection of the console keyboard to the printer is possible, too. (Useful if you want to enter titles on listings.) From within the F(ILER request a T(RANSFER from CONSOLE: to PRINTER:. Then type your message, header or other info and end it with a Control C. The control C signals end of file from the console and your message will be transferred to the printer.

7. When using L(INK you must specify the name you want followed by '.CODE'. Do this when you are prompted for the output file name. Otherwise, when you try to execute, you will get an error message.

Autostart ROM

Lots of things change when you plug in this new ROM chip. Some of the changes are nice and quite handy. Others can cause some inconvenience. (But only if you have had your Apple a year or more and like to use the monitor routines a lot.) Here are some of the features:

1. Automatic Basic selection if a disk drive is not installed.

2. Automatic booting if a drive is in slot 6 and a functioning diskette is in the drive.

3. Extended screen editing capability.

4. Reset returns to the Basic installed, not the monitor.

5. Stop a listing and start it again with a Control S. Allows you to examine any part of your program.

6. Suspend execution of a program with a Control S too.

Some of the differences caused with autostart in place are:

1. No direct access to the monitor. If the monitor routines are used a lot, you must use a call such as CALL-151 to get to the monitor each time reset is pressed. There are a couple of memory POKEs that can simplify this and let

the reset key return program to the monitor, too.

2. Some programs taking advantage of routines in the monitor may not run. Several utility routines were replaced with new ones for autostart features.

But, for most of us, the new autostart ROM will make using the Apple easier and quite foolproof. In a business environment, autostart provides complete load-and-go capability, a definite advantage for operator training and use requirements.

Applesoft Formatter

Apple chose to include graphics capability over formatting in their version of Microsoft Basic. Therefore, there is no PRINT USING command and corresponding imaging formatter. For most of us this is not a problem. Sometimes, though, you may want to line up columns containing dollars and cents values. Listing 1 illustrates a routine that will do this job. Also included in the routine are number length and format checks. And, the VAL and STR$ commands are used for string and real number conversions. Let's examine the program and see how it works.

• Line 1040 initializes the variables and dimensions the length of the dollars column. Change the DIM value to be

```
]LIST

1000   REM   **********************
1010   REM   * DOLLAR FORMATTER *
1020   REM   **********************
1030 :
1040   LET D = 1:T = 0: DIM D$(25)
: HOME
1050   PRINT D;" ";
1060   INPUT "DOLLARS - ";D$(D)
1070   IF D$(D) = "END" GOTO 1200
1080   IF D$(D) = "0" THEN D$(D) =
"0.00"
1090   IF  MID$ (D$(D), LEN (D$(D)
) - 2,1) = "." GOTO 1130
1100   PRINT "INCORRECT FORM !"
1110   PRINT
1120   GOTO 1050
1130   IF  LEN (D$(D)) =  < 7 GOTO
1170
1140   PRINT "NUMBER TOO LONG !"
1150   PRINT
1160   GOTO 1050
1170   REM
1180   LET T = T +  VAL (D$(D))
1185   LET D = D + 1
1190   GOTO 1050
1200   LET D = D - 1
1210   PRINT                  .
1220   FOR I = 1 TO D
1230   PRINT  TAB( 39 -  LEN (D$(I
)));D$(I)
1240   NEXT I
1250   PRINT :T$ =  STR$ (T)
1260   PRINT "TOTAL"; TAB( 30)"$";
 TAB( 39 -  LEN (T$));T$

]RUN
1 DOLLARS - 1234567
INCORRECT FORM !

1 DOLLARS - 123456.78
NUMBER TOO LONG !

1 DOLLARS - 1234.56
2 DOLLARS - 345.98
3 DOLLARS - 0
4 DOLLARS - 0.75
5 DOLLARS - 195.75
6 DOLLARS - END

                         1234.56
                          345.98
                            0.00
                            0.75
                          195.75

TOTAL            $ 1777.04
```

Listing

longer than your list.

• Input is accepted by lines 1050 thru line 1080. Line 1050 numbers the input line, 1060 accepts the input, 1070 checks to see if END was entered to terminate input and 1080 allows a '0' to be used if the entry has no value. My choice is to convert a no-value entry to 0.00 rather than leave it blank.

• Form is checked in line 1090. The position of the period is checked. I assumed that the form is standard 2 decimal place dollars and cents. If the entry is wrong the program returns to the input lines.

• Total length of the string of numbers is checked in line 1130. If greater than seven characters, this example program sends you back to the input lines. (The 1170 following line 1130 is part of the GOTO in line 1130.)

Note that you may want to check for alpha characters at this point. A string parsing routine can be used to check the ASCII value of each character. Of course, you can check the entry on the screen and change it before return is pressed. However, automatic error checking is more reliable; the computer doesn't get board or distracted.

• Line 1180 uses the VAL command to convert the D$ string to a real number. The value of T is adjusted with each entry and becomes the total sum of all the values entered.

• In line 1185, the counter D is incremented for each value entered. Make sure the counter is incremented **after** the total is adjusted, otherwise you will never get a correct total. Line 1190 returns to line 1050 for more input.

• When END is used to terminate input, the program branches to line 1200. Because the D counter was incremented and no additional input was made, the counter needs to be decremented by one.

• Lines 1220 to 1240 do the work of aligning all the inputs in a column. Each value is tabbed to some position, in this example 39, minus the length of the string D$.

• In line 1250, total value T is converted to a string by using the STR$ command. This was done so the total could also be tabbed into position under the column of numbers. The word TOTAL, a '$' and the value of the column are printed by line 1260.

With a disk based system, saving the input values as a file is quite straightforward. Consider how it might be done on tape using the STORE command. Hint: Remember the VAL and STR$ commands. Another program option would include the ability to subtract numbers and keep the total correct. □

Flip Your Disk
Apple I/O

Chuck Carpenter   *February, 1980*

The Diskette Craze

Several times over the past few months I've heard of people recording on both side of their diskettes. One source of software even ships their programs recorded this way. **This is a very risky practice.** Here's why:

- Single sided media is only certified on the normal recording side of the diskette.
- The uncertified side can have 'soft spots' that may not generate enough output to be read by the read head. Some drives will work OK, some won't.
- Diskettes spin in one direction. Dirt is collected on one side by the liner in the diskette jacket.
- When you turn the diskette over, it spins in the opposite direction. The dirt comes loose and passes under the head. Increased head and media wear is the result.
- A felt pad is used to load the head, under light pressure, against the diskette. In normal use, the pad collects dirt and bits of magnetic material.
- Pressed against the normally un-recorded side, the head load pad poses no problem. The resulting abrasion is on the unused side. You can guess what is going to happen to your programs when this abrasive pad is allowed to rub on both sides of your diskettes.

Note that two sided drives use read/ write heads loaded against each other. The diskette always spins in one direction. And, the media is certified on both sides. The diskettes that "fall out" or are marginal are used for single side applications.

Also, in order to use the media on both sides, a notch must be cut in the diskette jacket. If even the smallest plastic chip gets loose and wedges inside, the magnetic surface will be scraped bare. If you're lucky this will occur outside the recording area on the diskette (**if** you're lucky). Assuming you can cut the second notch without making chips, some of your easily replaced programs might be saved on both sides of a diskette. If you belong to a club with a large library or can easily get another copy of a non-critical program, there is little risk. If a particular program generates a unique data base, then don't take the risk. Any special programs you write or use should only be saved on the normal recording side of unmodified diskettes.

One more point: If you insist on using both sides of a diskette, have them checked. If you have access to the new language system, Pascal, use the BAD BLOCKS function to check diskette surfaces. The higher writing density of the Pascal DOS increases the chance of finding any bad spots, too. Doing some certifying on your own will significantly improve your odds against lost data.

These comments are the result of personal experiences with dozens of disk drives and hundreds of diskettes. A recent assignment of mine included subsystem responsibility for drives and media. Also, I made a specific point of discussing the problem with Shugart Field Engineers. Their comments concurred exactly with mine.

Apple's Easy I/O

Built into your Apple is a connector (a 16 pin socket) that will allow you to sense and control things in the "outside world." There are also 8 expansion connectors for pugging in all sorts of complex circuit boards (for instance, the disk drive controllers, the serial and parallel boards, the clock boards and so on). But using these connectors is not easy and we'll leave the expansion connectors to the serious hardware designer.

Easy input and output (I/O), is provided by the game paddle connector (GP I/O). You can control and monitor a wide variety of circuits and gadgets. The input and output pin voltages are all transistor transistor logic (TTL) levels. And, there are many inexpensive TTL devices available from computer shops and electronic supply stores. The maximum voltage for TTL circuits is 5 volts. As you will see, this supply voltage is conveniently provided on the GP I/O connection. Connectors are easily made to the pins of the GP I/O with a 16 pin component header. The signals available at the GP I/O connector are:

- Four latchable bits to turn things on and off.
- Three sense bits to check for switch closure and opening.
- Four analog inputs for sensing control positions, measuring temperature or whatever.
- One utility strobe so you can control things in time with the computer.
- Power, +5 volts and ground for low current applications.

All twelve signal ports (I/O pins) are controllable from programs. The following diagram shows the arrangement of the inputs and outputs on the 16 pin GP I/O connector.

Top View

NC	9	8	Ground
PDL1	10	7	PDL2
PDL3	11	6	PDL0
AN3	12	5	Strobe
AN2	13	4	SW2
AN1	14	3	SW1
AN0	15	2	SW0
NC	16	1	+5 Volts

Location J14   On The Apple Board
Figure 1

More information about GP I/O signals can be found on pages 126, 137, 138 and 150 in the old 'Apple II Reference Manual' (the red book) and pages 23 to 25 and 100 in the new 'Apple II Reference Manual.'

Some I/O Background

Now that you know this basic information, some background on circuits to connect to the I/O pins will get things started. One thing you could connect is more game paddles and another switch. The paddles and switches that come with your Apple are connected to PDLO, SWO, PDL1 and SW1. The game paddle and switch circuit looks like this:

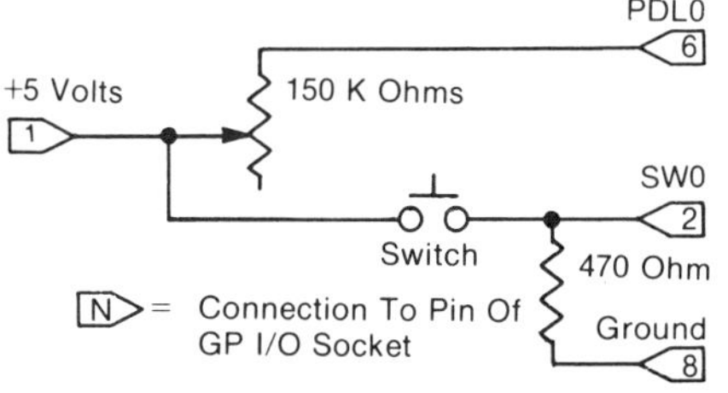

Typical Game Paddle Circuit

Program statements used to read the PDL and SW inputs are:

PEEK PDL (X); gives a number between 0 and 255 from one of the PDL inputs depending on the position of the variable resistor.

PEEK (addr); gives a number less than 127 if the switch is off and a number greater than 127 if the switch is closed. Using this command as an equality will test this condition. Here's one way:

IF PEEK(-16286) > 127 = 1 GOTO . . .

Another possibility is to connect a lamp or light emitting diode (LED) to one or more of the annunciator output pins, AN0 to AN3. A circuit to connect an LED looks like this:

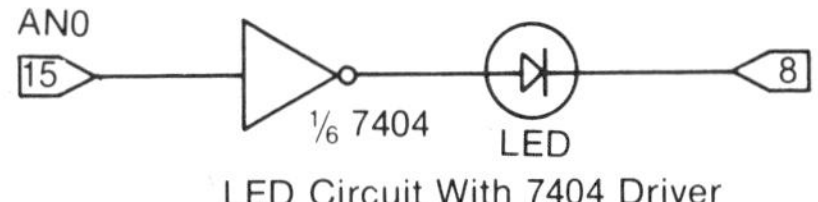

LED Circuit With 7404 Driver

or, a low current lamp can be connected like this:

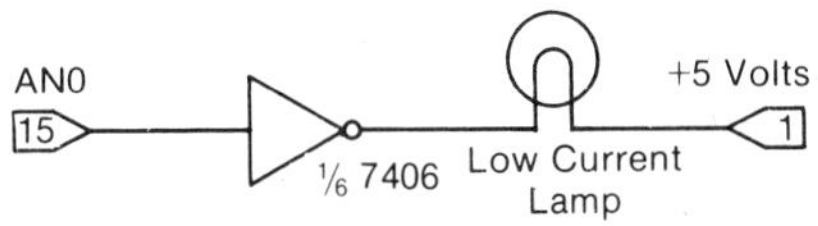

Lamp Circuit With 7406 Driver

The current available from the 5 volt supply pin is limited to 100 mA. The lowest current lamp I have found is a 6 volt, 25 mA unit from Radio Shack. Figure about 15 mA for an LED. This means that more LEDs can be connected to the AN(X) outputs with power left for the TTL buffer/amplifiers. Use of LED's will reduce the need for an external power supply. In all cases, use a TTL buffer/amplifier to drive the external circuits. You will

have more circuit flexibility and the circuits in your Apple will be protected from accidents.

The two TTL devices illustrated in the circuits above are inverting types. That is, the output signal is the opposite polarity of the input signal. It's not really necessary to invert in this application. These two TTL devices are popular and inexpensive. Both types include 6 individual circuits in the 14 pin package. The 7406 is an open collector device and should be used for driving low current lamps or relays. The 7404 will work as a driver for lower current devices like the LEDs and as a logic element and buffer.

Who's There

Monitoring a remotely located switch is one task you can accomplish through the SW input pins. For instance you can connect a switch as shown in the following circuit to monitor a remote location,

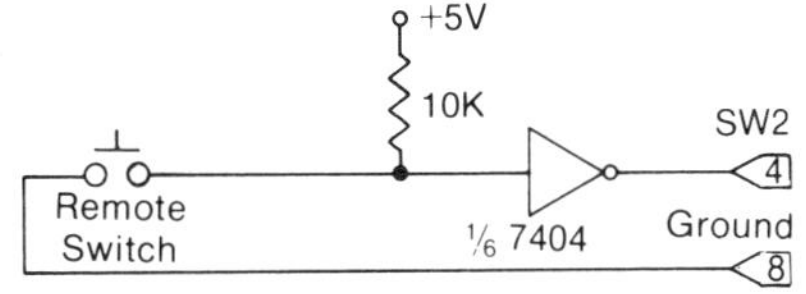

Switch Sensing With 7404 Buffer

With the switch open, the 10K pullup resistor insures that the input to the 7404 is not floating and is not affected by noise on the wires. The 7404 is an inverter, so the output is a zero or low when the input is at 5 volts. When the switch is closed, the input goes to zero or low and the output goes up or high. By using the PEEK command in a Basic program the SW2 input can be tested.

IF PEEK (-16285) > 127 = 1 GOTO . . .
REM : switch 3 is on when true

When the voltage at SW2, pin 4 is near zero, the PEEK statement is false. Closing the switch causes the input to SW2, pin 4 to go to a voltage level between 3 and 4 volts. The PEEK statement will now be true and you can cause your program to respond accordingly.

Apple Turns On

Pins 12 to 15 are the latchable outputs called annunciator ports. Each of these outputs can be set from within a program by using a POKE statement. When power is first turned on, the normal level is set by the power-on reset routines in the monitor ROM. For AN0 and AN1 this level is high. A POKE to the address representing the AN(X) set or reset condition will cause the voltage to change accordingly. For instance:

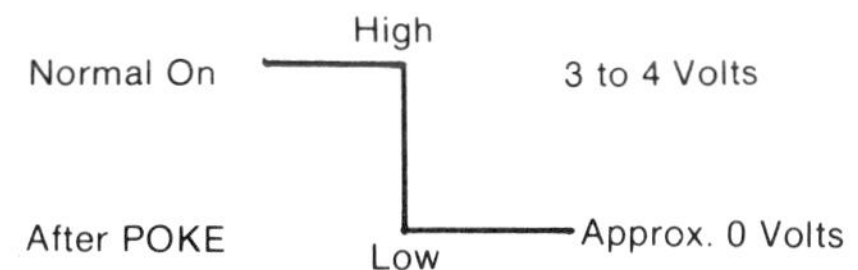

To switch the voltage back high, another POKE is required; this time to a different address. For output AN0 the POKEs required are like this:

POKE -16296,0 : REM — SET AN0 HI
POKE -16295,0 : REM — SET AN0 LO
POKE -16296,0 : REM — SET AN0 HI

Using three POKEs in a row like this will generate a pulse at the AN0 pin. It will be a fairly fast pulse and if the LED circuit shown previously were connected to AN0 the LED would blink.

To make the LED flash on and off use a FOR NEXT loop with suitable delays between POKEs. First, it's a good idea to make sure the AN0 output is at the desired starting level. Use a POKE in your initiating routine to assure that AN0 is set HI. Then, use a program segment something like this to flash the LED:

FOR I = 1 TO 10
POKE -16295,0 : REM — LED IS ON
FOR J = 1 TO 200 : NEXT J
POKE -16296,0 : REM — LED IS OFF
FOR J = 1 TO 200 : NEXT J
NEXT I
RETURN

The same routine can also be used to flash the lamp except the on and off conditions are reversed. Depending on your requirements, you can reverse the order of POKEs, add a 7404 inverter ahead of the 7406, or leave the circuit as is. More information on addresses to use for the other latchable outputs can be found on pages 75 and 137 in the red book and page 24 of the new reference manual.

Which Way and How Far

Analog inputs, such as the output voltage from a game paddle, can be 'read' by the PDL inputs. A voltage that varies continuously between 0 and 3 volts will be converted to numbers between 255 and 0 in the computer. A game paddle is the most usual gadget connected to PDL inputs but there are many other possibilities. One such possibility is a temperature checking circuit. Here's one idea:

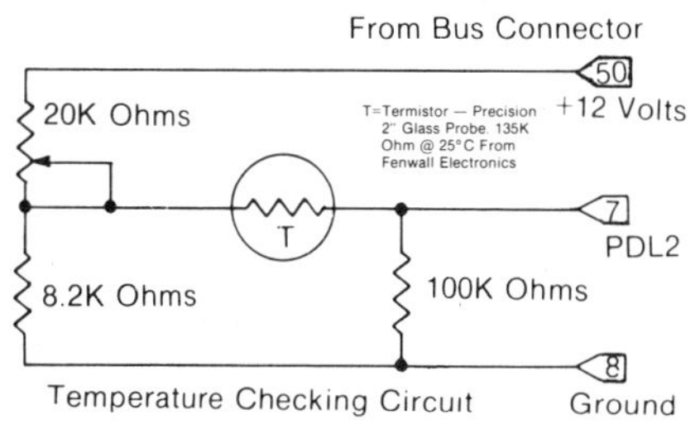

Temperature Checking Circuit

Poking Subroutines •Tone Routine Pause Routine •Sargon II

Chuck Carpenter

March, 1980

Put it There

Using the POKE command to put a byte of data into memory is quite useful. Examination of a variety of Apple programs will illustrate the point. Some programs which include musical segments for instance, use a series of POKEs to poke in the machine language routine that controls the pitch and duration values. This technique is fine for setting and resetting various program pointers and control bytes. But for longer routines, there are a couple of other techniques that are useful. One way is to use a combination of READ and DATA statements. Another is to use a string parsing routine to separate and POKE the data into memory. The economy of coding your program using a simple series of POKEs, or one of the other methods, will depend on how much work you want to do (or how much memory can be saved).

Just Plain POKEs

Using the tone generating routine as an example, the POKE statements required would take two program lines. Not too bad, but this routine is only 19 bytes long. Here's an example.

```
1500 REM
1510 REM   *** RANDOM TONES
1520 REM   ********************
1530 REM
1540 POKE 2,173: POKE 3,48: POKE
     4,192: POKE 5,136: POKE 6,208
     : POKE 7,4: POKE 8,198: POKE
     9,1: POKE 10,240
1550 POKE 11,8: POKE 12,202: POKE
     13,208: POKE 14,246: POKE 15
     ,166: POKE 16,0: POKE 17,76
     : POKE 18,2: POKE 19,0: POKE
     20,96
1560 CALL -936: VTAB 12: TAB 14:
     PRINT "RANDOM TONES"
1570 IF PEEK (-16286)>127=1 THEN
     RETURN
1580 IF PEEK (-16287)>127=1 THEN
     1600
1590 GOTO 1570
1600 P= RND (100)+20:D= RND (100
     )+20
1610 POKE 0,P: POKE 1,D: CALL 2
1620 GOTO 1570
```

The program segment first loads the machine language routine from the series of POKEs starting at memory location 2. Each POKE uses a data pair representing the decimal value of the memory location and the data byte to be put in that location. Note that it is necessary to convert hexadecimal values to decimal with this method.

Program lines 1560 to 1580 are used to control the routine. Line 1570 examines pushbutton 2. If it's off then button 1 is examined in line 1580. If neither button is pressed, the program loops back to line 1570 and keeps checking. If button 2 is pressed the program ENDs or RETURNs if it's used as a subroutine. Line 1600 generates a random value for the pitch and duration of the tone to be played. The values have been adjusted so that extremes are held to a reasonable audio range. Line 1610 then POKEs the values for pitch and duration into memory locations 0 and 1 and CALLs the machine language program at memory location 2.

As long as button 1 is held down and button 2 is not pressed, random tones of random duration will be heard from the speaker. A listing of this program from the Apple II disassembler looks like this.

```
0002-   AD 30 C0    LDA    $C030
0005-   88          DEY
0006-   D0 04       BNE    $000C
0008-   C6 01       DEC    $01
000A-   F0 08       BEQ    $0014
000C-   CA          DEX
000D-   D0 F6       BNE    $0005
000F-   A6 00       LDX    $00
0011-   4C 02 00    JMP    $0002
0014-   60          RTS
```

If you use this range of memory for other than integer Basic programs you can clobber some routines. Locate the program in page 3 starting at address $300 (decimal 768). There is usually space available here (after DOS is loaded) for short programs. To use this program with Applesoft, change the random value generators to: P=INT((RND(1)*100)+20) and D=INT((RND(1)*100)+20).

(See correction in upcoming issue.)

READ and DATA

To do the same thing with the Applesoft READ . . . DATA combination, write the program something like this:

```
1000   REM   ** POKE DATA **
1010   REM
1020   LET MEMRY = 768
1030   READ BYTE: IF BYTE = 256 GOTO
       1100
1040   POKE MEMRY,BYTE
1050   LET MEMRY = MEMRY + 1
1060   GOTO 1030
1070   DATA   173,48,192,136,208,4,
       198,1,240
1080   DATA     8,202,208,246,166,0,
       76,0,3,96
1090   DATA   256
1100   RESTORE : RETURN
```

With this technique, the DATA statements contain the machine language program. Memory start is specified in line 1020 and incremented in line 1050. (Note the use of MEMRY as a variable. MEMORY would have looked like MEM OR Y because OR is a reserved word.) As long as no Byte value is greater than 255 ($FF) then the program continues to loop at line 1060. Only one POKE statement is used at line 1040. The advantage of using this method is in the addition of more Bytes of data. It is only necessary to add more DATA statements to increase the program to any size. Don't forget to RESTORE the READ . . . DATA pointer. An OUT OF DATA error would result when you tried to use the routine again. Another way to write this type of routine is shown below.

```
1000   REM   ** POKE DATA **
1010   REM
1020   FOR I = 768 TO 786
1030   READ J
1040   POKE I,J
1050   NEXT I
1060   RETURN
1070   DATA   173,48,192,136,208,4,
       198,1,240
1080   DATA   88,202,208,246,166,0,
       76,0,3,96
```

With this variation, you need to know the start and end addresses. Only the start address is needed with the first routine. Remember to convert the hexadecimal values in the program to decimal before including them in the DATA statements. Also, it is not necessary, except for clarity, to leave the escape value (256) on a separate line. A disadvantage is not being able to POKE in random with this routine.

String Parsing

Another way to put machine language programs into memory

involves the use of strings. Again, using the tone generating program as an example, here's a way to write the program; first in Integer then in Applesoft.

```
1000   REM   ** Parse & POKE **
1010   REM
1020   LET LOC = 768
1030   DIM H$(32)
1040   LET H$ = "AD30C088D004C601F
       008CAD0F6A6004C"
1050   GOSUB 1100
1060   LET H$ = "000360"
1070   GOSUB 1100
1080   RETURN
1090   REM  POKE H$ values into me
       mory
1100   FOR I = 1 TO  LEN (H$) STEP
       2
1110   LET H1 =  ASC (H$(I)) - 176
1120   IF H1 =  > 9 THEN H1 = H1 -
       7
1130   LET H2 =  ASC (H$(I + 1)) -
       176
1140   IF H2 > 9 THEN H2 = H2 - 7
1150   POKE LOC,H1 * 16 + H2
1160   LET LOC = LOC + 1
1170   NEXT I: RETURN
```

For Applesoft, the string H$ does not have to be dimensioned so line 1030 will not be needed. Down to line 1090, the program otherwise remains the same. The string parsing routine has a couple of changes. This is how it looks:

```
1100   FOR I + 1 TO  LEN (H$) STEP 2
1110   LET H1 =  ASC ( MID$ (H$,I,
       1)) - 48
1120   IF H1 =  > 9 THEN H1 = H1 - 7
1130   LET H2 =  ASC ( MID$ (H$,I +
       1,1)) - 48
1140   IF H2 > 9 THEN H2 = H2 - 7
1150   POKE LOC,H1 * 16 + H2
1160   LET LOC + LOC + 1
1170   NEXT I: RETURN
```

In both examples, the beginning address called LOC is $300. Additional program lines are needed to provide the pitch and duration values. Store these at two memory locations at the beginning or end of the machine language routine. I left them at 00 and 01 in this program.

The parsing-POKEing subroutine does a number of things for you. First, it converts each character to the ASCII value in lines 1110 and 1130. Next, the value is adjusted to keep the number within the HEX range of 0 to 15. This is done in lines 1120 and 1140. In line 1150, the ASCII pairs are converted to HEX numbers and POKEd into memory at location LOC. The difference in the numbers subtracted in lines 1110 and 1120 comes from the way each version of Basic handles the keyboard strobe bit. Integer leaves it on the ASCII value; Applesoft does not. The process continues until all the data pairs represented in string(s) H$ are put in memory.

This routine has all the advantages of the READ . . . DATA routine. You can easily change the program being put in memory by changing the contents of the strings. Also, you do not have to convert the HEX values to decimal; the program does all conversions for you.

Be careful when entering the data into the strings. It's easy to get mixed-up because of the compacted form used. Enter one string of 32 characters at a time. Then check it carefully **before** you press RETURN to enter it.

Using a technique like this, you can overlay the same small area of memory with a variety of programs. CALL a subroutine and RUN it as an option within your main program. Each one would run from the memory space. Of course, you could just link the machine language program to your Basic program . . . but that's another story.

Hold it There

Reviewing a long list of data requires using some technique to keep the data on the screen from passing by too fast. One way is to count the number of data lines printed. Then stop the program after 20 or so lines are printed. Something like this:

```
1000   READ D$(I): IF D$(I) = "END
       " GOTO ....
1010   PRINT D$(I)
1020 C = C + 1
1030   IF C <  > 20 GOTO 1050
1040   VTAB 22: PRINT "PRESS RETUR
       N TO CONTINUE": GET A$: IF A
       $ <  > CHR$ (13) GOTO 1040
1050   NEXT I
```

This Applesoft routine assumes you have initialized a FOR . . . NEXT loop to READ a list of DATA statements. The statements in line 1040 use the GET command to halt the program for an input. To insure that only the RETURN key is used, use CHR$(13) to accept only that key. An equivalent halt feature in Integer Basic, uses PEEKs to read the keyboard strobe ($C000) and then POKEs to reset the strobe ($C010).

```
1180 X =  PEEK ( - 16384): IF X <
     128 THEN 1180
1190  POKE  - 16368,0
```

Another possibility in Applesoft would include the SPEED command. If the output needs to be read while being listed, then slow the printing speed down by using — 990 SPEED=150. Don't forget to set SPEED=255 after the list routine is completed.

Text Typer

To do an equivalent print speed control in Integer Basic, use a string parsing routine to print each character separately. A delay between printed characters will provide the desired speed control. Here's a short routine to illustrate one way to do it.

```
100 DIM TXT$(40):S=-16336: REM  Spkr
110 CALL -936: GOTO 210
120 REM   ** Text Typer **
130 REM
135 FOR D=1 TO 200: NEXT D
140 FOR I=1 TO LEN(TXT$)
150 PRINT TXT$(I,I);
160 IF TXT$(I,I)=" " THEN 180
170 SOUND= PEEK (S)- PEEK (S)
180 FOR D=1 TO 50: NEXT D
190 NEXT I
200 RETURN
210 REM  ** Text Strings **
220 TXT$="The text typer prints thes
    e strings"
230 PRINT
240 GOSUB 120
250 TXT$="one character at a time wi
    th sound."
260 PRINT
270 GOSUB 120
280 VTAB 22: END
```

Lines 100 and 110 initialize the program parameters, clear the screen and direct the program to the text strings. The strings are identified starting at line 210. Each string calls the typing routine at line 120 after being identified (or reidentified). Add as many strings as desired at this point. The text subroutine uses a FOR . . . NEXT loop to parse the string one character at a time. Line 160 checks for spaces, and if the character is not a space, line 170 toggles the speaker to make a tapping sound. A short delay is produced in line 180 to give the desired typing effect. Line 190 goes back for more characters and line 200 RETURNs to the main program when all strings have been printed. To use the same program in Applesoft, change lines 150 and 160 like this:

```
150   PRINT  MID$ (TXT$,I,1);
160   IF  MID$ (TXT$,I,1) = " "
      THEN 180
```

Also, you can use strings that are subscripted variables in Applesoft. A loop outside the print loop can then be used to call the strings. If you want to direct the output of these programs to a printer, be sure to cancel the effect of these routines. Otherwise, the already slow printer will become even slower.

More Stoppers

The buttons on the game paddle can be used as program stoppers too. To do this, use a program line something like this:

```
300   IF  PEEK ( - 16287) > 127
      THEN 300
```

Put this line at the beginning of the loop that reads and lists your program. Each time you press and hold the button on paddle 1, the program will halt. You might want to make it halt with one push and start on another.

One more way to halt a program uses the Applesoft WAIT command. Insert this routine in your listing program and use any key to suspend and start the listing.

```
410   IF  PEEK ( - 16384) > 127 THEN
      POKE  - 16368,0
420   WAIT  - 16384,128,0: POKE  -
      16368,0
```

Sargon II

If you have been looking for an excellent chess program, try Sargon II. Several problems were reported with Sargon. There was no evidence of them during the games played on this version. Version 2 has 6 levels of play ranging in time-to-make-a-move from several seconds to several hours. I only tried levels 2 and 4. The playing time at these levels was quite acceptable. Not being a world-rated player, I won't judge playing skill. Several other reviewers however, have rated Sargon II above average. I know I had to work quite hard and found it could be beaten by multi-pronged offense. Sargon II plays what I consider an aggressive game and no vague moves were made (by Sargon anyway).

Implementation is good. Graphics are well done and use the entire screen. Moves are entered on a text page and become a log of game moves. The ESCape key is used to switch from text to graphics. There were two things I didn't like. There is no sound made when 'check' occurs, and you can't make a back-up copy of the tape. Hayden uses a scrambled load-and-go technique with the tape. I'm not in favor of programs I can't copy. As for the non-audible check, it's a matter of paying attention. The text page shows that check has occurred and check is obvious by the position of the pieces. A little 'beep' would be nice though.

After playing a few games, moves were quite easy to make. The algebraic system is used and reference to a grid map became only occasionally necessary. Entry mistakes and illegal moves are audible. Evidence that the program is working is included on the text page. Gives you that 'warm feeling' that all is OK when the computer is doing a long deep search. Board set-up for trying those 'mate-in-two' challenges is provided, and correction of moves is possible if you made the wrong choice. The choice of moves being considered by Sargon II is displayed on the text page. Sargon II by Dan and Kathe Spracklen is available at $29.95 from Hayden Book Co. and most computer stores. I found Sargon II quite enjoyable, and I think you will too.

File Builder
Basic On Videotape

Chuck Carpenter

April, 1980

Simple File Builder

One of the most useful features associated with the Apple II DOS is the use of files. Files can include anything from a matrix of data as a result of mathematical calculations to a sophisticated Data Base Management System. Listing 1 is an example of a simple file builder and manager. Random access, fixed length files, are used in this example. At this level, sequential files, of fixed length, would have been just as easy to implement. But that's not part of this story.

Most of the elements required to manage a file system are used in this example. Here's what has been included:

- Initialization Routines
- Error Detection Routine
- An Operating System Section
- Building New Files
- Adding New Records
- List Records with Suspension
- Keyword Search
- Record Editing

The initializing and error detecting sections are transparent to the user. The others are included in the operating section as menu options. Other menu selections could include printer selection and control, and sorting. We'll leave these for the future. Let's examine each section of the Simple File Builder and see what it's all about.

Initialize

After clearing the screen with HOME, the program is directed to line 2720 if an error occurs. In one part of the program an error is forced, and used to change the flow of the program. Otherwise, if an error occurs, the program returns to the options menu. If you use control C the effect is the same as an error. The forced error, #5 in line 2720, is an out-of-data error. When a new file is named and you try to read it, this error occurs. There are no records to read. The error is trapped and the program directs you to the Build New Records option. More on this when we get to the Operating System. Other tasks handled in the initialization routine are setting up the control D required to identify DOS commands, dimensioning the number of records (R$) and setting the initial count of the record counter (C).

Line 1110 turns the NOMON controls on. Sometimes it is desirable to see some of the data passing to or from the disk. In this program, I turned everything off. In line 1120, my clock routine is loaded into memory for future use. If there is no routine there, an error will be generated and mess things up. Leave it out or substitute something else here. Lines 1130 to 1160 print a heading and ask for the name of a file. Enter the name of your first file — something like Inventory or Apple II Articles — and press RETURN. The program now passes on through the System Variables listing to the Operating System.

Operating System

The Operating System is a section of the program including an option selection menu and control for directing input requests. Line 1350 CALLs a Mountain Hardware clock output routine. The date and time is available each time the options menu is selected. An error will occur if you try to use this command without a legitimate routine to CALL. In fact, a CALL to nothing in particular will blow the program. Options for the file are printed by lines 1380 to 1430. Existence of a file is checked in lines 1440 through 1480. If the file, named in line 1150, previously existed, then the number of records are posted on the screen along with the name of the file. If the file named is a new file and no records existed, then error #5 is generated.

These lines (1440 - 1480) use DOS commands to make the test for a file. Line 1440 is used to OPEN the file F$ with a length of 40 characters in each record. The contents of record 0 are READ in line 1450 to INPUT the value C, the record count. It is at this point that the OUT OF DATA error, #5, occurs and Build New Records option is selected for a new file. If the MON I,O,C commands were left on at this point, you would see the error displayed on the screen. If there is an existing file, the file is CLOSED in line 1460. The number of records and the name of the file are displayed in line 1470. Input for the option selection is accepted in line 1480 and tested for range in lines 1490 and 1500. Numbers greater than 5 return the program back to the options list again. A zero POKEs the DOS error register back to zero, CLOSEs the file, sets SPEED back to the fastest value, and ENDs the program. Line 1510 sends the program to the program line number corresponding to the file option selected. Branches occur according to the value of S, like this:

    S=1,   GOTO 1520 - Build the File
    S=2,   GOTO 1620 - Add Records
    S=3,   GOTO 1900 - List Records
    S=4,   GOTO 2110 - Edit a Record
    S=5,   GOTO 2350 -
            Keyword Search

Because numbers greater than 5 are trapped and zero stops the program, branching to the requested option is quite reliable.

New and Bigger

Building a new file and adding records options do essentially the same thing. The new file has to start at one and new record adds start at the last record plus one. Otherwise, the file must first be OPENed and prepared for accepting records. Let's start with BUILD FILE and detail the steps used for this segment of the program.

To start the file building process, a short reminder of the option and file name are printed by line 1560. The named file is OPENed in line 1570 for a length of 40 characters. This length was chosen because the output is listed only on the screen. Next, line 1580 uses a control D to halt DOS action. Doing this prevents further program activity from creating garbage in the file. Line 1770 prints the current record number and waits for INPUT. A test for file END is included in line 1780. If the input is END, the program branches to line 1840 and record processing is concluded. Line 1790 makes DOS active again for a WRITE and line 1800 PRINTs (or WRITEs) the record to the DOS buffer. The buffer accepts up to 256 characters and then transfers them automatically to the disk. The buffer contents get transferred to the disk when the file is CLOSEd, too. DOS action is stopped again in line 1810, the record counter is incremented in line 1820 and the program returns for another record at line 1830. This loop

continues until the input equals END in line 1780 and the branch to line 1840 is taken.

No new record was added when END was typed. So the counter (C) is decremented and the result printed in line 1840. DOS is again activated and the current record count is written into record zero. Lines 1850 and 1860 do the record count work, and line 1870 CLOSEs the file. In line 1880, a GET command in combination with CHR$(13) is used to exclude all key input except RETURN. When RETURN is pressed, the program returns to the option menu.

Adding records uses two more steps than starting a new file. First, the previous record count is READ in from record zero. Then, the last record entered is READ. This is accomplished in lines 1700 and 1720. The record number and the record are printed in line 1740. Having this information on the screen provides a model for subsequent entries. The record count is incremented in line 1760 and the rest is the same as new record processing.

Listing Records

Up to line 2000, the List program functions are much the same as processing new and added records. Line 2010 starts a loop that lists the contents of the file. A file suspension routine using the WAIT command in combination with a PEEK at the keyboard and a POKE at the keyboard reset is included in line 2020. Each record is INPUT (READ) to the DOS buffer and printed on the screen. When all records are listed, the file is CLOSEd and control is returned to the options menu.

Use of the list option allows scanning the file for one or more records. Speed control is another feature that could be added for listing records. The suspension routine stops and starts the list routine. But, the records still go by quite fast on the screen. Include a line to set the Speed to 125 at the beginning of the listing loop. A header to describe the contents of the file is another possible option. Add a line to put titles on the fields and keep it on the screen with a POKE 34,N.

    1950 PRINT"DESCRIPTION....COST
         ...DATE PUR"
    1955 POKE 34,4
    .
    .
    .
    2006 SPEED=125
    .
    .
    .
    2096 POKE 34,0 : SPEED=255

New line 1955 holds the top of the screen at 4 lines until the listing is completed. Be sure to disable or reset

any special controls you use. You'll get some funny results otherwise.

Now, suppose you would also like to add the cost figures in the cost column. The records have been used as one continuous string, so something besides adding simple variables together is needed. In this example program, the cost figures start in column 22 and are 7 characters wide. Add lines to add the figures in these columns like this:

    2004 LET T=0
    .
    .
    2065 LET ST=VAL(MID$(R$,22,7)):
         T=T+ST
    .
    .
    2074 PRINT:PRINT TAB (24)"$";
         INT(T*100+.5)/100

Each time a record is READ, line 2055 extracts the VAL of the cost column as a subtotal (ST) and starts summing the total (T). When the list is complete, the final total is printed with a $ under the cost column. If you change the position of the cost field, be sure to adjust MID$ and Total TAB too.

Edit a Record

To edit a record with this very simple editor, you must know the number of the record(s) to be edited. The technique used **is** quite simple, but effective for short and simple records. After requesting the record number, the file is opened and prepared for reading records. The requested record will be displayed on the screen with the record number. After it's displayed, you get a chance to change it or leave it alone. If the record was the wrong one, just press N and the record is stored back on the disk unchanged. A Y to change the record displays the INPUT prompt (?) on the screen. You can then type in a new line, being careful to follow the exact format. Or, you can use escape D to move the cursor up to the displayed record. Then use the right arrow key to move to the part of the record to be changed. Retype the changes as needed and move the cursor to the end of the line. Press RETURN. The new record will be put on the disk in place of the old one. A bit more sophisticated approach would use VTAB and HTAB to position the INPUT prompt at the beginning of the line to be changed. The step to use escape D to move the cursor is not needed if this is done. After all changes are made, the program returns to the option menu. (Remember, I said it was a simple editor.)

Keyword Search

This routine is useful for finding all the items with the same name or things in the same year or month and so on. For most of the files I am using, I prefer to use a search rather than a sort. For nice ordered lists of things though, a sort is the only way. But, that's a story for another time. Keyword search was described in detail in the January '80 Apple Cart. Most of the detail included opening, reading and closing Apple II DOS files. These details have been covered here too, so on to the meat of the program.

After requesting the keyword to be located, the file is OPENed and prepared for READing records. A loop for calling-up each record starts at line 2510. Each record is then scanned, 1 character at a time, for the keyword. If a keyword is found, the record is displayed and a flag is set. The program returns for the next record and continues the search. If no keywords were found, a prompt to look for another keyword is displayed. If records were found containing the keyword, you are also given the option to make changes. The option to search for more keywords is also displayed. Answering No to both of the prompts returns the program to the option menu.

More Zing

Several times during this discussion the simplicity of the program has been emphasized. There are a number of features that would make using file more productive. Each improvement would make the program more confusing and difficult to explain. A program for cataloging magazine articles from Southeastern Software uses a number of clever features. The human factors of using the program were greatly improved by the techniques used. Inclusion of sort routines and more ideas for building records and formatting will be included in future columns.

Basic on Videotape

Videocassettes teaching computer applications and programming fundamentals are now available to businesses and schools. The concept, called Evolution 1 (TM), was created by Dr. Portia Isaacson of Electronic Data Systems (EDS) in Dallas.

Currently available are 4 tapes of interest to potential Apple owners (and other beginning Basic programmers). The videotape presentation, using familiar analogies, makes no assumptions about prior knowledge of computers or programming. Lesson 1 starts with instructions on getting the computer operating. The viewer is then taught to use several Basic programming commands in a refreshing, unhurried manner. By the end of the fourth tape, the viewer has acquired sufficient skill to proceed with confidence, to more advanced challenges. Each tape is accompanied by a study booklet. The booklets are easy to use and effectively reinforce learning through color highlighted text and representations of a video screen. The booklets could be used separately but all the supporting information from the tape presentation would be lost. Additional tapes, teaching more advanced Basic, are planned.

Other videotapes in the Evolution 1 (TM) series include 2 Point Of Sale (POS) tapes and 2 Business application tapes. The POS tapes are designed to support retail sales people with technical information. Business applications illustrate techniques for using a small computer in a small business. Three new lessons are planned for the business series too.

The newest entries include an 8 tape series titled 'Little Computers . . . See How They Run.' These tapes describe various microcomputer features and accessories including detail of the microprocessor chip itself.

Tapes are available to computer retailers, distributors, educational people and corporations on a lease basis. The lease rate is $35.00 per month per tape with a 6 tape minimum. Tapes can be mixed in combinations. These tapes can be exchanged during the year for a $40.00 fee. One set of study booklets comes with each tape series. Additional sets cost $10.00 to $20.00 per set.

For more information, call Evolution 1 at 800-527-0278 (in Texas, 214-661-4070), or write them at 14580 Midway Road, Dallas, TX 75234. Also, look for these videocassettes at your local computer store.

```
  RUN

HOME INVENTORY FILE MANAGER
----------------------------
ENTER THE FILE NAME - HOME.INVEN

1980 01/14 20:46:09.640

FILE OPTIONS:

  1. BUILD NEW RECORDS
  2. ADD MORE RECORDS
  3. LIST RECORDS
  4. EDIT A RECORD
  5. KEYWORD SEARCH
  0. END THE PROGRAM

FILE 'HOME.INVEN' CONTAINS 5 RECORDS !

WHICH NUMBER - 3

LIST TEXT FILE - HOME.INVEN

1     COUCH/DAY BED........1134.95..02/77
2     LOVE SEAT............0395.89..02/77
3     REFRIGERATOR........0895.79..09/78
4     WASHER..............0379.55..09/78
5     CASETTE DECK........1145.37..12/79

PRESS RETURN TO CONTINUE -
```

```
WHICH NUMBER - 3

LIST TEXT FILE - HOME.INVEN

1     COUCH/DAY BED........1134.95..02/77
2     LOVE SEAT............0395.89..02/77
3     REFRIGERATOR........0895.79..09/78
4     WASHER..............0379.55..09/78
5     CASETTE DECK........1145.37..12/79

                  $3951.55

PRESS RETURN TO CONTINUE -

WHICH NUMBER - 5

KEYWORD SEARCH - HOME.INVEN

KEYWORD - 09/78

3 REFRIGERATOR........0895.79..09/78

4 WASHER..............0379.55..09/78

DO YOU WANT TO EDIT ? Y/N ?N

TRY ANOTHER KEYWORD ? Y/N ?N

PRESS RETURN TO CONTINUE -
```

```
MASTER FILE: (6,2) DISCOGRAPHY DATA FILE.MST

FIELD #     DESCRIPTION             TYPE
-------     -----------             ----
    1       TITLE                   45,A
    2       ARTIST                  35,A
    3       COMPOSER                50,A
    4       PRODUCER                30,A
    5       LABEL                   20,A
    6       DATE                    6,N
    7       POSITION                3,N
    8       CONDITION               15,A
    9       REMARKS                 20,A


SORT #      DESCRIPTION
------      -----------
    1       TITLE
    2       ARTIST
            *LABEL
            **DATE
    3       LABEL
            *DATE
    4       POSITION
```

FIGURE 1

```
1000   REM ***********************
1010   REM * SIMPLE FILE BUILDER *
1020   REM * BY: CHUCK CARPENTER *
1030   REM ***********************
1040   :
1050   REM   ** INITIALIZE **
1060   REM   ***************
1070   :
1080   HOME
1090   ONERR  GOTO 2720
1100   LET D$ =  CHR$ (4): DIM R$(200):C = 1
1110   PRINT D$;"NOMON I,O,C"
1120   PRINT D$;"BLOAD B.TIME": REM   DATE & TIME
1130   HOME : VTAB (2): PRINT "HOME INVENTORY FILE MANAG
       ER"
1140   FOR I = 1 TO 27: PRINT "-";: NEXT I: PRINT
1150   INPUT "ENTER THE FILE NAME - ";F$
1160   :
1170   REM   ** SYSTEM VARIABLES **
1180   REM   ********************
1190   :
1200   REM   F$= FILE NAME
1210   REM   D$= CONTROL D
1220   REM   R$= FILE RECORD
1230   REM   A$= RETURN (CHR$(13))
1240   REM   Q$= LOCAL RESPONSE
1250   REM   I&J LOCAL VARIABLES
1260   REM   C = RECORD COUNT
1270   REM   S = OPTION SELECTION
1280   REM   R = RECORD # TO EDIT
1290   REM   K$= KEYWORD TO SEARCH
1300   REM   K = SEARCH FLAG
1310   :
1320   REM   ** OPERATING SYSTEM **
1330   REM   ********************
1340   :
1350   CALL 900: REM   DATE & TIME
1360   PRINT : PRINT "FILE OPTIONS:"
1370   PRINT
1380   PRINT " 1. BUILD NEW RECORDS"
1390   PRINT " 2. ADD MORE RECORDS"
1400   PRINT " 3. LIST RECORDS"
1410   PRINT " 4. EDIT A RECORD"
1420   PRINT " 5. KEYWORD SEARCH"
1430   PRINT " 0. END THE PROGRAM"
1440   PRINT : PRINT D$"OPEN";F$;",L40"
1450   PRINT D$"READ";F$;",R";0: INPUT C
1460   PRINT D$"CLOSE";F$;""
1470   PRINT "FILE '";F$;"' CONTAINS ";C;" RECORDS !"
1480   PRINT : INPUT "WHICH NUMBER - ";S
1490   IF S > 5 GOTO 1350
1500   IF S = 0 THEN  PRINT : PRINT : PRINT "DONE": POKE
       216,0: PRINT D$"CLOSE";F$;"": SPEED= 255: END
1510   ON S GOTO 1520,1620,1900,2110,2350
1520   :
1530   REM   ** BUILD THE FILE **
1540   REM   *******************
1550   :
1560   HOME : VTAB (2): PRINT "BUILD FILE - ";F$;" "
1570   PRINT D$"OPEN";F$;",L40"
1580   PRINT D$
1590   GOTO 1770
1600   :
1610   REM   ** ADD RECORDS **
1620   REM   ***************
1630   :
1640   HOME
1650   PRINT : VTAB (2): PRINT "ADD FILE RECORDS - ";F
       $;"": PRINT
1660   PRINT D$"OPEN";F$;",L40"
1670   PRINT D$"READ";F$;",R";0
1680   INPUT C
1690   PRINT D$"READ";F$;",R";C
1700   INPUT R$(C)
1710   PRINT D$: PRINT
1720   PRINT "R";C;"";: PRINT  TAB( 6)R$(C)
1730   PRINT
1740   LET C = C + 1
1750   :
1760   :
1770   PRINT "R";C;" ";: INPUT R$(C)
1780   IF R$(C) = "END" GOTO 1840
1790   PRINT D$"WRITE";F$;",R";C
1800   PRINT R$(C)
1810   PRINT D$
1820   LET C = C + 1
1830   GOTO 1770
1840   LET C = C - 1: PRINT : PRINT C: PRINT
1850   PRINT D$"WRITE";F$;",R";0
1860   PRINT C
1870   PRINT D$"CLOSE";F$;""
1880   PRINT : PRINT "PRESS RETURN TO CONTINUE - ";: GET
       A$: IF A$ =  CHR$ (13) THEN  HOME : VTAB (5): GOTO
       1350
1890   HOME : GOTO 1880
1900   :
1910   REM   ** LIST RECORDS **
1920   REM   ****************
1930   :
1940   HOME
1950   PRINT : PRINT "LIST TEXT FILE - ";F$;""
1960   PRINT
1970   PRINT D$"OPEN";F$;",L40"
1980   PRINT D$"READ";F$;",R";0
1990   INPUT C
2000   PRINT D$
2010   FOR I = 1 TO C
2020   IF  PEEK ( - 16384) > 127 THEN  POKE  - 16368,0:
       WAIT - 16384,128,0: POKE  - 16368,0
2030   PRINT D$"READ";F$;",R";I
2040   INPUT R$(I)
2050   PRINT D$
2060   PRINT I; TAB( 4)R$(I)
2070   NEXT I
2080   PRINT D$"CLOSE";F$;""
2090   PRINT : PRINT "PRESS RETURN TO CONTINUE - ";: GET
       A$: IF A$ =  CHR$ (13) THEN  HOME : VTAB (5): GOTO
       1350
2100   HOME : GOTO 2090
2110   :
2120   REM   ** EDIT A RECORD **
2130   REM   *****************
2140   :
2150   HOME
2160   PRINT : PRINT "EDIT FILE RECORD - ";F$;"": PRINT

2170   PRINT "ENTER RECORD NUMBER - ";: INPUT R: PRINT
2180   PRINT D$"OPEN";F$;",L40"
2190   PRINT D$"READ";F$;",R";R
2200   INPUT R$(R)
2210   PRINT D$
2220   PRINT "RECORD ";R;" CHANGES - 35 CHARACTERS MAX."

2230   PRINT : PRINT "RECORD ";R;" ="
2240   PRINT " ";: PRINT R$(R)
2250   PRINT : INPUT "DO YOU WANT TO CHANGE IT - Y/N ";Q
       $: PRINT : IF Q$ = "N" GOTO 2320
2260   INPUT R$(R)
2270   :
2280   PRINT D$"WRITE";F$;",R";R
2290   PRINT R$(R)
2300   PRINT D$"CLOSE";F$;""
2310   VTAB 17
2320   PRINT "ANY MORE RECORDS Y/N ";: INPUT Q$: IF Q$ =
       "Y" GOTO 2110
2330   PRINT : PRINT "PRESS RETURN TO CONTINUE - ";: GET
       A$: IF A$ =  CHR$ (13) THEN  HOME : VTAB (5): GOTO
       1350
2340   HOME : GOTO 2330
2350   :
2360   REM   ** KEYWORD SEARCH **
2370   REM   ******************
2380   :
2390   HOME
2400   PRINT : PRINT "KEYWORD SEARCH - ";F$;""
2410   PRINT : INPUT "KEYWORD - ";K$
2420   LET K = 0
2430   PRINT D$"OPEN";F$;",L40"
2440   PRINT D$"READ";F$;",R";0
2450   INPUT C
2460   PRINT D$
2470   FOR J = 1 TO C
2480   PRINT D$"READ";F$;",R";J
2490   INPUT R$(J)
2500   PRINT D$
2510   FOR I = 1 TO 40 -  LEN (K$)
2520   IF  MID$ (R$(J),I, LEN (K$)) <  > K$ GOTO 2550
2530   PRINT : PRINT J;: PRINT " ";: PRINT R$(J)
2540   LET K = K + 1
2550   NEXT I
2560   NEXT J: PRINT
2570   IF K > 0 GOTO 2610
2580   PRINT : PRINT "NOTHING FOUND - ": PRINT "TRY ANOT
       HER KEY WORD ? Y/N ";
2590   INPUT Q$: IF Q$ = "Y" GOTO 2350
2600   IF Q$ = "N" GOTO 2660
2610   PRINT D$"CLOSE";F$;""
2620   PRINT : PRINT "DO YOU WANT TO EDIT ? Y/N ";
2630   INPUT Q$: IF Q$ = "Y" GOTO 2110
2640   PRINT : PRINT "TRY ANOTHER KEYWORD ? Y/N ";
2650   INPUT Q$: IF Q$ = "Y" GOTO 2350
2660   PRINT : PRINT "PRESS RETURN TO CONTINUE - ";: GET
       A$: IF A$ =  CHR$ (13) THEN  HOME : VTAB (5): GOTO
       1350
2670   HOME : GOTO 2660
2680   :
2690   REM   ** ERROR ROUTINE **
2700   REM   *****************
2710   :
2720   IF  PEEK (222) <  > 5 THEN  PRINT "PROCESSING ERR
       OR": SPEED= 255: GOTO 1350
2730   IF  PEEK (222) = 5 THEN  PRINT : PRINT "THIS IS A
       NEW FILE": FOR I = 1 TO 5000: NEXT : GOTO 1520
2740   :
2750   REM   CRC - 5 JAN 1979
2760   :
```

LISTING 1

207

Apple II vs. Apple II Plus •Integer to Applesoft Beginner's Assembly Language Empirical Music

Chuck Carpenter

May, 1980

Apple II vs Apple II Plus

Confusion over the advantages and disadvantages of the two basic models of the Apple II has created problems for some buyers. The Apple II plus has been advertised as an "Improvement" of the Apple II. Whether or not there has been any real improvement, is a matter of opinion. Here's a summary of some of the features:

Apple II
- Integer Basic - standard
- Mini-assembler, disassembler
- Number range ±32767
- Whole number (integers) only
- Fast speed
- Direct assembly language access
- Sweet 16 interpreter
- Floating point assembly language routines
- Limited string functions for text

Apple II plus
- Applesoft Basic - standard
- Autostart ROM
- Floating point (decimal) numbers
- Number range ±9.99999999 E37
- Expanded string functions
- Extended programming commands

The significant difference is that you can't run Basic programs written for one on the other. And conversion from one to the other is not a simple task either. More on that later.

By adding a $200.00 language card to either unit, you can include all the features in one machine. Considering that most currently available software is written in Integer Basic, it appears that the Apple II with Applesoft in RAM (on tape or disk) is a better choice. That is, a better choice if you want to avoid the cost of a language card and your computing interest is only a hobby. For some business and scientific applications where the extended capabilities of Applesoft are needed, the Apple II plus is a better choice.

If you're interested in becoming familiar with and using assembly language, then buy the Apple II. The Apple II plus with autostart eliminates most of the useful assembly language capability. Of course, the use of assembly language is often an area of confusion for the newcomer. Assembly language programs are used frequently in parts of other programs and as complete operating systems. As you become more and more familiar with the capabilities of the Apple, the mysteries disappear. Don't limit your possibilities. Remember: everything is easy once you understand it.

One more point. Most computer retailers are selling both versions for the same price. There is really no difference in the hardware you get; just the language implemented in the basic machine. Have a serious talk with the store people (or buy elsewhere) if you're charged more for an Apple II plus.

Integer Basic Card

If you want to have all the features of both versions of the Apple, then get the Apple II plus with the Integer Basic cards. There are some advantages to doing this too—the Programmers Aid ROM is included. In addition to getting all the assembly language capability, you have all the useful features of the programmers aid ROM. For instance:

- Renumber and Append (Integer Basic)
- Tape verify (Basic)
- Tape verify (binary)
- Relocate (binary)
- RAM test program
- Music routines
- High Res graphics routines

With this combination, you can do anything an Apple can do. It's easy to switch from one language system to the other and you'll never be frustrated by not being able to use one of those really great programs.

Converting Integer to Applesoft

There have been several attempts to write a program to convert Integer Basic to Applesoft. For short, uncomplicated programs, this can sometimes be easily done. The more sophisticated the program (and the programmer) the more difficult the task is. The hard way is to type in the program, making syntax and command changes as you go. Provided, of course, that you're aware of all the differences. Another way creates a text file out of the Integer Basic program and recreates the same program in Applesoft. A way to do this was described in Apple's Contact #5. Here's how they did it (note that @ means Control D):

```
0 PRINT" @ OPEN X"
1 POKE 33,33
2 PRINT" @ WRITE X"
3 LIST
4 PRINT" @ CLOSE"
5 END
```

This program could have been written all on one line, too. Enter the routine anywhere in your Integer Basic program. A line 0 is most convenient. Don't forget, you need a Disk II system to do this. Once entered, RUN the new program. A file named "X" will be OPENed and the program you're working on will be listed into that file. After the disk stops, type FP to change to Applesoft and EXEC the file. Your program is now in Applesoft. Of course, you had to have both Basics in the Apple being used to do this (your own or a friend's). A program could be written to completely interpret from one language to the other. But I doubt that anyone would want to pay the price for it, and it probably wouldn't fit in an Apple anyway.

Now that you have gotten the Integer program in Applesoft, the real fun (?) begins. You will need to search for and change all the command and syntax differences. Let's look at a comparison list of these differences.

- Input commands
      IB - INPUT"APPLES", A use a comma
      AS-INPUT"APPLES"; A use a semicolon
- String commands
      IB - PRINT A$(I,I)
      AS - PRINT MID$(A$,I,1)
There is only one form of string command in Integer. Applesoft also includes the LEFT$, RIGHT$, VAL and STR$ commands.
- MOD functions
      IB - POKE 1, TRY MOD 256
      AS - POKE 1, TRY - INT(TRY/256) *256
      or
      IB - Z = X   MOD Y
      AS - Z = X-INT(X/Y)*Y
- IF statements
      IB - IF X THEN 200 : GOTO 500
      AS - IF X   THEN 200
            GOTO 500
In Integer, if X is false (0) the program reads the next statement following the colon. In Applesoft, if X is false the program drops to the NEXT line no.
- Inequalities
      IB - IF X#Y   THEN 500
      AS - IF X < > Y   THEN 500
Integer uses a # sign to mean does-not-equal.
- Variable names
      IB - TRY1 = TRY2 + TRY3
      AS - T1 = T2 + T3
Applesoft recognizes only the first 2

characters as the variable.
- Random numbers
      IB - X = RND(16)
      AS - X = INT(16*RND(1))
Another way to generate random integers in Applesoft uses the random variable format, X%.
      AS - X% = 16*RND(1)
- Integers
      IB -TRY1 = TRY2
      AS - T1% = T2%
This is the same result as changing to random integers in the previous example. It is not always necessary to change the variables to integers. The program will run faster and use less memory if you do.
- DIM statements
      IB - DIM A$(20)
means, 1 string 20 characters long.
      AS - DIM A$(20)
means, 20 strings up to 255 characters long. Remove all DIM statements from the program. You do need to dimension the quantity of AS strings if there are more than 10.
- TAB statements
Change all IB TAB statements to AS HTAB statements.
- Computed GOTO s
      IB - GOTO 1000 + X * 100
      AS - ON   X   GOTO   1100,1200, 1300,1400
If 4 program options exist, then branching will occur as a function of the selected option number (X = 1 to 4).
- Page 0
Relocate any machine code used by IB in page 0. Some of page 3 is usually available. Or, move LOMEM up to make room above $800. Change all CALLs accordingly.
Now you can see why I called it fun (?). If you are real serious about converting Integer to Applesoft, it can be done. But I would opt for the Integer Basic card if at all possible.

Assembly Language

With the built-in assembly language capability of the Apple, it seems a shame that a beginners guide is not available. There are a number of books available that describe assembly language for the type of microprocessor in the Apple II. All of them assume prior knowledge of fundamental principles. For those of you who would like to begin at the beginning, let's attempt a tutorial for the neophyte assembly language programmer.

Background

The differences between Apple II, with and without Autostart, and the

Apple II plus relative to using the Apple II monitor need to be known. The monitor is a collection of assembly language programs. Included in these programs are routines to handle input from the keyboard, translation of commands to computer functions and display of results on the video screen. In fact, the ease with which you can do things with your Apple is the result of programs in the monitor. Imagine if you had to enter each key stroke, one character at a time, with a group of panel switches. We'll get back to the monitor later.

Here's how to get the monitor with each version of the Apple. The result is to see the asterisk (*) prompt.

- Apple II - without Applesoft ROM; Power on and press Reset. Press Reset any other time too.
- Apple II - with Applesoft ROM; Press Reset as without ROM except make sure the switch on the ROM card is in the Integer Basic position (Press Control + B to check).
- Apple II - with autostart; Autostart will automatically put you in the resident Basic language. You will need to type CALL-151 + Return to get to the monitor. Same conditions with the ROM card switch.
- Apple II plus - with Integer card; It is also possible to get into the Apple monitor without the integer cards. But, you won't be able to write assembly language programs. There is no mini-assembler available. A CALL-151 will put you in the monitor. From this point you can dump memory, modify memory and move memory. But, without the Integer card, that's it. A future column will describe the use of an assembler. The use of a full fledged assembler will solve the problem in the Apple II plus without integer Basic capability.

Monitor Commands

A variety of commands is available for your use when the asterisk prompt is present.

- List and dump memory
- Modify and move memory
- Examine and verify memory
- Save to, and load from, cassette
- Hexadecimal arithmetic
- Mini-assembler (Integer system only)
- Many others

The various options and commands and other features of the Apple II monitor are found on pages 68 through 75 in the old Apple II Reference Manual (the red book). Even more information on the monitor can be found on pages 39 through 66 in the new Apple II Reference Manual. Incidentally, the new manual is great. If you're serious about learning the inner-workings of your computer, this is the book to have. Now, back to assembly language.

Binary and HEX

If you understand the relationships between binary, decimal and hexadecimal numbers, then the discussion of assembly language will be easier. The range of addresses used to define memory location is $0000 to $FFFF. The $ is used to indicate a HEX number. In decimal, the range is 0 to 65535 or 65536 memory locations. There is no need to consider the binary value of the address. Only the data found at the memory location are used. The address lets you find where the data **are**.

Data in a memory cell is called a byte. A byte is made up of 8 bits, and each bit is represented by a '1' or a '0.' A one means the bit is on; a zero means the bit is off. Four bits, called a nybble, represent a hexadecimal number. It takes two hexadecimal numbers—nybbles—to represent the binary data byte in a memory location. You will want to learn the relationships between binary, hexadecimal and decimal numbers. In assembly language programming, it is often necessary to know the binary pattern in a memory location. You will become comfortable using binary and hexadecimal numbers as you get more skilled with assembly language programming. Much more on computer number systems will be found in the listed references. Also, study the memory maps found in your Apple reference manuals and programming books. These will help you understand how Apple's memory is used.

Assembly Language

There are at least 2 ways you can enter assembly language into your Apple II. One is to hand write the program, hand assemble it and use monitor routines to enter it one byte at a time. The other uses the Apple II mini-assembler. Before we try to write and enter an assembly language program, some knowledge of the parts of a program is needed. Then, we will look at writing assembly language programs and converting them to machine language. Some of the features of the Apple's 6502 microprocessor will be examined, too.

The Instructions

Microprocessors use a set of codes for commands and instructions. The 6502 microprocessor has a set of instructions that has 55 codes. These codes are called **mnemonics** (ni-mon-ick—this means easy to remember). By themselves, the mnemonic instruction codes can't tell the 6502 what needs to be done. Additional information called an **operand** is used with most instruction codes.

Mnemonic	Operand
LDA	#$C1
JSR	$FDED
RTS	

This example is called an assembly language program. In order to use this little routine, it must be converted to machine language. This is the job of an assembler program. We will use the Apple II mini-assembler later in this article to write a program.

Operation Codes

Each instruction code also has a corresponding Hex value called an operation code. These opcodes (short for operation codes) are recognized by the system monitor and converted to binary values for the 6502. Actually, the computer only recognizes binary numbers. If you were to examine the memory cells during program execution, you would only find patterns of 1's and 0's. To make it easier for you to converse with the computer, binary has been converted to a coded machine language. One step above hexadecimal machine language is assembly language. Assembly language uses mnemonic instructions called opcodes, and data called operands to simplify programming. Pages 100 through 105 in the 'red book' and pages 118 through 128 in the new Reference Manual include all the 6502 instructions (mnemonics), opcodes and address modes. These are also included in the reference material.

Address Modes

Operands used with each instruction code identify which opcode to use for the instruction. Operands also tell the computer which address mode to use. Address modes instruct the computer to do something specific with the contents of the operand. There are several possible address modes that can be used with many of the instructions. Depending on the results and type of program, different address modes are possible with each instruction code. We will only use 3 address modes in the examples used here.

More About the 6502

Microprocessors, like the 6502, have internal read/write (RAM) memory called registers. These registers allow the programmer to move instructions and data into and out of the microprocessor. One register is called the accumulator (or A register). Two others are the X and Y registers. The accumulator is the most important register in the 6502. Many program steps will put data in the accumulator then put it into some memory location. Sometimes an operation is performed on the value in the accumulator directly. Two operations that occur in this process are called **load** and **store**. Load causes a value to be placed in a 6502 register. Store takes data from a 6502 register and puts it into an external memory location.

Instructions, Addresses and Opcodes

Instruction codes used for accumulator operations are LDA and STA. The three letter mnemonic is made up from characters in the instruction.

LDA (**L**oa**D** **A**ccumulator)
STA (**ST**ore **A**ccumulator)

The instruction LDA means two things: 1 - lead the value in the operand into the accumulator or, 2 - load the value found at the address in the operand into the accumulator. The 6502 knows which to do by the way you write the operand. Depending on the form used, the addressing mode is defined accordingly. Here are two examples for the LDA instruction.

1. LDA #$C1 (Immediate addressing mode)
2. LDA $0300 (Absolute addressing mode)

In example 1, the # sign (using 6502 conventions) indicates that the accumulator is to be loaded with $C1. (Remember that a $ in front of a number means HEX.) Example 2 indicates to the 6502 that it is to get the value found at memory location $0300, and load it into the accumulator.

Instruction STA means that the 6502 will take the value presently in the accumulator and store it in the address specified by the operand. For example, STA $0300 means take the value in the accumulator and store it in location $0300. Two other instructions we will use are JSR (**J**ump to **Sub**Routine) and RTS (**Re**Turn from **S**ubroutine).

Remember we said that mnemonic instruction codes could be represented by HEX opcodes. Here is a list of the codes used so far:

Opcode	Instruction	Address Mode
$A9	LDA	Immediate
$AD	LDA	Absolute
$8D	STA	Absolute
$20	JSR	Absolute
$60	RTS	Implied

As mentioned earlier, there are many instruction codes, addressing modes and opcodes in the 6502 instruction set. Check them out in the reference material.

Assembling a Program

Let's write a short program using everything discussed so far. Here's how to do it. First, select the starting point in memory. There is space for short programs at address $0300. So our program will start there. (Otherwise, use any space in memory not used by Apple programs; consult the memory maps.) Now write the assembly language part of the program with appropriate operands. Then look up the opcodes and hand assemble the machine code. The starting address of our program, $0300, is the beginning of page 3 of memory. (Page 0 starts at $0000 and ends at $00FF, page 1 is from $0100 to $01FF, page 2 from $0200 to $02FF, page 3 from $0300 to $03FF and so on. There are a total of 256,256-byte pages.)

New conventions introduced in the sample program will include the single byte, two byte and three byte instructions, and also the arrangement of the bytes in the three byte instruction. Depending on the instruction used and the data in the operand field, the opcode is assembled with the required number of data bytes. Immediate mode addressing uses the opcode (always first) then one byte of data. Absolute mode uses two bytes of data. Following the opcode, the least significant byte of the data in the operand is entered, then the most significant byte. Here's an illustration of the concept.

```
$C030 ←—Hex address (operand)
   └—Least significant byte
   └—Most significant byte
```

Implied mode (the RTS instruction, for example) uses only single byte opcodes. The instruction itself includes all the information needed for the desired end result. Instruction RTS is used when you call one program from another. The return from subroutine returns you back to

a point where you want to continue in your program (or subroutine).

Now, back to our program. The program we will write will:

1- load the accumulator (LDA with a value

2- jump to a subroutine (JSR) that prints the contents of the accumulator on the screen

3- jump to another subroutine (JSR) to beep the bell, and

4- end the program (RTS).

First, write the assembly language program that will do these things. I'll provide you with the value for the accumulator and the subroutine addresses for the operands to get things going (see Figure 1).

Our program will start at address $0300 and will use consecutive memory locations starting with the opcode for LDA immediate. The next memory location will contain the data in the operand. An opcode always has to be the first byte of data in your program. Otherwise. the computer won't be able to recognize legitimate instructions. Often, some form of LDA will be the first instruction. Let's begin.

```
0300- A9
0301- C1
```

Look up the opcodes for each of the other mnemonic instruction codes and write them down. (we did this earlier). Now, write the opcode for JSR in the next consecutive memory location, followed by the data in the operand. Remember the sequence of the bytes of data in the operand.

```
0302- 20
0303- ED
0304- FD
```

Now do the same thing with the next JSR and operand.

```
0305- 20
0306- E4
0307- FB
```

And, complete the program with the single byte instruction, JSR.

```
0308- 60
```

Of course, the complete program won't look like this in the Apple mini-assembler format. The following example represents how it will look.

```
*300L
```

	Machine Code	Assembly Code	
0300-	A9 C1	LDA	#$C1
0302-	20 ED FD	JSR	$FDED
0305-	20 E4 FB	JSR	$FBE4
0308-	60	RTS	

Note that the opcode follows each address and is followed by the data as defined by the operand.

Apple II mini-assembler

Now let's try the mini-assembler to write a program. In the following sequence, you will be typing in the underlined characters. Computer response is not underlined. Also, it is not necessary to use the $ character or leading zeros. The mini-assembler takes care of these things. The character Ƀ (slash b) means to type a blank with the space bar. Remember, too, to type Return when you want your entries to be accepted (see Figure 2).

You have just assembled a program starting at location $0300. Notice that it is not necessary to leave spaces in your entries either. The assembler can tell what is what.

Now run the program using the following sequence.

$300G   ; run program from assembler

    A   ; see an A, hear a beep

Figure 1

Inst.	Operand	Comment
LDA	#$C1	; load the accumulator with $C1
JSR	$FDED	; jump to character-out routine
JSR	$FBE4	; jump to bell routine
RTS		; make a definite return

Figure 2

Step	Action		Comments
1.	**F666G**		; enter mini-assem. at F666
2.	**!□**		; see prompt and cursor
3.	**300:LDA #C1**		; first line to assemble
4.	0300- A9 C1	LDA #$C1	; see assembled output
5.	**ƀJSR FDED**		; next line to assemble
6.	0302- 20 ED FD	JSR $FDED	; see assembled output
7.	**ƀJSR FBE4**		; next line to assemble
8.	0305- 20 E4 FB	JSR $FBE4	; see assembled output
9.	**ƀRTS**		; last line to assemble
10.	0308- 60	RTS	; see assembled output

What we just did was to run the program from inside the mini-assembler. This is what happened in the assembly process.

First, the start location in memory was selected. Address $0300 was the choice. Apple's mini-assembler assumes all addresses and data are in HEX. The only place the $ is used, in the disassembled listing, is in the operand. Next, the value $C1 was loaded into the accumulator. An immediate mode instruction did this. The HEX value $C1 represents the character A.

In steps 5 and 6, a JSR instruction was assembled. The operands used represent two subroutines in the Apple II monitor. A character output routine is at $FDED. This routine puts the value currently in the accumulator on the screen. Recall that our first instruction loaded the HEX value for A in the accumulator. A routine at address $FDE4 is called BELL2. This routine generates the beep heard in the speaker. The program we assembled ends with the RTS instruction. Note that any program you run from the monitor should end with the RTS instruction. The monitor command, such as 300G, is a jump (JRS) to the specified address. To get back to the monitor where you started, you must include the RTS. Otherwise.....CRASH!

When inside the mini-assembler, the $ is used to indicate a monitor command. Typing 300G and Return ran the program as though you were in the monitor, and that's what happened when you pressed Return. The computer went to address $0300 and followed the instructions found there. Each event occurred in the order it was written. **Remember**: The first instruction where you enter the program has to be an opcode. The program would abort or run wild if it did not use a legitimate sequence of instructions.

To exit from the mini-assembler press Reset, or if you have the autostart ROM type $FF69G and Return. Now type 300L and press Return. A listing of 20 disassembled lines will appear on the screen. Only the first 5 lines include our character output and bell ringing routine. You should be able to recognize them from previous examples. There may be other data listed there too, but it's not valid for this program.

Try One Yourself

You can run this program as often as you want by typing 300G and Return. Try experimenting with different values in the accumulator. Numbers 0 to 9 are values $B0 to $B9. Letters A to Z are values $C1 to $DA. A space is $A0 and a carriage return is $8D. Write a program to print out your name or the current date. Hint: Use LDA immediate for each character you want to print along with a JSR to the character output routine. End a line with a carriage return, and end the program with RTS. Explore these and experiment. You can't do anything more than mess-up your own programs.

Reference Material

Here's a short list of sources where you can find additional information on 6502 assembly language programming

1. **6502 Assembly Language Programming**, Leventhal, Osborne -1979
2. **6500 Programming Manual**, Rockwell, Synertech, Commodore
3. **Programming the 6502**, Zaks, Sybex -1978
4. **6502 Applications Book**, Zaks, Sybex -1979

We'll talk about indexing, assemblers and other assembly language fundamentals in future columns.

Empirical Music

Here's a useful routine for creating tones or musical notes contributed by Richard Ferri. He uses it to determine just the right sound needed for his programs. The program comes in two parts. The machine language tone generating routine and a Basic program to provide interactive input of values for the pitch (frequency) and duration. The values of A and B in the Basic program must be less than 255.

First, using monitor commands, enter the machine language.

```
0308- FF FF AD 30 C0 88 D0 05
0310- CE 09 03 F0 09 CA D0 F5
0318- AE 08 03 4C 0A 03 60
```

Second, type in this Applesoft program and run it.

```
100   REM   MACHINE LANGUAGE SUBROUTINE
110   HOME : PRINT : PRINT : PRINT
120   INPUT "WHAT IS THE VALUE OF 'A' (FREQUENCY)? ";A
130   PRINT : PRINT
140   INPUT "WHAT IS THE VALUE OF 'B' (DURATION)? ";B
150   POKE 776,A: POKE 777,B: CALL 778
160   VTAB 14: HTAB 15: PRINT "A= ";A
170   VTAB 16: HTAB 15: PRINT "B= ";B
180   GET X$: GOTO 100
```

And there you have it—empirical music. Anyone else with something to share?

Reset Guard •Speaker Volume Control
Pause Revisited •Applesoft/Integer Booting
Tone Routine Corrections
Telephone Software Connection
S-C Assembler •Apple II Simulators

Chuck Carpenter

July, 1980

Missed last month due to a heavy work schedule and a personal illness. My work schedule may cause me to miss a column from time to time. But, keep sending the letters. I will answer them all and as timely as the complexity of the answer permits.

Input From Readers

Here's a couple of ideas from Jim Levin. The first is a clever idea to protect the system from accidental reset. Figure 1 shows a diagram of the device. The material is heavy paper such as a 3x5 index card. (I

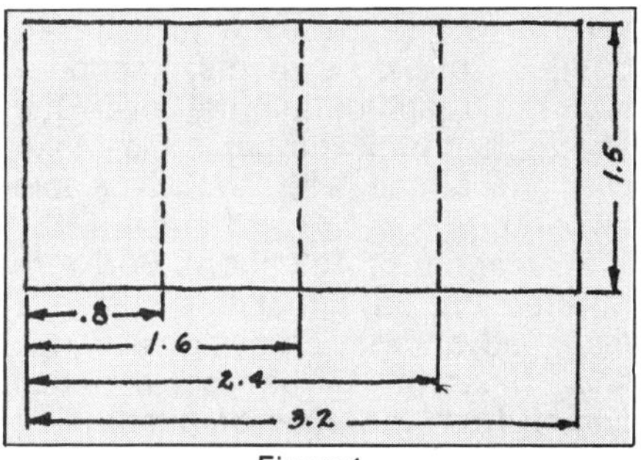

Figure 1

would also suggest certain types of light guage plastic). Cut the rectangle to size and fold it into a square tube 0.8 inches on a side. Tape the open edges together. Slide the tube down over the RESET key. And there

you have it; RESET protection with material cost less than 1 cent and installation time under 3 minutes. Jim suggests taping the sides away from the keys to the surface of the computer.

Jim's second idea puts a volume control on the speaker. By using an inexpensive trimmer type variable resistor, you can reduce speaker volume to any comfortable level. Connect the control as shown in Figure 2.

Mount the resistor so the screw-driver slot is accessible from one of the ventilation slots. Remember that this modification will void your warranty. Make your decision accordingly.

The volume control idea from Jim stimulated my thinking about my system. I have been using an external

speaker which I connect or disconnect depending on how late at night it is. I decided to make it a little more sophisticated by hooking things up as shown in Figure 3.

I mounted the switch and resistor by drilling 2¼ inch holes in the case. The jack for the external speaker is mounted on the rear apron. Now I can select either speaker with volume control. My external speaker is a Radio Shack mobile speaker. It's a 4 inch speaker in a plastic case. But it has good sound with lots of volume.

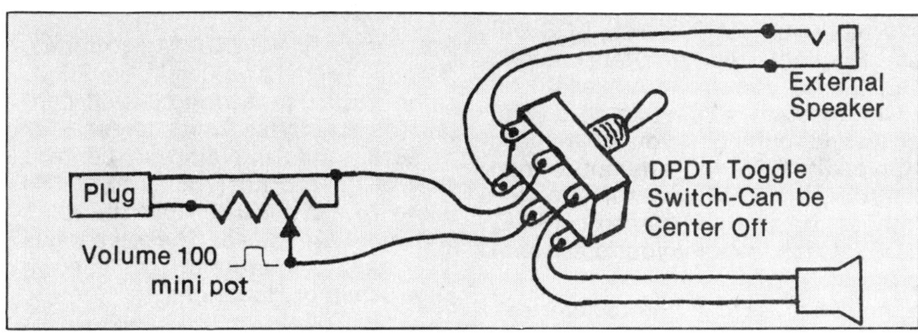

Figure 3

Again, these modifications will void your warranty.

Fred Gunther sent in another idea for program stoppers. He has solved the same problem another way. Fred suggests that you provide one of the following subroutines:

Integer Basic

```
50 PRINT"DEPRESS THE";:POKE 50,63:PRINT"RETURN";
55 POKE 50,255:INPUT"KEY TO CONTINUE.",IN$:RETURN
```

Applesoft

```
50 PRINT"DEPRESS THE";:INVERSE:PRINT"RETURN";
55 NORMAL:INPUT"KEY TO CONTINUE.",IN$:RETURN
```

Then in the main program, each time you want to pause, you need only:

```
...GOSUB 50
```

The inverse lettering for RETURN helps to make it obvious that the user

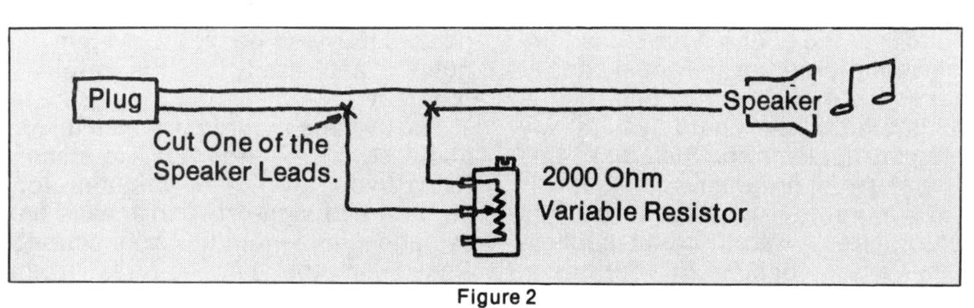

Figure 2

presses one key rather than type in 6 letters.

More Reader Input

This great idea from Bob Sander-Cederlof will help you with some of your booting problems. The problem is that the boot program, or the so-called HELLO program, must be in either Integer Basic or Applesoft. It cannot be both at the same time. So, if you use the Applesoft version, anyone using your disk without Applesoft gets the message, "LANGUAGE NOT AVAILABLE" when the disk is booted. Or, if you use an Integer Basic boot program, the person with an Apple II Plus and no Integer Basic gets the same message.

According to Bob, there is an answer. He discovered it by reading the documentation that comes with the Apple Writer Text Editing System. The key is to remember that if the boot program is written in Applesoft, and if, furthermore, there is no Applesoft in ROM in your machine, the DOS tries to load and run an Integer Basic file with the name APPLESOFT. So, INIT your disk with an Applesoft boot program written in Integer Basic and store it on the disk under the file name "APPLESOFT."

When you boot this disk, DOS will try to boot the program named HELLO. If you have Applesoft on ROM, this will succeed, and you will be up and running. If you do not have Applesoft, DOS will attempt to load it from the disk by running the Integer Basic file named APPLE-SOFT which is really your other boot program.

Another RESET protector idea comes from George Norkus. This one uses an "O" ring as a stiff spring to make reset harder to push. The O ring is a National AS-108. Remove the reset key cap and slide the O ring over the plunger stem. Reinstall the key cap. Now, the hard-to-push key won't allow accidental resets. Another option, in place of the O ring, is a piece of closed cell foam. A piece about an eighth of an inch thick and a half inch in diameter will do fine. Cut an X or cross in the middle. Slide this down over the plunger as with the O ring.

I've noticed that the new Apples have a much stiffer spring on the reset key. Also, an option is now available in which you have to use CONTROL and RESET together. The new features don't appear to be available for older models. So, the

ideas coming from readers will be helpful to many of us.

Feedback

In the March Apple Cart, there were several programs for loading assembly language into memory from Basic. I even went so far as to use the same zero page program in examples for page 3 use. *Can't be done!* The opcodes for instructions other than page 0 are different. The correct program for page 3 was sent to me by Thomas Giacchi. Here is his page 3 version of the Random Tones program:

Machine Language

```
300L

0300-    FF               ???
0301-    FF               ???
0302-    AD 30 C0    LDA   $C030
0305-    88          DEY
0306-    D0 05       BNE   $030D
0308-    CE 01 03    DEC   $0301
030B-    F0 08       BEQ   $0316
030D-    CA          DEX
030E-    D0 F5       BNE   $0305
0310-    AE 00 03    LDX   $0300
0313-    4C 02 03    JMP   $0302
0316-    60          RTS
```

Pokes

POKE 770,173	POKE 781,202
POKE 771,48	POKE 782,208
POKE 772,192	POKE 783,245
POKE 773,136	POKE 784,174
POKE 774,208	POKE 785,0
POKE 775,5	POKE 786,3
POKE 776,206	POKE 787,76
POKE 777,1	POKE 788,2
POKE 778,3	POKE 789,3
POKE 779,240	POKE 790,96
POKE 780,9	

In the READ...DATA routines, change the DATA values in the POKE commands. The string H$ will contain the data bytes from address $302 to $316. And the starting address should be 770, not 768. Thomas is using 768 and 769 to hold the pitch and duration values. These changes will allow the program to work in page 3 memory locations.

Software Over The Phone

Software for the stay-at-home shopper (and energy savers) is available over the phone. Several very useful and well done programs are now available from the Telephone Software Connection at (213) 329-3715. I have the phone answering program, the program to send a picture and the program to play Go Moku over the phone. I have used the answering program the most, and it makes your Apple respond like a miniature bulletin board system. My interests in electronic mail make this a most useful program.

On your first call, you will be asked to complete a short "credit application," which consists of your name, address, phone number(s), and Master Charge or Visa number. Then

you will be asked to select a password to protect your account from unauthorized purchases.

Immediately after answering the questions, you will be shown a list of the programs currently available, and you are invited to select any of the free programs that are on the system. After you make your selection, it will ask you to verify that it is correct and then it will attempt to transfer you the program. If you used a "dialer" program to call the system, it will detect this and ask you to get out of that program so it won't get in the way of the transfer process. If you aren't in Applesoft it will ask you to get into it. Then sit back and watch one of the slickest program transfers you will ever see, including the saving and locking of the program onto your disk.

The program selection is unique and, as far as I know, they are not available elsewhere. One is an answering machine program that will answer a modem phone line with your name 24 hours a day. It will also let you call in from a remote terminal to get your messages and operate your system. Included are some excellent security routines to prevent "crashers" and an outgoing message capability to let you leave messages that will be automatically given to selected friends, when they call in. Other programs let you send any type of program to another computer, send a 16 line message to selected bulletin board systems, send a high-res graphics picture over the phone, and play the game Go Moku over the phone with another Apple owner.

Ed Magnin of Telephone Software Connection, says that this system's main advantages are convenience and flexibility. The convenience comes from the ease of purchasing software at anytime of day or night without stepping out of your house, and without worrying whether they have just run out of your favorite program. The flexibility is that any new programs can be on line for sale the instant they are ready, complete with documentation (included as part of the program). If updates are ever needed they can be on the system as quickly and easily as the original program.

The average program for sale takes about seven minutes (13K) to transfer, if you add three minutes for sign-on and sign-off, that means an average ten minute connection. Based on the phone rates from California to Maine, this would cost less than $4.00 during the day, $3.00

after five or $2.00 after eleven or on weekends. That is less than most postage and handling charges, and those outside of California save the 6% sales tax.

The phone transfer system will work with the D.C. Hayes modem or the Comm. card and an acoustic modem. Be sure your first free program is the dial TSC program. Then when you call back for software, you can do it automatically. TSC is adding new things all the time. By the time you read this, there will be a nice selection of programs for you to try. And, the transfer process really is fascinating.

S-C Assembler II

In the May column, I mentioned using an assembler other than the mini-assembler in the Apple II. And, for those of you with the Apple II Plus, the only way you can do any machine language assembly is with an "external" program. I have used the S-C Assembler II for a couple of years now. There are a number of assemblers on the market, but none as easy to use by the casual user. The S-C Assembler II (S-C A2) includes many useful features for creating, editing, assembling, and testing your assembly language programs. Let's take a look at some of these features:

- Similarity to Basic - S-C A2 is completely integrated with Basic routines. If you are familiar with Basic in your Apple II and its syntax, you can easily understand the S-C A2. Works on all Apple models.

- Compatible with the Apple II mini-assembler-Input format and assembled output will be familiar to users of the mini-assembler. Those of you starting on the Apple II Plus will appreciate the standardized format. Machine language is made easier and more powerful with extensions such as labels, symbolic addressing and comments.

- Line Oriented - S-C A2 uses line numbers like Basic and has complete screen editing features and capability to renumber, you can add-to, delete and change your program easily and conveniently.

- Compact Size-The tape version will easily run, with lots of working space, on a 16K ma-

chine. The DOS version, because of DOS, requires more memory; a 24K system is the minimum.

- Cassette and DOS Support-Both the tape and DOS versions support standard Apple II I/O syntax. Also, both versions include an internal printer driver routine and/or the support of peripherals using the PR# command.

For the newcomer to the world of assembly language, the S-C A2 will provide a familiar way to start writing your own 6502 assembly language programs. Once you become more skilled, there are several S-C A2 extensions that will facilitate your program writing. For instance:

- Pseudo Opcodes-There are seven codes called assembler directives in the S-C A2. These codes allow you to define the origin (.OR), define a target address (.TA), define equates for address expressions (.EQ), define data (.DA), define ASCII strings (.AS), define HEX strings (.HS) and end the program or test segment (.EN).

There are 13 assembler commands that provide functional program development and control. The assembler is fully compatible with DOS 3.2, and all the Apple II monitor commands are usable inside S-C A2. I found using the assembler as easy to use as programming in Basic. I think you will find it enjoyable to use too. You can purchase the S-C Assembler II at many computer stores. If it is not available where you are, you can order by mail from S-C Software, P.O. Box 5537, Richardson, TX 75080. The price for the tape version is $25.00 and for the DOS version, $35.00. Both include a 40 page reference manual.

Apple II Silmulators

Using the Apple II as a development system for two popular microprocessors is now possible. An 8080 and an RCA 1802 simulator by Dann McCreary will do the job. The simulators allow you to enter opcodes and data using the format of the particular computer. The simulators then interpret the hexadecimal code as though a program was being executed on the particular computer.

Included in the package are a tape and supporting documentation. The tape includes the interpreter manual, the interpreter, a sample program and a disassembler for micro's assembly language code. The documentation includes a listing of the sample program, a summary of all

the instructions and commands found in the operators manual and a programmers reference card. The package is designed to run on a 16K or larger system.

To make effective use of the Apple II capabilities, Dann has created special codes for calling 6502 routines. This way you can develop your software and take advantage of Apple II features at the same time. Some of the vacant opcodes for the computer are used to include a mnemonic and corresponding opcode for 6502 calls. By using the opcode in your routines, a variety of programming options can be included.

Developing the particular code requires that you first hand assemble your program. Then, using the Apple II monitor routines, enter the HEX machine code into memory starting at address $1000. Now, call the simulator-interpreter at address $800 and execute the program using simulator commands. All the registers for the micros are displayed on the screen and complete editing and debugging commands are available. All I/O ports, external flags and interrupts are implemented by the simulators. Once the program is written and debugged, you can implement the code on your dedicated controller.

Both packages include instructions for customizing the programs to fit your system configuration. And, both are available for $21.50 from Dann McCreary, Software Design, Box 16435, San Diego, CA 92116.

The New Apple II Reference Manual

Those of you who have only recently purchased your Apples probably got one with it. The new reference manual replaces the "Red Book." For anyone interested in learning all about the innards of the Apple, the new reference manual is the book to have. Such infinitely useful items as schematics and complete pin-out data on all connectors are provided. Tables of page zero usage for each language are included. (Shows where all the spots are not used so you can tuck a byte or two of data away.) And, all the PEEKs, POKEs and CALLs to the game paddle and other I/O functions are tabulated for you. The differences between various revisions of Apple mother boards are discussed, and so are the features of the autostart ROM. There is much, much more, and if you didn't get the new reference manual with your Apple, it's an excellent addition to your Apple library. □

Disk Drives •Apple III •Super-Text
Integer Billboard •Pascal Flash and Inverse

Chuck Carpenter

August, 1980

Disk Drives

Problems of I/O Errors occurring during read/write operations have become more frequent. Experiences of others and my own involvement indicates cost-reduced production may be the problem. With the cost-reduced drives, you have to be very careful to get the diskette centered over the clamp. If the problem seems unduly severe, you may need to have the speed calibrated and the drive mechanism re-aligned. The drive used by Apple is a stripped-down Shugart SA-400. The repair manual for the SA-400 will provide the necessary data for the required adjust-ments. Realignment is not easy to do. Special diskettes and an oscilloscope are required to make the adjustments.

Head alignment can be part of the problem so make sure it's done by someone who understands the nature of these critical adjustments. Motor speed is easier to do. There is a tach disk attached to the spindle pulley. One bar-track is for 60Hz and one is for 50Hz. By shining a lamp on the tach disc, you can adjust the speed control pot (mounted on the small PCB at the back of the drive) for zero movement of the bars. Make sure this is done with a diskette in the drive. The torque load of the diskette will make a significant difference in motor speed. There is a procedure for making this adjustment with a frequency counter too. And, be sure to check the head load arm and the head load pad for proper operation and wear.

The overall quality of current disk drives is the more likely problem. I have had to insert a diskette several times, on the newer units, to get a proper read. This condition will cause a problem with a write to the diskette too. If the diskette was not centered, the system would not be able to read/write the catalog track correctly. It would be possible to clobber things if you tried to write to an off-center track. One way to check centering is to always read from the disk first; do a CATALOG, for instance. Also, if you are having problems with reads/writes and getting lots of I/O errors, write to the Manager of Quality Control at Apple. The address is on various manuals you have. Describe the specifics of the problem. Especially describe the details of the conditions when it happens, frequency and so on. Don't try to vent your frustrations, though. You'll get a lot more help if you're rational.

Apple III

Apple's newest entry into integrated personal computer systems has arrived. The systems will be available to dealers by the time you read this, and to customers during the following couple of months. Most all the things Apple II owners pay extra for, are now included as standard. Here's a summary of the functions and features:
- 80 character lines, upper and lower case.
- Numeric keypad, RESET removed from the keyboard.
- Four cursor keys for easier editing.
- Improved audio and an external jack.
- Language system, e.g., Pascal.
- Calendar/clock
- Memory management for up to 128K RAM.
- Built-in serial interface for printer or modem.
- Interface for Silentype printer.
- 4 channel A/D input.
- Video interfaces.
- A new Sophisticated Operating System (SOS).
- Emulation mode which runs Apple II software.

And, all this will be available to you for a cost of about $4300.00 for the minimum system.

Hardware

Apple III will use a 6502A running at 2 MHz. Included with the 6502 instruc-tion superset, are a relocatable base register page, a relocatable stack and a 128K byte address range (96K of memory is standard). Peripherals will function with full interrupt capability. A timer derived from the system clock can be programmed for durations up to 18 minutes. The power supply has been beefed-up and will allow 2 disk drives to be operated at the same time. A calendar/clock, integrated into the main circuit board, can be operated over 3 years on its battery. The new audio circuits use a 6 bit D-to-A converter to generate high quality sound to either the built-in speaker or through an external jack.

One drive is built into the Apple III with provisions to support up to 3 additional drives. The new drives will use a 16 sector system providing about 143K bytes of storage — about a 40% increase over DOS 3.2 (the new system is called DOS 3.3). An RS-232 communications interface port is built-in, too. Reference is made to its use with letter-quality printers. There is also a port for the Silentype thermal printer and provisions for an optional parallel printer card are provided too. Another connector on the back panel provides access to the 4 A/D inputs. The traditional joystick will be connected here. Since all connectors are now mounted on the rear panel, there is no longer any need to "lift the cover" to get inside.

The keyboard is detached and greatly expanded. There are 74 keys including a 13-key numeric pad. An alpha-lock key and a shift key are provided. RESET is behind the keyboard. Four cursor control keys are provided for easy cursor move-ment. And, the keyboard offers sculptured keys with textured surfaces. The keyboard has features obviously intended for such applications as word processing. A variety of video outputs are provided from black and white to high resolution in many colors. All video signals and voltages are available through a DB15 connector. Video display modes include 560 x 192 dot black and white, 280 x 192 dot hi-res color, 140 x 192 dot hi-res color, 80 column black and white text, 40 column color on color and all Apple II modes. Monitors will be the 12 inch Sanyo, 12 inch Hitachi and eventually Apple's custom 12 inch B&W monitor. An RF modulator can be used for connection to a television set.

Software

Apple's new Sophisticated Operating System is abbreviated SOS and pronounced SAUCE (I know!). The SOS is said to effectively manage these user and system functions:

- Running applications
- Accessing peripherals
- Accessing data
- Developing applications
- Developing languages
- Memory management
- Device management
- CPU scheduling
- File management
- Interrupt control

Features and Benefits of SOS

Apple's new Operating System maximizes system efficiency by controlling resource use and allocation. Software development is easier and program size and complexity is reduced through a powerful system interface for languages and applications. The flexible file system provides efficient system data storage and access, allowing applications to share data and faster access to information. Powerful new utilities provide complete application access to all of the advanced capabilities. To meet your system needs, SOS can be custom configured, even by the inexperienced operator, with the easy-to-use system configuration program. And, the system is designed to be easily expanded allowing you to further enhance the power and flexibility.

Visicalc III

An enhanced version of Visicalc, as sold for the Apple II, will be available exclusively from Apple for the Apple III. The package will take advantage of the 80 column screen, cursor controls and SOS file system. Incidentally, I saw a demonstration of Visicalc II recently. The capabilities of this system are super. If you're doing any financial planning or modeling, you can benefit from Visicalc. I'm getting a copy for my own use so I'll review it in a future column.

Additional Software

There will be a new Business Basic. It is intended to be the Apple standard and will feature formatting capabilities with PRINT USING, longer names for vari-

ables, fast disk access, nineteen-digit integer arithmetic and will support the IF-THEN-ELSE statements for enhanced program structure. (Sounds a lot like Microsoft Basic version 5.0.)

Pascal will be available too. The software will be upgraded for use with SOS. Pascal will feature improved performance and will be compatible with the Pascal file system on Apple II. Fortran, compatible with the Pascal file system, run-time package and program development tools will also be available. This will be an ANSI standard Fortran for compatibility with vast subroutine libraries for math, science, engineering and statistics. A Mail List Manager package will be available too. The program features:

- High speed entry of names, addresses and phone numbers.
- 970 names per diskette.
- Sorting a diskette in 75 seconds by either name or zip code.
- Merge capabilities allowing files to span diskettes.
- Flexible formatting and printing capability.
- Complete menu-driven user interface.

Apple III Packages

The Apple III will be sold as various application packages. These are intended to provide the nucleus of various user solution packages. With a variety of application software and hardware, the package becomes customized for individual customers. The three package groups identified at this time are: Information analyst, Word processor and Software development.

The information analyst includes:
- 96K Apple III
- SOS
- Apple Business Basic
- Visicalc III
- Mail List Manager
- 12 inch B&W monitor

The word processing system includes:
- 96K Apple III
- SOS
- Apple Business Basic
- Word Painter
- Training course to use Word Painter
- 12 inch B&W monitor
- Either a Silentype or letter quality printer

And, the software development system includes:
- 96K Apple III
- SOS
- Apple Business Basic
- Fortran
- Apple Pascal
- 12 inch B&W monitor
- Expansion drive

One final note. The system is packaged in a metal cabinet. There will be no more problems with radiation interference

from the high-speed microprocessor circuits.

Super-Text Word Processor

This column was developed and written with my new word processor. The package is great. I have been looking for a word processor that would work well with Apple's limited screen capacity. The processor allows free-form entry of text. This means that you don't have to concern yourself with the 40 column limit. Output formatting takes care of putting the text wherever you want it to go. Upper and lower case are easily controlled, and if you have the Paymar Lower Case Adapter, you can see the text on the screen the same as it will be printed. Here's a summary of some of the features:

- Full screen cursor editing.
- Scanning forward or reverse.
- Line scrolling both directions.
- Paragraph scrolling both directions.
- Add text (also begins text)
- Change text for deleting or correcting.
- Math mode
- Print mode
- Auto link — one program to another.
- Options program.
- Diablo type printer controls.
- Formatting, tabbing, centering, justifying, etc., etc.

And much more. I've just starting using the processor so I'm not aware of all the features. I know I like what I have been able to do so far. The ease of use is really impressive. I'll provide the details later. The package is about $100.00 and it's called Super-Text, The Professional Word Processor. It's distributed by Muse Software and should be available at your local computer store.

Readers Input

Here's a neat little program from Randi Rost. The program is called "Puffer" and it moves the characters across the screen in billboard fashion. Randi says this Integer Basic program appears to "puff" a message across the screen. You must put as many characters or spaces in A$ as it is dimensioned for. In this example, 40. The program is an endless loop as written. Line 80 could be an escape by testing for a processed key. You can change the delay time by changing line 40. See the listing and sample run of the program.

Rosa Pascal Sez

For those of you who are using Pascal, included are a couple of short utility routines sent in by Ron DeGroat. These routines will let you do a couple of things in Pascal that are in Basic but not in Pascal. Following is the text of Ron's letter essentially as it was written:

The assembly language procedures shown in Listing #1 allow the user to display text in FLASHing, INVERSE and NORMAL modes with Apple Pascal in much the same way that Applesoft Basic does.

These procedures may be directly linked to the Pascal host (see example program in Listing #2) or stored in a UNIT in the SYSTEM.LIBRARY along with other useful utilities (such as PEEK and POKE routines, q.v., "The Multi-Lingual Apple" column in the Feb. and Mar./Apr. 1980 issues of Call A.P.P.L.E.). For more information about the control codes ($C083 and $C088) see Appendix D of the Apple Language System Installation and Operating Manual.

It should also be noted that since the Apple uses the top two bits of the ASCII characer code to select INVERSE and FLASHing modes, lower-case letters cannot be displayed in these modes.

LISTING #1:   INVERSE, NORMAL & FLASH PROCEDURES

```
.PROC INVERSE
LDA ØCØ83 ;SELECT 2ND 4K BANK
LDA ØCØ83 ;AND WRITE-ENABLE
LDA #ØØ
STA ØD8ED ;CLEAR BITS 6 & 7
LDA ØCØ88 ;SELECT 1ST BANK & WRITE-
RTS       ;PROTECT, THEN RETURN
;- - - - - - - - - - - - - - - - - - - -
.PROC NORMAL
LDA ØCØ83
LDA ØCØ83
LDA #8Ø
STA ØD8ED ;SET BIT 7 FOR NORMAL MODE
LDA ØCØ88
RTS
;- - - - - - - - - - - - - - - - - - - -
.PROC FLASH
LDA ØCØ83
LDA ØCØ83
LDA #4Ø
STA ØD8ED ;SET BIT 6 FOR FLASH MODE
LDA ØCØ88
RTS
```

LISTING #2: EXAMPLE PASCAL PROGRAM

```
PROGRAM TESTSTUFF;

PROCEDURE INVERSE;   EXTERNAL;
PROCEDURE NORMAL;    EXTERNAL;
PROCEDURE FLASH;     EXTERNAL;

BEGIN
  GOTOXY(Ø,1Ø);
  WRITE ('THIS SHOULD BE ');
  FLASH;
  WRITELN ('FLASHING');
  NORMAL;
  WRITELN;
  WRITE ('AND THIS SHOULD BE ');
  INVERSE;
  WRITE ('INVERSE');
  NORMAL;
END.
```

Note: For Pascal newcomers, constants in Apple Pascal assembly language must start with an integer, 0 to 9. If the first digit is greater than 9, i.e., A, B, C, D, E or F, the number must be prefaced with a 0, as shown in Listing #1.)

How the Modification Works:

Listing #3 shows a section of code stored on disc in Block No. 4 of SYSTEM.APPLE file. When loaded into memory, this code resides in the second 4K bank of RAM, which must be selected and write-enabled with the control codes described above before any change can be made.

LISTING #3:   CODE EXCERPTS FROM SYSTEM.APPLE

```
D8E8: E9 2Ø SBC #2Ø ;CONVERT TO U.C.
D8EA: 29 3F AND #3F ;CHAR. MASK
D8EC: 9 8Ø ORA #8Ø ;MODE SELECT:
                    ; 4Ø = FLASH
                    ; ØØ = INVERSE
```

The character mask clears the top 2 bits of the character, and the next instruction sets the bit necessary for the mode selected. Thus, by changing the contents of memory location D8ED, as indicated, we can select either FLASHing, INVERSE or NORMAL modes. □

Listing and sample RUN of "Puff" program.

```
>LIST
   10 DIM A$(40): DIM B$(40)
   20 A$="ANY 40 CHARACTER STRING AT ALL IN HERE.."
   30 CALL -936: VTAB 10: PRINT A$
   40 FOR U=1 TO 200: NEXT U
   50 B$=A$(2,40)
   60 B$(40)=A$(1,1)
   70 A$=B$
   80 GOTO 30
   90 END

>RUN
ANY 40 CHARACTER STRING AT ALL IN HERE..
NY 40 CHARACTER STRING AT ALL IN HERE..A
Y 40 CHARACTER STRING AT ALL IN HERE..AN
 40 CHARACTER STRING AT ALL IN HERE..ANY
40 CHARACTER STRING AT ALL IN HERE..ANY
O CHARACTER STRING AT ALL IN HERE..ANY 4
 CHARACTER STRING AT ALL IN HERE..ANY 40
CHARACTER STRING AT ALL IN HERE..ANY 40
STOPPED AT 40
>
```

Hello Programs Menus
Disk-O-Tape •Lemonade Music Table
Applesoft Revealed

Chuck Carpenter

September, 1980

Reports from NCC are indicating lots of new products will be available for our Apple computers. My first new acquisition will be the Softcard from Microsoft. With this card I will be able to have a version of Basic that is more suitable for the kind of programming I like to do. There will be several other languages available for the Softcard system too. Check the ads in the magazines and at your computer store if you're interested. I'll be watching the ads and computer stores for any other new items, too. I have one slot left once I get Softcard, and will be looking for something to fill it. No, I'm not getting an Apple III. After lots of thinking on the subject, I decided that I would not be able to do many of the things that I like to do. With the Apple III, a lot of flexibility will be lost. With all the products being offered for the Apple II, and all the things you can do with the system on your own, it seemed foolish to me to start all over again. And, now that Mountain Hardware has announced an expander box, you can add 8 more slots to your Apple II. The next several months should bring us many interesting Apple II projects. I, for one, will be trying to check out each one.

Listings 1 and 2 are programs to turn your catalog listing into a menu. By including these programs in your HELLO program, you will see the catalog listed on the screen and then, as if by magic, changed to a menu. You can then press a corresponding key and RUN, LOAD, UNLOCK, or LOCK any file listed. Listing 1 is in Applesoft, and the selection options are displayed in billboard fashion. The Integer version in Listing 2 will not appear to be doing anything until you press one of the selection keys. Then you either RUN a program or do one of the other functions. If you have both Integer and Applesoft, you can use the technique of putting the Applesoft version in the HELLO program and the Integer version in a program called Applesoft. The procedure for doing this was described in last month's column. There is a limitation. You can only have up to 23 catalog entries showing on the screen at a time. If you have more than 23, only the last 23 will be included in the menu. These programs were written by Bob Sander-Cederlof for our local newsletter. I usually don't like to bother with gadget programs but these are quite useful. Seemed like something that you might like to have.

Lemonade Music

In the March 1980 column, I included a program for playing "music" with the Apple. The music-playing routine is a machine-language program from the red Apple II Reference Manual. This same music routine is used in the "Lemonade Stand" program being shipped with the newer Apples. I was able to find a copy on the master diskette of a friend's new machine. Why am I telling you all of this!?

Charles Kluepfel of New York City has sent along some interesting data relative to that program. The version I have was written in Applesoft and the program POKEs the machine language into page 3 of memory. Charles found this to be done in lines 10000 through 10190 of the Lemonade Stand program. The values for pitch and duration are POKEd into decimal memory locations 768 and 769. Charles has calculated the values to select the pitch. Here is his contribution.

Based on the tone values for "Raindrops Keep Falling on My Head" in line 11550 of "Lemonade Stand" — 152, 152, 152, 144, 152, 171, 192, 152 and the sheet music for that song, a knowledge that A (pitch) is inversely proportional to the frequency and that 12 half-tones make an octave (doubling of frequency), we get Table 1.

Note that 0 serves as 256 as it needs to be decremented 256 times to get back to zero. The formula used is: if x is the number of half-tones lower than C above middle C, use the nearest integer to:

$$128 * 2 \char94 (x/12)$$

Also, a value of 1 can be used for pauses, as the note produced is barely audible. To play all of Lemonade Stand's songs, load the program, GOSUB 10000 to POKE the

Table 1. Values for A to be POKEd for Pitch

	Low	Mid	High	High+
F	192	96	48	24
E	203	102	51	25
D#, Eb	215	108	54	27
D	228	114	57	29
C#, Db	242	121	60	30
C	0	128	64	32
B		136	68	34
A#, Bb		144	72	36
A		152	76	38
G#, Ab		161	81	40
G		171	85	43
F#, Gb		181	91	45

machine language program, delete line 115200, which has non-musical data, and repeatedly GOSUB 11700. You will get "Yes, We Have No Bananas," some glug, glug, glugs of a glass filling up, "Summertime, and the Living is Easy," "Raindrops Keep Falling on my Head," and "Singin' in the Rain." Charles notes further that if a value of 196 is used to represent middle C then the formula to use is:

```
A = 232.5 / 2 ~ (x/12)
```

All of these calculations will help those of you interested in making your own simple music interpreter. One gentleman, also from New York City, called to let me hear a very nice classical piece done with the tone generating routine. My thanks to both for an interesting application of a useful utility routine. Of course, you should write a program to make the calculations for you. I mean, after all!

Disk-O-Tape

Here's a new program that will allow you to copy your diskettes to cassettes. With Disk-O-Tape, you can copy an entire DOS 3.2 diskette to inexpensive cassettes. Up to 4 diskettes can be stored on both sides of a 60 minute tape. Considering the cost of disks, you can save the cost of several disks you now have tied up as archive or back-up storage. The program is designed to let you save a diskette to tape and, as desired, restore the contents back to an initialized diskette. Here are some of Disk-O-Tapes features:

- Copy an entire DOS 3.2 disk to tape.
- Comprehensive error detection during transfer.
- True read-after-write for reliability.
- Loading boot-strap saved with each copy.
- User-assigned naming of tapes.
- Copy time is a function of data on the disk.
- Copies all but the DOS tracks, 0-2.
- Pays for itself in media savings alone.

This is one program that should find a lot of use. Consider the ease with which you can mail the contents of a disk on a rugged cassette. Or, how many of your rarely used disks you can now use for other purposes. Disk-O-Tape is available for $12.00 postpaid from: Dann McCreary, Box 16534-Y, San Diego, CA 92116.

Applesoft Revealed

Analyzing how an Applesoft program is constructed in memory has several benefits. One is to append a program. Another might be to make special changes to certain memory locations. A third could be to include a machine language program in with your Basic program. Once you know how to directly modify a program in memory, your imagination can do the rest.

In the following discussion, all memory locations and data will be in hexadecimal. This can be confusing if you usually work with decimal numbers. And the 'Tokens' we will be talking about are decimal values in the Applesoft manual. When working directly with values in memory, only hexadecimal numbers are used. So, if you're not comfortable with HEX numbers, now's the time. (You should be able to easily convert back and forth because PEEKs and POKEs use decimal values.)

Clearing Memory

On page 140 in the appendix of the Applesoft manual, you can find that programs start at memory location 801 for the ROM version (3001 for the tape version). The page zero pointer to this location is in memory locations 67-68. To make sure we can know that our inputs are easily identified, let's put an easy-to-recognize character in several memory locations. The following sequence will let us do that:

```
]CALL-151

*800:FF

*801<800.87FM

*800.81F

0800- FF FF FF FF FF FF FF FF
0808- FF FF FF FF FF FF FF FF
0810- FF FF FF FF FF FF FF FF
0818- FF FF FF FF FF FF FF FF
```

The character 'F' is not likely to be found in pairs in this test, so I used it. This is what happened: From Applesoft, a CALL-151 is made to get to the monitor. Next, the value FF is loaded into memory location 800. The next step uses the monitor move cómmands to fill a range of memory with the value loaded into location 800. A memory dump of the program area we will be using is shown in the last step. I am showing less memory than the move command used because I already know how big my test program is. Now, press the <CTRL>B key sequence to get back to Applesoft.

A Test Program

Now let's write a short program and see what happens to the program space. To keep things easy to understand, only low line numbers and simple commands will be used. The following sequence, using a three line program, will do the job:

```
1   REM
2   X = 1
3   PRINT

]CALL-151

*69.6A

0069- 17 08
*
*800.81F

0800- 00 07 08 01 00 B2 00 0F
0808- 08 02 00 58 D0 31 00 15
0810- 08 03 00 BA 00 00 00 FF
0818- FF FF FF FF FF FF FF FF
```

After typing in the short program, we again make the CALL to the monitor. This time, from page 140, the memory locations in page zero containing the address of the end of the program are examined. A memory dump of locations 69 and 6A show us that the end of the program is at memory location 0817. It's customary to display the low address byte first and the high address byte last (adds to the challenge of learning new things). And, once more, we make a memory dump of the range where we expect the program to be.

Interpretation

And there it is. By examining the data in the memory dump, the contents of the program will be revealed. As you can see, the Applesoft interpreter replaced most of the Fs with program data. The first byte at address 800 is always 00 and is not part of the program. The next two bytes at address 801 & 802 contain the address of the next line at 0807. Next, bytes at addresses 803 & 804 are the number of the first line, 0001. Following the line number pair, the next byte represents the token for the REM in line 1. Tokens are used to represent keywords and commands. This way, only one byte is needed to represent commands that may use several letters. A complete list of tokens used in Applesoft can be found on page 121 in the Applesoft manual. You may want to convert these decimal values to hexadecimal for easy reference.

Following the REM token is the end of the line indicator. This is always 00. At location 0807 and 0808 are the bytes for the address of the next line, 080F. As you recall, the first line started with the byte pair for the address of this line which started at 0807 (whew). Addresses 0809 and 080A are the line number of this line, 2. The bytes 58, D0, and 31 represent the ASCII value for X, the token for =, and the ASCII value for 1. The end of line 00 byte is at 080E. Note that a table of ASCII values can be found on pages 138 and 139 in your Applesoft manual. You will find that a HEX 80 has to be added to the characters so the output will be in normal video when the value is printed on the screen.

The last line starts at addresses 080F and 0810. These bytes point to the next line address at 0815. In this case, the bytes at this address are the end of program bytes, 0000. At address 0811 and 0812 are the line number bytes, followed by the token for PRINT, then the end of line byte, 00. As mentioned before, the end of program bytes 0000 are at addresses 0815 and 0816. At the beginning, we said the end of the program was at 0817. This we determined by listing the contents of 69 and 6A. Actually, this is the address of the beginning of the variables table. Now, press the <CTRL>C combination to get back to Applesoft. Make sure it's C or the program will be wiped out. (Can you figure out how to restore the pointer to the end of the program yet?)

Variables Appear!

Because we have not run the program, the variables table has not been placed in memory. This is an important thing to remember. If you are going to make any changes to a program, don't run it until you have made all the changes you intend to make. Now, let's run the program:

```
]LIST

1  REM
2  X = 1
3  PRINT

]RUN


]CALL-151

*800.81F

0800- 00 07 08 01 00 82 00 0F
0808- 08 02 00 58 D0 31 00 15
0810- 08 03 00 BA 00 00 00 58
0818- 00 81 00 00 00 00 FF FF
```

Now go back to the monitor once again. Notice that the interpreter has now placed the variable table at the end of the program. Only two of the F's are left.

Signifying What?

Suppose you wanted to change line number 3 to something else. By changing the values in memory locations 0811 and 0812 to FF you would change line number 3 to 65535. Or, something that makes using machine language simpler, tack the code on the end of your Basic program.

- First, write the Basic program
- Second, determine the address of program end
- Next, load the program into memory
- Start it at the address of program end
- Remember this is at the location indicated by 69 & 6A
- Change the contents of 69 and 6A to the end of machine language
- Now go back to Basic and save the program.

Remember, don't run the program until after you have saved it.

When the machine language program is written, make a note of its length. Also, be sure it is written to run in the memory space where it will be included in your Basic program. Make sure to add the end of program 0000 bytes to your program too. There! Now doesn't that start your imagination humming? □

```
Listing 1
]LIST                           Applesoft Cataloger

100    TEXT : HOME :D$ =   CHR$ (4): PRINT D$"CATALOG":B =   PEEK (
       37) - 2: IF B > 22 THEN B = 22
110 T = 0:CH = 4: FOR CV = 0 TO 23: GOSUB 1000: IF C <  > 160 THEN
       POKE P - 1,219: POKE P,T + 193: POKE P + 1,221:T = T + 1:
    S = CV
120    NEXT CV: VTAB 24:A$ = "TYPE LETTER TO RUN, OR LOAD=1 LOCK=
       2 UNLOCK=3 DELETE=4 EXIT=5...."
130 B$ = "RUN": HTAB 1: PRINT  LEFT$ (A$,39)::A$ =   MID$ (A$,2)
        + LEFT$ (A$,1):K =   PEEK ( - 16384): IF K < 128 THEN   FOR
    K = 1 TO 75: NEXT K:K =   FRE (0): GOTO 130
140    POKE  - 16368,0:K = K - 176: IF K < 1 OR K > 5 THEN 300
200    HTAB 1: CALL  - 868: IF K = 5 THEN   END
210    PRINT " PRESS 'LETTER' YOU WISH TO ":: IF K = 1 THEN B$ =
       "LOAD"
220    IF K = 2 THEN B$ = "LOCK"
230    IF K = 3 THEN B$ = "UNLOCK"
240    IF K = 4 THEN B$ = "DELETE": FLASH
250    PRINT B$:: CALL  - 198: NORMAL : GET K$:K =   ASC (K$) - 48

300    IF K < 17 OR K > T + 16 THEN 130
310 CH = 1:CV = S - T + K - 16: GOSUB 1000: IF C = 194 AND (B$ =
       "RUN" OR B$ = "LOAD") THEN B$ = "B" + B$
320    FOR CH = 6 TO 39: GOSUB 1000:B$ = B$ +   CHR$ (C): NEXT CH:
        HTAB 1: CALL  - 868: PRINT B$: PRINT D$;B$: GOTO 100
1000 C1 =   INT (CV / 8):C2 = CV - C1 * 8:P = 1024 + 128 * C2 +
       40 * C1 + CH:C =   PEEK (P): RETURN
```

```
Listing 2
>LIST                          Integer Cataloger

   0 LOMEM:2048: POKE -16298,0: POKE -16300,0: TEXT
  10 DIM A$(40),B$(6):D$="": PRINT D$;"NOMONCIO": CALL -936: PRINT
     D$;"CATALOG"
  20 I=I+2: IF SCRN(4,I-1)=10 THEN 20:P=I/2
  30 VTAB P+Q: TAB 4: PRINT "[ ]":Q=Q+1:R=I+Q*2-2: COLOR=(Q+128
     )/16: PLOT 4,R-1: COLOR=(Q+128) MOD 16: PLOT 4,R-2
  40 IF SCRN(4,R+1)#10 THEN 30:T= PEEK (37): PRINT "RUN ?  LOCK=1 U
     NLOCK=2 DELETE=3 EXIT=4";:B$="RUN"
  50 K= PEEK (-16384): IF K>176 AND K<180 THEN 60: IF K=180 OR
     K>192 AND K<193+Q THEN 80: GOTO 50
  60 IF K=177 THEN B$="LOCK": IF K=178 THEN B$="UNLOCK": IF K=
     179 THEN B$="DELETE": VTAB T+1: TAB 1: CALL -868
  70 PRINT " PRESS "LETTER" YOU WISH TO ":: IF K=179 THEN POKE
     50,127: PRINT B$:: CALL -198
  80 POKE 50,255: POKE -16368,0: IF K>176 AND K<180 THEN 50: IF
     K=180 THEN END :I=I+(K-193)*2-2: IF SCRN(1,I)=2 AND B$="RUN"
     THEN B$="BRUN"
  90 FOR X=7 TO 39: POKE 2046+X, SCRN(X,I)+ SCRN(X,I+1)*16: NEXT
     X: PRINT : PRINT D$;B$;A$: GOTO 0
```

EXTRA IGNORED Ignored
Strings to Tape •More Apple I/O

Chuck Carpenter

October, 1980

A question came up recently about the software I review. I explained that I only review the stuff that seems to be well done. That is, the documentation does not leave you guessing, the programs have decent human factors, and that there appears to be reasonable support should there be any problems. In the case of software, I haven't reviewed anything unless I have used it for some time. Some of the packages that were sent to me were returned or discarded. As for hardware and such physical devices, my attitude is much the same. If I don't or can't use the device, I don't write a review of it. (Except for the Apple III which I did from Apple's release documentation.) Occasionally, when I personally know that several people are using a product with good results, I'll interview them and use the information in limited reviews.

So, if you are wondering about a particular piece of software or a hardware peripheral widget, check the other articles in *Creative Computing*. There are a number of reviews presented each month. And, if you have been following the letters, you will know that the reviews have provoked lots of replies because of their honesty. There is a bimonthly newspaper type publication, too, called Infoworld. A number of software packages are reviewed there every two weeks or so. The coverage is for more than just Apples, but a lot of Apple software is reviewed. Like any other review, *you* must be the final judge. Each of us has our personal biases and prejudices and reviews will reflect this. It appears to be contra-human to be totally objective. Which brings me to the review I did on Apple III in the August '80 Apple Cart. My report indicated the keyboard was detached. Not so! Well, so much for third-hand review information.

From Down Under

Alan Thomas from Tasmania, Australia sent this program back in March '80. My intention was to include it several months ago. I lost it, Alan has kindly replaced it, and now I can include it. To better understand Alan's routine, recall the significance of the ASCII values used in the CHR$ statements:

●CHR$(7) Control G(bell)

●CHR$(8) Control H(backspace) <--

●CHR$(13) Control M(return)

●CHR$(21) Control U(forward space)-->

●CHR$(32) Space bar

●CHR$(44) Comma

●CHR$(58) Colon

A complete list of the decimal values for all the ASCII characters can be found on pages 138-139 in the Applesoft Reference Manual. Here's the description sent by Alan for his program.

Alan relates . . . I am writing to describe a problem I have come across and to give a solution — refer to the program in Listing 1.

The problem is the statement INPUT A$ or, should I say, the problem is actually its inflexibility. On many occasions I have wanted to do things with INPUT characters, but the INPUT statement coldly allows you to do almost anything until you press RETURN and only then do you realize you have an EXTRA IGNORED error or you have accidentally put in more characters than you wished. The remedy is the subroutine from lines 10000-10025. Lines 10-30 are a small demonstration program, where GOSUB 10000 is equiva-

```
]LIST

10    TEXT : HOME
20    PRINT "ENTER STRING -"
30    PRINT
40    GOSUB 10000
50    PRINT : PRINT A$: END
10000 A$ = "":A1$ = "":A2$ = ""
10001 A3$ = CHR$ (7):A4$ = CHR$ (8):A5$ = CHR$ (13):
      A6$ = CHR$ (21):A7$ = CHR$ (32):A8$ = CHR$ (44)
      :A9$ = CHR$ (58)
10002 GET A$
10003 IF A$ = A6$ AND A1$ = "" AND A2$ < > "" THEN A$
      = LEFT$ (A2$,1): GOTO 10022
10004 IF (A$ = A6$ OR A$ = A7$) AND A1$ = "" THEN A$ =
      A7$: GOTO 10012
10005 IF A$ = A6$ AND LEN (A2$) > LEN (A1$) THEN A$ =
      MID$ (A2$, LEN (A1$) + 1,1):A1$ = A1$ + A$: GOTO
      10025
10006 IF A$ = A6$ THEN A$ = A7$: GOTO 10012
10007 IF A$ = A4$ AND A1$ = "" GOTO 10002
10008 IF A$ = A4$ AND LEN (A1$) = 1 THEN A1$ = "": GOTO
      10025
10009 IF A$ = A4$ THEN A1$ = LEFT$ (A1$, LEN (A1$) -
      1): GOTO 10025
10010 IF A$ = A8$ OR A$ = A9$ THEN PRINT A3$;: GOTO 1
      0002
10011 IF A$ = A5$ THEN A$ = A1$ + A$: PRINT : RETURN
10012 IF LEN (A1$) = 39 THEN PRINT A3$;: GOTO 10002
10022 A1$ = A1$ + A$
10023 IF LEN (A2$) > LEN (A1$) THEN A2$ = A1$ + RIGHT$
      (A2$, LEN (A2$) - LEN (A1$)): GOTO 10025
10024 A2$ = A1$
10025 PRINT A$;: GOTO 10002

] REM  BY: ALAN THOMAS : 7 MAR '80
```

Listing 1.

lent to INPUT A$, with a few additions. The subroutine uses GET A$, so that every character is checked as it is typed in.

Features

1. Using the backspace arrow key, you cannot move the cursor or print characters back beyond the first character position.

2. If you have already printed some characters, you may go back and forth as desired, using the arrow keys.

3. Line 10010 checks to see that you do not input the comma or colon; they are not legal input characters. A beep is announced (control G) to let you know. This is to save later frustration if you have, for example, written A$ into a disk record and subsequently read it back using the INPUT statement. You will then most likely see on your screen an unwanted ?EXTRA IGNORED. However, if you are not going to use an INPUT statement, but only the PRINT A$ statement, then the comma and colon are allowed as input characters and the error will not occur. For such functioning, just delete line 10010.

4. The INPUT statement does not allow you to print leading spaces (such as for headings in a central position), while this subroutine will allow you to fill with spaces to a desired position, using either the SPACE BAR or the right arrow key.

5. Lines 10012-10021 may be used to include your own input conditions. For instance, line 10012 has already been included to make sure that you do not input more than 39 characters.

6. You may type as fast as you like, or you may use the repeat key.

7. When you have finished typing your string, press the RETURN key and the string A$ will appear on your screen...

Alan's program is a good example of solving a programming limitation by use of other program functions. Since all the ASCII characters can be tested using CHR$, many other program options are possible.

Saving Strings on Tape

In the February '80 column, I mentioned (briefly) something about saving strings on tape. At the time, I hadn't a need to do this nor had I found a suitable program. The SAVE and RECALL commands are available but these are intended for numerical arrays. I recently purchased a *Best of Contact '78*. This is a collection of many of the programming ideas included in the 6 issues of *Contact* As you may recall, *Contact* was published briefly by Apple as a house newsletter. I found a copy of *'Best of'* in several of the local computer stores. For those of you living where computer stores are few and far between, try the Apple hot line or write to them for a mail source. There's some good info in the *'Best of'* so try to get a copy. Now back to saving string on tape.

```
1   :
2   REM : PROGRAM TO SAVE STRINGS TO
3   REM : CASSETTE TAPE.
4   REM : BY: R. WIGGINTON (6/78)
5   :
10  DIM A$(10)
20  PRINT "TYPE IN NINE STRINGS, SEPARATED BY": PRINT "C
    ARRIAGE RETURNS. "
30  FOR K = 1 TO 9: INPUT A$(K): NEXT K
38  :
40  REM  NOW SAVE A$ TO TAPE
42  :
50  GOSUB 1000
55  PRINT "STRINGS ARE NOW ON TAPE. TO RECALL,    TYPE
    'GOTO 100', REWIND AND START TAPE, AND PRESS 'RETUR
    N'."
58  PRINT "LET TAPE RUN UNTIL CURSOR RETURNS."
60  END
98  :
100  REM  THIS PART RECALLS THE STRINGS FROM TAPE.
102  :
110  DIM B$(10)
120  GOSUB 2000
130  FOR K = 1 TO 9: PRINT B$(K): NEXT K
140  END
148  :
1000  REM  STORE A$ TO TAPE.
1002  :
1004   PRINT "INSERT CLEAN TAPE, START RECORDING."
1006   PRINT "PRESS ANY KEY WHEN READY": GET Z$
1010 X =  FRE (0): STORE A$
1012  :
1020  REM  STORE A$ REALLY STORES POINTERS
1022  REM  IN ORDER FOR THIS PROGRAM TO WORK, HIMEM MUST
     BE AT THE SAME
1024  REM  VALUE WHEN THE STRINGS ARE RECALLED AS WHEN T
     HEY ARE STORED.
1026  :
1030 X =  PEEK (115) +  PEEK (116) * 256 -  PEEK (111) -
      PEEK (112) * 256
1040  GOSUB 2100
1050  POKE 30,X -  INT (X / 256) * 256: POKE 31,X / 256:
      CALL  - 307
1052  :
1054  REM  PUT (X) INTO LOCS 30&31, AND WROTE IT TO TAPE
1056  :
1060  REM  (X) IS  THE LENGTH OF THE STRING AREA.
1062  :
1070  POKE 60, PEEK (111): POKE 61, PEEK (112): POKE 62,
      PEEK (115): POKE 63, PEEK (116): CALL  - 307
1072  :
1080  REM  HAVE NOW WRITTEN EVERYTHING.
1082  :
1090  PRINT "O.K. ": RETURN
```

Listing 2A.

```
 LIST 2000-

2000  RECALL B$
2002  :
2004  REM  GOT POINTERS BACK.
2006  :
2010  GOSUB 2100: CALL  - 259
2012  :
2014  REM  GOT LENGTH OF STRING BACK
2016  :
2020 X =  PEEK (30) +  PEEK (31) * 256
2022  :
2024  REM  X IS LENGTH OF AREA TO READ IN
2026  :
2030 X =  PEEK (115) +  PEEK (116) * 256 - X
2040  POKE 60,X -  INT (X / 256) * 256: POKE 61,X / 256
2050  POKE 62, PEEK (115): POKE 63, PEEK (116): CALL  -
     259
2060  RETURN
2100  POKE 60,30: POKE 61,0: POKE 62,31: POKE 63,0: RETURN

2102  :
2104  REM  SET CASSETTE ROUTINE POINTERS

]
```

Listing 2B.

String Saving Program

Listing 2 is the program I found in *'Best of'* for saving and recalling strings from tape. The program is in Applesoft and was written by R. Wigginton from Apple Co. The program is divided into three major sections.

• String input, lines 20 & 30

- Saving the strings, lines 50 and 1000 to 1090
- Recalling the strings, lines 110 to 140 and 2000 to 2060

Most of the program is self-explanatory. At least as far as using it, that is. Some of the peeks and pokes are not so obvious, and a little discussion will be useful. First, remember that a PEEK is used to examine the contents of a memory location. A POKE is used to store a value into a memory location. The values used are the decimal equivalents of hexadecimal numbers.

The string input section in lines 30 and 40 lets you put in 9 strings. By changing the dimension, you can allow as many strings as you would need. So far so good. In line 50 the program jumps to line 1000. This line is the start of the program for saving the strings to tape. Lines 1003 and 1005 allow you to set-up the tape for recording. Once the tape is ready, start the recorder then press any key. Then in line 1010, the variable X is made equal to the amount of free memory left and stored on the tape as a pointer. You will notice that X is the only numeric variable used in this program. It is used, however, in such a way that there is never any conflict. This is a useful technique to remember if you want to save memory. Next in line 1030, X is made equal to the length of memory used to store the strings. Applesoft stores strings starting at high memory down. Decimal memory locations 115 and 116 (hex 73 & 74) contain the address of high memory. The pointer for the address of the start of string storage is in locations 111 and 112 (hex 6F & 70) and this value is subtracted from high memory.

These pointer locations are found on pages 140 and 141 in the Apple II Reference Manual. If you want to find the address, in decimal, stored at any location, use the pointers in direct commands like this.

    PRINT PEEK(LO)+256*PEEK(HI)

Where LO is the low number in the pointer and HI is the high number. Also realize that the opposite is true of the bytes of the actual address. The low number is the high byte and the high number is the low byte. Confusing isn't it! Let's continue with the save routines.

Line 1040 then jumps to a subroutine to set the cassette routine pointers. This is the same routine used when you type SAVE except it will be executed directly by this program. This step tells the routine where to find the data to be saved. On the RETURN, X, the length of the string area to be saved, is stored in two memory locations and then saved on tape. This is done with the command CALL –307. Next, the start and stop addresses of the string area are given to the tape save program and the entire string area is saved

with another call to –307. Note that –307 is the machine language address of the tape save program in the monitor. The hexadecimal address is $FECD.

Getting it All Back

Once you have the strings saved to tape, the next task is to retrieve them. In this program, GOTO 100 sets-up the routine to read the data back into memory. At line 110 the number of strings to be read is dimensioned. Then, the program jumps to line 2000 where the actual tape RECALL will occur. Note that it is not necessary to use the same string variable. Only the data was saved and as long as the pointers and lengths remain the same, any variable can be used. Line 2010 recovers the pointers to the area in memory where the data will be returned. A-tape read call to memory location –259 does this. Location –259 in the monitor is the tape read program. The hexadecimal address is $FEFD. The next two lines appear to be in conflict. To do what was done here you need to know how the interpreter works. In

line 2020 the variable X gets one value. Then, in line 2030, X gets another. The significance is that the value of X is not changed until all the steps following the equal sign are completed. Thus, there is no conflict and X winds up with the value it needs to read back the strings on the tape. After all the pokes are made in lines 2040 and 2050, the final tape-read is made with another call to –259. Following the return to line 130, the strings you stored are printed on the screen and the program ends at line 140.

The program works. After I typed it in and got rid of all my typos and mistakes, I succeeded in storing and recalling a list of strings. The problems will occur if you make any changes at all without rerunning the program segments that establish the pointers to memory and the string storage area length. These are critical. If you don't have a disk storage system, there are lots of possibilities for using this program. You could also connect a control circuit and drive the cassettes from the game paddle ports. Hmmm . . . Interesting idea for a future column.

```
JLIST

1000  REM **************************
1010  REM * DEMO AC CONTROL ROUTINE *
1020  REM *    BY* CHUCK CARPENTER   *
1030  REM **************************
1040  :
1050  REM  ** INITIALIZE **
1060  :
1070  REM * SET VARIABLES TO ZERO
1080  :
1090  LET L1% = 0:L2% = 0
1100  LET L3% = 0 * L4% = 0
1110  :
1120  REM * SET ANO TO AN3 HIGH
1130  :
1140  POKE  - 16295,0:  POKE  - 16293,0
1150  POKE  - 16291,0:  POKE  - 16289,0
1160  :
1170  REM  ** SET TEST LIMITS **
1180  HOME
1190  PRINT : PRINT "ENTER HIGH AND LOW TEST LIMITS"
1200  PRINT "----- ---- --- --- ---- ------"
1210  PRINT : INPUT "PDL-0 LOW TEST LIMIT....";L1%
1220  PRINT : INPUT "PDL-0 HIGH TEST LIMIT...";L2%
1230  PRINT : INPUT "PDL-1 LOW TEST LIMIT....";L3%
1240  PRINT : INPUT "PDL-1 HIGH TEST LIMIT...";L4%
1250  :
1260  REM   ** TEST OF SET LIMITS **
1270  :
1280  PRINT : PRINT : HOME
1290  PRINT "DISPLAY OUT-OF-RANGE TEST"
1300  PRINT "------- ------------ ----"
1310  PRINT : PRINT
1320  IF  PDL (0) < L1% OR  PDL (0) > L2% THEN  POKE  -
      16295,0:  POKE  - 16296,0:  POKE  - 16295,0:  PRINT :
      PRINT "PDL-0 TEST LIMIT OUT-OF-RANGE!"
1330  IF  PDL (1) < L3% OR  PDL (1) > L4% THEN  POKE  -
      16293,0:  POKE  - 16294,0:  POKE  - 16293,0:  PRINT :
      PRINT "PDL-1 TEST LIMIT OUT-OF-RANGE!"
1340  FOR I = 1 TO 1000: NEXT I
1350  :
1360  REM  ** ESCAPE ROUTINE **
1370  :
1380  REM * CHECK THE KEYBOARD
1390  :
1400  IF  PEEK ( - 16384) > 127 = 1 GOTO 1450
1410  :
1420  REM * RESET THE STROBE
1430  :
1440  POKE  - 16368,0: GOTO 1280
1450  POKE  - 16368,0
1460  HOME : PRINT "END OF AC CONTROL TEST PROGRAM.....
      "
```

Listing 3.

Apple Turn-on with Easy I/O

For the circuit tinkerer, here's an idea for turning things on and off with your Apple. The circuit diagram in Figure 1 and Program Listing 3 illustrate a simple AC circuit controller using the Easy I/O connections on the game paddle socket. This circuit and control program can be used to control low power AC devices. Up to 4 circuits are possible but only one will be shown here. Since they are all identical, just add as many more as you want. And this is not the only circuit possible. By using some of the integrated circuit (IC) devices now on the market you can use the 4 single bit output ports (AN0 to AN3) to control up to 16 devices. More on that later.

About the Circuit

A 555 IC is used to provide a timed pulse to the transistor driver. The solid state relay is used to control the AC device. Input to the 555 is provided from the game paddle connector pin 15. This is the AN0 port. Ports for AN1 to 3 are also available. A pulse of short duration is generated at pin 15 from a Basic program and this pulse in turn creates a longer pulse. The components connected to the 555 provide a 2 second output pulse in this circuit. By changing either R1 or C1, the timing of the pulse can be changed. For instance, if the resistor R1 were changed to 500K, the output pulse duration would be around 5 seconds. Should you choose to drive the circuit direct from the AN0 port, just leave out the 555. Then you need to change the direction of the driving voltage. Instead of the short negative going pulse, you would use a constant positive voltage. Again, your Basic program would provide the controlling signal. The dotted line shows the connection to make if the 555 is not used. With a direct connection to the transistor driver, you can turn the AC relay on for any length of time you choose.

About the Program

Listing 3 is a short program to illustrate using the AC control circuit. This program provides a short output pulse to AN0 and AN1. The game paddles are used to provide the control signals. These signals could just as easily be a temperature measuring device or other variable voltage source into the PDL(0) and PDL(1) ports. (Same for the other two game paddle ports too.) For demonstrations though, the game paddles are easily accessible. By setting up a range of high and low test voltages, a pulse is generated when the 'window' is exceeded on either end.

Lines 1050 through 1150 are used to initialize the variables and to set the ports high. Integer variables were used as represented by the % symbol. The pokes used represent the address of the output ports. These addresses set the voltages to the high value. Using an address represented by a higher number (absolute value) will set the ports to the low value. You can see this in lines 1320 and 1330 where the voltage goes from high to low and back to high with the pokes used. It may not be necessary to initialize these levels since they are used in the generation of the pulse. However, I like to know where I am starting.

Test limits are set in lines 1190 to 1240. Since the output range is 0 to 255, a test window range between these limits is selected. In the sample run, the low limit is 20 and the high limit is 200. For closer control, set the limits closer together. The limits can be skewed toward either end, too. Lines 1320 and 1330 are used to test the output values. If the window limits are exceeded, a short pulse is generated to the control circuit. This pulse triggers the 555 IC and a 2 second pulse is generated to drive the solid state relay. If you wanted to use the direct connected circuit, then you would want to change the poke sequence to drive the voltage high to activate the relay.

Then at some other point in the program, poke the voltage back to low to turn the relay off.

As long as you don't press any keys on the keyboard, the program will continue to loop and test input voltages. A delay loop is included in line 1340 to prevent flicker on the screen. To escape from the program, lines 1400 to 1450 test for the pressing of a key and reset the keyboard strobe. And, line 1460 ends it once a key is pressed.

I've used this control circuit and program for machine control. The possibilities for home control and game playing responses are numerous. As I mentioned at the beginning of this section, you can use other IC's for control of several devices. A 74150 TTL IC will provide control signals for 16 outputs. With the input connected to the 4 output ports — connected in binary coded decimal — you can generate pokes to turn any one of the 16 outputs on or off. The *TTL Cookbook* by Don Lancaster (Sams 21035) is a good source of information on TTL applications.

```
RUN

ENTER HIGH AND LOW TEST LIMITS
----- ---- --- --- ---- ------

PDL-0 LOW TEST LIMIT....20

PDL-0 HIGH TEST LIMIT...200

PDL-1 LOW TEST LIMIT....20

PDL-1 HIGH TEST LIMIT...200

DISPLAY OUT-OF-RANGE TEST
------- ------------ ----

PDL-0 TEST LIMIT OUT-OF-RANGE!

PDL-1 TEST LIMIT OUT-OF-RANGE!

DISPLAY OUT-OF-RANGE TEST
------- ------------ ----

DISPLAY OUT-OF-RANGE TEST
------- ------------ ----

PDL-0 TEST LIMIT OUT-OF-RANGE!

DISPLAY OUT-OF-RANGE TEST
------- ------------ ----

PDL-1 TEST LIMIT OUT-OF-RANGE!
END OF AC CONTROL TEST PROGRAM.....

]
```

Example Run of AC Control Test

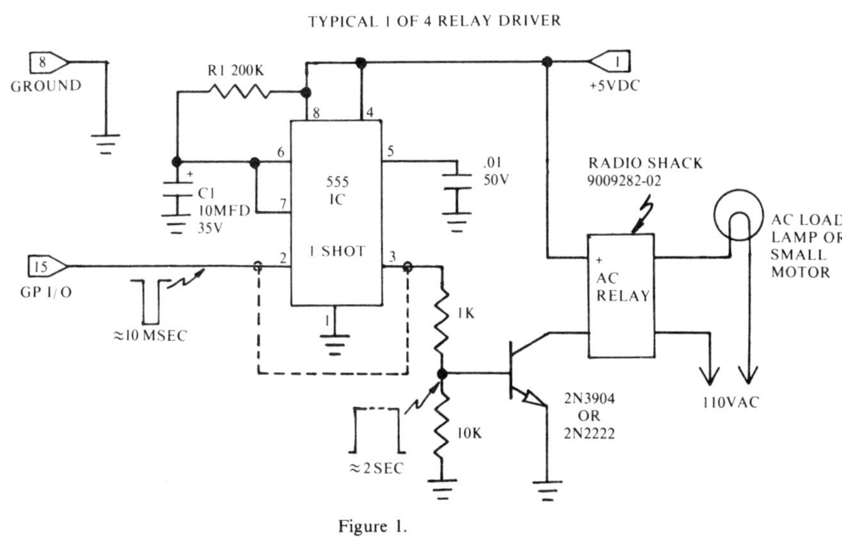

Figure 1.

Assembly Language — Addressing
Head Cleaners •Interrupts

Chuck Carpenter

November, 1980

In the May '80 issue, the Apple Cart column included a section on assembly language fundamentals. To continue with additional fundamentals, this column will describe the principals of indexing. Another 6502 microprocessor feature includes the use of interrupts. The second part of this column will describe simple interrupt control hardware (to monitor remote switches) and a machine language program featuring indexing. The circuit and program will let you monitor the "outside world" and run your favorite program at the same time.

Indexing Principals

Sequencing a data table to print character strings is easily handled in 6502 assembly language by "indexing" the table. Apple's 6502 microprocessor includes a variety of indexing instructions. Two of these, absolute indexing and one form of indirect indexing will be described here. Once the principals of indexing are understood, you can easily master each of the 6502 indexing modes. The examples

included will help you gain this understanding.

Absolute Indexing

Absolute indexing is accomplished by locating the characters in a table relative to the starting address of the table. To determine the relative position in the table, a displacement value is added to the starting address. In the 6502, there are 3 registers used for processing data in a program. One is the accumulator or A register and the others are the X and Y index registers. Absolute indexing uses the A register — to contain the base address — and the X or Y register to hold the offset or index value. In our examples, we'll use the X register. This sounds confusing so let's look at an example.

In this program line example, the main program starts at address $0800 (the $ symbol means a hexadecimal number). The assembled machine language represents the indexing opcode and starting address (operand) of the table. Remember that the operand determines the address

mode which modifies the instruction and establishes the final opcode. This operand indicates an indexing operation; address $0900 plus the current value of the X register. The character table starts at address $0900. Each character in the table will be found at the absolute value of X added to the base address $0900. The value of X is the displacement value.

Another View Point

One more example will help show the mechanism of absolute indexing. Let's examine a program segment that will display a character string. For instance, if you wanted to display your name and the year, you might set up a table as shown in Figure 1. First, you need to start with the offset value for the table in the X register. In this case we start with zero. The first character is at address $0900. So, we don't need a displacement for the first character. Then we load the accumulator with the character found at address $0900 plus the current value in the X register. The operand $0900, X indicates this condition. That is, the accumulator is to hold the character at base address $0900 indexed absolute by the value of the X register. The first time through, the character loaded in the accumulator will be the first letter of your name. This character is printed out on the screen by the monitor routine at address $FDED. Next the X value is compared to the value for the end of the list + one. Because the X register and the end-of-list value are not equal, the routine branches back to the label INDEX to get the next character in the table.

The second time through, the value in the X register is now $01 and the accumulator will be loaded with the character in $0901. The print-out, incre-

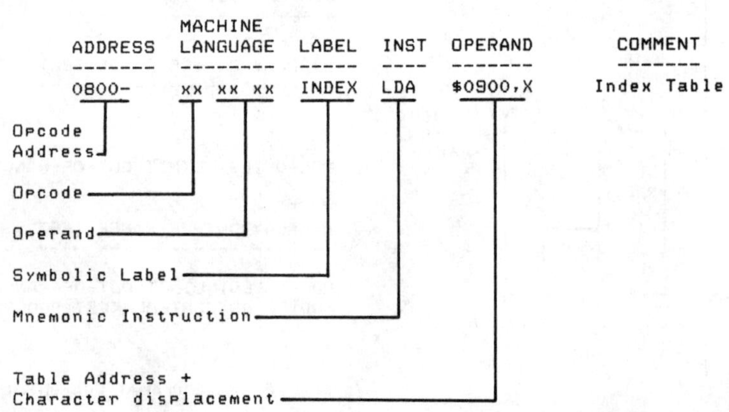

```
LABEL   INST    OPERAND         COMMENT
-----   ----    -------         -------
        LDX     #$00        ; index displacement
INDEX   LDA     $0900,X     ; read table
        JSR     $FDED       ; print character
        INX                 ; next character
        CPX     #$0E        ; table length + 1
        BNE     INDEX       ; back if not done
        RTS                 ; end it if it is

0900-  Y
0901-  O
0902-  U
0903-  R
0904-  spc
0905-  N
0906-  A
0907-  M
0908-  E
0909-  spc
090a-  Y
090b-  E
090c-  A
090d-  R
```

Figure 1.

Put as many characters as needed in the table. Use the ASCII value as shown on pages 138 and 139 of the Applesoft reference manual.

```
LABEL   INST    OPERAND         COMMENT
-----   ----    -------         -------
        LDX     #$04        ; 5 char. offset
INDEX   LDA     $0900,X     ; index table
        JSR     $FDED       ; print character
        DEX                 ; next character
        BPL     INDEX       ; back it not done
        RTS                 ; end it if it is

0900-  4F   (O)
0901-  4C   (L)
0902-  4C   (L)
0903-  45   (E)
0904-  48   (H)
```

Figure 2.
Short-table indexing.

menting, and comparing operations are carried out as before. The cycle is then repeated until the entire table is completed. When the compare is equal, the routine ends. Note that the characters all include the high-order bit. That is, a hex 80 is added to the ASCII value of the character. Otherwise, because of an Apple video characteristic, the output would be in reverse video. Indexing in this manner will allow up to 256 characters in a table. (Decrementing from $FF to $00 equals 256 steps.)

Try It This Way Too

To index a table longer than 256 bytes, you would need to use other techniques. One way would be to hold the index displacement constant and increment the memory locations. An example will be included with indirect indexing later. For shorter tables — less than 128 characters — a shorter program is possible. An example is shown in Figure 2. This version is similar to our previous example. Except, it's shorter and reversed.

The displacement value starts at the end of the table and the last character is read first. Rather than increment X we decrement it. And, the branch to get the next character is taken as long as X remains plus. Plus (or minus) is determined by the sign bit of the placement value. If the eighth bit is a zero, the value is plus. If the eighth is a one, the value is minus ($00 to $7F are plus — $80 to $FF are minus). When the value of X is decremented from $00 to $FF the sign bit becomes minus and the program ends. Because half the indexing values will be plus and the other half minus, this technique will only allow a 128 character table to be indexed.

This is the simplest form of indexing. By incrementing or decrementing the index register you can sequentially "pick" the data from your table. The operand (memory location plus the value in the index register) points to the character in the table.

Indirect Addressing

Indirect addressing does essentially the same thing as absolute except one more step is added. With indirect addressing, the operand, plus the index value, points to the memory location that points to memory where the table is. Simple, right! Here's a diagram to illustrate the technique.

```
0800-        LDY #$00
0802-        LDA ($0300),Y This operand
0805-        INY
  .
  .
0300-00      0900+Y       Points to this
0301-09                   Memory location
  .
  .
0900- 54 (T)              Which points to
0901- 41 (A)              the table
0902- 42 (B)
0903- 4C (L)
0904- 45 (E)
```

For simple table-reading programs, absolute indexing is adequate. Indirect indexing is more appropriate where code economy and speed of operation are important. For such applications, you must index from page zero. In the example above, the code is for pages 3, 8 and 9 (arbitrary for purposes of illustration). The next example shows the code to use for zero page indexing.

```
0800-        LDY #$00
0802-        LDA ($3A),Y
0804-        INY
  .
  .
```

Note that the indexing instruction implies a two-address indirect location; $0300-$0301 and $3A–$3B.

Another application of indirect addressing might be a block memory move. A typical example in the Apple II is the memory move command for the monitor. If you examine the code for this routine you will see a useful technique variation. Rather than increment or decrement an offset value, the memory addresses are incremented. Here's a short program to list a portion of memory. The routine at $FCBA is used by the memory move routine to compare byte counts.

```
MOVMEM
LDY #$00    ; index offset value
LDA (3C),Y  ; get the byte indirect
JSR $FDDA   ; print the byte in A
LDA #$A0    ; space character
JSR $FDED   ; print the character
              in A
JSR $FCBA   ; compare byte count
BCC MOVMEM  ; not done — go back
RTS         ; done — end it
```

Indexing in this example is page zero indirect. The index offset value is not changed. But, if you examine the monitor routine at $FCBA, you will see that the memory address is incremented. When the beginning address is equal to the ending address the carry flag is set. At this point the program is ended by the RTS.

If you set up a jump to the label MOVMEM address at $03F8 then the (CTRL) Y monitor function can be used. For instance, if $0800 is the starting address then at $03F8 to $03FA store 4C 00 08. To run the program enter the starting address a period and the ending

address; like this —
    MEMSTART.MEMEND.
Now press CTRL and Y. When you do the control Y, the monitor will jump to the program address stored at location #03F8 and the memory contents from MEM-START TO MEMEND will be printed on the screen. Again, if you read through the program at $FCBA in the listing of the monitor, you will find that the indirect memory location at $3C – $3B is incremented. The table being indexed is the range of memory you specify by MEM-START.MEMEND. (Note: *Indexing Principals* is rewritten from articles I wrote originally published in the Southeastern Software Newsletter.)

Head Cleaners

3M has developed a product to clean disk drive heads. Included in the kit are two special "diskettes" and a bottle of cleaning fluid. The kit allows you to clean the heads without opening the case. High-use systems should use the kit about once a month. Most of us only need to use it every 6 months or so (or if "funny" things happen to stored programs). Note that some diskettes cause more head contamination than others; especially the bargain types. In this case, you must use the kit more frequently. Order model 7440, the 5 inch size, for your Apple drives. You can get the kit from most 3M distributors or from Data Recording Products Division/3M, St. Paul, MN 55101. The cost is $30.00.

We Now Interrupt . . .

There are two types of interrupt capability in the Apple II. One is called a Non Maskable Interrupt (NMI) and the other is a Maskable Interrupt (IRQ). The interrupts are connected to the 6502 microprocessor in the Apple II. (NMI and IRQ are abbreviations for the name of the interrupt and not assembly language mnemonics.) Both will allow you to monitor some remote function while running a program. The NMI will halt the program regardless of any other condition. The IRQ (Interrupt request) will not halt the program unless you clear the interrupt flag allowing the interrupt to occur. Setting the interrupt flag will prevent an IRQ from taking control. From this discussion you can see that NMI is the highest priority interrupt.

Interrupt Access

Both of the interrupts are available from the expansion connectors; pins 29 and 30 for NMI and IRQ respectively. Usual access is made through the edge connector of a circuit board made to plug into the expansion connector. One such board is the Apple prototyping board. This is an expensive way to connect to just two

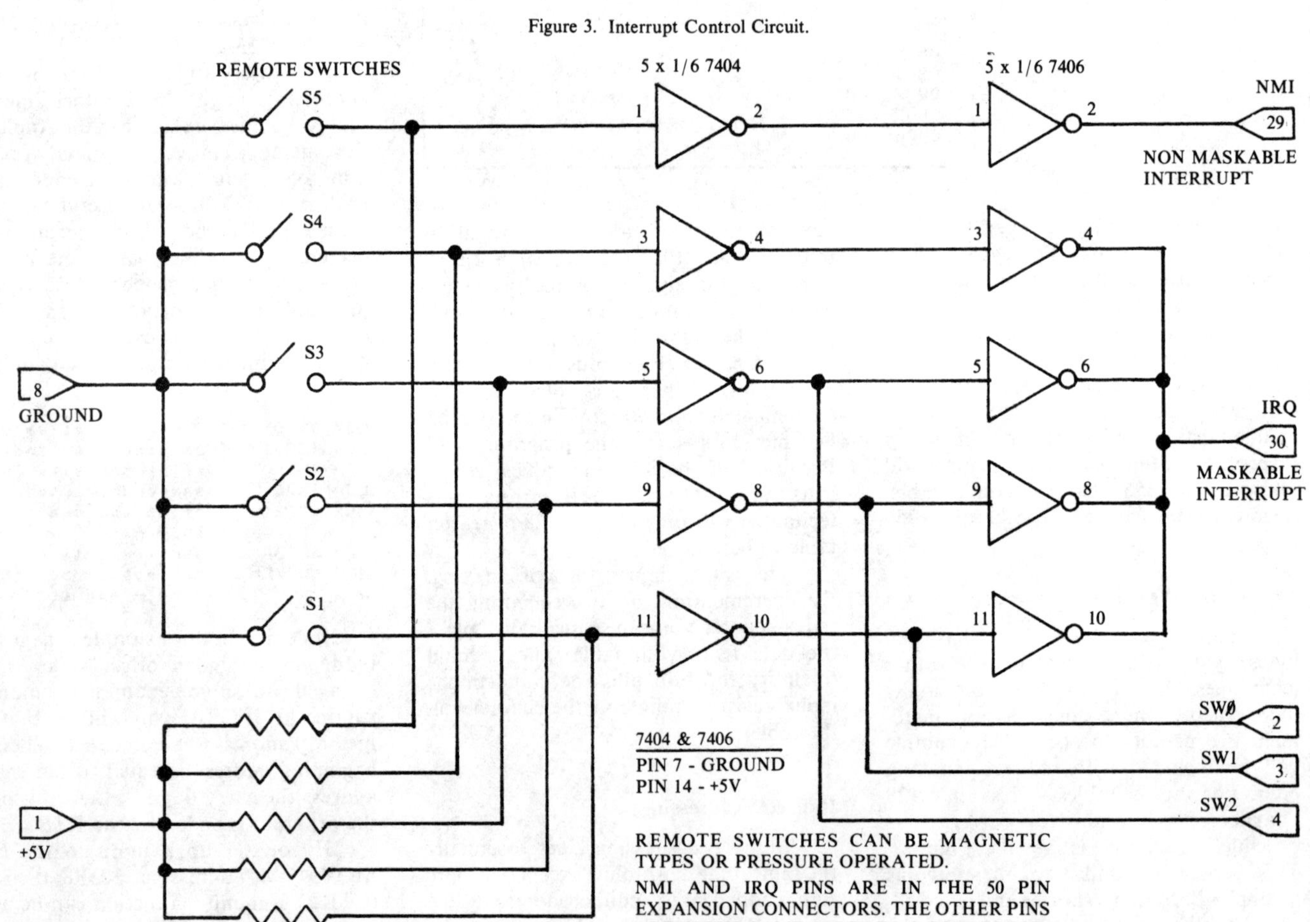

Figure 3. Interrupt Control Circuit.

USE A CONTROL PROGRAM LIKE LISTING 1 TO SENSE THE IRQ INPUTS. A SIMILAR PROGRAM AT A DIFFERENT MEMORY LOCATION CAN BE USED FOR NMI. THE MULTIPLE INTERRUPT INPUT COULD ALSO BE USED FOR NMI. JUST CONNECT THE 4-SWITCH CIRCUIT TO PIN 29 INSTEAD OF PIN 30. THE PROGRAM IN LISTING 1 WOULD BE THE SAME. THE S5 CIRCUIT CAN BE LEFT OFF IF ONLY ONE INTERRUPT TYPE IS USED.

pins. One idea would be to find a scrap circuit board with the proper edge connector. Cut the connector off and solder wires to the two interrupt pins. Connect these wires to a 16 pin component header plugged into the game paddle I/O socket. Use the two pins which are not connected to other circuits (9 and 16). Some of the other pins will be used for other interrupt monitoring connections.

Another possibility would be to remove the main circuit board and jumper the interrupt lines to the unused GP I/O socket pins. If you or someone you know has experience making jumpers on circuit boards, this is the best way. You could mess up the board so don't try it unless you know what you're doing. Doing this will void warranties, too. The connections to the GP I/O of the NMI and IRQ signal lines make it possible to make other simple connections for monitoring more than two devices. We'll get to that shortly.

Signal Levels

Both the interrupt lines have pull-up resistors. This means that an active low signal is required to cause an interrupt to occur. The NMI is edge sensitive. When an input of the proper direction occurs, the interrupt occurs. The duration of the input signal is not important. Only the leading edge of the signal is sensed. However, no other input to NMI can occur until the current interrupting signal returns from low to high. The IRQ on the other hand is level sensitive. A signal change to active low for some period of time is required to make the interrupt occur. The minimum amount of time is the length of the longest instruction cycle. This is because the interrupt does not happen until the current cycle is completed. Again, the signal must go away before any other maskable interrupts can occur. A useful reference on the discussion of 6502 interrupts can be found in *Micro* magazine for July 1980, page 47.

An Interrupt Program

Listing 1A is an assembly language program for polling a series of switches used in the circuit of Figure 3. This circuit allows monitoring of the non maskable interrupt as the priority input. It also provides for polling of 4 inputs to the maskable interrupt. Since we are using the three switch input bits in the GP I/O connector, we can have 4 input circuits, the assumption being that we can test three inputs directly and default to the fourth. The flow chart in Figure 4 illustrates the assumption. Before we continue with a discussion of the interrupt program, a short digression is needed to establish the maskable interrupt initialization (if you are to include this capability in a Basic program).

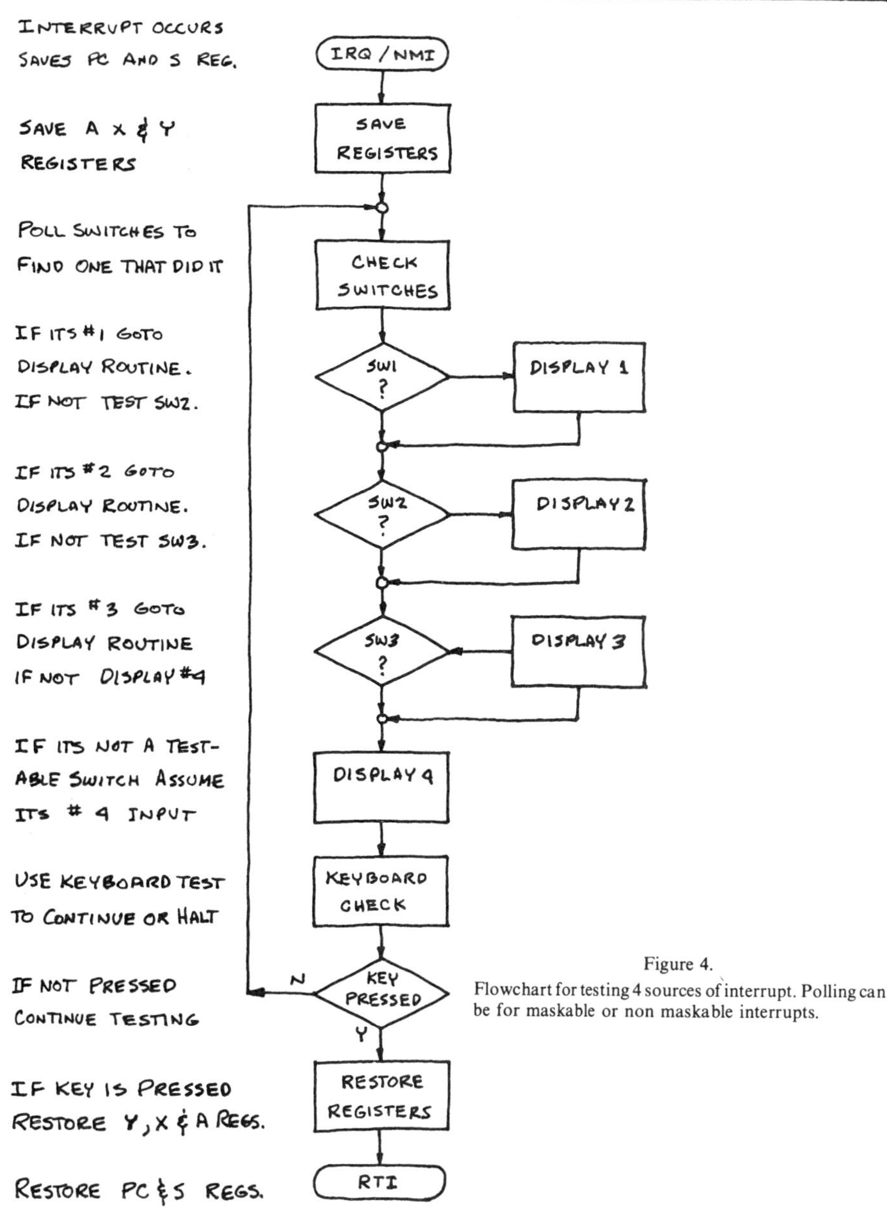

Figure 4.
Flowchart for testing 4 sources of interrupt. Polling can be for maskable or non maskable interrupts.

Initializing Interrupts

The Apple monitor is the first place where interrupts are processed. A jump indirect through the address stored at locations $03FE and $03FF occurs as the result of an IRQ input. The address of the interrupt handling routine would be stored at these addresses. Addresses $03FB to $03FD are used to contain a jump to the address of the program used to handle non maskable interrupts. The addresses can be the same or different depending on your needs for interrupt handling. Our example program in Listing 1 is for IRQ input. The handling requirements are similar so the program will serve as an illustration for IRQ and NMI application.

In addition to initializing the vector addresses to the handling programs, the IRQ flag must be set. The mnemonic instructions used to do this are CLI (58 hex, 88 dec) to allow the IRQ to interrupt the program, and SEI (78 hex, 120 dec) to prevent interrupts from the IRQ input. As you might guess, the mnemonics stand for clear interrupt and set interrupt. In a Basic program the initialization can be handled by a series of POKEs to memory. To poke the interrupt routine address use

    xxxx POKE 1022,00
    xxxx POKE 1023,03

to put the IRQ routine at address $0300. And, use

    xxxx POKE 1019,76
    xxxx POKE 1020,00
    xxxx POKE 1021,03

to put the NMI routine at address $0300. Note that 76 is the decimal value of the op code $4C (mnemonic JMP). Additionally, provide a way to set or clear the interrupt flag as desired when you start the program. You can use pokes to do this too.

Following an input line asking the program user which choice, use

    xxxx POKE 10,88:POKE 11,60
    xxxx CALL 10:RETURN

to allow interrupts and,

    xxxx POKE 10,120:POKE 11,60
    xxxxCALL 10:RETURN

to prevent interrupts. Again, use these as part of your initialization program. Addresses 10 and 11 ($A and $B) are used for the USR function. If your program includes the USR function find another pair of addresses to use.

The Program

Listing 1B is an assembly language program to poll several inputs to the single IRQ line. This program checks each of the three switch inputs. If one of them is not on, the assumption is made that it is the fourth. Whichever input causes the interrupt will be displayed on the screen. Should any other switch close, that input will be displayed too. All inputs must return to the normal open state before the cycle can be started over. Since this program and circuit are intended only for demonstration, no attempt was made to provide automatic reset. The program is somewhat self explanatory. Only a brief comment is required to clarify the function of each section.

The first section equates actual memory locations to symbolic names. This allows you to use the name in place of the memory location. The assembler will keep track of the locations at assembly time. Each of the switch input addresses, the keyboard, and monitor routines to be used are equated to labels. The program is then assigned the originating address of $0300. This address could be any place you have space for the interrupt handling routines.

Registers not saved by the IRQ (or NMI) are saved in this sequence. The status register and the program counter are saved as a result of the interrupt. To insure that other registers will be saved, they are pushed on the stack by this sequence. Once the routine is completed, the opposite sequence is performed to restore the registers. This is accomplished by the RESTOR sequence. Having saved and restored all the registers, you can return back to the interrupted program exactly where you left off.

Next, each switch is tested. If any switch is on, the program branches to a routine to display this fact on the screen. Three switches are tested and a default is made to the fourth interrupting device. The assumption is made that this routine is running because an interrupt occurred. Therefore, if it's not one of the testable switches, it must be the one left.

Having tested and displayed the switch indicating the interrupt source, the program returns and repeats the test of the inputs. But, not before the keyboard input is tested for a pressed key. If no key has been pressed, the routine continues. Should any other input switches close, they will be displayed too. Response to the reason for the interrupt can be made at this time. If a key is pressed, the program passes to the register restore section. The key-testing routine permits you to allow the interrupt condition to continue until you have made whatever action is necessary.

Following the restoring section is the common routine for displaying the response. Depending on the activated circuit, a register is loaded with the switch number. This number is then used by the following routine to display a message and indicate the switch number. The alarm message uses the absolute indexing method mentioned at the beginning of this column. The message is contained in an ASCII string at the end of the program. □

Listing 1A.

```
LIS 1000,1500

1000 ******************************
1010 * INTERRUPT POLLING ROUTINE *
1020 * BY: CHUCK CARPENTER  7/80 *
1030 ******************************
1040
1050 *   USES THE SYNTAX OF THE
1060 *   S-C ASSEMBLER II
1070
1080 *   SYMBOLIC ADDRESS ASSIGNMENTS
1090
1100 SW1    .EQ $C061   SWITCH-IN PIN2 GP I/O
1110 SW2    .EQ $C062   SWITCH-IN PIN3
1120 SW3    .EQ $C063   SWITCH-IN PIN4
1130 KEY    .EQ $C000   KEYBOARD DATA
1140 STROBE .EQ $C010   CLEAR KEYBOARD STROBE
1150 CHROUT .EQ $FDED   MONITOR CHARACTER OUT
1160
1170        .OR $0300   PAGE 3 ORIGIN
1180
1190 *   SAVE THE REGISTERS
1200
1210 SAVE   PHA         SAVE ACCUMULATOR ON STACK
1220        TXA         PUT X IN A
1230        PHA         SAVE X ON STACK
1240        TYA         PUT Y IN A
1250        PHA         SAVE Y ON STACK
1260
1270 *   CHECK THE SWITCHES AND DISPLAY
1280 *   THE ONES THAT ARE ON
1290
1300 CHK1   LDA SW1     CHECK SWITCH 1
1310        BPL CHK2    NOT ON-GOTO SW2
1320        JSR DISP1   ON-GOTO DISPLAY 1
1330 CHK2   LDA SW2     CHECK SWITCH 2
1340        BPL CHK3    NOT ON-GOTO SW3
1350        JSR DISP2   ON-GOTO DISPLAY 2
1360 CHK3   LDA SW3     CHECK SWITCH 3
1370        BPL CHK4    NOT ON - MUST BE 4
1380        JSR DISP3   ON-GOTO DISPLAY 3
1390 CHK4   JSR DISP4   DISPLAY BY DEFAULT
1400
1410 *   PRESS A KEY TO ESCAPE
1420 *   FROM POLLING ROUTINE
1430
1440 KYBD   LDA KEY     CHECK FOR PRESSED KEY
1450        BPL CHK1    NOT PRESSED-BACK TO SW TEST
```

```
1460        STA STROBE  PRESSED-CLEAR STROBE
1470
1480 *   RESTORE THE REGISTERS THEN
1490 *   BACK TO MAIN PROGRAM
1500
:
```

Listing 1B.

```
LIS 1510,1870

1510 RESTOR PLA         GET Y BACK TO A
1520        TAY         PUT A IN Y
1530        PLA         GET X BACK TO A
1540        TAX         PUT A IN X
1550        PLA         GET A BVACK
1560        RTI         GOTO MAIN PROGRAM
1570
1580 *   PUT THE SWITCH NUMBER INTO
1590 *   TEMPORARY STORAGE
1600
1610 DISP1  LDA #$31     SWITCH 1 ON
1620        STA $FA      STORE IN IN SCRATCH LCTN
1630        JMP CRT      JUMP TO DISPLAY RTNE
1640 DISP2  LDA #$32     SWITCH 2 ON
1650        STA $FA      STORE IT
1660        JMP CRT      JUMP TO DISPLAY
1670 DISP3  LDA #$33     SWITCH 3 ON
1680        STA $FA      STORE IT
1690        JMP CRT      JUMP TO DISPLAY
1700 DISP4  LDA #$34     SWITCH 4 ON
1710        STA $FA      STORE IT
1720
1730 *   PRINT THE ALARM MESSAGE
1740
1750 CRT    LDY #$0F     LOAD INDEX DISPLACEMENT
1760 CRT1   LDA TABLE,Y  PRINT THE MESSAGE
1770        ORA #$80     SET HI BIT - NORMAL VIDEO
1780        JSR CHROUT   PRINT THE CHARACTER IN A
1790        DEY          NEXT CHARACTER
1800        BPL CRT1     BACK FOR MORE TABLE
1810        LDA $FA      LOAD THE ON-SWITCH #
1820        JSR CHROUT   PRINT IT
1830        LDA #$8D     LOAD A CARRIAGE RETURN
1840        JSR CHROUT   PRINT IT
1850        RTS          BACK TO INTERRUPT ROUTINE
1860 TABLE  .AS " HCTIWS TA MRALA"
1870        .EN
:
```

Dos 3.3 •Applesoft Bug
Micro-Verter •Applesoft Billboard
Tips From Here and There •Microsoft Softcard

Chuck Carpenter

January, 1981

Well, here we are in another year. Lots of things have happened in the Apple world. And, I expect a lot more will happen. There are a dozen or so companies making accessories and many more writing software. I mentioned a directory of Apple products in last months column. This same company publishes a directory of Apple software. And, I have seen at least one other company offering a directory of Apple software. The magazine is called *Peelings II* and is dedicated to reviewing software for the Apple. Like any review, the contents are biased by the preference and interests of the reviewers. They claim to be impartial but we are, after all, human creatures. Even so, the magazine is a valuable source of information about the software and its general worth. *Peelings II*, at $15.00 for 6 issues, is available from Peelings II, 945 Brook Circle, Las Cruces, NM 88001; Phone (505) 523-5088 evenings. At this time (Sep. '80), the copy I have is Vol 1 No. 2. If you're interested, you may want to get all the back issues too.

DOS 3.3

This new Disk Operating System (DOS)from Apple converts your 13 sector system to a 16 sector system. You can still use your 13 sector disks as-is but the process is more awkward. You can't boot directly from 13 sector disks so you have to go through a 2 step process each time.

Included with the DOS 3.3 package are the following:
•Two new ROMS for the controller card
•A ROM puller tool
•The DOS Manual
•A 16 sector Master System diskette
•A Basics diskette
The ROMs are installed in place of 2 that come with the disk drive controller card. The programs in these ROMs allow the system to "read" the 16 sector diskettes. After you install them, you can no longer use 13 sector diskettes to boot the system. To use 13 sector disks, first boot the system with the Basics diskette. Then insert the 13 sector diskette and run. As long as no problems occur you can change from one diskette to another, If you're using the protected type diskettes (not copyable) you have to start over from the beginning to change to another diskette. Same thing if a loss of 13 sector DOS occurs. The 16 sector Basics disk has to be booted first, then run the 13 sector disk.

All is not lost though. Included on the 16 sector Master System diskette are programs to convert (move programs from) 13 sector disks to 16 sector disks. Since you gain about 23K more storage space on a diskette, there is some advantage. Also, the 16 sector system is compatible with the language card system and the new Softcard CP/M and MBasic system from Microsoft. (The ROMs used to convert the controller card are the same as those for the Language Card system.) Once you programs are moved from 13 to 16 sector diskettes, operation is the same as always. You could even initialize the diskettes with new volume numbers and HELLO programs before you transfer programs. (Dave Powell, now stationed in Germany, might appreciate this bit of information.) The transfer of programs is made easy with a program called MUFFIN. This program lets you transfer all types of individual files or complete catalogs with single or multiple drive systems.

Another program included on the System Master diskette is called FID (File Developer). This program has two functions. First, it lets you easily catalog, copy,delete, lock and unlock all types of DOS files. Second, it lets you copy from one diskette to another with only one disk drive. This program extends the capabilities of the system allowing you to more easily work with files and the DOS.

The DOS manual is a revised and expanded version of the original DOS 3.2 manual. Most of the information is the same. There are new sections covering operation using 16 sector diskettes. A section on Format of Diskettes Information is expanded as is the section on Using Machine Language Files, especially the RWTS (Read or Write a Track or Sector) subroutine. Other sections fully describe the features and use of the FID and MUFFIN programs.

I heard rumblings at one of our Apple Corps meetings that DOS 3.3 would work only on 48K systems. I can't tell you otherwise, since mine is 48K. Check it out first. You can get DOS 3.3 for about $60.00 from your Apple supplier.

Reader Input

Randy Reeves from Cypress, TX sends along a tip for relief of programmers eyes. He has found that the plastic material sold in auto stores for reducing glare in your car, works well for cutting down glare from the monitor. The effect can also be achieved by using the sun screen material sold at hardware stores. Randy is also recommending the Program Line Editor from Synergistic Software. This program is also available from *Call A.P.P.L.E.* if you are a member. The editor is being used by serveral of our club members and is claimed to cut down programming time. I have it but have not used it enough to make any knowledgeable comment.

In the August '80 column, I commented on the declining quality of disk drives being shipped by Apple. Apparently others have experienced problems similar to mine. From Otterbein College in Westerville, Ohio, David Deeve sent along his techiniques for dealing with the problem. He writes, "I've found it works well to insert the disk, close the door, reopen the door and close it again." (This centers the diskette on the clamp...C.C) And he continues, "Also, when first initializing or copying a disk I always remove it, reinsert it and try a CATALOG to assure me that the disk was properly written." David also included what he finds to be an undocumented Pascal item. "If you have a codefile named SYSTEM.STARTUP (not SYSTEM.STARTUP.CODE) it will run automatically when the disk is booted. That is, a turnkey or "HELLO" type program."

An Applesoft Bug

A letter from Joe Verzulli from Port Jefferson Station, NY, turned up an interesting little Applesoft Quirk. The problem has to do with the use of string variables when DOS is not in use. It was an interesting coincidence that the July/August issue of *Call A.P.P.L.E.* included a short piece describing the same problem. Joe's example program looks like this:

```
10 GET R$

20 T = VAL(R$)

30 PRINT T
```

If you type in a number less than 9 for the GET, you will see the number printed to the 16th power. If you add:

```
15 R$ = R$
```

The problem seems to go away. I got as far as determining that a second variable was added to string variable table. You can do this by examining the area of memory where string variables are stored. In Applesoft, this is from HIMEM down. As you will recall, without DOS, HIMEM is at 49152 or $BFFF (HEX). I puzzled over the reasons for a while and called for help. I called Bob Sander-Cederlof at S-C Software and described the problem. He had just seen the *Call A.P.P.L.E.* item too. After discussing it for a few minutes, I had a better understanding and sent along a reply to Joe. A couple of days later I received a more detailed analysis from Bob to include in the column.

The Details

If you have a 48k Apple, and start up Applesoft without DOS, the program included by Joe and similar ones by others will produce strange results. If the number 1 is entered, the value printed is 1,11111111E16. For 2 you will get 2.22222222E16 and for 9 it becomes 1E17. Continuing essentially as Bob wrote it, this is what happens.

"The VAL function in Applesoft has a bug. I looked into the code (from $E707 through $E745 in the ROMs), and here is what it does. It finds the string, and sets the address of the first byte of the string into $5E and $5F. (Remember that $ means a hexadecimal number...C.C.) Then it adds the length, and stores the address of the byte following the string in $60 and $61. The value stored in that byte is saved on the stack, and a zero put in its place. Then the FIN subroutine is called, to convert the string to a floating point value. After the conversion is finished, the original contents of that byte are restored from the stack.

"The problem is this. In our little program, GET(R$) creates the R$ string at location $BFFF. The byte following is $C000, but there is no memory there. In fact, $C000 is the input register from the Apple keyboard! When VAL tries to store a zero at $C000, nothing happens. The FIN subroutine reads the digit you typed once at $BFFF, and then 16 more times at $C000, $C001,..., $COOF. That is a total of 17 digits, like this: "11111111111111111". The value of such a string is truly 1,11111111E16, just like the Apple said. If you type a 9, the value is rounded up to 1E17.

"Inserting the statement R$=R$ causes Applesoft to create another copy of the string at $BFFE, which is a safe location. Safe, because the zero VAL inserts will go at $BFFF, which is a real memory location.

"Another way to avoid this problem is to use HIMEM:49151 instead of the normal 49152 that is automatically set up. Still another way is to be certain that R$ is not the first use of a string. But my preferred "fix" is to buy a disk drive or two and use DOS. When DOS is loaded (in a 48K machine), HIMEM is at $9600, and everything works fine!"

Bob and I also discussed what would happen in a machine with less than 48K. Our guess is that it will be garbage since there is nothing there. Or, it just might seem to work ok. If you have a less-than-48K machine, try it out. My thanks to Bob for sharing this in-depth analysis.

Micro-Verter

If you haven't bought a modulator for your Apple, try this one. The Micro-Verter by ATV Research is battery operated and requires only one connection to the video output connector on the Apple. No connection is required to the TV since the signal is radiated by a short antenna stub on the Micro-Verter. The modulator is designed to work in the UHF channel range. After I installed the batteries, I experimented with the tuning range. I found that it would tune from channel 14 to 21. The unit seemed to operate the best on channel 17. There was practically zero distortion and very clear color on this channel. My guess is that I was in the center of the tuning range. This would be likely to give the best balance of bandwidth and other desirable characteristics. Speaking of distortion, this unit provides the cleanest signal of all the modulators I have tried. Since you do not have to connect the unit to the TV set, the worms from computer switching harmonics are practically nonexistent. Another feature I found useful also relates to the freedom from connections. If you wanted to use several monitors for demonstration purposes, you can use the Micro-Verter with a 6in hairpin antenna connected to the stub. This way the signal can be used by several sets within a 10 foot or so radius of the modulator. Very handy in a classroom environment. I used it this way when I taught an assembly language class.

The unit is packaged in a metal box and includes all connectors, cables, and a battery holder inside. There is a power switch on the front. Even though the unit will last several months with the switch left on, the switch provides extended battery life. The battteries are not included with the modulator. One note of caution. Use a plastic screw driver to tune the unit to the desired operating channel. This is not mentioned in the instructions. A metal screw driver could distort the tuning and is likely to short the metal case. The Micro-Verter is $35.00 postpaid in the U.S. and Canada, from ATV Reasearch, 13N. Broadway, Dakota City, Nebraska 68731; phone (402) 987-3771.

From Here And There

As a result of collecting Apple information from all over, I have accumulated several clever and useful programming ideas. The first one is shown is listing 1. This is the control program from Southeastern Software's *Magazine Article File Program*. The program sets-up a menu of options. Then, you can use the escape key (ESC) to move the cursor over the selections. Several ASCII values are used in the program. You will see these in the CHR$ functions. These are:
•CHR$(4) (CTRL) D
•CHR$(13) (RETURN)
•CHR$(27) (ESC)
•CHR$(91) left bracket
You can find all the ASCII codes on pages 138 and 139 in the Applesoft reference manual.
Each of the menu options are posi-

```
0 D$ =  CHR$ (13) +  CHR$ (4)
20  HOME
30  PRINT D$;"NOMON C,I,O"
40  VTAB 2: HTAB 9: PRINT "SOUTHE
    ASTERN SOFTWARE"
42  HTAB 7: PRINT "MAGAZINE ARTIC
    LE PROGRAM"
50  PRINT "----------------------"
60  VTAB 8: PRINT " USE THE "; CHR$
    (91);"ESC] KEY TO MOVE THE C
    URSOR"
70  PRINT "TO YOUR SELECTION AND
    THEN TYPE 'RETURN'"
80  VTAB 12
90  PRINT " CREATE/ADD FILE"
100  PRINT " SEARCH FILE"
110  PRINT " CORRECT FILE"
120  PRINT " LIST CONTENTS OF EN
    TIRE FILE"
130  PRINT " TRANSFER FILE AND P
    OINTERS"
140  PRINT " END PROGRAM"
200 SE = 1:VT = 12
210  VTAB VT: GET SE$
220  IF SE$ =  CHR$ (13) THEN  VTAB
    20: GOTO 260
230  IF SE$ =  CHR$ (27) THEN VT =
    VT + 1:SE = SE + 1
240  IF SE = 7 THEN 200
250  GOTO 210
260  PRINT : VTAB VT: FLASH : PRINT
    "*": NORMAL
265  ON SE GOTO 300,310,320,330,3
    40,350
300  PRINT D$;"RUN CR MAG FILE"
310  PRINT D$;"RUN MAG FILE SRCH"

320  PRINT D$;"RUN CRRT MAG FILE"

330  PRINT D$;"RUN MAG FILE DUMP"

340  PRINT D$;"RUN MAG FILE EXCH"

350  VTAB 23: END
65535  REM
```
Listing 1

tioned on the screen in lines 80 to 140.
Lines 200 to 250 move the cursor from
selection to selection when the (ESC) key
is pressed. The GET command is used to
check for the (RETURN) key. When it is
pressed, the program branches to line 260
where a flashing asterisk is put next to
your selection. Then depending on the
selection number, a program is loaded
and run. This is also a good way to conserve memory. If all the menu options
were too large to fit in memory at once,
this technique overlays memory with the
current operating program. At the end of
the current option, you would run the
menu program again.

Here's another one from the Southeastern Software *Newsletter*. In the
August '80 issue I included an Integer
Basic program called 'puff'. This program
would scroll a message across the screen
billboard style. For those of you without
Integer Basic, here's one in Applesoft. It
was written by Dr. Romano and it
appeared in *Newsletter* number 7. See
Listing 2.

This program, also a billboard scrolling
program, is from *The Apple Gram*
(Dallas). It's called *Moving Title Demonstration* and was written by Bob Sander-
Cederlof. See Listing 3.

This program is a little less obvious so
I'll include the description that goes

alongwith it. First, the program clears the
screen, sets text mode and sets the variable 'Q' equal to the address of the
Apple's speaker. Next in line 30, two rows
of stars are printed. These are for the title
to pass through. In line 80 the title content is defined and made equal to the
length of the row of stars; 34 in this example. Moving the title is accomplished in
line 90. The title is centered by the limits
of the FOR loop, and sound is created by
the PEEK(Q) function. Line 95 is a delay
loop giving the user time to read the display. In line 110, the program is listed so
you don't have to do it.

Another one from *The Apple Gram*
and also by Bob, helps you ask questions
in the program. Here's how it goes...
Many times when you want to ask the
user of a program a question, they must
answer either "yes" or "no". I must have
written a thousand different versions of
this kind of question routine. Sometimes
I code them in line, and sometimes I am
smart enough to write a general subroutine to do it.

```
]LIST
1  HOME
3  VTAB 12
5  INPUT "........ THE BILLBOARD
     SHALL READ ...... ? ";A$
6 A$ = "
                     " + A$: REM *
    ** THE SPACE BETWEEN THE QUO
    TATION MARKS IS 40 SPACES
10  HOME
20 L =  LEN (A$)
30  FOR X = 1 TO L
40 S = L - X
50  VTAB 12
60  PRINT  MID$ (A$,X,40);
70  IF S < 40 THEN  PRINT  MID$ (
    A$,1,39 - S)
80  FOR T = 1 TO 150: NEXT T
90  NEXT X: GOTO 30
]
```
Listing 2

Finally, I hit upon a really neat subroutine for answering this kind of question while I was working on a text editor.
Here is the code:

```
100 PRINT Q$"(Y/N)";: GET A$:

    IF A$="Y THEN YES=1:RETURN

110 IF A$="N" THEN YES=0:RETURN

120 INVERSE:PRINT"PRESS 'Y' OR 'N'...":

    NORMAL:GOTO 100
```

To use the subroutine, you put the
question, without a question mark at the
end, into string Q$; then you call the
subroutine with a GOSUB. When the
subroutine returns, you test the value of
the boolean variable YES and take ap-
ropriate action. The subroutine handles
making sure the user does type either a
'Y' or an 'N', and will not return until this
is done. It tells them what to do, and
keeps on asking the question until they
do it. Here is an example of a calling line:

```
1910 Q$="DO YOU WANT TO SEE THE CATALOG":

GOSUB 100: IF YES THEN PRINT D$"CATALOG"
```

Notice that the IF statement tests the
boolean value of YES, by just "IF YES

THEN...". This is because the IF processor in Applesoft (as in Integer Basic) will
take the true branch if the value of the
expression is non-zero, and the false
branch if it is zero.

Microsoft Z80 Softcard

Well, I have the Softcard in my machine now, and so far, I am pleased with
it. I have found one problem that I believe to be a bug. You can't open a random file directly from the program. In
order to use a random file, it was necessary first to use a sequential file command. If the file did not already exist, the
random command would not open one.
You can work around it by adding one
line before you use the random
command:

```
100 OPEN "O",#1, filename:CLOSE
```

Also, I found some typos in the section
that explains the use of the file commands. There may be more but I haven't
found them yet. Another thing to be
aware of is the compatibility with other
cards. The Softcard will not work with
many of the accesory cards available for
the Apple. For instance, the Softcard
will not recognize the existence of the
D.C Hayes Modem. To use it with the
Softcard, special software will be required. If you should want to use this
system, you should check to see if you
can use other boards you may have.For
the most part, I find it has features similar
to the Language System. If you are using
the Language card and so on, The Softcard will be similar in it's relationship to
peripherals.

In addition to the Z80 based circuit
board, the system comes with 2 half page
manuals and two system diskettes. The
manuals are divided between the system
description and CP/M in one and Microsoft Basic version 5.0 in the other. The
manuals are about half-page size. They

```
]LIST
2  REM
MOVING TITLE DEMONSTRATION
5  REM
WRITTEN BY BOB SANDER-CEDERLOF
JULY 7, 1980
10 Q =  - 16336: TEXT : HOME
30  FOR J = 1 TO 2: VTAB J * 4 +
    2: HTAB 4: FOR I = 1 TO 34:
    PRINT "*";: NEXT I: PRINT :
    NEXT J

80 A$ = "MOVING TITLE DEMONSTRATI
    ON": REM            PUT YOUR
    OWN TITLE HERE
90  FOR I = 1 TO 19 +  LEN (A$) /
    2:P =  PEEK (Q) +  PEEK (Q):
    VTAB 8: HTAB 40 - I: PRINT
    LEFT$ (A$,I)" ": NEXT I
95  FOR I = 1 TO 3000: NEXT I: REM
    DELAY SO PEOPLE CAN READ THE
    TITLE
100  REM PUT THE REST OF YOUR PRO
    GRAM HERE.
110  HOME : LIST ,100: FOR I = 1 TO
    3000: NEXT I: END : REM  TO
    SAVE YOU THE TROUBLE...
]
```
Listing 3

233

prop nicely in front of you so you can view them easily. There is a lot of information in the manuals so expect to spend a lot of time becoming familiar with the contents. I have never worked with CP/M before, so it was all new to me. I have heard a lot of pros and cons about the merits of CP/M. Once you become familiar with one, no other ever seems quite right. There are a number of utilities to let you do many things that you can't do with the Apple operating system. So learn to use the tools and accept it as another part of the learning experience. Everything is easy once you understand it.

The Basic manual includes a description of the commands and functions of the language. It is intended for the experienced programmer. There are only occasional examples as required to emphasize a point. Also included in the manual are the requirements for calling 6502 routines from the Z80 system. The implementation seems to be well integrated into the two systems since you are not able to detect any interferences. All the keyboard inputs have to pass from the 6502 to the Z80 as do the screen functions and the links to your printer and so on.

Operation of the system is provided by programs included on two diskettes. One diskette is for the standard 13 sector DOS systems. With this disk you get CP/M and MBasic. This version of Basic includes low resolution graphics commands. When this disk is used and MBasic is loaded, you have a little over 14K of memory left. The other diskette is for use with the Language System or with DOS 3.3. The 16 sector system includes hi resolution graphics with Basic as well as the lo res version. In the 16 sector system, you have about 26.5K of memory with MBasic and 17.5K of memory with GBasic.

The system is sure to be well supported by Microsoft. And, eventually there will be Apple CP/M software. I'll be telling you more about the Softcard from time to time.

"In conclusion — advances in data communication technology will enhance cultural, economic and scientific interchange between nations; alleviate social stress by reducing the need to maintain large urban populations in support of centralized production facilities; and allow a lot of us to work at home in our 'jammies'."

Applesoft Mini Pilot
Super Text II

Chuck Carpenter

February, 1981

Programming languages for the Apple II come in all sizes. There are at least three versions of Basic available: Integer, Applesoft, and now Microsoft Basic-80 with the new Softcard. With the language card you can have Pascal and Fortran. Languages like Forth, XPL0 (experimental programming language zero) and Tiny Pascal are around too. Another language called Pilot is available from Apple and other sources. This language comes in a variety of sizes. Some are extended versions with lots of power. Others are less powerful. All versions of Pilot have common features; they use simple syntax and complicated command structures. The syntax of Pilot is elementary, non-mathematical, and lends itself readily to Computer Aided Instruction (CAI) programs. Included in this column is a version of Pilot that I call Mini Pilot. The language is easy to learn and is useful for teaching beginners the basics of programming.

MINI PILOT

Mini Pilot was written in 1978 by N. Dealy who has placed it in the public domain. I obtained a copy and made a couple of modifications to it. The Mini Pilot interpreter was coded to conform to a version of Pilot described on pages 56 to 60 in the Sept/Oct '77 issue of *People's Computers* magazine (now *Recreational Computing*). Charles Shapiro, a Junior in High School at the time, wrote his version of the interpreter in HP3000 Basic. It uses only six commands, a label designator and a designation for strings. The version to be described here is written in Applesoft Basic and uses a similar— Apple enhanced—format. I have added disk capability and a command to clear the screen. Here's how Mini Pilot works.

Program Features

Single letter commands are used to write programs. Other symbols used in programs are the asterisk (*) for labels and the dollar sign ($) for strings. An option in this version of Pilot uses the exclamation (!) to designate a remark. Listing 1 is a simple program written to illustrate the commands and symbols of Mini Pilot. Here are some of the features of Mini Pilot.

- Commands T:, A:, M:, J:, Y or N, E:, C:, and R:
- Subroutine labels and strings
- Disk SAVE, LOAD and REPLACE
- Named programs
- Soft entry to interpreter after exit with BYE
- Paddle (0) control of list speed
- Syntax error message
- Suspend listing with space bar
- Continue listing with any key
- Line length limit warning bell

Program Directives

These features provide you with functions to develop and use your Mini Pilot programs. The directives are prompted with REQUEST? followed by one of several options. The options are:

- NEW—Start of a new program, asks for a program name
- LIST—Lists the named program currently in memory
- EDIT—Allows changing a specified line number
- RUN—Runs the named program
- DSAVE—Saves the named program to disk
- DLOAD—Loads the named program from disk
- REPLACE—Replaces previous named program on disk with current program in memory
- BYE—Exits Pilot back to Basic

Because the interpreter includes disk commands, named programs are needed. A NEW input to REQUEST asks for a program name. Inputs LIST and RUN use the named program. EDIT lets you change any line in your program. The previous line is displayed on the screen too so you can see where you are. The disk command DSAVE, saves on the disk, as a text file, the current named program. REPLACE

```
REQUEST? RUN

RUN OF APPLE BLOSSOMS

HI...MY NAME IS APPLE II !
     WHAT IS YOUR NAME?

?CHUCK

DO YOU WANT TO TRY A VOWEL (V)
OR A CONSONANT (C)
TYPE A 'V' OR A 'C'

?V
NAME A VOWEL CHUCK !

?C

THAT IS NOT A VOWEL CHUCK !
NAME A VOWEL CHUCK !

?A

THAT IS CORRECT CHUCK ! ! !

DO YOU WANT TO TRY IT AGAIN ?
TYPE Y FOR YES OR N FOR NO.

?Y

DO YOU WANT TO TRY A VOWEL (V)
OR A CONSONANT (C)
TYPE A 'V' OR A 'C'

?C

NAME A CONSONANT CHUCK !

?R

THAT IS CORRECT CHUCK ! ! !

DO YOU WANT TO TRY IT AGAIN ?
TYPE Y FOR YES OR N FOR NO.

?N

THANKS FOR PLAYING CHUCK .
HOPE WE CAN DO IT AGAIN SOON.

BYE....

END OF RUN

REQUEST?
```

Sample Run of Apple Blossoms—Pilot Program.

exchanges the program on disk with the current program in memory. You DSAVE the program when it's NEW. After the first time, you REPLACE to resave a program. REQUEST of BYE exits the Apple II Mini Pilot interpreter and returns you to Applesoft Basic. If you don't do anything else to the interpreter program at this point, you can return to pilot via the soft entry point by typing—and executing—GOTO1230.

Other features listed earlier included: A syntax error message if you didn't start the line right; listing speed control with game paddle #1; listing suspension with the space bar and continuation by pressing any key; and a line limit warning bell to keep you from exceeding the 39 character line length limit.

```
REQUEST? LIST

        APPLE BLOSSOMS


 0   R:VOWELS AND CONSONANTS
 1   C:
 2   T:HI...MY NAME IS APPLE II !
 3   T:      WHAT IS YOUR NAME?
 4   T:
 5   A: $NAME
 6  *BEGIN
 7   T:
 8   T:DO YOU WANT TO TRY A VOWEL (V)
 9   T:OR A CONSONANT (C)
10   T:TYPE A 'V' OR A 'C'
11   T:
12   A:
13   M:V,'
14   JN:*CONSONANT
15  *VOWEL
16   T:NAME A VOWEL $NAME !
17   T:
18   A:
19   T:
20   M:A,E,I,O,U,'
21   TN:THAT IS NOT A VOWEL $NAME !
22   JN:*VOWEL
23   JY:*CORRECT
24  *CONSONANT
25   T:
26   T:NAME A CONSONANT $NAME !
27   T:
28   A:
29   T:
30   M:B,C,D,F,G,H,J,'
31   MN:K,L,M,N,P,Q,R,'
32   MN:S,T,V,W,X,Y,Z,'
33   TN:THAT IS NOT A CONSONANT $NAME !
34   JN:*CONSONANT
35   T:
36  *CORRECT
37   T:
38  ! SOME POSITIVE FEEDBACK
39   T:THAT IS CORRECT $NAME !!!
40   T:
41  !
42   T:
43   T:DO YOU WANT TO TRY IT AGAIN ?
44   T:TYPE Y FOR YES OR N FOR NO.
45   T:
46   A:
47   T:
48   M:Y,'
49   JY:*BEGIN
50   T:THANKS FOR PLAYING $NAME .
51   T:HOPE WE CAN DO IT AGAIN SOON.
52   T:
53   T:BYE....
54   END:

REQUEST?
```

Listing 1. Example Pilot Program.

Program Commands

Some of the single-letter commands were mentioned briefly under features. As indicated, the commands are single letters followed by a colon. Here is a description of each Instruction, conditioner, and variable used by Mini Pilot.

Instructions
•T: Type whatever is included on this line
•A: Ask a question and/or wait for input. String input is allowed with the A: command
•M: Match for characters/keywords from an input command
•J: Jump to a labeled line as a result of a Match test
•C: Clear the screen
•R: Remark or comment line
Conditioners
•Y Condition instruction with a positive match
•N Condition instruction with a negative match
Variables
•$= String included with the A: command. Requires a leading and trailing space
•*= Label or subroutine
•!= Alternate for remark—R:—or comment

The program in Listing 1 uses each of the commands listed and the sample run shows

```
REQUEST? NEW
PROGRAM NAME?LOOP

 0?*BEGIN
 1?T:THIS PROGRAM LOOPS
 2?J:BEGIN
 3?E:          E OR END-OK
 4?DONE

REQUEST? EDIT
STARTING AT LINE? 2
1 T:THIS PROGRAM LOOPS
2 J:BEGIN

                 FORGOT
 2?J:*BEGIN  ←   ASTERISK
 3?DONE

REQUEST? LIST

        LOOP


 0  *BEGIN
 1   T:THIS PROGRAM LOOPS
 2   J:*BEGIN
 3   E:

REQUEST? DSAVE

REQUEST? DLOAD
PROGRAM NAME?LOOP

REQUEST? REPLACE

REQUEST? RUN

RUN OF LOOP


THIS PROGRAM LOOPS
THIS PROGRAM LOOPS
THIS PROGRAM LOOPS
THIS PROGRAM LOOPS
                  CONTROL C
REQUEST? BYE
```

Figure 1. Example Programming Sequence and Use of Programming Directives.

what the program does. Since the program is quite simple, I have not included any detailed description. Note the use of an apostrophe character at the end of a match line. This delimiter is needed to show the program where the end of the match items are. Figure 1 is a short demo of a programming sequence. This example uses many of the program directives. There were many Pilot programs printed in *people's computers* magazine prior to mid 1979. If you can find a library of this magazine, you can see many examples of how Pilot is used. Listing 2 is the Mini Pilot interpreter.

The Interpreter

Organization of the interpreter is straightforward. Each section is highlighted by function. You can follow the program sequence starting with the operating system (Pilot O.S.). As you make selections from the REQUEST command line, a branch is taken to a corresponding section of the program. The actual coding and logic of each section is more obscure. Since I didn't write it, I'm not going to try and explain it. Analysis of the code detail is left to the reader. (Commonly called a cop out.)

Some changes are easily made though. For instance turning on a printer. Include code lines like the disk commands in lines 1340 to 1360. Then add a subroutine at a convenient spot in the program. Another example is the way I added the C: command for clearing the screen; lines 2030 to 2070. The disk and screen-clear changes did not affect any of the critical interpreter code. The interpreter is not too complicated. Make several copies of the program before you start experimenting. Have fun changing it and learning something about the construction of a programming language.

For those who would like to try Mini Pilot, I have a deal. If you will send me a good quality diskette and $2.50 for my time and return postage, I'll make a copy of the program and return it to you. Be sure to adequately package the diskette. I use Floppy Armor from Square One. You can use two pieces of fiber board from a box too. Cut two pieces about one-half inch larger than the diskette and jacket. Then tape the edges and put it in an envelope. If I don't get the money I'll keep the diskette until you send it. If you don't like typing in a long listing, I'll be as helpful as I can.

SUPER—TEXT II

I promised a review of the Super-Text word processor from Muse so here it is. Since I started using the word processor, a new enhanced version has been released. I have also had the chance to see a couple of others recently. My choice is still for Super-Text for the kind of word processing I do now. Super-Text is easy to learn, easy to use, and easy to remember. The new

Super-Text II is even easier to use. Many changes have been made to improve the human factors of the program. One change, the preview mode, was a waste of time as far as I am concerned. I can find no practical use for this mode. You have to do too many things to see line lengths greater than forty columns. Once you use the word processor for any length of time, you get quite good at judging how your output is going to look. It's less involved than trying to use the new preview mode.

What It Can't Do

In the comparable cost catagory, there are only a couple of things. There is no header, trailer or footnote capability. And, you can't move lines of text and paragraphs around easily. Another 'can't do' might include hyphenation. If you don't use right margin justification, you get very ragged, ragged right. I haven't seen this capability in other word processors either.

Documentation

Super-Text II comes packaged in a book-size three-ring binder. The binder includes two diskettes of premium quality and the manual. The manual is rewritten and re-arranged from the original version. Most of the changes make the instructions easier to follow. One change makes it harder to use. The old manual had summary sheets of all the control codes at the end. Now, these summary sheets are at the end of each related section. You have to thumb through the manual to find what used to be all in one place. My personal preference is for a users guide. Visicalc and others have used this approach. Once you have reasonably mastered the operation of the software, usually you only need a quick reference to bring something back to mind. It's much easier than thumbing through the manual.

The manual is divided into eleven sections. The introduction provides you with enough information to get you up and running. In subsequent sections you find out how to initialize data disks, learn the five modes of operation, develop your printer interface requirements, and use the trade marked AUTOLINK function. Also included are a copy program and section on loading non Super-Text files. This last section is only useful for loading you own binary print driver or files from an older compatible word processor. The manual claims to be prepared with Super-Text. I think the old one was but this one appears to be type-set. None-the-less, the manual is well done and easy to follow. I like the new bookshelf size. Also many of the new manuals designed to contain the diskettes have a new feature. The pocket is formed so the diskettes can't be damaged by the binder rings. Things are looking-up for the software buyer.

Human Factors

Operating the new Super-Text II is much easier the old version. You no longer have to be a programmer to set up the printer slot and change the program if you want to use lower case (assuming you have an adapter). These things can be done right from the master menu. Some help might be needed if you want to use the printing replacement table. This feature lets you include special control functions needed by your printer. For instance, my printer has two pitches, enhanced characters and two character sets. With the replacement table, I have included control characters to do these things in my manuscripts and letters. You need to exit the program and do some things in machine language to set-up a replacement table. The manual is pretty clear but will be confusing to the beginner. Apparently most people wanted the print mode more often than the math mode. The new software loads the print module first and initializes the printer for

you. I had to make changes in my old version to do this. If Muse would just come out with an 80 column version to work with my new Videx Videoterm board and make it work with DOS 3.3, things would be great. One more point. Some have found it awkward to use the various Super-Text modes. You have to exit one mode to use another. I have gotten used to this feature and now find it quite natural. Like anything else, it's easy once you understand it.

Operating Features

Earlier, five modes of operation were mentioned. Actually, there are only three. The add mode and the print mode are used in combination. The print mode is the most powerful of the operating modes. In this mode you use the format codes to make the printed output be whatever you need it to be. Within the physical restrictions of your system of course. The entry of text into the word processor is free-form. You do not have to be concerned

---

Some of the lines of the interpreter contain a bell (control G). Here is a listing of the specific lines. All these lines contain a bell between the quotes. Note that line 1450 is a control D. A null string is represented by all other quote pairs.

```
1290  "-BYE"              2490  ""
1570  "END OF RUN"        2570  "COMMAND ERROR"
2480  ""
```

```
 LIST                            Listing 2.
 300 L
 1000    REM ***************************
 1010    REM * MINI - PILOT INTERPRETER *
 1020    REM ***************************
 1030  :
 1040    REM CODING BY:N. DEALEY   1978
 1050    REM DISC MODS BY:
 1060    REM CHUCK CARPENTER 1979
 1070  :
 1080    SPEED= 175
 1090    TEXT : HOME : VTAB 6: FOR I = 1 TO 35: PRINT "*";:
         NEXT
 1100    VTAB 8: HTAB 11
 1110    PRINT "MINI - PILOT II"
 1120    HTAB 14: PRINT "REV. 3.00": PRINT : HTAB 13: FLASH
         : PRINT "MODS-BY-CRC": NORMAL
 1130    PRINT : FOR I = 1 TO 35: PRINT "*";: NEXT
 1140    PRINT
 1210    FOR W = 0 TO 5000: NEXT W: HOME
 1220    GOSUB 2860
 1230  :
 1240    REM *** PILOT .O.S. ***
 1250    REM *******************
 1260  :
 1270    PRINT
 1280    INPUT "REQUEST? ";R$
 1290    IF R$ = "BYE" THEN  POKE 216,0: SPEED= 255: VTAB  PEEK
         (37): HTAB 13: PRINT "-BYE": END
 1300    IF R$ = "RUN" THEN  GOSUB 1470
 1310    IF R$ = "EDIT" THEN  GOSUB 2130: GOSUB 2380
 1320    IF R$ = "LIST" THEN  GOSUB 2200
 1330    IF R$ = "NEW" THEN  GOSUB 2340
 1340    IF  LEFT$ (R$,7) = "REPLACE" THEN  GOSUB 2600
 1350    IF  LEFT$ (R$,5) = "DSAVE" THEN  GOSUB 2650
 1360    IF  LEFT$ (R$,5) = "DLOAD" THEN  GOSUB 2760
 1370    GOTO 1240
 1380  :
 1390    REM *** ERROR ROUTINE ***
 1400    REM *********************
 1410  :
 1420    SPEED= 255
 1430    IF  PEEK (222) = 255 OR  PEEK (222) = 5 GOTO 1240
 1440    PRINT : PRINT "SYSTEM ERROR #"; PEEK (222);"L:"; PEEK
         (218) +  PEEK (219) * 256: PRINT : GOTO 1240
 1450    LET D$ = ""
 1460  :
 1470    REM *** RUN ***
 1480    REM ***********
 1490  :
```

about the 40 column limitation of the screen. Words longer than the remaining length of the line are moved to a new line. Words are not broken at the end of a line. I have heard this called the 'mind-dump stream of consiousness' concept. The idea being that you can just type what you're thinking. The format can be easily added later. I do a combination of things. Sometimes I just type away so I don't lose my train of thought. Other times I put the paragraph and format markers in as I go. Additionally, the math mode is not used independently. You have to load the math module in place of the print module to use it.

The Cursor Mode

All of the other Super-Text modes are entered from the cursor mode. While in the cursor mode, there are forty-two key combinations to load and save files, move the cursor, move text, delete text, find and replace text, query the system, do block operations, use the split screen, do three special functions, enter other modes, and exit Super-Text to Basic. Don't be alarmed by the number of key combinations. Some are used infrequently and others are the same in other modes. You will find yourself using only a few combinations all the time and others only once in a while.

The Add and Print Modes

In the add mode, there are fourteen key combinations to use upper and lower case, start a new line or a paragraph, ditto and fill space, tabbing and justification, and exit the add mode. You return to the cursor mode by pressing the key marked ESC twice. Print mode is the mode that makes Super-Text powerful. Format and printer control are established in the add mode using seventeen key combinations. With these combinations, you can format and tab, number and text, turn the printer off and on under program control, and use the user definable replacement table.

There are also sixteen default conditions you can set from the main menu during initial boot. These options can be your most used requirements during printing. The format line can then be used to make local changes in the text during development.

Change Mode

In the change mode, you have thirteen key combinations for cursor movement (same as cursor mode and non-destructive), text movement, deleting text and changing text. The change mode is useful for editing text that is incorrect. Use the add mode to start new text or add more text into existing text.

Math Mode

This mode is used to perform calculations on numbers in a file or to act as a

```
1500   FOR I = 0 TO NV: FOR I1 = 0 TO 1:I$(I1,I) = "": NEXT
       : NEXT
1510  C1 = 0
1520   PRINT : PRINT "RUN OF ";CP$: PRINT : PRINT
1530   FOR A = 0 TO MX: IF  LEN (P$(0,A)) = 2 AND  RIGHT$
       (P$(0,A),1) <  > M$ GOTO 1560
1540   FOR C2 = 1 TO 6: IF  LEFT$ (P$(0,A),1) = S$(C2) THEN
       ON C2 GOSUB 1590,1660,1820,1940,2020,2090
1550   NEXT C2
1560   NEXT A
1570   PRINT : PRINT : PRINT "END OF RUN": RETURN
1580  :
1590   REM *** ASK ***
1600   REM ***********
1610  :
1620   FOR Z = 1 TO  LEN (P$(1,A))
1630   IF  MID$ (P$(1,A),Z,1) = "$" THEN I$(0,C1) =  MID$
       (P$(1,A),Z): HTAB 1: INPUT I$(1,C1):Z$ = I$(1,C1):C
       1 = C1 + 1: RETURN
1640   NEXT Z: HTAB 1: INPUT Z$: RETURN
1650  :
1660   REM *** TYPE ***
1670   REM ************
1680  :
1690   HTAB 1
1700   FOR Z = 1 TO  LEN (P$(1,A))
1710   IF  MID$ (P$(1,A),Z,1) = "$" GOTO 1730
1720   NEXT Z: GOSUB 1800: RETURN
1730   FOR Z1 = Z TO  LEN (P$(1,A)) + 1
1740   IF  MID$ (P$(1,A),Z1,1) = " " OR  MID$ (P$(1,A),Z1
       ,1) = "" GOTO 1760
1750   NEXT Z1: GOSUB 1800: RETURN
1760  V$ =  MID$ (P$(1,A),Z,Z1 - Z)
1770   FOR H = C1 - 1 TO 0
1780   IF V$ = I$(0,H) THEN  PRINT  MID$ (P$(1,A),1,Z - 1
       );I$(1,H); MID$ (P$(1,A),Z1, LEN (P$(1,A)) - Z1 + 1
       ): RETURN
1790   NEXT H: GOTO 1720
1800   PRINT P$(1,A): RETURN
1810  :
1820   REM *** MATCH ***
1830   REM *************
1840  :
1850  M$ = "N":E1 = 1
1860   FOR E = 1 TO  LEN (P$(1,A))
1870   IF  MID$ (P$(1,A),E,1) = D1$ GOTO 1890
1880   GOTO 1910
1890   IF  MID$ (P$(1,A),E1,E - E1) = Z$ THEN M$ = "Y": RETURN

1900  E1 = E + 1
1910   IF  MID$ (P$(1,A),E,2) = " " OR  MID$ (P$(1,A),E,1
       ) = "" THEN  RETURN
1920   NEXT E: RETURN
1930  :
1940   REM *** JUMP ***
1950   REM ************
1960  :
1970   FOR D = 0 TO MX
1980   IF P$(0,D) <  > "" GOTO 2000
1990   IF  MID$ (P$(1,A),1,40) =  MID$ (P$(1,D),1,40) THEN
       A = D: RETURN
2000   NEXT D
2010   PRINT : PRINT "JUMP TO UNFOUND LABEL FROM LINE #";
       A: POP : RETURN
2020  :
2030   REM *** CLEAR SCREEN ***
2040   REM ********************
2050  :
2060   PRINT : HOME
2070   RETURN
2080  :
2090   REM *** END ***
2100  :
2110  A = MX: RETURN
2120  :
2130   REM *** EDIT ***
2140   REM ***********
2150  :
2160   INPUT "STARTING AT LINE? ";C
2170   IF C > 0 THEN  PRINT C - 1; TAB( 2);P$(0,C - 1);D0
       $;P$(1,C - 1): PRINT C; TAB( 2);P$(0,C);D0$;P$(1,C)

2180   RETURN
2190  :
2200   REM *** LIST ***
2210   REM ***********
2220  :
2230   IF CP$ = "" THEN  RETURN
2240   PRINT : INVERSE : HTAB 8: PRINT CP$: NORMAL : PRINT
```

direct fifteen digit calculator. To use this mode you have to load it in place of the print module. This can be done from the menu by using a control L from the cursor mode. If your text requires computation of tabulated data then you will find this module useful. My work does not require calculations so I have not used the math mode.

Autolink

Here's another one I haven't used yet. An example would be if my column used more space than available memory (There is a little over 20K bytes available in RAM memory. This equates to about fifteen doubled spaced pages at ten characters per inch.) The Autolink feature would be used to link the next section to the first. This way you can make your text as many pages as a disk can hold. An example of a phone list linked from list to list is included on the disk. I've tried it so I know it works.

Conclusion

For my applications, I have found Super-Text more than adequate. I have not found a need for the more exotic and complicated features. The ease of use is a definite plus for this word processor. And the software is practically goof proof too. You can easily recover from a RESET. And going in and out of the program to make changes to the replacement table has always worked for me—no crashes. Muse has now adopted the policy of sending two diskettes with the system. This is a definite improvement over their previous policy. Should you damage a disk, you can keep going while you obtain a replacement. The replacement cost is with proof of purchase during the first year. You are on your own after that. Since I have calculated that a disk isn't likely to wear out for over eight years, this policy doesn't make sense. If you damage the disks after the first year, presumably you have to spend the full price all over again. Muse's replacement policy is as good as I've seen. However, support of software for more than a year at some nominal cost would be helpful. You can find Super-Text II at your computer for $150.

PROGRAMMING HELP

Several people have written to me asking for help on different programs included in the Apple Cart. I want to provide all the help I can but...Trying to analyze a program without seeing it is tough. It's got to be a lot like trying to diagnose a patient who's at home. If you are going to write, also include a diskette with a copy of the program on it. This way I can see what's happening as it happens. Also, most of the problems have been typos. If you will send the diskette with return postage, I'll try to find the problem, fix it if I can, and return it to you. We can both save a lot of time and your frustrations this way. □

```
2250    PRINT
2260    FOR A = 0 TO MX: IF  PEEK ( - 16384) > 127 THEN  POKE
        - 16368,0: WAIT  - 16384,128,0: POKE  - 16368,0
2270    IF P$(0,A) = "" AND P$(1,A) = "" GOTO 2320
2280    SPEED= 255 -  PDL (0): IF A <  = 9 THEN  HTAB 2
2290    IF P$(0,A) <  > "" THEN  PRINT A;: HTAB 5: PRINT P
        $(0,A);D0$;P$(1,A): GOTO 2310
2300    PRINT A;: HTAB 4: PRINT P$(1,A)
2310    NEXT A
2320    SPEED= 255: RETURN
2330    :
2340    REM *** NEW ***
2350    REM ***********
2360    :
2370    C = 0: INPUT "PROGRAM NAME?";CP$: FOR A = 0 TO MX: FOR
        A1 = 0 TO 1:P$(A1,A) = "": NEXT : NEXT
2380    PRINT : FOR A = C TO MX: IF A <  = 9 THEN  HTAB 2
2390    PRINT A;: HTAB 3: PRINT "?";
2400    A$ = " ": FOR I = 2 TO LL
2410    GET A1$: IF  ASC (A1$) = 8 AND I > 2 THEN  PRINT  CHR$
        (8);:I = I - 1: GOTO 2410
2420    IF  ASC (A1$) = 8 AND I <  = 2 THEN  PRINT : GOTO
        2390
2430    IF  ASC (A1$) = 3 THEN  PRINT : RETURN
2440    IF  ASC (A1$) = 21 THEN  POKE 36, PEEK (36) + 1: GOTO
        2480
2450    IF  ASC (A1$) = 13 GOTO 2500
2460    IF  ASC (A1$) >  = 97 AND  ASC (A1$) <  = 122 THEN
        A1$ =  CHR$ ( ASC (A1$) - 32)
2470    PRINT A1$;:A$ =  LEFT$ (A$,I - 1) + A1$ +  MID$ (A
        $,I + 1,36)
2480    IF I = LL - 5 OR I = LL - 1 THEN  PRINT "";
2490    NEXT I: PRINT ""
2500    PRINT :A$ =  RIGHT$ (A$, LEN (A$) - 1)
2510    IF A$ = "DONE" THEN  RETURN
2520    IF A$ = "EDIT" THEN  GOSUB 2130:A = C - 1: GOTO 25
        80
2530    IF  LEFT$ (A$,1) = "*" OR  LEFT$ (A$,1) = "!" THEN
        P$(0,A) = "":P$(1,A) = A$: GOTO 2580
2540    FOR B = 1 TO  LEN (A$)
2550    IF  MID$ (A$,B,1) = D0$ THEN P$(0,A) =  LEFT$ (A$,
        B - 1):P$(1,A) =  MID$ (A$,B + 1, LEN (A$) - B + 2)
        : GOTO 2580
2560    NEXT B
2570    PRINT "COMMAND ERROR":A = A - 1
2580    NEXT A: RETURN
2590    :
2600    REM *** REPLACE ***
2610    REM ***************
2620    :
2630    PRINT D$;"UNLOCK";CP$: PRINT D$;"DELETE";CP$
2640    :
2650    REM *** DISK SAVE ***
2660    REM *****************
2670    :
2680    FOR A = MX TO 0 STEP  - 1: IF P$(0,A) = "" AND P$(
        1,A) = "" THEN  NEXT
2690    PRINT D$;"OPEN";CP$
2700    PRINT D$;"WRITE";CP$
2710    FOR I = 0 TO A: PRINT P$(0,I): PRINT  CHR$ (34);P$
        (1,I); CHR$ (34): NEXT
2720    PRINT D$;"CLOSE";CP$
2730    PRINT D$;"LOCK";CP$
2740    RETURN
2750    :
2760    REM *** DISK LOAD ***
2770    REM *****************
2780    :
2790    INPUT "PROGRAM NAME?";CP$
2800    PRINT D$;"OPEN";CP$
2810    PRINT D$;"READ";CP$
2820    FOR I = 0 TO MX: INPUT P$(0,I),P$(1,I): NEXT I
2830    PRINT D$;"CLOSE";CP$
2840    RETURN
2850    :
2860    REM *** INITIALIZE ***
2870    REM ******************
2880    :
2890    ONERR  GOTO 1390
2900    D0$ = ":":D1$ = ","
2910    MX = 99:LL = 36:NV = 19
2920    DIM P$(1,99),I$(1,19),S$(7)
2930    LET D$ =  CHR$ (4): REM  (CTRL) D
2940    DATA     A,T,M,J,C,E
2950    FOR I = 1 TO 6: READ S$(I): NEXT
2960    PRINT
2970    PRINT D$;"NOMON I,O,C": HOME
2980    PRINT
2990    RETURN
]
```

Reset RESET •More Tips •Wandering Apples
Pascal Flash Continued •Direct Text
Rounded Applesoft •GET vs. INPUT
Integer Billboard Revisited •INPUT ASC II

Chuck Carpenter

April, 1981

Wow! Did anyone send in their $190,000 for the Radcom Plus+ FSK/CW board? (Dec '80 column.) I'm sure by now you know the price is $190.00. And, the program for it is not **called** Integer Basic — it's **written** in Integer Basic.

READER INPUT

This month I'm going to catch-up on all the reader contributions. I've been collecting them for a few months, and now have several. Which brings up a point. When I batch them like this, the ones received last get into the column right away. Those sent earlier don't get used for several months. So, from now on, anything sent to me will be used in the next column. It will still be 3 to 4 months before you see it. That's the cycle time from the time I write a column to the time it gets printed.

Reset Defense

Those of you having the Autostart ROM can use these suggestions from Douglas Dougherty (I didn't save his address). The first item is in response to a letter by Robin Ault in the June '80 issue. The letter claimed there was no software defense against accidentally pressing the RESET key. Douglas writes . . . "This is completely untrue! Since $3F2 contains the 'soft-entry vector', the RESET key can cause a jump to anywhere the programmer desires. To make a program reset proof, follow these steps!

1. Assemble the following program at location $300.

```
TSX                 ;GET STACK POINTER
LDA  102,X          ;FETCH HIGH BYTE
LDY  101,X          ;FETCH LOW BYTE
INY                 ;INCREMENT IT
TAX
JSR  $F940          ;PRINT Y - X
RTS
```

This routine will report its return address by reading it from the stack.

2. Get back into Basic and type CALL 768. You should see — 23 D8, showing that $D823 is the address to continue in Basic. (Note that the symbol $ indicates a hex number . . . CC)

3. If your system does not have a disk, that is, no DOS, follow these steps from the monitor.

```
* 3F2 : 23 D8        ;LOAD BASIC CONTINUE
* FB6FG              ;SET POWER UP BYTE
* 0G                 ;BACK TO BASIC
```

If you have DOS, the above will clobber it every time the RESET key is pressed. Therefore, DOS users should see that the original content of $3F2 is $9DBF, the address of a subroutine which re-enables DOS, and ends with a JMP ($9D5E). The address $9D5E contains $D43C, the normal continue-in-Basic address. So type *9D5E:23 D8 to set the new address. Now, if we type in the following Basic program, and run it, we shall see that it lives up to its claim.

```
10 PRINT "THIS PROGRAM IS RESET PROOF" :
   GOTO 10
```

However, if RESET is pressed repetitively, quickly enough, a ?SYNTAX ERROR will occur and halt the program. But, simply adding 5 ONERR GOTO 10, will solve this problem. The program becomes goof-proof against everything including using a CONTROL C. (If you want to trap the control C, use the associated error code in a code line. The error codes can be found on pages 114-115 of The DOS Manual . . . CC) Exceptions are turning the machine off and throwing a brick at your Apple. Incidentally, assuming you are running DOS, this all reduces to the following:

```
10 X=9*4096+13*256+5*16+14
20 POKE X,35 : POKE X+1,216
   : REM ENABLE RESET PROTECTION
30 POKE X,60 : POKE X+1,212
   : REM DISABLE IT
```

Douglas included two other items of interest in his letter. The first describes an interaction between the use of FRE(0) and the Applesoft Renumber/Append program. Second, he describes how to edit a program line without picking up extra spaces.

Use of the Applesoft FRE(0) function after using the Renumber/Append program — implemented with the & command — will produce disastrous results. Says Douglas, "I have not a clue as to why this is true, but if one says X=FRE(0) after any & (if & points at Renumber/Append, a very useful program, by the way), it will cause the screen to flash and the system to go bonkers, requiring you to turn it off and on again to recover. On one occasion this caused the clicking sound which signifies power supply failure, which in turn caused a disk file to get messed-up. I hope that Apple will notice this and fix it in the next version of Renumber/Append."

Continuing with multiple line statements, Douglas adds . . . "Any of you out there who, like me, try to pack as many statements as possible into a multiple statement line will have noticed what a pain it is to recopy them when editing a program. Due to the way Applesoft formats a listed line you will pick up extra spaces at the beginning and end of the lines . . . However, POKE 33,33 sets the line width down, and the extra format spaces will not be inserted. Hence the line can be copied exactly. The following program segment, which should be put into a text file, then EXECed into an existing program, when needed, will be of help in these situations:

```
1 HOME : POKE 33,33
2 LIST 00001
3 REM LIST IS AT 2067-2071
4 INPUT "#";L% : L$=STR$(L%)+100000
   : FOR I=2 TO 6 : POKE 2065+I,ASC(MID$(L$,I))
   : NEXT I : GOTO 2
```

Now type RUN then the program line to be listed and then CONTROL C (RETURN) to get out, and the program line will be ready to be copied. Use the escape codes to move the cursor as required."

My thanks to Douglas for sharing some of his discoveries and suggestions. This last example may be confusing to the beginner. The real reason for including it was to show the use of POKE 33,33. The normal window width stored at address 33 is 40. Applesoft, in formatting a listing, adds 7 spaces to lines that continue on another line. The lines look better with uncluttered line numbers. But, any text you type will include these spaces if you copy over them with the cursor. This will not occur with commands, equations or between multiple line statements; only text between quotes. You can simply type the POKE 33,33 as a direct command, too. To reset the window width after you have done your editing, type TEXT or POKE 33,40 (or even RESET). Remember to retype any control codes you have included in a line. Things like CONTROL D will not be copied when the cursor is passed over a line.

Wandering Apples

Do you have a need to provide some security for your Apple? This idea from Jim Levin at the University of California at San Diego will be helpful then. Jim suggests using an automotive ground strap, a bicycle cable, and a combination lock.

- First, loop the ground cable up through and back down through the ventilation slots in the bottom plate of the Apple. This will put the holes in the cable next to each other.
- Next, loop the bicycle cable around some secure object. A pipe or desk leg for instance.
- Finally, lock the ground cable and bicycle cable together with the padlock.

Jim acknowledges that this is not maximum security. But, it will keep the Apple from **walking away.** The parts are readily available and inexpensive. You may qualify for insurance this way too.

Jim has also included some Pascal information. The information is related to the Pascal programs included in the August '80 column. Procedures for Inverse, Normal and Flash were included.

The following Language Card Assembler routines demonstrate how Jim worked around some pecularities in his version of the assembler. He further points out that each .proc line has to end with ,0 and there has to be a .END at the end.

```
bk1. VIDEO.TEXT
        .PROC INVERSE,0
        LDA     0C083
        LDA     0C083
        LDA     #0
        STA     0D8ED
        LDA     0C088
        RTS

        .PROC NORMAL,0
        LDA     0C083
        LDA     0C083
        LDA     #080
        STA     0D8ED
        LDA     0C088
        RTS

        .PROC FLASH,0
        LDA     0C083
        LDA     0C083
        LDA     #040
        STA     0D8ED
        LDA     0C088
        RTS

        .END
```

Readers are left to their own devices to find out if these procedures work. My abilities in Pascal are limited (more than in Basic). So these procedures, included for your information, are untested.

Direct Text

Here's a little program from H. Owen Jones from Gormley Ont., Canada that lets you put characters directly in the text area of memory. Owen did this to determine how memory locations correspond with screen position. Here's the Applesoft program.

```
10 HOME
20 I=1024 : J=32
30 IF PEEK (-16384)>127 THEN END
40 POKE I,J+128
50 I=I+1 : J=J+1 : REM  INCREMENT MEMORY, NEXT ASCII
60 IF I<>2047 THEN 90 : REM OUT OF TEXT MEMORY?
70 I=1024 : HOME : GOTO 30 : REM YES, START OVER
90 IF J=95 THEN J=32 : REM RESTART ASCII SEQUENCE
100 GOTO 30
```

The program fills the screen with the available character set. Pressing any key will stop the program. Variables are initialized to the beginning of text memory (I) and the lowest ASCII value (J, decimal). Note that when the ASCII value is POKEd, the number 128 is added to it. This ensures that the display mode is NORMAL. If 128 is not added, the INVERSE mode is obtained.

Owen suggests a couple of enhancements, too. Adding this line:

```
35 POKE I-1,32+128
```

will display a single character. The character moves across the screen and changes as it does. The rest of the screen is filled with ASCII spaces. Add 40 to the initial value of I and add this line:

```
45 VTAB 1 : PRINT"ADDRESS : ";I
```

to see a display of the current memory location. You can slow the speed of the display down by using the SPEED command or inserting a delay loop. This routine demonstrates the possibilities of inserting text directly on the screen. It is not necessary to use the tab commands.

Some additional comments. I would change line 30 to read:

```
30 IF PEEK(-16384)> 127 THEN POKE -16368 : END
```

Having read the keyboard data (–16384), the keyboard strobe (–16368) should be reset. Do this to avoid problems reading the keyboard at some other point in a program. Note that these are addresses $C000 and $C010 respectively. For more information on the memory locations used for the screen display of text, see pages 16 and 82/83 of the Reference Manual. The last pages are actually the memory locations that are **not** used by text memory.

Rounded Applesoft

Geoff Puterbaugh from Sunnyvale, California contributed the program in Listing 1. He found that Apple insists on changing numbers from one form to another. For instance, Geoff typed in:

```
PRINT .001
```

and found that . . . "the gleeful response from the Apple is —

```
1E-03"
```

After several frustrating and futile attempts at rounding he found that any number less than 0.01 will be printed in exponential notation (a computerized form of engineering notation). This previously unnoticed "feature" of Applesoft was found on page 4 of the Applesoft Reference Manual. Since business programs don't require exponential notation, the program in Listing 1 was written to convert numbers to conventional decimal notation.

The subroutine is given a variable called "FLOTE" (your program should determine that this is less than 0.01 before calling the subroutine) and returns two variables; OUT$ and EFLAG. If EFLAG is zero there is a problem. The actual subroutine begins on line 100 and ends on line 290. The other lines simply call the subroutine with various values of FLOTE. A sample run of the program included with Geoff's letter showed how Applesoft would print a number and the results of using this program. Incidentally, the PRINT USING command in other versions of Basic keeps you from having to do this. (Microsoft Basic-80 that comes with the Z-80 Softcard for instance.)

GET vs INPUT

A program by Alan Thomas using the GET command in place of the INPUT command was included in the Oct. '80 column. Eric Shenk from Harrisonburg, Va. has found another way to do something similar. Eric, as have others, finds the lack of an LINPUT command one of Applesoft's problems. The LINPUT command, allows typing most anything into an INPUT statement. With Eric's program, the LINPUT command is effectively implemented in Applesoft. The program uses the keyboard input buffer ($200) and monitor routines to convert input into a string. See Listing 2.

```
LIST

10    GOTO 1000
100   OUT$ =  STR$ (FLOTE)
105   EFLAG = 0
110    FOR MARK = 1 TO  LEN (OUT$)
130    IF  MID$ (OUT$,MARK,1) = "E"
         THEN EFLAG = 1:EMARK = MARK
         :MARK =  LEN (OUT$)
140    NEXT MARK
150    IF EFLAG = 0 THEN 290
160   EXP =  VAL ( MID$ (OUT$,EMARK
         + 2,2)): REM   GET VALUE OF
         EXPONENT
170   MANTISSA$ =  MID$ (OUT$,1,EMA
         RK - 1): REM   PROBABLY HAS
         A DOT IN IT
180    IF EMARK = 2 THEN 200: REM
         THERE IS NO DECIMAL POINT IN
         THE MANTISSA
190   MANTISSA$ =  LEFT$ (MANTISSA$
         ,1) +  MID$ (MANTISSA$,3,EMA
         RK - 1): REM   REMOVING THE D
         ECIMAL POINT FROM THE MANTIS
         SA
200   NICE$ = "."
210    FOR MARK = 1 TO EXP - 1
220   NICE$ = NICE$ + "0"
230    NEXT MARK: REM   NICE$ IS NO
         W ".00" THRU ".0000000000---
         (EXP)"
250   NICE$ = NICE$ + MANTISSA$
290   OUT$ = NICE$: RETURN
1000   PRINT " *** VARIOUS IRREGUL
         AR SMALL NUMBERS *** "
1010   FOR FLOTE = 1 / 64000 TO .0
         1 STEP .00238
1020   GOSUB 2000
1030   NEXT FLOTE
1040   PRINT " *** REGULAR PATTERN
         OF SMALL NUMBERS *** "
1050   FOR FLOTE = .0004 TO .004 STEP
         .0002
1060   GOSUB 2000
1070   NEXT FLOTE
1080   END
2000   PRINT " APPLESOFT'S ORIGINA
         L IDEA FOR THIS NUMBER : ";F
         LOTE
2010   GOSUB 100: IF EFLAG = 0 THEN
         PRINT " ABORT!! ** APPLESOF
         T NOT BEHAVING": PRINT " AS
         ADVERTISED!!": END
2020   PRINT " REFORMATTED NUMBER
         IS                         : ";O
         UT$
2030   RETURN
```

Listing 1. Program by Geoff Peterbaugh to format numbers in decimal notation.

```
LIST

10    GOSUB 10000
20    PRINT A$
25    IF A$ = "STOP" THEN  STOP
30    GOTO 10
9998   REM
9999   REM
10000   CALL ( - 657)
10010 A$ = ""
10020   FOR J = 1 TO 256
10030   IF  PEEK (J + 511) = 141 THEN 10060
10040 A$ = A$ +  CHR$ ( PEEK (J + 511))
10050   NEXT J
10060   RETURN


]RUN
YOU NOTICE THAT, IT ACCEPTS COMMAS!
YOU NOTICE THAT, IT ACCEPTS COMMAS!
IT WILL ALSO ACCEPT ":", AND QUOTES AND JUST ABOUT ANYTHING ELSE!
IT WILL ALSO ACCEPT ":", AND QUOTES AND JUST ABOUT ANYTHING ELSE!
STOP
STOP
```

Listing 2. Program by Eric Shenk to Simulate the LINPUT Command in Applesoft Basic.

According to Eric . . . "The actual subroutine is lines 10000 to 10060, 7 very short lines. In the sample run, the first line is the input, while the computer prints the second line in verification. Of course, this won't allow quite as much flexibility as Mr. Thomas' program, in that, if you want to not accept certain characters, you can't throw them out immediately. (Although it would be no problem to throw out "illegal" characters by checking PEEK(J+511) between lines 10030 and 10040.) This routine has the following advantages:

1. It will accept any character — leading/trailing spaces, commas, colons, quotes, and control characters — except the carriage return.

2. Since it's using the monitor routines, all editing features (available on the Apple . . . CC) are automatically available without extra programming.

3. It will accept a full line of input and it's very short and totally not messy!

In short, it's exactly the same as an LINPUT statement (probably) would be in Applesoft."

And, I agree. The LINPUT command used in Microsoft Basic (Z-80 card) does just that. If you use this command, you can type whatever format you choose into the input line. Prevents you from having to use special formatting on dates and so on.

Another commend on Alan's program comes from Paula Hodgkinson (again, didn't save the address). She has been using the program quite a bit. A problem occurred though, when she used it in a program that saved the string to a disk. Paula says . . . "The problem is in line 10011. The RETURN at the end is added to the string. It becomes an invisible character that doesn't show up on the screen. When I saved the string to the disk the invisible RETURN at the end of the field (or record) became the next field (or record) read. This messed up everything after that.

I caught this by checking the length of my string and found out it was one longer than it should be. Once I realized what the problem was, fixing it was simple. Just change line 10011 to:

```
IF A$ = A5$ THEN A$ = A1$ : PRINT : RETURN
```

You don't need to add the RETURN to the end of the string."

Integer Cataloger

Here's a program from Norman Clarke from Hoffman Estates, Ill. This program combines the Puffer program from the Aug. '80 issue, and the Integer Basic Cataloger program from the Sept. '80 issue. The Integer program did not have the neat scrolling capability that the Applesoft version did. Norman's program uses the Puffer program to add the scrolling feature. See Listing 3.

```
1   DIM A$(70),B$(6),C$(70)
5   POKE -16298,0: POKE -16300,
    0: TEXT
7   P=0:Q=0:I=0
10  D$="": PRINT D$;"NOMONCOI":
    CALL -936: PRINT D$;"CATALOG"

20  I=I+2: IF SCRN(4,I-1)=10 THEN
    20:P=I/2
30  VTAB P+Q: TAB 4
31  PRINT "[ ]":Q=Q+1:R=I+Q*2-2
    : COLOR=(Q+128)/16: PLOT 4,
    R-1: COLOR=(Q+128) MOD 16: PLOT
    4,R-2
40  IF SCRN(4,R+1)#10 THEN 30:T=
    PEEK (37): GOSUB 200
45  GOSUB 200
50  K= PEEK (-16384): IF K>176 AND
    K<181 THEN 60: IF K=181 OR
    K>192 AND K<193+Q THEN 80: GOTO
    50
60  IF K=177 THEN B$="LOAD": IF
    K=178 THEN B$="LOCK": IF K=
    179 THEN B$="UNLOCK": IF K=
    180 THEN B$="DELETE"
61  VTAB 1: TAB 1: CALL -868
70  PRINT " PRESS 'LETTER' YOU WISH
    TO ";: IF K=180 THEN POKE 50
    ,127: PRINT B$;: CALL -198
80  POKE 50,255: POKE -16368,0:
    IF K>176 AND K<181 THEN 50
    : IF K=181 THEN END :I=I+(K-
    193)*2-2: IF SCRN(1,I)=2 AND
    B$="RUN" THEN B$="BRUN"
85  PRINT
90  FOR X=7 TO 39: POKE 2046+X,
    SCRN(X,I)+ SCRN(X,I+1)*16:
    NEXT X
92  PRINT D$;B$;A$
100 GOTO 5
200 A$="TYPE LETTER TO RUN, OR LOAD=
    1 LOCK=2 UNLOCK=3 DELETE=4 EXIT=
    5->"
210 B$="RUN"
220 VTAB 1: PRINT A$(24)
230 FOR U=1 TO 100: NEXT U
240 C$=A$(2,63)
250 C$(63)=A$(1,1)
260 A$=C$
270 K= PEEK (-16384): IF K<128 THEN
    220
280 RETURN
```

Listing 3. Integer Cataloger Revisited.

Again, my thanks to all who have sent ideas, programs, comments and suggestions. I'll use them whenever practicable and of course, more timely from now on.

INPUT TESTING

Someplace I read that Applesoft would not allow you to test the ASCII value of characters in an INPUT statement: Since I have been doing this in some of my programs, I don't have the foggiest notion what this person meant. The ASCII value of any character depends on the "on" bits (0-5) used to represent the particular character. As you probably know, ASCII is an acronym for the American Standard Code for Information Interchange. A unique value from 0 to 127 is assigned to each of 128 numbers, letters, special characters and control characters. Your Apple does not allow all the characters to be used. There is no direct lower-case capability for instance. Additionally, the Apple adds bits (6 & 7) to the code to provide inverse and flashing capability.

There are commands in Applesoft to let the programmer deal directly with the ASCII value of a character. If you want to 'generate' a specific character, you would use the CHR$(N) command. N represents the decimal equivalent of the ASCII value. To test the value of a character in a string, you would use the ASC (A$) command. The following routine is a modification of one I have used to test for input from a menu. See Listing 4.

```
JLIST
100    HOME : PRINT "INPUT A NUMBER
       0 - 6"
110    PRINT : PRINT "WHICH NUMBER
       DO YOU WANT...";: GET A$: IF
       ASC (A$) < 48 OR  ASC (A$) >
       57 THEN  PRINT : PRINT "ENTR
       Y IS NOT A NUMBER": FOR I =
       1 TO 3000: NEXT I: GOTO 100
120    S = VAL (A$)
130    IF S = 0 THEN  PRINT : PRINT
       "END": END
140    PRINT : PRINT : IF S < 1 OR
       S > 6 THEN  PRINT "INCORRECT
       SELECTION": FOR I = 1 TO 30
       00: NEXT I: HOME : GOTO 100
150    PRINT : PRINT : PRINT "THAT'
       S RIGHT": PRINT "YOU MADE IT
       PAST THE TRAPS."
]
```

Listing 4. Demo Program Illustrating the Use of the ASC Command to Test Input.

Lines 100 and 110 ask you to input a number from 0 to 6. The number is accepted into the program as a string. This is necessary in order to use the ASC command. Next, the value of the input is tested for correct ASCII range. If the range is not correct, a message is displayed for a few seconds and program control is returned to the input line. A correct range indicates that the input was a number. You could restrict the range to just the numbers you wanted. I didn't do that, choosing instead to check for correct numbers in another line. Line 120 converts the string to a real number. The integer command modifier could be used here if you wanted to be sure the number was an integer. I have never experienced any difficulty by not specifically using integers. In line 130 the program is ended if the number selected is zero. I usually use this to escape from my menu.

Correct number range is tested in line 140. Again, if the range is wrong, program control is returned to the input line. At this point my program usually uses an ON (X) GOTO statement. I like this approach for selecting the program segment to be used as a result of a menu selection. In this example, I tested for the input to be in the range of ASCII numbers and then for the correct number range. If these both occurred then a message was printed to say so. As you can see, whoever said Applesoft would not allow you to test for the ASCII value of a number was wrong. Pages 138 and 139 of the Applesoft Basic Programming Manual include the Applesoft ASCII character codes.

Out of Memory • 3.3 Master Disk • Double DOS
FRE(0) • Hi-Res Graphics Package
Lo-Res Block Letters • Best Billboard!
Yes/No Answers • Data Capture 4.0
Game Paddle I/O Expander • Microstick

Chuck Carpenter

May, 1981

Read any good disclaimers lately? Be sure to read some of the warranty disclaimers showing up in the documentation of software these days. You may decide not to buy just on the basis of what you read. My impression as I read them, is that the responsibility for use is the user's and nobody else's. If the software is useless as a result of incompetence or negligence or both, it's still the user's problem.

Sure, software suppliers want to protect themselves against people opening the drive door when a descriptor file is being written to the disk. And there are many of us who inadvertently bend, fold, staple, write on or otherwise multilate diskettes. But why not be reasonable with warranties; they sound as though the suppliers have no intention of supporting their products.

Why not have warranties that are positive? Let us know that the supplier will support the product. And, at the same time, let us know that the supplier will not be responsible for our blunders. After all, we are not a bunch of corporations! We are individuals supporting the desk-top computer and software industries.

RAMBLINGS

Recently, I was showing-off my computer by demonstrating games and Hi-Res graphics—most of them in Integer Basic. Several times when I tried to switch from one program to another, an OUT OF MEMORY error occurred. This happens when one program sets HIMEM or LOMEM or both and the next program doesn't reset these values. To the next program being loaded, it looks as though there is not enough memory to accept the program.

In the past, I have rebooted the system or tried to find the software switch addresses so I could reset the memory pointers. Suddenly, one day, it occured to me that there is an easier way. At least there is

with DOS. (DOS is the Disk Operating System.) All you need to do is type FP if you're in Integer, or INT if you're in Applesoft. Doing this resets all the pointers to initial boot status. Then switch back to the language you want to use or just run the program. With DOS, the correct language will be selected anyway. Oh yes, be very careful to not type INIT when you mean INT. You might wipe out a disk. You can find out more about the commands to switch languages in The DOS Manual, pages 28 and 29. Anyone have a good way to do it with a tape system?

Master Disk 3.3

DOS 3.3 includes a system disk with a number of utilities, demo programs and the programs required to boot the system. Because several system combinations are possible, all booting and language requirements are included on the Master System disk. Depending on your system, and whether you are using the language card, Applesoft or Integer Basic is loaded into the card. The boot programs called HELLO and APPLESOFT include tests for the presence of the language card. HELLO is an Applesoft program. APPLESOFT is the same program written in Integer Basic. If your system has Integer in ROM, Applesoft is loaded into the language card. Your Integer Apple tries to run the HELLO program, finds that it is in Applesoft, loads the APPLESOFT program and runs it. Since the Applesoft program is really in Integer Basic, the program is run like any other program. The reverse occurs if you have an Apple II Plus with Applesoft in ROM.

You do not need all the programs on the master disk to boot your system. You can save a lot of space if you include only those programs needed by your system. If you have an Apple II, you need the Integer

HELLO program (called APPLESOFT) and the FPBASIC program. The Applesoft HELLO program and INTBASIC programs are required for an Apple II Plus. To customize your working disks, try this:

First, initialize a diskette using the procedure from your DOS Manual. Notice how much faster you can INIT a diskette with DOS 3.3 than you can with 3.2.

Next, use the FID utility to transfer—from the master disk—the APPLESOFT program, and the FPBASIC program to the INITed diskette. Follow the procedure in The DOS Manual.

Now, before you do anything else, rename APPLESOFT, HELLO. Make a note of this change on the label. This disk will not boot on an Apple II Plus.

Be sure you make a copy of the master system disk, and use it, before you start this procedure. (The DOS 3.3 COPY program is faster than 3.2 too.)

At this point, you have a disk that will boot on an Apple II and load Applesoft into the language card RAM. The Integer Basic HELLO program looks for the language card, and if it's there, loads the FPBASIC program (Applesoft.) For those systems with only Applesoft in ROM and no Integer Basic card (standard Apple II Plus), a different set of programs is needed. In fact, if all that is available is Applesoft, use whatever INIT program you choose. There is no need to have programs that will look for the language card.

Another feature I added to my working copy of the system master is Double DOS. (Not the one we just made, the one with all the utilities.) With this program in memory you can switch easily from one DOS system to the other. Double DOS uses about 7K of memory, but it is very handy when you want to work interchangeably with the two systems. I modified the HELLO program to run Double DOS after Applesoft is loaded. Line 310 can be changed to read:

310 CALL -936 : VTAB 12: HTAB 10 : PRINT "RUNNING DOUBLE DOS"

Then add this line:

320 PRINT "*RUN DOUBLE DOS"

The asterisk means to type a CONTROL D as the first character inside the quotes. Now save the revised program by typing:

SAVE HELLO

If you don't have a copy of Double DOS, you can get one over the phone from the Telephone Software Exchange (213) 329-3715. Of course, you have to have a modem to do this, and a plastic money account number which to charge it to.

Another way to switch from one type of DOS to the other is to modify the hardware. Some enterprising souls have soldered one set of ROMs to the other. The pins to connect the supply voltage were lifted and left unsoldered. These pins were then connected to a DPDT switch. Lots of things can happen when you do this, so I don't recommend it. That's why I'm telling you about it.

Measuring Remaining Memory

When using Applesoft, all you need to do to find remaining memory is type PRINT FRE(0). However, if you have more than 32K of memory left, you will get a negative number. To convert the negative number to a positive number, add 65536 to it. The maximum amount of memory available in a 48K machine is 65536 bytes. As an immediate mode command, it would look like this:

PRINT 65536+FRE(0)

Should the amount of remaining memory be less than 32K however, you will get a larger positive number; something greater than 65536. To avoid the problem try this sequence.

    X = 65536+FRE(0)
    IF X > 65536 THEN X = X - 65536
    PRINT X

When you need to know the remaining RAM memory, use a subroutine like this in your program.

Programming Hi-Res Graphics

If you're just starting to write Hi-Res programs on your Apple II Plus, you may run into a limited program size problem. Floyd Goldstein from Bellmore, NY did and wrote to me about it. I checked it out and sure enough, for those of you using Applesoft, there can be a limited memory problem. Here's some historical background, that explains the problem.

In the beginning, the Apple II was available only with Integer Basic. Integer Basic, at least Apple Integer Basic, was written mostly to be a game programming language. And, graphics capability was included to make any game more dramatic and interesting. Integer Basic does not have many of the features included in Applesoft, but it is very fast. But, these are not the features that cause the problem. An Integer Basic program is stored differently in memory from the way an Applesoft Basic program is stored. The program is stored in memory starting from HIMEM, and grows in size toward LOMEM. Variables used in the program are stored starting at LOMEM and expanding upward. If you construct a memory map similar to the one included in the December '80 column, you can visualize the results better. Pages for Hi-Res graphics are located between high and low memory locations. For Integer Basic, this works well. Most of available memory is from the high end down. Applesoft stores programs from low memory up. If you use page one, there is about 4K of memory for a program. If you use only page two (HGR2) then about 12K of memory is available.

Machine language can be used to solve part of the problem. Write short Applesoft programs that call machine language stored in high memory locations. This assumes you can program in machine language. Another way is to buy the Integer Basic ROM card. Then you can write graphics programs the way the Apple II was designed to be used. The expense of the Integer card may make the latter approach unpopular. Having the Integer card though, makes it possible to do anything the Apple was designed to do.

Lo-Res Block Letters

Some time ago, I needed to make a series of slides using lo-res graphics. Mostly, the slides were words in block letters. Because I was presenting the Apple II, the words "Apple II" were on one of the slides. Listing 1 is a segment of the program used. Applesoft is the language and allowed the use of READ . . . DATA commands. First, quadrile paper was used to represent the 40 x 40 screen. Then, each letter was blocked out on this matrix. Next, each block was given a matrix location according to Apple screen conventions. The first number of each pair is the horizontal position, the second number is the vertical position. DATA statements were written to include the number pairs for each letter.

```
2000    HOME : GR : FOR I = 1 TO 99
2010    LET C =  INT ( RND (1) * 15) + 1
2020    IF C <  > 1 AND C <  > 2 AND C <  > 8 AND C <  > 9 AND C <  > 12 AND C <  > 13 THEN  GOTO 2010
2030    COLOR= C
2040    READ X,Y: PLOT X,Y
2050    NEXT I
2060    DATA  5,3,4,4,3,5,3,6,3,7,3,8,3,9,6,4,7,5,7,6,7,7,7,8,7,9,4,7,5,7,6,7
2070    DATA  10,3,10,4,10,5,10,6,10,7,10,8,10,9,11,3,12,3,13,3,14,4,14,5,14,6,13,7,12,7,11,7
2080    DATA  17,3,17,4,17,5,17,6,17,7,17,8,17,9,18,3,19,3,20,3,21,4,21,5,21,6,20,7,19,7,18,7
2090    DATA  24,3,24,4,24,5,24,6,24,7,24,8,24,9,25,9,26,9,27,9,28,9
2100    DATA  31,3,31,4,31,5,31,6,31,7,31,8,31,9,32,9,33,9,34,9,35,9,32,3,33,3,34,3,35,3,32,6,33,6,34,6
2110    DATA  16,12,17,12,18,12,18,13,18,14,18,15,18,16,18,17,18,18,17,18,16,18
2120    DATA  23,12,22,12,21,12,21,13,21,14,21,15,21,16,21,17,21,18,22,18,23,18
2130    RESTORE
2140    HOME : VTAB 23: HTAB 30: PRINT "SLIDE 1": GET A$
2150    GR : TEXT : HOME
```

Listing 1. An Applesoft program using READ and DATA statements to store and reproduce lo-res graphics characters.

In the program, line 2000 starts the sequence by clearing the screen, turning on the graphics mode, and beginning the plotting loop. Line 2010 generates a random number equal to the number of each possible color. The colors desired are the Apple colors, so line 2020 allows only those six colors. Line 2030 sets the color equal to the number selected, and line 2040 READs the data pairs from the DATA statements and PLOTs them on the screen. Beyond the DATA statements, one line RESTOREs the DATA pointer, another identifies the slide and holds it on the screen until a key is pressed. When desired, the slide is replaced with another after clearing the screen of graphics and text (line 2130). Since this segment could be a subroutine, a RETURN statement would be appropriate at this point.

READERS' INPUT

A billboard routine was included in the January '81 column. The program displayed a message in scrolling billboard fashion on the screen. Brian Winkel from Albion College in Albion, MI sent along his version shown in Listing 2. Brian feels his version is more interesting and useful since it will scroll your message indefinitely. One obvious modification, according to Brian, would be to use "many strings, one after the other, and scan a story across."

Rosa Pascal Sez

In response to a letter from Max Nareff from San Francisco, Ron DeGroat has come to my rescue once again. Max needed a Pascal program that would randomly generate all 26 alpha characters without repetition. The program in Listing 3 is Ron's reply. I'm not going to explain it, and will leave its use of those of you who are Pascal programmers. Max wrote back and said it worked, and that was good enough for me.

Yes/No Answers

One of the routines included in the January '81 column showed how to include a uniform question answering routine in your programs. Robin Ault from Newtonville, MA, has sent along additional information about this routine. It appears that a conflict occurs with the GET command and DOS commands. Robin's letter explains part of the problem. She says, "In the three-line subroutine for getting yes/no answers, I think an extra PRINT statement would help matters:

    100 PRINT Q$ "(Y/N)"; : GET A$:
PRINT A$: IF A$ = ...etc.

Or, the PRINT A$ could be just PRINT. Reasons: (1) as the routine stands, the error message in line 120 will be printed starting on the same line as the (Y/N) bit, right after it. With my added PRINT A$, it

```
2   REM   SOURCE: CREATIVE COMPUTING, JANUARY 1981 PAGE 174.
5   REM   WRITTEN BY BOB SANDER-CEDERLOF
6   REM   SOURCE SUPPLIED IDEA ONLY.
7   REM   TOTALLY MODIFIED AND WORKED UP BY BRIAN J. WINKEL, 7 JANUARY 1981
8   LG = 1: REM   DELAY BETWEEN LETTERS
9   B = 0: REM   INDICATOR SET LATER AS 1 IF MESSAGE IS > 40 LETTERS ELSE B = 0.
10  G = - 16336: TEXT : HOME : REM   G IS SPEAKER
15  REM   LINES 61 AND 146 ARE RANDOM CLICKS TO SIMULATE SOUND OF TICKER TAPE.
29  REM   PRINTING BORDERS
30  FOR J = 1 TO 2: VTAB J * 4 + 2: FOR I = 1 TO 40: PRINT "*";: NEXT I: PRINT : NEXT J
49  REM   MESSAGE TO TICKER TAPE AS STRING B$
50  B$ = "TICKER TAPE:...WINKEL AD AGENCY...THE BEST IN TOWN...YOUR MESSAGE IN LIGHT AND
       SOUND... SEE LINE 50...STRING B$...FOR YOUR VERY OWN MESSAGE!!...$50 PER LINE... CA
       LL 482-4350...IN NEW JERSY CALL COLLECT"
51  REM   LINES 52-55 PREPARING MESSAGE IN TWO CASES: LENGTH > OR <= 40.
52  IF  LEN (B$) > 40 THEN B = 1
53  IF  LEN (B$) < 40 THEN  GOTO 55
54  B$ = B$ + ".....": GOTO 60
55  FOR J = 1 TO 40 - LEN (B$):B$ = B$ + ".": NEXT J
59  REM   LINES 59-62 PRINTING MESSAGE STARTING WITH MESSAGES ENTERING FROM RIGHT SIDE OF
       SCREEN.
60  FOR I = 1 TO 40: VTAB 8: HTAB 41 - I: PRINT  LEFT$ (B$,I);" ": FOR K = 1 TO LG: NEXT
       K
61  FOR Z = 1 TO  INT (10 *  RND (1) + .5):P = P +  PEEK (G): FOR W = 1 TO 30: NEXT W: NEXT
       Z
62  NEXT I
89  REM   LINES 90-160 PRINT MESSAGE AFTER SCREEN LINE IS FILLED ONCE.
90  FOR I = 1 TO  LEN (B$)
100 VTAB 8
105 C$ =  MID$ (B$,I, LEN (B$) - 1) +  MID$ (B$,1,I - 1)
145 PRINT  LEFT$ (C$,40)
146 FOR Z = 1 TO  INT (10 *  RND (1) + .5) * P = P +  PEEK (G): FOR W = 1 TO 30: NEXT W
       : NEXT Z
150 FOR K = 1 TO LG: NEXT K
160 NEXT I
170 GOTO 90
```

Listing 2. A billboard program to continuously scroll a message. This routine is complete with sound.

```
PROGRAM RANDOMALFA;      (****************)

                         (*   WRITTEN BY *)

USES APPLESTUFF;         (* RON DEGROAT  *)

                         (* 15-DEC-1980  *)

VAR ALFA:STRING;         (****************)

    LETTER:STRING[1];

BEGIN

    LETTER:=' '; (*NULL STRINGS SHOULD*)

    ALFA:=' ';    (*USUALLY BE AVOIDED *)


    WHILE (LENGTH(ALFA) <= 26) DO

      BEGIN

        LETTER[1]:=CHR((RANDOM MOD 26)+65);


        IF (POS(LETTER,ALFA) =0)

          THEN ALFA:=CONCAT(ALFA,LETTER);

      END;


      DELETE(ALFA,1,1);   (*DELETE LEADING BLANK*)

      WRITELN(ALFA);

    END.
```

Listing 3. Pascal program to generate the 26 alpha characters randomly without repetition.

will start more normally, on a new line and, also, the user will be able to see what was just typed; (2) the sample application you gave, with a subroutine call from line 1910, may not work because the PRINT D$ "CATALOG" does not occur after a carriage return. So, unless the D$ is something like CHR$(13)+CHR$(4), DOS will not pick up the CATALOG command. (Note that CHR$(13) is a carriage return and CHR$(4) is a CONTROL D...CC.)

COMMUNICATIONS

Data Capture 4.0 from Southeastern Software enables the user with a Hayes Modem, to generate, send, receive and capture data from any compatible time-share system. I'm not sure what isn't compatible. It has worked with every time-share system to which I have access. And that inlcudes mainframes and bulletin boards.

Data Capture has been around for a while at various lower revision levels. I have 3.0 but didn't use it much; it was, in my opinion too awkward to use. Not so with version 4.0! All functions are controlled from a menu. The menu uses single character commands for each function. When the menu is displayed on the screen, pressing a related key will activate one of the 13 available choices. The T or Toggle function includes seven more options. Operation is controlled with the toggle choices and includes drive selection, baud rate, capture on/off, duplex half/full, local carrier on/off, special characters on/off, and transmit on/off.

Documentation

Operating instructions are included in 24 pages of documentation. There is no binder for the pages, but once you learn how to use the software they will hardly be needed. Operation is very friendly and usually only access to the menu is needed. You can file the instructions away in a folder and retrieve them when required.

Page one begins by telling you to make backup copies. Configuring the diskette for your system is described here and so are the special notes found throughout the documentation. Two and a half pages then describe in detail how to configure the diskettes to your system. Use of the systems is described in the remainder of the documentation. All the menu functions are discussed and many examples of what you should see or do are given. Human factors and friendliness—features I am tough about—are in the very good category.

Operation

Once you have the configuration completed, operation is simple. Just switch to the menu and select a function. You can compose text, do simple text editing, send the text, copy or capture text, save the text to disk, and list the text. Other functions include answering the phone, hanging up the phone, merging text, and printing text. More things than I've had any occasion to do. There is also a provision for entering and automatically dialing phone numbers. Even though the software is designed to work automatically with the Hayes Modem, provisions are made for manual operation with acoustic modems. Additionally, the software supports lower case only with an adapter. Without an adapter, only capital letters are possible.

Conclusions

I've used, or tried to use, previous versions of Data Capture. I have also used several other communications programs. Data Capture 4.0 is the easiest to use and most flexible so far. You can get Data Capture 4.0 for $65 from Southeastern Software, 6414 Derbyshire Dr., New Orleans, LA 70126. Phone (504) 246-7937/8438. If you want to have real lower case too, the Paymar Lower Case Adapter is available for $64.95.

GAME PADDLE I/O EXPANDER

CJM Enterprises is manufacturing an expander/extender for the Apple paddle socket. They call it the Microsystem and it includes an Applexpander, Microstick (joystick/game paddle), and an AC Control box. (See Figure 1.) You may have seen their ads in *Creative Computing* over the past few months. By itself, the CJM Applexpander is an extension of the game paddle socket with a lot of plusses. Here are the features:

16 pin extension cable to bring the socket connections outside the Apple II case.

Rugged sockets to accept the popular "Jones" style plugs. These won't wear out as less durable plugs do.

Electronically buffered connections to the circuits. Keeps things from being connected directly to your Apple and causing damage.

External speaker connections and a volume control. Note that this feature requires cutting wires in your Apple.

Once the Applexpander is plugged in, there is no longer any need to use the internal socket. Additional wear on the socket is eliminated. IC sockets are not designed for lots of insertions and removals, so one potential source of trouble is removed.

Microstick

Essentially, the Microstick is two game paddles in one package. Two rugged pushbuttons are included on the chassis too. The Applexpander will accept two of these, giving four game paddles at one time. Don't forget that you can still only have three switch inputs; that's all there are.

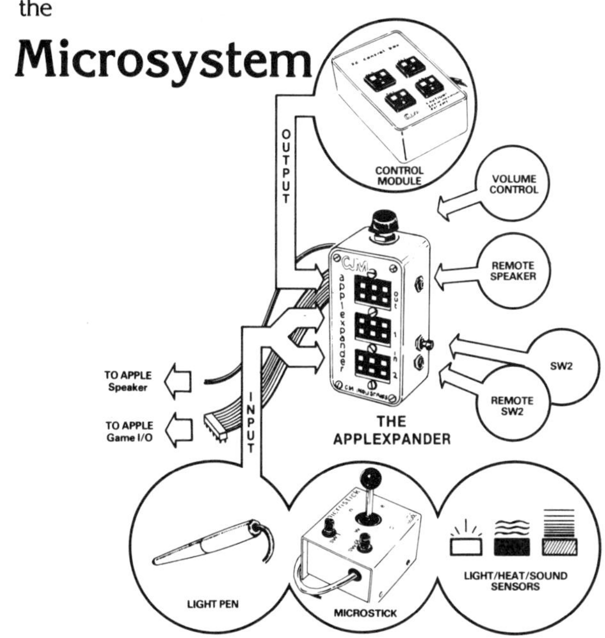

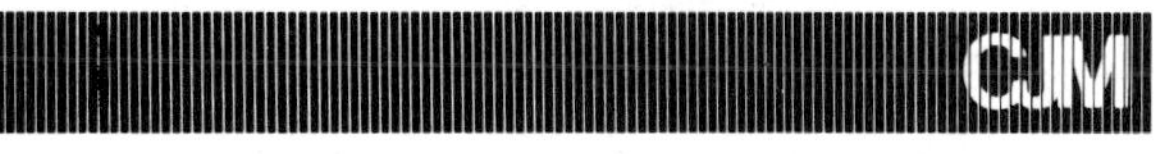

Figure 1. CJM's Game Paddle Expander System. For the hardware experimenter, this system provides an easy way to simplify interface problems.

A booklet is included with the system describing its uses and things you can do. There are examples of software showing how to use the inputs and outputs. Software examples are in Basic and machine language. There were several typos and exclusions in the booklet I received, some of which could mislead the less experienced user. These should be corrected by the time you read this.

If you're inclined to experiment with simple hardware ideas, this system can make the job easier. All the required interfacing and buffering is done. I didn't get the AC Control box so I can't tell you about it. The parts I did get are rugged and well packaged. The use of rugged parts is necessary to prevent wear and broken pins. You can get the system from CJM Industries, Inc., P.O. Box 2367, Reston, VA 22090. Phone (703) 620-2444, Microsystem is available as individual parts or as a complete system. Prices range from $74.95 for the Applexpander, $69.95 for the Microstick, and $109.95 for the AC Control box, to 169.95 for System I. System I is one each Applexpander, Microstick, paddle adapter kit, software (graphics kit and demo), and documentation. There are other system combinations to $399.95. CJM also lists several other items on the order form, including some devices to connect to the AC Control box.

PASCAL MANUALS

My new Pascal manuals came in the mail recently, and they were worth the wait. I sent in the card that came with my language system over a year ago. With the card, a new owner was to get the new manual(s) free when published. The single preliminary reference manual grew into two manuals. One is called the Language Reference Manual, and the other is called the Operating System Reference Manual. I'm not a serious Pascal programmer but I find them useful for anything I need to know about the system. The new Apple Fortran system also requires the user to have the information in the Operating System Reference Manual. That seems to be the reason for two manuals. Fortran comes with only the Fortran Language Reference Manual. If you bought the Language System, and sent in the card, you should have received the manuals by now.

More Machine Language • Random Numbers
Assembly Language References

Chuck Carpenter

June, 1981

NEW BOOK

For those of you interested in Apple Machine Language, a new book has been published, *Apple Machine Language* by Don and Kurt Inman. The book is published by Reston Publishing Co. Inc., Reston, VA.

This book may be the best ever for the beginner. It is profusely illustrated with examples, drawings and diagrams. Twelve chapters lead you through a review of Applesoft, the similarities between Basic and machine language, and several exercises in machine language. You learn about simple graphics, displaying text, Apple sounds, the Apple system monitor, and doing mathematics in machine language. The use of the mini-assembler is thoroughly discussed and a final chapter tells you how to put it all together. Included in the appendix are sections on Basic statements, machine language instructions, built-in subroutines, hex to decimal negative equivalents, how video memory is mapped, ASCII screen codes, color codes for low resolution graphics, and a very nice presentation of the 6502 instruction codes. The one shortcoming I saw is that it requires the availability of Integer Basic. My copy cost $15 at one of the local computer stores.

THE ASSEMBLY LINE

Also for the assembly/machine language programmer, a new newsletter. From S-C Software, the source of an excellent Apple-oriented Assembler, comes a 6502 assembly language newsletter. The February 1981 issue lists several "Apple Noises and Other Sounds." These included: simple tone, Apple 'bell' subroutine, machine-gun noise, laser 'swoop' sound, inch-worm sounds, touch-tones simulator, and Morse code output.

Other topics include: "Stuffing Object Code in Protected Places," "Multiplying on the 6502" and "A String Swapper for Applesoft."

Previous issues have included programs for converting certain keyboard keys to a 10-key system for data entry. Listing 1 is the program for the 10-key capability. A portion of the newsletter is devoted to updates, patches and other items of interest to users of the S-C Assembler II. Reviews of the assembler were included in the July and December '80 issues of *Creative Computing*. You can get the newsletter by sending $12 for one year (12 issues) to Apple Assembly Line, S-C Software, P.O. Box 5537, Richardson, TX 75080. Other countries add $6 per year for extra postage.

Continuing with more assembly language, here's a graphics routine by Tom Spidell from Milwaukee, WI. The program switches graphics pages and from one type of graphics to the other. The concepts included here can be used in your program to switch graphics pages. You can CALL the program from a basic routine as needed. Listing 2 shows the program using the syntax of the S-C Assembler II. Don't forget that a program located at address $0300 is activated by CALL 768.

One Liners

Listing 3 and 4 are graphics one liners from Bob Sander-Cederlof. One makes a quilt pattern and the other draws concentric patterns resembling the layers of an onion. Maybe that's why Bob calls it "Make an Onion." Both are high res graphics routines. Be sure to type them very carefully.

Does anyone else have one liners they would like to share? Send them to me and I will include them in the column.

QUESTIONS 'N ANSWERS

About Random Numbers—In the January '81 issue, there is a program to generate random color blocks. The program on page 144 is part of the "How to Solve It—With the Computer" series by Donald T. Piele. Here's the program:

```
10 GR
20 COLOR = 9
30 X = INT(40*RND(1))
40 Y = INT(40*RND(1))
50 PLOT X,Y
60 GOTO 30
70 END
```

The expected result is for the program to fill the screen—eventually—with blocks of color. Usually, the program seems to stop with the screen only partially filled.

Checking around, I found this is an anomaly with the Applesoft random number generator. The number used to seed the random number sequence gets stuck and the range becomes limited. My understanding stops right here, but not my curiosity. The description of Applesoft page zero usage in the Applesoft manual indicates that memory locations $C9 to $CD hold the random number. By modifying the original program slightly, I found that I could get the screen to fill every time. And, there was no noticeable similarity to the pattern. A line is added to poke another random number into one of the locations where the random number is stored. In decimal, these are locations 201 to 204. Here's the new program line:

```
25  POKE  201,PEEK(INT(255*RND
   (1)))
```

Then change line 60 to read:
```
60 GOTO 25
```
Line 25 is pulling a number randomly from page zero. These page zero values are often changing as the (any) program is running. Once this was done, the program never failed to fill the screen. If someone can provide an explanation, please do. Many readers and at least one columnist will be grateful.

About Assembly Language Indexing - Fundamentals of Indexing were described in the November '80 issue. Generally the information was well received but, there were a couple of questions. Here is some additional information to support the November '80 column.

First, some backup on operands and opcodes in assembly language. The operand is the key element used in the program to determine which of the opcodes will be used. Notice that absolute indexing uses the form $0900,X while indirect indexing uses the form ($3A),Y. These are only two of the indexing operands. Some others are ZP,X,ABS,Y, and (ZP,X) where ZP means Zero Page.

```
                     0900  * MULTIPLE SCREENS
                     0910  *
                     1000  * THIS PROGRAM WILL SHOW ALL OF THE
                     1010  * PAGES OF TEXT AND GRAPHICS
                     1020  * AT THE SAME TIME (IMPOSSIBLE
                     1030  * HUH?). ACTUALLY, THE VIDEO
                     1040  * MONITOR JUST CAN'T KEEP UP WITH
                     1050  * THE CHANGES AND SHOWS ALL THE
                     1060  * SCREENS. TYPE ANY KEY TO ROTATE
                     1070  * THE SCREEN.
                     1080  *
                     1090  * BY TOM SPIDELL
                     1100  * MILWAUKEE, WI
                     1110  *
0000-                1120  DUMMY      .EQ $00
C000-                1130  KEYBOARD   .EQ $C000
C050-                1140  GRMODE     .EQ $C050
C010-                1150  KEYCLEAR   .EQ $C010
C051-                1160  TXTMODE    .EQ $C051
C054-                1170  PG1        .EQ $C054
C055-                1180  PG2        .EQ $C055
C056-                1190  LORES      .EQ $C056
C057-                1200  HIRES      .EQ $C057
                     1210  *
                     1220  *------------------------------------
                     1230  *
                     1235            .OR $300
0300- AD 50 C0       1240  BEGIN     LDA GRMODE
0303- A1 00          1250            LDA (DUMMY,X) ;6 CLOCK CYCLES
0305- AD 56 C0       1260            LDA LORES
0308- A1 00          1270            LDA (DUMMY,X)
030A- AD 57 C0       1280            LDA HIRES
030D- A1 00          1290            LDA (DUMMY,X)
030F- AD 55 C0       1300            LDA PG2
0312- A1 00          1310            LDA (DUMMY,X)
0314- AD 51 C0       1320            LDA TXTMODE
0317- A1 00          1330            LDA (DUMMY,X)
0319- AD 54 C0       1340            LDA PG1
031C- B5 00          1350            LDA DUMMY,X ;4 CLOCK CYCLES
031E- AD 00 C0       1360            LDA KEYBOARD
0321- 10 DD          1370            BPL BEGIN
0323- AD 10 C0       1380            LDA KEYCLEAR
0326- 4C 00 03       1390            JMP BEGIN
                     1400            .EN
```

```
              SYMBOL TABLE

              0300- BEGIN
              0000- DUMMY
              C050- GRMODE
              C057- HIRES
              C000- KEYBOARD
              C010- KEYCLEAR
              C056- LORES
              C054- PG1
              C055- PG2
              C051- TXTMODE
```

Listing 1 Program to display all the graphics pages.

Each one accomplishes indexing a slightly different way. And, each one will use a different operand in the machine language code (generated during the assembly of an assembly language program).

The opcode is used by the instruction set, the 6502 microcode, to define what is to happen next in the program. When the indexing opcode or instruction is executed by the microprocessor, it knows whether to look for a byte of data *at* an address or *for* a two byte address. That's

```
                1000  *----------------------------------
                1010  *     NUMERIC KEY PAD FOR APPLE
                1020  *----------------------------------
                1030          .OR $300
                1040          .TF B.NKP
                1050  *----------------------------------
0300- A9 01     1060          LDA #1
0302- 8D 10 03  1070          STA TOGGLE
0305- A9 12     1080          LDA #NKP
0307- 85 38     1090          STA $38
0309- A9 03     1100          LDA /NKP
030B- 85 39     1110          STA $39
030D- 4C EA 03  1120          JMP $3EA
                1130  *----------------------------------
0310-           1140  TOGGLE .BS 1
0311-           1150  SAVEY  .BS 1
                1160  *----------------------------------
                1170  NKP
0312- 20 1B FD  1180          JSR $FD1B
0315- C9 93     1190          CMP #$93        CONTROL-S
0317- F0 1D     1200          BEQ .4
0319- 2C 10 03  1210          BIT TOGGLE
031C- 30 10     1220          BMI .2          NOT IN NUMERIC MODE
031E- 8C 11 03  1230          STY SAVEY
0321- A0 0B     1240          LDY #TBLSIZ-1
0323- D9 41 03  1250  .1      CMP CHRTBL,Y
0326- F0 07     1260          BEQ .3          FOUND IN TABLE
0328- 88        1270          DEY
0329- 10 F8     1280          BPL .1
032B- AC 11 03  1290          LDY SAVEY
032E- 60        1300  .2      RTS
032F- B9 4D 03  1310  .3      LDA ALIAS,Y
0332- AC 11 03  1320          LDY SAVEY
0335- 60        1330          RTS
0336- AD 10 03  1340  .4      LDA TOGGLE
0339- 49 80     1350          EOR #$80
033B- 8D 10 03  1360          STA TOGGLE
033E- 4C 0C FD  1370          JMP $FDOC
                1380  *----------------------------------
0341- AF CC A0
0344- CE CD AC
0347- C8 CA CB
034A- D9 D5 C9  1390  CHRTBL .AS -"/L NM,HJKYUI"
000C-           1400  TBLSIZ .EQ *-CHRTBL
034D- 8D        1410  ALIAS  .HS 8D
034E- AD B0 B1
0351- B2 B3 B4
0354- B5 B6 B7
0357- B8 B9     1420         .AS -"-0123456789"
SYMBOL TABLE    1430  *----------------------------------

034D- ALIAS
0341- CHRTBL
0312- NKP
.01=0323, .02=032E, .03=032F, .04=0336
0311- SAVEY
000C- TBLSIZ
0310- TOGGLE
```

Listing 2 Program from The Assembly Line showing how to use the Apple as a 10-key data entry keyboard.

```
100  REM
QUILT PATTERN
----------------
BOB SANDER-CEDERLOF
FEBRUARY 4, 1981
200  HGR2 : FOR A = 26 TO 156 STEP
     26: FOR C = A - 25 TO A: HCOLOR=
     A / 26: HPLOT 20,C TO 259,C:
     C = C + 1: FOR D = 20 TO 220
     STEP 40: HCOLOR= (D + 20) /
     40: HPLOT D,C TO D + 39,C: NEXT
     : NEXT : NEXT : FOR I = 1 TO
     5000: NEXT : TEXT : HOME : LIST
```

Listing 3 One-liner makes a quilt pattern in color.

```
100  REM MAKE AN ONION
110  CF = 1.15:XC = 140:YC = 96: HGR2
     : HCOLOR= 3: FOR N = 1 TO 48
     :R = 2 * N - 1:P = 6.2831853
     1 / N:C =  COS (P):S =  SIN
     (P):X = R:Y = 0: HPLOT XC +
     X * CF,YC: FOR I = 1 TO N:XN
     = X * C - Y * S:YN = X * S +
     Y * C:X = XN:Y = YN: HPLOT  TO
     XC + X * CF,Y + YC: NEXT : NEXT
     : FOR I = 1 TO 2000: NEXT : TEXT
     : END
120  REM BY BOB SANDER-CEDERLOF
```

Listing 4 One-liner draws onion-like concentric circles.

are a couple of books that I recommend (In addition to the new one in this column). The books are:

6502 Software Design, Leo J. Scanlon, Sams # 2156. (Good book for beginners.)

6502 Assembly Language Programming, Lance Leventhal, Osborne/ McGraw Hill. (Very detailed and complete.)

About Interpreters—For instructional purposes, I'm interested in Pascal and Fortran interpreters. I've looked for these in various ads but have not yet found one. Using a compiler for learning is painfully slow. For each little program segment the student is required to go through the entire compiling sequence to find out if the routine works. Compilers are definitely needed for large application programs and the student should know how to use them. But, during the initial instruction period getting familiar with the language would go much faster with an interpreter. It's sort of like learning to drive a car. It's a lot easier to teach the fundamentals of driving with a car equipped with an automatic transmission. A manual transmission creates too many distractions for the new driver.

Pascal or Fortran interpreters need not be fast. But they should be compatible with all the error message and functions of the compiled equivalent. If error messages could be generated with each typed line, all the better. A good example is the way Apple Integer Basic is handled. Each line is checked as it is typed in. This way, the student gets immediate feedback and doesn't have to wait for compile time or run time errors to find out what happened with the program. How about it, anyone want to become rich and famous?

---

why I used the statement that a two-address indirect location is implied. Since it takes two bytes to store a 16 bit address, the microcode program in the 6502 knows to look at two consecutive memory locations for the address of the table to be indexed.

Page zero addressing is implied in just the opposite way. The addresses are $0000 to $00FF. Because the first two bytes are always $00 the microcode interpretation of page zero instructions knows the first byte is always $00. Therefore, page zero instructions only need one byte—8 bits—to specify the usual 16-bit address. Since only one byte is needed, less code is used and the program will run faster because only half the page zero address must be decoded. (Notice too, that the low byte of the index table is stored in address $0300 and the high byte is stored in $0301. This is 6502 convention.)

In the May '80 issue of *Creative Computing* a discussion of Machine Language Fundamentals was included. Also, there

Graphics Book
GET vs. INPUT, Part 2 • Z-80 and Clock Boards
Memory Dump From MBASIC

Chuck Carpenter *July, 1981*

Voice recognition was featured at our computer club recently. The unit demonstrated was by Scott Instruments. You can see ads featuring this device in recent computer magazines. One ad appeared in the April '81 Complete Computer Catalog in *Creative Computing*. I had a chance to use this equipment, and it is fantastic. It can be used to do things like run Basic programs or control external devices. I was able to condition its input recognition to accept my voice only. We also conditioned the instrument to recognize either of the two voices. One use of a unit such as this is control of equipment without the use of hands. One example involved a lady who is a quadraplegic; with the Scott VET/2 Voice Entry Unit, and the Mountain Computer BSR Remote Controller, this lady could control her bed, the lights, and many things around her, as well as summon help. Now, this is a *real* micro computer application. The unit is more expensive than those you may have seen so far. But, it really works. The cost is $895. Scott Instruments, 815 North Elm, Denton, TX 76201. (817) 387-9514.

OOPS!

A program to simulate the LINE INPUT command from other versions of Basic was included in the April '81 issue (page 204, GET vs INPUT). As written, the program doesn't work. Craig Peterson wrote and explained why: "The PEEK function in line 10040 will gather the input with the high bit of each character set (*to one—CC*). Applesoft strings want this bit to be zero. Therefore, all the characters will look normal on the television (*or monitor—CC*) screen, but they will be wrongly represented internally. The resulting problem is that any Applesoft compares will be impossible to satisfy. The STOP used to stop the program doesn't work because 'STOP' in line 25 has the high bits off while A$ has them all set. The problem can be corrected by changing line 10040 to:

10040 A$=A$+CHR$(PEEK(J+511)-128)"

As Craig pointed out, had I run this program I would have noticed the problem. Since I had a listing with a sample run (???), I took a shortcut. Sigh!

Z-80 TELLS TIME

It's not immediately obvious, but the Mountain Computer clock board will work with the Microsoft Z-80 board. At least it does with a Microsoft Basic program I wrote. Some detective work was required first. The reason for this is that the Z-80 maps memory differently.

• Address 0000H for the Z-80 system is $1000 in the 6502 system. Notice that Z-80 convention uses the trailing H to indicate Hex. 6502 convention uses the $ to indicate Hex.

• High memory, from E000H to FFFFH, starts at 6502 address $0000. This is the same as page 0 through page 7 of the standard Apple.

• Some way was needed to find where things were in memory.

• Apple CALL commands are included in Microsoft Basic to call 6502 commands once you find out where they are.

Where Am I?

First, I needed to find out what was going on in memory. A dump routine is included with the CP/M operating system,

Graphics Book

Those of you interested in hi-res graphics will like this book. It's called *Computer Graphics Primer*, and it's by Mitchell Waite. The book has been on the market for a couple of years but I just "discovered" it. Chapters 1 and 2 are general information about graphics and graphics history. The rest of the book is about graphics programs, all of which were written on the Apple II. You learn how to use the graphics commands and how to make things seem to move on the screen. The programs work too. This book is one of the Sams Primer series. Mitchell Waite has written several of them; all well done. It's Sams publication number 21650, and the cost of the copy I have was $12.95.

```
100 HOME
110 INPUT"STARTING ADDRESS - ",X
120 INPUT"RANGE IN BYTES - ",Y
130 PRINT: PRINT"ADDR.";
140 PRINT"   0   1   2   3   4   5   6   7   8   9  10  11  12  13  14  15"
150 PRINT"-----";
160 PRINT"------------------------------------------------------------------"
170 GOSUB 250
180 FOR I=X TO X+Y-1
190 A$=HEX$(PEEK(I))
200 IF LEN(A$)=1 THEN A$="0"+A$
210 PRINT A$;" ";
220 N=N+1 : IF N=16 THEN PRINT :  N=0 : X=X+16 : GOSUB 250
230 NEXT I
240 END
250 PRINT USING "#####  ";X;
260 RETURN
```

Listing 1. Microsoft MBasic listing of memory dump program used to create the dump shown in Figures 1 and 2. Note the HEX$ and PRINT USING commands that are not available in Applesoft.

ADDR.	0	1	2	3	4	5	6	7	8	9	10	11	12	13	14	15
62208	00	00	00	00	00	00	00	00	00	00	00	00	00	00	00	00
62224	00	00	00	00	00	00	00	00	00	00	00	00	00	00	00	00
62240	00	00	00	00	00	00	00	00	00	00	00	00	00	00	00	00
62256	00	00	00	00	00	00	00	00	00	00	00	00	00	00	00	00
62272	00	00	00	00	00	00	00	00	00	00	3A	BB	F3	FE	03	C2
62288	0C	DB	3A	BE	E0	1F	9F	C9	CD	12	DB	E6	7F	C9	3A	BB
62304	F3	FE	03	C2	3E	DC	3A	BE	E0	E6	02	28	F9	79	32	45
62320	F0	21	7C	03	22	D0	F3	2A	DE	F3	77	C9	8D	BF	C0	60
62336	4A	F3	58	F3	12	DB	5E	F3	3E	DC	45	DD	45	DD	3F	DD
62352	3F	DD	EE	F2	2B	DD	20	1B	AA	D9	D4	A9	A8	1E	BD	0B
62368	0C	A0	00	0C	0B	1D	0E	0F	19	1E	1F	1C	0B	5B	00	7F
62384	02	5C	15	09	FF	FF	FF	FF	02	05	03	04	01	04	02	00
62400	AD	83	C0	AD	83	C0	8D	00	C7	AD	81	C0	20	3F	FF	20
62416	AA	C9	8D	81	C0	20	4A	FF	4C	C0	03	00	00	20	00	E7
62432	14	0B	00	CD	01	01	60	60	00	08	00	01	00	00	00	00
62448	C0	03	C0	03	A6	4C	C0	03	4C	C0	03	4C	C0	03	C0	03
62464																

Figure 1. Memory dump of page 3 of Apple memory. Address 62208 is Z-80 Address F300H. The equivalent 6502 address is $0300 or 768 decimal. Note the change in the vector addresses under control of the Z-80 starting at address 62448.

but, this is a slow procedure. You have to exit Basic, dump the program, and return to Basic. Or, you have to exit Basic, load the DDT program from CP/M and dump the range of memory you want, then exit the DDT program and return to Basic. Doing some of these things wipes out the range of memory you want to see.

What was needed was a program to dump memory from Basic. This is where some of the added power of MBasic comes in handy. There are a couple of commands that make the task much easier. The program in Listing 1 is an example of my results. The program uses decimal values to identify the memory locations. Further improvements of the program would do conversions for you. Other options would be to have the program do a disassembly of memory too. But that's another story.

Back to the dump routine. Lines 110 and 120 accept input for the starting address and the number of bytes to dump. Use the decimal equivalent of the starting address. You can use any number of bytes, but multiples of 16 up to 256 fit nicely on the screen. If you use only 40 columns, make it multiples of 8 up to 128 bytes per dump. Headers for the dump are provided by lines 130 to 160. Line 170 jumps to the address printing subroutine at line 250. This routine uses the PRINT USING command to format the address at the beginning of each row. A loop for printing the dump over the selected range starts at line 180. Line 190 converts the decimal value found by the PEEK to a hexadecimal number. The HEX$ command from MBasic is used to do this. In line 200, the program tests the length of the number. If the number is only one digit, a zero is appended to the front. In line 210, the hex number is printed along with a pair of spaces.

Line 220 does the rest of the work in the program. First it increments the address by one. Then it tests to see if 16 addresses have been printed. If not, control passes

to the NEXT I on the next line. If 16 bytes have been printed, then a print is issued to disconnect the semicolon at the end of line 210. Remember that a semicolon causes print statements to print things next to each other on the same line. Next in line 220, N is set back to zero and X is incremented by 16 bytes. The variable X is now equal to the beginning address of the next row of bytes. The address is printed and the routine continues until all the bytes requested are printed. The program ends with the address of the next memory location. An example of a dump is shown in Figure 1. This is 256 bytes of Z-80 memory at address F300H or $0300 of 6502 memory. Some of you will recognize this as page 3 of Apple's memory. Note that I changed the PRINT commands to LPRINT so that I could direct the dump to my printer.

Use of this hex dump routine allowed me to examine memory while I was in Basic. Since my goal was to find out what was going on from Basic, this program solved my problem. It also simplified the task. Now there was no need to exit Basic each time there was a need to examine changes. Eventually, I figured out that part of page 3 (Figure 1) never changed. No matter what else I did with various programs, those first 74 bytes remained zeros. Now, I was ready to find a way to use my Mountain Computer clock board (MCCB) from MBasic.

Running The Clock

There is a command in MBasic that is used to call 6502 routines. It is CALL %. I experimented with POKEs and the use of the CALL % command until I found the proper combination. First, the clock needed to be activated. Then a way was needed to retrieve the data generated by the clock. Some background on what the clock does will be helpful at this point.

To use the MCCB with machine language, you need to do the following:
• Load the keyboard switch high byte (KSWH at address $27) with the clock address high byte. I have my clock in slot 4 so this byte is C4.
• Jump to the starting address of the clock routine at $C400.
• Return from the program and translate the data stored by the MCCB.

I have a machine language program that does this, so I used the first 8 bytes. The program looks like this:

```
LDA  #$C4
STA  $27
JSR  $C400
RTS
```

Using the values assembled from this program, I POKEd them into the first 8 bytes of page 3. Then I used the CALL % command to attempt to run the clock. The output of the MCCB is stored at the high end of the keyboard buffer from $0281 to $0294 (F281H to F294H in Z-80 notation). By using my dump routine, this area of memory was checked. Sure enough, there was the output from the clock. The clock output is stored in reverse order. The month and day start at the highest address. One thousandth of a second is stored at the lowest address. All of this is described in detail in the MCCB manual. The program in Listing 2 was the result of my experiments. Here's how it works.

Using the Clock

After converting the hex data from the sort assembly program, the POKEs in lines 60000 and 60010 resulted. These lines insert the code in page 3 as shown in Figure 2, which is a dump of the first 16 bytes of memory showing our 8 byte clock calling routine. The next 2 lines, 60020 and 60030 set-up the CALL % to the 6502 routine

```
60000 POKE 62208!,169 : POKE 62209!,196 : POKE 62210!,133 : POKE 62211!,57
60010 POKE 62212!,32 : POKE 62213!,0 : POKE 62214!,196 : POKE 62215!,96
60020 CLOCK = &H300
60030 HOME : CALL % CLOCK
60040 VTAB(10) :
60045 POKE 62088!,58 : POKE 62091!,58
60050 FOR I=62100! TO 62081! STEP -1
60060 A$=CHR$(PEEK(I))
60070 PRINT A$;
60080 NEXT I
60090 VTAB (22) : PRINT
60100 FOR I=1 TO 1000 : NEXT I
60120 GOTO 60030
```

Listing 2. MBasic clock calling program. Program POKEs machine language then CALLs it with a special MBasic command.

```
ADDR.     0    1    2    3    4    5    6    7    8    9   10   11   12   13   14   15
---------------------------------------------------------------------------------------
62208    A9   C4   85   39   20   00   C4   60   00   00   00   00   00   00   00   00
62224
```

Figure 2. First 16 bytes of page 3 after using the clock program in Listing 2.

from MBasic. I used the illustration in the MBasic manual to do this. Note that the H indicating hex precedes the address. Just the opposite from the way it is done at Z-80 addresses. That is, you use the offset with Z-80 0000H at 6502 $1000. When you call a 6502 address with the CALL % command you use the actual 6502 address. Makes the job more challenging this way.

Line 60045 inserts colons in the output from the clock. Normally, these two locations contain semi-colons. This keeps the clock data from confusing Applesoft programs. Colons look better in a time printout so I used them. A loop to print the output starts at line 60050. Remember that the clock data is stored in reverse order. Hence, the reverse stepping of the loop. The data in each memory location is converted to it's decimal ASCII value in line 60070 and printed in line 60080. The cursor is moved out of the way by line 60090 and a delay is created by line 60100. (A value of 256 in this loop changes the display very close to once a second.) Line 60120 keeps the display going as long as you want. If the routine was to be used with a program, the GOTO 60030 would be changed to a RETURN from a subroutine call.

Thus ended my quest to make my MCCB work with the Z-80 board. Now that wasn't all that difficult, was it?

FROM OUT OF THE PAST

Jack Cowley asked a question. Why all the fuss about protecting the Apple from accidental RESET? Well, once upon a time, the Apple keyboard was different than it is now. In the early days of yesteryear there was no autostart ROM. More importantly, there was no neat little switch on the back of the keyboard with which to select the CONTROL RESET option. On the older units—the first 75,000 or so—when the reset button was pushed that was it. You might be able to recover your program if you were lucky. The Autostart ROM helped some when it came along after about a year and a half. You could then recover the program easily, but whatever was happening at the time of a reset was probably lost. Some of the routines you may have seen, direct the reset vector to a safe place. Such a routine was submitted by Douglas Dougherty and was included in the April '81 column.

Check which unit you have before ordering accessories for use with the keyboard. Most of the lower case units are designed to work with one or the other, but not both. I have the Keyboard Enhancer from Videoterm now. It is designed to provide the CONTROL RESET option on level 6 or earlier machines. If your unit has the switch on the back of the keyboard you would use the level 7 model. I'll be telling you more about the Keyboard Enhancer in a future column.

NEXT TIME

The next column will feature more input from readers, including a description of how to obtain the mini-assembler on machines that don't have Integer Basic. and how to get the mini-assembler on machines that don't have Integer Basic, Also, I'll tell how to get the mini-assembler on machines that don't have the language system. □

<hr>

Notes

Apple II — Mini Assembler

Chuck Carpenter

In the July '81 column, I mentioned that a mini-assembler would be included in a future column. This is it. Rushika Fernandopulle has provided the program.

Mini-Assembler

If you have an Apple II, you have the mini-assembler. Those of you with a II Plus don't. The program was located in ROM along with several other Integer Basic utilities. The use of Applesoft in the II Plus eliminated these programs. Rushika found a way to extract the program from the language card programs found on the System Master disk. Here's what Rushika had to say: "On the System Master I noticed a program (in machine language—a B, or binary, file) called INTBASIC. It is for use with a language card, and starts at $D000. I needed a mini-assembler, so I decided to use the one on the INTBASIC program by using these steps:

1. Boot DOS with the System Master and then type BLOAD INTBASIC, A$2000.

2. Insert another INITed disk and type BSAVE ASM1,A$4500,L$200.

3. Clear all memory, then type the program shown in Listing 1. (Note: To clear memory, use the monitor move command. First CALL-151 to get to the monitor.

```
JLIST
10 DATA  559,595,811,864
20 DATA  695,725,735
30 FOR T = 1 TO 4: READ A
40 POKE 21000 + A,84: NEXT
50 FOR T = 1 TO 3: READ A
60 POKE 21000 + A,85: NEXT
]
```

Listing 1. Program used to modify the mini-assembler for relocation at $5400.

Then at the asterisk prompt, type 801:0. Next, type 800 801.95FEM. This sequence will fill all of memory from 800 to 95FF with the 0 character. Address 95FF is the last address just below the beginning of DOS. Now type 3D0G to return to the Basic language in use. Remember to type RETURN at the right places so the computer knows what you want to do—CC)

4. Type BLOAD ASM,A$5400.

5. Run the program from Listing 1.

6. Type BSAVE MINIASSEMBLER, A$5400,L$200.

7. Run the mini-assembler by using a CALL21862 or in from the monitor use 5566G.

Now I can use the mini-assembler, and this makes machine language programming a lot easier."

Rushika's technique works. I used it to extract a version for use by anyone not having access to the programs mentioned. Listing 2 is my version of the process described above. Here's how it works.

More About Mini

To use the assembler in Listing 2, you first need to type it in to memory. Use the monitor commands to do this. I recommend that you don't enter more than two lines worth of characters at a time. First, get to the monitor as required by your machine. Press RESET or CALL-151—CALL-151 will work with any machine. If you are working with an early version of DOS, also do a 48:0 so you don't mess up the reentry to DOS later.

Once you have *carefully* typed in all the hex data, you can try it out. From the monitor, use 555EG. Now, all the mini-assembler commands shown in the Apple II Reference Manual will work. Follow the procedure shown there to use the assembler. Once you are sure it works, save it on a diskette. Type 3D0G and return to Basic. Now type BSAVE ASM1, A$5400,L$170. If all is well, you will save the program as a binary file.

Of course, you can save it under any name you choose. You may have noticed that the length of my version is shorter than the one described above. When Apple

Listing 2. Apple disassembly of the mini-assembler. Note that you can enter the program at $5492. The jump at $555E is easier to remember.

```
5400LLLLLLLLL
5400-   E9 81        SBC   #$81
5402-   4A           LSR
5403-   D0 14        BNE   $5419
5405-   A4 3F        LDY   $3F
5407-   A6 3E        LDX   $3E
5409-   D0 01        BNE   $540C
540B-   88           DEY
540C-   CA           DEX
540D-   8A           TXA
540E-   18           CLC
540F-   E5 3A        SBC   $3A
5411-   85 3E        STA   $3E
5413-   10 01        BPL   $5416
5415-   C8           INY
5416-   98           TYA
5417-   E5 3B        SBC   $3B
5419-   D0 6B        BNE   $5486
541B-   A4 2F        LDY   $2F
541D-   B9 3D 00     LDA   $003D,Y
5420-   91 3A        STA   ($3A),Y
5422-   88           DEY
5423-   10 F8        BPL   $541D
5425-   20 1A FC     JSR   $FC1A
5428-   20 1A FC     JSR   $FC1A
542B-   20 D0 F8     JSR   $F8D0
542E-   20 53 F9     JSR   $F953
5431-   84 3B        STY   $3B
5433-   85 3A        STA   $3A
5435-   4C 95 54     JMP   $5495

5438-   20 BE FF     JSR   $FFBE
543B-   A4 34        LDY   $34
543D-   20 A7 FF     JSR   $FFA7
5440-   84 34        STY   $34
5442-   A0 17        LDY   #$17
5444-   88           DEY
5445-   30 4B        BMI   $5492
5447-   D9 CC FF     CMP   $FFCC,Y
544A-   D0 F8        BNE   $5444
544C-   C0 15        CPY   #$15
544E-   D0 E8        BNE   $5438
5450-   A5 31        LDA   $31
5452-   A0 00        LDY   #$00
5454-   C6 34        DEC   $34
5456-   20 00 FE     JSR   $FE00
5459-   4C 95 54     JMP   $5495
545C-   A5 3D        LDA   $3D
545E-   20 8E F8     JSR   $F88E
5461-   AA           TAX
5462-   BD 00 FA     LDA   $FA00,X
5465-   C5 42        CMP   $42
5467-   D0 13        BNE   $547C
5469-   BD C0 F9     LDA   $F9C0,X
546C-   C5 43        CMP   $43
546E-   D0 0C        BNE   $547C
5470-   A5 44        LDA   $44
5472-   A4 2E        LDY   $2E
5474-   C0 9D        CPY   #$9D
5476-   F0 88        BEQ   $5400
5478-   C5 2E        CMP   $2E
547A-   F0 9F        BEQ   $541B
547C-   C6 3D        DEC   $3D
547E-   D0 DC        BNE   $545C
5480-   E6 44        INC   $44
5482-   C6 35        DEC   $35
5484-   F0 D6        BEQ   $545C

5486-   A4 34        LDY   $34
5488-   98           TYA
5489-   AA           TAX
548A-   20 4A F9     JSR   $F94A
548D-   A9 DE        LDA   #$DE
548F-   20 ED FD     JSR   $FDED
5492-   20 3A FF     JSR   $FF3A
5495-   A9 A1        LDA   #$A1
5497-   85 33        STA   $33
5499-   20 67 FD     JSR   $FD67
549C-   20 C7 FF     JSR   $FFC7
549F-   AD 00 02     LDA   $0200
54A2-   C9 A0        CMP   #$A0
54A4-   F0 13        BEQ   $54B9
54A6-   C8           INY
54A7-   C9 A4        CMP   #$A4
54A9-   F0 92        BEQ   $543D
54AB-   88           DEY
54AC-   20 A7 FF     JSR   $FFA7
54AF-   C9 93        CMP   #$93
54B1-   D0 D5        BNE   $5488
54B3-   8A           TXA
54B4-   F0 D2        BEQ   $5488
54B6-   20 78 FE     JSR   $FE78
54B9-   A9 03        LDA   #$03
54BB-   85 3D        STA   $3D
54BD-   20 34 55     JSR   $5534
54C0-   0A           ASL
54C1-   E9 BE        SBC   #$BE
54C3-   C9 C2        CMP   #$C2
54C5-   90 C1        BCC   $5488
54C7-   0A           ASL
54C8-   0A           ASL
54C9-   A2 04        LDX   #$04
```

Listing 2 continued on pg. 226.

wrote the original version, they put a jump address at an easy-to-remember location. Since this address changed anyway, I shortened the wasted space and used a new jump address. The actual entry address is $5492 and you can use this if you choose. I used this version of mini to make this listing, but there is no guarantee it is bugless. All effort was made to check it out. But, you're on your own.

When you write a program be sure to start and end it at safe locations. The programs you write can start at $0800 and end at $53FF. Or they can start at $555F and end at $95FF. Or the program can use any combination of the addresses between these two ranges. Any other addresses used may clobber the assembler, DOS or something else. Be sure you know where your program is located and what it is doing. Of course it's fun to experiment, too. The most that can happen is you will have to reload DOS and the assembler. Be sure you have the program saved and use a scratch disk to do the experimenting. You might do something that causes the system to write on the disk when you don't expect it.

BUGS

The column in the May '81 issue contained a billboard program by Brian J. Winkel. My word processor made a mistake and inserted some typos in Brian's program. (Doesn't everyone blame it on the computer?) Paul Raymer pointed out that JERSY line 50 should be JERSEY. He also pointed out that the *second* asterisk in line 146 should be a colon. The program will run as Brian intended it when you make the changes.

NEXT TIME

I'll talk about getting started with the Apple—its versatility, how to find good Apple software, what hardware and peripherals you should consider—and a whole lot more. □

"Believe me — you're making a mistake."


```
54CB-   0A            ASL
54CC-   26 42         ROL    $42
54CE-   26 43         ROL    $43
54D0-   CA            DEX
54D1-   10 F8         BPL    $54CB
54D3-   C6 3D         DEC    $3D
54D5-   F0 F4         BEQ    $54CB
54D7-   10 E4         BPL    $54BD
54D9-   A2 05         LDX    #$05
54DB-   20 34 55      JSR    $5534
54DE-   84 34         STY    $34
54E0-   DD B4 F9      CMP    $F9B4,X
54E3-   D0 13         BNE    $54F8
54E5-   20 34 55      JSR    $5534
54E8-   DD BA F9      CMP    $F9BA,X
54EB-   F0 0D         BEQ    $54FA
54ED-   BD BA F9      LDA    $F9BA,X
54F0-   F0 07         BEQ    $54F9
54F2-   C9 A4         CMP    #$A4
54F4-   F0 03         BEQ    $54F9
54F6-   A4 34         LDY    $34
54F8-   18            CLC
54F9-   88            DEY
54FA-   26 44         ROL    $44
54FC-   E0 03         CPX    #$03
54FE-   D0 0D         BNE    $550D
5500-   20 A7 FF      JSR    $FFA7
5503-   A5 3F         LDA    $3F
5505-   F0 01         BEQ    $5508
5507-   E8            INX
5508-   86 35         STX    $35
550A-   A2 03         LDX    #$03
550C-   88            DEY
550D-   86 3D         STX    $3D
550F-   CA            DEX
5510-   10 C9         BPL    $54DB
5512-   A5 44         LDA    $44
5514-   0A            ASL
5515-   0A            ASL
5516-   05 35         ORA    $35
5518-   C9 20         CMP    #$20
551A-   B0 06         BCS    $5522
551C-   A6 35         LDX    $35
551E-   F0 02         BEQ    $5522
5520-   09 80         ORA    #$80
5522-   85 44         STA    $44
5524-   84 34         STY    $34
5526-   B9 00 02      LDA    $0200,Y
5529-   C9 BB         CMP    #$BB
552B-   F0 04         BEQ    $5531
552D-   C9 8D         CMP    #$8D
552F-   D0 80         BNE    $54B1
5531-   4C 5C 54      JMP    $545C
5534-   B9 00 02      LDA    $0200,Y
5537-   C8            INY
5538-   C9 A0         CMP    #$A0
553A-   F0 F8         BEQ    $5534
553C-   60            RTS
553D-   20 7D F4      JSR    $F47D
5540-   A5 F8         LDA    $F8
5542-   10 13         BPL    $5557
5544-   C9 8E         CMP    #$8E
5546-   D0 F5         BNE    $553D
5548-   24 F9         BIT    $F9
554A-   10 0A         BPL    $5556
554C-   A5 FB         LDA    $FB
554E-   F0 06         BEQ    $5556
5550-   E6 FA         INC    $FA
5552-   D0 02         BNE    $5556
5554-   E6 F9         INC    $F9
5556-   60            RTS
5557-   A9 00         LDA    #$00
5559-   85 F9         STA    $F9
555B-   85 FA         STA    $FA
555D-   60            RTS
555E-   4C 92 54      JMP    $5492
5561-   FF            ???
5562-   FF            ???
5563-   FF            ???
5564-   FF            ???
5565-   FF            ???
*
```

ENTRY ADDRESS

Apple II — A Review

Chuck Carpenter

November, 1981

Since there are many newcomers to the world of Apple II, in this month's column I will share some thoughts about getting started with an Apple. Also, as I mentioned in the July '81 column, the mini-assembler will be discussed.

Getting Started

The Apple II is one of the most versatile of all personal computers. The reasons for this versatility are many:

• Ease of expansion. Sockets for RAM (Random Access-Read/Write Memory) are built-in—so are the sockets for up to seven peripherals. There is a socket for language expansion too.

• Capacity for up to 14 disk drives. If you only want to store data you can use all seven peripheral slots for disk drives.

• Color graphics. You can choose lo-res in 16 colors or hi-res in seven colors. The commands to manipulate graphics are built into the programming languages.

• Programmable sound. Music synthesis and special effects are possible. Out of one little speaker you can produce the sounds of space war or symphonies (with a little imagination).

• Game paddle I/O. This is more than just a game paddle connector. You can program three inputs for such things as sensing switches. There are four output bits that can be turned on and off under program control. A program is included in Listing 1 to let you drive a printer from one of these bits. Four analog inputs are available for game paddle controls. These inputs can be used for measuring any low speed device. Or, you can use them to make temperature measurement.

• Power supply. To power all of these things there is a high-quality switching power supply. This supply, of modern design technology, will provide all the power needed to run a fully loaded Apple II. There is no need to buy another supply for most of the available add-ons.

• Languages. The standard machine (Apple II Plus) comes with Applesoft Basic in ROM (Random Access—Read Only Memory). The language is always there when you turn the machine on. You can get the very fast Apple Integer Basic too. If you want UCSD Pascal or a version of Fortran 77, these are also available. The Apple Language System supports both of these languages.

With all this flexibility, it is no wonder that so many software packages and peripherals are available for the Apple II.

Software

Software packages are available to cover most any requirement. Apple supplies several, but many, many more are available from independent sources. There is so much software, in fact, that space is not available here to list it.

One way to see some of the software packages is to visit several computer stores. Visit as many as possible because none of them carry exactly the same ones. For those of you that have to shop by mail, the ads in magazines will be helpful. Another source of software information is catalogs. One such catalog is *The Apple Software Directory* from WIDL Video, 5245 West Diversity, Chicago, IL 60639, (312) 622-9606.

Once you find some interesting software, how do you know it's any good? If you buy at a store, ask to try it. If you buy by mail, you can't do that, but most reputable companies exchange defective software.

Reviews are a good source of information. Many magazines, such as *Creative Computing*, have regular reviews of Apple software. One magazine is devoted to Apple software reviews; it is called *Peelings II*, and you can get a subscription for $15 per year by writing to POB 188, Las Cruces, NM 88004. Or, you can phone (505) 526-8364. Some back issues are available.

Hardware

Hardware accessories range from disk drives to modems for communications to printers that permanently capture the electronic word. Each requires some type of interface between the computer and the peripheral device. Again, a search through the magazines will turn-up most of the possibilities.

Disk drive controllers are the usual first hardware option. The Apple II uses its own special controller. By doing this, Apple was able to use their own format and get more data on a diskette than most other systems. The disk drives are modified Shugart SA400s. I believe they are called an SA385 since they are stripped-down somewhat. You can't use the SA400, in any event. The Apple disk system puts 143K bytes on a single sided diskette. Most other systems only allow about 80 to 90K bytes. Several companies are now making more storage capacity available.

One company, Sorento Valley Associates (SVA), makes an Apple compatible controller that lets you use 8" drives. The capacity of a standard 8" disk is 250K bytes per side. There are other companies now offering more capacity in 5 1/4" drives too—these are the newer drives that use more than 35 tracks for storage. Some drives use 40 tracks, some use 70 tracks, and some now use 80 tracks. The 40-track drives from Shugart are modified SA400s. The track-per-inch density is still the same. The 80-track drives use higher track density and require special head positioning mechanisms. Consequently, the cost of these drives is much higher. You will be seeing many new controllers and drives with much higher capacity over the next year or so, and it won't be long before some company will offer a 5 1/4" rigid that will store 6 to 10 Megabytes. It might even be Apple.

Compatibility with the Apple Disk Operating System (DOS) is always a question. The only way to know for sure is to try your software on one of these systems. Most of the people that I know who have the SVA system, for instance, have had good luck with it. It's been around the longest. Check out the system of interest first. If the company has been in business for a couple of years they are probably doing a good job.

Printers

One peripheral that always causes confusion is the printer. There are so many types and sizes now that it is difficult to know where to start. Some of the options are: parallel or serial interface, dot matrix print font or formed character font, friction feed or tractor feed, upper case characters only or lower case with descenders. And, the list goes on and on.

Parallel interface printers send the character from the computer to the printer as a complete character. Serial printers send the character as a stream of data one element of the character at a time. Parallel printers require interface control called handshaking. Handshaking signals are used to tell the computer that the printer can accept characters into its input buffer. When the buffer is full, the computer is signaled to stop sending. The printer then prints out the characters and signals the computer that it is ready for more characters. The data can be transmitted to the printer as fast as the computer can send it.

Note that it is of no use to send the data faster than the printer can print it. An operating system that allows "spooling" or the equivalent is needed. Spooling is a technique for dumping the output to be printed into a special buffer storage area. The printing is done from the buffer while the computer goes off and does other things for the operator. The Apple operating system is not that sophisticated. You must wait for printing to be completed before you can do another task.

Serial printers are usually described as having an RS-232 interface. This interface defines the characteristics of the signals and the pins used for the signal and handshaking lines. Connectors for RS-232 compatible signals and handshaking are usually the 25-pin D type. Most printers use this configuration but not all. Serial printers often do not require handshaking to print. The electronics and printing mechanisms are designed to allow printing at some maximum speed. The head will actually move faster but the speed is controlled to allow for carriage returns without buffer overflow. If this were not done, some characters would be lost during the carriage return time. If you want to run the serial printer at maximum speed, handshaking is required. Typical speed of current printers is 30 to 45 characters per second. This is often translated as 300 to 450 baud. A baud is a transmission rate of so many bits of serial data in a given time period. Current use of the more or less outdated term is 10 bits per character.

Often too, the serial printer will allow simple interfacing to the computer. Many times, I have used a simple driver program to drive my DEC LA-34 from the game paddle connector. If the printer input uses modern electronics, it is often what is called TTL (Transistor Transistor Logic) compatible. These are the output voltages available from the game paddle I/O (input-output) pins. Figure 1 shows how to make the connections. A program to drive a serial TTL-compatible printer is shown in Listing 1. With this program, you never have to be concerned with the effect of tabs. Many of the interface boards, including Apple's, have problems with tabs that have to be handled with a special code. This program prints just what is in the code. It can also be used as a slow-list program.

Enter the hex code using the Apple monitor commands. These can be found on pages 40 to 66 of the Apple II Reference Manual. Specifically, use the instructions on pages 43 and 44. The program will run from the monitor using the instruction 39DG (RETURN). From a Basic program use CALL 925. To change the speed of the program, change the byte of data at location $038B. Notice that the value in the program is $D3. (The $ symbol is used to mean a hexadecimal number in 6502 microprocessor notation.) Change this value to $4D if your printer runs at 30 characters per second—or 300 baud. For higher speeds use smaller numbers. (This is the timing loop value for the delay between character elements.)

Other Features

Most of the less expensive printers use what is called a dot matrix. Each character is formed by an arrangement of dots. These dots are in a fixed pattern and are made by individual wires striking the paper through an inked ribbon. The dot matrix is often in a 5 x 7 or 7 x 9 arrangement. There are also special arrangements such as the N x 9 pattern used by my Centronics 737 printer. This arrangement is used for the proportional spacing feature.

Formed characters are found on the more expensive printers. The Xerox, NEC and similar printers are examples. A formed character is like that found on a typewriter. When the hammer strikes the paper a complete character is printed. With the printers mentioned, the characters are on the spokes of a printwheel. These spoked wheels are often called daisy wheels. Hence the term "Daisy Wheel Printers." Printers of the formed character type give much better quality print and are much more expensive. Note that some matrix printers do not have descenders. That is, certain characters do not go below the line. This is done to save the cost of more wires in the print-head. Most of the newer printers now have descenders of sorts. This helps to make the print more readable. Also watch to see if the lower case letters are raised. Some printers do this to give the appearance of descenders. But the character is actually raised above the line to keep it within a smaller matrix.

Printers to be used for graphics almost always have to have tractor feed. Tractor feed is used to maintain the position of the paper in relation to the print head. If you try to do graphics without being able to control the position of the paper, you may get gaps in the graphics being printed. Also, be sure there is software available to drive the printer you chose for graphics. It is not a simple matter of just having a printer with individual dot control. My 737 has that capability. But, as far as I know, there is no software available to let me use it for graphics.

Other considerations to be made include the choice of thermal or regular paper. Thermal paper is used with the Apple Silentype printer, which allows you to use the various plotting programs available. But, you have to use special coated paper. It is expensive and has a finite life. If it is not handled with care, your printed listings may discolor. Any heat will break it down. Plain paper printers, on the other hand, require frequent replacement of the ribbon. If you write for publication, the editors will insist on new ribbons—frequently. If you write only casually, you can get away with a lot of things. If you insist on using the blue thermal paper remember: it is very difficult to read the stuff and it is practically impossible to reproduce it with any optical system such as photography.

```
:ASM
              1000 ********************
              1010 * PRINTER DRIVER ROUTINE *
              1020 * BY: CHUCK CARPENTER   *
              1030 ********************
              1040
              1050 * TOGGLES TTL AN0-PIN 15
              1060
              1070        .OR $0360
              1080
0035-         1090 YSAV1  .EQ $35      SAVE Y
0036-         1100 PRINTL .EQ $36      USER PORT L
0037-         1110 PRINTH .EQ $37      USER PORT H
C058-         1120 MARK   .EQ $C058    AN0 SET HIGH
C059-         1130 SPACE  .EQ $C059    AN0 SET LOW
FDF0-         1140 CHROUT .EQ $FDF0    PRINT A CHAR.
FCA8-         1150 DELAY  .EQ $FCA8    DELAY ROUTINE
03EA-         1160 PRTDOS .EQ $03EA    DOS DRIVER HK
              1170
              1180 *   MAIN PROGRAM
              1190
0360- 84 35   1200 PRINTR STY YSAV1    CONTENTS OF Y
0362- 48      1210        PHA
0363- 20 7C 03 1220       JSR TOGGLE
0366- 68      1230        PLA
0367- C9 8D   1240        CMP #$8D     CARRIAGE RET.
0369- D0 0C   1250        BNE COUT
036B- A9 8A   1260        LDA #$8A     LINE FEED
036D- 20 7C 03 1270       JSR TOGGLE
0370- A9 58   1280        LDA #$58
0372- 20 A8 FC 1290       JSR DELAY    DELAY SOME
0375- A9 8D   1300        LDA #$8D     CARRIAGE RET.
0377- A4 35   1310 COUT   LDY YSAV1    GET Y VALUE
0379- 4C F0 FD 1320       JMP CHROUT   PRINT CHAR.
037C- A0 0B   1330 TOGGLE LDY #$0B
037E- 18      1340        CLC
037F- 48      1350 PUSH   PHA
0380- B0 05   1360        BCS TOGGL1
0382- AD 58 C0 1370       LDA MARK     MARK OUT
0385- 90 03   1380        BCC RATE
0387- AD 59 C0 1390 TOGGL1 LDA SPACE   SPACE OUT
038A- A9 D3   1400 RATE   LDA #$D3     BAUD RATE
              1410
              1420 * $D3=110   $4D=300
              1430
038C- 48      1440 PUSH1  PHA
038D- A9 20   1450        LDA #$20
038F- 4A      1460 SHIFT  LSR
0390- 90 FD   1470        BCC SHIFT
0392- 68      1480        PLA
0393- E9 01   1490        SBC #$01
0395- D0 F5   1500        BNE PUSH1
0397- 68      1510        PLA
0398- 6A      1520        ROR
0399- 88      1530        DEY
039A- D0 E3   1540        BNE PUSH
039C- 60      1550        RTS
              1560
              1570 * START PRINTER
              1580
039D- A9 60   1590 PRTON  LDA #PRINTR
039F- 85 36   1600        STA PRINTL
03A1- A9 03   1610        LDA /PRINTR
03A3- 85 37   1620        STA PRINTH
03A5- 4C EA 03 1630       JMP PRTDOS
              1640
              1650        .EN

SYMBOL TABLE
FDF0- CHROUT
0377- COUT
FCA8- DELAY
C058- MARK
0037- PRINTH
0036- PRINTL
0360- PRINTR
03EA- PRTDOS
039D- PRTON
037F- PUSH
038C- PUSH1
038A- RATE
038F- SHIFT
C059- SPACE
0387- TOGGL1
037C- TOGGLE
0035- YSAV1
:
```

Hex Code

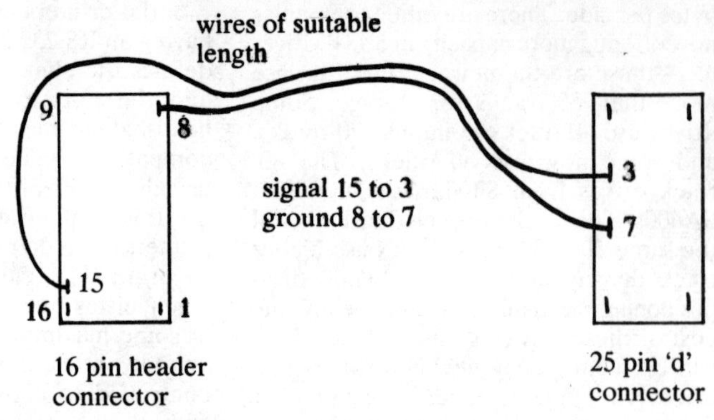

Figure 1. Connections from the 16 pin Apple game I/O connector to a TTL compatible serial printer. Use the program in Listing 1 to drive a printer connected as shown.

Lots More

Whole columns could be devoted to each of the peripheral options available for the Apple. One significant choice would be communications. You have several choices there. One is with the Apple communications card and an acoustic modem. Another is with the Hayes direct coupled modem. Each has its own special features and characteristics. My system uses the Hayes modem. You can do many things, such as dial from the keyboard and have unattended answering. Electronic mail and other technologies are also within the communications realm.

Amateur radio is possible with some of the equipment available. One company offers a card to let you send and receive morse code and teletype. And, how about video monitoring and control. There are peripheral cards to let you control a 3/4" video recorder. The list goes on and on. No brief treatment such as this could cover all the possibilities. Recent issues of some Apple magazines have talked about the use of the Apple computer in the making of major science fiction films, and, the Apple has been used in space exploration applications too.

Listing 1. Assembly of printer drive program in the format of the S-C ASSEMBLER II. Enter the hex code starting at address $0360 and ending at address $03A7. For some printers the mark and space addresses at $C058 and $C059 may need to be reversed. Load the program using APPLE Monitor commands. Run it with a 39DG from the monitor or a CALL 925 from a Basic program. Change the baud rate as shown in Line 1400 for 110 or 300 baud.

Information Sources

Softalk magazine is available to all Apple owners in the USA. If you are not getting your complimentary subscription, contact Softalk Publishing Inc., 11021 Magnolia Blvd., North Hollywood, CA 91601. (213) 980-5074.

Other magazines for Apple owners include:

• *Nibble*, Box 325, Lincoln, MA 01773. $17.50 for 8 issues.
• *Call-APPLE*, 304 Main Ave. S., Suite 300, Renton, WA 98055. Membership required. $25 one-time application fee; $15 yearly dues.

Other useful publications about the Apple include:
• *Beneath Apple DOS* by Don Worth and Peter Lechner, Quality Software, 6660 Reseda Blvd., Suite 105, Reseda, CA 91335. (213) 344-6599. An in-depth analysis of Apple DOS. Covers all versions of DOS concentrating on DOS 3.3. Sells for about $22 and is well worth the price.

• *Computer Station's Programmers Handbook to the Apple II*. Complete summary of all Apple commands. Includes DOS, Assembler/Editor, Basics, Pascal, Visicalc, CP/M, Basic-80, and much more. A useful reference for the serious Apple II programmer. About $20.
• *The Apple Monitor Peeled* by William E. Dougherty, 14349 San Jose St., Mission Hills, CA 91345. (213) 896-6553. Covers all the calls and subroutines in the Apple Monitor. Also useful for the serious Apple programmer. Especially if you're interested in assembly/machine language programming. About $10.
• *Apple Machine Language* by Don Inman and Kurt Inman, Reston Publishing Co. Inc., Reston, VA. This book covers the fundamentals of assembly language programming from an Apple point of view. Basic programs are used to explain machine language. The content is specifically Apple and covers the mini-assembler. I got my copy from a local computer store for about $20.

And Lots More

My intent here was to give the newcomer and potential owner some help with sources of Apple information. There was also an attempt to explain some of the more confusing aspects of peripherals. Please write to me if you have any questions. There is so much to be covered that I could not possibly do it here. Perhaps your imagaination has been stimulated though and that's good.

NEXT TIME

Lots of you wrote to me about the space problem with hi-res graphics also mentioned in the May '81 column. There were too many to mention each one. I'll summarize them and give credit to all. A couple responses included elaborate programs for helping to get more space for hi-res programs. But that's enough until next time. □

"... That's a great idea Starnes but in 10 seconds it's going to be obsolete ..."

Apple Hi-Res Books of Interest

Chuck Carpenter

Back in the May '81 issue, there was some discussion of limited memory space with hi-res graphics. Several readers sent me their techniques for handling the problem. Some of the techniques will be included in this column. And, we'll get into the specifics of the whats and whys for doing it. Also, several readers sent in some one-liner programs. Those will be included in this column, too. Since it's Christmas time again you may be looking for things to use with your Apple II. Several Apple-only books are included here with a brief discussion of the contents.

MISSING INFO

CP/M for the Apple was reviewed here in the Sept '81 issue. On page 146, in the paragraph titled *Documentation* I mentioned several sources of information. I said I would cover them later. Well, this is later! Actually, the intention was to include the info with the review. But...Anyway, here it is now.

Probably the most useful book you can get is the *CP/M Primer* by Mitchell Waite and Stephen Murtha (see photo). Most of the functions of the CP/M operating system are simply and effectively described. The Primer is a must for CP/M beginners. Then there's *The CP/M Handbook* by Rodnay Zaks and *CP/M Users Guide* by Thom Hogan. These are two very thorough books for the more advanced CP/M user. You can find these books at many computer stores or look for them in the magazine ads. Here's a list of the books and their publishers.

CP/M Primer
Howard W. Sam & Co., Inc.
4300 West 62nd St.
Indianapolis, IN 46268

CP/M Handbook
Sybex
2344 Sixth St.
Berkeley, CA 94710

CP/M Users Guide
Osborne/McGraw-Hill
630 Bancroft Way, Dept. L-13
Berkeley, CA 94710

Chuck Carpenter, 2228 Montclair Pl., Carrollton, TX 75007.

The 8 1/2 x 11 size CP/M Primer and the half-page size Volume 1 of the Microsoft documentation.

HI-RES MEMORY

In the April '81 column, was included a brief discussion of hi-res memory usage. The intent of that article was to illustrate why less memory is available to Applesoft programmers than to Apple Integer programmers. Since no attempt was made to show how to work around limited memory, several readers sent in a variety of solutions. We'll get to them but first some background.

Pointers and Things

In order for the Basic interpreter to know the size of a program, memory locations are used to contain various program addresses. These are called pointers (also pointer registers). Pointers contain the addresses for the beginning of the program, the end of the program, the end of variable tables and more. You can find the pointer data listed on pages 140 and 141 of your *Apple II Reference Manual*. These pages refer to zero page usage. It is conventional with 6502 programs to put often-used data in page 0. When this is done, machine language programs run faster. On page 140 you will find that the beginning of a program is stored at hex addresses $67 and $68 (decimal 103 and 104). Note that the $ symbol is used to show hexadecimal numbers in the 6502 microprocessor system.

Normally the values stored at these addresses are 01 and 08. They represent the hex address $0801. If you want to move the beginning of a Basic program, just change the programs to make more room. As I mentioned earlier, several readers contributed their techniques. They range from the uncomplicated to the sophisticated. Let's look at some examples.

The Uncomplicated

First, determine if you are going to use one or two hi-res pages. Next, POKE the new beginning-of-program pointers into memory locations 103 and 104. Now, to finish, POKE a zero into the memory location preceding the address used above. It will look something like this:

```
POKE 103,LOMEM LOBYTE+1
POKE 104,LOMEM HIBYTE
POKE LOMEM,0
```

If you wanted to set LOMEM and the program pointers to the top of hi-res page 2, do this:

```
POKE 103,1
POKE 104,96
POKE 24576,0
```

To set LOMEM to the top of hi-res page 1, use these POKEs:

```
POKE 103,1
POKE 104,64
POKE 16384,0
```

Going back to the start can be accomplished by typing TEXT then INT or FP. Use the one corresponding to the version of Basic you're using. Pressing RESET will work too. Be careful you don't lose your program.

Note the third POKE in the examples. This is done to tell Applesoft where the beginning of program space is. This version

```
10    TEXT : HOME
15    VTAB 3: HTAB 13
20    PRINT "LOMEM MODIFIER"
21    PRINT : PRINT "1. 16,384 OR $4000": PRINT "2. 24,576 OR $6000"
22    PRINT "3. 28,672 OR $7000": PRINT "4. ANOTHER LOCATION"
24    VTAB 10: PRINT "  WHERE DO YOU WANT LOMEM SET ";: GET A$
25    IF A$ = "1" THEN LO = 16384: GOTO 50
26    IF A$ = "2" THEN LO = 24576: GOTO 50
27    IF A$ = "3" THEN LO = 28672: GOTO 50
30    VTAB 10: PRINT "  WHERE DO YOU WANT LOMEM SET ";: INPUT A$
40    LET LO =  VAL (A$): IF LO < 2048 OR LO > 4900 THEN  HOME : GOTO 30
50    LET LO = LO + 1
100   LET I =  INT (LO / 256)
110   LET R = LO - I * 256
120   POKE 103,R
130   POKE 104,I
140   POKE LO - 1,0
200   HOME : VTAB 10
210   PRINT "LOMEM IS SET TO ";LO - 1
220   PRINT : PRINT "LOAD YOUR PROGRAM"
300   NEW
```

Listing 1. Program to POKE LOMEM for use with graphics programs.

```
10    REM  - BY: SHAUN HOPE,
             NORTHANTS, ENGLAND

20    GR : HOME :U = 1:S = 16:T = 2
      :E = 39:F = 40:Z = 0:C =  RND
      (1) * 15 + 1: FOR N = 0 TO 1
      00 STEP .015: COLOR= C:M =  ABS
      ( INT ( SIN (N) ^ T * F)):Q =
      Q + U - F * (Q = E):C = C *
      (Q > Z) + (Q = Z) *  RND (U)
      * S:X = E - Q:Y = E - M: PLOT
      M,Q: PLOT Q,M: PLOT X,Y: PLOT
      Y,X: PLOT M,X: PLOT X,M: PLOT
      Y,Q: PLOT Q,Y: NEXT : RUN
```

Listing 2. Lo-res routine to draw a pattern on the screen. Unique use of logic avoids use of IF-THEN statements.

```
10    REM  - BY: BOB WONG
             BROOKLYN, NY
20 C = 139:D = 95: HGR : POKE -
   16302,0: FOR Z = 1 TO 5000: FOR
   Y = 1 TO 50:E =  RND (1) * 7
   :A =  RND (1) * 269 + 10:B =
   RND (1) * 181 + 10: HCOLOR=
   E: HPLOT C,D TO A,B:S =  PEEK
   ( - 16336): NEXT :D = B:C =
   A: CALL  - 3082: NEXT : TEXT
   : END
```

Listing 3. Hi-res routine draws a pattern of lines in a variety of colors.

```
10    REM  - BY: SKENE MOODY
             SAN MARINO, CA
20    FOR N = 0 TO 49: HOME : VTAB
      24: HTAB 20: PRINT "N= ";N: HGR
      : HCOLOR= 3: HPLOT 279,79: FOR
      I = 0 TO 6.28318531 STEP .06
      28318531: HPLOT  TO COS (I)
      * 139 + 140, SIN (N * I) *
      79 + 79: NEXT : NEXT : TEXT
      : HOME : LIST
```

Listing 4. Hi-res routine produces lissajous figures. These figures will be familiar to long-time oscilloscope users.

of Basic, a dialect of Microsoft Basic, puts a zero at the beginning of program space. The next byte is the first byte of the program. It is also the first byte of the address of the next line in the program.

Several readers contributed similar info on this technique. They are: William J. Edmunds, Herbert McKinstry, Charles Kluepfel, Steven Kahn, John Bury, James F. Johnson, and Henry Hwong. (In no particular order.)

The Sophisticated

Using the POKE method is effective. But, the power of your computer is not being used to advantage. A more automated way was also contributed by William J. Edmunds. Listing 1 is his program to set the memory locations as required. William sez, "I've included a listing of a short program I am working on. With some modification, I can use it as a loader for completed programs that won't fit below the hi-res page.

"Option (1) will set lo-mem above hi-res page 1, option (2) above hi-res page 2, and option (3) above $7000. I use (3) for disk based Applesoft and the hi-res character generator available from Apple's contributed software bank. Option (4) lets you set lo-mem wherever you like, within reason.

"Back before I learned to do this, I struggled with disk-based Applesoft and hi-res page 2 (trying to keep my programs under 4K). This program really opened things up for me and is just as useful now that I have a RAM card."

William's program will be a help to those of you just starting with hi-res graphics and Applesoft. You can run this program as a boot program. Or, use it as-is each time your want to use hi-res graphics. A similar suggestion was made to do the task with an EXEC file. In *Call Apple* and *Nibble* magazines there have

been ways shown to link the low side of the graphics pages to the high side. There are lots of ideas and ways to solve hi-res problems. Experiment and find as many as you can.

ONE-LINERS

In the June '81 column I used a couple of one-liner programs. In response to a request for more, three readers replied. Listings 2, 3 and 4 are the resulting programs.

Listing 2 includes a lo-res program from Shaun Hope. This program uses logic in place of IF...THEN statements. As Shaun points out, "IF...THEN statements cannot be used in a one-liner. This makes a useful exercise in the use of logical statements. For instance:

$Q = Q + 1 : IF Q = 40 THEN Q = 0 : COLOR = RND(1) * 16 :$

Applesoft would skip to the next line (which we don't have in a one-liner) if the IF condition were false. Integer Basic would go on to the COLOR statement regardless.

The only way to get around this in a one-liner is to use two logical statements:

$Q = Q + 1 - 40 * (Q = 39) : C = C * (Q 0) + (Q = 0) * RND(1) * 16 :$

Notice the INT function is not necesssary on COLOR statements, and that variables are used (in the program) in an attempt to make the program a little faster."

Try Shaun's program with your color TV. You will see some interesting patterns.

Another program comes from Bob Wong. The program in Listing 3 is a hi-res graphics program. The program draws a pattern of lines in several colors.

Listing 4, a hi-res program from Skene Moody, produces some interesting patterns. Those of you who have worked with oscilloscopes will recognize the familiar lissajous figures. The vertical frequency is always 1 and the horizontal frequency changes from 1 to 49. Near the end of the range the figures look like amplitude modulated frequencies. (Or, something like a two-tone modulated transmitter output.)

Type these one-line programs carefully. I have to do some of them over several times. It's easy to leave out part of one line. What interesting variations can you think of? Send your ideas and programs and they will be included in a future column.

BOOKS TO BUY

Books written especially for use with the Apple became more available this past year. Here's a list of some of the ones I have.

About Machine Language

Apple Machine Language, by Don and Kurt Inman, Reston Publishing Co., Inc., Reston, VA 22090.

Twelve chapters integrate machine language with Basic and the Apple Mini-assembler. Chapters 1 to 7 review Basic and develop a Basic Operating System (BOS). The BOS is used to develop machine language programs. These programs do simple graphics, display text, and generate sounds. Chapter 7 combines sound with graphics.

Chapters 8, 9 and 10 explain some of the Apple System Monitor (SM). Most of these chapters deal with arithmetic processing. That's a shame because there are lots of things happening in the monitor besides mathematics. However, it is true that all the monitor functions are mathematical in nature. Some discussion of these functions in non-mathematical terms would have made learning about the monitor more friendly.

Apple's Mini-assembler is discussed in chapter 11. The mini-asembler is used to describe several of the 6502 indexing modes. One problem I see here is that the Apple II Plus machines don't have a mini-assembler. My Oct. '81 column described how to have the mini-assembler on any machine. So, if you want to do things described in the book, you can.

Chapter 12 is called "Putting It all Together." This chapter combines Basic, BOS, SM, and the mini-assembler.

Each chapter includes a summary, exercises, and answers to the exercises. The Appendix includes a section on Basic statements, Machine language instructions, built-in subroutines, and display symbols (prompts). Also included in the appendix are hex equivalents, video memory data, and the 6502 instruction codes. This is a good book for anyone interested in Apple machine language. There are some shortcomings. But, once this book is learned, it's easy to continue on with machine language.

About DOS

Looking for a book that will completely describe the Apple Disk Operating System? Here's one that will.

Beneath Apple DOS, by Don Worth and Pieter Lechner, Quality Software, 6660 Reseda Blvd., Suite 105, Reseda, CA 91335 (213) 244-6599.

This book is more for those in the advanced programming category. Don't overlook it as a source of information while you're learning though. It's a lot like learning algebra. You don't know why you're doing it until you take calculus.

Beneath Apple DOS is divided into 8 chapters and 3 appendices. The first two chapters are introductory; no real meat here. Chapter 3 discusses diskette formatting. Chapter 4 begins to tell you about the DOS details. In chapter 5, the structure of DOS is discussed. Using DOS from assembly language is included in chapter 6 and chapter 7 tells you how to customize DOS. DOS program logic is included in chapter 8. The appendices include example programs in appendix A, disk protection schemes in B and a Glossary in appendix B.

About Everything

There are a couple of books available that do just about that: tell you most everything. One of them is called the *Apple II User's Guide*. The other is called *Programmers Handbook to the Apple II*.

Apple II User's Guide, by Lon Poole with Martin McNiff and Steven Cook, 630 Bancroft Way, Berkeley, CA 94701.

Eight chapters and 12 sections to the Appendix make this a useful beginner's book. From introductory chapter 1 to the compendium of statements in chapter 8, this book covers the fundamentals of operating your Apple II. In chapter 2 you learn how to operate the Apple II. Chapter 3 begins the fundamentals of programming in Basic, with advanced Basic in chapter 4. Information about the disk is covered in chapter 5 and Graphics and Sound are included in chapter 6. Chapter 7 provides the beginner with some exposure to the Machine Language Monitor. The appendices include such extras as Useful PEEKS and POKES, Memory Usage, and ASCII Character Codes and Applesoft Reserved Word Tokens.

Generally, the book provides useful information to the newcomer. There are some problems though. For instance, on page 156 there is a table of Applesoft Basic Immediate Mode commands. These are actually deferred (or programmed) mode commands. As with anything you read use the contents as information-only until you can verify the accuracy. The book is well done otherwise and will be an asset to the beginners library.

Programmer's Handbook to the Apple II, Computer Station, Inc., 11610 Page Service Dr., St. Louis, MO 63141. (314) 432-7019.

This *Handbook* is a huge extension to Computer Station's Programmers Guide. There are 15 sections covering everything from the Monitor to References. This book is a compendium of the commands for most of the major programs used with the Apple II. Once you have learned the basics of a particular program, you can find the essence of the commands and statements in the *Handbook*. Included are the Basics, Pascal, Visicalc, and CP/M with Basic-80. This book is a useful reference to many of the programs used on the Apple II. □

Pascal Programs

Chuck Carpenter   *March, 1982*

Over the past months, I have received a few Pascal programs and comments. Some of the input was relative to previous items in the column (randomizing strings). One letter asked about how to print from a Pascal program. It seemed like it ought to be easy to do—it wasn't. Along with a variety of other Apple info, this column will include the semi-sometimes offerings from Rosa Pascal.

Rosa Pascal Sez

Printing from a Pascal program. For us mostly Basic programmers, that seems like it should be simple. Just use the equivalent of PR#1 or LPRINT or whatever works in the version of Basic you use. The question was asked by Jim Pittman. And, after much searching in the Apple manuals, no easily recognized way to print was found. By this time, there didn't seem to be an easy way to answer Jim's question. Then I started searching through the other manuals I have on Pascal programming. Nothing there either. The closest was a mention of the use of the write-in command with input/output routines. It was mentioned briefly in the *Pascal Primer* by David Fox and Mitchell Waite.

By this time I was almost desparate enough to call some of the local Pascal programmers. But not quite. Looking through several magazines for Pascal programs produced the answer. The programs found were documented well enough for me to understand how printing in Pascal is accomplished. So the techniques were sent along to Jim in hopes the question was answered. It was, and Jim returned a sample routine shown in Listing 1. Observe the last few lines of the program. These lines include the main program. This is how Pascal calls the various sub programs.

Listing 1.

```
(*                      James C. Pittman Jr.                      *)
(*                                                                *)
(*      Write out a table of ASCII characters to a printer        *)
(*                                                                *)
(*    This is a sample Pascal program to demonstrate printing input and *)
(* output from within a program.   See  article in NIBBLE, Vol 2, Nr 5, *)
(* (1981)  page 119,  and  the  Apple Pascal  Language Reference Manual, *)
(* pages  26-29 on  REWRITE,  RESET, and  CLOSE  procedures.  Thanks to *)
(* Chuck Carpenter for his suggestions.              18 October 1981 *)
(*                                                                *)
program     printest  (input,output);
var         x,y,z : integer;
            output : string[8];
            fid : interactive;

procedure   data;                                (*  Get "line width" input; *)
begin                                            (*   try "15" for example.  *)
  writeln(fid);  (* "fileid" or identifier of a previously declared file *)
  writeln(fid,'Enter an integer between 7 and 26, or 0 to stop. ');
  readln(z); write(fid,'  (',z,')')
end;

procedure   display;                             (*  Write some output  *)
begin
  y := 0;                                        (* Initialize "line width" *)
  writeln(fid);
  for x := 32 to 127 do                (* Print all the ASCII characters *)
  begin
    write(fid,' ',chr(x),' '); y := y + 1;
    if y > z then                                  (* Start new line *)
      begin
        y := 0;
        writeln(fid)
      end;
  end
end;

begin                                            (* Main part of program *)
  z := 1;
  while z <> 0 do                                (* Stop if z = zero *)
  begin
    writeln;
    writeln('Select either <console:> or <printer:> ');
    readln(output);                    (* Don't make a typing mistake here! *)
    reset(fid,output);
    data;                                        (* Do the first "subroutine" *)
    if z <> 0 then
    display;                                      (* Do the second "subroutine" *)
    close(fid);     (* Must close the file so can go back and select again *)
  end                                            (* End, z = zero *)
end.
```

Chuck Carpenter, 2228 Montclair Pl., Carrollton, TX 75007.

In the main program Jim has included a way to select the console: (Apple keyboard and monitor) or the printer. A sample run of the program is included in Figure 1.

In the May '81 column, a short program by Ron DeGroat was included showing a way to randomize a string of characters. Two programs were received showing how to do similar things. Listing 2, submitted by Ronald A. Thisted, included a detailed discussion. (Much too long to include here, however.) The program itself is well annotated and experienced programmers should be able to understand the routine. Another program, shown in Listing 3, was contributed by Fred W. Hansen. Again, the program is well annotated. Since my Pascal skill is limited, the programs are included for your interest without explanation.

Figure 1.

```
Enter an integer between 7 and 26, or 0 to stop.
   (15)
      !  "  #  $  %  &  '  (  )  *  +  ,  -  .  /
   0  1  2  3  4  5  6  7  8  9  :  ;  <  =  >  ?
   @  A  B  C  D  E  F  G  H  I  J  K  L  M  N  O
   P  Q  R  S  T  U  V  W  X  Y  Z  [  \  ]  ^  _
   `  a  b  c  d  e  f  g  h  i  j  k  l  m  n  o
   p  q  r  s  t  u  v  w  x  y  z  {  |  }  ~
Enter an integer between 7 and 26, or 0 to stop.
   (7)
      !  "  #  $  %  &  '
   (  )  *  +  ,  -  .  /
   0  1  2  3  4  5  6  7
   8  9  :  ;  <  =  >  ?
   @  A  B  C  D  E  F  G
   H  I  J  K  L  M  N  O
   P  Q  R  S  T  U  V  W
   X  Y  Z  [  \  ]  ^  _
   `  a  b  c  d  e  f  g
   h  i  j  k  l  m  n  o
   p  q  r  s  t  u  v  w
   x  y  z  {  |  }  ~
Enter an integer between 7 and 26, or 0 to stop.
   (0)
```

Listing 2.

```
PROGRAM JUMBLE (OUTPUT);
(*
                        WRITTEN 30-APRIL-81
                        BY RONALD A. THISTED

     THIS PROGRAM ILLUSTRATES A GENERAL SHUFFLING ALGORITHM THAT CAN BE
USED TO GENERATE RANDOM PERMUTATIONS OF ARBITRARY SETS OF OBJECTS.  IT
IS ILLUSTRATED HERE ON THE CHARACTERS OF THE ROMAN ALPHABET.

     IN GENERAL, THE N OBJECTS TO REARRANGE RESIDE IN AN ARRAY OF LENGTH
N; THE POINT IS TO SHUFFLE THE ITEMS IN THE ARRAY.  AT STEP 1, A RANDOM
ITEM IS SELECTED TO OCCUPY THE LAST POSITION IN THE ARRAY.  THIS
SELECTED ITEM IS THEN EXCHANGED WITH WHATEVER ITEM WAS ALREADY IN THE
LAST POSITION.  AT THIS POINT, ITEM NUMBER N IS IN ITS FINAL RESTING
PLACE, AND ALL OF THE REST OF THE ITEMS OCCUPY THE FIRST N-1 POSITIONS
OF THE ARRAY.  STEP NUMBER 2 SELECTS A RANDOM ITEM FROM THOSE REMAINING
TO OCCUPY THE NEXT TO LAST POSITION, AND THE CHOSEN ITEM IS THEN PLACED
THERE.  AFTER STEP 2, THE LAST TWO ITEMS ARE IN THEIR HOMES, AND THE
FIRST N-2 ITEMS REMAIN TO BE ASSIGNED A PLACE.  THIS CONTINUES UNTIL ALL
ITEMS HAVE BEEN ASSIGNED.

     THE ALGORITHM IS DUE TO MOSES AND OAKFORD (TABLES OF RANDOM
PERMUTATIONS, STANFORD UNIVERSITY PRESS, 1963).  THIS ALGORITHM AND
OTHERS RELATED TO IT ARE DISCUSSED IN KNUTH, THE ART OF COMPUTER
PROGRAMMING: SEMINUMERICAL ALGORITHMS, VOLUME 2, SECOND EDITION (1980),
ADDISON-WESLEY.                        *)

USES APPLESTUFF;
CONST
     SETSIZE = 26;    (* SIZE OF ROMAN ALPHABET *)
VAR
     I       : 1..SETSIZE; (* LOOP COUNTER *)
     POS     : 1..SETSIZE; (* POSITION OF SELECTED ITEM *)
     CH      : CHAR;       (* HOLDS AN ITEM TEMPORARILY *)
     OBJECTS : PACKED ARRAY [1..SETSIZE] OF CHAR;

BEGIN (* MAIN PROGRAM *)
     (* FIRST, INITIALIZE OUR SET OF OBJECTS AND GIVE THE APPLE RANDOM
        NUMBER GENERATOR A RANDOM STARTING POINT. *)

     OBJECTS := 'ABCDEFGHIJKLMNOPQRSTUVWXYZ'; RANDOMIZE;

     (* NEXT, WE SHUFFLE.  ORDINARILY THE INSTRUCTIONS THAT FOLLOW
        WOULD RESIDE IN A PROCEDURE WHICH WE WOULD CALL HERE. *)

     FOR I:= SETSIZE DOWNTO 2 DO
        BEGIN
        POS := 1 + RANDOM MOD SETSIZE; (* SELECT LUCKY ITEM GOING TO BIN I  *)
        CH := OBJECTS[I];              (* SAVE PRESENT OCCUPANT OF BIN I     *)
        OBJECTS[I] := OBJECTS[POS];    (* MOVE LUCKY ITEM TO ITS FINAL HOME  *)
        OBJECTS[POS] := CH             (* THEN RE-USE THE VACATED BIN        *)
        END;
(* FINALLY, PRINT OUT THE SHUFFLED SET TO CONVINCE THE SKEPTICS. *)
     WRITELN(OBJECTS)
     END.
```


More Info

Apple owners can find information about their systems from a new source. A summary of over 100 books and magazines about the Apple and the Apple 6502 microprocessor is included in the *Apple Owners Book List*. If you're looking for information about the Apple, you should be able to find much of it here. The uncopyrighted list is $2.00 per copy and is updated monthly. Use and dissemination of the list is encouraged, according to its editor. Get your copy from Bob Broedel, P.O. Box 20049, Tallahassee, FL 32304.

String Art

For those who are just getting started with graphics, here's a program you will find interesting. The program, called "String Art" was written by Daniel Rice. Listing 4 is the program. According to Daniel, this is how it works: "Here is a small Applesoft program that draws interesting "String Art" patterns. It actually draws consecutive ovals, each differing slightly in angle and location. Thus, with a large scale, interweaving straight-line effects are created. Typing CTRL-C during execution returns the program to line 110. Any other character temporarily stops the program until another key is pressed. A negative response to the question in line 160 ends the program. On an Apple II Plus, or an Apple II with Applesoft card or language system, line 200 may be changed to HGR:HCOLOR=7. Line 270 contains an invisible CTRL-G between the quotes. Occasionally, the program may 'refuse' to draw a certain pattern. The solution is merely to re-run the program, and try again."

There are a couple of interesting features in Daniel's program. In lines 120 and 130 are included a series of POKEs. Line 120 POKES 6 bytes of data into consecutive addresses starting at 768 decimal or $0300 hex. (Remember that the $ symbol means hex in 6502 microprocessor notation.) The two POKES in line 130 are to addresses 232 and 233 decimal or $E8 and $E9. These two addresses are the pointer to the beginning of a shape table for hi-res graphics. The shape table is included in the data starting at address $0300. So, the pointer at address $E8-$E9 will be used by this graphics program to point to the shape table needed to draw the consecutive ovals. You can find out more about creating and using shape tables on pages 92 to 100 in the Applesoft Reference manual.

Daniel's use of the shape table is novel and creative. The use of POKEs to enter the table ensures that it is loaded each time the program runs. It is not described this way in the pages mentioned above. Since page 3 of the Apple memory usually is free, it is ideal for storage of small programs and data. Apple DOS uses memory from $03D0 to $03F0 or so. Anyway, you can use the memory up to $030F for your own purposes such as the shape table in this program. For testing of keyboard input, line 240 looks for the carriage return. Decimal 141 is $8D, the ASCII value of a carriage return. Note that in the Apple II, the high bit is set on all normal video characters. Other video attributes are invoked when this bit is changed. Line 270 then resets the strobe with the POKE and rings the bell. In line 280 the program is halted until any key is pressed. The keyboard strobe is reset again in line 290 and the program continues back at line 250. Typing a CTRL-G invokes an error condition which is trapped by the ONERR command in line 100. As you can see, lots of things happen, even in small programs.

Listing 3.

```
(*   PROCEDURE RANDOMIZES THE CONTENTS OF ANY STRING PASSED TO IT.
**   IT REQUIRES "USES APPLESTUFF" AND "RANDOMIZE" IN THE MAIN PROGRAM
**   BLOCK.
**
**   AUTHOR: FRED W. HANSEN
**   DATE   : 05/27/81
**
**   NOTES:
**
**     1. BYPASS PROCESSING IF THE INPUT SOURCE STRING IS NULL OR ONLY
**        ONE CHARACTER LONG;
**     2. INITIALIZE THE WORK STRING TO NULL.
**     3. RANDOMLY SELECT A CHARACTER (BY POSITION) FROM THE INPUT SOURCE
**        STRING;
**     4. PLACE THE SELECTED CHARACTER ON THE END OF THE DESTINATION
**        STRING;
**     5. REMOVE THE SELECTED CHARACTER FROM THE SOURCE STRING;
**     6. REPEAT THE PROCESS UNTIL THERE ARE NO MORE CHARACTERS LEFT
**        IN THE SOURCE STRING;
**     7. THE SOURCE STRING BECOMES THE NOW-RANDOMIZED DESTINATION
**        STRING.
*)
PROCEDURE SCRAMBLE (VAR SOURCE:STRING);

        VAR
           SELECTEDCHAR  : INTEGER;
           DESTINATION   : STRING;


        BEGIN

(* 1 *)  IF LENGTH (SOURCE) <= 1 THEN
            EXIT (SCRAMBLE);

(* 2 *)  DESTINATION := '';

        REPEAT
(* 3 *)     SELECTEDCHAR := (RANDOM MOD LENGTH (SOURCE)) + 1;
(* 4 *)     DESTINATION  := CONCAT (DESTINATION,
                                    COPY (SOURCE, SELECTEDCHAR, 1));
(* 5 *)     DELETE (SOURCE, SELECTEDCHAR, 1);
(* 6 *)  UNTIL LENGTH (SOURCE) = 0;

(* 7 *)  SOURCE       := DESTINATION;

        END;     (* SCRAMBLE *)
```

Listing 4.

```
100  ONERR  GOTO 110
110  TEXT : HOME
120  POKE 768,1: POKE 769,0: POKE
     770,4: POKE 771,0: POKE 772,
     4: POKE 773,0
130  POKE 232,0: POKE 233,3
140  POKE  - 16368,0
150  ROT= 0
160  INPUT "STRING DESIGN # ?";A
170  POKE  - 16368,0
180  IF A < 0 THEN  END
190  SCALE= A
200  HGR2 : HCOLOR= 7
210  XDRAW 1 AT 140,95
220  FOR A = 1 TO 255
230  ROT= A: DRAW 1
240  IF  PEEK ( - 16384) = 141 THEN
     270
250  NEXT A
260  GOTO 220
270  POKE  - 16368,0: PRINT "";
280  IF  PEEK ( - 16384) < 128 THEN
     280
290  POKE  - 16368,0: GOTO 250
300  REM  BY DANIEL RICE
310  REM  "STRING ART"
]SAVER#0
```

Big Letters—Small Letters

My Apple II now has the Keyboard Enhancer in place of the Paymar Adapter. As an enhancement to the basic Apple II, you still need software to make the lower-case characters appear in your text. With the Videoterm 80-column board, you have instant upper-lower case capability. And it works without special control characters. If you are also using the Z-80 Softcard, you can have the equivalent of two computers in the same case. You can do any of the regular Apple II things, or you can boot-up the CP/M disk and use the 80 column capability with the expanded capability of the Z-80 board. Next time, I'll give a more comprehensive review of the Videx Keyboard Enhancer.   □

Apple — New Developments
Keyboard Enhancer

Chuck Carpenter

April, 1982

Anxiously, I opened the carton to my new Apple II. Quickly, I connected all the cables and leads. Then, with nervous anticipation, I turned on the power switch. I pressed the RESET key, heard the speaker 'beep,' and saw the asterisk prompt appear on the screen of my monitor. Everything seemed to be working. Now back to the Reference Manual. How do I make it do something? Wow! This manual is confusing! How can anyone understand all this information. These 50 pages of reference material are a lot for a beginner to learn.

That's how it all started in September 1977. My Apple II, serial number 333, is still the same. Disk drives and 32K more RAM were added. All the expansion slots are full, and connection to peripherals, like my Centronics 737 printer, is now a simple task. Connecting peripherals wasn't always so easy though. There were no peripheral boards available at first. One of my first computer articles described hooking up a Telpar 40-column thermal printer. I had to tell everyone how to make it work from the game paddle connector.

The program used to drive the printer was similar to the one included in the Dec. '81 column. Except back then, the hook to DOS (disk operating system) at $03EA wasn't needed. The only interface needed was a pair of wires from the game paddle connector. Later on, when the expanded Apple II Reference Manual (the 151-page red book) came along, a more sophisticated program to drive a teletype was included. This program would also drive serial printers (with TTL compatible inputs).

From Out of The Past

Lots of things happened over the following months and years. We learned ways

Chuck Carpenter, 2228 Montclair Pl., Carrollton, TX 75007.

to get programs on and off tape. (Our first exposure to the use of monitor routines.) And things like PR#1 and IN#1 to access an expansion slot were discovered, too. (What a discovery to learn that you didn't need to press RESET to turn a printer routine off; just type PR#0.) Before learning this simple operation, I had changed the printer routine to restore the data in addresses $36 and $37. Using PR#0 does this for you automatically. The ability of a user to hook input/output software through these addresses is one of the features that has made Apple so great. Apple never did try to hide anything from hardware or software developers. The number of peripheral boards and software packages available to the Apple owner is testimony to a great deal of foresight on the part of the Apple II creators.

Better and Better

Integer Basic was available almost immediately when you turned on your Apple, so was machine language. To use Basic, you typed CTRL +B (hard entry) or CTRL+C (soft entry). To return to the monitor for machine language you pressed RESET. The original Apples were designed with a very fast version of Basic included in ROM. Also included in ROM were utilities to work with machine language programs. You could assemble, disassemble, examine and change memory, and move programs around in memory. You could also access the speaker and the game paddle input/output pins directly. No other machine had this capability. If the lack of floating point arithmetic was a problem, there were routines in ROM for this too.

My Apple, a whopping 16K, also included the first version of Applesoft. It was a tape

version offered as an incentive to purchasers of 16K units and it had many bugs. But it included floating point arithmetic and I wanted that. My programming skills were more elementary then and I needed the extra programming power. The string handling capability was better, but it took me a while to find out why that made a difference. Eventually the tape version was improved and many hi-res graphics features were added. Soon after, the Applesoft ROM card became available. With only the "flick" of a switch, you could use all the capabilities of the Apple. Nowadays, all the Apple II Plus machines have the latest version of Applesoft resident in ROM.

And Still More

Following the development of Applesoft came the Programmers Aid ROM and then the Autostart ROM. Useable only with Integer Basic (it's in the $D000 ROM), the Programmers Aid ROM provides several utilities. You can test memory, make music, renumber and append Integer programs, and relocate machine language programs. There were also several routines for making hi-res graphics easier. The source code for all the utilities was also included. At the time, these were some of the more advanced aids available to the Apple II programmer.

You can still have the Aid ROM in your Apple II Plus. The Integer Basic card includes both the Aid ROM and the old monitor ROM. If you choose the Language System, the code in the ROMs is included on the Basic disks.

The Autostart ROM replaced the original monitor ROM. Once you made the replacement, you gained some features and lost some. Features lost included the mini-assembler and other machine language routines. Features gained included the auto boot or load-and-go capability, and some immunity from catastrophic RESET. With the old monitor, you frequently lost your program with an accidental RESET. The code in autostart was designed so you could recover most of the time—much more friendly for the programmer.

Note that with Integer Basic machines, you have both the old and new monitor ROMs in place. The Language system includes the new monitor on the 16K card. I read someplace that you could easily switch from one monitor to the other. I couldn't find the information to include it here, but I'll keep looking and use it in a future column.

And Into the Future

Several changes have been made to the main circuit board. Starting at level 0, the current level is now at 7. Most of these changes are transparent to the user. Some, like color killer, were obvious. Early machines would display text in blues and oranges when a color TV was used as a monitor. Color killer forced the signal to white. Other changes included international features, and removal of the 4K or 16K memory selection options. Since memory has become so inexpensive, you can now buy 32K for less than the cost of 4K in 1977.

Reset problems have been all but eliminated with the new keyboards. Early keyboards were longer than they are now. When you pulled open the top, the edge would push the top of the keyboard. Many keyboards were pried loose from their mountings this way. The first keyboard change was to make it shorter. The most recent keyboards have a piggy back board attached to them. This little board has the RESET saver switch on it. By setting this switch to the proper position, you have to press both the control and reset keys to do a RESET. You can also have the regular reset capability in the other switch position—a much needed improvement considering the precarious position of the reset key on the Apple II keyboard.

And how about all those older machines? How can they be protected from accidental resets? Several methods have been tried. They range from little hardware gadgets that protect the key from being pressed to software changes that direct the program to a safe place if reset is pressed accidentally. One of the best devices that I have tried is the Keyboard Enhancer. You get a combination of a lower-case adapter and reset protector when the Enhancer is installed.

Keyboard Enhancer

When I bought the Keyboard Enhancer, I had an ulterior motive. My 80-column board, also made by Videx, is directly compatible with the Enhancer. With the Enhancer installed, the Apple II keyboard works much like a typewriter. With no additional software, the shift keys shift from lower case to upper. Except for a non-standard keyboard layout, using the Enhancer with the Videoterm 80-column board gives me all the features of an 80-column terminal. By installing a short assembly language program, the same features, in the standard 40 columns, are provided. You also get the CTRL-RESET feature, and a character set with true descenders, but nine special characters are missing from the Apple keyboard.

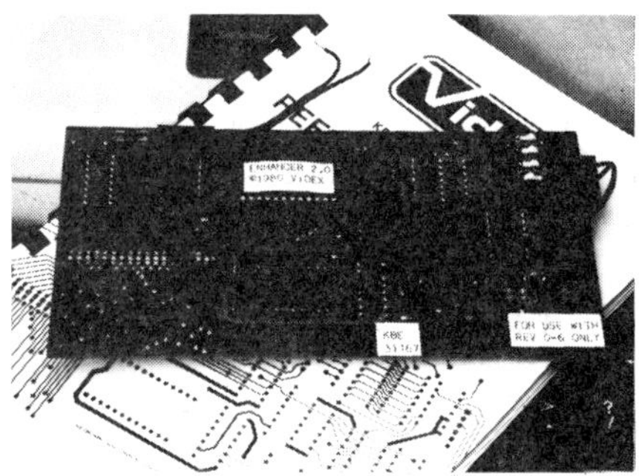

Keyboard Enhancer.

Hardware

Components and circuits are contained on a small board. There are two versions; one for machines made prior to revision 7 and one for revision 7 machines. Recall that revision 7 machines already have the control reset feature. Installing the board is an involved but uncomplicated process. You have to disassemble the Apple II.

To make the necessary corrections, the encoder chip on the keyboard has to be removed. The instructions are clear but if you are not used to doing these things you might get some help. Additionally, the character ROM on the main board is removed along with two control logic chips. The three devices removed are plugged into the Enhancer board and the board is plugged into the sockets vacated by the three devices. Once installed, everything is partially reassembled. A check-out procedure is included to help you find out if it is working. It's easier to do with the 80-column board—you don't need to enter the machine language program.

After check-out is completed the Apple is buttoned-up and you're in business. The circuit board is made with quality components: the material is epoxy fiberglass, the kind known as G10, and all sockets are high quality Augat parts. In the electronics industry, these are considered to be premium components. Assembly and workmanship are high quality too.

Software

About all the software you need is provided in a short machine language program. The program is not needed if you are using it only with the Videoterm 80-column board. To make sure it worked however, I loaded it and it did. Memory in page 3 is used for the program. If you have used this space (and many peripherals do) you will have to find a way of exchanging overlays or relocating the programs elsewhere in memory. There are several patches for the Apple Writer Word Processor. With these patches you can use the Enhancer lower case capability without special codes.

Enhancer is compatible with the Z-80 Softcard, The Hayes Modem, and, if you are using the Videoterm, it is compatible with the Language System. In addition, if you are inclined, you can change the character set to suit your needs. Information is included in the manual to help you develop and program your own character set.

Documentation

All you need to know about installing and using the Enhancer is included in the manual. Written by Curtis White, Paul Davis and Darrell Aldrich, the manual covers installation, check-out, use, and theory of operation. Special capabilities, such as remapping the keyboard, are also included. To help you remap the keyboard, both standard keyboard mapping and alternate mapping data tables are included. Some of you may be familiar with Darrell's work from other sources. He has developed software for many graphics programs currently on the market.

Documentation on other Videex products has not been as well done, and my reviews of these products have been critical in the area of documentation. However, there are no significant problems with this manual. The presentation from installation to use to rolling your own EPROMS is well done. And for those of you who like to tinker with the parts, there is a schematic of the board.

Using It

Once you have it connected and checked out, using it is quite simple. At installation you choose the mode you want it to come up in. One mode is the standard Apple on both sides. The result is similar to the magnetic tape used for audio recordings. Except, the magnetic integrity is more critical. Once the disk is coated and cut to size, it is tested for magnetic integrity. Several things are checked:

• Amplitude of the recorded signal—the output when read back cannot be below a certain level. This ensures that you will be able to read what you recorded on the disk.

• Missing bits—a test to make sure that voids do not occur in the magnetic surface.

- Extra bits—a test to make sure that data is erased. It is possible for a bit to be recorded and not erased. Not too good for your data integrity.

If any of these problems occur during testing, that side of the disk is not certified. As you can see, it is quite possible that one side will fail and the other will be good. These good-on-one-side disks are used for single-sided disks. Of course, with the present state of the art, it is also quite likely that both sides are good. It would seem then that merely checking to see if the other side is good is all that is necessary. Not so!

The Mechanism

Complete disk assemblies include the media inside a plastic jacket. The inside of the jacket is lined with a lint-free cleaning material. The purpose of the cleaning material is to keep dust and lint off the magnetic surface; as the diskette spins, the dirt is collected on one side of the liner.

Look at the photo of the two types of read/write head mechanisms. The one on the right is a single-side head. The other is a dual-side head. Single heads are designed to read only one side of the disk. What happens to the other side is a don't care situation. Dual side heads are different, of course. There are two heads to do the read/write job. As can be seen in the photo, one head is forced against the other with the media in between. Note that the mechanism is designed for the media to always be spinning in the same direction. The single side head is from drives like those used in the Apple II disk drives. The dual head is from a Shugart SA450 40-track drive.

Read/Write Heads.

Data is recorded on and read back from the media by the read/write head. As you can see in the photo, the read/write head is the thin black line across the white circle supporting the head. In the photo, notice the felt pad on the head load arm. This pad—the head load pad—is used to force the media against the head. As you use the disk drives this felt pad collects bits of magnetic material and dirt. In doing the job of forcing the media, the head load pad becomes abrasive.

Now, you can see what I am leading up to. If you use both sides of the diskette, several problems occur:

- Dirt collecting on the liner travels from side to side across the head, and added wear-and-tear on the head and the media results.

- The head load pad abrades both sides of the media increasing the wear there, too.

Because the magnetic coating is very durable, it may take a long time for any damage to show up. Shugart specifies qualified media at three million passes per track. Some time ago, I calculated that it would take eight years to reach this value (at two hours per day of use). But, by increasing the abrasion on the media with the head load pad, who can tell. All of a sudden one day you will have a problem with disks that you can't read. All your valuable data will be gone, and without warning. The Apple system does not have any read after write capability. (Except when you copy a disk, then the system does check what was written.)

Be Safe Not Sorry

If you do your own certification of the second side, you are likely to be safe under some conditions. If you use the disks for back-up there is little risk. And, for disks used only once in a while there is not too much risk. But for those disks you use frequently, use only one side. The risk of data loss is not worth the money saved by using both sides of any disk in a drive designed only for single-side recording. If you have a Language System, the Bad Blocks routine in the Pascal utilities will do a fair job of testing media integrity, and several utility programs are available to do media testing. Get one of them if you can. Or find someone who will help you do the job. For maximum peace of mind with the Apple disk system though, use only one side of your disks.

Next Time

The next column will feature a review of a program called Program Line Editor. Readers have submitted more programs and ideas. Some of them will be included. And, questions sent by readers will be answered. Also, a tutorial on how to convert Hex to decimal and the reverse will be included. □

Notes

Program Line Editor
Hex to Decimal Conversions
One Line Programs

Chuck Carpenter   *May, 1982*

As promised, a review of *Program Line Editor* (PLE) is included this month. A tutorial on converting hex to decimal and back is, too. Other items include one-liners and answers to questions from readers. The review of PLE was written by Barry Bayer. Some of you may recognize his name from articles and columns he has written in this and other magazines.

Barry wrote me a letter some time ago and asked me why I was still telling people to use POKE 33,33 to help with their editing, especially since this great PLE program was available. I have PLE but I have never gotten around to using it. When Barry was asked to help, he graciously consented. Here, only slightly edited, is a review of *Program Line Editor* by Barry Bayer.

Program Line Editor

One of the most irritating features of the Apple II is the clearly inadequate editor used when entering or modifying Integer Basic or Applesoft floating point Basic programs. Try to insert a letter or two into an Applesoft program, particularly with the old, non-autostart monitor ROM, and by the time you're finished with a complicated sequence of CTRL-As, CTRL-Bs, and all sorts of other controls, you can get a little disgusted with the whole thing.

When a line is listed, the editor automatically includes spaces between keywords, and at the end and beginning of each 34 column line, to make the whole thing more readable. Unfortunately, the only way to make a change in a line is to list it, copy it using the Right Arrow key until the point of change, and continue to copy it to the end.

Chuck Carpenter, 2228 Montclair Pl., Carrollton, TX 75007.

Unless one carefully advances the cursor with a CTRL A, (ESC K with the autostart monitor ROM) strings tend to be broken up and look terrible. By the time you get to the end, the editor decides that all of those spaces that it put in (that you didn't want to begin with) make the line too long, and issues a *** SYNTAX ERROR message, and ignores the entire modification.

Some problems (squaring the circle, the Middle-East situation) may never be solved. But there are two generally used methods to solve the Apple II editor problems. The first (as has previously been discussed in this column) is to narrow the text window to 34 characters, which eliminates the "prettyprinting" function of the editor (POKE 33,33 does it); the second is to use Neil Konzen's *Program Line Editor*, or PLE, as it is affectionately known.

PLE is a strange type of program that almost everyone has and uses, but nobody ever talks about. For the benefit of new Apple owners, and for you old timers who may not have heard of it, let me describe a program that is really indispensible.

PLE comes well documented, on a DOS 3.2 disk, and is both copyable and Muffinable (to DOS 3.3). It is available commercially through Synergistic Software, and would be well worth its suggested retail price of $40 if all it did was to solve the "line editing" problems outlined above.

When you run PLE, it lowers HIMEM and the DOS buffers (about 1500 bytes), changes the DOS pointers, and installs itself immediately below DOS and above the DOS buffers and new HIMEM. And there it stays, unaffected by FPs, INTs or even hard RESETs, always ready to do its stuff.

Load a program, in either Integer Basic

or Applesoft. Find a line that you wish to edit, and key in CTRL-E and the line number. Thus far, you have done the equivalent of a LIST line number. But now starts the fun.

The sequence of CTRL-F and any keyboard letter or number key, will find the next occurrence of the character in the line. Press the same key again, and the cursor goes to the next occurrence of that character. Press any other key to get out of the sequence. CTRL-N puts the cursor at the end of the line, and CTRL-B puts it at the beginning. CTRL-Z will ZAP from the current cursor position up to, but not including the character pressed after the CTRL-Z. (A CTRL-Z ":" sequence is an excellent way to eliminate a single statement in a multiple statement line. A second ":" will eliminate a second statement, and so forth.)

A CTRL-P will pack the line and remove all the spaces between tokenized words (just in case the line may be getting too long because of all of those extra spaces inserted by the Basic editor.) But the best thing about all of this is that, once the change is made, a Return is sufficient to enter the new line. *You don't have to recopy the whole thing.* (Note that a tokenized word is a reserved keyword like PRINT. The interpreter assigns a token of only one byte to each reserved word to conserve memory. See page 121 in the Applesoft Reference Manual.—CC).)

But there is more. Move to the place in the line where you wish to insert characters, press CTRL-I, and start typing. PLE moves everything over to the right to make room for your insertion, be it a character, a word, or a full statement or two. And of course, a CTRL-D will delete characters. CTRL-A performs a case change transformation, enabling the programmer to insert lower case within strings. (Lower case could also be placed into a program proper, but such characters will either be changed into upper case, or rejected by the Basic editor.) Of course your monitor screen will not show lower case unless you have modified your Apple by adding a lower case character generator of some sort. But, the feature can be used for text intended to be printed on a printer with lower case.

And that about finishes *Program Line Editor*. Except that Mr. Konzen has given us "overfull" measure for our money. He also added an Escape Create feature that enables each Apple owner to create macros which, in effect, enable special function keys. For example, after I load PLE, (it is part of the HELLO program on the system disk I usually boot with) I can type in the sequence ESC 1 to display a CATALOG of the disk loaded into drive 1.

ESC-T is the equivalent of typing in TEXT and Return, ESC-L does a LIST, and ESC-W does a relatively complicated set of PEEKs and calculations and then PRINTs the address and length (in decimal) of the last BLOADed program, and ESC — jumps eight columns to the right. RUN, PRINT, CALL-151, or just about anything else you can think of can be programmed into this Escape Create feature. All are transparent to the user. All are easily modifiable by the user.

And all for about 1500 bytes and $40 dollars. Just think. Never get a *** SYNTAX ERROR after misspelling CATALOG again.

But maybe I was too rash in my opening. *Program Line Editor* is *not* indispensible. It is possible in the Apple Basics without it. But just like central heating, electric refrigerators, and indoor plumbing, I would rather not be without it. And I am sure that after you try it, you won't want to get along without it, either. (Thanks Barry — CC.)

To Hex and Back — A Tutorial

Converting from one number base to another is a frequent requirement for programming applications. When you use PEEKs and POKEs you need to convert from hex (base 16) to decimal (base 10). Programs to POKE machine language into memory and to dump the contents of memory are examples of practical applications. We will discuss a useful POKE program later, but first, let's consider the techniques for making the conversions.

Hex to Decimal

To convert from one system to another, it is first necessary to understand the nature of the systems. In the Apple, all the characters on the keyboard (and more that aren't available) are assigned codes.

The code is known as ASCII — pronounced AS-KEY — which stands for American Standard Code for Information Interchange. There are other codes around, and IBM uses one of their own called EBCIDIC. But for anything we do within the Apple, the ASCII code is the only one with which we need to be concerned.

Get your Applesoft II Basic Programming Reference Manual and turn to page 138. Find the numbers 0 and 9 and observe that, in the DEC column, the value assigned is from 48 to 57. On the next page, find the letters A to F. The values assigned here are 65 to 70. Note that there are seven characters between the numbers and letters. Numbers 48 and 7 will be used in the conversions from one base to the other. These numbers are the differences between the code values, the positional values in the table, and the value of the characters we want to convert. Now, let's examine a program that uses these relationships.

Listing 1 is a short program to convert hex numbers to decimal. The program accepts a four-digit hex number, manipulates the digits, then sums the digits into the equivalent decimal number. Input is accepted in line 1000. There is no error checking included, so you will get funny results if you don't use correct characters. Then, a FOR...NEXT loop is set-up in lines 1010 to 1025. This loop steps through each of the four input characters and assigns the decimal value to the digit. First, the digit is converted to its ASCII value with the Applesoft string function ASC. Next, if the digit is a number, 48 is subtracted to put it into the range 0 to 9. If the digit is one of the letters A to F, an additional 7 is subtracted to put the value in the 10 to 15 range. Now we have the values stored in variables $D(1)$ to $D(4)$. Variable 1 is the most significant digit (MSD) and so on.

```
1000    INPUT "ENTER A 4-DIGIT HEX
        NUMBER - ";H$
1010    FOR I = 1 TO 4
1020 D(I) =  ASC ( MID$ (H$,I,1))
        - 48: IF D(I) > 9 THEN D(I)
        = D(I) - 7
1025    NEXT I
1030 D(1) = D(1) * 4096:D(2) = D(
     2) * 256
1040 D(3) = D(3) * 16:T = D(1) +
     D(2) + D(3) + D(4)
1050    PRINT : PRINT T
]
]
]
]RUN
ENTER A 4-DIGIT HEX NUMBER - FFFF
65535
]
]
]RUN
ENTER A 4-DIGIT HEX NUMBER - 9999
39321
```

Listing 1. Sample program showing use of FOR...NEXT loops in hex to decimal conversion.

In line 1030, each of the four variables is converted to its base 16 value. Position 1, the MSD, is 16 to the third power or 4096. Position 2 is 16 squared or 256. Position 3 is 16 to the first power or 16, and position 4 is the 1's position (16 to the 0 power). So each position is multiplied by its positional value and summed in line 1040. Line 1050 prints the results of all the manipulation. The output will be a five-digit number. Using the loop to break down (parse) the hex string makes this a compact conversion routine. Listing 3 is an example of how to do the same conversion without the use of FOR...NEXT loops.

```
1000    INPUT "ENTER 5-DIGIT NUMBER
        - ";H
1020    FOR I = 1 TO 4
1130 H1 =  INT (H / 16):D(I) = H -
     16 * H1:H = H1
1140    NEXT I
1150    FOR I = 4 TO 1 STEP  - 1
1155 H$ = H$ +  CHR$ (D(I) + 48 +
     7 * ((D(I) > 9)))
1160    NEXT I
1170    PRINT : PRINT "$";H$
]
]
]
]RUN
ENTER 5-DIGIT NUMBER - 65535
$FFFF
]
]
]RUN
ENTER 5-DIGIT NUMBER - 00100
$0064
```

Listing 2. Sample program showing use of FOR...NEXT loops in decimal to hex conversion.

```
90   HOME
100    INPUT "INPUT A 4 DIGIT HEX N
       UMBER - ";A$
110    PRINT : PRINT
130    LET H1 =  ASC ( LEFT$ (A$,1)
       ) - 48
135    IF H1 > 9 THEN H1 = H1 - 7
140    LET H2 =  ASC ( MID$ (A$,2,1
       )) - 48
145    IF H2 > 9 THEN H2 = H2 - 7
150    LET H3 =  ASC ( MID$ (A$,3,1
       )) - 48
155    IF H3 > 9 THEN H3 = H3 - 7
160    LET H4 =  ASC ( RIGHT$ (A$,1
       )) - 48
165    IF H4 > 9 THEN H4 = H4 - 7
170    LET H1 = H1 * 4096
180    LET H2 = H2 * 256
190    LET H3 = H3 * 16
200    LET H = H + H1 + H2 + H3 + H
       4
210    PRINT : PRINT "$";A$;"   =   "
       ;H;"   DECIMAL"
```

Listing 3. Another way to convert hex to decimal requiring more coding than the example in Listing 1.

Decimal to Hex

As you might expect, converting from decimal to hex is just the reverse of hex to decimal. Listing 2 is a short program that does this. Again, FOR...NEXT loops are used to minimize coding. Line 1000 accepts input of a five-digit base-10 number. As in the other example there is no error checking. The number should have five digits between 00000 and 65535. This is consistent with the range of memory addressable by the Apple 6502 microprocessor.

Line 1020 uses a loop to break the number into four elements representing the hex values. They are stored in four variables, D(1) to D(4).

Lines 1050 to 1060 are another loop to convert the digits back to their ASCII values. This is accomplished with the CHR$ string function. To complete the conversion, 48 is added to the value of the digit for the numbers. If it is a letter, an additional 7 is added. Note that line 1155 uses relational logic to test for the range of values. I was not able to make this work in line 1020 of Listing 1. The string H$ is built one character at a time until all four hex characters are accumulated (concatenated).

Line 1070 prints the string with the $ symbol at the front. In 6502 convention, the $ symbol is used to indicate a hex number.

All Together Now

Now that you understand how to make the conversions, a program is needed to put it all together. The program in Listing 4 is my example of a way to do it. Lines 1060 to 1160 set up a menu and the logic to make the selection. The hex conversion program is in lines 2000 to 2100. A couple of additional items were added.

The variables are zeroed in line 2000, and the ability to go back and do it over is included in lines 2080 to 2100. Decimal conversion in lines 3000 to 3110 includes the same additions. Note that there is still no error checking in the program.

You could test for the number of input characters for instance. You could also test to see if they are in the correct range. As they say in the text books, I'll leave this as an exercise for the reader.

Making it Work

Having a program to make these conversions is kind of fun. But as a more practical matter, you can't use them at the same time you're writing another program. You would need to do the conversions first, then use them in your program as you write it. Since the most usual case is to convert hex to decimal, an example of a program using the conversion is appropriate. The Mountain Computer Clock in my computer requires machine language to initialize it and generate the clock output. Since the machine language is in hex, it is easier to let the program do the conversion to decimal for the POKE statements. Listing 5 is an example of a program that will do this. Note that in this program only two

digits are to be converted. The FOR...NEXT loops used in the examples would take too much code here, so each digit is converted separately. The program is really two subroutines. Lines 1, 2 and 3 are used to call the routines to first, enable the clock and second, to read the clock output.

The machine language program is going to be POKEd into page 3 of memory, decimal locations 768 ($300) to 775. A READ...DATA combination is used to store and recall the hex machine language code.

```
1000    REM *******************
1010    REM PROGRAM TO CONVERT HEX
1020    REM  AND DECIMAL NUMBERS.
1030    REM  BY: CHUCK CARPENTER
1040    REM *******************
1060    HOME
1070    PRINT "SELECT OPTIONS"
1080    PRINT "————— —————"
1090    PRINT
1100    PRINT "   1.   HEX TO DECI
        MAL CONVERSION"
1110    PRINT "   2.   DECIMAL TO
        HEX CONVERSION"
1120    PRINT "   0.   END THE PRO
        GRAM"
1130    PRINT
1140    PRINT "ENTER YOUR CHOICE ";
        : INPUT S
1145    IF S > 2 GOTO 1000
1150    IF S = 0 THEN  HOME : PRINT
        "END OF PROGRAM...": END
1160    ON S GOTO 2000,3000
1180    REM - ** HEX TO DECIMAL **
1190    REM  *******************
2000    HOME :H$ = "":T = 0
2010    INPUT "ENTER A 4-DIGIT HEX
        NUMBER...";H$
2020    FOR I = 1 TO 4
2030    D(I) =  ASC ( MID$ (H$,I,1))
         - 48: IF D(I) > 9 THEN D(I)
         = D(I) - 7
2040    NEXT I
2050    D(1) = D(1) * 4096:D(2) = D(
        2) * 256
2060    D(3) = D(3) * 16:T = D(1) +
        D(2) + D(3) + D(4)
2070    PRINT : PRINT H$" = ";T;" D
        ECIMAL"
2080    PRINT "MORE HEX CONVERSIONS
        Y/N ";: INPUT A$
2090    IF A$ = "Y" GOTO 2000
2100    GOTO 1000
2120    REM - ** DECIMAL TO HEX **
2130    REM  *******************
3000    HOME :N = 0:H$ = "":H = 0
3010    INPUT "ENTER A 5-DIGIT BASE
        -10 NUMBER...";H:N = H
3020    FOR I = 1 TO 4
3030    H1 =  INT (H / 16):D(I) = H -
        16 * H1:H = H1
3040    NEXT I
3050    FOR I = 4 TO 1 STEP  - 1
3060    H$ = H$ +  CHR$ (D(I) + 48 +
        7 * ((D(I) > 9)))
3070    NEXT I
3080    PRINT : PRINT N;" = $";H$;"
        HEXADECIMAL"
3090    PRINT "MORE HEX CONVERSIONS
        Y/N ";: INPUT A$
3100    IF A$ = "Y" GOTO 3000
3110    GOTO 1000
```

Listing 4. Menu driven program to convert hex and decimal numbers. Combines examples of Listings 1 and 2.

Line 5010 reads each byte of the data as variable A$. Each digit of the hex byte is converted to its ASCII value in lines 5020 to 5040.

```
1    GOSUB 5000
2    GOSUB 6000
3    END
5000    REM - ENABLING CLOCK
5010    FOR I = 768 TO 775: READ A$
5020    D1 =  ASC ( LEFT$ (A$,1)) -
        48
5030    IF D1 > 9 THEN D1 = D1 - 7
5040    D2 =  ASC ( RIGHT$ (A$,1)) -
        48
5050    IF D2 > 9 THEN D2 = D2 - 7
5060    D1 = D1 * 16:T = D1 + D2: POKE
        I,T
5070    T = 0: NEXT I: RESTORE
5080    RETURN
5090    DATA A9,C4,85,39,20,00,C4,
        60
6000    REM - READING CLOCK
6005    CALL 768
6010    POKE 651,58: POKE 648,58
6020    FOR I = 653 TO 646 STEP  -
        1
6030    A$ =  CHR$ ( PEEK (I))
6040    PRINT A$;: NEXT I
6050    PRINT : RETURN
]
]
]RUN
08:01:55
```

Listing 5. Program example to demonstrate one technique to convert hex data to decimal and POKE the result into a memory location within a program.

Line 5060 multiplies the digits by their weighted positional values, adds them together and POKEs the result into the current memory location I. When all bytes of data are converted and POKEd, the program is terminated in line 5070 and the data pointer is RESTOREd.

Next, the subroutine to read the clock output is called. This routine starts by CALLing the machine language program in page 3. Next the two POKEs put colons in two memory locations. This clock puts semi-colons in between the data in a loop. The data is stored in reverse order, hence the step of -1. Each character is converted to its ASCII value in line 6030 and printed in line 6040. Each character is printed in turn through the range of the loop. The memory range of the loop is at the end of page 2. This range is used by the keyboard as an input storage buffer. Since most of the space is not used by normal keyboard input, it can be used to advantage for temporary storage.

A program such as this example illustrates one possibility for conversion within the program. Another would be a memory dump program. For instance, you can enter

```
]LIST
100  REM     HEX TO DECIMAL
110  REM       BY: BILL VON BENKEN
120  REM
200  A$ = "0123456789ABCDEF": FOR
     B = 1 TO 16: FOR A = 1 TO 16
     : FOR C = 1 TO 16: FOR I = 1
      TO 16:W$ =  MID$ (A$,B,1):Z
     $ =  MID$ (A$,A,1):Y$ =  MID$
     (A$,C,1):X$ =  MID$ (A$,I,1)
     : PRINT W$;Z$;Y$;X$,N:N = N +
     1: NEXT : NEXT : NEXT : NEXT


]
```

Listing 6. Single line program to display hex numbers and decimal equivalents.

Listing 7. One liner randomly generates colorful flower patterns.

```
]LIST
10  REM  - FLOWERS
12  REM     BY: STEVEN WONG
14  REM
20  P = 3.14: HGR2 : FOR L = 1 TO
     30:A =  RND (1) * 219 + 30:B
     =  RND (1) * 131 + 30: HCOLOR=
    3: HPLOT A,191 TO A,B:H =  INT
    ( RND (1) * 7) + 1: HCOLOR=
    H - (H = 4):S =  RND (1) * 2
    0 + 10: FOR T = .5 * P TO 2.
    5 * P STEP 2 * P / S:X = A +
     SIN (T) * S:Y = B -  COS (T
    ) * S: HPLOT A,B TO X,Y: NEXT
    : NEXT : GOTO 20

]
```

Listing 8. Colorful snowflake patterns with the sound of falling snow are generated by this one liner.

```
]LIST
10  REM  - SNOWFLAKES
12  REM     BY: STEVEN WONG
14  REM
20  P = 3.14: HGR2 : FOR Z = 1 TO
     99:A =  RND (1) * 261 + 9:B =
     RND (1) * 173 + 9: HCOLOR=
     RND (1) * 7 + 1:C =  RND (1
    ) * 5 + 4: FOR T = .5 * P TO
    2.5 * P STEP 2 * P / C:X = A
     +  SIN (T) * C:Y = B -  COS
    (T) * C: HPLOT A,B TO X,Y:V =
     PEEK ( - 16336): NEXT : NEXT
    : GOTO 20
]
```

the starting location directly in hex. Then, the program can do the conversion to decimal for the PEEKs at memory. Next you can have the program print both the hex and decimal values of memory locations being examined. You could also add the printable characters represented by the hex data. I recently wrote a program to do these things. A program like this in Basic is slow but very useful since it can be used to examine itself as well as all other memory locations. You don't need to exit from Basic to use a memory dump utility. But that's another story.

One Liners

Programs that are complete in one line have been part of past columns. These fun little programs have been mostly clever uses of graphics. This month, Listings 6, 7 and 8 include one that is not graphics and two that are. As I have cautioned before, type them very carefully. It is very easy to make a mistake. Listing 6 is appropriate (by coincidence) this month—it shows hex numbers and their decimal equivalents. The program comes from Bill Von Benken.

The other two from Steven Wong generate attractive hi-res graphics patterns. If you have a one liner that you would like to contribute, please do. I'll include them in future columns.

Questions and Answers

About Integer Basic and Applesoft Basic: Recently, several letters have asked similar questions about the use of and the differences between the two main programming languages for the Apple. The original Apples had an Integer-only version of Basic as the only programming language available. Soon, however, the popularity of the computer demanded a language with more "power" in areas of number handling (floating point arithmetic as it is called) and the ability to handle text through string manipulation. Thus Applesoft was made available for the Apple II.

Integer Basic is quite a bit different from Applesoft in several ways. In addition to several commands and the implementation of them, the interpreter handles programs differently in memory. Integer Basic, as the name implies, uses only integers (whole numbers) in the range of plus and minus

32767. To use numbers outside this range, special programming techniques must be employed. In addition, the integer interpreter places the program in memory starting at high memory. Variables are stored from low memory up. The Applesoft interpreter, on the other hand, puts the program at low memory, the numerical variables at the end of the program, and the string variables from high memory down. Mainly because of the interpreter differences, you cannot run integer programs with Applesoft or the other way around.

Lately, some of the questions about these languages have included problems relative to the Language Card. There are programs on the masterdisk, which comes with the system, to load the non-resident language into the language card. For instance, if you have an Apple II, Applesoft will be loaded since Integer Basic is the ROM resident language. With the Apple II Plus, Integer Basic is loaded into the Language Card. If you have no language card, or you don't have one of the corresponding ROM cards, you can run only programs using the resident language in your machine.

Again:
• Apple II has Integer Basic resident in ROM.
• Apple II Plus has Applesoft Basic resident in ROM.

To use (or have) both languages in the same machine, you need to add hardware/firmware. Slot 0 in the expansion slots is reserved for this purpose. You add an Integer card to the Apple II Plus. You add an Applesoft card to the Apple II. I have an Apple II and originally added an Applesoft card so I could use both languages. Applesoft became the more popular language so the Apple II Plus came about.

There is an alternative. This is where the programs INTBASIC (and FPBASIC) come into use (the ones on your master disk). You can also plug a 16K (or more) ROM card into slot 0. When you do this, the language that is not resident in ROM is loaded into the RAM card. The master disk will test for the presence of a RAM card and load the appropriate language (during the boot cycle).

If you have one of the ROM language cards in slot 0, nothing happens since the alternate language is already there. Note that to get all the available utilities, you need to have the alternate ROM card or the RAM card installed. Once you do this, you can do anything that it is possible to do with your Apple II.

Remember, you cannot directly run Integer Basic programs with Applesoft or the other way around. Indirectly, you can convert one to the other. But it's not a simple task. Several people including me (May '80) have written about making such conversions.

Next Time
Several readers have contributed short programs other than one liners (keep 'em short please). Some of them will be included next time. There will be more Questions and Answers too. Please write, I'm delighted to hear from you. And, to save time, write directly to me. □

"I've just programmed our computer to give surprise birthday parties."

Entry Points and Subroutines
Hi Res • Ram Cards
Fast Load Utility

Chuck Carpenter

June, 1982

Several readers have asked about machine language entry points for hi-res graphics. By coincidence, an excellent source of the entry points showed up at just the right time. We'll feature the hi-res entry points in the column this month. As we have in previous columns, one-liners from readers will be included, as will the questions 'n answers section. I'll also discuss a new software utility which I think you will like.

Hi-Res Entry Points

Applesoft Basic includes several commands and statements for writing hi-res graphics programs. Most of the time programs using these commands are quite adequate. Many times though, the programmer wants a quicker response. To achieve this, you can take advantage of the machine language routines included in the ROMs in the Applesoft Basic Interpreter. That is, if you know where the routines are located in memory. (Note that the routines are in the same place if you have Applesoft loaded into a RAM card, too.)

The December '81 issue of the *Apple Assembly Line* newsletter solved the problem, and with the permission of Bob Sander-Cederlof of S-C Software, the hi-res entry information is paraphrased here. But first, some preliminary information for those of you who are new to machine language.

6502 Registers

As you read through the descriptions of the hi-res routine memory locations and their use, you will see references to the A, X, and Y registers. These are internal 6502 microprocessor memory locations. These registers are used to process variables (data) during computing functions. The A register is the accumulator. The X and Y registers are called Index registers. As you will see in the descriptions, you must provide the values needed for the machine language programs to function. Your program must store the data in the appropriate register before the hi-res routine is called.

To better understand how this is done, a knowledge of machine language is required. Three tutorials have been included

in this column, one in the May '80 issue and two in the November '80 issue. There are also many good books on the subject, including *Apple Machine Language* by Don and Kurt Inman and *6502 Software Design* by Leo J. Scanlon. Since the first one is Apple oriented, it is an excellent book for the machine language beginner. Now, let's look at the hi-res subroutines in the Applesoft Interpreter.

Hi-Res Subroutines

Table 1 is a list of the important locations used in page zero. These locations help keep track of what is going on during the computation process.

Table 2 shows the major entry points you can use for your hi-res machine language.

One-Liners

This month, we have two one-liners from one of our junior programmers. The programs are hi-res and are shown in Listings 1 and 2. The first one draws random triangles

Table 1.

$1A,1B	Shape pointer used by DRAW and XDRAW
$1C	Last used color byte
$26,27	Address of byte containing x,y point
$30	Bit mask for bit in that byte
$E0,E1	X-coordinate (0-279)
$E2	Y-coordinate (0-191)
$E4	Color
$E6	Page ($20 if HGR, $40 if HGR2)
$E7	SCALE= value
$E8,E9	Address of beginning of shape table
$EA	Collision counter
$F9	ROT= value

Table 2.

HGR2	$F3D8	Initializes and clears hi-res page 2.
HGR	$F3E2	Initializes and clears hi-res page 1.
HCLR	$F3F2	Clears the current hi-res screen to black.
BKGND	$F3F6	Clears the current hi-res screen to the last plotted color (from $1C).
HPOSN	$F411	Positions the hi-res cursor without plotting a point. Enter with (A) = Y-coordinate, and (Y,X) = X-coordinate.
HPLOT	$F457	Calls HPOSN and tries to plot a dot at the cursor position. If you are trying to plot a non-white color at a complementary color position, no dot will be plotted.
HLIN	$F53A	Draws a line from the last plotted point or line destination to (X,A) = X-coordinate, and (Y) = Y-coordinate.
HFIND	$F5CB	Converts the position of the hi-res cursor's position to X- and Y-coordinates; stores X-coordinate at $E0-E1 and Y-coordinate at $E2.
DRAW	$F601	Draws a shape. Enter with (Y,X) = the address of the shape table, and (A) = the rotation factor. Uses the current color.
XDRAW	$F65D	Draws a shape by inverting the existing color or the dots the shape draws over. Same entry parameters as DRAW.
SETHCOL	$F6EC	Sets the hi-res color to (X), where (X) must be between 0 and 7.

```
      LIST
10    REM       ONE LINER
                BY: MIKE CAMERON

20    HGR2 : FOR A = 1 TO 100: HCOLOR=
      INT ( RND (1) * 7):X =  INT
      ( RND (1) * 250 + 10):Y =  INT
      ( RND (1) * 170 + 10): HPLOT
      X,Y TO X - 4,Y - 9 TO X + 4,
      Y - 9 TO X,Y:S =  PEEK ( - 1
      6336): FOR W = 1 TO 150: NEXT
      W: HCOLOR= 0: HPLOT X,Y TO X
      - 4,Y - 9 TO X + 4,Y - 9 TO
      X,Y: NEXT
```

Listing 1. Draws random diamonds in color with sound.

```
      ]LIST
10    REM       ONE LINER
                BY: MIKE CAMERON

20    HGR2 : HCOLOR=  INT ( RND (1)
      * 7): HPLOT 0,0: FOR Z = 1 TO
      300:X =  INT ( RND (1) * 279
      ):Y =  INT ( RND (1) * 191):
      HPLOT  TO X,Y: NEXT : FOR X
      = 1 TO 300: NEXT : GOTO 10
      ]
```

Listing 2. Draws random lines in color.

in random colors with sound. The second draws random lines in random color. My guess is that Mike was experimenting when these programs were written.

One note about typing one-liners. Enter the text of the program without spaces. Some of the programs have too many characters after being listed. The Basic Interpreter inserts spaces to make the program easier to read. Often the extra spaces make the program too long for direct entry. As you may recall, only 255 characters can be typed into the keyboard input buffer, but if you leave out the spaces, an apparently too long program will fit in the buffer.

A couple of one-page programs were sent to me too. They are called one-pagers because the entire program fits on the screen when listed. Since I had an extra day off because of an ice storm, I decided to enter the programs and include them here (remember the January '82 cold wave). Both are very interesting programs. I think you will especially enjoy the lo-res graphics program in Listing 4.

Listing 3 is an adaptation of the lo-res kaleidoscope program in the original Apple II Reference Manual. This book, known as the Red Book, included several Integer Basic programs, a couple of which were interesting games using lo-res graphics. This program is an interesting adaptation of the old lo-res program. The program runs very slowly, so give it plenty of time. The patterns that are developed are worth the wait. Bring your camera and take pictures.

How many Apple II Plus owners know about Integer Basic? If you have the Integer Card or a RAM card, I'm sure you have used Integer Basic. The language is the original Apple language and was developed for games and educational applications. It runs much faster than Applesoft for most applications—especially graphics programs.

The program in Listing 4 was written in Integer Basic and the results are fascinating. One of the features of the program is that it switches pages. That is, while you are looking at one page, a new display is being developed on the other. All of a sudden the display changes when the pages are switched. The process then continues on the other page. Fascinating!

When you first run the program, it displays two lines of text. Follow the instructions, set LOMEM and then type the GOTO. Now sit back and watch the display. It takes several seconds to get started, so give it a chance. I used my green-screen monitor and the results were very good, but it is much better viewed in color. If you would like to use this program in Applesoft you will need to change the INT statements. Otherwise the program should run properly. I'm not going to say what it does. Type it in and run it; you'll like it.

QUESTIONS 'N ANSWERS

Frequently, readers write to me and ask questions about all sorts of Apple related things. (Even about Apple and IBM!) The questions are often specific; something the individual reader is interested in. Other times the questions are general in nature and concern topics of interest to many readers. The questions asked most often are about connecting printers, adding on-line storage, and using RAM cards.

Listing 3. Hi-res version of the old Red Book Lo-Res Graphics program.

```
10    REM     HIGH RES KALEIDOSCOPE
20    REM     ADAPTED FROM LOW RES
22    REM     KALEIDOSCOPE (RED BOOK)

30    REM     BY: STUART RANKIN

40    E = 30: HGR2 : HOME : FOR W =
      3 TO 1000: FOR I = 0 TO 95: FOR
      J = 0 TO 95
100   K = I + J
110   A =  INT (2.65 * J / (I + 32)
      + I * W / E)
120   A =  ABS ( INT (A - .99999))
130   IF A > 7 THEN E = E * 50:A = 7
140   HCOLOR=  INT (A)
150   HPLOT I,K: HPLOT K,I: HPLOT
      278 - I,190 - K: HPLOT 278 -
      K,190 - I
160   HPLOT K,190 - I: HPLOT 278 -
      I,K: HPLOT I,190 - K: HPLOT
      278 - K,I
170   NEXT J,I,W: END
```

Listing 4. Lo-res graphics in Integer Basic. Draws on both pages and switches when complete. Very interesting program.

```
0     REM     ONE PAGER
              BY:  L. J. TIBBITTS

1     CALL -936: PRINT "LOMEM: 6000"
      : PRINT "GOTO 10": END
2     X= RND (14)*3:Y= RND (14)*3
      : IF X<Y THEN RETURN : GOTO 2
5     GOSUB 2:A=X:B=Y: GOSUB 2: FOR
      I=A TO B: COLOR=C: HLIN X,Y AT
      I: NEXT I: COLOR=0
7     VLIN A,B AT X: VLIN A,B AT
      Y: HLIN X,Y AT A: HLIN X,Y AT
      B: RETURN
10    CALL -936: GR : REM   TIBBITTS
102   COLOR= RND (15)+1: FOR I=1 TO
      28: HLIN 1,38 AT I: NEXT I:
      GOTO 124
110   C= RND (15)+1
120   FOR K=1 TO RND (10): GOSUB
      5: NEXT K: IF RND (10)>1 THEN
      110: POKE -16300,0
124   FOR J=0 TO 1024: POKE 2048+
      J, PEEK (1024+J): NEXT J
126   POKE -16299,0: GOTO 110
```

About Printers

Basically, printers come in two types. There are Receive Only (RO), and Keyboard Send/Receive (KSR). Generally, a KSR printer will have a keyboard attached to the printer. You can use the printer to send and to receive. An RO printer will only receive the data sent to it. Since there is no keyboard, RO printers are often more compact.

There are also serial printers and parallel printers available in both types. You can use some serial printers as-is, without any control signals other than the data lines. Other serial printers require handshaking, a term used to describe the way in which the computer and printer talk to each other. Parallel interface printers include handshaking as part of the computer-to-printer connections.

The DEC LA-34 is a KSR serial printer that does not require handshaking. You can use the Apple II High Speed Serial Interface Board with this printer, for instance. The LA-34 will print at 300 baud (30 characters per second), but runs as fast as 45 characters in the catch-up mode, after a carriage return.

The LA-34, since it is KSR with an RS-232 serial interface, can also be used with a modem to talk directly to a host computer. You can take advantage of the wide printing width to see output as it would be printed on an 80-character screen. You will use a great deal of paper, however. Be aware too, that you must switch the transmitted data and received data lines when a printer is used with a modem. Normally, these lines are pins 2 and 3 in the standard 25-pin connector.

Other serial printers can accept data at much higher speeds. For instance, my Epson MX-80 with a serial adapter, runs at 1200 baud (and will run as high as 9200 baud). The print head can't run at this speed, so the input buffer must tell the computer when it is full of characters. At this time the handshaking signals tell the computer to stop sending. When the buffer is cleared, another signal is sent to start the data again. Note that in this mode, it is of no advantage to send the data any faster than the print head can move.

If you have a system that allows spooling or buffering of data during the print cycle, the high speed transmission is more important. You can keep the spooling operation from loading other computing functions with higher transmission speeds. At least one manufacturer is making a card that will let you print and do other functions at the same time. Some word processors provide this capability too. Both functions slow down since the microprocessor must handle both functions. The faster the print buffer is filled, the sooner other functions are taken care of.

There are several serial interface cards on the market now which include handshaking. Since even the standard RS-232 serial interface allows many handshaking options, make sure the interface card and the printer are compatible.

Parallel printers, on the other hand, send the data as fast as the computer can send it all the time. Handshaking is built into the parallel interface. But not all parallel interfaces are the same.

My MX-80 and Centronics 737 are both parallel RO printers. The parallel card used for the 737 will not work with the MX-80. Manufacturers have tended to use the phrase "Centronics-compatible" but some are "more" compatible than others. Again, there are many parallel interface boards on the market now. Make sure the interface board works with the printer that you want to use.

About Disk Drives

Several companies are making expansion drives for the Apple system. Among these are Sorento Valley Associates (SVA), Vista, and Micro-Sci. The first two are offering controller cards and software for expansion to 8" drives. Micro-Sci claims to have 5 1/4" expansion drives and software for the Apple.

My experience has been only with SVA, a company which has a good reputation. With their controllers you can add up to 4 megabytes of on-line storage capacity in floppy drives. This capacity is provided through double-sided, double density controller capacity.

SVA has also announced controllers for 8" and 5 1/4" fixed (or rigid) drives. The software on the 8" system is integrated with DOS 3.3. You can have both the Apple controller card and the SVA controller card in the system at the same time.

The other two companies are new in the Apple disk drive business. Vista has been around a while, but I am not familiar with their products. Vista has announced a controller and Apple compatible software for 8" drives. The system is reported to be very much like the SVA units.

Micro-Sci started about a year ago and had problems. They advertise a 40-track drive and a 70-track drive. Software was reported to be the major problem by those with whom I have discussed the products. The 40-track drive does not offer much in the way of additional capacity. With the 70-track unit, you get about 1/4 megabyte of storage—about as much as a single-sided 8" disk. As I learn more about these disk drive memory expansion systems, I will keep you informed.

About RAM Cards

Adding a RAM card to the Apple brings us in a complete circle. Now you can "softload" many languages and utilities into addressable memory occupied by ROM. A few years ago, the rage was to have a computer that had the programming language in ROM. When you turned on the power, the language was ready to use immediately. Of course, if you had to load programs from tape, you could understand why programs in ROM were so desirable. Now, with fast access disk drives, the more flexible softload capability has gained popularity.

Apple's Language System included the first RAM card that I know of. It is part of the package you get when you buy Pascal. Several other manufacturers offer 16K RAM cards, most of which are quite similar to the Apple RAM card. You can load Integer Basic, Applesoft Basic, Pascal or Fortran, or use the Z-80 Softcard with them. The units have switches in software and hardware to connect or remove them from the memory circuits.

One supplier has a unit that has its own memory refresh circuits on it. This means that you don't have to remove any of the RAM chips on the main Apple board. However, my feelings are uneasy here; the logic is good, but there is always the possibility that refresh will occur at the wrong time. I prefer those boards which get their refresh timing from the same circuits the main Apple memory does.

Newer RAM boards now have capacities of 32K, 64K, and 128K bytes of memory. With this kind of capacity you could store the total contents of an Apple disk in RAM. In fact, that is the claim made for these memory giants. Other possibilities include moving DOS (the disk operating system) into this area of memory. You can get an additional 10K bytes of main memory for your programs this way. Note that the software must be compatible with DOS for these things to work properly.

A technique called bank switching is used to access a particular 16K section of the additional RAM memory. Addresses are used as bank switching registers. When a switching register is called, the appropriate 16K section is selected, and the programs stored there run accordingly. With just one 16K section, the usual result is to switch ROM with RAM. The result is similar to having Applesoft resident in ROM on the Apple main board, and an Integer Basic card in slot zero. You can switch one or the other on with the hardware switch, or make the switch with a software call. Most of the software available these days has the intelligence to make the analysis during boot time. That's how the master disk knows whether to load the non-resident language into a RAM card if it is installed in slot zero.

A Fast-Load Utility

Speaking of fast loading memory, a new utility called Universal Boot Initializer (UBI) will do this for you. As I mentioned above, loading programs from tape was sometimes agonizingly slow. When Applesoft was first available, it took 1.5 minutes to load it from tape. The same program takes 20 seconds from a disk. Now with UBI, you can load your system with the non-resident language in less than five seconds. Actually, if you measure only the one time it takes to load a RAM card, the time is less than two seconds.

UBI is a product of S&S Software, Box 5, Manvel, ND 52856. The utility is designed to provide the software developer or end user with universal boot capability. This means you can load DOS 3.2.1 or 3.3 from the same disk. In addition to the copy protected utility disk, the package includes a thorough training disk and a manual to help configure your own personal boot disk. Examples of single and dual language possibilities are included too, for a total of four sides of software.

There was only one thing I didn't like about the utility. You can't directly add the capability to an existing disk. However, once you initialize a blank disk, you can use a file transfer utility like FID on DOS 3.3 to move files from a slow boot disk to a UBI initialized disk.

The well organized manual includes more than most people want to know about how the utility works. In addition to the sections on customizing your own boot disk, the manual tells you how the UBI came about, and includes a complete section on how to copy the universal boot disk.

Because of a problem that occurs when you include both DOS 3.2.1 and 3.3 on the same disk, they become difficult to copy. The manual suggests ways to overcome the problem, including the FID method, and use of a bit copier.

Warranty and replacement policies are quite liberal. Defective disks are replaced at no charge within 30 days. User damaged disks are replaced for $15 with return of the original disk. A back-up copy of the original disk is available for $10 with return of the warranty card.

For the software developer, a software licensing agreement is available. The individual end-user does not need a license. UBI also includes a directory formatting capability. However, additional software is required to create the customized catalog.

The disks that I use frequently have been modified with UBI. I have been delighted with it since I first saw the prototype model in July '81. If you have felt that two-stage booting was more than you needed at times, then you will enjoy the fast-load, single-step capability offered with the UBI. The price is $49.95 plus $3 postage and handling. The phone number is (701)696-2574. □

"What'll it be, Herman? Boots, beans, bits, bait, booze, or bytes?"

Chapter VII
Software Reviews

Chapter VII — Software Reviews

In the past few years, *Creative Computing* has printed dozens of reviews of Apple software products. We could easily have made this book entirely from those reviews; but because there's so much other material in this chapter, we have given you simply a good cross-section of reviews. These describe the types of software that have been produced in the last few years.

Most of the reviews we've selected have been placed in the chapters relating to their particular applications. The reviews that follow round out our selections with fantasy, fiction, adventure, arcade games, and simulations. While not meant as a "buying guide," these reviews will give you an idea of the range of software available, and enough information to allow you to ask about other similar products that may exist. We have made sure the products here are still available, but some of the prices may have changed by the time you read this.

Special Notes For Chapter VII

● *The Sargon Chronicles,* by Theodore H. Ehara:

For those of you who enjoy a good game of chess, here is the story of Sargon. Ten years ago you may have considered the thought of playing against a computer to be a novelty. Several chess programs were in various stages of development on large computers at that time, and with the amount of computation power necessary and the almost endless chessboard variations possible, the thought of a "micro" chess-playing computer was still considered to be science fiction. As I recall, the thought of a hand-held electronic calculator was still somewhat futuristic. I was still using a slide rule . . . *(A what?).*

Some programs were capable of playing against novices, but it wasn't until Dan and Kathe Spracklen took their "Sargon" microcomputer chess program into a tournament dominated by the biggies and made a good showing that people realized that the day of microcomputer chess had arrived. Sargon II still remains one of the most respected micro-chess programs.

● *Three Mile Island,* by Victor Fricke:

Three Mile Island is now being sold in machine language, which makes it faster and compatible with an Apple II or Apple II Plus.

● *Soft Centered,* by David Lubar:

The review of Interactive Fiction in this article refers to the TRS-80. The programs are now available for the Apple also, and we think the idea is interesting.

It's dawn, and the sun is just beginning to show over the mountains to the east. You are in your sopwith Camel, checking your gear while the ground crew tops off your fuel tank. "Switch On" you call out, as the ground crewman spins your prop over, "Contact!" and your 130 h.p. engine coughs to life. You advance the throttle and taxi across the parking pad to the taxiway. Down the path, a left turn brings your plane to the east end of the airstrip. You throttle down, and poke the brakes lightly to bring your plane to a stop. After a quick check of the controls, you pour on the throttle and start rolling westward, faster and faster picking up speed as your plane starts to bob up and down, a slight pull on the stick and.... You're airborne! The ground drops away quickly as your altimeter winds upward.

Smoothly you move your stick to the left and your plane rolls easily toward the south. Your eyes are constantly scanning the horizon. Suddenly, your goal appears— the enemy fuel dump. As you fly toward it, bullets whiz by. Craning your neck, you see the Red Baron coming up quickly behind you! Cursing yourself for not being more observant you throw your plane into a dive hoping to lose him somehow... but you don't have a chance... you plane plummets to the ground and explodes! Are you dead? No, just upset! You reach over, press reset and start again. This time you'll get him..."CURSE YOU RED BARON!" Of course the reset button is on your Apple computer, and the reason you are still alive is because you have never left your chair. This has all been made possible by an excellent program from the people at Sub-Logic, 201 West Springfield, Champaign, Illinois ($25). The program comes as two parts:1) A three dimensional

Scott King, 7905 59th Ave. N., New Hope MI 55428.

flight simulator with through-the-windshield viewing and complete instrumentation and 2) British Ace, a WWI war game where your mission is to destroy the enemy fuel depot (which is guarded by a enemy airbase with 5 planes.)

The program loads very easily and is in machine language form, so it will run fast (updating the screen as often as 5 times/sec). Once loaded, it comes up running, with your plane sitting on the fueling pad at a British airbase in the N.E. corner of the world. The World is a 6 mile by 6 mile square of land. You can fly off the edge of the world, but if you go too far, you could get lost and not find your way back. The program contains two data bases. A low

> *Cursing yourself for not being more observant you throw your plane into a dive hoping to lose him somehow...but you don't have a chance...your plane plummets to the ground and explodes!*

level one gives you details of the airstrip for landing and taking off, and a high level one removes the detail work in order to increase the speed of the display. (You don't need to see the striped line on the runway from 10,000 feet anyway.) As you take off, you change data bases by using a landing gear switch. Although the Sopwith had rigid landing gear, this does make it easy to remember to switch data bases. Once in the air, your view out the windshield

shows the horizon, and a mountain range to the north. The view is set up as though you were leaning slightly forward, looking out and down over the nose of the plane. Below you see another airport.

This is the enemy airbase we've heard so much about in the previous paragraphs. The reason that the nasty ole Red Baron hasn't come up after us is because we aren't at war yet. It's easy though—just push a button "W" (not unlike these days in real life?) to go to war mode. Then you had better be ready to fight, because the bad guys are very hard to beat. But back to flying. Beneath the windscreen is a cockpit instrument panel with the minimum FAA required instruments, some of which are, Air Speed; Altimeter; Turn Rate; Compass heading; Rate of climb; and a bunch of engine monitoring gauges. Also included is a Radar Scope. (I'll bet you didn't expect a WWI plane to have Radar, did ya?) Well this was included because with the simulator, you don't have the ability to turn your head and look out the sides and back.

As far as performance goes, the plane is very easy to handle. The simulator has been designed around a WWI Sopwith F.1 Camel which just so happens to be very closely matched to a Piper Supercub 150 with a top speed of 150 mph and a maximum climb rate of 650 ft/mn. And for those of you who don't fly (I have never flown a small plane before either), you have nothing to worry about. The program comes complete with a manual that will teach you everything you need to know about flying and about flight in general. The manual explains what makes a plane fly, and what you can do to make it *not* fly! (CRASH!) The book suggests, (and I agree) that you should read the manual completely before you try to take off. I didn't and found myself upside down at 800 feet, the manual in one hand and the control stick in the

other. So read the manual before you fly!
(Better keep it close by for your first couple
of flights too.)

About the controls, the program is
designed to support keyboard input as well
as paddles. If you have a joystick *that will
plug into the connector*, all the better. But
it flys very well using the keyboard too. In
either case the simulation is very realistic.
There are a multitude of physical factors
thrown into a formula that determines the
responses and actions of your plane. A
few of these factors are: Aircraft Altitude;
Lift(Bernoulli); Lift(Angle of attack);
Forward push due to prop thrust; Forward
or rearward pull of gravity; Downward
pull of gravity; Drag(induced); Drag
(parasitic); Lift loss in turns; Momentum;
Side forces due to bank; Prop stalling;
Structural failure due to excessive speed
or G's; etc. (Whew!)

As you can see, there is a lot of computation going on in this program, and it
does it very fast too. The scene moving in
the windshield is very clean and smooth.

Conclusion

I have found that the A2-FS1 flight
simulation program is extremely well
written, and operates easily in a 16k Apple
II computer. The only addition I would
like to see, would be sound effects added
in to the program. I suspect that the reason
this was omitted was to keep the program
size small enough to fit a 16K machine.
Also at this time the low level data base
only contains the high resolution data for
the British air base, making it impossible
to land at the enemy base, or the civilian
one in the south side of the world. Once
again I feel that this was a question of
memory size. Perhaps in a later program
Sublogic will make an expanded version
for larger machines. But for the money, I
feel this is probably one of the better
programs on the market, and I highly
recommend it. ☐

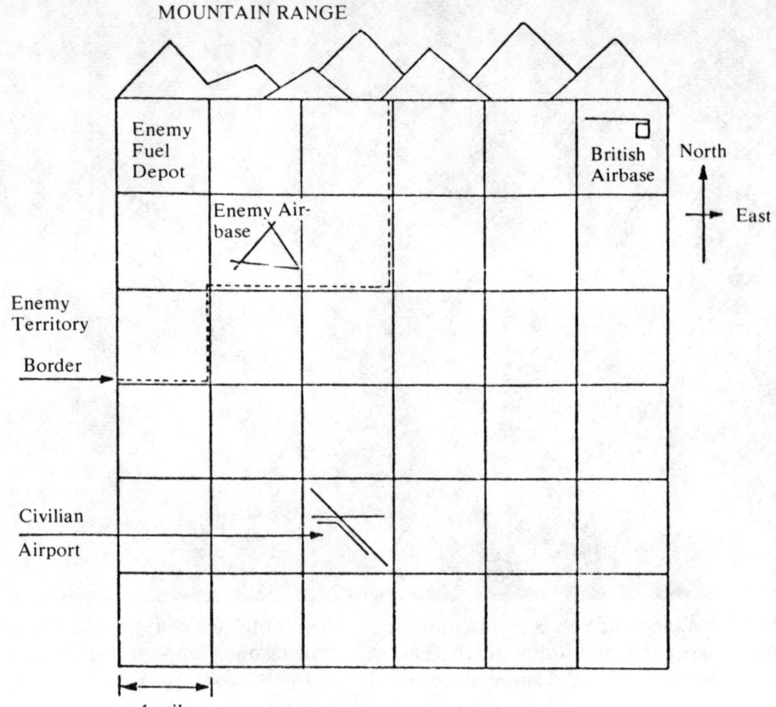

The world.

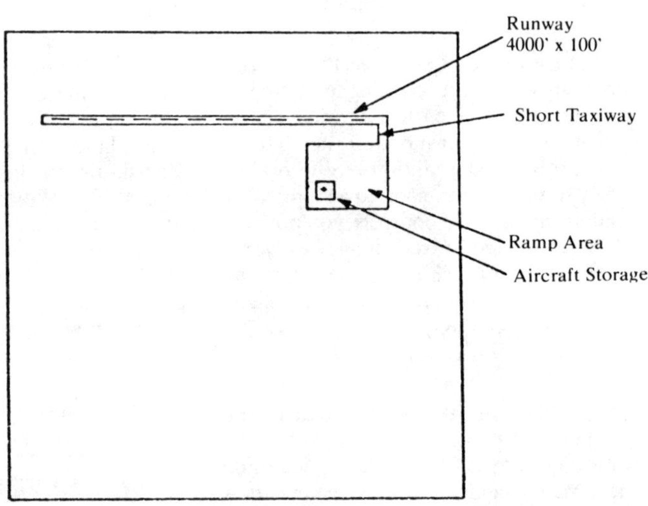

British airbase taxi chart.

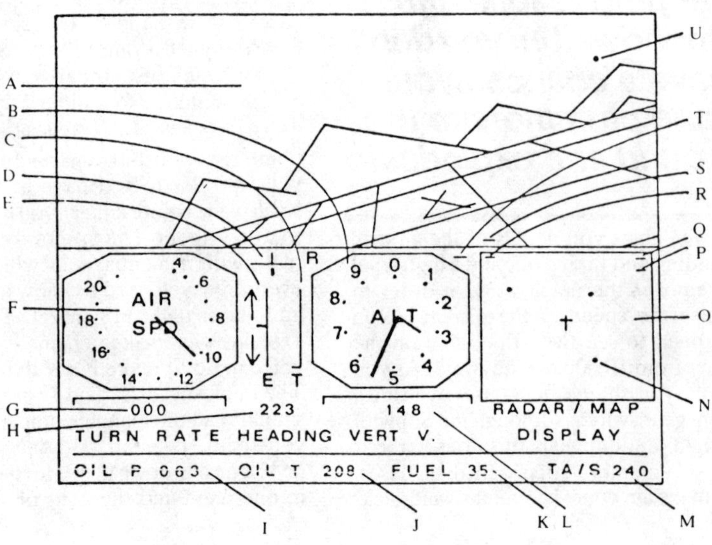

A   Three-dimensional out-the-windshield display.
B   Altimeter (feet)
C   Throttle indicator
D   Roll Rate indicator
E   Elevator position
F   Airspeed indicator (mph)
G   Turn Rate indicator (degrees per minute)
H   Heading indicator Gyro-
I   Compass (degrees)
J   Oil Pressure (psi)
K   Oil Temp (degrees F)
L   Fuel (gallons)
M   Vertical Velocity (feet per minute)
N   Tachometer (rpm x 10) or Score during game
O   Enemy aircraft on rador
P   Radar Display
Q   Enemy aircraft on radar
R   Enemy in Gun Range indicator
S   Enemy is Firing Guns indicator
T   Stall indicator
U   Enemy Aircraft on 3D display

New fantasy games are being produced at such a rate that if you were to line them up and march them through a computer one at a time, the line would never end. This presents a problem for the games addict with limited wealth, and for the reviewer with limited time. Some late sessions, killing dragons while the sun rose somewhere in the real world, solved the temporal problem. The financial problem can be eased by avoiding games that don't suit your tastes or fail to give you your money's worth.

The phrase "fantasy games" is a catch-all designed to encompass adventures, dungeons and dragons, role-playing games, and anything else of similar bent. Some of the programs come in versions for TRS-80, Apple and PET, others are only available for one computer. The settings range from castles and dungeons to outer space and strange islands, with interaction that ranges from sentences to single-letter commands.

Apshai and Others

The first campaign of this review will be through the deadly labrynths created by **Automated Simulations**. The games, with such exotic titles as *Temple of Apshai* and *The Datestones of Ryn* are all similar in basic format. The player moves through a series of rooms, gaining experience and treasures while fighting monsters. Throughout the game, fatigue and wound levels are displayed. If your fatigue gets too great, you can't fight or move. If the wounds hit bottom, you're finished (though ressurection plays a part in several of the programs).

The combat portion is nicely conceived. The player's character can attack, thrust, parry, or fire an arrow. But he has to be facing the opponent. This involves some quick moves and quick thinking, especially since you only have a certain amount of time to make any move. The monsters don't wait while you try to remember the command for turning around. There are two slight weaknesses in this combat portion. First, you have no indication of the status of the attacker. Since his wounds and fatigue aren't displayed, you don't know whether he is full of fight or at death's door. Thus you could waste a precious magic arrow on a monster that could easily be felled with a simple sword stroke. Also, a new command is held while the present move takes place. For example, while one attack is in progress, you can hit the key which fires an arrow. If the attack resulted in the death of the monster, the arrow will still be fired. This can be slightly annoying when you are running low on arrows.

The real-time aspect of the game presents a challenge to the new player. While you are looking through the manual for a command, room description, or treasure description, a skeleton might be hacking you to pieces. A few hours of play are sufficient to become familiar with the commands and treasures. After that, you can give full attention to the vampire bat or animated armor which is coming in for the kill.

The games vary mostly in purpose and treasures. *Temple of Apshai* is a four level dungeon. You wander, building characteristics and attempting to gather all twenty treasures. Whenever you leave the dungeon, the innkeeper can give you a list of collected treasures, and also sell you weapons, armor, and healing salves. The program does not keep track of a player's money. You have to look up the values of your treasures, then tell the inn keeper how much silver you have. Those who like to cheat at solitaire can make use of this to add a bit of unearned wealth to their character's coffers.

David Lubar

Morloc's Tower is designed to be an easier game. Here, the goal is to kill Morlock. The catch is that you have to find him first. On the way, you gather treasures, some of which are aids, some of which are designed to increase the mortality rate.

Datestones of Ryn is also designed for beginners, though pros will find some challenge here. The play field this time is a cavern with corridors and rooms. Hidden within are datestones. Each stone that is brought out of the cave earns you some points. Here, you are fighting not just monsters, but time itself. You only have twenty minutes.

Rescue at Rigel moves from fantasy to science fiction. Your sword and bow are replaced by blasters and other futuristic weapons. The treasures are now human captives which you must find and beam

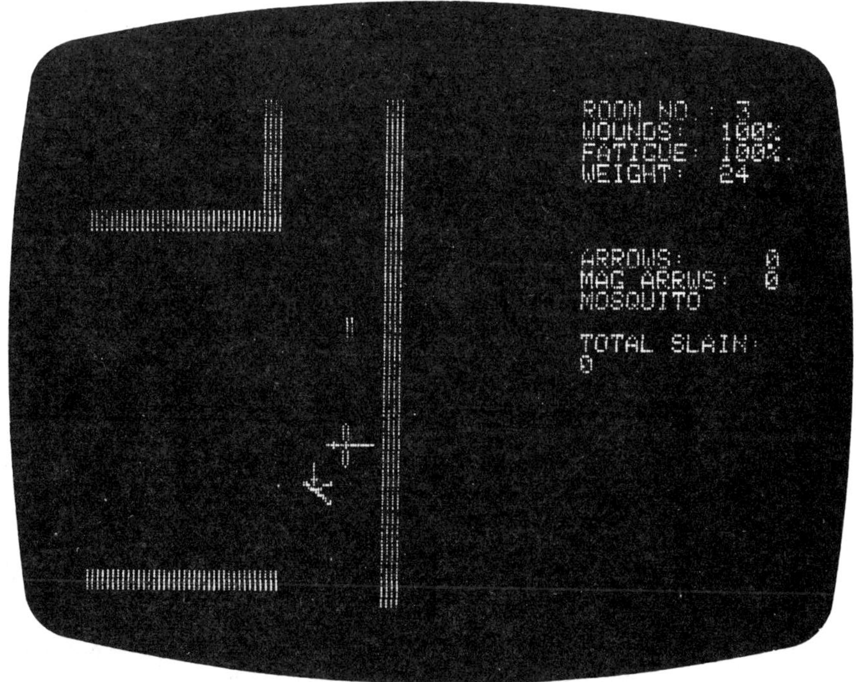

The hero fights a giant mosquito in a corridor of Apshai.

to safety. The multi-leveled alien ship has drop shafts, lift shafts, and teleport doors that make mapping a challenge.

Hellfire Warrior, the sequel to *Temple of Apshai*, extends the game potential greatly, adding new twists and improving some of the parts of play. For a closer look, see Dale Archibald's article, "Hellfire, Brimstone, and Fun," elsewhere in this issue.

A typical segment of play, using *Temple of Apshai* as an example, might run as follows. Your character, armed with a short sword, shield, and chain mail, has just left the inn and finds himself in a large room. There is a doorway to the East. After an unsuccessful search for secret doors, he moves forward. A treasure sits in the middle of the room. Before he can reach it, a giant rat attacks. The player sees he is out of line with the rat. Turning left, he moves up a few steps, then turns back and fires. The arrow strikes, but the rat keeps coming. Switching tactics, the player thrusts. The weakened rat strikes back, then succumbs to the wounds, leaving the adventurer to claim the treasure. He was slightly injured in the encounter, but doesn't yet want to use one of the few healing potions he managed to purchase. With a bit of experience under his belt, the brave fellow moves farther from the security of the exit, alert now for the next attack.

In design, concept, graphics, and entertainment, the games are good. The die-hard game player would probably want to own all of them. The person with only a mild interest in this area might find them too similar. Those who lie between these extremes would probably enjoy owning two or three of the games.

Now for prices and configurations. Note that all TRS-80 cassettes require a 16K Level II Model I system, TRS-80 disk versions need a 32K computer with TRSDOS, Apple versions on cassette require 32K and ROM Applesoft, Apple disk versions need 48K and ROM Applesoft. *The Datestones of Ryn*, at $19.95, is available on cassette for a TRS-80, Apple, or 16K PET. The disk version (same price) is available for a TRS-80 or Apple. *Morloc's Tower* ($19.95) comes on cassette for a TRS-80, Apple, or 24K PET. *Rescue at Rigel* ($29.95) is on cassette for the TRS-80, Apple, or 16K PET, with disk versions for the TRS-80 and Apple. *The Temple of Apshai* and *Hellfire Warrior* ($39.95 each) are on cassette for the TRS-80 or 32K PET, and on disk for the TRS-80 or Apple. **Automated Simulations** can be found at P.O. Box 4247, 1988 Leghorn St., Mountain View CA 94040. (Please add $1 for p&h, or they'll send a dragon to your doorstep.)

I Am Not a Number

If the above phrase brings a touch of nostalgia to your heart, you'll love **Edu-Ware's** psychological adventure set on an island prison. Based on the TV show, *The Prisoner*, this $29.95 disk for a 48K Apple with ROM Applesoft gives you a chance to escape from the island. For those who missed the series, it was a surreal story of a secret agent who had decided to resign from the service. Soon after posting his resignation, he found himself on a strange island populated by fellow inmates and members of the island hierarchy. During each episode, he tried to maintain his sanity and identity while trying to escape.

The program places you on an island with twenty rooms. You are given a special resignation code. If you reveal it, you lose. Each room on the island is a sort of mini-adventure. Usually there is more to discover than meets the eye. Some secrets are kept from you until you make the right move or acquire the necessary objects. While movement is accomplished though single-key commands, sections of the program allow full dialog between the player and the computer. The first room is a simple maze, though the walls aren't revealed until you bump into them. If you make certain mistakes, you get sent back to this room. After repeated trips, the maze becomes tedious, but this is good incentive not to make mistakes.

A full description of any of the rooms would spoil the fun, so they won't be discussed in detail. They include the hospital, library, diner, newsstand, and other facilities of the island. According to the instructions, the program makes use of devious psychological techniques such as subliminal messages. There is also a scoring system based on your ability to avoid conformity and submission. While it's nice to get a good score, your main goal is to escape. The game can be suspended at any point. When you return, you will start in the first room, but your score will be maintained, as will any possessions you have acquired.

A short segment of play might run this way. The Prisoner has left his room and is exploring the island. He wanders into a newsstand for a paper, then stops at the diner for some food. He tries to get into the library, but isn't admitted because he has no book to contribute. His next move puts him in the courthouse. The prosecutor speaks, then gives the Prisoner a chance to reply. He begins to type. At each keystroke, something is added to the picture on the screen. He pauses to think, then realizes the game his captors are playing. His next response proves his guess to be correct, but it is too late. He

loses the game and is returned to the first room.

The island can be reached by way of **Edu-Ware Services, Inc.**, 22035 Burbank 223, Woodland Hills CA 91367.

Almost Heaven

Avalon Hill, a leader in the field of war games, has expanded into the software market with half a dozen products, including a fantasy trip through the kingdom of Golconda. *Lords of Karma* ($20.00 plus $2.00 p&h) is sold as a single cassette containing 48K TRS-80, 32K PET, and 32K Apple versions of the program. The object of the game is to get to Heaven with as many Karma points as possible. These points are gained through acts of kindness, such as giving money to beggars, and acts of bravery, such as killing a giant spider. The display is straight text. You use the standard type of two-word commands, with single-letter entry for movements.

The program is large, and contains a lot of different locations, varying from underground mazes to open forest. After loading the machine-language tape, there is a wait of several minutes on the Apple and PET versions while the "board" is being set up. If you want to take a break, you can save the whole program back to tape, or save just the data. The instructions contain all the information necessary for doing this. The design of the program does have one flaw. When the game ends, you can't just run it again since the data contains an end-of-game condition. Instead, you have to go through the whole loading procedure again.   The length of the game varies greatly between plays. One time, I was zapped to Heaven with only 11 Karma points. Another time, I was up to 270 points with no sign of salvation. After a while, I found myself avoiding anything that might increase my Karma and end the game before I had explored all the tricks and traps of Golconda. A typical portion of play might run like this. You find yourself in the central square of Golconda. Hitting "L" for "LOOK" you are told what can be seen in all directions. Picking up a coin from the ground, you move north, passing through a gate into a narrow valley. You meet a beggar and give him the coin. Your Karma goes up. Moving off the path into the woods, you encounter a ruffian with a young woman. While attempting to speak with him, he stabs you. You are reborn on a mountain top, and must descend to the world below since you don't have enough Karma to go to heaven. For further enlightenment, contact **The Avalon Hill Game Company**, 4517 Harford Road, Baltimore MD 21214.　　□

Fantasy Games - Part 2

David Lubar

Still dazed from my first massive dose of fantasy games, I returned to the dungeons in search of the ultimate program. The path was strange and, at times, deadly, but there are treasures out there.

In the Beginning

Scott Adams was one of the first people to put major Adventures games into small computers, producing a series that has almost a cult following. His Adventures are text-oriented and accept one- or two-word commands such as "GO NORTH," "INVENTORY," or "KILL DRAGON." Each game has a specific motivation, ranging from greed to survival. In *Adventureland*, for instance, the object is to collect thirteen treasures hidden in a land abundant with magic and peril. In *Mission Impossible Adventure*, you have to save a nuclear reactor from terrorist sabotage while coping with an automated security system that doesn't like intruders. The attraction of such games rests in the ingenuity of the puzzles and problems encountered. Adventures make you think. Adams does well here, though, as in all games of this sort, some solutions won't work because the programmer didn't consider them. In a finite machine, this will always be the case.

Even when a solution doesn't work, the program should give an appropriate response. This, more than anything else, makes the difference between fun and frustration. The game shouldn't accept only the correct solution and ignore anything else. To give an example, let's say you have to break a window, and the required solution is to throw a stone idol at it. Suppose one of the items you are carrying is a violin. You might try playing a high note to shatter the window. In a poor game, the command "PLAY VIOLIN" would bring a response such as "WHAT?" In a good game, the response would be "NOTHING HAPPENS." In an excellent game, the reply would be something like "SORRY, THE NOTES PRODUCED AREN'T HIGH ENOUGH TO SHATTER THE WINDOW." This series of Adventures lies somewhere between good and excellent as far as handling improvised solutions. Some commands draw special responses, others draw stock replies. Not bad for games requiring between 16K and 24K.

The series begins with *Adventureland*, which includes extensive hints and clues for beginners. The second game, *Pirate Adventure*, also contains helpful hints, but it is a bit more difficult. As you move up the line, the games become even more difficult and devious, reaching a point where no hints are given.

The games can be saved at any point, which is a good idea in view of their linear nature. You usually have to do a specific series of things to get to a particular point. Saving the game can save a lot of time if you get killed or lose an essential item.

Another highlight of these games is the inclusion of humor. Adams has spiced the Adventures with comic moments, somewhat easing the pain of the high fatality rate encountered during play. I would recommend *Adventureland* or *Pirate Adventure* for the beginner. Old pros will want the additional challenge of the later games, especially since some of them introduce time factors. In *The Count*, the player begins to get drowsy after a while, and faces the prospect of becoming an unwilling blood donor in his sleep. Anyone journeying through *Ghost Town* must worry about finding accomodations before the fall of night. And that's the least of his troubles.

The entire Adventure series is available for the Apple, TRS-80, and Sorcerer. Some of the earlier games are also available for the PET or CP/M systems. Prices start at $14.95 for a 16K TRS-80 or 32K Apple tape. Disks with three Adventures for 32K TRS-80 or 48K Apple are $39.95. Adventure games are available from **Sensational Software**, P.O. Box 789-M, Morristown, NJ 07960.

Picture This

Adventures with hi-res graphics are a specialty of **On-Line Systems**, 36575 Mudge Ranch Rd., Coarsegold, CA 93614, and they have three such games on the market. The programs will run on any Apple with 48K and one disk drive. *Mission Asteriod* ($19.95), labeled "Hi-Res Adventure Number 0," is designed as a beginner's game, though parts of it present a challenge to the pro. The object is to save the Earth from an approaching asteroid. You have to get a flight plan and other essential items, then fly to the asteroid, destroy it, and survive the destruction, all the while fighting against a time limit. The scenes are presented with excellent graphics in full color. When you pick up an object, it disappears from the picture. If you drop something, it appears in the picture. The text occupies the bottom four lines of the screen, but you can toggle to a full-text page and back using the return key. *Mission Asteroid* is recommended for beginning adventurers who want to enjoy the game without getting too frustrated.

Hi-Res Adventure Number 1, *Mystery Mansion* ($24.95), places you in a locked house with a group of people who are dropping like flies. One of the guests in the mansion is a killer. The murderer wants the hidden jewels, and he isn't about to let you stand in his way. In this game, the graphics are black-and-white line drawings, but still full of detail. *Mystery Mansion* makes a great party game, allowing a group to play pseudo-sleuth in the comfort of a living room. And it's nice to have other suggestions around when you come to the tricky parts.

The beauty and potential of this type of adventure is brought to a new high with *The Wizard and the Princess* ($32.95). I have mixed feelings about portions of it; nevertheless it was one of my favorites, and one of the most enjoyable games. It was also the most frustrating. While some players have been known to breeze through the game, others keep on running into trouble. **Advanced adventurers shouldn't miss this challenge.** You start in the town of Serenia, which borders the desert. The goal is to find and rescue an abducted princess. The first obstacle is finding the way across the desert. While the solution can be stumbled on through luck or careful thought, many people get hung up here. Once past the desert, there is a forest, an island, mountains, and a castle. Each major area contains a large collection of locations, giving the adventurer much ground to

covered wonders beyond your reach. The other problem is that once the game is solved, there is nothing left to do with it. Since it is linear, you will have encountered every obstacle and seen every location after a successful play. On the other hand, finding the solutions and conquering the obstacles is a pleasure. For all the frustration encountered, the program made me think, and provided hours of fun.

Shades of Gygax

Many programs are designed to let the computer take the role of Dungeon Master. *Wizardry* from **Siro-Tech Software**, 6 Main St., Ogdensburg, NY 13669, does this better than any program I have seen. Written in Apple Pascal by Robert Woodhead and Andrew Greenberg, it will be sold in a run-time version that will work on any 48K

can be resurrected, and a trading post. At the trading post, characters can be equipped with whatever weapons they can afford. Certain characters can't use certain weapons. For example, Priests cannot use edged weapons. From the Tavern, the characters go to the Camp, then into the dungeon. The dungeon is displayed with three-dimensional graphics in the upper left of the screen. You walk through using keys for moving and turning. There are secret doors that only appear at certain times, and plenty of monsters. During each round of combat, you can fight, parry, use a spell, or run. The status of each character is displayed during combat. If a character is killed, there are two ways to get him back. You can go to the temple and pay a fee, or you can go to the training grounds and reroll him. If the entire party is killed, the characters are lost.

The program is full of nice features. Each character is stored with a password, so only his creator can bring him into the game. There is an inn where characters can rest and recover from their wounds. During play, characters age, and their performance is affected.

A group of hard-core D&D players tested the game and liked it very much, with a few reservations. The monsters encountered were much stronger on the first level than those in most dungeons. Also, it was not apparent how the characteristics affected play beyond determining the nature of the character.

All in all, *Wizardry* is an excellent program, and the possibility of future scenarios makes it a good investment for anyone in need of a Dungeon Master.

From Dungeons to Oceans

Synergistic Software, 5221 120th Ave. S.E., Bellevue, WA 98006 has three fantasy disks available for the Apple. *Doom Cavern* ($20) represents an excellent concept that is, unfortunately, limited by its own ambitious scope. The 48K Integer Basic program takes three characters into the dungeons of Hammardoom. As the player moves through this dungeon, a map is drawn in hi-res, and encounters occur. Many of the encounters bring in new programs, thus limiting the space on the disk and allowing for only one dungeon level. So then, the game is challenging, but too short. Solving the first level doesn't take that long. At the end, the author hinted he would be creating future levels. If so, the game could be outstanding. As it is, despite its brevity, the play was highly enjoyable. On the same disk is *Sorcerer's Challenge* in which two wizards duel. This is a strategy game with fantasy trappings, the object being to surround your opponent with spells, preventing him from moving.

The second disk contains *Wilderness Campaign* and *Dungeon Adventure*. These programs are also available on tape. *Dungeon Adventure* is a nice lo-res romp

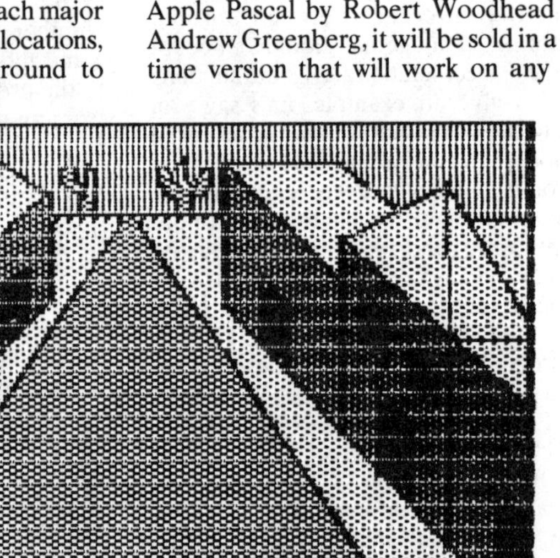

The Wizard and the Princess begins in the town of Serenia.

cover. Why did I say I had mixed feelings? On the good side are the graphics, the ingenuity of the program, and the internal logic in all the solutions. The bad side is tied in with the ingenuity. In a sense, this is a linear adventure. Without object A, you can't get object B. Without object B you can't get to a new location, and so on. If you get stuck at any point, you can't go on to new areas. True, that's part of the rules in this universe, but it can be frustrating, especially when you know there are undis-

Apple with DOS 3.3. The boot disk and initial scenario will cost $40; other scenarios will be available in the $20 to $30 range.

One or more can play, and each person can control several characters. Characters are produced at the training grounds, where characteristics are rolled. The character can be one of six types, including human, elf, and halfling. After the training grounds, the characters go to the Tavern. From here they have access to an inn where they can rest, a temple where dead members through four levels of dungeons, where the goal is to collect as much treasure as possible. Various beasts are encountered in these depths. The most dangerous are dragons that follow you and gulp down members of your party whenever they get hungry. *Wilderness Campaign* moves to a hi-res screen. Here, the goal is to gather enough troops to defeat the evil wizard. You wander the area, entering tombs and castles while encountering monsters and other hazards. There are towns where you can buy supplies and arms. The combat portion will interest those who enjoy role-playing games. On each round, the weapon value of the attacker and armor value of the defender is displayed, along with other points for special weapons, luck, and other factors. The problem with the combat is that the enemy is always reduced by half on each turn. This gets a bit tedious and predictable. The nice feature is that you control the "dice" using the spacebar. Despite the drawback in combat, the game is enjoyable, and each game is different.

Both programs come with Applesoft and Integer versions. *Wilderness Campaign* requires 48K for either tape ($17.50) or disk ($20). *Dungeon Adventure* requires 16K for tape ($15) and 32K for disk ($17.50). A 48K disk containing both programs costs $32.50.

Combat is much improved in *Odyssey, the Compleat Adventure*. The entire concept of the adventure is expanded into four separate programs. You start out on an island, attempting to acquire enough money for a ship, and enough men to man it. During your romp through this hi-res region, you'll encounter sealed tombs, abandoned castles, wandering soldiers, wizards, warlocks, monsters, and scads of hazards. Your actions will affect your alignment toward good or evil, and your alignment will affect the way others react to you. Wizards, for instance, will help those who are aligned with good and fight those aligned with evil. Warlocks behave in an opposite manner. This portion in itself is a fine game. But there is more.

Once you have a ship, you have to learn how to sail it, and venture to other islands in search of the orb. Changing winds, shifting currents, fog, and storms complicate matters for the adventurer at sea. A few unpleasant monsters have also been known to inhabit the deep. One of the islands contains an underground cave, thus bringing in another program. Some legends hold that the orb is beneath the ground. Others say it is in the sea. Those who know refuse to tell. After finding the orb, you must find the island of the evil usurper and defeat him. Here, some of the items previously found or purchased come into play. The initial portion takes the longest time, especially when you are new to the game and still struggling to survive this hostile land. Sailing also takes a fair amount of time; there are plenty of hazards to slow the adventurer or end his trip entirely. In comparison, the portion in the caves and on the last island are brief. Since the game ends by giving you your score, you have something to shoot for on the next run through. *Odyssey* is very good, highly enjoyable, and replayable. The 48K disk requires Integer Basic in ROM and costs $30. It is well worth the price.

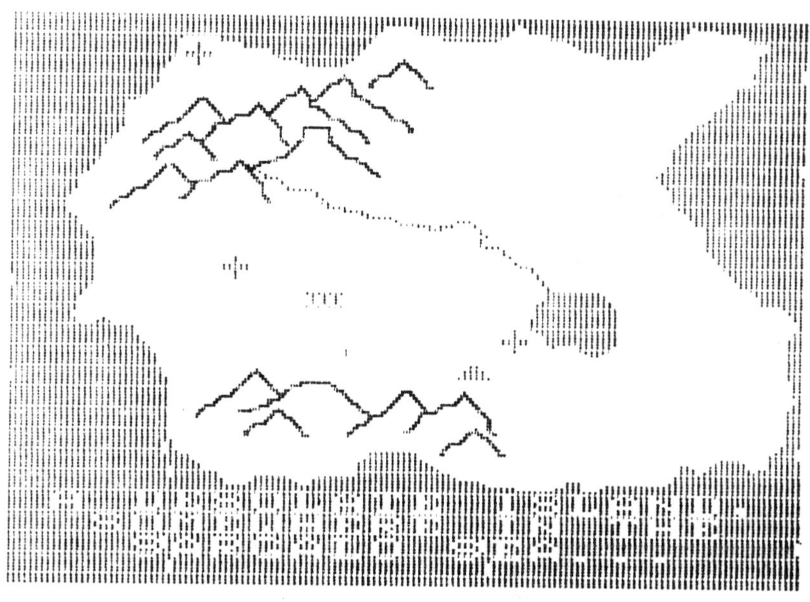

The first island encountered in *Odyssey.*

The Sargon Chronicle

Theodore H. Ehara

Creative Computing: How many hours do you put into Sargon?

Dan Spracklen: A DAY? (Chuckles) A lot!

Kathe Spracklen: Sixteen.

Dan Spracklen: Sometimes ten — sixteen hours.

Kathe Spracklen: He eats and sleeps.

Dan Spracklen: You know, it's something I like to do, so I do it a lot.

If you were standing in the tournament hall of the 9th Annual Tournament for the North American Com-

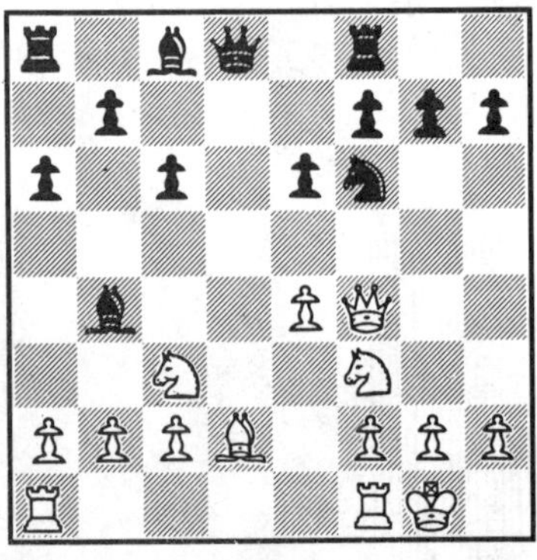

FIGURE 1

puter Chess Championship, you might have seen Dan Spracklen walking into the hall with a Jupiter computer in his arms. This electronic box would soon be loaded with a tough little chess-playing program known as Sargon II that was developed by Dan and his wife Kathe. However, if you had even a little knowledge of computer chess, you would realize that portable computers had a very poor chance against programs that were run on multi-

Theodore H. Ehara, 1004 Hinman Ave., Evanston, IL 60202.

million dollar machines. The speed of a larger computer gave it a distinct advantage in brute force (i.e., the ability to look ahead). Since a six-fold increase in speed gives the program an extra half move to look at, the more successful programs were always run on the fastest machines available.

Kathe (back to camera) and Dan Spracklen (far right) listen to David Cahlander (squatting) from Chess 4.9, as David Kittinger of Mychess waits for his program to move during the recent North American Computer Chess Championship. Sargon 2.5 is contained beneath the chess board and indicates its moves by LED lights on the board.

It was no laughing matter when Sargon II found itself matched against AWIT.

Perhaps an observer would have thought that Sargon would be better off playing in a microcomputer tournament, like the 1st San Jose Micro-Tournament, where computers were divided up into three classes (8K or greater memory, less than 8K and Basic programs). However, the four month old Sargon I program had won all of its five games to win that tournament. Now the Spracklens were looking for stronger competition.

They would find that competition at the North American Computer Chess Championship. While the San Jose tournament had computers ranging from $6,000 to a home-made

collection of circuits priced at $85, the 9th NACCC had the real big boys, computers priced in the millions, air-conditioned, bolted to the floor monsters that made moves by phone to terminals at the tournament site. Yes, the Spraklens had found strong competition for Sargon II.

Sargon — the name for an ancient king in Assyria.

"There were actually two Sargons," related Dan. "One was Sargon II. He was the king of Assyria, about 700 B.C. Sargon I was the king of Akkad, which was ancient Sumaria, about 2,000 B.C."

The name itself means 'Declared King' since Sargon I was not himself born king, but was crowned in adulthood," said Kathe.

"Of course we didn't know this, we knew that the name had ancient historical connotations, but we picked it because it sounded suave." She added with a laugh, "Then we had to go back and learn about it, since everybody kept asking us."

However, it was no laughing matter when Sargon II found itself

FIGURE 2

matched against AWIT. AWIT was running on an Amdahl 470 V6 computer that was located in the computer room at the University of Alberta. One of the "big boys." Some of the tournament spectators felt that this obvious mismatch would be quickly conceded to AWIT.

Three minutes to figure out the pitfall in the position or else Sargon II would lose the game by exceeding the time limit.

"The secret to the successful chess program," reflected Dan, "is putting this chess knowledge and combining it with brute force. You have to look ahead and you have to use knowledge while you're doing that. It's an integrated approach."

"A lot of people who are knowledge-based advocates," stated Kathe, "are, in some sense, against using a look-ahead. Whereas I feel that you might as well use a look-ahead, since it will refine anything you know. Why limit yourself arbitrarily?"

The difference between Sargon II and AWIT could be summed up in one word — staggering. The AWIT program was ten years old compared to Sargon's one. The Amdahl used a high-level language, ALGOL-W. The Wavemate Jupiter was using a primitive dialect of assembly language. Add in the difference in speed and memory capacity that a $5,000,000 computer would have against a $1,500 computer and you might understand why microcomputers could have a rough time in the NACCC.

Choosing a king's pawn opening, Sargon II found itself playing the Silician Defense. This particular opening chosen by AWIT was known for its sharp struggle since Polerio introduced it to the chess world in 1564. According to the Encyclopedia of Chess Openings, a standard reference among tournament players, AWIT could easily have equalized the position on the third move (3. ..., NQb3). AWIT did and the battle raged back and forth until the resulting end-game (see Table 1) was reached.

Although the winning technique might seem simple to a human chess player, computers were notorious for their sloppy end-game play. Basically, this was because of the difficulty in programming the concepts of the end-game, where different values are placed on pieces and positions. Furthermore, Sargon II had three minutes to make time-control. Three minutes to

Sargon II —	AWIT		
		33. N–B4+	K–N4
		34. N×R	B×P
1. P–K4	P–QB4	35. N×P	B×BP
2. P–Q4	P×P	36. N×P	B–N6
3. Q×P	N–QB3	37. N–B5	B–Q4
4. Q–K3	N–B3	38. P–KN3	B–B6
5. N–KB3	P–K3	39. N–N3	P–N5
6. N–B3	B–N5	40. N–Q4	B–K5
7. B–N5	P–QR3	41. P–B3	B–N2
8. B×N	QP×B	42. K–B2	P–R3
9. B–Q2	N–N5	43. K–K3	B–Q4
10. Q–B4	N–B3	44. N–B2	P–N6
11. 0–0	0–0 (See Fig. 1)	45. N–Q4	K–N3
12. QR–Q1	P–QN4	46. K–Q3	K–R2
13. B–K3	Q–R4	47. P–B4	K–N1
14. B–Q4	B×N	48. K–B3	K–N2
15. B×B	Q×P	49. N×P	B×N
16. B×N	P×B	50. K×B	K–B3
17. Q×P	Q–B5	51. K–B4	K–K2
18. Q–N5+	K–R1	52. P–QN4	K–Q2
19. Q–B6+	K–N1	53. K–Q5	P–R4
20. Q–N5+	K–R1	54. P–N5	K–B2
21. R–Q8	R×R	55. K–B5	K–N2
22. Q–B6+	K–N1	56. P–N6	K–N1
23. Q–N5+	K–B1	57. K–B6	K–B1
24. Q×R+	K–N2	58. P–N7+	K–N1
25. Q–N5+	K–B1	59. K–N6	P–R5
26. Q–Q8+	K–N2	60. P×P	P–B3
27. Q–Q4+	Q×Q	61. P–R5	P–B4 (See Fig. 2)
28. N×Q	B–N2	62. K–B6	K–R2
29. R–K1	K–N3	63. K–B7	K–R3
30. R–K3	R–Q1	64. P–N8=Q	K–R4
31. R–Q3	P–QB4	65. Q–N3	K–R3
32. N×KP	R×R	66. Q–R4 mate	

TABLE 1.

figure out the pitfall in the position or else Sargon II would lose the game by exceeding the time limit. Using half of its alloted time, Sargon II came up with the correct move and proceeded to win against AWIT.

Sargon II ended the tournament tied for third place. Although it was clearly beaten by the winner, BELLE from Bell Labs and runner-up, Chess 4.7 from Northwestern University, Sargon II could be considered the moral victor. It had proved, over the board, that hardware is not the only criteria needed to evaluate the performance of a chess program.

When asked later about their feelings on the Sargon II - AWIT game, Kathe replied, "It was kind of the high point in our lives." She laughed and continued, "It made the hard work worth it."

Although Dan and Kathe originally placed Sargon II at the 1500 level (Class C tournament strength) Sargon played five exhibition games under tournament conditions at the Paul Masson Open last July. The program ended its five games with a 3½ - 1½ result, giving it a provisional rating based on the games at 1640 (low Class B).

However, there has been a report of Sargon playing a Class A player who, according to rumor, played weaker than his rating. Perhaps this human was simply "psyched out" at the thought of playing a computer, or maybe he heard about what Sargon did to AWIT. □

Sargon I is available for TRS-80 (Level II) and Apple II computers in cassette form. If you'd rather program it yourself, you can buy **Sargon** written by Dan and Kathe Spracklen. Between moves, you might like to take a look at **Introduction to 8080 and Z-80 Assembly Language Programming** by Kathe Spracklen.

Sargon II is also available in cassette form for TRS-80 (Level II), Apple II and will soon be available for CP/M, SORCERER and Pet. Both books and tapes are available from Hayden Books.

If you don't have a computer (?) you can still play against Sargon II. Boris, a chess-playing processor made by Chafitz Inc., will be incorporating the Spracklen's programming into their newer models. Working along with Larry Atkin and David Slate, creators of Chess 5.0 — the current World Computer Chess Champion, the Spracklens are developing the recent models of Boris that will be sold this fall.

With the recruitment of the Spracklens to Chafitz's staff, the company has announced it plans to sign-up Boris for the next North American Computer Chess Championship.

Wars In Space

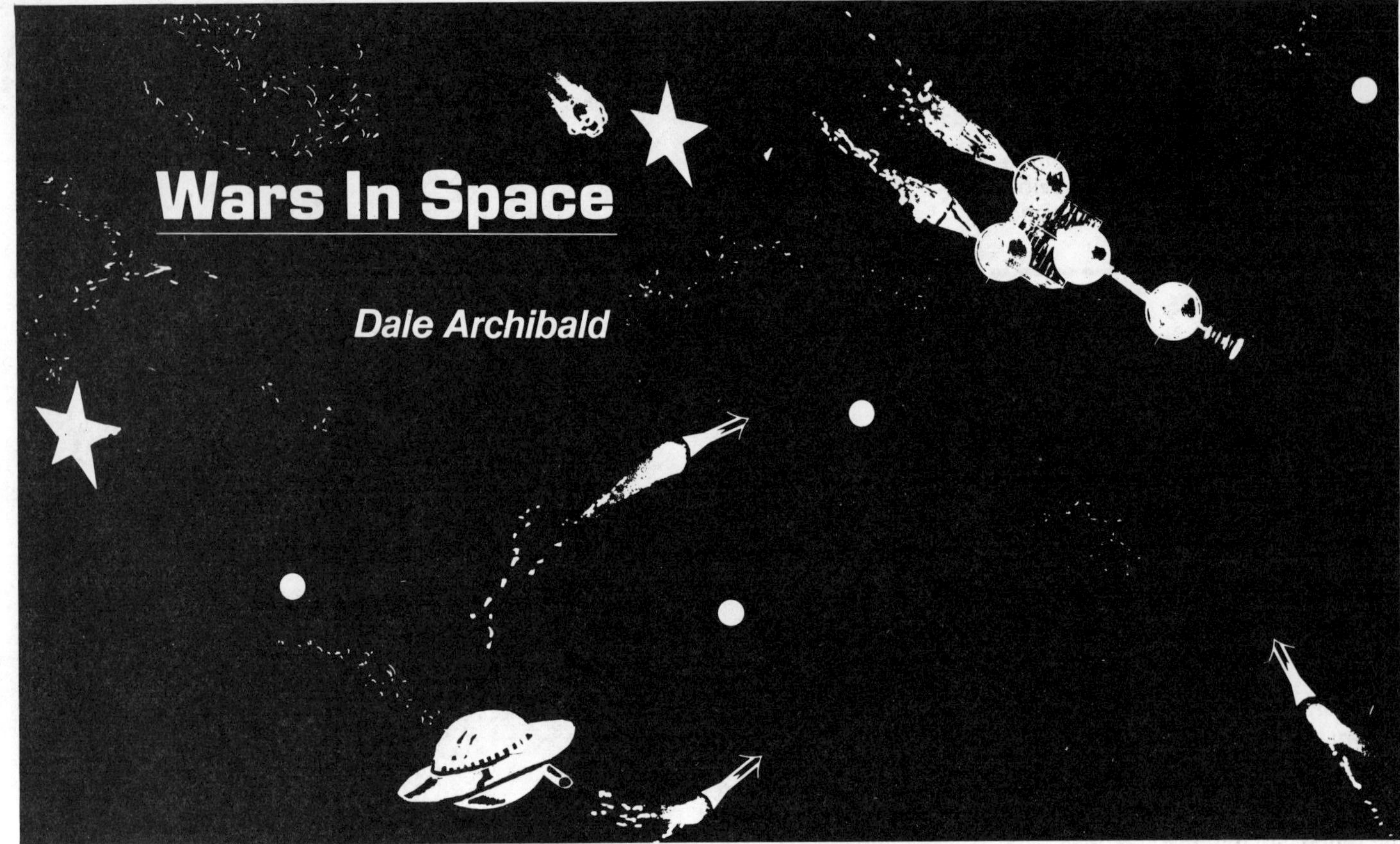

Dale Archibald

I enjoy space programs—and I don't mean N.A.S.A. or Buck Rogers. I admit part of the reason is that such flights of fancy feel so appropriate played on a home computer. Thus they're fun for several reasons, not the least of which is knowing such enjoyment would have been unavailable to me just five years ago.

Of course I'm referring to the games that use outer space as the background, from arcade shoot'em-ups to the new space strategy gems. Galaxy (P.O. Box 22072, San Diego, CA 92122) and Broderbund Software (Box 3266, Eugene, OR 97403) both offer good strategic space games.

I don't have a color monitor or TV set yet, even though most of the newer games for 48K Apple II Plus use high resolution color graphics. I'm sure I miss a lot of vibrancy, but most of the time color isn't essential.

I say most of the time, because in **Galaxy Space War 1**, if it isn't essential it sure is handy. Frank Tarkeny spent 11 months working on this game, and it was time well spent.

War 1 is a strategy game on disk for the 48K Apple II with Applesoft in ROM, or the Apple II Plus. It can be played solitaire, or by two people. It seems there is a war raging between opposing galaxies, the red and the green, each of which has a certain amount of energy and a certain number of building blocks with which to build a fleet.

Two modes of play are available. One mode allows total knowledge: that is, the

Dale Archibald, 1817 Third Ave. N., Minneapolis, MN 55405.

player can see all ships of both fleets, and their placement on the 17x33 sector grid.

More interesting is the "sensor knowledge" mode. Using this, the opposing craft aren't seen until—and here's where color is necessary—they're within sensor range. At that point, the four dots at the affected corners of the sector turn violet. So sensor knowledge allows the opponents to play blind until something blunders close. This is a fine example of what wargamers call "fog of war"; that is, in the confusion of combat, it isn't always possible to see and know everything that's happening on a battlefield. A computer is ideal for simulating this.

Play begins with shipbuilding. Ships are built by selecting the size, shape, and total energy. Each is designed according to individual taste, as long as the blocks—each filling a sector—touch one another. Each combatant can have a fleet of up to 26 ships, composed of from one to nine blocks, with between 100 and 999 energy units.

The instructions take up six pages and a summary sheet. They're a bit convoluted, but understandable after several readings.

For instance, the total energy a ship has is divided into quarters, each of which is allocated either to screen/detection or attack/move. Thus, if screens are set at 0 (zero per cent) detection is also set at 0, but the ship can move 4 sectors (doubled with hypermove) and/or attack with beams as far as 4 sectors away. If the screens are set at 4 (100 per cent), a ship can detect an enemy up to 4 sectors away, but can neither move nor attack.

If screen/detection is set at 1 (25 per cent), that leaves 3 sectors to move and/or attack. Each move costs attack energy points, one point for a one-sector move, two for a hypermove.

Screens can be changed at any time, but after that the ship can only attack until the end of that move. A ship with half its energy allocated to screen/detect could move up to 4 sectors (on hypermove), change its screen from 2 to 0, and attack up to 4 sectors away.

During an attack, the screen energy of the prey is first affected on a one-to-one basis; its attack energy is drained two units for every unit with which you attack. For example, if a defending ship has 100 energy units divided between screens and attack energy, you would expend 50 units to burst the screens and 25 to drain its attack energy.

Two other unusual features are the Plan Battle command and the Kill. Plan Battle gives the attacker a readout on the amount of power needed to destroy a defender with screens at the various settings. Kill lets a player clear the screen of the energy-drained husks of ships. There's also a Save Game feature.

When two players are battling each other, there are some shortcomings. First, whichever player is at the computer can attack without his opponent knowing which ship was hit until he returns to the keyboard. There is no defense except having screens on full. Then, too, a player can find out—by calling up the Galaxy summaries—how his fleet compares to the opponent's in terms of number of ships, blocks used, power, etc. (My opponent and I agreed not to look at that report or one another's ship reports.) The best strategy on the games I've played so far seems to be a very conservative one. That is, let your opponent use energy moving toward your galaxy. Then strike!

The Galactic Saga line put out by Broderbund is a whole new concept in games, different from any I've seen until now. They consist of **Galactic Empire, Galactic Trader,** and **Galactic Revolution.** The fourth, **Tawala's Last Redoubt,** is in the works. All programs are by Douglas G. Carlston, and they're very good. All are available for the TRS-80 Level II 16K on cassette, 32K disk, and on disk for the 48K Apple II Plus, or Apple II with Applesoft in ROM.

Your mission is to conquer and hold the 20 inhabited worlds of the system.

The story begins with you in command of Galactica's Imperial Forces. Your mission is to conquer and hold the 20 inhabited worlds of the system. Some worlds are primitive; others are equal in sophistication to Galactica, but many have larger or smaller populations; yet others may be technologically more advanced. You have 1,000 years to accomplish your mission.

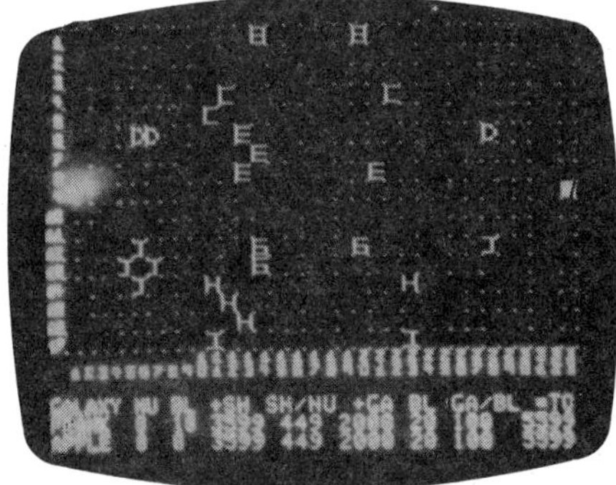

Galaxy War I

When you begin, you only have information about one planet: Galactica. You must order Lieutenant Starbuck to send out scouts to investigate the other planets and return. Their reports will bring your computer up-to-date on their status. (That can change over the years, remember.)

Computer Central will give you star maps of the local area and the galaxy, plus a rangefinder for the light years between two stars. If you'd rather have the planetary

directory, that will relate information about the planets from which probes have returned. Status reports tell you when and where probes will return, or when fighters, transports, or probes you've ordered are due to arrive, and where.

Besides Starbuck, other officers are Navigator Kirman, Lieutenant Bayliss (responsible for taxation, enlistments, and ordering ships), and Doctor Henderson (quick with a sleep needle).

The sound and graphics are good, albeit simple. The planets appear and disappear, star trails move toward you as your fleet travels through space. The battle scenes are simply readouts of the odds of winning.

The entire game is one of logistics. First conquer weak planets near Galactica, then tax them to build your forces back up. Primitive planets can only supply troops, while more advanced planets can supply ships as well. You're forced to shuttle back and forth between the occupied planets to collect taxes (once per visit), buy ships, and enlist troops. When you're ready, you go on to the next target, and, upon arrival, attack. Depending upon circumstances, you either win or retreat when the odds are bad.

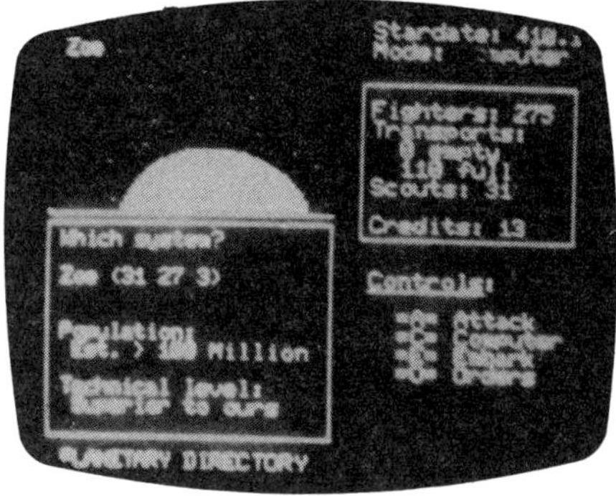

Galactic Empire

As you expand the empire, you can gather more taxes to build more ships. Time, however, is not always on your side. After all, the galaxy takes 60 years to cross and there are 19 planets to conquer.

Careful planning is the key to winning the game. Patience, too, is important. Each move deducts time from the 1,000 years you have. When you are not traveling or in suspended animation a year takes four minutes.)

The game runs quite a while. It's lucky there's a Save Game feature.

I wish there were a Save Game on **Galactic Trader** and **Galactic Revolution.** In **Galactic Trader,** the Emperor Tawala Mungo has removed you from your command. He has also, it is rumored, set assassins on your trail.

Computer Central has stayed true to you, as has your navigator, Kirman. Now you begin with a ship, 1,000 credits and 1,000 millits of fuel.

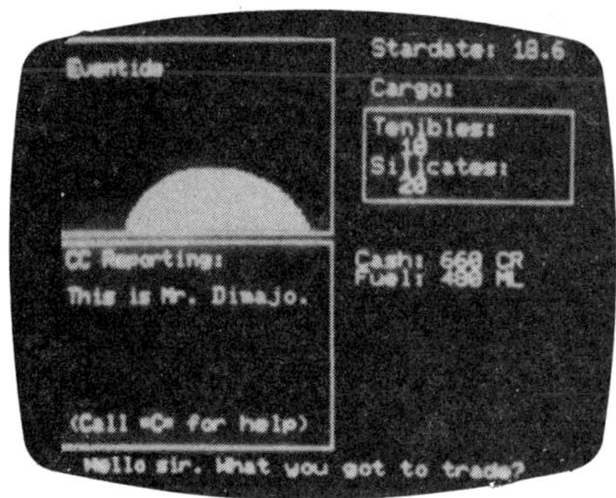

Galactic Trader

Unfortunately, you don't know where products originate, where they're most valuable, or the rates of barter (no trader will accept coin except on Galactica). By slow, cautious trading, you try to amass a fortune. Never retrace your steps, however, because if one of the trading companies discovers you've found a profitable route, it will steal it from you.

Every time you return to Galactica, by the way, the chances are better an assassin will earn blood money.

Computer Central will help you with star maps, trading records, and fuel use computations. You feed in the amount of cargo you have and where you want to go, and the computer shows how much fuel it will require. If you're forced to buy from the fuel cartel, however, you'll only get about half-price for your goods. You don't want to end up lost in space. You also don't want to make an error on a transaction with a trader. The results are very messy.

Last is **Galactic Revolution.** By the time this scenario begins, you've made your fortune. Tawala Mungo has pretty well hashed up the Empire you earned for him and now you feel the time is right to make your move. Unfortunately, despite his cruelty, he still has a great deal of support

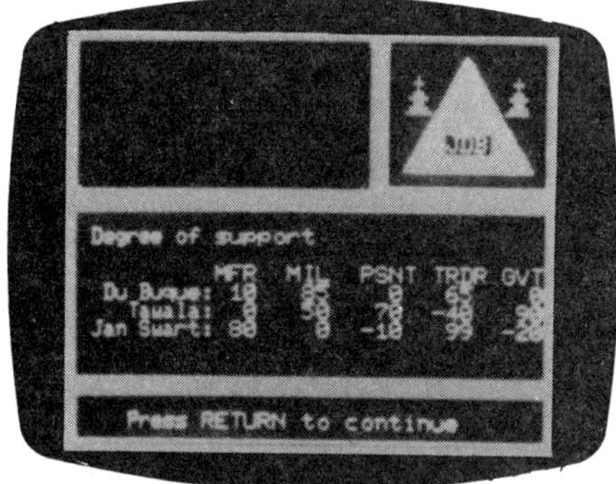

Galactic Revolution

from the peasantry, almost all the bureaucracy, and half the military.

In additon to Tawala, you are faced with the trader leader, Jan Swart. His constituency is strong among manufacturers and traders, but he is disliked by peasants and bureaucrats both.

Your only advantage is that no one hates you. You also have strong support from the military, and some from the traders.

Each of you is faced with the same problem: how to sway the public opinion on planets in your favor?

Every planet has five power groups: manufacturers, military, peasants, traders, and bureaucrats. In the solitaire game, there are no alliances. In the two and three player games, there can be alliances. There can also be blockades against planets to prevent taxation by an opponent if you make the wrong diplomatic moves, and force it away from your camp. In some cases, you might even want to declare war as a last resort.

When the game starts, there are seven independent planets, each with a different power structure. Each character also has a power base, with varying numbers of planets, troops, arms, and ships.

The key to winning a planet is administrative action. You may implement land reform or collectivize farm and factory; reduce or increase tariffs; institute univeral conscription or abolish the draft; or take any of four other actions. Each action will strengthen one or two groups and weaken others.

Tawala, for instance, might increase tariffs because it would weaken traders. He might lose some points among the peasants because imported goods would cost more, but it would increase his popularity among the manufacturers and give more strength to the bureaucracy that would be collecting the taxes.

DuBuque, the hero, might choose universal conscription on one planet because it would strengthen the military, which is strongly for him, and at the same time weaken both the peasantry and the traders (they're fine pilots).

This is a great wheeler-dealer game, with enough twists and turns to delight Machiavelli. The witty instruction book outlines strategies such as the Straw Man Maneuver, e.g. taking administrative actions to throw a planet to a very weak opponent, then declaring war against it. Win the planet back, change the administrative actions back—you're more popular than ever, and have "new credentials as a war hero."

How do you win? As Gary Carlston writes in the manual, "Well, you win if you get control of all 18 worlds. You'll even get a score, based on the amount of time it took you to take control and the resources you preserved at the end. No bells and whistles though. Winning isn't everything." If only it would Save Game. □

"No, I wish I had an Apple. Mine's a lemon."

The Warp Factor

David Lubar

This Alliance cruiser needed two successive MS (move ship) commands to describe this S-curve. The first MS command turns the ship to bearing 90° for 5 time units. The second command alters course to 0° for six time units. At least one more MS commands would be required to complete the remaining 5 time units of the turn.

creative computing
SOFTWARE PROFILE

Name: The Warp Factor

Type: Space Fight Simulation

System: 48K Apple with Rom Applesoft, Disk Drive

Format: Disk

Language: Applesoft

Summary: Excellent strategy game

Price: $39.95

Manufacturer: Strategic Simulations
465 Fairchild Drive
Suite 108
Mountain View, CA
94043

The early programs from **Strategic Simulations** had a reputation for a long lag time between turns. In complex situations, there could be waits of half an hour or more while combat results were produced. Thus, when *The Warp Factor* arrived for review, I was hesitant to look at it myself. I just couldn't envision spending hours in space fights that didn't take place in real time. Luckily, I did take a look at the game. *Warp Factor* is great. Those of you who liked playing Star Trek, but got bored with the simplicity and redundancy of the game, have a new addiction in store.

Warp Factor places you in command of a starship or fleet of ships. You can be part of any of six interstellar nationalities; Alliance, Reman Marauder, Imperial Pirate, Klargon Empire, Independent Starbase or Freeman. Different nations have different ships at their command. Each ship has a specific type of armament and shields, as well as a different turning rate, acceleration, and mass. This is no simple aim-and-shoot simulation. The ship must be commanded with skill and intelligence, integrating all features and capabilities of the vessel into each decision.

Play proceeds in phases. After choosing a scenario, and getting your ship or ships, you go through a series of commands. Let's assume you are controlling an Alliance Heavy Cruiser. The first command, after checking the status of the ship is Set Display. The display can be centered either on the ship or at galactic coordinate 0,0. The view can be in any of eleven magnifications from a close-up minus 5 to a wide-angle plus 5. Once you see the location of the enemy, you can make battle plans. Energy is allocated to shields, weapons, transporters, electronic counter measures, and electronic counter counter measures. Certain weapons have to be charged for several turns before they can be fired. Each ship has six shields, which can be individually reinforced. During energy allocation, you also choose the speed of the ship for that turn.

The next key area is the Fire Weapons command. In this segment, you choose which weapons to fire in up to three separate salvos. For example, the Alliance Heavy Cruiser can fire three phasers and two torpedoes during the first salvo. Then it can fire its remaining phasers and torpedoes at a different target during the second salvo, and fire nothing during the third. For each salvo, you have a choice of firing according to range, time, or last moment. This is where skill truly enters the game. Let's say you are close to an enemy ship. You might have already completed a portion of your movement phase (more on that later) and noticed that you fly past the ship on time segment eight. Using the specific-time option of the Fire Weapons command, you could choose to fire all rear-facing weapons at time-segment eight. Most weapons have a limited field of aim, and it does no good to fire a weapon forward if the target ship is behind you. Some weapons hit (or miss) their targets in the turn they are fired, others, such as drones and plasma torpedoes, might travel for more than one turn before reaching their target.

The final crucial command area is Move Ship. Here, you can specify direction of movement for up to sixteen time segments. After any move, the position of the ship is replotted. You can move a part of the distance, see where you end up, then go to the Fire Weapons command. Your turn is over after the last move segment has been entered.

Then comes your opponent's turn. If you are playing another human, he will go through the same command series. If you are playing against the computer, it will take a minute or so to enter commands.

Next come the results. The computer will think about things for a minute or so. If there is combat, it will inform you and ask you to hit return. This is nice since it allows you to leave the room and not miss anything. Combat results are reported as text, and there might be a wait of several more minutes between segments of the report. But the wait never seemed unduly long.

I first tried the game with one ship against a computer ship. Next, to see how much longer the wait became, I played with four ships against four on the computer. Surprisingly, the wait didn't increase much.

There are five scenarios available, four of which are for one player. Most scenarios allow a choice of ships, thus greatly expanding play possibilities. Along with the disk, you also get a thirteen-page instruction manual, and a set of sheets illustrating and describing the available ships.

Warp Factor is excellent. A lot of thought, strategy, and planning is required if you want any chance to beat the computer. The control over the ship, and the many facets of navigation and combat, make the game extremely challenging. If you have a bit of patience and don't mind waiting a few minutes for results, and if you want to take part in a contest requiring plenty of thought and skill, *Warp Factor* is definitely worth buying. □

Through Space And Turf on the Apple II Plus

David Lubar

Generally, it's nice to have a theme behind software reviews. In this case, there were some good games sitting around which really couldn't be tied together. Rather than wait for more games to come in, it seemed best to flaunt form and style by doing a themeless review. So, let the games begin.

Tuesday Night Football is a well-constructed game designed for one player. TNF (as its creator, Charles Anderson, calls it) contains several programs, including one for kicking practice. The human player has to do his own punting and make his own field goals. These feats are accomplished on a nicely-designed low-resolution field. The kicked ball rises up, wobbles against air currents, then drops down field. A bit of skill is required to get a decent kick.

During the game, the player has a choice of many different offense or defense moves. The field is displayed as a grid on the text screen, populated with X's and O's. Don't let the lack of animation hold you back. Mr. Anderson, having the option of designing an animated, paddle-controlled, limited game or a strategic contest, wisely chose the second option. This is a thinker's game, demanding strategy and skill.

Each play is given with color commentary. A scoreboard, first down marker, and ball marker are displayed during play. The game is rich in detail and variety. There are injuries, penalties, and fumbles. The player has to react quickly to recover a fumble. There is also a marker on the scoreboard that indicates which team has momentum.

The documentation is great. It is written in a pleasant, humorous style, not cranked out by someone in love with jargon. Instructions are included for changing the DATA statements so any two teams, real or imaginary, can play. ("Kirk hands off to Plato who is tackled by Capote and Mailer."

TNF is too rich in detail to be fully described here. If you like football, give it a try. TNF comes on cassette for $13.95 and on disk for $17.95. If you order directly from ShoeString Software (1235 Candlelight, Houston TX 77018) there is an additional charge of $1 for postage and handling. The game requires Applesoft in any flavor and 26K of free memory.

After a hard game of football, you can command another team in *A Stellar Trek* from Rainbow Computing. The program boldly goes where no Trek has gone before, allowing an incredible number of options. The game is thorough and challenging. A high-resolution display, mixing graphics and text, depicts the Enterprise and other vessels in full color. Animation is used whenever the ship moves or fires a weapon. The numerous commands are explained in 22 pages of instructions. Among the commands are options which allow the player to beam down a crew and mine dilithium crystals. How's that for detail?

At the opening of the game, you get to choose the names of the crew members. Trek aficianados can stick to the correct nomenclature; deviants can be as sacrilegious as they want. The names are saved on the disk for use in later games. There is a choice of game length, skill level, and regular or tournament play. Tournament play allows several persons to play, one at a time, against the same setup. In this mode, identical actions will produce identical results.

At any point, a game in progress can be saved. While Rainbow suggests that the other side of the disk can be used to save the game, this is not a good idea. Considering the minimal cost of disk space, and the chance of losing data by using both sides, it's better to splurge and save the game on a different disk.

That's it for the reviews. Perhaps there is a theme after all; both games are the result of hours of work, careful programming, and nice touches. ☐

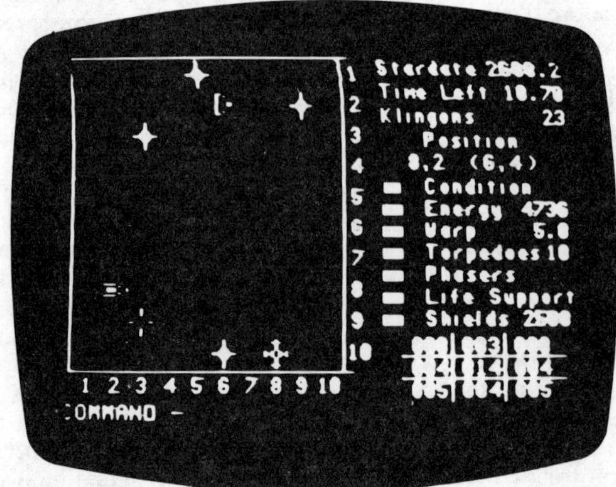

The Enterprise (lower left) prepares to take on a Klingon vessel at the top of the screen.

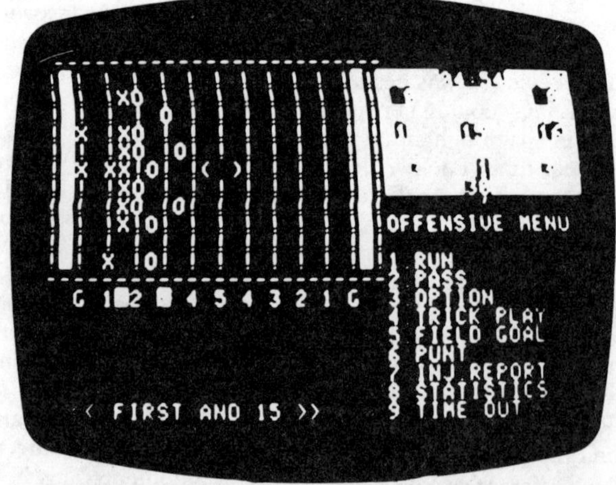

A delay-of-game penalty put the offense in trouble in this scene from TNF.

Three Mile Island

I am sure by now nearly everyone has heard aout what happened at the Three Mile Island nuclear power plant. I am especially familiar with the details of what transpired. I have been at TMI nearly full time since the accident, helping on the recovery effort.

After many weeks away from my family, home, friends and my Apple, I arrived home recently to discover a copy of MUSE NEWS, a publicity blurb from the MUSE Company, among my giant pile of unopened mail. Right across the top was a stylized drawing of the place from which I had just returned, and the frequently heard question, "Could it have been prevented?"

It was an announcement for a new program from MUSE for the Apple-II. The program was described as a realistic simulation of a pressurized nuclear reactor. This got me excited, because this was one of the ideas on my "later list." You know what I mean; program ideas to work on "later," when you have the time to do it. Somehow, "later" is a long time in arriving. Oh, well...

Needless to say, I placed an order for the program. I was really surprised at the size of the package when it arrived. It was big enough to hold 10 copies of the Apple DOS manual. When I opened the box, the surprise gave way to admiration. Inside was a diskette, a 36 page instruction booklet, and hundreds of foam excelsior "peanuts." MUSE Company, I am impressed by your care in seeing that the disk arrived undamaged.

The program is truly massive in size. It needs a full 48K system, and uses practically all the available memory. A ticking clock is provided, and the simulation proceeds at one minute intervals of sim-time, which occur in about 4 seconds of real time.

When you run the program, you become the operator at the controls of a nuclear power plant. The object is to run the plant in a safe and profitable manner. Naturally, there

Victor R. Fricke, 325 Ramapo Valley Road, Mahwah, NJ 07430

are hindrances and aids to this objective.

One thing that makes it difficult is that the demand for electricity varies over a wide range on a daily cycle. This forces you to change the operational status of equipment and to open and close valves. You also have to change the temperature of the reactor core by moving control rods.

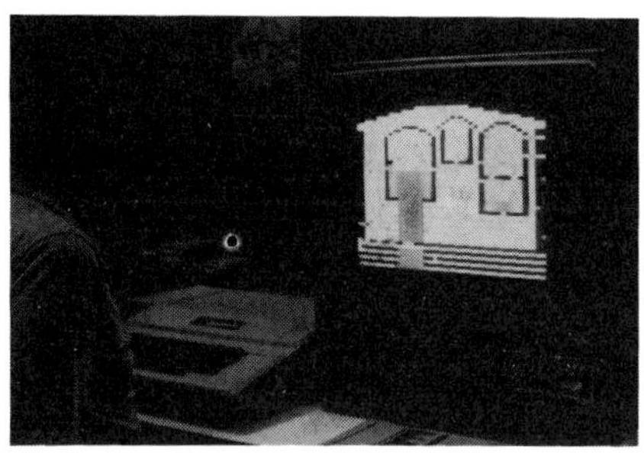

Another problem is that equipment fails frequently. Consequently, you have to change equipment status to deal with this, too. Valves fail as is; that is, a valve cannot be closed if it fails when it is open, and vice versa.

Another hindrance to successful operation is that the gnomes in Washington at the Nuclear Regulatory Commission are continually issuing safety bulletins. These bulletins tell you that their computer simulations indicate your gauges may be faulty and request you submit them for inspection. If you comply, the gauges are unavailable for a length of time, and you have to "fly it blind."

The aids you have in operating the plant are excellent. They include four graphical views of portions of the plant, an instrument panel, a financial summary and an equipment status and failure log.

Victor Fricke

The animation in each of the four graphic views of the plant is excellent. An open valve is represented by a green square, closed is red and out of service is black. Similarly for pumps, a red rectangle represents an idle pump, and green means running. This is the same color convention used on status panels in a real power plant.

When fluid is flowing in pipes, they are shown in appropriate colors; blue for cooling water, yellow for steam, pink for radioactive gas, etc. When there is no flow in the pipe, it changes to grey.

The way you start or stop a piece of equipment is to first call up the graphic display in which it is shown. Then, for example, if you want to close a valve, you press cntl-v, and a display of valve ID tags is shown beneath each valve. Just press the letter which identifies the appropriate valve, and it will flip from open to closed. A similar routine is used for other equipment; cntl-t for turbines, cntl-f for filters, etc.

Another aid is the instrument panel. On it are ten instruments which show the operating parameters of the plant, and several annunciators which warn of trouble.

The equipment status and failure log shows the operational status of each pump, valve, turbine and filter in the plant, and a prediction of when it will fail. Also, for equipment which is out for repairs, it shows when it will become available again.

The financial summary shows the electric output of the plant, the electric demand, and the profits and operating costs up to the present. If the profits become sufficiently negative, you are allowed to petition the Public Utilities Commission for a rate increase. If the losses are too great, your operating license is terminated for fiscal irresponsibility. When you petition for a rate increase, it is only granted 5% of the time.

As a simulation, Three Mile Island is excellent. As a game it is fascinating to me. Of course, what interests a nuclear engineer may not interest everybody. I am disturbed, however, by the model of plant systems chosen by the author. This game will probably leave a very false impression that it is a touchy thing to be able to operate a nuclear power plant safely.

For example, when experimenting with the program, I found that if the pressure inside containment rises to the point where the contain-ment is automatically sealed, then it becomes impossible to prevent a meltdown. When the program isolates the containment, it does so by closing all the valves. In practice, some of the valves remain open in a real plant. The steam and feedwater flow is not interrupted, because then there is no way to use the steam generator to remove the heat from the reactor.

Another example of departure from reality: the containment isolation in the game occurs at 5000 pounds per square inch pressure. In a real plant it occurs at 3 or 4 psi. There is no way the pressure could ever rise to such a high level. The highest pressure expected in a postulated accident is only 40 to 70 psi, depending on containment volume.

Indeed, the laws of thermodynamics are not followed in this game, since the 5000 psi cloud of steam is supposed to come from the 2400 psi pressurizer when its relief valve opens.

The game also gives the impression that there is only one emergency core cooling system, when in an actual plant there are usually at least three separate systems.

However, those criticisms do not detract from Three Mile Island as a game. As such, it is fascinating and fun to play. Indeed, if reality were modeled, it would be very boring. In routine operaton of nuclear power plants absolutely nothing changes for weeks on end; a computer gamester would soon tire of it and return to Startrek or Hunt The Wumpus.

□

ABM

Inciting the Cuss Factor

Dale Archibald

Dadblast it. There I was, solemnly dedicating my day to hard work writing, and the mailman innocently dropped a bomb in my hands. Bah!

The product announcement proclaimed, "Invader and Asteroids move over...ABM has arrived!" So it has. From Muse, 347N. Charles St., Baltimore, MD 21201. It sells for $24.95 on disk, and requires 32K, Applesoft ROM.

Your goal is to protect the cities of the eastern seaboard from Boston to Richmond against guided missile attacks that stream in from the top of the screen.

You see a green vapor trail begin, if you have color. Control the crosshairs with the game paddles (or I imagine a joystick would be better), and launch either 1- or 5-kiloton anti-ballisic missiles. But you must lead the correct distance: if you miss, the missile streaks on in to explode with a roar and hi-res color graphics.

Some incoming missiles are multiple warhead jobs. That is, they reach a certain

point and split into five or six; then those may split into five or six; then those may split yet again. At first, the game is fairly easy. The farther into it you get, however, the more missiles rain down on you.

My 0 paddle is rather worn from playing invader and asteroid games and "Computer Quarterback," so I wasn't able to cover the entire visible screen.

The beginning instructions allow you to calibrate your paddles, but it didn't work on mine. That is, the program didn't adjust for the lack of resistance in the paddle. It did allow me to select the direction in which I wanted to use the two paddles. I ended up with the 0 paddle controlling up and down movement while the 1 controls horizontal moves.

I chose to put the untouchable section at the top of the screen: I can't fire when I first see the missile, after all. I have to wait until I can lead it properly.

Sometimes a fireball will spread to stop other incoming warheads (or your ABMs). I've found the best strategy is to just keep protecting everything as long as possible. When the bombardment gets too heavy, focus on one area and try to protect that until the final explosion goes off.

The game even keeps track of the highest score achieved, lest you stop striving for self-improvement!

This is another arcade game suitable for Archibald's Law: The more you cuss it, the better it is. This monster's *highly* cussable.

Dale Archibald, 1817 Third Ave. N., Minneapolis, MN 55405.

Soft Centered

David Lubar

Battles in space and on Earth seem to be strong categories in the new software releases. This is a continuation of the computer-as-arcade-machine style, and I have to admit a fondness for it. No matter what other uses there are for computers, games will always represent a major portion of the new software. One such game is

> **A clever, logical solution to a problem might not work because the programmer never thought of it.**

covered below. Another popular area is adventure-type games. The original concept has spawned several programs that, while bearing a kinship to Adventure, are only distant cousins. One will be discussed below.

Winging it

Dogfight ($29.95), from **Micro Lab**, 811 Stonegate, Highland Park, IL 60035 has several game variations on one Apple disk. This 32K machine-language program puts you in control of a jet plane flying against enemy jets and helicopters. At the start, you have the option of using keys, paddles, or one or two joysticks for control. Next, you can select from six modes. The single-

player option allows you to play by yourself. With two players, you can play as partners or play as opponents. There are also two demo modes (one without sound) and a mode that lets up to eight players fly in competition. The game starts at level one. The player faces a single jet or helicopter. The enemy craft flies a random pattern, firing bullets. You must evade these bullets while making your own attack. A shot fired from a distance is less likely to down the enemy. Generally, you have to get rather close to the target. If you hit it, it explodes. Sometimes, the pilot will parachute from the plane. If you don't shoot him, he gets another plane and continues to fly. If you are hit, you have a chance to jump. Once the plane or helicopter is

destroyed, you move to the next level. Each level either adds another craft or increases the speed at which the crafts fly and shoot. As mentioned in their ads, Micro Lab will award special certificates to the first ten persons who score 10,000 points. It might be some time before those certificates are claimed.

Dogfight is a good game. The helicopter is one of the nicest pieces of graphics programming I have seen. Two things should be mentioned. The disk will only boot if the drive controller card is in slot six. Also, when the game comes up, you'll see some extra text on the screen along with the title. There is nothing wrong with your Apple, those random-seeming letters are supposed to be there.

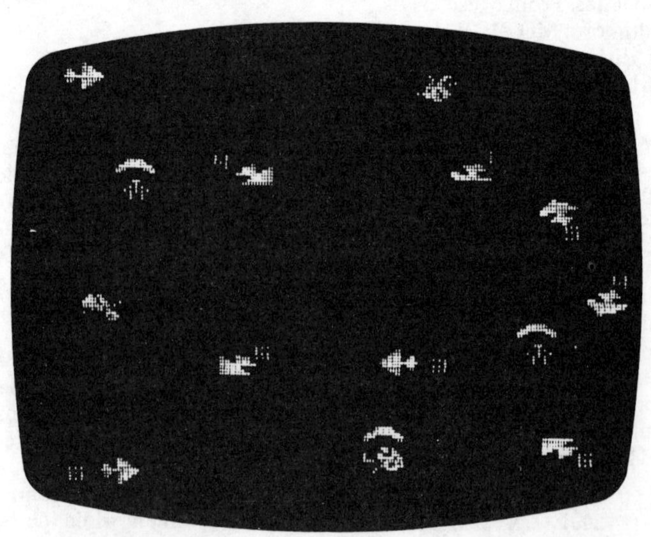

Interactive Literature   *Ted Nelson*

Bob Lafore's *Interactive Fiction* is a new genre he's invented. And it's great.

Unlike standard Adventure games, obsessed with knapsacks and secretive about the commands that make them work, *Interactive Fiction* is an adventure in a literary setting—a narrated story in which you are a character. Your chances for action consist mainly in deciding what to say when asked, but these interactive stories are generally vivacious and exciting. They are also excellent for parties, and for computer beginners and literati who do not find conventional Adventure games attractive. (And speaking as a jaded vetern, these were the most fun I've had with computers in a long time.)

Essentially *Interactive Fiction* is a Dialogue Adventure, a combination of Adventure and Eliza—since the programs behind the stories must parse your replies and branch appropriately.

Each story begins with a longish introduction—over-long, perhaps—but gets you wide awake with something like, "And we hope you are ready to become a fictional character." This really grabs you (—especially if, like most of us, you sometimes suspect you *are* a fictional character.)

Then the story begins—excruciatingly stylized, a combination of mood, whimsy and nostalgia—and soon you have your first chance to reply.

Each time you reply, it's a temptation just to go for keywords—but if you have any love of story-telling, you're more likely to reply in full sentences, befitting your station as a character.

The dialogue format, it must be ad-

Essentially Interactive Fiction is a Dialogue Adventure.

---

mitted, is sometimes awkward; but it's a nice prompt. (And the whirring disk, the first part of the computer's response, creates a nice conversational tempo.)

And what you say has consequences. You live or die, find the murderer or not, achieve fame or disgrace. And all in the framework of delightful story-telling and purple prosody:

"...As you raise the head droplets of coffee in Rodney's beard glisten in the light from the dirty window."

Lafore has thought through his format beautifully. By careful stacking of the stories, he gives you neat choices of action, but not so many as to make the story unwieldy. (The respones that lurk ready to pounce on *your* utterances are often choice.) Sometimes he will surprise you by speaking for you; sometimes he lets you off the hook, as in "Two Sides of the Coin," where you can ask your Dr. Watson to take over if your own initiatives don't work.

For a Swarthmore alumnus, Lafore unfortunately slips us a surprising number of misspellings—I noted "governement," "trolly," "reasonalby," "imaginitive," and the arresting "douchess." He is also not consistent in the spelling of the characters' names. But no matter.

Bob Lafore is obviously a talented writer with a nice command of atmosphere, fictional action and structure; not content to be merely a swell teller of conventional tales, we can be glad he favors us with an entire new system of interactive writing.

Never mind the swords and sacks of souvenirs; I'd rather curl up with a good interactive story.   □

You are There

Interactive Fiction. The phrase does a good job of describing the product. These programs by Robert LaFore, on disk for a TRS-80, are stories where the player has a chance to take part in the development of the plot. This is done through dialogue. Throughout each story, the player has a chance to put words in the mouth of a character. The choice of words affects the outcome of the story. This approach has several ramifications. As with all interactive programs, you can succeed only with solutions that have been anticipated by the author. In other words, you are working within a well-defined universe. Part of the fun is in discovering the laws of this universe. Part of the frustration is in being unable to transcend these laws. A clever, logical solution to a problem might not work because the programmer never thought of it. Another important feature of these games is that you only get out of them what you put in. A user can approach *Interactive Fiction* as a contest between him and the computer, where the goal is to find the vocabulary and overcome the program. For instance, in *Interactive Fiction* you can enter sentences consisting not of real dialogue but of a string of potential keywords. This approach might reveal the design of the program, but it kills all the fun.

The early disks were structured in such a way that the drive was accessed fairly often. The programs vary in interest and quality. *Six Micro Stories* ($14.95) is one of the best. The player takes part in short stories, each with many outcomes. In one, you are a spy attending a German party during World War II. Another story involves a meeting with a young women in a park. The novel *Two Heads of the Coin* ($19,95) is a Holmes-and-Watson type affair. Billed as one of the more difficult programs to solve, it is clever, but not that tough. Again, the main thing is getting into the spirit of the program. Even after you've solved the story, you can go back and look at other branches.

The most recent release, *His Majesties Ship Impetuous*, takes a slightly different approach. There are fewer interruptions for disk access and the story is more linear, ing on decisions made earlier. As the captain of the Impetuous, you have many choices to make, each of which could come back to haunt you later. Whether you end in fame or infamy, you can always take another run through the game. This raises another interesting point. Since there is a goal (namely, ending in fame and glory), players might be discouraged from exploring all the avenues since many are obviously losers. But what seems obvious might not be correct. Besides being fun as games, these programs are a good way to show off your computer the next time someone asks, "What do you do with that thing?"

Computer Bismarck

Randy Heuer

It is difficult to determine just what features make a computer simulation enjoyable. Using very vague terms, a computer simulation should be challenging but not impossible, and of course should be something that would ordinarily be difficult to do without the aid of the computer.

Perhaps one of the first "good" computer simulations was the classic "Star Trek" game. The commander of the *Enterprise* was faced with two separate challenges in each game. One was the strategic problem of the overall destruction of the entire Klingon fleet in a given amount of time. The other was the tactical challenge of handling the combat situation in each quadrant.

Admittedly, most "Star Trek" type games are generally not difficult to win after several sessions, but the length of time "Star Trek" has endured attests to its popularity. Some more recent good computer simulations that come to mind — although not all conflict simulations — are *Galactic Empire* (Softside), *Three Mile Island* (Muse) and *Air Traffic Controller* (Creative Computing). All of these simulations feature an overall problem that is overcome by solving many small problems. It is this two-step thought process that makes these games interesting.

Now there is a new simulation on the market which again confronts the player with an overall problem that can only be solved through the solution of many small problems. *Computer Bismarck* is perhaps one of the most complex home computer simulations produced to date. Its level of complexity may be too much for some; however, for those who find most computer games dull after a few sessions, *Computer Bismarck* may provide the challenge they've been seeking.

The Historical Perspective

For those not familiar with World War II naval history, I'll briefly outline the situation that *Computer Bismarck* attempts to simulate.

At the beginning of the war, the German battleship *Bismarck* was probably the finest battleship afloat. Although the British possessed a greater number of capital ships, none of her battleships could match the *Bismarck*.

In late May 1941, the *Bismarck* and the cruiser *Prinz Eugen* left port from Bergen, Norway. Their mission: to intercept Allied merchant convoys supplying England with vital war supplies. The U-boats had already deeply hurt the British war effort, and these immensely powerful German surface ships loose in the Atlantic could completely disrupt this tenuous link.

The next few days would prove to be fateful for both sides. In the first engagement between the German duo and the British battleships *Hood* and *Prince of Wales,* an early salvo from the *Bismarck*

The diversification of the German player's possible strategy also makes it difficult to determine whether the computer is really playing a good game or randomly wandering about the map.

penetrated the *Hood's* deck, exploding the ship's main ammunition magazine. In a matter of seconds, the *Hood* sank and over 1400 men died. The *Bismarck* then escaped the shadowing British cruisers.

However, fate soon turned against the *Bismarck:* a lucky hit from a British Swordfish torpedo plane disabled the *Bismarck's* steering while she was steaming toward France. With the *Bismarck* practically helpless, the British engaged the German ship with a sizable force of ships, and after a few hours the *Bismarck* went down with over 2200 men.

The Simulation

So much for what really happened. The computer simulation, though, lets us explore the many things that *might* have happened. In *Computer Bismarck,* players take the role of the commander of either the British or German fleets. Or a lone player may command the British fleet while the computer controls the German forces.

Two versions of the program are presently available. The one reviewed here is the 48K Apple version (for ROM Applesoft). This package requires a disk drive and retails for $59.95. (A less sophisticated cassette version for a 16K TRS-80 is also available, but since I have not seen it I cannot say what the similarities and differences are from the Apple version. The TRS-80 version sells for $49.95.)

The Apple version comes packaged in a rather oversized box about the size of many of those "bookcase" games from Avalon Hill and others. Rattling around inside are an instruction booklet, two sets of playing charts, a pair of very nice maps laminated in plastic, two grease pencils and the diskette. The multi-colored maps are coated with plastic so players may make notations on the maps with the grease pencils and then later erase them.

The rules are long and fairly complex; however, it is important that the players become totally familiar with the rules before attempting to play *Computer Bismarck.* I know that many people reach right for the diskette after buying a software package, but this is one of those games where not having a very clear understanding of the rules and their implications will be disastrous. In fact, I think I can safely say that most people will find this simulation impossible to play without reading the rules and having them nearby the first few games. The separate playing charts are also very helpful; indeed, unless you memorize all the necessary values, it's imperative that these also be on hand while playing the game.

For those people unfamiliar with conflict simulations (such as any of several published in board-game form by companies such as Avalon Hill, Simulation Publications, etc.), a grid is placed over a map of the field of play to facilitate movement. In *Computer Bismarck* a 20 x 18 grid is superimposed on a map of the North Atlantic. Each of the ships and planes involved is assigned a series of numerical ratings to represent characteristics such as speed, endurance, firepower, ability to absorb damage, detectability and search capabilities. On a given turn, a player may usually move any or all of his units up to their movement limits. Thus the simulation is much more dynamic (and realistic) than games such as chess. Another feature unique to conflict simulations is that the element of chance may effect the outcome of a particular battle, although the player with superior forces will usually win. But nothing is guaranteed.

Perhaps the most unusual feature of *Computer Bismarck* is the fact that neither side is aware of the location of the other's forces except when a sighting occurs. The computer keeps track of the necessary numbers and determines whether opposing units can see and attack each other. Thus the players get the feel of the total blindness that the actual commanders must have experienced. It is this feature that makes *Computer Bismarck* unique among computer games and board games alike. Experienced wargamers will find this element particularly satisfying and frustrating at the same time.

The Program

We now get to the software itself (finally).

The game is played entirely on the monitor or TV screen. Before each player moves his units, a high-resolution map, with the present locations of the player's units, is displayed on the screen. The map itself is very well done, and the only small complaint I can register is that the movement-grid is not also superimposed; I believe this could have been done without serious program modification.

This is one of those games where not having a very clear understanding of the rules and their implications will be disastrous.

It's also a bit difficult from looking at the screen to determine which unit is which, as all the battleships are represented by B's, all the cruisers (light and heavy) are represented by C's, etc. Given the resolution problem of small computers, I don't know how this problem could be handled effectively. One solution might be to provide the players with cardboard counters like those in board games and let the players move them about on the laminated maps. I suppose people could make their own. (I should point out that if a player forgets the location of a particular unit, there are a couple of commands that provide either the present position of the unit when given the unit's name, or list the names of the units at a given gridpoint.) Despite these minor complaints, the display is fairly functional after one masters the command lists.

Players control the movement and actions of their units via a two-level command system. The player enters a two-character code for whatever action or display he wishes. To move his units, the player enters the appropriate code and then refers to the second command menu. The ships or planes that may move at this turn are then listed one at a time, and the player may enter the appropriate movement commands. As the player enters the movement commands, the units are moved about the screen — although a player may change any or all of his moves until he enters the DM (done move) command. At this point the other player moves his units via the same process. The actual updating of positions is done simultaneously by the computer after both players are finished.

Neither player is aware of the location of the opposing units unless a sighting occurs. This is accomplished by displaying only the player's own units on the screen

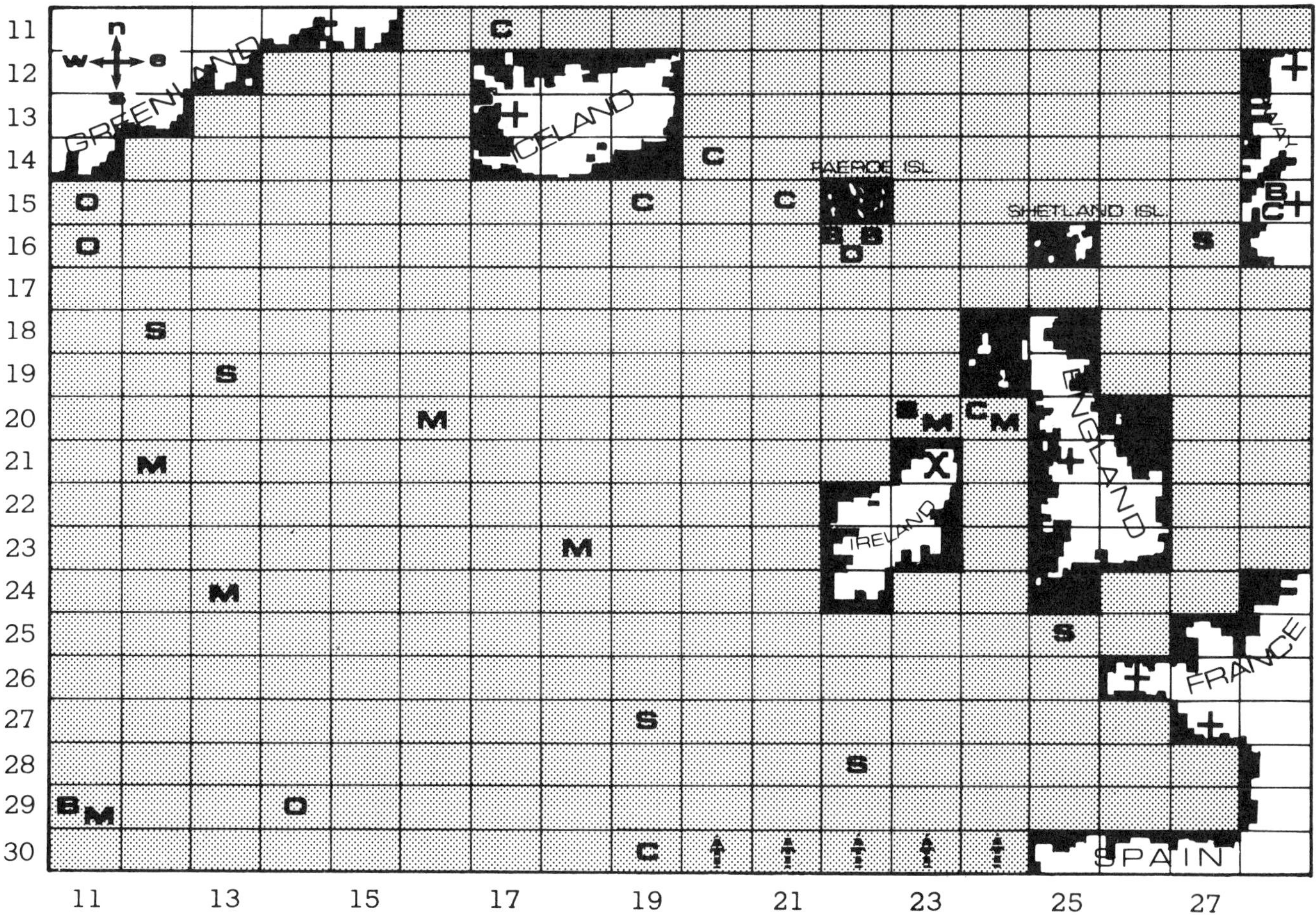

during each player's turn. Before the game, each player enters a secret password so that his opponent can't see his map (unless the opponent knows his password). This is a worthwhile feature, although one player must leave the room on the other's turn.

The computer opponent (nicknamed "Otto Von Computer, Simulated Admiral") is also worth commenting on. Perhaps the biggest problem most wargamers face is finding an equally fanatical opponent to play against. *Computer Bismarck* solves this problem by providing a series of subroutines to play the role of the German commander.

"Otto" appears to play a fairly respectable game. I say *appears to,* since with the hidden-movement rule (and the fact that the program is LIST protected), I can judge "Otto's" ability only from the limited experience of a few games. The diversification of the German player's possible strategy also makes it difficult to determine whether the computer is really playing a good game or randomly wandering about the map. Generally speaking, "Otto" makes particularly good use of his U-boats and seems to use good judgment as to when to attempt to break his surface ships out into the Atlantic.

The typical game of *Computer Bismarck* lasts from two to five hours.

Fortunately for those of us who rarely have a continuous block of time like that, a game may be saved on diskette at the end of any turn. Thus a single game can be played over a period of days. This feature is absolutely necessary with computer games of such duration.

Neither side is aware of the location of the other's forces except when a sighting occurs.

The only major complaint I have about *Computer Bismarck* is the missing tactical-warfare element. Although a player may decide whether to attempt to withdraw a ship, which target to fire upon and whether to fire torpedoes, very few other choices are left to the player once a combat situation occurs. Hits and misses just happen and the player has little control over this action.

In some ways this "missing" tactical combat phase may be somewhat of a blessing for many people who find the strategic portion of *Computer Bismarck* enough of a challenge. However, I find it disappointing that players have so little control over this part of the game after the complete control they've had up to this point. Maneuvering your forces in the decisive battle would add so much to the game.

Final Remarks

I suppose the final question is whether *Computer Bismarck* is worth the rather considerable cost. The answer really depends upon your taste in software. *Computer Bismarck* is probably not for everyone.

The point which I probably cannot emphasize enough is that it is an extremely complex simulation. In most computer games only one piece may move each turn. In this simulation, however, as many as thirty units may move on a turn. Changing weather conditions, fuel supplies, combat damage, and of course the clock, must all be accounted for in determining a player's overall move. Some people may find this extent of sophistication too much to handle.

However, for those ready for a challenging computer simulation, I enthusiastically recommend *Computer Bismarck*. These people will enjoy the complex problems that this game presents, at times frustrating and bewildering.

For more information on *Computer Bismarck,* contact Strategic Simulations, Inc., P.O. Box 5161, Stanford, CA 94305. □

Notes

New Games for the Apple

David Lubar

Among the software to cross this desk recently are several new games for the Apple II. They are all worth covering, though each might appeal to a different section of the Apple community.

A Shoe in the Works

On-Line Systems has done it again with *Sabotage*, a highly captivating game that will put blisters on anyone's paddle finger. The player has a small cannon at the bottom of the screen. Aiming and firing can be controlled either through a paddle or the keyboard. The player attempts to defend his cannon against helicopters that drop parachutists, and against planes that drop bombs. If enough saboteurs reach the ground, they destroy the cannon in a very amusing manner. If a bomb lands, the cannon is blown to pieces. The player has the option of using steerable shells which curve as the cannon is rotated. With paddle control, a stream of shells can be fired by holding the button down.

If the game sounds too easy, add the fact that each shot costs a point. The player can hose the helicopters with a stream of shells, but that strategy won't contribute much to his score. Once saboteurs reach the ground, they can't be shot. But there is a way to get rid of them. If the parachute is shot away from an attacker in the air, he will fall to the ground with a splat. A saboteur unfortunate enough to be beneath the plummetting paratrooper will be eradicated. The game starts out at an easy pace with just one or two helicopters on the screen at any time. After a while, the planes appear. When the heli-

copters return, they drop more saboteurs. The shrapnel from struck helicopters can wipe out other helicopters or paratroopers, and it's possible, in this way, to get two or three helicopters with one shot.

The game keeps track of high score during individual runs, but doesn't store the high score on disk. *Sabotage* is a very good game with fine graphics and high replayability.

On the Circuit

International Gran Prix Racing is everything an Apple game should be, and more. Written by Richard Orban, who created *Three Mile Island*, it is one of the few driving games that successfully solves the paddle problem. Namely, how can a player shift, accelerate, decelerate, and steer without getting hopelessly tangled in a jumble of paddles and keys? The solution in *Gran Prix* is absolutely elegant. The player uses only one paddle. The paddle controls steering. If the button is held, the car accelerates. If the button is quickly released and pressed, the car will shift to the next gear, assuming high enough engine revs have been reached. Releasing the button causes the car to decelerate. During deceleration, a press and release of the button is used for downshifting. If the player desires, he can switch to automatic transmission. There is even a cruise control.

---

creative computing

SOFTWARE PROFILE

Name: Sabotage

Type: Arcade Game

System: 48K Apple, Disk Drive

Format: Disk

Language: Machine Language

Summary: Excellent game

Price: $24.95

Manufacturer:
On-Line Systems
36575 Mudge Ranch Rd.
Coarsegold, CA 93644

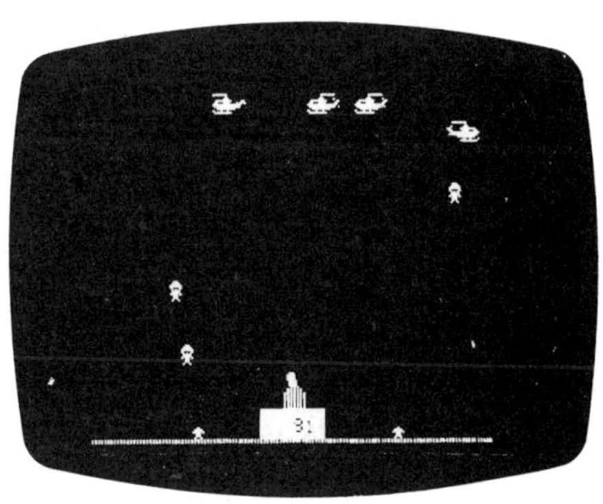

Sabotage.

---

creative computing

SOFTWARE PROFILE

Name: International Gran Prix

Type: Road race game

System: 48K Apple, Disk Drive, Paddles

Format: Disk

Language: Machine Language

Summary: Best road race on the market

Price: $30

Manufacturer:
Riverbank Software, Inc.
Smith's Landing Road
P.O. Box 128
Denton, MD 21629

All this merely scratches the surface of an excellent game. The program is basically a road race game, similar to the arcade game *280-ZAP*, where the screen displays roadposts flashing by the car. The icing on the cake comes in the form of five Gran Prix courses. At the start of the game, the player selects a course, then chooses the number of laps he wants to drive (from 1 to 10). Next, the amount of fuel is selected, followed by the skill level.

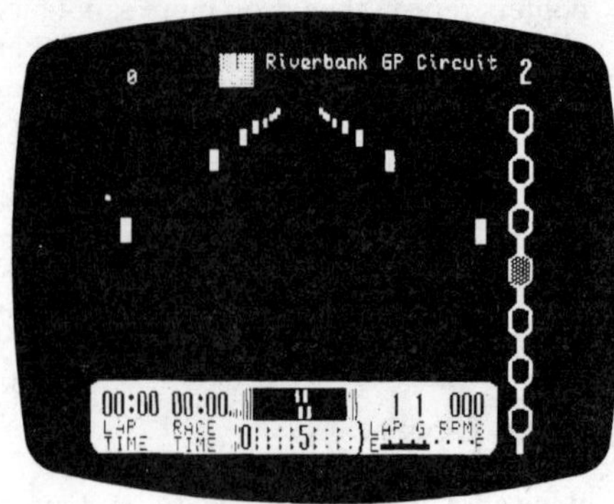

International Gran Prix.

There are eight levels. At the easiest, the car barely drifts; in middle levels, it skids; at the top level, the road turns to Teflon.

The dashboard display includes speedometer, tachometer, a timer for current lap and total time, and indicators showing the relation of the tires to the posts. Whenever the car moves dangerously close to the posts, a clicking warns the driver. Collisions are accompanied by a weird sound that seems to defy the limitations of the Apple speaker. The player's best lap time and total time for any course and skill level are stored and displayed by the game. All the curves have names, and these names are displayed on the screen when the car approaches.

Beyond great graphics and superb design, the game also simulates driving with nearly total realism. Whatever algorithms the author used, he did a good job. The car handles very accurately. It can accelerate through curves, go into controlled skids, and fishtale if the player oversteers. *Gran Prix* is a winner.

That Familiar Glow

Fighting its way through the plethora of Missile Command clones, *Norad*, from Western MicroData, emerges as a new

twist on the theme. The player has a hi-res map of the good old USA, dotted with ten cities and ten missile bases. Each base has a number. Press that number on the keyboard and a missile leaves the base. The arrow keys control the horizontal motion of the missile. The space bar detonates the missile. If it is detonated close to an incoming warhead, all is well. If not, the warhead hits a city or a base. Cities hit twice are destroyed. Bases are wiped out with one hit. At intervals throughout the game, the cities are rebuilt, and any eradicated bases near a surviving city are replaceo. The surviving cities also stock the silos with extra missiles. Silos start with ten missiles. The player receives bonus points for unused missiles.

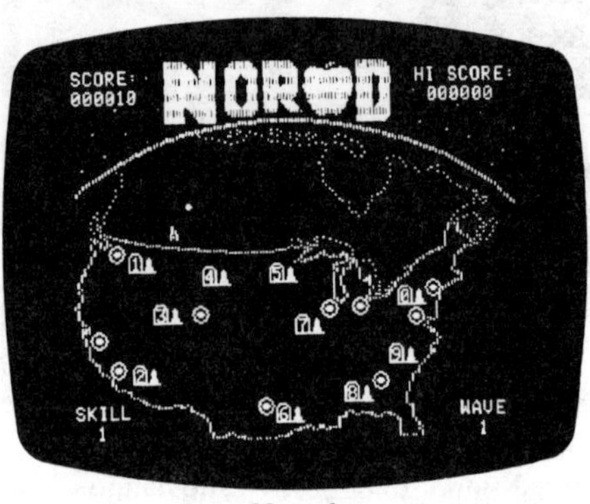

Norad.

There are three skill levels. Higher levels start with faster attacks, and throw more waves of attack at the player. On each level, the player wins if he survives a specific number of waves. At a certain point, the player is also given an MX missile site which can be moved across the map. The lowest skill level is good for learning the game. The highest level is very tough.

Raiders of the Lost Star

Strongly resembling a certain Atari classic, *Space Raiders* is a search-and-destroy game. Using a joystick or keys, the player moves through galactic quadrants, blasting enemy ships. The strong point of the game is the motion of the stars. The field moves toward the player and shifts realistically when he turns. The question is whether to compare it to the Atari version, or to view it as a game in itself. By comparison, it just doesn't offer the same graphics or sound. What works for the Atari won't necessarily work on the Apple, and vice versa. As a game, it is interesting, but rather repetitive. Only one ship attacks at a time. Basically, the player goes into a sector, destroys all the enemy ships, goes into the next sector, and so on. The player can also dock at a starbase when he needs more energy. The target has to be in the center of the crosshairs to be hit, adding a bit of difficulty to the

game. If Atari Star Raiders appeals to you, this is as good a version as is likely to be produced for the Apple.

Treking On

Rainbow has made improvements to *A Stellar Trek* (reviewed Oct., 1980), producing *Super Stellar Trek*. The game offers a hi-res, real-time fight against Klingons and other baddies. The most obvious improvement is the elimination of constant disk access. In the original version, the program went to the disk after every command. Now, the routines remain in RAM, speeding up play and lowering disk wear. The first time a user plays the game, he is asked to name all the officers. From then on, this information is used to add color to the game, with reports coming to the bridge from the officers.

Overall play is in the basic StarTrek format; the player has a limited amount of time in which to find and destroy the Klingons, using photon torpedos and phasers. Extensive commands are available for such exotic actions as mining dilithium crystals. Those who enjoy Trek games will like this one.

Ashes to Apples

An arcade game dealing with a certain mythical bird has found its way to the Apple in the form of *Falcons*. The game seems fairly easy for the first ten seconds or so. Several rows of ships move above the player, firing down at his base. This part is reminiscent of Invaders. Then a few ships break formation and swoop down. Now it seems a bit like Galaxian. The similarity vanishes as the attacking ships begin to fly in strange patterns, moving below the screen and attacking the player from below. A transformation suddenly occurs. The ship changes to a falcon and flies evasive patterns. It's worth more points now, but harder to hit. If the player clears the field, he gets another with a different formation. After this second field is cleared, the hard part begins. Small blue dots appear on the screen, weaving back and forth.

creative computing
SOFTWARE PROFILE

Name: Falcons

Type: Arcade Game

System: 48K Apple II or Apple III, Disk Drive

Format: Disk

Language: Machine Language

Summary: Superb and challenging game

Price: $29.95

Manufacturer:
Picadilly Software
89 Summit Ave.
Summit, NJ 07901

They start to grow, becoming large dots, then huge falcons. They swoop at the player, moving at high speed. If hit straight on, the falcon is destroyed. If only winged, it returns. If the player gets through this field without losing his allotment of three ships, he gets a second field of dots that grow into falcons. Survivors are given a chance to destroy the mother ship. Make that MOTHER SHIP. The thing is huge.

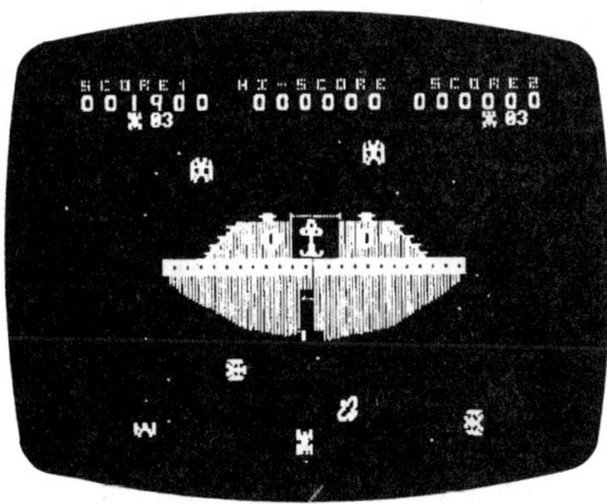

Attacking the mother ship in Falcons.

To destroy it, the player first has to blast a hole through the bottom. Next, a hole has to be made in a revolving rim. Once there is a clear path for a shot to the inside, the ship can be destroyed. But the mother ship shoots back. And groups of small ships hover above it, swooping down on the player. If the player destroys the mother ship, the game cycles back through the five levels again.

Beside firing, the player has the option of using shields. A shield lasts for about four seconds, then can't be used again for about five seconds. Shields are great for destroying swooping falcons since the birds are killed on contact with the force field. The game can be played with keys, paddles, or a joystick. There was one rough edge noticeable when fighting the mother ship. Occasionally, one of the attackers wouldn't be entirely erased from the screen when destroyed. But this barely detracts from the appeal of the game. *Falcons* is tough, fun and very well done.

Killer Robots, Drones, and Low-Life Storm Troopers

Mission Escape arrived here two days ago and has already taken control of the staff. They've been lining up to play this one. It is a cross between the arcade game, *Berzerk*, and some high-adrenalin contest that might be thought of as death chess. The player starts at one of four doors to a room containing robots, drones, and storm troopers. His object is to get to the specified exit, and thus, to the next level. The storm troopers fire lasers that do damage to the player's armor. The drones also fire lasers but, if shot, explode with enough force to destroy anything adjacent to them. The robots fire missiles that always kill with one shot. Against this arsenal, the player has three weapons. He can fire a laser, fire a burst of three laser shots, or fire a missile. The missiles and rapid-fire bursts are limited, single laser shots are unlimited.

creative computing
SOFTWARE PROFILE

Name: Mission Escape

Type: Strategy and Action Game

System: 48K Apple, Applesoft, Disk Drive

Format: Disk

Language: Machine Language

Summary: Highly replayable game

Price: $24.95

Manufacturer:
CE Software
801 73rd. St.
Des Moines, IA 50312

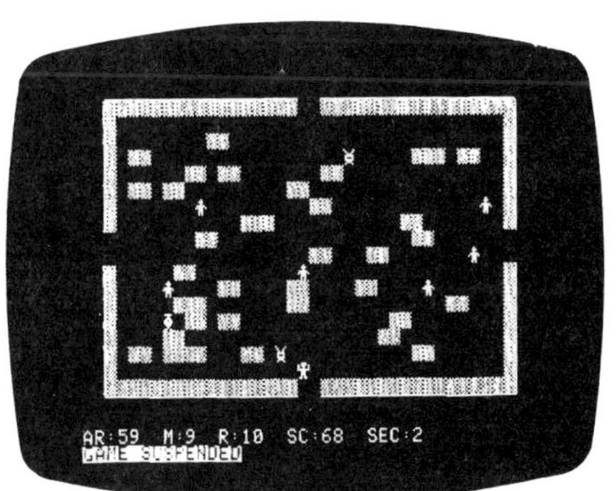

Mission Escape.

The player and the enemy alternate turns. The player has ten seconds to issue up to three orders. Movement and firing are controlled from the keyboard. While some keyboard-controlled games are unexciting, *Mission Escape* is definitely not dull. Despite the alternation of turns, there is a real-time feel to it. As an extra touch, the top five scores are kept on the disk. *Mission Escape* is highly recommended.

It Isn't Raining Rain

Finally, in an attempt to make up for not reviewing it sooner, one more game deserves mention in this roundup. *Alien Rain* pits the player against a swarm of hovering, swooping attackers. They start out placidly enough, just moving back and forth across the top of the screen, letting the player pick them off with his ship. Then one or more of the critters comes swooping down, flying a drunken path and raining missiles. Attackers that make it to the bottom wrap around to rejoin the formation at the top. There are two flagships that are worth bonus points if shot while swooping. If the player clears the board, he gets another screenful. If he scores 3000 points, he gets an extra ship.

creative computing
SOFTWARE PROFILE

Name: Alien Rain

Type: Arcade Game

System: 48K Apple, Disk Drive

Format: Disk

Language: Basic

Summary: Tough and fast moving

Price: $24.95

Manufacturer:
Broderbund Software
Box 3266
Eugene, OR 97403

The animation here is very smooth, and the game is tough enough for most players. For those who have it mastered, Broderbund also offers *Alien Typhoon* with more aliens and faster action. □

Painter Power

David Lubar

Eric Podietz held an audience enthralled with a dynamic creation of abstract art. The demonstration of his real-time graphics system was one of the highlights of the 1980 Personal Computer Arts Festival in Philadelphia. Using angled lines and shapes for brushes, Mr. Podietz put patterns on the screen, creating images reminiscent of weavings, abstract landscapes, and Escher stairways. He used an S-100 system and worked in black and white. But that was last year. During that time, he was not idle. He was busy creating an Apple version, adding extensions that make full use of color graphics and other Apple features. The result is *Painter Power*, a software package unlike anything else on the market. Two versions come with the disk; beginner and advanced. The beginner version gets the user going right away. The advanced version adds more power and a bit more complexity.

To use the beginner version, the painter selects a background color and a speed and gets down to creating. Using keys or paddles, the direction of the moving brush is controlled, putting marvelous images on the screen. If the brush is not to the user's liking, it can be changed easily. During creation, brush color can be changed, the brush can be lifted or set down, or the program can be frozen, allowing changes at the user's leisure. With wraparound set, the brush will reappear opposite the point at which it leaves the screen, and continue

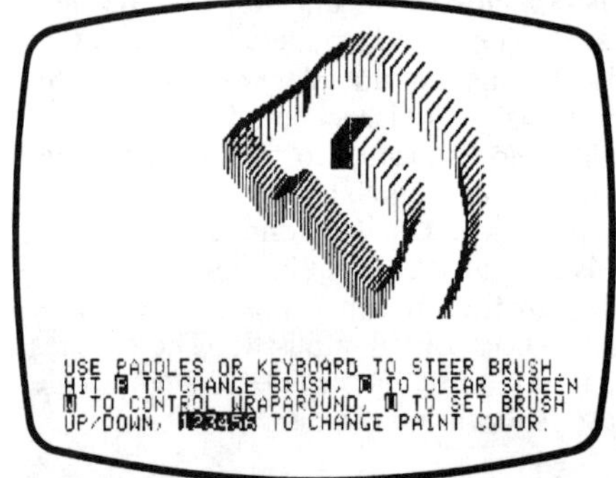

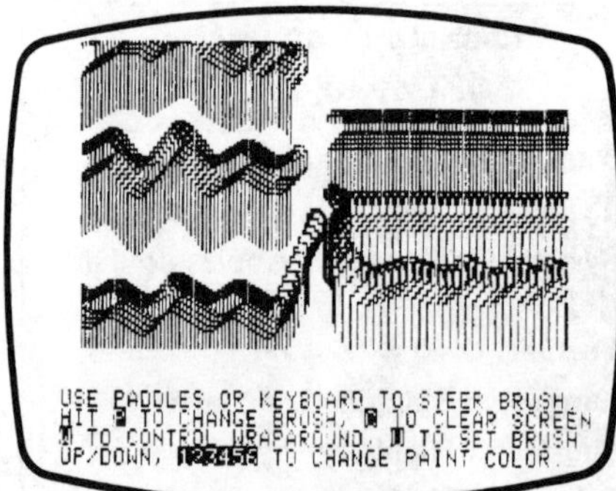

Simple examples of designs created with Painter Power. The first uses the pre-defined brush from the beginner mode, the second was done with a user-defined brush in the shape of a question mark.

painting. With wraparound off, an image of the brush reappears, allowing the user to keep track of its relative location, but will not paint until it is returned to the actual screen. In essence, the painter (player?) has a neat little imagination box that seems to offer an infinite variety of images. Finished scenes can be created and saved to disk, or users can follow in the footsteps of Mr. Podietz and give real-time performances (with an appropriate musical accompaniment). Those who tested the program enjoyed it immensely, even in the beginner version.

Advanced *Painter Power* adds all the extras that users of the beginner version might begin to wish for. While this version takes a bit more effort on the part of the user, the return is well worth the time spent learning the system. Not only can brushes be created, they can also be saved to disk. There is even the capability to create a special "Quickstroke" where a brush traces a predetermined pattern. And for those with a mathematical bent, a special routine allows the creation of brushes based on math functions. The location of the brush is displayed numerically at the bottom of the screen, aiding the user in keeping track of the brush when wraparound is turned off. There are many more features in the advanced system, and it would take days to explore all of them.

How does *Painter Power* differ from other painting programs? While you can probably reproduce its results with other systems, the fluidity and symmetry obtained by the moving brush make it the easiest system available for abstract designs. The strength of the program is its dedication to a specific area of graphics, and the ease with which it implements that approach.

While *Painter Power* deals with the abstract and is obviously not for everyone, it will delight anyone who is interested in creating patterns and designs, or just finding another way to have fun with the Apple.

Other Graphics

Several other Apple graphics programs arrived here too late to be covered in this issue. Notable among them is a graphics editor from SubLogic, that works in conjunction with their 3-D packages. The A2-GE includes a motion programmer. It will be reviewed here in the near future. Also, several vendors have new packages for shape table creation, animation, and other areas of graphics. These, too, will be explored in detail in upcoming issues. □

Applesoft Compilers:
A Comparative Evaluation

Helmar Herman

Many Apple owners have waited with great anticipation for an Applesoft Basic compiler. Now, within a span of a few months, four companies have released Applesoft compilers.

Why this interest in Applesoft compilers? And what is an Applesoft compiler anyway?

To understand what a compiler is, and what it can do for you, you must first understand how your Applesoft Basic works.

Interpreter

Applesoft is an interpretive language. Each time a Basic statement is to be executed by Applesoft, Applesoft must re-examine the statement to determine what to do. (Please refer to the sample program in Listing 1.)

```
10 INPUT 'ENTER A NUMBER';NUM
20 PRINT SQR(NUM)
30 GOTO 10
```

Listing 1. Sample Applesoft program.

Every time the program logic goes to a new line, Applesoft must examine the statement. For example, in line 10, Applesoft must determine that it is an INPUT request, that ENTER A NUMBER is to be displayed prior to prompting the operator, and that the response is to be placed in NUM.

When a number is entered, Applesoft will then examine statement 20 and perform the specified action (PRINT). Applesoft will then examine the next statement, 30, and perform the GOTO request.

Whenever a new line is encountered, Applesoft must re-examine the line as though it has never seen it before. It is because of this constant re-examination of statements that interpretive languages are slow.

Another problem with interpretive languages is that whenever program control is to transfer to a new statement (statement

30), Applesoft must spend time looking for the statement to which transfer is to be made. In a large program, this can take a considerable amount of time.

Compiler

A compiler transforms the Basic program into a machine language program. Each statement is examined by the compiler and is converted (compiled) into machine language instructions that perform the specified action.

When the program is run, the compiled machine language program is executed directly by the hardware, without a software interpreter having to examine each line.

When program control is to be transferred to a new statement, the address of the new statement is compiled into the machine language program, thus eliminating the need to search for the statement to which transfer is to be made.

Advantages and Disadvantages

There are various trade-offs with interpreters and compilers. See Figure 1 for a list.

In general, interpreters are much better when developing programs because of the ease and speed of program modification

and debugging. Compilers are better when the program is ready for production work because of the speed advantage.

Four Systems Examined

The four systems being examined are Expediter II from On-line Systems, TASC from Microsoft Inc., Applesoft Compiler from Hayden Publications, and Speed Star from Southwestern Data Systems.

In examining these systems, important items to look for are:

1. *Accuracy*. The compiled programs should run *exactly* as the interpreted programs do.

2. *Compatibility*. All functions of the Applesoft interpreter should be supported.

3. *Program Optimization*. The faster and smaller the compiled program, the better.

4. *Communication*. Compiled programs should be able to pass information to and from other compiled programs.

5. *Program Size*. Compiled programs will normally be larger than the interpreted version. If the compiler generates excessively large programs, its usefulness may be limited.

Item	Interpreter	Compiler
Ease of program development	Here the interpreter is far superior. A change to a program can be made and the results tested in just a few seconds.	Whenever a change is made to a program, the program must be re-compiled before testing can proceed.
Speed	Interpreted programs run relatively slowly.	Compiled programs run relatively fast.
Size	In general, interpreted programs are smaller.	Compiled programs are generally two to three times larger than interpreted programs.
Remarks	Remarks are to be avoided because they make the program larger and slower. On the other hand, programs without remarks are very difficult to modify.	Since remarks are removed during the compilation process, they may be used as needed.

Figure 1. Tradeoffs between interpreters and compilers.

Helmar Herman, Creative Computer Applications, 19 Shadwell Rd., Nashua, NH 03062.

Slightly less important items of interest are:

1. *Speed of Compilation*. Since (in theory) compilation is performed only after the program has been debugged, the program won't be compiled very often. A fast compile is nice, but not a critical factor.

2. *Ease of Use*. The compiler should be easy to use and forgiving in nature. It should be fairly safe to assume, however, that most persons using an Applesoft compiler must be familiar with Applesoft and know how to program.

Also of interest to software authors who may want to market compiled programs is the policy of the compiler company toward distribution of compiled code.

Expected Problems

Programs that call other programs that have been compiled will have to be changed to do a BRUN XXXXXXXX (or BLOAD XXXXXXXX:CALL YYYY) instead of a RUN XXXXXXXX.

Programs that depend on timing loops will have to be modified. For example, suppose a program uses the following statement to pause for a few seconds: 10 FOR X=1 TO 1000:NEXT X. With an interpreted version, this may take 2-3 seconds. With a compiled version, however, it may take only a fraction of a second.

Real-time games will have to be modified to adjust for the speed increase. How would you like it if all of a sudden the balls in your favorite game started whizzing by at five times the speed you're used to?

```
5 REM TEST A
10 REM STRING MINIPULATION TEST AND TRY TO CAUSE APPLESOFT FR
20   HOME : INPUT "HIT RETURN TO BEGIN TEST";X$
100  REM  FILL THE STRINGS
105 TEST$ = "A"
110 X$ = "x":Y$ = "x":Z$ = "x"
140  FOR COUNT = 0 TO 250
150 X$ = X$ + "x"
160 Y$ = Y$ + "x"
170 Z$ = Z$ + "x"
175  GOSUB 2000
180  NEXT COUNT
200  REM  FILL ARRAYS WITH THE STRINGS
201  VTAB 12: HTAB 15: PRINT "          ";
205 TEST$ = "B"
210  DIM X$(20),Y$(20),Z$(20)
220  FOR COUNT = 0 TO 19
230 X$(COUNT) = X$
240 Y$(COUNT) = Y$
250 Z$(COUNT) = Z$
255  GOSUB 2000
260  NEXT COUNT
300  REM  STRIP DOWN THE CHARACTERS
301  VTAB 12: HTAB 15: PRINT "          ";
305 TEST$ = "C"
307  FOR COUNT = 1 TO  LEN (X$) - 1
310 X$ =  LEFT$ (X$, LEN (X$) - 1)
320 Y$ =  LEFT$ (Y$, LEN (Y$) - 1)
330 Z$ =  LEFT$ (Z$, LEN (Z$) - 1)
335  GOSUB 2000
340  NEXT COUNT
1000  PRINT "TEST COMPLETE"
1010  END
2000  REM  ROUTINE TO DISPLAY CURRENT TEST AND COUNT
2010  VTAB, 12: HTAB 15
2020  PRINT TEST$,COUNT;
2030  RETURN
```

Listing 2. String manipulation test.

```
5 REM TEST B
10 REM PROGRAM SIZE TEST
100 A=1
1010 END
```

Listing 3A. Program size test.

```
5 REM TEST B
10 REM PROGRAM SIZE TEST
100 A=1
110 B=2
1010 END
```

Listing 3B. Program size test.

```
5   REM  TEST C
10   REM  TEST OF A BUBBLE SORT
20   HOME : INPUT "HIT RETURN TO BEGIN TEST";X$
30   DIM A(100)
100  REM  FILL THE ARRAY
105 TEST$ = "A"
110  FOR COUNT = 1 TO 100
120 A(COUNT) = 101 - COUNT
125  GOSUB 2000
130  NEXT COUNT
200  REM  SORT THE ARRAY
201  VTAB 12: HTAB 15: PRINT "          ";
205 TEST$ = "B"
210  FOR X = 99 TO 1 STEP  - 1
215 COUNT = X: GOSUB 2000
220  FOR Y = 1 TO X
230  IF A(Y) <  = A(Y + 1) THEN 270
240 A = A(Y)
250 A(Y) = A(Y + 1)
260 A(Y + 1) = A
270  NEXT Y
280  NEXT X
1000  PRINT "TEST COMPLETE"
1010  END
2000  REM  ROUTINE TO DISPLAY CURRENT TEST AND COUNT
2010  VTAB 12: HTAB 15
2020  PRINT TEST$,COUNT;
2030  RETURN
```

Listing 4. Bubble sort test.

```
5 REM TEST D
10   REM  SPEED TEST FOR HEAVY DISK I/O PROGRAM
20   HOME : INPUT "HIT RETURN TO BEGIN TEST";A$
30 D$ =  CHR$ (4)
40 TEST$ = "A"
100  REM  OUTPUT THE FILE
110  PRINT D$;"OPEN TESTFILE,D1"
120  FOR COUNT = 1 TO 100
130  PRINT D$;"WRITE TESTFILE"
140  PRINT "THIS IS THE SAMPLE RECORD,";COUNT
150  GOSUB 2000
160  NEXT COUNT
170  PRINT D$;"CLOSE TESTFILE"
200  REM  READ THE FILE BACK
210 TEST$ = "B"
220  PRINT D$;"OPEN TESTFILE"
230  FOR CCOUNT = 100 TO 1 STEP  - 1
240  PRINT D$;"READ TESTFILE"
250  INPUT Z$,COUNT
260  GOSUB 2000
270  NEXT CCOUNT
280  PRINT D$;"CLOSE TESTFILE"
1000  PRINT "TEST COMPLETE"
1010  END
2000  REM  ROUTINE TO DISPLAY CURRENT TEST AND COUNT
2005  PRINT D$
2007  VTAB 12: HTAB 17: PRINT "          ";
2010  VTAB 12: HTAB 15
2020  PRINT TEST$,COUNT
2030  RETURN
```

Listing 5. Speed test for heavy disk I/O program.

Test A (Listing 2) is a string manipulation test. Being tested is the speed of the compiled version and its vulnerability to Applesoft frees. Since string manipulation requires a fair amount of work by the computer, I would expect a significant time improvement in this test. An Applesoft free, by the way, is a problem that arises in large programs that do a great deal of string manipulation. As the area reserved for strings fills up, Applesoft periodically condenses the strings (also called garbage collection) to free up room at the end for more strings.

Test B (Listings 3A and 3B) is a test to see how large a single statement program is and how much it grows by adding one simple statement. Listing 3A will show you how much overhead each program will have. To this overflow you then add the amount of storage taken by each compiled program statement. The lower the overhead, the better.

Test C (Listing 4) is a general speed test. It uses a bubble sort (one of the slowest) to test the speed of a logic-bound program.

Test D (Listing 5) tests the speed of a heavy disk I/O program. I expect that compiled programs will run at about the same speed as interpretive programs.

See Figure 2 for the results of the tests.

All the compilers tested shared the following features:

1. The compilers produce machine language object code that can be loaded and run with the BRUN command.

2. The compiled program can be placed anywhere in memory. Once compiled for a particular place, it can only run there.

3. Figure 3 shows what commands are not supported by which compilers.

4. Special compiler directive commands are supported via REM statements.

5. Compiled programs cannot be interrupted with Ctl-C.

6. They support local or global variables. Global variables allow you to pass information from one compiled program to another (but not from an un-compiled program to a compiled one).

7. Once started, the compilers can only be interrupted with the Reset key.

Expediter II

Expediter II comes with two disks. One for DOS 3.2, and the other for DOS 3.3. The disks are copy protected.

Rather than just producing a machine language program which is then BRUN, the compiler produces a one statement Applesoft program. The one statement is usually 1 CALL 4352. The machine language portion of the program is attached to this single line Basic program. You can thus SAVE, LOAD, and RUN the program exactly as you would any other Basic program.

If you *must* have a BLOADable version of the compiled code, there are instructions on how to accomplish this.

You can also leave "holes" in your compiled code to provide room for such things as the hi-res areas.

One potentially difficult problem is in the method used for string manipulation. Applesoft treats all strings as variable length strings. Thus a 5-byte string and a 60-byte string would take 65 bytes (plus overhead). Expediter treats all strings as fixed length strings. Before compilation you must specify how long the strings are to be. All strings will then be that length. Thus a 5-byte string would still occupy 60 bytes (or whatever string length was specified).

TEST	LENGTH	SPEED (C1)	(C2)	
A(I)	717	23	••	Listing 2.
A(O)	3465	30!	33	
A(M)	4797	13	98	
A(H)	2500	(*1)	14	
A(S)	3222	17	1	
B(I)	38	••	••	Listing 3A.
B(O)	2362	••	11	
B(M)	4028	••	62	
B(H)	376	••	10	
B(S)	2101	••	1	
B(I)	46	••	••	Listing 3B.
B(O)	2384	••	11	
B(M)	4048	••	62	
B(H)	395	••	10	
B(S)	2124	••	1	
C(I)	464	124	••	Listing 4.
C(O)	2964	27	23	
C(M)	5049	40	94	
C(H)	2622	24	15	
C(S)	3070	53	1	
D(I)	594	36	••	Listing 5.
D(O)	3275	32	27	
D(M)	4642	30	94	
D(H)	1937	30	13	
D(S)	2730	30	1	

The top numbers (I) are the interpreter figures;
(O) are the On-Line compile figures;
(M) are the Microsoft compiler figures;
(H) are the Hayden compiler figures;
(S) are the Southwestern compiler figures.

Note—the compiled lengths for each compiler are calculated differently. Length comparisons may not be completely accurate.

(O) compiled length excludes variables.
(M) compiled length includes variables.
(H) compiled length includes non-string variables.
(S) compiled length includes variables.

(C1) is the program run speed.
(C2) is compilation speed (how long does it take the compile).

*When Listing 2 was compiled and run on the Hayden compiler, an error occurred after the 147th loop of test A. The error was OUT OF MEMORY ERROR IN MODULE $0803. In accordance with a suggestion from the manual, I added the following line the program: 145 X=FRE(0). The program then ran in 15 seconds.

Figure 2. Test results.

The good part of this is that there is never any garbage collection. Also, in theory, string operations should be faster. In practice, however, they appear to be slower.

The bad part is that if you have many strings, they must all be as long as the longest one, which may cause a storage problem.

Worse, is that you are not notified if you exceed a string length. The program just keeps on running, wiping out who knows what variables until eventually something vital is destroyed and the program fails.

There is an unusual restriction with this system. All arrays must be defined in the program *physically* ahead of the first use rather than *logically* ahead of the first use. Thus the following program is invalid:

10 GOSUB 100
20 A(20)=5
30 END
100 DIM A(20)
110 RETURN

The DIM statement at 100 must physically precede the first use at statement 20 even though statement 100 will be executed before statement 20.

Because of this restriction, and because of the common practice of placing DIM statements at the end of programs (for speed), inexperienced users may have trouble with Expediter when compiling off-the-shelf programs.

As far as speed and length of programs, the Expediter sits comfortably between the extremes produced by the tests, though it created the slowest code for the string program. On the other hand it has the fewest unsupported Basic statements of any of the compilers tested.

An annual charge of five times the list price is charged for distribution of compiled code.

On-line Systems, 36575 Mudge Ranch Rd., Coarsegold, CA 93614. $99.

TASC (The AppleSoft Compiler)

The version of TASC that I tested was a pre-release Beta test version, and all test results should be viewed in that light.

TASC is distributed on a DOS 3.2 disk. It can be muffin'd to produce a DOS 3.3 version. The disk I have is not copy protected, and Microsoft has indicated that they have not yet decided whether or not they will copy protect the final production version.

TASC was written in Basic and then used to compile itself—a very intriguing concept.

The output from TASC is a relatively small BLOADable file. The size of the object program is deceptive, however, because in order to run the program, you must first BLOAD the file RUNTIME. RUNTIME contains execution time sub-routines which are called by your compiled program. It is approximately 4K long.

It is a slight inconvenience to have to BLOAD RUNTIME every time you want to run a compiled program. On the other hand, the amount of disk space required for each program is reduced.

For frequently used programs, you can simply write an Applesoft program that BLOADs the runtime package and then BRUNs your compiled program.

Unlike the other compilers, TASC can be gracefully interrupted while compiling.

Whenever the program pauses for user information, such as program name, you can enter DOS command by prefixing the response with a Ctl-D.

TASC fared worst in compilation speed, but did reasonably well in execution time. While the runtime routines take a fair chunk of space, the compactness of the compiled code could make up for this in long programs. TASC had more unsupported statements than any of the other compilers.

Microsoft, Inc., 10800 NE Eighth Suite 819, Bellevue, WA 98004. (206) 455-8080. $150.

Hayden Applesoft Compiler

The Hayden compiler is currently available only in 3.2.1 format. Hayden indicates that a 3.3 version is coming and will be shipped free to users who have returned their warranty cards.

Although the disk is not copy protected, the system is shipped with a special "protection device" that must be installed in the game I/O socket.

Hayden was not specific about charges for re-distribution of compiled code. The impression I got was that each request will be handled on an individual basis.

Two extra programs are supplied with the system. The first is the only full color, low-res, single disk copy program I've ever seen. It's quite entertaining. Second is a program to "de-muffin" programs from DOS 3.3 to DOS 3.2. I expect that the second program will disappear on DOS 3.3 versions.

Unsupported Statement	On-line	Microsoft	Hayden		Southwestern
CONT	U	U	S		U
DEF FN	S	*	*		S
DEL	U	U	U		U
HIMEM	U	S	S		S
IF X$ THEN	S	***	S	S	S
LIST	U	U	U		U
LOAD	S	U	U		U
LOMEM	U	U	S		S
NEXT	**	S	S		S
NOTRACE	S	U	U		S
RECALL	U	U	U		U
RESUME	U	S	S		U
SAVE	S	U	U		U
SHLOAD	S	U	U		S
STORE	U	U	U		U
TRACE	S	U	U		S
&	S	U	S		****

U = Unsupported
S = Supported

*DEF FN may be defined, but not re-defined.

**A FOR may have one and only one corresponding NEXT. The following program would be invalid:
```
10 FOR X=1 TO 10
20 IF X=5 THEN NEXT X:GOTO 40
30 PRINT X:NEXT X
40 END
```

***Strings may not be used as a logical argument. Statements such as IF A$+B$ THEN 100 are illegal. Statements such as IF A+B THEN 100 are legal.

****Makes the compiler crash.

Figure 3. Unsupported Applesoft statements.

This compiler was the second fastest in compilation and registered favorable execution speeds. On the other hand, each time you want to re-compile a program, you must re-boot! If you are already booted, there is no way to invoke the compiler without booting again. Also, when the compile is done, you must hit the Reset key to exit—a rather strange idea.

The ability to pass data from compiled program to compiled program is limited. All numeric variables must be referenced in the respective programs in exactly the same order. If string variables are shared, then FRE() statements must be inserted into the programs at strategic points.

Like the Microsoft compiler, this one also generates a set of runtime subroutines. These subroutines can either be included in the program or be declared EXTERNAL. If they are external, then they must be BLOADed before execution.

Speed Star

The version of Speed Star that I tested was also a pre-released test version. All test results should be viewed in that light.

Like the Hayden compiler, this one is protected by a device inserted into the game socket. According to Southwestern, the final version will allow you to plug your game paddles into the protection device, thus allowing both to be attached at the same time.

This compiler is lightning fast. The test compiles were done almost instantaneously. Also, repeat compiles are quick because you don't have to reload the compiler each time. However, comparative execution speed varied considerably from test to test. The compiler locates itself at location X'7200' and is invoked with the "8" key.

The address at which Speed Star runs is HIMEM for a 32K system. Unfortunately, it still loads there on a 48K system. The extra 16K does not appear to be useable during the compile process, thus limiting the size of your program.

One nice feature is the ability to include Ctl-C checking logic in the object program automatically. Also, you can have the system check subscripting ranges. These checks, of course, do not come free. They result in a decrease in storage and a slight speed degradation.

There are many times when a significant speed increase can be accomplished just by having one or two Applesoft sub-routines converted to machine language and leaving the rest of the program interpretive. This was the only compiler that allowed interpreter programs to call and pass variables to and receive variables from compiled programs. Although I didn't actually try this feature, it seemed fairly simple, based on the documentation.

Southwestern Data Systems, P.O. Box 582-S, Santee, CA 920071 (714) 562-3670. $85 (introductory price).

Conclusions

I ran one other test on all four of the compilers in which I tried to compile the menu program from The CCA Data Management System. The program works perfectly in interpretive mode. After compiling, I got the following results:

Microsoft: It worked for a while. I was able to define the system configuration, but then it crashed into the monitor.

Online: The screen went blank and then nothing.

Hayden: The menu was displayed, but whenever I tried to enter a number for a valid function, the system beeped and rejected it. Then when I entered an invalid function, the program got an Applesoft error.

Southwestern: The configuration portion ran, but instead of displaying the menu, the program terminated.

Just as an educated guess, I suspect that the compilers are having trouble with the ONERR routines.

I recompiled with the Microsoft compiler and specified inclusion of the RESUME logic. The program worked much better and operated correctly with one minor exception.

At about this time, Microsoft sent me some fixes to their compiler, and wonder of wonders, the problem was solved. The menu now worked perfectly.

I was encouraged by this and tried compiling the SORT portion of the system. A dramatic success. The compiled program ran perfectly and was substantially faster than the interpretive program. I did have to modify the program to change the dynamically dimensioned arrays to statically dimensioned arrays.

The above experience illustrates my concluding statements and conclusions:

The larger and more complex a program is, the less likely it will compile successfully without modification (for example, dynamic arrays).

For one reason or another, off-the-shelf programs will probably not compile successfully without modification and effort.

Recommendation

Before I applied the patches to the Microsoft compiler, I was not ready to recommend any of the compilers.

After running the fixed program, however, the Microsoft compiler would be my recommendation. Although it is by far the slowest, the programs it compiles seem more likely to run successfully. It appears that once again, the tortoise has beaten the hares!

If you have programs that are too large to compile, you may want to consider the Southwestern compiler. It is the only one to support the compilation of subroutines with full data transfer capabilities. As was evidenced with the CCA DMS main menu, however, you may have to fiddle with your program to get it to work. □

Apple Disk Utilities

David Lubar

The Apple disk operating system (DOS) is, of course, useful for storing and retrieving programs, but this is just the leading edge of its abilities. One can also access and change disk data at the byte level. Such operations are useful in many ways. Unfortunately, Apple DOS by itself doesn't contain the full set of commands and utilities required for these manipulations. To fill the void, several programs have appeared which allow the user to read, edit, and write disk sectors. Two such programs are discussed below. One is specifically designed for working just with disk data, while the other includes a wealth of added functions.

Dakin's Dozen

The *Dakin5 Programming Aids 3.3* is the Cadillac of disk utilities. It contains just about every utility the serious programmer might need. Let's take the routines

in the order in which they appear in the menu. The Lister allows you to configure listings specifically for your printer. You can specify line length and page length. If desired, page numbers will be added. The list is headed with the program name, the date and title. The program is smart enough to reject bad data such as a time entry containing more than 59 minutes. The last date used is stored on the disk and is kept as a default value. It can be changed at any time. The Lister can handle both full and partial listings.

Line Cross Reference produces a list of all referenced lines. The information can be sent to the printer or the screen. Another nice feature is revealed when you use this program. A message is placed at the top of the screen telling you how to load a program and then give a CALL to run the cross reference. This message is protected since the program lowers the top of the scroll window. You can get a catalog, list to the screen, or do anything else that causes scrolling without losing the message. During execution, a keypress halts the display, allowing users without printers a chance to see the information. The Variable Reference program functions in a similar manner, producing a list of all variables and the lines where they occur.

The Peeker is a handy program that prints the contents of random access files. Either an entire file or just a partial series of records can be printed or sent to the screen.

The Patcher is used for reading, editing, and writing disk sectors. You can specify a specific track and sector, or enter a file name. If a file name is entered, the program moves sequentially through sectors containing that file. If a specific sector is requested, only that one is displayed. After

any changes are made the program asks for the next track and sector number. Changes can be entered either as hex code, ASCII data with the hi bit off, or ASCII data with the hi bit on. Changes are entered by giving the relative address of the byte within the sector, followed by the desired data. A single byte or series can be changed at any time. The changes are sent to disk unless escape is pressed. While this method works well enough, it is not the easiest way to edit sectors, and is best used for making minor changes.

The Copier program is similar to FID, which comes with Apple DOS 3.3. Copier allows you to copy files, using two drives, but doesn't allow wild cards in file names, or offer any of the other extras that come with FID. Diskette Copy is a dual-drive copy program that initializes the destination disk and verifies all files. It also allows you to initialize a disk without placing DOS on it. These two programs are nice additions to the package, but don't really offer anything special.

The Array Editor creates and edits text files. Any sequential text file with fewer than 91 characters per record and fewer than 201 records can be manipulated with this utility. The most obvious use for this would be to create EXEC files. It could also be handy for correcting errors in files created by Basic programs or for fixing partially clobbered files.

The calculator is a machine-language subroutine for doing addition, subtraction, multiplication and division with twenty-place accuracy. To use the Calculator with Basic programs, you BLOAD it and set HIMEM to 36864. The numbers used in the operation must be stored as strings, with no non-numeric characters. Thus, only integers can be passed since decimal points are not allowed. The required routine is CALLed from Basic, and executes very quickly. On return, the answer is stored as a string. If there is a remainder in a division problem, it is stored in a separate string. Though applications requiring floating-point answers will require extra work on the programmer's part, the Calculator routine can be very helpful to anyone who needs high precision arithmetic at high speeds. If the user commits an error in defining the operation, the program doesn't bomb, but returns to Basic. A location can be PEEKed to obtain the error code.

The next utility is one about which Apple should have thought when they were designing the computer. It's called the Screen Printer, and it dumps the text screen to a printer. The code for this sits in page 3 of RAM, out of the way of most programs. Printout is obtained by hitting Control-Z whenever the keyboard is active. This routine was used to obtain hard copy of the sector display shown in Figure 1. Anyone who has ever tried to obtain a sample run of a program that doesn't print sequentially to the screen can appreciate the value of this routine.

The Prompter is another program which is designed to be used as a subroutine. It allows you to specify the format and restrictions of data received through INPUT statements. Among other things, it allows default values to be specified, prints optional commas and leading zeroes in numeric input, and allows special user-defined input restrictions as well as restrictions on length of input. Users wishing to incorporate Dakin5 subroutines in their own commercial software should contact the company about licensing.

Finally, we have the Cruncher. This powerful tool compresses Applesoft programs, removing unneeded spaces, deleting unreferenced REMs, and removing the comments from referenced REMs. After running the Cruncher, you load a program and give a call to the monitor. A Geiger-counter sound comes from the Apple speaker; the longer it clicks, the more the program is being crunched. Not only will crunched programs take up less space, they will run faster than uncompressed versions. The routine works quickly, and produced a substantial reduction in the programs on which it was tested.

The Dakin5 Programming Aids 3.3 is the Cadillac of disk utilities.

The entire Dakin5 package shows evidence of much thought and care. The instructions, packaged in a ring binder, are thorough and understandable. Anyone involved in software development should be able to get a great deal of mileage from this disk.

creative computing
SOFTWARE PROFILE

Name: Disk Fixer
Type: Utility
System: 32K Apple II, Disk Drive
Format: DOS 3.2 Disk (can be muffinned to 3.3)
Language: Machine Language
Summary: Excellent read/write program for disks.
Price: $29.95
Manufacturer:
Image Computer Products, Inc.
615 Academe Dr.
Northbrook, IL 60062

The Image of Perfection

Disk Fixer is designed solely for reading and editing disk sectors, but it does a superb job. The program, which can handle any flavor of DOS from 3.2 up, combines sector display with powerful screen editing capabilities, making it easy to use and extremely versatile. So many functions are provided that they can't all be covered here.

Basically, you start most operations by pulling a sector into the main buffer. This is done using the R command (for Read a sector). The current track and sector are listed at the top of the screen. When you hit R, the cursor moves up to these

Figure 1. A directory sector displayed by the 20 Patcher.

```
         ** THE PATCHER **


   TRACK 11     SECTOR 0F


00- 00 11 0E 00 00 00 00 00 ........
08- 00 00 00 0E 01 02 C8 C5 ......HE
10- CC CC CF A0 A0 A0 A0 A0 LLO
18- A0 A0 A0 A0 A0 A0 A0 A0
20- A0 A0 A0 A0 A0 A0 A0 A0
28- A0 A0 A0 A0 03 00 13 0F     ....
30- 00 D4 C5 D3 D4 A0 A0 A0 .TEST
38- A0 A0 A0 A0 A0 A0 A0 A0
40- A0 A0 A0 A0 A0 A0 A0 A0
48- A0 A0 A0 A0 A0 A0 A0 02        .
50- 00 14 0F 02 C2 D2 C5 C1 ....BREA
58- CB A0 A0 A0 A0 A0 A0 A0 K
60- A0 A0 A0 A0 A0 A0 A0 A0
68- A0 A0 A0 A0 A0 A0 A0 A0
70- A0 A0 02 00 15 0F 04 CD    .....M
78- D0 C9 C3 A0 A0 A0 A0 A0 PIC

UPDATE :
```

Figure 2. VTOC map from Disk Fixer.

```
-------------- DISKFIXER --------------
TRACK $11/SECTOR $00/VOLUME $FE/BYTE $08
----------------------------------------
$00! ***::::::::::::I:$::E:::::::::F:G:H
$01! ***::::::::::::I:$::E:::::::::F:G:H
$02! ***::::::::::::I:$::E:::::::::F:G:H
$03! ***::::::::::::I:$::E:::::::::F:G:H
$04! ***::::::::::::I:$::EE::::::::F:G:H
$05! ***::::::::::::I:$::EE::::::::F:G:H
$06! ***::::::::::::I:$::EE::::::::F:G:H
$07! ***:::::::::::IIH$::EE::::::::F:GGH
$08! ***:::::::::::IIH$::EE::::::::FFGGH
$09! ***:::::::::::IIH$::EED:::::::FFGGH
$0A! ***:::::::::::IIH$:CEED:::::::FFGGH
$0B! ***:::::::::BJIIH$ACEED:::::::FFGGH
$0C! ***:::::::::BJIIH$ACEED:::::::FFGGH
----------------------------------------
VTOC 0123456789ABCDEF0123456789ABCDEF012

----------------------------------------
B0
(13-SECTOR)                   FILTER ON

PRESS SPACE TO CONTINUE...             #
```

numbers, which are changed merely by typing the new track and sector. The sector is brought into the main buffer and also into the edit buffer, which appears on the screen. All changes are made to the edit buffer. You move through the screen using the I, J, K, and M keys. There are also commands to move to the top of the screen or to any specified byte. Other keys allow you to bring in the next sector. The display offers many options. You can have a half sector displayed in hex with ASCII equivalents on the side, a full sector in hex, or a full sector in ASCII. There is a filter which can be used to mask the hi bit of ASCII displays. Numbers can be entered in either hex or decimal.

While this alone would constitute a full utility, Image Computer Products provides much more. There are special commands to view and manipulate the disk catalog. You can change filenames, sort files, or scan through all sectors of a specific file. When requesting files, Disk Fixer allows the wildcard entries found in FID.

Another set of routines manipulates the volume table of contents (VTOC). When the VTOC is accessed, Disk Fixer provides a display of free and used sectors on the disk. Beyond this, it can map the VTOC, displaying not only the sectors in use, but also showing which programs occupy which sectors. An example of this is shown in Figure 2. Another command fixes any errors in the VTOC, locking out sectors that are in use but marked as free in the bit map and freeing locked sectors that aren't in use.

There are special commands to view and manipulate the disk catalog.

A set of special commands is included for various functions. Any display can be sent to the printer using Control-P. You can switch between 13 and 16 sector disks with a keystroke. You can exit the program and get into the monitor with Control-Q, then return to the program with Control-Y. The program also contains a line editor which is handy for entering ASCII data. For example, it allows you to put control characters in file names.

To put any data back to the disk, you have to move the edit buffer back to the working buffer and issue a write command. These steps help protect against unwanted writes. There is little chance of destroying a sector by sending bad or incorrect data to it.

The manual is clear, and contains some applications notes showing how to use the program to resurrect a dead file, change a binary file to a text file, and other tricks. Disk Fixer is a superb program.

Choices

The Dakin5 program works only with DOS 3.3, thus those with older versions of DOS will be unable to use it. The Image program works with either DOS, but contains fewer utilities. The programmer who needs to do a large amount of specialized work on sectors, or who doesn't require the other utilities, would probably do best buying Disk Fixer. If you need a wide range of utilities, and you don't plan to do extensive work on disk sectors, the Dakin5 package would be the best purchase. Those who need all the utilities and who also want to do a lot of sector work might consider investing in both packages.

Disk Fixer and Dakin5 Programming Aids are quality pieces of software which perform as promised. They are two utilities that can make life easier for the Apple owner. □

"I picked up that thousand-item multiple regression analysis that you've been working on for two months. Here's the output."

JUST FOR KICKS

Dale Archibald

I never expected to see a computer game this good—at least not so soon. Designed by Jay Sullivan (who also designed Hi-Res Football for On-Line), this game is a screamer. Rather, it's a cusser, especially when one of the strikers sends the ball floating toward your net and you send the goalie in the wrong direction.

Sullivan has designed it so that each player controls the movements of eight soccer players with the game paddles. The angle of an arrow drawn on the paddle determines the direction in which a figure runs. So your figures are constantly scrambling across the screen. I should have such boundless energy.

The player in the green jersey dribbled the ball down the field, deftly evading the rushes and lunges of his purple-clad opponents. At the last second, faking a kick to draw the goalie toward him, he passed the ball to a teammate who drove it between the bars for a score.

The player who has the ball dribbles it with his feet. The paddle setting also controls the direction of the kick—in one of 28 directions. With a little practice, you learn how to pass the ball back and forth between players; how to fake the goalie out; how to carom a pass into the goal off the sidelines in the beginner's game; where to have your goalie put a goal kick; and how to keep from being demolished by the Apple team in solitaire games.

To simulate balls being kicked into the air, some kicks can't be caught immediately: a rebound off the solitaire goalie delays one second, as does a throw-in when the ball is kicked out of bounds to the top or bottom (advanced game only). A corner kick occurs when a team kicks the ball out of bounds on the side of the field on which its goal is located; the opposing team gets to kick it in from the corner, with a two second delay. Finally, a goalie can kick with a two-and-a-half second delay if the opposing team kicks the ball out of bounds on his side.

There are three levels of play when two people play, one for solitaire play. At the beginner level, the ball bounces off all four sides of the field. For intermediates it bounces off the top and bottom but goes out of bounds to left and right, and in advanced play the ball can go out of bounds anywhere.

On color sets, the players are green and purple. On black and white, they're gray vs. black and white stripes.

It's hilarious to see the players run headlong across the field, steal the ball away from each other and intercept passes. The goalie even glides to catch the ball between his legs on attempted scores.

Don't expect to get the hang of it right away, either. I've been beaten by scores of 42 to 14, 24 to 6, etc. It took me several days of practice before I finally beat the game 5 to 3.

The game is divided into two halves of any length up to 45 minutes. The one bad thing about it is that there is no way to get a time-out to answer the telephone or any other call. □

Dale Archibald, 1817 Third Ave. N., Minneapolis, MN 55405.

On the Rocks

David Lubar

Ever since Bruce Wallace wrote the Apple version of Asteroids in Space (available from Quality Software), new versions of asteroids have appeared with startling regularity. At least four versions were sent to us in the past year. None was reviewed since none was as good as the original Wallace program. Now, a new asteroids game has appeared. Expecting yet another rehash, I was pleasantly surprised with the program. While *Apple-oids*, from **California Pacific**, is basically another version of the familiar arcade game, the program has nice touches and additions that make it worth owning.

The most obvious change is the use of floating apples (the fruit, not the computer) instead of asteroids. The apples, when shot, break up into smaller apples, and these smaller apples break up further when hit. You start out with six large apples. Clear them and you get a field of eight. Each successive field has ten apples.

There are two enemy ships that can appear with alarming frequency. The large ship shoots in a pattern rather than aiming for you. Destroying this ship earns you 200 points. The small ship goes for blood and is worth 1000 points. The point values of the apples vary according to size. You start with three ships, and win an extra ship for each 10,000 points.

So far, this all seems fairly standard. But there is more. One of the problems with Asteroids is the method of controlling the ship. *Apple-oids* seems to have taken a fairly sensible approach. Paddle number 1 controls rotation of the ship. The button on that paddle controls thrust. The ship will keep going after you release the button, but it will also decelerate and stop after a while. Firing is controlled from the keyboard. Any key from 0 to 9 fires a shot.

Any other key puts you in hyperspace. There is a chance that the ship will explode on emergence from hyperspace. There is also a chance of emerging from hyperspace right on an asteroid. Such occurences are fatal.

The ship rotates smoothly with a turn of the paddle. When the paddle is at either extreme, it sends the ship into a continuous spin. This avoids the problem encountered when the paddle is fully turned and you want to continue rotating.

The game displays the score and high score in hi-res numbers on the side of the screen. The number of ships remaining is represented pictorially at the bottom.

As a bonus, the disk also contains *Chipout*, which, as you've surely guessed, is a version of breakout. Done in hi-res, the program will satisfy breakout fans. There is one very nice touch. You start out with five balls. They are stored in a horizontal slot on the left wall. Each time a new ball comes into play, it slides from the slot, moves across the screen, then drops.

Simply put, *Apple-oids* is very good. The game is fun, highly replayable, and excellent graphically. California Pacific has come out with another winner. □

creative computing
SOFTWARE PROFILE

Name: Apple-oids

Type: Arcade game

System: 32K Apple, Disk Drive

Format: Disk

Language: Machine Language

Summary: Fun to play

Price: $29.95

Manufacturer:
California Pacific Computer Co.
7700 Edgewater Dr.
Oakland, CA 94621

Apple/UCSD Pascal 1.1: A User's Evaluation

Ross M. Tonkens

Having lived with Apple's newly updated version of UCSD Pascal (Pascal Ver. 1.1) for over a month, now, I feel a few observations are in order.

First, let me say that the manuals alone are worth the $60 update cost, for those of us who have had to live with the infamous "White Book" for the last year and a half. Just the sight of a real index (spanning more than seven pages!) brought tears of joy to my eyes.

In fact the system consists of over two manuals and four disks. I say "over two"

Ross M. Tonkens, M.D., 6221 Wilshire, Suite 607, Los Angeles, CA 90048.

manuals because there are two full-fledged reference manuals, one for the operating system, and one for Apple's implementation of UCSD Pascal. Both manuals are of the outstanding glossy quality to which we have become accustomed from Apple. I might add in passing that the graphic artwork gracing the covers of the manuals would sell briskly as poster art. In addition, three 9- to 16-page pamphlets are included. One describes differences between the old and new versions of Apple/UCSD Pascal; one is an addendum to the new operating system reference manual; and the third is an addendum to the new Pascal language reference manual.

Perhaps the best features of the current update are found only in these addenda. Among them were EXEC files, chaining capability, built in upper and lower case text generation without hardware add ons, much faster compile times, new compiler options, and an explicit list of previous bugs, fixed in this new version. Also contained in one of these little pamphlets is, at last, a lucid description of how program segmentation is accomplished by the compiler which clears up many mysteries left unresolved by even monk-like study of previous documentation.

This is all fine, but "how well does it wear?" as the saying goes. In short, "very well, indeed." All of the inconsistencies in how the operating system previously handled files with the special suffixes, ".text" and ".code" have been resolved. Combined with the addition of EXEC file capability, this has increased my productivity by at least 100%.

Now the user can define a common sequence of operating system commands, for example, those steps taken to compile and link a UNIT and install it in a library, or the commands issued to compile, link, and run a program, and have the computer perform them automatically in sequence, rather like a job control language. Instead of having to watch the computer full time, I now simply call up an EXEC file and take a break while the boring processes of compilation, linking, and test running all take place unattended.

EXEC files almost make up for my lack of a hard disk drive in terms of the increase in throughput achieved. About the only new problem the changes have created is temporary obsolescence of any memory-sensitive software, since the old memory map on which such software would have been based has been changed. This problem should be only temporary, as the update will involve simply altering the CONSTANT declarations of any Pascal 1.0 program which referenced memory directly once the new memory map is published by Apple. This brings me to my only complaint, namely that the new Pascal 1.1 manual did not already contain this information.

While the new Apple/UCSD Pascal Ver. 1.1 still has its idiosyncrasies, Apple seems to have distilled out those problems which were truly intolerable, while adding numerous conveniences which make it a truly serious software development system at last.

Now if I could just save the money for that hard disk.... □

GRAPHS
From Your Apple II

Robert Plamondon

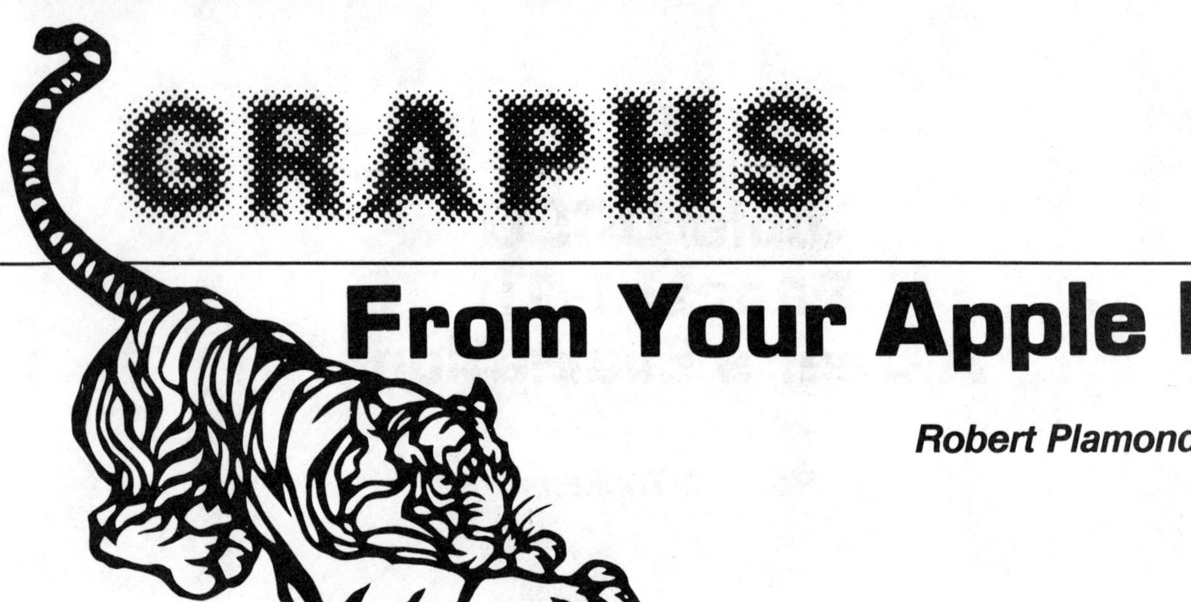

The high resolution graphics capability of the Apple II is a versatile feature, indeed. Graphics are used for such varied purposes as space games, custom character sets, and, or course, graphs.

In the past the use of Apple-generated graphs was limited by the scarcity of programs to generate them, and the means to make permanent copies. Most printers lacked the ability to print graphs, and those that did required machine-language driver programs. Thus, graphic output from the Apple was used only by those who had both a suitable printer and a good deal of programming experience.

Fortunately, those days are now gone. Several popular printers, such as the Paper Tiger, Epson MX-70, and some daisy-wheel printers have graphics capability, either as a standard feature or as an inexpensive option. In addition, several software houses have released programs which allow you to create and print your own graphs.

Scientific Plotter

Scientific Plotter from Interactive Microware and Creative Computing Software is available on diskette for 48K Apples with ROM Applesoft, and comes with about 30 pages of mildly confusing documentation.

This package is designed specifically for lab scientists who want to be able to make neat graphs of experimental data.

Robert Plamondon, 667 SW 15th Street, Corvallis, OR 97330.

<table>
<tr><td>

creative computing

SOFTWARE PROFILE

Name: Scientific Plotter

Type: 48K Apple, Applesoft, Disk drive

Format: Disk

Language: Applesoft

Summary: Quality graphing program

Price: $24.95

Manufacturer:

Interactive Microware, Inc.
P.O. Box 771
State College, PA 16801
or
Creative Computing Software
39 E. Hanover Ave.
Morris Plains, NJ 07950

</td></tr>
</table>

The only kind of graph it makes is the x-y plot; if you want bar graphs or pie charts, this is not the program for you.

Scientific Plotter produces a graph of your data points, with each point represented by a circle, square, cross, or star. Each of these symbols is available in four sizes. You can add error bars if you like, and the points can be connected by straight lines, or not, at your option.

The great advantage of the program is that it lets you play with the format of your graph, and scale it exactly to your needs. When drawing graphs by hand, your choices of format and scale are limited by the types of graph paper you have at your disposal. Drawing graphs by hand is also tedious and error-prone—just the kind of thing you'd like to fob off onto a computer.

Scientific Plotter has an impressive array of options. You can type in data points by hand, calculate them in subroutines, or pull them off a disk file. You have full control of the size of the graph, the location of the axes, the scale, and the color of the

> **Drawing graphs by hand is also tedious and error-prone — just the kind of thing you'd like to fob off onto a computer.**

data points. The format of the graph, the data, and the graph itself can be saved and retrieved from the data. Labels can be placed anywhere on the graph in any of four orientations and in any hi-res color. And there are many other useful features; too many to cover in a review.

The program works by asking you a series of questions. It starts by printing:

```
NAME OF FORMAT FILE ()?
<NONE>
```

Format files hold all the information on scaling, labels, and whatnot that the program needs to make a graph. The two parentheses generally hold the range of

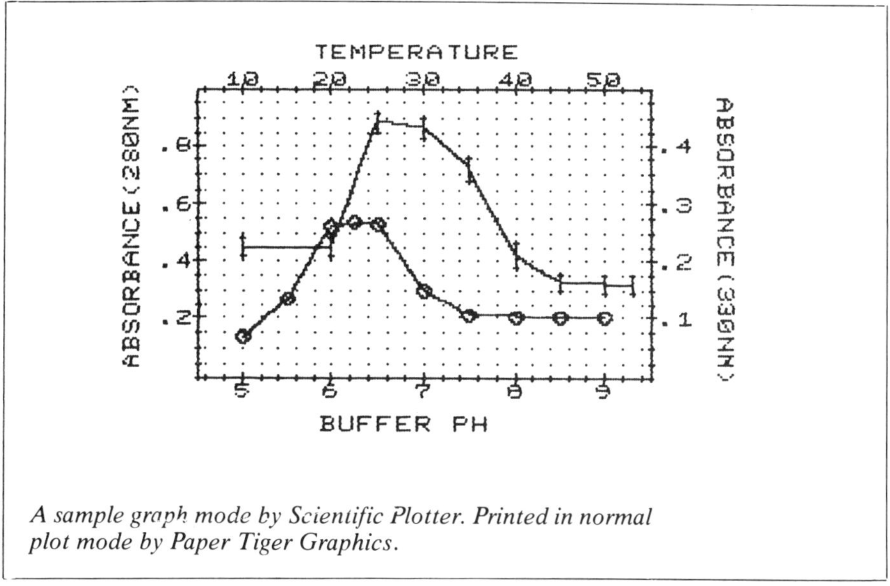

A sample graph mode by Scientific Plotter. Printed in normal plot mode by Paper Tiger Graphics.

values an answer can take; in this case, your response can be anything you want, so there are no limits shown. The "NONE" indicates that if you hit return without typing anything, the program assumes you don't want to load a format file. "NONE" is the default answer.

There are quite a few questions, and answering all of them (if only by the default value) can take a long time, especially when you make mistakes. Fortunately, the default value is equal to the last value you have entered, so you type only the corrections, and hit return on all the other questions. If you read in a format file at the beginning of the cycle, the values in the file become defaults. This can also save time, since most graphs have many parameters in common.

As a final time-saver, Control-A causes the program to step through the questions automatically, assigning the default value to each quantity. This can be stopped by hitting any key. This feature lets you flash past the routine questions and stop only where changes must be made.

As the questions are answered, the program gets the information it needs to start the graph. As soon as you input the position of the x-axis, the program displays the hi-res graphics page, draws the x-axis, and returns to text mode. This sequence of input, plotting, and return to text mode occurs every time the program puts something on the graph, and lets you see what you are building.

Unfortunately, there is no way to back up to fix a mistake on the previous question. Instead, you must start over. This is the worst flaw in the program.

The labeling feature is very flexible; labels can be placed in any of four orientations, anywhere on the screen. A ridiculously large number of labels can be placed on a graph.

One method of placing labels and axes on the graph is the Cursor command which places a small cross on the hi-res display. This cross can be moved by game paddles or a joystick, and is used to designate the starting position of a label or a coordinate axis without guessing x and y values.

My initial reaction to this program was massive frustration at the difficulty of correcting errors, followed by great satisfaction at the quality of my graphs. Once I had a few format files on disk, I found that I could make graphs with a few non-default values, and everything moved very quickly.

I have found Scientific Plotter to be a very useful program, and a genuine bargain at $25.

Paper Tiger Graphics

Enhanced Paper Tiger Graphics Software from Computer Station provides a way to transfer the contents of the hi-res graphics screen to your printer, assuming that you have a Paper Tiger 440 or 445 with graphics, as I do. Computer Station also sells graphic dump programs for the Paper Tiger 460G, Anadex 9501 and the NEC Spinwriter, which I assume are similar to the one for the Paper Tiger 440G.

Computer Station takes the problem of putting the contents of the screen onto a piece of paper, solves it elegantly, and wraps a truly foolproof control section around it. The program gives you a printout very quickly; its speed is limited mostly by the speed of the printer interface card. The program is menu-driven, and the menu is the best I have ever seen. The whole program is a joy to use.

The only fly in the ointment is that you have to tell it what kind of interface card you have, and in which slot it is located. If you have trouble remembering the card you have, and where you put it, this can slow you down.

The labeling feature is very flexible.

Let the Games Begin

David Lubar

Apple games are proliferating at an astounding rate. The stack seems to grow daily, with a large selection to dazzle consumers. While it is impossible to cover every program being released, the following gives a good idea of what is available for the game-hungry Apple owner.

Coming on Strong

On-Line Systems is alive and well, which is good news for game lovers. The best of their latest releases is *Threshold*. Given only a casual glance, the game seems to be nothing more than another shoot-em-up space battle. The player has a ship at the bottom and fires at enemy creatures above. The creatures are birds that flap their wings and fly evasive formations while shooting at the player. Get through the birds and another set of enemies appears. They move differently. The game begins to shine. A third formation appears, then a fourth. If the player hasn't lost all five of his ships at this point, he gets more fuel from the mother ship. New attackers appear. There are many, and it is not likely that anyone will see all of them.

Not only are there a variety of enemies, but each group exhibits substantial differences. They move in different ways, combine in different patterns, and attack differently. Many of the shapes are internally animated. There are wheels that spin, ships that tilt sideways into slim profiles, and objects that twirl like falling maple leaves.

Beyond this, there is still more to *Threshold*. The player can fire rapidly, but his laser tends to heat up. If it overheats, he will be unable to fire until it cools. If fuel runs out before a set of four screens is destroyed, the player loses the game. Finally, the player has a special option that can be used once per ship. By hitting a key, the enemy objects are slowed down for a while,

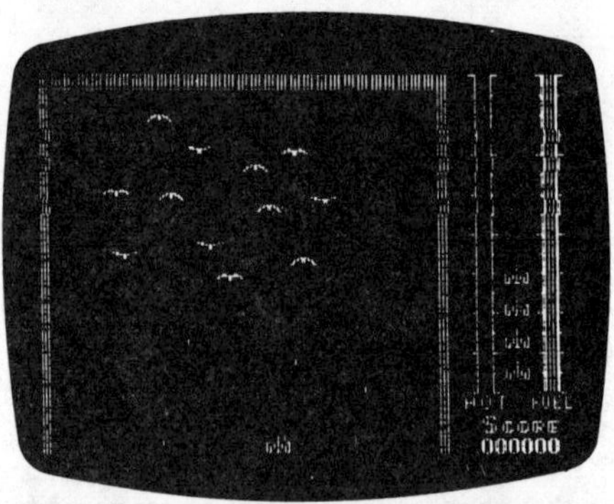

The first of many screens in Threshold.

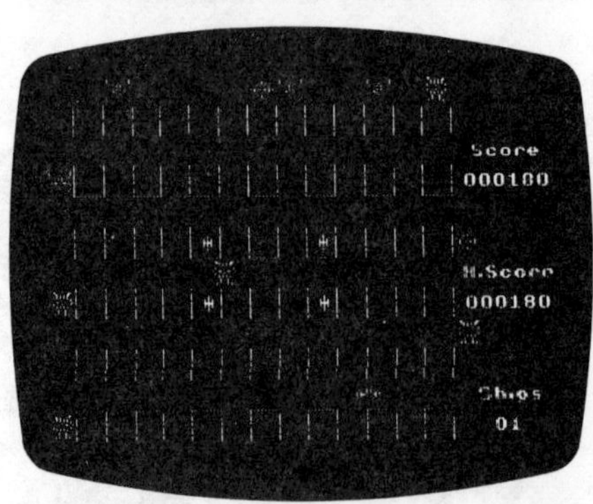

In Crossfire, there is no safe place to hide.

giving the player a brief advantage. Either paddles or keyboard controls can be used in this multi-faceted duel.

The animation in *Threshold* is superb, the game is challenging, and it is unlikely that anyone will tire of playing while the mystery of future screens lies ahead.

Crossfire is another arcade game from On-Line. Using keys, the player moves around a grid of squares, avoiding the shots of creatures that also move through the grid. The player can fire back, though his bullets are limited. The key controls are a bit tough to master. One set of four keys moves the player, another set is used for shooting. Rather than using a combination such as I,J,K, and M, the programmer chose I,J,K, and L, with K for down. Having the down key between left and right, rather than below it, is a bit confusing at first. Once the player has mastered the controls, he can concentrate on wiping out the enemy. His reward is another set of attackers, and a smaller supply of bullets. *Crossfire*, like *Threshold*, contains good animation, quick

---

creative computing

SOFTWARE PROFILE

Name: Threshold

Type: Arcade game

System: 48K Apple, Disk Drive

Format: Disk

Language: Machine Language

Summary: Highly challenging and full of surprises

Price: $39.95

Manufacturer:
On-Line Systems
36575 Mudge Ranch Rd.
Coarsegold, CA 93614

---

creative computing

SOFTWARE PROFILE

Name: Crossfire

Type: Arcade game

System: 48K Apple, Disk Drive

Format: Disk

Language: Machine Language

Summary: The enemy attacks from all sides

Price: $29.95

Manufacturer:
On-Line Systems
36575 Mudge Ranch Rd.
Coarsegold, CA 93614

response to controls, and a challenge to the player.

Good Bet

Draw Poker from Softape has some of the finest graphics ever done for the Apple. Though the game has been around for a while, it has that quality touch associated with the newest software. The program consists of five card draw for one player against the computer. While a two-player version of poker isn't quite as thrilling as a contest among five or six players, the graphics are so well done and entertaining that the game deserves a look. For each hand, the cards are spread, cut, assembled and shuffled. Each action, except for shuffling, is displayed graphically with a beautiful set of cards. The programmer did a really smooth job. When a bet is made, the chips appear on the screen. When the player or computer wins a hand, the chips are slid to the winner's side of the table.

The one weakness is in the betting system. The only unit of currency is the five dollar chip. Each bet and raise must be five dollars, no more or less. This allows less flexibility

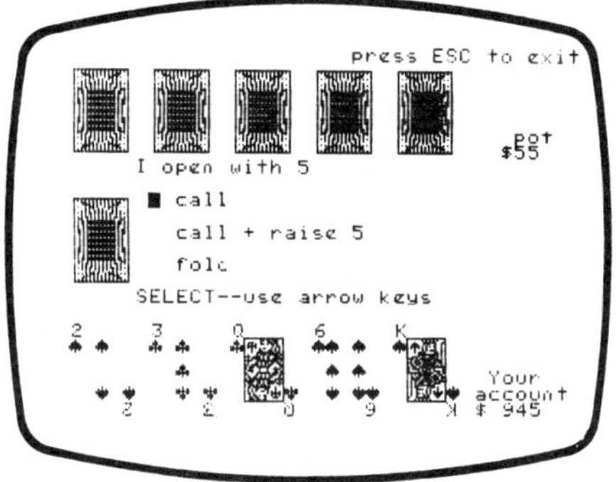

A hand from Draw Poker.

"...I said he's programmed to return serves,...not drop shots..."

creative computing
SOFTWARE PROFILE

Name: Draw Poker

Type: Card game
System: 32K Apple, Disk Drive

Format: Disk
Language: Machine Language
Summary: Superb graphics
Price: $29.95
Manufacturer:
    Softape
    10432 Burbank Blvd.
    North Hollywood, CA 91601

in strategy than when the player has a range to work with. While *Draw Poker* doesn't take the place of four friends and a six pack, it will give the poker addict a willing opponent, and also provide a great way to show off the power of Apple graphics.

Follow the Bouncing Ball

Datamost gives players a dose of pulse-driving action in the guise of *Thief*. The player must make his way through a series of rooms, avoiding such dangers as collision with walls, fire from enemy robots, and an indestructible smiling bouncing ball. In defense, the player has a gun. Control is through a joystick. Moving the stick moves the player. Holding the button while moving the stick points the gun. If the button is released while the stick is held to any side or corner, a bullet fires. A self-centering joystick is highly recommended for this one.

At the start, the player is in a green room, and the robots don't shoot. After a

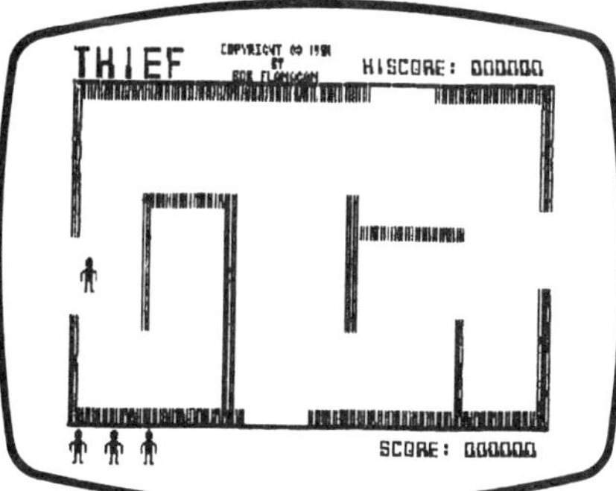

Slow humanoids don't last long in Thief.

certain score, the rooms become blue and the robots fire back. Later, the room becomes orange and the robots fire more frequently. Some of us have even had a brief peek at violet walls before being blown away. Unlike the arcade version, the robots in *Thief* can't be tricked into colliding

creative computing
SOFTWARE PROFILE

Name: Thief

Type: Arcade game

System: 48K Apple, Disk Drive, Joystick

Format: Disk

Language: Machine Language

Summary: Highly addictive and hard
        to beat

Price: $29.95

Manufacturer:
    Datamost
    19273 Kenya St.
    Northridge, CA 91326

with walls. But they can be destroyed by the bouncing ball. This is a game that can't be played just once. No one here has been able walk away from it without "just one more try." Since its arrival, *Thief* has stolen a great deal our time.

Two Can Play as Cheaply as One

In *Star Thief* from Cavalier, the thieves are the enemy. They are trying to steal power pods that the player must guard.

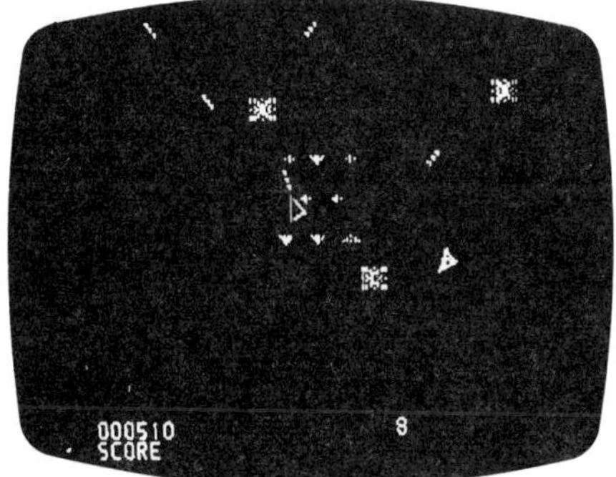

Two players can work together in Star Thief.

The player, using a paddle, can shoot and fly. He has an unlimited number of ships, but a limited supply of pods. The strength of the game is that it can be played by two people. If they cooperate, working together to guard the pods, the game can last a long time. Even when played solo, the game is good. The thieves aren't hard to shoot, but they keep coming. And whenever the player is hit, he must wait a few seconds for a new ship.

Controlling the ship with a single paddle is not difficult. The paddle rotates the ship and the button, if held, supplies thrust. A jab of the button produces a burst of missiles. This allows players to concentrate on the game without worrying about the keyboard. *Star Thief* is a fine addition to the small supply of two-player cooperative games for the Apple.

<table>
<tr><td>

creative computing
SOFTWARE PROFILE
Name: Star Thief

Type: Arcade game

System: 48K Apple, Disk Drive, Paddles

Format: Disk

Language: Machine Language

Summary: Fun for one or two players

Price: $29.95

Manufacturer:
   Cavalier Computer
   P.O. Box 2032
   Del Mar, CA 92014

</td></tr>
</table>

Uplifting Experience

3-D Skiing from Continental Software pairs Slalom and Ski Jump, making a fun package for sports fans. The jump is presented as a side view. From one to four players can compete in up to 99 jumps. Each jump starts with a press of the paddle button which gets the skier moving. Another button press at the right time launches him from the end of the ramp.

Once in the air, the lean of the skier is controlled by the paddle. A proper lean stretches out the jump. If the player leans too far, he loses balance. This can result in a spill that is almost as violent as the famous "agony of defeat" segment from *Wide World of Sports*. The player must also straighten out to land. If he doesn't, he finishes the ride sitting down. While a good technique can be developed for jumping, it is not so easy to master that it becomes automatic.

Slalom offers three courses, three levels of difficulty, and short and long versions of each course. The game gives a view of the back of the skier, looking down hill. The object is to ski through all the flags without hitting any or taking a spill. A paddle controls the direction the skis are pointed. If they are straight, the player

<table>
<tr><td>

creative computing
SOFTWARE PROFILE
Name: 3-D Skiing

Type: Sport game

System: 48K Apple, Disk Drive, Paddles

Format: Disk

Language: Machine Language

Summary: The jump is a killer

Price: $24.95

Manufacturer:
   Continental Software
   12101 Jefferson Blvd.
   Culver City, CA 90230

</td></tr>
</table>

moves forward, picking up speed. Turning the skis results in the skier turning in that direction. Turning also cuts down speed. Thus, the player who cuts the flags at the narrowest angle will get the best time, though he also runs the greatest risk of hitting a flag.

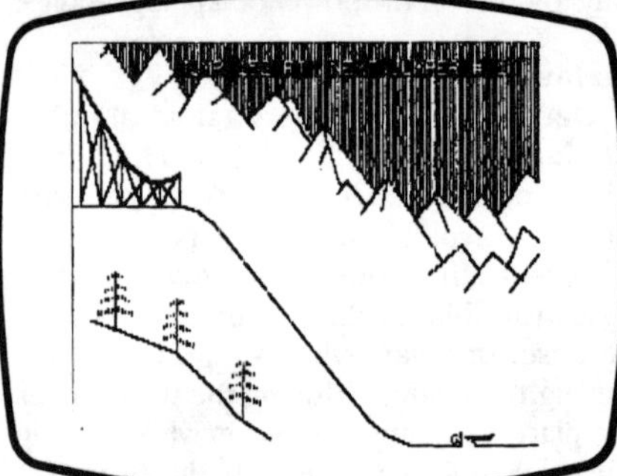

Ski Jump gives a new meaning to fear of flying.

The only weak point of Slalom is that the player cannot change courses or levels without rebooting the disk. This option would have been a nice addition. Except for this, *3-D Skiing* is fun to play and fun to watch.

Sudden Terror

Red Alert from Broderbund is a fast-paced, frantic game that has the player defending the bottom of the screen from a mass of attackers. Instead of just defending the standard ship or base, the player protects a series of installations, including radar, missiles, and a shield repair system. Above these facilities is the shield and above the shield are the attackers. They rain down missiles that eat away the shield. The player moves a crosshair, firing simultaneously from two guns at either side of the screen. The shots burst out in a circular pattern, destroying anything that enters the perimeter of fire. Once both guns have been destroyed, the game is over. The player can launch a special missile that destroys everything on the screen. He gets a new missile every 2500 points, but if the missile launcher is destroyed, no more missiles can be earned. Radar increases the spread

of the player's fire. The repair unit mends the shield at 10,000 points, and again at higher values. Once any of these specialized units is destroyed, it is gone for good unless

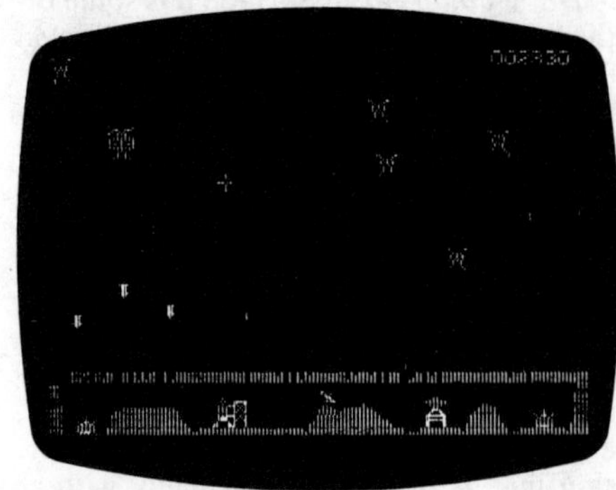

The player's shield is quickly destroyed in Red Alert.

the player is lucky enough to shoot one of the rare supply ships that zips across the screen.

The standard attack comes from swooping, dodging creatures that drop small missiles. Occasionally, a larger creature, looking somewhat like an Apple from *Apple Panic*, comes along and drops a cluster of larger missiles. These really do a job on the shield.

<table>
<tr><td>

creative computing
SOFTWARE PROFILE
Name: Red Alert

Type: Arcade game

System: 48K Apple, Disk Drive,
        Joystick (Recommended)

Format: Disk

Language: Machine Language

Summary: Fast-paced and tough

Price: $29.95

Manufacturer:
   Broderbund Software
   2 Vista Wood Way
   San Rafael, CA 94901

</td></tr>
</table>

The game demands total concentration from start to finish. There is no chance to relax for a second. Some will find it too fast paced, but those who have mastered its predecessors will find a real challenge in *Red Alert*.

Words for the Wise

Cross Clues from SRA is an original word game designed for the computer. Two players take turns trying to guess words in a crossword-style grid. On each turn, a player first tries for a complete word. If he is correct, he gets another guess. If the word is incorrect, any letters in the correct position are kept, and any correct consonants are also displayed wherever else they appear on the grid. Next, the player gets to select a single consonant. This is also displayed wherever it occurs in the grid. Points are scored for each occurrence of a letter. Each turn is also restricted by a time limit, and good players have their time cut in half.

A game of Cross Clues in progress.

Though the puzzles contain a fair number of short words, the vocabulary is sophisticated, and even puzzle experts will find the game to be a test of their skills. The disk contains 50 puzzles. An option for creating new puzzles would have been thoughtful. As is, owners of the game will have to wait and see if SRA will be releasing new puzzle disks.

Call in the Bouncer

While I try, in the interest of avoiding conflicts, to refrain from reviewing many programs from Creative Computing Software, there's a new game that is just too good to keep quiet about. *Blisterball* starts with the traditional ship at the bottom of the screen, but takes off from there in a different direction. High above, in an enclosed area, balls bounce. When the game starts, one ball drops, bouncing off the floor and walls. The player must avoid being hit, and try to shoot the ball. If he succeeds, two balls drop. After this come three, then four, and finally five. If the player is still alive, he gets to try for five bonus balls which drop one at a time. These balls are worth ten times as much as the others, but they fall faster and don't bounce. In the next round, the balls are

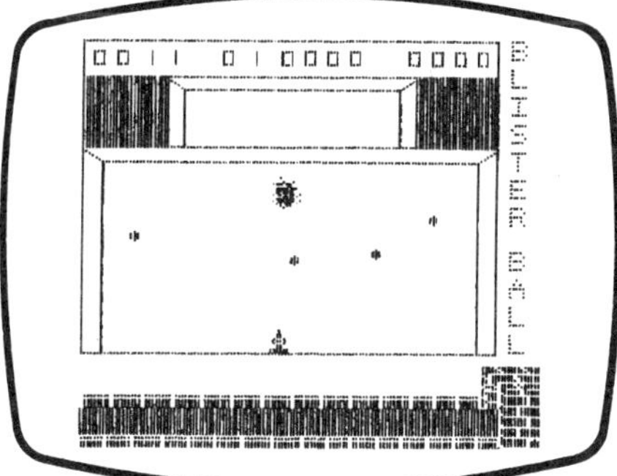

As one ball dies the others keep bouncing in Blisterball.

worth more, but they don't bounce as high. With each round, they lose elasticity. In each bonus round, the balls fall more quickly, requiring fast reflexes and a good aim. When the balls get too low, the walls begin to close in.

The game has two skill levels, and options for play by one person, two playing as a team, or two playing in competition. Almost everyone who has tried the game, including arcade addicts, has been quickly destroyed the first few times. A ship can take three hits before being knocked into the gutter. Those hits come pretty quickly when dealing with the multiple bouncing balls. On the weak side, the program doesn't save the high score to disk. Aside from this, *Blisterball* is a fine arcade game that offers good play value.

The package also contains *Mad Bomber*, a game where one or two players attempt to shoot bombs dropping from overhead racks. The racks start out empty, then quickly begin to fill. Whenever a rack has four bombs, it drops one. The player has a limited amount of ammunition, but can reload by moving all the way to the side of the screen. If a bomb hits a player, he loses ten rounds of ammunition. When ten bombs hit the ground, the game is over. Though not as strong as *Blisterball*, *Mad Bomber* is a lot of fun in the two-player cooperative mode, and very challenging as a solo game. □

Chapter VIII
Programs —
Ready to Run

Chapter VIII — Programs Ready to Run

In this section, you will find games to play, Christmas trees to light, plane landings to simulate, and power plants to blow up. These programs include lo-res or hi-res graphics, and have sounds ranging from ticks and tocks in Apple clocks to murderous ;meltdowns in nuclear power plants. Others will graph your own data as pie charts, or your own functions as polar coordinates.

For those who want to change some of the Integer BASIC programs to Applesoft BASIC, or conversely, some equivalent expressions are outlined below:

Integer	Applesoft
1) CALL -936	1) HOME
2) RND (3)	2) INT(3*RND(1))+1
3) K MOD 2	3) K-INT(K/2)*2
4) Y=TIME/12+3	4) Y=INT(TIME/12)+3
5) IF..THEN..:IF..THEN..	5) Only if put on TWO lines in Applesoft.
6) #	6)
7) INPUT "...",N$	7) (INPUT) ".......";N$

For additional comments regarding the differences between Integer and Applesoft BASIC, see the article on "Chess Clock".

Special Notes For Chapter VIII

● *Lit'l Red Bug,* by Bob Bishop:

The first program simulates driving a race car on a winding stretch of pavement. The faster you go, the more points you win or lose, depending on whether you are on the track or not. It uses Integer BASIC and some machine code. Directions for the novice for typing in the latter are included below. (Note: This program will **not** work as it is given here if you have Applesoft only.)

To enter the data table:
1) First, turn on your Apple so that you have the Integer BASIC prompt (=).
2) Next, type 'CALL - 151'. This allows you to have access to machine language, which uses the asterisk prompt.
3) Now type '1000: 00 08 00 08 00 08 00 80' and push Return.
4) Then type '1008: 28 A8 28 A8 28 A8 28 A8'.
5) Continue typing the list as it appears in the article until you reach the end of line 1038.
6) To check this listing, type '1000.103F' (This lists all values between the two numbers separated by the period.)

Then, to enter the first machine language program:
1) Type in "10AE: A213 BD 00 10" and push return.
2) Next, type in "10B3: 85 02 BD 20 10 85 03" and push Return.
3) Continue by starting each line with one of the numbers in the left column, followed by a colon (not the dash) and then typing in only the numbers in the second, third, and fourth columns (assuming there are six columns altogether.)
4) There does not have to be any particular number of two-character entries following the line number, but keeping the number small allows for easier error correction.
5) Your last line of this first program will be '1006: 00'.

To enter the second machine language program:
1) Enter '10EE: A5 00 85 02 68 48'.
2) Next, enter '10F4: C6 02 D0 FA'.
3) Continue the typing of this listing just as in the first program: line number, then colon, then two digit character pairs from the appropriate columns.
3) End this listing with the last line '1160: 4C EE 10'.
5) To check these last two programs, type in '10AEL' and what appears on the screen will be in the same format as that used in the article. If you would like to see more lines in the same format, type 'L' and push return.

For Disk storage, type 'BSAVE TITLE, A$1000,L$164' (interpretation: save the Binary file under the name of TITLE, starting in memory at the hexadecimal location of 1000 and with a hexadecimal length of 164 bytes!) To return to Integer BASIC, type '3D06' or CTRL-C and then hit return.

• *Grandapple Clock,* by Christopher Howerton:

This program simulates the old grandfather clock with ticks and tocks and alarms and chimes (all made soundless, optionally). It is written in Applesoft using hi-res graphics for the clock face, the moving hands, and the swinging pendulum. The novice may see some strange creatures such as Integer variables (those ending in a percent sign, such as A% or B% (I)). This will save on the space reserved for the array variables. Even for the more advanced, the ROT and XDRAW functions may be new. (For another example of the XDRAW function, see the Christmas tree program.) However, the logic of the program is well explained using flow diagrams and a line-by-line description.

The P. Lutus sound routine referred to may not be generally available, so an adaptation is listed below:

```
100 REM Applesoft program to duplicate the P. Lutus sound routine from the
200 REM old red Apple II reference manual.
250 REM adaptation by J. B. Tate *810722* with the help of M. W. Pelczarski
300 GOSUB 32000
350 HTAB 20
400 PRINT "TYPE 0 FOR PITCH, TO END."
450 INPUT "Pitch (10-250)";F
460 INPUT "DURATION (1-255)";D
470 IF f=0 THEN GOTO 800
500 POKE 768,F: POKE 769,D
600 CALL 770
650 GOTO 350
800 END
32000 FOR I=770 to 790
32010 READ J: POKE I,J
32020 NEXT I
32030 DATA 173,48,192,136,208,5,206,1,3,240
32040 DATA 9,202,208,245,174,0,3,76,2,3,96
32050 RETURN
```

• *Chess Clock,* by Christopher Howerton:

Chess Clock is written in Integer BASIC and uses lo-res graphics to form the characters for a digital clock. The time displayed includes both minutes and seconds. The many REM statements will not only aid your understanding of the program, but will also allow you to customize it to your own specifications.

See the notes at the beginning of this chapter for some of the differences between Integer BASIC and Applesoft BASIC.

• *Caesar's Watch,* by Paul Raymer:

The Romans, known for their extensive water canals, might have used water to record the passage of time. At least Paul Raymer's references seem to indicate that was the case. This Applesoft program uses lo-res graphics so you can "get the picture", and is well documented, with REM statements dividing it nicely into sections. The drips silently fill the second vessel, which empties into the minute vessel, and which empties into the hour vessel (which must be thrown out after twelve hours.)

• *Apple Pie,* by N. B. McBurney II:

In most any news magazine you will find pictorial statistics in the form of bar graphs or colored charts. This Applesoft program, using hi-res graphics, also shows comparisons — but as parts of a circle or 'pieces of a pie.' The well-placed REM statements and the variable list at the end, cross-referenced with the appropriate lines in the program, will allow most programmers to follow the logic of the program.

• *Apple Nuclear Power Plant,* by Stephen R. Berggren:

This program simulates the performance of a water-pressurized nuclear power plant. The program is written in Applesoft and is small enough to fit into 16K. It uses lo-res graphics to draw the water tower, reactor core, turbine. For example, one section limits input to only the digits 0-9 and keyboard entries to only four keystrokes. The author states, "The program is almost entirely crashproof." (Should "crashproof" be allowed to have any modifiers?) Note the REM statements at the end of the program which explain the program by sections.

- *Landing Simulator,* by Jake Jacobs:

The screen displays the pilot's view of the runway in hi-res graphics and the instrument panel — showing altitude, rate of climb, velocity, power and the distance (to the runway.) This program uses the game paddles for controlling the 'stick' and the power, and incredibly fits into 16K. Only similar triangle mathematics is used to explain the calculations in the program. Suggested extensions follow sufficient documentation to allow a personal version to evolve.

- *Ten to the Thirty-Eighth,* by William Bradford:

From Martin Gardener's game of GOOGOL, which is ten to the one-hundredth power, has sprung "Ten to the Thirty-Eight." (To give you an indication of the size of these numbers, it has been estimated that the number of grains of sand on Coney Island is approximately only ten to the twentieth. A Googol may adequately represent the number of atoms in the universe.) The computer chooses up to 14 random numbers, ranging from very small to very large (the latter being defined as ten to the thirty-eighth). You choose to see the numbers, one at a time, until you believe the largest has been displayed. You must take the last number displayed. From one to four players may play at the same time, with time given for each to place their bets on their own choices. A formula is given in the article that can be used to analyze a winning strategy.

- *Teachers! A Social Science Survey Program,* by Dr. James Owens:

Questionnaires about various and sundry topics are a part of almost everyone's life. They usually inquire about your sex, age and other things — with the results sometimes appearing on TV or in the news the following week. This program shows how results can be tallied and analyzed in fourteen different ways. It was written two years ago, when 48K of memory was unheard of, and therefore omits the REM statements for the different sections, allowing the program to fit into 4K of memory. The 'DATA x,y,a,b,c' statements in the program represent the following:

x = 2 if male or 3 if female

y = 5 if under 30 years of age or 4 if over

a = response to question one and ranges from 1 (disagree strongly) to 9 (agree strongly)

b = response to question two

c = response to question three

The program also has a nice rounding function used to control output to two places and avoids division by zero without an IF . . . THEN . . . (just add IE-04 to the denominator).

- *The Intricate Graphs of the Polar Functions,* by Richard T. Simoni, Jr.:

Mathematics teachers and students, rejoice! One of the most unique but arithmetically frustrating topics — polar graphing — is now easily within your grasp. This program, though very short and simple, uses hi-res graphics to draw wonderful polar curves. Changing the parameters in any one equation is easily done and can be used to illustrate topics such as bounds, extent and symmetry. Unusual graphs, never before attempted, such as: r = Cos(2*Sin(q)) yield surprising results.

- *What to Name the Baby?* by Paul Raymer:

Write out a list of all possible four-letter words (there are 456,976 ways so it may take a while!) or use this Applesoft program to do it for you. With 16 words per line (you need a space between each word) and 80 characters per line, that's 28,561 lines or 433 pages (with 66 lines per page). With an Epson MX-80 printer it would take a little less than 8 hours.

Although some mathematics classrooms have signs that warn against speaking any four letter words (such as inch, foot, yard, etc.) there are some more respectable ones such as 'love' and 'nice.' Who knows, you might also find out what to name the baby.

- *Weather Station,* by Paul Raymer:

Just to show your friends that computer programs can have whimsical applications, try running "Weather Station" for them. This program will ". . . bring your computer in touch with the real world, without expensive electronic coupling devices or complex meteoroligical equipment."

Requiring only one extra piece of equipment (an 8 by 10 sheet of paper), this program is well documented and uses NO hi-res or lo-res graphics. However, due to copyright restrictions, it may not be used by local radio stations without specific permission.

- *Christmas Tree,* by Stephen R. Berggren:

Are you tired of cleaning up dry needles, and putting away the lights, tinsel, and Christmas tree stand? Perhaps this program is for you.

Written in Applesoft, it displays a Christmas tree with up to 200 lights that you place using the game paddles. You have the options of choosing the color of the lights and whether they are to be flashing or non-flashing. Once more, we have an example of a shape table and the XDRAW function in an interesting program. (This was also used in the Grandapple Clock program.)

Lit'l Red Bug

Bob Bishop

Lit'l Red Bug is a game of skill in which you must drive your Volkswagen along a road without going off the pavement. The faster you go, the more points you get...unless you leave the road. Off the road, you begin to lose points. The faster you go, the more points you lose!

If you don't have a color display, you might want to change the last part of line 10 to read: CAR=15 instead of: CAR=1.

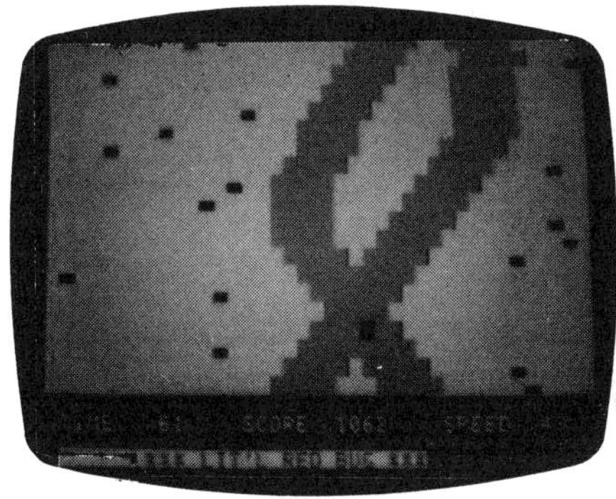

This will change the color of the "bug" to white so that it will show up better on a black and white set.

The program is written in Apple-II integer Basic with just a touch of machine language for class.

Bob Bishop, Apple Computer, 10260 Brandley Dr., Cupertino, CA 95014.

Note: Besides the Basic portion of *Lit'l Red bug*, there are three portions of machine code which have to be entered; two programs and one data table. The easiest way to enter this code is through direct hex entry in the monitor. For the table, just type 1000: followed by the data. If RETURN is used, begin the next line with another colon. Once this table is entered, the two short programs can be entered in two ways. Either the assembler can be used, or more simply, the hex code in the second column can be entered. For each program, enter the starting address, followed by a colon, then start typing the groups of numbers in the second column. Again, when you hit return, type another colon. After entering all the code, check the results by typing the first address followed by an L. This should cause the screen to display exactly what is shown in the listing. To save the data on cassette, use 1000.1163W. To save it on disk, use BSAVE TITLE, A$1000, L$164.

Second note: The author, Bob Bishop, is the lesser-known brother of a certain mythical figure who works deep in the halls of the Elppa Computer Company.

```
*1000.103F

1000-   00 80 00 80 00 80 00 80
1008-   28 A8 28 A8 28 A8 28 A8
1010-   50 D0 50 D0 50 D0 50 D0
1018-   00 00 00 00 00 00 00 00
1020-   04 04 05 05 06 06 07 07
1028-   04 04 05 05 06 06 07 07
1030-   04 04 05 05 06 06 07 07
1038-   00 0A 0A 0A 0A 08 0B 0A

10AE-   A2 13          LDX   #$13
10B0-   BD 00 10       LDA   $1000,X
10B3-   85 02          STA   $02
10B5-   BD 20 10       LDA   $1020,X
10B8-   85 03          STA   $03
10BA-   CA             DEX
10BB-   BD 00 10       LDA   $1000,X
10BE-   85 00          STA   $00
10C0-   BD 20 10       LDA   $1020,X
10C3-   85 01          STA   $01
10C5-   A0 27          LDY   #$27
10C7-   B1 00          LDA   ($00),Y
10C9-   91 02          STA   ($02),Y
10CB-   88             DEY
10CC-   10 F9          BPL   $10C7
10CE-   8D FF FF       STA   $FFFF
10D1-   E0 00          CPX   #$00
10D3-   D0 DB          BNE   $10B0
10D5-   60             RTS
10D6-   00             BRK

10EE-   A5 00          LDA   $00
10F0-   85 02          STA   $02
10F2-   68             PLA
10F3-   48             PHA
10F4-   C6 02          DEC   $02
10F6-   D0 FA          BNE   $10F2
10F8-   8D 30 C0       STA   $C030
10FB-   C6 01          DEC   $01
10FD-   D0 EF          BNE   $10EE
10FF-   60             RTS
1100-   A9 9D          LDA   #$9D
1102-   85 00          STA   $00
1104-   A9 40          LDA   #$40
1106-   85 01          STA   $01
1108-   20 EE 10       JSR   $10EE
110B-   A9 74          LDA   #$74
110D-   85 00          STA   $00
110F-   A9 57          LDA   #$57
1111-   85 01          STA   $01
1113-   20 EE 10       JSR   $10EE
1116-   A9 50          LDA   #$50
1118-   85 00          STA   $00
111A-   A9 61          LDA   #$61
111C-   85 01          STA   $01
111E-   20 EE 10       JSR   $10EE
1121-   A9 40          LDA   #$40
1123-   85 00          STA   $00
1125-   A9 00          LDA   #$00
1127-   85 01          STA   $01
1129-   20 EE 10       JSR   $10EE
112C-   A9 50          LDA   #$50
112E-   85 00          STA   $00
1130-   A9 61          LDA   #$61
1132-   85 01          STA   $01
1134-   20 EE 10       JSR   $10EE
1137-   A9 40          LDA   #$40
1139-   85 00          STA   $00
113B-   A9 00          LDA   #$00
113D-   85 01          STA   $01
113F-   20 EE 10       JSR   $10EE
1142-   A9 40          LDA   #$40
1144-   85 00          STA   $00
1146-   A5 00          LDA   $00
1148-   85 01          STA   $01
114A-   20 EE 10       JSR   $10EE
114D-   A9 40          LDA   #$40
114F-   85 00          STA   $00
1151-   A9 00          LDA   #$00
1153-   85 01          STA   $01
1155-   20 EE 10       JSR   $10EE
1158-   A9 40          LDA   #$40
115A-   85 00          STA   $00
115C-   A5 00          LDA   $00
115E-   85 01          STA   $01
1160-   4C EE 10       JMP   $10EE
```

```
5 X=Y=L=DL=R=DR=SPEED=POS=TOT=TIME=Z=BACK
10 ROAD=5:FIELD=12:BUSH=4:CAR=1
20 DOWN=4096+174
40 GOSUB 2000
60 TOT=0:TIME=425:Y=TIME/12+3
70 POS=1500:X=POS/75:BACK=ROAD
80 L=16:DL=0:R=20:DR=0
100 COLOR=BACK: VLIN Y-1,Y AT X
150 CALL DOWN
160 Z= PEEK (-16336):Z= PEEK (-16336)
200 POS=POS+ PDL (0)-128: IF POS<0 THEN POS=0: IF POS>2999
    THEN POS=2999

220 TIME=TIME-1:Y=TIME/12+3
230 X=POS/75:BACK= SCRN(X,Y)
250 COLOR=CAR: VLIN Y-1,Y AT X
300 COLOR=FIELD: HLIN 0,39 AT 1: HLIN 0,39 AT 0
310 COLOR=BUSH: PLOT RND (40),1
320 COLOR=ROAD: HLIN L,L+4 AT 1: HLIN R,R+4 AT 1: HLIN L,L+4
    AT 0: HLIN R,R+4 AT 0
350 Z= PEEK (-16336):Z= PEEK (-16336)
400 IF NOT RND (5) THEN DL= RND (3)-1
410 IF NOT RND (5) THEN DR= RND (3)-1
420 IF L=1 THEN DL=1: IF L=33 THEN DL=-1
430 IF R=1 THEN DR=1: IF R=33 THEN DR=-1
450 L=L+DL:R=R+DR
480 SPEED=(255- PDL (1))/5
490 FOR K=0 TO SPEED: NEXT K
500 TOT=TOT+60-SPEED
520 IF BACK=FIELD THEN 1000
540 Z= PEEK (-16336):Z= PEEK (-16336)
550 VTAB 22: TAB 9: PRINT TIME/6;" ";: TAB 22: PRINT TOT;
    " ";: TAB 37: PRINT 90-SPEED
600 IF TIME>0 THEN 100
700 TEXT : CALL -936: VTAB 5
710 TAB 12: PRINT "--- GAME OVER ---"
720 VTAB 12: PRINT " YOUR SCORE OF ";TOT;" IS ";
730 IF TOT>10000 THEN 750
740 PRINT "TERRIBLE!": PRINT : IF TOT<5000 THEN PRINT "(YOU
    SHOULD BE ASHAMED OF YOURSELF!)"
750 IF TOT>10000 AND TOT<=15000 THEN PRINT "PRETTY BAD!"
760 IF TOT>15000 AND TOT<=19000 THEN PRINT "ABOUT AVERAGE."
770 IF TOT>19000 AND TOT<=22000 THEN PRINT "VERY GOOD!"
780 IF TOT>22000 THEN PRINT "EXCELLENT!"
790 IF TOT>24000 THEN CALL 4352
800 FOR K=1 TO 1000: NEXT K
810 VTAB 20: PRINT "PUSH EITHER PADDLE BUTTON TO PLAY AGAIN"
820 IF PEEK (-16286)<128 AND PEEK (-16287)<128 THEN 820
850 GOSUB 2050
900 GOTO 60
1000 FOR K=1 TO 20:Z= PEEK (-16336): NEXT K
1010 TOT=TOT-5*(50-SPEED):TIME=TIME-1
1020 IF TOT<0 THEN TOT=0
1050 GOTO 550
2000 TEXT : CALL -936
2010 VTAB 10: TAB 10: PRINT "*** LIT'L RED BUG ***"
2020 PRINT : TAB 19: PRINT "BY"
2030 PRINT : TAB 15: PRINT "BISH BOBHOP"
2040 FOR K=1 TO 1500: NEXT K
2045 GOSUB 3000
2050 GR : POKE -16298,0
2060 VTAB 22: PRINT " TIME:";: TAB 15: PRINT "SCORE:";:
     TAB 30: PRINT "SPEED:
     "
2070 POKE 50,63: VTAB 24: TAB 2: PRINT " *** LIT'L RED BUG ***
     ";: POKE 50,255
2100 FOR K=0 TO 39
2110 COLOR=FIELD: HLIN 0,39 AT K
2120 COLOR=BUSH: IF K MOD 2 THEN PLOT RND (40),K
2130 COLOR=ROAD: HLIN 16-K/8,24+K/8 AT K
2140 NEXT K
2200 RETURN
3000 CALL -936: TAB 10: PRINT "*** LIT'L RED BUG ***"
3010 PRINT : PRINT : PRINT "THE OBJECT OF THIS GAME IS TO
     DRIVE YOUR"
3020 PRINT "LITTLE RED VOLKSWAGEN DOWN THE ROAD AS"
3030 PRINT : PRINT "FAST AS YOU CAN WITHOUT GOING OFF THE"
3040 PRINT : PRINT "PAVEMENT.  GAME PADDLE 0 IS YOUR STEER-"
3050 PRINT : PRINT "ING WHEEL, AND PADDLE 1 IS YOUR ACCELER-"
3060 PRINT : PRINT "ATOR.  HAVE A NICE RIDE!"
3090 FOR K=1 TO 1000: NEXT K
3100 VTAB 22: PRINT "PUSH EITHER GAME PADDLE BUTTON TO BEGIN"
3110 IF PEEK (-16286)<128 AND PEEK (-16287)<128 THEN 3110
3120 IF PEEK (-16286)>127 OR PEEK (-16287)>127 THEN 3120
3200 CALL -936: RETURN
```

"Where do you want it?"

Grandapple Clock

Christopher Howerton

The enclosed program was written by William B. Smith of Gambier Island, British Columbia. Here is his description.

This program is an attempt to humanize the computer a little by having it perform the old-fashioned functions of a grandfather clock. Using the Grandapple clock has certain advantages over a regular clock:

1) it will keep the Apple II working 24 hours a day rather than gathering dust in a corner, or (if switched on) maybe figuring out how to program itself.
2) allows for operation of a a grandfather clock regardless of gravity -- a useful feature when visiting the moon
3) costs less than a real grandfather clock (not counting the computer, of course)

Other uses of the Grandapple clock include store display, timing games, and showing modern day children what clocks used to look like in the analog era.

The program displays, graphically, a clock face on the monitor, using the high resolution graphics facilities of the Apple. It uses Roman numerals to mark the hours, has a long and a short hand, and has gothic style columns on either side of the clock face just to balance the display.

The menu at the start of the program allows the user to have sound effects (chimes, ticks and tocks with a visual pendulum and an alarm.)

To Use
a) This program requires 24K bytes of RAM.
b) Load Applesoft Basic (cassette version)
c) Load the program in the usual manner, and type 'RUN'

Christopher Howerton, 13572 92 Avenue, Surrey, B.C. Canada V3V 1H7.

d) Now follow the instructions in the menu.
e) To stop the clock, hit any key
f) To turn off the alarm, hit any key.

Note that the program simulates the clock without use of any special hardware. This is done by using timing loops. This program uses the simple tone routine by P. Lutas which is in the red Apple Manual.

Line by line description:

Lines 0-99	were originally reserved for REMs, but Murphy's Law regarding program size expanding to fit available memory applied!
100-149	are the basic timekeeping loop. The variable E allows for the different subroutine options (e.g. chimes) to have the amount of time they use deducted from the variable which keeps the clock accurate. Line 120 branches the program to the "tick tock" routine, which has its own timing loop. Line 130 allows the user to exit the program by depressing any key.
150-199	keep the minutes, hours and am/pm flags updated. Line 160 also branches to the "alarm" routine, if the alarm is set, to check whether it is time to ring the alarm. This occurs once each minute.
200-299	draw and erase the minute and hour hands. The several IF statements control the display of the hands when they pass each other pm% new position of minute hand ph% new position of hour hand

opm% old position of minute hand
xph% old position of hour hand

Line 285 branches program to "chimes" routine once per hour if the flag is set

300-349	control the "tick tock" and pendulum features. If this option is being used, lines 305-315 control the timekeeping loop. Lines 325&335 call for the tick and the tock noise. Lines 330&340 draw, and lines 347 & 348 erase the pendulum. The variable B keeps track of whether the clock ticked or tocked last time.
350-399	are the chimes option. Lines 350-363 call for a little tune. Lines 365-385 chime the number of hours. Line 390 keeps account of the time used for the above.
400-499	are the alarm option. Lines 400-415 are checked once each minute, if the alarm is set, to see if it is time to start ringing. The remaining lines produce an interrupted tone until any key is depressed.
500-599	provide the data for the short tune, the various shapes, and the position of these shapes on the hgr2 display page.
600-699	are mostly read statements to draw the clock face. Line 690 makes a machine code program for sounds (written by P. Lutas).
700-799	include the menu and and input statements.
800-849	are the exit from the program after any key is depressed.

```
>PR#0##############

]LIST GRANDAPPLE CLOCK

3   HIMEM: 16277
4   DIM ZD$(1),ZC$(1),ZB$(1),ZA$(1
    )
5   GOTO 700
90  E = 420 + (H * 140)
119 E = 1
120 IF  ASC (ZC$) = 89 THEN  GOTO
    300
125 FOR A = E TO 4862
130 IF  PEEK ( - 16384) > 127 THEN
    GOTO 800
140 NEXT A
160 MIN = MIN + 1: IF  ASC (ZD$) =
    89 THEN  GOSUB 400
165 IF MIN < 60 THEN  GOTO 200
170 MIN = 0:HOUR = HOUR + 1
172 IF  ASC (ZB$) = 89 THEN FLAG
    = 1
175 IF HOUR < 12 GOTO 200
180 HOUR = 0: IF PM = 1 THEN PM =
    0: GOTO 200
185 IF PM = 0 THEN PM = 1: GOTO
    200
200 SCALE= 12
205 PM% = MIN * 64 / 60: ROT= PM%
    : GOSUB 290
210 PH% = (HOUR * 64 + PM%) / 12:
    ROT= PH%: GOSUB 295
215 IF PH% = XPH% THEN  ROT= PH%
    : GOSUB 295
220 IF PM% = PH% THEN  ROT= PH%:
    GOSUB 295
225 IF B = 0 THEN  GOTO 285
230 ROT= OPM%: GOSUB 290
235 ROT= XPH%: GOSUB 295
240 IF OPM% = PH% THEN  ROT= PH%
    : GOSUB 295
241 IF HOUR = 6 AND MIN = 34 THEN
    ROT= PH%: GOSUB 295
245 IF XPH% = PM% AND XPH% < >
    PH% THEN  ROT= PM%: GOSUB 29
    5
246 IF PM% = XPH% AND PH% = PM% +
    1 THEN  ROT= PM%: GOSUB 295
250 IF PH% = XPH% THEN  ROT= XPH
    %: GOSUB 295
285 OPM% = PM%:XPH% = PH%:B = 1:E
    = 1: IF FLAG = 1 THEN  GOSUB
    350
286 FLAG = 0: IF R = 0 THEN  GOTO
    120
287 GOTO 160
290 XDRAW 1 AT 140,80: RETURN
295 XDRAW 2 AT 140,80: RETURN
300 ROT= 7: DRAW 7 AT 80,180:G =
    19
305 FOR A = E TO 4862 STEP 67:Q =
    1
```

Flowchart to Grandapple Clock

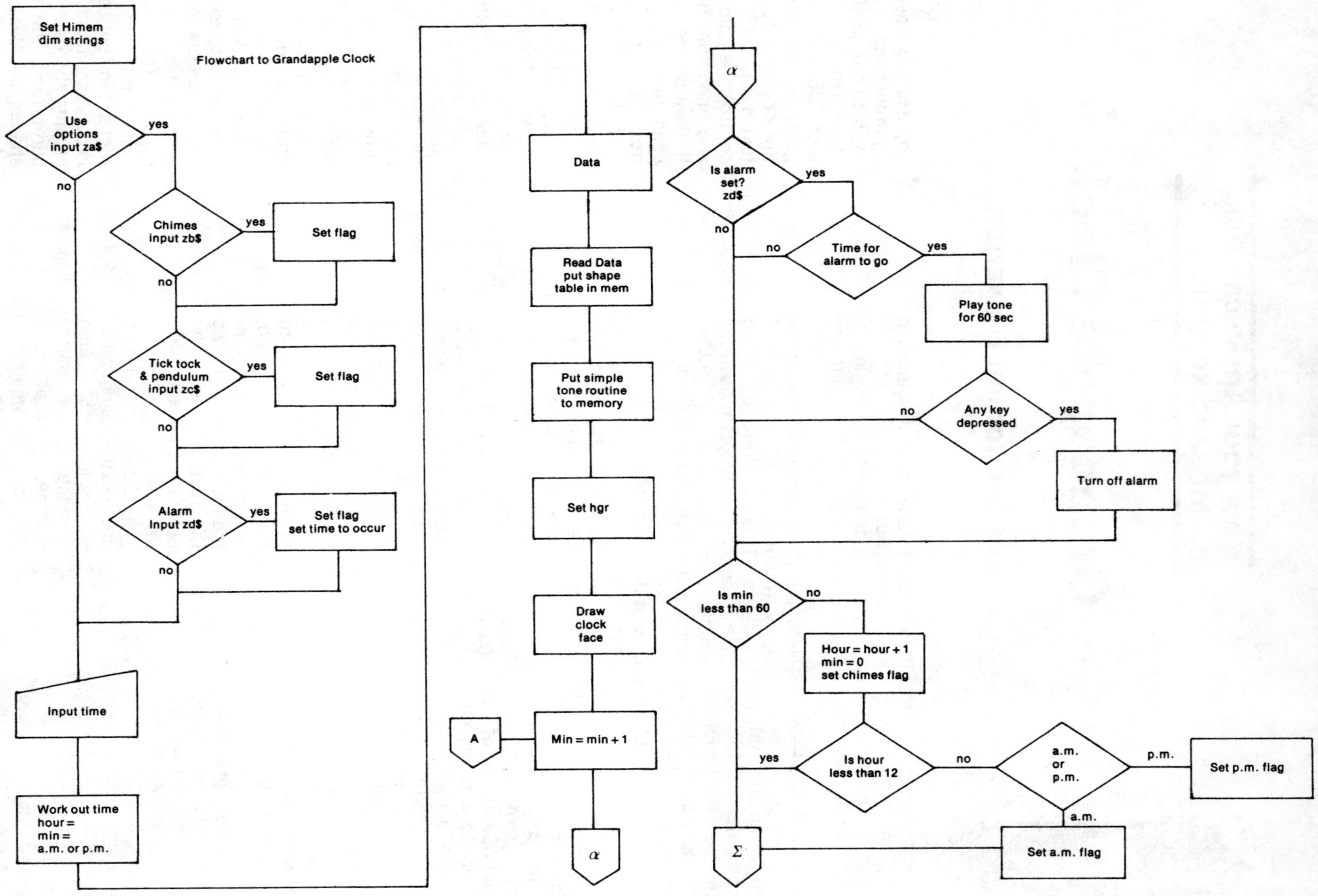

```
307 FOR F = G TO 60
310 IF  PEEK ( - 16384) > 127 THEN
     GOTO 800
315 NEXT F
320 IF B = 1 GOTO 335
325 POKE 768,100: POKE 769,03: CALL
     770
330 DRAW 7 AT 80,180:B = 1: XDRAW
     7 AT 168,180: GOTO 345
335 POKE 768,70: POKE 769,03: CALL
     770
340 DRAW 7 AT 168,180: XDRAW 7 AT
     80,180:B = 2
345 G = 1: NEXT A
347 IF B = 1 THEN  XDRAW 7 AT 80
     ,180
348 IF B = 2 THEN  XDRAW 7 AT 16
     8,180
349 E = 1: GOTO 160
350 RESTORE
355 FOR A = 0 TO 3: READ E
360 POKE 768,E: POKE 769,50: CALL
     770: FOR F = 1 TO 200: NEXT
     F: NEXT A
361 IF A = 8 GOTO 365
362 FOR F = 1 TO 400: NEXT F
363 FOR A = 4 TO 7: READ E: GOTO
     360
365 FOR A = 1 TO 1000: NEXT A
370 H = HOUR: IF HOUR = 0 THEN H =
     12
375 FOR E = 1 TO H: POKE 768,250
     : POKE 769,100: CALL 770
380 FOR F = 1 TO 800: NEXT F
385 NEXT E
390 E = 500 + (H * 133)
395 RETURN
400 IF MIN = 60 THEN ALARM = (HO
     UR + 1) * 100: GOTO 405
403 ALARM = HOUR * 100 + MIN
405 IF PM = 1 THEN ALARM = ALARM
     + 1200
410 IF ALARM = SET GOTO 420
415 E = 4: RETURN
420 SET = SET + 1:E = 1:R = 1

435 FOR A = E TO 87
440 IF  PEEK ( - 16384) > 127 THEN
     ZD$ = "N":R = 0: GOTO 455
445 POKE 768,255: POKE 769,255: CALL
     770
450 NEXT A
455 POKE  - 16368,0
465 RETURN
500 DATA  100,150,100,250,100,15
     0,50,150
505 DATA  08,00,18,00,22,00,25,0
     0,32,00,44,00,70,00,73,00,77
     ,00

510 DATA  36,36,36,00
515 DATA  36,36,00
520 DATA  54,54,54,54,54,14,00
525 DATA     118,118,118,118,118,
     05,100,100,100,100,100,12,0
530 DATA  14,14,14,14,14,14,14,1
     4,14,14,222,219,219,27,96,12
     ,12,12,12,12,12,12,12,12,12,
     00
535 DATA  53,39,00
540 DATA  44,62,00
545 DATA   63,63,54,45,53,62,62,
     62,54,53,53,62,62,46,46,54,5
     5,55,46,46,46,54,63,55,46,45
     ,5,0
550 DATA     144,1,148,1,178,14,
     200,40,204,40,208,74,212,74,
     216,74,216,74,200,110,146,14
     8,98,136,102,136,74,110,78,1
     10,82,110,60,73,100,13
555 DATA  204,110,178,136,132,14
     8,84,136,60,110,64,74,70,40,
     86,14,130,2,138,16,170,24,19
     2,46,200,78,192,110,170,132,
     138,140,106,132,84,110,76,78
     ,84,46,106,24
580 DATA  173,48,192,136,208,5,2
     06,1,3,240,9,202,208,245,174
     ,0,3,76,2,3,96
600 FOR A = 1 TO 8: READ B: NEXT
     A
605 FOR A = 16278 TO 16382: READ
     B: POKE A,B: NEXT A
610 HGR2 : HCOLOR= 3: SCALE= 1: ROT=
     0
620 POKE 232,150: POKE 233,63
630 HIMEM: 16277
640 FOR A = 1 TO 18: READ B,C: DRAW
     3 AT B,C: NEXT A
650 FOR A = 1 TO 5: READ B,C: DRAW
     4 AT B,C: NEXT A
660 FOR A = 1 TO 4: READ B,C: DRAW
     5 AT B,C: NEXT A
670 FOR A = 1 TO 12: READ B,C: DRAW
     6 AT B,C: NEXT A
680 SCALE= 5: DRAW 8 AT 25,16: DRAW
     8 AT 252,16: ROT= 32: DRAW 8
     AT 26,141: DRAW 8 AT 253,14
     1
690 FOR A = 770 TO 790: READ B: POKE
     A,B: NEXT A
695 A = 0:B = 0:C = 0:XPH% = 65:X
     PM% = 65: GOTO 160
700 CALL  - 936
701 PRINT "(THIS PROGRAM WRITTEN
     BY BILL SMITH,     GAMBIER
     ISLAND, B.C. CANADA)": PRINT
     : PRINT

705 PRINT "HI,I'M APPLES GRANDFA
     THER CLOCK": PRINT  SPC( 40)
706 PRINT "DO YOU WANT ME TO CHI
     ME THE HOURS OR USEMY OTHER
     FACILITIES ?": PRINT " "
707 INPUT "PLEASE TYPE Y OR N,TH
     EN HIT 'RETURN'KEY";ZA$
710 IF  ASC (ZA$) < > 89 THEN  GOTO
     765
714 CALL  - 936
715 PRINT "WHICH OF THE FOLLOWIN
     G WOULD YOU LIKE?,"
716 PRINT "JUST PRINT Y OR N,
                         (DON'T
     FORGET TO HIT THE RETURN KEY
     )"
717 PRINT "        "
718 PRINT " "
720 INPUT "CHIMES?";ZB$
725 INPUT "TICK TOCK?";ZC$
730 INPUT "ALARM?";ZD$
732 IF  ASC (ZD$) < > 89 THEN  GOTO
     770
735 PRINT " ": INPUT "WHAT TIME
     DO YOU WANT THE ALARM TO GO
     OFF?
                            PL
     EASE USE 24 HOUR NOTATION,FO
     R EXAMPLE 1340 AND NOT TWENT
     Y TO TWO";SET
736 GOTO 770
765 ZB$ = "N":ZC$ = "N":ZD$ = "N"

770 CALL  - 936
771 INPUT "WHAT IS THE PRESENT T
     IME PLEASE? USE 24 HOUR NOTA
     TION, FOR EXAMPLE 1340 AND N
     OT TWENTY TO TWO";A
772 CALL  - 936: PRINT "HANG ON,
     WHILST I WIND THIS APPLE UP"

773 A = A - 1
774 FOR Q = 1 TO 999: NEXT Q
775 MIN = ( INT ((A / 100 -  INT
     (A / 100)) * 100 + .05) *  SGN
     (A / 100))
780 IF A > 1200 THEN A = A - 120
     0: PM = 1
785 HOUR = (A - MIN) / 100:A = 0
790 IF HOUR = 12 THEN HOUR = 0
795 GOTO 500
800 TEXT : CALL  - 936
810 PRINT "STOP PLAYING WITH THE
     APPLE !!!!, GO AND TELL DAD
     TO WIND UP THE CLOCK AND ST
     ART IT AGAIN"
```

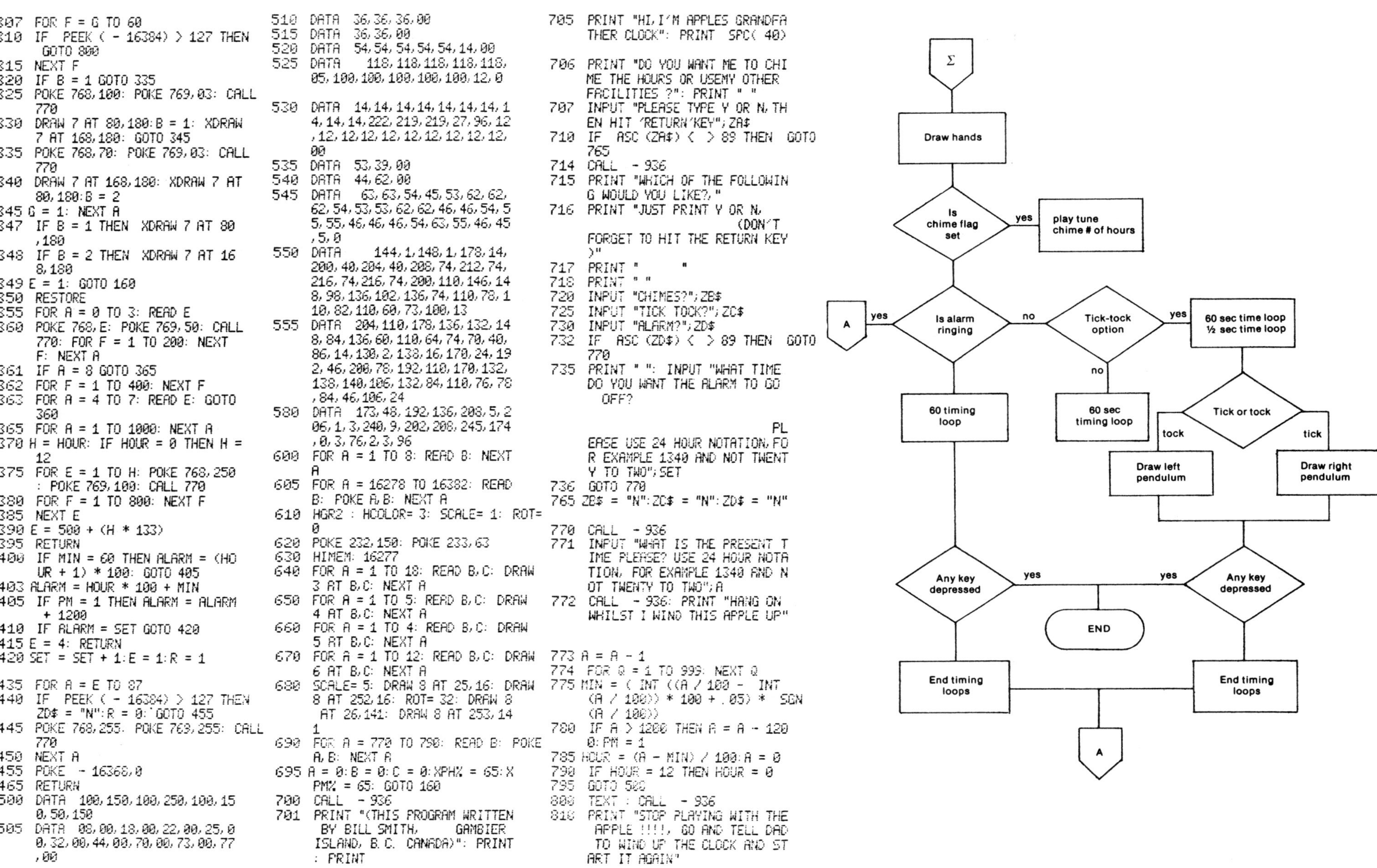

Watch Those Typos, Folks!

Dear Editor:

I have received many letters saying there are bugs in Bill Smith's "Grandapple Clock" (Jan '80 p. 104), and have spent many hours finding typing errors in people's listings (usually the data statements have a number or two added, missing, or incorrect).

If typed as it appeared in *Creative Computing,* the program works. The code may be imperfect, but it works.

Although most people asked me to do syntax checks, some people did write to say they enjoyed Mr. Smith's first program. I was particularly impressed with two writers: Larry Fitzpatrick and John McKillan. These two gentlemen obviously took the time to read what was being typed and came up with reasonable suggestions for improvement. These changes follow.

A lot of the stylistic weaknesses have been improved by Gary Little (president of "Apples British Columbia," #101-2044 West Third Ave., Vancouver, B.C., V6J 1L5).

In conclusion, I would like to thank those who took the time to type in the program and even improve it. As for those who swore there were bugs (probably put in on purpose as Wine Yellow would say), I can only note that Microsoft has a fine typing tutor . . .

Larry Fitzpatrick's changes: 1629 Elizabeth Street, Melbourne, FL 32901:

a. omit line 119

b. change line 286 to read: 286 Flag=0:IF R=0 Then GOTO 90

John McKillan's changes: 817 Lavonne Dr., Santa Monica, CA 93454:

a. In Line 695, replace XPM% with OPM%

b. Change line 795 to read: 795 Goto 600

c. The alarm will not go off if "SET" in line 735 is greater than 1200. To fix this problem:

  1. Change line 736 to 737, i.e., delete 736, add: 737 Goto 770

  2. Add: 736 IF Set $\geq$ 1200 then Set = Set – 1200

Christopher Howerton
13572 92 Avenue
Surrey, B.C.
Canada V3V 1H7

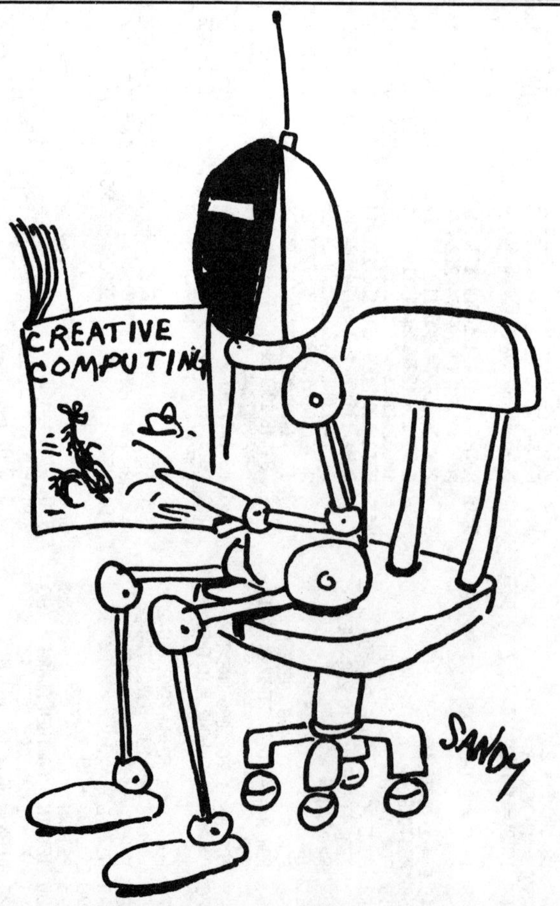

Is speed chess your game? Well, don't go out and buy a chess clock when you can use your computer to time moves.

Chess is an interesting intellectual game, but it lacks action. Many people do not play chess simply because it takes so long. Well, if you want to put real action into your chess game, then this program is for you.

A chess clock is basically two stop watches connected in such a way that exactly one of the stop watches is running at any instant. While a player is deciding on his move, his clock is running. As soon as he moves his piece, and is happy with his chosen move, the player presses a button which stops his clock and starts his opponent's clock.

Unlike regular chess, a player may alter a move which he has made, so long as he hasn't pressed the button. The game ends with a checkmate as in regular chess, or when someone runs out of time. By alloting a weaker player more time for his game, a chess clock can effectively handicap a game. However, a chess clock is also used in speed chess. To play speed chess, allow each player four minutes of playing time. You will find that this time limit puts action into a chess game. It also drives some players mad.

Mechanical chess clocks have been in existence for many years, but are expensive enough that I couldn't justify buying one at my level of play. Then, late (after the Tonight show) one Friday evening, the need for a chess clock again arose as Jeff, Dave and I simultaneously developed a craving for a game of speed chess. Fortunately, one of us (exactly whom is lost in the mists of time) noticed that in that very room was a general purpose, stored program, electronic digital computer. We greeted the rising sun with a working chess clock. The version presented here is almost totally re-written, but the basic ideas and algorithms were developed that night by the three of us.

This program is written using Apple's Integer Basic, and takes advantage of that language's low-resolution graphics facilities. Integer Basic is a simple language, so there should be no trouble converting this program to other Basics, provided these differences are taken into account:

1. Variable names in Integer Basic are allowed to be more than 2 characters long. You will have to shorten variables such as PLAYER.

2. CALL −936 clears the screen and homes the cursor.

3. Lines 560-570, 1560-1570 and 1470-1480 are equivalent to GET (receiving input without hitting the RETURN key).

4. PEEK(−16336) is used to make a little beep on the Apple's speaker.

5. In low-resolution graphics mode, the screen is broken into a 40 x 40 grid. The top left-hand corner is (0,0). The top right-hand corner is (39,0). The lower right-hand corner is (39,39). PLOT is used to color in a single grid square. VLIN n,m AT z draws a vertical line from (z,n) to (z,m). HLIN n,m AT z draws a horizontal line from (n,z) to (m,z).

6. In low-resolution graphics mode, all the graphing described in (5) is done in whatever color the variable COLOR currently represents. It should be an integer between 0 and 15.

The digits displayed on the clock are represented using a 7 segment display. Lines 820-880 "light" the correct segments for a given digit "N." Figure 1 shows which segment each of these lines light.

FIGURE 1		
Segment	Program Line Drawn at:	
1	820	
2	830	
3	840	
4	850	
5	860	
6	870	
7	880	

I believe that the program is quite understandable and "trick" free. It is quite long at first glance, but you will notice that one half of the program consists of REM statements to help you understand it. When you make your copy, please retain the credits in lines 390-520.

Christopher Howerton, 13572 92 Ave., Surry, BC.

```
>LIST CHESS TIMER
   10 REM      YE MIGHTY CHESS CLOCK
   20 REM
   30 REM     IF THERE ARE ANY PROBLEMS
   40 REM    OR SUGGESTIONS, CONTACT:
   50 REM
   60 REM          JEFF BONNYCASTLE
   70 REM          12881-99 AVE
   80 REM          SURREY B. C.   CANADA
   90 REM          V3T-1E6
  100 REM
  110 REM
  120 REM   N0$    :FIRST PLAYER'S NAME
  130 REM   N1$    :OTHER PLAYER'S NAME
  140 REM   L$     :STRING VARIABLE FOR
  150 REM           GATHERING INPUT AND
  160 REM           PRINTING THE LOSER
  170 REM   COLOUR:15 FOR ONE PLAYER
  180 REM           0 FOR THE OTHER ONE
  190 REM   YPOS  :Y POSITION OF THE
  200 REM           TWO TIME DISPLAYS
  210 REM   TIME  :SECONDS REMAINING
  220 REM           FOR EACH PLAYER
  230 REM   CLOCK :HOLDS THE 10 DIGITS
  240 REM           CURRENTLY DISPLAYED
  250 REM   CLCK2 :HOLDS THE 5 DIGITS
  260 REM           FOR THE TIME OF THE
  270 REM           PLAYER WHOSE CLOCK
  280 REM           IS MOVING
  290 REM
  300 REM
  310 DIM N0$(200),N1$(200),L$(200
      )
  320 DIM COLOUR(1),YPOS(1),TIME(
      1),CLOCK(9),CLCK2(4)
  330 REM
  340 REM
  350 REM CLEAR SCREEN, PRINT CREDITS
  360 REM
  370 REM
  380 CALL -936
  390 PRINT "         YE MIGHTY CHESS
      CLOCK"
  400 PRINT : PRINT : PRINT
  410 PRINT "DEVELOPED IN THE DEAD OF
      NIGHT, WITH"
  420 PRINT "WEREWOLVES BAYING AT THE
      DOOR, AND"
  430 PRINT "VARIOUS OTHER BEASTIES AL
      READY INSIDE,"
  440 PRINT "BY:"
  450 PRINT
  460 PRINT : PRINT "CHRISTOPHER E. HO
      WERTON"
  470 TAB 5: PRINT "ALLAN D. BOOTH"
  480 TAB 9: PRINT "JEFFREY J. BONNYCA
      STLE"
  490 PRINT
  500 PRINT "WE ALMOST DIDN'T MAKE IT.
      . . "
  510 VTAB 20
  520 PRINT "        HIT ANY KEY TO CONTI
```

```
530 REM
540 REM WAIT FOR ANY KEY TO BE HIT
550 REM
560 IF PEEK (-16384)<=127 THEN
    560
570 POKE -16368,0
580 GOTO 980
590 REM
600 REM
610 REM
620 REM THIS SUBROUTINE PRINTS A
630 REM DIGIT "N" AT POSITION X,Y
640 REM USING A 7 SEGMENT DISPLAY
650 REM
660 REM
670 REM
680 REM FIRST ERASE ALL 7 SEGMENTS
690 REM
700 COLOR=2
710 VLIN Y,Y+8 AT X
720 VLIN Y,Y+8 AT X+4
730 HLIN X,X+4 AT Y
740 HLIN X,X+4 AT Y+4
750 HLIN X,X+4 AT Y+8
760 REM
770 REM NOW PRINT THE DIGIT AT THE
780 REM CORRECT POSITION, WITH THE
790 REM CORRECT COLOUR.
800 REM
810 COLOR=COLOUR(PLAYER)
820 IF (N=0 OR N=2 OR N=3 OR N=
    5 OR N>6) THEN HLIN X,X+4 AT
    Y
830 IF (N=0 OR N=4 OR N=5 OR N=
    6 OR N>7) THEN VLIN Y,Y+4 AT
    X
840 IF (N<5 OR N>6) THEN VLIN Y,
    Y+3 AT X+4
850 IF (N<>1 AND N<>7) THEN HLIN
    X+1,X+4 AT Y+4
860 IF (N=0 OR N=2 OR N=6 OR N=
    8) THEN VLIN Y+4,Y+8 AT X
870 IF (N<>2) THEN VLIN Y+4,Y+8 AT
    X+4
880 IF (N=0 OR N=2 OR N=3 OR N=
    5 OR N=6 OR N=8) THEN HLIN
    X,X+4 AT Y+8
890 RETURN
900 REM
910 REM
920 REM          INITIALIZATION
930 REM MAKE NICE BLUE BACKGROUND,
940 REM PUT IN THE COLONS, AND DRAW
950 REM THE DIVIDING LINE.
960 REM
970 REM
980 GR
990 MOVES=0
1000 COLOR=2: FOR Z=0 TO 39: VLIN
     0,39 AT Z: NEXT Z
1010 COLOUR(0)=15:COLOUR(1)=0
1020 YPOS(0)=4: YPOS(1)=25
1030 COLOR=COLOUR(0)
1040 PLOT 7,7: PLOT 7,8: PLOT 7,
     10: PLOT 7,11: PLOT 24,7: PLOT
     24,8: PLOT 24,10: PLOT 24,11
1050 HLIN 1,38 AT 19
1060 COLOR=COLOUR(1)
1070 HLIN 1,38 AT 20
1080 PLOT 7,28: PLOT 7,29: PLOT
     7,31: PLOT 7,32: PLOT 24,28
     : PLOT 24,29: PLOT 24,31: PLOT
     24,32
1090 REM
1100 REM

1110 REM       MORE INITIALIZATION
1120 REM GET THE PLAYERS' NAMES AND
1130 REM THEIR RESPECTIVE GAME TIMES
1140 REM
1150 REM
1160 FOR I=0 TO 9:CLOCK(I)=-1: NEXT
     I
1170 FOR PLAYER=0 TO 1
1180 PRINT : PRINT : PRINT
1190 IF PLAYER=0 THEN INPUT "WHO'S PL
     AYING WHITE? ",N0$
1200 IF PLAYER=1 THEN INPUT "WHO'S PL
     AYING BLACK? ",N1$
1210 PRINT "HOW MUCH TIME DO YOU WANT
     ? "
1220 PRINT
1230 INPUT "HOURS",H
1240 IF H>=0 AND H<=8 THEN 1280
1250 PRINT "SORRY, BUT YOU CAN ONLY H
     AVE 8 HOURS"
1260 GOTO 1220
1270 PRINT
1280 INPUT "MINUTES",M
1290 IF M>=0 AND M<=59 THEN 1330
1300 PRINT "YOU MUST HAVE BETWEEN 0 A
     ND 59 MINUTES"
1310 GOTO 1270
1320 PRINT
1330 INPUT "SECONDS",S
1340 IF S>=0 AND S<=59 THEN 1370
1350 PRINT "YOU MUST HAVE BETWEEN 0 A
     ND 59 SECONDS"
1360 GOTO 1320
1370 TIME(PLAYER)=S+60*M+3600*H
1380 GOSUB 2020
1390 NEXT PLAYER
1400 PLAYER=0
1410 PRINT "HIT ANY KEY TO START THE
     TIMER": PRINT
1420 REM
1430 REM   WAIT FOR A KEY TO BE HIT
1440 REM   THEN CLEAR STROBE AND
1450 REM   START WHITE'S CLOCK
1460 REM
1470 IF ( PEEK (-16384)<=127) THEN
     1470
1480 POKE -16368,0
1490 GOTO 1600
1500 REM
1510 REM   IF ANY KEY HAS BEEN HIT,
1520 REM   CLEAR THE STROBE, BEEP,
1530 REM   STOP ONE CLOCK, AND START
1540 REM   THE OTHER CLOCK.
1550 REM
1560 IF ( PEEK (-16384)<=127) THEN
     GOTO 1710
1570 POKE -16368,0
1580 FOR I=1 TO 8: II= PEEK (-16336
     )+ PEEK (-16336)+ PEEK (-16336
     ): NEXT I
1590 PLAYER= ABS (PLAYER-1)
1600 MOVES=MOVES+1
1610 PRINT : PRINT
1620 PRINT "          MOVE NUMBER
     ";(MOVES+1)/2
1630 PRINT
1640 REM
1650 REM REDUCE PLAYER'S TIME BY 1
1660 REM AND SEE IF HE HAS ANY TIME
1670 REM LEFT.   IF HE DOESN'T, BEEP
1680 REM AND POINT OUT THAT HE HAS
1690 REM LOST THE GAME.
1700 REM
1710 TIME(PLAYER)=TIME(PLAYER)-1
1720 IF TIME(PLAYER)>-1 THEN 1900
1730 FOR I=1 TO 500: II= PEEK (-16336

): NEXT I
1740 L$=N1$
1750 IF PLAYER=0 THEN L$=N0$
1760 PRINT L$(1, LEN(L$));" LOSES ON
     TIME AT MOVE NUMBER ";(MOVES+
     1)/2
1770 PRINT : INPUT "DO YOU WANT ANOTH
     ER GAME? ",L$
1780 PRINT : PRINT : PRINT
1790 IF L$(1,1)="Y" THEN 900
1800 TEXT : CALL -936
1810 VTAB 8: PRINT "GOOD-BYE, ";
     N0$;" AND ",N1$
1820 VTAB 20: TAB 8: PRINT "FOR NOW A
     NYWAY..."
1830 END
1840 REM
1850 REM WE GET HERE ONLY IF A
1860 REM PLAYER'S DISPLAYED CLOCK IS
1870 REM TO BE DECREMENTED BY ONE
1880 REM SECOND.
1890 REM
1900 GOSUB 2020
1910 GOTO 1560
1920 REM
1930 REM
1940 REM THIS SUBROUTINE DECREMENTS
1950 REM A PLAYER'S CLOCK BY ONE
1960 REM SECOND.
1970 REM
1980 REM FIRST, DETERMINE WHAT EACH
1990 REM OF THE PLAYER'S CLOCK'S
2000 REM DIGITS SHOULD BE
2010 REM
2020 T=TIME(PLAYER)
2030 CLOCK2(0)=T/3600
2040 CLOCK2(1)=(T-CLOCK2(0)*3600)/
     600
2050 CLOCK2(2)=(T-CLOCK2(0)*3600-CLOCK2(
     1)*600)/60
2060 CLOCK2(3)=(T-CLOCK2(0)*3600-CLOCK2(
     1)*600-CLOCK2(2)*60)/10
2070 CLOCK2(4)=(T-CLOCK2(0)*3600-CLOCK2(
     1)*600-CLOCK2(2)*60-CLOCK2(3)
     *10)
2080 REM
2090 REM NOW FIND THE Y COORDINATE
2100 REM OF THE PLAYER'S CLOCK.
2110 REM THEN REDRAW ANY DIGIT
2120 REM WHICH HAS CHANGED.
2130 REM
2140 Y=YPOS(PLAYER):P=PLAYER*5
2150 X=1:N=CLOCK2(0)
2160 IF N<>CLOCK(P) THEN GOSUB 690
2170 X=9:N=CLOCK2(1)
2180 IF N<>CLOCK(P+1) THEN GOSUB
     690
2190 X=17:N=CLOCK2(2)
2200 IF N<>CLOCK(P+2) THEN GOSUB
     690
2210 X=26:N=CLOCK2(3)
2220 IF N<>CLOCK(P+3) THEN GOSUB
     690
2230 X=34:N=CLOCK2(4)
2240 GOSUB 690
2250 FOR I=0 TO 4
2260 CLOCK(P+I)=CLOCK2(I)
2270 NEXT I
2280 REM
2290 REM THIS IS THE TIMING LOOP
2300 REM WHICH WE MUST USE SO THAT
2310 REM THE CLOCK IS RELATIVELY
2320 REM ACCURATE.
2330 REM
2340 FOR I=1 TO 220: NEXT I
2350 RETURN
2360 END
```

CAESAR'S WATCH

Paul Raymer

The discovery recently at the Gelati digs—where an ancient pizzaria was uncovered by horologists at the University of Nevada in cooperation with the State Historical Society and Wine Tasting Association of Manjare, Italy—is the source of the reference material on this wonderful program.

Evidence gathered by examining bits of chard and thyme and verifying that material with the carbon-zinc dating equipment by Ray-O-Vac proves within a shadow of a doubt that the materials were those of either Julius or Augustus Caesar or some other famous Roman.

While some artistic license was taken to translate the ancient documents—many of them written in a foreign language which made them hard to understand—the recreation of what the author honestly believes is either the pocket watch of Julius Caesar, or the floor plan of a barbaric hovel in Rome, has been attempted. Encouraged by his research, the author proceeded on the basis that it was indeed a pocket watch, and comparisons between the resultant diagrams and Roman water clocks show a faint resemblance.

Unfortunately, because of limited financial resources and the refusal of the Rand Corporation to provide a grant, the author was unable to get final copyright releases from the Caesar family and hopes the heirs (in Las Vegas, Lake Tahoe and Atlantic City) will understand and provide their tacit approval by not taking any legal action. Because all of the original documents were carefully studied, the author believes the resultant program is as authentic and accurate as any of his other programs.

In accordance with tradition, the program has been translated to run on an Apple Computer to take full advantage of the low resolution graphics of that computer. Although it is surprisingly accurate for a water clock, provisions have been made for moderate time adjustments. This was, of course, not included in the original plans by Mr. Caesar since it wasn't really critical whether a battle started at 6:00 or 6:10. Of even less import was whether the lions were admitted to the arena at 8:00 or 8:15—certainly of interest neither to the Christians nor the lions.

The clock, of course, is based on a 12-hour cycle and resets itself automatically. This, according to historical data, is because of the marvelous system of viaducts originated by the Romans so long ago, in the olden days.

Because the plans upon which this clock are built were prior to Pope Gregory's fooling around with the calendar, the alert computerist will note a gap of 11 days. However, with inflation and the state of the economy, it may not be that bad after all.

How the Program Works

Lines 100-250 are the introduction to the program—a reversed image title. This is a lazy way of having the info ordinarily used as REM statements become your title.

Lines 260-300 clear the screen and read data which will later be used to translate arabic numbers to Roman numerals. Values are established for variables LL, T and TT to be defined later.

Lines 300-420, in effect, explain how the time adjustment variables may be changed, if necessary. Please note that only the first two letters of the variables are actually used. Full use of Roman names is because of the author's involvement in Latin as a student many (many, many) years ago.

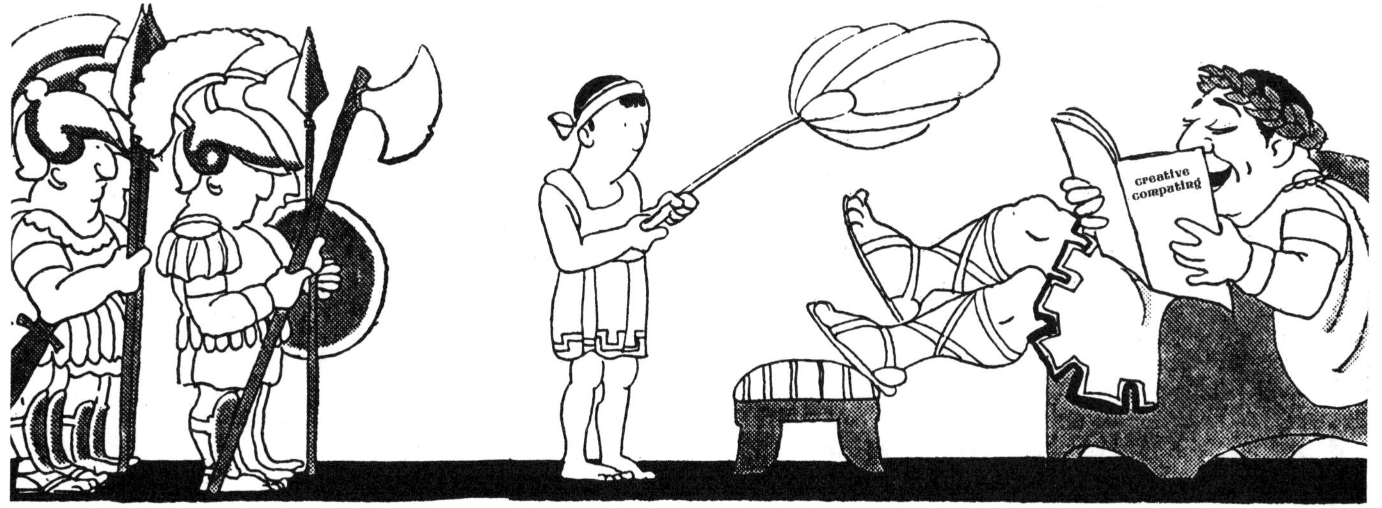

Lines 430-460 accept your input to start clock on time, and begin graphics mode.

Lines 470-590 start graphics to build water spigot and containers to receive water drops.

Lines 600-630 start clock to match input of hours. This input will be corrected at the "minute" routine and then again when the "hour" change takes place. This enables you to correlate the program with real time.

Lines 640-1080 start "water dripping" routine which will fill up the "seconds" vessel. When 60 drops have fallen, the cycle will shift to emptying the vessel.

Lines 1990-2430 empty the "seconds" vessel and start to fill the "minutes" container. The contents are emptied from the bottom of the "seconds" container to fill the "minutes." Ports which are opened during the transfer of water are then closed upon completion of this exchange. The time is printed, after having been converted from Arabic to Roman with the use of the R$(H) and R$(M). Both use the same data since the figures are actually the same, for this reason the Dim was set originally at R$(60) to provide for this contingency.

Lines 3000-3070 start the "hour-making" subroutine. These lines remove all image from the "minutes" vessel.

Lines 3080-3120 provide the graphics to begin the "hour" bottle.

Lines 3130-3310 add one hour to the hour bottle for each hour indicated in program. Gingerbread allows for a bar to cross over the screen to apparently "fill" the bottle. A time delay is established at this point to enable the action to be seen.

Lines 3320-4120 adjust the hour. When time exceeds 12 (limit of the program) all variables are returned to zero to start new cycle. This enables the program to run continuously, with a fair degree of accuracy.

5000-5050 are the data statements which are used to translate the Arabic (decimal, we call them) to Roman numerals . . . the easy way.   □

```
100    TEXT : HOME : CLEAR
110    INVERSE
120    PRINT "                              "
130    PRINT " ***************************** "
140    PRINT " *                         * "
150    PRINT " *     CAESAR'S WATCH      * "
160    PRINT " *                         * "
170    PRINT " *    THE BARGAIN BOX      * "
180    PRINT " *      PO BOX 42831       * "
190    PRINT " *    LAS VEGAS NEVADA     * "
200    PRINT " *         89104          * "
210    PRINT " *                         * "
220    PRINT " ***************************** "
230    PRINT "                              "
240    REM
250    FOR W = 1 TO 3000: NEXT W: NORMAL
260    HOME
270    DIM R$(60)
280    FOR X = 1 TO 60: READ R$(X): NEXT X
290 LL = 5:T = - 1:TT = - 1
300    REM
310    REM    TIME ADJUST
320    REM    JULIUS=SECOND EMPTY
330    REM    AUGUSTUS=FILLING
340    REM    OCTAVIUS=HOUR ADJUST
350    REM
360 JULIUS = 9:AUGUSTUS = 10:OCTAVIUS = 100
370    REM
380    REM    ROMAN WATER CLOCK
390    REM    ORIGINAL CONCEPT BY
400    REM    PAUL RAYMER
410    REM    VIII/IX/MCMLXXX
420    REM
430    INPUT "HOW MANY MINUTES PAST THE HOUR? ";M
440    INPUT "WHAT IS THE HOUR? ";H
450    HOME
460    GR
470    COLOR= 15
480    FOR X = 0 TO 39: HLIN 0,4 AT X: NEXT X
490    HLIN 0,8 AT 38: HLIN 0,8 AT 39
500    VLIN 18,39 AT 8
510    FOR X = 10 TO 15: HLIN 5,17 AT X: NEXT X
520    FOR X = 16 TO 21: HLIN 13,17 AT X: NEXT X
530    COLOR= 1
540    HLIN 12,13 AT 35: HLIN 12,13 AT 34
550    HLIN 30,32 AT 35: HLIN 30,32 AT 34
560    VLIN 34,39 AT 14: VLIN 34,39 AT 30
570    HLIN 14,30 AT 38: HLIN 14,30 AT 39
580    COLOR= 7
590    REM
600    REM    START CLOCK
610    REM
620    GOSUB 3000
630    GOSUB 2390
640    R = 37:D = 22
650    PLOT 15,D
660    FOR W = 1 TO AUGUSTUS: NEXT W
670    D = D + 1: IF D = R + 1 THEN    GOSUB 1000
680    IF R = 33 THEN    GOSUB 2000
690    COLOR= 0
700    PLOT 15,D - 1
710    COLOR= 7
720    GOTO 650
1000    REM
1010    REM    SECOND MAKER
1020    REM
1030    P = P + 1
1040    PLOT 14 + P,R
1050    IF P = 15 THEN R = R - 1:P = 0
1060    COLOR= 7
1070    D = 22
1080    RETURN
1990    REM
2000    REM    MINUTE MAKER
2010    COLOR= 15
2020    FOR X = 8 TO 13: PLOT X,39: NEXT X
2030    COLOR= 0
2040    R = R + 1
2050    PP = 15
2060    FOR X = 1 TO 60
2070    PP = PP - 1
2080    PLOT 15 + PP,R
2090    IF PP = 0 THEN R = R + 1:PP = 15
2100    COLOR= 7
2110    PLOT 14,37: FOR W = 1 TO JULIUS: NEXT W
2120    COLOR= 0: PLOT 14,37
2130    COLOR= 7
2140    PLOT 13,37: FOR W = 1 TO JULIUS: NEXT W
2150    COLOR= 0: PLOT 13,37
2160    COLOR= 7
2170    PLOT 13,38: FOR W = 1 TO JULIUS: NEXT W
2180    COLOR= 0: PLOT 13,38
2190    COLOR= 7
2200    FOR V = 11 TO 5 STEP - 1
2210    COLOR= 7: PLOT V,38
2220    FOR W = 1 TO JULIUS: NEXT W
2230    COLOR= 0: PLOT V,38
```

```
2240    NEXT V
2250    NEXT X
2260 T = T + 1
2270    COLOR= 7: PLOT LL,37 - L:LL = LL + 1
2280    IF LL = 8 THEN LL = 5:L = L + 1
2290    IF L = 21 THEN LL = 5:L = 0
2300    IF M > T THEN 2260
2310 R = R - 1
2320    COLOR= 1: PLOT 14,37
2330    COLOR= 15: PLOT 8,38
2340    HLIN 0,8 AT 38
2350    COLOR= 0
2360    FOR X = 9 TO 13: PLOT X,39: NEXT X
2370 M = M + 1: IF M = 60 THEN H = H + 1:M = 0: GOSUB 3000
2380    IF H = 13 THEN  GOSUB 4000: GOSUB 3000
2390    HOME : PRINT  TAB( 2)"MINUTES"; TAB( 20)"SECONDS";
        TAB( 35)"HOURS"
2400    PRINT
2410    PRINT  TAB( 13)"TEMPUS EST ";R$(H); CHR$ (32);R$(M)
2420    COLOR= 3
2430    RETURN
3000    REM
3010    REM   HOUR MAKER
3020    REM
3030    COLOR= 0
3040    FOR X = 17 TO 38
3050    HLIN 5,7 AT X
3060    FOR W = 1 TO AUGUSTUS: NEXT W
3070    NEXT X
3080    COLOR= 15
3090    VLIN 14,39 AT 36: VLIN 14,39 AT 39
3100    HLIN 36,39 AT 14
3110    PLOT 34,28
3120    HLIN 34,35 AT 29
3130    REM
3140    REM   ADD AN HOUR
3150    REM
3160    COLOR= 0
3170    VLIN 18,27 AT 8
3180    COLOR= 15
3190    HLIN 8,33 AT 27
3200    FOR W = 1 TO 50: NEXT W
3210 TT = TT + 1
3220    IF TT = 13 THEN 3360
3230    COLOR= TT + 1
3240    PLOT 37,39 - (2 * TT)
3250    PLOT 38,39 - (2 * TT)
3260    COLOR= 15
3270    HLIN 36,39 AT 39
3280    COLOR= 0: HLIN 8,34 AT 27
3290    COLOR= 15: VLIN 18,28 AT 8
3300    IF H > TT THEN 3140
3310 T = T - 1
3320    REM
3330    REM   ADJUST HOUR
3340    FOR W = 1 TO OCTAVIUS: NEXT W
3350    REM
3355 LL = 5:L = 0
3360    RETURN
4000    REM
4010    REM   CLEAR TO ONE AFTER 12
4020    REM
4030    COLOR= 0
4040    FOR X = 15 TO 38
4050    HLIN 37,38 AT X
4060    FOR W = 1 TO AUGUSTUS: NEXT W
4070    NEXT X
4080 TT = 0
4090 H = 1
4100 R = 37
4110 LL = 5:L = 0
4120    RETURN
5000    REM
5010    REM   ARABIC TO ROMAN
5020    REM
5030    DATA   I,II,III,IV,V,VI,VII,VIII,IX,X,XI,XII,XIII
        XIV,XV,XVI,XVII,XVI II,XIX,XX
5040    DATA   XXI,XXII,XXIII,XXIV,XXV,XXVI,XXVII,XXVIII,
        XXIX,XXX,XXXI,XXXII, XXXIII,XXXIV,XXXV,XXXVI,
        XXXVII,XXXVIII,XXXIX,XL
5050    DATA   XLI,XLII,XLIII,XLIV,XLV,XLVI,XLVII,XLVIII,
        XLIX,L,LI,LII,LIII,L IV,LV,LVI,LVII,LVIII,LIX,LX
5060 FINIS
```

APPLE PIE

N. B. McBurney II

Exploit the high resolution graphics capability of your Apple to display easy-to-understand pie charts.

One of several reasons that I purchased an Apple as a personal computer, over the others on the market, was Apple's high-resolution color graphics capability. An excellent use for this capability is the generation of pie charts.

Pie charts, sometimes called circle or sector charts, are used to illustrate component parts in relation to their total by the use of radial sections of circular areas. Pie charts are a very effective graphic illustration technique for:

1. Illustrating percentage data.

2. Displays with a smaller number of plotted values.

3. Displays of data relationships that must be quickly and easily grasped by potentially unsophisticated audiences.

4. Illustrations where relative amounts are to be emphasized, as opposed to data trends.

Pie charts also have the distinct advantage of being much easier to program than grid-based routines (while the accompanying listing may look intimidating at first glance, the bulk of it is comment statements — for which I have no apologies). The key to pie charts is in the use of the trigonometric functions SIN and COS coupled with a little polar and cartesian geometry. In polar geometry a circle centered at the polar coordinate system origin is achieved by holding the radius (r) constant and varying the angle through 360 degrees (i.e., r=c). To convert to the cartesian coordinate system, that we need to use the Apple's HIRES screen:

$$x = r \cos \theta$$
$$y = r \sin \theta$$

N. R. McBurney II, 2561 Stockbridge Rd., Marietta, GA 30062.

Finally, by adding constants to x and y we can move the center of the circle to any valid coordinates on the HIRES screen. This is exactly what happens in lines 1700-1780 and 1860. In fact, once the requisite variables are initialized the instructions in lines 1700-1780 and 1860 are all that are required to generate the pie chart. The rest of the program is concerned with input, labeling, error detection and general beautification of the display.

The program allows up to ten input values to be specified along with two title lines of up to forty characters each. The titles are entered in the DATA statements in lines 2690 and 2700. Titles will be automatically centered by the program. The title lines are followed by up to ten more DATA statements (lines 2720-2760 in the accompanying listing) contain three fields each. The first field is the amount the sector is to represent. The second field is a short description of the sector that will be used to label the graph. The third and final field is the color for the sector. Colors will vary depending on your TV display and how it is adjusted. On my set the following values for the color field results in the associated sector color:

    1 = Green
    2 = Blue
    3 = White
    4 = Black
    5 = Orange

You will want to experiment with the color field. I've found that some color combinations give strange results when drawn next to each other (e.g., orange next to green). My local

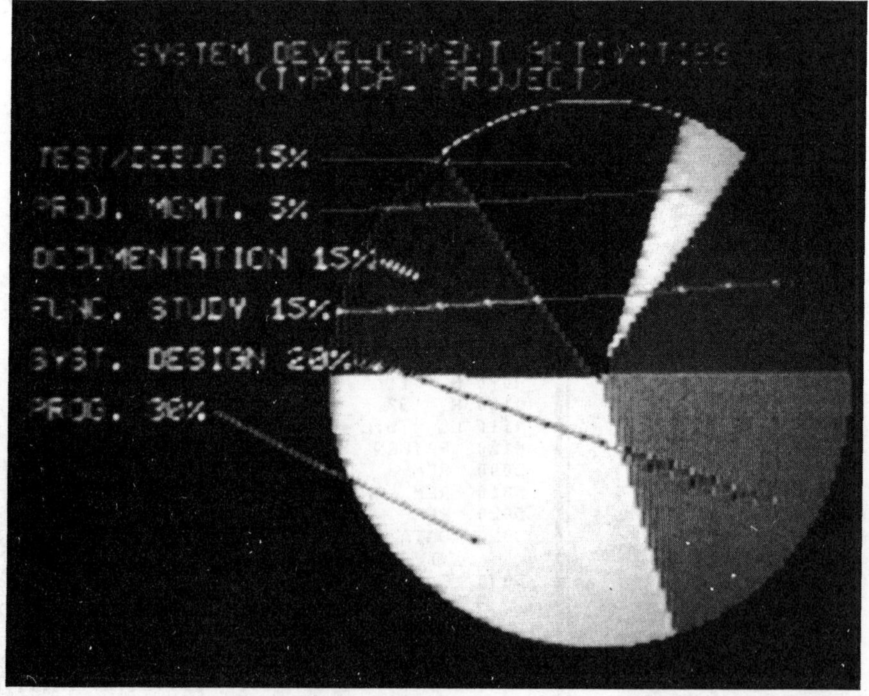

FIGURE 1

"

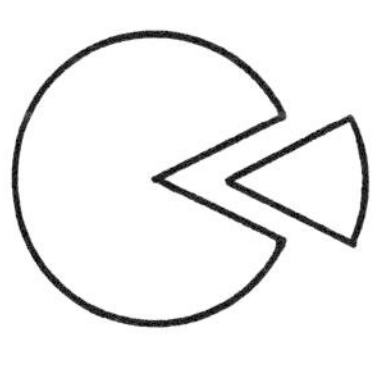

4. Automatic sector color assignment (i.e., work out what color combinations work).

5. Draw the pie as a coin seen from an oblique angle.

6. Forget the whole color thing and do it in black and white with lines instead of shading.

7. Modify the input section to select graph data from disk, cassette or enter interactively.

While you're considering all this I'll go get a piece of pie — Apple pie at that! □

FIGURE 2

computer shop explained it away as 'color flip' but I wasn't about to show my ignorance and ask what that was.

The DATA statement at line number 2680 specifies rotation and labeling mode. The first field will rotate the pie chart in a clockwise (or counterclockwise if negative) direction. The second field specifies the labeling mode. If the second field equals one then the labels are printed to the left of the display with a line drawn to each corresponding sector. The program attempts to order the display of the labels such that none of these lines will cross. This is done in lines 2060-2170. The program is not always completely successful at this, but by rotating the graph (field-1) and adjusting the length of the sector labels, crossed lines can be avoided. The display shown in Figure 1 was generated by the data statements in the attached listing and uses this mode of labeling.

If the second field of the first DATA statement is two, then each sector is labeled with a character from A to J, and the same character plus a '=' is prepended to the label when it is displayed. This mode of labeling is illustrated in the display shown in Figure 2. Figure 2 was generated with the following DATA statements:

```
DATA 15,2
DATA PROJECTED US POPULA-
        TION AGE DISTRIBUTION
DATA ———1990———
DATA 52005,< 14 YRS.,1
DATA 12771,14 - 17,2
DATA 25148,18 - 24,3
DATA 41086,25 - 34,4
DATA 36592,35 - 44,5
DATA 25311,45 - 54,1
DATA 20776,55 - 64,4
DATA 17804,65 - 74,3
DATA 12021,> 74 YRS.,2
```

The program was written in ROM Applesoft on a 48K RAM system but should run on a smaller system.

Labeling is done with the High Resolution Character Generator and Table by Christopher Espinosa in the **Apple Software Bank Contributed Volumes 3-5.** This software has the distinct advantage of price — it's free from your local Apple dealer! You just provide the blank disk or cassette (the manual did cost me $2.00). These software routines are read into RAM from disk by the statements in lines 1870-1940. If you are using a cassette simply load the character generator at $6000 and the character table at $6800 or wherever you have room. There are limitations on the starting addresses of this software so be sure to check Apple's documentation (mentioned above) before rearranging things. Once the routines are loaded, delete lines 1870-1940 and run the program.

Other than the above comments, the program is fairly simple and the liberal comments should prove adequate to walk your way through the program.

Some enhancements the reader may want to consider are:

1. Displaying the percent in each sector.

2. Writing logic so that lines from labels to sectors would only be drawn for sectors too small to label with a character key.

3. Detaching a specified sector to

```
1000  REM   +------------------------------------------+
1010  REM   :            PIE CHART GENERATOR            :
1020  REM   :                    BY                     :
1030  REM   :              N.R. MCBURNEY                 :
1040  REM   :              FEBUARY 1980                 :
1050  REM   +------------------------------------------+
1060  REM   : DATA FORMAT:                             :
1070  REM   :  LINE# DATA ANGLE,LABEL MODE             :
1080  REM   :     WHERE:                               :
1090  REM   :         ANGLE=ANGLE OF ROTATION          :
1100  REM   :               (DEGREES CLOCKWISE)        :
1110  REM   :         LABEL MODE=1, DRAW POINTER TO    :
1120  REM   :                   EACH SECTION           :
1130  REM   :                 =2, LETTER CODE          :
1140  REM   :                   EACH SECTION           :
1150  REM   :  LINE# DATA FIRST LINE OF TITLE          :
1160  REM   :  LINE# DATA SECOND LINE OF TITLE         :
1170  REM   :  LINE# DATA VALUE,LABEL,COLOR            :
1180  REM   :     WHERE:                               :
1190  REM   :         VALUE=PORTION OF TOTAL FOR PIE SECTOR :
1200  REM   :         LABEL=SECTOR LABEL               :
1210  REM   :         COLOR=SECTOR COLOR (1-5)         :
1220  REM   +------------------------------------------+
1230 R = 87:PI = 3.141593 * 2:X1 = 279 - R:Y1 = 192 - R
1240  REM   +----------------------------------+
1250  REM   : READ IN ANGLE AND LABELING MODE :
1260  REM   +----------------------------------+
1270  READ GAMMA,MODE
1280  IF MODE = 1 OR MODE = 2 THEN 1310
1290  PRINT "ERROR-LABELING MODE MUST BE 1 OR 2"
1300  STOP
1310 GAMMA = PI / 4 - GAMMA / 360 * PI
1320  DIM Z(10),LABEL$(10),C(10)
1330  DIM X2(10),Y2(10)
1340  DIM A(10),TITLE$(2)
1350  REM   +--------------------+
1360  REM   : READ IN THE TITLES :
1370  REM   +--------------------+
1380  FOR I = 1 TO 2
1390  READ TITLE$(I)
1400 TITLE$(I) =  LEFT$ (TITLE$(I),40)
1410  NEXT I
1420  REM   +----------------------+
1430  REM   : INPUT PIE CHART DATA :
1440  REM   +----------------------+
1450  ONERR  GOTO 1560
1460  READ Z(NSECT + 1),LABEL$(NSECT + 1),C(NSECT + 1)
1470 NSECT = NSECT + 1
1480  IF C(NSECT) > 0 AND C(NSECT) < 7 THEN 1510
1490  PRINT "ERROR-COLORS MUST BE IN THE RANGE 1-6"
1500  STOP
1510 T = T + Z(NSECT)
1520  GOTO 1460
1530  REM   +----------------------+
1540  REM   : CHECK FOR END OF DATA :
1550  REM   +----------------------+
1560  IF  PEEK (222) = 42 THEN 1600
1570 L =  PEEK (218) +  PEEK (219) * 256
1580  PRINT "APPLE ERROR NUMBER "; PEEK (222);" IN LINE #";L
1590  STOP
1600  POKE 216,0
1610  REM   +----------------------------+
1620  REM   : NORMALIZE THE INPUT VALUES :
1630  REM   +----------------------------+
1640  FOR I = 1 TO NSECT
1650 A(I) = Z(I) / T * PI
1660  NEXT I
1670  REM   +--------------------+
1680  REM   : DRAW THE PIE CHART :
1690  REM   +--------------------+
1700  HGR2
1710  FOR I = 1 TO NSECT
1720 ALPHA = BETA
1730 BETA = BETA + A(I)
1740  FOR J = ALPHA TO BETA STEP 0.01
1750  HCOLOR= C(I)
1760 X = X1 + R *  COS (J - GAMMA)
1770 Y = Y1 + R *  SIN (J - GAMMA)
1780  HPLOT X1,Y1 TO X,Y
1790  IF C(I) < > 0 AND C(I) < > 4 THEN 1820
1800  HCOLOR= 3
1810  HPLOT X,Y
1820  NEXT J
1830 SI = (ALPHA + BETA) / 2 - GAMMA
1840 X2(I) = X1 + R / 1.3 *  COS (SI)
1850 Y2(I) = Y1 + R / 1.3 *  SIN (SI)
1860  NEXT I
```

```
1870  REM     +---------------------------------------------+
1880  REM     : READ IN THE CHARACTER GENERATOR AND TABLE :
1890  REM     : AND LABEL THE PIE CHART                    :
1900  REM     +---------------------------------------------+
1910 D$ =  CHR$ (4)
1920  PRINT D$;"BLOAD HI-RES CHARACTER GENERATOR,A$6000"
1930  PRINT D$;"BLOAD CHARACTER TABLE,A$6800"
1940  PRINT D$
1950  POKE 54,0: POKE 55,96: REM  TURN ON PRINT TO HIRES SCREEN
1960  FOR I = 1 TO 2
1970  VTAB I
1980  HTAB (42 -  LEN (TITLE$(I))) / 2
1990  PRINT TITLE$(I)
2000  NEXT I
2010  HCOLOR= 6
2020  REM     +-----------------------+
2030  REM     : SELECT LABELING MODE :
2040  REM     +-----------------------+
2050  ON MODE GOTO 2090,2310
2060  REM     +---------------------------------------+
2070  REM     : SORT BY Y VALUE OF CENTER OF SECTION :
2080  REM     +---------------------------------------+
2090  VTAB 4:YC = 20
2110  FOR I = 1 TO NSECT
2120 K = 200
2130  FOR J = 1 TO NSECT
2140  IF Y2(J) >  = K THEN 2170
2150  IF Y2(J) = 0 THEN 2170
2160 K = Y2(J):L = J
2170  NEXT J
2180  REM     +--------------------+
2190  REM     : LABEL EACH SECTION :
2200  REM     +--------------------+
2210  PRINT
2220 Y2(L) = 0
2230  PRINT LABEL$(L)
2240 YC = YC + 16
2250  HPLOT 3 +  LEN (LABEL$(L)) * 7,YC TO X2(L),K
2260  NEXT I
2270  GOTO 2520
2280  REM     +-------------------------------------+
2290  REM     : LABEL EACH SECTION WITH LETTER CODE :
2300  REM     +-------------------------------------+
2310 J =  ASC ("A") - 1
2320  FOR I = 1 TO NSECT
2330  PRINT
2340  PRINT  CHR$ (J + I);"=";LABEL$(I)
2350 CV =  PEEK (37) + 1
2360  VTAB Y2(I) / 8 + 1
2370  HTAB X2(I) / 7 + 1
2380 Y2(I) =  INT (Y2(I) / 8) * 8 + 2
2390 X2(I) =  INT (X2(I) / 7) * 7 + 3
2391  REM     +---------------------------------------+
2392  REM     : FIRST DRAW BLACK BACKGROUND FOR LETTER KEY :
2393  REM     +---------------------------------------+
2400  HCOLOR= 0
2410  IF C(I) = 5 THEN  HCOLOR= 4
2420  FOR K = 1 TO 16
2430  HPLOT X2(I) - 8,Y2(I) - 8 + K TO X2(I) + 8,Y2(I) - 8 + K
2440  NEXT K
2450  PRINT  CHR$ (J + I)
2460  HTAB 1
2470  VTAB CV
2480  NEXT I
2490  REM     +---------------------------------------------+
2500  REM     : TYPE ANY CHARACTER TO RETURN TO TEXT MODE :
2510  REM     +---------------------------------------------+
2520 X =  PEEK ( - 16384)
2530  IF X < 128 THEN 2520
2540  POKE  - 16368,0
2550  PR# 0
2560  TEXT
2570  END
2580  REM     +-----------------------------------------+
2590  REM     : BEGIN INPUT DATA                        :
2600  REM     +-----------------------------------------+
2610  REM     : COLOR=1 GREEN (DEPENDS ON TV)           :
2620  REM     : COLOR=2 BLUE (DEPENDS ON TV)            :
2630  REM     : COLOR=3 WHITE                           :
2640  REM     : COLOR=4 BLACK                           :
2650  REM     : COLOR=5 DEPENDS ON TV (ORANGE ON MINE)  :
2660  REM     : COLOR=6 RESERVED FOR POINTER            :
2670  REM     +-----------------------------------------+
2680  DATA  19,1
2690  DATA  SYSTEM DEVELOPMENT ACTIVITIES
2700  DATA  (TYPICAL PROJECT)
2710  DATA  5,PROJ. MGNT. 5%,3
2720  DATA  15,FUNC. STUDY 15%,1
2730  DATA  20,SYST. DESIGN 20%,2
2740  DATA  30,PROG. 30%,3
2750  DATA  15,DOCUMENTATION 15%,5
2760  DATA  15,TEST/DEBUG 15%,4
```

Name	Line references
A	1340 1650 1730
ALPHA	1720 1740 1830
BETA	1720 1730 1740 1830
C	1320 1460 1480 1750 1790 2410
CV	2350 2470
D$	1910 1920 1930 1940
GAMMA	1270 1310 1760 1770 1830
I	1380 1390 1400 1410 1640 1650 1660 1710 1730 1750 1790 1840 1850 1860 1960 1970 1980 1990 2000 2110 2260 2320 2340 2360 2370 2380 2390 2410
J	1740 1760 1770 1820 2130 2140 2150 2160 2170 2310 2340 2450
K	2120 2140 2160 2250 2420 2430 2440
L	1570 1580 2160 2220 2230 2250
LABEL$	1320 1460 2230 2250 2340
MODE	1270 1280 2050
NSECT	1460 1470 1480 1510 1640 1710 2110 2130 2320
PI	1230 1310 1650
R	1230 1760 1770 1840 1850
SI	1830 1840 1850
T	1510 1650
TITLE$	1340 1390 1400 1980 1990
X	1760 1780 1810 2520 2530
X1	1230 1760 1780 1840
X2	1330 1840 2250 2370 2390 2430
Y	1770 1780 1810
Y1	1230 1770 1780 1850
Y2	1330 1850 2140 2150 2160 2220 2360 2380 2430
YC	2090 2240 2250
Z	1320 1460 1510 1650

Notes

Apple Nuclear Power Plant

Stephen R. Berggren

The safety, usefulness and desirability of nuclear power plants is a subject that has recently been a very "hot" topic of conversation. It seems that almost everyone has an opinion about what should be done about nuclear power plants. It's too bad that only a very few people have actually been at the controls of one of the big generating plants to get a firsthand feel for how it works.

That's all I wanted to do; to run my own nuclear power plant. Unfortunately, I did not have several hundred million dollars or a license from the Nuclear Regulatory Commission. Neither did I want to wait the ten years it would take to build a power plant. I was therefore forced to use what I did have, my Apple II computer. This wasn't such a bad alternative. After all, on a computer the worst thing that could result from my mismanagement would be a software crash. I would be completely safe from explosions, radiation and irate protesters.

My efforts at a safe study of nuclear power have resulted in a program that simulates the performance of a pressurized water nuclear power plant. The program is designed to be educational, as well as challenging and fun. It starts with a simple description of the workings of a plant I designed. This is followed by an animated diagram of the plant and its operation in color graphics. Then instructions are provided on how to operate the controls. Finally the plant starts operation with a daily status report appearing on the screen. The keyboard is used to adjust the controls and then move to the next day. Within the

Stephen R. Berggren, 104 Ridgeway Ave. Louisville,KY 40207

program, a series of equations simulates the response of the reactor and power system and presents the next day's status. Warnings are provided when the plant is not operating properly or when any damage is done. This report is a much simplified version of the computerized status reporting used in most nuclear power plants.

I did not have several hundred million dollars or a license from the Nuclear Regulatory Commission. I was therefore forced to use what I did have, my Apple II computer.

As with a real power plant, the object is to produce as much electrical power as possible without injuring anyone or damaging the equipment. This plant can produce up to two megawatts of power before overloading, but the average power output depends on how close to this maximum the plant is operated and how long the plant is down for maintenance. When the plant's nuclear fuel is exhausted (after about 120 days) the program evaluates the operator's performance based on the average power output and the damage sustained by the plant. Of course, if the plant's operation should result in a meltdown, the operator should consider his performance rather poor.

A Disastrous Sample Run

In the sample program run, you can see that at day one the plant was in cold shutdown and everything was at 25 (degrees centigrade). Of course, the control rods were fully inserted and all coolant flow was stopped. I started the plant by pulling out the control rods. As the reactor

heat went up, primary and secondary coolant flow was started to cool the reactor and run the generator turbine. By day 15, the plant's temperatures had settled down and the plant was running well, although not very close to its maximum power output. That's the trick; keeping the power output high and the temperatures in the operating ranges.

At day 19, a small coolant leak developed, but I decided not to shut down just to fix it. However, by day 23 things had really turned sour, and I had to try for a maintenance shutdown. With all coolant systems on full and the control rods in, the reactor cooled quickly and then entered the automatic maintenance shutdown mode. It took 32 days to repair the damage but then the plant was ready to start again. But I made a mistake. I tried to heat the reactor too quickly and went beyond the safe temperature range. Then, I tried to compensate by increasing the primary coolant flow and got into more trouble. Before I could get the emergency coolant on, the reactor went out of control and disaster struck. Too bad, but I deserved it. At least no one was hurt.

The program is written in a very straightforward manner and only the keyboard input and operating algorithms should be at all hard to understand. Lines 955 to 985 demonstrate the keyboard input. The key is entered as A$ and filtered in line 965 to allow only (space), (return) and 0 thru 9 to pass through. The (space) will skip to the next variable while the (return) will allow the program to continue to the next day's report. A$ is then concatenated to B$ whose VAL becomes the new input variable. The FOR statement in line 955 limits the input to four keystrokes. The program is almost entirely crashproof. *(Famous last words.—Ed.)*

If you are really interested in the operating algorithm, lines 1280 to 1395 simulate heat flow equations that have been simplified slightly. Don't feel too bad if you don't understand exactly how they work. They do work. The REM statements at the end of the program give the prefixes and suffixes used to create the variables. They also describe what each section is supposed to do.

Program Details

The program is written in Applesoft, Apple's floating point Basic, and fits in a 16K memory. Translation should be very easy with some exceptions. The diagram routines use color graphics. If your system does not have graphics, delete lines 6000 to 7060. You must also fix lines 220 and 222, since calling a deleted subroutine is an easy way to crash. The program also makes extensive use of logic evaluations within expressions. For example, (A<100) equals one if true, and zero if false. This is a quick and easy way to avoid IF statements. If your system does not have this capability, convert each of these expressions to IF statements. Many of the variables have percent signs following them. This is Applesoft's way of saying 'integer variable.' I used them to keep fractions out of the numbers printed in the status report. If your system can easily control the number of decimal places printed, forget the percent signs.

> **Before I could get the emergency coolant on, the reactor went out of control and disaster struck. Too bad, but I deserved it.**

In Applesoft, the PEEK in line 910 returns the vertical position of the cursor. If you can't find your cursor, you will have to think up another way to input the control variable. Finally, the instructions and the status report are made to fit a 40 by 24 character screen. These can be easily modified to fill a wider screen.

I have some final words to engineers, nuclear technicians and other qualified readers. No, I have never seen a real power plant that was designed like this. Yes, I know it takes much less than a day for a reactor to respond to changes in coolant flow and control rod position. Besides, who ever heard of a reactor with only one emergency cooling system, and that one with a limited supply of coolant? And, blasphemy of blasphemies, no SCRAM mechanism? I am sure your list of discrepancies is far more complete. What I have tried to do is to incorporate characteristics and responses of a simplified and idealized nuclear power plant into a computer simulation game. Several concessions to accuracy were made in order to create a simulation that would provide realistic responses to simple inputs and make an interesting and instructive game. □

```
10    HOME
20    PRINT  SPC( 8)"APPLE NUCLEAR POWER PLANT"
30    PRINT  SPC( 9)"BY STEPHEN R. BERGGREN
40    PRINT
50    PRINT "THIS PROGRAM SIMULATES THE OPERATION OF"
60    PRINT "A NUCLEAR POWER REACTOR.   THE OBJECT"
70    PRINT "IS TO OPERATE THE PLANT AT A MAXIMUM"
80    PRINT "AVERAGE POWER OUTPUT WITHOUT CAUSING"
90    PRINT "A REACTOR MELTDOWN."
100   PRINT
110   PRINT "THE CONTROL RODS ADJUST THE AMOUNT OF"
120   PRINT "HEAT PRODUCED BY THE REACTOR.   PRIMARY"
130   PRINT "COOLANT TRANSFERS THIS HEAT TO THE HEAT"
140   PRINT "EXCHANGER.   SECONDARY COOLANT TRANSFERS"
150   PRINT "HEAT FROM THE HEAT EXCHANGER TO THE"
160   PRINT "TURBINE, WHERE POWER IS PRODUCED, AND"
170   PRINT "FINALLY TO THE COOLING TOWER.   THE"
180   PRINT "EMERGENCY COOLANT IS USED TO HELP SHUT"
190   PRINT "DOWN THE REACTOR WHEN OTHER SYSTEMS"
200   PRINT "FAIL.   UNLIKE THE OTHER COOLANTS, "
210   PRINT "EMERGENCY COOLANT IS NOT RECYCLED."
220   PRINT : INPUT "ENTER 'D' TO SEE REACTOR DIAGRAM    ENTER 'I' FOR WORKIN
G INSTRUCTIONS          ENTER 'S' TO START OPERATION       ";A$
221     IF A$ = "D" THEN  GOSUB 6000: GOTO 220
222     IF A$ = "S" THEN 390
225   TEXT : HOME
230   PRINT "THE CONTROLS ARE OPERATED BY TYPING IN"
235   PRINT "THE DESIRED CONTROL ROD SETTING AND"
240   PRINT "FLOW RATES. (USE VALUES FROM 0 TO 100)"
245   PRINT "IF NO ENTRY IS MADE, THE VALUES WILL"
250   PRINT "NOT CHANGE.   USE THE SPACE BAR TO STEP"
255   PRINT "TO THE DIFFERENT FUNCTIONS.   WHEN THE"
260   PRINT "DESIRED ENTRIES HAVE BEEN MADE, USE THE"
265   PRINT "'RETURN' KEY TO ADVANCE TO THE NEXT DAY."
270   PRINT "THE REACTOR CAN BE OPERATED UNTIL A"
275   PRINT "MELTDOWN OCCURS OR THE REACTOR FUEL IS"
280   PRINT "EXHAUSTED.   THE FUEL WILL LAST FOR"
285   PRINT "ABOUT 100 TO 150 DAYS.   WHEN THE FUEL"
290   PRINT "IS EXHAUSTED, YOUR PERFORMANCE WILL BE"
295   PRINT "EVALUATED.
298   PRINT : INPUT "   (PRESS RETURN TO CONTINUE)";A$: HOME
300   PRINT : PRINT "IF YOU WANT TO REPAIR DAMAGE OR REPLACE"
305   PRINT "COOLANT, BRING THE REACTOR TEMPERATURE"
310   PRINT "DOWN BELOW 100 AND SHUT OFF THE COOLANT"
315   PRINT "FLOWS.   THIS WILL CAUSE AN AUTOMATIC"
320   PRINT "MAINTENANCE SHUTDOWN AND ALL COOLANT"
325   PRINT "WILL BE REPLENISHED AND REPAIRS MADE."
330   PRINT "THE GREATER THE DAMAGE, THE LONGER THE"
335   PRINT "REPAIRS WILL TAKE."
340   PRINT
350   PRINT "       WARNING: THIS POWER PLANT HAS"
360   PRINT "       NO AUTOMATIC SAFETY DEVICES!!"
370   PRINT
380   GOTO 220
390   REM   INITIATE
400   GOSUB 2000
410 RH = 0
420 RL = 0
430 DAY% = 0
440 TT = 0
450 DMGE% = 0
455 A% = 0:A1% = 0:A2% = 0
460   REM WRITE REPORT
470   TEXT : HOME
475 DAY% = DAY% + 1
480   PRINT  SPC( 7)"APPLE NUCLEAR POWER PLANT"
490   PRINT  SPC( 8)"STATUS REPORT - DAY ";DAY%
500   PRINT
510   PRINT "WARNINGS:"
520   IF RT% > 800 THEN  PRINT " REACTOR OVERHEATED":RD% = RD% + 1 + (RT%
      > 850) + (RT% > 900) + 2 * (RT% > 950):PD% = PD% + 1:ED% = ED% + 1
      + (RT% > 850)
530   IF XT% > 500 THEN  PRINT " HEAT EXCHANGER OVERHEATED":XD% = XD% + 1
      + (XT% > 600):PD% = PD% + 1:SD% = SD% + 1
540   IF GO% > 2000 THEN  PRINT " TURBINE OVERLOADED":TD% = TD% + 1 + (GO%
      > 2500  ):SD% = SD% + 1
550   IF CT% > 300 THEN  PRINT " COOLING TOWER OVERHEATED":SD% = SD% + 1
560   IF GO% < 1000 THEN  PRINT " POWER OUTPUT LOW"
570   IF EV% < 200 THEN  PRINT " EMERGENCY COOLANT LOW"
580   IF PV% < 100 THEN  PRINT " PRIMARY COOLANT LOW":PD% = PD% + 1
590   IF SV% < 100 THEN  PRINT " SECONDARY COOLANT LOW":SD% = SD% + 1
600   PRINT
610   PRINT "DAMAGE:"
620   IF RD% > 3 THEN  PRINT " REACTOR CORE DAMAGED"
630   IF PD% > 4 THEN  PRINT " PRIMARY COOLANT LEAK - ";PD%;"/DAY":PV% =
      (PV% - P
D%) * ((PV% - PD%) > 0)
640   IF SD% > 4 THEN  PRINT " SECONDARY COOLANT LEAK - ";SD%;"/DAY":SV% =
```

```
      (SV% -  SD%) * ((SV% - SD%) > 0)
650   IF ED% > 2 THEN  PRINT " EMERGENCY COOLANT LEAK - ";2 * ED%;"/DAY":
      EV% = (E V% - 2 * ED%) * ((EV% - 2 * ED%) > 0)
660   IF PB% THEN  PRINT " PRIMARY COOLANT PUMP FAILURE - ";10 * PD% *
      (PD% < 10)  + 100 * (PD% >  = 10);"%"
670   IF SB% THEN  PRINT " SECONDARY COOLANT PUMP FAILURE - ";10 * SD% *
      (SD% < 1 0) + 100 * (SD% >  = 10);"%"
680   IF XB% THEN  PRINT " HEAT EXCHANGER FAILURE"
690   IF GB% THEN  PRINT " TURBINE FAILURE"
700   PRINT
710   IF RD% > 5 THEN  PRINT "      MELTDOWN!  MELTDOWN!  MELTDOWN!":
      GOTO 3000
720   PRINT "INDICATORS:"
730   PRINT " REACTOR TEMP. (MAX 800) ";RT%
740   PRINT " HEAT EXCHANGER TEMP. (MAX 500) ";XT%
750   PRINT " COOLING TOWER TEMP. (MAX 300) ";CT%
760   PRINT " POWER OUTPUT (MAX 2000KW) ";GO%;"KW"
765 KW% = TT / DAY%
770   PRINT " AVERAGE POWER OUTPUT  ";KW%;"KW/DAY
800   PRINT " CONTROL RODS- ";A%
810   PRINT " COOLANTS"
820   PRINT "  EMERGENCY  LEVEL- ";EV%;"  FLOW- ";EF%
830   PRINT "  PRIMARY    LEVEL- ";PV%;"  FLOW- ";PF%
840   PRINT "  SECONDARY  LEVEL- ";SV%;"  FLOW- ";SF%
850   IF (100 - RL) < 5 THEN  PRINT : PRINT : PRINT "REACTOR FUEL
      EXHAUSTED": GOT O 4000
900   REM GET NEW CONTROL VALUES
910 P = PEEK (37)
920   VTAB (P - 3)
930   HTAB (20)
950 A2% = A1%:A1% = A%
955 B$ = "": FOR I = 1 TO 4
960   GET A$:Z = ASC (A$)
965   IF (Z <  > 13 AND Z <  > 32) AND (Z > 57 OR Z < 48) THEN 960
970 B$ = B$ + A$: IF Z = 13 THEN 1170
975   IF Z = 32 THEN 990
980 A% =  VAL (B$):A% = A% + (100 - A%) * (A% > 100)
985   PRINT A$;: NEXT I
990   VTAB (P - 1)
1000   HTAB (35)
1005 B$ = "": FOR I = 1 TO 4
1010   GET A$:Z = ASC (A$)
1015   IF (Z <  > 13 AND Z <  > 32) AND (Z > 57 OR Z < 48) THEN 1010
1020 B$ = B$ + A$: IF Z = 13 THEN 1170
1025   IF Z = 32 THEN 1050
1030 EF% =  VAL (B$):EF% = EF% + (100 - EF%) * (EF% > 100)
1035   IF EF% > EV% THEN EF% = EV%
1040   PRINT A$;: NEXT I
1050   VTAB (P)
1060   HTAB (35)
1065 B$ = "": FOR I = 1 TO 4
1070   GET A$:Z = ASC (A$)
1075   IF (Z <  > 13 AND Z <  > 32) AND (Z > 57 OR Z < 48) THEN 1070
1080 B$ = B$ + A$: IF Z = 13 THEN 1170
1085   IF Z = 32 THEN 1110
1090 PF% =  VAL (B$):PF% = PF% + (100 - PF%) * (PF% > 100)
1100   PRINT A$;: NEXT I
1110   VTAB (P + 1)
1120   HTAB (35)
1125 B$ = "": FOR I = 1 TO 4
1130   GET A$:Z = ASC (A$)
1135   IF (Z <  > 13 AND Z <  > 32) AND (Z > 57 OR Z < 48) THEN 1130
1140 B$ = B$ + A$: IF Z = 13 THEN 1170
1145   IF Z = 32 THEN 1165
1150 SF% =  VAL (B$):SF% = SF% + (100 - SF%) * (SF% > 100)
1160   PRINT A$;: NEXT I
1165   HTAB (1): VTAB (P - 3): CALL  - 958: GOTO 800
1170   IF PF% = 0 AND SF% = 0 AND RH < 1 AND RT% < 100 AND A% = 0 THEN
      GOSUB 200 0: HTAB (1): VTAB (24): CALL  - 922: PRINT "
      MAINTENANCE SHUTDOWN - ";MD%;" D
1180   IF EF% > EV% THEN EF% = EV%
1200   REM DAMAGE ASSESSMENT AND OPERATION CALCULATIONS
1205 EV% = EV% - EF% - 2 * ED% * (ED% > 3)
1210 PD% = PD% + (PF% > 90) * ( RND (20) > .95)
1220 SD% = SD% + (SF% > 90) * ( RND (20) > .92)
1230 PB% = PD% > 5
1240 SB% = SD% > 5
1250   IF PF% > (100 - PD% * 10) AND PB% THEN PF% = (100 - PD% * 10) *
      (100 - PD%  * 10 > 0)
1260   IF SF% > (100 - SD% * 10) AND SB% THEN SF% = (100 - SD% * 10) *
      (100 - SD%  * 10 > 0)
1270 RL = RL + RH / 50
1280 RH = (A% * 30 + A1% * 60 + A2% * 10) / 2500 * (100 - RL)
1300 PH = PF% * (100 * (PV% > 100) + PV% * (PV% <  = 100)) / 350
1310 EH = EF% / 200 * (RT% - 25)
1320 RT% = RT% + RH - EH - PH - 5 * (RT% > 25)
1325 RT% = 25 + (RT% - 25) * (RT% > 25)
1330 XT% = ((RT% - 25) * PF% + (CT% - 25) * SF%) / (PF% + SF% + 1) + 25
```

```
1340   IF XB% THEN XT% = RT% * .8 + 5
1350 SH = SF% * (100 * (PV% > 100) + PV% * (PV% <  = 100)) / 350 *
     (XT% - CT%)
1360   IF XB% THEN SH = SH * .2
1370 GO% = SH / XT% * (XT% - CT%) * 2 / 3
1375   IF GO% > 2600 THEN GO% = 2600
1380 GO% = GO% * (GO% > 0) * (GB% = 0)
1390 CT% = 25 + ((XT% - 25) * (SH - GO%) / (SH + 1) * .75)
1395 CT% = 25 * (CT% <  = 25) + CT% * (CT% > 25)
1400   IF XB% < 1 THEN XB% = (XD% > 2) * ( RND (4) > .9)
1410   IF GB% < 1 THEN GB% = (GD% > 4) * ( RND (4) > .9)
1420 TT = TT + GO%
1430   GOTO 470
2000   REM MAINTENANCE REPAIR SUBROUTINE
2010 EV% = 300
2020 PV% = 120
2030 SV% = 120
2040 RT% = 25
2050 XT% = 25
2060 CT% = 25
2070 DMGE% = DMGE% + 2 * RD% + ED% + PD% + XD% + SD% + GD%
2080 MD% = 5 + 3 * (10 * (RD% > 3) + (ED% > 3) + (PD% > 3) + (SD% > 3)
     + 2 * PB%  + 2 * SB% + 3 * XB% + 3 * GB%):DAY% = DAY% + MD%
2090 RD% = 0
2100 ED% = 0
2110 PD% = 0
2120 XD% = 0
2130 SD% = 0
2140 GD% = 0
2150 PB% = 0
2160 SB% = 0
2170 XB% = 0
2180 GB% = 0
2190 EF% = 0:PF% = 0:SF% = 0
2195 GO% = 0
2200   RETURN
3000   REM  MELTDOWN ENDING
3010   PRINT
3020   IF RD% > 6 THEN 3100
3030   PRINT "THE REACTOR CORE HAS BEEN DISTROYED BY"
3040   PRINT "UNCONTROLLED THERMAL RUNAWAY.  HOWEVER,"
3050   PRINT "THE CONTAINMENT BUILDING HAS NOT YET"
3060   PRINT "RUPTURED.
3070   PRINT
3080   PRINT "INITIATE YOUR EVACUATION PLAN."
3090   GOTO 5000
3100   PRINT "THE REACTOR CORE HAS MELTED DOWN AND"
3110   PRINT "PRODUCED A STEAM EXPLOSION.   THE"
3120   PRINT "CONTAINMENT BUILDING HAS RUPTURED."
3130   PRINT "LETHAL RADIOACTIVE GASES AND DEBRIS"
3140   PRINT "HAVE ESCAPED."
3150   PRINT
3160   PRINT "INITIATE YOUR EVACUATION AND RADIATION"
3170   PRINT "CLEANUP PLANS AND GET MEDICAL"
3180   PRINT "ASSISTANCE."
3190   GOTO 5000
4000   REM  EVALUATION OF GAME RESULTS
4010   PRINT
4020   PRINT "OVER A PERIOD OF ";DAY%;" DAYS, YOU HAVE"
4030   PRINT "PRODUCED AN AVERAGE POWER OUTPUT OF"
4040   PRINT KW%;" KILOWATTS PER DAY."
4050 AKW% = 1 + (KW% > 1000) + (KW% > 1200) + (KW% > 1500) + (KW% > 1800)
4060   PRINT
4070   PRINT "YOUR AVERAGE POWER PRODUCTION RATE IS"
4080   ON AKW% GOTO 4090,4100,4110,4120,4140
4090   PRINT "HORRIBLE! FIND A LESS DEMANDING JOB.": GOTO 4200
4100   PRINT "WAY BELOW YOUR AREA'S POWER NEEDS.": GOTO 4200
4110   PRINT "ADEQUATE. YOU COULD DO BETTER.": GOTO 4200
4120   PRINT "EXCELLENT! POWER COSTS IN YOUR AREA"
4130   PRINT "WILL NOT BE INCREASED.": GOTO 4200
4140   PRINT "NEAR THE MAXIMUM!  POWER COSTS IN YOUR"
4150   PRINT "AREA WILL DROP SIGNIFICANTLY."
4200   REM DAMAGE EVALUATION
4210   PRINT
4215   GOSUB 2000
4220 D% = 1 + (DMGE% > 10) + (DMGE% > 20) + (DMGE% > 30)
4230   PRINT "THE EQUIPMENT DAMAGE SUSTAINED DURING"
4240   PRINT "THIS PERIOD WAS ";
4250   ON D% GOTO 4260,4270,4280,4290
4260   PRINT "VERY LIGHT.": GOTO 5000
4270   PRINT "MODERATE.": GOTO 5000
4280   PRINT "HEAVY.": GOTO 5000
4290   PRINT "SEVERE."
5000   REM END
5010   PRINT
5020   PRINT "WOULD YOU LIKE TO TRY AGAIN? (Y OR N)";
5030   INPUT A$
5040   IF A$ = "" THEN 5030
5050   IF A$ = "Y" THEN  GOSUB 2000: GOTO 390
5060   HOME
5070   END
5100 B$ = ""
```

```
5105   FOR I = 1 TO 4
5110   GET A$
5130   IF  ASC (A$) <  > 32 THEN 5140
5134   IF B$ = "" THEN  RETURN
5136 OUT% =  VAL (B$)
5138   RETURN
5140   IF  ASC (A$) = 13 THEN  POP : GOTO 1170
5150 B$ = B$ + A$
5160   PRINT A$;
5170   NEXT I
5180   RETURN
6000   GR : COLOR= 15: FOR I = 0 TO 39: HLIN 0,39 AT I: NEXT I
6005 DE = 6000
6010   HOME : VTAB 23
6020   PRINT "  THIS IS THE REACTOR VESSEL"
6030   RESTORE
6035   COLOR= 1
6040   FOR I = 1 TO 29
6050   READ X1,X2,Y
6060   HLIN X1,X2 AT Y
6070   NEXT I
6080   DATA 7,9,6,15,17,6,6,18,7,5,19,8,5,7,9,17,19,9,5,6,10,18,19,10,5,6,
       11,18,19,11,5,6,12,18,19,12,5,6,13,18,19,13,5,6,14
6090   DATA 18,19,14,5,6,15,18,19,15,5,6,16,18,19,16,5,6,17,18,19,17,5,6,
       18,18,19 ,18,5,7,19,17,19,19,6,18,20,7,17,21,8,16,22
6100   COLOR= 0
6110   HLIN 13,14 AT 6
6120   COLOR= 12
6130   HLIN 14,15 AT 5
6140   HLIN 14,16 AT 4
6150   HLIN 15,16 AT 3
6160   FOR I = 1 TO DE: NEXT I
6170   VTAB 23
6180   PRINT "  THIS IS THE REACTOR CORE       "
6190   COLOR= 8
6200   FOR I = 9 TO 15
6210   VLIN 11,17 AT I
6220   NEXT I
6230   FOR I = 1 TO DE: NEXT I
6240   VTAB 23
6250   PRINT "  THESE ARE THE CONTROL RODS    "
6260   COLOR= 13
6270   VLIN 2,17 AT 11
6280   VLIN 2,17 AT 13
6290   FOR I = 1 TO DE: NEXT I
6300   VTAB 23
6310   PRINT " THE EMERGENCY COOLANT CAN COOL THE"
6320   PRINT " REACTOR IN AN EMERGENCY."
6330   COLOR= 2
6340   FOR I = 1 TO 36
6350   READ Y,X
6360   PLOT X,Y
6370   FOR J = 1 TO 200: NEXT J
6380   NEXT I
6390   DATA 4,2,4,4,5,2,5,3,5,4,6,2,6,3,6,4,7,3,8,3,9,3,10,3,11,3,12,3,
       12,4,12,5, 12,6,12,7,12,8,12,9
6400   DATA 13,9,14,9,15,9,16,9,16,8,16,7,16,6,16,5,16,4,16,3,17,3,18,3,
       19,3,20,3 ,22,3,24,3
6410   FOR I = 1 TO DE: NEXT I
6420   HOME : VTAB 23
6430   PRINT " THE PRIMARY COOLANT CARRIES HEAT FROM"
6440   PRINT " THE REACTOR CORE TO THE HEAT EXCHANGER"
6450   FOR I = 1 TO 52
6460   READ Y,X
6470   PLOT X,Y
6480   FOR J = 1 TO 200: NEXT J
6490   NEXT I
6500   FOR I = 1 TO DE: NEXT I
6510   DATA 4,25,4,27,5,25,5,26,5,27,6,25,6,26,6,27,7,26,8,26,9,26,10,26,
       11,26,12 ,26,12,25,12,24,12,23,12,22,12,21,12,20,12,19
6515   DATA 12,18,12,17,12,16,12,15,13,15,14,15,15,15,16,15,16,16,16,
       17,16,18
6520   DATA  16,19,16,20,16,21,16,22,16,23,16,24,16,25,16,26,16,27,16,28,
       16,29,16 ,30,15,30,14,30,13,30,13,30,12,30,12,29,12,28,12,27
6540   HOME : VTAB 23
6550   PRINT " THIS IS THE HEAT EXCHANGER"
6560   COLOR= 5
6570   HLIN 28,34 AT 10
6580   VLIN 10,18 AT 34
6590   HLIN 28,34 AT 18
6600   VLIN 10,18 AT 28
6605   COLOR= 2: PLOT 28,12: PLOT 28,16: COLOR= 5
6610   FOR I = 1 TO DE: NEXT I
6620   VTAB 23
6630   PRINT " THIS IS THE GENERATOR TURBINE"
6640   HLIN 5,18 AT 30
6650   VLIN 30,36 AT 18
6660   HLIN 5,18 AT 36
6670   VLIN 30,36 AT 5
```

```
6680  COLOR= 0
6690  HLIN 2,17 AT 33
6700  FOR I = 7 TO 15 STEP 2
6710  PLOT I,34: PLOT I + 1,32
6720  NEXT I
6730  FOR I = 1 TO DE: NEXT I
6740  VTAB 23
6750  PRINT " THIS IS THE COOLING TOWER         "
6760  COLOR= 5
6770  VLIN 23,25 AT 24
6780  VLIN 23,25 AT 36
6790  VLIN 25,26 AT 25
6800  VLIN 25,26 AT 35
6810  VLIN 26,28 AT 26
6820  VLIN 26,28 AT 34
6830  VLIN 28,36 AT 27
6840  VLIN 28,36 AT 33
6850  PLOT 34,36
6860  PLOT 26,36
6870  HLIN 25,35 AT 38
6880  FOR I = 1 TO DE: NEXT I
6890  VTAB 23
6900  PRINT " THE SECONDARY COOLANT CARRIES HEAT"
6910  PRINT " FROM THE HEAT EXCHANGER TO THE "
6920  PRINT " TURBINE AND THEN TO THE COOLING TOWER"
6925  COLOR= 2
6930  FOR I = 1 TO 123
6940  READ Y,X
6950  PLOT X,Y
6960  FOR J = 1 TO 200: NEXT J
6970  NEXT I
6980  DATA 4,35,4,37,5,35,5,36,5,37,6,35,6,36,6,37,7,36,8,36,9,36,10,36,
      11,36,12,36,12,35,12,34,12,33,12,32,13,32,14,32,15,32,16,32
6990  DATA 16,33,16,34,16,35,16,36,17,36,18,36,19,36,20,36,20,35,20,34,
      20,33,20,32,20,31,20,30,20,29,20,28,20,27,20,26,20,25,20,24,20,23,
      20,22,20,21
7000  DATA 21,21,22,21,23,21,24,21,25,21,26,21,27,21,27,20,27,19,27,18,
      27,17,27,16,27,15,27,14,27,13,27,12,27,11,27,10,27,9,27,8,27,7
7010  DATA 28,7,29,7,30,7,31,7,32,7,34,10,32,13,34,16,35,16,35,17,35,18,
      35,19,35,20,35,21,35,22,35,23,35,24,35,25,35,26,35,27,35,28
7020  DATA 34,28,34,29,34,30,35,30,35,31,35,32,34,32,34,33,34,34,34,35,
      34,36,34,37,34,38,33,38,32,38,31,38,30,38,29,38,28,38,27,38,26,38,
      25,38,24,38,23,38
7030  DATA 22,38,21,38,20,38,19,38,18,38,17,38,16,38,15,38,14,38,13,38,
      12,38,12,37
7040  HOME : VTAB 23
7060  RETURN
9000  REM VARIABLE PREFIXES
9010  REM A-CONTROL RODS, C-COOLING TOWER, E-EMERGENCY COOLANT,
      G-TURBINE, P-PRIMARY COOLANT, R-REACTOR, S-SECONDARY COOLANT,
      X-HEAT EXCHANGER
9020  REM VARIABLE SUFFIXES
9030  REM B-BROKEN, D-DAMAGE, F-FLOW RATE, H-HEAT FLOW, L-LIFE, O-OUTPUT,
      T-TEMPERATURE, V-VOLUME
9040  REM OTHER VARIABLES TOT-TOTAL POWER OUTPUT, KW-AVERAGE POWER
      OUTPUT, DAY-DAY OF OPERATION, DMGE-TOTAL EQUIPMENT DAMAGE
9050  REM PROGRAM DISCRIPTION BY LINE NUMBER
9060  REM 10-220 INTRODUCTION
9070  REM 225-380 INSTRUCTIONS
9080  REM 390-455 VARIABLE INITIATION
9090  REM  460-850 WRITE REPORT AND ASSESS DAMAGE
9100  REM  900-1165 INPUT NEW CONTROL VARIABLES
9110  REM 1170 MAINTENANCE SHUTDOWN EVALUATION
9120  REM 1200-1260 PUMP FAILURE ASSESSMENT
9130  REM 1270-1430 PLANT OPERATING ALGORITHMS
9140  REM 2000-2200 MAINTENANCE SHUTDOWN SUBROUTINE
9150  REM 3000-3190 MELTDOWN ENDING
9160  REM 4000-4290 EVALUATION OF GAME RESULTS
9170  REM 5000-5070 END
9180  REM 6000-7060 PLANT DIAGRAM SUBROUTINE
9190  REM 9000-9190 REMARKS
9200  REM   APPLE NUCLEAR POWER PLANT
9210  REM  BY STEPHEN R BERGGREN

RUN
          APPLE NUCLEAR POWER PLANT
            BY STEPHEN R. BERGGREN


THIS PROGRAM SIMULATES THE OPERATION OF
A NUCLEAR POWER REACTOR.  THE OBJECT
IS TO OPERATE THE PLANT AT A MAXIMUM
AVERAGE POWER OUTPUT WITHOUT CAUSING
A REACTOR MELTDOWN.

THE CONTROL RODS ADJUST THE AMOUNT OF
HEAT PRODUCED BY THE REACTOR.  PRIMARY
COOLANT TRANSFERS THIS HEAT TO THE HEAT
EXCHANGER.  SECONDARY COOLANT TRANSFERS
HEAT FROM THE HEAT EXCHANGER TO THE
TURBINE, WHERE POWER IS PRODUCED, AND
FINALLY TO THE COOLING TOWER.
```

THE EMERGENCY COOLANT IS USED TO HELP SHUT
DOWN THE REACTOR WHEN OTHER SYSTEMS
FAIL. UNLIKE THE OTHER COOLANTS,
EMERGENCY COOLANT IS NOT RECYCLED.

ENTER 'D' TO SEE REACTOR DIAGRAM   ENTER 'I' FOR WORKING INSTRUCTIONS
ENTER 'S' TO START OPERATION
THE CONTROLS ARE OPERATED BY TYPING IN
THE DESIRED CONTROL ROD SETTING AND
FLOW RATES.(USE VALUES FROM 0 TO 100)
IF NO ENTRY IS MADE, THE VALUES WILL
NOT CHANGE. USE THE SPACE BAR TO STEP
TO THE DIFFERENT FUNCTIONS. WHEN THE
DESIRED ENTRIES HAVE BEEN MADE, USE THE
'RETURN' KEY TO ADVANCE TO THE NEXT DAY.
THE REACTOR CAN BE OPERATED UNTIL A
MELTDOWN OCCURS OR THE REACTOR FUEL IS
EXHAUSTED. THE FUEL WILL LAST FOR
ABOUT 100 TO 150 DAYS. WHEN THE FUEL
IS EXHAUSTED, YOUR PERFORMANCE WILL BE
EVALUATED.

        (PRESS RETURN TO CONTINUE)

IF YOU WANT TO REPAIR DAMAGE OR REPLACE
COOLANT, BRING THE REACTOR TEMPERATURE
DOWN BELOW 100 AND SHUT OFF THE COOLANT
FLOWS. THIS WILL CAUSE AN AUTOMATIC
MAINTENANCE SHUTDOWN AND ALL COOLANT
WILL BE REPLENISHED AND REPAIRS MADE.
THE GREATER THE DAMAGE, THE LONGER THE
REPAIRS WILL TAKE.

        WARNING: THIS POWER PLANT HAS
        NO AUTOMATIC SAFETY DEVICES!!

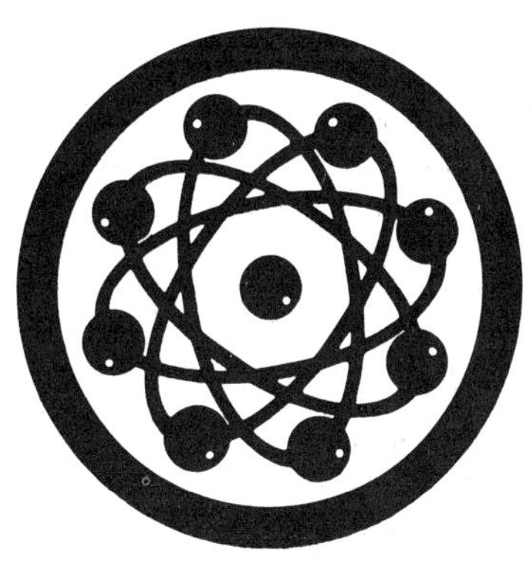

ENTER 'D' TO SEE REACTOR DIAGRAM   ENTER 'I' FOR WORKING INSTRUCTIONS
ENTER 'S' TO START OPERATION   S
        APPLE NUCLEAR POWER PLANT
          STATUS REPORT - DAY 1

WARNINGS:
 POWER OUTPUT LOW

DAMAGE:

INDICATORS:
 REACTOR TEMP. (MAX 800) 25
 HEAT EXCHANGER TEMP. (MAX 500) 25
 COOLING TOWER TEMP. (MAX 300) 25
 POWER OUTPUT (MAX 2000KW) 0KW
 AVERAGE POWER OUTPUT 0KW/DAY
 CONTROL RODS- 0
 COOLANTS
  EMERGENCY   LEVEL- 300   FLOW- 0
  PRIMARY   LEVEL- 120   FLOW- 0
  SECONDARY   LEVEL- 120   FLOW- 01
          STATUS REPORT - DAY 2

WARNINGS:
 POWER OUTPUT LOW

DAMAGE:

INDICATORS:
 REACTOR TEMP. (MAX 800) 26
 HEAT EXCHANGER TEMP. (MAX 500) 25
 COOLING TOWER TEMP. (MAX 300) 25
 POWER OUTPUT (MAX 2000KW) 0KW
 AVERAGE POWER OUTPUT 0KW/DAY
 CONTROL RODS- 1
 COOLANTS
  EMERGENCY   LEVEL- 300   FLOW- 0
  PRIMARY   LEVEL- 120   FLOW- 0
  SECONDARY   LEVEL- 120   FLOW- 0100

        APPLE NUCLEAR POWER PLANT
          STATUS REPORT - DAY 19

WARNINGS:

DAMAGE:
 SECONDARY COOLANT LEAK - 5/DAY

INDICATORS:
 REACTOR TEMP. (MAX 800) 778
 HEAT EXCHANGER TEMP. (MAX 500) 465

COOLING TOWER TEMP. (MAX 300) 254
POWER OUTPUT (MAX 2000KW) 1858KW
AVERAGE POWER OUTPUT   1478KW/DAY
CONTROL RODS- 9
COOLANTS
  EMERGENCY   LEVEL- 300   FLOW- 0
  PRIMARY   LEVEL- 120   FLOW- 70
  SECONDARY   LEVEL- 105   FLOW- 100
       STATUS REPORT - DAY 20

      APPLE NUCLEAR POWER PLANT
       STATUS REPORT - DAY 23

WARNINGS:
  HEAT EXCHANGER OVERHEATED
  COOLING TOWER OVERHEATED
  POWER OUTPUT LOW
  SECONDARY COOLANT LOW

DAMAGE:
  SECONDARY COOLANT LEAK - 11/DAY
  SECONDARY COOLANT PUMP FAILURE - 100%

INDICATORS:
  REACTOR TEMP. (MAX 800) 783
  HEAT EXCHANGER TEMP. (MAX 500) 667
  COOLING TOWER TEMP. (MAX 300) 327
  POWER OUTPUT (MAX 2000KW) 790KW
  AVERAGE POWER OUTPUT   1487KW/DAY
  CONTROL RODS- 9
  COOLANTS
   EMERGENCY   LEVEL- 300   FLOW- 0
   PRIMARY   LEVEL- 120   FLOW- 70
   SECONDARY   LEVEL- 76   FLOW- 20

      APPLE NUCLEAR POWER PLANT
       STATUS REPORT - DAY 30

WARNINGS:
  POWER OUTPUT LOW
  EMERGENCY COOLANT LOW
  PRIMARY COOLANT LOW
  SECONDARY COOLANT LOW

DAMAGE:
  PRIMARY COOLANT LEAK - 7/DAY
  SECONDARY COOLANT LEAK - 19/DAY
  PRIMARY COOLANT PUMP FAILURE - 70%
  SECONDARY COOLANT PUMP FAILURE - 100%
  HEAT EXCHANGER FAILURE

INDICATORS:
  REACTOR TEMP. (MAX 800) 96
  HEAT EXCHANGER TEMP. (MAX 500) 81
  COOLING TOWER TEMP. (MAX 300) 25
  POWER OUTPUT (MAX 2000KW) 0KW
  AVERAGE POWER OUTPUT   1140KW/DAY
  CONTROL RODS- 0
  COOLANTS
   EMERGENCY   LEVEL- 0   FLOW- 0
   PRIMARY   LEVEL- 82 FLOW- 0
   SECONDARY   LEVEL- 0 . FLOW- 0
        MAINTENANCE SHUTDOWN - 32 DAYS

      APPLE NUCLEAR POWER PLANT
       STATUS REPORT - DAY 63

      APPLE NUCLEAR POWER PLANT
       STATUS REPORT - DAY 69

WARNINGS:
  REACTOR OVERHEATED
  TURBINE OVERLOADED

DAMAGE:
  REACTOR CORE DAMAGED
  EMERGENCY COOLANT LEAK - 10/DAY

     MELTDOWN! MELTDOWN! MELTDOWN!

THE REACTOR CORE HAS MELTED DOWN AND
PRODUCED A STEAM EXPLOSION.   THE
CONTAINMENT BUILDING HAS RUPTURED.
LETHAL RADIOACTIVE GASES AND DEBRIS
HAVE ESCAPED.

INITIATE YOUR EVACUATION AND
RADIATION CLEANUP PLANS AND
GET MEDICAL ASSISTANCE.

WOULD YOU LIKE TO TRY AGAIN?
(Y OR N)?N

". . . and I wish you would stop referring to this cold
as my down time!"

LANDING SIMULATOR

Jake Jacobs

I have always wanted to learn how to fly an airplane but never took the time. After I had my Apple computer for a few weeks and had impressed myself with its capabilities, I undertook the task of developing a simple landing simulator in Applesoft Basic. To keep it simple and also to minimize the flicker on the screen I eliminated banking and turning. The controls are the "stick" which moves only forwards and backwards (not left or right) and the 'throttle' which controls power from 0 to 100 percent. Both controls are simulated by the game paddles. Paddle 0 is the stick and paddle 1 is the throttle.

The screen displays the pilot's view of the runway using hi-res graphics. The lower four text lines simulate the pilot's instruments. These are: ALTitude in feet, rate of CLIMB or descent, in feet/minute, VELocity in knots, DME (distance measuring equipment) which indicates the distance in nautical miles from the front

Jake Jacobs, 1903 Fordham Way, Mountain View, CA 94040.

end of the runway, and percent POWER applied by the throttle. There is also a glide-slope indicator which shows the pilot whether he or she is on the 3.5 degree glide slope when approaching the runway.

There are two principle parameters to be computed: distance from the runway

---

I undertook the task of developing a simple landing simulator in Applesoft Basic.

(X) and altitude (ALT). The program is a continuous loop. During every pass through this loop the program calculates the new values of X and ALT from the old values. For example X is calculated from the old X by the statement $X = X + V$, where V is the current velocity. Similarly, the new

altitude is calculated by adding the rate of climb to the old altitude. These values are derived from the two input variables, the stick and the throttle. Once the values of X and ALT are computed, the view of the runway as seen by the pilot is then calculated and displayed in hi-res graphics. But first the old image of the runway is erased by redrawing it with HCOLOR set equal to 0.

The runway appears as a trapezoid in most cases. Since banking and turning are not simulated, the view of the runway is always symmetrical about an imaginary vertical line down the center of the screen (see Photo 1). Therefore only four values have to be calculated: the vertical positions of the horizontal lines which simulate the rear and front of the runway, and the widths of the rear and front of the runway.

Interestingly, no trigonometric functions have to be used. Only the simple geometry of similar triangles is applied. Figure 1 depicts a side view of the aircraft and the runway. The pilot's eye is assumed to be one foot away from the windshield

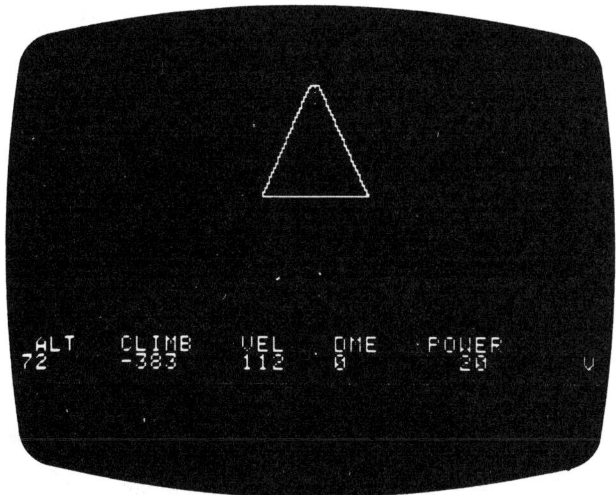

Photo 1. View of the runway as the aircraft is about to land. Note the negative rate of CLIMB.

Photo 2. Photograph of author's "stick" and "throttle" box which replaces the game paddles. However the game paddles work just fine so you need not build your own box.

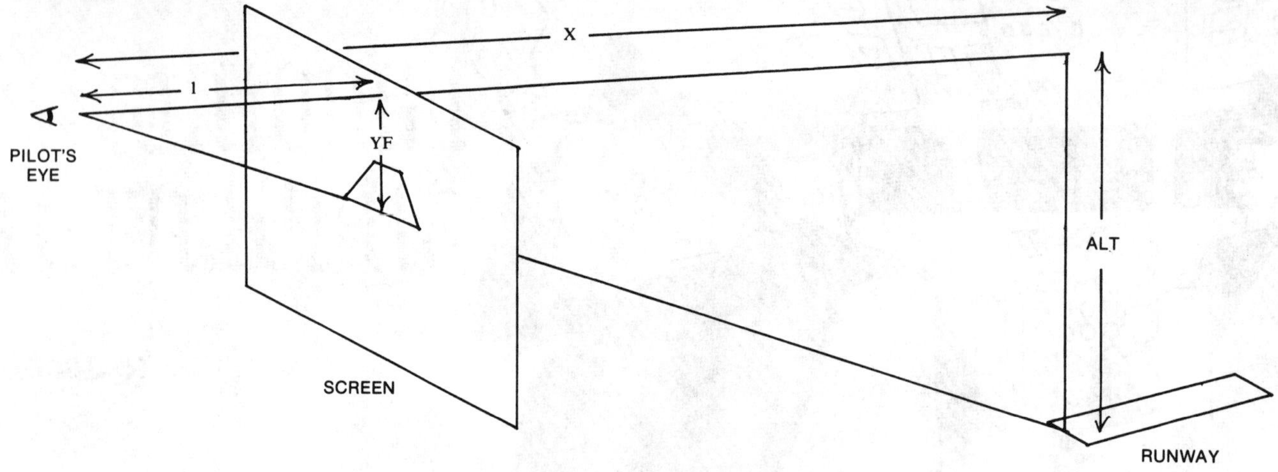

Figure 1. Side view of aircraft illustrating how the screen position of the front of the runway, YF, is calculated. Only simple similar triangles are used.

(i.e., the TV monitor, but you don't have to sit that close to your screen; the one foot is for calculation purposes only). Therefore the Y offset from the top of the screen (YF) of the front of the runway view is calculated from similar triangles as follows:

$$\frac{YF}{1} = \frac{ALT}{X}$$

YF must be scaled by multiplying it by 159, the maximum Y value that can be HPLOTed. If you have followed this so far, you will realize that for some values of X and ALT, YF could have a value that would plot off the bottom of the screen. In fact much of the program loop is taken up calculating what parts of the view of the runway are off the screen and correcting for this so that the HPLOT statements do not "blow up."

In a similar fashion, YR, the Y offset of the rear of the runway, is calculated. The same principle of similar triangles is employed to calculate the widths of the front and rear of the runway, and will not be described here.

A word about programming. Note that all constants used in the program are actually variables that are initialized at the beginning of the program. This was done for three reasons.

1. During run-time, variables are accessed faster than the time it takes for numeric constant strings to be evaluated.

2. When writing the program it was much easier to change a single assignment statement at the beginning of the program than to find all occurences of a particular constant throughout the program.

3. Using variables instead of numeric constants makes the program much more readable and self documenting. Note that some constants have the same value as others, but are given different names. (Remarks were included in the original program but many were deleted for this article to allow the program to run on a 16K machine.)

Here we introduce exponential smoothing, which is a fancy term for something quite simple.

If, for example, one wished to change the length of the runway from 4000 feet to 6000 feet, one would merely change the assignment statement 280 to RW = 6000. All occurences of the "constant" RW (and there are many) will be changed correctly.

Flying the Airplane

You start at a random distance from the runway and at a random altitude. The runway starts out as a small dot or line on the screen. As you approach the runway it will become larger and take on the appearance of a trapezoid. The program is calculating what the runway should really look like from your given altitude and distance from the runway. The throttle controls primarily your rate of climb and descent. The stick controls primarily your airspeed but also your rate of climb and descent. This is just the opposite of what most people think, but that is how an airplane really works. The best way to "fly" the plane is to place paddle 1 (throttle) on the table and put the stick (paddle 0) in your left hand and control it with your right hand. Then you can reach up to the table to adjust the throttle with your right hand. The author has built a "stick" and "throttle" in a small metal box as shown in Photo 2, but the game paddles work just fine.

The ALTitude and CLIMB indicators work together. Your altitude is shown in feet (from the ground) and the CLIMB indicator shows your rate of climb in feet per minute if positive or descent if negative. The VELocity indicator shows airspeed in knots or nautical miles per hour. A nautical mile is 6000 feet. The DME indicator is the Distance Measuring Equipment and indicates your distance from the front end of the runway in nautical miles. After you pass over the front of the runway the DME will begin to increase in value, rather than decrease as you approach the runway, because you are moving away from the front of the runway. The POWER indicators merely parrots the throttle setting from 0 to 100 percent. The last indicator on the right is the glide-slope indicator. Imagine an invisible line with a 3.5 degree slope raising towards you from the front of the runway. As you land you should stay on this imaginary line. The glide-slope indicator tells you if you are on this line and if not, what you should do:

- — means you are on the glide-slope
- ʌ means that you should climb (you are too low)
- v means that you should go down (you are too high).

When you are very close to the runway, you should ignore the glide-slope indicator since it applies to the front of the runway and you never actually land at the very front of the runway.

There are three markers on the runway, one every 1000 feet. These give you some idea how much runway you have left when landing. If you decide to change the length of the runway (see below), the markers will space themselves correctly ¼, ½ and ¾ the distance down the runway.

When cruising your throttle should be set at about 75 percent. When climbing you should be at 100 percent throttle. When landing, 20 percent is about right. You must land with a descent of less than 150 feet/minute, otherwise you will crash. If your velocity falls below 60 knots you will stall and your rate of descent will become –2000 feet/minute. But you can recover by pushing the stick foward to increase your lift. You can crash in other ways. If you hit the ground before you are over the runway you have crashed. If you touchdown on the runway but there is too little runway remaining you will crash off the end of the runway. And of course you can always fly over the runway and not touch down at all. All of these conditions are indicated by messages on the screen.

The Program

Lines 10 through 410 initialize variables that are used as constants. Some that might be of interest if you wish to modify the program are Line 310, VM — stall velocity, Line 380, AM — minimum altitude, below which you are considered to be on the ground, and Line 400, RC — crash descent, above which you have landed too hard. Lines 450 and 460 establish the initial values for X and ALT. You may choose to change the algorithms for these initial conditions.

Line 500 starts the main loop of the program, which runs down to line 840. This loop is for a trapezoidal runway view. There are a couple of branches to lines 850 or 1040 if the runway view is partially off of the screen. The main loop calculates and plots the runway view. Subroutine 1200 is the main subroutine in the program. It sets P0 and P1 to the paddle values and uses these to calculate a new velocity, V, from the old V. Here we introduce exponential smoothing, which is a fancy term for something quite simple. Smoothing creates lag or inertia into some variables. For example, the velocity should not change instantaneously (nor should the rate of change of altitude or the pitch angle of the aircraft). These variables are permitted to change only gradually. Let us look at a simplified version of line 1240 for calculating V.

$$V = .95 \, V + .05 \, DV$$

where DV is the change of velocity (based on the stick and throttle positions) and is used here for illustrative purposes only. The new velocity is the old velocity plus the change in velocity, DV. But we only let the DV term influence 5 percent of the new velocity and let the old velocity influence

```
0   REM  VARS. FO, HO, RO, XO: SECOND CHARACTER IS A LETTER "OH"; PO: SECOND
    CHARACTER IS DIGIT "ZERO"
10   TEXT : HOME
20   GOSUB 1700
30   REM CONSTANTS
40   CZ = 2
50   C1 = 0
60   C2 = .03
70   C3 = .7
80   C4 = .09
90   C5 = .39
100  C8 = 30
110  C9 = .09
120  DC = 100
130   REM EXPONENTIAL SMOOTHING
140  D = .95
150  DD = 1 - D
160  E = .8
170  EE = 1 - E
180  F = .8
190  FF = 1 - F
200  H1 = .3
210  P5 = .055
220  P7 = .065
230   REM HI-RES CONSTANTS
240  CE = 139.5
250  VE = 191
260  HO = 279
270   REM RUNWAY LENGTH
280  RW = 4000
290  M2 = RW / 2:M1 = RW / 4:M3 = M1 + M2
300   REM STALL VEL.
310  VM = 60
320  VC = 1
330  ST = 20
340  Q1 = 255
350  Q3 = 3
360  Q6 = 600
370   REM STALL DESCENT
380  AM = 5
390   REM CRASH DESCENT
400  RC = 150
410  C = 7000
420   REM INITIAL CONDX.
430  V = 100
440  HR = H1 * (Q1 - PDL (0))
450  X = 20000 + 20000 * RND (1)
460  ALT = 1000 + 1000 * RND (1)
470  X1 = 0:X2 = X1:X3 = X1:X4 = X1:Y1 = X1:Y2 = Y1:Y3 = Y1:Y4 = Y1:X5 = X1:Y5
    = Y1
480   HGR
490   HOME
500   REM START MAIN LOOP
510   IF ALT < AM THEN 1400
520   YR = ALT / X * VE + HR
530   IF YR > VE OR YR < 0 THEN YR = VE
540   YF = ALT / (X - RW) * VE + HR
550   F1 = 0:F2 = F1:F3 = F1
560   R1 = ALT / (X - M1) * VE + HR: IF R1 > 0 AND R1 < VE AND X > M1 THEN
    F1 = 1
570   R2 = ALT / (X - M2) * VE + HR: IF R2 > 0 AND R2 < VE AND X > M2 THEN
    F2 = 1
580   R3 = ALT / (X - M3) * VE + HR: IF R3 > 0 AND R3 < VE AND X > M3 THEN
    F3 = 1
590   IF X - RW < ALT THEN YF = VE
600   FO = (C / (X + ALT / Q3))
610   RO = C / (X + ALT / Q3)
620   IF X - RW < ALT THEN FO = C / (ALT + ALT / Q3)
630   IF RO < 0 THEN RO = CE
640   FL = CE - FO
650   FR = CE + FO
660   RL = CE - RO
670   RR = CE + RO
680   IF RO > = CE GOTO 1570
690   IF FO > CE THEN 850
700   IF YF > VE THEN 1040
710   HCOLOR= 0
720   IF E1 THEN  HPLOT CE,N1
730   IF E2 THEN  HPLOT CE,N2
740   IF E3 THEN  HPLOT CE,N3
750   HPLOT X1,Y1 TO X2,Y2 TO X3,Y3 TO X4,Y4 TO X1,Y1: IF Y5 < VE THEN  HPLOT
    0,Y5 TO HO,Y5
760   HCOLOR= COL
770   IF F1 THEN  HPLOT CE,R1
780   IF F2 THEN  HPLOT CE,R2
790   IF F3 THEN  HPLOT CE,R3
800   HPLOT RL,YR TO RR,YR TO FR,YF TO FL,YF TO RL,YR
810   X1 = FL:Y1 = YF:X2 = RL:Y2 = YR:X3 = RR:Y3 = YR:X4 = FR:Y4 = YF:Y5 =
    VE
820   N1 = R1:N2 = R2:N3 = R3:E1 = F1:E2 = F2:E3 = F3
```

```
830   GOSUB 1200
840   GOTO 500
850   REM
860   YB = YF - (YF - YR) * (FO - CE) / (FO - RO)
870   IF YB < 0 THEN YB = 0
880   IF YB > VE THEN 1040
890   HCOLOR= 0
900   IF E1 THEN  HPLOT CE,N1
910   IF E2 THEN  HPLOT CE,N2
920   IF E3 THEN  HPLOT CE,N3
930   HPLOT X1,Y1 TO X2,Y2 TO X3,Y3 TO X4,Y4 TO X1,Y1: IF Y5 < VE THEN  HPLOT
      0,Y5 TO HO,Y5
940   HCOLOR= COL
950   IF F1 THEN  HPLOT CE,R1
960   IF F2 THEN  HPLOT CE,R2
970   IF F3 THEN  HPLOT CE,R3
980   HPLOT 0,YB TO RL,YR TO RR,YR TO HO,YB
990   IF YF < VE THEN  HPLOT 0,YF TO HO,YF
1000  X1 = 0:Y1 = YB:X2 = RL:Y2 = YR:X3 = RR:Y3 = YR:X4 = HO:Y4 = YB:Y5 =
      YF
1010  N1 = R1:N2 = R2:N3 = R3:E1 = F1:E2 = F2:E3 = F3
1020   GOSUB 1200
1030   GOTO 500
1040   REM
1050  XO = (VE - YR) * (FO - RO) / (YF - YR) + RO
1060   HCOLOR= 0
1070   IF E1 THEN  HPLOT CE,N1
1080   IF E2 THEN  HPLOT CE,N2
1090   IF E3 THEN  HPLOT CE,N3
1100   HPLOT X1,Y1 TO X2,Y2 TO X3,Y3 TO X4,Y4 TO X1,Y1: IF Y5 < VE THEN  HPLOT
      0,Y5 TO HO,Y5
1110   HCOLOR= COL
1120   IF F1 THEN  HPLOT CE,R1
1130   IF F2 THEN  HPLOT CE,R2
1140   IF F3 THEN  HPLOT CE,R3
1150   HPLOT CE - XO,VE TO RL,YR TO RR,YR TO CE + XO,VE
1160  X1 = CE - XO:Y1 = VE:X2 = RL:Y2 = YR:X3 = RR:Y3 = YR:X4 = CE + XO:Y4
      = VE
1170  N1 = R1:N2 = R2:N3 = R3:E1 = F1:E2 = F2:E3 = F3
1180   GOSUB 1200
1190   GOTO 500
1200   REM MAIN SUBROUTINE
1210  P1 =  PDL (1)
1220  PW =  INT (P1 * C5)
1230  PO =  PDL (0)
1240  V = D * V + DD * (PO * C3 + C8 + C4 * P1)
1250  CL = DC * DALT
1260  ALT = ALT + DALT
1270  VV = V * VC
1280   VTAB 22: HTAB 1
1290   PRINT  TAB( 2);"ALT"; TAB( 8);"CLIMB"; TAB( 16);"VEL"; TAB( 22);"DME";
      TAB( 28);"POWER"
1300   VTAB 23: HTAB 1
1310  AR$ = "-"
1320   IF ALT > P7 *  ABS (X - RW) THEN AR$ = "V"
1330   IF ALT < P5 *  ABS (X - RW) THEN AR$ = "^"
1340   PRINT  TAB( 1); INT (ALT); TAB( 8); INT (CL); TAB( 16); INT (VV); TAB(
      22); INT ( ABS ((X + ALT / Q3 - RW) / Q6)) / 10; TAB( 30);PW;" "; TAB(
      38);AR$
1350  X = X - V
1360  DALT = E * DALT + EE * (C2 * P1 - V * C1 - C9 * PO + CZ)
1370   IF V < VM THEN DALT =  - ST
1380  HR = F * HR + FF * H1 * (Q1 - PO)
1390   RETURN
1400   REM LANDED!
1410   IF X > RW GOTO 1510
1420  X = X - 10 * V
1430   IF X < 0 GOTO 1630
1440   IF CL <  - RC GOTO 1780
1450   PRINT "YOU LANDED AT "; INT (VV);" MPH AND STOPPED "
1460   PRINT  INT (X);" FEET FROM THE END OF THE RUNWAY."
1470   PRINT "YOU WERE DESCENDING AT ";  - INT (CL);" FEET/MINUTE."
1480   GET Z$
1490   TEXT : HOME
1500   GOTO 20
1510   REM
1520   TEXT : HOME
1530   GOSUB 1850
1540   PRINT "YOU CRASHED "; INT (X - RW);" FEET SHORT"
1550   PRINT "OF THE RUNWAY AT "; INT (VV);" MPH..TRY AGAIN"
1560   GOTO 20
1570   REM
1580   TEXT : HOME
1590   PRINT "YOU OVERFLEW THE RUNWAY AT "; INT (VV)
1600   PRINT "MPH AT AN ALTITUDE OF "; INT (ALT)
1610   PRINT "FEET.  TRY AGAIN!!!"
1620   GOTO 20
1630   REM
1640   TEXT : HOME
1650   GOSUB 1850
```

the new velocity 95 percent. This puts lag into the rate at which the velocity can change which tends to simulate the real world. You can change the smoothing constants in lines 140, 160, and 180.

The main subroutine calculates the instrument values and displays them in line 1340. The pitch angle of the aircraft is simulated by variable HR in line 1380 which offsets the view of the runway on the screen. This offset calculation is highly simplified and is a function of the stick only. In a real aircraft the pitch angle is a function of airspeed, throttle, and other variables. You may wish to try a more realistic expression for HR here.

Finally, there are a number of terminating messages. You have "landed" when your altitude is less than AM (line 510). Line 1400 begins the checks of what kind of landing you made (normal or crash). Line 1410 checks if you are short of the runway. Line 1420 assumes it takes ten times your velocity to stop and then line 1430 checks if you flew off the end of the runway. Finally line 1440 checks if you landed too hard. If you get past these checks, lines 1450 through 1470 print the safe landing message. Line 680 checks to see if you have flown off the end of the runway.

Program Modifications

The author has made many variations of this program such as adding instrument approach (where you cannot see the runway until you are very close to it), visual only approach (where the instruments do not work), a visual marker two miles from the runway, a marker which flashes an indicator when the plane is five or a half mile from the runway, and so on. One variation allows you to take off from one runway and land at another. You may want to experiment with such variables as

RW — runway length (4000 feet)
X   — starting distance from runway
ALT — starting altitude
V   — velocity (make a jet!)

Try changing various constants in expressions for V and DALT (rate of climb). (Do not delete any remarks in the program because some remarks are GOTO targets.)

Sublogic Company (201 W. Springfield Ave., Champaign, IL 61820) has on the market the FS-1 Flight Simulator which is fantastic. It simulates turns, banks, and much more. I highly recommend it if you want to "fly." But since FS-1 is written in assembly language with no listings supplied, you cannot learn much about how it works (although their rather extensive operating manual has block diagrams of the simulator's structure). I started writing my Flying Simulator before I had heard of FS-1, but have to admit I spend more time "flying" FS-1 than my own. Happy landings. □

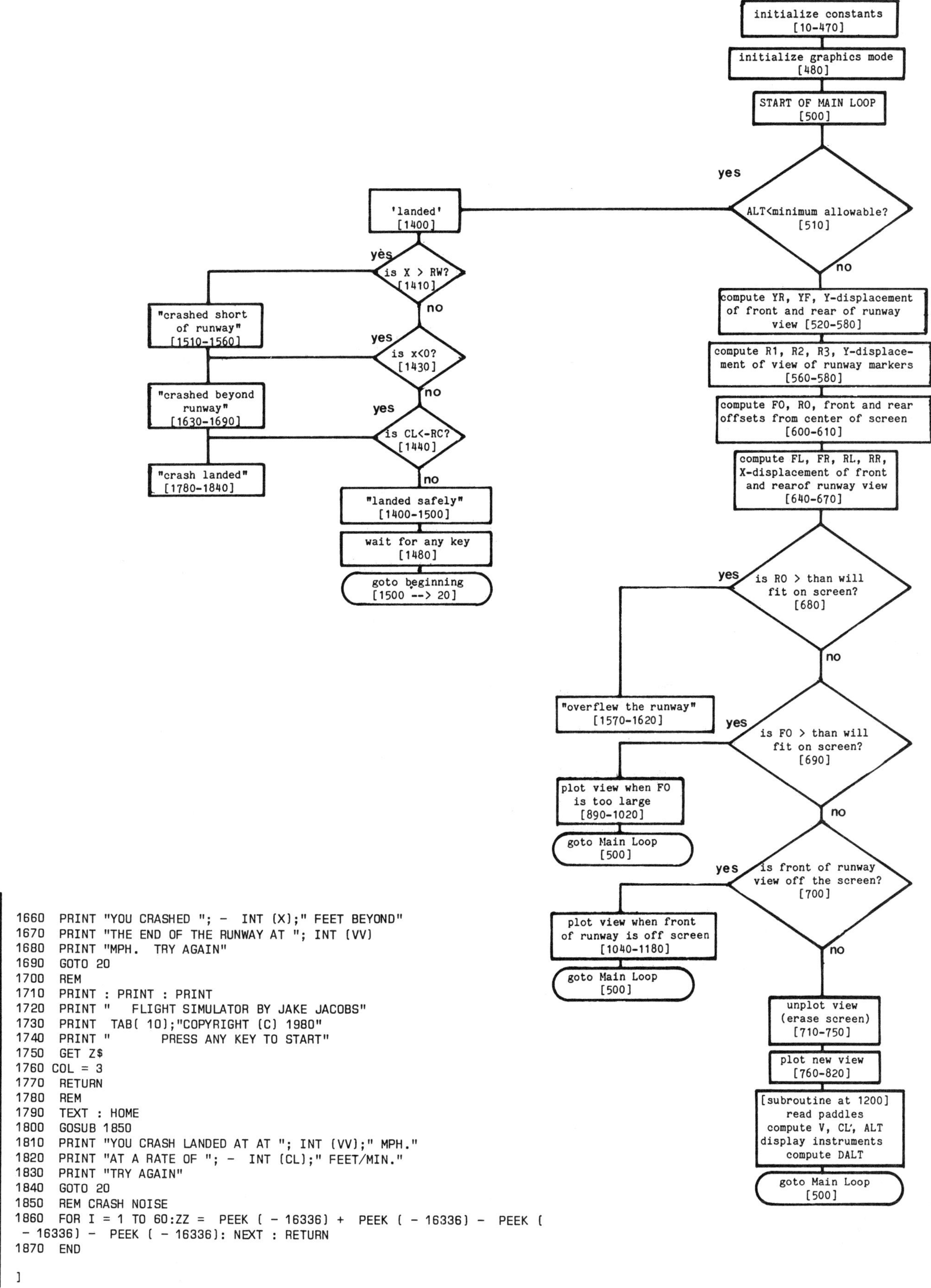


```
1660  PRINT "YOU CRASHED "; - INT (X);" FEET BEYOND"
1670  PRINT "THE END OF THE RUNWAY AT "; INT (VV)
1680  PRINT "MPH.  TRY AGAIN"
1690  GOTO 20
1700  REM
1710  PRINT : PRINT : PRINT
1720  PRINT "   FLIGHT SIMULATOR BY JAKE JACOBS"
1730  PRINT  TAB( 10);"COPYRIGHT (C) 1980"
1740  PRINT "        PRESS ANY KEY TO START"
1750  GET Z$
1760 COL = 3
1770  RETURN
1780  REM
1790  TEXT : HOME
1800  GOSUB 1850
1810  PRINT "YOU CRASH LANDED AT AT "; INT (VV);" MPH."
1820  PRINT "AT A RATE OF "; - INT (CL);" FEET/MIN."
1830  PRINT "TRY AGAIN"
1840  GOTO 20
1850  REM CRASH NOISE
1860  FOR I = 1 TO 60:ZZ = PEEK ( - 16336) + PEEK ( - 16336) - PEEK (
     - 16336) - PEEK ( - 16336): NEXT : RETURN
1870  END

]
```

Ten to the Thirty-Eighth

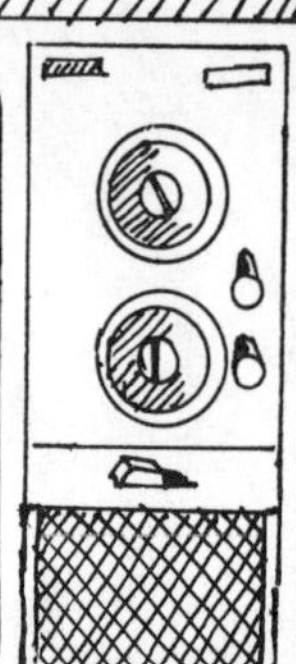

William Bradford

Readers of Martin Garner's book "New Mathematical Diversions from Scientific American," may recognize the game described here. It is a version of the game "Googol," discussed in Gardner's book. I will explain later why I changed the name of the game. I have also added some twists which you may find of interest.

A googol is the number ten multiplied by itself one hundred times.

Invention of the original game of Googol is attributed to John H. Fox, Jr. and L. Gerald Marnie. As described in Garnder's book, the game is played by having someone (the computer in this case) select a number of slips of paper. On the back of each slip, a positive number is written which you are not allowed to see. The values of the numbers range from small fractions up to numbers the size of a "googol" or larger. A googol is the number ten multiplied by itself one hundred times, or "ten-to-the-one-hundredth." The game thus derives its name from the not very ridgidly defined upper limit to the numbers written on the slips.

When all the numbers have been written down, the slips are randomized and placed face down. You then turn the slips face up, one at a time. The object is to stop when you turn up the number which you guess to be the largest. The last slip which you choose to turn up is your guess. You may not go back to a previously re-

William Bradford, 7868 Naylor Avenue, Los Angeles, CA 90045.

vealed slip. Should you turn over all the slips, the last one must be your guess.

The program described here follows the original game closely. However, the largest number which can be represented in Applesoft II is 10^{38} (ten to the thirty-eighth), hence the name of this version. Also, you get to choose the number of slips to use (from 3 to 14). These two facts tend to help you since you know that with a small number of slips to choose from, a number of 10^{37} or greater is almost certainly the largest. In the original game, the googol is not necessarily the upper limit, so that you are never certain of any large number.

I will not go into the detailed analysis of the odds of your finding the highest number. I'll only quote the results of the argument attributed to L. Moser and J. R. Pounder. You may derive it for yourself or refer to Gardner's book.

The strategy is to select p slips out of the n available. Note the largest value among the p slips and then continue selecting from the remaining slips until you find a larger number. The following formula gives the probability of finding the largest number in n slips;

$$\frac{p}{n}\left(\frac{1}{p} + \frac{1}{p+1} + \frac{1}{p+2} \cdots + \frac{1}{n-1}\right)$$

Given n, p is determined by picking a value for p which gives the largest value to the above expression. For example, if n = 10 then p = 3. For other values of n, you are urged to determine p for yourself. (You didn't buy that computer just to play Star Trek, did you?) Of course, as I mentioned above, the fact that you know the upper bound to the possible values does put the odds a little more in your favor.

While writing the program to play this game, it occurred to me that it might be interesting to skew the odds a little. Since the computer is turning over the slips, it is possible for it to lie to you about the value of any slip. The false value you get is chosen at random, so it may be higher or lower than the true value. If knowing that the machine may be lying to you is not enough, you can have it tell you when it is lying. Of course, it won't tell you until after you have made a bet or chosen another slip.

You now know the essential facts about the game. The program was written for an Apple II in Applesoft II, so it should be fairly portable to other machines using Microsoft's Basic. The program is set up to handle from one to four players. Players make their bets before selecting a slip to turn over. Only one slip is turned over at a time, so players should work out who does the selecting. When a slip is turned over, each player is offered the chance to stop. All players may continue to bet until all the players have chosen. Bets may not be decreased, but they may remain fixed at any value. When the last player has selected, all of the strips are revealed with their true values. The slip with the

The googol is not necessarily the upper limit

largest value is shown in flashing mode. Wins and losses are computed and displayed and the players' funds adjusted accordingly. At this time new players may be added, the number of slips changed, or the game option may be changed.

The program shown in the accompanying listing has some features which are designed with the Apple II video output in mind. The strips are shown in the INVERSE video mode, while the bets and available funds are shown in the NORMAL video mode.

When a player wins, the word WIN is shown in FLASHING mode above his bet. Similarly, the winning number is shown as a flashing number. If hard copy output is desired, several statements (205, 403, 406, 1207 and 1314) will require some modification. In fact, for a hard copy only device, statements 1200 through 1220 can be deleted.

Since the computer is turning over the slips, it is possible for it to lie to you about the value of any slip.

In the course of writing this article, it occurred to me that it would be interesting to see a version of the game where the computer is a player. Perhaps an interested reader could contribute a program to do so to Creative Computing. Another option would be to have the computer display a blank slip instead of lying. The slip would not be turned over until all bets were in. Other possibilities include more sophisticated schemes for having the computer lie, such as telling you that it has lied when it really hasn't. Of course, we humans can generally lie better than a computer (at least until a HAL 9000 type of computer shows up), so there are many such variations. Take advantage of the "Input/Output" column to share your ideas. In any case, the idea is to have a little fun with your brain and its extension, your computer.

For those of you who are wondering about the origin of the term "googol," is was invented by a nine year old child, a nephew of mathematician Dr. Edward Kasner. Dr. Kasner, a respected teacher, is noted as having given lectures on the mathematics of infinity, topology and other advanced mathematical subjects to kindergarten-age children. The reasoning of Dr. Kasner's nephew concerning the finite value of googol is interesting, and is described in the selection by Drs. Kasner and Newman referenced below. □

References

Gardner, Martin, New Mathematical Diversions from Scientific American, Simon and Schuster, New York, 1966, Chapter 3, Problem 3.

Kasner, Edward and James R. Newman "New Names for Old" in The World of Mathematics, Simon and Schuster, New York, 1956, Volume 3, page 2009.

SAMPLE RUN

```
RUN
10↑38
(TEN TO THE THIRTY-EIGHTH)
A BETTING GAME FOR THE APPLE II
PROGRAMMED BY L. W. BRADFORD
DO YOU WANT INSTRUCTIONS? (Y/N)N

GAME OPTIONS
  1STRAIGHT UP GAME (I DON'T LIE)
  2'RUSSIAN ROULETTE'(I LIE TO YOU)
  3LIKE NO. 2, BUT I TELL YOU WHEN
  I AM DEALING A BOGUS NUMBER
IF THIS ISN'T CLEAR,SEE THE INSTRUCTIONS
WHICH? 3

HOW MANY PLAYERS? (1 TO 4) 1

YOU'RE OUT OF CASH NO. 1
DO YOU WISH TO BORROW SOME? Y
OK, HOW MUCH? (LIMIT IS $1000) 1000
    HOW MANY SLIPS OF PAPER DO YOU WISH TO  PICK FROM? (MAX = 14)
?9

BETS   0
FUNDS 1000
TIME TO PLACE YOUR BETS!
HOW MUCH DO YOU WISH TO WAGER NO. 1 ?
?5
BETS   5
FUNDS 1000
WHICH STRIP DO YOU WISH TO SEE?5
695520.399
DO YOU WISH TO STOP NOW NO. 1?N
TIME TO PLACE YOUR BETS!
HOW MUCH DO YOU WISH TO WAGER NO. 1 ?
?5

BETS   5
FUNDS 1000
WHICH STRIP DO YOU WISH TO SEE?2

2.40168801
DO YOU WISH TO STOP NOW NO. 1?N
TIME TO PLACE YOUR BETS!
HOW MUCH DO YOU WISH TO WAGER NO. 1 ?
?10

BETS   10
FUNDS 1000
WHICH STRIP DO YOU WISH TO SEE?7
.055058695
DO YOU WISH TO STOP NOW NO. 1?N
TIME TO PLACE YOUR BETS!
HOW MUCH DO YOU WISH TO WAGER NO. 1 ?
?10

BETS   10
FUNDS 1000
WHICH STRIP DO YOU WISH TO SEE?8

3.51407399E+29
DO YOU WISH TO STOP NOW NO. 1?Y


ALL BETS ARE NOW IN
4328953.03
2.40168801
4952400.91
7.5659165
695520.399
133182.867
.055058695
3.51407399E+29

47.9456399
THE CORRECT NUMBER WAS 3.51407399E+29 !
WIN
10
FUNDS
1010
?

DO YOU WISH TO CHANGE GAME OPTION?N
DO YOU WANT TO CHANGE THE NUMBER OF PLAYERS?N
BETS   0
FUNDS 1010
    HOW MANY SLIPS OF PAPER DO YOU WISH TO  PICK FROM? (MAX = 14)
?3
```

BETS 0
FUNDS 1010
TIME TO PLACE YOUR BETS!
HOW MUCH DO YOU WISH TO WAGER NO. 1 ?
?1000

BETS 1000
FUNDS 1010
WHICH STRIP DO YOU WISH TO SEE?2

5.866947E+27
DO YOU WISH TO STOP NOW NO. 1?Y

ALL BETS ARE NOW IN
.427343843   1
5.866947E+27   2

1701507.38   3
THE CORRECT NUMBER WAS 5.866947E+27 !
WIN
1000
FUNDS
2010
?

```
1    TEXT : HOME :Y$ = "Y":N$ = "N"

2    DIM S(15),B(4),F(4),CH(4)
3 NG = 0: GOTO 3000
100   REM  PRINT BETS AND FUNDS AV
AILABLE AND HEADERS FOR THEM

101   POKE 34,16: POKE 35,19
105   VTAB 16: HTAB 1: PRINT "BETS
";
106   FOR R = 1 TO PM
107   PS = R * 8
108   VTAB 16: HTAB PS: PRINT B(R)

110   NEXT R
112   VTAB 18: HTAB 1: PRINT "FUND
S ";
114   FOR R = 1 TO PM
115   PS = R * 8
116   VTAB 18: HTAB PS: PRINT F(R)

118   NEXT R
120   RETURN
198   REM  PRINT OUT THE NUMBER FO
R STRIP ST IF VALUE IS NEGAT
IVE THEN STRIP HAS BEEN TURN
ED OVER ALREADY

200   IF S(ST) < 0 THEN 250
201   R = INT ((ST + 1) / 2)
202   CL = ST - 2 * (R - 1)
203   POKE 34,0: POKE 35,16
204   VTAB R * 2 - 1:PS = 22 * (CL
 - 1): IF PS = 0 THEN PS = 4
205   : HTAB PS: INVERSE : PRINT ABS
(S(ST))
206   NORMAL : POKE 34,20: POKE 35
,23
207   XP = XP + 1:ERR = 0
208   HOME : VTAB 20
209   S(ST) = - S(ST)
210   RETURN
211   REM  TEST FOR GAME OPTION, P
RINT MESSAGE FOR LIE (IF NEE
DED)
212   IF W = 1 THEN  RETURN
213   IF ST < > L THEN  RETURN
214   IF W = 2 THEN 230
216   PRINT "THE VALUE JUST SHOWN
IS NOT A TRUE ONE!"
218   GOSUB 990
230   S(L) = - TE
234   RETURN
250   PRINT "THAT NUMBER HAS ALREA
DY BEEN SHOWN"
252   GOSUB 990
253   ERR = 1
254   RETURN
298   REM  A CHOICE HAS BEEN MADE
BY PLAYER R. IF HE STOPS SET
 HIS CHOICE FLAG.
300   FOR R = 1 TO PM
302   IF CH(R) < > 0 THEN 320
303   HOME
304   PRINT "DO YOU WISH TO STOP N
OW NO. ";R;: INPUT A$
306   IF A$ < > Y$ AND A$ < > N$
THEN 304
308   IF A$ = N$ THEN 320
310   CH(R) = ST
314   WS = WS + 1
320   NEXT R
330   RETURN
398   REM  TEST FOR WINNERS. BALAN
CE THE PLAYERS' FUNDS
400   FOR R = 1 TO PM
401   PS = R * 8
402   Q = CH(R): IF S(Q) < > MX THEN
406
403   VTAB 15: HTAB PS: FLASH : PRINT
"WIN"
405   SG = 1: GOTO 410
406   VTAB 15: HTAB PS: INVERSE : PRINT
"LOSE"
407   SG = - 1: HTAB PS: PRINT B(R)
410   VTAB 16: HTAB PS: PRINT B(R)

412   F(R) = F(R) + SG * B(R)
414   VTAB 18: HTAB PS: NORMAL : PRINT
"      ": VTAB 18: HTAB PS: NORMAL
 : PRINT F(R)
416   B(R) = 0: NEXT R
420   RETURN
598   REM  BANKING ROUTINE  SET UP
 LOANS AND CLEAR ACCOUNTS
600   R = 1: IF F(R) > 0 THEN  RETURN

605   POKE 34,20: POKE 35,23: HOME
 : PRINT "YOU'RE OUT OF CASH
NO. ";R: INPUT "DO YOU WISH
TO BORROW SOME? ";A$
606   IF A$ < > Y$ AND A$ < > N$
THEN 605
608   IF A$ = Y$ THEN 620
610   F(R) = - 1: PRINT "OK! BE SE
EING YOU!"
612   RETURN
620   INPUT "OK, HOW MUCH? (LIMIT
IS $1000) ";F(R)
621   IF F(R) < 0 THEN 621
622   IF F(R) < 1000.01 AND F(R) >
0 THEN  RETURN
624   IF F(R) > 1000 THEN 630
626   INPUT "DO YOU WISH TO QUIT?
";A$
627   IF A$ < > Y$ AND A$ < > N$
THEN 626
628   IF A$ = Y$ THEN 610
630   PRINT "LET'S TRY AGAIN": GOTO
620

650   I = 1
654   IF F(I) < > - 1 THEN 664
656   FOR R = I TO PM - 1
658   B(R) = B(R + 1):CH(R) = CH(R +
1):F(R) = F(R + 1)
660   NEXT R
662   PM = PM - 1:PO = PM
664   I = I + 1: IF I > PM THEN  RETURN

670   GOTO 654
698   REM  TAKE BETS  A BET OF 0 (
ZERO) DEALS YOU OUT (HOWEVER
, YOU ARE ASKED TO CONFIRM Y
OUR DESIRE TO QUIT)
700   POKE 34,20: POKE 35,23
705   HOME : VTAB 21
710   PRINT "TIME TO PLACE YOUR BE
TS!"
720   PRINT "HOW MUCH DO YOU WISH
TO WAGER NO. ";I;" ?": INPUT
AZ
721   IF AZ < 0 THEN 720
722   IF AZ > F(I) OR AZ > 1000 THEN
730
723   IF AZ = 0 AND B(I) < > 0 THEN
RETURN
724   IF AZ < B(I) THEN 780
725   IF AZ = 0 AND B(I) = 0 THEN
750
726   B(I) = AZ: RETURN
730   PRINT "YOU CAN'T WAGER THAT
MUCH, TURKEY!": PRINT "TRY A
GAIN"
732   GOSUB 990
734   GOTO 720
750   INPUT "DO YOU WISH TO QUIT?"
;A$
751   IF A$ < > N$ AND A$ < > Y$
THEN 750
754   IF A$ = N$ THEN 770
756   F(I) = - 1
758   RETURN
770   PRINT "YOU MUST PLACE A BET
OR QUIT!"
772   GOTO 720
780   PRINT "YOU CAN'T DECREASE YO
UR BET!"
782   GOSUB 990
784   GOTO 720
990   FOR SS = 1 TO 300: NEXT SS
992   RETURN
996   REM  NOW BEGIN PLAY SET UP O
PTIONS ON LIES  BRANCH TO GE
T NUMBER OF PLAYERS
1000  PO = 0
1001  TEXT : HOME
1005  NG = 1
1010  VTAB 2: HTAB 14: PRINT "GAM
E OPTIONS"
1012  VTAB 6: PRINT " 1";: HTAB 5
: PRINT "STRAIGHT UP GAME (I
DON'T LIE)"
1014  VTAB 8: PRINT " 2";: HTAB 5
: PRINT "'RUSSIAN ROULETTE'(
I LIE TO YOU)"
1016  VTAB 10: PRINT " 3";: HTAB
5: PRINT "LIKE NO. 2, BUT I
TELL YOU WHEN": VTAB 11: HTAB
7: PRINT " I AM DEALING A BO
GUS NUMBER"
1020  VTAB 18: PRINT "IF THIS ISN
'T CLEAR,SEE THE INSTRUCTION
S"
1022  VTAB 21: INPUT "WHICH? ";W
1024  IF W > 3 OR W < 1 THEN 1022

1026  HOME : GOTO 1100
1030  POKE 34,0: POKE 35,16: HOME

1032  VTAB 2: PRINT "  HOW MANY S
LIPS OF PAPER DO YOU WISH TO
   PICK FROM? (MAX = 14)"
1033  VTAB 5: INPUT NP: IF NP < 2
OR NP > 14 THEN 1033
1040  Z = RND (1):MX = - 1:IM =
15
1042  FOR I = 1 TO NP:X = RND (2
)
1044  Y = INT (38 * RND (3) * RND
(4)):S(I) = X * (10 ^ Y)
1045  IF S(I) < MX THEN 1047
1046  IM = I:MX = S(I)
1047  NEXT I
```

```
1048   IF W = 1 THEN  RETURN
1050   L =  RND (4): IF L < .1 THEN
 1050
1052   L = 100 * L:ZZ =  INT ((L /
NP -  INT (L / NP)) * NP + .
 05):L = ZZ
1054   TE = S(L):X =  RND (2):Y =  INT
 (38 *  RND (5) *  RND (6))
1056   S(L) = X * (10 ^ Y)
1060   RETURN
1098   REM   GET THE NUMBER OF PLAY
ERS
1099   REM   THEN INITIALIZE FUNDS.
 THEN HOW MANY STRIPS, THEN
TAKE BETS (CONVOLUTED, BUT I
T WORKS)
1100   VTAB 10: INPUT "HOW MANY PL
AYERS? (1 TO 4) ";PM
1101   IF PM < 1 OR PM > 4 THEN 11
00
1102   IF PM = P0 THEN 1111
1103   IF P0 = 0 THEN 1109
1104   FOR I = PM TO P0: GOSUB 600
: NEXT I
1106   P0 = PM: GOTO 1111
1109   P0 = PM
1110   FOR I = 1 TO PM: GOSUB 600:
 NEXT I
1111   GOSUB 650: GOSUB 1030: GOSUB
 100
1112   FOR I = 1 TO PM: GOSUB 700:
 NEXT I
1115   GOSUB 650
1119   REM   INITIALIZE CHOICE MEMO
RY
1120   FOR I = 1 TO PM:CH(I) = 0: NEXT
 I
1130   WS = 0
1198   REM   THIS SECTION PRINTS OU
T THE DISPLAY FOR APPLE VIDE
O. STRIPS ARE WHITE BLOCKS (
INVERSE BLANKS)
1200   TEXT : HOME
1202   N = 0:PP = 0
1204   FOR J = 1 TO 14 STEP 2
1206   VTAB J: HTAB 1: FOR K = 1 TO
 2
1207   NORMAL : PRINT " ";: INVERSE
 : PRINT " ";
1208   N = N + 1: IF N = NP THEN 12
10
1209   NEXT K
1210   PQ = J + 1: FOR K = J TO PQ:
 VTAB J:PS = 38 * (K - J)
1212   IF PS = 0 THEN PS = 1
1214   NORMAL : HTAB PS: PRINT K: IF
 K = NP THEN 1220
1216   NEXT K
1218   NEXT J
1220   NORMAL
1222   POKE 34,17: POKE 35,19
1229   REM   DISPLAY BETS AND TOTAL
S
1230   GOSUB 100
1250   POKE 34,20: POKE 35,23
1252   HOME : VTAB 21
1254   PRINT "WHICH STRIP DO YOU W
ISH TO SEE";: INPUT ST
1255   IF ST > NP THEN 1252
1256   GOSUB 200: IF XP = NP THEN
1290
1257   IF ERR = 1 THEN 1252
1258   GOSUB 300
1260   IF WS = PM THEN 1300
1261   REM   WS=PM MEANS ALL PLAYER
S HAVE CHOSEN
1265   GOSUB 212
1269   REM   CHANGE BETS?
1270   FOR I = 1 TO PM
1272   GOSUB 700
1275   NEXT I
1277   GOSUB 650
1280   GOTO 1230
1288   REM   OKAY ALL STRIPS HAVE B
EEN SHOWN. IF NO CHOICE HAS
BEEN MADE, THEN THE CHOICE M
UST BE THE REMAINING STRIP
1290   FOR I = 1 TO PM: IF CH(I) <
 > 0 THEN 1296
1292   CH(I) = ST
1296   NEXT I
1298   REM   ALL BETS ARE IN, PRINT
 OUT THE REAL VALUES FOR ALL

THE STRIPS, FLASH THE LARGE
ST
1300   POKE 34,20: POKE 35,23: HOME
1301   VTAB 20
1302   PRINT "ALL BETS ARE NOW IN"
1303   GOSUB 230
1304   POKE 34,0: POKE 35,15
1306   FOR ST = 1 TO NP
1308   GOSUB 201
1309   S(ST) =  ABS (S(ST))
1310   IF S(ST) <  > MX THEN 1320
1312   VTAB R * 2 - 1:PS = 22 * (C
L - 1): IF PS = 0 THEN PS =
4
1314   HTAB PS: FLASH : PRINT S(ST
)
1320   NEXT ST
1330 : POKE 34,20: POKE 35,23
1331   HOME : VTAB 20
1332   PRINT "THE CORRECT NUMBER W
AS ";MX;" !"
1339   REM   SETTLE THE BETS
1340   GOSUB 400
1342   XP = 0
1345   PRINT H$;: INPUT A$
1350   TEXT : HOME
1354   VTAB 10: INPUT "DO YOU WISH
 TO CHANGE GAME OPTION?";A$
1356   IF A$ <  > N$ AND A$ <  > Y
$ THEN 1354
1358   IF A$ = Y$ THEN 1005
1360   VTAB 12: INPUT "DO YOU WANT
 TO CHANGE THE NUMBER OF PLA
YERS?";A$
1362   IF A$ <  > N$ AND A$ <  > Y
$ THEN 1360
1364   IF A$ = Y$ THEN 1100
1366   HOME
1368   GOSUB 100
1370   GOTO 1111
1372   REM
1374   REM   LOOP THROUGH THE PROGR
AM
1376   REM
1400   REM   PRINT HEADER FOR PROGR
AM, ASK IF INSTRUCTIONS ARE
NEEDED
1500   REM
3000   VTAB 8: HTAB 17: PRINT "10^
38": VTAB 10: HTAB 8: PRINT
"(TEN TO THE THIRTY-EIGHTH)"
: VTAB 12: HTAB 5: PRINT "A
BETTING GAME FOR THE APPLE I
I"
3002   VTAB 16: HTAB 6: PRINT "PRO
GRAMMED BY L. W. BRADFORD"
3004   VTAB 22: INPUT "DO YOU WANT
 INSTRUCTIONS? (Y/N)";A$
3005   IF A$ <  > Y$ AND A$ <  > N
$ THEN 3006
3006   IF A$ = N$ THEN 1000
4000   TEXT : HOME
4001   H$ = "HIT RETURN TO CONTINUE
"
4002   PRINT "10^38 IS BASED ON 'G
OOGOL', A GAME THAT IS DESCR
IBED BY MARTIN GARDNER IN HI
S  BOOK 'NEW MATHEMATICAL D
IVERSIONS FROM  SCIENTIFIC A
MERICAN'."
4003   PRINT : PRINT
4004   PRINT "THE GAME WAS ORIGINA
TED BY JOHN H. FOX  AND L. G
ERALD MARNIE, IN 1958."
4005   PRINT
4006   PRINT : PRINT "THE GAME DES
CRIBED HERE IS ESSENTIALLY
THE SAME, BUT WITH SOME 'TWI
STS' TO IT."
4008   PRINT : PRINT "A GOOGOL IS
10 MULTIPLIED BY ITSELF 100
TIMES.  THE ORIGINAL GAME HA
D THAT       VALUE AS AN UPPE
R LIMIT."
4009   PRINT "THE LIMIT FOR THIS G
AME IS 10^38, WHICH EXPLAINS
 THE NAME"
4010   VTAB 22: PRINT H$;: INPUT A
$
4020   HOME : PRINT "THE BASIC GAM
E IS PLAYED AS FOLLOWS;": PRINT

"THE PROGRAM PICKS SOME RAND
OM POSITIVE"
4022   PRINT "NUMBERS (FROM 0 TO A
BOUT 10^38).": PRINT "THE NU
MBERS ARE WRITTEN ON THE BAC
K OF": PRINT "SOME STRIPS OF
 PAPER."
4023   PRINT
4024   PRINT : PRINT "THE NUMBER O
F STRIPS OF PAPER TO BE USED
 IS UP TO YOU.": PRINT "BUT
YOU MUST CHOOSE AT LEAST 3 A
ND NOT MORE THAN 14."
4026   PRINT : PRINT "WHEN YOU SEL
ECT A STRIP, IT WILL BE
'TURNED OVER' TO DISPLAY THE
 NUMBER."
4028   VTAB 22: PRINT H$;: INPUT A
$
4040   HOME : PRINT "THE GAME IS P
LAYED BY TURNING THE STRIPS
OVER ONE AT A TIME";: PRINT
" UNTIL YOU COME"
4042   PRINT "TO THE STRIP WHICH Y
OU GUESS TO BE THE    LARGEST
 OF THE BUNCH."
4044   PRINT : PRINT "YOU MUST TAK
E THE LAST STRIP YOU TURNED
 OVER, YOU CAN'T GO BACK TO
ANOTHER."
4046   PRINT "FROM ONE TO FOUR PEO
PLE MAY PLAY AT ANY  ONE TIM
E.": PRINT : PRINT "PLAYERS
MAKE BETS ON THEIR OWN CHOICE
S."
4048   PRINT "IF A PLAYER MAKES A
CHOICE, THE OTHERS   MAY CONT
INUE SEARCHING.": PRINT "BET
TING CONTINUES UNTIL ALL PLA
YERS     HAVE CHOSEN"
4050   PRINT : PRINT "TO HOLD AT A
 PARTICULAR BET, ENTER A
ZERO FOR THE BET.": PRINT "Y
OU MUST, HOWEVER, MAKE SOME B
ET OF AT"
4052   PRINT "LEAST $1.00"
4058   VTAB 22: PRINT H$;: INPUT A
$
4060   HOME : VTAB 2: PRINT "TO TH
ROW A LITTLE CONFUSION INTO
MATTERS THE COMPUTER CAN LI
E TO YOU."
4062   PRINT : PRINT "TWO OPTIONS
ARE PROVIDED TO THE BASIC  G
AME.": PRINT "IN THE FIRST O
PTION, THE COMPUTER WON'T TE
LL YOU"
4064   PRINT : PRINT "THE SECOND O
PTION IS NOT FOR THE FAINT
OF HEART.": PRINT "THE COMPU
TER WILL TELL YOU IF IT HAS
    LIED ABOUT THE LAST NUMB
ER."
4066   PRINT : PRINT "SO, IF YOU'V
E JUST BET ON IT, YOU MAY
LOSE OR YOU MAY WIN BUT YOU
WON'T BE     SURE"
4068   PRINT "BUT THEN NEITHER WIL
L ANYBODY ELSE."
4070   VTAB 22: PRINT H$;: INPUT A
$
4072   HOME : VTAB 3: PRINT "THE R
EAL CHALLENGE OF THE GAME IS
   TO     FIND A WAY TO OPTIMIZ
E YOUR BETTING."
4074   PRINT : PRINT "MARTIN GARDN
ER DISCUSSES THE STRATEGY
FOR THE NORMAL GAME IN HIS B
OOK,"
4076   PRINT : PRINT "  'NEW MATH
EMATICAL DIVERSIONS FROM
"       SCIENTIFIC AMERICAN"

4078   PRINT : PRINT "THE ANALYSIS
 OF THE SITUATIONS WHERE THE
COMPUTER LIES TO YOU IS LEF
T TO THE     INTERESTED READE
R."
4080   VTAB 20: INPUT "HIT RETURN
TO START PLAY";A$
9000   TEXT : HOME
9100   GOTO 1000
9999   END
```

Teachers!
A Social Science
Survey Program!

Dr. James Owens

This program will add a whole new dimension to social science classes . . . from elementary school to college! All you need is an inexpensive 4K microcomputer.

Dr. James Owens, Professor of Management, The American University, Washington, D.C.

Many teachers, especially high-school and college teachers, can easily use a small computer (even one with as little as 4K of RAM memory) to conduct and process professional-type social science surveys. Obviously, such surveys and studies contribute to the teacher's research, and publication-record in the "publish or perish" academic world. More importantly (and interestingly), social science surveys of a teacher's own classroom students, when quickly tabulated and processed, provide rich material for enhancing and making *relevant* course topics. For example, the function of the Social Security program in the USA can be rescued from dull abstraction in classroom lectures by a survey question forcing the student to record his own opinion and discuss it within the context of the tabulated opinions and statistical conclusions of the class population as a whole. The same is true for a multitude of other routine high-school and college course topics such as the ERA amendment, function of taxation in the USA, corporation profits, political voting patterns and more. Such classroom applications are virtually infinite in number and potential course subject areas.

The "Survey" program described here was developed and used with an Ohio Scientific 6502 computer providing 8K BASIC in ROM and 20K of RAM memory. However, the essential values of the "social science survey" in classroom use can be achieved in as little as 4K of RAM memory and most BASIC-IN-ROM systems (e.g., other Microsoft BASIC systems such as the Level II TRS-80, Apple II, Sorcerer, PET).

The Questionnaire

The program permits a highly refined graduation of questionnaire responses ranging from *very strong* agreement to *very strong* disagreement with all items on the questionnaire (including provision for "no opinion" responses). Figure 1 presents the basic format of such a questionnaire. The program here dimensions fifty rows for fifty questions or fewer. Depending on memory available, the program can process about forty full DATA lines, including 1K of memory for the RUN, within the contraints of a typical 4K RAM memory system. A 4K system, therefore, can handle a survey of, for example, a forty-person sample with twenty-five questions in the questionnaire, a 100-person sample with ten questions in the questionnaire, or any proportionate combination of sample number and question number between the two extremes exampled. Conserving memory, as this program does, any user, restricted to 4K of RAM, will still find room in memory for very useful research or classroom-oriented social science survey projects. It should be noted that a large survey, for example a 100-person sample with 50 questions in the questionnaire, will require about 20K of RAM.

The Video Display—
or Output—of the Program

The program generates for each row of output-information (each row being equivalent to a particular question in the questionnaire) a full twenty-one "columns" of calculated values. Since, however, it would be a rare conventional page of paper or computer video screen that could list twenty-one horizontal columns, the programmer has the choice of arraying the columns closely (using a ';') or vertically (using no punctuation at all in the Line 490 PRINT statement) or, as used in this program, completing the PRINT statement with a comma. Only the latter programming tactic emerges as useful in terms of esthetics, styling and *readability* — and, thus, is used here. The "comma," ending Line 490, produces for each Question/Item number an easily readable and systematically consistent array of 'columns' in five vertical rows as illustrated in Figure 2. Use of the full twenty-one 'columns' permits calculation output of professional-type values such as standard deviation for the sample total as well as internal sample elements such as "males" vs "females" or "age 30 or over" vs "age 29 or under." Most importantly, calculations of the standard error of the difference between "means" (such as between the mean for Males and the mean for Females or the mean for those over age 30 vs those under age 29) become possible — as well as reports on the "significance of the difference between means" (as in Figure 2 columns #18 and #20). Note: Many users of this program may not need, or want, all of the calculations-results produced in the RUN output; in which case, unwanted lines can easily be deleted from the program. Also, the 21-column output display formatted as in Figure 2 requires a video display of 64 characters per line available with many small systems such as Radio Shack's TRS-80, OSI's C2 Challenger series of systems and others; if your system provides fewer than 64 characters/line display, a semi-colon — or no punctuation at all — at the end of line 490 will position the twenty-one columns in a more readable format than the comma used in the program here.

Just prior to the video display of the first question (as in Figure 2), the program generates a display summarizing the sample and its subsamples, as follows:

Total Sample	= 9
Total Males	= 4 Total Females = 5
Total Age 30+	= 5 Total Age 29- = 4

The Program Methodology and Documentation

An explicit goal of the program development was to economize memory use to a minimum. One main method was, of course, to eliminate all documentation (REM statements) from the program lines. That documentation will, therefore, be presented here in line-order by line number (or groups of lines).

Line 10 rounds off all decimals to two only for purposes of readability.

Figure 1. Typical questionnaire form.

Directions: Please enter in the column at the right a number from "1" to "9" for each question/item indicating your degree of agreement or disagreement on the 1-9 scale where:

1 = "I disagree very strongly."
2 = "I disagree strongly."
3 = "I disagree substantially."
4 = "I disagree slightly."
5 = "No Opinion or Preference"
6 = "I agree slightly."
7 = "I agree substantially."
8 = "I agree strongly."
9 = "I agree very strongly."

For Reference please check appropriate categories: Male ✓ Female

Age 30 or over ✓ Age 29 or under

#	QUESTION/ITEMS	Enter 1-9 in this Column
1.	The Social Security System, including premiums and payments, should be abolished.	1
2.	The "ERA" amendment should be ratified and become law.	2
3.	All taxes, including Federal and State income taxes, should be decreased.	9
4.	Etc.	

Figure 2. Illustration of typical video display of calculations (question #1 is illustrated). Note: In the actual video display generated by the program the column numbers and descriptions above are deleted (to conserve memory) and only the calculated values are printed. See Figure 3 for actual video display output.

Column # 1 Question #	Column # 2 Males' Score	Column # 3 Females' Score	Column # 4 Age 30+ Score	Column #5 29- Score
1	21	17	12	26

Column # 6 Mean for Total Sample	Column # 7 Mean for Males	Column # 8 Mean for Females	Column # 9 Mean for 30+	Column #10 Mean for 29-
4.22	5.25	3.4	2.4	6.5

Column # 11 Standard Deviation for Total Sample	Column # 12 Standard Deviation for Males	Column # 13 Standard Deviation for Females	Column # 14 Standard Deviation 30+	Column #15 Standard Deviation 29-
2.44	2.68	1.85	1.5	1.12

Column # 16 Number of "No Opinion"	Column # 17 Standard Error of the Difference between the Male vs Female Means	Column # 18 Significance of the M/F Difference (3 = 99% level of confidence)	Column # 19 Standard Error of Difference between 30+ vs 29- Means	Column #20 Significance of 30+/29- Difference
2	1.58	1.17	.87	4.7

Column # 21 % of "No Opinion				
.22				

Note: In the actual video display generated by the program the column numbers and descriptions above are deleted (to conserve RAM memory) and only the calculated values in the order above are printed. See figure 3 for actual numerical video display output for Question/items #2 and 3.

Without this function the video display becomes overcrowded with useless decimal expressions of six or more digits (such as 4.2247653). The "FNH" in 490 implements the function.

Line 20 dimensions an array of fifty rows, each row consisting of twenty-one columns. As mentioned above, each row (1,2,3 etc.) represents a single, particular survey question identified by the same question number and row number (thus, Row 1's displayed calculations display the calculated results for Question 1 of the survey, as in Figure 2). Remember, too, that within each row, as displayed on the video screen, the row's twenty-one columns are themselves formatted into five vertical elements ("rows" within the basic Row) and five horizontal columns (Figure 2).

Lines 30 to 80 enter the row (or question) number, from 1 to 50, into the first column of each row and set all twenty remaining columns for each row at zero.

Lines 90 to 230 place survey responses (numerical values) into Columns 2, 3, 4 and 5 for each question (row). The variable P reads either a 2 or a 3 (2 = Male, 3 = Female) from the first DATA entry in each DATA line (Line 901) and keeps a count of total males and females; the variable R does the same count for respondents aged 30 and over vs those aged 29 and under (30+ vs 29–) as read from the second datum from each line (every data line representing one individual respondent). The variable R reads either a 4 or a 5 (4 = age 30+, 5 = age 29–). Although obvious, it may be of interest to many readers that the P and R variables can be used, *with no structural change in the program*, to record and calculate a variety of "categories" such as smokers vs non-smokers, liberal vs conservatives, Protestants vs non-Protestants, Yankee baseball fans vs their opposite and so on. Also, if only a single discrimination of sample categories is needed, or none at all, then simply eliminate the program lines which involve the P variable and the R variable respectively. Line 95 registers dummy data to move the program toward its end. Lines 180 and 210 calculate and total the sums of squared values needed for the later standard deviation calculation and store these temporarily in Columns 17 and 20. After the standard deviation calculations are completed, and the sums of the squared values no longer relevant, Columns 17 through 20 are "erased" and used to record, and display, meaningful values as in the Figure 2 format. Although a bit intricate, or "tricky," the loops in 170 through 220 minimize memory use by quantum proportions as compared to a series of GOTO's. Line 190 records "no opinion" responses for their total as displayed in Column 16.

Lines 250 through 290 calculate the averages (arithmetic means) for, respectively, the total sample, males, females, age 30+ and age 29–, while line 300 records the sample total. (See Figure 2.)

Lines 310 through 350 calculate the standard deviations for, respectively, the total sample, males, females, age 30+ and age 29– (see any standard Statistics text for statement and explanation of the formula for the standard deviation). Results are displayed in Columns #11 through #15, respectively, as in Figure 2.

Lines 360 and 370 calculate the *standard error of the difference*

```
-----------------------------------------------------------------------
TOTAL SAMPLE =  9
TOTAL MALES =  4              TOTAL FEMALES =  5
TOTAL AGE 30+ = 5             TOTAL 29- = 4
=======================================================================
1                 21                17              12              26
4. 22             5. 25             3. 4            2. 4            6. 5
2. 44             2. 68             1. 85           1. 5            1. 12
2                 1. 58             1. 17            . 87           4. 7
0

***********************************************************************
2                 12                36              27              21
5. 33             3                 7. 2            5. 4            5. 25
2. 62             1. 58             1. 6            2. 42           2. 86
2                 1. 07             3. 94           1. 79            . 08
0

***********************************************************************
3                 30                35              37              28
7. 22             7. 5              7               7. 4            7
1. 47             1. 5              1. 41           1. 36           1. 58
2                  . 98              . 51           1                . 4
0

***********************************************************************
4                 0                 0               0               0
0                 0                 0               0               0
0                 0                 0               0               0
0                 0                 0               0               0
0

***********************************************************************
5                 0                 0               0               0
0                 0                 0               0               0
0                 0                 0               0               0
0                 0                 0               0               0
0

***********************************************************************
6                 0                 0               0               0
0                 0                 0               0               0
0                 0                 0               0               0
0                 0                 0               0               0
0

***********************************************************************
7                 0                 0               0               0
0                 0                 0               0               0
0                 0                 0               0               0
0                 0                 0               0               0
0
```

Figure 3. Actual program output (for 3 sample questions from DATA statements in Program A). Note: The underlining of 3.94 in Question 2 and .51 and .4 in Question 3 is to draw attention to an *enormous statistical significance* in the difference between "male" and "female" responses to Question 2. This, contrasted with virtually no significant differences in Question 3 ("males" and "females" of all ages indicate a preference for lower taxes).

between the Means for males vs females and age 30+ vs 29–, respectively, recording these values for printing in Columns 17 and 19 for each question/item (see Figure 2). (Formula is available in any standard Statistics text.)

Lines 380 and 390 calculate the *significance of the difference between means* (where 2 = a 95% statistical confidence level, 3 = a 99% statistical confidence level, etc.). For example, in the hypothetical and illustrative data here, there is virtually *no significance* in the difference between male and female responses on "abolishing the Social Security System" (Q 1) but a *very* significant difference in the responses of respondents *over and under age 30* (Column 20 for Q 1 shows a "4.7" value, meaning 4.7 standard errors of difference or a *greater than 99% probability* that the difference is *real* rather than due to any kind of sampling chance). In Q 2, regarding the ERA amendment, Column 18 shows a similar huge significance of difference between *male* and *female* responses (3.94) while, in Q 3, no significant differences appear in either Columns 18 (males vs females) or 20 (age 30+ vs 29−), meaning that there is not much difference among the categories about the desire for tax reduction.

Lines 420 through 550 are the printing routine. Again, please note the comma ending Line 490.

In each DATA line, one for each survey respondent, the first datum indicates sex, the second datum indicates age, the third datum indicates numerical response to the first question, the fourth datum indicates response to the second question and the fifth datum indicates response to the third question. *Important Note*: In actual use, the user will want more than the three "questions" illustrated here; thus, Line 150 must be changed to establish the *exact* number of questions such as 150 FOR Q = 1 TO 10 (for a survey of ten questions) or 150 FOR Q = 1 TO 50 (for a survey of fifty questions).

The last DATA line must end with a −1 dummy data to move the program to an end.

A special note about the .0001 in lines 380 and 390: the .0001 assures a RUN and avoidance of an occasional "division by zero" error message without affecting the substantial results produced in Columns 18 and 20 for each row (question) number.

Varieties of Application

With minor changes in the basic program, a user can obtain professional-type statistical results for a large variety of combinations of sample categories, number and type of questions in a questionnaire, statistical calculations and video display. ∎

```
3   REM -------------------------------------
4   REM     SOCIAL SCIENCE SURVEY PROGRAM
5   REM        BY DR. JAMES OWENS
7   REM
8   REM     CREATIVE COMPUTING MAGAZINE
9   REM -------------------------------------
10  DEF FNH(X)=INT(X*100+.5)/100
20  DIM S(50,21)
30  FOR R=1 TO 50
40  LET S(R,1)=R
50  FOR C=2 TO 21
60  LET S(R,C)=0
70  NEXT C
80  NEXT R
90  READ P
95  IF P=-1 THEN GOTO 240
100 IF P=2 THEN LET M=M+1
110 IF P=3 THEN LET F=F+1
120 READ R
130 IF R=4 THEN LET O=O+1
140 IF R=5 THEN LET U=U+1
150 FOR Q=1 TO 3
160 READ A
170 LET S(Q,P)=S(Q,P)+A
180 LET S(Q,P+15)=S(Q,P+15)+A^2
190 IF A=5 THEN LET S(Q,16)=S(Q,16)+1
200 LET S(Q,R)=S(Q,R)+A
210 LET S(Q,R+15)=S(Q,R+15)+A^2
220 NEXT Q
230 GOTO 90
240 FOR R=1 TO 50
250 LET S(R,6)=(S(R,2)+S(R,3))/(M+F)
260 LET S(R,7)=S(R,2)/M
270 LET S(R,8)=S(R,3)/F
280 LET S(R,9)=S(R,4)/O
290 LET S(R,10)=S(R,5)/U
300 LET T=M+F
310 LET S(R,11)=SQR(((S(R,17)+S(R,18))/T)-S(R,6)^2)
320 LET S(R,12)=SQR((S(R,17)/M)-S(R,7)^2)
330 LET S(R,13)=SQR((S(R,18)/F)-S(R,8)^2)
340 LET S(R,14)=SQR((S(R,19)/O)-S(R,9)^2)
350 LET S(R,15)=SQR((S(R,20)/U)-S(R,10)^2)
360 LET S(R,17)=SQR((S(R,12)^2/M)+(S(R,13)^2/F))
370 LET S(R,19)=SQR((S(R,14)^2/O)+(S(R,15)^2/U))
380 LET S(R,18)=ABS((S(R,7)-S(R,8)))/(S(R,17)+1E-04)
390 LET S(R,20)=ABS((S(R,9)-S(R,10)))/(S(R,19)+1E-04)
400 NEXT R
420 PRINT "-------------------------------------"
430 PRINT"TOTAL SAMPLE = ";T
440 PRINT"TOTAL MALES = ";M,"TOTAL FEMALES = ";F
450 PRINT"TOTAL AGE 30+ =";O,"TOTAL 29- =";U
460 PRINT"====================================="
470 FOR R=1 TO 50
480 FOR C=1 TO 21
490 PRINT FNH(S(R,C)),
500 NEXT C
510 PRINT
520 PRINT
530 PRINT
540 PRINT"*************************************"
550 NEXT R
560 END
901 DATA 2,4,1,2,8
902 DATA 2,4,5,4,9
903 DATA 3,4,2,9,5
904 DATA 3,4,3,7,7
905 DATA 3,4,1,5,8
906 DATA 2,5,8,1,5
907 DATA 2,5,7,5,8
908 DATA 3,5,6,9,6
909 DATA 3,5,5,6,9,-1
```

Program A. Social Science Survey Program. (With the exception of the title, REM statements do not appear in the program in order to conserve memory. Documentation for the program statements is provided in the article. The program lines, excepting DATA, use 1.4K of memory.)

The Intricate Graphs of the Polar Functions

Richard T. Simoni, Jr.

For those of us who could never get past trigonometry as taught in the schools, let alone make it into analytic geometry, the personal computer and its graphic display offer new hope for understanding — Here's a nice introduction.

Most graphics-generating devices which can be interfaced with personal computers depend upon the generation of several rectangular ordered pairs (x,y) for the plotting of points. Therefore, most of us tend to stick rigidly with the rectangular coordinate system, forgetting that other interesting coordinate systems can be used just as well and converted to rectangular coordinates for use with the graphics devices. One of the most interesting type of function to plot on graphics hardware are polar coordinate functions. Their fascination lies in analyzing the intriguing designs and patterns that these functions create.

What Are Polar Functions?

To get a basic understanding of polar functions, one must first look at the polar coordinate system itself. Instead of determining the position of a point in a plane by vertical and horizontal distances from an origin, points are located by the distance r from the point to the origin and the angle 0 between one axis and the ray from the origin to the point, as shown in Figure 1. While the rectangular system uses ordered pairs (x,y), the polar system uses ordered pairs (r,0). Positive angles are measured counterclockwise from the positive axis; negative angles are measured clockwise. Similarly, a negative distance r will locate the point in the quadrant opposite that of the specified angle 0, as in the example in Figure 2. This

Richard T. Simoni, Jr., 29 Farnham Park Drive, Houston, TX 77024.

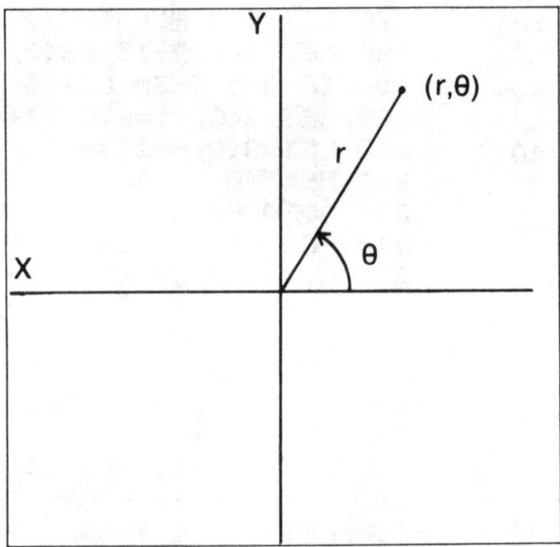

Figure 1

Points are located by a distance r from the origin and an angle 0 in the polar coordinate system. These points are written as ordered pairs (r,0).

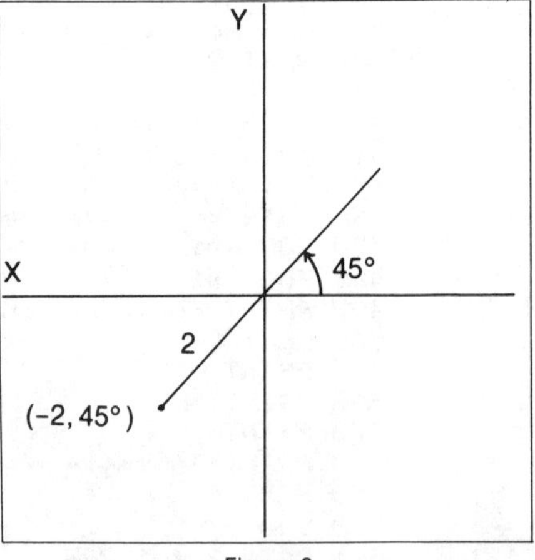

Figure 2

The point specified by the ordered pair (−2, 45°) is located in the third quadrant since 45° is in the first quadrant and r is negative.

quadrant shift is one of the main reasons many polar functions plot so beautifully.

The method used in graphing polar functions is similar to that used in rectangular graphing. Just as a function f(x) can be graphed by trying different values of x and solving for y, so can the function f(0) be graphed by

trying different values of 0 and solving for 4. Of course, in order to plot these polar functions on to many graphics devices, the polar coordinates must be converted to rectangular coordinates.

Luckily, the transition is easily made from radius and angular data to standard x and y values. As seen in Figure 3, a line is drawn from the origin of the graph to the desired point. Another line is then drawn from the point down perpendicular to the x-axis, forming the altitude of a triangle whose trigonometric properties can be used to solve for the x and y coordinates of the point.

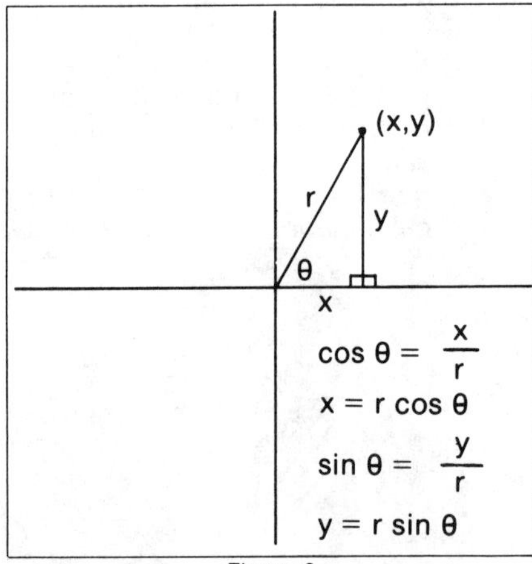

$$\cos \theta = \frac{x}{r}$$
$$x = r \cos \theta$$
$$\sin \theta = \frac{y}{r}$$
$$y = r \sin \theta$$

Figure 3

Equations for converting the radius r and angle 0 into their equivalent rectangular coordinates.

Polar functions, just like their rectangular counterparts, are generally written with one variable isolated, most often the distance r, thus expressing the function in terms of 0. Some advantages are to be gained by using polar functions in certain applications. For example, the general formula of a circle with its center at the origin, $x^2+y^2=r^2$, is reduced to a simple r=a in polar form.

A Computer Program to Graph Polar Functions

Almost without exception, the most interesting polar function graphs involve those functions which are periodic, that is, those whose values repeat after a certain interval. The most common periodic functions that can be introduced to the polar system are the trigonometric properties of sine and cosine. They are perfectly suited for application of both polar functions (which are expressed in terms of an angle 0) and small-computers Basic interpreters (most of which employ the intrinsic functions SIN and COS). Since both sin(x) and cos(x) have periods of 2π radians, solving for the corresponding value of r, and converting the angle and radius data into x and y coordinates for the graphics display device.

The program presented here is written for the Apple II computer, which has the capability to display graphics on a television monitor with a resolution of 280 x 180. The program is written in Applesoft II Basic, which is compatible with most other small-computer Basics. The function to be plotted is defined in the first line of the program, and must be expressed in terms of 0, which has been called Q in the program for lack of a better symbol.

After defining the function, the user is asked to input a step and a scale. The step is the interval in degrees that the program uses in incrementing 0 and 0 to 2π radians. In choosing the appropriate step, the user must decide whether the interest lies in the accuracy of the graph or in the speed with which it is drawn. A smaller step will plot the function more accurately, but with less speed than would be the case with a higher step value. Usually, a step value of 1° is the best tradeoff between speed and accuracy. A step value of 0.1° is usually sufficiently small to provide the best possible accuracy on the Apple's

```
1Ø DEF FNR(Q)=COS(4*Q)
2Ø W=Ø
3Ø HOME : INPUT "STEP? ";A
4Ø INPUT "SCALE? ";S
5Ø HOME
6Ø INPUT "DO YOU WANT TO SEE THE X-Y AXES? ";A$
7Ø IF A$="YES" OR A$="Y" THEN W=1
8Ø HGR2
9Ø IF W<>1 THEN 13Ø
1ØØ HCOLOR=2
11Ø HPLOT Ø,96 TO 279,96
12Ø HPLOT 14Ø,Ø TO 14Ø,191
13Ø HCOLOR=3
14Ø FOR I=Ø TO 36Ø STEP A
15Ø T=I/57.3
16Ø Y=FNR(T)*SIN(T)
17Ø X=FNR(T)*COS(T)
18Ø Y=INT(Y*S) : X=INT(X*S)
19Ø IF I=Ø THEN HPLOT 14Ø+X,96-Y
2ØØ HPLOT TO 14Ø+X,96-Y
21Ø NEXT I
22Ø END
```

Listing 1
The Applesoft II Basic program which graphs a given polar function on the screen. The function to be plotted is specified in line 10.

Photo 1a
The graph of the equation R=COS(4*Q).

Photo 1b
The graph of R=SIN(4*Q). Note the phase shift between this graph and the graph of Photo 1a.

display, while a step value of 3° will provide excellent speed for quick viewing of the graphs. The scale is a relative factor which is altered by the user to allow the pattern to fill most of the screen. Without this factor, some functions might appear too small on the screen, while others might be too large to plot. The proper scale will be between 10 and 100 for most functions. After supplying a step and scale, the user has to specify whether or not the x and y axes should be included in the screen display. While the axes are sometimes useful in understanding why a particular function produces a certain pattern, they are not always aesthetically pleasing.

The program begins its plot routine with the FOR statement in line 140. This loop increments the angle through 360 degrees by the step value input earlier by the user. Line 150 converts the angle to radians for use with the intrinsic trigonometric functions. Lines 160 and 170 calculate the distance r and combine it with the angle T to generate the equivalent rectangular coordinates. Line 180 sizes the coordinates in accordance with the scale as previously input by the user. Lines 190 and 200 plot the coordinates on the screen.

If the program immediately stops before plotting anything, it is likely that the program has attempted to plot a point which is not physically on the

screen. This can usually be remedied by running the program with a different scale value.

Several interesting comparisons can be made between some of the resulting patterns which represent the graphs of the given functions. Photos 1a and 1b dramatically show the inherent phase shift between the trigonometric functions sine and cosine. While the x and y axes virtually split the "leaves" of one graph, the "leaves" of the other graph fall directly between the axes. Photos 2a and 2b

Photo 2a
The graph of R=COS(2*SIN(Q)).

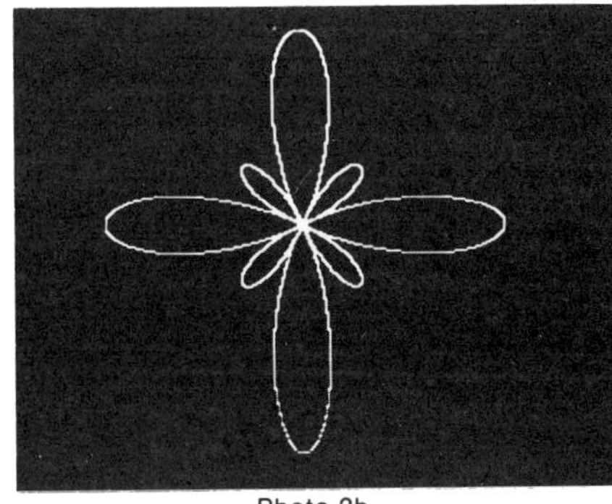

Photo 2b
The graph of R=COS(2*SIN(2*Q)). Note in comparison with Photo 2a that doubling the angle's coefficient also doubles the number of times the pattern is repeated.

illustrate that doubling the angle's coefficient in the function also doubles the number of times the pattern is repeated through the full 360 degrees of the circle. Photos 3a and 3b serve to illustrate the importance of the step value. Though both patterns were generated from the same function, a definite difference can be detected in

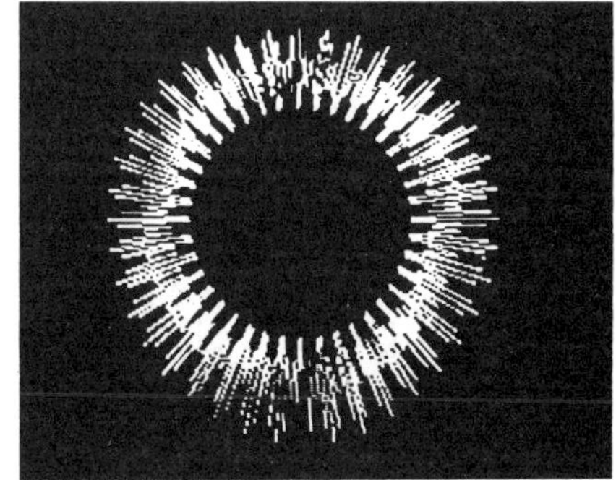

Photo 3a
The graph of R=COS(SIN(100*Q)), with a step value of 1 degree.

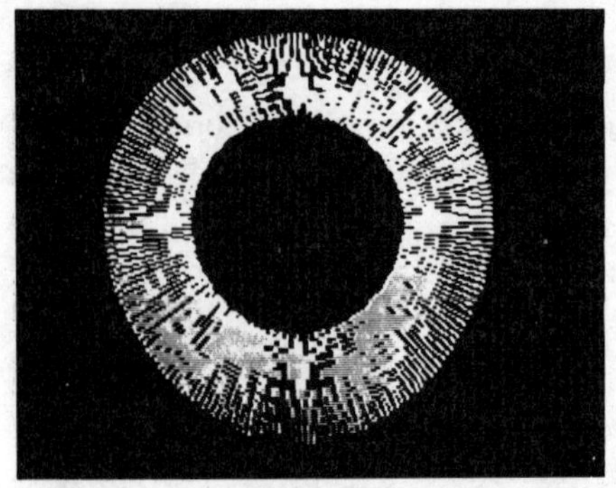

Photo 3b
A more accurate graph of R=COS(SIN(100*Q)), generated with a step value of 0.1 degree.

Photo 4
The graph of R=COS(SIN(8*Q)).

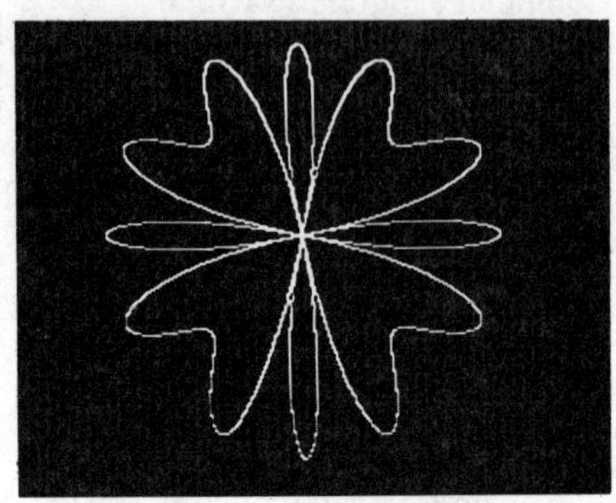

Photo 5
The graph of R=COS(4*SIN(2*Q))

the pattern of Photo 1a (step value = 1 degree) and the pattern of the more accurate Photo 1b step value = .1 degree). In this case, the speed gained by using a higher step value caused a severe reduction in the accuracy of the final graph. Photos 4 and 5 are further examples of aesthetically pleasing designs that can be produced by this program.

While the mathematics involved has its interesting aspects, the real attraction of this program is the exploration of the infinite number of patterns which can be produced through the use of different functions. Almost nothing can match the enjoyment of watching the line being plotted take an unusual and unexpected turn which ultimately produces an even more complex and mind-stimulating pattern than the one before it. It is yet another example of man's interest in mathematics and its products.   □

"You remembered!"

What to Name the Baby?

Paul Raymer

I had just finished several hours at my two computers, watching the Apple and the TRS-80 battle out a series of Tic-Tac-Toe games, with pretty much the usual results. The Apple was far superior in play because of its high resolution graphics and color, but the TRS-80 won its games by cheating, using the old keyboard bounce gimmick.

Then I realized that I had really not done any creative computing since my two best-selling programs, "Adventure in the Sin Palace" and "Universe Reversed."

You may recall my version of "Adventure," with its series of 101 erotic rooms, how you experienced the delights of each room, and its varied occupants, before dying of exhaustion with a smile on your face; and "Universe" where the entire solar system is reversed in its orbit, and one must determine the resulting action upon the tides and ocean currents, The Los Angeles Dodgers and the Snail Darters.

Then the brilliant idea came to me—"What to name the Baby?"

The idea evolved into a simple program to find all the possible names for a baby, using four letters, names which would work for boys or girls or whatever.

The idea evolved into a simple program to find all the possible names for a baby, using four letters, names which would work for boys or girls or whatever.

Then, after running, testing, debugging and listing the program, a sudden and frightening realization came upon me. First, I realized that the program was actually producing four-letter words that would not only not be suitable for a child's name but hardly suitable for a truck driver, Marine sergeant or computer programmer — names not normally used in mixed company, and, in fact, used only in current best-selling movies and books. And second, I realized that we were not expecting a child in the near future.

This program, dear reader, is

Paul Rayner, 3464 Townhouse Dr., Las Vegas, NV 89121

therefore dedicated to you for your use, amusement and modification and/or destruction. The program listing is for Applesoft Basic. It can easily be adapted for other Basics, TRS-80 Level II or merely discarded.

Explanation Of Listing

Lines 100-250 are preliminary introduction information. Mostly this "dresses up" the listing, but primarily it makes the writer of the program feel quite important. Most people who run programs never see this stuff at all anyhow. Line 250 is the most important line in the program. It contains every element used in the printout and is instrumental to the success of the program. The author fondly refers to this line as a "string"

and claims that when properly used this "string" could print out all of William Shakespeare's plays. Lines 260-310 do all the manipulation of the "string" and form the actual printout. The tough part follows... Lines 340-370 do the tricky stuff. Makes each column do its thing, then starts the next column. Line 370 just prints the total number of words. Not necessary, but informative if you quit in the middle of the program you may want to PRINT T and see how close you got to the possible total of 456,976 names (words). Lines 410-680 are gingerbread put into the program because the author found out that magazines pay by the word. Actually they are not required for running the program, but make it look more impressive than it really is.

```
]LIST

100   HOME
110   VTAB 12: HTAB 12: PRINT "FOU
      R LETTER WORDS": FOR M = 1 TO
      2000: NEXT M
120   HOME : GOTO 400
130   TEXT : HOME : CLEAR
140   REM
150   REM  **********************
160   REM  *                    *
170   REM  * FOUR LETTER WORDS  *
180   REM  *                    *
190   REM  *     PAUL RAYMER    *
200   REM  *      BOX 42831     *
210   REM  * LAS VEGAS NV 89104 *
220   REM  *                    *
230   REM  **********************
240   REM
250   A$ = "ABCDEFGHIJKLMNOPQRSTUVW
      XYZ"
260   W = 1:X = 1:Y = 1:Z = 1
270   T = T + 1
280   W$ =  MID$ (A$,W,1)
290   X$ =  MID$ (A$,X,1)
300   Y$ =  MID$ (A$,Y,1)
310   Z$ =  MID$ (A$,Z,1)
320   PRINT W$;X$;Y$;Z$; CHR$ (32)
      ;
330   W = W + 1
340   IF W > 26 THEN X = X + 1:W =
      1
350   IF X > 26 THEN Y = Y + 1:X =
      1
360   IF Y > 26 THEN Z = Z + 1:Y =
      1
370   IF Z > 26 THEN  PRINT : PRINT
      "TOTAL WORDS: ";T
380   GOTO 270
390   END
400   FOR P = 1 TO 10: PRINT  CHR$
      (7);: NEXT P
410   CALL  - 384
420   VTAB 10: HTAB 16: PRINT " WA
      RNING! "
430   CALL  - 380
440   VTAB 20: PRINT "THIS PROGRAM
      TAKES MORE THAN FIVE HOURS"
450   PRINT "TO COMPLETE!"
460   PRINT : PRINT "ARE YOU UP TO
      IT? (YES/NO)"
470   GET D$
480   IF  LEFT$ (D$,1) = "N" THEN
      670
490   CALL - 936: CALL - 384
500   PRINT "
                       "
510   PRINT " SOME OF THESE WORDS
      ARE JUST AWFUL       "
520   PRINT " AND SHOULD NOT BE SE
      EN BY KIDS OR        "
530   PRINT " NICE PEOPLE OR ANYON
      E SINCE THEY ARE     "
540   PRINT " REALLY X-RATED WORDS
      .                    "
550   PRINT "
                       "
560   PRINT " ONE OF THE WORDS IS
      ACTUALLY 'XXXX'!     "
570   PRINT "
                       "
580   PRINT " IF IT GETS TOO DIRTY
      FOR YOU WHILE        "
590   PRINT " THE PROGRAM IS RUNNI
      NG -- JUST PRESS     "
600   PRINT " RESET OR 'CONTROL/C'
      -- OR PULL THE       "
610   PRINT " PLUG OUT OF THE WALL
      SOCKET TO SHUT       "
620   PRINT " OFF THE COMPUTER!
                       "
630   PRINT "
                       "
640   CALL  - 380
650   VTAB 22: PRINT "STILL WISH T
      O CONTINUE? (YES/NO)": GET D
      $
660   IF  LEFT$ (D$,1) = "Y" THEN
      GOTO 130
670   HOME : PRINT "I DON'T BLAME
      YOU!"
680   FOR M = 1 TO 2000: NEXT M: HOME
      : END

]RUN
            FOUR LETTER WORDS
               WARNING!
THIS PROGRAM TAKES MORE THAN FIVE HOURS
TO COMPLETE!

ARE YOU UP TO IT? (YES/NO)

   SOME OF THESE WORDS ARE JUST AWFUL
   AND SHOULD NOT BE SEEN BY KIDS OR
   NICE PEOPLE OR ANYONE SINCE THEY ARE
   REALLY X-RATED WORDS.

ONE OF THE WORDS IS ACTUALLY 'XXXX'!

IF IT GETS TOO DIRTY FOR YOU WHILE
THE PROGRAM IS RUNNING -- JUST PRESS
RESET OR 'CONTROL/C' -- OR PULL THE
PLUG OUT OF THE WALL SOCKET TO SHUT
OFF THE COMPUTER!

STILL WISH TO CONTINUE? (YES/NO)
AAAA BAAA CAAA DAAA EAAA FAAA GAAA HAAA
IAAA JAAA KAAA LAAA MAAA NAAA OAAA PAAA
QAAA RAAA SAAA TAAA UAAA VAAA WAAA XAAA
```

WEATHER STATION

Paul Raymer

The most pressing problem the average computer owner faces is the weather. Some folks may feel that developing new algorithms, testing out logic problems, running simulation and adventure games or performing complex mathematical tasks have a greater priority, but when I asked the two people I know who have computers, they agreed with me, it *was* weather.

The following "Weather Station" program will bring your computer in touch with the real world, without expensive electronic coupling devices or complex meteorological equipment. No hardware modifications to your computer will be required.

You will need only a plain white piece of paper, approximately 8½" x 11" (21.59 x 27.94 cm) and a pencil and a pad for writing down certain scientific data. No prior knowledge of weather forecasting is required, but such knowledge may prove to be helpful.

Although this program is written for the Apple II in Applesoft Basic, it can easily be translated to any Microsoft Basic dialect with a few dozen simple, but tedious, changes.

The program and listing is restricted to personal use only and may not be used by local radio and/or television stations for forecasting the weather, without permission. □

Paul Raymer, P.O. Box 42831, Las Vegas, NV 89104.

```
JPR#0
JPRINT""
JLIST
100  REM
110  REM    ********************
120  REM    *                  *
130  REM    * WEATHER  STATION *
140  REM    *                  *
150  REM    *    PAUL RAYMER    *
160  REM    *     POB 42831     *
170  REM    * LAS VEGAS NEVADA  *
180  REM    *       89104       *
190  REM    *                  *
200  REM    ********************
210  REM
220  REM    I/XXIX/MCMLXXX
230  REM
240  REM    THIS PRINTS THE TITLE NEATLY
250  REM
260  TEXT : HOME : CLEAR
270  VTAB 10: HTAB 12: PRINT "WEATHER STATION"
280  FOR M = 1 TO 2000: NEXT M
290  CALL - 936
300  REM
310  REM    INSTRUCTIONS FOR USE
320  REM
330  PRINT "YOU NOW HAVE THE ABILITY TO INTERFACE"
340  PRINT "YOUR COMPUTER WITH THE OUTSIDE WORLD,": PRINT
350  PRINT "TAKE AN ORDINARY SHEET OF PAPER ABOUT"
```

```
360   PRINT "8-1/2 X 11 (ORDINARY TYPING PAPER WILL"
370   PRINT "DO) AND PLACE IT OUTDOORS FOR FIVE"
380   PRINT "MINUTES.": PRINT
390   PRINT "THE COMPUTER WILL NOW GO INTO A HOLDING"
400   PRINT "PATTERN FOR ABOUT FIVE MINUTES OR SO..."
410   FOR X = 1 TO 10000: NEXT X
420   CALL  - 936: FOR X = 1 TO 5: PRINT  CHR$ (7): NEXT X
430   PRINT "WHEN READY PRESS SPACE BAR TO GET THE "
440   PRINT "WEATHER REPORT ";: GET A$
450   CALL  - 936: FOR X = 1 TO 1000: NEXT X
460   REM
470   REM   HUMAN INTERACTION WITH REFERENCE MATERIAL
480   REM
490   PRINT "PLEASE ANSWER THE FOLLOWING QUESTIONS"
500   REM
510   REM   DELAY LOOPS GIVING TIME FOR HUMANS TO THINK
520   REM
530   GOSUB 1170
540   PRINT "WITH EXTREME ACCURACY TO INSURE MOST"
550   GOSUB 1170
560   PRINT "SCIENTIFIC RESULTS.": PRINT
570   GOSUB 1170
580   GOSUB 1210
590   INPUT "WAS THE PAPER STILL OUTSIDE? ";S$
600   GOSUB 1170
610   GOSUB 1210
620   INPUT "WAS THE PAPER WET?";R$
630   GOSUB 1170
640   GOSUB 1210
650   INPUT "DID THE PAPER MOVE?";W$
660   GOSUB 1170
670   GOSUB 1210
680   REM
690   REM   NOTE CLEVER USE OF 'IF' STATEMENT
700   REM
710   IF  LEFT$ (W$,1) = "Y" THEN  PRINT "IN WHICH DIRECTION? ";: INPUT D$
720   GOSUB 1170
730   GOSUB 1210
740   IF  LEN (D$) > 0 THEN  PRINT "HOW FAR? ";: INPUT F$
750   GOSUB 1170
760   GOSUB 1210: GOSUB 1210: CALL  - 936
770   REM
780   REM   USE OF FOLLOWING SLOW PRINTOUT OPTIONAL WITH SKILL IN UNDERSTAND
      ING METEOROLOGICAL INFORMATION
790   REM
800   SPEED= 100
810   PRINT "HERE IS TODAY'S WEATHER REPORT BASED ON"
820   PRINT "SCIENTIFIC DATA YOU HAVE ENTERED INTO"
830   PRINT "THE COMPUTER...": PRINT
840   REM
850   REM   DOING METEORLOGICAL STUDY OF DATA AND OTHER STUFF FED INTO COMPU
      TER
860   REM
870   REM
880   REM   EXTREME HIGH WIND INDICATOR
890   REM
900   IF  LEFT$ (S$,1) = "N" THEN  PRINT "TORNADO APPROACHING!"
910   REM
920   REM   MOISTURE FACTOR ANALYZER
930   REM
940   IF  LEFT$ (R$,1) = "Y" THEN  PRINT "RAIN PROBABILITY 90% -- SHOWERS L
      IKELY  TOMORROW"
950   REM
960   REM   WIND VELOCITY SCALE
970   REM
980   IF  VAL (F$) > 0 THEN X1$ = " MILD"
990   IF  VAL (F$) = 3 THEN X1$ = " MODERATE"
1000  IF  VAL (F$) > 3 THEN X1$ = " STRONG"
1010  REM
1020  REM   ELECTRONIC WIND SOCK
1030  REM
1040  IF  LEFT$ (W$,1) = "Y" THEN X2$ = " WIND"
1050  IF  LEFT$ (D$,1) = "E" THEN X3$ = " WEST"
1060  IF  LEFT$ (D$,1) = "W" THEN X3$ = " EAST"
1070  IF  LEFT$ (D$,1) = "N" THEN X3$ = " SOUTH"
1080  IF  LEFT$ (D$,1) = "S" THEN X3$ = " NORTH"
1090  IF  LEFT$ (W$,1) = "Y" THEN  PRINT "A";X1$;X2$;" IS BLOWING FROM THE
      ";X3$
1100  REM
1110  REM   NICE WEATHER DATA BANK
1120  REM
1130  IF  LEFT$ (R$,1) = "N" THEN  PRINT "WEATHER CLEAR AND DRY"
1140  IF  LEFT$ (W$,1) = "N" THEN  PRINT "AIR IS CALM AT PRESENT"
1150  SPEED= 255
1160  END
1170  FOR M = 1 TO 100: NEXT M: RETURN
1180  REM
1190  REM   CHEAP WAY TO MAKE TALKIES OUT OF YOUR SILENT WEATHER REPORTS
1200  REM
1210  FOR X = 1 TO 3: PRINT  CHR$ (7): NEXT X: RETURN
```

CHRISTMAS TREE

Stephen R. Berggren

One of the most enjoyable jobs of the Christmas season is decorating the Christmas tree. It is unfortunate that this pleasant and satisfying task can only be done once each year. Besides, how can you be any good at something you do only once a year? You should be able to decorate a Christmas tree whenever you want to. Can a personal computer solve a problem like this? Of course, it can! Using the *Christmas Tree* program you can decorate and display your own Christmas tree any time you want to.

The *Christmas Tree* program displays a Christmas tree and allows you to decorate it with up to 200 colored lights. Game paddles control the placement of the lights. The colors may be red, green, blue, violet or white. A delete function can be used to erase any mistakes. Once the tree is decorated to your satisfaction, it can be displayed with either flashing or non-flashing lights.

The program was written for the Apple II computer. The language used is Applesoft, the floating point version of Basic used in the Apple II. The program can operate under either the ROM or RAM versions of this language. However, under the RAM version, the number of lights used may be limited to about 150. Using any more lights may overwrite the graphics screen. Removing the REM statements will allow more lights to be used. The program makes use of the hi-resolution color graphics, game paddle inputs and shape table drawing routines of this system. Other systems with color graphics such as the Atari or the Compucolor should be able to run the program after changing the drawing and cursor routines. Of course, the data used to draw the tree must be modified to fit the different screen sizes.

The program itself is really very simple. Line 10 sets aside memory for the X and Y position and color of each light. The "%" sign means that they are integer

values. After providing directions in lines 200 to 370, it uses lines 600 to 710 to draw the outline of a Christmas tree in green on the hi-resolution graphics screen. The data table at lines 150 and 160 provides the shape. Note that it draws the shape twice with the second shape right next to the first. This just makes a wider line. Next, a very simple shape table is put into the memory using data at line 840. This shape is a tiny square made up of four dots. This shape table is used to draw the lights and is also the cursor that shows where the lights will be placed. Its size is just large enough to show clearly on the screen. Now the program uses lines 1010 to 1060 to put a cursor on the screen in a place determined by the two paddle controls. The

---

Once the tree is decorated to your satisfaction, it can be displayed with either flashing or non-flashing lights.

XDRAW commands at lines 1030 and 1050 reverse the colors of the background at that position. Since two reversals leave the screen looking just as it did, this procedure does not erase anything. The cursor may be moved anywhere without leaving a trail.

As the cursor is being drawn, the program uses line 1040 to see if a key has been pressed. If one has, lines 2040 to 2080 determine what key was pressed and branch to the needed routines. Line 2035 is simply a warning that all 200 lights have been put on the tree. Lines 2088 to 2130 put the light on the screen at the cursor position and put the position and color into memory. If a light is to be removed, the program jumps down to lines 6000 to 6030. This subroutine checks the position of the cursor square against the positions in memory. If it finds a match, it changes the color in memory to black and erases the light from the screen.

When the Christmas tree is finished, a "Control-N" key will send the program to lines 5000 to 5040. There the cursor square is removed and the program waits for a carriage return while the tree remains displayed. If a "Control-F" is typed instead, the program goes to lines 3000 to 4060. The cursor is first removed. Then a light is selected at random and turned on while another light is selected at random and turned off. This process is repeated very rapidly and gives the effect that the lights are flashing. The flashing continues until interrupted by a "Control-C" or "reset."

Several modifications to the program might be interesting. First, by saving the arrays that hold the light colors and positions a particularly pleasing tree might be kept indefinitely. Second, shape tables for stars, candy canes or bells could be included to allow for decorations besides lights. Finally, a means for drawing lines could be included to draw in background and unique decorations.

Decorating is part of the fun of the Christmas season. With this *Christmas Tree* program your computer can contribute to this fun by displaying a beautiful Christmas decoration designed by you. Merry Christmas! □

```
]RUN

      C H R I S T M A S   T R E E

         BY STEPHEN R BERGGREN

THIS PROGRAM ALLOWS YOU TO DECORATE
AND DISPLAY A CHRISTMAS TREE.  YOU MAY
PUT UP TO 200 LIGHTS ON THE TREE AND
MAKE THEM FLASH OR GLOW STEADILY.

TO PUT LIGHTS ON THE TREE, MOVE THE
FLASHING DOT TO THE RIGHT POSITION AND
PRESS A COLOR KEY.  WHEN FINISHED,
PRESS 'CTRL-F' FOR FLASHING LIGHTS OR
'CTRL-N' FOR NORMAL.  THESE ARE THE
AVAILABLE COLORS.  'DELETE' REMOVES
THE LIGHT UNDER THE CURSER.

     W = WHITE        G = GREEN

     R = RED          V = VIOLET

     B = BLUE         D = DELETE

   <PRESS RETURN TO BEGIN>
```

Stephen R. Berggren, 2347 Duncan Drive, Dayton, Ohio 45324.

```
LIST

10    DIM XN%(200),YN%(200),CN%(200
      )
20    REM   XN%() = X POSITION OF LI
      GHT
30    REM   YN%() = Y POSITION OF LI
      GHT
40    REM   CN%() = COLOR OF LIGHT
140    REM   DATA TO DRAW TREE
150    DATA 180,124,180,70,148,86,1
      50,80,118,96,120,90,88,106,9
      0,100,58,116,60,110,28,126,2
      0,128
160    DATA 28,130,60,146,58,140,90
      ,156,88,150,120,166,118,160,
      150,176,148,170,180,186,180,
      132,190,132
200    HOME
210    PRINT "      C H R I S T M A
      S   T R E E"
220    PRINT : PRINT "          BY ST
      EPHEN R BERGGREN"
230    PRINT : PRINT "THIS PROGRAM
      ALLOWS YOU TO DECORATE"
240    PRINT "AND DISPLAY A CHRISTM
      AS TREE.  YOU MAY"
250    PRINT "PUT UP TO 200 LIGHTS
      ON THE TREE AND"
260    PRINT "MAKE THEM FLASH OR GL
      OW STEADILY."
270    PRINT : PRINT "TO PUT LIGHTS
       ON THE TREE, MOVE THE"
280    PRINT "FLASHING DOT TO THE R
      IGHT POSITION AND"
290    PRINT "PRESS A COLOR KEY.  W
      HEN FINISHED, "
300    PRINT "PRESS 'CTRL-F' FOR FL
      ASHING LIGHTS OR"
310    PRINT "'CTRL-N' FOR NORMAL.
       THESE ARE THE"
315    PRINT "AVAILABLE COLORS.  'D
      ELETE' REMOVES"
318    PRINT "THE LIGHT UNDER THE C
      URSER."
320    PRINT : PRINT "     W = WHIT
      E     G = GREEN"
330    PRINT : PRINT "     R = RED
           U = VIOLET"
340    PRINT : PRINT "     B = BLUE
           D = DELETE"
370    PRINT : INPUT "   (PRESS RET
      URN TO BEGIN)";A$
590    HGR2
595    REM   DRAW TREE
600    HCOLOR= 1
610    HPLOT 124,190 TO 124,180
620    FOR I = 1 TO 24
630    READ Y,X
640    HPLOT   TO X,Y
650    NEXT I
660    HPLOT 123,189 TO 123,178
670    RESTORE
680    FOR I = 1 TO 24
690    READ Y,X
700    HPLOT   TO X - 1,Y - 1
710    NEXT I
720    HCOLOR= 0
790    REM   LOAD THE SHAPE TABLE FO
      R THE LIGHTS
800    FOR I = 768 TO 774
810    READ SHAPE
820    POKE I,SHAPE
830    NEXT I
840    DATA   1,0,4,0,37,55,0
850    POKE 232,0: POKE 233,3
860    ROT= 0
870    SCALE= 1
880 N = 0
1000    REM   DRAW CURSOR DOT, LOOK
       FOR KEY INPUT
1010    XP = 256 -   PDL (0) + 15
1020    YP =   PDL (1): IF YP > 189 THEN
       YP = 189
1030    XDRAW 1 AT XP,YP
1040    KEY =   PEEK ( - 16383): IF K
      EY > 127 THEN 2000
1050    XDRAW 1 AT XP,YP
1060    GOTO 1010
1990    REM   TEST THE KEY INPUT
2000    POKE  - 16368,0
2010    IF KEY = 142 THEN 5000
2020    IF KEY = 134 THEN 3000
2030    IF KEY = 196 THEN   GOSUB 60
      00: GOTO 1050
2035    IF N = 200 THEN   PRINT  CHR$
      (7) CHR$ (7) CHR$ (7): GOTO
      1050
2040    IF KEY = 215 THEN CN%(N) =
      3: GOTO 2090
2050    IF KEY = 194 THEN CN%(N) =
      6: GOTO 2090
2060    IF KEY = 214 THEN CN%(N) =
      2: GOTO 2090
2070    IF KEY = 210 THEN CN%(N) =
      5: GOTO 2090
2080    IF KEY = 199 THEN CN%(N) =
      1: GOTO 2090
2085    GOTO 1050
2088    REM   DRAW A NEW LIGHT
2090    HCOLOR= CN%(N)
2100    DRAW 1 AT XP,YP
2110    XN%(N) = XP:YN%(N) = YP
2120    N = N + 1
2130    GOTO 1010
2990    REM   REMOVE THE CURSOR DOT
3000    HCOLOR= 0
3010    DRAW 1 AT XP,YP
3990    REM   FLASH THE LIGHTS BY RA
      NDOMLY TURNING ONE ON AND ON
      E OFF
4000    P =   INT ( RND (1) * N)
4010    HCOLOR= CN%(P)
4020    DRAW 1 AT XN%(P),YN%(P)
4025    P =   RND (1)
4030    P =   INT ( RND (1) * N)
4040    HCOLOR= 0
4050    DRAW 1 AT XN%(P),YN%(P)
4060    GOTO 4000
4990    REM   REMOVE THE CURSOR DOT
      AND QUIT WITH ALL LIGHTS ON
5000    HCOLOR= 0
5010    DRAW 1 AT XP,YP
5020    INPUT A$
5030    TEXT
5040    END
5990    REM   ERASE THE DOT UNDER TH
      E CURSOR
6000    FOR I = 0 TO N
6010    IF XP = XN%(I) AND YP = YN%
      (I) THEN   HCOLOR= 3:CN%(I) =
      0: DRAW 1 AT XP,YP: PRINT  CHR$
      (7)
6020    NEXT I
6030    RETURN
```

Randy Jensen

Welcome to Stoneville Manor. This dream mansion can be yours, all yours, once you have obtained the deed. To get the deed, you need only open the safe. To open the safe you need only . . . . Well, we'll let you find that out for yourself. It will suffice to say that there are many surprises along the way.

Stoneville Manor is written in Applesoft, and requires 16K of *free* memory. Since this adventure might take some time to complete, a save-game feature is included which allows you to store the present status of the game on disk. To do this, give the command SAVE GAME. Whenever a new game is started, the combination of the safe changes. Good luck, and may all your deeds be legal.

Randy Jensen, 12501 Doons Dr., Oklahoma City, OK 73132.

```
10   HOME :L = 9
50   DIM I$(33),O$(33),O(33),L$(37
     ),D$(3,37),D(3,37)
100  VTAB (11): HTAB (12)
110  PRINT "STONEVILLE MANOR"
400  FOR X = 1 TO 33
410  READ I$(X),O$(X),O(X)
420  NEXT X
430  FOR X = 1 TO 37
440  READ L$(X)
450  NEXT X
460  FOR Y = 1 TO 37: FOR X = 1 TO
     3
470  READ D$(X,Y),D(X,Y)
480  NEXT X: NEXT Y
490  FOR X = 1 TO 3
500  READ P$(X)
510  NEXT X
520  FOR X = 1 TO 8
530  READ VE(X)
540  NEXT X
550  FOR X = 1 TO 3
560  Z =  INT (89 *  RND (1)) + 11
570  N$(X) =  STR$ (Z)
580  NEXT X
590  FOR X = 1 TO 3
600  Z =  INT (3 *  RND (1)) + 1
610  IF S(Z) = Z THEN 600
620  S$(Z) = N$(X):S(Z) = Z
625  NEXT X
630  HOME : VTAB (10)
640  PRINT  SPC( 15)"CREATED BY"
650  PRINT  SPC( 14)"RANDY JENSEN
     "
660  VTAB (22): HTAB (8)
670  INPUT "DO YOU WANT INSTRUCTI
     ONS?";C$
```

```
680   IF  LEFT$ (C$,1) = "Y" THEN
      GOSUB 7500
700   HOME : VTAB (12): HTAB (2)
710   INPUT "DO YOU WANT TO CONTIN
      UE AN OLD GAME?";C$
720   IF  LEFT$ (C$,1) = "Y" THEN
      GOSUB 8300
1000  HOME
1010  PRINT : INVERSE : PRINT "LO
      CATION:": NORMAL : PRINT L$(
      L)
1020  PRINT : INVERSE : PRINT "DI
      RECTION:": NORMAL
1030  FOR X = 1 TO 3
1040  GOSUB 5000
1050  NEXT X
1060  PRINT : INVERSE : PRINT "VI
      SABLE OBJECTS:": NORMAL
1070  IF L = 30 AND O(13) < > 0 THEN
      1190
1075  IF L = 31 AND O(13) < > 0 THEN
      1190
1085  FOR X = 1 TO 33
1090  IF O(X) = L THEN  PRINT O$(X)
1100  NEXT X
1110  GOSUB 5200
1190  PRINT : INPUT "NOW WHAT?";C
      $
1220  IF  LEFT$ (C$,3) = "GET" THEN
      2030
1225  IF C$ = "DROP SNORKEL" THEN
      3640
1230  IF  LEFT$ (C$,4) = "DROP" THEN
      2190
1240  IF  LEFT$ (C$,8) = "TAKE IN
      V" THEN 2350
1260  IF C$ = "ENTER VENT" THEN 2 395
1270  IF C$ = "ENTER BALLOON" THEN
      2540
1280  IF C$ = "ENTER LAKE" THEN 2
      600
1290  IF C$ = "ENTER DOOR" THEN 2
      650
1300  IF C$ = "ENTER STORE" THEN
      2680
1320  IF  LEFT$ (C$,5) = "ENTER" THEN
      2750
1340  IF  LEFT$ (C$,8) = "EXAMINE
      " THEN 2840
1350  IF  LEFT$ (C$,5) = "LOOK " THEN
      2850
1360  IF  LEFT$ (C$,6) = "GO JOG"
      THEN 3000
1370  IF  LEFT$ (C$,4) = "GO E" AND
      L = 32 THEN 3950
1380  IF  LEFT$ (C$,4) = "GO O" THEN
      3030
1390  IF  LEFT$ (C$,2) = "GO" THEN
      3080
1400  IF C$ = "PET SERVAL" THEN 3
      130
1410  IF C$ = "FEED SERVAL" THEN
      3150
1420  IF C$ = "GIVE TROUT" THEN 3
      150
1430  IF  LEFT$ (C$,8) = "CUT TRE
      E" THEN 3190
1435  IF  LEFT$ (C$,10) = "CLIMB
      TREE" THEN 3800
1440  IF  LEFT$ (C$,9) = "CHOP TR
      EE" THEN 3190
1450  IF  LEFT$ (C$,4) = "DIVE" THEN
      3210
1460  IF C$ = "END GAME" THEN  HOME
      : END
1470  IF  LEFT$ (C$,3) = "BUY" AND
      L = 10 THEN 2850
1475  IF C$ = "REMOVE COVER" THEN
      3250
1480  IF  LEFT$ (C$,9) = "OPEN VE
      NT" THEN 3250
1485  IF C$ = "OPEN BOOK" THEN 28
      50
1490  IF C$ = "OPEN DOOR" THEN 32
      95
1495  IF C$ = "OPEN CREDENZA" THEN
      2850
1500  IF C$ = "OPEN BAG" THEN 285

1510  IF C$ = "OPEN SAFE" THEN 70
      00
1520  IF C$ = "UNLOCK DOOR" THEN
      3295
1540  IF C$ = "INFLATE RAFT" THEN
      3350
1550  IF C$ = "INFLATE BALLOON" THEN
      3380
1560  IF C$ = "BUILD BALLOON" THEN
      3380
1570  IF C$ = "FLY BALLOON" THEN
      3460
1580  IF C$ = "SAIL BALLOON" THEN
      3460
1590  IF C$ = "READ WILL" AND F =
      1 THEN 7200
1600  IF C$ = "READ BOOK" THEN 28
      50
1605  IF C$ = "READ SIGN" THEN 39
      00
1610  IF C$ = "SAVE GAME" THEN 84
      00
1620  IF C$ = "CLEAR SCREEN" THEN
      1000
1990  PRINT "DON'T UNDERSTAND": GOTO
      1190
2030  IF C$ = "GET TROUT" AND L =
      29 AND O(10) < > 0 THEN  PRINT
      "IT SLIPPED OUT OF YOUR HAND
      S": GOTO 1190
2035  IF C$ = "GET PICTURE" AND L
      = 16 THEN  PRINT "TO VALUAB
      LE": GOTO 1190
2040  IF L = 10 THEN  PRINT "CAN
      ONLY BUY FROM STORE": GOTO 1
      190
2045  IF C$ = "GET TABLE" AND L =
      37 THEN  PRINT "IT'S NAILED
      DOWN": GOTO 1190
2050  IF S = 1 THEN 6000
2055  IF I = 4 THEN  PRINT "INVEN
      TORY TO HEAVY": GOTO 1190
2060  IF C$ = "GET MASK" THEN 615
      0
2065  IF C$ = "GET SNORKEL" THEN
      6100
2070  FOR X = 1 TO 19
2080  G =  LEN (I$(X))
2090  IF  MID$ (C$,5,G) = I$(X) AND
      O(X) = 0 THEN  PRINT "ALREAD
      Y HAVE OBJECT": GOTO 1190
2100  IF  MID$ (C$,5,G) = I$(X) AND
      O(X) = L THEN O(X) = 0:I = I
      + 1: GOTO 1000
2110  NEXT X
2120  IF C$ = "GET SERVAL" AND O(
      30) = L THEN 6200
2130  IF C$ = "GET CREDENZA" AND
      L = 14 THEN  PRINT "CAN'T LI
      FT IT": GOTO 1190
2140  IF C$ = "GET CASE" AND O(26
      ) = L THEN  PRINT "NOT THIRS
      TY": GOTO 1190
2150  IF C$ = "GET SAFE" AND O(25
      ) = L THEN  PRINT "SAFE IS S
      ECURED TO WALL": GOTO 1190
2170  GOTO 1990
2190  FOR X = 1 TO 19
2200  G =  LEN (I$(X))
2210  IF  MID$ (C$,6,G) = I$(X) AND
      O(X) = 0 THEN 2240
2220  NEXT X
2230  GOTO 1990
2240  IF X = 8 AND L = 28 THEN O(
      8) = 5:I = I - 1: FLASH : PRINT
      "RAFT DRIFTS AWAY": FOR X =
      1 TO 3000: NEXT X: NORMAL : GOTO
      1000
2245  IF X = 8 AND L = 29 THEN O(
      8) = 5:I = I - 1: FLASH : PRINT
      "RAFT DRIFTS AWAY": FOR X =
      1 TO 3000: NEXT X: NORMAL : GOTO
      1000
2270  I = I - 1
2280  IF L = 28 THEN O(X) = 30: GOTO
      1000
2290  IF L = 29 THEN O(X) = 31: GOTO
      1000
2300  O(X) = L: GOTO 1000

2350  FOR X = 1 TO 19
2360  IF O(X) = 0 THEN  PRINT O$(
      X)
2370  NEXT X
2380  GOTO 1190
2395  FOR X = 1 TO 8
2400  IF VE(X) = L THEN 2415
2405  NEXT X
2410  GOTO 1990
2415  IF O(8) = 0 AND R = 1 THEN
      PRINT P$(2): GOTO 1190
2420  FOR X = 1 TO 4
2425  IF O(X) = 0 THEN  PRINT P$(
      2): GOTO 1190
2430  NEXT X
2450  IF L = 13 AND C1 = 0 THEN PRINT
      P$(1): GOTO 1190
2460  IF L = 14 AND C2 = 0 THEN PRINT
      P$(1): GOTO 1190
2470  IF L = 17 AND C3 = 0 THEN PRINT
      P$(1): GOTO 1190
2480  IF L = 18 AND C4 = 0 THEN PRINT
      P$(1): GOTO 1190
2485  IF W = 0 THEN  PRINT "YOU W
      EIGH TO MUCH": GOTO 1190
2490  IF L = 13 AND C1 = 1 THEN L
      = 21: GOTO 1000
2500  IF L = 14 AND C2 = 1 THEN L
      = 24: GOTO 1000
2510  IF L = 17 AND C3 = 1 THEN L
      = 26: GOTO 1000
2520  IF L = 18 AND C4 = 1 THEN L
      = 27: GOTO 1000
2530  GOTO 1990
2540  IF H = 0 THEN  PRINT "NOT R
      EADY YET": GOTO 1190
2550  IF L = 8 THEN L = 34: GOTO
      1000
2560  IF L = 36 THEN L = 35: GOTO
      1000
2570  PRINT "CAN'T FIND": GOTO 11
      90
2600  IF L < > 5 THEN 1990
2610  IF O(8) < > 0 THEN  PRINT
      "NEED SOMETHING TO FLOAT ON"
      : GOTO 1190
2630  IF R = 0 THEN  PRINT "RAFT
      IS TO FLAT": GOTO 1190
2640  L = 28: GOTO 1000
2650  IF L = 16 AND K = 0 THEN  PRINT
      "DOOR IS LOCKED": GOTO 1190
2655  IF L = 20 THEN L = 16:K = 1
      : GOTO 1000
2660  IF L = 16 THEN L = 20: GOTO
      1000
2670  GOTO 1990
2680  IF L < > 9 THEN  GOTO 1990

2690  FOR X = 1 TO 19
2700  IF O(X) = 0 THEN  PRINT "CA
      N'T ENTER STORE WITH INVENTO
      RY": GOTO 1190
2710  NEXT X
2720  L = 10: GOTO 1000
2750  IF C$ = "ENTER MANOR" AND L
      = 9 THEN L = 12: GOTO 1000
2760  IF C$ = "ENTER MANOR" AND L
      = 1 THEN L = 17: GOTO 1000
2770  IF C$ = "ENTER HOSPITAL" AND
      L = 9 THEN L = 11: GOTO 1000
2780  IF C$ = "ENTER TUNNEL" AND
      L = 31 AND O(13) = 0 THEN L =
      32: GOTO 1000
2790  IF C$ = "ENTER CREEK" AND L
      = 4 THEN  FLASH : PRINT "YO
      U SLIPPED AND FELL": FOR X =
      1 TO 3000: NEXT X: NORMAL :S
      = 1:L = 11: GOTO 1000
2800  IF C$ = "ENTER GORGE" AND L
      = 8 THEN  PRINT "TO STEEP":
      GOTO 1190
2810  IF C$ = "ENTER SHACK" AND L
      = 36 THEN L = 37: GOTO 1000
2820  GOTO 1990
2840  G =  LEN (C$) - 8:O$ =  MID$
      (C$,9,G): GOTO 2860
2850  G =  LEN (C$) - 5:O$ =  MID$
      (C$,6,G)
```

```
2860  FOR X = 1 TO 33
2870  IF Q$ = I$(X) AND O(X) = L THEN
      2900
2875  IF Q$ = I$(X) AND O(X) = 0 THEN
      2900
2880  NEXT X
2890  GOTO 1990
2900  IF Q$ = "BOTTLE" THEN  PRINT
      P$(3);N$(1): GOTO 1190
2910  IF Q$ = "GOBLET" THEN  PRINT
      P$(3);N$(2): GOTO 1190
2920  IF Q$ = "TABLE" THEN  PRINT
      "ON TOP IS A NOTE WITH THE N
      UMBER ";N$(3): GOTO 1190
2930  IF Q$ = "CASE" THEN  PRINT
      "ONE BOTTLE IS MISSING": GOTO
      1190
2940  IF Q$ = "BOOK" THEN 6550
2950  IF Q$ = "CREDENZA" AND O(13
      ) = 40 THEN  PRINT "INSIDE I
      S A SWIM MASK": GOTO 1190
2960  IF Q$ = "BAG" AND O(19) = 4
      0 THEN  PRINT "INSIDE IS A S
      NORKEL": GOTO 1190
2970  IF Q$ = "PICTURE" THEN  PRINT
      "BEHIND PICTURE IS A SAFE":E
      = 1: GOTO 1190
2980  PRINT "NOTHING UNUSUAL": GOTO
      1190
3000  IF O(11) <  > 0 THEN  PRINT
      "NEED SHOES": GOTO 1190
3010  IF L > 9 THEN  PRINT "CAN'T
      JOG HERE": GOTO 1190
3015  W = 1: PRINT "WHEW!...DONE":
      GOTO 1190
3020  IF L = 28 THEN L = 5: GOTO
      1000
3025  GOTO 1990
3030  IF S = 1 THEN  PRINT "NOT W
      ELL": GOTO 1190
3040  IF L = 21 AND C1 = 0 THEN PRINT
      P$(1): GOTO 1190
3050  IF L = 24 AND C2 = 0 THEN PRINT
      P$(1): GOTO 1190
3060  IF L = 26 AND C3 = 0 THEN PRINT
      P$(1): GOTO 1190
3070  IF L = 27 AND C4 = 0 THEN PRINT
      P$(1): GOTO 1190
3080  IF  LEFT$ (C$,4) = "GO E" AND
      L = 18 THEN 6300
3090  FOR X = 1 TO 33
3100  IF  MID$ (C$,4,1) = D$(X,L)
      THEN L = D$(X,L): GOTO 1000
3110  NEXT X
3120  PRINT "DIRECTION NOT CLEAR"
      : GOTO 1190
3130  IF V = 0 AND L = 18 THEN 62
      00
3140  GOTO 1990
3150  IF V = 1 THEN 1990
3160  IF L <  > 18 THEN 1990
3170  IF O(14) <  > 0 OR L <  > 1
      8 THEN  PRINT "NEED FOOD": GOTO
      1190
3180  FLASH : PRINT "SERVAL TOOK
      TROUT AND ESCAPED": IF O(14)
      = 0 THEN I = I - 1
3185  V = 1:O(14) = 40:O(30) = 40:
      FOR X = 1 TO 3000: NEXT X:
      NORMAL : GOTO 1000
3190  IF L = 2 AND O(12) = 0 OR O
      (12) = L THEN O(4) = 2: GOTO
      1000
3200  GOTO 1990
3210  IF L = 28 AND O(8) = 0 AND
      O(19) = 0 THEN O(8) = 5:I =
      I - 1:L = 30: FLASH : PRINT
      "RAFT DRIFTS AWAY": FOR X =
      1 TO 3000: NEXT X: NORMAL : GOTO
      1000
3215  IF L = 29 AND O(8) = 0 AND
      O(19) = 0 THEN O(8) = 5:I =
      I - 1:L = 31: FLASH : PRINT
      "RAFT DRIFTS AWAY": FOR X =
      1 TO 3000: NEXT X: NORMAL : GOTO
      1000
3220  IF L = 28 AND O(19) = 0 THEN
      L = 30: GOTO 1000
3225  IF L = 29 AND O(19) = 0 THEN
      L = 31: GOTO 1000

3230  IF L = 28 OR L = 29 THEN PRINT
      "NEED SNORKEL": GOTO 1190
3240  GOTO 1990
3250  IF L = 13 THEN C1 = 1: GOTO
      1000
3255  IF L = 21 THEN C1 = 1: GOTO
      1000
3260  IF L = 14 THEN C2 = 1: GOTO
      1000
3265  IF L = 24 THEN C2 = 1: GOTO
      1000
3270  IF L = 17 THEN C3 = 1: GOTO
      1000
3275  IF L = 26 THEN C3 = 1: GOTO
      1000
3280  IF L = 18 THEN C4 = 1: GOTO
      1000
3285  IF L = 27 THEN C4 = 1: GOTO
      1000
3290  GOTO 1990
3295  IF L = 16 OR L = 20 THEN 33
      05
3300  GOTO 1990
3305  IF L = 16 AND K = 0 THENPRINT
      "CAN'T DOOR IS LOCKED FROM O
      THER SIDE": GOTO 1190
3310  PRINT "OK": GOTO 1190
3350  IF L <  > 5 THEN  PRINT "NO
      T HERE": GOTO 1190
3360  IF R = 1 THEN  PRINT "ALREA
      DY INFLATED": GOTO 1190
3370  PRINT "OK":R = 1: GOTO 1190

3380  IF L <  > 8 THEN  PRINT "NO
      T HERE": GOTO 1190
3390  FOR X = 1 TO 6
3395  IF O(X) = 0 OR O(X) = 8 THEN
      HB = HB + 1
3400  NEXT X
3405  IF HB = 6 THEN 3420
3410  PRINT "NOT READY":HB = 0: GOTO
      1190
3420  FOR X = 1 TO 6
3425  IF O(X) = 0 THEN I = I - 1
3430  O(X) = 40
3440  NEXT X
3450  H = 1: GOTO 1000
3460  IF H = 0 THEN  PRINT "NOT R
      EADY": GOTO 1190
3470  IF L = 8 OR L = 36 THEN  PRINT
      "NEED TO GET IN FIRST": GOTO
      1190
3480  IF L = 34 THEN 3500
3485  IF L = 35 THEN 3570
3490  GOTO 1990
3500  Z = 13:Y = 5: GOSUB 6400
3510  Z = 8:Y = 11: GOSUB 6400
3520  Z = 3:Y = 17: GOSUB 6400
3530  Z = 8:Y = 23: GOSUB 6400
3540  Z = 13:Y = 29: GOSUB 6400
3550  HOME
3560  L = 35: GOTO 1000
3570  Z = 13:Y = 29: GOSUB 6400
3580  Z = 8:Y = 23: GOSUB 6400
3590  Z = 3:Y = 17: GOSUB 6400
3600  Z = 8:Y = 11: GOSUB 6400
3610  Z = 13:Y = 5: GOSUB 6400
3620  HOME
3630  L = 34: GOTO 1000
3640  IF O(19) <  > 0 THEN  PRINT
      "DON'T HAVE": GOTO 1190
3650  IF L > 27 AND L < 32 THENPRINT
      "YOU QUICKLY GRAB IT BACK!":
      GOTO 1190
3660  O(19) = L:I = I - 1: GOTO 10
      00
3800  IF L <  > 2 THEN 1990
3810  FLASH : PRINT "YOU FELL OFF
      ": FOR X = 1 TO 3000: NEXT X
      : NORMAL :S = 1:L = 11: GOTO
      1000
3900  IF O(9) = 0 OR O(9) = L THEN
      PRINT "SIGN SAYS:AN APPROPR
      IATE PLACE": GOTO 1190
3910  PRINT "CAN'T FIND": GOTO 11
      90
3950  IF O(19) = 0 THEN 3080
3960  PRINT "NEED SNORKEL": GOTO
      1190
5000  REM  DIRECTION

5010  IF D$(X,L) = "-" THEN  RETURN
5020  IF D$(X,L) = "O" THEN  PRINT
      "OUT": RETURN
5030  IF D$(X,L) = "N" THEN  PRINT
      "NORTH": RETURN
5040  IF D$(X,L) = "E" THEN  PRINT
      "EAST": RETURN
5050  IF D$(X,L) = "S" THEN  PRINT
      "SOUTH": RETURN
5060  IF D$(X,L) = "W" THEN  PRINT
      "WEST": RETURN
5070  IF D$(X,L) = "U" THEN  PRINT
      "UP": RETURN
5080  IF D$(X,L) = "D" THEN  PRINT
      "DOWN": RETURN
5200  REM  OBJECTS
5210  IF O(13) = 0 AND L = 31 THEN
      PRINT "AN UNDERWATER TUNNEL
      ": RETURN
5220  IF L = 13 OR L = 14 OR L =
      17 OR L = 18 THEN  PRINT "VE
      NT"
5230  IF L = 13 AND C1 = 1 THEN  PRINT
      "VENT COVER": RETURN
5240  IF L = 14 AND C2 = 1 THEN  PRINT
      "VENT COVER": RETURN
5250  IF L = 17 AND C3 = 1 THEN  PRINT
      "VENT COVER": RETURN
5260  IF L = 18 AND C4 = 1 THEN  PRINT
      "VENT COVER": RETURN
5270  IF H = 1 AND L = 8 OR L = 3
      6 THEN  PRINT "HOT AIR BALLO
      ON": RETURN
5280  Z =  INT (10 * RND (1)) + 1

5290  IF L = 6 AND Z = 1 THEN  PRINT
      "THE BUTLER WITH TWO STICKS
      OF DYNAMITE": RETURN
5300  IF L = 3 AND Z = 3 THEN  PRINT
      "THE MAID WITH A PACK OF BLO
      ODHOUNDS": RETURN
5310  IF L = 7 AND Z = 5 THEN  PRINT
      "THE GARDNER WITH A BULLDOZE
      R": RETURN
5320  IF L = 33 AND Z < 5 THEN  PRINT
      "A BAT PASSES CLOSE BY": RETURN
5330  IF L = 27 AND Z < 3 THEN  PRINT
      "YOU HAVE COBWEB IN YOUR HAI
      R": RETURN
5340  IF L = 25 AND Z < 3 THEN  PRINT
      "A RODENT BRUSHES YOUR LEG":
      RETURN
5350  IF L = 4 AND Z = 7 THEN  PRINT
      "A TOAD JUMPS ACROSS THE CRE
      EK": RETURN
5360  IF L = 28 AND O(14) = 0 AND
      Z < 5 THEN  PRINT "A HUNGRY
      GULL CIRCLES OVERHEAD": RETURN

5370  IF L = 2 AND Z = 8 THEN  PRINT
      "A PRIMATE WATCHES FROM ABOV
      E": RETURN
5390  RETURN
6000  IF C$ = "GET WELL" THEN S =
      0: PRINT "RECOVERED": GOTO 1
      190
6020  GOTO 1990
6100  IF O(19) = 0 THEN  PRINT "A
      LREADY HAVE OBJECT": GOTO 11
      90
6115  IF O(19) = 40 AND O(7) = 0 THEN
      O(19) = 0:I = I + 1: GOTO 10
      00
6120  IF O(19) = 40 AND O(7) = L THEN
      O(19) = 0:I = I + 1: GOTO 10
      00
6130  IF O(19) = L THEN O(19) = 0
      :I = I + 1: GOTO 1000
6140  GOTO 1990
6150  IF O(13) = 0 THEN  PRINT "A
      LREADY HAVE": GOTO 1190
6160  IF O(13) = 40 AND L = 14 THEN
      O(13) = 0:I = I + 1: GOTO 10
      00
6170  IF O(13) = L THEN O(13) = 0
      :I = I + 1: GOTO 1000
6180  GOTO 1990
```

```
6200  REM  SERVAL ATTACK
6210  FLASH : PRINT "YOU HAD JUST
      ENOUGH STRENGTH TO GET AWAY
      ": FOR X = 1 TO 3000: NEXT X
      : NORMAL :S = 1:L = 11: GOTO
      1000
6300  IF V = 0 THEN  PRINT "SERVA
      L WON'T LET YOU": GOTO 1190
6310  L = 19: GOTO 1000
6400  REM  BALLOON
6410  HOME : VTAB (Z)
6420  PRINT  TAB( Y)"- - -"
6425  PRINT  TAB( Y - 1)"-     -"
6430  PRINT  TAB( Y - 2)"=========="
6440  PRINT  TAB( Y - 1)"-     -"
6445  PRINT  TAB( Y)"-   -"
6450  PRINT  TAB( Y + 1)".-."
6455  PRINT  TAB( Y + 1)". ."
6460  PRINT  TAB( Y + 1)"---"
6470  PRINT  TAB( Y + 1)"***"
6480  PRINT  TAB( Y + 1)"---"
6485  FOR X = 1 TO 1000: NEXT X
6490  RETURN
6500  FOR X = 1 TO 20:SO = PEEK
      ( - 16336): FOR Y = 1 TO 50:
      NEXT Y: NEXT X
6510  RETURN
6550  HOME
6560  PRINT : PRINT  TAB( 5)"HOW
      TO BUILD A HOT AIR BALLOON"
6570  PRINT : PRINT  TAB( 8)"#1 B
      ALLOON"
6575  PRINT  TAB( 8)"#2 HEAT SOUR
      CE"
6580  PRINT  TAB( 8)"#3 FUEL"
6585  PRINT  TAB( 8)"#4 GONDOLA O
      R CONTAINER"
6590  PRINT  TAB( 8)"#5 CABLE OR
      TWINE"
6595  PRINT  TAB( 8)"#6 MATCHES O
      R LIGHTER"
6600  PRINT "BUILD BALLOON AT AN
      APPROPRIATE PLACE"
6605  VTAB (22): HTAB (8)
6610  INPUT "PRESS RETURN TO CONT
      INUE ";C$
6620  GOTO 1000
7000  REM  SAFE
7010  IF E = 0 THEN  PRINT "CAN'T
      FIND": GOTO 1190
7030  IF L < > 16 THEN  PRINT "N
      OT HERE": GOTO 1190
7040  PRINT "COMBINATION LOCK"
7050  INPUT "ENTER FIRST NUMBER -
      -";F$(1)
7055  GOSUB 6500
7060  IF F$(1) < > S$(1) THEN  PRINT
      "NOT CORRECT": GOTO 1190
7070  INPUT "ENTER SECOND NUMBER
      --";F$(2)
7075  GOSUB 6500
7080  IF F$(1) + F$(2) < > S$(1)
      + S$(2) THEN  PRINT "NOT CO
      RRECT": GOTO 1190
7090  INPUT "ENTER LAST NUMBER --
      ";F$(3)
7095  GOSUB 6500
7100  IF F$(1) + F$(2) + F$(3) <
      > S$(1) + S$(2) + S$(3) THEN
      PRINT "NOT CORRECT": GOTO 1
      190
7105  F = 1
7110  PRINT "CLICK!.............
      ...INSIDE IS A WILL": GOTO 1
      190
7200  HOME
7210  VTAB (6)
7220  PRINT " *************************
      *******************"
7225  PRINT " *"; SPC( 36);"*"
7230  PRINT " *                    WI
      LL          *"
7235  PRINT " *
                           *"
7240  PRINT " * I,MR. STONE,LEAVE
      ALL MY WORLDLY  *"
7245  PRINT " * POSSESSIONS TO WH
      OMEVER OPENS THIS *"
7250  PRINT " * SAFE.
                         *"
7255  PRINT " *"; SPC( 36);"*"
7260  PRINT " *************************
      *******************"
7265  PRINT
7270  PRINT "            <<<CONGRATU
      LATIONS>>>": END
7500  HOME : PRINT
7510  PRINT "WELCOME TO STONEVILL
      E.YOU HAVE RECENTLY"
7520  PRINT "LEARNED THAT WEALTHY
      MR.STONE DIED AND"
7530  PRINT "RUMOR HAS IT THAT TH
      IS ECCENTRIC MISER"
7540  PRINT "HAS LEFT HIS ENTIRE
      ESTATE TO WHOMEVER"
7550  PRINT "FINDS AND OPENS HIS
      SAFE.": PRINT
7570  PRINT "TO PLAY,YOU MUST MAN
      IPULATE OBJECTS AND"
7580  PRINT "EXPLORE YOUR SURROUN
      DINGS BY USING TWO"
7590  PRINT "WORD COMMANDS.FOR EX
      AMPLE, 'GET BASKET'"
7600  PRINT "OR 'GO SOUTH'.TO SPE
      ED UP DIRECTIONAL"
7605  PRINT "MOVEMENT,'GO' COMMAN
      DS MAY BE SHORTENED"
7610  PRINT "TO INCLUDE ONE LETTE
      R SUCH AS 'GO S'.": PRINT
7615  PRINT "THE COMMAND 'SAVE GA
      ME' WILL PRESERVE"
7620  PRINT "YOUR PROGRESS FOR PL
      AY AT A LATER TIME"
7625  PRINT "OR IF YOU PREFER TO
      JUST END THE GAME"
7630  PRINT "THEN ENTER 'END GAME
      '.AND, IF NEEDED,"
7640  PRINT "'CLEAR SCREEN' WILL
      RESET YOUR LOCATION. "
7670  VTAB (22): HTAB (8)
7680  INPUT "PRESS RETURN TO CONT
      INUE";C$: RETURN
8000  DATA "BALLOON","FALLEN WEAT
      HER BALLOON",3,"STOVE","SMAL
      L WOOD BURNING STOVE",1,"BAS
      KET","LARGE WICKER BASKET",1
      2
8010  DATA "LOGS","LOGS",40,"TWIN
      E","ROLL OF TWINE",17,"MATCH
      ES","BOOK OF MATCHES",15
8020  DATA "BAG","BURLAP BAG",18,
      "RAFT","INFLATABLE RAFT",1,"
      SIGN","SIGN",8
8030  DATA "NET","FISH NET",7,"SH
      OES","JOGGING SHOES",10,"AXE
      ","AXE",10
8040  DATA "MASK","SWIM MASK",40,
      "TROUT","TROUT",29,"GOBLET",
      "CRYSTAL GOBLET",19
8050  DATA "BOTTLE","EMPTY BOTTLE
      OF CHABLIS",33,"BOOK","BOOK
      ",14,"PICTURE","PICTURE OF M
      R STONE",16
8060  DATA "SNORKEL","SNORKEL",40
      ,"MANOR","STONEVILLE MANOR",
      9,"MANOR","STONEVILLE MANOR"
      ,1
8070  DATA "SHACK","OLD ABANDONED
      SHACK",36,"TABLE","WOODEN T
      ABLE",37,"CREDENZA","WALNUT
      CREDENZA",14
8080  DATA "SAFE","SAFE",40,"CASE
      ","CASE OF CHABLIS",18,"TREE
      S","TREES",2
8090  DATA "DOOR","DOOR",20,"DOOR
      ","DOOR",16,"SERVAL","AN IMP
      ORTED SERVAL",18
8100  DATA "STORE","GENERAL STORE
      ",9,"STAIRWAY","STAIRWAY",19
      ,"HOSPITAL","HOSPITAL",9
8110  DATA "IN THE COURTYARD","IN
      A WOODED AREA","IN A MEADOW
      ","ALONG A SLIPPERY CREEK","
      ON THE BANK OF A LAKE","IN A
      BARREN FIELD","ON A ROCKY T
      RAIL"
8120  DATA "AT THE EDGE OF A  GORGE", "ON MAIN
      STREET",  "INSIDE THE GENERAL STORE",  "INSIDE
      THE HOSPITAL", "IN THE FOYER","IN THE PARLOR"
8130  DATA "IN THE STUDY","IN AN
      ORIEL","IN THE GALLERY","IN
      THE ATRIUM","IN THE WEST WIN
      G OF THE WINE CELLAR","IN TH
      E EAST WING OF THE WINE CELL
      AR"
8140  DATA "AT THE TOP OF A STAIRWAY","AT AN OUTLET
      IN THE DUCT", "AT A TURN IN THE  DUCT", "AT
      A FORK IN THE  DUCT","AT AN OUTLET IN  THE
      DUCT", "AT A TURN IN THE  DUCT"
8150  DATA "AT AN OUTLET IN THE D
      UCT","AT AN OUTLET IN THE DU
      CT","ON THE LAKE","IN THE SO
      UTHERN BAY","UNDER THE SURFA
      CE OF THE LAKE","UNDER THE S
      URFACE OF THE LAKE"
8160  DATA "ALONG AN UNDERGROUND
      RIVER","INSIDE A CAVERN","IN
      A HOT AIR BALLOON","IN A HO
      T AIR BALLOON","ON TOP OF A
      PLATEAU","INSIDE THE SHACK"
8170  DATA  "W",2,"S",4,"-",0,"E"
      ,1,"S",3,"N",9,"N",2,"E",4,"
      -",0,"W",3,"E",5,"N",1,"W",4
      ,"-",0,"-",0,"S",9,"E",7,"-"
      ,0,"W",6,"E",8,"-",0
8180  DATA  "W",7,"-",0,"-",0,"S"
      ,2,"N",6,"-",0,"O",9,"-",0,"
      -",0,"O",9,"-",0,"-",0,"O",9
      ,"S",13,"-",0,"N",12,"E",14,
      "S",17,"W",13,"E",15,"S",16
8190  DATA "W",14,"-",0,"-",0,"N"
      ,14,"W",17,"-",0,"O",1,"N",1
      3,"E",16,"E",19,"-",0,"-",0,
      "W",18,"U",20,"-",0,"D",19,"
      -",0,"-",0,"O",13,"S",22,"-"
      ,0,"N",21,"E",23,"-",0
8200  DATA  "W",22,"N",24,"S",25,
      "O",14,"S",23,"-",0,"N",23,"
      W",26,"-",0,"O",17,"D",27,"E
      ",25,"O",18,"U",26,"-",0,"O"
      ,5,"S",29,"-",0,"N",28,"-",0
      ,"-",0
8210  DATA  "U",28,"S",31,"-",0,"
      U",29,"N",30,"-",0,"E",31,"W
      ",33,"-",0,"E",32,"-",0,"-",
      0,"O",8,"-",0,"-",0,"O",36,"
      -",0,"-",0,"-",0,"-",0,"-",0
      ,"O",36,"-",0,"-",0
8220  DATA "VENT IS COVERED","SOM
      ETHING IS TO BIG","INSIDE IS
      A NOTE WITH THE NUMBER "
8230  DATA  13,14,17,18,21,24,26,
      27
8300  REM  RETRIEVE
8310  D$ =  CHR$ (4)
8320  PRINT D$;"OPEN GAME"
8330  PRINT D$;"READ GAME"
8340  INPUT L,W,S,I,F,H,R,K,E,V
8350  INPUT C1,C2,C3,C4
8360  INPUT N$(1),N$(2),N$(3),S$(
      1),S$(2),S$(3)
8370  FOR X = 1 TO 33
8380  INPUT O(X)
8390  NEXT X
8395  PRINT D$;"CLOSE GAME": RETURN
8400  REM  SAVE
8410  D$ =  CHR$ (4)
8420  PRINT D$;"OPEN GAME"
8430  PRINT D$;"WRITE GAME"
8435  PRINT L: PRINT W: PRINT S: PRINT
      I: PRINT F
8440  PRINT H: PRINT R: PRINT K: PRINT
      E: PRINT V
8445  PRINT C1: PRINT C2: PRINT C
      3: PRINT C4
8450  PRINT N$(1): PRINT N$(2): PRINT
      N$(3)
8460  PRINT S$(1): PRINT S$(2): PRINT
      S$(3)
8470  FOR X = 1 TO 33
8480  PRINT O(X)
8490  NEXT X
8495  PRINT D$;"CLOSE GAME"
8500  HOME : END
```

Chapter IX
Tips for
Easier Programming

Chapter IX — Tips for Easier Programming

By this time, you're probably eager to apply what you've learned to your own programs. Here are some articles to sharpen your own programming skills.

Special Notes for Chapter IX

● *On Effective Documentation,* by Michael Robinson:

What is needed in order to change a program that you wrote some time ago? How can you best explain your program to your computer instructor or just your best friend (they may be the same person)? The answer to both questions is one word — documentation. The first lines of your program should be REM statements that explain: a) what the program does, b) what each section does, and c) who did it and when the last revision was.

● *Bombproof Data Entry,* by Greg Kielian:

Programmers and gamesters please note — a good program should allow for entry of information without one seeing "SYNTAX ERROR or EXTRA IGNORED." Also, do your programs allow either a 'Y', 'YES', or 'YEAH' in answer to a question? This article — and the next two — show how to eliminate many kinds of problems and allow for more varied responses. Also, read the *Strings and Things* article (in this chater) for more good tips.

For Applesoft users: the PRINT@ command (for TRS-80) can be done with HTAB and VTAB commands. In the example below, note that what is printed by line 90 blanks out what is printed by line 65 due to the HTABs and VTABs.

```
 50 REM ** Input Routine No. 4 **
 60 HTAB 10 : VTAB 20
 65 PRINT "ARE YOU READY TO CONTINUE";
 70 INPUT R$
 80 IF LEFT$(R$,1)="Y" THEN 110
 85 HTAB 10 : VTAB 20
 90 PRINT "INVALID RESPONSE, PLEASE RETYPE."
100 FOR I=1 TO 500: NEXT
105 GOTO 60
110 REM ** The rest of the program **
```

● *The Challenge of Error Trapping,* by Mike Summers and John Willett:

Robin Ault, in Letters to the Editor, *Creative Computing,* June 1980, made some additional suggestions that specifically apply to the Apple.

1) Before using 'Input Routine No. 5,' check for an empty input (i.e., if only return was input), otherwise an Apple error occurs here.
2) ONERR GOTO can be used to check on a range of wrong values typed in.
3) Restricting the INPUT text window to one line will automatically clear the system-generated error messages.
4) Use GET A$, which allows only single character input, and check against an array of allowed characters.
5) Because RESET always gets you out of the program, include a safe, neutral entry point in your program so you can type 'GOTO 500,' for example, after a RESET without input data loss.

● *Displaying Numbers in Tabular Format,* by Melvyn Magree:

Would you like to line up your numerical output so:

```
1.23                 1.23
456.1   looks like   456.1
0.75                 0.75
```

Try adding this simple subroutine to your program for an improved output.

● *Divide N-Conquer,* by John Barry:

Calculators and computers initially share one common fault: numeric answers are only given to a fixed number of places, and then the answer is truncated. For example, 67344 divided by 9074 equals 7.4627659574468085106, approximately, with no repeat in sight! (My calculator printed 7.46259, with no rounding.) This article shows you to keep as many places as you would like. To those who ask, "Why?" I respond, "Why not?"

For a different method and format, see the next article, *Unlimited Precision Division for Real Number BASIC,* by Pat Fitzgerald.

• *Strings and Things: BASIC String Manipulations,* by Tom Badgett:

Here is help for those who LEN, MID$, RIGHT$, and LEFT$ leave out in left field. No more "type 1 for yes and 2 for no". Also, read the "Bombproof Data Entry" articles in this chapter.

• *Apple Strings,* by Rick Geiger:

This is a more technical article than *Strings and Things,* and uses a machine language subroutine to do an equivalent INSTR function. For example, 'LET X=INSTR(A$,B$)' stands for: IN STRing A$ search for the substring, B$. The value of X will be zero, if not found, and N, if found — starting in the Nth position.

Additional information relating to this article can be found in the I/O column of the August 1980, *Creative Computing.* James Webb, from Pulaski, Virginia, states: "When a statement such as X$=X$ is executed, the two position name is changed from X$ to a coded representation of that name and stored in $81 and $82." Listed below is the coded representation of each, which is also used in the variable table.

Used in Basic	Coded Name (in hex)
x%	D8 80
xx%	D8 D8
x	58 00
xx	58 58
x$	58 80
xx$	58 D8

Guy Lyle, from Lake Zurich, Illinois, writes: "Applesoft keeps a pointer to the last-used variable in locations $83 and $84. This pointer points at the third byte of the variable descriptor (for string variables, the length byte). We can access any number of variables within the variable tables, as long as we know their exact order and position within the tables. This is managed by having BASIC refer to the parameter variables in the order they are expected to be seen in the variable table, before any access, use, or definition of any other variables. The Applesoft simple variable table pointer at $69 and $6A points to the very beginning of the variable table. Entries for each variable are seven bytes apart, a fact that Rick used in his GET ADDRESS routine. One may simply use indexed-Y addressing to look up the values of any of the variables (or pointers, in the case of string variables). A word of caution: integer values are stored by Applesoft high-byte-first as opposed to the normal low-byte-first 6502 convention. Also, there is an error in the Applesoft II reference manual: string variable names are denoted by a positive first byte and a negative second byte.

• *Letters from the Dump,* by David Lubar

This article describes a simple way to find and display ASCII characters in machine language programs. (And you thought it couldn't be done!)

• *Disk Power: How to Use it:*

Here is a beginner's guide to sequential or direct access (random) data files. The programs given as examples are written in both Integer and Applesoft BASIC.

• *Executive Privilege,* by Leland D. Young:

Here we present a simple example of using the EXEC command for maintaining backup files. The necessary PEEKS and POKES are very well explained. For additional help in typing in a machine language subroutine, see the notes at the beginning of chapter VIII for "Lit'l Red Bug" article.

• *The "Tiny" Interpreter Exercise,* by Philip Tubb:

This article explains what is actually happening in your Apple after you type RUN. You know that no machine can understand a high level language, such as BASIC, so how does the program written in BASIC really work? The short answer is: the program must pass through an interpreter that changes it into a machine readable format, which is on a different "level." Changing FORTRAN into BASIC is similar to a human interpreter changing Spanish into English — since both are on the same "level." If you then changed the English to numeric equivalent statements, (that is let C=67, A=65, and T=84, so CAT= 676584!) you are going one step further and changing "levels."

Applesoft BASIC is an "interpretive" language, as opposed to a "compiled" language. Each time a line in a BASIC program is reached (during a RUN), the approximate machine code is executed. (A compiler changes all the BASIC code into machine instructions and then that is executed, not the original program.) Since most interpreters are written in machine language, it is difficult to understand what is really happening unless you first understand a lot about machine code. This tiny interpreter, written in Applesoft, is developed by asking the right questions, and could actually be used to interpret simple BASIC programs.

• *Apple II: Reading Data From Tape,* by Bruno B. Wolff, Jr.:
   This article is for those with Integer BASIC and cassette recorders who need to create data files on tape.

• *The Quest for the Perfect Printer,* by George Blank:
   This article gives a good rundown of what's available in printers: the types of printers, the options, and an approximate cost range. The comparison chart tells you if a specific printer has been reviewed by *Creative Computing,* and if so, in which issue. I notice that on the chart the Apple Silentype is listed at a price of $635. Just recently they reduced that to $399. As with the rest of the products in this book, the prices should be treated as estimates, since they tend to fluctuate with competition and demand.

• *The Dynatyper Typewriter Interface,* by Jim Cavuoto:
   We included this one because it's quite different in approach from the other "printers."

• *Chatsworth Mark Sense Card Reader,* by Keith Schlarb:
   For most people, a mark sense card reader won't make any sense. But for certain applications where a lot of data must be gathered and then entered into the computer, or for classroom applications (where on-line time is at a premium), this device could be a real blessing.

On Effective Documentation

Michael Robinson

Here's a pleasant Saturday-afternoon task: take a program, not a simple one and not one of your own, and write complete documentation for it. The fewer remarks it has before you begin, the better. After you finish your documentation, give it to a novice user and see how well he understands it. Or, read it yourself, and see how well *you* understand it.

I would expect very few people to jump right up and spend their days doing what I just suggested. I said it to make a point: if you for any reason were to hunt for an obscure, complex, poorly-documented program, you would not have to look very far. Hundreds of them exist: programs written by someone who had insufficient regard for the usefulness (and the importance) of good, effective documentation. After the coding and debugging of a program is finished, all too many programmers quit, and unwittingly leave the job half-done. What did they forget? Documentation.

Not all programs need a user manual. Most programs, in fact, do not. But *all* programs need some sort of documentation, some form of explanation showing both how to use the program and how the program works. This explanation may be brief, or it may be verbose. But it must be present, and it must be clear. Even if the program is not to be distributed, it should be documented. Few programmers remember the fine details of their programs for very long after they finish them. But if the need arises to trap an obscure bug, or just to make the program a little bit better, the amount and clarity of documentation provided in initial and subsequent coding efforts will make a great deal of difference in how quickly and how easily the work is done. Everyone needs a reminder, or a re-explanation, now and then. It saves thinking the problem through again. And if a program is to be distributed, then documentation becomes vastly more important. Now, instead of writing for

Michael D. Robinson, Route 4, Box 70, Ringgold, GA 30736.

someone already fairly familiar with the code, you must write for someone who has never seen it! It is no easy task.

Possibly the greatest problem in writing effective documentation is the fact that the programmer who created the program often finds himself assuming that the reader knows a great deal more than he actually does. The programmer may find it difficult to explain the program in terms that someone else can easily understand. Being the author, and thus knowing well the background and details of the program's usage and operation, he tends to omit those details from his documentation and assume that the reader already knows and understands them. In fact, he probably does not.

Documentation is not an incidental task, to be done when everything else is finished; it is a basic and very important part of programming.

All documentation is written with the assumption that the reader knows a certain amount of information already. This amount does vary. The Level I Basic manual for the TRS-80, for example, was a strictly tutorial affair, assuming no programming knowledge whatsoever from its reader. The Level II Basic manual for that same computer, on the other hand, assumed that the reader was already familiar with Basic (from the Level I manual, perhaps?), and said so right at the beginning.

Documentation for personal users must also be written with an understanding of the sequence of use that personal programs undergo. The reader will probably first experiment with the system, becoming familiar with it through the more tutorial segments of the manual, and then begin actually to use the system for his

particular task. Later, he will want answers to specific questions, without having to read a bunch of material he has already examined. He will then want to find quick definitions and summarizations — reference material, not tutorial material.

Thus, good documentation must contain all of these: quick-reference summaries, detailed descriptions, and textual discussions of the material. In many documentation manuals, the quick-reference summaries appear at the beginning, with references to more detailed discussions which are presented later in the manual. The experienced user can flip to the summaries and be satisfied, while the less-experienced user can refer to the text discussions.

Besides information for the user of the program, all documentation should contain a description of how the program operates. This information can, of course, be much more technical and less user-oriented than the user documentation, since the programmer to whom the technical documentation is addressed can be assumed to possess skill comparable to that of the original programmer, but the documentation must nevertheless be equally clear. All major program modules must be identified, preferably by remarks contained in the program itself. This is one reason that documentation should always include a listing of the program.

Much documentation consists of comments and annotations in the source code. The programmer can get a good, leisurely look at the program, and easily see from the contained comments what the program as a whole is doing as well as what any given section of the program is doing. Therefore the documentation should also contain an identification and description of all major variables, labels, and procedures in the program, and a concise description of the data base used by the program.

Documentation should identify the name of the program, begin with the programmer's name, the date the program was originally written, the current version of the program, and its date. The program should contain this information in header comments, and any manuals should contain the information, as in: "For Version 6.03 of MAILIST, by Ima Good Programmer, written 6/14/79, last updated on 6/22/79 by Ima G. Programmer." (Patches should also be denoted by remarks, including who put the patch in, when it was inserted, and what error the patch was intended to correct — especially since patches are usually last-minute insertions and can be rather difficult to understand.)

The experienced user can flip to the summaries and be satisfied.

Documentation should thus consist of four distinct sections: (1) an introduction, to tell the user in simple, non-technical terms what the program is doing; (2) a quick-reference guide to let the experienced user of the program get answers to questions quickly; (3) a more in-depth explanation of the program's operation and use, intended more for the less-experienced program user; and (4) a technical description of how the program works to allow other programmers to easily service the material.

Documentation is not an incidental task, to be done when everything else is finished; it is a basic and very important part of programming. It makes the difference between a mediocre program and a good one. Documentation is the difference between a job half-done and a job well-done. □

"It can't actually think, but when it makes a mistake,
it can blame it on some other computer."

Bombproof Data Entry

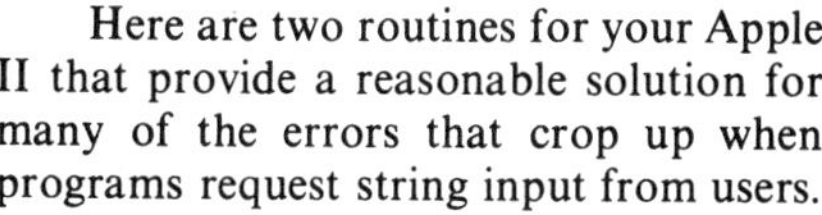

Greg Kielian

Here are two routines for your Apple II that provide a reasonable solution for many of the errors that crop up when programs request string input from users.

These routines allow all alphanumeric characters to be typed in, including commas (no more '?EXTRA IGNORED')! Characters such as 'control C' are filtered out. Each word or string entry has a fixed maximum length which is used to prompt the operator. This fixed length is handy for formatting files, tables, etc. The strings can, if need be, be converted to numbers after entry. Both routines were written in Applesoft Basic.

The first routine inputs data in a conventional echoing mode, with the cursor moving rightword. The second

The second offers an unusual and attractive leftward motion of the input string, with a fixed cursor.

offers an unusual and attractive leftward motion of the input string, with a fixed cursor. Each of these can be used as subroutines, to act as very effective filters and error traps for your user-oriented programs.

Two important variables are:
L — Maximum length of string to be input.
B$ — Where the entered data will reside at the end of the routine.

Forward-Stepping Input (Program 1)

The most important lines of the program are:
200 — Display prompting. Also depends on lines 180, 190, 210, 220 and 330. HTAB values are dependent on the length of the prompt line. In this case line 150 or "LAST NAME:" which is ten characters long and requires a minimum HTAB of 11 (or 10 + I where I is greater than 0).

Greg Kielian, P.O. Box 1084, Longmont, CO 80501.

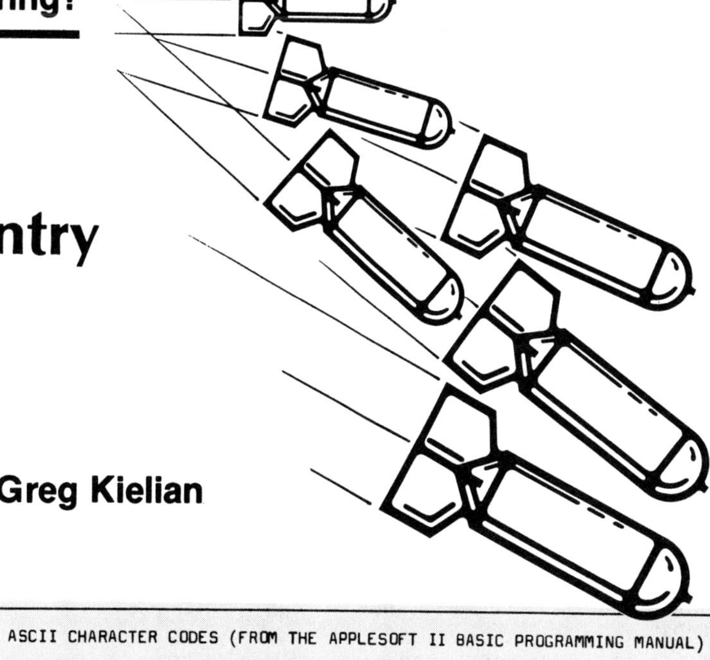

ASCII CHARACTER CODES (FROM THE APPLESOFT II BASIC PROGRAMMING MANUAL)

```
DEC  = ASCII DECIMAL CODE
HEX  = ASCII HEXADECIMAL CODE
CHAR = ASCII CHARACTER NAME
N/A  = NOT ACCESSIBLE DIRECTLY FROM THE APPLE II KEYBOARD
```

DEC	HEX	CHAR	WHAT TO TYPE	DEC	HEX	CHAR	WHAT TO TYPE
Ø	ØØ	NULL	CTRL @	48	3Ø	Ø	Ø
1	Ø1	SOH	CTRL A	49	31	1	1
2	Ø2	STX	CTRL B	5Ø	32	2	2
3	Ø3	ETX	CTRL C	51	33	3	3
4	Ø4	ET	CTRL D	52	34	4	4
5	Ø5	ENQ	CTRL E	53	35	5	5
6	Ø6	ACK	CTRL F	54	36	6	6
7	Ø7	BEL	CTRL G	55	37	7	7
8	Ø8	BS	CTRL H OR ←	56	38	8	8
9	Ø9	HT	CTRL I	57	39	9	9
1Ø	ØA	LF	CTRL J	58	3A	:	:
11	ØB	VT	CTRL K	59	3B	;	;
12	ØC	FF	CTRL L	6Ø	3C	<	<
13	ØD	CR	CTRL M OR RETURN	61	3D	=	=
14	ØE	SO	CTRL N	62	3E	>	>
15	ØF	SI	CTRL O	63	3F	?	?
16	1Ø	DLE	CTRL P	64	4Ø	@	@
17	11	DC1	CTRL Q	65	41	A	A
18	12	DC2	CTRL R	66	42	B	B
19	13	DC3	CTRL S	67	43	C	C
2Ø	14	DC4	CTRL T	68	44	D	D
21	15	NAK	CTRL U OR →	69	45	E	E
22	16	SYN	CTRL V	7Ø	46	F	F
23	17	ETB	CTRL W	71	47	G	G
24	18	CAN	CTRL X	72	48	H	H
25	19	EM	CTRL Y	73	49	I	I
26	1A	SUB	CTRL Z	74	4A	J	J
27	1B	ESCAPE	ESC	75	4B	K	K
28	1C	FS	N/A	76	4C	L	L
29	1D	GS	CTRL SHIFT-M	77	4D	M	M
3Ø	1E	RS	CTRL ↑	78	4E	N	N
31	1F	US	N/A	79	4F	O	O
32	2Ø	SPACE	SPACE	8Ø	5Ø	P	P
33	21	!	!	81	51	Q	Q
34	22	"	"	82	52	R	R
35	23	#	#	83	53	S	S
36	24	$	$	84	54	T	T
37	25	%	%	85	55	U	U
38	26	&	&	86	56	V	V
39	27	'	'	87	57	W	W
4Ø	28	(	(	88	58	X	X
41	29	)	)	89	59	Y	Y
42	2A	*	*	9Ø	5A	Z	Z
43	2B	+	+	91	5B	[	N/A
44	2C	,	,	92	5C	\	N/A
45	2D	-	-	93	5D	]	] (SHIFT-M)
46	2E	.	.	94	5E	↑	↑
47	2F	/	/	95	5F	←	N/A

Table 1.

230 — GETs character as it's typed.
240 — Checks character to see if it's a carriage return. If it is, control passes to line 370 and the routine is finished.
250 — Checks character to see if it's a back arrow. If it is, lines 260 and 290 remove the last character entered.
300 — If the character has passed the first two tests, the number of characters entered is checked. If it's equal to the maximum number allowed (L), control is sent back to line 210 for a carriage return or back arrow.
310 — If the character is illegal and has an ASCII value less than 32 (refer to Table 1), control is sent back to line 180 and another character is input.
320 — At this point the character has finally passed through the entire filter and is concatenated onto 'B$'.
340 — The character count is incremented and control is sent to fetch another character.
380 — 'B$' is trimmed to the specified length. The program (or subroutine) could be ended at this point, with the desired data in 'B$'.

```
100    HOME
110 M$ = "--------------------"
120 S$ = "                    "
130 L = 10
140    VTAB 10
150    PRINT "LAST NAME:";
160    PRINT  MID$ (M$,1,L)
170 I = 1
180    VTAB 10
190    HTAB (10 + I)
200    PRINT "-"
210    VTAB 10
220    HTAB (10 + I)
230    GET X$
240    IF X$ =  CHR$ (13) THEN 370
250    IF X$ <  >  CHR$ (8) THEN 300
260    IF I = 1 THEN 180
270 B$ =  MID$ (B$,1, LEN (B$) - 1)
280 I = I - 1
290    GOTO 180
300    IF I = L + 1 THEN 210
310    IF  ASC (X$) < 32 THEN 180
320 B$ = B$ + X$
330    PRINT X$
340 I = I + 1
350    IF I = L + 1 THEN 210
360    GOTO 180
370    CALL  - 868
380 B$ = B$ + S$
390 B$ =  MID$ (B$,1,L)
400    VTAB 15
410    HTAB 1
420    PRINT B$
430    END
```

Routine 1. Forward-Stepping Cursor.

```
100    HOME
110 M$ = "--------------------"
120 S$ = "                    "
130 L = 10
140 B$ =  MID$ (M$,1,L)
150    VTAB 10
160    PRINT "LAST NAME:";
170 I = 1
180    VTAB 10
190    HTAB 11
200    PRINT  MID$ (B$, LEN (B$) - L + 1, LEN (B$))
210    VTAB 10
220    HTAB (11 + L)
230    GET X$
240    IF X$ =  CHR$ (13) THEN 350
250    IF X$ <  >  CHR$ (8) THEN 300
260    IF I = 1 THEN 180
270 B$ =  MID$ (B$,1, LEN (B$) - 1)
280 I = I - 1
290    GOTO 180
300    IF I = L + 1 THEN 180
310    IF  ASC (X$) < 32 THEN 180
320 B$ = B$ + X$
330 I = I + 1
340    GOTO 180
350 B$ =  MID$ (B$, LEN (B$) - I + 2, LEN (B$))
360 B$ =  MID$ (S$,1,L -  LEN (B$)) + B$
370    VTAB 15
380    HTAB 1
390    PRINT B$
400    END
```

Routine 2. Backward-Stepping String.

Back-Sliding Input (Program 2)

This program operates in much the same way as the first, with the following differences:
140 — 'B$' is initialized with dashes instead of being blank or empty.
200 — Display prompting that resembles backward scrolling. This format also depends on lines 180, 190, 210 and 220. Again HTAB values are dependent on line 160 or "LAST NAME:" which is ten characters long and requires an HTAB of 11.

Examples

Using Routine 1, and entering the name "JOHNSON," gives a display corresponding to the following:
(Note: ∧ indicates cursor position)

Step	Display
1	LAST NAME: _________∧
2	LAST NAME: J ________∧
3	LAST NAME: JO _______∧
4	LAST NAME: JOH ______∧
5	LAST NAME: JOHS _____∧ Note that a mistake was made.
6	LAST NAME: JOH ______∧ Back arrow was typed.
7	LAST NAME: JOHN _____∧ Mistake was corrected.
8	LAST NAME: JOHNS ____∧
9	LAST NAME: JOHNSO ___∧
10	LAST NAME: JOHNSON __∧

At step ten a RETURN was typed and a 'B$' contains "JOHNSON   ." Notice the blanks in the last three character positions.

Using Routine 2, and entering the name "STITTSWORTH," results in the following display: (Note: ∧ indicates cursor position)

Step	Display
1	LAST NAME: ----------∧
2	LAST NAME: ---------S∧
3	LAST NAME: --------ST∧
4	LAST NAME: -------STI∧
5	LAST NAME: ------STII∧
6	LAST NAME: -------STI∧ Back arrow was typed.
7	LAST NAME: ------STIT∧ Mistake was corrected.
8	LAST NAME: -----STITT∧
9	LAST NAME: ----STITTS∧
10	LAST NAME: ---STITTSW∧
11	LAST NAME: --STITTSWO∧
12	LAST NAME: -STITTSWOR∧
13	LAST NAME: STITTSWORT∧

At step 13 the only characters recognized are carriage return or back arrow. Since the word didn't fit, it could be modified by retyping it *before* it's actually accepted by the machine. If a RETURN had been typed at step nine, 'B$' would contain " STITTS." Notice the blanks in the first four character positions. □

Bombproof Data Entry—A Revision

Susan Luca

At the time I read Greg Kielian's article "Bombproof Data Entry" in the November 1980 issue of *Creative Computing*, I was dealing with a similar problem. However, I found that his approach was not adequate for my needs since the routine does not allow back spacing to one character while maintaining the other data.

The problem I was dealing with required the entry of notational text which could be from one to three lines, with a line containing up to 36 characters. Another criterion was that a "beep" should be heard at thirty spaces to signal that five more letters could be input on that line. I found that the back spacing which erased all input letters it back spaced over was very frustrating when trying to change one letter near the beginning of the line.

Therefore, I decided to incorporate an array with the get statement. By using the array input the backspace and forward space could be used without losing any correct data.

The elements of the array are not concatenated until the "return" is pressed or until the end of the line is reached; in this case the line has a maximum of 36 characters. The following is a line-by-line explanation of the routine, which is written in Basic for the Apple II Plus.

10 Dimensions the array.
20 Clears the screen.
30 Prints information on the screen.
40 Sets the cursor to edge of screen.
50 Sets the counters to 1. "B" is the line indicator. "T" is the number of input letters or spaces.
60 Sets the number of lines to 3.
70 Prevents the array counter from being less than 1.
75 Gets the input letter. Puts the letter in an array and prints the letter.
80 Checks for a backspace and returns to get a new input.
80 Checks for a forward space and returns to get a new input.
100 Checks for control character inputs which are not accepted.
110 Looks for a return at less than thirty spaces. This would end the input. The array is then concatenated.
120 Looks for the return and concatenates the array.
130 Sounds the "beep" at thirty characters.
140 If the input reaches 36 characters the line is ended and the next line is started.
150 The counter is increased and the program returns to get another input.
160 The screen is cleared.
170 The first line is printed.
180 Second line is printed.
190 Third line is printed.
200 The routine ends.

```
5    REM   DATA INPUT BY ARRAY
6    REM   SUSAN LUCA
10   DIM DX$(38)
20   HOME
30   VTAB 9: HTAB 5: PRINT "ITEM:"
40   VTAB 11: HTAB 1
50   B = 1:T = 1
60   IF B > 3 THEN  GOTO 160
70   IF T = 0 THEN T = 1
75   GET DX$(T): PRINT DX$(T);
80   IF   ASC (DX$(T)) = 8 THEN T = T - 1: GOTO 70
90   IF   ASC (DX$(T)) = 21 THEN T = T + 1: GOTO 70
100   IF   ASC (DX$(T)) < 32 AND   ASC (DX$(T)) <  > 13 THEN  GOTO 70
110   IF   ASC (DX$(T)) = 13 AND T < 30 THEN  FOR S = 1 TO T - 1:DES$(B) = D
      ES$(B) + DX$(S): NEXT S: GOTO 160
120   IF   ASC (DX$(T)) = 13 THEN  FOR S = 1 TO T - 1:DES$(B) = DES$(B) + DX
      $(S): NEXT S:B = B + 1:T = 1: GOTO 60
130   IF T = 30 THEN  PRINT "";
140   IF T = 36 THEN  FOR S = 1 TO T:DES$(B) = DES$(B) + DX$(S): NEXT S:B =
      B + 1:T = 1: PRINT : GOTO 60
150 T = T + 1: GOTO 60
160   HOME
170   VTAB 5: HTAB 1: PRINT DES$(1)
180   VTAB 6: HTAB 1: PRINT DES$(2)
190   VTAB 7: HTAB 1: PRINT DES$(3)
200   END
```

Susan Luca, GSP Computer Resources, Inc., 9 Ash St., Hollis, NH 03049.

The Challenge of Error Trapping

Mike K. Summers

John B. Willett

Introduction

In the School of Education at the University of Hong Kong we are designing and evaluating a variety of Computer-Assisted Learning (CAL) packages for use with low-cost microcomputers at school and university level. A typical CAL package consists of a computer program together with a student workbook and a teacher's guide. The teacher's guide should contain full program documentation together with a description of the educational aims of the package and suggestions for integrating the CAL work for the particular topic into the curriculum. Under the general guidance of the teacher, the student uses the microcomputer in an interactive mode to investigate problems posed in the student workbook. It is the interactive nature of the relationship between learner and machine that often creates problems for both the user and the CAL package designer. This is because the packages themselves must be user-proof. When the program requests the student to input information, inappropriate or incorrect responses (for example, typing errors) must be trapped. A trap is simply a

> **It is the interactive nature of the relationship between learner and machine that often creates problems for both the user and the CAL package designer.**

program routine which checks the validity of the user's response to the computer's request for input. In the case of inappropriate or incorrect responses the trapping routine will inform the student of the nature of his error and suggest corrective action. In the absence of such a trap it is perfectly possible for an unwitting user to interrupt the program or even delete sections of it. This article is concerned with the general problem of trapping. Although the discussion below origi-

John Willett, Mike Summers, School of Education, University of Hong Kong, Hong Kong.

nates from work on computer-assisted learning, the information is of general interest since nearly all software designed for small computers involves some form of direct user-computer interaction (for example, gaming, simulation, computer art, small business applications and so on). The particular examples of trapping techniques described in this article refer to the Radio Shack TRS-80 microcomputer with Level II BASIC and 16K RAM, since this is the machine for which we are designing CAL materials. However, most of the practical experiences and suggestions are equally applicable to other inexpensive microcomputer systems with extended BASIC interpreters.

The need for traps

When running a CAL program, the student is often required to input data. This data can be either NUMERICAL or ALPHABETIC. Depending on the nature of the data, a different type of input routine must be used. A typical routine asking for numerical input is listed below:

```
50 REM **** INPUT ROUTINE
   #1 ****
60 PRINT "WHICH STUDY DO
   YOU REQUIRE. TYPE 1 OR 2"
70 INPUT X
80 IF X = 1  THEN 100
90 IF X = 2  THEN 300
100 REM **** START OF STUDY
    ONE ****
'
'
'
'
'
'
300 REM **** START OF STUDY
    TWO ****
```

Obviously, this type of routine satisfies the essential requirements of a CAL package in which the student is offered a choice of two studies. In practice, however, such a simple routine cannot guard against the possibility of erroneous inputs. For example, if the student responds with any number other than 1 or 2, lines 80 and 90 will fail to detect the input and the program will automatically run to line 100 (the start of study one). If the student inputs

alphabetic data, then the BASIC interpreter (which is expecting numerical input) returns its own error message. In the case of the TRS-80, the message REDO? appears on the screen. A further problem arises if the student inputs punctuation marks. With the TRS-80, a semicolon input produces a REDO? message, while commas and colons produce the error message EXTRA IGNORED (after which the program runs on to line 100). The trouble with messages of this kind is that they are either in poor English, or

> **A simple routine cannot guard against the possibility of erroneous inputs.**

are abbreviations which may be totally incomprehensible to the package user. However, there is a more important reason for designing programs which prevent machine error messages of this kind appearing. The advent of cheap microcomputers with memory-mapped video displays and graphics facilities allows the designer of CAL packages to present information to the student page-by-page. Such a page mode of operation should be contrasted with the Teletype in which output is printed sequentially line by line. In the Teletype mode, the entire display scrolls up when the screen is full, so that information is eventually lost from the top of the screen. A microcomputer with graphics and memory-mapped video used in the paged mode allows very rapid presentation of information (a whole screen of information can be generated almost instantaneously) in a visually captivating form, and is ideal for CAL. An important focus of CAL program design is then to plan whole pages of attractive and interesting information with which the student is to interact. However, if an unforeseen machine error message such as REDO? is generated by the computer during program use, a carefully designed and attractive display can be destroyed. In the case of the TRS-80, REDO? may erase previously generated lines of display. More seriously, REDO?

causes the whole page to scroll upwards, so that planned information is premanently lost from the top of the screen. To avoid the problems, the CAL program designer must include trapping routines which not only check the validity of user inputs, but also print comprehensible corrective messages in good English at appropriate places on the screen. In other words, all input errors should be trapped by the CAL program itself so that the BASIC interpreter is never required to display its own error messages.

Alpha and Numeric INPUTS

Consider now an input routine designed for accepting alphabetic data. The routine below, for example, uses alphabetic data to 'turn the pages' of a video display:

```
50 REM **** INPUT ROUTINE
   #2 ****
60 PRINT "DO YOU WISH TO
   CONTINUE"
70 INPUT R$
80 IF R$ = "YES" THEN 100
90 IF R$ = "NO" THEN 999
100 REM **** START OF NEXT
    PAGE ****
999 END
```

This routine is similar to the first one in that if the user responds correctly (in this case, with "YES" or "NO") the computer reacts appropriately. Also, if the user inputs any other alphabetic string (for example, "PERHAPS"), neither lines 80 nor 90 recognize R$ and the program automatically runs to line 100 where the page is turned. However, this input routine has one very important advantage over the routine designed to accept numerical input. If the user accidentally inputs numeric data, then the computer reacts in the same way as when an incorrect alphabetic string is input. This illustrates an important assymetry in the computer's handling of input data. In the case of the first input routine, an accidental alphabetical input when the computer is expecting numerical data results in an error message. In the second routine, an accidental numerical input when the computer is expecting alphabetic data produces no machine error message. This is simply a reflection of the fact that it is quite legitimate to store numbers in string form, but it is most definitely not legitimate to store alphabetic inputs as numbers. In both cases the user inputs are invalid, but the second routine does not upset the screen display with the unwanted REDO? error message. This fact is exploited in some of the trapping routines described later. The reaction of the second routine to punctuation mark inputs is similar but not identical

to that of the first routine. This time commas, colons and semicolons all allow the program to run to line 100 where the page is turned without user permission. As before, the comma and the colon produce the error message EXTRA IGNORED, but this time the semicolon does not produce the disruptive REDO?.

The above discussion of problems which can arise from erroneous user inputs in interactive programs without traps, used two very simple input routines to provide examples. However, it should be noted that more sophisticated input routines can lead to even more catastrophic results. For example, the sophisticated programmer might decide to delete lines 80 and 90 from the first of the above input routines and replace them by the single line

```
85 ON X GOTO   100,300
```

However, if the user now responds to the input request with a negative number, the TRS-80 prints the error message ?FC ERROR IN 85, indicating an illegal function call (the ON expression GOTO line number, line number - statement is not valid for negative X) and the computer returns to the command mode. The program run is interrupted and the user confused. But potentially, there is a far greater problem than this. If, as a result of this confusion, the user now inputs a positive number, the corresponding line number will be deleted. Although situations of this kind are unlikely to arise, the CAL program designer must guard against all such eventualities to the best of his ability. This means he must devise as near-perfect trapping routines as possible.

The CAL program designer must include trapping routines which not only check the validity of user inputs, but also print comprehensible corrective messages in good English at appropriate places on the screen.

Types of trap

We will distinguish between two types of trap, and discuss them separately. The first is concerned with trapping invalid user responses to the computer's request for alphabetic input, while the second deals with invalid responses to requests for numerical input.

1. Alphabetic input

A modification of INPUT ROU-

TINE #2 which works reasonably well is given below:

```
50 REM **** INPUT ROUTINE
   #3 ****
60 PRINT "ARE YOU READY
   TO CONTINUE"
70 INPUT R$
80 IF R$ = "YES" THEN 110
90 PRINT "INVALID RE-
   SPONSE. PLEASE RETYPE"
100 GOTO 70
110 REM **** START OF NEXT
    PAGE ****
```

It is most definitely not legitimate to store alphabetic inputs as numbers.

In lines 60 and 70 the computer requests alphabetic input. Line 80 tests for the positive response ("YES") which, if detected, results in a jump to the new page beginning at line 110. All other inputs, including both numbers and letters (or combinations), result in display of the corrective message INVALID RESPONSE. PLEASE RE-TYPE. Line 100 then causes a jump back to line 70 where the computer again waits for a valid user entry. In the case of the TRS-80, the only way the user can defeat this trap is by responding to the input request with a comma or a colon. The computer then returns the error message EXTRA IGNORED, but program execution proceeds correctly (the INVALID RESPONSE message is displayed). However, a spurious and undesired error message will have been generated and, in the paged mode, this may completely spoil a carefully designed display.

Marginal improvements of the above trap are possible using a combination of the TRS-80 statements PRINT @ **position, item list** and CHR$ (expression), together with judicious use of semicolons. We will first briefly review the function of these two statements and of the semicolon. The PRINT @ **position, item list** statement allows information to be printed starting at any one of 1024 separate locations on the memory-mapped screen. Existing lines can be overwritten, so that a message asking for user input can be replaced by a message indicating on invalid response, at exactly the same screen location. The CHR$ **expression** statement returns a one-character string whose character has the specified decimal ASCII code. For example, CHR$ (65) would return the letter A, since the decimal ASCII code for A is 65. The interesting thing about this statement is that it can also be used with the ASCII codes for control functions. Of particular use is CHR$ (30), where 30 is the ASCII code for the control function which erases to the end of the line (later). A semicolon at the end of a program line indicates to the computer that, when the line has been executed, the cursor should not move to the next line of output display, but should wait at the end of the current line of display. If, for example, the program line prints a request for user input on the screen, the cursor does not move to the next line to accept that input but waits at the end of the sentence requesting input. Let us now see how the above can be combined to produce a better trap:

```
50 REM **** INPUT ROUTINE
   #4 ****
60 PRINT @448, "ARE YOU
   READY TO CONTINUE";
70 INPUT R$
80 IF R$ = "YES" THEN 110
85 PRINT @448, CHR$ (30)
90 PRINT @448, "INVALID
   RESPONSE. RETYPE";
100 GOTO 70
REM **** START OF NEXT
   PAGE ****
```

As before, lines 60 and 70 request alphabetic input. However, this time both the question and user response occur one after the other on the same line (the line beginning at screen location 448) because of the semicolon at the end of line 60. Line 80 detects the positive response ("YES") and causes a jump to the new page starting at line 110. If the user inputs an invalid response, the existing question and the response are erased by line 85 and replaced (beginning at the same screen location i.e. 448) by the IN-VALID RESPONSE message of line 90. The interesting thing about this trap is that it is almost foolproof. All inputs except commas and colons are trapped as with input routine #3. As before, comma and colon inputs result in the error message EXTRA IGNORED, but with input routine #4 this is immediately erased, and the trap continues to operate correctly (the INVALID RE-SPONSE message is displayed). We leave it to the more perverse reader to discover why this trap is only **almost** foolproof!

Another interesting trap for either alphabetic or numeric input is one in which the user response is searched (parsed) for particular alphanumeric characters or combinations of characters. Consider the following input routine:

```
50 REM **** INPUT ROUTINE
   #5 ****
60 PRINT "INPUT YOUR
   RESPONSE"
70 INPUT R$
80 FOR N = 1 to LEN (R$)
90 K$ = MID$ (R$, N, 1)
100 IF K$ = "E" THEN 140
110 NEXT N
120 PRINT "INVALID RE-
   SPONSE. RETYPE"
130 GOTO 70
140 REM **** CONTINUATION
   OF PROGRAM ****
```

This routine searches the user input string to see if it contains the letter E in any position. Program execution is only allowed to continue if an E is detected. The core of the trap is contained in lines 80 through 110 which search the input string one letter at a time looking for the letter E. If this is detected, there is a jump from line 100 to line 140, where the program continues. Use is made of two statements found in many extended BASICs (LEN (string) and MID$ (string, x, y)). Len (string) returns the number of characters in the string in decimal form. MID$ (string, x, y) returns a substring extracted from the specified string. This substring is of length y and is extracted starting at position x (i.e., x characters from the start of the specified string). In the above routine, each character of the string R$ is extracted in turn and becomes the substring K$. This substring is compared to the letter "E" in line 100, and if equivalence is not detected, the INVALID RESPONSE message is displayed and the program returns to line 70 and awaits a new input. Such a trap is useful in some CAL programs, but more obviously in word, spelling and code-type games.

Several interesting modifications of input routine #5 are possible. One modification involves use of the TRS-80 statement ASC (string), which returns the decimal ASCII code of the first character of the specified string. This, for example, allows replacement of line 100 of input routine #5 by

```
100 IF ASC(K$) = 69  THEN 140
```

since the decimal ASCII code for the letter E is 69. In this particular instance there is no advantage in such a modification, but there are cases where use of ASC (string) can be of great value. One example might be a program in which the user response to the computer's request for input must consist only of alphabetic characters in a particular range (e.g., G through P). This can be achieved by rewriting line 100 as:

```
100 IF ASC (K$) > = 71 AND
    ASC (K$) < = 80 THEN 140
```

Since the decimal ASCII codes of the characters G and P are the numbers 71 and 80 respectively, the trap will only let through combinations of letters in the allowed range.

A final point to note about input routine #5 is that it suffers from the same pitfalls as input routine #3 described earlier. However, use of the modifications included in input routine #4 will render the various forms of input routine #5 virtually foolproof.

2. Numerical input

Earlier we noted an important assymetry in the reaction of the computer to different types of input. An accidental alphabetic input when the computer is expecting numerical input results in display of the machine error message REDO?, but accidental input of numeric data when alphabetic input is expected produces no such

The search for the perfect trap goes on!

message. This assymetry can be usefully exploited when designing effective traps for numerical input. Consider the following:

```
50 REM **** INPUT ROUTINE
   #6 ****
60 PRINT "WHICH STUDY DO
   YOU REQUIRE. TYPE 1 OR 2"
70 INPUT R$
80 R = VAL (R$)
90 IF R = 1 THEN 130
100 IF R = 2 THEN 300
110 PRINT "INVALID RE-
   SPONSE. RETYPE"
120 GOTO 70
130 REM **** START OF
   STUDY 1 ****
   '
   '
   '
   '
300 REM *** START OF STUDY
   2 ****
```

In line 70 the computer is expecting a string input, and when a number is input it is stored as the string R$. It is, of course, quite legitimate to store numbers in string form and no machine error message is returned. Likewise, line 70 will accept accidental alphabetic inputs without display of a machine error message, but these will not be allowed through the trap. This is because line 80 extracts the numerical value of the input string using the VAL (string) statement, where VAL (string) automatically returns a numerical value of zero for string characters other than numbers. Lines 90 and 100 detect the allowed inputs 1 or 2, while other inputs result in display of the INVALID RESPONSE message of line 110. A combination of the above input routine with input routine #4 produces a trap for numerical input which is highly user-proof.

Final point

Although none of the traps described in this article are completely user-proof, some are very nearly so. By appropriate combination of the various techniques, the prospective program author should be able to design an effective trap suited to his needs. However, let there be no doubt, the search for the perfect trap goes on! □

Displaying Numbers in Tabular Format

Melvyn D. Magree

Some Basics do not have a PRINT USING capability. The subroutine described here converts a floating-point number into a string with integer and fractional parts of pre-defined lengths.

Basic prints all numbers with the most significant digit in the leftmost position of the field. If there is a fractional part to the number, all of the digits to represent it completely are displayed. If you wish to display a table, the result may be ragged like this:

```
1.23
456.1
0.75
-90.123
```

But the result that you really want is

```
  1.230
456.100
  0.780
-90.123
```

This latter form is particularly useful when displaying sums of money. Nobody writes a check for 54.3 dollars!

Some Basics do provide a PRINT USING feature, which allows you to give a string which tells Basic how you would like the number displayed. If you have such a Basic, you need read no further. If you do not, a subroutine which handles most cases follows. It is written using Microsoft Basic for the OSI C4P-MF, but it can be used as is for the Apple and many other Basics.

This subroutine rounds the number, separates it into an integer part and a fractional part, places any leading and trailing zeros on the fractional part, converts each part to a string, places any minus sign in front of the integer part, puts the two strings together with a decimal point between them, and pads the resulting string with any required leading spaces.

Melvyn D. Magree, 5925 Magnolia Lane, Plymouth, MN 55442.

Explanation

To understand the subroutine in more detail, let us step through it with an example, say N=123.456, IP=4, and FP=2.

Line 100 saves the sign of N as plus or minus 1 or as 0 if N is 0. Line 102 determines the number to be used for rounding and for ensuring that leading and trailing zeros are in the fractional part. Thus, we have S=1 and N2=100.

Line 104 removes the sign from the number and rounds it to the desired significant figures. Our example is already positive and adding .5/100 to it gives us N1=123.461. If our example had been negative, N1 would have been the same, but the sign would have been saved as S=-1 in line 100.

Lines 106 and 108 separate the rounded, absolute number into an integer part and an augmented fractional part. IP in our case becomes 123. The fractional part is converted to an integer and any leading zeros are preserved. N1-IP is 0.461, multiplying by 100 gives us 46.1, and taking the integer part of that and adding 100 gives us FP=146. The last operation preserves any leading zeros; the extra digit will be removed later.

Line 110 converts the integer part to a string. The STR$ function leaves one position for the sign which we are not interested in at the moment; the last two statements of this line remove this leading space. For our example D$="123" and L=3.

Line 112 is a "fudge" for the case when the integer part is 0 and is not to be displayed. This does not apply for our number. If IP had been zero, D$ from line 110 would have been "0"; if no integer part were to be displayed, D$ should be a null string.

Line 114 places any required minus sign on the string. The second IF statement in the line handles the case where the integer part is zero and only one space had been requested for it. If our number had been negative, we would have had D$="-123" and L=4.

Line 116 is the only error check in the subroutine and is for the most likely error case, a number larger than can be held in the specified fields. Several years ago, I heard of a large scientific computer installation that had changed vendors. When they ran some of the programs they had been using for years, several of the results were given as asterisks rather than as numbers. The second vendor replaced all the numbers that were too big for the given field with asterisks whereas the first vendor truncated the numbers to fit! The installation had been using these truncated numbers as if they were accurate! For our use this problem is not so important, especally if you consider the way that we have constructed the string and the way that we will probably use it. The most probable worst case is that the complete number will be displayed but the line may be extended to the right. I would advise keeping this test so that you are warned about possible errors in your program that give larger results than you expected.

Line 118 places any required spaces in front of the integer part of our number. The technical term for this operation is right-justify and space-fill. D$ for our example is now " 123."

Line 120 places the decimal point and the rounded fractional part to the right of the integer part. The STR$ function converts FP to " 146," and the RIGHT$ function gives us the desired "46." The IF statement is included for two reasons. First, Basic considers it an error if you try to extract a substring of length zero and stops your program. Second, if you specified a fractional part of length zero, I presume that you do not want decimal point. D$ is now our desired result of " 123.46." If N had been negative, we would have had "-123.46."

Line 124 processes the error case detected at line 116. D$ is set to a string of asterisks. The length of this string is the sum of the requested lengths of the integer and fractional parts plus one for the decimal point.

If our number had been 12345.67, then we would have had a result of seven asterisks; that is, D$="*******."

Please note that no error checks are made for specification of negative or unusually large part lengths. Your Basic will probably stop at some point in this subroutine if that does happen.

Although this subroutine is not as fast as it might be if it were provided in ROM or in machine code, it is reasonably fast for many applications. The example was run 100 times on an OSI C4P-MF in 4.5 seconds. This means each execution of the subroutine takes less than 45 milliseconds.

If you do not need the flexibility, you can customize the subroutine and gain some speed. For example, if all of your numbers will be positive, you can delete lines 100 and 114. If you always use a given length fractional part, say 2 for cents, then you can replace line 102 with N2=100. This will probably make the most significant improvement. The above test was run with this last change in 4.15 seconds. ☐

The Program

Input: N - number to be converted
               IL - length for integer part
               FL - length for fractional part
Output: D$ - string of length IL+FL+1
Error case: If integer part requires more than IL digits, set D$ to a string of IL+FL+1 asterisks (*).
Uses: S, N1, N2, IP, FP, and L

```
100 S=SGN(N)
102 N2=10 ↑ FL
104 N1=ABS(N)+.5/N2
106 IP=INT(N1)
108 FP=INT(N2*(N1-IP))+N2
110 D$=STR$(IP):L=LEN(D$)-1:D$=RIGHT$(D$,L)
112 IF IL=0 AND IP=0 THEN D$="":L=0
114 IF S< 0 THEN L=L+1:D$="-"+;D$:IF IP=0 AND IL=1 THEN D$="-":L=1
116 IF IL< L THEN 124
118 IF IL > L THEN D$=" "+D$:L=L+1:GOTO 118
120 IF FL > 0 THEN D$=D$+"."+RIGHT$(STR$(FP),FL)
122 RETURN
124 D$="*":FOR N1=1 TO IL+FL:D$=D$+"*":NEXT:RETURN
```

Notes

Divide N~Conquer

John E. Bailey

For many of us, the hardest part of programming is developing the algorithms needed to perform the tasks that will produce the desired results. Presented here is the development of an algorithm to perform long division. Although it may not be very useful for more than demonstration purposes, the technique presented here may be helpful in developing more complex and meaningful algorithms.

One of the things that makes a computer so powerful is its ability to perform a given function many many times. We can use this capability with the example above and develop a program to perform long division.

Consider the two integers $A = 7$ and $B = 3$. If we divide A by B we get 2.333333. Depending upon the accuracy of our Basic, the result may be carried out to 6 or more digits. This amount of accuracy is generally all that is necessary. But even so, the degree of accuracy can be improved by using the long division technique that is taught in grade school. For example:

```
       2.333333------
      ________________
   3 | 7.000000
       6
      ____
       10
        9
      ____
       10
        9
```

This process can continue for as many digits as desired. In this example, 3 is called the divisor, 7 is called the dividend, and 2.333333--- is called the quotient. Dividing 7 by 3 gives a quotient of 2 with a remainder of 1. The remainder is then multiplied by 10. This result becomes the new dividend, and the division process continues.

One of the things that makes a computer so powerful is its ability to perform a given function many many times. We can use this capability with the example above and develop a program to perform long division. To do this, we need to develop an algorithm to simulate long division. This is where programmers sometimes bog down and quit. But the process is really very simple if it is approached in a logical fashion. Let's return to the original example. We let $A = 7$ be the dividend and $B = 3$ be the divisor. We will also let C be the quotient and R be the remainder. Now,

John E. Bailey, 1108 Post Oak #1, Sulphur, LA 70663.

```
10 INPUT "ENTER VALUE FOR DIVIDEND A =",A
20 INPUT "ENTER VALUE FOR DIVISOR B =",B
30 INPUT "ENTER VALUE FOR NUMBER OF DECIMAL PLACES N =",N
40 LET C=INT(A/B)
50 PRINT A," /",B;" =",C,".",
60 FOR I=1 TO N
70 LET R=A-(B*C)
80 LET A=R*10
90 LET C=INT(A/B)
100 PRINT C,
110 NEXT I
120 END

RUN

ENTER VALUE FOR DIVIDEND A =7
ENTER VALUE FOR DIVISOR B =3
ENTER VALUE FOR NUMBER OF DECIMAL PLACES N = 25
 7 / 3 = 2. 3 3 3 3 3 3 3 3 3 3 3 3 3 3 3 3 3 3 3 3 3 3 3 3 3

RUN

ENTER VALUE FOR DIVIDEND A =67344
ENTER VALUE FOR DIVISOR B =9024
ENTER VALUE FOR NUMBER OF DECIMAL PLACES =350
 67344 / 9024 = 7. 4 6 2 7 6 5 9 5 7 4 4 6 8 0 8 5 1 0 6 3 8 2 9 7 8 7 2
 3 4 0 4 2 5 5 3 1 9 1 4 8 9 3 6 1 7 0 2 1 2 7 6 5 9 5 7 4 4 6 8 0 8 5 1
 0 6 3 8 2 9 7 8 7 2 3 4 0 4 2 5 5 3 1 9 1 4 8 9 3 6 1 7 0 2 1 2 7 6 5 9
 5 7 4 4 6 8 0 8 5 1 0 6 3 8 2 9 7 8 7 2 3 4 0 4 2 5 5 3 1 9 1 4 8 9 3 6
 1 7 0 2 1 2 7 6 5 9 5 7 4 4 6 8 0 8 5 1 0 6 3 8 2 9 7 8 7 2 3 4 0 4 2 5
 5 3 1 9 1 4 8 9 3 6 1 7 0 2 1 2 7 6 5 9 5 7 4 4 6 8 0 8 5 1 0 6 3 8 2 9
 7 8 7 2 3 4 0 4 2 5 5 3 1 9 1 4 8 9 3 6 1 7 0 2 1 2 7 6 5 9 5 7 4 4 6 8
 0 8 5 1 0 6 3 8 2 9 7 8 7 2 3 4 0 4 2 5 5 3 1 9 1 4 8 9 3 6 1 7 0 2 1 2
 7 6 5 9 5 7 4 4 6 8 0 8 5 1 0 6 3 8 2 9 7 8 7 2 3 4 0 4 2 5 5 3 1 9 1 4
 8 9 3 6 1 7 0 2 1 2 7 6 5 9 5 7 4 4 6 8 0 8 5 1 0 6 3 8 2 9 7 8 7 2 3
```

Figure 1

$$\begin{array}{r} C \\ B \,\overline{)\, A} \\ B*C \\ \hline A-(B*C)*10 \end{array}$$

Here we divide the dividend A by the divisor B and get the quotient C. Following the procedure used in the example, we then multiply B times C; then subtract that product from A to get the remainder A–(B*C); then multiply the remainder by 10 to get the new dividend A–(B*C)*10. The process then begins to repeat itself. This repetition can continue for as many times as we want it to.

Now let's develop a program that implements the algorithm to simulate long division. The first thing to do is to define the variables.

```
10 LET A=7
20 LET B=3
30 LET N=25
```

Here again, A is the dividend, B is the divisor, and N is the number of times we want to repeat the division, i.e., the number of digits we want to the right of the decimal. Next, define the initial quotient and print that result.

```
40 LET C=INT(A/B)
50 PRINT C,".",
```

Now set up a For/Next loop to perform the process N number of times.

```
60 FOR I=1 TO N
```

Now implement the algorithm developed earlier.

```
70 LET R=A-(B*C)
80 LET A=R*10
90 LET C=INT(A/B)
100 PRINT C,
110 NEXT I
120 END
```

Line 70 computes the remainder. Line 80 multiplies the remainder by 10 and replaces the old dividend with the new dividend. Line 90 computes the new quotient and Line 100 prints it. The process continues N number of times.

The technique shown here in developing the long division algorithm may be used in developing much more complex ones. The method is simple. Define your variables. Define how they interact with each other by using an example. Define the intermediate results and logically make them produce the final result.

The program presented here makes an interesting demo. Lines 10, 20 and 30 should be changed to input statements so that the variables A, B and N can be made any desired values. Explain to your friends what the program does, plug in some values, and watch the result fly across the screen.

It should be emphasized that the values for A, B and N must be integers. Figure 1 shows the fully developed program and a run example. □

"I know you did a speedy installation — that's the problem!"

Unlimited Precision Division for Real Number Basic

Pat Fitzgerald

In computer division the result is expressed in one of two ways, either as a real number or a real number multiplied by a power of 10. The transition from one form to the other is dependent on the size of the computer word. However, by suitable programming, it is possible to divide two numbers and obtain all digits of the answer provided that neither the divisor nor the dividend are greater than the computer's power to express numbers without going into exponential notation. This article describes a simple method to do this using Basic.

To fix ideas, the program has been written for a PDP 11/10 minicomputer which can express numbers in the range 1 E − 7 to 1 E 7 without using exponential notation. The program has obvious modifications to suit other versions of Basic. After asking for the number to be divided and the divisor, the program checks to see if the numbers and initial division are within the required range, this is achieved in lines 25 to 30 through the subroutine in lines 200 to 215. Line 40 requests the number of decimal places and, as the program produces these numbers in groups of 7, the number input is divided by 7. Each successive division is tested in line 80 to see if the result is equal to zero. If it is the program prints the message in line 260.

Practically all versions of Basic suppress leading zeros, so if the division is to produce the correct result the program must supply these.

The number of each division after the first is checked to see how many digits it has by calculating the logarithm to base 10 of the number by the use of the function defined in line 10, the integer value of this is taken and one added to it. This gives the number of digits in the answer. If the answer is less than or equal to 6, the subroutine in line 130 is called up to print the suppressed zeros. After each division the program returns to line 15 for another run. The best printout on our machine is 7 groups of 7, any more and untidy printing results with groups being split between lines. For this reason the number N1 in line 60 is decremented by one each time a group is printed. When it reaches zero a new line is called and N1 set to 7 by the subroutine in line 240. The program is given in Listing 1 and examples of its output are given in Listing 2. □

Pat Fitzgerald, Winchmore Irrigation Research Station, Private Bag, Ashburton, New Zealand.

Listing 1

```
1 REM*****************************************************************************
2 REM PROGRAM FOR FAST UNLIMITED PRECISION DIVISION USING REAL NUMBERS.
3 REM
4 REM      ====      PAT FITZGERALD      ====      SEPTEMBER 1979
5 REM
6 REM*****************************************************************************
10 DEF FNL(U) = LOG(U)/LOG(10)
15 PRINT "TYPE NUMBER TO BE DIVIDED AND DIVISOR";
20 INPUT X,Y
25 LET Z = X: GOSUB 200
30 LET Z = Y: GOSUB 200
35 LET Z = X/Y: GOSUB 200
40 PRINT "NUMBER OF DECIMAL PLACES REQUIRED.";
45 INPUT N
50 LET N = N/7
55 LET Q = INT(X/Y)
60 LET N1=7
65 PRINT Q;".";
70 LET X = (X-Q*Y)*1E7
75 LET Q = INT(X/Y)
80 IF Q= 0 THEN GOTO 260
85 LET Q1 = INT(FNL(Q)) + 1
90 IF Q1 < = 6 THEN GOSUB 130
95 IF Q1 <  = 6 THEN GOTO 105
100 PRINT Q;
105 LET N1 = N1-1
110 IF N1 = 0 THEN GOSUB 240
115 LET N= N - 1
120 IF N > 0 THEN 70
125 PRINT:PRINT:PRINT:GOTO 15
130 REM SUBROUTINE TO PRINT SUPRESSED LEADING ZEROS.
135 IF Q1 = 1 THEN PRINT  "000000"Q;
140 IF Q1 = 2 THEN PRINT   "00000"Q;
145 IF Q1 = 3 THEN PRINT    "0000"Q;
150 IF Q1 = 4 THEN PRINT     "000"Q;
155 IF Q1 = 5 THEN PRINT      "00"Q;
160 IF Q1 = 6 THEN PRINT       "0"Q;
190 RETURN
200 REM SUBROUTINE TO TEST WHETHER NUMBERS ARE IN RANGE.
205 IF ABS(Z) > 1E7   THEN 220
210 IF ABS(Z) < 1E-7 THEN 220
215 RETURN
220 PRINT"AS RESULT OF DIVISION WILL INVOLVE FLOATING POINT NUMBERS"
225 PRINT"THE PROGRAM WILL NOT WORK PROPERLY."
230 PRINT:PRINT:PRINT
235 GOTO 15
240 PRINT
245 LET N1 = 7
250 RETURN
260 PRINT:PRINT:PRINT
265 PRINT "ALL REMAINING DIGITS ARE ZERO."
270 PRINT:PRINT:PRINT
275 GOTO 15
280 END
```

Listing 2

```
RUN
TYPE NUMBER TO BE DIVIDED AND DIVISOR?145,35
NUMBER OF DECIMAL PLACES REQUIRED.?500
 4 . 1428571  4285714  2857142  8571428  5714285  7142857  1428571
   4285714  2857142  8571428  5714285  7142857  1428571  4285714
   2857142  8571428  5714285  7142857  1428571  4285714  2857142
   8571428  5714285  7142857  1428571  4285714  2857142  8571428
   5714285  7142857  1428571  4285714  2857142  8571428  5714285
   7142857  1428571  4285714  2857142  8571428  5714285  7142857
   1428571  4285714  2857142  8571428  5714285  7142857  1428571
   4285714  2857142  8571428  5714285  7142857  1428571  4285714
   2857142  8571428  5714285  7142857  1428571  4285714  2857142
   8571428  5714285  7142857  1428571  4285714  2857142  8571428
   5714285  7142857
```

```
TYPE NUMBER TO BE DIVIDED AND DIVISOR?20,2
NUMBER OF DECIMAL PLACES REQUIRED.?49
 10 .

ALL REMAINING DIGITS ARE ZERO.

TYPE NUMBER TO BE DIVIDED AND DIVISOR?25,13
NUMBER OF DECIMAL PLACES REQUIRED.?98
 1 . 9230769  2307692  3076923 0 769230  7692307  6923076  9230769
 2307692  3076923 0 769230  7692307  6923076  9230769  2307692

TYPE NUMBER TO BE DIVIDED AND DIVISOR?123456789,12
AS RESULT OF DIVISION WILL INVOLVE FLOATING POINT NUMBERS
THE PROGRAM WILL NOT WORK PROPERLY.

TYPE NUMBER TO BE DIVIDED AND DIVISOR?.001,12
NUMBER OF DECIMAL PLACES REQUIRED.?49
 0 .0000 833  3333326  9765625

TYPE NUMBER TO BE DIVIDED AND DIVISOR?123,321
NUMBER OF DECIMAL PLACES REQUIRED.?49
 0 . 3831775  7009345  7912772  5856697  8193146  4174454  8286604

TYPE NUMBER TO BE DIVIDED AND DIVISOR?1,3227
NUMBER OF DECIMAL PLACES REQUIRED.?56
 0 .000 3098  8534242  3321970  8701580  4164859 00 24790  8273938
 6445615

TYPE NUMBER TO BE DIVIDED AND DIVISOR?1971,9791
NUMBER OF DECIMAL PLACES REQUIRED.?28
 0 . 2013073  2304156  8791747  5229292

TYPE NUMBER TO BE DIVIDED AND DIVISOR?1979,9791
NUMBER OF DECIMAL PLACES REQUIRED.?28
 0 . 2021244

ALL REMAINING DIGITS ARE ZERO.
```

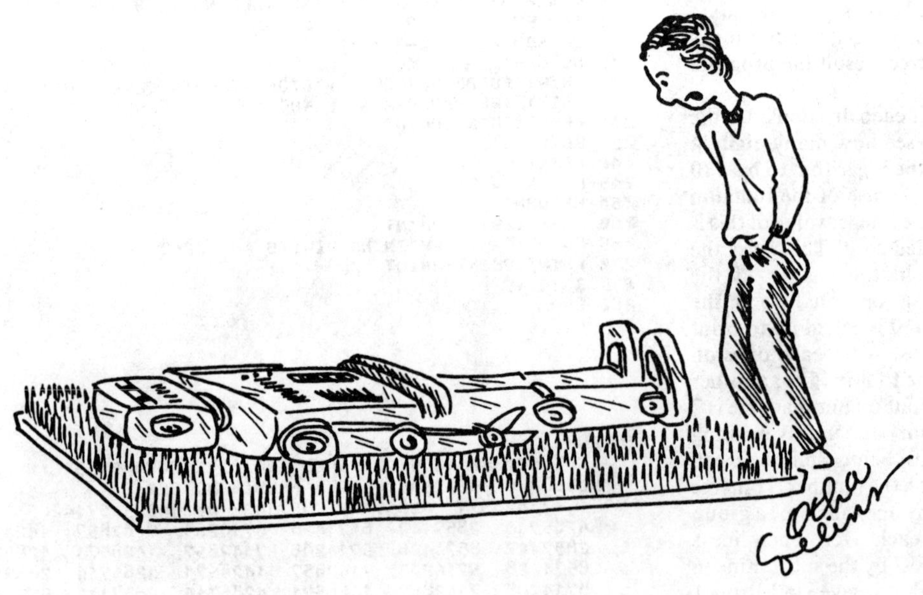

" — Oh sure — that's easy for you to do!"

Strings and Things: BASIC string manipulations

J. Tom Badgett

STRINGS & THINGS:
Basic String Manipulation

My computer should do all the work it can. Judging from the software available for most microcomputers and the operating systems many companies design, I may be in the minority. Nevertheless, I do everything I can to ensure that all my own software includes check routines, redundancies and hand holding; so, even months later, I can run a program without having to list it first or refer to a printed manual for instructions.

If I make a mistake (which I do more often than not), I expect my computer to be smarter than I am. It should be able to catch my mistakes, tell me what I did wrong, and prompt me in correcting the error. BASIC has some useful functions to help a programmer install these kind of routines in his software. A complete tutorial on data checking and hand holding is beyond the scope of this article, but I'd like to cover in some detail how I use BASIC's string functions to improve my software.

J. Tom Badgett, 400 Albemarle St., Bluefield, W. VA 24701.

I'm using Ohio Scientific Instrument's 9-digit BASIC, written by Microsoft. It uses fairly standard commands and functions (very similar to the Altair BASIC which was almost a standard in microcomputing for so long; the OSI BASIC also is similar to the Radio Shack Level-II BASIC). Refer to Table I for a list of the functions we'll be discussing. You can use this information to convert to your own BASIC.

Table I

Function	Description
ASC(X$)	Returns the ASCII value, in Decimal, of the first Character in the string.
CHR$(I)	Converts the ASCII value of a letter, number or symbol to the proper letter, number or symbol. A numerical value for I results in the character the decimal value of I represents.
LEFT$(X$,I)	Gives the leftmost I characters of X$. Begins reading X$ from the left and forms a new string with the length of I.
RIGHT$(X$,I)	Works the same as LEFT$, but reads from the rightmost side of the string, X$.
MID$(X$,I,J)	Forms a new string from X$ by reading X$ beginning at the character I spaces from the left of the string and continuing for J characters. If the value of J is omitted it will read to the end of the string beginning with the Ith character.
LEN(X$)	Gives the length of X$ in Bytes. If X$ has five characters then LEN(X$) = 5.
STR$(X)	Converts a number to a string. If X = 3 then STR$(X) forms a string of "3".
VAL(X$)	Opposite of STR$(X). Converts a string to a number. If X$ = "3" then VAL(X$) = 3.

A Definition Please

First, what is a string? It can be considered a statement, usually defined by quotation marks, that the computer takes literally. That is, the computer will accept a string statement as you define it, store it away, print it on command, etc., but performs no calculations on the string.

Consider the program line:

```
10 PRINT "THIS IS AN EXAMPLE OF A STRING."
```

The information enclosed in quotes in the above example is a string. If this string information is something you will be using fre-

String variables can be added; they can be stored and recalled; they can be printed; they can be compared.

quently in your program, you may define it further so programming will be easier:

```
10 A$="THIS IS AN EXAMPLE OF A STRING."
20 PRINT A$
```

The string statement is defined in line 10, using the variable "A" and the string identifier "$." Hereafter in the program, "A$" always will equal "THIS IS AN EXAMPLE OF A STRING." unless it is changed to something else. If the first example were changed to:

```
10 PRINT "5 + 3"
```

The computer will print exactly what is between the quotation marks (5 + 3) and not the computation of five plus three (8).

Except for this very important difference, string statements and string variables can be used in BASIC programs like any other variable. String variables can be added; they can be stored and recalled; they can be printed; they can be compared. This, then, gives the programmer a powerful tool for program development. Next, consider this example:

```
10 INPUT A
```

When this statement is encountered in a program everything comes to a halt while the computer waits for input from the keyboard or other input device. When a numerical variable such as "A" is asked for, any alphabetic characters will not be accepted. If letters are input in response to the INPUT A statement, BASIC will return something like REDO FROM START. After the number is entered you can compare it for size (too large or too small), or you can compare it to another known value, but that's about the only checking you can do with a numerical value.

I prefer to use a string INPUT, even if I'm looking ultimately for a numerical value. This increases program versatility';

```
10 INPUT A$
20 IF A$="HELP" THEN GOSUB 2000:GOTO 40
30 IF A$="MENU" THEN 1000:REM
      PROGRAM CHOICES
40 A=VAL(A$)
```

The numerical value the program is seeking is input in line 10 as A$. If I want to jump to another area of the program, an INPUT statement of this form gives me a chance. Suppose I'm into the program and realize it is the wrong one, or that I've forgotten how to enter the data. With an INPUT statement structured as a string I can build into the program a wide variety of options. In line 40 the string is converted to a number for further manipulation by the program.

I use the same strategy for invoices and purchase orders. When my invoice printing program asks for the quantity (a value the program uses to figure the extended price) the quantity is entered as a string. This allows me to answer the computer's prompt, "QUANTITY?," with "2 Boxes" or "3 cases" when items are priced and delivered by the box or case. When the string is converted to a number with the VAL statement, BASIC strips off the number (2 or 3 in the examples above) and uses that value in its computations. You might wish to add some additional coding, however, to check for an entry that has no numerical value. Such an entry would return a zero as the cost of an item (0 boxes times a unit price will give 0). Line 50 below will request additional input when a zero value is detected in the string:

```
40 INPUT A$
50 IF VAL(A$)=0 THEN PRINT
      "INVALID-REENTER:GOTO 40"
```

Again, by using string input you have the option of adding additional coding to allow a jump to another portion of the program. With the invoice printing program, suppose you discover you've made an improper entry only after typing RETURN. With the proper coding you could type REPEAT on the next input statement and the previous sequence would be erased and you would have a chance to enter the information again.

BASIC's ability to manipulate strings is truly amazing and helpful.

String Manipulations

Now, perhaps, you're beginning to see the value of using string input statements. But this is only the beginning. BASIC's ability to manipulate strings is truly amazing and helpful. One of the uses frequently suggested for a microcomputer is mailing list maintenance...just the kind of redundant, repetitive work a computer does well. With the proper use of BASIC's string functions you can enhance your mailing lists. If you want to use your mailing list to send personalized letters to a number of individuals you can write a program to search the data files for the names, print the heading of the letter, then use the string functions to construct a salutation from the full name in the address list. A portion of such a program is reproduced in Listing I.

This routine uses what may be one of the most powerful and useful of all the string functions, the MID$. The MID$ function usually takes the form: MID$(A$,I,J). This constructs a new string from A$ by looking at A$'s Ith character and reading for J characters. That's not as complicated as it sounds. Consider this string:

```
A$="TESTING"
  1234567
```

Listing I

```
50 N$="Mr. John Jones"
100 FOR J=LEN(N$) TO 1 STEP -1
110 N1$=MID$(N$,J,1)
120 IF N1$=" " THEN 450
130 NEXT J
450 IF MID$(N$,4,1)="." THEN N=5: GOTO 500
460 IF MID$(N$,4,1)="s" THEN N=5: GOTO 500
475 N=4
500 N2$=LEFT$(N$,N)+RIGHT$(N$,LEN(N$)-J)
510 PRINT "Dear ";N2$;":"
```

Line 50 introduces N$, a value which likely would come from a disk file or some other part of the program. At line 100 the dissection of the string begins. Line 100 sets up a loop which will execute for the number of characters in N$ in descending order. Line 110 establishes a second string N1$, which is the single character in N$ at location J. N1$ will equal "s" the first time through the loop, "e" the second time, etc. until the space before the last name is encountered. Then line 120 will cause a jump to line 450 where a check is made for a period. If the period occurs 4 characters over from the beginning of the string, then the first word is "Mrs." and line 500 must construct a string using the first five characters in the string ("Mrs." plus a space). A check is made in line 460 for the title "Miss". If the fourth character in the string is "s" then again five characters are stripped off the original string to form the new string to be used in the salutation or in the body of the letter ("Miss" plus a space). If there is no period then the first word must be "Mr." or "Ms." and the first part of the string need only be four characters long ("Mr." or "Ms." plus a space). N is set to 4 in line 475 before the new string is constructed with the LEFT$ and RIGHT$ functions in line 500. You can use many variations of this technique to search a string for certain characters and to build new strings from an original string. Line 510 shows how you might format the newly formed string for use in the salutation of the letter.

This string, A$, has seven characters as I've indicated with the numbers under the string, "TESTING." The numbers are not actually a part of A$. Now, if the following program is executed, B$ is found to be "TING."

```
10 A$="TESTING"
20 B$=MID$(A$,4,4)
30 PRINT B$
```

MID$(A$,4,4) started with the fourth character of A$, the second T in this case, and read for four characters to form the new string, B$. You could achieve the same results in this example by replacing Line 20 with; B$ = MID$(A$,4). When the value of J in the MID$ function is eliminated it reads to the end of the specified string.

This string function is useful in changing names in a mailing list as in Listing I. By applying a MID$ search to a name you can construct another string to use as the salutation. With the program in Listing I you can start with a string that is a full name, such as Mr. John Jones, and construct a new string such as Mr. Jones or John to use in the body of your letter.

Two more common string operators work similarly. The LEFT$ and RIGHT$ functions are used when you want to strip off a portion of a string beginning at the right or left side for a specified number of characters. In the previous program example, B$ could have been constructed to equal "TING" using the RIGHT$ function:

```
10 A$="TESTING"
20 B$=RIGHT$(A$,4)
30 PRINT B$
```

Again, B$ = "TING" because the RIGHT$ and LEFT$ functions start with the rightmost or leftmost character in the string and read for the number of characters specified. If B$ = LEFT$(A$,4) then B$ = "TEST." These can be used when you don't want the versatility of looking at a single character at a time, as is necessary with the routine in Listing I. RIGHT$ and LEFT$ work well, however, only if you want to compare the first or last character in a string or the first several or last several characters in a string. This is sometimes the case when the computer asks for a "YES" or "NO" answer. Rather than comparing A$ to "YES" and "NO," I use the following form:

```
10 INPUT "DO YOU WANT TO CONTINUE";A$
20 IF LEFT$(A$,1)="Y" THEN 1000
30 IF LEFT$(A$,1)<>"N" THEN PRINT
    "I'M SORRY,";:GOTO 10
40 PRINT "OK. THANKS.": END
```

With this form, you don't have to answer with a full "YES" or "NO." Also, I've included in the example a simple "check" routine to look for undefined input. Here the program is looking for either a "YES" or a "NO." If the operator accidentally enters something else, the program would end if you didn't have line 30.

From Numerical to Alpha and Back and Back Again

There are other string functions you may not use as frequently as MID$, LEFT$, and RIGHT$, but they, too, are useful. VAL(A$) returns a number value of A$. If A$ = "10" then VAL(A$) = 10. If A$ = "TEST" then VAL (A$) = 0 because words don't have numerical significance. In fact, the VAL(A$) function can be used anywhere the value A can be used. If A$ is a negative number, VAL(A$) will return a negative number. If, however, A$ = " + 22," VAL(A$) is simply 22, without the plus sign.

The inverse of the VAL(A$) function is the STR$(A) function. If A = 22 then STR$(A) returns a string which is "22." Consider the following program lines:

```
10 A=22
20 A$=STR$(A)
30 PRINT A$
```

At line 30 the program would print 22, which is the value of A$. Why would you ever want to convert a number to a string? I use this function when I want to search for a number or if I want to modify a number. Once the number is converted to a string, remember, you can apply the MID$ search to it and examine individual digits in a long number. This technique sometimes is helpful in program security or in generating a random number. Example:

```
10 A=23450
20 A$=STR$(A)
30 B=VAL(MID$(A$,2,2))
40 C$=LEFT$(A$,1)
50 OPEN "KEY"+C$,1
60 PN=VAL(RIGHT$(A$,LEN(A$)-1))
```

With this routine you can start with a number, A (returned from another part of the program), and create a random number, B, to use in computations somewhere else. Then you can construct C$ from A$ (line 40) and use this as an identifier for a data file. In line 50 the command OPEN "KEY" + C$,1 opens a data file with the name "KEY3." In this manner you can reduce the length of data files you have to search for information by catagorizing them according to the leading number returned in the value A. I have an inventory program, for example, that classifies inventory into 5 classes. The part numbers for these parts always start with a 1,2,3,4 or 5, depending on which class they fall in. Once that class number is stripped off, the actual part number becomes the number that is left (line 60 in the example above).

This sample program routine introduces other string concepts. First, in line 50, notice that the string "KEY" can be added to C$ (or vice versa) to form a new string. We could have added another program step at line 45: K$ = "KEY." Then line 50 would have become: 50 OPEN K$ + C$,1. Either way, the strings would be added. Suppose the program were set up for data file names with a dash before the number, then use a statement like:

```
50 OPEN "KEY-"+C$,1
```

or like this:

```
50 OPEN K$+"-"+C$,1
```

Either form would give a file name of "KEY-2." Notice the use of the VAL statement in line 30 coupled with a MID$ search. If you're careful about placement of parentheses you can "nest" such functions as much as you wish. Line 60 is an example of this nesting and also introduces another string function, LEN. Remember that we want to strip off the leading

number to use as a class number to determine which data file to open. That is done in line 40. Now the rest of the number must be isolated for use as the part number. By doing it like the example in line 60, you're not limited to a certain number of characters in the string. Starting at the right of the string, the computer searches all the characters in the string except the left most character and forms a new string, which is then converted to a number, PN, via the VAL function. LEN returns the length of the string, so a string that is a number of five digits has a length (LEN) of five. In this example, we don't want the first number in the string, so I've specified a search for the length of A$-1 (LEN(A$-1)). Line 60 in this example could have been written like this:

```
60 PN=VAL(MID$(A$,2))
```

The LEN function counts spaces as part of the length of the string, so that a string, "THIS IS A STRING," has a length of 16. Another reason for using string input in the inventory example above is the ability it provides of using alphabetic as well as numeric codes for the part numbers.

LEN returns the length of the string, so a string that is a number of five digits has a length (LEN) of five.

There are two more commonly used string functions we haven't discussed: CHR$ and ASC. You've probably seen CHR$ used in some programs. It is a covenient way of printing a character from a program variable and for sending control codes to a terminal or printer. It takes the form (CHR$(1), where 1 is the numerical representation of an ASC11 character in decimal. The character "A," for example, is 65 in decimal, so if the computer sees a program line like this:

```
10 PRINT CHR$(65)
```

the letter "A" will be printed.

You may have seen programs that use the CHR$ function with a table of variables to print a message, such as a program heading, without using conventional PRINT statements. Programmers sometimes use this technique when they want to make it difficult for anyone to strip off their copyright statement or other information at the head of the program run. Consider this program:

```
5 DIM L(34)
10 FOR J= 1 TO 34
20 READ L(J)
25 PRINT CHR$(L(J));
30 NEXT J
40 END
50 DATA 84,72,73,83,32,73,83,32,65,32
60 DATA 84,69,83,84,32,79,70,32,84,72
70 DATA 69,32,85,83,69,32,79,70,32,67
80 DATA 72,82,36,46
```

This program demonstrates how the CHR$ function works. The data statements contain the decimal ASCII values of letters and symbols. These values are read in a loop in line 20, then converted to their alphabetic or symbolic form with the CHR$ function. The message that results is: THIS IS A TEST OF THE USE OF CHR$. Many printers and video terminals use ASCII control codes to change certain operating parameters. In this case the CHR$ function can be used as part of a BASIC program to turn off and on these operating options.

The ASC string function can be considered the opposite of CHR$. It returns the ASCII value of the first letter in a string, so that if A$ = "TEST," ASC(A$) would be 84. Computers with graphics capabilities frequently use this function to print letters or symbols in specific positions on the screen. By breaking a string down into individual letters (using the MID$ function), you can POKE the ASCII value of the string away in a specific memory location, either a video memory or simply any portion of RAM. See Listing II and III for short programs you can have some fun with. They demonstrate both the ASC and CHR$ BASIC functions in a way that could be used as a code for computerists to communicate with each other.

Listing II

```
10 A$="TEST*"
20 X=1
30 A(X)=ASC(MID$(A$,X,1))
35 IF A(X)=42 THEN 45
40 X=X + 1: GOTO 30
45 I=1
50 FOR J= 8000 TO 8000+X
60 POKE J,A(I)
65 I=I + 1
70 NEXT J
100 DISK!"SA 50,1=8000/1
110 END
```

Line 30, Listing II, searches the string defined in 10 and converts each letter to its ASCII equivalent. Line 35 checks for the string limiter "*", and dumps out of the closed loop when it is found. Lines 50-70 POKE these values away in a free portion of memory. Line 100 puts the information away on disk. By prearranging with someone else which track of the disk the information is on and the length of A$, you could use the

Listing III

```
10 X=4:    REM  LENGTH OF A$
15 DISK!"CA 8000=50,1
20 FOR J= 0 TO X-1
30 PRINT CHR$(PEEK(8000 + J));
40 NEXT J
50 END
```

program in Listing III to recall the hidden information and print it out. This is not really a super secret code, but it'll help you understand the ASC and CHR$ functions. You can probably see the value of this kind of disk routine when writing software you hope to sell. Somewhere in the depths of your program stick away a routine similar to this one, using for A$ some command or instruction within the body of the program. You can key the disk to specific users this way or check for unauthorized copying of the program.

Making Comparisons

We've covered the usually available string functions in BASIC. Let's consider some of the finer points of their use. Remember at the beginning I said strings may be manipulated in much the same way as numerical variables. The operators =, <, >, < =, > =, and + may be used with strings as you would use them with numbers. There are some conventions to remember, however, that make strings behave slightly differently from numbers.

In using the "<"and">" comparators, remember that the length of the string is the determining factor. The string "A," thererore, is shorter than the string "A," since trailing spaces are considered in determining string length. If you are using strings in data statements and plan to compare them for length, you might wish to put each string inside quotes as part of the data statements, even though this is not normally necessary for the data statements to function properly. By enclosing data statements with strings in quotes, leading spaces will be retained and BASIC's string limiters won't operate on the string. Check your BASIC manual for details on string limiters. The Microsoft BASIC I'm using automatically limits a string when it sees a comma (,) or a colon (:). There are ways around this problem if you're not using a ROM BASIC. With the Ohio Scientific Instruments OS 65U disk operating system, for example, the following program lines will allow commas and colons to be included in strings:

```
10 POKE 2972,13
20 POKE 2976,13
```

This is useful when entering city and state information from the keyboard. If your program doesn't need to keep these two variables separate you'll have to construct a third string from the city and state, or store the data away as two separate strings. By POKEing off the string limiters you can enter such data, complete with commas, in a single string. You probably can find a similar POKE to turn off string limiters in your BASIC.

Disk Data Files

Pay special attention to handling of string information with disk data files. Generally, it is desireable to completely fill a data field even if the string to be stored there isn't as long as the field established for it. If your operating system doesn't handle this housekeeping chore automatically, add spaces to string data being written to disk files to erase previous information in that field and to ensure that all strings from the same field in different records are the same length. You'll need to do the same thing when searching a data field for information stored as string information. If your program asks the operator to INPUT a string to be used for comparison, the next line in the program must fill out the string to the length of the data field, otherwise the trailing spaces in the string stored on disk will denote a different string from the one being sought. Perhaps an example will make this idea clearer.

Suppose one of your data fields is 10 characters long. To write a string shorter than 10 characters to the disk in this field, you should add spaces to the string to make it 10 characters long before it is written to the disk:

```
10 A$="TEST"
20 IF LEN(A$)<10 THEN A$=A$+" ":GOTO 20
```

Then write the information to the proper field. By adding spaces to all strings written to the same field in different records, all strings in that field will be the same length. Do the same thing when searching for a string in that field:

```
10 INPUT "STRING FOR SEARCH";A$
20 IF LEN(A$)<10 THEN A$=A$ + " ": GOTO 20
```

When the computer begins checking the disk files for comparison, the string you have asked it to find is always the same length as the one in the field it is searching.

You might want to use some "special case" comparisons with the strings. Just be sure to try out these examples with your version of BASIC to be sure they function the same way as with the Microsoft version I'm using. I've already shown some examples using IF/THEN comparisons with strings. What about a program line like: IF A$ THEN 200? In this case the program will jump to line 200 only if A$ has something in it. That is, if A$ is anything but " " (space) a jump will occur. You can check for numerical value by using: IF VAL(A$) THEN 200. In this line, a jump will occur on any value of A$ except zero. You may use the AND function with VAL(A$) in a similar way: IF VAL(A$) AND VAL(B$) THEN 200. This statement can be useful if you want to determine whether a string has numerical value or contains only text. If either A$ or B$ is text, then the result of the AND operation is zero and no branch will occur. Indeed, a jump happens with this statement only when the value of the AND operation is something other than zero. This is another somewhat sneaky operation to help throw would-be program stealers off the track. It can be extremely difficult to determine exactly what the programmer was looking for in these statements.

Finally, you can use the NOT function in the same way: IF NOT VAL(A$) THEN 200. Any value of A$ greater than or equal to zero, less than or equal to -1 will cause a jump to 200. You can use a statement like this to look for a value between zero and -1, either returned from another part of the program or used as a trace element or security technique in your program.

Summary

BASIC handles alphabetic information well—better than some other high level languages. Sometimes, however, it is easy to forget this fact as we program from a numerical orientation. I have found that using strings in my programs makes them more versatile, easier to adapt and more user-oriented. As computers proliferate, the ability of software to help the user and make computer use easier will become more and more important. There's little excuse any more for programs that ask for user input in this form: "TYPE 1 FOR YES AND 0 FOR NO," which was common in the early days of microcomputing. Memory prices are low enough that users can afford to use strings and not worry about space conservation as much as before.

Become familiar with the string functions of your BASIC—then use them. Programming is more fun and the computer is easier to use.   □

Notes

Apple Strings

Rick Geiger

There are distinct advantages to developing application programs in a higher level language such as Applesoft, but all too frequently Applesoft is either too slow or just won't do what you want. When this has happened to me, I have either revised my program or written it in assembly language. While short assembly language subroutines can be used, the difficulties in passing parameters back and forth restricts their use, especially for string processing.

Recently I've been working on a program to manipulate data in text files that reside on the Apple mini-floppy. Since Applesoft does not include an INSTR function, there is no straightforward way to locate a substring within a larger string. I also wanted to be able to use an old block mode CRT so I could create and edit a screenful of data using the editing functions of the CRT and then transmit them to the Apple.

After the return, the Applesoft program can use the modified variable like any other string variable.

My first program attempt was written entirely in Applesoft but it was so slow that characters were lost in the data transmission, and the lengthy wait for a substring search was intolerable. What to do now? I considered writing the whole program in assembly language, but I needed to do a lot of disk I/O and one look at the read/write track/sector routines documented in the DOS 3.2 manual convinced me that I didn't want to write **that** much code.

Richard G. Geiger, 901 Holiday Ct., Concord, CA 94518.

So the only solution was to develop a convenient way of passing strings back and forth to some assembly language subroutines. That way I could program the serial interface code and the substring search code in assembler and still do the disk I/O in Applesoft.

The first method I tried was to dedicate an area of memory as a string buffer and use an Applesoft POKE loop to store the string and a PEEK loop to read it. The POKEing worked okay, but the PEEK loop appended each PEEKed character, and the string concatenation overhead was murder! I tried pre-allocating the string and storing the PEEKed character into the middle of it, but the whole process was still too slow. Finally, I decided to try using the Applesoft string pointers and just pass the address of the string to the assembly language subroutines. I have seen other programs that used similar techniques, but they almost always require that only one variable be used and that it be the first one defined in the program.

The subroutine listed below will work with any string variable and set up the parameters needed for an assembler subroutine. The routine is called GET ADDRESS and makes use of the fact that the name of the last referenced variable in Applesoft is stored in locations $81 and $82 (hex). Applesoft references each string by means of a runtime descriptor that includes all of the necessary information. The address where this table of string (and other variable type) descriptors begins is contained in loca-

tions $69 and $6A. The format of a string descriptor is:

```
byte    contents

+0 first character of the variable name
+1 second character of the variable name
+2 length of the string
+3 low address byte
+4 high address byte
+5 0
+6 0
```

The call to the GET ADDRESS subroutine is immediately preceded by a variable reference that places the variable name you want into $81 and $82. A convenient one that executes quickly is:

```
100 X$+X$:CALL<subroutine address>
```

Upon return from GET ADDRESS, a location in page zero contains the string address, another page zero location contains the address of the variable pointer, and the length of the string is stored in a defined location in the GET ADDRESS subroutine.

With this information, an assembly language subroutine can access the string by indirect indexing from the page zero location containing the string address. For example, to get the third character (assuming, of course, that the string had at least three characters) you might use the following instructions:

```
LDY #2          ;LOAD OFFSET TO THE THIRD CHARACTER
LDA (STARTL),Y  ;GET THE CHARACTER
```

where STARTL is the page zero location containing the address of the string.

The availability of the address of the pointer (in addition to the address of the string) means that you can pass a string from an assembly language subroutine to an Applesoft program. For instance, if you just received a string of characters from the serial I/O interface that you wanted to write to the disk, you would call GET ADDRESS just after referencing the string variable that you want to receive the string. Your assembly language subroutine could then use the following instructions to modify the variable pointer to map over the input buffer:

```
LDY #4        ;LOAD OFFSET TO HIGH ADDRESS BYTE OF POINTER
LDA #H,INBUF  ;LOAD HIGH BYTE OF BUFFER ADDRESS
STA (PTRL),Y  ;STORE HIGH ADDRESS BYTE INTO POINTER
DEY           ;DECREMENT OFFSET TO POINT TO LOW ADDRESS BYTE
LDA #L,INBUF  ;GET LOW BYTE OF BUFFER ADDRESS
STA (PTRL),Y  ;STORE LOW ADDRESS BYTE INTO POINTER
DEY           ;DECREMENT OFFSET TO POINT TO LENGTH BYTE
TXA           ;TRANSFER LENGTH FROM X-REG TO A-REG
STA (PTRL),Y  ;STORE LENGTH INTO POINTER
RTS           ;RETURN
```

After the return, the Applesoft program can use the modified variable like any other string variable. In the above example the buffer where the string was stored is INBUF, the page zero location holding the address of the variable descriptor is PTRL. The notation used to designate the high and low bytes of the buffer address is for the C. W. Moser 6502 assembler.

How The Subroutine Works

The call to GET ADDRESS should be directly preceded by a reference to the string variable you want. The instruction:

```
100 A$=A$ : CALL <address of GET
              ADDRESS subroutine>
```

works nicely and makes sure that Applesoft doesn't later clobber the string. The only other thing to be careful of is that the variable you use (A$ in the example above) must not be a null string. If the instruction given above as an example is the first reference to the string variable, the GET ADDRESS routine will fail.

The operand of the CALL instruction must be an address, *not* a variable containing the address. If the operand is a variable, that variable will become the last variable referenced and GET ADDRESS will not do what you intended. So, assemble the GET ADDRESS subroutine and CALL the specific address at which you locate it.

The subroutine starts by clearing the index into the variable descriptor space. This index is saved by the next instruction because in the code that follows, several parts of the descriptor need to be checked. If any of the checks fail it is convenient to branch to a single place·to increment the Y-REG to look at the next descriptor. Since Y-REG may have been changed during the checking and we don't want to add the logic that would be necessary to know which check failed, we simply restore the initial value from the save area.

Indirectly referencing the page zero location $69 (VTBL) we get the first character of the variable name from the variable descriptor. This is checked against the contents of $81 (CHAR1), the first character of the name of the last referenced variable. If they are not the same, we immediately go look at the next descriptor (GANXT).

If the first characters match, we bump the variable descriptor index (Y-REG) and compare the second characters. Again, if they don't match, we go look at the next descriptor. Even if the first two characters match, more checking is necessary to ensure that we have located the right variable. Real, integer and string variables may all have the same names but be distinct and separate variables. Although the documentation in the Applesoft manual would seem to indicate that you

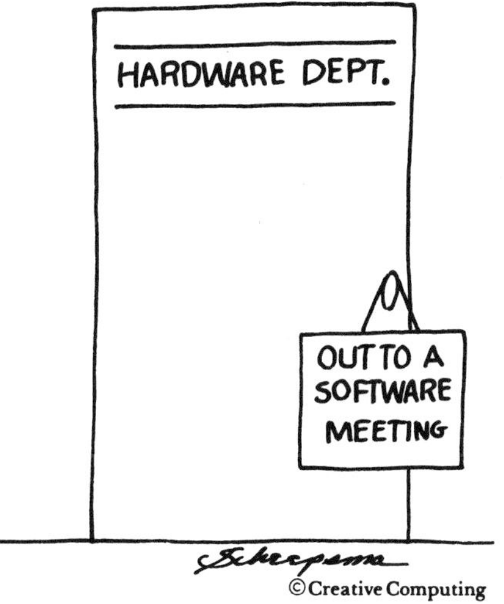

©Creative Computing

should be able to distinguish string descriptor from a real or integer descriptor by the sign bits on the name characters, I did not find this reliable.

Next, we bump the index (Y-reg) to look at the high address byte of the pointer. Since no strings can be located in page zero, this byte cannot be zero if this is a string descriptor. Then we bump the index to look at the last byte of the descriptor which *must* be zero.

The Applesoft manual seems to indicate that you should be able to distinguish a string descriptor from a real or integer descriptor by the sign bits on the name characters.

If any of the tests fail, we retrieve the initial index from the save area (YSAV) and increment it by 7 to look at the next descriptor. $FC is the final value possible in Y-REG before the index rolls over. So far I haven't found it necessary to add code to look at possible variable descriptors beyond this, but it may be required for some programs. We then transfer the incremented index into Y-REG and go through the checks for the new descriptor.

If all the checks are passed, we back up the index and extract the high address byte of the string data and store it in the page zero location STARTH. Then we back up again and store the low address byte in STARTL. Another decrement positions the index at the length byte which we extract and store in LENGTH.

In order to allow other assembler routines to modify the descriptor, we must save its address. First we compute the absolute address by adding the offset we ended up with in our search (which is in YSAV) and the starting address of the descriptor space in VTBL. We store the high and low bytes resulting from the addition in the page zero locations PTRL and PTRH.

If properly called, this routine should not fail, but just in case all the descriptors fail the checks by the time we get to an offset of $FC, we set up an error indication to tell the calling program that the search failed.

I hope these routines prove useful in augmenting your Applesoft programs with assembly language subroutines.   □

```
0250  ;
0260  ; PAGE ZERO ADRESSES
0270  ;
0280  STARTL       .DE 6          ;BASE ADDRESS FOR STRINGS
0290  STARTH       .DE 7
0300  VTBL         .DE $69        ;CONTAINS STARTING ADDR OF VRBL POINTERS
0310  CHR1         .DE 129        ;CONTAINS FIRST CHARACTER OF LAST USED VRBL NAME
0320  CHR2         .DE 130        ;SECOND CHR OF LAST USED VRBL NAME
0330  PTRL         .DE 8          ;CONTAINS ADDR OF POINTER FOR LAST USED@VRBL
0340  PTRH         .DE 9          ;CONTAINS ADDR OF POINTER FOR LAST USED VRBL
0350  ;
0360  ;GET ADDRESS
0370  ;
0380  GETADD       LDY #0         ;CLEAR TABLE INDEX
0390  GASRCH       STY YSAV       ;SAVE INDEX INTO VRBL TABLE
0400               LDA (VTBL),Y         ;GET FIRST CHR OF VRBL NAME FROM POINTER
0410               CMP CHR1       ;IS IT THE ONE?
0420               BNE GANXT      ;BR IF NO
0430               INY  ;BUMP INDEX TO LOOK AT NEXT CHR
0440               LDA (VTBL),Y         ;GET 2ND CHR FROM POINTER
0450               CMP CHR2       ;ARE 2ND CHRS THE SAME?
0460               BNE GANXT      ;BR IF NO
0470               INY  ;BUMP INDEX BY 3 TO LOOK AT HIGH
0480               INY  ;ADDR BYTE. IF THIS IS A STRING POINTER
0490               INY  ;BYTE MUST=0
0500               LDA (VTBL),Y         ;GET HIGH ADDR BYTE
0510               BEQ GANXT      ;BR IF 0=>N_T0Q STRVNG
0520               INY  ;BUMP INDEX BY02 TO LOOK QT LAST BYTE
0530               INY  ;WHICH MUST BE 0
0540               LDA (VTBL),Y         ;GET LAST BYTE
0550               BEQ GAGOT      ;IF 0 THEN WE HAVE IT
0560  GANXT        LDA YSAV       ;GET INDEX TO PREVIOUS POINTER
0570               CLC
0580               ADC #7         ;BUMP INDEX TO NEXT OINTER
0590               CMP #252       ;ARE WE DONE
0600               BEQ GAERR      ;BR IF AT END
0610               TAY  ;TRANSFER NEW INDEX TO X-REG
0620               BNE GASRCH     ;GO LOOK AT NEW POINTER
0630  GAGOT        DEY  ;BACK UP BY 2 TO GET HIGH ADDR
0640               DEY
0650               LDA (VTBL),Y         ;GET HIGH ADDR BYTE OF STRING
0660               STA STARTH     ;SAVE
0670               DEY  ;BACK UP TO LOW ADDR BYTE
0680               LDA (VTBL),Y         ;GET LOW ADDR
0690               STA STARTL     ;STORE IT
0700               DEY  ;BACK UP TO LENGTH
0710               LDA (VTBL),Y         ;GET LENGTH
0720               STA LENGTH     ;STORE IT
0730               CLC
0740               LDA VTBL       ;GET LOW BYTE OF POINTER TABLE ADDRESS
0750               ADC YSAV       ;ADD INDEX INTO THE TABLE
0760               STA PTRL       ;STORE LOW BYTE OF POINTER ADDR
0770               LDA VTBL+1     ;GET HIGH BYTE OF OINTER TABLE ADDR
0780               ADC #0         ;ADD CARRY IF THERE WAS ONE
0790               STA PTRH       ;STORE HIGH BYTE OF POINTER ADDR
0800               LDA #0         ;LOAD SUCCESSFUL RETURN CODE
0810               BEQ GARET      ;RETURN
0820  ;
0830  ;SINCE WE ARE SEARCHING THE VRBL TBL FOR THE LAST USED VRBL IT SHOULD NOT
0840  ;BE POSSIBLE FOR THIS ROUTINE TO FAIL, BUT JUST IN CASE HERE IS THE
0850  ;ERROR HANDLING CODE
0860  ;
0870  GAERR        LDA #255       ;LOAD NO FIND ERROR
0880  ;
0890  ; RETURN
0900  ;
0910  GARET        STA RTCODE     ;STORE RETURN CODE
0920               RTS
```

We're trying to get away from machine language, but this is awfully useful — especially for finding out what commands are valid in Adventure games without a lot of silly guesswork.

Programs written in Basic are fairly easy to read. You can locate characters which will be printed just by scanning the listing in search of PRINT statements. In a long machine-language program, the process is more complicated since printed characters are represented in memory as hex data. The following article describes a short, simple routine for finding and displaying ASCII characters in machine-language programs. The routine is written for the Apple II, but could easily be modified to use with any other 6502 system.

There are a number of uses for this type of routine. If you want to modify the printout of a program, this routine will simplify the process. It can help find the

If the program is stopped, the location of the last characters printed can easily be determined.

keywords that are recognized by an interactive program.

First, decide on a location to enter the routine. It can be placed either above or below the program you want to examine. In the following example, location 300 (hex) will be used. With the target program already in memory, enter the monitor's assembler by typing F666G. After entering the first line, remember to put one space before each of the remaining lines. If you aren't familiar with the monitor, don't worry; just type exactly what is listed below and ignore the strange things that

happen to each line after you hit RETURN.

Following the ! prompt, type

```
        300:LDA 800
(space)  JSR FDF0
         LDA #A0
         JSR FCA8
         INC 301
         BNE 300
         INC 302
         JMP 300
```

That's all there is to it. The routine is ready to run. *CAUTION:* this routine contains self-modifying code. Normally, this is a poor programming technique and should be avoided. In this case, there is a reason for self-modification.

To use the routine, hit RESET, then enter the command 300G. A lot of meaningless characters will flow by, but all the words contained as data will also appear. If, at any point, you wish to determine where the data on the screen is stored, just hit RESET. This will stop the dump. Then, enter 300L. The first line of the routine will now be

    LDA XXXX

where XXXX is the address of the next byte to be printed.

How does it work? First, the hex data from location $800 is put into the accumulator. (If the program starts higher up, you would replace 800 with the value of the first line of the program.) Then, the monitor's print routine (located at FDF0) is used to put the byte on the screen as an ASCII character. Since the routine is quite fast, a pause is needed before printing the next character. This is done by putting A0 into the accumulator and using the monitor's WAIT subroutine (located at FCA8). To increase or decrease the pause, just increase or decrease A0. Now for the self-modifying part.

The computer stores the command LDA 800 in three bytes at locations 300-

302. 300 contains the hex code for LDA. 301 contains the lo byte of the operand and 302 contains the hi byte. The command INC 301 increases the value of location 301 by one. In other words, the program changes the value of one of its own commands. At this point, LDA 800 has become LDA 801. The value of the lo byte will go from 0-FF. After this, it will become 0 again. The BNE (branch on result not equal to 0) will keep sending control back to 300 until the command becomes LDA 8FF. At this point the branch condition will become false, so the program will move on to the next line (after incrementing FF to 00). Now, the hi byte is incremented, and the command at 300 becomes LDA 900. From then on, the cycle continues, increasing the lo byte from 00-FF, then increasing the hi byte by one. If the program is stopped, the location of the last characters printed can easily be determined.

A lot of meaningless characters will flow by, but all the words contained as data will also appear.

Remember, if you use this routine at a different location, you will have to change the values of the last four lines. Change the BNE and JMP to the value of the start of the routine, and change the INC commands to one byte (for the first INC) and two bytes (for the second INC) beyond the start of the routine.

Due credit dept. Thanks go to Richard Corcoran for suggesting the use of the WAIT subroutine, and for providing numerous bits of helpful input.

Happy dumping.   □

Disk Power: How to Use It
Apple's new disk system

Carl Swenson

Using Apple's new disk system, and others, will be a lot easier if you have an understanding of reading and writing files. The techniques presented below should be helpful ... especially for Apple owners.

Carl Swenson, Seattle University, Seattle, WA 98112

Photo by Carolyn Kozo

A disk for your computer is enough to make your head spin. The luxury of loading and saving programs instead of fighting a cantankerous cassette player is next to heaven, and the real power of computing is now available through the disk.

A disk enables you to write and use programs which have large amounts of stored information; for example, mailing lists, business records, nutritional values of foods and inventories. These programs require disk file reading and writing from within a program. This article gives examples, hints and warnings on use of the disk commands for data file creation and maintenance. Unfortunately, disk file commands vary greatly from BASIC to BASIC. We're going to be discussing the format and techniques for the APPLE II DISK II.

The Data File

Since most of us speak BASIC, this new concept, data file manipulation, might best be thought of as an extension of the READ — DATA operation. A data file can be thought of as a huge data statement which can be read from or written to by the program. However, it doesn't need to be stored as part of the program in RAM like a DATA statement. The data file stays out on the disk and the disk becomes a secondary, slower than RAM, memory. Presto, you have a 100K machine; and with a quick change of a disk, you get a new 100K.

In BASIC, variables of the READ list are read in sequence from the DATA list. Each successive variable takes the next piece of data. Similarly, a disk file is first OPENed, which starts any read or write at the first piece of data in the file. When finished with a file it is always CLOSED. Each time the file is opened, the result is like a RESTORE in the DATA statement; data starts fresh from the first entry.

Sequential Files

The method of starting at the beginning of a file and reading and writing in order is called sequential processing. In many situations, sequential processing is adequate and desirable. For example, programs are stored sequentially. One need only know where the file begins and ends and there is no need to know where a given line is stored. There is little muss or fuss where each line of the program or piece of data is stored because it is in order.

An example of the use of a sequential data file would be to store transactions for a personal finances program. Each transaction might require six entries:

1) transaction number,
2) date,
3) vendor code,
4) check number if a bill is paid, or date due if a bill is received,
5) account affected,
6) amount of transaction.

The transactions would be stored one after the other. When the end of the month arrives and it is time to produce the balance sheet, the transactions are read back sequentially one at a time and processed. This type of file needs controls to signal the end of the file, as well as insure that a new transaction is written after the last transaction and

404

not over any previous transactions. A suitable way to accomplish this is to store the transaction number (with, say, exactly 3 digits) of the last transaction of the file as the first entry of the file. This first number can be read and then an IF-THEN statement can check each subsequent transaction to see if it is the last one. Reaching the last transaction signals the end of processing, or if you are entering transactions it signals that it is in the correct position to write the next new transaction. The use of a transaction number that does not change in length (here, exactly 3 digits) is necessary in some machines (like APPLE) because of the file structure. This will be a later topic.

Direct Access Files

The solution to the limitations of sequential file manipulation is to use direct accessing (sometimes called random access). As a practical example, suppose you have a mailing list with over 2,000 names and addresses and Cher keeps sending in address changes (or name changes). You don't want to use sequential files since this could mean the entire list would need to be read and rewritten to the disk. Sequential processing does not lend itself to single actions or simple changes.

If you knew where Cher's address is stored in memory, then no read is required, and you could write over her old address with a single write and be done. The question is: At what byte is her name and address? The answer is: In the beginning there was organization (Thank God!). You decide that each name, address and city/state/zip will be 30 characters long. Thus the three lines of 30 characters will take up 93 characters (90 characters plus 3 separators). Each new name is started on a 93 byte boundary. Now if you know Cher is 20th on the list, her name will start at 20 * 89 + 1 = 1801. Notice that you do pay a price for direct access; you waste space, since few names or addresses take up all 30 characters.

In many cases there is a combination of the two methods. For example, a file might be a set of financial accounts, and each financial account might be a record having its name, the twelve monthly balances and the year to date accumulation. Thus each account will be a record ready to be accessed directly, while inside the record the balances will be stored sequentially.

Now it's time for the real thing. What follows are examples using the Apple II Disk II.

DISK II Command Subroutines

The Disk II documentation for the READ and WRITE operations leaves many questions unanswered. There are no complete examples, and if you have seen or used other BASIC file commands you realize that APPLE'S are somewhat different.

In order to avoid the recognition of several new reserved words, APPLE'S disk commands have been put in a print statement that starts with a "CONTROL-D." This can make the disk commands sometimes cumbersome and hard to read. Program 1 in integer BASIC shows how subroutines can make a READ or WRITE to the disk more readable. Notice that line 10-70 can be the first part of any of your integer BASIC programs that include READ and WRITE to files. The subroutines 20-50 are placed first to speed up the program.

A write to a file requires four things to be done:

1) GOSUB OPEN. The file must be opened. This means the file name is assigned a buffer area in RAM and the file pointer is set to the first piece of data in the file.
2) GOSUB WRITE. This creates readiness for a file write, as opposed to a display write. That is, any subsequent PRINT statements before the next DOS command will write to the file and not appear on the screen. (To debug, it is possible to see on the screen the values that are being written to the disk by turning on the monitor.)
3) PRINT. The value is written to the file via the buffer. Remember, the write DOS command traps all print statements until any other DOS statement is executed.
4) GOSUB CLOSE. The file is closed, meaning that all the data in the buffer has been written to disk and that the buffer area is now free to be reassigned. The write to file is turned off.

In Program 1, a simple write is accomplished in lines 200-230. Similarly, a READ is shown in lines 300-330. Since F$ was defined in line 210, it could have been deleted from line 310 as long as no changes were made to F$ before 310.

The disk commands and input/output of the disk file can be monitored (made to appear on the screen) by using the MON and NOMON commands which are explained in the Disk II documentation. Having the monitor on is a good way to see the disk file manipulations in the learning or debugging states. A perfected program usually has at its beginning the NOMON command to turn off the monitor.

The following two notes refer to integer BASIC.

Note #1: You may wonder why Statement 220 does not use PRINT X1, X2, X$. It is an unfortunate thorn in the DOS which requires a separate PRINT statement for each entry, since otherwise a data separator is not printed on the file between the data entries. For example, PRINT 1,2 will put "12" on file as a single entry. In other words, PRINT A,B will not have the same effect as PRINT A: PRINT B if you are in the disk write mode. However, the same is not true for a disk read; INPUT A,B is identical to INPUT A: INPUT B.

Note #2: Keeping D$ ="" (see 70) alone on a separate line is a safety measure. The CONTROL-D does not appear in the screen (but it is there if you put it there), and if the line were copied over using the Apple editing wizardry the CONTROL-D would be lost.

File Structure

There are some limitations to sequential file processing. Consider the case where you find a transaction for $119.58 to be incorrect — it should be $9.58. This requires that all subsequent transactions of the file will have to be moved because the $9.58 takes up less space.

To understand this, let's see precisely how files are set up byte by byte. In Apple files, numbers are stored as a string; 119.58 would take up six bytes, and 9.58 would take up only four. E-notation numbers are real hogs, and at worst they might take up 15 bytes. Strings are stored a character per byte.

```
>LIST

   0 REM       ----------PROGRAM 1--------------
   1 REM
   2 REM    WRITTEN IN INTEGER BASIC
   3 REM
   5 REM    READ/WRITE FILE EXAMPLE
   6 REM
  10 GOTO 60
  20 PRINT D$; "OPEN"; F$:  RETURN
  30 PRINT D$; "READ"; F$:  RETURN
  40 PRINT D$; "WRITE"; F$:  RETURN
  50 PRINT D$; "CLOSE"; F$:  RETURN
  60 OPEN=20:READ=30:WRITE=40:CLOSE=50
  70 DIM D$(1):D$=""
  80 REM
  90 REM
 100 DIM X$(7),A$(7),F$(5)
 110 X1=5:X2=10:X$="EXAMPLE"
 180 REM
 190 REM
 200 REM   SEQUENTIAL WRITE EXAMPLE
 210 F$="FILE1": GOSUB OPEN
 220 GOSUB WRITE: PRINT X1: PRINT X2: PRINT X$
 230 GOSUB CLOSE
 280 REM
 290 REM
 300 REM    SEQUENTIAL  READ  EXAMPLE
 310 F$="FILE1": GOSUB OPEN
 320 GOSUB READ: INPUT A1, A2, A$
 330 GOSUB CLOSE
 380 REM
 390 REM
 400 PRINT A1, A2, A$
 410 END
```

As any number or string is written to the disk, a 1 byte mark is placed to separate it from other numbers or strings. Thus, a number or string takes up its length plus one. See Figure 1 for an illustration of a file.

If you want to write the 9.58 value in the file where the 119.58 is now located, you would need to use the B parameter provided in the disk READ format. After the file has been opened, the command below will accomplish the write, to the file names TF.

PRINT D$; "WRITE TF, B29"

However, the file now has an extra number (8 at byte 35) as shown in Figure 2. This throws the sequence totally out of whack since a sequential read would incorrectly read 8 to be the transaction number of the second transaction. Now you can see why the subsequent transactions would all need to be moved back two bytes.

Since you can move anywhere with the B parameter, the R and L might seem superfluous. However, using R and L is usually more convenient. Let's use the mailing list as an example. The R would be the record number (a name and address), the L would be the length of each entire record, and the B is used to move inside a record. The length of a record in this case is 93. The direct access operates by using the current L (given in OPEN), the current R and B (given in WRITE or READ), and moves to the L * R + B + 1th byte. This is an absolute count from the beginning of the file.

Program 2 shows a simplistic program to create and change a data file, using direct access manipulations. In particular it solves the problem of quickly and easily changing Cher's name or address. Since the data is all character string, the program could have been written in integer BASIC. However, to exhibit the modifications necessary for programs with floating point data, program 2 is written in APPLESOFT II.

If a listing is not requested, program 2 can be used to fill a data file. If a listing is requested of a record which has not been previously written to, an error will occur. This program is not set up to protect records, so that you can use it to input records longer than 90 bytes and then use the list to see how it clobbered the next record. It is also not intended to be an actual application program, since it has no search or sort capabilities. However, by modifying and exercising it in various ways, you will be able to discover the ins and outs of file transactions.

Note #3: While APPLESOFT II is an extended language, it does not allow a variable for a line number in a GOSUB statement even though this is permissible in integer BASIC. While this makes

Figure 1

```
                    Transaction 1
          ┌──────────────────────────────────────┐
108■101■092778■SHELL■156■450■119.58■102■...
  ↑    ↑      ↑
 separator
```

Figure 2

```
                    Transaction 1
          ┌──────────────────────────────────────┐
108■101■092778■SHELL■156■450■9.58■8■102■...
                                   ↑
                                 Byte 35
```

```
]LIST
0  REM ------PROGRAM 2------------
1 :
2  REM  WRITTEN IN APPLESOFT II
3 :
5  REM  DIRECT ACCESS FILE EXAMPLE
6 :
10  GOTO 60
20  PRINT D$; "OPEN"; F$; ",L"; L: RETURN
30  PRINT D$; "READ"; F$; ",R"; R; ",B"; B: RETURN
40  PRINT D$; "WRITE"; F$; ",R"; R; ",B"; B: RETURN
50  PRINT D$; "CLOSE"; F$: RETURN
60 D$ =  CHR$ (4)
80  DIM A$(2):L = 93
90  INPUT "FILE NAME="; F$
100  INPUT "RECORD NUMBER="; R
110  INPUT "DO YOU WANT A LISTING (Y/N)?"; T$
120  IF T$ < > "Y" THEN 180
125  REM  --------PRINT RECORD--------------
130  GOSUB 20: REM  OPEN
140  FOR J = 0 TO 2
150  :::B = J * 31: GOSUB 30: REM  READ
155  :: INPUT A$(J)
160  NEXT
165  GOSUB 50: REM  CLOSE
170  PRINT : PRINT A$(0): PRINT A$(1): PRINT A$(2): PRINT
175  REM  -------INPUT OR CHANGE ENTRIES-------
180  PRINT "HIT RETURN WHEN NO CHANGE REQUIRED"
190  INPUT "NEW NAME= "; A$(0)
200  INPUT "NEW STREET ADDRESS="; A$(1)
210  INPUT "NEW CITY/STATE/ZIP="; A$(2)
215  GOSUB 20:: REM  OPEN
220  FOR J = 0 TO 2
230  :: IF  LEN (A$(J)) = 0 THEN 250
240  :::B = J * 31: GOSUB 40: REM   WRITE
245  :: PRINT A$(J)
250  NEXT
260  GOSUB 50: REM CLOSE
265  REM -------EXIT OR NEXT RECORD----------
270  PRINT : INPUT "(-1 TO END) NEXT RECORD="; R
280  IF R > = 0 THEN 110
290  END
```

Figure 3

```
>LIST                              >LIST
  10 REM    EXAMPLE A               10 REM    EXAMPLE B
  20 DIM D$(1),A(5):D$=""           20 DIM D$(1),A(5):D$=""
  30 PRINT D$; "OPEN F"             30 PRINT D$; "OPEN F"
  40 FOR I=1 TO 5                   40 FOR I=1 TO 5
  50 PRINT D$; "READ F"             50 PRINT D$; "READ F, B0"
  60 INPUT A(I)                     60 INPUT A(I)
  70 PRINT A(I)                     70 PRINT A(I)
  80 NEXT I                         80 NEXT I
  90 PRINT D$; "CLOSE F"            90 PRINT D$; "CLOSE F"
 100 END                          100 END
```

the subroutine technique a little cumbersome, it is suggested that the GOSUB still be used but be followed by a remark to make it clear.

Note #4: In APPLESOFT II the print A,B not being equal to PRINT A: PRINT B is still with us. An exception is if A is long enough to cause PRINT A,B to print B on a new line of the screen then a separator is written. It is easiest to forget the exception and consistently use PRINT A: PRINT B.

Note #5: This program could trigger one of the early DOS bugs. If it will not execute past line 250, see your dealer or recent publications for the DOS patch.

Note #6: On the positive side, APPLESOFT II allows the comfort of seeing the previously hidden CONTROL-D. (See line 70.) A further welcome feature is the repeated colon acceptability as a means of indenting. All structured programmers please stand, applaud and whistle!

Note #7: If you want to input values to be written to the disk, the INPUT statement must be before the GOSUB WRITE, or else the input prompt (question mark) will be written to file and screw up the whole operation. Notice how the input was done prior to the write in Program 2. No error will result from using a PRINT after a GOSUB READ and before the INPUT statement.

Note #8: There is a record 0 which could have been used by the first record. However, having record 5 (for example) in position number 4 is awkward. Secondly, and more important, record 0 is a prime location to store maintenance information, such as the number of records in the file. A common and useful technique in many business programs is to store a copy of the last record of the file in this record 0 location.

Note #9: If a record has never had some of its bytes written upon these bytes will be end-of-file marks. This occurs even though there is more data down the road in another record.

Note #10: Files are dynamic so you don't need to worry about opening a small file and then later, as it grows, having it write over another file. Only when the disk is full does a problem occur. This is rare but could sneak up on you, since you might not know how big a file really is. The CATALOG command does list all files with a file size number, but it does not work properly, and the Gospel According to Apple is to simply ignore the file size number.

Note #11: Should you need a relative move (like move 10 more each time), the POSITION command will accomplish this and can be added as a subroutine just like the other commands have subroutines.

Note #12: Sequential file processing can take place only when there is no R and/or B parameter in the READ or WRITE. For example, in Figure 3 (Example A) the first five values in the file will be read. However, in Example B the same first value in the file will be repeatedly read for all five inputs. Thus if your program uses both sequential and direct access it is not possible to use the direct access set up and put R = 0 and b = 0 to create the sequential mode. The sequential read and write can have and use their own individual subroutines.

With the direct and sequential access to large data bases, you are now able to do some heavy data processing. Let the Disk II allow you to take a big bite of data, and remember the slogan: "Old Apple users never die, they just lose their byte." ∎

"What kind of computer error?"

Executive Privilege

Leland D. Young

Have you ever felt a little uneasy about using the Exec text file feature that is available on your Apple DOS 3.2 to increase the flexibility of your programs? Maybe my experience can help.

The Problem

My experimenting with Exec was prompted by a problem I faced with a program I was writing. This program, Flog, maintained golf handicap data in files which were stored on the same disk as the program. Good practice to protect such data files required that they be placed on a separate backup disk. In addition to this requirement, I wanted the backup disk to have the full capabilities of the original disk. That is, the backup disk would contain not only the data files, but also Flog and any other programs necessary to make the backup disk perform exactly as the original. Not much of a problem for a dual disk drive system, but more complicated with only one drive available, which was my case.

The original programs presented here serve as good examples for learning some of the inner-workings of a 48K Apple II. As written originally, the sequence of programs would run as follows: The main program (Flog) would update and maintain data files on golf players and place these files on the original disk. When the use of Flog ended, it would automatically load backup, take the data files from the original disk, load them into memory and, before pausing, display a message on the TVT such as "REMOVE ORIGINAL DISK - INSERT BACKUP DISK." When the backup disk was in the drive unit the data files in memory would then be transferred to the backup disk. After the transfer operation was completed, Backup then created an Exec file called Chek. At this point the backup disk would still be in the disk drive. After the creation of Chek, it was automatically run. This was done by the last statement shown in Listing 1.

Leland D. Young, 12603 Forest Hills Dr., Tampa, FL 33612.

During the execution of Chek, each line would be evaluated by the computer and the proper action taken. Backup, as shown in Listing 1, is not the complete program with the capability of transferring data files. Instead, the Backup listing only shows the portion containing the Exec file Chek.

The purpose of Chek is to determine if Flog and Backup are on the backup disk (which is now in the drive unit). If, for example, Flog is not on the backup disk, then Chek proceeds to display the message "REMOVE BACKUP DISK - INSERT ORIGINAL" and wait for the "Return" key to be hit. When the original disk is in place and the "Return" is hit, Flog is loaded into memory from the original disk. When loading is complete, the message "REMOVE ORIGINAL DISK - INSERT BACKUP" is displayed and the computer again waits for a "Return." When the backup disk is in place and the "Return" key is hit, Chek then determines if Backup is on the backup disk. If it is not, then the same steps as explained above for Flog are taken. When all CHEK statements are evaluated the message "BACKUP OPERATION COMPLETED - END PROGRAM" is displayed on the TVT unless the sequence of inserting the original and backup disks is altered. If this occurs, the statement "END PROGRAM - INVALID SEQUENCE" is displayed instead and all operations cease.

This article will describe how Chek operates. The logic of Chek in the use of IF statements and the flow of the statements will not be covered. The use of Call statements, memory locations and subroutines and how they can be used with Exec will be discussed.

The EXEC File

With the Exec command you can create a sequential text file that may contain commands or program lines (numbered or unnumbered) including Basic statements. These statements, when executed, control the computer as if the same information were typed on the keyboard. Exec does not delete a program that is already in memory. These features enable Chek to function.

CHEK Preliminaries

When writing an Exec file, a format of sorts should be followed. In its most fundamental form, the format requires: 1) the definition of the Control-D character, 2) the use of the OPEN and WRITE statements preceding the file, 3) the contents of the file and 4) the use of the CLOSE statement.

The Control-D character is defined so that the DOS commands OPEN, WRITE and CLOSE can be executed by the program.

I noticed a peculiarity about the Control-D during my trials with Chek. The DOS version 3.2 Instruction and Reference Manual, in discussing its example Exec file DOIT on page 75, states that the commands which are PRINTed into the file, for later EXECing, are not preceded by a Control-D. I found that this can be done if a line contains only the DOS command and nothing else. However, if anything precedes a DOS command, the Control-D character becomes necessary. See Listing 1, line 20080, for an example of where the Control-D is needed. Also, I found it best not to have any statements following a DOS command on the same line. When this is done, the statements following the DOS command on the line are ignored.

Notice in line 20010 of Listing 1 the definition of Q$ where CHR$(32) is the ASCII code for a quotation mark. Review Listing 1 to see how it is used in Chek to prepare strings for printing, as in lines 20140, 20150, 20170, etc.

Checking for a Program

When Chek is executed, it immediately determines if the program Flog is stored

```
10   REM BACKUP
20   REM L.D.YOUNG  APPLESOFT
40 C1$ = "('RETURN' TO CONTINUE)"

60 DD$ =  CHR$ (4): REM CNTRL-D
20000   REM
20010 Q$ =  CHR$ (34):L = 0:Y = 0
20020   PRINT DD$"BLOAD MESSG"
20030   PRINT DD$"MON C,I,O"
20040   PRINT DD$"OPEN CHEK"
20050   PRINT DD$"DELETE CHEK"
20060   PRINT DD$"OPEN CHEK"
20070   PRINT DD$"WRITE CHEK"
20080   PRINT "POKE6,0:PRINTDD$"Q$
     "LOCK FLOG"Q$
20090   PRINT "X=PEEK(43619):IFX<>
     7THENL=1"
20100   PRINT "IFL=1THENCALL778:VT
     AB20:PRINTTAB(9)C1$:CALL768"
20110   PRINT "IFL=1THENPOKE6,1:CA
     LL832"
20120   PRINT "DD$=CHR$(4)"
20130   PRINT "L=PEEK(6):IFL=1THEN
     Y=PEEK(43619)"
20140   PRINT "IFL=1ANDY=1THENPRIN
     TDD$"Q$"SAVE FLOG"Q$
20150   PRINT "IFL=1ANDY=1THENPRIN
     TDD$"Q$"LOCK FLOG"Q$
20160   PRINT "IFL=1ANDY=1THENL=0:
     POKE6,0:NEW"
20170   PRINT "IFY=1THENPRINTDD$"Q
     $"LOCK BACKUP"Q$
20180   PRINT "IFY=1THENX=PEEK(436
     19)"
20190   PRINT "IFY=1ANDX<>7THENL=1
     "
20200   PRINT "IFY=1ANDL=1THENCALL
     778:VTAB15:PRINTTAB(9)C1$:CA
     LL768"
20210   PRINT "IFY=1ANDL=1THENPOKE
     6,2:CALL832"
20220   PRINT "L=PEEK(6):IFL=2THEN
     Y=PEEK(43619):L=1"
20230   PRINT "IFY=1ANDL=1THENCALL
     783:VTAB20:PRINTTAB(9)C1$:CA
     LL768"
20240   PRINT "IFY=1ANDL=1THENPRIN
     TDD$"Q$"SAVE BACKUP"Q$
20250   PRINT "IFY=1ANDL=1THENPRIN
     TDD$"Q$"LOCK BACKUP"Q$
20260   PRINT "IFY=1ANDL=1THENNEW"
20270   PRINT "IFY=0ORY=1THENCALL-
     198:HOME:VTAB9:PRINTTAB(10)"
     Q$"BACKUP OPERATION COMPLETE
     "Q$":PRINT:PRINTTAB(16)"Q$"E
     ND PROGRAM"Q$
20280   PRINT "IFY<>0ANDY<>1THENHO
     ME:CALL-198:VTAB9:PRINT"Q$"E
     ND PROGRAM - INVALID SEQUENC
     E"Q$
20290   PRINT DD$"CLOSE CHEK"
20300   PRINT DD$"EXEC CHEK"
```

Listing 1.

on the backup disk. This check can be done by using other statements (RENAME, for example) but I chose to use the LOCK statement. When Flog is placed on a disk it is also LOCKed, so the logic for the test is that if Flog can't be found it cannot be locked, and the error statement FILE NOT FOUND will be printed by DOS. Of course, if the file is on the backup disk, LOCK will ensure the

program is locked. Conveniently, if Flog is locked already, using LOCK will not cause an error. Looking at line 20090 in Listing 1, if X ≠ 7 (see Table 1) then Flog is assumed not to be on the disk.

	MEMORY LOCATION	
	$AA63	43619
ERROR/STATUS	(Hex)	(Dec)
LOAD	01	1
CATALOG	06	6
LOCK	07	7
LANGUAGE NOT AVAILABLE	18	24
FILE NOT FOUND	4B	75
FILE LOCKED	77	119
FILE TYPE MISMATCH	A9	169

Table 1. Codes and memory location for 48K system.

Making a Pause

Next I had to find out how to make Chek pause until the operator was ready for the computer to continue. If the check for Flog showed it was not on the backup disk, the program would have to wait for the backup disk to be removed and original disk inserted in the drive unit, displaying the proper instructions to the operator.

The pause subroutine is shown in Listing 2 at hexadecimal (denoted by $ preceding the number) locations $0300-$0309. This subroutine is called by the statement CALL 768, where 768 is the decimal equivalent of $0300. The ASCII characters used in the assembly language subroutines were taken from the ASCII Screen Character Set, Table 7 of the Apple Reference Manual. From this Set, $A0 represents a "space", and $8D represents a "Return."

The pause subroutine functions by putting a "space" character ($A0) into the accumulator then jumping to location $FD1B which is the start of a subroutine that looks for an input from the keyboard. When a key is pressed the subroutine then returns to $0305 with the accumulator containing the character entered at the keyboard. The contents of the accumulator is then compared with a "Return" character ($8D). If the two are not equal the subroutine moves to $0300 and repeats the procedure again. If the key pressed is a "Return" the subroutine then returns to the main program. This subroutine would function acceptably if $A0 were not placed in the accumulator initially, but a character may be displayed on the TVT if the "Return" is not the first key hit.

Displaying a Message

When the pause subroutine is in operation, there should also be a message displayed on the TVT directing the operator to perform some task. In our case, if Flog is not on the backup disk Chek must pause

for a response from the operator afer displaying a message. The initial message is "REMOVE BACKUP DISK—INSERT ORIGINAL." Also the statement "('RETURN' TO CONTINUE)" is displayed at the bottom of the TVT. Referring to Listing 1, this sequence of events is handled by line 20100 where CALL 778 ($030A) causes the initial disk message to be displayed. CALL 768 causes the pause subroutine to operate until a "Return" is entered at the keyboard.

Detecting an Error

When an Exec file does not execute statements using line numbers, error detecting is different from that normally used in Basic programs. Chek is such a program. Although line numbers are used in Backup (which creates Chek), the execution of Chek is done in the order of the statements contained in the file and not as determined by line numbers. Line numbers, however, can be given to the statements easily. For examples of both possibilities see lines 20120 and 20130 of Listing 1.

When Chek is executed, only the information contained within the quotation marks will be executed. But line numbers could be assigned to the statements if desired as in the following example:

20120 PRINT"150 DD$ = CHR$(4)"
20130 PRINT"160 L=PEEK(6):IF L=1
    THEN Y=PEEK(43619)"

The problem with assigning line numbers is that these lines become a part of any program that may be in memory. That is, if Flog is in memory, and Chek is created with line numbers, as in the above example, these line numbers belonging to Chek are treated by the computer as part of Flog. So if Flog is then SAVEd, the saved version of Flog will contain not only the Flog statements but also the numbered Chek statements. Flog is then altered and if run could function improperly. For this reason Chek was developed without using line numbers.

The absence of line numbers in Chek solved one problem but created another. That is, how can errors be detected by Chek? If the ONERR statement could be used, a code would be placed in decimal location 222 ($DE) when an error occurred. But ONERR can't be used as there are no line numbers to reference. Another location then must be found.

After searching magazine articles, reviewing the DOS subroutines and experimenting, I was able to find a location that consistently contains a code associated with a particular status or error. This location (in a 48K system) is decimal 43619 ($AA63). Codes placed in this location are listed in Table 1. I have not verified this, but my guess is that in a

```
0300-    A9. AO       LDA    #$AO      *PUT A 'SPACE' IN ACCUMULATOR
0302-    20 1B FD     JSR    $FD1B     *GET CHAR. FROM KEYBOARD
0305-    C9 8D        CMP    #$8D      *SEE IF IT'S A 'RETURN'
0307-    D0 F7        BNE    $0300     *IT ISN'T.  TRY AGAIN
0309-    60           RTS              *IT IS.  GOTO CALLING ROUTINE
030A-    A2 00        LDX    #$00      *SET UP MESSAGE "REMOVE BACKUP DISK - INSERT ORIGINAL "
030C-    4C 11 03     JMP    $0311
030F-    A2 01        LDX    #$01      *SET UP MESSAGE "REMOVE ORIGINAL DISK - INSERT BACKUP"
0311-    20 9D 03     JSR    $039D     *HOME, CLEAR & SET VERT.TAB TO 8
0314-    20 3A FF     JSR    $FF3A     *SOUND 'BELL'
0317-    18           CLC              *CLEAR CARRY
0318-    8A           TXA              *PUT CONTENTS X-REG.IN ACCUM.
0319-    A2 00        LDX    #$00      *ZERO X-REG.FOR 1ST LOCATION OF MESSAGE
031B-    C9 01        CMP    #$01      *COMPARE ACCUM W/ 1
031D-    F0 0E        BEQ    $032D     *IF ACCUM=1 THEN BRANCH TO $032D
031F-    BD A6 03     LDA    $03A6,X   *LOAD ACCUM. W/ INDEXED MEMORY CONTENT
0322-    C9 DB        CMP    #$DB      *SEE IF CHAR. IS A [
0324-    F0 15        BEQ    $033B     *IT IS.  BRANCH TO $033B
0326-    20 ED FD     JSR    $FDED     *IT ISN'T.  PRINT IT
0329-    E8           INX              *INCREMENT X-REG. FOR NEXT INDEXED CHAR.
032A-    4C 1F 03     JMP    $031F     *GOTO $031F TO CONTIN.MESSAGE
032D-    BD CB 03     LDA    $03CB,X   *LOAD ACCUM. W/ INDEXED MEMORY CONTENT
0330-    C9 DB        CMP    #$DB      *SEE IF CHAR. IS A [
0332-    F0 07        BEQ    $033B     *IT IS.  BRANCH TO $033B
0334-    20 ED FD     JSR    $FDED     *IT ISN'T.  PRINT IT
0337-    E8           INX
0338-    4C 2D 03     JMP    $032D
033B-    A9 00        LDA    #$00      *SET UP.CURSOR TO LEFT SIDE OF SCREEN
033D-    85 24        STA    $24       *PUT 0 IN LOCATION $24 (CURSOR HORIZ.POSITION)
033F-    60           RTS              *RETURN TO CALLING ROUTINE
0340-    AD 58 9D     LDA    $9D58     *STORE CONTENTS OF $9D58 (LO BYTE ADDR.)
0343-    85 07        STA    $07       *INTO $07
0345-    AD 59 9D     LDA    $9D59     *STORE CONT. OF $9D59 (HI BYTE ADDR.)
0348-    85 08        STA    $08       *INTO $08
034A-    A9 57        LDA    #$57      *PUT LO BYTE OF $0357 (I.E. $57)
034C-    8D 58 9D     STA    $9D58     *INTO $9D58
034F-    A9 03        LDA    $03       *PUT HI BYTE OF $0357 (I.E. $03)
0351-    8D 59 9D     STA    $9D59     *INTO $9D59
0354-    20 D1 A4     JSR    $A4D1     *JUMP TO 'RUN' SUBROUTINE
0357-    20 0F 03     JSR    $030F     *JUMP TO 'MESSAGE' SUBROUTINE
035A-    20 00 03     JSR    $0300     *JUMP TO 'PAUSE' SUBROUTINE
035D-    A5 07        LDA    $07       *PLACE CONTENTS BACK INTO
035F-    8D F8 9D     STA    $9D58     **$9D58 AND $9D59 THAT
0362-    A5 08        LDA    $08       *WERE REMOVED
0364-    8D 59 9D     STA    $9D59     *EARLIER
0367-    60           RTS              *RETURN TO CALLING ROUTINE
  .
  .
  .
039D-    20 58 FC     JSR    $FC58     *HOME AND CLEAR SCREEN
03A0-    A9 08        LDA    #$08
03A2-    20 5B FB     JSR    $FB5B     *SET VERT. TAB TO 8
03A5-    60           RTS              *RETURN TO CALLING ROUTINE
```

Listing 2. "MESSG."

32K system the equivalent decimal location would be 27235 ($6A63).

Loading from Exec

Some problems arose in the early stages of troubleshooting Chek when it loaded Flog into memory. Referring to Listing 1 the original statement used in line 20110 was

20110 PRINT"IFL=1THENPOKE 6,1: PRINTDD$"Q$"LOAD FLOG"Q$

This functioned properly in loading Flog into memory, but when loading was completed, a program popped up related to the way in which the computer executes an Exec file. When an Exec file is created it is stored on disk. When the Exec file is executed, it is read from the disk into the file buffer of the Apple by sector and each field in succession is examined and acted upon. When the last field contained in the file buffer is handled, the next sector on disk is then read into the file buffer. It must be remembered that the Exec file Chek was created and placed only on the backup disk.

Let us recap the sequence of things. Chek has checked for Flog on the backup disk. It discovers that Flog is not there so it displays a message on the TVT telling the operator to replace the backup disk in the drive unit with the original disk (which has Flog on it) and pauses until the "Return" key is hit. Now the original disk, which does not contain the Exec file Chek, is in the disk drive. The program Flog is loaded into memory as required by the statement in line 20110. After this, the computer tries to read the next field (Chek statement) that is in the file buffer. In my case, nearly all of the statements in the file buffer were executed so that after Flog had been loaded, the computer had only one or two more fields to read. After reading these last remaining fields in the buffer the computer then tried to read the next sector of the Chek file from the disk. This could not be done as the original disk, which did not have Chek stored on it, was in the drive unit and everything came to a halt after a few irrelevant characters were printed on the screen.

To make things function properly it was necessary to get the backup disk into the drive unit before the computer tried to read the next sector of Chek. This is why I settled on line 20110 shown in Listing 1. The CALL 832 is the machine language subroutine that takes care of loading a program, displaying appropriate messages and pausing the program to enable the backup disk to be placed in the drive unit before things go awry. The CALL 832 subroutine is shown in Listing 2 at memory location $0340-$0367.

410

Loading with CALL 832

During my review of various publications, trying to get a handle on memory locations and subroutines that would be helpful to me, I found a memory map listing of the Apple II DOS 3.2 which showed the beginning addresses of many DOS subroutines for a 48K system. This memory map listing shows that the LOAD routine begins at decimal location 42003 ($A413). I was unable to use this subroutine successfully. If would load the program satisfactorily, but at its completion it would ignore Chek and return to the monitor. Rather than try to jump into the depths of the subroutine and figure out what memory locations needed to be modified, I took some time to see how the RUN routine beginning at decimal location 42193 ($A4D1) would work. RUN loads a program into memory then jumps unconditionally to another routine that executes the program just loaded. Thus, the trick was to change the destination address of this last jump so that instead of running the program just loaded, a routine of my choosing (i.e. the message routine at $030F) would be executed and Chek would not be side-stepped as in the LOAD routine.

The RUN routine, shown in Listing 4, is located at memory locations $A4D1-$A4E4. The unconditional jump, beginning at $A4E2, causes the routine to jump to the address contained in locations $9D58 and $9D59 where $9D58 holds the low byte address and $9D59 holds the high byte address of the routine that will run the program just loaded into memory.

The plan in using CALL 832 is to load the desired program (Flog in this case) using the loading part of the RUN routine in Listing 4 (locations $A4D1-$A4E1) but placing the beginning address into $9D58 and $9D59. In this case the address is

```
A4D1-    AD  B6  AA      LDA      $AAB6
A4D4-    F0  03          BEQ      $A4D9
A4D6-    8D  B7  AA      STA      $AAB7
A4D9-    20  13  A4      JSR      $A413
A4DC-    20  C8  9F      JSR      $9FC8
A4DF-    20  51  A8      JSR      $A851
A4E2-    6C  58  9D      JMP      ($9D58)
```

Listing 4. Run subroutine.

$0357 which is shown in Listing 2. By having the RUN routine jump to $0357, the desired message and pause subroutines can be run.

One way of placing the address $0357 into $9D58 and $9D59 is to take the contents of $9D58 and $9D59 and store them for the time being in safe locations, $07

and $08 in this case. Next the low and high bytes of $0357 itself (low byte, $57; high byte, $03) are placed in $9D58 and $9D59 respectively. See Listing 2 locations $0340-$0353 for this procedure.

When the unconditional jump is made to $0357, a jump to the message subroutines is made. After the message is displayed, the subroutine then returns to $035A and execution continues with the pause subroutine (beginning at $0300) which waits for the operator to exchange the disks and hit the "Return" key. Now we have the backup disk in the drive unit again and the computer can read all the sectors it wants without causing any problems.

Before leaving the CALL 832 subroutine, however, a little housekeeping is in order. It seems, if for no other reason than good practice, that the original contents should be returned to $9D58 and $9D59. This is done in locations $035D-$0366. Location $0367 returns the CALL 832 subroutine to Chek.

General

Some of the things used in Backup (Listing 1) should probably be explained a little further. Line 20020 loads the machine language routines found in Listing 2. These routines could be loaded by another program (such as Flog) and used as needed no matter what Basic program or Exec file happened to be in the computer. These machine language routines will not be disturbed unless the programmer does so deliberately or DOS is booted again.

Lines 20040 and 20050 of Listing 1 clear Chek to make sure no information contained in it from a previous use will interfere with its proper functioning. If this is not done it is possible that Chek could accumulate statements and characters that would adversely affect its proper execution.

Zero page locations $06, $07 and $08 have been used because they are apparently free for programmer use. I say this in reference to the memory maps depicted in the Apple manuals which show these locations free from use by any functions of the Apple. According to the Apple II Reference Manual, $09 is also available. Additionally, a portion of page three can be used safely by the programmer in locations $0300-$03EF.

Line 20120 of Listing 1 is necessary because the process of loading a program clears variables. The POKE and PEEK functions are used with location $06 to maintain variable information after the LOAD routine is used also.

The NEW command in lines 20160 and 20260 is used to remove from memory Basic programs loaded into memory. This is done to ensure that the backup operation is completed with no program in memory that can be run. The Control-D character is not needed for NEW as it is not a DOS command.

Listing 3 is included to show the complete file "MESSG." The message used by the subroutines beginning at $031F and $032D use the characters stored in locations $03A6-$03CA and $03CB-$03EF respectively. The character set used was taken from Table 7 of the Reference Manual where $C1=A, $C2=B, etc.

The way a message is displayed by "MESSG" can be seen by looking at the locations $031F-$032A of Listing 2 and locations $03A6-$03CA of Listing 3.

```
0300-  A9 AO 20 1B FD C9 8D DO
0308-  F7 60 A2 00 4C 11 03 A2
0310-  01 20 9D 03 20 3A FF 18
0318-  8A A2 00 C9 01 FO OE BD
0320-  A6 03 C9 DB FO 15 20 ED
0328-  FD E8 4C 1F 03 BD CB 03
0330-  C9 DB FO 07 20 ED FD E8
0338-  4C 2D 03 A9 00 85 24 60
0340-  AD 58 9D 85 07 AD 59 9D
0348-  85 08 A9 57 8D 58 9D A9
0350-  03 8D 59 9D 20 D1 A4 20
0358-  0F 03 20 00 03 A5 07 8D
0360-  58 9D A5 08 8D 59 9D 60
0368-  00 00 00 00 00 00 00 00
0370-  00 00 00 00 00 00 00 00
0378-  00 00 00 00 00 00 00 00
0380-  00 00 00 00 00 00 00 00
0388-  00 00 00 00 00 00 00 00
0390-  00 00 00 00 00 00 00 00
0398-  00 00 00 00 00 20 58 FC
03A0-  A9 08 20 5B FB 60 D2 C5
03A8-  CD CF D6 C5 AO C2 C1 C3
03B0-  CB D5 DO AO C4 C9 D3 CB
03B8-  AO AD AO C9 CE D3 C5 D2
03C0-  D4 AO CF D2 C9 C7 C9 CE
03C8-  C1 CC DB D2 C5 CD CF D6
03D0-  C5 AO CF D2 C9 C7 C9 CE
03D8-  C1 CC AO C4 C9 D3 CB AO
03E0-  AD AO C9 CE D3 C5 D2 D4
03E8-  AO C2 C1 C3 CB D5 DO DB
*
```

Listing 3. Machine language listing of "MESSG."

CALL -198 executes a subroutine that sounds the "bell."

Conclusion

I hope that this article has provided you with some insight into how Exec can be used, and that the not-too-obvious subroutines will be useful. Once you get into these areas you may uncover some of the secrets of the Apple computer yourself and share them with other Apple users. □

Apple Pascal

Steve North

For the last several months I have been using the Apple/UCSD Pascal system, and I'd like to share my impressions with you.

To run Pascal on the Apple II, you must plug in a Language System board in slot 0, and insert a 16-pin jumper into a memory chip socket. This allows the 48K Apple to think it has 64K of RAM, or to switch back to normal mode (with Basic in ROM). You must also replace your old disk bootstrap ROMs on the disk controller card to accommodate the higher-density disk format Pascal (and the new Basic DOS) use. After replacing the disk-boot ROMs, you can directly boot Pascal or DOS 3.3, and can convert old Basic disks to the new format or boot them by a two-step process. One should reasonably have at least two disk drives to run Pascal.

Apple Pascal is not only a language compiler, but a complete operating system with utilities and libraries. It is screen-oriented (with lots of paging instead of scrolling) and meshes in a pleasing way with the Apple's graphics, sound effects,

Steve North, 35A Orchard Street, Summit, NJ 07901.

game paddles, and plug-in I/O cards. However, this monolithic style of software design — making one giant self-contained system to Do It All — can be more restrictive than very open-ended designs incorporating many very small (sometimes disposable) software tools. (While there are no absolutes, CP/M follows this philosophy much more closely, and this

---

Pascal is easy to learn and almost forces one to write logical, readable, understandable programs.

---

helps explain why it is so popular and there is so much CP/M compatible software.) Certainly Apple Pascal presents the user with a much more integrated view of the system, but at a price.

The Choices

When Pascal is booted, it displays a menu of commands, each activated by a single keypress. The following are available:

E) Edit a file. The editor is screen-oriented — you have a cursor you move around within the file to do insertions, changes, and deletions — but it is more slanted toward program development than letter-writing. For example, it has an auto-indent mode to encourage the writing of structured programs, and it can also be told to discriminate between quoted text and Pascal code. The editor and the rest of

the system can default to a "current work file," which is very convenient for sessions of editing, compiling, and debugging.

F) File system. This subsystem gives you access to another set of commands for listing directories, copying files, testing for bad disk sectors, scrunching free space on disks, and the like. Disks can be accessed symbolically (by a name like GAMES or XYZ98) rather than by physical device number, a feature that would be welcome in other systems. The operating system is also smart about allowing you to change disks (and even asks you to do it when necessary), unlike other operating systems which throw up their hands in despair when disks have been changed without rebooting.

C) Compile. The compiler is the heart of the Pascal system. The compiler and library incorporate almost all of the stuff in the Jensen and Wirth *Pascal User Manual and Report,* and adds some very welcome extensions, such as Logo-like turtle-graphics, without any kludging. *(Editor's note: "turtles" are hypothetical reptiles with pens in their beaks that rotate and crawl on the screen under program control.)*

Pascal itself (as a language, not speaking of any implementation in particular) is a very nice, cleanly designed language for both simple and complex programming. Designed by Wirth in Europe, some Americans found it Teutonic and restrictive. Its only major competitor for this kind of programming on personal computers is C, another "structured" language. Most compupeople seem to agree that C is a somewhat more powerful language than Pascal, especially for systems software writing, but it is harder to learn and allows one to get in trouble much more quickly. Pascal is easy to learn and almost forces one to write logical, readable, understandable programs. (Of course, you could also get C up on your Apple by buying the BD Software or Whitesmith's C compiler for the Z-80 along with a Microsoft Z-80 Softcard, but that's another adventure of dubious merit for another article.)

The Compiler

The compiler recognizes the data type STRING, not really in the original Pascal specification (a blunder), which is the same old array of characters that standard Pascal has, but with a length attribute magically tacked on. Compile-time toggles allow you to turn on/off the checking of I/O errors (why would you want to turn them off?), range errors, and the internal swapping of the compiler. the user can include an externally stored text file with special routines or definitions in it.

Anyway, we should mention in passing that the compiler handles errors more gracefully than ANY OTHER we've tried, by allowing you to jump immediately into the editor with the cursor over the offending code, and a description of the problem at the top of the screen. The compiler also generally finds where the error really is, which isn't always easy to do.

The compiler handles errors more gracefully than ANY OTHER we've tried, by allowing you to jump immediately into the editor with the cursor over the offending code.

R) Run a program. This causes the current workfile to be compiled (if necessary), linked (if necessary), and executed.

X) This command executed a named code file (output of assembler or compiler).

A) A 6502 assembler with many juicy pseudo-ops is also included in the package.

Subroutines in 6502 machine language can be called from Pascal.

L) The linker can be explicitly called by the user for user-written non-standard libraries.

Gripes

Since there is no debugger in the Pascal system, fixing programs is done the horrible way, by inserting WRITE statements all over the place to try to decipher what's happening. Debuggers for high-level languages are usually primitive at best, but it's sometimes helpful to be able to look at the stack or see a traceback or set breakpoints. Another moderate annoyance is that Pascal wants to run on an 80 column screen, and the plain-old-vanilla flavored Apple II has only 40 columns (whereas the space-age Apple III has 80 columns). The attempted solution for the Apple II was to split the 80 column screen into two imaginary 40-column screens and then you can either flip back and forth between them or scroll horizontally. This technique works OK but if it bothers you, it is also possible to connect an external terminal or use an 80-column video card. This links us to another minor problem — the Pascal system is a bit fussy about talking to non-Apple I/O cards (in particular it did not recognize the SSM Apple RS-232 I/O card which entailed great fussing with user-written I/O drivers).

The documentation is good, but a few items fell between the cracks. In particular, there did not seem to be any specific information in the reference manual on how parameters are passed to assembly language subroutines. Also, the documentation on what's happening in the system at the nuts and bolts level is missing (perhaps for proprietary reasons).

For those curious about details of the implementation, Apple/UCSD is a "portable" (a little bit) compiler which is apparently reworked Zurich p-code. That is, the compiler and operating system and everything else wonderful but not Apple-dependent is written in a machine language for a hypothetical stack architecture processor, which is simulated by the 6502 in the Apple. This might sound inefficient but the p-machine is highly optimized toward running Pascal object code and thus is very reasonable in its use of time and memory.

Overall, Pascal is a very very nice language, and this is a very very nice implementation. If you're a teacher, and have an Apple, perhaps you should be teaching your students Pascal instead of Basic, which encourages bad programming practices and looks backward, not forward. If you're a personal computer user, you'll find Apple Pascal to be fast, powerful, and a pleasure to use. Absolutely get one of these if you can afford the $500 list price.

□

What a P-Machine Is

Since good computer software is so difficult to develop it's worthwhile to make it as portable as possible. This is hard enough to do with application software written in a "high-level" language like Microsoft Basic, but the difficulties are compounded when writing system software since it is tied more closely to one particular machine. Further, efficiency (of both cpu and memory usage) are often more critical in system programs.

So, let's say you've cooked up a really super Pascal system written in assembly language for the Z-80, and now you want to move it to the Apple which has a 6502 processor. You could always recode the entire Pascal system for the 6502, but it would be almost as much work as starting from scratch. Or, you could write a Z-80 simulator for the 6502. This would be easier than re-writing all the Z-80 code, but the trade-off is a loss of speed and a few K of memory because of the overhead of this added layer of interpretation. But what makes the Z-80 (or the 6800 or the Z-8000 or any other particular processor) especially great for writing a Pascal compiler and operating system? Well, nothing. As long as we're interpreting one machine on another, then, it makes sense to design a hypothetical processor which would be a nice home for running Pascal- with built-in instructions for doing Pascal-type things.

Guess what, computer fans, that's how UCSD Pascal works. Merely by implementing the infamous p-machine by interpreting it on an existing microprocessor, the entire Pascal compiler and operating system and utilities can be moved. So when you think the Apple is running Pascal, in fact, it is running a simulation of a computer which is running Pascal object programs.

Of course, if you want a real code crunching compiler that can squeeze every cycle and every spare byte out of the object code, then a compiler that makes executable native code for the host processor is in order. This approach is taken by Ithaca Intersystems pascal and Leor Zolman's BD C compiler, for instance. But neither of these compilers could be made to run on another microprocessor too quickly.

An alternative approach to make portable compilers (and other software) is to write everything, including the compiler itself, in a high-level language, let's say on machine A. Then, to move everything to machine B, we need only rewrite to code generator in the compiler on machine A so that it makes programs for machine B, run everything through the new compiler, and transport the resulting programs to machine B. Alas, writing good code generators is a tricky, art-not-a-science thing, and this approach has not been applied much to personal computers.

—SN

413

Q & A
The "Tiny" Interpreter Exercise

Philip Tubb

Over the years there have been numerous requests for an article describing the internal workings of interpreters. The following will provide an interesting self-teaching exercise for individuals wanting to explore interpreters and should also be an ideal classroom exercise. The experimentation and learning shouldn't stop after entering and running the program in the article. Go ahead and add new features and commands to the "Tiny" Interpreter... and really start learning.

A new column, "Operating Systems Q&A" by John Craig, began in the November-December 1978 issue. Many questions were sent in which weren't limited to operating systems, and ultimately I was asked to do a general questions and answers column.

One question particularly struck me as interesting. John Thompson of Monee, Illinois asked about "...that never-never land between machine language and a high level language like BASIC..." and wanted to know how interpreters are written. Most users of personal computers use high level languages, but few know exactly how they work or how they are written. Since most users are familiar with BASIC, I decided to answer the question by writing an interpreter for a small BASIC-like language. Rather than writing the interpreter in machine language as is usually done, I've decided to write it in BASIC since most readers will then be able to follow the programming logic.

The writing of interpreters is a complex subject, but is of sufficient interest to warrant a detailed explanation. So, this first Q&A column will be a bonus double-size single-topic issue. Henceforth I'll try to answer several questions in each column (unless I find another worthy topic). There is no extra charge for this special issue, so enjoy!

The "Tiny Interpreter" Specs

First, it is important to decide what the language will be like. I'll pick a few BASIC statements, just enough to illustrate some key interpreter con-

Phil Tubb is President of ALF Products, Inc. (1448 Estes, Denver, CO 80215), manufacturers of music synthesizer boards for the Apple computer.

cepts: LET, INPUT, PRINT, GOTO and IF. An interpreter needs a command set such as LIST, RUN and RENUMBER. Most BASICs include a very complex floating-point arithmetic package, which is too elaborate for this example (and is really a different subject entirely). I'll stick to add, subtract, less than and equal to with integers from -9999 to 9999. In traditional interactive-interpreter style, I'll write a line oriented editor which allows lines to be added, deleted and replaced by line number.

The next step is to define the exact syntax of the language. I prefer to use a modified form of BNF (an acronym for Backus Naur Form - a notation for describing the syntax of languages). First, I define the element <program>. The definition is approximately:

<program>: :<line>[<program>]

The ": :" is read "is defined as" (this is a slight variation from the standard symbol, ": : =", because it is easier to type). Anything in brackets is optional. In English the definition above is: "a program is defined as a line optionally followed by a program or, in other words, one or more lines" which is why BNF is used instead.

Next, we dive in and define the elements used in the definition of <program>. In this case the only one is <line>:

<line>: :<line number><statement><return

It is not necessary to define the ASCII character return , since this is for our own use. Let's continue defining elements until there are none left to define:

<line number>: : an integer from 1 to 9999

Although an integer from 1 to 9999 can be defined in BNF, it is much easier to read in English. We can use a slash (/) to indicate "or":

<statement>: :<LET>/<INPUT>/<PRINT>/<GOTO>/<IF>

<LET>: :<variable>" = "<value>

<INPUT>: : "INPUT"<variable list>

<PRINT>: : "PRINT"<value list>

GOTO : : "GOTO" line number

IF : : "IF" value "THEN" statement

<variable>: :<A-Z>[<characters>]
   Note 1

<value>: :(<variable>/<number>) [<binary op×value>]

<number>: : an integer from -9999 to 9999

<binary op>: :" +"/"-"/"<"/" ="

<variable list>: :<variable>["；" <variable list>]

<value list>: :<value>["；" value list>]

That's all, but most languages run on for pages. Anything in quotes is typed literally.<A-Z>is not defined because it's fairly obvious that it's a letter from A to Z. "Note 1" for the<variable>definition would explain that < characters> is one or more ASCII characters not including " +", "-", "<", " =", or "；", that there is some maximum variable name length, and that the name may not contain the word "THEN". One might also wish to mention that for convenience variable names beginning with "INPUT", "PRINT", "GOTO", or "IF" should not be chosen since they cannot be assigned values with a LET statement. (The reasons behind this will be explained as we go along). The use of parentheses in the definition of <value>is to clarify that the definition is "a variable or a number, optionally followed by a binary operator and a value," rather than "a variable, or a number optionally followed by a

```
1 LET
2 INPUT
3 PRINT
4 GOTO
5 IF
```

Table 1.

binary operator and a value."

Next, we grind the syntax down into something easy to work with. There are five statement types, and they are shown in Table 1. All statements start with a keyword (such as "PRINT"; except LET. All are composed of combinations of 8 key syntax elements, shown in Table 2. This allows us to make a simple syntax list with the keyword, the statement type number, and its key syntax elements (see Table 3). This will be useful when actually writing the interpreter. Although this language is so small it may not be necessary to approach syntax formats in a "key syntax elements" scheme, in conventional (larger) languages it is often the easiest way to go.

Usually one must determine the function of each statement in detail, but since this language is essentially BASIC we'll assume the intended function is already known.

How To Write The Interpreter

There are countless ways to write interpreters. There are many factors

---

Everyone likes fast interpreters, but fast interpreters tend to be large or to be for limited languages.

---

which must be balanced. Everyone likes fast interpreters, but fast interpreters tend to be large or to be for limited languages. For example, a machine language could probably run faster than a high level language, but who would want an interpreter for a machine language? Everyone likes to see syntax errors printed right when they type in the line, but some languages cannot be syntaxed on entry. Should the lines be stored in text form, or changed to a more compact form? These questions, and many others, must be worked out based on the intended application of the language. The scheme which I prefer is not the most efficient, although it is very efficient; it is not the fastest, although it is very fast; it does not have the most compact storage format, although it is very compact; and it is not easy to write, although there are harder schemes to write. Probably the biggest disadvantage to this scheme is that it makes the interpreter itself harder to write than many other schemes. One should bear in mind, though, that the interpreter need only be written once (or a few times) and must be used countless times.

I prefer to analyze the syntax of each line as it is entered and store it in a special, easy-to-use format. All line numbers will be stored as integers from -9999 to -1 (the opposite of the number actually typed). Each line will be a line number, then a number from 1 to 5 indicating the statement type, then one or more numbers that will differ from statement to statement, and finally a -10000 to mark the end of the line. "THEN" will be stored as -10001, as will semicolons in value lists. Binary operators will be stored with the numbers shown in Table 4.

Nothing else will be stored except variables. Variables are interesting things to work with. Obviously one would wish to have multi-character variable names (like "SUM"). Another common desire is for names followed by an integer (like "SUM1", "SUM2" and "SUM3"). Apple owners are familiar with the problems associated with multi-character variable names. In Apple's Integer BASIC, the whole variable name is stored as text, requiring a great deal of storage when long names are used frequently. Further, each time a variable is referenced, Integer BASIC scans a long variable value table for a matching name. This takes a long time, so the shorter the name is, the better. Applesoft (Apple's Microsoft BASIC) works somewhat differently. It also stores the whole variable name as text, requiring a great deal of storage. Table search time is reduced by limiting the search to the first two letters of the name. Unfortunately, this makes SUM1 and SUM2 the same variable, since they both start with SU. Rather primitive, I'd say. I like to build a table of variable names. When a line is entered which contains a variable, the interpreter scans through the table. If the name is not already in the table, it is added to the end. To store the variable reference, one need only store an integer which indicates the variable's place in the table. Room can be reserved in the table for the variable's value, too. This scanning takes place only when a line is entered, not while the program is running, so execution speed is kept high (in fact, the integer which indicates the variable's location in the table is quite useful for determining where the value should be stored or read.) With this scheme you get fast execution, and the space required for any variable typed in a line is the same, regardless of the number of letters in the name (except that the name must be stored once in the table).

The storage format just described is useful for (a) reducing the amount of memory required to store a line, and (b) increasing program execution speed since the interpreter need only look at numbers like "3" rather than strings of characters like "PRINT". However, there remains one particularly tedious operation which must still be done during program execution. "GOTO 50" would require that line 50 be located. Fortunately, there is a simple solution to this problem. At the beginning of RUN, we just zip through the program finding all the lines, and replace the stored numbers with an integer that indicates the

location of the line. These "pointers" will be stored as non-negative numbers, so as to not be confused with actual numbers, which are stored as negative numbers. This scheme has at least two advantages: (a) it speeds up program execution, and (b) it allows one to be notified of all non-existent line references (e.g., GOTO 50 when there is no line 50) at once, without waiting for the particular line with the error to be executed.

The main disadvantage of all this string/number crunching is that it takes time. Some people claim that it takes additional programming in the interpreter but I'm not sure just how much extra, if any, is required. Fortunately, it's not too bad to take time at this particular point because (a) each line need only be crunched once, rather than each time it is run,

```
1 (variable)
2 (value)
3 (variable list)
4 (value list)
5 "="
6 (line number)
7 "THEN"
8 (statement)
```

Table 2.

and (b) the user may not even notice the slight pause when he presses return because he is preparing to type the next line, and if he is using a printer the crunching can almost always be done while the printer is doing the line feed.

Microsoft: The Good and the Bad

Now we're ready to begin writing. In real life I wrote the interpreter once, threw it away, and began again with a good idea of what would be coming up (this is my standard practice). Since I happen to have an Apple II computer handy, the interpreter is written in Applesoft. I would like to digress momentarily to discuss some difficulties I had using Applesoft. I started programming several years ago with Hewlett-Packard 2000 Timeshare BASIC, which is an excellent BASIC. HP's strings are far easier to use than Microsoft's LEFT$, RIGHT$ and MID$ (plus, HP's method is preferred in recent proposed ANSI standards). For example, to delete the first character in a string, you use: 100 A$ = A$(2). With Microsoft, you must use: 100 IF LEN(A$) = 1 THEN A$ = " " : GOTO 120 and 110 A$ = RIGHT$(A$, LEN(A$)-1). I wouldn't even begin to translate HP's 100 A$(4,7) = B$(20,23), especially if the length of B$ might be 21 characters. These string operations got to be so tedious, that in the rewrite I decided to give up and avoid using Applesoft's strings at all (which will probably give you a better idea of how it's done in machine language anyway). Another difficulty I had was that if I used 100 FOR A = 1 TO B in HP BASIC, and B is less than 1, the body of the loop (between the FOR and the NEXT) would not be done at all, but with Applesoft it will be done once anyway. Generally I solve this by adding an IF statement which should be unnecessary (according to the infallible Phil Tubb). Just to give you an idea how useful a zero-times-through loop can be, we'll put three asterisks (***) in the text each place it would have been useful. I found it necessary to move all my subroutines to the beginning of the program because Applesoft doesn't use the pre-scan GOTO technique discussed previously. Normally, I like to place my subroutines at the end of the program (who doesn't?). There were some instances where variable names mixed with keywords; I'll point those out later for those of you who enjoy seeing others make interesting mistakes. Finally, I had originally planned to separate variable names or values with commas (like 10 INPUT SUM1, SUM2, SUM3) but Applesoft doesn't allow strings with commas to be input. "Surprise" doesn't even begin to describe my emotions. Programming of this sort deserves nothing but contempt; if I had written it I would hide in shame.

Initial Housekeeping

Onward with the actual interpreter example program. First we need to set some limits on variable size and similar parameters. By gathering all such parameters together to the beginning of the program, the parameters can be easily changed later if needed. We need to know the maximum program size (MPROG), the maximum line length (MLINE), the maximum variable table size (MTABLE), the maximum variable name length in characters (MVAR) and the maximum input line length in characters (MIN). We also need to dimension arrays and set a few initial variable values. A pointer is needed to the next available space in PROG%, the program array (NPROG); a pointer to the next available space in TABLE%, the variable table (NVAR); a flag for run mode/syntax mode (RFLAG); and a temporary NVAR variable (QNVAR). The BASIC programming is as follows:

```
10 MPROG = 500 : MLINE = 40 :
   MTABLE = 500 : MVAR = 40 :
   MIN = 80
```

```
20 DIM IN(MIN + 3),T1(MLINE-1),
   T2(MVAR-1),PROG%(MPROG),
   TABLE% (MTABLE-1) :
   NPROG = 0 : NVAR = 0 :
   RFLAG = 0 : QNVAR = 0 : GOTO
   5000
```

Arrays T1 and T2 are used as temporaries. The PROG% and TABLE% arrays would be all available unused memory if programming in machine language. (For those not familiar with Microsoft BASIC, the % indicates an integer array which requires less storage than a regular floating-point array.)

The first step is to obtain an input line from the user. A subroutine will be used to input a string and convert it into an array of numbers. In machine language, the string would normally appear as a list of numbers. The programming is quite simple:

Applesoft doesn't allow strings with commas to be input. "Surprise" doesn't even begin to describe my emotions.

```
110 INPUT " ",A$ : IF MIN<
    LEN(A$) THEN PRINT "INPUT
    LINE TOO LONG." : GOTO 110
```

```
114 IN(0) = 0 : I = 0 : IF LEN(A$)
    THEN FOR A = 1 TO LEN(A$) : IN(A-1)
    = ASC(MID$(A$,A,1)) : NEXT A :
    IN(A-1) = 0
```

```
116 RETURN
```

I originally typed IF LEN(A$)>MIN THEN... since that is far more clear, but it turned into IF LEN(A$)>M INT HEN. Also *** in 114. A zero is placed as the last item in the array as an end marker (in machine language this might just be the ASCII return character instead). The variable I is set to the first character, and will be advanced as the processing for each character is finished.

The first thing to do with the input line is to check to see if the first character is a digit. If it is, a line is being input; otherwise, it is a command.

```
5000 NVAR = QNVAR : PRINT
     "-"; : GOSUB 110 : IF IN(I)<48
     OR IN(I)>57 THEN 5200
```

Let's assume for the moment that the input line begins with a digit and, therefore, line 5000 doesn't branch to 5200. The first thing to do with a line number is to translate the ASCII characters into a number (like 1, 2 and 3 into 123). Since numbers are used in various places, a subroutine is appropriate. This one will accept numbers from -9999 to 9999.

```
80 N = 0 : N1 = 1 : IF IN(I) = 45
   THEN N1 = -1 : I = I + 1
```

```
90 N2 = IN(I)-48 : IF N2<0 OR
   N2>9 OR N*10 + N2 9999 THEN
   N = N*N1 : GOTO 30
```

```
100  N = N*10 + N2 : I = I + 1 :
     GOTO 90
```

The ASCII value for "-" is 45, and the code for "0" is 48. Exit from the routine is to line 30, which is a subroutine to delete spaces (ASCII value 32):

```
30 IF IN(I) = 32 THEN I = I + 1 :
   GOTO 30
```

```
40 RETURN
```

The reason for this is that something must be done about spaces. Most BASICs ignore all spaces not in quotes or REM statements, which leads them into such follies as turning MIN THEN into MINTHEN and into M INT HEN. I prefer to allow (and ignore) spaces only between syntax elements. Since a number is essentially a syntax element, the subroutine at line 30 is used to consume any spaces following the number.

Line Numbers

You will recall that only positive numbers are allowed for line numbers, and that they are stored using negative numbers. The subroutine at line 80 returns N as the integer, which must be checked for being positive and stored. The line currently being entered will be stored in the T1 temporary array, and PNT will point to the next available element. Since line numbers are also used by GOTO, a subroutine is required to translate and store a line number:

```
50 GOSUB 80 : N = N : IF N>=0
   THEN POP : PRINT "ILLEGAL
   LINE NUMBER." : GOTO 5000
```

```
60 IF PNT = MLINE THEN POP :
   PRINT "LINE TOO LONG." :
   GOTO 5000
```

```
70 T1 (PNT) = N : PNT = PNT + 1
   : RETURN
```

Line 60 is a handy subroutine that stores N into the T1 array, first checking to be sure the line isn't too long. Note that POP causes Applesoft to forget that we're in a subroutine, and allows a return directly to line 5000 (where a new line will be input).

How does this store-a-line-number routine get called? First, we have to check to see if any of the line numbers have been changed to pointers. If so, they must be changed back to line numbers because if a new line is added the locations of existing lines may change. RFLAG will be set to non-zero when pointers are present, and zero when they aren't, so we use:

```
5010 IF RFLAG THEN GOSUB
340
```

This will call a subroutine at line 340 (which coverts pointers back to line numbers) if RFLAG is non-zero. Now for the line number:

```
5020 PNT = 0 : GOSUB 50 : IF
NOT IN(I) THEN PNT = 0 : GOTO
5090
```

If the end marker is found after the line number then a statement is to be deleted and the line shown above branches to line 5090.

At this point a new or replacement statement is being checked. It must be syntaxed (checked for proper format and identified as to type) and stored. Since all statements begin with a keyword except LET, the first step is to check to see if the line begins with any of the known keywords. If it doesn't we'll assume it is a LET statement. The syntax of the various statements, shown in Table 3, is represented in DATA statements as follows:

```
9000 DATA 5,73,78,80,85,84,2,3,255
9010 DATA 5,80,82,73,78,84,3,4,255
9020 DATA 4,71,79,84,79,4,6,255
9030 DATA 5,71,79,32,84,79,4,6,255
9040 DATA 2,73,70,5,2,7,8,0
9050 DATA 1,1,5,2,255
```

```
        (LET) 1 ; 1, 5, 2
        INPUT 3 ; 4

        (LET) 1 ; 1, 5, 2
        INPUT 2 ; 3
        PRINT 3 ; 4
        GOTO 4 ; 6
        IF 5 ; 2, 7, 8

        Table 3.
```

The first number in each line is the number of letters in the keyword. This is followed by that many numbers which indicate the ASCII characters of the keyword. Following these numbers are the numbers given in Table 3. Note that line 9030 is the same as 9020 except it contains an extra letter (ASCII 32) in the keyword. This allows GOTO to be entered as either GOTO (line 9020) or GO TO (line 9030). Each syntax list ends with either 255 or 0, and following the 255 or 0 the next statement type begins. The 0 indicates that the next statement is LET which has no keyword.

First the data must be restored in case this is not the first time a statement is being deciphered. Then the length of the keyword is read and checked to see if it matches the keyword used in the input line:

```
5030 RESTORE
5040 READ L : FOR A = 0 TO L-1
: READ B : IF IN(I + A) = B THEN
NEXT A : GOTO 5070
```

Line 5040 will branch to line 5070 if there is a keyword match. Otherwise, the read continues until a 0 or a 255 is found. If a 255 is found we go back to 5040 to try the next statement type.

```
5050 READ L : IF L = 255 THEN
5040

5060 IF L THEN 5050
```

Now, at line 5070, the statement type is known. The next number in the DATA statements will indicate the statement number, then its syntax. "L" is the number of characters in the keyword, or 0 if no keyword was found (and thus a LET statement is assumed). The data for LET (in line 9050) contains no keyword information and therefore begins with the statement number (1). The next step is to skip over the keyword (if any) in the input line and also skip over any spaces found. Then the statement number must be read from the DATA and stored:

```
5070 I = I + L : GOSUB 30 : READ
N : GOSUB 60
```

Next the syntax can be read and an ON GOSUB used to branch to the appropriate routines. This will be done repeatedly until a 255 is found in the syntax list.

```
5080 READ N : IF N <> 255 THEN
ON N GOSUB 120,220,260,280,
300,50,320,330 : GOTO 5080
```

When a 255 is found, it falls through to the next line which stores the -10000 end-of-line marker. If the input line doesn't end, then an error is printed.

```
5085 N = -10000 : GOSUB 60 : IF
IN(I) THEN PRINT "END OF LINE
EXPECTED." : GOTO 5000
```

Syntax Elements

Now for a look at each of the key syntax elements. The first (and most complicated) one is a "variable." The name must be isolated by looking for the first illegal character or the word THEN. The illegal characters are " + ", "-", "<", " = ", and ";". The first four are illegal because they are binary operators, and we want "SUM1 + SUM2" to be taken as the variable "SUM1", the operator " + ", and the

variable "SUM2". Semicolon is illegal because we want "INPUT A; B" to be taken as "INPUT", the variable "A", the separator ";", and the variable "B". If semicolon was a legal variable name character it would be taken as "INPUT" and the variable "A; B".

Most BASICs ignore all spaces not in quotes or REM statements, which leads them into such follies as turning MIN THEN into MINTHEN and then into M INT HEN.

THEN must be excluded so that "IF SUM1 THEN" will exclude the THEN from the variable name, thus making the variable "SUM1" rather than "SUM1 THEN". Further, variables are allowed to start only with letters. This is a rather arbitrary restriction, the main use of which is to avoid taking "-5" or "16" as a variable. The programming for all this begins by checking to see if the first character of the variable name is a letter:

```
120 VPNT = 0 : IF IN(I)<65 OR
IN(I)>90 THEN POP : PRINT
"ILLEGAL VARIABLE." : GOTO
5000
```

"VPNT" will point into temporary array T2 where the variable name will be constructed (copied from the input line). It will also be useful for determining the number of characters in the name. Each character must now be checked for illegal characters and THEN.

```
130 A = IN(I) : IF NOT A OR A = 43
OR A = 45 OR A = 60 OR A = 61
OR A = 59 OR A = 84 AND IN(I +
1) = 72   AND   IN(I + 2) = 69 and
IN(I + 3) = 78 THEN 150

140 T2(VPNT) = A  :  I = I + 1  :
VPNT = VPNT + 1  :  IF  VPNT
MVAR THEN 130
```

Note that 0 must also be considered an illegal character since it marks the end of the line. The checking process continues until an illegal character or THEN is found, or until the maximum number of characters allowed have been accumulated. If there are no characters in the name (e.g., the name started with THEN), an error must be printed. If not, trailing spaces must be removed.

```
150 IF NOT VPNT THEN IN(I) = 0
: GOTO 120

155 IF T2(VPNT-1) = 32  THEN
VPNT = VPNT-1 : GOTO 155
```

Now we must check to see if the variable name is already in TABLE%. The first item in TABLE% is the value of the first variable. The next item is the length of the variable name in characters. This is followed by the variable name, and then all this information repeats for the next variable. TABLE% begins with element 0.

```
1 +
2 -
3 =
4 =
```
Table 4.

160 FOR A = 1 TO NVAR-1 : IF TABLE%(A) < >VPNT THEN 190

If the lengths don't match, it can't be the right name. If they do match, each character must be checked:

170 FOR B = 1 TO VPNT : IF TABLE%(A + B) < > T2(B-1) THEN 190

180 NEXT B : N = A + 9999 : GOSUB 60 : GOTO 30

When a match is found, the pointer value is stored and the variable subroutine is exited through line 30. The stored value minus 9999 will point to the length of the variable name, and the stored value minus 10000 will point to the value of the variable. If the name does not match, the next name must be checked:

190 A = A + TABLE%(A) + 1 : NEXT A

If it isn't in the table, we check to see that there is enough room to add it. If so, it is copied into the table, setting the initial value to zero.

200 IF NVAR + NPNT>MTABLE-2 THEN POP : PRINT "TOO MANY VARIABLES."
: GOTO 5000

210 TABLE%(NVAR) = 0 : TABLE%(NVAR + 1) = VPNT : FOR A = 0 TO VPNT-1 : TABLE% (NVAR + A + 2) = T2(A) : NEXT A : N = NVAR + 10000 : NVAR = NVAR + VPNT + 2 : GOSUB 60 : GOTO 30

Originally line 200 read NVAR + NPNT + 2>MTABLE THEN which is a little easier to understand, but the end of which becomes MTAB LET HEN. (Note that this cannot happen with the variable subroutine just described, even if a check was being made for LET rather than THEN, because the space between MTABLE and THEN would prevent the formation of LET.)

The next key syntax element is "value." Often this is referred to as an "expression" or an "arithmetic expression" but "value" is much easier to say and type. We begin by checking for "-" (ASCII 45) and the digits (ASCII 48 through 57). If one of these is found, the item must be a number, otherwise it must be a variable.

220 IF IN(I) = 45 OR IN(I)>47 AND IN(I)<58 THEN GOSUB 80 : GOSUB 60 : GOTO 240

The subroutine to translate a number already exists at line 80. The number is then stored using the subroutine at line 60. If it is a variable rather than a number, a store-a-variable subroutine is used at line 120:

230 GOSUB 120

Next, for either a number or a variable, a check is made for a binary operator. If there isn't one, the value is finished. Otherwise, the operator is stored and we go back up to find a number or a variable.

240 A = IN(I) : N = (A = 43) + 2* (A = 45) + 3*(A = 60) + 4*(A = 61) : IF NOT N THEN RETURN

250 GOSUB 60 : I = I + 1 : GOSUB 30 : GOTO 220

One would normally use DATA for the various operators rather than a sum of logicals (in line 240), but Applesoft doesn't seem to have any way to RESTORE data beginning at a certain

---

Variables are allowed to start only with letters. This is a rather arbitrary restriction, the main use of which is to avoid taking "-5" or "16" as a variable.

line, and I didn't want to RESTORE all the data and then read through the syntax data just to get to the operator data.

The next key syntax type is a "variable list." The syntaxing is quite simple and mostly just calls the "variable" subroutine (line 120). Semicolons (ASCII 59) separate the variables and are checked for, but there is no need to store them.

260 GOSUB 120 : IF IN(I) < > 59 THEN 30

270 I = I + 1 : GOSUB 30 : GOTO 260

"Value list" is quite similar, but calls "value" (line 220). Semicolons must be stored lest small positive numbers be confused with operators.

280 GOSUB 220 : IF IN(I) < > 59 THEN 30

290 I = I + 1 : GOSUB 30 : N = -10001 : GOSUB 60 : GOTO 280

The next syntax element is just the equal sign in the LET statement. It is noted but not stored:

300 IF IN(I) < > 61 THEN POP : PRINT " = EXPECTED." : GOTO 5000

310 I = I + 1 : GOTO 30

The next element is "line number" which simply calls the subroutine already present at line 50. (See the ON GOSUB in line 5080.) THEN is next, which is noted and stored as -10001 :

320 IF IN(I) < > 84 OR IN(I + 1) < > 72 OR IN(I + 2) < > 69 OR IN(I + 3) < >78 THEN POP : PRINT "THEN EXPECTED." (GOTO 5000 325 I = I + 4 : GOSUB 30 : N = -10001 : GOTO 60

Finally, we have "statement." All that is necessary is to forget that a subroutine was called (in line 5080) and start over again at the "statement" routine. Since PNT has been advanced, the statement will automatically be stored after the beginning of the IF statement already stored (since IF is the only statement which uses the syntax element "statement").

330 POP : GOTO 5030

Line Processing

When the line is finally all syntaxed and stored in temporary array T1 as a series of numbers, we're ready to insert it in the proper place within the PROG% array which holds the whole program. T1(0) contains the line number, whether adding a line or deleting one, when we arrive at line 5090. PNT indicates the length of the line (and is 0 when deleting a line). This will be copied into L (for "length") because at one point we will need a variable which indicates the amount of extra space needed, which may be different than PNT if a line is being replaced with a longer line. If there are no lines in the program at the moment, a skip is made down to line 5160 (***). Otherwise, a scan through PROG% is used to find the proper position for the line.

5090 A = 0 : PA = -10000 : L = PNT : IF L AND NOT NPROG THEN 5160

5100 FOR A = 0 TO NPROG-1 : IF PA = -10000 and PROG%(A)< = T1(0) THEN 5120

5110 PA = PROG%(A) : NEXT A : PROG%(A) = 0

The "PA" stuff is to get around the fact that most BASICs don't allow

PROG%(A-1) if A = 0, and I was foolish enough to actually use element 0 of the array. If I had started using PROG% at element 1, PROG%(0) could have been set to -10000 and then we could change "IF PA = -10000 AND PROG%(A)< = T1(0)" to the more rational "IF PROG%(A-1) = -10000 AND PROG%(A)< = T1(0)" and avoid using PA at all. PROG%(0) need only be set at the very beginning of the program. However, being more used to machine language (where "arrays" are imaginary and you can start the "subscripts" at any number you like), I didn't notice this difficulty until it was well entrenched in the program. It is a very sloppy technique, but it doesn't matter very much so I'm leaving it in, just to give everyone something to sneer at.

If the proper line isn't found at all, then the first unused element in PROG% is set to 0 (in line 5110) to avoid "replacing" a line that isn't there. If a line with a higher line number than the new line is found, or if the end of the program is found, we wind up at line 5120, with A pointing to the higher-numbered line or the first unused element in PROG%.

If the line number at element A in PROG% matches the line number of the new line, a line is to be replaced or deleted. If it doesn't match, then a line is to be inserted or the line to be deleted doesn't exist. An error message is printed if the line doesn't exist:

    5120 IF PROG%(A) = T1(0) THEN 5170

    5130 IF NOT PNT THEN PRINT "NO SUCH LINE." : GOTO 5000

Line 5140 is where a line is inserted, and line 5170 will be where a line is replaced or deleted. If a line is to be inserted, then first a check is made to see if there is enough space for it. If so, a "hole" will be expanded into the PROG% array by line 5150 (***), and the line will be copied into this hole (line 5160 ***).

    5140 IF NPROG + L>MPROG THEN PRINT "PROGRAM TOO LARGE." : GOTO 5000

    5150 IF L THEN FOR B = NPROG -1 TO A STEP -1 : PROG%(B + L) = PROG%(B) : NEXT B

    5160 NPROG = NPROG + L : QNVAR = NVAR : IF PNT THEN FOR B = 0 TO PNT-1 : PROG% (A + B) = T1(B) : NEXT B

    5165 GOTO 5000

A somewhat obscure item in line 5160 is the "QNVAR = NVAR". A similar obscurity occured way back at line 5000 ("NVAR = QNVAR"). This is mainly due to a problem in BASIC called the "implied LET" statement. I had originally intended to name QNVAR PNVAR (for "previous NVAR") but that conflicts with PNT (grumble). When a syntax error occurs, NVAR will be set back to the previous NVAR (QNVAR) by line 5000. This deletes all variables added to TABLE% during processing of the illegal line. However, when a valid line is entered, line 5160 sets QNVAR equal to NVAR so line 5000 won't change the value of NVAR (thus keeping all the variables added to TABLE%). What does all this have to do with the LET statement? Well, suppose I type in 10 GOSUB 50. There isn't any GOSUB in this language, therefore, since GOSUB doesn't match any of the keywords, a LET statement is assumed. GOSUB 50 is a legal variable name so it is added to the TABLE%. However, since " = " is expected but not found, " = EXPECTED." message will be printed. (This is rather cryptic for an error message, but it is what the syntaxer is "thinking." You can jazz the errors up quite a bit just by adding a PRINT LEFT$(A$,I + 1); in front, like PRINT LEFT$(A$,I + 1);" = EXPECTED.". This can be done to all the syntax errors. In this case, it would print "10 GOSUB 50 = EXPECTED.", and if you fill in the equal by typing 10 GOSUB 50 = , then it would print "10 GOSUB 50 = ILLEGAL VARIABLE." assuming you fixed up the other messages. Then you just supply a legal variable like: 10 GOSUB 50 = SUM1, and (presto!) you get a legal statement. It will probably begin to dawn on you that it thinks "GOSUB 50" is a variable.) It would be crude to fill the TABLE% up with all these screwball variable names, so the simple QNVAR trick prevents it.

To get back to finished line processing, line 5170 is the place where lines are replaced or deleted. The old line, or the line to be deleted, is pointed to by A. It is now necessary to determine the length of the old line. Usually people begin each line by storing the length, for a variety of good reasons. In this case I didn't.

Now all that remains is to execute the three commands. If the first letter of the input line is an L, then it must be the list command.

    5170 FOR B = 1 TO NPROG : IF PROG%(A + B-1) < > -10000 THEN NEXT B

The length of the old line is now in B. If the new line is larger than the old line (or the same size), we can use the routine already written for "inserting" a Line must be set to the difference in lengths and it will then make a hole big enough for the increased size.

    5180 IF B<= PNT THEN L = PNT -B : GOTO 5140

Line 5140 will even check to make sure there is enough room to add the longer line. If the new line is shorter than the old, or if a line is being deleted we have to squeeze PROG% down to eliminate the difference in size (or the whole line). Then we can use line 5160 to copy the new line in (if any).

    5190 FOR L = A + B TO NPROG-1 : PROG%(L-B + PNT) = PROG%(L) : NEXT L : L = PNT-B : GOTO 5160

L must be set to the difference in length so NPROG w be correctly updated.

More Housekeeping

That's it for syntaxing! We now have a program which will accept statements, grind them down to numbers and store them away in the proper order. Now we need a couple of subroutines to convert line numbers from numbers to pointers and vice-versa. The subroutine to convert numbers into pointers looks like this:

    410 PA = -10000 + NOT NPROG : FOR A = 0 TO NPROG-1 : IF PA<> -10000 THEN 500

    415 L = A

    420 A = A + 1 : IF PROG%(A) = 4 THEN IF PROG%(A + 1) 0 THEN 460

    430 IF PROG%(A)<> 5 THEN 500

    440 A = A + 1 : IF PROG%(A)< > -10001 THEN 440

    450 GOTO 420

    460 C = PROG%(A + 1) : PA = -10000 : FOR B = 0 TO NPROG-1 : IF PA = -10000 AND PROG%(B) = C THEN 490

    470 PA = PROG%(B) (NEXT B : IF RFLAG = 1 THEN POP : PRINT "UNDEFINED REFERENCE IN LINE";-PROG%(L); "." : GOTO 5000

    480 GOTO 500

    490 PROG%(A + 1) = B

    500 PA = PROG%(A) : NEXT A : RETURN

The + NOT NPROG in line 410 checks for a null program (***). Line 420 checks for statement type 4, which is GOTO (the only statement which can have a line number reference). If found, line 460 changes the number to a pointer reference, if it wasn't one already. Line 430 checks for statement type 5 (IF) since it contains a statement which could be a GOTO (or another IF). One obscure item is the check of RFLAG in line 470. For now, it is sufficient to know that the RUN command will set RFLAG to 1.

The subroutine which will undo all of this looks like:

```
340 PA = -10000 + NOT NPROG :
    FOR A = 0 TO NPROG-1 : IF PA<>
    -10000 THEN 400

350 A = A + 1 : IF PROG%(A) = 4
    THEN IF PROG%(A + 1)>=0
    THEN 390

360 IF PROG%(A)<>5 THEN 400

370 A = A + 1 : IF PROG%(A)<>
    -10001 THEN 370

380 GOTO 350

390 PROG%(A + 1) = PROG%
    (PROG%(A + 1))
```

Everyone knows that renumber is particularly difficult to do, because you have to change all the GOTO references. In fact, it's so difficult that most personal computer BASICs don't have it at all.

```
400 PA = PROG%(A) : NEXT A :
    RFLAG = 0 : RETURN
```

Again (line 340), + NOT NPROG checks for a null program (***). You may recall that this subroutine was called way back in line 5010. Line 400 sets RFLAG to 0 so this routine won't be called by line 5010 again until it is necessary.

Now all that remains is to execute the three commands. If the first letter of the input line is an L, then it must be the list command. (This command syntax checker is pretty crude, but it is not significant to this example.) If there is no program to list, then line 5205 goes back to the line input routine (***).

```
5200 IF IN(I)<>76 THEN 5420

5205 IF NOT NPROG THEN 5000
```

(Line 5420 is where we wind up if the first letter isn't L.) For each line, the line number must be printed:

```
5210 PRINT : FOR A = 0 TO
     NPROG-1

5215 PRINT -PROG%(A);" "; :
     A = A + 1
```

Now the data is run through (the same data used in syntaxing an input line), search for a matching statement type number and print the keyword.

```
5220 RESTORE

5230 READ L : FOR B = 1 TO L :
     READ T1(B) : NEXT B : READ B :
     IF B = PROG%(A) THEN 5260

5240 READ L : IF L < > 255 AND L
     THEN 5240

5250 IF L THEN 5230

5255 READ B
```

The statement keyword has been found by the time we get to line 5260. It has been stored in temporary array T1. L is the length of the keyword (or zero for LET), and the next data item to be read is the syntax of the statement. First, the keyword (***) is printed:

```
5260 IF L THEN FOR B = 1 TO L :
     PRINT CHR$(T1(B)); : NEXT B :
     PRINT " ";

5265 A = A + 1
```

Now we simply read the syntax out of the data, and list the rest of the line. An ON GOSUB is used to call a subroutine for each syntax type.

```
5270 READ L : IF L < > 255 THEN
     ON L GOSUB 5290,5300,5340,
     5360,5380,5390,5410,5415    :
     GOTO 5000
```

Line 5280 is used when the whole line is finished. Now for a look at each syntax item.

The first syntax item is "variable". A variable (L) is set to the location of the length and name, then the name is printed.

```
5290 L = PROG%(A)-9999 : FOR
     B = 1 TO TABLE%(L) : PRINT
     CHR$(TABLE%(B + L)); : NEXT
     B : A = A + 1 : RETURN
```

Next, we have "value." If the first item is greater than 9999, it is a variable and the above subroutine is used. Otherwise, it is a number and is just printed.

```
5300 IF PROG%(A)>9999 THEN
     GOSUB 5290 : GOTO 5320

5310 PRINT PROG%(A); :
     A = A + 1

5320 IF PROG%(A)<0 THEN
     RETURN
```

At line 5320, a value less than zero means the end of the "value." Otherwise, there is a binary operator and the whole thing starts over.

```
5330 A$ = " +-<= " : PRINT MID$
     (A$,PROG%(A),1); : A = A + 1 :
     GOTO 5300
```

Next, we have "variable list" which is rather trivial:

```
5340 GOSUB 5290 : IF PROG%
     (A)<>-10000 THEN PRINT ";"; :
     GOTO 5340

5350 RETURN
```

Similarly, for "value list" the values are printed separated by semi-colons until the end of line marker (-10000) is reached.

```
5360 GOSUB 5300 : IF PROG%(A)
     < > -10000 THEN PRINT ";"; :
     A = A + 1 : GOTO 5360

5370 RETURN
```

Here's a real tricky one for the LET statement's equal sign:

```
5380 PRINT " = "; : RETURN
```

The next item is "line number", and we must take into account that line numbers are stored either as negative numbers or as non-negative addresses. We could have just done GOSUB 340 to change them all to negative numbers but that would be crude.

```
5390 IF PROG%(A)<0 THEN
     PRINT -PROG%(A); : A = A + 1 :
     RETURN

5400 PRINT -PROG%(PROG%
     (A)); : A = A + 1 : RETURN
```

Next, we have another devious subroutine:

```
5410 A = A + 1 : PRINT "THEN ";
     : RETURN
```

Finally, we do "statement" in the usual manner:

```
5415 POP : GOTO 5220
```

Line 5420 is where we wind up if a command is typed that doesn't start with the letter L. If it doesn't start with R either, then there is something wrong.

```
5420 IF IN(I) < > 82 THEN PRINT
     "COMMAND ERROR." : GOTO
     5000
```

Now we have a choice of RUN or RENUMBER. If the second letter is E then the command is renumber, otherwise we'll branch to run.

```
5430 A = IN(I + 1); : IF A < > 69
     THEN 5460
```

You may be wondering why I choose to include **renumber**. Everyone knows that renumber is particularly difficult to do, because you have to change all the GOTO references. In fact, it's so difficult that most personal computer BASICs don't have it at all. I think we'll just do it an easy way to spite them all. First, we'll call the same routine run will use to turn line numbers into pointers then just change the line numbers and forget about the GOTO references.

```
5440 RFLAG = 2 : GOSUB 410 :
L = -10 : PA = -10000 : FOR A = 0
TO NPROG-1 : IF PA = -10000
THEN PROG%(A) = L : L = L-10
5450 PA = PROG%(A) : NEXT A :
GOTO 5000
```

Setting RFLAG to 2 causes the 410 subroutine to just ignore any undefined references and leave them as negative numbers (when called by run with RFLAG = 1, an error message will be printed for undefined references). Since the GOTO line numbers just point to the real line numbers and we've just changed all those, the line numbers in the GOTO statements will be changed without having to bother with them. Undefined references will be left alone, which is preferable. (The above routine numbers by 10's starting with 10, but could be modified for more complex numbering.) Clean living has its benefits.

Now at line 5460 we have the run command. It looks like this:

```
5460 IF A <> 85 THEN IN(I) = 0 :
GOTO 5420
5470 RFLAG = 1 : GOSUB 410 :
PNT = 0 : GOTO 620
```

Line 5460 makes sure the second letter of the command is a U. For obvious reasons we have put most of the run command near the beginning of the program.

At line 620 the pointer (PNT) has been copied to the current line number into LINE for future reference. If there are no more lines to run a branch is made to the line input section (line 5000).

```
620 LINE = PNT : PNT = PNT + 2
: IF LINE = NPROG THEN 5000
```

PNT is advanced by 2 so as to point to the first parameter (past the statement type number). An ON GOTO statement will be used to branch to the appropriate statement's routine:

```
630 ON PROG%(PNT-1) GOTO
670,680,740,760
```

The IF statement must determine the value of a given "value." A subroutine (beginning at line 510) to evaluate a value and return the answer in N will be used.

```
510 GOSUB 590 : N = A
```

Line 590 will return the value of a number or variable in A.

```
520 B = PROG%(PNT) : IF B<0
THEN RETURN
```

The value is complete if no binary operator follows. Otherwise, the second number/variable is evaluated and an ON GOSUB goes to the proper arithmetic routine.

```
530 PNT = PNT + 1 : GOSUB 590 :
ON B GOSUB 550,560,570,580 :
IF ABS(N)<10000 THEN 520
540 POP : PRINT "OVERFLOW
IN LINE";-PROG%(LINE);"." :
GOTO 5000
550 N = N + A : RETURN
560 N = N-1 : RETURN
570 N = N<A : RETURN
580 N = N = A : RETURN
590 A = PROG%(PNT) : PNT =
PNT + 1 : IF A<10000 THEN
RETURN
600 A = TABLE%(A-10000) : RE-
TURN
```

Once the IF statement value has been determined we continue with the statement that follows "THEN" if the value is non-zero:

```
640 GOSUB 510 : PNT = PNT + 2 :
IF N THEN 630
```

Otherwise, skip down to the next line:

```
650 PNT = PNT + 1 : IF PROG%
(PNT-1)<>-10000 THEN 650
660 GOTO 620
```

The LET statement is quite simple. L is the pointer to the destination variable.

```
670  L = PROG%(PNT)-10000  :
PNT = PNT + 1 : GOSUB 510 :
TABLE%(L) = N : GOTO 610
```

Line 610 is a general purpose line that increments PNT and then falls through to line 620:

```
610 PNT = PNT + 1
```

The input statement reads in a line (using the subroutine at line 110). If the first letter of the input is an S, program execution is stopped and we branch to the line input section (line 5000).

```
680 PRINT "?"; : GOSUB 110 : IF
IN(I) = 83 THEN PRINT
"STOPPED AT LINE";-PROG%
(LINE);"." : GOTO 5000
```

Next, we check to see if there are any letters left in the input line. If not, go back up and get some more.

```
690 IF NOT IN(I) THEN 680
```

If the first character is not a "-" (ASCII 45) or a digit (ASCII 48 through 57), an error message is printed and another line is asked for.

```
700 IF IN(I) <> 45 AND (IN(I)<48
OR IN(I)>57) THEN PRINT "BAD
INPUT." : GOTO 680
```

Otherwise, we translate the number (line 80) and store it in the proper variable. If there are no more variables to input, we're done (branch to line 610).

```
710 GOSUB 80 : TABLE%
(PROG%(PNT)-10000) = N : PNT
= PNT + 1 : IF PROG%(PNT) =
-10000 THEN 610
```

Otherwise, a check is made for a semicolon in the input line, and we go do the next variable. (Semicolons are used in the input string to separate numeric values. I would prefer commas, but they are not allowed in Applesoft.)

```
720 IF IN(I) <> 59 THEN IN(I) = 0 :
GOTO 700
730 I = I + 1 : GOTO 690
```

The print statement is quite simple:

```
740 GOSUB 510 : PRINT N;""; :
IF PROG%(PNT) = -10000 THEN
PRINT : GOTO 610
750 PNT = PNT + 1 : GOTO 740
```

The GOTO statement is also simple:

```
760    PNT = PROG%(PNT)    :
GOTO 620
```

Conclusion

That's it. In real life it is much more complicated, of course, but this interpreter is intended only to show some basic concepts. You can type the interpreter in and try it if you like, but it is really only to show the exact process. (I've tested it, of course.) If you do run it, you'll notice that it takes quite a while to syntax a line when it is typed in. Keep in mind that a well written interpreter (written in machine language rather than BASIC) can easily do this in a very small fraction of a second. This will put the speed of the RUN command in proper perspective.

Do you have questions related to microcomputers? Send them to this address:

Questions & Answers
Creative Computing Magazine
P.O. Box 789-M
Morristown, N.J. 07960

Please try to keep questions general, like "What is an RS-232 printer interface?" rather than, "How do I connect a Cray-30 terminal into my Hyperdata 80 CPU?"   □

Apple II: Reading Data From Tape

You have an Integer Basic program which has relatively large arrays of data. For instance, you have financial data to read into an analysis program; or, as I do, a baseball program which needs repeated updating of player records; or a table of department names that needs periodic updating.

Although Integer Basic does not have a DATA statement, there are three other ways to get these data into your program. First, you can assign each element individually. If you have lots of memory and the data will not change, this is not a bad way to do it. Second, you can enter data using the INPUT operator in your program. This is fine if you have a relatively small amount of data to enter each time you want to run the program.

Finally, for large amounts of data or for data that need periodic updating, you can read data into your program using the techniques I will describe.

Follow these steps to create, write, and read the data.

1. Create the data with a separate program.

2. Write the created data to tape from the data creation program.

3. Read the data into your execution program.

That sounds easy, so let's see how to do it using a simple example.

First create the data. Start by setting the write arrays as your first statement.

```
100 DIM A(10),B(10)
```

This act sets up memory location starting at $800 (hex address 800, decimal 2048) to store the data.

Now let's write a simple input program.

```
110 FOR J = 1 TO 10
120 INPUT "KEY IN DATA ITEM 1",C
```

Bruno B. Wolff, Jr., 2004 E. Kensington Blvd., Shorewood, WI 53211.

Bruno B. Wolff, Jr.

We'll add a simple edit step to prevent a 32767 error.

```
130 IF C < 328 THEN 150
140 PRINT "DATA ITEM TOO LARGE":
    GO TO 120
150 INPUT "KEY IN DATA ITEM 2",D
160 A(J)=(C*100+5)/D
170 B(J)=J+100
180 NEXT J
```

Now you need to determine two important locations in memory — the starting address of the area of memory you want to write and the ending address of that area. Since Integer Basic starts assigning variables to memory at $800 (unless you change it by changing LOMEM), you know the starting address right off. You can find

---

Now you need to determine two important locations in memory — the starting address of the area of memory you want to write and the ending address of that area.

---

the ending address two ways. One, you can calculate it: or, two, you can read it by looking at the memory location with the monitor.

First let's calculate it. Integer Basic needs one byte for each character in the variable name. (You may want to refer to page 35 and following in the red book.) Then it has a byte for the DISPLAY option. Then two bytes for the next variable address. Then there are two bytes for each element in the array. The number of elements is the dimension number plus 1 since element 0 is the first element. So we have

1+1+2+22 (for A) and 1+1+2+22 (for B) or a total of 52 locations, i.e., 34 hex.

Now we add the number of bytes needed to our starting location minus 1 to get the ending address.

Hexadecimal	Decimal
800	2048
+ 34	+ 52
− 1	− 1
833	2099

A second way to find the starting and ending address is to use the monitor. To do this you have to RUN the program. The program will run to line 120. Then hit the reset key. You'll get the monitor prompt "*."

Input 800.803 to see the first four bytes of variable memory. The computer will respond:

```
800  C1 00 1A 08
```

"C1" is the hex notation for "A." "00" says the display option is off. "1A 08" says the next variable starts at $81A.

Next input 81A.81D to display the variable "B" and the location of the next variable. The machine will respond 81A C2 00 34 08. "C2" is the hex notation for "B." "00" shows the display option is off, and "34 08" says the next variable starts at $834. From that we conclude the last location we want to write is one less than $834 or $833.

Now Control C back into Basic.

Now that we know the start and end addresses, we have to put them into the computer.

The starting address is loaded in decimal locations 60 (low order) and 61 (high order). The ending address is loaded into 62 (low order) and 63 (high order).

Take the hex starting address of 800 and separate the low order and high order bytes. Low order = 00, high order = 8. The decimal equivalent of 00 is 0, and 8 is 8. Simple enough.

Now take the ending location 833. The decimal equivalent of the low order byte 33 is 51(3*16+3). The high order byte 8 converts easily to 8 decimal.

```
190 POKE 60,0
200 POKE 61,8
210 POKE 62,51
220 POKE 63,8
```

Another way to compute the poke address is to take the decimal address and compute the low-order byte by using the MOD function with 256 as modulus and divide the decimal address by 256 to find the high order byte. So an alternative way is to POKE as follows:

```
170 POKE 60,2048 MOD 256
180 POKE 61, 2048/256
190 POKE 62, 2099 MOD 256
200 POKE 63, 2099/256
```

There are two ways of looking at the same thing. One is just as good as the other. If you look at the monitor, the first method is easier. If you count, the second way is easier.

The next thing we have to do is CALL the program that writes to the tape. First let's give ourselves a message to position our tape and put the program on hold until we're ready.

```
230 DIM A$(1)
240 PRINT "POSITION TAPE AND SET IN
    RECORD MODE"
250 INPUT "HIT RETURN WHEN READY",A$
260 CALL-307
270 PRINT "WRITE COMPLETED"
280 END
```

Now that wasn't too bad, was it?

The final thing we have to do now is write the program that will use the data created in program 1.

We'll do a simple program to read and print the data we read in. The most important thing to remember is that the create-data program and the use-data program must start out with the same dimension statement.

```
100 DIM A(10),B(10)
```

Now we POKE the read addresses we already computed when setting up the write program.

```
110 POKE 60,0
120 POKE 61,8
130 POKE 62,51
140 POKE 63,8
```

Then we set up to read in the arrays.

```
150 DIM A$(1)
160 PRINT "POSITION TAPE AN
    PLAY MODE"
170 INPUT "WHEN READY START TAPE AND
    HIT RETURN", A$
180 CALL-259
190 PRINT "READ COMPLETED"
```

Now we'll clear the screen and print the data, adding a delay so you can read the message in 190.

```
200 FOR J=1 TO 300: NEXT J
210 CALL-936
220 PRINT "B        A"
230 PRINT
240 FOR J = 1 TO 10
250 PRINT B(J);
260 PRINT "   "; A(J)
270 NEXT J
280 END
```

There you have it. A few points to remember: to compute the variable length be sure to add one byte for each letter in your variable name and the number of bytes includes subscript 0. For string variables each variable has one byte for each cell plus a termination byte (set to 1E) which marks the end of the string.

To review, then, for numeric variables the total number of bytes is:

```
        L letters in a name
       +1 display byte
       +2 address of next variable
+(N+1) * 2 two bytes for each cell
           (Dimension N plus 1).
```

For strings:

```
        L letters in name
       +1 display byte
       +2 address of next variable
+(N+1) one byte for each cell
           (dimension N plus one)
       +1 termination byte
```

Also remember that both programs must start with the same dimension statements and have the same read and write addresses.

I think you'll find these routines useful. Now you can build your own Integer Basic programs to read and write data. □

<hr>

Notes

WIZARDRY

with the System Monitor

Richard T. Simoni, Jr.

When I first purchased my Apple II two years ago and started programming in Integer Basic, I thought about a myriad of small editing features which would make my life as a programmer easier. I tried in vain to implement the features, and simply concluded, "Well, it must be beyond the capabilities of the Apple." That was before I learned some rudimentary 6502 assembly language and discovered a tricky little feature tucked into the System Monitor of the Apple.

The feature is called the "character output switch" (CSW), and is included in the Apple design to allow character output to be sent to a peripheral card PROM driver program (which might then send the output to a printer, for example). The essence of the CSW is memory locations $36 and $37, individually called CSWL (CSW Low) and CSWH (CSW High), respectively. At any one time, these locations hold the starting address of the current character output routine. When you press Reset and enter the System Monitor, this address is $FDFO, the starting address of the COUT1 routine in the Apple Monitor. This routine takes the number stored in the accumulator (A-register) and displays its ASCII equivalent on the screen at the current cursor position. Every time the Apple wants to print a character on the screen, execution branches to the address stored in the CSW.

Now the big question comes up: "How do I use these CSW locations to make my Apple do strange and wonderful things it couldn't do before?" Well, the solution is to change the address stored in the CSW from the location of the Apple's output

Richard T. Simoni, Jr., #29 Farnham Park Dr., Houston, TX 77024.

```
*3EFL

03EF-    A9 00        LDA    #$00
03F1-    85 36        STA    $36
03F3-    A9 03        LDA    #$03
03F5-    85 37        STA    $37
03F7-    60           RTS
03F8-    4C EF 03     JMP    $03EF
```
———————— Listing 1. ————————

routine to the location of your own machine language routine. After accomplishing its purpose, your routine can then jump to Apple's output routine, and you've fooled the Apple. It'll never know the difference!

Of course, before writing sneaky routines that control the cursor, list programs with continuous user control over the speed of the output, etc., we must devise a method to replace the address stored in locations $36 and $37 with the address of our own routine. Since page three of memory can be used for machine language programs in both the Integer Basic and Applesoft II Basic memory map, I have chosen to start our routines at memory location $300. Our routine will then be "activated" by storing the address $300 in

the CSW (locations $36 and $37). This can be accomplished in a number of ways, such as the Monitor command:

*36:00 03 (return)

I personally prefer to use the short assembly language program shown in Listing 1. This program is executed by typing the Monitor CTRL-Y command. Once this program and our routine are entered, therefore, all that is needed to "activate" the routine is:

*(CTRL-Y) (return)

This main control program can be used with each of the routines described in this article.

Stoplist

Enough of the preliminaries. Let's plunge into some actual wizardry. The first routine is named Stoplist, and is shown in Listing 2. After entering this routine along with the main control program (I will assume from here on that you have already done this), the CTRL-Y command will activate Stoplist. Try listing some memory (*000.FFF) and touch a key as the data scrolls by. The display will freeze until you press another key. The routine

Listing 2.

```
*300L

0300-    48           PHA                     ;SAVE A-REG
0301-    AD 00 CO      LDA    $C000            ;WAS KEY PRESSED?
0304-    10 08         BPL    $030E            ;NO, BRANCH TO END
0306-    AD 10 CO      LDA    $C010            ;CLEAR KEYBOARD
0309-    AD 00 CO      LDA    $C000            ;WAIT UNTIL ANOTHER
030C-    10 FB         BPL    $0309            ;  KEY IS PRESSED
030E-    AD 10 CO      LDA    $C010            ;CLEAR KEYBOARD
0311-    68           PLA                      ;RESTORE A-REG
0312-    4C FO FH      JMP    $FDFO            ;SEND CHAR TO SCREEN
```

SUBROUTINE	ADDRESS	FUNCTION
PREAD	$FB1E	lets Y-register=PDL(X-register)
ADVANCE	$FBF4	advances cursor
BS	$FC10	backspaces cursor
UP	$FC1A	moves cursor up
LF	$FC66	moves cursor down (line feed)
COUT1	$FDF0	displays ASCII character in A-register at current cursor position
IOSAVE	$FF4A	saves all registers in page zero locations
IOREST	$FF3F	restores all registers from these locations

Table 1.

NAME	LOCATION	FUNCTION
CSWL	$36	character output switch (see text)
CSWH	$37	
ACC	$45	temporary storage for the A-register
XREG	$46	temporary storage for the X-register
IN	$200	first location in the line input buffer
KBD	$C000	keyboard data entry location
KBDSTRB	$C010	clear keyboard strobe when accessed

Table 2.

```
*300L

0300-   20 4A FF    JSR   $FF4A    ;SAVE REGISTERS
0303-   A2 00       LDX   #$00
0305-   20 1E FB    JSR   $FB1E    ;LET Y-REG=PDL(0)
0308-   C0 00       CPY   #$00     ;IS Y-REG=0?
030A-   F0 0B       BEQ   $0317    ;YES, GO TO END
030C-   A2 FF       LDX   #$FF     ;NO, ENTER X-REG LOOP
030E-   CA          DEX
030F-   E0 00       CPX   #$00
0311-   D0 FB       BNE   $030E    ;END OF X-REG LOOP
0313-   88          DEY            ;Y-REG=Y-REG-1
0314-   4C 08 03    JMP   $0308    ;GO BACK TO Y-REG LOOP
0317-   20 3F FF    JSR   $FF3F    ;RESTORE REGISTERS
031A-   4C F0 FD    JMP   $FDF0    ;SEND CHAR TO SCREEN
```

Listing 3.

will remain in effect if you enter either Basic, but if you press Reset, the Apple will put its own address back in the CSW and you will have to re-activate with the CTRL-Y command.

The Stoplist routine brings up a few points which must be needed when writing routines for use with the CSW feature. You must protect the 6502 registers! Don't forget, when your routine is called, the ASCII equivalent of the letter or symbol to be displayed will be stored in the accumulator. If you want this character to make it to the screen, you must make certain the value in the accumulator is the same upon exiting your routine as it was upon entry. In the Stoplist routine, this is accomplished by pushing the A-register on to the stack (PHA instruction)

at the beginning of the routine and then pulling it back (PLA instruction) before jumping to the screen output routine of the Monitor.

Stoplist is also similar to most routines using the CSW feature in that it references some hardware-dependent memory addresses and jumps to some routines in the System Monitor. The Monitor subroutines called by the programs presented in this article are listed in Table 1. Special hardware-dependent memory locations used by the programs presented in this article are listed in Table 2.

Slowlist

Let's say after using Stoplist for a while, you decide that you don't actually want to stop the listing; you just want to slow it

down a bit so you can read it as it goes by. Our next routine, named Slowlist and shown in Listing 3, is for you. After keying in the routine and activating it, you will find that the speed of all screen output is governed by the position of paddle 0. This allows you to speed past the sections of the listing you don't care about, and slow down to digest the good parts.

Slowlist works by reading the paddle position (using the PREAD subroutine in the Monitor) and then creating a delay proportional to that position. After the delay, the routine sends the next character to the Monitor COUT1 routine to be displayed on the screen. Note again that Slowlist makes sure to protect the registers. Since the routine changes the X and Y registers, simply pushing the accumulator on the stack as we did in Stoplist will not protect the registers. Luckily, a simple call to the monitor IOSAVE routine stores all the registers in memory locations set aside for this purpose in page zero. When all is done and the registers must be restored, a call to IOSAVE's sister routine, IOREST, restores the registers to their original state.

Cursor Control

Often, when editing programs in either Integer Basic or Applesoft II Basic, I find myself confronted with a seemingly unending string of key sequences using the ESCape key to position the cursor just where I want it. The only problem with this is that each cursor move takes two keystrokes instead of one, not to mention that the cursor cannot be moved up or down with the Repeat key. Cursor Control, shown in Listing 4, takes care of these problems. Once activating the routine, the cursor can be controlled by holding down the CTRL key and pressing the A, B, C, or D keys to move the cursor right, left, down, or up, respectively. While this also requires two keystrokes to move the cursor a single postion, additional moves are made by continuing to hold the CTRL key down until the cursor is in the desired position on the screen. These control character movements are also compatible with the Repeat key.

While the method used by Cursor Control to accomplish its tasks is fairly straightforward, some of the instructions near the end of the routine are rather confusing. This section erases the control character typed by the user from the input line buffer. This buffer starts at location $200 and holds the ASCII value of each character typed into the input line. Although a typed control character goes into the buffer, it is not shown on the screen, and therefore would not normally have to be eliminated from the buffer. Unfortunately, any control character inserted within an Applesoft statement

```
*300LL

0300-   20 4A FF    JSR   $FF4A    ;SAVE REGISTERS
0303-   A5 45       LDA   $45      ;GET CHARACTER
0305-   C9 84       CMP   #$84     ;CTRL-D PRESSED?
0307-   D0 06       BNE   $030F    ;NO, GO TO NEXT CHECK
0309-   20 1A FC    JSR   $FC1A    ;MOVE CURSOR UP
030C-   4C 2A 03    JMP   $032A    ;END, ERASE CTRL-D
030F-   C9 83       CMP   #$83     ;CTRL-C PRESSED?
0311-   D0 06       BNE   $0319    ;NO, GO TO NEXT CHECK
0313-   20 66 FC    JSR   $FC66    ;MOVE CURSOR DOWN
0316-   4C 2A 03    JMP   $032A    ;END, ERASE CTRL-C
0319-   C9 82       CMP   #$82     ;CTRL-B PRESSED?
031B-   D0 06       BNE   $0323    ;NO, GO TO NEXT CHECK
031D-   20 10 FC    JSR   $FC10    ;MOVE CURSOR LEFT
0320-   4C 2A 03    JMP   $032A    ;END, ERASE CTRL-B
0323-   C9 81       CMP   #$81     ;CTRL-A PRESSED?
0325-   D0 17       BNE   $033E    ;NO, GO TO END
0327-   20 F4 FB    JSR   $FBF4    ;MOVE CURSOR RIGHT
032A-   AD 00 02    LDA   $0200    ;GET CHAR INPUT
032D-   C9 85       CMP   #$85     ;CTRL CHARACTER?
032F-   B0 05       BCS   $0336    ;NO, BRANCH
0331-   A9 A0       LDA   #$A0     ;REPLACE CTRL
0333-   8D 00 02    STA   $0200    ;WITH SPACE
0336-   A5 46       LDA   $46      ;GET LINE LENGTH
0338-   C9 00       CMP   #$00     ;LENGTH=0?
033A-   F0 02       BEQ   $033E    ;YES, DON'T DECREMENT
033C-   C6 46       DEC   $46      ;NO, SUBTRACT ONE
033E-   20 3F FF    JSR   $FF3F    ;RESTORE REGISTERS
0341-   4C F0 FE    JMP   $FDF0    ;SEND CHAR TO SCREEN
```

— Listing 4. —

```
*300L

0300-   C9 A0       CMP   #$A0     ;NON-CTRL CHAR?
0302-   B0 07       BCS   $030B    ;YES, GO TO END
0304-   C9 8D       CMP   #$8D     ;RETURN CHARACTER?
0306-   F0 03       BEQ   $030B    ;YES, GO TO END
0308-   38          SEC
0309-   E9 40       SBC   #$40     ;MAKE CTRL FLASHING CHAR
030B-   4C F0 FD    JMP   $FDF0    ;SEND CHAR TO SCREEN
```

— Listing 5. —

will cause a "SYNTAX ERR" message (except in a PRINT statement, of course). In order to keep the routine compatible with Applesoft (Integer Basic doesn't have this problem), I wrote Cursor Control such that all control characters were eliminated from the input buffer.

The last routine I will present here is of use primarily to Disk II owners. When I first came home with my brand new disk drive, I plugged it in and wrote a short program in Basic to save on my crisp new diskette. (Just to see if it would work.) In my excited frenzy to think of a suitable name under which to save the program, I made the irrational decision to type in quickly a random series of letters as the file name. So I had a program named "AFDYUOISIIS" on my diskette catalog. Much to my dismay, I found I couldn't reload the program or even access it in order to delete the strange name from my diskette. After repeatedly seeing the "FILE NOT FOUND" message, I realized that when I originally saved the program, I had inadvertently inserted a control character into the file name. Since control characters don't show themselves on the screen, I didn't know which character I had typed, and I didn't know where in the name I had typed it.

This horrible situation prompted me to write Ctrl-flash (shown in Listing 5), another CSW-oriented routine which displays all control characters as flashing characters on the screen. After activating the routine, try typing some control characters. They will "flash before your eyes."

The method used in Ctrl-flash is simple. If the program detects the character code in the accumulator to be a control character, the program subtracts just enough from the character's ASCII code to pull it down into the range of numbers the Apple displays as flashing letters.

I hope you will be able to use the techniques presented here to further explore some of the inner capabilities of the Apple hidden deep within its circuits. With some imagination, you should be able to write your own routines to suit your own needs. CSW routines have a habit of becoming extremely useful to the programmer who uses them! □

Chapter X
Branches

Chapter X — Branches

Once you grow tired of your Apple just sitting there on its own, you can always buy the little "extras." There are printers, of course, which most people eventually consider a necessity. There are also lots of little plug-in boards to make it play music (see Chapter II), keep time, talk, or enhance the video display (see Chapter IV). You can add a second microprocessor (a Z-80, on Microsoft's Softcard), and as a result, several new languages like FORTRAN, COBOL, and an extended BASIC — or you can add an extra 16K of RAM (Random Access Memory) that will give you Apple's Pascal or FORTRAN, and extra room for programs such as *Visicalc*. As we are writing this we can also see that soon you'll be able to add a RAM module that will give you the equivalent of two disk drives . . . all in RAM. And if the Apple talking to its own little family of peripherals isn't enough, you can also make it talk to all of your home appliances, or you can let it talk to any of thousands of other computers via the telephone. This can bring you everything from newspapers and stock prices to over-the-phone games.

In this chapter, we've compiled articles from *Creative Computing* that discuss some of the add-ons not already mentioned in this book, and some of the services that they may bring to you. Be sure to watch their pages for reviews of more peripherals, because each issue brings word of something new.

Special Notes For Chapter X

• Apple as Time-Sharing User, by James Parr:

This article describes one of the modems available for the Apple. The D.C. Hayes Micromodem is a direct-connect modem, meaning that it plugs into your phone's wall outlet. There are also acoustic modems available for a little less money into which you place the handset from your phone (it has to be a standard handset, not one of the new compact or fancy phones) — and information is passed by means of audio tones.

• *A Home Control System,* by Paul Daro:

There are several interfaces you can use to control the BSR X-10 home controller described in this article. Mountain Hardware's Introl X-10 is one of them. Micro Mint also makes a similar product, the "Busy Box," and Thunderware makes a clock board — Thunderclock — that has an optional controller for the X-10 system available. No matter which option you choose, make sure there is some kind of software included, unless you want to write your own. Also, in most cases it makes little sense to buy one if you don't have a clock board on your computer. Control via the computer keyboard is not any better than manual control through BSR's control unit. An exception would be in instances when you have some other software or input device hooked in and want to control various appliances on conditional input (e.g., if a window is opened, a sensor triggers a signal to the computer, and the computer signals the BSR unit to turn on all the lights. If you want to get fancy, you'd then have your modem respond by placing a call to the police — and your voice synthesizer would tell them what the problem is!).

Apple as Time-Sharing User

James Parr

Introduction

A properly equipped personal computer (such as the Apple II) can not only do computations of its own; it can be used as a terminal to a time-sharing system, and can communicate with the time-sharing system even when not acting as a terminal. This allows such applications as: transmitting your data or programs to the time-sharing system; transferring time-sharing files to your disk or tape, where they can be used by your computer as programs or data, or just saved as an archive to be restored to the time-sharing system later; having programs in your computer reference data from the time-sharing system or use time-sharing programs as subroutines. In short, almost all of the facilities of the time-sharing system are made available to the personal computer, and vice-versa.

This article presents some examples of techniques and programs for communication between an Apple II microcomputer and the Educational Computing Network (ECN), a CDC-based time-sharing network for some state universities in Illinois. With small modifications, these techniques should work on other time-sharing systems. Adaptation to other personal computers is more difficult, since the Apple programs are tailored to the peculiarities of Applesoft Basic and the Apple operating system.

To make use of these techniques, you need an Apple II computer with Applesoft

J. T. Parr, Mathematics Department, Illinois State University, Normal, IL 61761.

Basic, and either a modem and modem card, such as the Apple communications card and modem, or the D.C. Hayes Micromodem II (total retail about $1600, if you already have a TV or monitor). The last program uses a disk drive, but it could be adapted for cassette storage, or to use data directly instead of storing it on a file.

Making Contact: Apple As Terminal

Terminals and time-sharing systems operate in either full duplex or half duplex mode. A time-sharing system operating full duplex sends back ("echoes") to the terminal for every character it receives; the terminal in full duplex mode doesn't print

> ## Almost all of the facilities of the time-sharing system are available to the personal computer.

the character when it is typed at the keyboard, but only when it is sent back by the system. In half duplex mode, the terminal prints each character, and the system does not echo it back. If the duplex modes of the terminal and the system do not match, each letter typed will be printed twice, or not at all. On ECN, the command FULL or HALF can be entered to change the system from one duplex mode to the other. The extra input to the Apple from the echoing makes it a little more difficult to write programs to communicate with a full duplex system, so we shall want the system in half duplex mode for all of this work.

The following series of commands turns your Apple into a half-duplex terminal, ready to dial up a time-sharing system. Replace MSLOT with the number of the Apple slot your modem card is in. This procedure is for the Apple communications card and modem. (For more detail or a different modem, consult your modem manual.)

```
]PR# MSLOT

]PRINT

]PR# 0

]POKE 2040 + MSLOT, 9

]IN# MSLOT

]ctrl-A ctrl-H
```

The switches on the CAT modem should be set to O and F. The POKE sets the data format; different systems use different formats, so consult your manuals.

The Apple has a few peculiarities as a terminal: Its screen is only forty characters wide. The keyboard has no underscore, left bracket, or backslash, although these characters will be printed on the screen if sent by the system, and can be transmitted by an Apple program using the CHR$ function. Sending the break character is done by pressing ctrl-A ctrl-S, and cancelled by pressing any key.

Once in half-duplex terminal mode, the Apple responds to a keypress only by printing it on the screen and sending it out through the modem, with two exceptions: RESET and control sequences starting with ctrl-A. Pressing ctrl-A ctrl-X takes the Apple out of terminal mode and back to normal functioning ("local mode" or "local control"). So does RESET, but sometimes with undesirable side effects. If this is done without logging off from ECN, ECN will wait on the line up to its usual time limit while you use the Apple to run Applesoft, save or load programs, etc. Then you can reenter terminal mode with the sequence

```
]POKE 2040 + MSLOT, 9

]IN# MSLOT

]ctrl-A ctrl-H
```

and resume working with the Apple as a terminal; ECN will still be on the line. If the system has sent anything while the Apple was in local mode, some characters or blank lines may appear on the screen as soon as you enter IN# MSLOT. Sometimes the IN command undoes the POKE.

If you can't get any response from the system but ILLEGAL COMMAND, go back to local mode and repeat the sequence starting with the POKE.

While the Apple is in local mode, a PR# MSLOT command causes all subsequent output to be sent through the modem as well as to the screen, until a PR# O or RESET cancels it. An IN# MSLOT causes the Apple to ignore keyboard input except for RESET and ctrl-A sequences, and listen only to the modem until the next IN# O or RESET. These commands can be used directly or in programs to communicate with ECN while the Apple remains under local control, running Applesoft programs or responding to direct commands from the keyboard.

If you use the IN and PR commands in a program running under DOS, they can disconnect the disk I/O. This can be corrected by following each PR# O with POKE 54, 189: POKE 55, 158, and each IN# O with POKE 56, 129; POKE 57, 158. The DOS manual recommends putting the PR and IN commands in PRINT statements. Then the POKEs aren't necessary, but the program will work only under DOS, and you must be sure NOMON C is in effect before each PR# MSLOT, or you may send those commands as output through the modem. There is no difficulty with IN# and PR# as direct commands, since direct commands are all handled through DOS anyway.

Sending Program Output

Here is a program which sends its output to the time-sharing system:

```
100   REM    TIME-SHARING
102   REM    GRADEBOOK
104   REM ---------------
110   LET MSLOT = 2
120   POKE 2040 + MSLOT, 9
130   PR# MSLOT
140   PRINT "    NAME";
150   PRINT  TAB( 20);"SCORES";
160   PRINT  TAB( 30);"AVERAGE"
170   FOR T = 1 TO 100:NEXT
180   PRINT
190   PR# 0
200   REM ---------------
210   FOR N = 1 TO 200
220   : INPUT "NAME, SCORES?
      ";N$,S1,S2
225   : IF N$ = "" THEN 290
230   : LET AV = .5 * (S1 + S2)
235   : PR# MSLOT
240   : PRINT N; TAB( 4);N$;
245   : PRINT  TAB( 20);S1;
      TAB( 25);S2;
250   : PRINT  TAB( 30);AV
255   : PR# 0
260   : NEXT N
290   REM
300   END
```

When this program is run with the Apple in half duplex mode, everything that appears on the screen while PR# MSLOT is in effect will also be sent through the modem to the time-sharing system. Commas in PRINT statements do not provide automatic tabbing as they do on the screen, but

semicolons, TAB and SPC give their usual results. Notice that the INPUT statement is not within the scope of a PR# MSLOT; if it were, its prompt and the user's response would also be sent through the modem. ECN requires a pause after a carriage return (a PRINT that does not end in a comma or semicolon) before it is ready to receive more output from the Apple; for FOR-loop in line 170 provides the necessary delay before the following PRINT statement, and the INPUT command inside the loop assures a pause before the next PRINT.

To prepare ECN to receive the output, we use ECN's TEXT mode, which causes it to put all characters it receives into the primary file. While addressing ECN as a half-duplex terminal, enter

```
NEW,name of file to receive output

TEXT

ctrl-A ctrl-X

]RUN
```

```
list

   80/03/24. 15.48.22.
PROGRAM    ASEND

1000   REM ************************
1001   REM    ASEND              *
1002   REM COPIES ANY TEXT FILE  *
1003   REM TO AN ECN TEXT FILE.  *
1004   REM ECN MUST BE IN TEXT   *
1005   REM MODE TO USE IT.       *
1006   REM                       *
1007   REM    J. T. PARR         *
1008   REM   MATHEMATICS DEPT    *
1009   REM    ILL. ST. UNIV.     *
1010   REM   VERSION 3/13/80     *
1011   REM ************************
1080   :
1110   LET MSLOT = 2
1120   LET DFMT = 9
1130   LET D$ = CHR$ (4)
1140   LET CA$ = CHR$ (1) + CHR$ (1)
1150   INPUT "FILE TO BE COPIED? ";F$
1190   :
1200   REM -- D O S  COMMANDS
1210   PRINT
1220   PRINT D$;"NOMON C,I,O"
1230   PRINT D$;"OPEN ";F$
1240   PRINT D$;"READ ";F$
1250   SPEED= 255
1260   ONERR  GOTO 1400
1290   :
1300   REM -- C O P Y
1310   FOR C = 1 TO 1E30
1320   : GET C$
1330   : PRINT CA$;
1340   : POKE 2040 + MSLOT,DFMT
1350   : PR# MSLOT
1360   : PRINT C$;
1370   : PR# 0
1375   : POKE 54,189: POKE 55,158
1380   : IF  ASC (C$) = 13 THEN  FOR
       T = 1 TO 500: NEXT
1390   : NEXT C
1395   :
1400   REM -- C L O S E   U P
1410   PR# MSLOT
1420   POKE 2040 + MSLOT,DFMT
1430   PRINT  CHR$ (3);
1440   PR# 0
1445   POKE 54,189: POKE 55,158
1450   PRINT
1460   PRINT D$;"CLOSE ";F$
1470   PRINT "EXITED TEXT MODE."
1480   PRINT "DON'T FORGET TO PACK."
9999   END
READY.
```

Listing 1

Since the Apple has been left in half duplex mode, the program output will now be seen on the screen, along with the INPUT prompts and responses, while the output without the prompts and responses is also being sent into the ECN file. When you get the Applesoft prompt again, enter

```
]POKE 2040 + MSLOT, 9

]IN# MSLOT

]ctrl-A ctrl-H

 ctrl-C
```

The ctrl-C takes ECN out of TEXT mode, and gets you the message EXIT TEXT MODE. In TEXT mode several invisible "end-of-record marks" will have been inserted in the file. They are removed by entering the PACK command. Enter NOSORT and LNH to see the results. You can then SAVE or XEDIT the file.

Listing A Program To ECN

Suppose you have a program in Apple memory which you would like to send to an ECN file, and that it has no line numbers less than 10. Then add these lines to the program. Replace MSLOT with your modem slot number.

```
1 SPEED = 80: POKE 33,33
2 POKE 2040 + MSLOT, 9
3 PR# MSLOT
4 LIST 10,
5 FOR T = 1 TO 100 : NEXT
6 PRINT CHR$(3)
7 PR# 0
8 SPEED = 255: POKE 33,40
9 END          (or, DEL 1,9)
```

Now get in contact with ECN as a half-duplex terminal, and enter

```
NEW,name of file to receive listing

TEXT

ctrl-A ctrl-X

]RUN
```

This runs lines 1-9. When line 4 lists your program, PR# MSLOT is in effect, so the listing goes out through the modem to ECN. The POKE 33,33 sets the Apple screen width to 33, which keeps the listing routine from inserting extra carriage returns into the listing. (They can also be avoided by using ctrl-A ctrl-F to put the Apple, but not ECN, into full duplex mode; but then the listing will not show oin the Apple screen.) SPEED = 80 is to help keep ECN from dropping a character after each carriage return. The listing will take quite a while: two and half minutes for a program of eighty-five short lines. Eventually, you will get the Applesoft prompt back. Line 6 sent a ctrl-C to ECN, so it will be out of TEXT mode already. Enter

```
]POKE 2040 + MSLOT, 9

]IN# MSLOT

]ctrl-A ctrl-H

 PACK
```

```
80/03/24. 15.50.04.
PROGRAM    RECEIVE

100   REM   --------------------
110   REM   RECEIVES TEXT FILE
120   REM   FROM CDC BASIC PGM
130   REM   BSEND.
140   REM
150   REM   J T PARR
160   REM   MATHEMATICS DEPT
170   REM   ILLINOIS STATE UNIV.
180   REM   VERSION 3/14/80
199   REM   --------------------
200   REM   C O N S T A N T S
205   REM   --------------------
210   LET DUMMY$ = '*'
220   LET D$ =  CHR$ (4)
230   PRINT 'NAME OF FILE TO COPY TO';
240   INPUT F$
250   LET MSLOT = 2
260   LET DFMT = 9
290   REM   --------------------
300   REM   D O S   C O M D S
310   REM   --------------------
320   PRINT D$;'MON C,I,O'
330   PRINT D$;'OPEN ';F$
340   PRINT D$;'DELETE ';F$
350   PRINT D$;'OPEN ';F$
390   REM   --------------------
400   REM   I N P U T   L O O P
410   REM   --------------------
420   ONERR  GOTO 900
430   FOR L = 1 TO 1E20
440   : LET L$ = ''
445   REM -- GIVE GOAHEAD
450   : PR# MSLOT
460   : POKE 2040 + MSLOT,DFMT
470   : PRINT 1
480   : PR# 0
490   : POKE 54,189: POKE 55,158
500   REM   --------------------
501   REM   L O A D   L$
502   REM   --------------------
505   : IN# MSLOT
510   : FOR C = 1 TO 1E20
520   :: GET C$
530   :: IF  ASC (C$) = 13 THEN 560
540   :: LET L$ = L$ + C$
550   :: NEXT C
560   : REM    G E T   P R O M P T
565   : GET P$: IF P$ = '' THEN 565
570   : PRINT
580   : IN# 0
590   :
600   REM   --------------------
601   REM   P R I N T   L$
602   REM   --------------------
640   : PRINT D$;'WRITE ';F$
650   : PRINT L$
660   : PRINT D$
675   : IF P$ = DUMMY$ THEN L = 1E30
680   : NEXT L
690   :
700   REM   --------------------
710   REM   C L O S E   U P
720   REM   --------------------
725   POKE 216,0
730   IN# 0
740   PR# 0
750   POKE 54,189: POKE 55,158
755   PRINT
770   PRINT D$;'CLOSE'
780   END
799   REM   --------------------
900   REM    E R R O R
909   REM   --------------------
910   PRINT
920   PRINT 'ERROR # '; PEEK (222)
930   PRINT '(FOR TABLES OF
      ERROR NUMBERS'
935   PRINT 'SEE APPLESOFT
      & DOS MANUALS)'
940   POKE 216,0
950   PR# MSLOT
960   PRINT 'STOP'
990   GOTO 700
995   :
READY.
```

There will be a blank line at the top of the listing, and if ECN was not able to keep up after the carriage returns, first digits of some line numbers will be missing. These problems can be corrected with the editing package, giving a good copy of the program on an ECN file to save, print, edit, etc. Lines of more than 150 characters are not accepted by ECN.

If you put lines 1-9 above on a disk text file, you can EXEC the file. If you have included the line numbers on the file, those lines will be appended to the beginning of your program. If you left the line numbers off the file, the commands will be executed directly; in that case, some of them may be printed on the file along with the program listing.

There is a more roundabout way which you might prefer if you have a disk. List your program to a disk file, making sure that POKE 33,33 or NOMON O is in effect to avoid those extra carriage returns. This listing won't take so long, at SPEED = 255. Then use the Apple ASEND program to send the text file with the listing on it to ECN. With the Apple in half duplex mode,

---

If the duplex modes of the terminal and the system do not match, each letter typed will be printed twice, or not at all.

---

the listing will be displayed on the screen as it is being sent. The ASEND program uses a delay loop after each carriage return, so it can send each line at SPEED = 255 without ECN missing any characters, and without taking so long to send the listing.

Copying Disk Text Files To ECN

The Applesoft program ASEND (Listing 1) can be used to transfer any Apple disk text file to an ECN file. The following steps will accomplish the move. Get DOS operating and connect with ECN as a half-duplex terminal.

```
NEW,name of file to write to

TEXT

ctrl-A ctrl-X

Insert disk with ASEND.

]LOAD ASEND

Insert disk with text file.

]RUN

Enter name of file to be copied.

]IN# MSLOT

]ctrl-A ctrl-H

ctrl-C

PACK

SAVE
```

```
100   REM**************************
110   REM BSEND: CDC BASIC PGM    *
120   REM  SEND TEXT FILE TO      *
130   REM  APPLE II MICROCPTR     *
140   REM  FROM ECN.              *
150   REM                         *
181   REM     J T PARR            *
182   REM    MATHEMATICS          *
183   REM     ILLINOIS STATE UNIV. *
184   REM VERSION 6/11/80         *
190   REM**************************
200   REM    S E T    U P
210       FILE #1 = 'TEXT'
220       DELIMIT #1, (CR)
230       RESTORE #1
240       MARGIN 0
300   REM    T R A N S M I T
310       FOR L=1 TO 1E30
315         IF END #1 THEN 400
320         INPUT G
330         INPUT #1, L$
340         PRINT L$
350         NEXT L
400   REM   S I G N   O F F
410       PRINT '*'
999       END
READY.
```


Copying Files To Apple Disk

Since the Apple lacks the equivalent of the ECN TEXT mode, we use an Apple program RECEIVE (Listing 2) to receive text being sent by ECN and write it onto a disk file. If you don't have a disk, a program including some of the techniques of RECEIVE could receive the data and use it directly or STORE it on a cassette. The sending is done by a CDC Basic program BSEND (Listing 3), which sends a line of the file each time RECEIVE signals that it is ready. BSEND is very simple and straightforward, while the idiosyncracies of Apple DOS and the communications card make the RECEIVE program more complicated.

The following sequence shows how to use the BSEND and RECEIVE programs. We assume that DOS is in effect and that the Apple is connected to ECN as a half-duplex terminal.

```
OLD,BSEND

GET,TEXT=name of file to be copied

RNH

Wait for ? prompt, then press
ctrl-A ctrl-X

Insert the disk containing RECEIVE.

]LOAD RECEIVE

Insert the disk you want the file
copied to.

]RUN
```

Answer the prompt with the name you wish the disk copy of the file to have. When you get the Applesoft prompt again, the copy is complete. You may then return to terminal mode and log off. Most errors that occur will be intercepted by an error-handling routine in RECEIVE, but if somehow the Apple should "hang" so that it is necessary to RESET, be sure to enter a CLOSE command to safeguard the file and your disk.

If the file you have copied contains a Basic program and you want to use it as such instead of as data, the command EXEC filename will enter it into the Apple memory as a program, where you can edit it, run it, and save it.

Notes On The Program

In order to be able to deal with all characters, including commas and quote marks, the Apple programs ASEND and RECEIVE use the GET command instead of INPUT. The GET command causes the next PRINT command to lose characters; hence the extra PRINT statements following each series of GET commands. Not only may some output be lost, but if it happens to be the CHR$(4) preceding a DOS command, then DOS will not receive the command. The manual recommends printing an extra CHR$(1) character as the one to be lost, but in some cases that seems not to be sufficient, so ASEND uses two before each PRINT to the modem, and a carriage return before the CLOSE command. You can use INPUT instead of GET, if your application is compatible with INPUT's treatment of blanks, commas, and quotes.

In BSEND, the DELIMIT statement cancels commas and quote marks as delimiters, allowing the INPUT statement to read into L$ the entire next line of the file, no matter what it contains. MARGIN 0 allows BSEND to transmit lines of arbitrary length without inserting carriage returns. The sequence of events in the loop in BSEND is critical for correct synchronization with RECEIVE. RECEIVE has to intercept the BSEND prompt right after it has received a line. If it were to do so later, the prompt might already have been sent by the time the GET is executed, and it would wait indefinitely for a prompt. If ECN is responding quickly, getting P$ could be skipped, and the prompt would just be lost while the Apple writes L$ to the file; but a delay on the part of ECN could then cause the ? to be got as part of the next L$. The loop for getting the prompt flushes out null characters sent by ECN after each carriage return. □

"By golly, Sims, when it gets to vibrating like that I do believe it's laughing at us."

A Guide to Data Banks

The growing trend in data banks is for the industry to divide into producers (assemblers) and distributors (vendors). The producers are usually small companies that don't have the capacity to sell and service their products; they make agreements with distributors, who are better equipped to handle the marketing and installation of the equipment.

The following chart lists alphabetically major distributors of data banks with a wide selection of subject matter. Pricing information is not included because it depends on variables that are too numerous to place in a chart. For example, the Value Line data bank, containing stock-market and related financial data on more than 1,500 companies, is available from producer Arnold Bernhard and Co. for a $5,000 annual subscription fee. Value Line is also available from seven different distributors; these distributors charge the $5,000 fee plus their own fees for frequency of use and length of time used. Some distributors charge by the minute, others by 15-minute slots; and still others have minimum-time requirements. Sometimes more than one data bank is offered for the price of one subscription fee. To illustrate, the distributor Rapidata offers both the Flow of Funds data bank (on the money flow through various sectors of the United States economy) and the RAPIDQUOTE data bank (of price and volume data on 14,000 securities) to subscribers of its other data banks at no extra charge.

ADP Network Services, Inc. P.O. Box 2190 175 Jackson Plaza Ann Arbor, MI 48106 (313) 369-6800	A large distributor offering computational data banks in: Agriculture, Autos, Commodities, Demographics, Economics, Finance, Insurance, and International Business. Its main suppliers are Chase Econometric Associates and Standard & Poor's.
Bibliographic Retrieval Services, Inc. Corporation Park Building 702 Scotia, NY 12303 (518) 374-5011	A large distributor offering bibliographic data banks in: Agriculture, Business, Education, Environment, General News Publications, Science, and Social Science. Its suppliers are various trade associations and governmental groups.
CompuServe Network 5000 Arlington Centre Blvd. Columbus, OH 43220 (614) 457-8600	A distributor offering statistical data banks in: Demographics, Economics, and Finance. Its suppliers include Citibank, Value Line (Arnold Bernhard and Co.), and Standard & Poor's.
The Computer Co. 1905 Westmoreland St. Richmond, VA 23230 (804) 358-2171	A statistical data-bank vendor specializing in the Airline Industry. Its main supplier is the Civil Aeronautics Board.
Data Resources, Inc. 29 Hartwell Ave. Lexington, MA 02173 (617) 861-0165	A large vendor offering data banks in: Agriculture, Banking, Commodities, Construction, Economics, Energy, Finance, Insurance, International Business, Securities, and the Steel and Transportation Industries. In addition, detailed U.S. regional, national, and international economic, demographic, and financial indicators are tracked. Compustat, Value Line, and Standard & Poor's are sources.
Dow Jones News/Retrieval Service 22 Cortlandt St. New York, NY 10007 (212) 285-5000	A bibliographic data bank compiling *The Wall Street Journal*, *Barron's*, and the Dow Jones News Service. Dow Jones compiles its own data bank, which is updated immediately after appearing on the ticker and then maintained for ninety days.
General Electric Information Services Co. 401 N. Washington St. Rockville, MD 20850 (301) 340-4000	A computational data-bank vendor covering: Economics, Energy, Finance, and International Business. Its suppliers include the University of California and Value Line.

Infomart One Yonge St. Toronto, ON Canada M5E 1E5 (416) 366-3904	A large Canadian vendor with data banks covering: Agriculture, Business, Education, Energy, Engineering, Environment, Foundations, General News Publications, Government, Patents, Pharmaceuticals, and Science.
Informatics Inc. 6 Kingsbridge Rd. Fairfield, NJ 07006 (201) 575-2800	A statistical data-bank vendor covering: Demographics, Energy, Environment, and Transportation. Suppliers include governmental groups and the John Hopkins University Medical Center.
Interactive Data Corp. 486 Totten Pond Rd. Waltham, MA 02154 (617) 890-1234	A large computational data-bank distributor covering: Agriculture, Autos, Banking, Commodities, Demographics, Economics, Energy, Finance, International Business, and Insurance. Its main suppliers are Chase Econometric Associates, Standard & Poor's, and Value Line.
Lockheed Information Systems 3251 Hanover St. Palo Alto, CA 94304 (415) 493-4411	The largest bibliographic distributor, offering over 75 different data banks in: Agriculture, Business, Economics, Education, Energy, Engineering, Environment, Foundations, General News Publications, Government, International Business, Patents, Pharmaceuticals, Science, and Social Sciences. Its economic source is Predicasts Terminal Systems, Inc.; it relies on many trade associations and governmental groups for other data bases.
Mead Data Central, Inc. Courthouse Place, N.E. Dayton, OH 45463 (513) 222-6323	A bibliographic data-bank vendor specializing in: General News Publications and Legal Literature. Mead compiles its own data banks.
National CSS, Inc. 542 Westport Ave. Norwalk, CT 06851 (203) 853-7200	A financial vendor of computational data banks covering: Autos, Commodities, Economics, and Finance. Its main suppliers are Merrill Lynch Economics, and Value Line.
The New York Times Information Service, Inc. 1719A Rte. 10 Parsippany, NJ 07054 (201) 539-5850	A bibliographic data-bank vendor covering: Advertising, General News Publications, and Public Opinion Indexes. The New York Times Information Service maintains its own data banks.
Rapidata, Inc. 20 New Dutch Lane P.O. Box 1049 Fairfield, NJ 07006 (201) 227-0035	A statistical data-bank vendor covering: Economics and Finance. Rapidata compiles some of its own data banks and uses Citibank, Telrate and the Federal Reserve Board as additional suppliers.
SDC Search Service 2500 Colorado Ave. Santa Monica, CA 90406 (213) 820-4111	One of the largest bibliographic distributors, offering over 50 different data banks in: Agriculture, Business, Education, Energy, Engineering, Environment, Foundations, General News Publications, Government, Industry, Science, and Social Science. Its suppliers are various trade associations and governmental groups.
Service Bureau Co. 500 W. Putnam Ave. Greenwich, CT 06830 (203) 622-2000	A statistical data-bank distributor covering: Agriculture, Banking, Demographics, Economics, Engineering, Finance, and Insurance. Its suppliers include Standard & Poor's, Data Resources, Inc., and Telstat.
I.P. Sharp Associates Ltd. 145 King St. W. Toronto, ON Canada M5H 1J8 (416) 364-5361	A Canadian distributor with Canadian and American statistical data banks covering: Airlines, Banking, Commodities, Demographics, Economics, Environment, Finance, and International Business. Its suppliers include the Bank of Canada, Citibank, and the International Monetary Fund.
Time Sharing Resources, Inc. 777 Northern Blvd. Great Neck, NY 11022 (516) 487-0101	A statistical data-bank vendor covering: Commodities, Economics, and Finance. Its suppliers include the U.S. Department of Labor, Citibank, and the Federal Reserve Board.
Uni-Coll Corp. 3401 Science Center Philadelphia, PA 19104 (215) 387-3890	A computational data-bank vendor covering: Agriculture, Commodities, Economics, and Finance. The Wharton Economic Forecast supplies most of its data banks.
United Computing Systems, Inc. 2525 Washington Ave. Kansas City, MO 64108 (816) 221-9700	A statistical data-bank vendor covering: Demographics and Finance. Its suppliers include CACI and Standard & Poor's.

A Home Control System

Paul Daro

One of the first applications of mini and microcomputers to gain widespread use was in commercial control systems. Computers were, and still are, quite useful for constantly monitoring and controlling electrical and mechanical systems. With recent developments in the microcomputer industry driving processor and peripheral costs down, we are now starting to see products that provide household computerized control. The Introl/X-10 system for the Apple Computer is one such product. It is a system for controlling an entire household of electrical appliances and devices.

In addition to performing its control functions, certain configurations of the Introl/X-10 system allow for another feature not commonly found in home systems - simultaneous execution of two different programs. The interrupt-driven Introl/X-10 performs its control function in the upper part of Apple memory, leaving room at the bottom for the user's own program (even BASIC).

The Introl X/10 system consists of a hardware/software package. The hardware provides the interface from the Apple to the outside world; the software enables the user to set up a real-time 'schedule' for controlling AC devices. The system is complete - no further programming is necessary to make it control a house, although there is BASIC interface that allows advanced users to set up more sophisticated applications than the software package provides.

The Hardware

There are 3 basic functional units that make up the Introl system. At one

Paul Daro, 436 Trevethan Ave., Santa Cruz, CA. 95062.

end, a Mountain Hardware Introl/X-10 controller board provides an interface between Apple programs and the other 2 functional units; it sends out control commands via an ultrasonic transducer. These commands are received by the second unit, a BSR Command Console. The Command Console then transmits the commands over existing household AC power lines to the third functional unit, a BSR remote module. A single Command Console can control an unlimited number of remote modules, and each remote module controls one appliance (up to 1500 watts) or several lamps (up to 300 watts).

The Introl/X-10 circuit board can be mounted in any of the Apple II peripheral slots (except 0, of course). It has an on-board ROM program that controls the transmission of pulses to the BSR Command Console. The board is activated by the BASIC PR# command, and information is passed to the ROM program using conventional PRINT statements.

In addition to receiving Apple commands and sending them out to the remote modules, the Command Console also has a keyboard, enabling the user to send commands manually. The Command Console

and remote modules are sold by BSR, Ltd. as the System X-10, a centralized electrical control system. Mountain Hardware has added the Apple peripheral board, thus facilitating centralized computer control, and creating the Introl/X-10 system.

In order to fully understand the Introl/X-10 system, one should understand how commands are sent. On the side of each remote module is a "unit code" dial. This dial has 16 different positions, numbered 1 to 16. This dial identifies the remote module. Commands are issued from the Command Console either manually or using the Introl board. They are issued by first sending a unit code and then a function code - the unit code selects the electrical device, and the function code identifies the action to take place. Suppose you sent the sequence 6, ON. Then all electrical devices plugged into remote modules with the unit code dial set at 6 would be turned on. There are also function codes for turning devices off, making lights dimmer and brighter, and 2 global codes 'ALL LIGHTS ON' and 'ALL LIGHTS OFF,' which turn all lights on or all lights and appliances off regardless of the unit code dial setting.

This simple scheme provides for alot of flexibility, as several different devices can be controlled together even though they are plugged into different remote modules - all you need do is dial up the same unit code for each and one command turns them all on. This could prove useful for controlling several outside lights located around the house, or perhaps to control room heaters in each bedroom. At the same time, the 16 different settings on the unit code dial provide the capability to independently control 16 different groups of devices. This should be more than adequate for any home application, especially when one considers that each of the 16 groups can have an unlimited number of devices dialed to it.

The Software

So far only the rudiments of the system have been explained. The following is by far the most powerful part of the Mountain Hardware package - a software system for setting up and running a schedule of device ON/OFF/DIM commands.

With this software package, the user runs one program to set up a schedule that contains information for each device concerning what day and time the device is to be turned on, off, or dimmed. The he/she runs a second program which loads this schedule and then executes the commands at the appropriate times, allowing the individual to walk away and leave the computer running - control is fully automated from then on. This program also keeps an accumulated total of the time a given device group was turned on, and the total amount of power it consumed.

Setup Program

The schedule setup program is written in Applesoft BASIC, and needs at least 32K of RAM to run. The program uses menus to interact with the user. This makes the setup process a simple one, requiring limited prior knowledge of the setup process from the user.

Basically, there are two ways in which someone might want to set up a schedule for a given device. The first approach deals with events that occur on some sort of regular basis. For example, you want to turn the coffee pot on every weekday at 8:00, so your coffee is ready when you get up. Or, perhaps you want to turn your lawn spinkler on for 2 hours every Tuesday and Friday. These types of events occur regularly every week, and you want them to occur at the specified time as long as your computer is running. Events like these have been termed regular events.

The other type of event specification is used in cases where you want something to happen only once. For instance during the weekend of the 14th, you are going away and want some lights to come on in the evening and go off in the morning. You want your regular schedule to run all the time, but in addition, on the 14th and 15th you want some additional events to occur. Events such as these are termed special events, and the system provides a means for entering these as well. Using the setup program, the user creates a separate schedule for each module group. (A module group is the set of all remote modules dialed to the same unit.)

Running the Setup Program

When the program is first run, the user chooses between creating a new schedule and updating an old one previously saved on disk. From this point, the setup process has two principle modes - the primary or executive mode and the edit mode. In the primary mode, the following options are available:

ASSIGN - With this option, the user makes up a name for each module group and inputs the total power consumption in watts for each group. The name and wattage is then assigned to the unit code number of the module group. Unused unit code numbers may be left unassigned, but a number must be assigned before a schedule may be created for it. This option exists primarily to help the user keep track of which module group contains which devices.

DISPLAY - This option displays for all 16 groups the module group numbers, names and wattages as they were entered.

SWAP SCHEDULES - This switches the schedules of two module groups. This function is used when you switch the unit code setting on a remote - you can do the swap function to reassign the schedule, instead of retyping it.

REMOVE SCHEDULE - This deletes the schedule for one entire module group.

SAVE SCHEDULE - This saves the entire schedule table for all 16 groups onto a user-specified disk file.

COMPUTE FILE SPACE - This tells how much room is left in the schedule table, giving the user an idea of how much more schedule information may be entered.

In the edit mode, individual group schedules are modified/updated; concurrently a schedule table in memory is updated. Upon entering the edit mode, the user specifies which module group he wishes to work on. He then has the option to add events to the schedule, remove events from the schedule and display the entire schedule for a given module group.

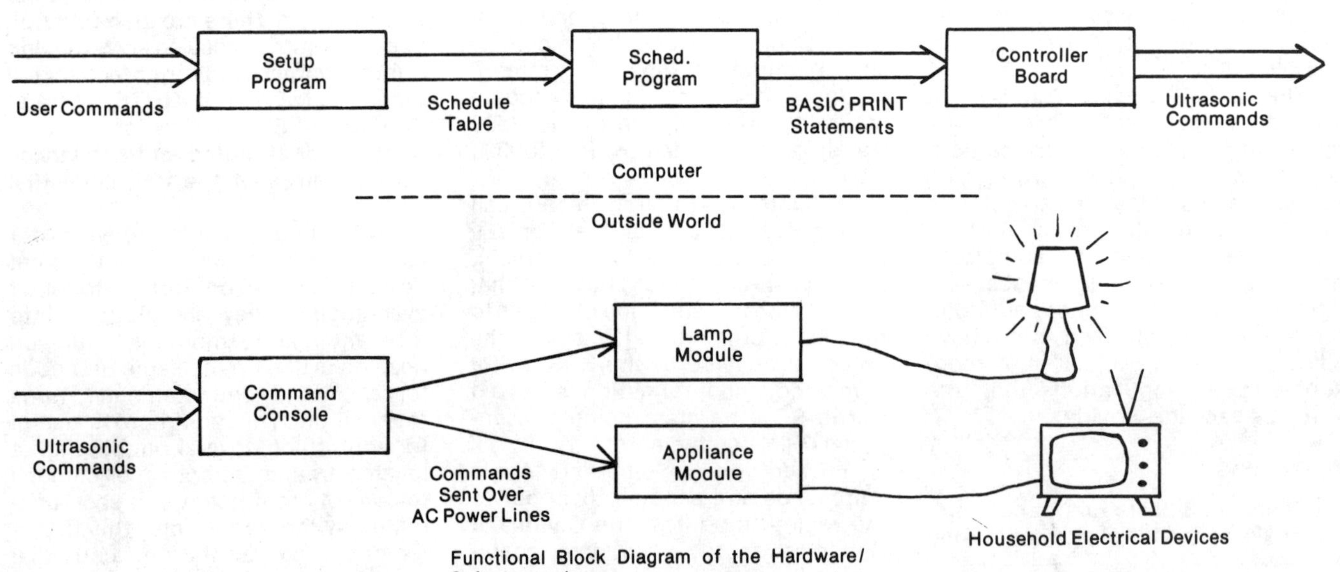

Functional Block Diagram of the Hardware/ Software package.

In adding events, there are different specifications for regular and special events. Regular events are specified by entering the day(s) on which it occurs, time at which it occurs and the desired function. Special events also have a date(s) associated with the event occurrence. In each case, the user is prompted for each parameter (day, time, etc.) separately.

The time parameter is specified by typing in the time much as it would be displayed on a digital clock. For example, "12:30A" would mean the 80th minute after midnight. Furthermore, there is a feature which allows specification of an event to occur randomly within a given interval. For example, if you went on vacation for a month and wanted lights turned on in the evening, you could use the random time function to have them come on at a random time between 6:00 and 8:00 every night. This helps to confuse anyone who might be staking out your house since the lights are not coming on in any recognizable pattern. This would be specified as "6:00P-8:00P."

The days parameter specifies on which days the events will happen. Days can be entered singly, separated by commas, or as a range of days, separated by a dash. For example, "MON,TUES,THU" would specify Monday, Tuesday and Thursday. On the other hand, "TUES-SAT" would be interpreted as Tuesday, Wednesday, Thursday, Friday and Saturday.

The function specification is one of three functions: ON, OFF, or DIM. ON and OFF are self-explanatory. The DIM function has a parameter associated with it; the DIM level. The DIM level is a number in the range 1 to 9, and specifies the final brightness of the light. The DIM function really means "turn on the lamp and then dim it to the given level." For example, if at 9:00 you wanted to turn a light on and dim it down to level 9 (most dim), the function would be "DIM 9." If at 9:10 you wanted to brighten it up by 3 DIM levels, the function would be "DIM 6."

Thus, a complete regular event specification consists of a time, days and a function entry. For example, to turn your heater on every morning at 8 and off at 10, two events would be entered:

    8:00A SUN-SAT ON
    10:00A SUN-SAT OFF

To make sure your TV was always turned off at night (for those who like

to fall asleep in front of it), you might enter:

    1:00A SUN-SAT OFF

Special events are entered just like regular events, but in addition there is a date specification. The date specification consists of a month and dates within the month. For example, "FEB 10-20" means February 10th through February 20th. Or "FEB 10, 12, 14, 16, 25" means February 10th, 12th, etc. So if you want your lawn spinkler to come on every Monday and Thursday while you are away in the last 2 weeks of July, the following special event entry would do it:

    3:00P MON,THU JULY 14-28 ON
    5:00P MON,THU JULY 14-28 OFF

By combining special and regular events, all possible needs are provided for. In the previous heater example, to keep the heater from going on while you are away, the following special event entry would do the trick:

    8:00A MON-SUN JULY 14-28 OFF

In fact, even if the heater were to come on many times during a day, this one special event entry would take care of all the regular events, since a special event overrides the entire regular schedule for a given day.

The Scheduler Program

After the schedule has been created and saved, the schedule can be loaded and executed by the second program. This second program, the scheduler, performs the events as they were specified in the setup program. The first thing the scheduler does is load the table. It then turns off all connected devices and then determines the on/off/dim status of each device, bringing each device to its appropriate status. This initialization has interesting implications for Apple configurations that have the autoboot feature and a Mountain Hardware Apple Clock. Suppose you are away on vacation with your Apple at home minding the house. Suddenly, the power goes off for a few seconds, then returns. Ordinarily, the program would die and all your devices would stay in whatever state they were in until you came home. But, with an auto-boot program that executes the scheduler, this problem is alleviated. The scheduler loads in the table again, re-initializes all the devices and, presto, you are right back where you were.

In configurations without a Mountain Hardware Clock, the scheduler is interrupted once per second by the Introl/X-10 board. After the user types in the initial date and time, the scheduler keeps track of the time and date from there; so the scheduler program will work in minimally configured systems. However, the auto boot feature described above will not work because once power goes down, the scheduler loses track of its accumulated time. Then when the power comes back, there is no one around to re-initialize the time. Also, without a Mountain Hardware Apple Clock, the foreground/background feature is not available. Many foreground programs would do disk accesses and other functions that require interrupts to be turned off for periods of 1 second or more. When this happens, the scheduler would lose some of the 1-second interrupts and thus would start to lose time.

With the Mountain Hardware Apple Clock, the scheduler is capable of actually reading the date and time from the clock board. Even when interrupts are disabled for several seconds, no time is lost because the clock keeps its own accumulated time. This enables the scheduler program to run in the background, while a foreground BASIC or machine language program has primary control.

Since most of the time the scheduler is merely waiting for events to occur, there is not much of a delay in response time when running in foreground/background. However, if many events were all scheduled to happen at the same time, there might be a 10 or 20 second delay while the schedule was busy sending out commands to the devices. However, this situation would most likely occur once or twice a day if at all. Since the schedule table resides in memory at scheduler run-time, the setup program could be run as a foreground program. Thus, you could update the schedule while the scheduler was executing it. This gives you the convenience of modifying the currently running schedule without having to stop and re-start everything.

Memory Considerations

The software package needs an Apple configured with a minimum of 32K of RAM. A 32K system will allow a schedule that contains up to 150 events, while a 48K system can handle up to 700 events. In foreground/background mode, a 32K setup will have room enough for a foreground program of up to 18K; in 48K systems the foreground programs can use 28K. In all cases, the DOS software is left intact.

Direct Interface

For the ambitious programmer, there is an optional direct interface to the ROM driver program. Thus the devices can be controlled directly from a BASIC program. The statement below activates the board:

PR#n, n = slot number of board

Once this has been done, PRINT statements are sent to the board, which interprets them and sends them out. For example, the statement below would turn on module group 1:

PRINT "1 ON"

Using this simple interface, the sophisticated user can set up a scheduling scheme. A direct interface program might be written to work in conjunction with the scheduler program to get a combination of straightforward scheduling and more complex timing functions for special devices.

Conclusion

Overall, the system is quite easy to install and run. The setup program is very user-oriented since its use doesn't require programming knowledge and the multi-tasking feature makes the Introl /X10 an extremely flexible control system. It is also inexpensive - $279.00 buys the entire system including software, controller board, Command Console and three remote modules (additional remotes are $16.00 each). $279.00 for a practical system for computerized home control. □

Notes

The Quest for the Perfect Printer

George Blank

The right printer is easier to recognize than the Holy Grail. During my three years on a fruitless quest, dozens of people have described it to me. It is compact, lightweight, fast, quiet, reliable, easy to service, easy to load with paper, uses plain paper of various widths with or without holes along the sides, has typewriter quality print, uses cheap ribbons, and costs less than $500.

During the first score of months on my quest, I believed that it also had excellent graphics. I have since learned that this is not so. There is a fundamental incompatibility between quality graphics and a printer that will be used for correspondence. A high resolution graphics printer, such as Integral Data Systems' excellent later models, must have tractor feed for precise registration. Every dot must be printed in exactly the right place. The tractor feed is the most expensive part of a good graphics printer. But a correspondence printer must accept ordinary stationery, typewriter paper, and even envelopes. Tractor feed stationery is hard to get, expensive, and has annoying unfinished edges when you tear off edges. I suppose tractor feed envelopes are available somewhere, but are even more difficult to find.

I am adamant about the price. I see no reason why a decent printer should cost more than the computer to which it is connected.

The print quality may or may not be negotiable. I have no quarrel with attractive high density dot matrix characters like those of the Epson MX-80 or the Centronics 737 printers for 98% of my printer use. But it does seem tacky to address Christmas Cards or apply for a job using dot matrix print.

In my opinion, one thing that is absolutely non-negotiable is true descenders on the lower case characters. This means that the tails on lower case g, j, p, q, and y must extend below the line of other letters.

439

I have talked to more than a dozen printer manufacturers who have told me that the public doesn't demand descenders. My personal experience does not support that view. For I have talked to well over a hundred people looking for printers, and quality lower case type was high on everyone's preference list. Any printer without descenders is unacceptable to me, and the manufacturer who doesn't believe they are necessary may be in for a rude awakening.

The Tin Cup Theory

Even if you are on a quest for the Holy Grail, you must stop occasionally for a drink. A tin cup may not be as satisfactory as the Grail, but it sure beats sticking your head in the river for a drink. Many of the printers I have used have been in the "tin cup" category, and I have received varying degrees of service and satisfaction from them as I continued my quest.

Actually, I would like to group the printers I have used into three categories, and compare them to tin cups, plastic cups, and sterling silver goblets. My primary needs for printers fall into three categories: software development, normal writing, and quality correspondence.

Printers that are satisfactory for software development may be compared to a tin cup. They are for my personal use only, get heavy use, and print quality, perhaps even true descenders, can be sacrificed for low cost, reliability or high speed. Printers that are acceptable for everyday writing, including letters and magazine articles, can be compared to the plastic dinnerware that many people use for family dining. The output of such printers must be read by other people, and while typewriter quality is not a must, it should come close. The printers that I must currently use for important correspondence can be compared to silver goblets. While they are necessary when you are sending resumes to the Fortune 500 asking for a position as Chairman of the Board, they tend to be oversized, overpriced, and hard to maintain. Personally, I never liked polishing silver.

My perfect printer does not fall into any of these categories. I would rather compare it to an ordinary china cup. Only a china cup does a good job of keeping my coffee warm without adding any unpleasant tastes or burning my fingers, and while I may use a cup made out of tin, plastic, styrofoam, glass, pewter, or even silver, it is not by choice.

"Tin Cup" Printers

In the tin cup category of printers I have used, I include the Radio Shack Quick Printer II, the Eaton LRC 7000+ and the Centronics 730 and 779. Since the Centronics 730 is so close in price and features to the 737, which belongs in the next category, I will not describe it. Anyone to whom the 730 appeals should get the 737.

Radio Shack Quick Printer II

This delightful little printer has three main strengths. It is cheap, very portable, and eligible for Radio Shack service. I know of no other printer that sells for less than $220 brand new and comes equipped with an RS-232 serial and a Centronics parallel port, not to mention a special port for the TRS-80 bus. It is so small and light that I was able to carry my TRS-80 keyboard, cassette recorder, and the printer in a small suitcase, substituting the printer for a video monitor. It has very few parts, and I never had any trouble with it. But even if it fails, Radio Shack offers the least expensive and most readily available printer servicing I know about. It is very quiet and the paper is reasonably cheap.

There are also significant drawbacks to this printer. It uses hard-to-read electrostatic paper, and the print width on the paper is only 2". A long listing is sheer murder to read, and since it only prints 32 characters per line, I would not want to use it for assembly language programming. Also, the paper just sits in a groove, and I have often sent it unrolling across the floor when moving the printer from place to place.

The Eaton LRC 7000 (Atari 820)

This is quite a step up from the Quick Printer II for only a little more money. While it lists for $389, it is frequently discounted, and often sells for less than $300. It takes an ordinary cheap typewriter ribbon and plain paper, though you must use 4 1/4" wide roll paper. While it normally comes configured for 40 characters per line, there is a version, the 7000+, with a 64-character line that is ideal for use with the TRS-80. The mechanism is very rugged,

```
ATARI 820 (Eaton LRC)
abcdefghijklmnopqrstuvwxyz
ABCDEFGHIJKLMNOPQRSTUVWXYZ
```

and was used for years in cash registers, so service should not be frequent. A serial version of the same printer, with a smart controller for the Atari Bus, is sold as the Atari 820 printer. The newly announced price is $299.95. The print is easy to read, and is a good cheap printer for software development work.

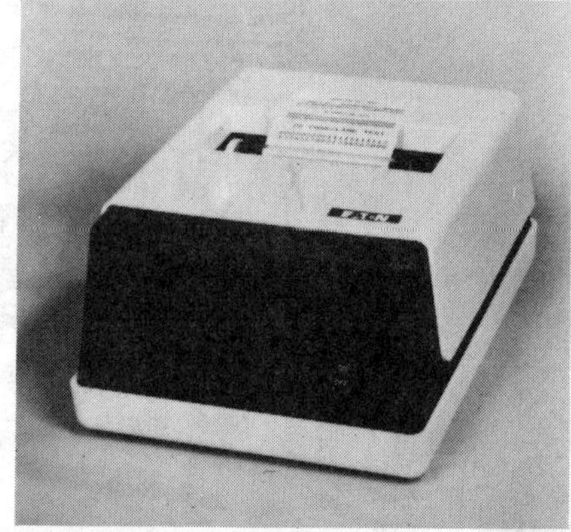

The Eaton printers have three serious drawbacks. The narrow paper width is insufficient for many uses, it is quite noisy, and it is very slow. On short listings, the speed is acceptable, but on long listings, the mechanism heats up and must stop to cool off. When this first happened to me, I thought the printer was broken, but later realized that it was normal for it to print a couple of lines, cool off for 10 seconds, print a couple more lines, cool off again, etc. It is also significantly larger and heavier than the Quick Printer II, though smaller than the rest of the printers to be discussed.

The Centronics 779 (Radio Shack Line Printer I)

This rugged, dependable old timer is the pack mule of the computer industry. The list price is around $1395, but it is almost always discounted, and is frequently available used. Radio Shack seems to be

```
Centronics 779 (Radio Shack Line Printer I)
with Service Technologies lower case kit
    abcdefghijklmnopqrstuvwxyz
    ABCDEFGHIJKLMNOPQRSTUVWXYZ
```

closing out the similar 781 (same printer without adjustable character size) at $789, and Radio Shack service is much cheaper and easier to find than Centronics service. It does not come with lower case, but several companies, including Service Technologies (32 Nightingale Rd., Nashua,

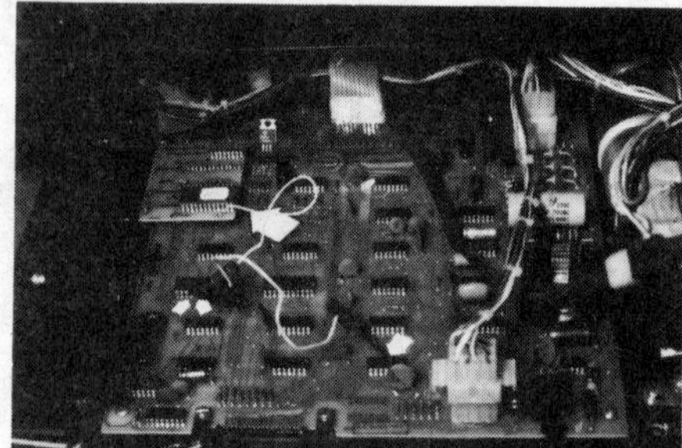

The Service Technologies lower case modification (small board in upper left) installed in a Centronics 779 printer.

Comparison Chart of 35 Popular Printers

Printer	Reviewed	Price	Paper	Print Mode	Feed	Columns	Graphics	Interfaces	Lower Case
Anadex DP-9501	6/81	$1595	Plain	Dot Matrix	T	80-220	Dot	P	Descenders
Apple Silentype (Trendcom 200)		$ 635	Thermal	Dot Matrix	R	40	Dot	Apple	Raised
Atari 820 (Eaton LRC)	7/81	$ 299	Plain	Dot Matrix	R	40	Partial	A	Raised
Atari 825 (Centronics 737)	4/81 7/81	$ 799	Plain	Dot Matrix	L,P,R,S	72-132	No	A	Descenders
Base 2 800 MST	2/81	$ 699	Plain	Dot Matrix	T	64-132	Dot	C P S	Raised
Centronics 737	4/81 7/81	$ 995	Plain	Dot Matrix	L,P,R,S	72-132	No	P	Descenders
Centronics 779 (781)	6/80 7/81	varies	Plain	Dot Matrix	L,R,S,T	64-132	No	P	(Need Kit)
Commodore CBM 2022	5/80 12/80	$ 995	Plain	Dot Matrix	T	80	Character	C	Raised
Comprint 912	6/80	$ 659	Elect.	Dot Matrix	R	80	No	P,S	Descenders
Diablo 1640		$3195	Plain	Daisy Wheel	L,R,S,T	132	No	S	Typewriter
Eaton LRC	7/81	$ 389	Plain	Dot Matrix	R	40 (64)	No	P S	Raised
Escon E-A Interface	6/80	$ 675	(Kit for IBM Selectric Typewriter)				No	C P S	Typewriter
Epson MX-80	7/81	$ 645	Plain	Dot Matrix	P	80-132	Character	P	Descenders
Heath H-14	6/80	$ 625	Plain	Dot Matrix	P	80	No	S	Raised
Howard Industries Typrinter 221		$2850	Plain	Type Ball	S	132	No	S	Typewriter
Integral Data 460		$1395	Plain	Dot Matrix	T	80-132	Dot	P,S	Descenders
Integral Data 560		$1695	Plain	Dot Matrix	T	80-132	Dot	P,S	Descenders
Malibu 160	12/79 6/80	$2395	Plain	Dot Matrix	T	80	Dot	S	Descenders
Micro Computer Devices Selectraterm	12/79 6/80	$2495	Plain	Type Ball	L,S,T	132	No	P,S	Typewriter
Micro Peripherals Inc. 88G	4/81	$ 749	Plain	Dot Matrix	L,R,S,T	80-132	Dot	A	Raised
NEC Spinwriter	7/81	$3055	Plain	Thimble	L,R,S,T	132	No	P,S	Typewriter
Okidata Microline 82	7/81	$ 649	Plain	Dot Matrix	F,P	132	Block	P,S	Raised
Qume Sprint 5	12/79 6/80	$2995	Plain	Daisy Wheel	L,R,S,T	132	No	P,S	Typewriter
Radio Shack Daisy Wheel II		$1960	Plain	Daisy Wheel	L,S,T	132	No	P	Typewriter
Radio Shack Line Printer I	6/80 7/81	$1395	Plain	Dot Matrix	L,R,S,T	132	No	P	(Need Kit)
Radio Shack Line Printer IV	4/81 7/81	$ 995	Plain	Dot Matrix	L,P,R,S	80-132	Dot	A,P,T	Descenders
Radio Shack Line Printer VI	2/81	$1160	Plain	Dot Matrix	L,P,R,S	80-132	Character	P	Raised
Radio Shack Line Printer VII		$ 399	Plain	Dot Matrix	P	80	No	P	Raised
Radio Shack Quick Printer II	11/79 7/81	$ 219	Elect.	Dot Matrix	R	16,32	No	P,S	Raised
Rochester Data Dynatyper	7/81	$ 499	(Attaches to electric typewriter)				No	C,P,S	Typewriter
Starwriter Daisy Wheel	7/81	$1795	Plain	Daisy Wheel	L,S	132	No	P,S	Typewriter
Teletype Model 43	12/79 6/80	$1095	Plain	Dot Matrix	T	132	No	S	Descenders
Texas Instruments 810	12/79 6/80	$1895	Plain	Dot Matrix	T	132	No	P,S	Optional
Trendcom 100	6/80	$ 375	Thermal	Dot Matrix	R	40	Dot (Opt)	P	Raised
Vista V300 - 25	7/81	$1895	Plain	Daisy Wheel	L,S	132	No	P,S	Typewriter

KEY: **Paper Feed** (L) Labels (P) Pin Feed (R) Roll (S) Sheets (T) Tractor Feed (F) Friction
Interfaces Available (A) Atari (C) CBM/PET (IEEE 488) (P) Centronics Parallel (TRS-80, Apple) (S) Serial

NH 03062, $125) and Digital Systems Engineering (12503 Kings Lake Dr., Reston VA 22091, $95 and $135) offer modification kits. I used the Service Technologies kit and installed it in five minutes using only a screwdriver.

Since these printers can have either platen feed (like a typewriter) or tractor feed, they are very flexible, although the platen feed does not seem to grip uniformly, particularly on small labels. The print speed is relatively fast, and I have seen about a dozen of these in heavy use over a period of years, with few service problems. If I could get true descenders on the lower case characters, this would come quite close to my ideal printer. As it is, I do not object strongly to letters and articles done on the 779 printer. It is great for line listings, whether Basic or Assembly language.

The Service Technologies 779 lower case conversion kit. (Pen is not included.)

In addition to the lack of true descenders and the poor platen grip, this printer is moderately noisy, heavy, and takes up a great deal of room, but that is not enough to keeep it from being my favorite "tin cup" printer.

Moving up to Melmac

There are two printers in the "plastic cup" category, the Epson MX-80 and the Centronics 737, both of which are distinguished by "correspondence" quality print with true descenders on lower case. They use a high density dot matrix print that is close enough to typewriter quality for many uses. They are also small and lightweight. At the moment, these two printers come closer to the ideal printer for home use than anything else available.

The Epson MX-80

This is my first choice among currently available printers. I have used one at home, and we have had three at Creative Computing in almost constant use for nearly a year. One of them is connected to our typesetting system, and nearly every article, book, and piece of software documentation we have printed since July of last year has

been printed on it for proofreading—often several times. The only problem we have experienced has been an occasional paper jam caused by paper catching on the wire rack that supports the paper coming out of the printer. This can be corrected if you catch it as soon as it happens, but it does mean that one can't leave the printer unattended when printing out a long listing.

The MX-80 is quiet, rugged, moderately fast, has attractive print, and even has a good price. While it lists for $645, I have frequently seen it discounted. One dealer at the West Coast Computer Faire was selling it at a price so low that I don't dare print it. He could hardly keep up with the demand.

The only real drawbacks to the MX-80 are the lack of true typewriter quality print and its limitation to pin feed only. I cannot give an answer about service availablity or price, for though I have used four of them extensively, the most drastic service ever needed has been a change of ribbon or addition of more

paper. The company is working on a platen feed model which they hoped to demonstrate at the National Computer Conference in May and have available this summer. The price has not been determined at this writing, but most people who are buying a printer will want to check this one out.

**The Centronics 737
(Atari 825, Radio Shack Line Printer IV)**

This thousand dollar printer has even nicer print quality than the MX-80, particularly in its condensed and proportional type modes. It will handle both pin feed and plain paper. With the right software (currently unavailable, unless you use control characters from your own Basic program), it will offer proportional

spacing, underlining, superscripts and subscripts. It will print up to 132 columns, and the Centronics version is often discounted well below the $995 list price. Here again, I recommend the Radio Shack version for the service, but if you can get good service at a computer store on another version, buy it there.

I think service is more important on this printer than any of the others I have mentioned so far. I have experienced problems with several of them, usually with the print head carrier traveling over to the right and locking, or burning up the print head. In addition, I find the paper difficult to feed in, and have had

frequent paper jams, which are sometimes difficult to clear. They are usually caused by the paper folding over and feeding back into the paper feed. I don't like the design of the bus connector, because you don't know which way to plug in the cable until you try a "smoke test." I haven't damaged a printer by plugging the cable in wrong, but I have burned my fingers unplugging the connector after discovering it was upside down.

The platen is made of hard plastic with spaced ridges and does not hold narrow forms or labels well. The pin feed mechanism is not adjustable, and is set up for 9 1/2" paper. I have been told that the most serious problems, locking up and the burned up heads, have been corrected in later models, but I would insist on an iron-clad guarantee before buying one of these printers. I can say that our Atari 825 printer, about a month old, has given us no trouble at all.

Sterling Silver—The Real Thing?

True letter-quality printers tend to be expensive, large, heavy, and prone to servicing problems. Let us consider the best first, and after recognizing that only businessmen (it is tax deductible for them) and the independently wealthy can afford it, move on to the others.

The NEC Spinwriter

The list price on this majestic printer is indeed royal: from $3,055 to $4,255 depend-. ing on the options. It is much like a typewriter, with fixed width print characters, 132 columns across at 10 characters per inch. It is rugged, durable, and for a letter quality printer, reasonably fast at 55 characters per second. Most of my line listings printed in "Outpost: Atari" before

I moved to New Jersey in March were done on this printer, and the print quality is excellent. I have experience with only one of them, but it was in frequent use for more than a year without any problems except a small crack in the outer case when somebody dropped it down the stairs.

It is big, heavy, and noisy. I wouldn't allow it in my office because of the noise, but always took my important correspondence over to it. Not only is it expensive to buy, but the ribbons are costly as well. With a quality platen and adjustable tractors, it is a very versatile printer. I do think it has too many features. It was a nuisance trying to defeat the paper empty indicators when I just wanted to print an address on an envelope. However, if I could afford any printer I wanted, it would be a Spinwriter.

The Vista 25 CPS Printer (Starwriter Daisy Wheel)

The printer that now sits in my office is an $1895 Vista. My limited experience with it has not been entirely satisfactory. Though I have had it for over a month, I have been unable, despite repeated calls, to get a manual for it. This is a serious

---

```
      Vista V300-25

abcdefghijklmnopqrstuvwxyz

ABCDEFGHIJKLMNOPQRSTUVWXYZ

This is the Vista V300-25 using

Superscript's Diablo printer

driver with underlining,

superscripts, subscripts,

Boldface, slash 0, elite spacing,

and pica spacing.
```

---

problem, for it has many built-in features controlled by software control codes, and without a manual you don't even know what they are, much less how to work them. In addition, it is out of adjustment, and does vertical line feeds unevenly, leaving a line of extra space every few lines.

The specifications are quite impressive. It has high quality print, and uses standard print wheels. It will give variable line heights, boldface, subscripts and superscripts, variable spacing, and probably a bunch of other features that I would know about if I had a manual. It is significantly quieter than the Spinwriter, though less than half as fast at 25 characters per second. There is also a 45 character per second model available.

The same printer, which is made in Japan, is available as the Starwriter Daisy Wheel Printer. I think that this would probably be a good buy if you could get it from a dealer that would stand behind it and service it at a reasonable price, but it is definitely not the kind of printer to buy through the mail.

During the last 15 months, Creative Computing has reviewed many other printers. All of these printers plus those above are listed in the chart. Back issues with these reviews are available for $2.50 each postpaid or $2.00 each for 3 or more issues. □

Notes

The Dynatyper
Typewriter Interface

Jim Cavuoto

Of all the possible uses of computers, word processing probably has the most potential for luring new people into the growing family of computer owners. But there is one factor which may still inhibit many of these people: the cost of a letter-quality printer, which is likely to be two to four times the cost of the computer itself.

There is another, perhaps psychological, barrier preventing people—especially writers, or would-be writers—from investing in computer equipment for word processing. For these people, the typewriter has become the cornerstone, the articulator of their creative efforts, and to give it up in favor of a complicated, untested new system would certainly be a risky venture—not to mention a waste of the money they have already invested in a good electric typewriter.

Fortunately, there is a product that helps overcome both the financial and psychological resistance to using computers for word processing. It is the Dynatyper typewriter interface from Rochester Data Inc., a device which rests on the typewriter keyboard and accepts output supplied by the computer. For about one-fifth the cost of a letter-quality printer, it is possible to turn your typewriter into a component in your computer system. But how well does it work? I hope to show in this review that it works quite well.

Jim Cavuoto, 2004 Curtis Ave. #A, Redondo Beach, CA 90278.

My first reaction when I saw a picture of the Dynatyper sitting on top of a typewriter was to chuckle—"do they really expect me to believe this is going to work?" It does. I've been using it for several months with my Apple and IBM Selectric typewriter, with excellent results. It will work with any electric typewriter—I've even

For about one-fifth the cost of a letter-quality printer, it is possible to turn your typewriter into a component in your computer system.

seen it power a portable Smith Corona that was almost smaller than the Dynatyper itself. The advertisements boast that the Dynatyper lifts on and off in five seconds, but this is wrong. It takes me three and a half seconds. This feature, plus the fact that no modification to your typewriter is required, is a major selling point to writers who want to preserve the sanctity of their typewriters.

Theory of Operation

The Dynatyper consists of a lightweight case housing 52 "plungers," each of which rests in a solenoid. It is these plungers, which are half delryn and half metal, that physically strike the keys on the typewriter. A plunger is activated when current flows through its corresponding solenoid, setting up a magnetic field that thrusts the plunger downward and hits the key on the typewriter. It is this ingenious mechanism that gives the Dynatyper its excellent performance, pleasing simplicity and high reliability. For although the unit may at first seem like an electromechanical product with all the pitfalls inherent in moving parts, the only movement is produced by electromagnetic forces—there are no linkages or connections causing movement. So essentially, as long as Maxwell's equations of physics remain in force, the plungers will be activated with high reliability. Reports from people who have been using the Dynatyper for a year or more indicate that few, if any, malfunctions can be anticipated.

The Dynatyper also comes with an external power supply, a parallel interface card and a cassette tape with the operating software. This is, perhaps, the only drawback to the system: operating the Dynatyper requires loading a 300-byte binary driver that controls the unit. As an alternative Rochester Data has just come out with a serial interface for the unit that eliminates the need for the operating software; however, this option costs about $200 extra.

The plungers protruding from the underside of The Dynatyper press the keys of the typewriter.

Two plastic washers, located on either side of the spacebar, are the only indication that the typewriter is being used as a printer.

Software

The operating software accompanying the parallel interface is embedded in a Basic program that allows the user to change the values of the delay constants affecting typing speed and also to locate the binary driver at a convenient location in the memory map. This may be a bit too much flexibility, however; for every time a user wishes to load the program, he must first set HIMEM so the binary driver can be safely tucked away, and then answer a series of questions concerning changing the delay constants. Normally, a user would want to set the appropriate values once, and then not have to worry about resetting them every time he uses the Dynatyper.

So I've found that a better solution is to substitute my selected values directly into the binary driver and save only the assembly language program, which can then be inserted as a subroutine in any program that would require the Dynatyper. Inci-dentally, this is what must be done if you want to use the Dynatyper with any of the existing word processing software packages on the market; these programs will not work unmodified with the Dynatyper. Fortunately, most suppliers of word processing software have agreed to modify or at least reveal how to modify their programs so they can be used with the Dynatyper. The manufacturers of Easy Writer, Apple Writer, and Magic Window have all been eager to cooperate.

My solution was to write my own word processing program which incorporates the Dynatyper's operating software.

Performance

To insure a high level of performance from the Dynatyper, it is important that it be initially aligned properly on your typewriter. Otherwise, you may lose characters during output. Initial alignment only takes about a half hour, but it does require some experimentation to get the best configuration.

The first thing that must be done is to mount two white plastic washers on either side of the space bar of the typewriter using the cardboard template supplied. These two washers are the only indication that your typewriter is being used as a printer, and since they are attached with double-sided tape, they are easily removed. Into these two washers are placed the two bottom screws of the Dynatyper. The two top screws rest directly on the typewriter in such a way that the unit is held securely in place. With the cover off, these four screws are then adjusted by trial and error until every plunger, when pushed manually, activates its corresponding key on the typewriter. The plungers come in three different heights so the Dynatyper can be converted to different typewriters.

When the alignment is complete, you must determine the typing speed and setting of the separate delay constants. Although the Dynatyper can reliably activate its plungers at a rate of up to 50 cps, most typewriters are limited to a maximum typing speed of 15 cps before characters begin dropping out. Also, the return, tab and backspace keys should be made to delay many times longer than the other keys since they require longer activation times. I've found it best to operate my unit at 12 cps to reduce wear on my typewriter. At this speed, which cor-responds to 140 words per minute, there are very rarely any missed characters.

Thus, for word processing applications where high speed output is not the most important concern, the Dynatyper interface is an effective and low cost alternative to a letter-quality printer. The Dynatyper sells for $499 for Apple and TRS-80 versions and slightly more for PET, OSI, Northstar and HP-85 versions. Included in the purchase price is a one-year, all-inclusive warranty and a set of thriftily produced manuals.

(Rochester Data Inc., 3000 Winton Road South, Rochester, NY 14623.) □

445

Chatsworth Data
Mark Sense Card Reader

Keith Schlarb

Shown are the interface, card reader and AC/DC adapter.

Educators, rejoice! Have you wanted to use a computer in your classroom, but found data entry through a single keyboard next to impossible? You know the story; one student entering data and 25 waiting in line. I had the same dilemma, until I purchased the Chatsworth Data MR-500 Mark Sense Card Reader. The card reader has made it possible to handle student programs from an entire class with one microcomputer. A student simply marks his line numbers and Basic statements on the programming cards by shading in the appropriate areas of the card. When finished, the cards are fed through the reader and the program is entered into the computer. The program can then be processed by cards appropriately marked, "RUN," "LIST," etc. Time required to enter each student's program is drastically cut, since cards are read as fast as they can be placed in the reader. Also, most students can shade in the program cards as fast as they are able to hen peck in their program on the keyboard. A short program, 10 to 15 lines, can be entered and run in 30 seconds. An ad-

Keith Schlarb, 5617 Indianolia Ave., Worthington, OH 43085.

Figure 1. Sample of the first 7 columns of a mark sense programming card. The cards have a total of 40 columns.

Mountain Hardware ROMPLUS+

Steve North

Mountain Hardware's ROMPLUS+ board is an EPROM memory board for the Apple II with a capacity of 12K bytes. The board also has 255 bytes of on-board scratchpad RAM and two TTL inputs for user applications. The ROMPLUS+ also has an onboard control ROM that allows the other ROM software to be accessed easily via ordinary input and output commands.

All this is very nice, but not especially useful unless you're going to develop your own ROM-based software. However, Mountain Hardware also has an optional plug-in ROM for the ROMPLUS+ board, the Keyboard Filter, which takes advantage of this hardware to expand the I/O features of the Apple.

The Keyboard Filter generally interacts with the user and the other system software much more gracefully than other packages.

Like the other character generators we previously reviewed for the Apple, the Keyboard Filter draws software-defined character fonts on the high resolution graphics screen of the Apple to provide upper and lower case characters or anything else that can be drawn in a 7x9 dot matrix. The Keyboard Filter has some other interesting features which the other character generators do not, though, and it generally interacts with the user and the other system software much more gracefully than other packages. For example, the Keyboard Filter software can be activated by typing PR#5 (to get the attention of the control ROM) and then control-shift-M 1 (to turn on the Keyboard Filter installed in ROM socket 1). This is easier than loading a program stored on cassette or disk and also eliminates some fussing around to avoid memory collisions with other programs.

The Keyboard Filter processes input and output by intercepting and processing characters like any other I/O device (such as a disk or printer). Most of its special functions are accessed by outputting control characters, either by PRINT statements or echoing them from the keyboard. The functions include selection of character fonts, colored and inverse video text, cursor movement, overstrike and "keyboard macros" (single-stroke shorthand entry of longer character sequences).

One of the TTL inputs on the ROMPLUS+ may be connected to the shift key on the Apple so that it can operate with some semblance to a normal typewriter keyboard. Since the Apple keyboard is normally uppercase only, the alternative is to define some particular control character to mean "toggle upper/lower case." It's much more people-oriented to type with the shift key. So, by looking at the status of the shift key the Keyboard Filter software can determine if the user is entering upper or lower case. Unfortunately, the Apple keyboard has the exponent and at-sign over the N and P keys respectively, so to type these symbols, if you've made the shift-key modification, you have to type a control character to toggle into "raw mode" to enter the symbol, and then type the control character again to get back into normal upper/lower case. Since these two symbols are not entered frequently, it's a very reasonable tradeoff to make.

The documentation for the hardware and software was better than average. It will provide the casual user with enough information to access the Keyboard Filter from Basic, and if you're interested in machine language programming or making your own ROMs, there's also enough documentation of low-level bit diddling. The ROMPLUS+/Keyboard Filter behaved nicely with Integer and Applesoft Basic in ROM and also talks with Applesoft in RAM. However, it cannot be activated at the same time as other peripherals that overlap the address space at C800-CFFF (such as the D.C. Hayes Micromodem).

The quality of the hardware and software is what we've come to expect from Mountain Hardware. It's sophisticated, flexible, and easy to use. However, before buying one, consider that the software you write with embedded Keyboard Filter commands may not be very transportable to other Apples without this add-on. Also, it's a bit on the expensive side since you can get software character generators for about $20 (although they are not as powerful or convenient, and don't have the shift-key modification). Still, for

The quality of the hardware and software is what we've come to expect from Mountain Hardware.

designing your own custom software or funny little programs in Basic, we recommend the ROMPLUS+/Keyboard Filter if you can justify the price.

The ROMPLUS+ with Keyboard Filter is available for $200.00 from Mountain Hardware, Inc., 300 Harvey West Blvd., Santa Cruz, CA 95060. (408) 429-8600. □

Keyboard Filter Control Codes

A No function
B No function
C Normal function — stops programs
D Normal function — DOS commands
E Turns on cursor movement mode
F Font switching — followed by number of desired font
G Normal function — bell
H Normal function — backspace
I Toggle inverse mode
J No function
K Select input from peripheral — followed by slot number
L Toggle shift lock
M Normal function — carriage return
N No function
O Toggle overstrike mode
P Switch page being displayed
Q Select output to peripheral — followed by slot number
R Toggles raw mode
S Prints keyboard macro — followed with key for desired macro
T Selects color — followed by number of desired color
U No function
V Toggles shift key usage in modified Apples
W Copy to end of line (for editing)
X Normal function — delete line
Y No function
Z Clears current page

ditional advantage to educators is using the card reader to grade multiple choice tests. A special test scoring card is used which allows for 100 questions, each with 5 possible answers. Students shade in the appropriate answer on the card as they take the test. The cards are then fed through the reader and are graded by using a test scoring program which is furnished by Chatsworth Data on request, at time of purchase.

The Chatsworth Card Reader is compact in size, 4.6"(width) x 4.3" (height)x4.5" depth, and weighs only 4 pounds. It is composed of the main reader housing, with motor to drive the reader, an AC/DC converter and an interface board and all are included in the purchase of the reader.

It was a simple task to get the reader up and running with my Apple Plus II. The interface board was plugged into slot 4 of the Apple and the other end of the interface cord was attached to the reader. The AC/DC adapter was plugged into an electrical outlet and the reader was ready for its first performance. The computer was ready to accept information from the card reader after the "IN#4" command was typed and the return key hit. Returning to keyboard use was accomplished by marking a card with the "IN#0" command and feeding it through the reader. The "IN#4" and "IN#0" commands may also be used within programs to enter data from the reader.

Marking Programming Cards

Figure 1 shows a portion of a programming card, drawn to an enlarged size. When marking a program, columns 1-4 are used for the line number. Columns 5-40 are marked for the Basic statement. The cards are marked using the standard Hollerith Code and a #2 pencil. Figure 2 shows the card symbols, symbol location within the boxes and the appropriate marking for the symbols. The following are a few

examples of the correct markings required to enter data by card: To enter 0-9 numbers simply shade in the appropriate box of the number. Letters A-I are marked by shading the (&) box plus the box containing the letter. Examples are letter C marked by (&3), and F by (&6). Letters J-R are marked by the (-) box and the corresponding letter. Letter K is (- 2) with Q being a (- 8). Letters S-Z are marked in a similar way, shown in Figure 2. The symbols appearing at the bottom center of the boxes, below the numbers, are marked by a combination of (8) and the appropriate box. An equal sign, for example, is a (6 8) mark combination. The symbols to the right of the boxes are marked by combinations of one of the following (& - 0) plus (8) and the appropriate box containing the desired symbol. See Figure 2 for the exact combinations.

Entering Data

Entering a program is a simple procedure. Using the "IN#4" command the computer looks for information from the reader. Input all the cards, with the last being the "IN#0" command to return to the keyboard, and the program is ready to run. If it is desired to run the program by using the reader, then do not use the "IN#0" card and enter instead the "RUN" statement.

Several methods are available for entering variables into an existing program. I have found the easiest method to input a long list of variables is through the use of data statements. Mark the variables on a card, always using the same program line, so as not to accidentally destroy another line of the program. Enter the data statement before running the program. This procedure can easily be adapted for programs you already have by changing "INPUT" statements to "READ" statements through the program.

A second method of using the reader to input variables is to use the the "IN#4" and "IN#0" commands

Shown is the correct marking for the statement 10 A = B + C.

within the program. The variables are entered through the reader when requested. If the program statement "INPUT A.B.C.D.E" is used, then an equal number of variables may be entered on a single card. However, each variable must be separated by a comma.

A third method to input variables is the use of a FOR-NEXT loop, again with the "IN#4" and "IN#0" commands within the program. See Figure 3 for a sample program using the FOR-NEXT loop. Use of the loop, however, requires that only one variable be marked on each card. This could lead to using a large number of cards.

```
400 IN#4
410 FOR I = 1 TO 10
420 PRINT "INPUT CARD"
430 INPUT A(I)
440 NEXT I          Figure 3.
450 IN#0
```

The FOR-NEXT loop above can be used to input variables into a program. The IN#4 command allows the computer to accept data from the reader and line 450 returns control to the keyboard.

Cost

Chatsworth Data is presently advertising the card reader, AC/DC converter and interface at $750. The cost of programming cards is $15/1000.

Thus far I have had no problems with the reader. It is a fantastic piece of computer equipment. Obviously I still use the keyboard to enter programs, but the card reader has made it possible for one microcomputer to handle programs from a full classroom of students. So, unless your school system can afford a dozen microcomputers, or you don't mind having 25 students waiting in line, you may want to join me as a rejoicing owner of a Chatsworth Data MR-500 Mark Sense Card Reader. □

Chatsworth Data Corporation
20710 Lassen Street
Chatsworth, California 91311
(213) 341-9200

SYMBOL LOCATION	SYMBOLS	MARKING
Center of Box	1 2 3 4 5 6 7 8 9 0	appropriate box
Top Left of Box	A B C D E F G H I	appropriate box plus (&)
Center Left of Box	J K L M N O P Q R	appropriate box plus (-)
Bottom Left of Box	/ S T U V W X Y Z	appropriate box plus (0)
Bottom Center of Box	: # @ = "	appropriate box plus (8)
Top Right of Box	[. < (+ !	appropriate box plus (&) plus (8)
Center Right of Box	] $ *) ; ↑	appropriate box plus (-) plus (8)
Bottom Right of Box	/ ' % ← > ?	appropriate box plus (0) plus (8)
Carriage Return & 5 8 9		
Line feed 0 5 9		

Figure 2. Other ASC II characters can also be marked on the cards. An entire list with the correct marking codes are furnished with the reader instructions.